To Page Potter,
with admiration and great
personal regards,
Wm. Van Alstyne
Sept. 9, 1991

University Casebook Series

June, 1991

ACCOUNTING AND THE LAW, Fourth Edition (1978), with Problems Pamphlet (Successor to Dohr, Phillips, Thompson & Warren)

George C. Thompson, Professor, Columbia University Graduate School of Business.
Robert Whitman, Professor of Law, University of Connecticut.
Ellis L. Phillips, Jr., Member of the New York Bar.
William C. Warren, Professor of Law Emeritus, Columbia University.

ACCOUNTING FOR LAWYERS, MATERIALS ON (1980)

David R. Herwitz, Professor of Law, Harvard University.

ADMINISTRATIVE LAW, Eighth Edition (1987), with 1989 Case Supplement and 1983 Problems Supplement (Supplement edited in association with Paul R. Verkuil, Dean and Professor of Law, Tulane University)

Walter Gellhorn, University Professor Emeritus, Columbia University.
Clark Byse, Professor of Law, Harvard University.
Peter L. Strauss, Professor of Law, Columbia University.
Todd D. Rakoff, Professor of Law, Harvard University.
Roy A. Schotland, Professor of Law, Georgetown University.

ADMIRALTY, Third Edition (1987), with Statute and Rule Supplement

Jo Desha Lucas, Professor of Law, University of Chicago.

ADVOCACY, see also Lawyering Process

AGENCY, see also Enterprise Organization

AGENCY—PARTNERSHIPS, Fourth Edition (1987)

Abridgement from Conard, Knauss & Siegel's Enterprise Organization, Fourth Edition.

AGENCY AND PARTNERSHIPS (1987)

Melvin A. Eisenberg, Professor of Law, University of California, Berkeley.

ANTITRUST: FREE ENTERPRISE AND ECONOMIC ORGANIZATION, Sixth Edition (1983), with 1983 Problems in Antitrust Supplement and 1990 Case Supplement

Louis B. Schwartz, Professor of Law, University of Pennsylvania.
John J. Flynn, Professor of Law, University of Utah.
Harry First, Professor of Law, New York University.

BANKRUPTCY, Second Edition (1989), with 1990 Case Supplement

Robert L. Jordan, Professor of Law, University of California, Los Angeles.
William D. Warren, Professor of Law, University of California, Los Angeles.

BANKRUPTCY AND DEBTOR–CREDITOR LAW, Second Edition (1988)

Theodore Eisenberg, Professor of Law, Cornell University.

UNIVERSITY CASEBOOK SERIES—Continued

BUSINESS ASSOCIATIONS, AGENCY, PARTNERSHIPS, AND CORPORATIONS (1991)
William A. Klein, Professor of Law, University of California, Los Angeles.
Mark Ramseyer, Professor of Law, University of California, Los Angeles.

BUSINESS CRIME (1990)
Harry First, Professor of Law, New York University.

BUSINESS ORGANIZATION, see also Enterprise Organization

BUSINESS PLANNING (1991)
Franklin Gevurtz, Professor of Law, McGeorge School of Law.

BUSINESS PLANNING, Temporary Second Edition (1984)
David R. Herwitz, Professor of Law, Harvard University.

BUSINESS TORTS (1972)
Milton Handler, Professor of Law Emeritus, Columbia University.

CHILDREN IN THE LEGAL SYSTEM (1983) with 1990 Supplement (Supplement edited in association with Elizabeth S. Scott, Professor of Law, University of Virginia)
Walter Wadlington, Professor of Law, University of Virginia.
Charles H. Whitebread, Professor of Law, University of Southern California.
Samuel Davis, Professor of Law, University of Georgia.

CIVIL PROCEDURE, see Procedure

CIVIL RIGHTS ACTIONS (1988), with 1990 Supplement
Peter W. Low, Professor of Law, University of Virginia.
John C. Jeffries, Jr., Professor of Law, University of Virginia.

CLINIC, see also Lawyering Process

COMMERCIAL AND DEBTOR–CREDITOR LAW: SELECTED STATUTES, 1990 EDITION

COMMERCIAL LAW, Second Edition (1987)
Robert L. Jordan, Professor of Law, University of California, Los Angeles.
William D. Warren, Professor of Law, University of California, Los Angeles.

COMMERCIAL LAW, Fourth Edition (1985), with 1991 Case Supplement
E. Allan Farnsworth, Professor of Law, Columbia University.
John Honnold, Professor of Law, University of Pennsylvania.

COMMERCIAL PAPER, Third Edition (1984), with 1991 Case Supplement
E. Allan Farnsworth, Professor of Law, Columbia University.

COMMERCIAL PAPER, Second Edition (1987) (Reprinted from COMMERCIAL LAW, Second Edition (1987))
Robert L. Jordan, Professor of Law, University of California, Los Angeles.
William D. Warren, Professor of Law, University of California, Los Angeles.

COMMERCIAL PAPER AND BANK DEPOSITS AND COLLECTIONS (1967), with Statutory Supplement
William D. Hawkland, Professor of Law, University of Illinois.

UNIVERSITY CASEBOOK SERIES—Continued

COMMERCIAL TRANSACTIONS—Principles and Policies, Second Edition (1991)

Alan Schwartz, Professor of Law, Yale University.
Robert E. Scott, Professor of Law, University of Virginia.

COMPARATIVE LAW, Fifth Edition (1988)

Rudolf B. Schlesinger, Professor of Law, Hastings College of the Law.
Hans W. Baade, Professor of Law, University of Texas.
Mirjan P. Damaska, Professor of Law, Yale Law School.
Peter E. Herzog, Professor of Law, Syracuse University.

COMPETITIVE PROCESS, LEGAL REGULATION OF THE, Revised Fourth Edition (1991), with 1989 Selected Statutes Supplement

Edmund W. Kitch, Professor of Law, University of Virginia.
Harvey S. Perlman, Dean of the Law School, University of Nebraska.

CONFLICT OF LAWS, Ninth Edition (1990)

Willis L. M. Reese, Professor of Law, Columbia University.
Maurice Rosenberg, Professor of Law, Columbia University.
Peter Hay, Professor of Law, University of Illinois.

CONSTITUTIONAL LAW, Eighth Edition (1989), with 1990 Case Supplement

Edward L. Barrett, Jr., Professor of Law, University of California, Davis.
William Cohen, Professor of Law, Stanford University.
Jonathan D. Varat, Professor of Law, University of California, Los Angeles.

CONSTITUTIONAL LAW, CIVIL LIBERTY AND INDIVIDUAL RIGHTS, Second Edition (1982), with 1989 Supplement

William Cohen, Professor of Law, Stanford University.
John Kaplan, Professor of Law, Stanford University.

CONSTITUTIONAL LAW, Eleventh Edition (1985), with 1990 Supplement (Supplement edited in association with Frederick F. Schauer, Professor, Harvard University)

Gerald Gunther, Professor of Law, Stanford University.

CONSTITUTIONAL LAW, INDIVIDUAL RIGHTS IN, Fourth Edition (1986), (Reprinted from CONSTITUTIONAL LAW, Eleventh Edition), with 1990 Supplement (Supplement edited in association with Frederick F. Schauer, Professor, Harvard University)

Gerald Gunther, Professor of Law, Stanford University.

CONSUMER TRANSACTIONS, Second Edition (1991), with Selected Statutes and Regulations Supplement

Michael M. Greenfield, Professor of Law, Washington University.

CONTRACT LAW AND ITS APPLICATION, Fourth Edition (1988)

Arthur Rosett, Professor of Law, University of California, Los Angeles.

CONTRACT LAW, STUDIES IN, Fourth Edition (1991)

Edward J. Murphy, Professor of Law, University of Notre Dame.
Richard E. Speidel, Professor of Law, Northwestern University.

CONTRACTS, Fifth Edition (1987)

John P. Dawson, late Professor of Law, Harvard University.
William Burnett Harvey, Professor of Law and Political Science, Boston University.
Stanley D. Henderson, Professor of Law, University of Virginia.

UNIVERSITY CASEBOOK SERIES—Continued

CONTRACTS, Fourth Edition (1988)

    E. Allan Farnsworth, Professor of Law, Columbia University.
    William F. Young, Professor of Law, Columbia University.

CONTRACTS, Selections on (statutory materials) (1988)

CONTRACTS, Second Edition (1978), with Statutory and Administrative Law Supplement (1978)

    Ian R. Macneil, Professor of Law, Cornell University.

COPYRIGHT, PATENTS AND TRADEMARKS, see also Competitive Process; see also Selected Statutes and International Agreements

COPYRIGHT, PATENT, TRADEMARK AND RELATED STATE DOCTRINES, Third Edition (1990), with 1989 Selected Statutes Supplement and 1981 Problem Supplement

    Paul Goldstein, Professor of Law, Stanford University.

COPYRIGHT, Unfair Competition, and Other Topics Bearing on the Protection of Literary, Musical, and Artistic Works, Fifth Edition (1990), with 1991 Statutory and Case Supplement

    Ralph S. Brown, Jr., Professor of Law, Yale University.
    Robert C. Denicola, Professor of Law, University of Nebraska.

CORPORATE ACQUISITIONS, The Law and Finance of (1986), with 1990 Supplement

    Ronald J. Gilson, Professor of Law, Stanford University.

CORPORATE FINANCE, Third Edition (1987)

    Victor Brudney, Professor of Law, Harvard University.
    Marvin A. Chirelstein, Professor of Law, Columbia University.

CORPORATION LAW, BASIC, Third Edition (1989), with Documentary Supplement

    Detlev F. Vagts, Professor of Law, Harvard University.

CORPORATIONS, see also Enterprise Organization and Business Organization

CORPORATIONS, Sixth Edition—Concise (1988), with 1990 Case Supplement and 1990 Statutory Supplement

    William L. Cary, late Professor of Law, Columbia University.
    Melvin Aron Eisenberg, Professor of Law, University of California, Berkeley.

CORPORATIONS, Sixth Edition—Unabridged (1988), with 1990 Case Supplement and 1990 Statutory Supplement

    William L. Cary, late Professor of Law, Columbia University.
    Melvin Aron Eisenberg, Professor of Law, University of California, Berkeley.

CORPORATIONS AND BUSINESS ASSOCIATIONS—STATUTES, RULES, AND FORMS (1990)

CORRECTIONS, SEE SENTENCING

CREDITORS' RIGHTS, see also Debtor-Creditor Law

UNIVERSITY CASEBOOK SERIES—Continued

CRIMINAL JUSTICE ADMINISTRATION, Fourth Edition (1991)
Frank W. Miller, Professor of Law, Washington University.
Robert O. Dawson, Professor of Law, University of Texas.
George E. Dix, Professor of Law, University of Texas.
Raymond I. Parnas, Professor of Law, University of California, Davis.

CRIMINAL LAW, Fourth Edition (1987)
Fred E. Inbau, Professor of Law Emeritus, Northwestern University.
Andre A. Moenssens, Professor of Law, University of Richmond.
James R. Thompson, Professor of Law Emeritus, Northwestern University.

CRIMINAL LAW AND APPROACHES TO THE STUDY OF LAW, Second Edition (1991)
John M. Brumbaugh, Professor of Law, University of Maryland.

CRIMINAL LAW, Second Edition (1986)
Peter W. Low, Professor of Law, University of Virginia.
John C. Jeffries, Jr., Professor of Law, University of Virginia.
Richard C. Bonnie, Professor of Law, University of Virginia.

CRIMINAL LAW, Fourth Edition (1986)
Lloyd L. Weinreb, Professor of Law, Harvard University.

CRIMINAL LAW AND PROCEDURE, Seventh Edition (1989)
Ronald N. Boyce, Professor of Law, University of Utah.
Rollin M. Perkins, Professor of Law Emeritus, University of California, Hastings College of the Law.

CRIMINAL PROCEDURE, Third Edition (1987), with 1990 Supplement
James B. Haddad, Professor of Law, Northwestern University.
James B. Zagel, Chief, Criminal Justice Division, Office of Attorney General of Illinois.
Gary L. Starkman, Assistant U. S. Attorney, Northern District of Illinois.
William J. Bauer, Chief Judge of the U.S. Court of Appeals, Seventh Circuit.

CRIMINAL PROCESS, Fourth Edition (1987), with 1990 Supplement
Lloyd L. Weinreb, Professor of Law, Harvard University.

DAMAGES, Second Edition (1952)
Charles T. McCormick, late Professor of Law, University of Texas.
William F. Fritz, late Professor of Law, University of Texas.

DECEDENTS' ESTATES AND TRUSTS, See also Family Property Law

DECEDENTS' ESTATES AND TRUSTS, Seventh Edition (1988)
John Ritchie, late Professor of Law, University of Virginia.
Neill H. Alford, Jr., Professor of Law, University of Virginia.
Richard W. Effland, late Professor of Law, Arizona State University.

DISPUTE RESOLUTION, Processes of (1989)
John S. Murray, President and Executive Director of The Conflict Clinic, Inc., George Mason University.
Alan Scott Rau, Professor of Law, University of Texas.
Edward F. Sherman, Professor of Law, University of Texas.

DOMESTIC RELATIONS, see also Family Law

DOMESTIC RELATIONS, Second Edition (1990)
Walter Wadlington, Professor of Law, University of Virginia.

UNIVERSITY CASEBOOK SERIES—Continued

EMPLOYMENT DISCRIMINATION, Second Edition (1987), with 1990 Supplement

Joel W. Friedman, Professor of Law, Tulane University.
George M. Strickler, Professor of Law, Tulane University.

EMPLOYMENT LAW, Second Edition (1991), with Statutory Supplement

Mark A. Rothstein, Professor of Law, University of Houston.
Andria S. Knapp, Visiting Professor of Law, Golden Gate University.
Lance Liebman, Professor of Law, Harvard University.

ENERGY LAW (1983) with 1986 Case Supplement

Donald N. Zillman, Professor of Law, University of Utah.
Laurence Lattman, Dean of Mines and Engineering, University of Utah.

ENTERPRISE ORGANIZATION, Fourth Edition (1987), with 1987 Corporation and Partnership Statutes, Rules and Forms Supplement

Alfred F. Conard, Professor of Law, University of Michigan.
Robert L. Knauss, Dean of the Law School, University of Houston.
Stanley Siegel, Professor of Law, University of California, Los Angeles.

ENVIRONMENTAL POLICY LAW, Second Edition (1991)

Thomas J. Schoenbaum, Professor of Law, University of Georgia.
Ronald H. Rosenberg, Professor of Law, College of William and Mary.

EQUITY, see also Remedies

EQUITY, RESTITUTION AND DAMAGES, Second Edition (1974)

Robert Childres, late Professor of Law, Northwestern University.
William F. Johnson, Jr., Professor of Law, New York University.

ESTATE PLANNING, Second Edition (1982), with 1985 Case, Text and Documentary Supplement

David Westfall, Professor of Law, Harvard University.

ETHICS, see Legal Profession, Professional Responsibility, and Social Responsibilities

ETHICS OF LAWYERING, THE LAW AND (1990)

Geoffrey C. Hazard, Jr., Professor of Law, Yale University.
Susan P. Koniak, Professor of Law, University of Pittsburgh.

ETHICS AND PROFESSIONAL RESPONSIBILITY (1981) (Reprinted from THE LAWYERING PROCESS)

Gary Bellow, Professor of Law, Harvard University.
Bea Moulton, Legal Services Corporation.

EVIDENCE, Sixth Edition (1988 Reprint), with 1990 Case Supplement (Supplement edited in association with Roger C. Park, Professor of Law, University of Minnesota)

John Kaplan, Professor of Law, Stanford University.
Jon R. Waltz, Professor of Law, Northwestern University.

EVIDENCE, Eighth Edition (1988), with Rules, Statute and Case Supplement (1990)

Jack B. Weinstein, Chief Judge, United States District Court.
John H. Mansfield, Professor of Law, Harvard University.
Norman Abrams, Professor of Law, University of California, Los Angeles.
Margaret Berger, Professor of Law, Brooklyn Law School.

UNIVERSITY CASEBOOK SERIES—Continued

FAMILY LAW, see also Domestic Relations

FAMILY LAW Second Edition (1985), with 1991 Supplement

Judith C. Areen, Professor of Law, Georgetown University.

FAMILY LAW AND CHILDREN IN THE LEGAL SYSTEM, STATUTORY MATERIALS (1981)

Walter Wadlington, Professor of Law, University of Virginia.

FAMILY PROPERTY LAW, Cases and Materials on Wills, Trusts and Future Interests (1991)

Lawrence W. Waggoner, Professor of Law, University of Michigan.
Richard V. Wellman, Professor of Law, University of Georgia.
Gregory Alexander, Professor of Law, Cornell Law School.
Mary L. Fellows, Professor of Law, University of Minnesota.

FEDERAL COURTS, Eighth Edition (1988), with 1990 Supplement

Charles T. McCormick, late Professor of Law, University of Texas.
James H. Chadbourn, late Professor of Law, Harvard University.
Charles Alan Wright, Professor of Law, University of Texas, Austin.

FEDERAL COURTS AND THE FEDERAL SYSTEM, Hart and Wechsler's Third Edition (1988), with 1989 Case Supplement, and the Judicial Code and Rules of Procedure in the Federal Courts (1989)

Paul M. Bator, Professor of Law, University of Chicago.
Daniel J. Meltzer, Professor of Law, Harvard University.
Paul J. Mishkin, Professor of Law, University of California, Berkeley.
David L. Shapiro, Professor of Law, Harvard University.

FEDERAL COURTS AND THE LAW OF FEDERAL–STATE RELATIONS, Second Edition (1989), with 1990 Supplement

Peter W. Low, Professor of Law, University of Virginia.
John C. Jeffries, Jr., Professor of Law, University of Virginia.

FEDERAL PUBLIC LAND AND RESOURCES LAW, Second Edition (1987), with 1990 Case Supplement and 1990 Statutory Supplement

George C. Coggins, Professor of Law, University of Kansas.
Charles F. Wilkinson, Professor of Law, University of Oregon.

FEDERAL RULES OF CIVIL PROCEDURE and Selected Other Procedural Provisions, 1991 Edition

FEDERAL TAXATION, see Taxation

FIRST AMENDMENT (1991)

William W. Van Alstyne, Professor of Law, Duke University.

FOOD AND DRUG LAW, Second Edition (1991)

Peter Barton Hutt, Esq.
Richard A. Merrill, Professor of Law, University of Virginia.

FUTURE INTERESTS (1970)

Howard R. Williams, Professor of Law, Stanford University.

FUTURE INTERESTS AND ESTATE PLANNING (1961), with 1962 Supplement

W. Barton Leach, late Professor of Law, Harvard University.
James K. Logan, formerly Dean of the Law School, University of Kansas.

UNIVERSITY CASEBOOK SERIES—Continued

GOVERNMENT CONTRACTS, FEDERAL, Successor Edition (1985), with 1989 Supplement

John W. Whelan, Professor of Law, Hastings College of the Law.

GOVERNMENT REGULATION: FREE ENTERPRISE AND ECONOMIC ORGANIZATION, Sixth Edition (1985)

Louis B. Schwartz, Professor of Law, Hastings College of the Law.
John J. Flynn, Professor of Law, University of Utah.
Harry First, Professor of Law, New York University.

HEALTH CARE LAW AND POLICY (1988)

Clark C. Havighurst, Professor of Law, Duke University.

HINCKLEY, JOHN W., JR., TRIAL OF: A Case Study of the Insanity Defense (1986)

Peter W. Low, Professor of Law, University of Virginia.
John C. Jeffries, Jr., Professor of Law, University of Virginia.
Richard C. Bonnie, Professor of Law, University of Virginia.

INJUNCTIONS, Second Edition (1984)

Owen M. Fiss, Professor of Law, Yale University.
Doug Rendleman, Professor of Law, College of William and Mary.

INSTITUTIONAL INVESTORS, (1978)

David L. Ratner, Professor of Law, Cornell University.

INSURANCE, Second Edition (1985)

William F. Young, Professor of Law, Columbia University.
Eric M. Holmes, Professor of Law, University of Georgia.

INSURANCE LAW AND REGULATION (1990)

Kenneth S. Abraham, University of Virginia.

INTERNATIONAL LAW, see also Transnational Legal Problems, Transnational Business Problems, and United Nations Law

INTERNATIONAL LAW IN CONTEMPORARY PERSPECTIVE (1981), with Essay Supplement

Myres S. McDougal, Professor of Law, Yale University.
W. Michael Reisman, Professor of Law, Yale University.

INTERNATIONAL LEGAL SYSTEM, Third Edition (1988), with Documentary Supplement

Joseph Modeste Sweeney, Professor of Law, University of California, Hastings.
Covey T. Oliver, Professor of Law, University of Pennsylvania.
Noyes E. Leech, Professor of Law Emeritus, University of Pennsylvania.

INTRODUCTION TO LAW, see also Legal Method, On Law in Courts, and Dynamics of American Law

INTRODUCTION TO THE STUDY OF LAW (1970)

E. Wayne Thode, late Professor of Law, University of Utah.
Leon Lebowitz, Professor of Law, University of Texas.
Lester J. Mazor, Professor of Law, University of Utah.

JUDICIAL CODE and Rules of Procedure in the Federal Courts, Students' Edition, 1989 Revision

Daniel J. Meltzer, Professor of Law, Harvard University.
David L. Shapiro, Professor of Law, Harvard University.

UNIVERSITY CASEBOOK SERIES—Continued

JURISPRUDENCE (Temporary Edition Hardbound) (1949)

Lon L. Fuller, late Professor of Law, Harvard University.

JUVENILE, see also Children

JUVENILE JUSTICE PROCESS, Third Edition (1985)

Frank W. Miller, Professor of Law, Washington University.
Robert O. Dawson, Professor of Law, University of Texas.
George E. Dix, Professor of Law, University of Texas.
Raymond I. Parnas, Professor of Law, University of California, Davis.

LABOR LAW, Eleventh Edition (1991), with 1991 Statutory Supplement

Archibald Cox, Professor of Law, Harvard University.
Derek C. Bok, President, Harvard University.
Robert A. Gorman, Professor of Law, University of Pennsylvania.
Matthew W. Finkin, Professor of Law, University of Illinois.

LABOR LAW, Second Edition (1982), with Statutory Supplement

Clyde W. Summers, Professor of Law, University of Pennsylvania.
Harry H. Wellington, Dean of the Law School, Yale University.
Alan Hyde, Professor of Law, Rutgers University.

LAND FINANCING, Third Edition (1985)

The late Norman Penney, Professor of Law, Cornell University.
Richard F. Broude, Member of the California Bar.
Roger Cunningham, Professor of Law, University of Michigan.

LAW AND MEDICINE (1980)

Walter Wadlington, Professor of Law and Professor of Legal Medicine, University of Virginia.
Jon R. Waltz, Professor of Law, Northwestern University.
Roger B. Dworkin, Professor of Law, Indiana University, and Professor of Biomedical History, University of Washington.

LAW, LANGUAGE AND ETHICS (1972)

William R. Bishin, Professor of Law, University of Southern California.
Christopher D. Stone, Professor of Law, University of Southern California.

LAW, SCIENCE AND MEDICINE (1984), with 1989 Supplement

Judith C. Areen, Professor of Law, Georgetown University.
Patricia A. King, Professor of Law, Georgetown University.
Steven P. Goldberg, Professor of Law, Georgetown University.
Alexander M. Capron, Professor of Law, University of Southern California.

LAWYERING PROCESS (1978), with Civil Problem Supplement and Criminal Problem Supplement

Gary Bellow, Professor of Law, Harvard University.
Bea Moulton, Professor of Law, Arizona State University.

LEGAL METHOD (1980)

Harry W. Jones, Professor of Law Emeritus, Columbia University.
John M. Kernochan, Professor of Law, Columbia University.
Arthur W. Murphy, Professor of Law, Columbia University.

UNIVERSITY CASEBOOK SERIES—Continued

LEGAL METHODS (1969)
  Robert N. Covington, Professor of Law, Vanderbilt University.
  E. Blythe Stason, late Professor of Law, Vanderbilt University.
  John W. Wade, Professor of Law, Vanderbilt University.
  Elliott E. Cheatham, late Professor of Law, Vanderbilt University.
  Theodore A. Smedley, Professor of Law, Vanderbilt University.

LEGAL PROFESSION, THE, Responsibility and Regulation, Second Edition (1988)
  Geoffrey C. Hazard, Jr., Professor of Law, Yale University.
  Deborah L. Rhode, Professor of Law, Stanford University.

LEGISLATION, Fourth Edition (1982) (by Fordham)
  Horace E. Read, late Vice President, Dalhousie University.
  John W. MacDonald, Professor of Law Emeritus, Cornell Law School.
  Jefferson B. Fordham, Professor of Law, University of Utah.
  William J. Pierce, Professor of Law, University of Michigan.

LEGISLATIVE AND ADMINISTRATIVE PROCESSES, Second Edition (1981)
  Hans A. Linde, Judge, Supreme Court of Oregon.
  George Bunn, Professor of Law, University of Wisconsin.
  Fredericka Paff, Professor of Law, University of Wisconsin.
  W. Lawrence Church, Professor of Law, University of Wisconsin.

LOCAL GOVERNMENT LAW, Second Revised Edition (1986)
  Jefferson B. Fordham, Professor of Law, University of Utah.

MASS MEDIA LAW, Fourth Edition (1990)
  Marc A. Franklin, Professor of Law, Stanford University.
  David A. Anderson, Professor of Law, University of Texas.

MUNICIPAL CORPORATIONS, see Local Government Law

NEGOTIABLE INSTRUMENTS, see Commercial Paper

NEGOTIATION (1981) (Reprinted from THE LAWYERING PROCESS)
  Gary Bellow, Professor of Law, Harvard Law School.
  Bea Moulton, Legal Services Corporation.

NEW YORK PRACTICE, Fourth Edition (1978)
  Herbert Peterfreund, Professor of Law, New York University.
  Joseph M. McLaughlin, Dean of the Law School, Fordham University.

OIL AND GAS, Fifth Edition (1987)
  Howard R. Williams, Professor of Law, Stanford University.
  Richard C. Maxwell, Professor of Law, University of California, Los Angeles.
  Charles J. Meyers, late Dean of the Law School, Stanford University.
  Stephen F. Williams, Judge of the United States Court of Appeals.

ON LAW IN COURTS (1965)
  Paul J. Mishkin, Professor of Law, University of California, Berkeley.
  Clarence Morris, Professor of Law Emeritus, University of Pennsylvania.

PENSION AND EMPLOYEE BENEFIT LAW (1990)
  John H. Langbein, Professor of Law, University of Chicago.
  Bruce A. Wolk, Professor of Law, University of California, Davis.

PLEADING AND PROCEDURE, see Procedure, Civil

UNIVERSITY CASEBOOK SERIES—Continued

POLICE FUNCTION, Fifth Edition (1991)

Reprint of Chapters 1–10 of Miller, Dawson, Dix and Parnas's CRIMINAL JUSTICE ADMINISTRATION, Fourth Edition.

PREPARING AND PRESENTING THE CASE (1981) (Reprinted from THE LAWYERING PROCESS)

Gary Bellow, Professor of Law, Harvard Law School.
Bea Moulton, Legal Services Corporation.

PROCEDURE (1988), with Procedure Supplement (1991)

Robert M. Cover, late Professor of Law, Yale Law School.
Owen M. Fiss, Professor of Law, Yale Law School.
Judith Resnik, Professor of Law, University of Southern California Law Center.

PROCEDURE—CIVIL PROCEDURE, Sixth Edition (1990), with 1991 Supplement

Richard H. Field, late Professor of Law, Harvard University.
Benjamin Kaplan, Professor of Law Emeritus, Harvard University.
Kevin M. Clermont, Professor of Law, Cornell University.

PROCEDURE—CIVIL PROCEDURE, Fifth Edition (1990)

Maurice Rosenberg, Professor of Law, Columbia University.
Hans Smit, Professor of Law, Columbia University.
Rochelle C. Dreyfuss, Professor of Law, New York University.

PROCEDURE—PLEADING AND PROCEDURE: State and Federal, Sixth Edition (1989), with 1990 Case Supplement

David W. Louisell, late Professor of Law, University of California, Berkeley.
Geoffrey C. Hazard, Jr., Professor of Law, Yale University.
Colin C. Tait, Professor of Law, University of Connecticut.

PROCEDURE—FEDERAL RULES OF CIVIL PROCEDURE, 1991 Edition

PRODUCTS LIABILITY AND SAFETY, Second Edition, (1989), with 1989 Statutory Supplement

W. Page Keeton, Professor of Law, University of Texas.
David G. Owen, Professor of Law, University of South Carolina.
John E. Montgomery, Professor of Law, University of South Carolina.
Michael D. Green, Professor of Law, University of Iowa

PROFESSIONAL RESPONSIBILITY, Fifth Edition (1991), with 1991 Selected Standards on Professional Responsibility Supplement

Thomas D. Morgan, Professor of Law, George Washington University.
Ronald D. Rotunda, Professor of Law, University of Illinois.

PROPERTY, Sixth Edition (1990)

John E. Cribbet, Professor of Law, University of Illinois.
Corwin W. Johnson, Professor of Law, University of Texas.
Roger W. Findley, Professor of Law, University of Illinois.
Ernest E. Smith, Professor of Law, University of Texas.

PROPERTY—PERSONAL (1953)

S. Kenneth Skolfield, late Professor of Law Emeritus, Boston University.

PROPERTY—PERSONAL, Third Edition (1954)

Everett Fraser, late Dean of the Law School Emeritus, University of Minnesota.
Third Edition by Charles W. Taintor, late Professor of Law, University of Pittsburgh.

UNIVERSITY CASEBOOK SERIES—Continued

PROPERTY—INTRODUCTION, TO REAL PROPERTY, Third Edition (1954)

Everett Fraser, late Dean of the Law School Emeritus, University of Minnesota.

PROPERTY—FUNDAMENTALS OF MODERN REAL PROPERTY, Second Edition (1982), with 1985 Supplement

Edward H. Rabin, Professor of Law, University of California, Davis.

PROPERTY, REAL (1984), with 1988 Supplement

Paul Goldstein, Professor of Law, Stanford University.

PROSECUTION AND ADJUDICATION, Fourth Edition (1991)

Reprint of Chapters 11–26 of Miller, Dawson, Dix and Parnas's CRIMINAL JUSTICE ADMINISTRATION, Fourth Edition.

PSYCHIATRY AND LAW, see Mental Health, see also Hinckley, Trial of

PUBLIC UTILITY LAW, see Free Enterprise, also Regulated Industries

REAL ESTATE PLANNING, Third Edition (1989), with Revised Problem and Statutory Supplement (1991)

Norton L. Steuben, Professor of Law, University of Colorado.

REAL ESTATE TRANSACTIONS, Revised Second Edition (1988), with Statute, Form and Problem Supplement (1988)

Paul Goldstein, Professor of Law, Stanford University.

RECEIVERSHIP AND CORPORATE REORGANIZATION, see Creditors' Rights

REGULATED INDUSTRIES, Second Edition, (1976)

William K. Jones, Professor of Law, Columbia University.

REMEDIES, Second Edition (1987)

Edward D. Re, Chief Judge, U. S. Court of International Trade.

REMEDIES, (1989)

Elaine W. Shoben, Professor of Law, University of Illinois.
Wm. Murray Tabb, Professor of Law, Baylor University.

SALES, Second Edition (1986)

Marion W. Benfield, Jr., Professor of Law, University of Illinois.
William D. Hawkland, Chancellor, Louisiana State Law Center.

SALES AND SALES FINANCING, Fifth Edition (1984)

John Honnold, Professor of Law, University of Pennsylvania.

SALES LAW AND THE CONTRACTING PROCESS, Second Edition (1991)

(Reprinted from Commercial Transactions, Second Edition (1991)
Alan Schwartz, Professor of Law, Yale University.
Robert E. Scott, Professor of Law, University of Virginia.

SECURED TRANSACTIONS IN PERSONAL PROPERTY, Second Edition (1987) (Reprinted from COMMERCIAL LAW, Second Edition (1987))

Robert L. Jordan, Professor of Law, University of California, Los Angeles.
William D. Warren, Professor of Law, University of California, Los Angeles.

UNIVERSITY CASEBOOK SERIES—Continued

SECURITIES REGULATION, Sixth Edition (1987), with 1990 Selected Statutes, Rules and Forms Supplement and 1990 Cases and Releases Supplement

Richard W. Jennings, Professor of Law, University of California, Berkeley.
Harold Marsh, Jr., Member of California Bar.

SECURITIES REGULATION, Second Edition (1988), with Statute, Rule and Form Supplement (1988)

Larry D. Soderquist, Professor of Law, Vanderbilt University.

SECURITY INTERESTS IN PERSONAL PROPERTY, Second Edition (1987)

Douglas G. Baird, Professor of Law, University of Chicago.
Thomas H. Jackson, Dean of the Law School, University of Virginia.

SECURITY INTERESTS IN PERSONAL PROPERTY (1985) (Reprinted from Sales and Sales Financing, Fifth Edition)

John Honnold, Professor of Law, University of Pennsylvania.

SELECTED STANDARDS ON PROFESSIONAL RESPONSIBILITY, 1991 Edition

SELECTED STATUTES AND INTERNATIONAL AGREEMENTS ON UNFAIR COMPETITION, TRADEMARK, COPYRIGHT AND PATENT, 1989 Edition

SELECTED STATUTES ON TRUSTS AND ESTATES, 1991 Edition

SOCIAL RESPONSIBILITIES OF LAWYERS, Case Studies (1988)

Philip B. Heymann, Professor of Law, Harvard University.
Lance Liebman, Professor of Law, Harvard University.

SOCIAL SCIENCE IN LAW, Second Edition (1990)

John Monahan, Professor of Law, University of Virginia.
Laurens Walker, Professor of Law, University of Virginia.

TAXATION, FEDERAL INCOME (1989)

Stephen B. Cohen, Professor of Law, Georgetown University

TAXATION, FEDERAL INCOME, Second Edition (1988), with 1990 Supplement (Supplement edited in association with Deborah H. Schenk, Professor of Law, New York University)

Michael J. Graetz, Professor of Law, Yale University.

TAXATION, FEDERAL INCOME, Seventh Edition (1991)

James J. Freeland, Professor of Law, University of Florida.
Stephen A. Lind, Professor of Law, University of Florida and University of California, Hastings.
Richard B. Stephens, late Professor of Law Emeritus, University of Florida.

TAXATION, FEDERAL INCOME, Successor Edition (1986), with 1991 Legislative Supplement

Stanley S. Surrey, late Professor of Law, Harvard University.
Paul R. McDaniel, Professor of Law, Boston College.
Hugh J. Ault, Professor of Law, Boston College.
Stanley A. Koppelman, Professor of Law, Boston University.

UNIVERSITY CASEBOOK SERIES—Continued

TAXATION, FEDERAL INCOME, OF BUSINESS ORGANIZATIONS (1991)
> Paul R. McDaniel, Professor of Law, Boston College.
> Hugh J. Ault, Professor of Law, Boston College.
> Martin J. McMahon, Jr., Professor of Law, University of Kentucky.
> Daniel L. Simmons, Professor of Law, University of California, Davis.

TAXATION, FEDERAL INCOME, OF PARTNERSHIPS AND S CORPORATIONS (1991)
> Paul R. McDaniel, Professor of Law, Boston College.
> Hugh J. Ault, Professor of Law, Boston College.
> Martin J. McMahon, Jr., Professor of Law, University of Kentucky.
> Daniel L. Simmons, Professor of Law, University of California, Davis.

TAXATION, FEDERAL INCOME, OIL AND GAS, NATURAL RESOURCES TRANSACTIONS (1990)
> Peter C. Maxfield, Professor of Law, University of Wyoming.
> James L. Houghton, CPA, Partner, Ernst and Young.
> James R. Gaar, CPA, Partner, Ernst and Young.

TAXATION, FEDERAL WEALTH TRANSFER, Successor Edition (1987)
> Stanley S. Surrey, late Professor of Law, Harvard University.
> Paul R. McDaniel, Professor of Law, Boston College.
> Harry L. Gutman, Professor of Law, University of Pennsylvania.

TAXATION, FUNDAMENTALS OF CORPORATE, Third Edition (1991)
> Stephen A. Lind, Professor of Law, University of Florida and University of California, Hastings.
> Stephen Schwarz, Professor of Law, University of California, Hastings.
> Daniel J. Lathrope, Professor of Law, University of California, Hastings.
> Joshua Rosenberg, Professor of Law, University of San Francisco.

TAXATION, FUNDAMENTALS OF PARTNERSHIP, Second Edition (1988)
> Stephen A. Lind, Professor of Law, University of Florida and University of California, Hastings.
> Stephen Schwarz, Professor of Law, University of California, Hastings.
> Daniel J. Lathrope, Professor of Law, University of California, Hastings.
> Joshua Rosenberg, Professor of Law, University of San Francisco.

TAXATION OF CORPORATIONS AND THEIR SHAREHOLDERS (1991)
> David J. Shakow, Professor of Law, University of Pennsylvania.

TAXATION, PROBLEMS IN THE FEDERAL INCOME TAXATION OF PARTNERSHIPS AND CORPORATIONS, Second Edition (1986)
> Norton L. Steuben, Professor of Law, University of Colorado.
> William J. Turnier, Professor of Law, University of North Carolina.

TAXATION, PROBLEMS IN THE FUNDAMENTALS OF FEDERAL INCOME, Second Edition (1985)
> Norton L. Steuben, Professor of Law, University of Colorado.
> William J. Turnier, Professor of Law, University of North Carolina.

TORT LAW AND ALTERNATIVES, Fourth Edition (1987)
> Marc A. Franklin, Professor of Law, Stanford University.
> Robert L. Rabin, Professor of Law, Stanford University.

TORTS, Eighth Edition (1988)
> William L. Prosser, late Professor of Law, University of California, Hastings.
> John W. Wade, Professor of Law, Vanderbilt University.
> Victor E. Schwartz, Adjunct Professor of Law, Georgetown University.

UNIVERSITY CASEBOOK SERIES—Continued

TORTS, Third Edition (1976)
Harry Shulman, late Dean of the Law School, Yale University.
Fleming James, Jr., Professor of Law Emeritus, Yale University.
Oscar S. Gray, Professor of Law, University of Maryland.

TRADE REGULATION, Third Edition (1990)
Milton Handler, Professor of Law Emeritus, Columbia University.
Harlan M. Blake, Professor of Law, Columbia University.
Robert Pitofsky, Professor of Law, Georgetown University.
Harvey J. Goldschmid, Professor of Law, Columbia University.

TRADE REGULATION, see Antitrust

TRANSNATIONAL BUSINESS PROBLEMS (1986)
Detlev F. Vagts, Professor of Law, Harvard University.

TRANSNATIONAL LEGAL PROBLEMS, Third Edition (1986) with 1991 Revised Edition of Documentary Supplement
Henry J. Steiner, Professor of Law, Harvard University.
Detlev F. Vagts, Professor of Law, Harvard University.

TRIAL, see also Evidence, Making the Record, Lawyering Process and Preparing and Presenting the Case

TRUSTS, Sixth Edition (1991)
George G. Bogert, late Professor of Law Emeritus, University of Chicago.
Dallin H. Oaks, President, Brigham Young University.
H. Reese Hansen, Dean and Professor of Law, Brigham Young University.
Claralyn Martin Hill, J.D. Brigham Young University.

TRUSTS AND ESTATES, SELECTED STATUTES ON, 1991 Edition

TRUSTS AND WILLS, See also Decedents' Estates and Trusts, and Family Property Law

UNFAIR COMPETITION, see Competitive Process and Business Torts

WATER RESOURCE MANAGEMENT, Third Edition (1988)
The late Charles J. Meyers, formerly Dean, Stanford University Law School.
A. Dan Tarlock, Professor of Law, IIT Chicago-Kent College of Law.
James N. Corbridge, Jr., Chancellor, University of Colorado at Boulder, and Professor of Law, University of Colorado.
David H. Getches, Professor of Law, University of Colorado.

WILLS AND ADMINISTRATION, Fifth Edition (1961)
Philip Mechem, late Professor of Law, University of Pennsylvania.
Thomas E. Atkinson, late Professor of Law, New York University.

WRITING AND ANALYSIS IN THE LAW, Second Edition (1991)
Helene S. Shapo, Professor of Law, Northwestern University
Marilyn R. Walter, Professor of Law, Brooklyn Law School
Elizabeth Fajans, Writing Specialist, Brooklyn Law School

University Casebook Series

EDITORIAL BOARD

DAVID L. SHAPIRO
DIRECTING EDITOR
Professor of Law, Harvard University

EDWARD L. BARRETT, Jr.
Professor of Law, University of California, Davis

ROBERT C. CLARK
Dean of the School of Law, Harvard University

OWEN M. FISS
Professor of Law, Yale Law School

GERALD GUNTHER
Professor of Law, Stanford University

THOMAS H. JACKSON
Dean of the School of Law, University of Virginia

HARRY W. JONES
Professor of Law, Columbia University

HERMA HILL KAY
Professor of Law, University of California, Berkeley

PAGE KEETON
Professor of Law, University of Texas

ROBERT L. RABIN
Professor of Law, Stanford University

CAROL M. ROSE
Professor of Law, Yale University

CASS R. SUNSTEIN
Professor of Law, University of Chicago

SAMUEL D. THURMAN
Professor of Law, Hastings College of the Law

FIRST AMENDMENT

Cases and Materials

By

WILLIAM W. VAN ALSTYNE
William R. & Thomas S. Perkins Professor of Law
Duke University School of Law

Westbury, New York
THE FOUNDATION PRESS, INC.
1991

COPYRIGHT © 1991 By THE FOUNDATION PRESS, INC.
615 Merrick Ave.
Westbury, N.Y. 11590

All rights reserved
Printed in the United States of America

Library of Congress Cataloging-in-Publication Data

Van Alstyne, William W.
    First Amendment : cases and materials / by William W. Van Alstyne.
    p. cm. — (University casebook series)
    Includes index.
    ISBN 0–88277–879–X
    1. United States—Constitutional law—Amendments—1st—Cases.
2. Freedom of speech—United States—Cases. 3. Freedom of Religion—
United States—Cases. 4. Freedom of the press—United States—
Cases. 5. Civil rights—United States—Cases. I. Title.
II. Series.
KF4558 1st.V36 1991
342.73'085—dc20
[347.30285]
                                                        91–9180

Van Alstyne First Amendment UCB

*This book is dedicated
to
James Madison, Thomas Jefferson,
and John Stuart Mill*

PREFACE

Twenty years ago, cases and materials devoted to the fourth, fifth, and sixth amendments to the Constitution became separated from basic courses in constitutional law. The same trend is now well underway in respect to the first amendment—the amendment that concerns our rights of free speech, of peaceable assembly, petition, and of the press, of religion, and of the separation of church and state. As we mark the beginning of the third century of the Bill of Rights in 1991, the first amendment has become something of a subject unto itself. Now it, too, tends to be taught subsequent to the basic constitutional law course.

The cases and materials presented here respond to this trend. Their aim is to capture the principal lines of historical, philosophical, and doctrinal first amendment development, and the primary first amendment case law of the Supreme Court. They mean to be serviceable in a separate two or three hour semester course on the constitutional law of church and state, and of speech and press in the United States.

At the same time, these materials sometimes refer to connecting cases and doctrines of constitutional law covered in a basic first year course. These connecting references are meant to be helpful in providing a sense of fit between the first amendment and that larger body of fundamental law. The first amendment, to paraphrase John Donne, is not an island. It is rather, a piece of a continent, a part of the main. Because that is so, I think it is a mistake to isolate first amendment cases and materials too completely from the main body of constitutional law. There are strong consistencies of jurisprudence in nearly every constitutional system. There are—or ought to be—certain common constitutional themes that recur in our courts that need an accounting as much in respect to first amendment adjudications as they do in other settings, whether they go to such technical matters as standing, or to such general matters as separation of powers, federalism, equal protection, or proper standards of judicial review. Those ties are reflected in these materials as well.

This is not a treatise, of course, but primarily a classroom resource. In keeping with this purpose, the principal cases (approximately 120) are edited sparingly. The point is to permit these cases to stimulate, rather than to substitute for, a generous and critical discussion in class. An additional number of cases—approximately 250 more—are supplied in footnotes where they properly belong. Secondary sources are provided at intervals, and so, too, with various questions and comments. The organization of the book is equally straightforward. Its aim is to track the historical and adjudicative evolution of first amendment doctrines with at least ordinary fidelity to the manner in which they have appeared during two centuries of judicial review. The point in proceeding in this way is not to eschew critical judgment of one's own. Rather, it is to

PREFACE

reserve to each teacher and student their own worthy opinion as to whether these doctrines and developments are truly sound, once they come to terms with the Supreme Court's own approach. Insofar as it provides some useful basis for doing so, it will fulfill its task.

WILLIAM VAN ALSTYNE

Durham, North Carolina
December 15, 1990

SUMMARY OF CONTENTS

	Page
PREFACE	xxi
TABLE OF CASES	xxxi
CASES CITED IN FOOTNOTES	xxxv
CONSTITUTION OF THE UNITED STATES	xli

CHAPTER 1. AN INTRODUCTION TO THE FIRST AMENDMENT 1

Continuity With the Basic Course in Constitutional Law I and the Argument Favoring Absolute Protection of Free Speech 1
The Argument of the Amendment as a [Mere] Common Law Clause 6
The Uncertainties of the First Amendment When Adopted 17
Coda to "The Introduction to the First Amendment": *Other* Clauses Related to Freedom of Speech and of the Press 21

CHAPTER 2. THE FIRST AMENDMENT IN FORMATIVE TRANSITION AND THE CENTRALITY OF UNTRAMMELED SOCIAL ADVOCACY IN THE UNITED STATES 29

A. "Bad Tendency and Legislative Deference" versus "Clear and Present Danger" 29
B. Politics, Privacy, Libel, and Tort Law 155
C. Politics and "Symbolic" Dissent 224

CHAPTER 3. THE FIRST AMENDMENT IN SPECIFIC ENVIRONMENTS 287

A. The Government as Employer, Contractor, Purchaser of Services, and Provider of Benefits 287
B. A Return to the Early Holmes and the Right-Privilege Distinction of *McAuliffe v. Mayor of New Bedford* 291
C. The Unconstitutional Conditions Doctrine 292
D. A Reprise on the Problem: Applying the *"Connick"* Test 328
E. The Government's Management of Public Property: First Amendment Rights of Access and Use 382
F. Coerced Expression and Freedom Not to Speak 535
G. Equalizing Freedom of Speech by Leveling Expenditures and Contributions—Regulating the Uses of Money and Speech 559

CHAPTER 4. THE FIRST AMENDMENT AND THE LESSER PROTECTION OF NONPOLITICAL SPEECH IN THE UNITED STATES 601

A. Commercial Speech 601
B. The Uncertainties of Regulating or Criminalizing the "Obscene" 669

SUMMARY OF CONTENTS

Page

CHAPTER 5. AN INTRODUCTION TO THE CHURCH–STATE CLAUSES OF THE FIRST AMENDMENT 760

Introduction 760

CHAPTER 6. "CONGRESS SHALL MAKE NO LAW RESPECTING AN ESTABLISHMENT OF RELIGION. . ." 767

A. The General Test(s) 767
B. The General Test Refined 802
C. The General Test Modified and in Dispute 861

CHAPTER 7. ". . . OR PROHIBITING THE FREE EXERCISE THEREOF" 929

A. The General Test 929
B. The General Test Modified and in Dispute 953

CHAPTER 8. DEFINING "RELIGION" 1022

Introductory Note 1022

Index 1043

TABLE OF CONTENTS

	Page
Preface	xxi
Table of Cases	xxxi
Cases Cited in Footnotes	xxxv
Constitution of the United States	xli

CHAPTER 1. AN INTRODUCTION TO THE FIRST AMENDMENT 1

Continuity With the Basic Course in Constitutional Law I and the Argument Favoring Absolute Protection of Free Speech 1
    The Unqualified Language of First Amendment Text 1
    The Comparison with other National Constitutions 3
    The Comparison with other Bill of Rights Clauses 5
    The Views of Justice Hugo Black 5
The Argument of the Amendment as a [Mere] Common Law Clause .. 6
    Patterson v. Colorado (1908) 6
    Blackstone's Commentaries on Freedom of the Press 11
    Qualified Language of First Amendment Text 13
The Uncertainties of the First Amendment When Adopted 17
    A Restriction on Congress, Not on the States 18
    A Summary of Three Graphically Distinct Orientations 20
Coda to "The Introduction to the First Amendment": *Other* Clauses Related to Freedom of Speech and of the Press 21

CHAPTER 2. THE FIRST AMENDMENT IN FORMATIVE TRANSITION AND THE CENTRALITY OF UNTRAMMELED SOCIAL ADVOCACY IN THE UNITED STATES 29

A. "Bad Tendency and Legislative Deference" versus "Clear and Present Danger" 29
    Schenck v. United States 29
    The Clear and Present Danger Test: Pitfalls and Problems .. 31
    Masses Publishing Co. v. Patten 35
    Abrams v. United States 41
    Gitlow v. People of New York 49
    Notes on the Answer Provided by *Gitlow v. New York* to the Unaddressed Question in *Patterson v. California* 54
    Whitney v. California 69
    Bridges v. California 75
    A Brief Summary Note on *Bridges v. California* 85
    Sheppard v. Maxwell 87
    Wood v. Georgia 93
    Nebraska Press Association v. Stuart 99
    Seattle Times Company v. Rhinehart 106

TABLE OF CONTENTS

Page

A. "Bad Tendency and Legislative Deference" versus "Clear and Present Danger"—Continued
- *New York Times Company v. United States* — 111
- Note — 122
- *Dennis v. United States* — 122
- A Brief Note on the *Dennis* Case — 140
- *Brandenburg v. Ohio* — 142
- *Hess v. Indiana* — 147
- *Cohen v. California* — 149

B. Politics, Privacy, Libel, and Tort Law — 155
- *New York Times Company v. Sullivan* — 158
- Note — 171
- *Time, Inc. v. Hill* — 173
- Note — 179
- *Gertz v. Robert Welch, Inc.* — 182
- *Dun & Bradstreet, Inc. v. Greenmoss Builder, Inc.* — 197
- *Miami Herald Publishing Company v. Tornillo* — 205
- *Hustler Magazine v. Falwell* — 209
- Note — 215
- *American Booksellers Association, Inc. v. Hudnut* — 218

C. Politics and "Symbolic" Dissent — 224
- *Tinker v. Des Moines Independent Community School District* — 224
- *United States v. O'Brien* — 233
- *Clark v. Community for Creative Non-Violence* — 240
- A Note on "Symbolic Expression" and the "*O'Brien* Test" — 251
- *Schacht v. United States* — 256
- *Spence v. State of Washington* — 259
- *Texas v. Johnson* — 268
- Notes on Protecting the Flag of the United States — 284

CHAPTER 3. THE FIRST AMENDMENT IN SPECIFIC ENVIRONMENTS — 287

A. The Government as Employer, Contractor, Purchaser of Services, and Provider of Benefits — 287

B. A Return to the Early Holmes and the Right-Privilege Distinction of *McAuliffe v. Mayor of New Bedford* — 291
- *Scopes v. Tennessee* — 291

C. The Unconstitutional Conditions Doctrine — 292
- *Pickering v. Board of Education* — 294
- *United States Civil Service Commission v. National Association of Letter Carriers* — 301
- *Mt. Healthy City School District Board of Education v. Doyle* — 308
- *Givhan v. Western Line Consolidated School District* — 311
- *Connick v. Myers* — 313
- *Rankin v. McPherson* — 321

TABLE OF CONTENTS

	Page
D. A Reprise on the Problem: Applying the "*Connick*" Test	328
Board of Education v. Pico	333
Snepp v. United States	348
United States v. Robel	354
Elrod v. Burns	358
Branti v. Finkel	371
E. The Government's Management of Public Property: First Amendment Rights of Access and Use	382
1. Government-Held Property and Free Speech Access and Use: Public Forum Doctrine and the First Amendment	383
Davis v. Commonwealth	387
Hague v. Committee for Industrial Organization	390
Schneider v. State	394
Note	398
2. Time, Place, and Manner Regulation	399
Niemotko v. Maryland	399
Kunz v. New York	404
Feiner v. New York	410
Note	415
United States v. Grace	415
City Council v. Taxpayers for Vincent	421
Ward v. Rock Against Racism	431
3. Forum Analysis	440
Southeastern Promotions, Ltd. v. Conrad	440
Perry Education Association v. Perry Local Educators' Association	447
Cornelius v. NAACP Legal Defense & Educational Fund	457
Hazelwood School District v. Kuhlmeier	471
4. A "Forum" Discussion and Review	481
United States v. Kokinda	484
5. Who Owns the Airwaves?	486
Red Lion Broadcasting Co. v. FCC	486
6. Notes on *Red Lion* and "Public Forum" Use	490
7. The First Amendment as a "Freedom of Information" Act	498
Houchins v. KQED, Inc.	498
Richmond Newspapers, Inc. v. Virginia	507
8. The Blurred Boundary Between Private and Public Property	517
Marsh v. Alabama	517
Note	520
Hudgens v. NLRB	522
PruneYard Shopping Center v. Robins	527
F. Coerced Expression and Freedom Not to Speak	535
West Virginia Board of Education v. Barnette	535
Wooley v. Maynard	544
Abood v. Detroit Board of Education	549
Note	557

TABLE OF CONTENTS

Page

G. Equalizing Freedom of Speech by Levelling Expenditures and Contributions—Regulating the Uses of Money and Speech 559
    Buckley v. Valeo 559
    Citizens Against Rent Control v. Berkeley 587
    Federal Election Commission v. National Conservative Political Action Committee 591
    Note 599

CHAPTER 4. THE FIRST AMENDMENT AND THE LESSER PROTECTION OF NONPOLITICAL SPEECH IN THE UNITED STATES 601

A. Commercial Speech 601
    Commercial Speech in the Supreme Court 601
    Valentine v. Christensen 604
    Bigelow v. Virginia 605
    Virginia State Board of Pharmacy v. Virginia Citizens Council 610
    Zauderer v. Office of Disciplinary Counsel of the Supreme Court of Ohio 625
    Central Hudson Gas & Electric Corporation v. Public Service Commission 636
    Bolger v. Youngs Drug Products Corporation 650
    Posados de Puerto Rico Associates v. Tourism Company of Puerto Rico 659
    Note 667
B. The Uncertainties of Regulating or Criminalizing the "Obscene" 669
    "Obscenity" and the First Amendment 669
    Roth v. United States 678
    Alberts v. California 678
    Smith v. California 692
    Kingsley International Pictures Corporation v. Regents of the University of the State of New York 698
    A Book Named "John Cleland's Memoirs of a Woman of Pleasure" v. Attorney General of Massachusetts 700
    Ginzburg v. United States 708
    Mishkin v. New York 715
    Redrup v. New York 718
    Stanley v. Georgia 720
    Miller v. California 726
    Paris Adult Theatre I v. Slaton 735
    New York v. Ferber 741
    Jenkins v. Georgia 753
    A Concluding Note 756

TABLE OF CONTENTS

CHAPTER 5. AN INTRODUCTION TO THE CHURCH–STATE CLAUSES OF THE FIRST AMENDMENT 760
Introduction 760
   Frothingham v. Mellon 762
   Flast v. Cohen 762

CHAPTER 6. "CONGRESS SHALL MAKE NO LAW RESPECTING AN ESTABLISHMENT OF RELIGION..." 767
A. The General Test(s) 767
   Everson v. Board of Education 767
   Notes on the *Everson* Opinions 784
     1. Other Clauses *re* Religion 784
     2. The Blaine Amendment, State Constitutions, and the Controversy Respecting the Fourteenth Amendment 785
     3. The *Everson* Test 787
   Illinois Ex Rel. McCollum v. Board of Education 789
   Zorach v. Clauson 792
   Engel v. Vitale 796
B. The General Test Refined 802
   School District of Abington Tp. v. Schempp 802
   Lemon v. Kurtzman 822
   Tilton v. Richardson 830
   Walz v. Tax Commission of the City of New York 835
   Board of Education of Central School District v. Allen 845
   Wolman v. Walter 854
C. The General Test Modified and in Dispute 861
   Mueller v. Allen 861
   Notes on the Establishment Clause and "Theocracy" 869
     1. Enforcing God's Laws as the Law of the Civil State 869
   McGowan v. Maryland 873
   Note 887
     2. Religion in Government 889
   Marsh v. Chambers 889
   Lynch, Mayor of Pawtucket v. Donnelly 898
   County of Allegheny v. American Civil Liberties Union 912
   Note 926

CHAPTER 7. "... OR PROHIBITING THE FREE EXERCISE THEREOF" 929
A. The General Test 929
   Reynolds v. United States 929
   Cantwell v. Connecticut 933
   Prince v. Massachusetts 939
   United States v. Ballard 946

TABLE OF CONTENTS

	Page
B. The General Test Modified and in Dispute	953
Wisconsin v. Yoder	953
Sherbert v. Verner	966
An Extended Note on *Sherbert v. Verner*	974
Goldman v. Weinberger	979
Lyng v. Northwest Indian Cemetery Protective Association	990
Jimmy Swaggart Ministries v. Board of Equalization of California	999
Employment Division, Department of Human Resources of Oregon v. Smith	1006

CHAPTER 8. DEFINING "RELIGION" 1022

Introductory Note 1022
Torcaso v. Watkins 1025
United States v. Seeger 1027
Welsh v. United States 1032

Index 1043

TABLE OF CASES

Principal cases are in italic type. Non-principal cases are in roman type. References are to Pages. Cases cited in text only.

Abood v. Detroit Bd. of Educ., 549, 557
A Book Named 'John Cleland's Memoirs of a Woman of Pleasure' v. Attorney General of Com. of Mass., 674, 700
Abrams v. United States, 41, 85, 388
Adamson v. People of State of California, 56, 57, 58, 59, 60, 62, 63
Alberts v. California, 678
Allegheny, County of v. American Civil Liberties Union Greater Pittsburgh Chapter, 912
American Booksellers Ass'n, Inc. v. Hudnut, 218

Ballard, United States v., 946
Bates v. State Bar of Arizona, 669
Bigelow v. Virginia, 605
Board of Airport Com'rs of City of Los Angeles v. Jews for Jesus, Inc., 483
Board of Ed. of Central School Dist. No. 1 v. Allen, 845
Board of Educ., Island Trees Union Free School Dist. No. 26 v. Pico, 333
Bolger v. Youngs Drug Products Corp., 650
Brandenburg v. Ohio, 142, 156
Branti v. Finkel, 371
Braunfeld v. Brown, 975
Bridges v. California, 75, 85, 122, 140
Buckley v. Valeo, 559, 599
Burleson, United States ex rel. Milwaukee Social Democratic Pub. Co. v., 390

Cantwell v. Connecticut, 933
Carolene Products Co, United States v., 603
Central Hudson Gas & Elec. Corp. v. Public Service Com'n of New York, 636, 668, 669, 671
Chaplinsky v. State of New Hampshire, 669, 670, 671, 672, 673
Chicago, B. & Q. R. Co. v. City of Chicago, 67
Citizens Against Rent Control/Coalition for Fair Housing v. City of Berkley, Cal., 587
Clark v. Community for Creative Non-Violence, 240
Clayton by Clayton v. Place, 887
Cohen v. California, 149
Commonwealth of (see name of Commonwealth)
Connick v. Myers, 313, 328, 330

Cornelius v. NAACP Legal Defense and Educational Fund, Inc., 457
County of (see name of county)

Davis v. Massachusetts, 382, 388, 390
Dennis v. United States, 122, 140, 141
Dun & Bradstreet, Inc. v. Greenmoss Builders, Inc., 197

Elrod v. Burns, 358
Employment Div., Dept. of Human Resources of Oregon v. Smith, 1006
Engel v. Vitale, 796
Epperson v. Arkansas, 887
Everson v. Board of Education of Ewing Tp., 766, 767, 784, 786, 788, 1024

Falwell v. Flynt, 216
Federal Election Com'n v. National Conservative Political Action Committee, 591, 599
Feiner v. People of State of New York, 410
Flast v. Cohen, 763, 764, 765, 766
Freedman v. Maryland, 677
Frost v. Railroad Commission of State of California, 293
Frothingham v. Mellon, 262, 763, 764

Gertz v. Robert Welch, Inc., 182
Ginzburg v. United States, 674, 708
Gitlow v. People of State of New York, 49, 54, 55, 56, 57, 58, 63, 64, 65, 67, 68, 85, 122
Givhan v. Western Line Consol. School Dist., 311, 330
Goldman v. Weinberger, 979
Grace, United States v., 415
Griswold v. Connecticut, 2

Hague v. Committee for Industrial Organization, 382, 390, 398
Hazelwood School Dist. v. Kuhlmeier, 471
Hess v. Indiana, 147
Hicklin, Regina v., 675
Houchins v. KQED, Inc., 498
Hudgens v. N. L. R. B., 522
Hustler Magazine v. Falwell, 209, 217

In re (see name of party)

Jenkins v. Georgia, 753, 757

xxxi

TABLE OF CASES

Jimmy Swaggart Ministries v. Board of Equalization of California, 999

Keller v. State Bar of California, 557
Kingsley Intern. Pictures Corp. v. Regents of N.Y.U., 698
Kokinda, United States v., 484
Kunz v. People of State of New York, 404

Lemon v. Kurtzman, 822, 873
Lochner v. People of State of New York, 603
Lovell v. City of Griffin, Ga., 398
Lynch v. Donnelly, 898
Lyng v. Northwest Indian Cemetery Protective Ass'n, 990

Marsh v. Chambers, 889
Marsh v. State of Alabama, 517, 520, 521, FWJ 473
Massachusetts, Com. of v. Mellon, 292, 762, 763
Masses Pub. Co. v. Patten, 35
McAuliffe v. Mayor, Etc., of City of New Bedford, 291, 292, 387
McDaniel v. Paty, 871
McGowan v. Maryland, 873, 887, 975
Members of City Council of City of Los Angeles v. Taxpayers for Vincent, 421
Miami Herald Pub. Co. v. Tornillo, 205, 386, 490, 491, 492, 493, 494
Miller v. California, 674, 675, 676, 726, 757
Milwaukee Social Democratic Pub. Co., United States ex rel. v. Burleson, 390
Mishkin v. State of New York, 715
Mt. Healthy City School Dist. Bd. of Ed. v. Doyle, 308, 330
Mueller v. Allen, 861

Nebbia v. People of State of New York, 603
Nebraska Press Ass'n v. Stuart, 99
New York v. Ferber, 741
New York Times Co. v. Sullivan, 157, 158, 171, 173, 180, 216, 290, 328, 491, 603
New York Times Co. v. United States, 111
Niemotko v. State of Maryland, 399

O'Brien, United States v., 233
Ohralik v. Ohio State Bar Ass'n, 669

Paris Adult Theatre I v. Slaton, 675, 676, 735, 757
Patterson v. People of State of Colorado ex rel. Attorney General of State of Colorado, 6, 11, 14, 15, 17, 20, 21, 54, 58, 65, 85, 387
Pell v. Procunier, 501
People of State of Illinois ex rel. McCollum v. Board of Education of School Dist. No. 71, Champaign County, Ill., 789
Perry Educ. Ass'n v. Perry Local Educators' Ass'n, 447, 482

Pickering v. Board of Ed. of Township High School Dist. 205, Will County, Illinois, 294, 328, 330
Posadas de Puerto Rico Associates v. Tourism Co. of Puerto Rico, 659, 667, 668, 669
Prince v. Commonwealth of Massachusetts, 939, 975
PruneYard Shopping Center v. Robins, 527

Railway Express Agency v. People of State of New York, 603, 671
Rankin v. McPherson, 321, 328, 330
Red Lion Broadcasting Co. v. F. C. C., 486, 490, 491, 492, 493, 494, 495, 497
Redrup v. State of New York, 718
Regina v. ——— (see opposing party)
Reynolds v. United States, 929
Richmond Newspapers, Inc. v. Virginia, 507
Robel, United States v., 354
Roe v. Wade, 2
Roth v. United States, 675, 678

Schacht v. United States, 256
Schenck v. United States, 29, 33, 34, 85, 388
Schneider v. New Jersey, 394, 398, 399
School Dist. of Abington Tp., Pa. v. Schempp, 802
Scopes v. State, 291, 292
Seattle Times Co. v. Rhinehart, 106
Seeger, United States v., 1027
Sheppard v. Maxwell, 87
Sherbert v. Verner, 966, 974, 977, 979, 1010
Slaughter–House Cases, In re, 83 U.S. 36, p. 68
Slaughter–House Cases, In re, 77 U.S. 273, p. 786
Smith v. People of the State of California, 677, 692
Snepp v. United States, 348
Southeastern Promotions, Ltd. v. Conrad, 440
Spence v. Washington, 259
Stanley v. Georgia, 720
Stone v. Graham, 887

Texas v. Johnson, 268, 284, 285
Thomas v. Review Bd. of Indiana Employment Sec. Div., 1010
Tilton v. Richardson, 830
Time, Inc. v. Hill, 173, 180, 182
Tinker v. Des Moines Independent Community School Dist., 224
Torcaso v. Watkins, 1025

United States v. ——— (see opposing party)
United States Civil Service Commission v. National Ass'n of Letter Carriers, AFL–CIO, 301
United States ex rel. v. ——— (see opposing party and relator)

TABLE OF CASES

Valentine v. Chrestensen, 603, 604, 669, 671
Virginia State Bd. of Pharmacy v. Virginia Citizens Consumer Council, Inc., 610, 668, 671

Walz v. Tax Commission of City of New York, 835
Ward v. Rock Against Racism, 431
Welsh v. United States, 1032
West Virginia State Board of Education v. Barnette, 535

Whitney v. People of State of California, 69, 85, 122
Wisconsin v. Yoder, 953
Wolman v. Walter, 854
Wood v. Georgia, 93
Wooley v. Maynard, 544

Zauderer v. Office of Disciplinary Counsel of Supreme Court of Ohio, 625, 669
Zorach v. Clauson, 792

CASES CITED IN FOOTNOTES

Cases cited in footnotes only.

Abrams v. United States, 17, 32, 69, 76, 156, 389
Adamson v. California, 55, 57, 60, 62
Adderley v. Florida, 228, 383, 427
Adler v. Board of Education of the City of New York, 293, 363
Africa v. Pennsylvania, 1023
Alberts v. California, 673, 677
Allgeyer v. Louisiana, 67
Amalgamated Food Employees Union v. Logan Valley Plaza, 386
American Arab Anti-Discrimination Committee v. Meese, 65
American Booksellers Ass'n, Inc. v. Hudnut, 758
American Communications Association v. Douds, 363
Apodaca v. Oregon, 57
Arnett v. Kennedy, 288
Ashwander v. TVA, 1031
Austin v. Michigan Chamber of Commerce, 600

Bailey v. Richardson, 293, 672
Bantam Books, Inc. v. Sullivan, 388, 677
Banzhaf v. FCC, 619
Barenblatt v. United States, 5
Barron v. Baltimore, 18, 60
Bates v. State Bar of Arizona, 631, 639, 669
Beauharnais v. Illinois, 113, 223
Beckley Newspapers Corp. v. Hanks, 172
Bethel School District No. 403 v. Fraser, 331
Blackwell v. Issaquena County Board of Education, 225
Board of Airport Commissioners v. Jews for Jesus, Inc., 481
Board of Education v. Barnette, 360, 374
Board of Education v. Pico, 383, 385
Boos v. Barry, 271
Bowers v. Hardwick, 759, 873
Boyd v. United States, 24
Brandenburg v. Ohio, 156, 483
Branzburg v. Hayes, 505
Braunfeld v. Brown, 975, 979
Brenneman v. Madigan, 504
Bridges v. California, 65, 79, 85, 94, 95, 513
Briscoe v. Reader's Digest Ass'n, 180
Broadrick v. Oklahoma, 639
Brotherhood of R.R. Trainmen v. Virginia, 27
Brown v. Glines, 984
Brown v. Louisiana, 228, 249, 383

Brown v. Oklahoma, 672
Buckley v. Valeo, 374, 587, 600, 763
Burnet v. Coronado Oil & Gas Company, 65
Burnside v. Byars, 225
Burstyn, Inc. v. Wilson, 759
Burton v. Crowell Pub. Co., 216
Burton v. Wilmington Parking Authority, 520, 521
Busey v. District of Columbia, 940
Butler v. Michigan, 655, 675, 709

Cafeteria Workers v. McElroy, 374
California v. LaRue, 758
California Motor Transport Company v. Trucking Unlimited, 27
Camarano v. United States, 266
Cantrell v. Forest City Publishing Company, 180
Cantwell v. Connecticut, 620, 670, 672
Capital Broadcasting Company v. Acting Attorney General, 664
Capital Broadcasting Company v. Mitchell, 664
Capital Cities Cable, Inc. v. Crisp, 664
Carroll v. President and Commissioners of Princess Anne County, 388, 678
CBS v. Democratic National Committee, 494, 495
Central Hudson Gas & Electric Corporation v. Public Service Comm'n of New York, 654, 672
Chaplinsky v. New Hampshire, 669, 672, 943
Chicago, Burlington and Quincy Railroad Company v. Chicago, 66, 67
Citizens Against Rent Control v. Berkeley, 600
City Council of Los Angeles v. Taxpayers for Vincent, 249, 250, 251, 483
City of Lakewood v. Plain Dealer Publishing Company, 385, 388
City of Madison, Jt. Sch. Dist. v. Wisconsin Public Employment Relations Commission, 449
City of Newport v. Iacobucci, 758
Clancy v. Daily News Corporation, 179
Clark v. Community for Creative Non-Violence, 254
Clayton v. Place, 888
Cleveland City Board of Education v. Loudermill, 288
Cohen v. California, 141, 399, 483, 672, 759
Collin v. Smith, 223

Commonwealth v. Davis, 387
Commonwealth v. Holmes, 702
Connick v. Myers, 328, 672
Consolidated Edison Co. v. Public Service Comm'n, 638
Cornelius v. NAACP Legal Defense & Education Fund, 483, 672
County of Allegheny v. ACLU, 787, 926
Cox v. Louisiana, 228
Cox v. New Hampshire, 943
Cox Broadcasting Corporation v. Cohn, 110, 181
Crowell v. Benson, 1031

Davidson v. New Orleans, 66, 67
Davis v. Beason, 935
Davis v. Commonwealth, 387, 388, 672
Debs v. United States, 32
De Jonge v. Oregon, 27, 28
Dean Milk Company v. Madison, 414
Den v. Hoboken Land & Development Company, 65
Dennis v. United States, 144, 389, 483
Donaldson v. Read Magazine, 619
Doubleday & Company v. New York, 689
Doyle v. Continental Insurance Company, 293
Dred Scott v. Sandford, 59, 65
Dun & Bradstreet, Inc. v. Grove, 619
Dunagin v. City of Oxford, Miss., 664
Duncan v. Louisiana, 57, 62
Dworkin v. Hustler Magazine, Inc., 217

E.F. Drew & Company v. FTC, 619
Eastern R.R. Presidents Conference v. Noerr Motor Freight, 27
Edwards v. Aguillard, 1023
Edwards v. South Carolina, 228
Eisenbadt v. Baird, 653
Elrod v. Burns, 367, 375, 378
Engel v. Vitale, 578, 922
Entick v. Carrington, 24
Epperson v. Arkansas, 873
Estate of Thornton v. Calder, 978
Evans v. Newton, 520
Everson v. Board of Education, 578, 766, 975

Falwell v. Flynt, 215
FCC v. Pacifica Foundation, 251, 494
Feiner v. New York, 402
Fellowship of Humanity v. County of Alameda, 1026
First English Evangelical Lutheran Church of Glendale v. County of Los Angeles, 67
First National Bank of Boston v. Bellotti, 65, 600
Flast v. Cohen, 762
Florida Star v. B.J.F., 181
Fort Wayne Books, Inc. v. Indiana, 677
Founding Church of Scientology v. United States, 1024

Frazee v. Illinois Department of Employment Security, 979
Freedman v. Maryland, 388, 642, 677, 678
Frohwerk v. United States, 32
Frost & Frost Trucking Company v. Railroad Commission, 293, 330
Frothingham v. Mellon, 762, 801
FTC v. Standard Education Society, 619

Gardiner v. A.H. Robins Co., 629
Gardner v. Los Angeles Board, 363
Garrison v. Louisiana, 114, 171
Gerende v. Board of Supervisors, 363
Gertz v. Robert Welch, Inc., 180, 200
Gibson v. Florida Legislative Investigation Committee, 355
Ginsberg v. New York, 675, 758
Ginzburg v. United States, 675, 758
Gitlow v. New York, 32, 57, 69, 262
Givhan v. Western Line Consolidated School District, 316, 318
Gooding v. Wilson, 672
Green v. McElroy, 355
Greer v. Spock, 383
Griffin v. California, 57
Griswold v. Connecticut, 1, 2, 3, 5, 653, 760
Groppi v. Wisconsin, 104

Hague v. CIO, 27, 414, 672
Halter v. Nebraska, 262, 267, 275
Hammond v. South Carolina State College, 228
Hannegan v. Esquire, Inc., 389
Harmon v. Drener, 771
Harris v. McRae, 288, 385
Hartsville Cotton Mill v. South Carolina Employment Security Commission, 971
Hazelwood School District v. Kuhlmeier, 331
Heffron v. International Society for Krishna Consciousness, Inc., 249
Heller v. New York, 24
Helvering v. Griffiths, 536
Herbert v. Lando, 110
Herndon v. Lowry, 939
Hobbie v. Unemployment Commission of Florida, 979
Hudgens Hardware v. NLRB, 386
Hustler Magazine v. Falwell, 172, 672
Hutchinson v. Proxmire, 22
Hyde v. City of Columbia, 181

Illinois State Employees Union v. Lewis, 365
Interstate Railway v. Massachusetts, 772

Ex parte, Jackson, 688
Jacobellis v. Ohio, 731
Jacobson v. Massachusetts, 942
Jamison v. Texas, 940
Jenkins v. Georgia, 676, 758
Judd v. Board of Education of Union Free School District, 870

CASES CITED IN FOOTNOTES

Judson Mills v. South Carolina Unemployment Compensation Commission, 971

Katz v. United States, 491
Keeton v. Hustler Magazine, Inc., 172
Keller v. State Bar of California, 549
Kennedy v. Mendoza-Martinez, 238
Keyishian v. Board of Regents, 293, 363
Kingsley Intern. Pictures Corp. v. Regents of Univ. State of N.Y., 758, 759
Kunz v. New York, 388, 402, 638, 672

Lamont v. Postmaster General, 390, 506, 676
Largent v. Texas, 940
Lathrop v. Donohue, 577
Layne v. Tribune Company, 179
Lemon v. Kurtzman, 873, 903
Lewis v. New Orleans, 672
Linmark Associates, Inc. v. Willingsboro, 654
Liverpool, N.Y. & P.S.S. Company v. Commissioners of Emigration, 768
Lochner v. New York, 2, 67
Lovell v. Griffin, 388
Lynch v. Donnelly, 924, 926

Machinists v. Street, 551, 577
Maher v. Roe, 385
Malloy v. Hogan, 57
Malnak v. Yogi, 1024
Marcus v. Search Warrant, 24
Marsh v. Alabama, 250, 386, 521
Marsh v. Chambers, 765
Martin v. Struthers, 250
Massachusetts v. Mellon, 288, 293
Masses Publishing Company v. Patten, 32, 73, 141, 156
Mathews v. Eldridge, 532
McAuliffe v. Mayor of New Bedford, 291, 330, 672
McCollum v. Board of Education, 1040
M'Cullouch v. Maryland, 3
McDaniel v. Paty, 870, 872, 1010
McGowan v. Maryland, 975
McMullen v. Carson, 325
Meachum v. Fano, 532
Memoirs v. Attorney General of Massachusetts, 674
Meyers v. Nebraska, 291
Miami Herald Publishing Company v. Tornillo, 173, 181, 619
Mishkin v. New York, 759
Miklovich v. Lorain Journal Company, 216
Miller v. California, 674, 675, 676, 677, 750, 751, 758
Milwaukee Social Democratic Publishing Company v. Burleson, 389, 688
Missouri Pacific Railway v. Nebraska, 66
Monitor Patriot Company v. Roy, 179
Monroe v. State Court of Fulton County, 271

Mt. Healthy City Board of Education v. Doyle, 317, 337, 672
Murdock v. Pennsylvania, 940
Musser v. Utah, 33

NAACP v. Alabama, 162
NAACP v. Button, 27
National Commission on Egg Nutrition v. FTC, 652
Near v. Minnesota, 68, 937
Nebbia v. New York, 2, 688
New York v. Ferber, 675
New York v. P.J. Video, Inc., 24
New York State Liquor Auth. v. Bellanca, 758
New York Times Company v. Sullivan, 5, 113, 171, 172, 180, 182, 223, 328, 531, 578, 619, 671
New York Times Company v. United States, 619
Newcomb v. Brennan, 377
Niemotko v. Maryland, 388
NLRB v. General Motors, 551
Noto v. United States, 140

Oklahoma Telecasters Association v. Crisp, 664
Olmstead v. United States, 491
Olsen v. Iowa, 1020

Pacific Gas & Electric Company v. City of Berkeley, 587
Palko v. Connecticut, 63
Palmore v. Sidoti, 1010
Papish v. Board of Curators of University of Missouri, 331, 474
Parducci v. Rutland, 331
Paris Adult Theatre I v. Slaton, 675, 676, 728
Patterson v. Colorado, 13, 17, 25, 68, 78
Pell v. Procunier, 512
Pennsylvania State Board of Pharmacy v. Pastor, 616
Perry Local Educators' Association v. Hohlt, 457, 481, 483
Pickering v. Board of Education, 330, 672
Pierce v. Society of Sisters, 670
Pinkus v. United States, 675
Pittsburgh Press Company v. Human Relations Commission, 619, 631
Pope v. Illinois, 758
Powell v. McCormack, 872
Princeton University v. Schmid, 386
Pruneyard Shopping Center v. Robins, 386
Public Clearing House v. Coyne, 688
Public S.R. Company v. Public Utility Commissioners, 772

Quaker Action Group v. Morton, 249
Quantity of Books v. Kansas, 24
Queensgate Investment Company v. Liquor Control Commission, 664

CASES CITED IN FOOTNOTES

Railway Employees' Department v. Hanson, 551
Railway Express Agency v. New York, 602
Red Lion Broadcasting Company v. FCC, 494
Redrup v. New York, 673, 720, 759
Renwick v. News and Observer Pub. Co., 180
Retail Clerks v. Schermerhorn, 555
Rex v. Secretary of Home Affairs, *Ex parte* O'Brien, 73
Reynolds v. United States, 769, 935, 975
Rochin v. California, 56
Roe v. Wade, 1, 3, 5
Rosenfeld v. New Jersey, 672
Roth v. United States, 69, 113, 673, 674, 677, 726, 727
Rowan v. Post Office Department, 390
Rutan v. Republican Party of Illinois, 367

Sable Communications of California, Inc. v. FCC, 675, 1010
Saia v. New York, 388
St. Amant v. Thompson, 172
San Francisco Arts & Athletics v. Olympic Committee, 275
Saxbe v. Washington Post Company, 512
Scales v. United States, 140
Schaefer v. United States, 76
Schenck v. United States, 33, 939
Schneider v. State, 262, 414, 439, 457, 654
School Dist. of Abington tp., Pa. v. Schempp, 893
Scopes v. State, 287, 291, 330, 672
Selective Draft Law Cases, 541
Sellers v. Johnson, 414
Shelley v. Kraemer, 531
Sherbert v. Verner, 975, 976, 979, 1039
Shuttlesworth v. Birmingham, 388
Skokie v. National Socialist Party, 672
Slaughterhouse Cases, 27, 56
Smith v. California, 677
Smith v. Goguen, 263, 270, 273
Snepp v. United States, 288
South Dakota v. Dole, 289
Southeastern Promotions, Ltd. v. Conrad, 388, 439
Spence v. Washington, 275, 545
Stanford v. Texas, 24
Stanley v. Georgia, 673, 674, 759
State v. Henry, 759
State v. Kool, 264
State v. Schmid, 386
Staub v. Baxley, 388
Steward Machine Company v. Davis, 289
Stone v. Graham, 873
Street v. New York, 267

Terminiello v. Chicago, 414, 672
Texas v. Johnson, 141, 251
Thomas v. Collins, 388
Thomas v. Review Board of Indiana Employment Security Division, 979

Thompson v. Wilson, 162
Thornhill v. Alabama, 939
Time, Inc. v. Hill, 180
Times Film Corporation v. Chicago, 677
Times-Picayune Pub. Corporation v. Schulingkamp, 105
Tinker v. Des Moines School Dist., 249, 383, 399, 486
Tobacco Institute, Inc. v. FCC, 619
Torcaso v. Watkins, 871, 1010, 1038
Trans World Airlines, Inc. v. Hardison, 978
Trop v. Dulles, 238
Twining v. New Jersey, 56

Ullmann v. United States, 1031
United Public Workers v. Mitchell, 365, 379
United Public Workers v. Mitchell, 364
United States v. Abney, 249
United States v. Ballard, 170
United States v. Brewster, 22
United States v. Burr, 22
United States v. Butler, 289
United States v. Cruikshank, 27, 62
United States v. Eichman, 285
United States v. Fontana, 73
United States v. General Motors Corporation, 529
United States v. Grace, 249
United States v. Helstoski, 22
United States v. Johnson, 22, 23
United States v. Lovett, 238
United States v. 95 Barrels of Vinegar, 619
United States v. O'Brien, 234, 247, 251, 263, 271, 362, 545, 672, 759
United States v. Robel, 361, 389
United States v. Rush, 1020
United States v. Scott, 65
United States v. Thirty-Seven Photographs, 748
United States Civil Service Comm'n v. National Ass'n of Letter Carriers, 328, 330, 364
United States Postal Service v. Greenburgh Civic Associations, 427

Valentine v. Chrestensen, 651
Valley Forge Christian College v. Americans United, 762
Virginia Pharmacy Board v. Virginia Citizens Consumer Council, 639, 642, 671
Vitek v. Jones, 532

Wallace v. Jaffree, 765, 982
Walz v. Tax Commission of the City of New York, 1040
Washington v. Davis, 1010
Washington Ethical Society v. District of Columbia, 1026
Webster v. Reproductive Health Services, 873
West Ohio Gas Company v. Public Utilities Commission, 640

CASES CITED IN FOOTNOTES

West Virginia Board of Education v. Barnette, 68, 761, 975
Whalen v. Roe, 110
Whitney v. California, 32, 68, 76, 141, 156
Widmar v. Vincent, 449
Wieman v. Updegraff, 363, 374
Wimberly v. Labor & Industrial Relations Commission, 976
Wisconsin v. Yoder, 975
Womack v. Eldridge, 210
Women Strike for Peace v. Morton, 249
Wooley v. Maynard, 761

Worsham v. A.H. Robins Company, 629
Wynehamer v. People, 66

Yates v. United States, 113, 140, 144, 389

Zacchini v. Scripps-Howard Publishing Company, 182
Zemel v. Rusk, 505
Zenith Radio Corporation v. Matsushita Electric Industrial Company, 110
Zorach v. Clauson, 785
Zurcher v. Stanford Daily, 22

*

THE CONSTITUTION OF THE UNITED STATES OF AMERICA 1787

We the people of the United States, in Order to form a more perfect Union, establish Justice, insure domestic Tranquility, provide for the common defence, promote the general Welfare, and secure the Blessings of Liberty to ourselves and our Posterity, do ordain and establish this Constitution for the United States of America.

Article I

Section 1. All legislative Powers herein granted shall be vested in a Congress of the United States, which shall consist of a Senate and House of Representatives.

Section 2. The House of Representatives shall be composed of Members chosen every second Year by the People of the several States, and the Electors in each State shall have the Qualifications requisite for Electors of the most numerous Branch of the State Legislature.

No Person shall be a Representative who shall not have attained to the Age of twenty five Years, and been seven Years a Citizen of the United States, and who shall not, when elected, be an Inhabitant of that State in which he shall be chosen.

[Representatives and direct Taxes shall be apportioned among the several States which may be included within this Union, according to their respective Numbers, which shall be determined by adding to the whole Number of free Persons, including those bound to Service for a Term of Years, and excluding Indians not taxed, three fifths of all other Persons.][1] The actual Enumeration shall be made within three Years after the first Meeting of the Congress of the United States, and within every subsequent Term of ten Years, in such Manner as they shall by Law direct. The Number of Representatives shall not exceed one for every thirty Thousand, but each State shall have at Least one Representative; and until such enumeration shall be made, the State of New Hampshire shall be entitled to chuse three, Massachusetts eight, Rhode Island and Providence Plantations one, Connecticut five, New-York six, New Jersey four, Pennsylvania eight, Delaware one, Maryland six, Virginia ten, North Carolina five, South Carolina five, and Georgia three.

When vacancies happen in the Representation from any State, the Executive Authority thereof shall issue Writs of Election to fill such Vacancies.

The House of Representatives shall chuse their Speaker and other Officers; and shall have the sole Power of Impeachment.

---

1. Changed by section 2 of the Fourteenth Amendment.

Section 3. The Senate of the United States shall be composed of two Senators from each State, [chosen by the Legislature thereof,] [2] for six Years; and each Senator shall have one Vote.

Immediately after they shall be assembled in Consequence of the first Election, they shall be divided as equally as may be into three Classes. The Seats of the Senators of the first Class shall be vacated at the Expiration of the second Year, of the second Class at the Expiration of the fourth Year, and of the third Class at the Expiration of the sixth Year, so that one third may be chosen every second Year; [and if Vacancies happen by Resignation, or otherwise, during the Recess of the Legislature of any State, the Executive thereof may make temporary Appointments until the next Meeting of the Legislature, which shall then fill such Vacancies.] [3]

No Person shall be a Senator who shall not have attained to the Age of thirty Years, and been nine Years a Citizen of the United States, and who shall not, when elected, be an Inhabitant of that State for which he shall be chosen.

The Vice President of the United States shall be President of the Senate, but shall have no Vote, unless they be equally divided.

The Senate shall chuse their other Officers, and also a President pro tempore, in the Absence of the Vice President, or when he shall exercise the Office of President of the United States.

The Senate shall have the sole Power to try all Impeachments. When sitting for that Purpose, they shall be on Oath or Affirmation. When the President of the United States is tried, the Chief Justice shall preside: And no Person shall be convicted without the Concurrence of two thirds of the Members present.

Judgment in Cases of Impeachment shall not extend further than to removal from Office, and disqualification to hold and enjoy any Office of Honor, Trust or Profit under the United States: but the Party convicted shall nevertheless be liable and subject to Indictment, Trial, Judgment and Punishment, according to Law.

Section 4. The Times, Places and Manner of holding Elections for Senators and Representatives, shall be prescribed in each State by the Legislature thereof; but the Congress may at any time by Law make or alter such Regulations, except as to the Places of chusing Senators.

The Congress shall assemble at least once in every Year, and such Meeting shall be [on the first Monday in December,] [4] unless they shall by Law appoint a different Day.

Section 5. Each House shall be the Judge of the Elections, Returns and Qualifications of its own Members, and a Majority of each shall

---

2. Changed by the Seventeenth Amendment.

3. Changed by the Seventeenth Amendment.

4. Changed by section 2 of the Twentieth Amendment.

constitute a Quorum to do Business; but a smaller Number may adjourn from day to day, and may be authorized to compel the Attendance of absent Members, in such Manner, and under such Penalties as each House may provide.

Each House may determine the Rules of its Proceedings, punish its Members for disorderly Behaviour, and, with the Concurrence of two thirds, expel a Member.

Each House shall keep a Journal of its Proceedings, and from time to time publish the same, excepting such Parts as may in their Judgment require Secrecy; and the Yeas and Nays of the Members of either House on any question shall, at the Desire of one fifth of those Present, be entered on the Journal.

Neither House, during the Session of Congress, shall, without the Consent of the other, adjourn for more than three days, nor to any other Place than that in which the two Houses shall be sitting.

Section 6. The Senators and Representatives shall receive a Compensation for their Services, to be ascertained by Law, and paid out of the Treasury of the United States. They shall in all Cases, except Treason, Felony and Breach of the Peace, be privileged from Arrest during their Attendance at the Session of their respective Houses, and in going to and returning from the same; and for any Speech or Debate in either House, they shall not be questioned in any other Place.

No Senator or Representative shall, during the Time for which he was elected, be appointed to any civil Office under the Authority of the United States, which shall have been created, or the Emoluments whereof shall have been encreased during such time; and no Person holding any Office under the United States, shall be a Member of either House during his Continuance in Office.

Section 7. All Bills for raising Revenue shall originate in the House of Representatives; but the Senate may propose or concur with Amendments as on other Bills.

Every Bill which shall have passed the House of Representatives and the Senate, shall, before it becomes a Law, be presented to the President of the United States; If he approves he shall sign it, but if not he shall return it, with his Objections to that House in which it shall have originated, who shall enter the Objections at large on their Journal, and proceed to reconsider it. If after such reconsideration two thirds of that House shall agree to pass the Bill, it shall be sent, together with the Objections, to the other House, by which it shall likewise be reconsidered, and if approved by two thirds of that House, it shall become a Law. But in all such Cases the Votes of both Houses shall be determined by Yeas and Nays, and the Names of the Persons voting for and against the Bill shall be entered on the Journal of each House respectively. If any Bill shall not be returned by the President within ten Days (Sundays excepted) after it shall have been presented to him, the Same shall be a

Law, in like Manner as if he had signed it, unless the Congress by their Adjournment prevent its Return, in which Case it shall not be a Law.

Every Order, Resolution, or Vote to which the Concurrence of the Senate and House of Representatives may be necessary (except on a question of Adjournment) shall be presented to the President of the United States; and before the Same shall take Effect, shall be approved by him, or being disapproved by him, shall be repassed by two thirds of the Senate and House of Representatives, according to the Rules and Limitations prescribed in the Case of a Bill.

Section 8. The Congress shall have Power To lay and collect Taxes, Duties, Imposts and Excises, to pay the Debts and provide for the common Defence and general Welfare of the United States; but all Duties, Imposts and Excises shall be uniform throughout the United States;

To borrow Money on the credit of the United States;

To regulate Commerce with foreign Nations, and among the several States, and with the Indian Tribes;

To establish an uniform Rule of Naturalization, and uniform Laws on the subject of Bankruptcies throughout the United States;

To coin Money, regulate the Value thereof, and of foreign Coin, and fix the Standard of Weights and Measures;

To provide for the Punishment of counterfeiting the Securities and current Coin of the United States;

To establish Post Offices and post Roads;

To promote the Progress of Science and useful Arts, by securing for limited Times to Authors and Inventors the exclusive Right to their respective Writings and Discoveries;

To constitute Tribunals inferior to the supreme Court;

To define and punish Piracies and Felonies committed on the high Seas, and Offences against the Law of Nations;

To declare War, grant Letters of Marque and Reprisal, and make Rules concerning;

To raise and support Armies, but no Appropriation of Money to that Use shall be for a longer Term than two Years;

To provide and maintain a Navy;

To make Rules for the Government and Regulation of the land and naval Forces;

To provide for calling forth the Militia to execute the Laws of the Union, suppress Insurrections and repel Invasions;

To provide for organizing, arming, and disciplining, the Militia, and for governing such Part of them as may be employed in the Service of the United States, reserving to the States respectively, the Appointment of the Officers, and the Authority of training the Militia according to the discipline prescribed by Congress;

To exercise exclusive Legislation in all Cases whatsoever, over such District (not exceeding ten Miles square) as may, by Cession of particular States, and the Acceptance of Congress, become the Seat of the Government of the United States, and to exercise like Authority over all Places purchased by the Consent of the Legislature of the State in which the Same shall be, for the Erection of Forts, Magazines, Arsenals, dock-Yards, and other needful Buildings;—And

To make all Laws which shall be necessary and proper for carrying into Execution the foregoing Powers, and all other Powers vested by this Constitution in the Government of the United States, or in any Department or Officer thereof.

Section 9. The Migration or Importation of such Persons as any of the States now existing shall think proper to admit, shall not be prohibited by the Congress prior to the Year one thousand eight hundred and eight, but a Tax or duty may be imposed on such Importation, not exceeding ten dollars for each Person.

The Privilege of the Writ of Habeas Corpus shall not be suspended, unless when in Cases of Rebellion or Invasion the public Safety may require it.

No Bill of Attainder or ex post facto Law shall be passed.

[No Capitation, or other direct, Tax shall be laid, unless in Proportion to the Census or Enumeration herein before directed to be taken.] [5]

No Tax or Duty shall be laid on Articles exported from any State.

No Preference shall be given by any Regulation of Commerce or Revenue to the Ports of one State over those of another; nor shall Vessels bound to, or from, one State, be obliged to enter, clear, or pay Duties in another.

No Money shall be drawn from the Treasury, but in Consequence of Appropriations made by Law; and a regular Statement and Account of the Receipts and Expenditures of all public Money shall be published from time to time.

No Title of Nobility shall be granted by the United States: and no Person holding any Office of Profit or Trust under them, shall, without the Consent of the Congress, accept of any present, Emolument, Office, or Title, of any kind whatever, from any King, Prince, or foreign State.

Section 10. No State shall enter into any Treaty, Alliance, or Confederation; grant Letters of Marque and Reprisal; coin Money; emit Bills of Credit; make any Thing but gold and silver Coin a Tender in Payment of Debts; pass any Bill of Attainder, ex post facto Law, or Law impairing the Obligation of Contracts, or grant any Title of Nobility.

---

5. Changed by the Sixteenth Amendment.

No State shall, without the Consent of the Congress, lay any Imposts or Duties on Imports or Exports, except what may be absolutely necessary for executing its inspection Laws: and the net Produce of all Duties and Imposts, laid by any State on Imports or Exports, shall be for the Use of the Treasury of the United States; and all such Laws shall be subject to the Revision and Control of the Congress.

No State shall, without the Consent of Congress, lay any Duty of Tonnage, keep Troops, or Ships of War in time of Peace, enter into any Agreement or Compact with another State, or with a foreign Power, or engage in War, unless actually invaded, or in such imminent Danger as will not admit of delay.

Article II

Section 1. The executive Power shall be vested in a President of the United States of America. He shall hold his Office during the Term of four Years, and, together with the Vice President, chosen for the same Term, be elected, as follows

Each State shall appoint, in such Manner as the Legislature thereof may direct, a Number of Electors, equal to the whole Number of Senators and Representatives to which the State may be entitled in the Congress: but no Senator or Representative, or Person holding an Office of Trust or Profit under the United States, shall be appointed an Elector.

[The Electors shall meet in their respective States, and vote by Ballot for two Persons, of whom one at least shall not be an Inhabitant of the same State with themselves. And they shall make a List of all the Persons voted for, and of the Number of Votes for each; which List they shall sign and certify, and transmit sealed to the Seat of the Government of the United States, directed to the President of the Senate. The President of the Senate shall, in the Presence of the Senate and House of Representatives, open all the Certificates, and the Votes shall then be counted. The Person having the greatest Number of Votes shall be the President, if such Number be a Majority of the whole Number of Electors appointed; and if there be more than one who have such Majority, and have an equal Number of Votes, then the House of Representatives shall immediately chuse by Ballot one of them for President; and if no Person have a Majority, then from the five highest on the List the said House shall in like Manner chuse the President. But in chusing the President, the Votes shall be taken by States, the Representative from each State having one Vote; A quorum for this Purpose shall consist of a Member or Members from two thirds of the States, and a Majority of all the States shall be necessary to a Choice. In every Case, after the Choice of the President, the Person having the greatest Number of Votes of the Electors shall be the Vice President.

But if there should remain two or more who have equal Votes, the Senate shall chuse from them by Ballot the Vice President.] [6]

The Congress may determine the Time of chusing the Electors, and the Day on which they shall give their Votes; which Day shall be the same throughout the United States.

No Person except a natural born Citizen, or a Citizen of the United States, at the time of the Adoption of this Constitution, shall be eligible to the Office of President; neither shall any Person be eligible to that Office who shall not have attained to the Age of thirty five Years, and been fourteen Years a Resident within the United States.

[In Case of the Removal of the President from Office, or of his Death, Resignation, or Inability to discharge the Powers and Duties of the said Office, the Same shall devolve on the Vice President, and the Congress may by Law provide for the Case of Removal, Death, Resignation or Inability, both of the President and Vice President, declaring what Officer shall then act as President, and such Officer shall act accordingly, until the Disability be removed, or a President shall be elected.] [7]

The President shall, at stated Times, receive for his Services, a Compensation, which shall neither be encreased nor diminished during the Period for which he shall have been elected, and he shall not receive within that Period any other Emolument from the United States, or any of them.

Before he enters the Execution of his Office, he shall take the following Oath or Affirmation:—"I do solemnly swear (or affirm) that I will faithfully execute the Office of President of the United States, and will to the best of my Ability, preserve, protect and defend the Constitution of the United States."

Section 2. The President shall be Commander in Chief of the Army and Navy of the United States, and of the Militia of the several States, when called into the actual Service of the United States; he may require the Opinion, in writing, of the principal Officer in each of the executive Departments, upon any Subject relating to the Duties of their respective Offices, and he shall have Power to grant Reprieves and Pardons for Offences against the United States, except in Cases of Impeachment.

He shall have Power, by and with the Advice and Consent of the Senate, to make Treaties, provided two thirds of the Senators present concur; and he shall nominate, and by and with the Advice and Consent of the Senate, shall appoint Ambassadors, other public Ministers and Consuls, Judges of the supreme Court, and all other Officers of the United States, whose Appointments are not herein otherwise provided for, and which shall be established by Law: but the Congress may by

---

6. Changed by the Twelfth Amendment.
7. Changed by the Twenty-fifth Amendment.

Law vest the Appointment of such inferior Officers, as they think proper, in the President alone, in the Courts of Law, or in the Heads of Departments.

The President shall have Power to fill up all Vacancies that may happen during the Recess of the Senate, by granting Commissions which shall expire at the End of their next Session.

Section 3. He shall from time to time give to the Congress Information of the State of the Union, and recommend to their Consideration such Measures as he shall judge necessary and expedient; he may, on extraordinary Occasions, convene both Houses, or either of them, and in Case of Disagreement between them, with Respect to the Time of Adjournment, he may adjourn them to such Time as he shall think proper; he shall receive Ambassadors and other public Ministers; he shall take Care that the Laws be faithfully executed, and shall Commission all the Officers of the United States.

Section 4. The President, Vice President and all civil Officers of the United States, shall be removed from Office on Impeachment for, and Conviction of, Treason, Bribery, or other high Crimes and Misdemeanors.

Article III

Section 1. The judicial Power of the United States, shall be vested in one supreme Court, and in such inferior Courts as the Congress may from time to time ordain and establish. The Judges, both of the supreme and inferior Courts, shall hold their Offices during good Behaviour, and shall, at stated Times, receive for their Services, a Compensation, which shall not be diminished during their Continuance in Office.

Section 2. The judicial Power shall extend to all Cases, in Law and Equity, arising under this Constitution, the Laws of the United States, and Treaties made, or which shall be made, under their Authority;—to all Cases affecting Ambassadors, other public Ministers and Consuls;—to all Cases of admiralty and maritime Jurisdiction;—to Controversies to which the United States shall be a Party;—to Controversies between two or more States;—between a State and Citizens of another State;—between Citizens of different States;—between Citizens of the same State claiming Lands under Grants of different States, [and between a State, or the Citizens thereof, and foreign States, Citizens or Subjects.][8]

In all Cases affecting Ambassadors, other public Ministers and Consuls, and those in which a State shall be Party, the supreme Court shall have original Jurisdiction. In all the other Cases before mentioned, the supreme Court shall have appellate Jurisdiction, both as to Law and Fact, with such Exceptions, and under such Regulations as the Congress shall make.

---

8. Changed by the Eleventh Amendment.

The Trial of all Crimes, except in Cases of Impeachment, shall be by Jury; and such Trial shall be held in the State where the said Crimes shall have been committed; but when not committed within any State, the Trial shall be at such Place or Places as the Congress may by Law have directed.

Section 3. Treason against the United States, shall consist only in levying War against them, or in adhering to their Enemies, giving them Aid and Comfort. No Person shall be convicted of Treason unless on the Testimony of two Witnesses to the same overt Act, or on Confession in open Court.

The Congress shall have Power to declare the Punishment of Treason, but no Attainder of Treason shall work Corruption of Blood, or Forfeiture except during the Life of the Person attained.

Article IV

Section 1. Full Faith and Credit shall be given in each State to the public Acts, Records, and judicial Proceedings of every other State. And the Congress may by general Laws prescribe the Manner in which such Acts, Records and Proceedings shall be proved, and the Effect thereof.

Section 2. The Citizens of each State shall be entitled to all Privileges and Immunities of Citizens in the several States.

A Person charged in any State with Treason, Felony, or other Crime, who shall flee from Justice, and be found in another State, shall on Demand of the executive Authority of the State from which he fled, be delivered up, to be removed to the State having Jurisdiction of the Crime.

[No Person held to Service or Labour in one State, under the Laws thereof, escaping into another, shall, in Consequence of any Law or Regulation therein, be discharged from such Service or Labour, but shall be delivered up on Claim of the Party to whom such Service or Labour may be due.][9]

Section 3. New States may be admitted by the Congress into this Union; but no new State shall be formed or erected within the Jurisdiction of any other State; nor any State be formed by the Junction of two or more States, or Parts of States, without the Consent of the Legislatures of the States concerned as well as of the Congress.

The Congress shall have Power to dispose of and make all needful Rules and Regulations respecting the Territory or other Property belonging to the United States; and nothing in this Constitution shall be so construed as to Prejudice any Claims of the United States, or of any particular State.

Section 4. The United States shall guarantee to every State in this Union a Republican Form of Government, and shall protect each of them

---

9. Changed by the Thirteenth Amendment.

against Invasion; and on Application of the Legislature, or of the Executive (when the legislature cannot be convened) against domestic Violence.

Article V

The Congress, whenever two thirds of both Houses shall deem it necessary, shall propose Amendments to this Constitution, or, on the Application of the Legislatures of two thirds of the several States, shall call a Convention for proposing Amendments, which, in either Case, shall be valid to all Intents and Purposes, as Part of this Constitution, when ratified by the Legislatures of three fourths of the several States, or by Conventions in three fourths thereof, as the one or the other Mode of Ratification may be proposed by the Congress; Provided that no Amendment which may be made prior to the Year One thousand eight hundred and eight shall in any Manner affect the first and fourth Clauses in the Ninth Section of the first Article; and that no State, without its Consent, shall be deprived of its equal Suffrage in the Senate.

Article VI

All Debts contracted and Engagements entered into, before the Adoption of this Constitution, shall be as valid against the United States under this Constitution, as under the Confederation.

This Constitution, and the Laws of the United States which shall be made in Pursuance thereof; and all Treaties made, or which shall be made, under the Authority of the United States, shall be the supreme Law of the Land; and the Judges in every State shall be bound thereby, any Thing in the Constitution or Laws of any State to the Contrary notwithstanding.

The Senators and Representatives before mentioned, and the Members of the several State Legislatures, and all executive and judicial Officers, both of the United States and of the several States, shall be bound by Oath or Affirmation, to support this Constitution; but no religious Test shall ever be required as a Qualification to any Office or public Trust under the United States.

Article VII

The Ratification of the Conventions of nine States, shall be sufficient for the Establishment of this Constitution between the States so ratifying the Same.

Done in convention by the Unanimous consent of the States present the Seventeenth Day of September in the Year of our Lord one thousand seven hundred and Eighty seven and of the Independence of the United States of America the Twelfth In Witness whereof We have hereunto subscribed our Names.

THE CONSTITUTION OF THE UNITED STATES

Amendments to the Constitution of the United States of America

Articles in Addition To, and Amendment Of, the Constitution of the United States of America, Proposed by Congress, and Ratified by the Legislatures of the Several States Pursuant to the Fifth Article of the Original Constitution

Amendment I [10]

Congress shall make no law respecting an establishment of religion, or prohibiting the free exercise thereof; or abridging the freedom of speech, or of the press; or the right of the people peaceably to assemble, and to petition the Government for a redress of grievances.

Amendment II

A well regulated Militia, being necessary to the security of a free State, the right of the people to keep and bear Arms, shall not be infringed.

Amendment III

No Soldier shall, in time of peace be quartered in any house, without the consent of the Owner, nor in time of war, but in a manner to be prescribed by law.

Amendment IV

The right of the people to be secure in their persons, houses, papers, and effects, against unreasonable searches and seizures, shall not be violated, and no Warrants shall issue, but upon probable cause, supported by Oath or affirmation, and particularly describing the place to be searched, and the persons or things to be seized.

Amendment V

No person shall be held to answer for a capital, or otherwise infamous crime, unless on a presentment or indictment of a Grand Jury, except in cases arising in the land or naval forces, or in the Militia, when

---

10. The first ten amendments to the Constitution of the United States were proposed to the legislatures of the several States by the First Congress, on the 25th of September 1789. They were ratified by the following States, and the notifications of ratification by the governors thereof were successively communicated by the President to Congress: New Jersey, November 20, 1789; Maryland, December 19, 1789; North Carolina, December 22, 1789; South Carolina, January 19, 1790; New Hampshire, January 25, 1790; Delaware, January 28, 1790; Pennsylvania, March 10, 1790; New York, March 27, 1790; Rhode Island, June 15, 1790; Vermont, November 3, 1791, and Virginia, December 15, 1791. The legislatures of Connecticut, Georgia, and Massachusetts ratified them on April 19, 1939, March 18, 1939 and March 2, 1939, respectively.

in actual service in time of War or public danger; nor shall any person be subject for the same offence to be twice put in jeopardy of life or limb; nor shall be compelled in any criminal case to be a witness against himself, nor be deprived of life, liberty, or property, without due process of law; nor shall private property be taken for public use, without just compensation.

Amendment VI

In all criminal prosecutions, the accused shall enjoy the right to a speedy and public trial, by an impartial jury of the State and district wherein the crime shall have been committed, which district shall have been previously ascertained by law, and to be informed of the nature and cause of the accusation; to be confronted with the witnesses against him; to have compulsory process for obtaining Witnesses in his favor, and to have the Assistance of Counsel for his defence.

Amendment VII

In Suits at common law, where the value in controversy shall exceed twenty dollars, the right of trial by jury shall be preserved, and no fact tried by a jury, shall be otherwise reexamined in any Court of the United States, than according to the rules of the common law.

Amendment VIII

Excessive bail shall not be required, nor excessive fines imposed, nor cruel and unusual punishments inflicted.

Amendment IX

The enumeration in the Constitution, of certain rights, shall not be construed to deny or disparage others retained by the people.

Amendment X

The powers not delegated to the United States by the Constitution, nor prohibited by it to the States, are reserved to the States respectively, or to the people.

Amendment XI [11]

The Judicial power of the United States shall not be construed to extend to any suit in law or equity, commenced or prosecuted against one of the United States by Citizens of another State, or by Citizens or Subjects of any Foreign State.

---

11. The Eleventh Amendment was ratified February 7, 1795.

THE CONSTITUTION OF THE UNITED STATES

Amendment XII [12]

The Electors shall meet in their respective states, and vote by ballot for President and Vice-President, one of whom, at least, shall not be an inhabitant of the same state with themselves; they shall name in their ballots the person voted for as President, and in distinct ballots the person voted for as Vice-President, and they shall make distinct lists of all persons voted for as President, and of all persons voted for as Vice-President, and of the number of votes for each, which lists they shall sign and certify, and transmit sealed to the seat of the government of the United States, directed to the President of the Senate;—The President of the Senate shall, in the presence of the Senate and House of Representatives, open all the certificates and the votes shall then be counted;—The person having the greatest number of votes for President, shall be the President, if such number be a majority of the whole number of Electors appointed; and if no person have such majority, then from the persons having the highest numbers not exceeding three on the list of those voted for as President, the House of Representatives shall choose immediately, by ballot, the President. But in choosing the President, the votes shall be taken by states, the representation from each state having one vote; a quorum for this purpose shall consist of a member or members from two-thirds of the states, and a majority of all the states shall be necessary to a choice. [And if the House of Representatives shall not choose a President whenever the right of choice shall devolve upon them, before the fourth day of March next following, then the Vice-President shall act as President, as in the case of the death or other constitutional disability of the President.] [13] The person having the greatest number of votes as Vice-President, shall be the Vice-President, if such number be a majority of the whole number of Electors appointed, and if no person have a majority, then from the two highest numbers on the list, the Senate shall choose the Vice-President; a quorum for the purpose shall consist of two-thirds of the whole number of Senators, and a majority of the whole number shall be necessary to a choice. But no person constitutionally ineligible to the office of President shall be eligible to that of Vice-President of the United States.

Amendment XIII [14]

Section 1. Neither slavery nor involuntary servitude, except as a punishment for crime whereof the party shall have been duly convicted, shall exist within the United States, or any place subject to their jurisdiction.

---

12. The Twelfth Amendment as ratified June 15, 1804.

13. Superseded by section 3 of the Twentieth Amendment.

14. The Thirteenth Amendment as ratified December 6, 1865.

Section 2. Congress shall have power to enforce this article by appropriate legislation.

Amendment XIV [15]

Section 1. All persons born or naturalized in the United States, and subject to the jurisdiction thereof, are citizens of the United States and of the State wherein they reside. No State shall make or enforce any law which shall abridge the privileges or immunities of citizens of the United States; nor shall any State deprive any person of life, liberty, or property, without due process of law; nor deny to any person within its jurisdiction the equal protection of the laws.

Section 2. Representatives shall be appointed among the several States according to their respective numbers, counting the whole number of persons in each State, excluding Indians not taxed. But when the right to vote at any election for the choice of electors for President and Vice President of the United States, Representatives in Congress, the Executive and Judicial officers of a State, or the members of the Legislature thereof, is denied to any of the male inhabitants of such State, being twenty-one years of age, and citizens of the United States, or in any way abridged, except for participation in rebellion, or other crime, the basis of representation therein shall be reduced in the proportion which the number of such male citizens shall bear to the whole number of male citizens twenty-one years of age in such State.

Section 3. No person shall be a Senator or Representative in Congress, or elector of President and Vice President, or hold any office, civil or military, under the United States, or under any State, who, having previously taken an oath, as a member of Congress, or as an officer of the United States, or as a member of any State legislature, or as an executive or judicial officer of any State, to support the Constitution of the United States, shall have engaged in insurrection or rebellion against the same, or given aid or comfort to the enemies thereof. But Congress may by a vote of two-thirds of each House, remove such disability.

Section 4. The validity of the public debt of the United States, authorized by law, including debts incurred for payment of pensions and bounties for services in suppressing insurrection or rebellion, shall not be questioned. But neither the United States nor any State shall assume or pay any debt or obligation incurred in aid of insurrection or rebellion against the United States, or any claim for the loss or emancipation of any slave; but all such debts, obligations and claims shall be held illegal and void.

Section 5. The Congress shall have power to enforce, by appropriate legislation, the provisions of this article.

---

15. The Fourteenth Amendment was ratified July 9, 1868.

Amendment XV [16]

Section 1. The right of citizens of the United States to vote shall not be denied or abridged by the United States or by any State on account of race, color, or previous condition of servitude.

Section 2. The Congress shall have power to enforce this article by appropriate legislation.

Amendment XVI [17]

The Congress shall have power to lay and collect taxes on incomes, from whatever source derived, without apportionment among the several States, and without regard to any census or enumeration.

Amendment XVII [18]

The Senate of the United States shall be composed of two Senators from each State, elected by the people thereof, for six years; and each Senator shall have one vote. The electors in each State shall have the qualifications requisite for electors of the most numerous branch of the State legislatures.

When vacancies happen in the representation of any State in the Senate, the executive authority of such State shall issue writs of election to fill such vacancies: Provided, That the legislature of any State may empower the executive thereof to make temporary appointments until the people fill the vacancies by election as the legislature may direct.

This amendment shall not be so construed as to affect the election or term of any Senator chosen before it becomes valid as part of the Constitution.

Amendment XVIII [19]

Section 1. After one year from the ratification of this article the manufacture, sale, or transportation of intoxicating liquors within, the importation thereof into, or the exportation thereof from the United States and all territory subject to the jurisdiction thereof for beverage purposes is hereby prohibited.

Section 2. The Congress and the several States shall have concurrent power to enforce this article by appropriate legislation.

Section 3. This article shall be inoperative unless it shall have been ratified as an amendment to the Constitution by the legislatures of the

---

16. The Fifteenth Amendment was ratified February 3, 1870.

17. The Sixteenth Amendment was ratified February 3, 1913.

18. The Seventeenth Amendment was ratified April 8, 1913.

19. The Eighteenth Amendment was ratified January 6, 1919. It was repealed by the Twenty-First Amendment, December 5, 1933.

Amendment XIX [20]

The right of citizens of the United States to vote shall not be denied or abridged by the United States or by any State on account of sex.

Congress shall have power to enforce this article by appropriate legislation.

Amendment XX [21]

Section 1. The terms of the President and Vice President shall end at noon on the 20th day of January, and the terms of Senators and Representatives at noon on the 3d day of January, of the years in which such terms would have ended if this article had not been ratified; and the terms of their successors shall then begin.

Section 2. The Congress shall assemble at least once in every year, and such meeting shall begin at noon on the 3d day of January, unless they shall by law appoint a different day.

Section 3. If, at the time fixed for the beginning of the term of the President, the President elect shall have died, the Vice President elect shall become President. If a President shall not have been chosen before the time fixed for the beginning of his term, or if the President elect shall have failed to qualify, then the Vice President elect shall act as President until a President shall have qualified; and the Congress may by law provide for the case wherein neither a President elect nor a Vice President elect shall have qualified, declaring who shall then act as President, or the manner in which one who is to act shall be selected, and such person shall act accordingly until a President or Vice President shall have qualified.

Section 4. The Congress may by law provide for the case of the death of any of the persons from whom the House of Representatives may choose a President whenever the right of choice shall have devolved upon them, and for the case of the death of any of the persons from whom the Senate may choose a Vice President whenever the right of choice shall have devolved upon them.

Section 5. Sections 1 and 2 shall take effect on the 15th day of October following the ratification of this article.

Section 6. This article shall be inoperative unless it shall have been ratified as an amendment to the Constitution by the legislatures of three-fourths of the several States within seven years from the date of its submission.

---

20. The Nineteenth Amendment was ratified August 18, 1920.

21. The Twentieth Amendment was ratified January 23, 1933.

Amendment XXI [22]

Section 1. The eighteenth article of amendment to the Constitution of the United States is hereby repealed.

Section 2. The transportation or importation into any State, Territory, or possession of the United States for delivery or use therein of intoxicating liquors, in violation of the laws thereof, is hereby prohibited.

Section 3. This article shall be inoperative unless it shall have been ratified as an amendment to the Constitution by conventions in the several States, as provided in the Constitution, within seven years from the date of the submission hereof to the States by the Congress.

Amendment XXII [23]

Section 1. No person shall be elected to the office of the President more than twice, and no person who has held the office of President, or acted as President, for more than two years of a term to which some other person was elected President shall be elected to the office of the President more than once. But this Article shall not apply to any person holding the office of President when this Article was proposed by the Congress, and shall not prevent any person who may be holding the office of President, or acting as President, during the term within which this Article becomes operative from holding the office of President or acting as President during the remainder of such term.

Section 2. This article shall be inoperative unless it shall have been ratified as an amendment to the Constitution by the legislatures of three-fourths of the several States within seven years from the date of its submission to the States by the Congress.

Amendment XXIII [24]

Section 1. The District constituting the seat of Government of the United States shall appoint in such manner as the Congress may direct:

A number of electors of President and Vice President equal to the whole number of Senators and Representatives in Congress to which the District would be entitled if it were a State, but in no event more than the least populous State; they shall be in addition to those appointed by the States, but they shall be considered, for the purposes of the election of President and Vice President, to be electors appointed by a State; and they shall meet in the District and perform such duties as provided by the twelfth article of amendment.

Section 2. The Congress shall have power to enforce this article by appropriate legislation.

---

22. The Twenty-First Amendment was ratified December 5, 1933.

23. The Twenty-Second Amendment was ratified February 27, 1951.

24. The Twenty-Third Amendment was ratified March 29, 1961.

Amendment XXIV [25]

Section 1. The right of citizens of the United States to vote in any primary or other election for President or Vice President, for electors for President or Vice President, or for Senator or Representative in Congress, shall not be denied or abridged by the United States or any State by reason of failure to pay any poll tax or other tax.

Section 2. The Congress shall have power to enforce this article by appropriate legislation.

Amendment XXV [26]

Section 1. In case of the removal of the President from office or of his death or resignation, the Vice President shall become President.

Section 2. Whenever there is a vacancy in the office of the Vice President, the President shall nominate a Vice President who shall take office upon confirmation by a majority vote of both Houses of Congress.

Section 3. Whenever the President transmits to the President pro tempore of the Senate and the Speaker of the House of Representatives his written declaration that he is unable to discharge the powers and duties of his office, and until he transmits to them a written declaration to the contrary, such powers and duties shall be discharged by the Vice President as Acting President.

Section 4. Whenever the Vice President and a majority of either the principal officers of the executive departments or of such other body as Congress may by law provide, transmit to the President pro tempore of the Senate and the Speaker of the House of Representatives their written declaration that the President is unable to discharge the powers and duties of his office, the Vice President shall immediately assume the powers and duties of the office as Acting President.

Thereafter, when the President transmits to the President pro tempore of the Senate and the Speaker of the House of Representatives his written declaration that no inability exists, he shall resume the powers and duties of his office unless the Vice President and a majority of either the principal officers of the executive department or of such other body as Congress may by law provide, transmit within four days to the President pro tempore of the Senate and the Speaker of the House of Representatives their written declaration that the President is unable to discharge the powers and duties of his office. Thereupon Congress shall decide the issue, assembling within forty-eight hours for that purpose if not in session. If the Congress, within twenty-one days after receipt of the latter written declaration, or, if Congress is not in session, within twenty-one days after Congress is required to assemble, determines by two-thirds vote of both Houses that the President is unable to discharge

---

[25] The Twenty-Fourth Amendment was ratified January 23, 1964.

[26] The Twenty-Fifth Amendment was ratified February 10, 1967.

THE CONSTITUTION OF THE UNITED STATES

the powers and duties of his office, the Vice President shall continue to discharge the same as Acting President; otherwise, the President shall resume the powers and duties of his office.

Amendment XXVI [27]

Section 1. The right of citizens of the United States, who are eighteen years of age or older, to vote shall not be denied or abridged by the United States or by any State on account of age.

Section 2. The Congress shall have power to enforce this article by appropriate legislation.

---

27. The Twenty-Sixth Amendment was ratified July 1, 1971.

FIRST AMENDMENT

Cases and Materials

*

Chapter 1
AN INTRODUCTION TO THE FIRST AMENDMENT

I.

Coverage of the first amendment was omitted from the basic course in constitutional law, principally because the demands of the basic course are thought to leave too little time to address the first amendment adequately, and because the subject matter of the first amendment looks sufficiently distinctive to lend itself to separate study in a compact, three-hour course. Even so, some of the materials in the basic course were doctrinally related to the first amendment, including some popular cases that provide a natural introduction for starting our work here. Specifically, *Griswold v. Connecticut*[1] and *Roe v. Wade*[2] ought to suggest an orientation to an easy approach to free speech and free press. Accordingly, we begin our brief introductory review with the very suggestion your work in the first year course would most strongly endorse.

A.

Whatever casebook and instructor one may have had as a guide to *Griswold* and *Roe,* one will recall that the starting point was the determination of the proper standard of judicial review. What was different in the Court's treatment of those cases was, most of all, the *strict scrutiny* standard the Supreme Court applied. Beginning with *Griswold,* the Court required that the state demonstrate a *compelling* interest in regulating the birth control practices of married couples. And it required also that the state demonstrate not only a *compelling* interest in regulating what was otherwise regarded as a highly protected subject of intensely personal concern, but that it also show that *no less intrusive* a form of regulation could avoid the social evil or kind of harm that the state sought to avoid.[3] The same generic approach was

---

1. 381 U.S. 479, 85 S.Ct. 1678, 14 L.Ed.2d 510 (1965).

2. 410 U.S. 113, 93 S.Ct. 705, 35 L.Ed.2d 147 (1973).

3. So, as you will recall, the state of Connecticut argued that the criminal ban on any device preventing conception would act as a useful additional deterrent to adultery—by putting adulterous persons at personal risk—but the Court held that even assuming the state's interest (in the avoidance of adulterous relations) was "compelling," the complete outlawry of birth control devices was too sweeping and draconian under the circumstances, i.e. the state would have to proceed by narrower means of control (e.g., by increasing the criminal penalties for adultery), to avoid unreasonably interfering with the private intimate relations of married couples under the circumstances.

applied in *Roe*.[4] You will recall, too, that the rationale for demanding *greater* justification and *tighter* boundaries on state or national laws affecting the kinds of personal liberties involved in *Griswold* and in *Roe*, than other kinds of personal liberties involved in certain other cases,[5] was rooted in a set of observations by the Court regarding "penumbras" and the Bill of Rights.

The Court defended the objectivity of requiring more justification by government for burdening some "rights" (e.g., relations within marriage) than other "rights" (e.g., conditions of conducting one's business enterprise—economic rights) by reference to several clauses, and many cases, arising under the first, fourth, and fifth amendments. Its point was [6] that the Constitution itself expressly singled out certain interests for protection against abridgment, as to which there was simply no question of the Court's duty to see they were upheld (it specifically mentioned "freedom of speech" as an example). It then noted that while related rights might not themselves be as fully protected as these rights were fully protected, still, to the extent that they *were* related (e.g., connected to them in some way), they were to that extent more-of-a-piece with these explicitly guaranteed rights than other kinds of rights claims. Recall that one of Justice Douglas's examples, in *Griswold,* was the "right of association." Justice Douglas noted that the Court had previously struck down certain state laws interfering with political rights of association, applying a stern standard of judicial review, and explaining the use of the standard partly in terms of the relatedness of being able to associate freely with others for political purposes to the right of free speech and peaceable assembly. So, while "the right of association" as such is not an enumerated first amendment right, still, its "penumbra" status gained a textual connection into the first amendment itself. And on that basis, even pre-existing cases (i.e. cases predating *Griswold*) had applied strict scrutiny review.

The point of this brief recapitulation, of course, is not to revisit Con Law I. It is, rather, to suggest that in one sense we have already had an introduction of one sort to the first amendment. What that introduction would seem to suggest is this: if even certain rights not in the first amendment are *highly* protected merely on the strength of having some penumbral consanguinity with that amendment but nothing

---

4. Indeed, recall that the case remains highly controversial not because the standard of judicial review was necessarily regarded as improper, but because of disagreement by many with the Court's view that the Texas statute did not meet that standard (namely, whether the protection of fetal life from destruction prior to the point of *ex utero* viability, was a sufficiently "compelling" interest to disallow abortion except when necessary to protect the pregnant woman from life-imperiling risks of carrying the fetus to full term).

5. E.g., Nebbia v. New York, 291 U.S. 502, 54 S.Ct. 505, 79 L.Ed. 940 (1934) (sustaining a state price-fixing law forbidding the sale of milk at retail for less than nine cents a quart) (repudiating Lochner v. New York, 198 U.S. 45, 25 S.Ct. 539, 49 L.Ed. 937 (1905), and holding generally that economic liberties will receive only *minimal* due process review).

6. See Justice Douglas's elaboration specifically in Griswold v. Connecticut, 381 U.S. 479, 85 S.Ct. 1678, 14 L.Ed.2d 510 (1965).

more,⁷ and such seems to be the case, as we have seen, *then presumably the rights that are expressly provided for by that amendment will be altogether strictly respected* by the Supreme Court, i.e. not subject to being balanced away (by the judiciary) or traded off at all.⁸

B.

The same conclusion might also seem well warranted on the following grounds as well, namely: a comparison of the first amendment in the Constitution of the United States with the more compromised style of equivalent provisions made in other constitutions respecting freedom of speech and of the press. Here are several examples. Note how they differ from our own:

Norway (1814), Article 100: There shall be liberty of the Press. No person may be punished for any writing, whatever its contents, which he has caused to be printed or published, *unless* he willfully and manifestly has either himself shown, or incited others to, disobedience to the laws, contempt of religion, morality or the constitutional powers, or resistance to their orders, *or* has made false and defamatory accusations against anyone.⁹

The People's Republic of China (1982), Article 35: Citizens of the People's Republic of China enjoy freedom of speech, of the press, of assembly, of association, of procession and of demonstration.¹⁰

The Soviet Union (1978), Article 50: *In accordance with the interests of the people and in order to strengthen and develop the socialist system,* citizens of the USSR are guaranteed freedom of speech, of the press, and of assembly, meetings, street processions and demonstrations.¹¹

England ( ), Article ( ):

---

7. I.e. if they are protected under the very demanding standard of judicial review reflected in cases such as Griswold v. Connecticut, 381 U.S. 479, 85 S.Ct. 1678, 14 L.Ed.2d 510 (1965), and Roe v. Wade, 410 U.S. 113, 93 S.Ct. 705, 35 L.Ed.2d 147 (1973) (and note how far removed the kinds of interests *actually* involved in both those cases seem to be from anything facially suggested by the first amendment itself).

8. Additionally, one might also take for granted that, given the Court's generous notion of "penumbras" of the first amendment, the amendment's own terms will of course be very generously construed, e.g., be deemed to cover varieties of expression though not themselves literally "speech" in the narrowest dictionary sense (e.g., armbands, flags, sculptures). Indeed, the usual presumption that dates at least from McCulloch v. Maryland, 17 U.S. (4 Wheat.) 316, 4 L.Ed. 579 (1819) (Marshall's famous dictum that it is a Constitution that is being expounded, one intended to endure and to be equal to circumstances only dimly foreseen, and thus not grudgingly to be construed), ought also apply to the first amendment especially since, freedom of speech and of the press being explicitly mentioned liberties in the Bill of Rights, they are among the "preferred" liberties the Constitution enshrines.

9. The Constitution of Norway is the second oldest in the world, i.e. it is antedated only by our own. (Nearly 160 countries currently operate under written constitutions, incidentally, but the majority of these national constitutions have been adopted only since 1970, and scarcely a half-dozen predate 1900.)

10. But see also Article 51 ("The exercise by citizens * * * of their freedoms * * * may not infringe upon the interests of the state, of society and of the collective * * *.").

11. See also Article 59 ("Citizens of the USSR are obliged to * * * comply with the standards of socialist conduct * * *.").

[ ]¹²

Denmark (1953), Article 77: Any person shall be entitled to publish his thoughts in printing, in writing, and in speech, *provided* that he may be held answerable in a court of justice.¹³

Germany (Federal Republic) (1949), Article V: (1) Everyone shall have the right freely to express and disseminate his opinion by speech, writing and pictures and freely to instruct himself from generally accessible sources * * * (2) *These rights are limited by the provisions of the general laws* * * *¹⁴

The United States (1791), First Amendment: Congress shall make no law abridging the freedom of speech or of the press.¹⁵

Note how these provisions tend to fall into three or, at most, four, categories. Roughly, they may be described in the following way. First, most characteristically, the constitutional protection furnished freedom of speech and of the press from government regulation is *significantly qualified* in some way. Or, second, there is just *no* constitutional protection provided at all. The Norwegian, Soviet, and West German provisions all seem on their face to be of the first, substantially qualified (Catch 22?) sort. As an example of the second sort, the English have no written constitution and thus no clauses protecting free speech and press to apply. Or, third, the constitutional provision may seem on its face to be of a sort that is merely assertive rather than prohibitory against legislative power. The provision from the 1982 Constitution of China seems to be of this sort, i.e. it merely makes a claim that may or may not be actually true.¹⁶ And, as noted in the footnote accompanying the principal provision even in this modern Constitution of The People's Republic of China, that provision is also heavily qualified by other provisions elsewhere found in the same Constitution. Among the three types (nonexistent, heavily qualified, or precatory), the *likely* protection to be furnished in litigation seeking to forestall the application of acts adopted by the national legislature may be pretty limited and uncertain, may it not?

Additionally, even in respect to these *qualified* clauses protecting freedom of speech and of the press (note, once again, for instance, the qualifying clause in the Constitution of the Federal German Republic), some may turn out to be even less substantial in practice than one might suppose. Such would be the case, for instance, if the clause in question is *not one the courts are deemed authorized to enforce* (a Catch 22 of a different sort).—As it happens, this turns out to be the case in respect to the relevant clauses in the respective constitutions of China

---

12. The English have no constitutional provision respecting freedom of speech or of the press—they have no written constitution at all.

13. See also Article 79 ("The citizen shall without previous permission be entitled to assemble unarmed [but] open-air meetings may be prohibited when it is feared that they may constitute a danger to the public peace.")

14. See also Article 18 ("Whoever abuses the freedom of expression * * * in order to attack the free, democratic basic order, shall forfeit these basic rights.")

15. I.e. Congress shall make NO law abridging the freedom of speech or of the press. "NO LAW" at all.

16. E.g., recall the events in the streets of Beijing, in the summer of 1989, in Tiananmen Square.

and the Soviet Union. Indeed, it is true of *most* constitutions throughout the world. So, while such constitutional clauses are not necessarily useless (these kinds of express constitutional clauses may provide some sense of self-restraint within the respective national assemblies of those countries that have adopted them), they are not very reassuring, substantively, on their face.

In contrast, the one uncompromised, stand-alone clause not captured in any of these three categories is the last and also the earliest, i.e. that of the Constitution of the United States, dating, as it does, unchanged, from 1791. To be sure, the first amendment says nothing about what state legislatures or even local city councils may be free to do (a problem we shall need to worry about).[17] But, as to *Congress,* well, it seems to be quite plain and absolutely unequivocal: "Congress shall make NO law abridging the freedom of speech or of the press," i.e. not just "not many laws," not just "laws unreasonably" abridging the freedom of speech, but NO laws at all, absolutely, positively, NONE.[18] So, we start in this brief course on the first amendment with that very notion.[19] For the reasons we have now briefly canvassed,[20] it would

17. Note, too, that on its face it also says nothing to restrain either *the courts* or *the executive* from interfering with freedom of speech or of the press (i.e. it is directed solely to Congress). Might this pose some problem also?

18. Justice Hugo L. Black, who served on the Supreme Court during the most active period of the Court's first amendment doctrinal developments (1937–1971), entirely agreed. See, e.g., Barenblatt v. United States, 360 U.S. 109, 141–43, 79 S.Ct. 1081, 1100–02, 3 L.Ed.2d 1115, 1137–39 (1959) (dissenting opinion) ("I do not agree that laws * * * abridging First Amendment freedoms can be justified by a congressional or judicial balancing process. * * * Not only does this violate the genius of our *written* Constitution, but it runs expressly counter to the injunction to Court and Congress made by Madison when he introduced the Bill of Rights.") (Emphasis in original.) New York Times Co. v. Sullivan, 376 U.S. 254, 293, 295, 84 S.Ct. 710, 733, 734, 11 L.Ed.2d 686, 716, 717 (1964) (concurring opinion) ("In my opinion the Federal Constitution * * * has grant[ed] the press an *absolute* immunity for criticism of the way public officials do their public duty.") (Emphasis added.) For a well written defense of Justice Black's textual literalism in matters of constitutional interpretation, see Black, Mr. Justice Black, The Supreme Court and the Bill of Rights, Harper's, Feb. 1961, at 63. See also T. Yarbrough, Mr. Justice Black and His Critics 130–150, 164–197 (1988); Black, The Bill of Rights, 35 N.Y.U. L.Rev. 865, 867 (1960); Cahn, Justice Black and First Amendment "Absolutes": A Public Interview, 37 N.Y.U.L.Rev. 549 (1962); Kalven, Upon Rereading Mr. Justice Black on the First Amendment, 14 UCLA L.Rev. 428 (1967); Reich, Mr. Justice Black and the Living Constitution, 76 Harv.L.Rev. 673 (1963).

19. In support of that notion, moreover, consider the following observation as well, namely, that just as the first amendment in the U.S. Constitution differs on its face from the more mannered (i.e. "qualified") types of clauses typically found in other, less protective, constitutions abroad, so, too, note it is also more absolute in its terms than are other amendments and other provisions that secure certain other rights even in the Bill of Rights itself. See, e.g., the fourth amendment (securing the right of the people only from "unreasonable" searches and seizures), the fifth amendment (providing for "due" process of law), the eighth amendment (prohibiting "cruel and unusual" punishments and "excessive" fines or bail).

20. The "reasons," again, in summary, are these. First, we already know that some rights merely penumbral to the first amendment are highly protected (*Griswold, Roe*) simply on the strength of that penumbral relationship, and even though those rights are not expressly protected; presumably, express first amendment rights ("the freedom of speech and of the press") will be protected more fully than such penumbral rights already highly protected though not explicitly enumerated at all. Second, the first amendment itself acknowledges no overriding conditions that would provide excuse for any Act of Congress abridging the freedom of speech or of

seem to be exactly the right place to start. The following figure may capture this perspective quite well:

Justice Black's First Amendment

```
┌─────────────────────────────────────┐
│                                     │
│        [Protected Absolutely]       │
│                                     │
│        The Freedom of Speech        │
│                                     │
│           and of the Press          │
│                                     │
└─────────────────────────────────────┘
```

There now follow some materials, however, that tend to show what became of this view, relatively early on.

II.

PATTERSON v. COLORADO

Supreme Court of the United States, 1907.[21]
205 U.S. 454, 27 S.Ct. 556, 51 L.Ed. 879.

MR. JUSTICE HOLMES delivered the opinion of the court.

the press. Third, the first amendment differs in this respect from other amendments that acknowledge some excusing condition in respect to some other express preferred rights (e.g., a search that is not an "unreasonable" search is not forbidden by the terms of the fourth amendment—the first amendment has no equivalently excusing phrase). Fourth, the first amendment differs in the same way from "free speech" provisions in other constitutions, too, i.e. unlike them, it does not provide that there are occasions and circumstances when one's freedom of speech must yield to other social interests of a more compelling good. In short, to paraphrase Justice Black, *the framers did all the "balancing" when they adopted the first amendment in the absolute form Madison proposed.* It is, therefore, not for the courts to "interpret" the first amendment to read into it phantom exceptions, qualifications, or limitations. It is, rather, their obligation to apply it, until such time as it may be changed. *Quod Erat Demonstrandum* (Q.E.D.), the first amendment absolutely protects free speech.

21. [Thomas Patterson was a director, officer, and the principal shareholder of the News–Times Pub. Co., which owned The Rocky Mountain News and The Denver Times, and Patterson was manager and editor-in-chief of both newspapers. Colorado had adopted an amendment to the state constitution changing certain political processes, pursuant to which Democrats were elected in Denver. The state supreme court ruled the amendments invalid, in effect restoring the political mechanism as it had been prior to the amendments. In a series of articles, cartoons, and editorials, the News and the Times condemned the decision, suggested that it was without any proper basis, and implied that the judges

This is a writ of error to review a judgment upon an information for contempt. The contempt alleged was the publication of certain articles and a cartoon, which it was charged, reflected upon the motives and conduct of the Supreme Court of Colorado in cases still pending and were intended to embarrass the court in the impartial administration of justice. There was a motion to quash on grounds of local law and the state constitution and also of the Fourteenth Amendment to the Constitution of the United States. This was overruled and thereupon an answer was filed, admitting the publication, denying the contempt, also denying that the cases referred to were still pending, except that the time for motions for rehearing had not elapsed, and averring that the motions for rehearing subsequently were overruled, except that in certain cases the orders were amended so that the democratic officeholders concerned could be sooner turned out of their offices. The answer went on to narrate the transactions commented on, at length, intimating that the conduct of the court was unconstitutional and usurping, and alleging that it was in aid of a scheme, fully explained, to seat various republican candidates, including the governor of the State, in place of democrats who had been elected, and that two of the judges of the court got their seats as a part of the scheme. Finally, the answer alleged that the respondent published the articles in pursuance of what he regarded as a public duty, repeated the previous objections to the information, averred the truth of the articles, and set up and claimed the right to prove the truth under the Constitution of the United States. Upon this answer the court, on motion, ordered judgment fining the plaintiff in error for contempt.

The foregoing proceedings are set forth in a bill of exceptions, and several errors are alleged. The difficulties with those most pressed is that they raise questions of local law, which are not open to reëxamination here. The requirement in the Fourteenth Amendment of due process of law does not take up the special provisions of the state constitution and laws into the Fourteenth Amendment for purposes of the case, and in that way subject a state decision that they have been complied with to revision by this court. French v. Taylor, 199 U.S. 274, 278; Rawlins v. Georgia, 201 U.S. 638, 639; Burt v. Smith, 203 U.S. 129, 135. For this reason, if for no other, the objection that the information was not supported by an affidavit until after it was filed cannot be considered. See further Ex parte Wall, 107 U.S. 265. The same is true of the contention that the suits referred to in the article complained of were not pending. Whether a case shall be regarded as pending while it is possible that petition for rehearing may be filed, or, if in an appellate court, until the remittitur is issued, are questions which the local law can settle as it pleases without interference from the Constitu-

reached the decision on crass political grounds favoring corporate interests and the Republican Party. (E.g., one early editorial, after lambasting the decision, then concluded: "What next? If somebody will let us know what next the utility corporations of Denver and the political machine they control will demand, the question will be answered.") In criminal contempt proceedings brought in the State Supreme Court by the Attorney General, the Court held Patterson guilty of common law criminal contempt as charged in the Attorney General's unverified information, imposing a fine of $1,000, and ordering "a committal until the payment thereof." The full case is reported at 35 Col. 253–461 (1906).] [Ed. note.]

tion of the United States. It is admitted that this may be true in some other sense, but it is not true, it is said, for the purpose of fixing the limits of possible contempts. But here again the plaintiff in error confounds the argument as to the common law, or as to what it might be wise and humane to hold, with that concerning the State's constitutional power. If a State should see fit to provide in its constitution that conduct otherwise amounting to a contempt should be punishable as such if occurring at any time while the court affected retained authority to modify its judgment, the Fourteenth Amendment would not forbid. Virginia v. Rives, 100 U.S. 313, 318; Missouri v. Dockery, 191 U.S. 165, 171.

* * *

It is argued that the articles did not constitute a contempt. In view of the answer, which sets out more plainly and in fuller detail what the articles insinuate and suggest, and in view of the position of the plaintiff in error that he was performing a public duty, the argument for a favorable interpretation of the printed words loses some of its force. However, it is enough for us to say that they are far from showing that innocent conduct has been laid hold of as an arbitrary pretense for an arbitrary punishment. Supposing that such a case would give the plaintiff in error a standing here, anything short of that is for the state court to decide. What constitutes contempt, as well as the time during which it may be committed, is a matter of local law.

The defense upon which the plaintiff in error most relies is raised by the allegation that the articles complained of are true and the claim of the right to prove the truth. He claimed this right under the constitutions both of the State and of the United States, but the latter ground alone comes into consideration here, for reasons already stated. In re Kemmler, 136 U.S. 436. We do not pause to consider whether the claim was sufficient in point of form, although it is easier to refer to the Constitution generally for the supposed right than to point to the clause from which it springs. We leave undecided the question whether there is to be found in the Fourteenth Amendment a prohibition similar to that in the First. But even if we were to assume that freedom of speech and freedom of the press were protected from abridgment on the part not only of the United States but also of the States, still we should be far from the conclusion that the plaintiff in error would have us reach. In the first place, the main purpose of such constitutional provisions is "to prevent all such *previous restraints* upon publications as had been practiced by other governments," and they do not prevent the subsequent punishment of such as may be deemed contrary to the public welfare. Commonwealth v. Blanding, 3 Pick. 304, 313, 314; Respublica v. Oswald, 1 Dallas, 319, 325. The preliminary freedom extends as well to the false as to the true; the subsequent punishment may extend as well to the true as to the false. This was the law of criminal libel apart from statute in most cases, if not in all. Commonwealth v. Blanding, ubi sup.; 4 Bl.Com. 150.

In the next place, the rule applied to criminal libels applies yet more clearly to contempts. A publication likely to reach the eyes of a jury, declaring a witness in a pending cause a perjurer, would be none the less a contempt that it was true. It would tend to obstruct the administration of justice, because even a correct conclusion is not to be reached or helped in that way, if our system of trials is to be maintained. The theory of our system is that the conclusions to be reached in a case will be induced only by evidence and argument in open court, and not by any outside influence, whether of private talk or public print.

What is true with reference to a jury is true also with reference to a court. Cases like the present are more likely to arise, no doubt, when there is a jury and the publication may affect their judgment. Judges generally, perhaps, are less apprehensive that publications impugning their own reasoning or motives will interfere with their administration of the law. But if a court regards, as it may, a publication concerning a matter of law pending before it, as tending toward such an interference, it may punish it as in the instance put. When a case is finished, courts are subject to the same criticism as other people, but the propriety and necessity of preventing interference with the course of justice by premature statement, argument or intimidation hardly can be denied. Ex parte Terry, 128 U.S. 289; Telegram Newspaper Co. v. Commonwealth, 172 Mass. 294; State v. Hart, 24 W.Va. 416; Myers v. State, 46 Ohio St. 473, 491; Hunt v. Clarke, 58 L.J.Q.B. 490, 492; Rex v. Parke [1903], 2 K.B. 432. It is objected that the judges were sitting in their own case. But the grounds upon which contempts are punished are impersonal. United States v. Shipp, 203 U.S. 563, 574. No doubt judges naturally would be slower to punish when the contempt carried with it a personally dishonoring charge, but a man cannot expect to secure immunity from punishment by the proper tribunal, by adding to illegal conduct a personal attack. It only remains to add that the plaintiff in error had his day in court and opportunity to be heard. We have scrutinized the case, but cannot say that it shows an infraction of rights under the Constitution of the United States, or discloses more than the formal appeal to that instrument in the answer to found the jurisdiction of this court.

Writ of error dismissed.

MR. JUSTICE HARLAN, dissenting.

I cannot agree that this writ of error should be dismissed.

By the First Amendment of the Constitution of the United States, it is provided that "Congress shall make no law respecting an establishment of religion, or abridging the freedom of speech, or of the press, or of the right of the people peaceably to assemble and to petition the Government for redress." In the Civil Rights Cases, 109 U.S. 1, 20, it was adjudged that the Thirteenth Amendment, although in form prohibitory, had a reflex character in that it established and decreed universal civil and political freedom throughout the United States. In United States v. Cruikshank, 92 U.S. 542, 552, we held that the right of the people peaceably to assemble and to petition the Government for a redress of grievances—one of the rights recognized in and protected by the First Amendment against hostile legislation by Congress—was an attribute of "national citizenship." So the First Amendment, although in form prohibitory, is to be regarded as having a reflex character and as affirmatively recognizing freedom of speech and freedom of the press as rights belonging to citizens of the United States; that is, those rights are to be deemed attributes of national citizenship or citizenship of the United States. No one, I take it, will hesitate to say that a judgment of a Federal court, prior to the adoption of the Fourteenth Amendment, impairing or abridging freedom of speech or of the press, would have been in violation of the rights of "citizens of the United States" as guaranteed by the First Amendment; this, for the reason that the rights of free speech and a free press were, as already said, attributes of national citizenship before the Fourteenth Amendment was made a part of the Constitution.

Now, the Fourteenth Amendment declares, in express words, that "no State shall make or enforce any law which shall abridge the privileges or immunities of citizens of the United States." As the First Amendment guaranteed the rights of free speech and of a free press against hostile action by the United States, it would seem clear that when the Fourteenth Amendment prohibited the States from impairing or abridging the privileges of citizens of the United States it necessarily prohibited the States from impairing or abridging the constitutional rights of such citizens to free speech and a free press. But the court announces that it leaves undecided the specific question whether there is to be found in the Fourteenth Amendment a prohibition as to the rights of free speech and a free press similar to that in the First. It yet proceeds to say that the main purpose of such constitutional provisions was to prevent all such "*previous* restraints" upon publications as had been practiced by other governments, but not to prevent the subsequent punishment of such as may be deemed contrary to the public welfare. I cannot assent to that view, if it be meant that the legislature may impair or abridge the rights of a free press and of free speech whenever it thinks that the public welfare requires that to be done. The public welfare cannot override constitutional privileges, and if the rights of free speech and of a free press are, in their essence, attributes of national citizenship, as I think they are, then neither Congress nor any State since the adoption of the Fourteenth Amendment can, by legislative enactments or by judicial action, impair or abridge them. In my judgment the action of the court below was in violation of the rights of free speech and a free press as guaranteed by the Constitution.

I go further and hold that the privileges of free speech and of a free press, belonging to every citizen of the United States, constitute essential parts of every man's liberty, and are protected against violation by that clause of the Fourteenth Amendment forbidding a State to deprive any person of his liberty without due process of law. It is, I think, impossible to conceive of liberty, as secured by the Constitution against hostile action, whether by the Nation or by the States, which does not embrace the right to enjoy free speech and the right to have a free press.

* * *

B.

In assessing the very different view of the first amendment reflected in the majority opinion in *Patterson v. Colorado,* from the first "absolute" view with which we began, consider once again the following excerpt by Justice Holmes. Note, particularly, the citation of authority provided at the end:

> We leave undecided the question whether there is to be found in the Fourteenth Amendment a prohibition similar to that in the First. But even if we were to assume that freedom of speech and freedom of the press were protected from abridgment on the part not only of the United States but also of the States, still we should be far from the conclusion that the plaintiff in error would have us reach. In the first place, the main purpose of such constitutional provisions is "to prevent all such *previous restraints* upon publication as had been practiced by other governments," and they do not prevent the subsequent punishment of such as may be deemed contrary to the public welfare. * * * The preliminary freedom extends to the false as to the true; the subsequent punishment may extend as well to the true as to the false. * * * 4 Bl.Com. 150.

C.

The reference at the end (4 Bl.Com. 150) is citation shorthand for volume 4 of William Blackstone's Commentaries on the Laws of England. A reference to that work confirms Justice Holmes' impression. Here it is, with Blackstone's own summary, following the page cited by Holmes:

W. Blackstone, IV Commentaries on the Laws of England 151–52 (1769):

> "In this [review of criminal libel just discussed on the preceding page, p. 150, namely, *libelli famosi*], and the other instances which we have lately considered, where blasphemous, immoral, treasonable, schismatical, seditious, or scandalous libels are punished by the English law, some with a greater, others with a less degree of severity, the *liberty of the press,* properly understood, is by no means infringed or violated. The liberty of the press is indeed essential to the nature of a free state: but this consists in laying no *previous* restraints upon publications, and not in freedom from censure for criminal matter when published. Every freeman has an undoubted right to lay what sentiments he pleases before the public; to forbid this, is to destroy the freedom of the press: but if he publishes what is improper, mischievous, or illegal, he must take the consequence of his own temerity. To subject the press to the restrictive power of a licenser, as was formerly done,

both before and since the revolution,* is to subject all freedom of sentiment to the prejudices of one man, and make him the arbitrary and infallible judge of all controverted points in learning, religion, and government. But to punish (as the law does at present) any dangerous or offensive writings, which, when published, shall on a fair and impartial trial be adjudged of a pernicious tendency, is necessary for the preservation of peace and good order, of government and religion, the only solid foundations of civil liberty. Thus the will of individuals is still left free; the abuse only of that free will is the object of legal punishment. Neither is any restraint hereby laid upon freedom of thought or enquiry: liberty of private sentiment is still left; the disseminating, or making public, of bad sentiments, destructive of the ends of society, is the crime which society corrects. A man (says a fine writer on this subject) may be allowed to keep poisons in his closet, but not publicly to vend them as cordials. And to this we may add, that the only plausible argument heretofore used for restraining the just freedom of the press, "that it was necessary to prevent the abuse of it," will entirely lose its force, when it is shewn (by a reasonable exertion of the laws) that the press cannot be abused to any bad purpose, without incurring a suitable punishment: whereas it never can be used to any good one, when under the control of an inspector. So true will it be found,

---

* The art of printing, soon after its introduction, was looked upon (as well in England as in other countries) as merely a matter of state, and subject to the coercion of the crown. It was therefore regulated with us by the king's proclamations, prohibitions, charters of privilege and of licence, and finally by the decrees of the court of star chamber; which limited the number of printers, and of presses which each should employ, and prohibited new publications unless previously approved by proper licensers. On the demolition of this odious jurisdiction in 1641, the long parliament of Charles 1, after their rupture with that prince, assumed the same powers as the starchamber exercised with respect to the licensing of books; and in 1643, 1647, 1649, and 1652, issued their ordinances for that purpose, founded principally on the starchamber decree of 1637. [These licensings practices and acts were] continued to 1692. It was then continued for two years longer by statute, 4 W. & M. c. 24, but though frequent attempts were made by the government to revive it, in the subsequent part of that reign * * * yet the parliament resisted it so strongly, that it finally expired, and the press became properly free, in 1694; and has ever since so continued. [Footnote by Blackstone.]

[In 1644, a half-century before Parliament allowed the last press licensing law to expire without renewing it (as Blackstone notes supra), John Milton wrote his famous *Areopagitica*. The title is taken from "Areopagus," the council of ancient Athens and the place where petitions were presented to that council—the areopagus stands on a slight hill nearby the agora, the place where popular assemblies met. One may recall from Milton's compelling prose his moving passages on freedom of speech and of the press. ("Give me the liberty to know, to utter, and to argue freely according to conscience, above all liberties. * * * And though all the windes of doctrin were let loose to play upon the earth, so Truth be in the field, we do injuriously by licensing and prohibiting to misdoubt her strength. Let her and Falsehood grapple; who ever knew Truth put to the wors, in a free and open encounter. Her confuting is the best and surest suppressing.") Milton's essay was addressed to Parliament. It was directed to licensing, and it is thus titled ("For the Liberty of *Unlicenc'd* Printing"). (Emphasis added.) ("I mean not tolerated Popery, and open superstition, which as it extirpats all religions and civil supremacies, so it self should be extirpat * * * that also which is impious or evil absolutely either against faith or manners no law can possibly permit, that intends not to unlaw it self * * *.").] [Ed. note.]

that to censure the licentiousness, is to maintain the liberty, of the press."

D.

The Court's treatment of the first amendment in Patterson v. Colorado [22] is surely startling, especially when coupled with the extracts we have added from Blackstone's Commentaries on which Holmes, for the Court, relied in deciding the case, finding no reversible error in the conviction and fine of Patterson for common law criminal contempt.[23] How does the Court understand the first amendment? And how does *Patterson* square with our first, "absolute," view? Evidently, the answer to both questions is found in a single solution. It is found by taking a more measured view of that amendment, reading it in the following way:

Congress shall make NO law abridging *the* freedom of speech or of the press—and by suggesting that "the" freedom of speech and "the" freedom of the press is coterminous with that freedom as it was understood as of 1769, which it was the sole design of the first amendment to give constitutional status as of 1791.[24]

If this is correct, there is nonetheless very little problem in squaring *Patterson* with the first amendment. Ironically, there is also no problem squaring it with the literalist views of Justice Black, either. Neither is there any problem in squaring it with our preliminary review, comparing the first amendment with other constitutional clauses. Rather, the suggested resolution is simple. It is this. The first amendment *is* unqualified, i.e. it *is* absolute: Congress shall, indeed, make no law abridging the freedom of speech or of the press, whether for a compelling reason or for any other reason. If it does, the Court is

---

22. 205 U.S. 454, 27 S.Ct. 556, 51 L.Ed. 879 (1907).

23. Note, among other elements: (1) There was no statute Patterson was alleged to have violated. (2) He was subjected to trial though no grand jury had determined suitable cause. (3) He was tried without benefit of jury [a significant matter—in the history of free speech and press, jury nullification played a powerful role]. (4) He was tried and sentenced by persons with a direct interest in the case. (5) The case on which the newspaper published its comments had *already* been concluded on the merits (only a motion for rehearing following final judgment was still pending). (6) The published statements alleged to constitute criminal contempt were obviously expressions of Patterson's opinion, i.e. an account of what, in his view, explained what had taken place. (7) Factual truth itself was ruled not to matter, i.e. *to be irrelevant as a matter of law.* (8) The court may also have not adhered even to state law. (On which of these issues would a different result be reached today? In England? In the United States? Why?)

24. To be sure, *Patterson* is a case reviewing "the freedom of *the press* " (rather than "the freedom of *speech* "), i.e. it refers (even as Blackstone does) to what "the liberty of the press" consists of (namely, the absence of prior restraints, not protection from post-publication amercement) (and note Holmes' point,—that "[t]he preliminary freedom extends as well to the false as to the true; *the subsequent punishment may extend as well to the true as to the false.* "). But there is no reason to suppose the point of reference for determining "the freedom of speech" would be a different one, is there? Presumably it will be the same: the legal legacy of England, roughly speaking as of 1769, which it was the design of the first amendment to give constitutional status against such acts of Congress as might seek to abridge it. In brief, what was protected in English law as of 1769, but not more (for it is *that* freedom of speech which is understood by "the" freedom of speech), is protected by the first amendment.

quite prepared to strike it down. But, that which Congress is (unqualifiedly) forbidden to make any law abridging is simply "the" freedom of speech and of the press, i.e. "the" freedom referred to by the amendment. Thus, so long as Congress makes no law abridging "the" freedom of speech or of the press (i.e. the freedom of speech or of the press referred to by the amendment itself), it does nothing to offend the first amendment *at all.* The Court is not called upon to "balance" any interests, moreover, any more than Justice Black supposed. Rather, it is merely to determine objectively, even as Holmes did in *Patterson,* whether there was any congressional trespass on "the" freedom of speech or of the press to which the amendment itself refers. To be sure, "the" freedom of speech and of the press thus secured by the first amendment may not be known without reference to something lying outside the Constitution itself, but once the proper reference is made (and its content objectively supplied and accordingly filled in), the amendment fully applies. The reference is to the freedom of speech and of the press as it was known to have developed roughly as of the date the first amendment was adopted, *nothing less,* albeit, of course, also *nothing more.* [25]

E.

Does this view of the first amendment effectively trash the amendment? Does it, for instance, make the first amendment virtually no better than what the English have (namely, no first amendment at all)? Clearly, it does not, in the following sense. The difference is that, lacking our first amendment, the English continue to be dependent upon the sufferance of Parliament even today to preserve the enjoyment of such freedom of speech and of the press as they had secured as of 1769 (the date of Blackstone's Commentaries). In the United States, the first amendment protects that complement of free speech and free press from congressional interference, albeit, perhaps, nothing more. Presumably, if Parliament wished, Parliament could even now reinstate a requirement of press licensing although it has had no such system since 1694. In the United States, presumably because of the first amendment, Congress could do nothing of the sort.[26] Still, even allowing for this difference, one would agree that the first amendment as thus construed falls far short of providing the absolute bulwark we earlier supposed.

---

25. Additional protection for freedom of the press and of speech would be sought in positive legislation, i.e. the first amendment merely establishes the minimum, not the maximum Congress (or each state) might affirmatively provide.

26. Presumably Congress could not do so, moreover, regardless of how "compelling" the circumstances and regardless of how few, or easy, the conditions of securing such a license might be. (Query, however: if it is true at a minimum that at least the first amendment flatly forbids any act of Congress from imposing a licensing system on freedom of speech or of the press, how can one square the constitutionality of the Federal Communications Act of 1934, insofar as that act of Congress makes it a criminal offense to broadcast without a license granted by the FCC, subject to grant, renewal, and cancellation, under such standards as are provided for in the act? Is CBS *not* a part of "the press"? Is Dan Rather *less* engaged in free speech than George Will? Is the FCA not a modern example of exactly the kind of licensing system even a pure "Blackstone" view of the first amendment forbids?)

III.

Note that the dissent by Justice Harlan in *Patterson*, was directed mainly to the question of the extent to which the fourteenth amendment did or did not pull over the protections of the first amendment into the privileges and immunities clause of the fourteenth amendment, rather than to the additional question, namely, assuming that it did, what then? If the first amendment would not preclude a federal criminal contempt prosecution in a like set of circumstances as those involved in the *Patterson* case (and where is Justice Harlan's demonstration that it would?), what does his dissent come to, in the end? The equivalency, if there is one, between the fourteenth amendment and the first amendment, is unquestionably highly consequential.[27] Even so, i.e. even under Justice Harlan's view, water does not rise higher than the source from which it flows. Accordingly, the fourteenth amendment will not provide more protection from state court contempt sanctions than the first amendment would provide in like circumstances from federal court sanctions, for the fourteenth amendment does not rise "higher" than the first. If, then, the first amendment would not apply so to forbid an equivalent federal criminal contempt prosecution, the dissent fails to show how the fourteenth amendment forbids such a prosecution in a state court setting even by its own test. So the main issue seems to be the one we have examined here, as the important one, after all. And, treating that issue straightforwardly, as we have now tried to do, fairly and fully, it has brought us to a rather disappointing place.

It may seem odd that the conclusion we have reached seems to be what it is. What it suggests is that to understand the first amendment (and also, therefore, to study for this course), all one needs best to do is to read Blackstone's Commentaries on the Laws of England, principally volume iv of the 1769 edition. As according to Blackstone, the criminal contempt prosecution of an editor in Patterson's position was entertainable at common law (and "the *liberty of the press,* properly understood, is by no means [thereby] infringed or violated"),[28] we would proceed in the same fashion in every case, including all cases involving acts of Congress such as the Sedition Act of 1798 [29] were it re-enacted even

---

27. We have already noted that the vast majority of likely abridgments of free speech and of the press will numerically arise as a consequence of state, city, and county laws and practices, rather than from Congress; it is no coincidence that the vast majority of "first amendment" cases decided by the Supreme Court during the past fifty years arise under state or local laws. So of course the so-called "incorporation" debate (i.e. the extent to which the fourteenth amendment pulls across the Bill of Rights for purposes of equal protection against the states) is highly consequential. We shall look at it, again, in due course.

28. We are merely quoting here from the passages from Blackstone reproduced earlier. (Emphasis in the original.)

29. The Act referred to may be found in 1 Stat. 596. Patterned after the English law of seditious libel, it was adopted in response to the seeming imminence of war with France, just seven years after the first amendment was ratified. It was applied a number of times and sustained against constitutional objection in the lower courts, but the Supreme Court never addressed it (though several of the Supreme Court Justices were involved in the cases in which it was used, in their role as circuit court judges), and it expired by its own terms, in 1801. Shortly after coming to office as President, Jefferson issued unconditional

now. If, by the same reference, i.e. to Blackstone, *the* liberty of the press "properly understood" would not have been regarded as thereby infringed by any equivalent criminal prosecution for seditious libel at common law, in England, around 1769, neither would it be objectionable here, pursuant to an act of Congress, so far as the first amendment is concerned. If, but only if, by the same reference, such a prosecution would have been regarded as infringing "the" liberty of the press, according to Blackstone's report, then neither may it be pursued here, and an act of Congress presuming to authorize it would be void. Both ways, evidently, our proposition will hold. *Quod Erat Demonstrandum:* studying Blackstone is the proper, objective measure of the first amendment and of this course.[30]

Moreover, if this proposition does hold, neither should it matter if that study should turn out to yield a rather disappointing content.[31] And neither should it matter if that study would show that the first amendment is a more weakly enacted restriction on national acts of speech and press regulation than even the foreign constitutional provisions we were tentatively (and unfavorably) comparing earlier on. So far as either may be true, still, to take Justice Black's own point seriously—that the first amendment is to be respected by the courts until such time as it is altered by amendment—it is obviously not for the courts to "balance" the claims of free speech or press differently than was done by the Constitution. It is, rather, for the courts to apply the Constitution, no more, no less, as it is.[32] One may put the same point more aggressively in the following way: If one were inclined to

pardons to all those convicted under the act, answering in correspondence to an inquiry by Abigail Adams, John Adams' wife, that he did so because in his view the Sedition Act was unconstitutional and invalid under the first amendment. (The prosecutions and convictions had been obtained during John Adams' administration.) The principal provision was this: *"If any person shall write, print, utter or publish any false and malicious writing against the government of the United States, or either house of congress, or the president, with intent to defame them, or either of them, or to bring them or either of them into contempt, or disrepute; or to excite against them or either of them, the hatred of the good people of the United States, then such person, being thereof convicted before any court of the United States having jurisdiction thereof shall be punished by a fine not exceeding two thousand dollars, and by imprisonment not exceeding two years."*

30. Just so, Leonard Levy concludes: "If * * * a choice must be made between two propositions, first, that the [freedom of speech and press] clause substantially embodied the Blackstonian definition and left the law of seditious libel in force, or repudiated Blackstone and superseded the common law, *the evidence points strongly in support of the former proposition."* (Emphasis added.) L. Levy, Emergence of a Free Press 281 (1985).

31. It would yield "a rather disappointing content," incidentally, even as is well illustrated by the *Patterson* case. If one will take the time to read Blackstone's coverage of the common law and of parliamentary discretion to limit speech and press in England (to avoid all speech and publication of a "pernicious tendency" as noted in one part of the excerpt we have already earlier quoted), as of 1769, one will find not a great deal that could not be done. Indeed, it raises a fair question of why an amendment doing no more than to enact Blackstone would have been thought worthwhile to bother with at all. Certainly there is no suggestion that there was otherwise such likelihood that Congress might somehow embark on a press licensing system as to explain it on that account, i.e. that it was proposed to head off some imminent or feared possibility of such a system.

32. The framers, we might say, did all the balancing when they adopted the first amendment in the Blackstone form, as they did. Such alterations as may come, must come—if at all—solely pursuant to article V.

rally to this view respecting the role and duty of the Supreme Court when one held the view that the first amendment was "actually" very strong and highly protective, what inconsistency now moves you to desert it, merely seeing the mistake you had laid up in your earlier hopes?

B.

Yet, before leaving this discussion as though it were now quite complete, if the Harlan opinion seems not convincing re the scope of the first amendment (i.e. not convincing to show that the amendment meant to repudiate Blackstone [33]), on the other hand, in fairness to Harlan, the Holmes' opinion may not be much better to show the opposite, i.e. that the amendment meant merely to shield speech and press from certain kinds of prior restraints it might be feared Congress might be tempted to impose.[34] Rather, Holmes also seemed to take much for granted, didn't he, but did not pursue the matter as he is clear that, in any event, the fourteenth amendment (which is all that is involved in the *Patterson* case) may not incorporate the first amendment—so the exact field of the first amendment isn't important—in *Patterson*—to decide.

Actually, the scholarship that has examined the "Blackstone-enactment" view of the first amendment, including Leonard Levy's own (excellent) work, is quite mixed.[35] What it may show is, principally, that there was very considerable apprehension of what Congress might

---

33. And if to repudiate Blackstone, then, instead, to enact *what?* I.e. if one were to succeed in showing that there is no convincing evidence that the first amendment deliberately used the phrase "the freedom of speech and of the press" with any such limited reference in mind as "the extent of protection generally respected in England and/or among the colonies and states as of 1769 or 1789 protecting freedom of speech and of the press from prior restraints *but not otherwise*" [which, in a nutshell, was Blackstone's view of the law of England], what then? Nothing else follows per se. (E.g., does it follow from that that therefore an act of Congress, say, forbidding an interstate dealer in pork bellies knowingly to misrepresent the nutritional benefits of pork bellies, on pain of civil sanctions to be imposed by the FTC (Federal Trade Commission) after a full and fair due process hearing reviewable on appeal, is obviously a violation of the first amendment? Literally, under Justice Black's view, it would seem to be so. Is it arguable, however, that "something in between" Blackstone and Black can logically be worked out? (But how will one determine what that "something in between" is?)

34. Both of the cases cited by Justice Holmes in *Patterson* were themselves also state cases (*Oswald* is a 1788 state criminal contempt case decided by the Pennsylvania supreme court; *Blanding* is an 1825 case from Massachusetts.) Neither involved any act of Congress or the first amendment as such. As you will see early on in the cases, moreover, Holmes substantially changed his mind about this matter. See, e.g., Abrams v. United States, 250 U.S. 616, 630–31, 40 S.Ct. 17, 22, 63 L.Ed. 1173, 1180 (1919); Bogen, The Free Speech Metamorphosis of Mr. Justice Holmes, 11 Hofstra L.Rev. 97 (1982); Rabban, The Emergence of Modern First Amendment Doctrine, 50 Chi.L.Rev. 1205, 1303–20 (1983).

35. For three critical reviews of Levy, see Anderson, The Origins of the Press Clause, 30 UCLA L.Rev. 455 (1983) (replied to, 32 UCLA L.Rev. 177 (1984); Mayton, Seditous Libel and the Lost Guarantee of a Freedom of Expression, 84 Colum.L.Rev. 91 (1984) (replied to, 37 Stan.L.Rev. 767); Rabban, The Ahistorical Historian: Leonard Levy on Freedom of Expression in Early American History, 37 Stan.L.Rev. 795 (1985). For two of the best historical works on freedom of speech and of the press in England and in early America, see E. Hudon, Freedom of Speech and Press in America (1963); F. Siebert, Freedom of the Press in England 1476–1776 (1952). The standard work in support of the view that the first amendment repudiated, rather than assimilated, Blackstone and the common law of seditious libel is Z. Chafee, Free Speech in the United States (1942).

presume to do once launched under its new, larger set of enumerated powers just then granted in the new Constitution of 1789. And what it may also show is that there was a widespread unwillingness to trust to earlier assurances that Congress would, even without any first amendment,[36] simply have no power whatever in respect to speech or press.[37] The several states in fact treated freedom of speech and of the press quite variously. The first amendment may well have reflected a widespread resolve that however much that state of affairs would continue even after the Constitution went into effect, *Congress* (in contradistinction to the several states) should have little or no role to play.[38] And, if that were so, then certainly a reference to Blackstone

36. The first amendment, incidentally, was originally the third amendment within the original list of twelve amendments Congress submitted for ratification by the states, in 1789. The first two amendments did not achieve a sufficient number of state ratification votes to become part of the Constitution. (The original first amendment would have fixed a certain formula for the number of Representatives. The original second amendment provided that "No law, varying the compensation for the services of Senators and Representatives, shall take effect, until an election for Representatives shall have intervened.")

37. Alexander Hamilton, in Federalist No. 84, pressed this argument as a reason for not proposing anything resembling the first amendment. He argued that whatever form of words might be used in framing some section of the Constitution, or some amendment to the Constitution, respecting protection of freedom of the press, would be confusing: "For why declare that things shall not be done which there is no power to do? Why, for instance, should it be said, that the liberty of the press shall not be restrained, when no power is given by which restrictions may be imposed?" Hamilton's argument was only a partial and temporary success. Others pointed out that Article I, Section 9 of the Constitution already enumerated a short list of positive restrictions on Congress, thus the precedent for taking additional express precautions was already set. The absence of a more elaborate Bill of Rights held up ratification in a number of states including New York and Virginia (both states were considered crucial even if nine other states might ratify); in North Carolina, ratification was delayed until the Bill of Rights was actually introduced. As reflected in St. George Tucker's observations (see next note infra), the fact that no express power was granted to Congress to regulate speech or press was deemed insufficient; the concern was that the power would be claimed indirectly, e.g., as an incident to regulate commerce among the several states or as an incident of other powers enumerated in Article I.

38. For example, in his appendix to his 1803 edition of Blackstone's Commentaries, St. George Tucker (Professor of Law at William & Mary) distinguished the pertinence of Blackstone in just this way (at p. 29): "The danger justly apprehended by those states which insisted that the federal government should possess no power, directly *or indirectly*, over the subject, was, that those who were entrusted with the administration might be forward in considering every thing as a crime against the government, which might operate to their own personal disadvantage; it was therefore made a fundamental article of the federal compact, that no such power should be exercised, or claimed by the federal government; leaving it to the state governments to exercise such jurisdiction and control over the subject, as their several constitutions and laws permit." (Emphasis added.) Levy acknowledges that this was consistently James Madison's view. (p. 318). ("The amendment, Madison declared, was intended to have the broadest construction on freedom of the press as well as religion. It 'meant a positive denial to Congress of any power whatever on the subject.'") In proposing the Bill of Rights in the first Congress, moreover, Madison also recorded his expectation of judicial enforcement as well. Address by James Madison before the United States House of Representatives, June 8, 1789, reprinted in 5 The Writings of James Madison 389 (G. Hunt ed. 1904) ("If they are incorporated into the constitution, independent tribunals of justice will consider themselves in a peculiar manner the guardians of these rights.") See also Van Alstyne, Congressional Power and Free Speech: Levy's Legacy Revisited, 99 Harv. L.Rev. 1089 (1986). The concern of the Bill of Rights was emphatically a concern to restrict Congress, see Barron v. Mayor and City Council of Baltimore, 32 U.S. (7 Pet.) 243, 8 L.Ed. 672 (1833). ("[I]t is universally understood, it is a part of the history of the day, that the great revolution which estab-

would be a very poor guide in understanding the stringency of the first amendment enacted as a restriction on *Congress,* or on the national government, understanding that it would have no implications for the several states.

C.

Between such words as "little" and "no" (i.e. as in the phrase that the first amendment meant that "Congress should have *little or no* role" in regulating free speech or the free press in the United States), however, there is still an equivocation, isn't there, respecting what Congress may or may not be able to do. So, what shall one do about that?[39] One might just eliminate the weasel word, "little," of course. That would take care of the problem. It would also be consistent with some things we have covered in Part I—as well as greatly shorten this course. There are, however, two sorts of problems, if we do: one that perhaps ought not trouble us, intellectually, but the other of which probably will.

The first is merely the practical problem that the courts (including the Supreme Court) have never been willing to read the first amendment as disarming Congress of *all* power to legislate in reference to things spoken or printed. Even worse, despite the review we have attempted here, it is difficult to find an archimedean point strong enough to insist that the first amendment so demands.[40] Some of the

lished the constitution of the United States, was not effected without immense opposition. Serious fears were extensively entertained, that those powers which the patriot statesmen, who then watched over the interests of the country, deemed essential to union, and to the attainment of those invaluable objects for which union was sought, might be exercised in a manner dangerous to liberty. In almost every convention by which the constitution was adopted, amendments to guard against the abuse of power were recommended. These amendments demanded security against the apprehended encroachments of the general government—not against those of the local governments. In compliance with a sentiment thus generally expressed, to quiet fears thus extensively entertained, amendments were proposed by the required majority in congress, and adopted by the states. These amendments contain no expression indicating an intention to apply them to the state governments.")

39. I.e. well, which is it, "little" or "no" role [for Congress to play]?—And if "little" (rather than "no") role, just *how* little, and as determined by *whose* opinion, and by *what* standards?

40. Footnote 33 supra provided an example of an act of Congress regulating speech of a sort (an act authorizing Federal Trade Commission cease and desist orders against false and misleading advertising of commercial goods and services in interstate commerce, after full hearing, with full judicial review). Doubtless such an act may raise substantial first amendment questions. Still, it is difficult to find support for the argument that Congress has no power (but, rather, is forbidden by the first amendment) to provide *any* remedies for interstate commercial fraud committed by means of oral or printed speech. Consider also acts of Congress such as these: an act subjecting one to federal criminal prosecution for committing perjury as a sworn witness in a federal court; an act making it a federal felony to solicit another to kill the President of the United States. Each is an instance of "speech" specifically criminalized by act of Congress. Does the first amendment invalidate the congressional act? Does it forbid either act from being applied? Would the act punishing criminal solicitation be valid only if the solicitation were actually acted upon?—But why should that make any difference, either way?

The book most often credited with presenting the historical case for a strong first amendment (in contrast with the Levy book, previously cited), is Z. Chafee, Free Speech in the United States (1942) (also cited in note 35 supra). Yet, Professor Chafee's own presentation falls very short of adopting the "absolute" form of the first amendment. (Id. at 145, 149–50: "We can all agree that the free speech clauses do

problems that beset the first amendment are apparently quite genuine. They will not all, easily, just "go away." If that is so, however, then where are we? At worst we are simply better prepared, more intelligently to begin on our work, once again.

Indeed, one might struggle with these things even as you will now do, conscientiously, as a student. It may well be the case that the first amendment did not just enact Blackstone into constitutional status. As we shall see, moreover, the Supreme Court eventually agreed. *Patterson v. Colorado* is not the last word. As to the many other questions we have now raised for purposes of introduction, the cases we shall be studying show a long series of provisional answers, many of which are highly contestable as, indeed, we shall see. Even so, despite all its difficulties, this is a serious and worthy subject—there may be none personally more absorbing or overall more significant,[41] to pursue. We shall have too little time to consider the full subject in every detail. Still, we shall come to terms with most of the basic field.[42] So far as our introductory tour is concerned, we have taken the measure of two very different views of the first amendment, neither of which appears quite to have worked out:

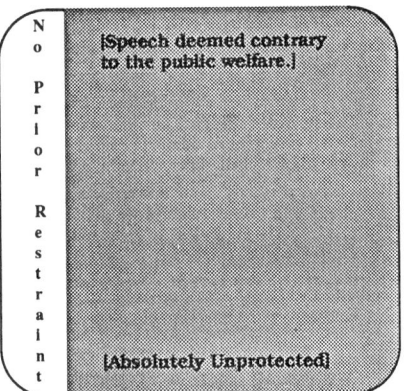

not wipe out the common law as to obscenity, profanity, and defamation of individuals. * * * [O]bscenity, profanity, and gross libels of individuals * * * fall outside the protection of the free speech clauses as I have defined them [as do criminal solicitation or even talking scurrilously about the flag].") Actually, there is good reason to disagree with Professor Chafee on some of these matters, as to Congress, as we shall see in this course. The point remains, however, that Chafee's examples gave him some difficulty nonetheless.

41. It is an idle pastime, a child's game, perhaps, to say which portions of the entire Constitution one might regard as most critical (e.g., the equal protection clause?—the clauses protecting one's right to vote?—that which provides for amendments?—

those enabling Congress to act?). Taking the world all in all, however, a good case can be made that the most vital clauses may be article I, section 9's provision for habeas corpus and the first amendment clause on free speech and free press. The first may enable one to be released from prison when wrongfully held. The second enables one freely to speak one's mind. Grant people guarantees such as these to live by and they may be able to move the world.

42. The latter third of these materials takes up the first amendment clauses addressed to religion ("Congress shall make no law respecting an establishment of religion or prohibiting the free exercise thereof"). A separate introduction is provided in due course.

We now begin again, with a somewhat more complex figure that will look more like the following one:

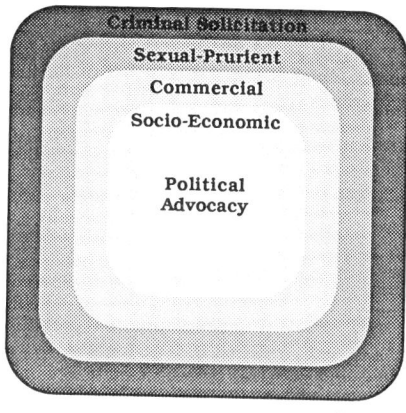

Before embarking on the modern case law of the first amendment, however, it may be helpful to review the following brief Coda on other constitutional clauses—clauses closely related to each other and to the first amendment, in the constitutional history of freedom of speech and of the press, both in England and in the United States.

CODA TO "THE INTRODUCTION TO THE FIRST AMENDMENT": *OTHER* CLAUSES RELATED TO FREEDOM OF SPEECH AND OF THE PRESS

The constitutional clauses interpreted in *Patterson v. Colorado* were drawn from the first and fourteenth amendments, as will routinely be true throughout this course. There are, however, several other clauses in the Constitution one should want to know more about because they, too, may bear on the subject in which we are engaged. Because this course does not provide time to deal with these other clauses in any systematic way, and because not all of them are necessarily treated in other courses for their relevance to the subject we are particularly concerned with in this course, it is useful at least to be aware of them, now. There may be times when reference to one or another of these clauses would usefully provide argumentative support buttressing a direct first amendment question as such (i.e. there may be a synergy among several clauses [43]). Thus this very brief additional review.

---

43. For example, to the extent that the fourth amendment (discussed infra) has a distinctive history linked to the development of freedom of the press, it is worthwhile to bear that connection in mind in considering police practices of search and seizure of newspaper files, in the investigation of crimes. Arguably, the standard fourth amendment requirements for search warrants, sufficient in other circumstances, ought not always be deemed sufficient when the police seek to capture and search through newspaper files when their interest—and application for a search war-

I.

There is in fact a free speech clause in the Constitution that antedates the First Amendment. It is found in article I, section 6. This clause enacts for the protection of Congress what in England had already been gained by Parliament's hard-won freedom from subordination to the monarchy: a freedom not to have its members seized and locked in the Tower of London by crown order, for remarks made in the course of parliamentary debate.[44] The relevant clause provides as follows: [45]

> For any Speech or Debate in either House, they [i.e. the Senators and Representatives] shall not be questioned in any other Place.[46]

The Speech and Debate clause protects a member of Congress from having to answer elsewhere in respect to what he or she says in Congress. Insofar as a member of Congress may repeat the same remarks elsewhere, however, e.g., as in issuing a news release, the absolute immunity may be lost.[47] Additionally, despite the shield furnished by the clause providing that one need not answer for any debate or vote in Congress, the clause does not immunize members of Congress from criminal prosecution for alleged bribe taking or bribe solicitation.[48]

---

rant—has been triggered by a published news report of matters of general political and public concern. See, e.g., Zurcher v. Stanford Daily, 436 U.S. 547, 98 S.Ct. 1970, 56 L.Ed.2d 525 (1978) (especially the concurring opinion by Justice Powell and the dissenting opinion by Justice Stevens). An argument in the Supreme Court is an argument about a whole case and not simply an argument addressed to different points of law lined up inside one's brief like dominoes where one pushes on one and then moves freshly to the next, pushing on it in turn. A different way of putting the same proposition is that the strength of one's case is equal to the sum of its parts and not just the sum divided all over again by the number of parts. For a useful general review, see C. Black, Structure and Relationship in Constitutional Law (1969).

44. See, for a brief review and discussion, United States v. Johnson, 383 U.S. 169, 178, 86 S.Ct. 749, 754, 15 L.Ed.2d 681, 687 (1966); D. Bogen, Bulwark of Liberty: The Court and the First Amendment 8–10 (1984).

45. Note its close similarity to the provision in the English Bill of Rights, enacted in 1689, "That the freedom of speech and debates in Parliament ought not to be impeached or questioned in any court or place out of Parliament." 1 W. & M. Sess. 2, c. 2.

46. Relatedly, the habeas corpus clause (article I, section 9) has a connecting thread. In part, the habeas corpus clause's origin tracks back to the successful effort by Parliament to insure that persons held in crown custody must be held pursuant to the common law or pursuant to an act of Parliament, and not by executive fiat alone. The Habeas Corpus Act in England was itself a means by which anyone seized for remarks made in Parliament might have special legal process to get released. See, e.g., W. Duker, A Constitutional History of Habeas Corpus 45, 62 (1980) ("As long as the executive retained authority to imprison arbitrarily, Parliament remained subordinate."); The Constitution of the United States, Analysis and Interpretation 651 (J. Killian, ed. 1987) ("At the English common law, habeas corpus was available to attack pretrial detention and confinement by executive order; it could not be used to question the conviction of a person pursuant to the judgment of a court with jurisdiction over the person.").

47. See, e.g., Hutchinson v. Proxmire, 443 U.S. 111, 99 S.Ct. 2675, 61 L.Ed.2d 411 (1979) (private civil libel action sustained over demurrer by Senator Proxmire re "Golden Fleece" award identifying plaintiff in news release ridiculing plaintiff's government-funded research, though the same remarks would have been absolutely privileged when made on Senate floor).

48. See United States v. Helstoski, 442 U.S. 477, 99 S.Ct. 2432, 61 L.Ed.2d 12 (1979); United States v. Brewster, 408 U.S. 501, 92 S.Ct. 2531, 33 L.Ed.2d 507 (1972).

II.

One will note that "treason" is a crime defined in the Constitution, and the punishment for treason is also limited, in article III, section 3:

> Treason against the United States, shall consist only in levying War against them, or in adhering to their Enemies, giving them Aid and Comfort. No person shall be convicted of Treason unless on the Testimony of two Witnesses to the same overt Act, or on Confession in open Court.
>
> The Congress shall have Power to declare the Punishment of Treason, but no Attainder of Treason shall work corruption of Blood, or Forfeiture except during the Life of the Person attainted.

This narrow, constitutionally-entrenched definition of treason—and the special proof the crime requires and the limitation on punishment—is related to the history of printing and to possible prosecution for what one writes down as a private record of one's thoughts. According to Blackstone,[49] there was a species of treason in the common law called "constructive treason," namely, compassing or imagining the death of the king. The offense of constructive treason was separate from the offense of seditious libel. Conviction of constructive treason required proof of an overt act, but the act of putting pen to paper, even in an unsent, speculative letter, was at one time held to suffice as an overt act. On the other hand, oral discourse disclosing a state of mind of a like character, while punishable as seditious libel, was not per se deemed to be a sufficient overt act for this highly extended definition of treason as such.[50] In one respect, then, the treason clause reflects its own (albeit limited) concern for a free press.[51]

Cf. United States v. Johnson, 383 U.S. 169, 86 S.Ct. 749, 15 L.Ed.2d 681 (1966).

49. Vol. 4 at 99–104. See also Mayton, Seditious Libel and the Lost Guarantee of a Freedom of Expression, 84 Colum.L.Rev. 91, 98–102 (1984).

50. Treason was a most heinous offense, and it was specially punished, by "drawing and quartering" (manacling the condemned person to be dragged through the streets behind horses until nearly dead, and, while alive, disemboweled before his own eyes, his innards burnt, his body then to be hacked into quarters, to be scattered, the head to be put atop a pikestaff along the public way), all goods and estates to be forfeited, all relatives deprived of inheritance and support. The constitutionally narrowed definition of treason, incidentally, was singularly responsible for saving Aaron Burr from conviction for treason during the Jefferson administration. (At trial before John Marshall, presiding as trial judge on circuit, Burr was determined as a matter of law not to have engaged in sufficient overt acts. See United States v. Burr, 8 U.S. (4 Cranch) 470 app. n. B (1807).) (The *Burr* case is additionally interesting because it involved an early use and testing of claims of "executive privilege." Burr claimed that a letter in President Thomas Jefferson's possession would tend to exonerate him; after initially resisting the court's request to submit the letter to the court, Jefferson, reluctantly, complied.)

51. For a stronger view, namely, that the treason clause reflexively restricts seditious libel as a possible alternative crime, see J. Hurst, The Law of Treason in the United States 152 (1971). ("[T]he record does suggest that the clause was intended to guarantee nonviolent political processes against prosecution under any theory or charge, the burden of which was the allegedly seditious character of the conduct in question.") See also Mayton, Seditious Libel and the Lost Guarantee of a Freedom of Expression, 84 Col.L.Rev. 91, 95, 98, 116 (1984). ("In the United States we have devised criminal statutes in the nature of constructive treason, but have instead characterized them as sedition or espionage laws, and thereby have avoided one of our own constitutional safeguards—the

III.

Relatedly, the Fourth Amendment has a First Amendment tie as well. Briefly, it is this. Recall that the Fourth Amendment provides:

> The right of the people to be secure in their persons, houses, papers, and effects, against unreasonable searches and seizures, shall not be violated, and no Warrants shall issue, but upon probable cause, supported by Oath or affirmation, and particularly describing the place to be searched, and the persons or things to be seized.

General writs of assistance and general warrants of search had figured prominently in English history, respecting the licensed press. The licensing system was enforced by ferreting out unlicensed print presses; their discovery and seizure proceeded pursuant to general writs of assistance and general warrants of search. The fourth amendment is, in part, a reaction to such practices; it disallows general warrants of search.[52]

IV.

Additionally, there is strong suggestion in press history literature that the assurances of trial by jury (article III and the sixth amendment) drew partly from freedom of press concerns:

> The Trial of all Crimes, except in Cases of Impeachment, shall be by Jury

* * *

> In all criminal prosecutions, the accused shall enjoy the right to a speedy and public trial, by an impartial jury of the State and district wherein the crime shall have been committed.

---

treason clause—against such laws. * * * The recorded discussion of the treason clause shows a common understanding of the clause as a free speech provision.")

52. Perhaps the most famous English case is Entick v. Carrington, 19 Howell's State Trials 1030, 95 Eng. 807 (1705), cited and relied upon by our Supreme Court in Boyd v. United States, 116 U.S. 616, 626, 6 S.Ct. 524, 530, 29 L.Ed. 746, 749 (1886). Entick, an associate of John Wilkes, successfully sued state officers who broke into his house and seized a mass of charts and pamphlets owned by Entick (Wilkes had published polemical pamphlets attacking crown policies and the king), pursuant to a general warrant, issued without a record of probable cause. The particularity requirement of the fourth amendment has been given its most stringent application when first amendment protected political materials have been the object of search warrants. See, e.g., Stanford v. Texas, 379 U.S. 476, 85 S.Ct. 506, 13 L.Ed.2d 431 (1965). Additionally, in respect to seizure of books and films, prior review by the warrant-issuing magistrate of each item may be specially required, seizures incidental to an otherwise lawful arrest may be disallowed (because no magistrate will have made an independent determination re their first amendment status), and an exceedingly prompt post-seizure adversary hearing may have to be provided to test "obscenity" seizures of allegedly criminally contraband materials as against the claim that they are not "obscene" by first amendment standards of law. See, e.g., Marcus v. Search Warrant, 367 U.S. 717, 81 S.Ct. 1708, 6 L.Ed.2d 1127 (1961); A Quantity of Copies of Books v. Kansas, 378 U.S. 205, 84 S.Ct. 1723, 12 L.Ed.2d 809 (1964); Heller v. New York, 413 U.S. 483, 93 S.Ct. 2789, 37 L.Ed.2d 745 (1973). But see New York v. P.J. Video, Inc., 475 U.S. 868, 875, 106 S.Ct. 1610, 1615 n. 6, 89 L.Ed.2d 871, 880 n. 6 (1986) (no higher standard of probable cause required than in other cases).

The assurance of trial by jury might mitigate the rigor of "the law."[53] A jury may decline to apply a law it finds unduly harsh though a judge, in a bench trial, would not.[54] In modern free speech and free press cases, the issue may also arise respecting the extent to which the jury determines whether the first amendment's legal standard (whatever it is) has or has not been met by the prosecutor in a speech or press case, i.e. that that issue is not solely for the judge to decide but, rather, the jury must itself be persuaded that that standard has been met. There is also a related question that can be important, namely, whether the trial jury cannot be required to return a special verdict but only a general (i.e. overall) verdict failing which the defendant cannot be held.[55]

V.

Finally, in completing this circle of other constitutional provisions specially entwined with the first amendment provisions on freedom of speech and of the press, it is fitting to return to the full first amendment itself. That amendment has two linked provisions at its end, each of which may have an independent and a synergistic litigative use:

Congress shall make no law * * * abridging the freedom of speech, or of the press; or *the right of the people peaceably to*

---

53. In seditious libel cases at common law, incidentally, the jury's role was very narrow; the jury was confined to determining whether the accused was in fact the printer or author of the indicted material, and whether the publication identified the aspersed party, as alleged. On the other hand, whether the material was "libelous" and "malicious" were deemed to be questions of law solely for the judge's determination, nor was a proffer of evidence in behalf of the accused respecting the truth of any factual statement admissible as a matter of law, nor was the jury to determine the law at all. Even so, despite a judge's clear instructions on these several points, juries sometimes acquitted in the teeth of the evidence. (They had no "right" to do so, albeit they possessed the "power" to do so, as the distinction was said to be). Several famous trials (e.g., Peter Zenger's trial in 1735) saved printers from serving prison terms solely by force of jury nullification. (For an excellent review of Zenger's case, see L. Levy, Emergence of a Free Press 37–44 (1985).) (Query: how, if at all, would any of this apply to *Patterson?* Was Patterson entitled to trial by jury? In a similar case today, would the fourteenth amendment be construed to entitle someone in Patterson's position to trial by jury?)

54. In an earlier footnote, the critical provisions of the Sedition Act of 1798 were quoted. Section 3 of the Sedition Act, however, did provide for two safeguards that common law trials for seditious libel had lacked, namely, (a) an expanded jury role, and (b) truth as an affirmative defense. Specifically, section 3 of the Sedition Act provided: "*And be it further enacted and declared,* That if any person shall be prosecuted under this act, for the writing or publishing any libel aforesaid, it shall be lawful for the defendant, upon the trial of the cause, to give in evidence in his defense, the truth of the matter contained in the publication charged as a libel. And the jury who shall try the cause, shall have a right to determine the law and the fact, under the direction of the court, as in other cases."

55. If the jury can be directed by the court to report serially, and only on each of the factual questions submitted to it, and not overall, i.e. not any general verdict (such as, "we find the defendant guilty," or, "we find the defendant not guilty"), the imposition of that procedure might significantly cut down on jury nullification practice. If judgment cannot be passed on the accused by the court unless the jury does find the defendant "guilty," and the jury is willing to find only that the defendant published the material as alleged in the information or indictment (but not that the defendant is "guilty"), again the defendant will effectively have won. The tie-in between the right to jury trial and the first amendment, was, historically, quite important. Arguably, in some settings, it still is.

assemble, and to petition the Government for a redress of grievances.

The right to petition the government for a redress of grievances dates from 1215, and Magna Carta,[56] which provided (in chapter 61) as follows:

> If we * * * offend in any respect against any man, or transgress against any of the articles of the peace * * * and the offense is made known to four of the twenty-five barons [who shall be elected to secure the king's continuing compliance with Magna Carta itself], they shall come to us—or in our absence from the kingdom to the chief justice—to declare it and claim immediate redress. If we, or in our absence abroad the chief justice, make no redress within forty days, * * * the four barons shall refer the matter to the twenty-five barons, who may * * * assail us in every possible way, with the support of the whole community of the land, by seizing our castles [etc.] until they have secured such redress as they have determined upon.

In 1669, the right of petition was confirmed by Parliament as a right vested in every English commoner "in case of grievance" to petition Parliament itself for redress, although Parliament reserved the privilege to determine to its own satisfaction whether the petition was fit to be received.[57] In 1689, following the Glorious Revolution, the Bill of Rights asserted the right of subjects to petition the King, and "all commitments and prosecutions for such petitioning" were made illegal.[58]

An interesting link between the right to petition the national government as assured by the first amendment, and the privileges and immunities clause of the fourteenth amendment, should be noted.

---

56. Chapters 39 and 40 of the Magna Carta, incidentally, are the familiar source of other portions of our Bill of Rights (e.g., the fifth and sixth amendments). Respectively, they provide:

"39. No free man shall be seized or imprisoned, or stripped of his rights or possessions, or outlawed or exiled, or deprived of his standing in any other way, nor will we proceed with force against him, or send others to do so, except by the lawful judgment of his equals or by the law of the land.

"40. To no one will we sell, to no one deny or delay right or justice."

57. Additionally, Blackstone's Commentaries (vol. 4 at 147, 1769 ed.) describes the crime of *tumultuous petitioning*. The crime consisted of appending more than twenty names to any petition to the king or to either house of Parliament, or the delivery of a petition by a company of more than ten persons. The offense applied even when the petition sought "any alteration of matters established by law in church or state," i.e. even when the petition sought a change in the substantive law through an act by Parliament itself. Evidently, the number of names on the petition, or the number of persons involved in delivering the petition, were felt to be unduly threatening or intimidating if they exceeded the specified maximum numbers. Similarly, with respect to freedom of peaceable assembly, Blackstone (iv at 142) notes the crime of *riotous assembly*. It consisted of an assembly by twelve or more persons failing to disperse when commanded to do so by proclamation of a peace officer (thus, the origin of the phrase, "to read the riot act"). The offense might arise though the assembly had as its object "to change the laws of the kingdom," and the act providing for the offense also granted immunity from liability to persons who might be called on to help disperse the "mob" once the proclamation was made requiring them to disperse.

58. 12 Encyclopedia of the Social Sciences 98 (1934).

From the beginning, the fourteenth amendment privileges and immunities clause [59] was very narrowly construed by the Supreme Court in the *In re Slaughter–House Cases*.[60] Even so, "the privilege" of assembling in order to frame a petition for redress of felt grievances *addressed to Congress* or to the national government (e.g., to have a law changed or a law enacted by Congress in response to what citizens of the United States deem to be a just grievance), was regarded as a privilege expressly conferred by the first amendment on all citizens of the United States and, as such, a privilege protected from abridgment by the states.[61] To this extent, freedom of political association, assembly, and speech, do not depend upon the general debate regarding the extent to which the first amendment and/or the whole Bill of Rights is or is not "incorporated" into the fourteenth amendment. Rather, the framing of grievances addressed to powers Congress possesses, or to powers the President possesses under Article II (e.g., the responsibility to take care that the laws of the United States be faithfully executed, the power to issue pardons, the qualified power to veto legislative acts, etc.) is a part of the first amendment assembly-and-redress-petition privilege, the exercise of which, by citizens of the United States,[62] the states may not seek to abridge. Additionally, the clause has also been construed to apply to petitions for redress of grievances to be brought in the courts, or federal agencies, of the United States.[63]

The "peaceably to assemble" clause, moreover, may have a distinct significance, too. In one aspect, it shelters an activity (namely, meeting with others, assembling in numbers) not explicit either in freedom of speech as such, freedom of the press as such, or the right to petition for a redress of grievances, as such. And as the clause nestles among its

59. *No State shall make or enforce any law which shall abridge the privileges or immunities of citizens of the United States * * *.*

60. 83 U.S. (16 Wall.) 36, 21 L.Ed. 394 (1872) (distinguishing privileges and immunities of national citizenship from general liberty, infringements of which are not forbidden by this clause). Subsequent cases, identifying selective absorption or incorporation of the Bill of Rights into the fourteenth amendment by way of the "due process" clause rather than the privileges and immunities clause, create the textual awkwardness of using a clause that reads virtually the same as merely one fifth amendment clause to embrace much more than that fifth amendment clause itself.

61. See, e.g., Hague v. CIO, 307 U.S. 496, 515, 59 S.Ct. 954, 963–64, 83 L.Ed. 1423, 1436 (1939) ("The privilege of a citizen of the United States to use the streets and parks for communication of views *on national questions* * * * must not, in the guise of regulation, be abridged or denied.") (emphasis added); De Jonge v. Oregon, 299 U.S. 353, 57 S.Ct. 255, 81 L.Ed. 278 (1937); United States v. Cruikshank, 92 U.S. 542, 552–53, 23 L.Ed. 588, 591–92 (1876) ("The right of the people peaceably to assemble for the purpose of petitioning Congress for a redress of grievances, or for anything else connected with the powers or the duties of the *National Government*, is an attribute of national citizenship * * *.") (emphasis added).

62. Note, therefore, that aliens are not similarly protected according to this view (since they are not citizens of the United States), and probably neither are corporations as such (i.e. the clause is limited to natural persons).

63. See, e.g., Brotherhood of R.R. Trainmen v. Virginia, 377 U.S. 1, 84 S.Ct. 1113, 12 L.Ed.2d 89 (1964); NAACP v. Button, 371 U.S. 415, 83 S.Ct. 328, 9 L.Ed.2d 405 (1963) (first amendment petition clause relied upon in holding invalid application of state ban on use of lay solicitors by NAACP to secure test cases for desegregation cases to be filed in federal court); California Motor Transport Co. v. Trucking Unlimited, 404 U.S. 508, 510, 92 S.Ct. 609, 611, 30 L.Ed.2d 642, 646 (1972); Eastern R.R. Presidents Conf. v. Noerr Motor Freight, 365 U.S. 127, 81 S.Ct. 523, 5 L.Ed.2d 464 (1961).

neighbors within the first amendment, it may give them (and take from them) a synergistic effect, i.e. assembling peaceably for the purpose of discussing political matters, framing resolutions seeking redress of felt grievances, and the like.[64] It may also be useful in elaborating a basis for objecting to laws that (unreasonably?) restrict who may meet, the auspices of the meeting, the number that may be permitted to be present, or the place where peaceable assembly is disallowed, i.e. laws that do not on their face restrict what may be said and thus do not, in a strict sense, abridge freedom of speech. The "peaceably to assemble" clause, linked with the petition for a redress of grievances clause, may also have something to say about *public forum* doctrine, i.e. the extent to which streets, parks, auditoriums, etc., may not be disallowed by positive law as rallying places or places for demonstrations. In an extended sense, it may provide some ground also for identifying some sort of first amendment "right" of political association as well.

To be sure, all of this is highly preliminary. But precisely because from now on our sharper focus is nominally on the free-speech-and-free-press clause (as well, of course, as the fourteenth amendment's relationship to that clause), it is useful to see how these other clauses may have: (a) a separate significance; and (b) an integrative or synergistic significance, with the free speech and free press clauses, even as we have also noted with reference to several other clauses we have now briefly reviewed. To the extent that some of these clauses seem intimately concerned with processes of *political* involvement (e.g., the assembly and petition clauses, freedom of debate within Congress itself), and delimitations on *political* crimes (e.g., treason), moreover, they may lend some weight and point to the peculiar diagram featured in the earlier materials placing political speech at the core of the first amendment itself.

---

64. See, e.g., De Jonge v. Oregon, 299 U.S. 353, 365, 57 S.Ct. 255, 260, 81 L.Ed. 278, 284 (1937) ("The holding of meetings for peaceable political action cannot be proscribed.")

Chapter 2

THE FIRST AMENDMENT IN FORMATIVE TRANSITION AND THE CENTRALITY OF UNTRAMMELED SOCIAL ADVOCACY IN THE UNITED STATES

A. "Bad Tendency and Legislative Deference" versus "Clear and Present Danger" with strict case-by-case independent judicial review. An original alternative proposed by Learned Hand. The strengthening addition by Brandeis to the clear and present danger test. A comparison of the first and fourteenth amendments, with differentiating federalism considerations playing a role. The "Gravity of Evil" balancing formula also proposed by Learned Hand. The fusion of the original Hand and Holmes–Brandeis tests in the *Brandenburg* case.

SCHENCK v. UNITED STATES
Supreme Court of the United States, 1919.
249 U.S. 47, 39 S.Ct. 247, 63 L.Ed. 470.

Mr. Justice Holmes delivered the opinion of the Court.

This is an indictment in three counts. The first charges a conspiracy to violate the Espionage Act of June 15, 1917, * * * by causing and attempting to cause insubordination, &c., in the military and naval forces of the United States, and to obstruct the recruiting and enlistment service of the United States when the United States was at war with the German empire, to-wit, that the defendants wilfully conspired to have printed and circulated to men who had been called and accepted for military service under the Act of May 18, 1917, a document set forth and alleged to be calculated to cause such insubordination and obstruction. The count alleges overt acts in pursuance of the conspiracy, ending in the distribution of the document set forth. The second count alleges a conspiracy to commit an offence against the United States, to-wit, to use the mails for the transmission of matter declared to be non-mailable by Title XII, § 2 of the Act of June 15, 1917, to-wit, the above mentioned document, with an averment of the same overt acts. The third count charges an unlawful use of the mails for the transmission of the same matter and otherwise as above. The defendants were found guilty on all the counts. They set up the First

Amendment to the Constitution forbidding Congress to make any law abridging the freedom of speech, or of the press, and bringing the case here on that ground have argued some other points also of which we must dispose.

It is argued that the evidence, if admissible, was not sufficient to prove that the defendant Schenck was concerned in sending the documents. According to the testimony Schenck said he was general secretary of the Socialist party and had charge of the Socialist headquarters from which the documents were sent. He identified a book found there as the minutes of the Executive Committee of the party. The book showed a resolution of August 13, 1917, that 15,000 leaflets should be printed on the other side of one of them in use, to be mailed to men who had passed exemption boards, and for distribution. Schenck personally attended to the printing. On August 20, the general secretary's report said "Obtained new leaflets from printer and started work addressing envelopes" &c.; and there was a resolve that Comrade Schenck be allowed $125 for sending leaflets through the mail. He said that he had about fifteen or sixteen thousand printed. There were files of the circular in question in the inner office which he said were printed on the other side of the one sided circular and were there for distribution. Other copies were proved to have been sent through the mails to drafted men. Without going into confirmatory details that were proved, no reasonable man could doubt that the defendant Schenck was largely instrumental in sending the circulars about. As to the defendant Baer there was evidence that she was a member of the Executive Board and that the minutes of its transactions were hers. The argument as to the sufficiency of the evidence that the defendants conspired to send the documents only impairs the seriousness of the real defence.

* * *

The document in question upon its first printed side recited the first section of the Thirteenth Amendment, said that the idea embodied in it was violated by the Conscription Act and that a conscript is little better than a convict. In impassioned language it intimated that conscription was despotism in its worst form and a monstrous wrong against humanity in the interest of Wall Street's chosen few. It said "Do not submit to intimidation," but in form at least confined itself to peaceful measures such as a petition for the repeal of the act. The other and later printed side of the sheet was headed "Assert Your Rights." It stated reasons for alleging that any one violated the Constitution when he refused to recognize "your right to assert your opposition to the draft," and went on "if you do not assert and support your rights, you are helping to deny or disparage rights which it is the solemn duty of all citizens and residents of the United States to retain." It described the arguments on the other side as coming from cunning politicians and a mercenary capitalist press, and even silent consent to the conscription law as helping to support an infamous conspiracy. It denied the power to send our citizens away to foreign shores to shoot up the people of other lands, and added that words could not express the condemnation such cold-blooded ruthlessness deserves, &c., &c., winding up "You must do your share to maintain, support and uphold the rights of the people of this country." Of course the document would not have been sent unless it had been intended to have some effect, and we do not see what effect it could be expected to have upon persons subject to the draft except to influence them to obstruct the carrying of it out. The defendants do not deny that the jury might find against them on this point.

But it is said, suppose that that was the tendency of this circular, it is protected by the First Amendment to the Constitution. Two of the strongest expressions are said to be quoted respectively from well-known public men. It well may be that the prohibition of laws abridging the freedom of speech is not confined to previous restraints, although to prevent them may have been the main purpose, as intimated in Patterson v. Colorado, 205 U.S. 454, 462. We admit that in many places and in ordinary times the defendants in saying all that was said in the circular would have been within their constitutional rights. But the character of every act depends upon the circumstances in which it is done. Aikens v. Wisconsin, 195 U.S. 194, 204, 206. The most stringent protection of freedom of speech would not protect a man in falsely shouting fire in a theatre and causing a panic. * * * The question in every case is whether the words used are used in such circumstances and are of such a nature as to create a clear and present danger that they will bring about the substantive evils that Congress has a right to prevent. It is a question of proximity and degree. When a nation is at war many things that might be said in time of peace are such a hindrance to its effort that their utterance would not be endured so long as men fight and that no Court could regard them as protected by any constitutional right. It seems to be admitted that if an actual obstruction of the recruiting service were proved, liability for words that produced that effect might be enforced. The statute of 1917 in § 4 punishes conspiracies to obstruct as well as actual obstruction. If the act, (speaking, or circulating a paper,) its tendency and the intent with which it is done are the same, we perceive no ground for saying that success alone warrants making the act a crime. Goldman v. United States, 245 U.S. 474, 477. Indeed that case might be said to dispose of the present contention if the precedent covers all *media concludendi*. But as the right to free speech was not referred to specially, we have thought fit to add a few words.

* * *

Judgments affirmed.

---

1. The Clear and Present Danger Test: Pitfalls and Problems

1. What alteration, if any, does *Schenck* represent in the common law (un)protection of free speech?—Surely not the second part. The second part, i.e. the requirement that the "substantive evils" sought to

be prevented must be of a kind "that Congress has a right to prevent" merely reiterates the standard requirement of federalism. Whenever Congress legislates, it must do so pursuant to some expressly enumerated or implied power vested in Congress in article I or elsewhere. So much of *Schenck* is thus simply an ordinary matter of federalism review. In no respect is it peculiar to first amendment cases as such.

On the other hand, the requirement that "the words used [must be] used in such circumstances and [must be] of such a nature as to create a clear and present danger" of such an evil, does seem new. It implies that when a statute punishing criminal conspiracies is applied simply to written or to spoken advocacy, the first amendment forbids the common law standard of intent (to obstruct) plus some material step (mailing the leaflets) to suffice for conviction. Rather, the advocacy must also pose a clear and present danger of actual interference, nothing less. Otherwise the defendant is to go free. But why should this be so?

If one is satisfied beyond reasonable doubt that Schenck (a) mailed his leaflets to persons who had already received draft notices, and (b) that he did so at least partly to persuade them to refuse to report when called (and not merely to share with them his strong objections to the draft and to the war), why ought this not be enough to convict him of attempting to obstruct the draft?[1] Why, moreover, should the government have to prove that the "danger" to unobstructed military recruitment presented by Schenck's specific mailing was not only a "clear" danger but also a "*present*" danger, i.e. what of significance is provided by this addition to the test?[2]

2. Despite the evident innovation made in *Schenck* ("that the prohibition of laws abridging the freedom of speech is not confined to previous restraints" but extends to social advocacy and to political criticism absent circumstances and words creating a clear and present danger of a preventable wrong akin to the false shouting of fire in a crowded theater causing a panic), does it appear that any actual obstruction to recruitment was in fact proved? Does it appear that there was evidence to support a claim that, at least, such actual obstruction was highly likely in fact?[3]

---

1. In the ordinary law of criminal attempts, is it usually necessary to prove the likelihood of the attempt to succeed in fact in order to hold the attempt punishable?

2. For partial answers to both sets of questions, see the Holmes and Brandeis opinions infra (in Abrams v. United States, 250 U.S. 616, 40 S.Ct. 17, 63 L.Ed. 1173 (1919); Gitlow v. New York, 268 U.S. 652, 45 S.Ct. 625, 69 L.Ed. 1138 (1925); and Whitney v. California, 274 U.S. 357, 47 S.Ct. 641, 71 L.Ed. 1095 (1927)). See also the next opinion by Judge Hand in Masses Publishing Co. v. Patten, 244 Fed. 535 (S.D. N.Y.1917).

3. Note the accompanying statements in the opinion re the "tendency" of the circular (a tendency to obstruct the draft, or a tendency to create a clear and present danger of obstruction?) See also Debs v. United States, 249 U.S. 211, 39 S.Ct. 252, 63 L.Ed. 566 (1919); Frohwerk v. United States, 249 U.S. 204, 39 S.Ct. 249, 63 L.Ed. 561 (1919) (sustaining convictions, Opinion by Holmes). For other criticism and comment, see Freund, The Debs Case and Freedom of Speech, 40 U.Chi.L.Rev. 239 (1973), reprinted from The New Republic, May 3, 1919, p. 13; Kalven, Ernest Freund and the First Amendment Tradition, 40 U.Chi. L.Rev. 235 (1972); Rabban, The First Amendment in Its Forgotten Years, 90 Yale L.J. 514 (1981).

Ch. 2 INDEPENDENT JUDICIAL REVIEW 33

3. The clear and present danger test is perhaps rightly thought to be relatively more protective of free speech than anything that preceded it. Nevertheless, it has been subject to the (seemingly odd?) criticism that even clear proof of clear and present danger of inducing illegal acts or violent acts by one's speech, is not sufficient to meet an appropriate first amendment test. Why might that be so? Consider the following observation by Justice Rutledge:

> It is axiomatic that a democratic state may not deny its citizens the right to criticize existing laws and to urge that they be changed. And yet, in order to succeed in an effort to legalize polygamy [as an example], it is obviously necessary to convince a substantial number of people that such conduct is desirable. But conviction that the practice is desirable has a natural tendency to induce the practice itself. Thus, depending on where the circular reasoning is started, the advocacy of polygamy may either be unlawful as inducing a violation of law, or be constitutionally protected as essential to the proper functioning of the democratic process.[4]

Justice Rutledge seems to propound a conundrum, even after adjusting the words of this quoted paragraph to take full account of the "clear and present danger" test, put forth by Holmes, in *Schenck v. United States*.[5] So, similar to the case Justice Rutledge put, to the extent that one desires a change in the law such that the preferential hiring of women [6] would be allowed, obviously one must first persuade people that that practice would be—and in fact is—desirable, though contrary to the view reflected in existing law.[7] To the extent that one's advocacy of the practice is persuasive, however, some, on becoming persuaded—seeing no good but rather, only harm in the present law that disallows such preferential hiring—may jump the gun, i.e. they will not wait for the change in the law but, rather, they will engage in the practice itself. If one's advocacy of the practice or of its desirability creates a "clear and present danger" of just such third party reaction, may it be prohibited and punished on that account? May it be prohibited and punished at least insofar as the speaker knows or should know of that danger? Why not, assuming the danger can be established as a matter of fact? If the advocacy stops short of specifically advocating violating the existing law, should it be deemed protected

---

4. Musser v. Utah, 333 U.S. 95, 101–02, 68 S.Ct. 397, 400, 92 L.Ed. 562, 567 (1948) (Rutledge, J., dissenting).

5. I.e. in the quoted paragraph, Rutledge adverts to the "natural tendency" to induce the practice itself, rather than of a "clear and present danger" that the practice may be engaged in. We may agree that, according to Holmes, the latter would have to be shown, i.e. that prevention of the mere "tendency" would not be enough, under the *Schenck* test.

6. Alternatively, substitute "men" for the word "women" in this sentence. Alternatively, still, substitute "blacks" or "whites." (In responding to the questions subsequently raised here, will it make any difference to you *which* object of advocacy is being pressed? Cf. J.S. Mill, On Liberty (1859) and see quotation, footnote 11 *infra*.)

7. E.g., contrary to some valid state statute forbidding employment discrimination based on sex, or contrary to the provision in Title VII of the Civil Rights Act of 1964, forbidding employment discrimination based on race, sex, religion, or national origin.

even though it has the effect of foreseeably inducing actual violations?[8] If the advocacy included advocacy of violating the existing law, then, though in fact it did not produce that effect, and, moreover, cannot be shown even to have created a clear and present danger of inducing a violation, how should it fare? Ought it be prohibitable because it sought a forbidden end (i.e. "discrimination") and also urged a forbidden act (i.e. violation of "the law")?

Is there, or ought there to be, a constitutional distinction between, say, an essay persuasive to the reader that women ought preferentially to hire other women[9] (such that some then presume to do so regardless of the existing law), and another that indeed urges them to take the law into their own hands? The clear and present "danger" may be as real in the one case as in the other, even as the author may well be aware. So why distinguish the two situations for first amendment purposes? Justice Rutledge's conundrum surely poses a good point.

The following case,[10] though not from the Supreme Court, proposed an answer from a different point of view. The author, Judge Learned Hand, thought the test expressed in his opinion in this case to be a better one than that which Holmes laid down in *Schenck*. Do you agree? Just how would it help, and how would it work?[11] Is it vulnerable to a weakness not found in Holmes's test? Does either one—or even both combined—seem sufficient for the adequate protection of free speech?

---

8. Incidentally, what does it mean to "advocate the violation of an existing law," or even to advocate the desirability of a certain practice not now allowed by law, for purposes of first amendment review? What would you say about Marc Anthony's address in Shakespeare's *Julius Caesar*? (Was Marc Anthony advocating that the crowd attack Brutus and the others involved in Caesar's assassination, or was he merely suggesting that Caesar's death ought to be seen as less than a deserved fate?)

9. Or, indeed, that men ought preferentially to hire other men, or that members of some racial group ought preferentially to hire those (racially) like themselves.

10. Reversed on appeal, 246 Fed. 24 (2d Cir.1917). Discussed and compared with Holmes' early standard, in Blasi, Learned Hand and the First Amendment, 61 Col.L. Rev. 1 (1990); Gunther, Learned Hand and the Origins of Modern First Amendment Doctrine: Some Fragments of History, 27 Stan.L.Rev. 719 (1975).

11. Cf. also the opening footnote to J.S. Mill, On Liberty (1859) (probably the single most influential essay ever written on Free Speech):

> If the arguments of the present chapter are of any validity, there ought to exist the fullest liberty of professing and discussing, as a matter of ethical conviction, any doctrine, however immoral it may be considered. It would, therefore, be irrelevant and out of place to examine here, whether the doctrine of tyrannicide deserves that title. I shall content myself with saying that the subject has been at all times one of the open questions of morals; that the act of a private citizen in striking down a criminal, who, by raising himself above the law, has placed himself beyond the reach of legal punishment or control, has been accounted by whole nations, and by some of the best and wisest men, not a crime, but an act of exalted virtue; and that, right or wrong, it is not of the nature of assassination, but of civil war. As such, I hold that the instigation of it, in a specific case, may be a proper subject of punishment, but only if an overt act has followed, and at least a probable connection can be established between the act and the instigation.

MASSES PUBLISHING COMPANY v. PATTEN

United States District Court for the Southern District of New York, 1917.
244 Fed. 535.

In Equity. Suit by the Masses Publishing Company against T.G. Patten, Postmaster of the City of New York. On motion for preliminary injunction. Motion granted.

The plaintiff applies for a preliminary injunction against the postmaster of New York to forbid his refusal to accept its magazine in the mails under the following circumstances: The plaintiff is a publishing company in the city of New York engaged in the production of a monthly revolutionary journal called "The Masses," containing both text and cartoons, each issue of which is ready for the mails during the first ten days of the preceding month. In July, 1917, the postmaster of New York, acting upon the direction of the Postmaster General, advised the plaintiff that the August number to which he had had access would be denied the mails under the espionage Act of June 15, 1917. Though professing willingness to excerpt from the number any particular matter which was objectionable in the opinion of the Postmaster General, the plaintiff was unable to learn any specification of objection, and thereupon filed this bill, and now applies for a preliminary injunction upon a statement of the facts.

Upon return of the rule to show cause the defendant, while objecting generally that the whole purport of the number was in violation of the law, since it tended to produce a violation of the law, to encourage the enemies of the United States, and to hamper the government in the conduct of the war, specified four cartoons and four pieces of text as especially falling within sections 1 and 2 of title 12 of the act and by the reference of section 1 as within section 3 of title 1. These sections are quoted in the margin.[1]

1.

TITLE I.

Espionage.

Sec. 3. Whoever, when the United States is at war, shall willfully make or convey false reports or false statements with the intent to interfere with the operation or success of the military or naval forces of the United States or to promote the success of its enemies and whoever when the United States is at war, shall willfully cause or attempt to cause insubordination, disloyalty, mutiny, or refusal of duty, in the military or naval forces of the United States, or shall willfully obstruct the recruiting or enlistment service of the United States, to the injury of the service or of the United States, shall be punished by a fine of not more than $10,000 or imprisonment for not more than twenty years, or both.

TITLE XII.

Use of Mails.

Section 1. Every letter, writing, circular, postal card, picture, print, engraving, photograph, newspaper, pamphlet, book, or other publication, matter or thing, of any kind, in violation of any of the provisions of this act is hereby declared to be nonmailable matter and shall not be conveyed in the mails or delivered from any post office or by any letter carrier: Provided, that nothing in this act shall be so construed as to authorize any person other than an employé of the dead letter office, duly authorized there to, or other person upon a search warrant authorized by law, to open any letter not addressed to himself.

Section 2. Every letter, writing, circular, postal card, picture, print, engraving, photograph, newspaper, pamphlet, book, or other publication, matter or thing, of any kind, containing any matter advocating or urging treason, insurrection, or forcible resistance to any law of the United States, is hereby declared to be nonmailable.

The four cartoons are entitled respectively "Liberty Bell," "Conscription," "Making the World Safe for Capitalism," "Congress and Big Business." The first is a picture of the Liberty Bell broken in fragments. The obvious implication, taking the cartoon in its context with the number as a whole, is that the origin, purposes, and conduct of the war have already destroyed the liberties of the country. It is a fair inference that the draft law is an especial instance of the violation of the liberty and fundamental rights of any free people.

* * *

The challenged text, omitting the excerpts just mentioned, total about one page out of a total of 28. Throughout the rest are sprinkled other texts designed to arouse animosity to the draft and to the war, and criticisms of the President's consistency in favoring the declaration of war.

The defendant attaches to its papers as well copies of the June and July numbers of The Masses and a number of Mother Earth, a magazine edited by Emma Goldman and Alexander Berkman, recently convicted in this court for a conspiracy to resist the draft. The earlier copies of The Masses contain inflammatory articles upon the war and conscription in revolutionary vein, some of which go to the extent of counselling those subject to conscription to resist. This case does not concern them except in so far as the defendant's position is correct that in the interpretation of the August number the purpose of the writers may be inferred from what preceded, and that an audience addressed in the earlier numbers would put upon the later number a significance beyond what the contents would naturally bear if it stood alone. It is not necessary for a determination of this case to set forth in detail the contents of these numbers. The copy of Mother Earth also need not be referred to.

* * *

LEARNED HAND, DISTRICT JUDGE (after stating the facts as above). [1] It is well settled that this court has jurisdiction to review the act of the postmaster. * * * If it appears that his proposed official course is outside of the authority conferred upon him by law, the court cannot escape the duty of so deciding, just as in the case of any other administrative officer. * * *

* * *

[2] Coming to the act itself, it is conceded that the defendant's only direct authority arises from title 12 of the act, §§ 1 and 2. His position is that under section 1 any writing which by its utterance would infringe any of the provisions of other titles in the act becomes nonmailable. I may accept that assumption for the sake of argument and turn directly to section 3 of title 1, which the plaintiff is said to violate. That section contains three provisions. The first is, in substance, that no one shall make any false statements with intent to interfere with the operation or success of the military or naval forces of the United States or to promote the success of its enemies. The defendant says that the cartoons and text of the magazine, constituting,

as they certainly do, a virulent attack upon the war and those laws which have been enacted to assist its prosecution, may interfere with the success of the military forces of the United States. That such utterances may have the effect so ascribed to them is unhappily true; publications of this kind enervate public feeling at home which is their chief purpose, and encourage the success of the enemies of the United States abroad, to which they are generally indifferent. Dissension within a country is a high source of comfort and assistance to its enemies; the least intimation of it they seize upon with jubilation. There cannot be the slightest question of the mischievous effects of such agitation upon the success of the national project, or of the correctness of the defendant's position.

All this, however, is beside the question whether such an attack is a willfully false statement. That phrase properly includes only a statement of fact which the utterer knows to be false, and it cannot be maintained that any of these statements are of fact, or that the plaintiff believes them to be false. They are all within the range of opinion and of criticism; they are all certainly believed to be true by the utterer. As such they fall within the scope of that right to criticise either by temperate reasoning, or by immoderate and indecent invective, which is normally the privilege of the individual in countries dependent upon the free expression of opinion as the ultimate source of authority. The argument may be trivial in substance, and violent and perverse in manner, but so long as it is confined to abuse of existing policies or laws, it is impossible to class it as a false statement of facts of the kind here in question. To modify this provision, so clearly intended to prevent the spreading of false rumors which may embarrass the military, into the prohibition of any kind of propaganda, honest or vicious, is to disregard the meaning of the language, established by legal construction and common use, and to raise it into a means of suppressing intemperate and inflammatory public discussion, which was surely not its purpose.

[3] The next phrase relied upon is that which forbids any one from willfully causing insubordination, disloyalty, mutiny, or refusal of duty in the military or naval forces of the United States. The defendant's position is that to arouse discontent and disaffection among the people with the prosecution of the war and with the draft tends to promote a mutinous and insubordinate temper among the troops. This, too, is true; men who become satisfied that they are engaged in an enterprise dictated by the unconscionable selfishness of the rich, and effectuated by a tyrannous disregard for the will of those who must suffer and die, will be more prone to insubordination than those who have faith in the cause and acquiesce in the means. Yet to interpret the word "cause" so broadly would, as before, involve necessarily as a consequence the suppression of all hostile criticism, and of all opinion except what encouraged and supported the existing policies, or which fell within the range of temperate argument it would contradict the normal assumption of democratic government that the suppression of hostile criticism does not turn upon the justice of its substance or the decency and propriety of its temper. Assuming that the power to

repress such opinion may rest in Congress in the throes of a struggle for the very existence of the state, its exercise is so contrary to the use and wont of our people that only the clearest expression of such a power justifies the conclusion that it was intended.

The defendant's position, therefore, in so far as it involves the suppression of the free utterance of abuse and criticism of the existing law, or of the policies of the war, is not, in my judgment, supported by the language of the statute. Yet there has always been a recognized limit to such expressions, incident indeed to the existence of any compulsive power of the state itself. One may not counsel or advise others to violate the law as it stands. Words are not only the keys of persuasion, but the triggers of action, and those which have no purport but to counsel the violation of law cannot by any latitude of interpretation be a part of that public opinion which is the final source of government in a democratic state. The defendant asserts not only that the magazine indirectly through its propaganda leads to a disintegration of loyalty and a disobedience of law, but that in addition it counsels and advises resistance to existing law, especially to the draft. The consideration of this aspect of the case more properly arises under the third phrase of section 3, which forbids any willful obstruction of the recruiting or enlistment service of the United States, but, as the defendant urges that the magazine falls within each phrase, it is as well to take it up now. To counsel or advise a man to an act is to urge upon him either that it is his interest or his duty to do it. While, of course, this may be accomplished as well by indirection as expressly, since words carry the meaning that they impart, the definition is exhaustive, I think, and I shall use it. Political agitation, by the passions it arouses or the convictions it engenders, may in fact stimulate men to the violation of law. Detestation of existing policies is easily transformed into forcible resistance of the authority which puts them in execution, and it would be folly to disregard the causal relation between the two. Yet to assimilate agitation, legitimate as such, with direct incitement to violent resistance, is to disregard the tolerance of all methods of political agitation which in normal times is a safeguard of free government. The distinction is not a scholastic subterfuge, but a hard-bought acquisition in the fight for freedom, and the purpose to disregard it must be evident when the power exists. If one stops short of urging upon others that it is their duty or their interest to resist the law, it seems to me one should not be held to have attempted to cause its violation. If that be not the test, I can see no escape from the conclusion that under this section every political agitation which can be shown to be apt to create a seditious temper is illegal. I am confident that by such language Congress had no such revolutionary purpose in view.

It seems to me, however, quite plain that none of the language and none of the cartoons in this paper can be thought directly to counsel or advise insubordination or mutiny, without a violation of their meaning quite beyond any tolerable understanding. I come, therefore, to the third phrase of the section, which forbids any one from willfully obstructing the recruiting or enlistment service of the United States. I am not prepared to assent to the plaintiff's position that this only refers to acts other than words, nor that the act thus defined must be shown to have been successful. One may obstruct without preventing, and the mere obstruction is an injury to the service; for it throws impediments in its way. Here again, however, since the question is of the expression of opinion, I construe the sentence, so far as it restrains public utterance, as I have construed the other two, and as therefore limited to the direct advocacy of resistance to the recruiting and enlistment service. If so, the inquiry is narrowed to the question whether any of the challenged matter may be said to advocate resistance to the draft, taking the meaning of the words with the utmost latitude which they can bear.

As to the cartoons it seems to me quite clear that they do not fall within such a test. Certainly the nearest is that entitled "Conscription," and the most that can be said of that is that it may breed such animosity to the draft as will promote resistance and strengthen the determination of those disposed to be recalcitrant. There is no intimation that, however hateful the draft may be, one is in duty bound to resist it, certainly not that such resistances is to one's interest. I cannot, therefore, even with the limitations which surround the power of the court, assent to the assertion that any of the cartoons violate the act.

The text offers more embarrassment. The poem to Emma Goldman and Alexander Berkman, at most, goes no further than to say that they are martyrs in the cause of love among nations. Such a sentiment holds them up to admiration, and hence their conduct to possible emulation. The paragraph in which the editor offers to receive funds for their appeal also expresses admiration for them, but goes no further. The paragraphs upon conscientious objectors are of the same kind. They go no further than to express high admiration for those who have held and are holding out for their convictions even to the extent of resisting the law. It is plain enough that the paper has the fullest sympathy for these people, that it admires their courage, and that it presumptively approves their conduct. Indeed, in the earlier numbers and before the draft went into effect the editor urged resistance. Since I must interpret the language in the most hostile sense, it is fair to suppose, therefore, that these passages go as far as to say:

> "These men and women are heroes and worthy of a freeman's admiration. We approve their conduct; we will help to secure them their legal rights. They are working for the betterment of mankind through their obdurate consciences."

Moreover, these passages, it must be remembered, occur in a magazine which attacks with the utmost violence the draft and the war. That such comments have a tendency to arouse emulation in others is clear enough, but that they counsel others to follow these examples is not so plain. Literally at least they do not, and while, as I have said, the words are to be taken, not literally, but according to their full import, the literal meaning is the starting point for interpretation. One may admire and approve the course of a hero without feeling any duty to follow him. There is not the least implied intimation in these words that others are under a duty to follow. The most that can be said is that, if others do follow, they will get the same admiration and the same approval. Now, there is surely an appreciable distance between esteem and emulation; and unless there is here some advocacy of such emulation, I cannot see how the passages can be said to fall within the law. If they do, it would follow that, while one might express admiration and approval for the Quakers or any established sect which is excused from the draft, one could not legally express the same admiration and approval for others who entertain the same conviction, but do not happen to belong to the society of Friends. It cannot be that the law means to curtail such expressions merely, because the convictions of the class within the draft are stronger than their sense of obedience to the law. There is ample evidence in history that the Quaker is as recalcitrant to legal compulsion as any man; his obstinacy has been regarded in the act, but his disposition is as disobedient as that of any other conscientious objector. Surely, if the draft had not excepted Quakers, it would be too strong a doctrine to say that any who openly admire their fortitude or even approved their conduct was willfully obstructing the draft.

When the question is of a statute constituting a crime, it seems to me that there should be more definite evidence of the act. The question before me is quite the same as what would arise upon a motion to dismiss an indictment at the close of the proof: Could any reasonable man say, not that the indirect result of the language might be to arouse a seditious disposition, for that would not be enough, but that the language directly advocated resistance to the draft? I cannot think that upon such language any verdict would stand. Of course, the language of the statute cannot have one meaning in an indictment and another when the case comes up here, because by hypothesis, if this paper is nonmailable under section 3 of title 1, its editors have committed a crime in uttering it.

After the foregoing discussion it is hardly necessary to speak of section 2 of title 12. The plaintiff insists that refusal to comply with the provisions of the draft cannot be classed as forcible resistance; that such a refusal is, at most, only inaction, the neglect of an affirmative duty even to the extent of submitting to imprisonment. It may be plausibly contended that by forcible resistance Congress meant more than passive resistance, but even if this be not true, the result is the same, because, so construed, the section goes no further than the last phrase of section 3 of title 1 as I have construed it here. What was therefore said upon that section will serve here.

The defendant's action was based, as I understand it, not so much upon the narrow question whether these four passages actually advocated resistance, though that point was distinctly raised, as upon the doctrine that the general tenor and animus of the paper as a whole were subversive to authority and seditious in effect. I cannot accept this test under the law as it stands at present. The tradition of English-speaking freedom has depended in no small part upon the merely procedural requirement that the state point with exactness to just that conduct which violates law. It is difficult and often impossible to meet the charge that one's general ethos is treasonable; such a latitude for construction implies a personal latitude in administration which contradicts the normal assumption that law shall be embodied in general propositions capable of some measure of definition. The whole crux of this case turns indeed upon this thesis. I make no question of the power of Congress to establish a personal censorship of the press under the war power; that question, as I have already said, does not arise. I am quite satisfied that it has not as yet chosen to create one, and with the greatest deference it does not seem to me that anything here challenged can be illegal upon any other assumption.

Finally, the question arises as to how far the earlier numbers of the paper should be considered. The theory is that the August number covertly refers to the explicit counsel of resistance in the numbers of June and July. A priori such a reference might legitimately incorporate the earlier expressions; I do not doubt that the memory of those expressions may in fact remain in the minds of readers and that they may be revived by the sympathy and accord with conscientious objectors expressed in the August number. Yet the plaintiff is still entitled to ask, whatever the results of its past utterance may be, that some words be pointed out which by some reference fairly inferable from the words themselves relate back to earlier and more explicit statements. I think there are no words in the four passages which admit of such an interpretation.

It follows that the plaintiff is entitled to the usual preliminary injunction.

ABRAMS v. UNITED STATES

Supreme Court of the United States, 1919.
250 U.S. 616, 40 S.Ct. 17, 63 L.Ed. 1173.

MR. JUSTICE CLARKE delivered the opinion of the Court.

On a single indictment, containing four counts, the five plaintiffs in error, hereinafter designated the defendants, were convicted of conspiring to violate provisions of the Espionage Act of Congress (§ 3, Title I, of Act approved June 15, 1917, as amended May 16, 1918, 40 Stat. 553).

Each of the first three counts charged the defendants with conspiring, when the United States was at war with the Imperial Government of Germany, to unlawfully utter, print, write and publish: In the first count, "disloyal, scurrilous and abusive language about the form of Government of the United States;" in the second count, language "intended to bring the form of Government of the United States into contempt, scorn, contumely and disrepute;" and in the third count, language "intended to incite, provoke and encourage resistance to the United States in said war." The charge in the fourth count was that the defendants conspired "when the United States was at war with the Imperial German Government, * * * unlawfully and wilfully, by utterance, writing, printing and publication, to urge, incite and advocate curtailment of production of things and products, to wit, ordnance and ammunition, necessary and essential to the prosecution of the war." The offenses were charged in the language of the act of Congress.

It was charged in each count of the indictment that it was a part of the conspiracy that the defendants would attempt to accomplish their unlawful purpose by printing, writing and distributing in the City of New York many copies of a leaflet or circular, printed in the English language, and of another printed in the Yiddish language, copies of which, properly identified, were attached to the indictment.

All of the five defendants were born in Russia. They were intelligent, had considerable schooling, and at the time they were arrested they had lived in the United States terms varying from five to ten years, but none of them had applied for naturalization. Four of them testified as witnesses in their own behalf and of these, three frankly avowed that they were "rebels," "revolutionists," "anarchists," that they did not believe in government in any form, and they declared that they had no interest whatever in the Government of the United States. The fourth defendant testified that he was a "socialist" and believed in "a proper kind of government, not capitalistic," but in his classification the Government of the United States was "capitalistic."

It was admitted on the trial that the defendants had united to print and distribute the described circulars and that five thousand of them had been printed and distributed about the 22d day of August, 1918. The group had a meeting place in New York City, in rooms rented by defendant Abrams, under an assumed name, and there the subject of printing the circulars was discussed about two weeks before the defendants were arrested. The defendant Abrams, although not a printer, on July 27, 1918, purchased the printing outfit with which the circulars were printed and installed it in a basement room where the work was done at night. The circulars were distributed some by throwing them from a window of a building where one of the defendants was employed and others secretly, in New York City.

The defendants pleaded "not guilty," and the case of the Government consisted in showing the facts we have stated, and in introducing in evidence copies of the two printed circulars attached to the indictment, a sheet entitled "Revolutionists Unite for Action," written by the defendant Lipman, and found on him when he was arrested, and another paper, found at the headquarters of the group, and for which Abrams assumed responsibility.

Thus the conspiracy and the doing of the overt acts charged were largely admitted and were fully established.

On the record thus described it is argued, somewhat faintly, that the acts charged against the defendants were not unlawful because within the protection of that freedom of speech and of the press which is guaranteed by the first amendment to the Constitution of the United States, and that the entire Espionage Act is unconstitutional because in conflict with that Amendment.

This contention is sufficiently discussed and is definitely negatived in Schenck v. United States and Baer v. United States, 239 U.S. 47; and in Frohwerk v. United States, 249 U.S. 204.

The claim chiefly elaborated upon by the defendants in the oral argument and in their brief is that there is no substantial evidence in the record to support the judgment upon the verdict of guilty and that the motion of the defendants for an instructed verdict in their favor was erroneously denied. A question of law is thus presented, which calls for an examination of the record, not for the purpose of weighing conflicting testimony, but only to determine whether there was some evidence, competent and substantial, before the jury, fairly tending to sustain the verdict. * * * [S]ince the sentence imposed did not exceed that which might lawfully have been imposed under any single count, the judgment upon the verdict of the jury must be affirmed if the evidence is sufficient to sustain any one of the counts. * * *

The first of the two articles attached to the indictment is conspicuously headed, "The Hypocrisy of the United States and her Allies." After denouncing President Wilson as a hypocrite and a coward because troops were sent into Russia, it proceeds to assail our Government in general, saying:

> His [the President's] shameful, cowardly silence about the intervention in Russia reveals the hypocrisy of the plutocratic gang in Washington and vicinity.

It continues:

> He [the President] is too much of a coward to come out openly and say: 'We capitalistic nations cannot afford to have a proletarian republic in Russia.'

Among the capitalistic nations Abrams testified the United States was included.

Growing more inflammatory as it proceeds, the circular culminates in:

> The Russian Revolution cries: Workers of the World! Awake! Rise! Put down your enemy and mine!
>
> Yes! friends, there is only one enemy of the workers of the world and that is CAPITALISM.

This is clearly an appeal to the "workers" of this country to arise and put down by force the Government of the United States which they characterize as their "hypocritical," "cowardly" and "capitalistic" enemy.

It concludes:

> "Awake! Awake, you Workers of the World!
>
> "REVOLUTIONISTS".

The second of the articles was printed in the Yiddish language and in the translation is headed, "Workers—Wake up." After referring to "his Majesty, Mr. Wilson, and the rest of the gang; dogs of all colors!", it continues:

"Workers, Russian emigrants, you who had the least belief in the honesty of *our* Government," which defendants admitted referred to the United States Government, "must now throw away all confidence, must spit in the face the false, hypocritic, military propaganda which has fooled you so relentlessly, calling forth your sympathy, your help, to the prosecution of the war."

The purpose of this obviously was to persuade the persons to whom it was addressed to turn a deaf ear to patriotic appeals in behalf of the Government of the United States, and to cease to render it assistance in the prosecution of the war.

It goes on:

> With the money which you have loaned, or are going to loan them, they will make bullets not only for the Germans, but also for the Workers Soviets of Russia. *Workers in the ammunition factories, you are producing bullets, bayonets, cannon, to murder not only the Germans, but also your dearest, best, who are in Russia and are fighting for freedom.*

It will not do to say, as is now argued, that the only intent of these defendants was to prevent injury to the Russian cause. Men must be held to have intended, and to be accountable for, the effects which their acts were likely to produce. Even if their primary purpose and intent was to aid the cause of the Russian Revolution, the plan of action which they adopted necessarily involved, before it could be realized, defeat of the war program of the United States, for the obvious effect of this appeal, if it should become effective, as they hoped it might, would be to persuade persons of character such as those whom they regarded themselves as addressing, not to aid government loans and not to work in ammunition factories, where their work would produce "bullets, bayonets, cannon" and other munitions of war, the use of which would cause the "murder" of Germans and Russians.

Again, the spirit becomes more bitter as it proceeds to declare that—

> America and her Allies have betrayed (the Workers). Their robberish aims are clear to all men. The destruction of the Russian Revolution, that is the politics of the march to Russia.
>
> *Workers, our reply to the barbaric intervention has to be a general strike! An open challenge* only will let the Government know that not only the Russian Worker fights for freedom, but also *here in America lives the spirit of Revolution.*

This is not an attempt to bring about a change of administration by candid discussion, for no matter what may have incited the outbreak on the part of the defendant anarchists, the manifest purpose of such a publication was to create an attempt to defeat the war plans of the Government of the United States, by bringing upon the country the paralysis of a general strike, thereby arresting the production of all munitions and other things essential to the conduct of the war.

This purpose is emphasized in the next paragraph, which reads:

> Do not let the Government scare you with their wild punishment in prisons, hanging and shooting. We must not and will not betray the splendid fighters of Russia. *Workers, up to fight.*"

After more of the same kind, the circular concludes:

> Woe unto those who will be in the way of progress. Let solidarity live!

It is signed, "The Rebels."

That the interpretation we have put upon these articles, circulated in the greatest port of our land, from which great numbers of soldiers were at the time taking ship daily, and in which great quantities of war supplies of every kind were at the time being manufactured for transportation overseas, is not only the fair interpretation of them, but that it is the meaning which their authors consciously intended should be conveyed by them to others is further shown by the additional writings found in the meeting place of the defendant group and on the person of one of them. One of these circulars is headed: "Revolutionists! Unite for Action!"

After denouncing the President as "Our Kaiser" and the hypocrisy of the United States and her Allies, this article concludes:

> Socialists, Anarchists, Industrial Workers of the World, Socialists, Labor party men and other revolutionary organizations *Unite for action* and let us save the Workers' Republic of Russia!
>
> *Know you lovers of freedom that in order to save the Russian revolution, we must keep the armies of the allied countries busy at home.*

Thus was again avowed the purpose to throw the country into a state of revolution if possible and to thereby frustrate the military program of the Government.

The remaining article, after denouncing the president for what is characterized as hostility to the Russian revolution, continues:

> We, the toilers of America, who believe in real liberty, shall *pledge ourselves,* in case the United States will participate in that bloody conspiracy against Russia, *to create so great a disturbance that the autocrats of America shall be compelled to keep their armies at home, and not be able to spare any for Russia.*

It concludes with the definite threat of armed rebellion:

> If they will use arms against the Russian people to enforce their standard of order, *so will we use arms,* and they shall never see the ruin of the Russian Revolution.

These excerpts sufficiently show, that while the immediate occasion for this particular outbreak of lawlessness, on the part of the defendant alien anarchists, may have been resentment caused by our Government sending troops into Russia as a strategic operation against the Germans on the eastern battle front, yet the plain purpose of their propaganda was to excite, at the supreme crisis of the war, disaffection, sedition, riots, and, as they hoped, revolution, in this country for the purpose of embarrassing and if possible defeating the military plans of the Government in Europe. A technical distinction may perhaps be taken between disloyal and abusive language applied to the *form* of our government or language intended to bring the *form* of our government into contempt and disrepute, and language of like character and intended to produce like results directed against the President and Congress, the agencies through which that form of government must function in time of war. But it is not necessary to a decision of this case to consider whether such distinction is vital or merely formal, for the language of these circulars was obviously intended to provoke and to encourage resistance to the United States in the war, as the third count runs, and, the defendants, in terms, plainly urged and advocated a resort to a general strike of workers in ammunition factories for the purpose of curtailing the production of ordnance and munitions necessary and essential to the prosecution of the war as is charged in the fourth count. Thus it is clear not only that some evidence but that much persuasive evidence was before the jury tending to prove that the defendants were guilty as charged in both the third and fourth counts of the indictment and under the long established rule of law hereinbefore stated the judgment of the District Court must be

Affirmed.

MR. JUSTICE HOLMES, dissenting.

This indictment is founded wholly upon the publication of two leaflets which I shall describe in a moment. The first count charges a conspiracy pending the war with Germany to publish abusive language about the form of government of the United States, laying the preparation and publishing of the first leaflet as overt acts. The second count charges a conspiracy pending the war to publish language intended to bring the form of government into contempt, laying the preparation and publishing of the two leaflets as overt acts. The third count alleges a conspiracy to encourage resistance to the United States in the same war and to attempt to effectuate the purpose by publishing the same leaflets. The fourth count lays a conspiracy to incite curtailment of production of things necessary to the prosecution of the war and to attempt to accomplish it by publishing the second leaflet to which I have referred.

* * *

No argument seems to me necessary to show that these pronunciamentos in no way attack the form of government of the United States, or that they do not support either of the first two counts. What little I have to say about the third count may be postponed until I have considered the fourth. With regard to that it seems too plain to be denied that the suggestion to workers in the ammunition factories that they are producing bullets to murder their dearest, and the further advocacy of a general strike, both in the second leaflet, do urge curtailment of production of things necessary to the prosecution of the war within the meaning of the Act of May 16, 1918, c. 75, 40 Stat. 553, amending § 3 of the earlier Act of 1917. But to make the conduct criminal that statute requires that it should be "with intent by such curtailment to cripple or hinder the United States in the prosecution of the war." It seems to me that no such intent is proved.

I am aware of course that the word intent as vaguely used in ordinary legal discussion means no more than knowledge at the time of the act that the consequences said to be intended will ensue. Even less than that will satisfy the general principle of civil and criminal liability. A man may have to pay damages, may be sent to prison, at common law might be hanged, if at the time of his act he knew facts from which common experience showed that the consequences would follow, whether he individually could foresee them or not. But, when words are used exactly, a deed is not done with intent to produce a consequence unless that consequence is the aim of the deed. It may be obvious, and obvious to the actor, that the consequence will follow, and he may be liable for it even if he regrets it, but he does not do the act with intent to produce it unless the aim to produce it is the proximate motive of the specific act, although there may be some deeper motive behind.

It seems to me that this statute must be taken to use its words in a strict and accurate sense. They would be absurd in any other. A patriot might think that we were wasting money on aeroplanes, or making more cannon of a certain kind than we needed, and might advocate curtailment with success, yet even if it turned out that the curtailment hindered and was thought by other minds to have been obviously likely to hinder the United States in the prosecution of the war, no one would hold such conduct a crime. I admit that my illustration does not answer all that might be said but it is enough to show what I think and to let me pass to a more important aspect of the case. I refer to the First Amendment to the Constitution that Congress shall make no law abridging the freedom of speech.

I never have seen any reason to doubt that the questions of law that alone were before this Court in the cases of *Schenck, Frohwerk* and *Debs,* 249 U.S. 47, 204, 211, were rightly decided. I do not doubt for a moment that by the same reasoning that would justify punishing persuasion to murder, the United States constitutionally may punish speech that produces or is intended to produce a clear and imminent danger that it will bring about forthwith certain substantive evils that the United States constitutionally may seek to prevent. The power undoubtedly is greater in time of war than in time of peace because war opens dangers that do not exist at other times.

But as against dangers peculiar to war, as against others, the principle of the right to free speech is always the same. It is only the present danger of immediate evil or an intent to bring it about that warrants Congress in setting a limit to the expression of opinion where private rights are not concerned. Congress certainly cannot forbid all effort to change the mind of the country. Now nobody can suppose that the surreptitious publishing of a silly leaflet by an unknown man, without more, would present any immediate danger that its opinions would hinder the success of the government arms or have any appreciable tendency to do so. Publishing those opinions for the very purpose of obstructing however, might indicate a greater danger and at any rate would have the quality of an attempt. So I assume that the second leaflet if published for the purposes alleged in the fourth count might be punishable. But it seems pretty clear to me that nothing less than that would bring these papers within the scope of this law. An actual intent in the sense that I have explained is necessary to constitute an attempt, where a further act of the same individual is required to complete the substantive crime, for reasons given in Swift & Co. v. United States, 196 U.S. 375, 396. It is necessary where the success of the attempt depends upon others because if that intent is not present the actor's aim may be accomplished without bringing about the evils sought to be checked. An intent to prevent interference with the revolution in Russia might have been satisfied without any hindrance to carrying on the war in which we were engaged.

I do not see how anyone can find the intent required by the statute in any of the defendants' words. The second leaflet is the only one that affords even a foundation for the charge, and there, without invoking the hatred of German militarism expressed in the former one, it is evident from the beginning to the end that the only object of the paper is to help Russia and stop American intervention there against the popular government—not to impede the United States in the war that it was carrying on. To say that two phrases taken literally might import a suggestion of conduct that would have interference with the war as an indirect and probably undesired effect seems to me by no means enough to show an attempt to produce that effect.

I return for a moment to the third count. That charges an intent to provoke resistance to the United States in its war with Germany. Taking the clause in the statute that deals with that in connection with the other elaborate provisions of the act, I think that resistance to the United States means some forcible act of opposition to some proceeding of the United States in pursuance of the war. I think the intent must be the specific intent that I have described and for the reasons that I have given I think that no such intent was proved or existed in fact. I also think that there is no hint at resistance to the United States as I construe the phrase.

In this case sentences of twenty years imprisonment have been imposed for the publishing of two leaflets that I believe the defendants had as much right to publish as the Government has to publish the Constitution of the United States now vainly invoked by them. Even if I am technically wrong and enough can be squeezed from these poor and puny anonymities to turn the color of legal litmus paper; I will add, even if what I think the necessary intent were shown; the most nominal punishment seems to me all that possibly could be inflicted, unless the defendants are to be made to suffer not for what the indictment alleges but for the creed that they avow—a creed that I believe to be the creed of ignorance and immaturity when honestly held, as I see no reason to doubt that it was held here, but which although made the subject of examination at the trial, no one has a right even to consider in dealing with the charges before the Court.

Persecution for the expression of opinions seems to me perfectly logical. If you have no doubt of your premises or your power and want a certain result with all your heart you naturally express your wishes in law and sweep away all opposition. To allow opposition by speech seems to indicate that you think the speech impotent, as when a man says that he has squared the circle, or that you do not care whole-heartedly for the result, or that you doubt either your power or your premises. But when men have realized that time has upset many fighting faiths, they may come to believe even more than they believe the very foundations of their own conduct that the ultimate good desired is better reached by free trade in ideas—that the best test of truth is the power of the thought to get itself accepted in the competition of the market, and that truth is the only ground upon which their wishes safely can be carried out. That at any rate is the theory of our Constitution. It is an experiment, as all life is an experiment. Every year if not every day we have to wager our salvation upon some prophecy based upon imperfect knowledge. While that experiment is part of our system I think that we should be eternally vigilant against attempts to check the expression of opinions that we loathe and believe to be fraught with death, unless they so imminently threaten immediate interference with the lawful and pressing purposes of the law that an immediate check is required to save the country. I wholly disagree with the argument of the Government that the First Amendment left the common law as to seditious libel in force. History seems to me against the notion. I had conceived that the United States through many years had shown its repentance for the Sedition Act of 1798, by repaying fines that it imposed. Only the emergency that makes it immediately dangerous to leave the correction of evil counsel to time warrants making any exception to the sweeping command, "Congress shall make no law * * * abridging the freedom of speech." Of course I am speaking only of expressions of opinion and exhortations, which were all that were uttered here, but I regret that I cannot put into more impressive words my belief that in their conviction upon this indictment the defendants were deprived of their rights under the Constitution of the United States.

Mr. Justice Brandeis concurs with the foregoing opinion.

GITLOW v. PEOPLE OF NEW YORK

Supreme Court of the United States, 1925.
268 U.S. 652, 45 S.Ct. 625, 69 L.Ed. 1138.

Mr. Justice Sanford delivered the opinion of the Court.

Benjamin Gitlow was indicted in the Supreme Court of New York, with three others, for the statutory crime of criminal anarchy. New York Penal Laws, §§ 160, 161. He was separately tried, convicted, and sentenced to imprisonment. The judgment was affirmed by the Appellate Division and by the Court of Appeals. * * *

The contention here is that the statute, by its terms and as applied in this case, is repugnant to the due process clause of the Fourteenth Amendment. Its material provisions are:

> § 160. *Criminal anarchy defined.* Criminal anarchy is the doctrine that organized government should be overthrown by force or violence, or by assassination of the executive head or of any of the executive officials of government, or by any unlawful means. The advocacy of such doctrine either by word of mouth or writing is a felony.
>
> § 161. *Advocacy of criminal anarchy.* Any person who:
>
> 1. By word of mouth or writing advocates, advises or teaches the duty, necessity or propriety of overthrowing or overturning organized government by force or violence, or by assassination of the executive head or of any of the executive officials of government, or by any unlawful means; or,
>
> 2. Prints, publishes, edits, issues or knowingly circulates, sells, distributes or publicly displays any book, paper, document, or written or printed matter in any form, containing or advocating, advising or teaching the doctrine that organized government should be overthrown by force, violence, or any unlawful means * * *,

"Is guilty of a felony and punishable" by imprisonment or fine, or both.

The indictment was in two counts. The first charged that the defendant had advocated, advised and taught the duty, necessity and propriety of overthrowing and overturning organized government by force, violence and unlawful means, by certain writings therein set forth entitled "The Left Wing Manifesto"; the second that he had printed, published and knowingly circulated and distributed a certain paper called "The Revolutionary Age," containing the writings set forth in the first count advocating, advising and teaching the doctrine that organized government should be overthrown by force, violence and unlawful means.

The following facts were established on the trial by undisputed evidence and admissions: The defendant is a member of the Left Wing Section of the Socialist Party, a dissenting branch or faction of that party formed in opposition to its dominant policy of "moderate Socialism." Membership in both is open to aliens as well as citizens. The Left Wing Section was organized nationally at a conference in New York City in June, 1919, attended by ninety delegates from twenty different States. The conference elected a National Council, of which the defendant was a member, and left to it the adoption of a "Manifesto." This was published in The Revolutionary Age, the official organ of the Left Wing. The defendant was on the board of managers of the paper and was its business manager. He arranged for the printing of the paper and took to the printer the manuscript of the first issue which contained the Left Wing Manifesto, and also a Communist Program and a Program of the Left Wing that had been adopted by the conference. Sixteen thousand copies were printed, which were delivered at the premises in New York City used as the office of the Revolutionary Age and the headquarters of the Left Wing, and occupied by the defendant and other officials. These copies were paid for by the defendant, as business manager of the paper. Employees at this office wrapped and mailed out copies of the paper under the defendant's direction; and copies were sold from this office. * * *

There was no evidence of any effect resulting from the publication and circulation of the Manifesto.

No witnesses were offered in behalf of the defendant.

* * * Coupled with a review of the rise of Socialism, [the Manifesto] condemned the dominant "moderate Socialism" for its recognition of the necessity of the democratic parliamentary state; repudiated its policy of introducing Socialism by legislative measures; and advocated, in plain and unequivocal language, the necessity of accomplishing the "Communist Revolution" by a militant and "revolutionary Socialism", based on "the class struggle" and mobilizing the "power of the proletariat in action," through mass industrial revolts developing into mass political strikes and "revolutionary mass action", for the purpose of conquering and destroying the parliamentary state and establishing in its place, through a "revolutionary dictatorship of the proletariat", the system of Communist Socialism. The then recent strikes in Seattle and Winnipeg [3] were cited as instances of a development already verging on revolutionary action and suggestive of proletarian dictatorship, in which the strike-workers were "trying to usurp the functions of municipal government"; and revolutionary Socialism, it was urged, must use these mass industrial revolts to broaden the strike, make it general and militant, and develop it into mass political strikes and revolutionary mass action for the annihilation of the parliamentary state.

* * *

The Court of Appeals held that the Manifesto "advocated the overthrow of this government by violence, or by unlawful means."

* * *

* * * The sole contention here is, essentially, that as there was no evidence of any concrete result flowing from the publication of the Manifesto or of circumstances showing the likelihood of such result, the statute as construed and applied by the trial court penalizes the mere utterance, as such, of "doctrine" having no quality of incitement, without regard either to the circumstances of its utterance or to the likelihood of unlawful sequences; and that, as the exercise of the right of free expression with relation to government is only punishable "in circumstances involving likelihood of substantive evil," the statute

---

3. There was testimony at the trial that "there was an extended strike at Winnipeg commencing May 15, 1919, during which the production and supply of necessities, transportation, postal and telegraphic communication and fire and sanitary protection were suspended or seriously curtailed."

contravenes the due process clause of the Fourteenth Amendment. The argument in support of this contention rests primarily upon the following propositions: 1st, That the "liberty" protected by the Fourteenth Amendment includes the liberty of speech and of the press; and 2nd, That while liberty of expression "is not absolute," it may be restrained "only in circumstances where its exercise bears a causal relation with some substantive evil, consummated, attempted or likely," and as the statute "takes no account of circumstances," it unduly restrains this liberty and is therefore unconstitutional.

The precise question presented, and the only question which we can consider under this writ of error, then is, whether the statute, as construed and applied in this case by the state courts, deprived the defendant of his liberty of expression in violation of the due process clause of the Fourteenth Amendment.

* * *

For present purposes we may and do assume that freedom of speech and of the press—which are protected by the First Amendment from abridgment by Congress—are among the fundamental personal rights and "liberties" protected by the due process clause of the Fourteenth Amendment from impairment by the States. * * *

It is a fundamental principle, long established, that the freedom of speech and of the press which is secured by the Constitution, does not confer an absolute right to speak or publish, without responsibility, whatever one may choose, or an unrestricted and unbridled license that gives immunity for every possible use of language and prevents the punishment of those who abuse this freedom * * *

That a State in the exercise of its police power may punish those who abuse this freedom by utterances inimical to the public welfare, tending to corrupt public morals, incite to crime, or disturb the public peace, is not open to question. * * *

And, for yet more imperative reasons, a State may punish utterances endangering the foundations of organized government and threatening its overthrow by unlawful means. These imperil its own existence as a constitutional State. Freedom of speech and press, said Story does not protect disturbances to the public peace or the attempt to subvert the government. * * *

By enacting the present statute the State has determined, through its legislative body, that utterances advocating the overthrow of organized government by force, violence and unlawful means, are so inimical to the general welfare and involve such danger of substantive evil that they may be penalized in the exercise of its police power. That determination must be given great weight. Every presumption is to be indulged in favor of the validity of the statute. Mugler v. Kansas, 123 U.S. 623, 661. And the case is to be considered "in the light of regulations required in the interest of public safety and welfare;" and that its police "statutes may only be declared unconstitutional where they are arbitrary or unreasonable attempts to exercise authority vested in the State in the public interest." Great Northern Ry. v. Clara

City, 246 U.S. 434, 439. That utterances inciting to the overthrow of organized government by unlawful means, present a sufficient danger of substantive evil to bring their punishment within the range of legislative discretion is clear. Such utterances, by their very nature, involve danger to the public peace and to the security of the State. They threaten breaches of the peace and ultimate revolution. And the immediate danger is none the less real and substantial, because the effect of a given utterance cannot be accurately foreseen. The State cannot be reasonably required to measure the danger from every such utterance in the nice balance of a jeweler's scale. A single revolutionary spark may kindle a fire that, smouldering for a time, may burst into a sweeping and destructive conflagration. It cannot be said that the State is acting arbitrarily or unreasonably when in the exercise of its judgment as to the measures necessary to protect the public peace and safety, it seeks to extinguish the spark without waiting until it has enkindled the flame or blazed into the conflagration. It cannot reasonably be required to defer the adoption of measures for its own peace and safety until the revolutionary utterances lead to actual disturbances of the public peace or imminent and immediate danger of its own destruction; but it may, in the exercise of its judgment, suppress the threatened danger in its incipiency. In People v. Lloyd, [304 Ill. 23, 35, 136 N.E. 512], it was aptly said: "Manifestly, the legislature has authority to forbid the advocacy of a doctrine designed and intended to overthrow the government without waiting until there is a present and imminent danger of the success of the plan advocated. If the State were compelled to wait until the apprehended danger became certain, then its right to protect itself would come into being simultaneously with the overthrow of the government, when there would be neither prosecuting officers nor courts for the enforcement of the law."

We cannot hold that the present statute is an arbitrary or unreasonable exercise of the police power of the State unwarrantably infringing the freedom of speech or press; and we must and do sustain its constitutionality.

This being so it may be applied to every utterance—not too trivial to be beneath the notice of the law—which is of such a character and used with such intent and purpose as to bring it within the prohibition of the statute.

* * *

And finding, for the reasons stated, that the statute is not in itself unconstitutional, and that it has not been applied in the present case in derogation of any constitutional right, the judgment of the Court of Appeals is

Affirmed.

Mr. Justice Holmes, dissenting.

Mr. Justice Brandeis and I are of opinion that this judgment should be reversed. The general principle of free speech, it seems to me, must be taken to be included in the Fourteenth Amendment, in view of the scope that has been given to the word 'liberty' as there used, although perhaps it may be accepted with a somewhat larger latitude of interpretation than is allowed to Congress by the sweeping language that governs or ought to govern the laws of the United States. If I am right, then I think that the criterion sanctioned by the full Court in Schenck v. United States, 249 U.S. 47, 52, applies. "The question in every case is whether the words used are used in such circumstances and are of such a nature as to create a clear and present danger that they will bring about the substantive evils that [the State] has a right to prevent." It is true that in my opinion this criterion was departed from in Abrams v. United States, 250 U.S. 616, but the convictions that I expressed in that case are too deep for it to be possible for me as yet to believe that it and Schaefer v. United States, 251 U.S. 466, have settled the law. If what I think the correct test is applied, it is manifest that there was no present danger of an attempt to overthrow the government by force on the part of the admittedly small minority who shared the defendant's views. It is said that this manifesto was more than a theory, that it was an incitement. Every idea is an incitement. It offers itself for belief and if believed it is acted on unless some other belief outweighs it or some failure of energy stifles the movement at its birth. The only difference between the expression of an opinion and an incitement in the narrower sense is the speaker's enthusiasm for the result. Eloquence may set fire to reason. But whatever may be thought of the redundant discourse before us it had no chance of starting a present conflagration. If in the long run the beliefs expressed in proletarian dictatorship are destined to be accepted by the dominant forces of the community, the only meaning of free speech is that they should be given their chance and have their way.

If the publication of this document had been laid as an attempt to induce an uprising against government at once and not at some indefinite time in the future it would have presented a different question. The object would have been one with which the law might deal, subject to the doubt whether there was any danger that the publication could produce any result, or in other words, whether it was not futile and too remote from possible consequences. But the indictment alleges the publication and nothing more.

NOTES ON THE ANSWER PROVIDED BY *GITLOW v. NEW YORK* TO THE UNADDRESSED QUESTION IN *PATTERSON v. COLORADO*

The question the Court left unaddressed in *Patterson v. Colorado,* was whether (or to what extent, if any) the fourteenth amendment applies the first amendment to the states. The answer provided by *Gitlow,* in the majority Opinion, is that the fourteenth amendment fully applies the free speech and free press clause of the first amendment to the states, by force of the due process clause contained in § 1.

This feature of *Gitlow v. New York* has continued to be cited and to be relied upon by the Supreme Court, ever since 1925. Indeed, *Gitlow* is probably more frequently cited for the proposition, "that the first amendment applies equally to the states by force of the due process clause of the fourteenth amendment," than for anything else,[12] and more frequently than any other case is similarly cited for the same proposition. *Gitlow* also is frequently [13] cited as the first case "incorporating" some express clause in the Bill of Rights into the due process clause of the fourteenth amendment. For this reason especially (i.e. its prominence in more general disputes respecting the alleged relationship between the Bill of Rights and the fourteenth amendment), it is very much at the heart of one of the major, enduring controversies respecting the Supreme Court's entire jurisprudence in respect to the fourteenth amendment: the identification of the due process clause as an "incorporation" clause of the Bill of Rights. Here is a brief review of several different, strongly held views.

I.

Between the incorporation of the Fourteenth Amendment into the Constitution and the beginning of the present membership of the Court—a period of seventy years—the scope of that Amendment was passed upon by forty-three judges. Of all these judges, *only one,* who may respectfully be called an eccentric exception, *ever indicated the belief that the Fourteenth Amendment was a shorthand summary of the first eight Amendments theretofore limiting only the Federal Government, and that due process incorporated those eight Amendments as restrictions upon the powers of the States.* * * * *It ought not to require argument to reject the notion that "due process of law" meant one thing in the Fifth Amendment and another in the Fourteenth.*

This blunt paragraph is from an opinion written by Justice Felix Frankfurter.[14] It appears in *Adamson v. California,*[15] a criminal procedure case decided in 1947, two decades after *Gitlow v. New York.* The "seventy years" to which Justice Frankfurter is referring are the seventy years between 1868 and 1938. The "membership" of the Court to which he refers includes the New Deal members of the Supreme Court, including himself and Justice Black, both of whom were appoint-

---

12. Indeed, as we shall see, its substantive holding was subsequently undermined and abandoned, i.e. later cases adopt the Holmes–Brandeis dissent, respecting the application of the first amendment to the facts of the case.

13. But mistakenly (see discussion infra).

14. "The immigrant son of Austrian Jews, Felix Frankfurter acquired a legendary reputation as a lawyer, law professor, intellectual gadfly, and presidential adviser even before President Franklin D. Roosevelt named him to the Supreme Court in 1939. * * * In addition to institutional self-restraint, Frankfurter found in Federalism—perhaps the oldest of our constitutional values—a major, articulate premise of his jurisprudence. His concern for maintaining the vitality of local government units distinguished him sharply from most other post-1937 Justices. * * * A great many of Frankfurter's conflicts with other Justices, often viewed as disputes over civil liberties or judicial self-restraint, actually focused for him upon questions of federalism." Parrish, Felix Frankfurter, in Encyclopedia of The American Constitution 764–68 (Levy, Karst & Mahoney eds. 1986).

15. 332 U.S. 46, 62, 67 S.Ct. 1672, 1680–81, 91 L.Ed. 1903, 1914 (1947). (Emphasis added.)

ed by Franklin D. Roosevelt. The *Adamson* case occupies eighty pages in the U.S. Reports. *Adamson* constitutes the single most elaborate judicial examination and most emphatic rejection of the thesis that the fourteenth amendment incorporates the Bill of Rights. It also raises a fair question whether the turn taken in *Gitlow,* was or was not in error. The *Adamson* case itself was not one concerning free speech. But it did yield a discussion that raises the question of finding anything more in the due process clause of the fourteenth amendment, applicable to the states, than one is prepared to find in the due process clause of the fifth amendment, applicable to the United States.

In *Adamson,* the Supreme Court rejected a claim that the clause in the fifth amendment that immediately precedes the fifth amendment due process clause, namely, the clause that *"no person shall be compelled in any criminal case to be a witness against himself,"* was also applicable to the states via the fourteenth amendment. Frankfurter's point, in concurring in that decision was, obviously, that the fourteenth amendment does track and, indeed, does repeat that part of the fifth amendment providing for due process. But the fourteenth amendment does not track, indeed, it does not repeat, any other part of the fifth amendment. Much less does it track or repeat any other portion of the Bill of Rights.

Accordingly, he suggested, while fourteenth amendment "due process" might very well provide protection from physically coerced confessions (e.g., confessions extracted by torture, beatings, prolonged isolation, sensory privations, etc.),[16] it does not excuse one from being compelled by judicial process to take the stand in an open, public courtroom to give evidence in one's own case. That different kind of protection arises in federal court from the special provision in the fifth amendment. The fourteenth amendment does not copy that special provision, that no person shall be compelled in any criminal case to be a witness against himself, but, rather, copies only the provision respecting due process. The latter, not the former, was made binding upon the states.[17]

16. See, e.g., Rochin v. California, 342 U.S. 165, 72 S.Ct. 205, 96 L.Ed. 183 (1952) (convicting a person on the strength of evidence physically coerced from the accused is not due process of law).

17. *Adamson* was a first degree murder, death penalty case from California. Reversal of Adamson's conviction was sought (unsuccessfully) on the ground that the prosecutor was unconstitutionally permitted by state law to comment in the course of the trial on the failure of the defendant to explain or to deny evidence against him, a procedure the majority of the Court assumed the fifth amendment disallowed "if this were a trial in a court of the United States under a similar law," which it was not. The Court disposed of Adamson's claim of alleged constitutional error in the following way.

First, relying upon an earlier decision (Twining v. New Jersey, 211 U.S. 78, 29 S.Ct. 14, 53 L.Ed. 97 (1908)), the Court rejected Adamson's claim that the privilege against self-incrimination was a privilege of national citizenship states were forbidden to abridge under the fourteenth amendment privileges and immunities clause (*Twining* is, on this point, an elaboration of the *Slaughterhouse Cases* you studied in Con Law I, a holding that remains undisturbed even today). Second, the Court next held that the privilege was as such not subsumed, either, within the due process clause of the fourteenth amendment. (Justice Frankfurter's point quoted in the text supra, was expressly addressed to Adamson's due process claim.) Accordingly, the Court held there was no error in the state procedure, and the judgment of the California Supreme Court, af-

If Justice Frankfurter's position makes good sense to you, in this brief excerpt from *Adamson,* then how does one account for the position the Supreme Court took in *Gitlow v. New York?* There, the majority of

firming the conviction and death penalty, was affirmed. (We reserve comment here on Justice Black's lengthy dissenting opinion in *Adamson.* It is, rather, taken up infra, in the text.)

Despite the outcome in *Adamson v. California,* however, seventeen years later, in Malloy v. Hogan, 378 U.S. 1, 84 S.Ct. 1489, 12 L.Ed.2d 653 (1964), a majority of the Supreme Court concluded differently, i.e. it held that the privilege against self-incrimination is applicable to the states under the due process clause as part-and-parcel of a fair trial. In so holding, moreover, it also declared that the scope of the privilege would be measured by "the same standards that [are used to measure that scope] against federal encroachment" (id. at 10, 84 S.Ct. at 1494–95, 12 L.Ed.2d at 660–61) (emphasis added). Effectively, then, in *Malloy v. Hogan,* the Supreme Court announced two kinds of change. It now regarded the fourteenth amendment's due process clause as absorbing a fifth amendment privilege against self-incrimination. And it regarded that privilege, moreover, as fully fungible with (i.e. as equally broad as) the express fifth amendment privilege itself. (In passing, it also twice cited *Gitlow v. New York* as having already accepted the same proposition in respect to state laws abridging the freedom of speech or of the press. See id. at 5, 10, 84 S.Ct. at 1489–90, 1494–95, 12 L.Ed.2d at 657–58, 660–61). Justice Brennan's clinching statement (Malloy, 378 U.S. at 10–11, 84 S.Ct. at 1494–95, 12 L.Ed.2d at 660–62 was this: "The Court thus has rejected the notion that the Fourteenth Amendment applies to the States only a 'watered-down subjective version of the individual guarantees of the Bill of Rights.'" Thus the notion that insofar as the fourteenth amendment absorbs some provision within the Bill of Rights albeit incidental to its own due process clause, when it does so, it does so literally "jot-for-jot," and "title-for-tittle."

Shortly following *Malloy v. Hogan,* in Griffin v. California, 380 U.S. 609, 85 S.Ct. 1229, 14 L.Ed.2d 106 (1965), a case came to the Court dealing with the same aspect of the privilege against self-incrimination as was also involved in the *Adamson* case itself (namely, the permissibility of prosecutorial comment to the jury on the failure of the accused to explain or to deny evidence against him, as would not be permitted in a federal proceeding consistent with long-standing interpretations of the fifth amendment self-incrimination clause). The Court applied the new view announced in the *Malloy* case. On the jot-for-jot, tittle-for-tittle thesis (of fungible equivalence between fourteenth amendment due process and the express fifth amendment self-incrimination privilege), it reversed Griffin's conviction because of the permitted prosecutorial comment. It also expressly overruled *Adamson* itself. In passing also, in *Malloy* (id. at 4, 84 S.Ct. at 1491, 2 L.Ed.2d at 656–57), Justice Brennan noted that as of its date, 1964, the number of Justices expressing themselves as supporting the view that the fourteenth amendment incorporates *all* of the first eight amendments, had risen to ten. (Cf. Frankfurter's number, quotation in text supra).

Of course, even as of 1964 Justice Brennan was referring to ten Justices overall, not ten *at any one time.* In fact, even today at no one time has the total number of Justices holding this view ever constituted a majority of the Court. Specifically, neither the second amendment, the third, the seventh, nor even one part of the fifth amendment itself (namely, the very first part requiring any trial of a capital or other infamous offense to be preceded by grand jury indictment), has yet been held applicable to the states.

Moreover, despite the general statement in *Malloy* and its application in the *Griffin* decision, it is not true that whenever a provision from the Bill of Rights has been deemed applicable to the states via the due process clause of the fourteenth amendment, that the scope of the particular provision in the Bill of Rights has been applied coextensively to the state. See, e.g., Apodaca v. Oregon, 406 U.S. 404, 92 S.Ct. 1628, 32 L.Ed.2d 184 (1972) (per Powell, J., at 369–79, 92 S.Ct. at 1637–38, 32 L.Ed.2d at 163–65, the sixth amendment may require unanimous jury verdicts (as part of the express sixth amendment right to trial by jury), but the fourteenth amendment, although interpreted as assimilating a right to trial by jury in serious cases as a requirement of due process (Duncan v. Louisiana, 391 U.S. 145, 88 S.Ct. 1444, 20 L.Ed.2d 491 (1968), permits a state to provide for jury verdict by less than unanimous vote (nine-of-twelve)). The sixth amendment and fourteenth amendment trial-by-jury standards are thus not necessarily coextensive nor is the sixth amendment necessarily carried over "jot-for-jot" and "tittle-for-tittle" into the due process clause of the fourteenth amendment. Might that possibility also apply as between the first amendment and the fourteenth amendment, as well?

the Court, even while sustaining Gitlow's state law conviction, nevertheless also did say the following:

> For present purposes we may and do assume that freedom of speech and of the press—which are protected by the First Amendment from abridgment by Congress—are among the fundamental personal rights and "liberties" *protected by the due process clause* of the Fourteenth Amendment from impairment by the States * * *

And Holmes (writing for himself and for Justice Brandeis), while dissenting on the outcome, also concurred albeit in the following qualified way:

> The general principle of free speech, it seems to me, must be taken to be included in the Fourteenth Amendment, in view of the scope that has been given to the word "liberty" as there used, although perhaps it may be accepted with a somewhat larger latitude of interpretation than is allowed to Congress by the sweeping language that governs or ought to govern the laws of the United States.

Gitlow is thus the case that answers the question the Court found unnecessary to decide in *Patterson v. Colorado*. But how satisfactory is that answer?

In *Adamson v. California*, Justice Frankfurter says that it seems very odd to read the first of these next-quoted clauses as equivalent to the second, five-part provision of which it repeats only one part:

> Nor shall any State *deprive any person of life, liberty, or property, without due process of law*
>
> (fourteenth amendment)
>
> *No person shall be* held to answer for a capital, or otherwise infamous crime, unless on a presentment or indictment of a Grand Jury [etc.]; nor shall any person be subject for the same offence to be twice put in jeopardy of life or limb, nor shall be compelled in any criminal case to be a witness against himself, nor be *deprived of life, liberty, or property, without due process of law;* nor shall private property be taken for public use without just compensation.
>
> (fifth amendment)

If reading even any one or more of the other four provisions [18] of the fifth amendment into the one look-alike provision (the due process provision) of the fourteenth amendment would seem strange, doesn't the Court's even bolder approach, in *Gitlow,* seem more strange by far? The fifth amendment "due process" clause might, conceivably, be thought of as itself embracing some of the other, explicitly-enumerated fifth amendment rights, since their particular enumeration within the fifth amendment might be thought of as precautionary enumerations of

---

18. I.e. the (1) grand jury provision, (2) the double jeopardy provision, (3) the self-incrimination provision, and (4) the just-compensation-for-private-property-takings provision, apart from (5) the due process provision.

due process, i.e. as examples of due process of law.[19] But even with that sort of stretching of fifth amendment interpretation, it hardly seems sufficient also to go beyond the boundaries of the fifth amendment, i.e. to absorb the first amendment—or the second amendment, or the third amendment—as well. And, indeed, as Justice Frankfurter suggests in *Adamson,* it would be a most remarkable fact of the Constitution if the mere due process clause of the fifth amendment were somehow understood to be, miraculously, a compact sort of shorthand for everything else in the Bill of Rights! Yet, unless the fifth amendment due process clause somehow does this (or unless it at least picks up the first amendment), how can it possibly be argued that the mere due process clause of the fourteenth amendment nonetheless does do that task in respect to the states?

Consider the matter in the following way. "Water," we have previously observed in these materials, "does not naturally rise higher than its source." If the antecedent referent of the post Civil War fourteenth amendment due process clause is the fifth amendment due process clause,[20] how, then, can the fourteenth amendment due process clause absorb the first amendment *when the fifth amendment due process clause obviously does no such thing?* Frankfurter's acerbic observations in *Adamson* thus surely do provide an occasion for pause. And once the issue has been raised in this fashion, how does one propose to work it out? Here is an alternative, proposed by Justice Black.

II.

My study of the historical events that culminated in the Fourteenth Amendment, and the expressions of those who sponsored and favored, as well as those who opposed its submission and passage, persuades me that one of the chief objects that the provisions of the Amendment's *first section,* separately, and *as a whole,* were intended to accomplish *was to make the Bill of Rights, applicable to the states.*[5] With full knowl-

19. One might try to argue that protection from double jeopardy, protection from trial without indictment by grand jury, and protection from compelled self-incrimination, are themselves merely examples of "due" process of law. (But in that case, probably one would also expect the notion to be reflected in the fifth amendment itself, i.e. that the due process clause would say "nor be otherwise deprived of life, liberty, or property, without due process of law," etc., rather than to read as it does.) (Moreover, as already observed in a previous footnote, in fact the Supreme Court has not regarded indictment by grand jury to be a feature of fourteenth amendment due process, *even now.* Yet, if the prerequisite of indictment by grand jury is to be seen as merely a specified example of due process, rather than as a separate fifth amendment requirement apart from due process as such, this approach by the Court seems very odd. A clause closely neighboring on the due process clause itself within the fifth amendment—the grand jury clause—is not deemed to be absorbed within the counterpart fourteenth amendment due process clause binding upon the states, but a clause found four amendments away, namely the speech and press clause in the first amendment, though having nothing to do with due process as such, is deemed, in *Gitlow,* to be thus absorbed. How come?)

20. And if it is not, despite its identity of language, then to what does it refer for the content of the protection it supplies?

5. [Footnote in Justice Black's opinion.] Another prime purpose was to make colored people citizens entitled to full equal rights as citizens despite what this Court decided in the Dred Scott case. *Scott v. Sandford,* 19 How. 393.

edge of the import of the *Barron* decision,[21] the framers and backers of the Fourteenth Amendment proclaimed its purpose to be to overturn the constitutional rule that case had announced. This historical purpose has never received full consideration or exposition in any opinion of this Court interpreting the Amendment.

These sentences appear in Justice Hugo Black's lengthy dissenting opinion in *Adamson*.[22] Among other sources reviewed in the Appendix to that opinion, Justice Black quoted elaborately from the Congressional Globe, i.e. the record of debates in Congress on the proposed fourteenth amendment, in 1866. Here is one of his more telling references, reproduced from *Adamson* itself:[23]

On May 23, 1866, Senator Howard introduced the proposed amendment to the Senate in the absence of Senator Fessenden who was sick. Senator Howard prefaced his remarks by stating:

"I * * * present to the Senate * * * the views and the motives [of the Reconstruction Committee].

"The first section of the amendment * * * submitted for the consideration of the two Houses relates to the privileges and immunities of citizens of the several States, and to the rights and privileges of all persons, whether citizens or others, under the laws of the United States * * *

"It will be observed that *this is a general prohibition upon all the States, as such, from abridging the privileges and immunities of the citizens of the United States. That is its first clause, and I regard it as very important.* It also prohibits each one of the States from depriving any person of life, liberty, or property without due process of law, or denying to any person within the jurisdiction of the State the equal protection of its laws.

* * *

"It would be a curious question to solve what are the privileges and immunities of citizens of each of the States in the Several States * * * I am not aware that the Supreme

---

A comprehensive analysis of the historical origins of the Fourteenth Amendment, Flack, The Adoption of the Fourteenth Amendment 94 (1908), concludes that "Congress, the House and the Senate, had the following objects and motives in view for submitting the first section of the Fourteenth Amendment to the States for ratification:

"1. To make the Bill of Rights (the first eight Amendments) binding upon, or applicable to, the States.

"2. To give validity to the Civil Rights Bill.

"3. To declare who were citizens of the United States."

21. (Justice Black's reference here is of course to Barron v. Baltimore, 32 U.S. (7 Pet.) 243, 8 L.Ed. 672, the 1833 decision we already noted, holding that the Bill of Rights was a set of limitations only on the new national government and not on the states).

22. Adamson v. California, 332 U.S. 46, 67 S.Ct. 1672, 91 L.Ed. 1903 (1947) (the quoted sentences appear at 71–72, 67 S.Ct. at 1686, 91 L.Ed. at 1919–20 (Emphasis added).

23. Id. at 104–107, 67 S.Ct. 1104–07, 91 L.Ed. at 1936–38 (Emphasis added).

Court has ever undertaken to define either the nature or extent of the privileges and immunities thus guaranteed. * * * But we may gather some intimation of what probably will be the opinion of the judiciary by referring to Corfield *vs.* Coryell [Here Senator Howard quoted at length from that opinion].

"Such is the character of the privileges and immunities spoken of in the second section of the fourth article of the Constitution. *To these privileges and immunities whatever they may be*—for they are not and cannot be fully defined in their entire extent and precise nature—to these *should be added the personal rights guarantied and secured by the first eight amendments of the Constitution; such as the freedom of speech and of the press; the right of the people peaceably to assemble and petition the Government for a redress of grievances, a right appertaining to each and all the people;* the right to keep and to bear arms; the right to be exempted from the quartering of soldiers in a house without the consent of the owner; the right to be exempt from unreasonable searches and seizures, and from any search or seizure except by virtue of a warrant issued upon a formal oath or affidavit; the right of an accused person to be informed of the nature of the accusation against him, and his right to be tried by an impartial jury of the vicinage; and also the right to be secure against excessive bail and against cruel and unusual punishments.

"Now, sir, here is a mass of privileges, immunities, and rights, some of them secured by the second section of the fourth article of the Constitution, which I have recited, *some by the first eight amendments of the Constitution;* and it is a fact worthy of attention that the course of decision in our courts and the present settled doctrine is, that all these immunities, privileges, rights, thus guarantied by the Constitution or recognized by it, are secured to the citizens solely as a citizen of the United States and as a party in their courts. They do not operate in the slightest degree as a restraint or prohibition upon State legislation. States are not affected by them, and it has been repeatedly held that the restriction contained in the Constitution against the taking of private property for public use without just compensation is not a restriction upon State legislation, but applies only to the legislation of Congress.

"Now, sir, there is no power given in the Constitution to enforce and to carry out any of these guaranties. They are not powers granted by the Constitution to Congress, and of course do not come within the sweeping clause of the Constitution authorizing Congress to pass all laws necessary and proper for carrying out the foregoing or granted powers, but they stand simply as a bill of rights in the Constitution, without power on the part of Congress to give them full effect; while at the same time the States are not restrained from violating the principles embraced in them except by their local constitutions, which may be altered from year to year. *The great object of the first section of this amendment is, therefore, to restrain the power of the States and compel them at all times to respect these fundamental guarantees.*"

In agreement with these rather emphatic expressions by Senator Howard, as Justice Black indicated in his footnote, was an early work by Horace Flack, written in 1908. In agreement also is a strongly argued, re-researched modern work by Michael Curtis, exactly to the same effect.[24] The latter, moreover, provides several examples in which the privileges and immunities clause was referred to during the state-by-state ratification process as prospectively protecting free speech, free press, and peaceable assembly, in particular, from state abridgments.[25] In contrast, a much-relied upon article by Charles Fairman, written after the *Adamson* case, argued strongly that Justice Black was mistaken.[26] And Raoul Berger, responding further to this seemingly endless debate, has insisted that Curtis is equally mistaken as was Justice Black.[27]

24. M. Curtis, No State Shall Abridge: The Fourteenth Amendment and the Bill of Rights (1987). See also 2 W. Crosskey, Politics and the Constitution chs. xxxi, xxxii (1953); H. Abraham, Freedom and the Court 40 (1982); Guthrie, The Fourteenth Article of Amendment to the Constitution of the United States (1898); H. Hyman & W. Wiecek, Equal Justice Under Law 386–438 (1982); J. James, The Framing of the Fourteenth Amendment (1956); Avins, Incorporation of the Bill of Rights: The Crosskey–Fairman Debates Revisited, 6 Harv.J. on Legis. 1 (1968); Boudin, Truth and Fiction About the Fourteenth Amendment, 16 N.Y.U.L.Q.Rev. 19 (1938); Crosskey, Charles Fairman, "Legislative History," and the Constitutional Limitations on State Authority, 22 U.Chi.L.Rev. 1 (1954).

25. M. Curtis, No State Shall Abridge: The Fourteenth Amendment and the Bill of Rights 138–40, 148–49 (1987). (The examples are from pro-ratification speeches deploring the manner in which abolitionist speech was suppressed in the secessionist states, a condition the speaker insisted would end once the fourteenth amendment was approved.) See also J. James, The Ratification of the Fourteenth Amendment 46, 162 (1984) (same). Cf. United States v. Cruikshank, 92 U.S. 542, 23 L.Ed. 588 (1876).

26. Fairman, Does the Fourteenth Amendment Incorporate the Bill of Rights?, 2 Stan.L.Rev. 5 (1949). (See also R. Stevens, Frankfurter and Due Process (1987).) In 1967, however, Justice Black expressed himself as under whelmed by the Fairman article Justice Harlan relied on in dissenting in Duncan v. Louisiana, 391 U.S. 145, 171, 88 S.Ct. 1444, 1458–59, 20 L.Ed.2d 491, 508–09 (1968). ("My Brother Harlan's objections to my *Adamson* dissent history, like that of most of the objectors, relies most heavily on a criticism written by Professor Charles Fairman * * *. I have read and studied this article extensively, including the historical references, but am compelled to add that in my view it has completely failed to refute the inferences and arguments that I suggested. * * * The historical appendix to my *Adamson* dissent leaves no doubt in my mind that both its sponsors and those who opposed it believed the Fourteenth Amendment made the first eight Amendments of the Constitution (the Bill of Rights) applicable to the States.") (Id. at 165, 88 S.Ct. at 1455–56, 20 L.Ed.2d at 505.)

And, further to avoid the trap of being accused of discovering all of the Bill of Rights in only that part of the fourteenth amendment worded the same as but one part of the fifth amendment (i.e. the due process clause), Justice Black added the following footnote (Id. at 166, 88 S.Ct. at 1456, 20 L.Ed.2d at 505–06) (emphasis in original): "My view has been and is that the Fourteenth Amendment, *as a whole,* makes the Bill of Rights applicable to the States. This would certainly include the language of the Privileges and Immunities Clauses, as well as the Due Process Clause."

27. R. Berger, The Fourteenth Amendment and the Bill of Rights (1989). (In Mr. Berger's view, the fourteenth amendment was limited to the constitutionalizing of the Civil Rights Act of 1866. See R. Berger, Government by Judiciary: The Transformation of the Fourteenth Amendment (1977).)

Still, however one may consider the matter, it is surely plain that resolution of the first amendment-fourteenth amendment relationship question obviously does not in fact require that one hinge the scope of first amendment protection from state law abridgments merely, or even more importantly, to the "due" process clause, as the Court in *Gitlow* presumed to do, does it? And to that extent, criticism aimed against applying the fourteenth amendment to free speech cases, on that basis, itself would seem seriously misspent, because one's freedom of speech need not be seen as an aspect of "liberty" not to be taken away without "due process," but, rather, as a protected privilege and immunity of national citizenship no state may make or enforce any law to abridge—a privilege and immunity as strongly protected against state action as the first amendment protects it against acts of Congress, at least if one believes Justice Black's view.

But alas, for our immediate purposes, this embarrassment, so far as it undercuts Justice Frankfurter's point, cuts both ways in view of *Gitlow v. New York* itself. The embarrassment cuts both ways because, to return to the point where we began this discursive review, i.e. to *Gitlow v. New York,* it was on the pedigree of the due process clause (i.e. the due process clause alone rather than the privileges-and-immunities clause, or rather than the first section of the fourteenth amendment "as a whole") upon which the majority of the Court as well as Justices Holmes and Brandeis did rely in *Gitlow v. New York.* And seemingly, that reliance, for the reasons canvassed incidental to our review of Frankfurter's opinion in *Adamson v. California,* does seem to be rather shaky.[28] Indeed, except for the Supreme Court, few have been willing to read the fourteenth amendment's due process clause as, all by itself, a per se shorthand for the Bill of Rights.[29]

As we already observed elsewhere in these materials, moreover, it could make some real difference which clause—if any—in the fourteenth amendment is regarded as the proper anchor for the protection of free speech. The one clause, the privileges and immunities clause, shields those who are "citizens of the United States," a limited class defined in the opening sentence of the fourteenth amendment itself.

---

28. Indeed, as we have seen, Justice Black did not himself embrace it (and note the title to the M. Curtis book—an obvious reference to the privileges and immunities clause and not to the due process clause).

29. Moreover, as we saw in an earlier footnote, even the Supreme Court does not now treat all of the first eight amendments as thus absorbed through the due process clause of the fourteenth amendment and thus made applicable to the states; some (e.g., the second, third, seventh and part of the fifth amendment itself) are not even yet deemed to apply, and other parts of other amendments may not apply wholly, in the Court's view. Rather, the Court majority's position has been one of so-called selective absorption or partial incorporation of some but not all of the provisions of the first nine amendments through the due process clause of the fourteenth amendment, as you may recall from Con Law I. The rationale, according to which the selection of some but not all is required, appears in its best known form in an opinion by Justice Cardozo, in Palko v. Connecticut, 302 U.S. 319, 58 S.Ct. 149, 82 L.Ed. 288 (1937); such rights or privileges as seem so essential to be "ranked as fundamental" in "the very essence of a scheme of ordered liberty" are identified also to the fourteenth amendment and limit the state governments as they limit the national government, but not all rights or privileges found in the first nine amendments are necessarily deemed to be of this kind. The rationale continues to sit uncomfortably astride the bench.

The other, the due process clause, shields all who are "persons," whether or not they are citizens as well. By no means, then, is it a small matter to say which clause is to do what kind of work.[30] The tie the *Gitlow* case makes, between the first amendment and the due process clause (rather than between the first amendment and the privileges and immunities clause), is not a mere technician's or aesthetician's cavil on which nothing turns.

Indeed, to pursue the distinction we have been examining within the fourteenth amendment, it may be thought that it would be eminently logical to regard certain enumerated substantive rights as rights of citizenship protected from state abridgment by the privileges and immunities clause of the fourteenth amendment, but certain procedural rights (e.g., to a fair trial) as rights shared more generally, by all persons within a state's jurisdiction, whether or not all such persons are also citizens of the United States. Consider the particular free speech cases thus far reviewed in this course in light of such a possible distinction. These have been speech cases, each involving some kind of political agitation including open public advocacy urging resistance to the law itself. That prerogative of complaining about the laws might be found suitable for citizens of the polity, i.e. a protected prerogative of one's citizenship status. Would it necessarily belong to those not citizens? Consider the obvious comparison of finding oneself a visitor or a resident alien in France or in England, or in some other foreign country in a like case.

One might not be greatly surprised if one were not regarded as a sufficient member of the French national polity to have the same latitude of political agitation freedom while within France as French citizens within France might be constitutionally guaranteed. As an alien, assigned, say, to the Paris office of an American law firm even for three, four, five years, or indefinitely, for instance, one might also lack the right to vote. Yet, one might still expect that insofar as one were charged with committing a crime while within France, or even were one sued civilly in France, the kind of trial one received would be conducted unexceptionably, i.e. with the same due process the French provide their own citizens in any like case. In brief, one might not be surprised were one's freedom to participate substantively in French politics (by voting or by speech) deemed to be more circumscribed substantively by French law, consistent with a Constitution written even in the same terms as our own Constitution, even while one might still receive equal protection in the French courts of all due process French courts are otherwise constitutionally expected to observe under provisions like those expressly found in our fifth and fourteenth amendments—providing a uniform standard of due process for persons (whether or not "citizens"). Providing a uniformity of due process would be quite consistent, jurisprudentially speaking, with wholly dis-

---

30. Nor, because of the difference in respect to the different classes respectively protected by the privileges and immunities clause vis-a-vis the due process clause, may one avoid making a specific selection of the proper clause by saying merely that freedom of speech, press, assembly, and petition are protected by the first section of the fourteenth amendment "as a whole."

tinguishing privileges and immunities of citizenship as such. Perhaps that is just what the fourteenth amendment provides in separating the privileges and immunities clause from the due process clause, and, in doing so, moreover, carries over a like distinction between the first and fifth amendments themselves.[31]

III.

All of the above having been considered, however, it is not sufficient to leave the *Gitlow* answer to the (previously-unaddressed) *Patterson* question behind us without some few paragraphs more. The linkage of one's substantive freedom of speech to the due process clause of the fourteenth amendment (rather than, if at all, to the privileges and immunities clause of the same amendment) does seem tenuous,[32] and it is consequential.[33] Still, despite all that, it is not without its own history that gives it a certain quasi-support. Here is just a bit of that history, recalled partly from Con Law I.

In two cases arising under the fifth amendment prior to the Civil War (and thus prior also to the fourteenth amendment), the Supreme Court had already declared that an act of Congress adversely affecting private property as a virtual taking or deprivation of an identifiable person's property was subject to judicial check and nullification in the Supreme Court according to the terms of the fifth amendment due process clause rather than the "takings" clause as such.[34] In 1896,

---

31. But see Bridges v. California, 314 U.S. 252, 62 S.Ct. 190, 86 L.Ed. 192 (1941). (Harry Bridges was a citizen of Australia and not a citizen of the United States.) See also American Arab Anti-Discrimination Com. v. Meese, 714 F.Supp. 1060 (C.D. Cal.1989) (Act of Congress providing for deportation of nonimmigrant aliens who publish or distribute material advocating or teaching opposition to all organized government or doctrines of world communism, held unconstitutional on first amendment grounds).

32. Despite one's impatience with worrying about such matters once Supreme Court precedent appears to entrench a certain point of view so that its original constitutional integrity no longer seems to matter as a practical concern, moreover, there is the sense that, eventually, others may scratch the itch of even entrenched error until it is no longer bearable. There is a resentment that stubborn truth harbors against falsehood. (The Court has overruled its own constitutional decisions on more than 120 occasions.) Despite the special place of precedent (*stare decisis*) in Anglo–American law, moreover, the Court has itself asserted that the force of *stare decisis* is less, rather than more, compelling in constitutional cases. See, e.g., United States v. Scott, 437 U.S. 82, 101, 98 S.Ct. 2187, 2199, 57 L.Ed.2d 65, 80–81 (1978); Burnet v. Coronado Oil & Gas Co., 285 U.S. 393, 406–08, 52 S.Ct. 443, 447–48, 76 L.Ed. 815, 823–25, (1932) (Brandeis, J., dissenting). But see Monaghan, Stare Decisis and Constitutional Adjudication, 88 Colum.L. Rev. 723 (1988).

33. Notice that the location of free speech protection to the privileges and immunities clause rather than to the due process clause might also affect the first amendment standing of corporations—they are not "citizens of the United States" within the meaning of the relevant clause of the fourteenth amendment. (Regarded as "persons," corporations have been sheltered as having rights of free speech. See, e.g., First National Bank of Boston v. Bellotti, 435 U.S. 765, 98 S.Ct. 1407, 55 L.Ed.2d 707 (1978) (state restriction on commercial corporate expenditures to influence ballot referendum struck down).

34. Den v. Hoboken Land & Improvement Co., 59 U.S. (18 How.) 272, 276, 15 L.Ed. 372, 374 (1856); Dred Scott v. Sandford, 60 U.S. (19 How.) 393, 450, 15 L.Ed. 691, 719 (1857) ("[A]n Act of Congress which deprives a citizen of the United States of his liberty or property, merely because he came himself or brought his property into a particular Territory of the United States, and who had committed no offense against the laws, *could hardly be dignified with the name of due process of law.*") (Emphasis added.) (Thus, the Court suggested in *Dred Scott*, an act of Congress that would work a divestiture of

following these precedents, the Court applied those fifth amendment, substantive "due process" clause restrictions to the states via the parallel due process clause of the fourteenth amendment.[35] Indeed, in a critical follow-up case that did so, the Court treated the fourteenth amendment due process clause as doing even more than foreclosing any substantively arbitrary restrictions on private property as such; rather,

a slaveowner's property in his slave merely by crossing over into a state with his slave for a short time and then exiting again, would affront the fifth amendment due process clause and would be held unconstitutional.) Additionally, certain pre-fourteenth amendment state supreme court cases applied state constitutional due process clauses as furnishing substantive limitations on state legislative power. The leading example is Wynehamer v. People, 13 N.Y. 378 (1856). (A recent and comprehensive tracing of substantive due process in American legal history is provided in F. Strong, Substantive Due Process (1986). See also Corwin, The Doctrine of Due Process of Law Before the Civil War, 24 Harv. L.Rev. 366 (1911).)

35. The transition is commonly associated with dicta in Davidson v. New Orleans, 96 U.S. 97, 24 L.Ed. 616 (1878). The Court discussed the jurisprudence of due process from Magna Carta forward, concluding: "It seems to us that a statute which declared in terms, and without more, that the full and exclusive title of a described piece of land, which is now in A, shall be and is hereby vested in B, would, if effectual, deprive A of his property without due process of law, within the meaning of the constitutional provision [of the fourteenth amendment]." Missouri Pacific Ry. Co. v. Nebraska, 164 U.S. 403, 417, 17 S.Ct. 130, 135, 41 L.Ed.2d 489, 495 (1896), applied Justice Miller's dictum in this way, and did so for a unanimous court. ("The taking by a State of the private property of one person or corporation, without the owner's consent, for the private use of another, is not due process of law, and is a violation of the Fourteenth Article of Amendment of the Constitution of the United States.") Chicago, Burlington and Quincy R.R. Co. v. Chicago, 166 U.S. 226, 235, 17 S.Ct. 581, 584, 41 L.Ed. 979, 984 (1896) treats the dictum in *Davidson* in just this way, too. (But see the concurring opinion by Justice Bradley in *Davidson* itself, id. at 107, 24 L.Ed. at 620, which, while concurring in the judgment sustaining the state law challenged in the case, dissented from Justice Miller's discussion of the due process clause on the ground that, as Bradley appeared to understand Justice Miller's own opinion, it did not interpret the due process clause this way. "I think," Justice Bradley opined (in contrasting his own view with Miller who wrote for the Court) "we are entitled under the fourteenth amendment, not only to see that there is some process of law, but 'due process of law,' provided by the State law when a citizen is deprived of his property; and that, in judging what is 'due process of law,' respect must be had to the cause and object of the taking, whether occurring under the taxing power, the power of eminent domain, or the power of assessment for local improvements, or none of these: and if found to be suitable or admissible in the special case, it will be adjudged to be 'due process of law;' but if found to be arbitrary, oppressive, and unjust, it may be declared to be not 'due process of law.'" Justice Miller's statement was that an act providing for the transfer of land from A to B "without more" would be vulnerable to due process objection, but there is an ambiguity about what is the "without more," to which he refers. He may, as Justice Bradley appeared to understand him, be referring not to some due process acceptability of the reason of the legislature to force the transfer, but only to some requirement that, insofar as A believes he has some ground other than fourteenth amendment due process on which to base an objection, provision must be made by the state for some kind of hearing or some kind of court in which he may be heard on those objections, i.e. failure to provide any forum in which to assert those other objections— whatever they might be—would be a failure to provide due process of law. Id. at 104–05, 24 L.Ed. at 619–20 (emphasis added), Miller also says: "[W]henever by the laws of a State, or by State authority, a tax, assessment, servitude, or other burden is imposed upon property for the public use, whether it be for the whole State or of some more limited portion of the community, and those laws provide for a mode of confirming or contesting the charge thus imposed * * * the judgment in such proceedings cannot be said to deprive the owner of his property without due process of law, however obnoxious it may be to other objections." And he adds at once the following observation: "If private property be taken for public uses without just compensation, it must be remembered that, when the fourteenth amendment was adopted, the provision on that subject, in immediate juxtaposition in the fifth amendment with the one we are construing, was left out, and this was taken.")

it held that due consideration of the owner's interests also implied a duty of compensation insofar as some appropriative public use (or third party use) was involved, to satisfy the imperatives of due process as such.[36] So, the fourteenth amendment, though having no just compensation clause like that expressly found in the fifth amendment,[37] was deemed to absorb such a clause as of 1897, as a feature of (substantive) due process of law.

Chicago, Burlington and Quincy Railroad Co. v. Chicago, decided by the Court in 1897, rather than *Gitlow v. New York*, is actually the first example of substantive due process absorption from a technically distinct part of the Bill of Rights (specifically, the takings clause of the fifth amendment) into the due process clause of the fourteenth amendment. Yet, the roots of that decision do seem to extend in some logical and traceable manner from sources located in the Court's own pre-fourteenth amendment substantive due process case law, namely, fifth amendment "substantive" due-process-clause case law. To this extent, then, the association of some cognate fourteenth amendment substantive due process rights separately identified within the Bill of Rights (e.g., the takings clause that adjoins the fifth amendment due process clause), has an integrated logic that antedates *Gitlow* by nearly thirty years, and a pre-fourteenth amendment due process history as well, linked into the fifth amendment due process clause itself.

These were, of course, property cases. But, as with "property" and substantive due process constraints upon legislative powers, so also with "liberty" and substantive due process constraints as well, i.e. the two are of a piece, so far as the due process clause is concerned. So, in *Lochner v. New York*,[38] as you will doubtless recall, insofar as the due process clause of the fourteenth amendment had already been applied to enforce its limits on legislative invasions of private property, the same clause, on its face equally protecting "liberty" as much as "property," was applied to liberty of a kind.[39] And so, in this fashion, the

---

36. Chicago, Burlington and Quincy R.R. Co. v. Chicago, 166 U.S. 226, 235, 239, 241, 17 S.Ct. 581, 584, 585–86, 586, 41 L.Ed. 979, 984, 985–86, 986 (1897). ("In our opinion, a judgment of a state court, even if it be authorized by statute, whereby private property is taken for the State or under its direction for public use, without compensation made or secured to the owner, is, upon principle and authority, wanting in the due process of law required by the Fourteenth Amendment of the Constitution of the United States * * *."). (The court then went forward to determine whether the compensation paid the railroad in the case satisfied the "just compensation" demanded by consistency with its view of the imperatives of substantive due process, finally concluding that it was.) *Applied*, so to require compensation for a temporary "taking," in First English Evangelical Lutheran Church v. County of Los Angeles, 482 U.S. 304, 107 S.Ct. 2378, 96 L.Ed.2d 250 (1987). The Court's opinion in *First English Evangelical* twins the fifth amendment takings clause with the fourteenth amendment due process clause, i.e. treats them as fungible, jot-for-jot, tittle-for-tittle, suggesting no distinction between the two.

37. Cf. the discussion of the Miller and Bradley opinions in Davidson v. New Orleans, 96 U.S. 97, 24 L.Ed. 616 (1878). See also the discussion in note 35 supra.

38. 198 U.S. 45, 25 S.Ct. 539, 49 L.Ed. 937 (1905). See also Allgeyer v. Louisiana, 165 U.S. 578, 17 S.Ct. 427, 41 L.Ed. 832 (1897).

39. The "liberty" involved in *Lochner* was one's liberty to make contracts. The question treated in the Supreme Court was the question of the extent to which a state legislature might substantively restrict that liberty. The majority thought the answer was "not much," while Holmes, dissenting, thought the answer was "pretty much as the legislature prefers." The

circle of our discussion begins to close. It is obviously this larger framework of substantive due process legal history the majority accepts in *Gitlow v. New York,* when it says:

> For present purposes we may and do assume that freedom of speech and of the press—which are protected by the First Amendment from abridgment by Congress—are among the fundamental personal rights and "liberties" protected by the due process clause of the Fourteenth Amendment from impairment by the States.[40]

And it is that same legal history Holmes (with Brandeis) also took into account concurringly,[41] in saying, as he did:

> The general principle of free speech, it seems to me, must be taken to be included in the Fourteenth Amendment, in view of the scope that has been given to the word "liberty" as there used, although perhaps it may be accepted with a somewhat larger latitude of interpretation than is allowed to Congress by the sweeping language that governs or ought to govern the laws of the United States.

What became of the original, robust controversy, therefore, was that it became attenuated and virtually mooted in practice. The due process clause (rather than the privileges and immunities clause—abandoned in the *Slaughterhouse Cases*), absorbed the chief work of fourteenth amendment, substantive free speech, state action review.[42] In turn, the first amendment, while not usually spoken of as though literally "incorporated," is regarded as informing that review, and, indeed, as setting its basic standards in the Supreme Court.[43] In that

three other Justices in dissent thought that the legislative latitude lay somewhere in between the majority view and Holmes' view, but found it sufficient to cover the case at hand.

40. (*Applied in* Near v. Minnesota, 283 U.S. 697, 51 S.Ct. 625, 75 L.Ed. 1357 (1931), holding a state statute invalid as interpreted to authorize an injunction against future publication of scandalous or defamatory matter, and declaring that "[i]t is no longer open to doubt that the liberty of the press and of speech is within the liberty safeguarded by the due process clause of the Fourteenth Amendment from invasion by state action.")

41. Note also that Justice Harlan, dissenting in 1907, in *Patterson v. Colorado,* declined to rely wholly upon the privileges and immunities clause although that clause was for him (as later on, for Justice Black) the principally relevant text. Still, he added: "It is, I think, impossible to conceive of liberty, as secured by the Constitution against hostile action, whether by the Nation or by the States, which does not embrace the right to enjoy free speech and the right to have a free press," and referred expressly to the fourteenth amendment clause "forbidding a State to deprive any person of his liberty without due process of law."

42. In Whitney v. California, 274 U.S. 357, 373, 47 S.Ct. 641, 647, 71 L.Ed. 1095, 1104–05 (1927), Justice Brandeis mused for one last time on the general problem we have addressed, in the setting of a free speech case. ("Despite arguments to the contrary which had seemed to me persuasive, it is settled that the due process clause of the Fourteenth Amendment applies to matters of substantive law as well as to matters of procedure.")

43. In West Virginia Bd. of Educ. v. Barnette, 319 U.S. 624, 639, 63 S.Ct. 1178, 1186, 87 L.Ed. 1628, 1638 (1944), Justice Jackson expressed the matter in the following way: "The test of legislation which collides with the Fourteenth Amendment, because it also collides with the principles of the First, is much more definite than the test when only the Fourteenth is involved. Much of the vagueness of the due process clause disappears when the specific prohibitions of the First become its standard. * * * It is important to note that while it is the Fourteenth Amendment which bears directly upon the State it is the more specific limiting principles of the First Amendment that finally govern this case."

sense, Justice Black has, more-or-less, won out for his own views as well. Even so, not every member of the Court has regarded first and fourteenth amendment cases interchangeably, and not all of them find a full tight fit of jot-for-jot (and tittle-for-tittle?) equivalency between the first amendment and the fourteenth amendment. For some quite distinguished judges, the concrete facts of a case may make a real difference, including such "facts" as which level of government presumed to author the objectionable law, and what is the range of its effects.[44] You will doubtless have noted, moreover, that both Holmes and Brandeis likewise reserved some leeway for first and fourteenth amendment distinctions to be drawn, though both were strongly committed to the political imperatives of free speech.[45] But we have concluded about as much as we can on the questions that first raised this inquiry, at least for the moment, and it is time to resume where we left off.

WHITNEY v. CALIFORNIA

Supreme Court of the United States, 1927.
274 U.S. 357, 47 S.Ct. 641, 71 L.Ed. 1095.

MR. JUSTICE SANFORD delivered the opinion of the Court.

By a criminal information filed in the Superior Court of Alameda County, California, the plaintiff in error was charged, in five counts, with violations of the Criminal Syndicalism Act of that State. Statutes, 1919, c. 188, p. 281. She was tried, convicted on the first count, and sentenced to imprisonment. The judgment was affirmed by the District Court of Appeal.

* * *

---

44. See, e.g., Justice Harlan dissenting in Roth v. United States, 354 U.S. 476, 506, 77 S.Ct. 1304, 1320, 1 L.Ed.2d 1498, 1519 (1957). (Federal obscenity statutes should be judged under the first amendment by a more stringent standard than state or local obscenity statutes under the fourteenth amendment—the national government has only a very limited enumerated power to concern itself with matters of morality, the subject is primarily confided via the tenth amendment to the diversity of the states. A uniform act of Congress, moreover, has a more sweeping effect than any state law. Its impact is wider, and its consequences much more far-reaching. A state statute runs no further than the state's boundaries and leaves to the population next door a freedom to choose differently. Consequently, the triangulation of the first amendment, federalism, and the tenth amendment counsels a very strong standard of judicial review of acts of Congress in this field, resulting in the invalidation of some acts of Congress the Court might appropriately sustain if limited merely as an act of a state.)

45. I.e. note the manner in which Holmes cast his language in the case, and the distinction he also drew: "The general principle of free speech, it seems to me, must be taken to be included in the Fourteenth Amendment, in view of the scope that has been given to the word 'liberty' as there used, although perhaps it may be accepted with a somewhat larger latitude of interpretation than is allowed to Congress by the sweeping language that governs or ought to govern the laws of the United States." Note, also, however, that it was Holmes and Brandeis (rather than the majority of the Court), who voted to hold the state statute invalid in Gitlow v. New York itself; their test, even under the fourteenth amendment, was far more stringent than the majority used and, indeed, the same as Holmes employed in Abrams v. United States.

The pertinent provisions of the Criminal Syndicalism Act are:

Section 1. The term 'criminal syndicalism' as used in this act is hereby defined as any doctrine or precept advocating, teaching or aiding and abetting the commission of crime, sabotage (which word is hereby defined as meaning wilful and malicious physical damage or injury to physical property), or unlawful acts of force and violence or unlawful methods of terrorism as a means of accomplishing a change in industrial ownership or control, or effecting any political change.

Sec. 2. Any person who: * * * 4. Organizes or assists in organizing, or is or knowingly becomes a member of, any organization, society, group or assemblage of persons organized or assembled to advocate, teach or aid and abet criminal syndicalism * * *

Is guilty of a felony and punishable by imprisonment.

The first count of the information, on which the conviction was had, charged that on or about November 28, 1919, in Alameda County, the defendant, in violation of the Criminal Syndicalism Act, "did then and there unlawfully, wilfully, wrongfully, deliberately and feloniously organize and assist in organizing, and was, is, and knowingly became a member of an organization, society, group and assemblage of persons organized and assembled to advocate, teach, aid and abet criminal syndicalism."

* * *

4. Nor is the Syndicalism Act as applied in this case repugnant to the due process clause as a restraint of the rights of free speech, assembly, and association.

That the freedom of speech which is secured by the Constitution does not confer an absolute right to speak, without responsibility, whatever one may choose, or an unrestricted and unbridled license giving immunity for every possible use of language and preventing the punishment of those who abuse this freedom; and that a State in the exercise of its police power may punish those who abuse this freedom by utterances inimical to the public welfare, tending to incite to crime, disturb the public peace, or endanger the foundations of organized government and threaten its overthrow by unlawful means, is not open to question. Gitlow v. New York, 268 U.S. 652, 666–668, and cases cited.

By enacting the provisions of the Syndicalism Act the State has declared, through its legislative body, that to knowingly be or become a member of or assist in organizing an association to advocate, teach or aid and abet the commission of crimes or unlawful acts of force, violence or terrorism as a means of accomplishing industrial or political changes, involves such danger to the public peace and the security of the State, that these acts should be penalized in the exercise of its police power. That determination must be given great weight. Every presumption is to be indulged in favor of the validity of the statute, Mugler v. Kansas, 123 U.S. 623, 661; and it may not be declared unconstitutional unless it is an arbitrary or unreasonable attempt to exercise the authority vested in the State in the public interest. Great Northern Railway v. Clara City, 246 U.S. 434, 439.

The essence of the offense denounced by the Act is the combining with others in an association for the accomplishment of the desired ends through the advocacy and use of criminal and unlawful methods. It partakes of the nature of a criminal conspiracy.

* * *

The order dismissing the writ of error will be vacated and set aside, and the judgment of the Court of Appeal

Affirmed.

MR. JUSTICE BRANDEIS, concurring.

Miss Whitney was convicted of the felony of assisting in organizing, in the year 1919, the Communist Labor Party of California, of being a member of it, and of assembling with it. These acts are held to constitute a crime, because the party was formed to teach criminal syndicalism. The statute which made these acts a crime restricted the right of free speech and of assembly theretofore existing. The claim is that the statute, as applied, denied to Miss Whitney the liberty guaranteed by the Fourteenth Amendment.

The felony which the statute created is a crime very unlike the old felony of conspiracy or the old misdemeanor of unlawful assembly. The mere act of assisting in forming a society for teaching syndicalism, of becoming a member of it, or of assembling with others for that purpose is given the dynamic quality of crime. There is guilt although the society may not contemplate immediate promulgation of the doctrine. Thus the accused is to be punished, not for contempt, incitement or conspiracy, but for a step in preparation, which, if it threatens the public order at all, does so only remotely. The novelty in the prohibition introduced is that the statute aims, not at the practice of criminal syndicalism, nor even directly at the preaching of it, but at association with those who propose to preach it.

Despite arguments to the contrary which had seemed to me persuasive, it is settled that the due process clause of the Fourteenth Amendment applies to matters of substantive law as well as to matters of procedure. Thus all fundamental rights comprised within the term liberty are protected by the Federal Constitution from invasion by the States. The right of free speech, the right to teach and the right of assembly are, of course, fundamental rights. See Meyer v. Nebraska, 262 U.S. 390; Pierce v. Society of Sisters, 268 U.S. 510; Gitlow v. New York, 268 U.S. 652, 666; Farrington v. Tokushige, 273 U.S. 284. These may not be abridged. But, although the rights of free speech and assembly are fundamental, they are not in their nature absolute. Their exercise is subject to restriction, if the particular restriction proposed is required in order to protect the State from destruction or from serious injury, political, economic or moral. That the necessity which is essential to a valid restriction does not exist unless speech would produce, or is intended to produce, a clear and imminent danger of some substantive evil which the State constitutionally may seek to prevent has been settled. See Schenck v. United States, 249 U.S. 47, 52.

It is said to be the function of the legislature to determine whether at a particular time and under the particular circumstances the formation of, or assembly with, a society organized to advocate criminal syndicalism constitutes a clear and present danger of substantive evil; and that by enacting the law here in question the legislature of California determined that question in the affirmative. Compare Gitlow v. New York, 268 U.S. 652, 668–71. The legislature must obviously decide, in the first instance, whether a danger exists which calls for a particular protective measure. But where a statute is valid only in case certain conditions exist, the enactment of the statute cannot alone establish the facts which are essential to its validity. Prohibitory legislation has repeatedly been held invalid, because unnecessary, where the denial of liberty involved was that of engaging in a particular business. The power of the courts to strike down an offending law is no less when the interests involved are not property rights, but the fundamental personal rights of free speech and assembly.

This Court has not yet fixed the standard by which to determine when a danger shall be deemed clear; how remote the danger may be and yet be deemed present; and what degree of evil shall be deemed sufficiently substantial to justify resort to abridgement of free speech and assembly as the means of protection. To reach sound conclusions on these matters, we must bear in mind why a State is, ordinarily, denied the power to prohibit dissemination of social, economic and political doctrine which a vast majority of its citizens believes to be false and fraught with evil consequence.

Those who won our independence believed that the final end of the State was to make men free to develop their faculties; and that in its government the deliberative forces should prevail over the arbitrary. They valued liberty both as an end and as a means. They believed liberty to be the secret of happiness and courage to be the secret of liberty. They believed that freed to think as you will and to speak as you think are means indispensable to the discovery and spread of political truth; that without free speech and assembly discussion would be futile; that with them, discussion affords ordinarily adequate protection against the dissemination of noxious doctrine; that the greatest menace to freedom is an inert people; that public discussion is a political duty; and that this should be a fundamental principle of the American government.[2] They recognized the risks to which all human institutions are subject. But they knew that order cannot be secured merely through fear of punishment for its infraction; that it is hazard-

---

2. Compare Thomas Jefferson: "We have nothing to fear from the demoralizing reasonings of some, if others are left free to demonstrate their errors and especially when the law stands ready to punish the first criminal act produced by the false reasonings; these are safer corrections than the conscience of the judge." Quoted by Charles A. Beard, The Nation, July 7, 1926, vol. 123, p. 8. Also in first Inaugural Address: "If there be any among us who would wish to dissolve this union or change its republican form, let them stand undisturbed as monuments of the safety with which error of opinion may be tolerated where reason is left free to combat it."

ous to discourage thought, hope and imagination; that fear breeds repression; that repression breeds hate; that hate menaces stable government; that the path of safety lies in the opportunity to discuss freely supposed grievances and proposed remedies; and that the fitting remedy for evil counsels is good ones. Believing in the power of reason as applied through public discussion, they eschewed silence coerced by law—the argument of force in its worst form. Recognizing the occasional tyrannies of governing majorities, they amended the Constitution so that free speech and assembly should be guaranteed.

Fear of serious injury cannot alone justify suppression of free speech and assembly. Men feared witches and burnt women. It is the function of speech to free men from the bondage of irrational fears. To justify suppression of free speech there must be reasonable ground to fear that serious evil will result if free speech is practiced. There must be reasonable ground to believe that the danger apprehended is imminent. There must be reasonable ground to believe that the evil to be prevented is a serious one. Every denunciation of existing law tends in some measure to increase the probability that there will be a violation of it.[3] Condonation of a breach enhances the probability. Expressions of approval add to the probability. Propagation of the criminal state of mind by teaching syndicalism increases it. Advocacy of law-breaking heightens it still further. But even advocacy of violation, however reprehensible morally, is not a justification for denying free speech where the advocacy falls short of incitement and there is nothing to indicate that the advocacy would be immediately acted on. The wide difference between the advocacy and incitement, between preparation and attempt, between assembling and conspiracy, must be borne in mind. In order to support a finding of clear and present danger it must be shown either that immediate serious violence was to be expected or was advocated, or that the past conduct furnished reason to believe that such advocacy was then contemplated.

Those who won our independence by revolution were not cowards. They did not fear political change. They did not exalt order at the cost of liberty. To courageous self-reliant men, with confidence in the power of free and fearless reasoning applied through the processes of popular government, no danger flowing from speech can be deemed clear and present, unless the incidence of the evil apprehended is so imminent that it may befall before there is opportunity for full discussion. If there be time to expose through discussion the falsehood and fallacies, to avert the evil by the processes of education, the remedy to be applied is more speech, not enforced silence. Only an emergency can justify repression. Such must be the rule if authority is to be reconciled with freedom.[4] Such, in my opinion, is the command of the

---

3. Compare Judge Learned Hand in Masses Publishing Co. v. Patten, 244 Fed. 535, 540; Judge Amidon in United States v. Fontana, Bull. Dept. of Justice No. 148, pp. 4–5; Chafee, "Freedom of Speech," pp. 46–56, 174.

4. Compare Z. Chafee, Jr., "Freedom of Speech," pp. 24–39, 207–221, 228, 262–265; H.J. Laski, "Grammar of Politics," pp. 120, 121; Lord Justice Scrutton in Rex v. Secretary of Home Affairs, Ex parte O'Brien, [1923] 2 K.B. 361, 382: "You really believe in freedom of speech, if you are willing to

Constitution. It is therefore always open to Americans to challenge a law abridging free speech and assembly by showing that there was no emergency justifying it.

Moreover, even imminent danger cannot justify resort to prohibition of these functions essential to effective democracy, unless the evil apprehended is relatively serious. Prohibition of free speech and assembly is a measure so stringent that it would be inappropriate as the means for averting a relatively trivial harm to society. A police measure may be unconstitutional merely because the remedy, although effective as means of protection, is unduly harsh or oppressive. Thus, a State might, in the exercise of its police power, make any trespass upon the land of another a crime, regardless of the results or of the intent or purpose of the trespasser. It might, also, punish an attempt, a conspiracy, or an incitement to commit the trespass. But it is hardly conceivable that this Court would hold constitutional a statute which punished as a felony the mere voluntary assembly with a society formed to teach that pedestrians had the moral right to cross unenclosed, unposted, waste lands and to advocate their doing so, even if there was imminent danger that advocacy would lead to a trespass. The fact that speech is likely to result in some violence or in destruction of property is not enough to justify its suppression. There must be the probability of serious injury to the State. Among free men, the deterrents ordinarily to be applied to prevent crime are education and punishment for violation of the law, not abridgment of the rights of free speech and assembly.

* * *

Whether in 1919, when Miss Whitney did the things complained of, there was in California such clear and present danger of serious evil, might have been made the important issue in the case. She might have required that the issue be determined either by the court or the jury. She claimed below that the statute as applied to her violated the Federal Constitution; but she did not claim that it was void because there was no clear and present danger of serious evil, nor did she request that the existence of these conditions of a valid measure thus restricting the rights of free speech and assembly be passed upon by the court or a jury. On the other hand, there was evidence on which the court or jury might have found that such danger existed. I am unable to assent to the suggestion in the opinion of the Court that assembling with a political party, formed to advocate the desirability of a proletarian revolution by mass action at some date necessarily far in the future, is not a right within the protection of the Fourteenth Amendment. In the present case, however, there was other testimony which tended to establish the existence of a conspiracy, on the part of members of the International Workers of the World, to commit present serious crimes; and likewise to show that such a conspiracy would be furthered by the activity of the society of which Miss Whitney was a member. Under

allow it to men whose opinions seem to you wrong and even dangerous; * * *" compare Warren, "The New Liberty Under the Fourteenth Amendment," 39 Harvard Law Review, 431, 461.

these circumstances the judgment of the state court cannot be disturbed.

* * *

MR. JUSTICE HOLMES joins in this opinion.

BRIDGES v. CALIFORNIA

Supreme Court of the United States, 1941.
314 U.S. 252, 62 S.Ct. 190, 86 L.Ed. 192.

MR. JUSTICE BLACK delivered the opinion of the Court.

* * * All of the petitioners were adjudged guilty and fined for contempt of court by the Superior Court of Los Angeles County. Their conviction rested upon comments pertaining to pending litigation which were published in newspapers. In the Superior Court, and later in the California Supreme Court, petitioners challenged the state's action as an abridgement, prohibited by the Federal Constitution, of freedom of speech and of the press; but the Superior Court overruled this contention, and the Supreme Court affirmed. The importance of the constitutional question prompted us to grant certiorari. 309 U.S. 649; 310 U.S. 623.

In brief, the state courts asserted and exercised a power to punish petitioners for publishing their views concerning cases not in all respects finally determined, upon the following chain of reasoning: California is invested with the power and duty to provide an adequate administration of justice; by virtue of this power and duty, it can take appropriate measures for providing fair judicial trials free from coercion or intimidation; included among such appropriate measures is the common law procedure of punishing certain interferences and obstructions through contempt proceedings; this particular measure, devolving upon the courts of California by reason of their creation as courts, includes the power to punish for publications made outside the court room if they tend to interfere with the fair and orderly administration of justice in a pending case; the trial court having found that the publications had such a tendency, and there being substantial evidence to support the finding, the punishments here imposed were an appropriate exercise of the state's power; in so far as these punishments constitute a restriction on liberty of expression, the public interest in that liberty was properly subordinated to the public interest in judicial impartiality and decorum.

* * *

It is to be noted at once that we have no direction by the legislature of California that publications outside the court room which comment upon a pending case in a specified manner should be punishable. As we said in Cantwell v. Connecticut, 310 U.S. 296, 307, 308, such a "declaration of the State's policy would weigh heavily in any challenge of the law as infringing constitutional limitations." Id. 308. Cf. Herndon v. Lowry, 301 U.S. 242, 261–264. For here the legislature of

California has not appraised a particular kind of situation and found a specific danger sufficiently imminent to justify a restriction of a particular kind of utterance. The judgments below, therefore, do not come to us encased in the armor wrought by prior legislative deliberation. Under such circumstances, this Court has said that "it must necessarily be found, as an original question," that the specified publications involved created "such likelihood of bringing about the substantive evil as to deprive [them] of the constitutional protection." Gitlow v. New York, 268 U.S. 652, 671.

How much "likelihood" is another question, "a question of proximity and degree"[4] that cannot be completely captured in a formula. In *Schenck v. United States,* however, this Court said that there must be a determination of whether or not "the words used are used in such circumstances and are of such a nature as to create a clear and present danger that they will bring about the substantive evils." We recognize that this statement, however helpful, does not comprehend the whole problem. As Mr. Justice Brandeis said in his concurring opinion in Whitney v. California, 274 U.S. 357, 374: "This Court has not yet fixed the standard by which to determine when a danger shall be deemed clear; how remote the danger may be and yet be deemed present."

Nevertheless, the "clear and present danger" language[5] of the *Schenck* case has afforded practical guidance in a great variety of cases in which the scope of constitutional protections of freedom of expression was in issue. * * *

Moreover, the likelihood, however great, that a substantive evil will result cannot alone justify a restriction upon freedom of speech or the press. The evil itself must be "substantial," Brandeis, J., concurring in Whitney v. California, *supra,* 374; it must be "serious," *id.* 376. And even the expression of "legislative preferences or beliefs" cannot transform minor matters of public inconvenience or annoyance into substantive evils of sufficient weight to warrant the curtailment of liberty of expression. Schneider v. State, 308 U.S. 147, 161.

What finally emerges from the "clear and present danger" cases is a working principle that the substantive evil must be extremely serious and the degree of imminence extremely high before utterances can be punished. Those cases do not purport to mark the furthermost constitutional boundaries of protected expression, nor do we here. They do no more than recognize a minimum compulsion of the Bill of Rights.

---

4. Schenck v. United States, 249 U.S. 47, 52.

5. Restatement of the phrase "clear and present danger" in other terms has been infrequent. Compare, however: " * * * the test to be applied * * * *is not the remote or possible effect.*" Brandeis, J., dissenting in Schaefer v. United States, 251 U.S. 466, 486. " * * * we should be eternally vigilant against attempts to check the expression of opinions that we loathe and believe to be fraught with death, *unless they so imminently threaten immediate interference with the lawful and pressing purposes of the law that an immediate check is required to save the country.*" Holmes, J., dissenting in Abrams v. United States, 250 U.S. 616, 630; "To justify suppression of free speech *there must be reasonable ground to fear that serious evil will result* if free speech is practiced. *There must be reasonable ground to believe that the danger apprehended is imminent.*" Brandeis, J., concurring in Whitney v. California, 274 U.S. 357, 376. The italics are ours.

For the First Amendment does not speak equivocally. It prohibits any law "abridging the freedom of speech, or of the press." It must be taken as a command of the broadest scope that explicit language, read in the context of a liberty-loving society, will allow.

II

Before analyzing the punished utterances and the circumstances surrounding their publication, we must consider an argument which, if valid, would destroy the relevance of the foregoing discussion to this case. In brief, this argument is that the publications here in question belong to a special category marked off by history,—a category to which the criteria of constitutional immunity from punishment used where other types of utterances are concerned are not applicable. For, the argument runs, the power of judges to punish by contempt out-of-court publications tending to obstruct the orderly and fair administration of justice in a pending case was deeply rooted in English common law at the time the Constitution was adopted. That this historical contention is dubious has been persuasively argued elsewhere. Fox, Contempt of Court, passim, *e.g.,* 207. See also Stansbury, Trial of James H. Peck, 430. * * *

More specifically, it is to forget the environment in which the First Amendment was ratified. In presenting the proposals which were later embodied in the Bill of Rights, James Madison, the leader in the preparation of the First Amendment, said: "Although I know whenever the great rights, the trial by jury, freedom of the press, or liberty of conscience, come in question in that body [Parliament], the invasion of them is resisted by able advocates, yet their Magna Carta does not contain any one provision for the security of those rights, respecting which the people of America are most alarmed. The freedom of the press and rights of conscience, those choicest privileges of the people, are unguarded in the British Constitution." 1 Annals of Congress 1789–1790, 434. And Madison elsewhere wrote that "the state of the press * * * under the common law, cannot * * * be the standard of its freedom in the United States." VI Writings of James Madison 1790–1802, 387.

There are no contrary implications in any part of the history of the period in which the First Amendment was framed and adopted. No purpose in ratifying the Bill of Rights was clearer than that of securing for the people of the United States much greater freedom of religion, expression, assembly, and petition than the people of Great Britain had ever enjoyed. It cannot be denied, for example, that the religious test oath or the restrictions upon assembly then prevalent in England would have been regarded as measures which the Constitution prohibited the American Congress from passing. And since the same unequivocal language is used with respect to freedom of the press, it signifies a similar enlargement of that concept as well. Ratified as it was while the memory of many oppressive English restrictions on the enumerated liberties was still fresh, the First Amendment cannot reasonably be taken as approving prevalent English practices. On the contrary, the only conclusion supported by history is that the unqualified prohibitions laid down by the framers were intended to give to liberty of the press, as to the other liberties, the broadest scope that could be countenanced in an orderly society.

* * *

We are aware that although some states have by statute or decision expressly repudiated the power of judges to punish publications as contempts on a finding of mere tendency to interfere with the orderly administration of justice in a pending case, other states have sanctioned the exercise of such a power. (See Nelles and King, loc. cit. supra, 536–562, for a collection and discussion of state cases.) But state power in this field was not tested in this Court for more than a century.[13] Not until 1925, with the decision in Gitlow v. New York, supra, 268 U.S. 652, did this Court recognize in the Fourteenth Amendment the application to the states of the same standards of freedom of expression as, under the First Amendment, are applicable to the federal government. And this is the first time since 1925 that we have been called upon to determine the constitutionality of a state's exercise of the contempt power in this kind of situation. Now that such a case is before us, we cannot allow the mere existence of other untested state decisions to destroy the historic constitutional meaning of freedom of speech and of the press.

History affords no support for the contention that the criteria applicable under the Constitution to other types of utterances are not applicable, in contempt proceedings, to out-of-court publications pertaining to a pending case.

* * *

No suggestion can be found in the Constitution that the freedom there guaranteed for speech and the press bears an inverse ratio to the timeliness and importance of the ideas seeking expression. Yet, it would follow as a practical result of the decisions below that anyone who might wish to give public expression to his views on a pending case involving no matter what problem of public interest, just at the time his audience would be most receptive, would be as effectively discouraged as if a deliberate statutory scheme of censorship had been adopted. Indeed, perhaps more so, because under a legislative specification of the particular kinds of expressions prohibited and the circumstances under which the prohibitions are to operate, the speaker or publisher might at least have an authoritative guide to the permissible scope of comment, instead of being compelled to act at the peril that judges might find in the utterance a "reasonable tendency" to obstruct justice in a pending case.

This unfocussed threat is, to be sure, limited in time, terminating as it does upon final disposition of the case. But this does not change its censorial quality. An endless series of oratoria on public discussion,

---

13. Patterson v. Colorado, 205 U.S. 454, the only case before this Court during that period in which a state court's power to punish out-of-court publications by contempt was in issue, cannot be taken as a decision squarely on this point. Cf.: "We leave undecided the question whether there is to be found in the Fourteenth Amendment a prohibition similar to that in the First." Id. 462.

even if each were very short, could hardly be dismissed as an insignificant abridgement of freedom of expression. And to assume that each would be short is to overlook the fact that the "pendency" of a case is frequently a matter of months or even years rather than days or weeks.

For these reasons we are convinced that the judgments below result in a curtailment of expression that cannot be dismissed as insignificant. If they can be justified at all, it must be in terms of some serious substantive evil which they are designed to avert. The substantive evil here sought to be averted has been variously described below.[15] It appears to be double: disrespect for the judiciary; and disorderly and unfair administration of justice. The assumption that respect for the judiciary can be won by shielding judges from published criticism wrongly appraises the character of American public opinion. For it is a prized American privilege to speak one's mind, although not always with perfect good taste,[16] on all public institutions. And an enforced silence, however limited, solely in the name of preserving the dignity of the bench, would probably engender resentment, suspicion, and contempt much more than it would enhance respect.

The other evil feared, disorderly and unfair administration of justice, is more plausibly associated with restricting publications which touch upon pending litigation. The very word "trial" connotes decisions on the evidence and arguments properly advanced in open court. Legal trials are not like elections, to be won through the use of the meeting-hall, the radio, and the newspaper. But we cannot start with the assumption that publications of the kind here involved actually do threaten to change the nature of legal trials, and that to preserve judicial impartiality, it is necessary for judges to have a contempt power by which they can close all channels of public expression to all matters which touch upon pending cases. We must therefore turn to the particular utterances here in question and the circumstances of their publication to determine to what extent the substantive evil of unfair administration of justice was a likely consequence, and whether the degree of likelihood was sufficient to justify summary punishment.

The Los Angeles Times Editorials. The Times–Mirror Company, publisher of the Los Angeles Times, and L.D. Hotchkiss, its managing editor, were cited for contempt for the publication of three editorials. Both found by the trial court to be responsible for one of the editorials,

---

15. Cf.: " * * * said telegram * * * had an inherent tendency * * * to *embarrass and influence the actions and decisions of the judge* before whom said action was pending." Bridges v. Superior Court, supra, 14 Cal.2d at 471; "The published statement was not only *a criticism of the decision of the court* in an action then pending before said court, but was *a threat* that if an attempt was made to enforce the decision, the ports of the entire Pacific Coast would be tied up." Id. 488; " * * * the test * * * is whether it had a reasonable tendency *to interfere with the orderly administration of justice.*" Id. 110. The italics are ours.

16. Compare the following statements from letters of Thomas Jefferson as set out in Padover, Democracy, 150–151: "I deplore * * * the putrid state into which our newspapers have passed, and the malignity, the vulgarity, and mendacious spirit of those who write them. * * * These ordures are rapidly depraving the public taste.

"It is however an evil for which there is no remedy, our liberty depends on the freedom of the press, and that cannot be limited without being lost."

the company and Hotchkiss were each fined $100. The company alone was held responsible for the other two, and was fined $100 more on account of one, and $300 more on account of the other.

The $300 fine presumably marks the most serious offense. The editorial thus distinguished was entitled "Probation for Gorillas?" After vigorously denouncing two members of a labor union who had previously been found guilty of assaulting nonunion truck drivers, it closes with the observation: "Judge A.A. Scott will make a serious mistake if he grants probation to Matthew Shannon and Kennan Holmes. This community needs the example of their assignment to the jute mill." Judge Scott had previously set a day (about a month after the publication) for passing upon the application of Shannon and Holmes for probation and for pronouncing sentence.

The basis for punishing the publication as contempt was by the trial court said to be its "inherent tendency" and by the Supreme Court as its "reasonable tendency" to interfere with the orderly administration of justice in an action then before a court for consideration. In accordance with what we have said on the "clear and present danger" cases, neither "inherent tendency" nor "reasonable tendency" is enough to justify a restriction of free expression. But even if they were appropriate measures, we should find exaggeration in the use of those phrases to describe the facts here.

From the indications in the record of the position taken by the Los Angeles Times on labor controversies in the past, there could have been little doubt of its attitude toward the probation of Shannon and Holmes. In view of the paper's long-continued militancy in this field, it is inconceivable that any judge in Los Angeles would expect anything but adverse criticism from it in the event probation were granted. Yet such criticism after final disposition of the proceedings would clearly have been privileged. Hence, this editorial, given the most intimidating construction it will bear, did no more than threaten future adverse criticism which was reasonably to be expected anyway in the event of a lenient disposition of the pending case. To regard it, therefore, as in itself of substantial influence upon the course of justice would be to impute to judges a lack of firmness, wisdom, or honor,—which we cannot accept as a major premise.

* * *

The Bridges Telegram. While a motion for a new trial was pending in a case involving a dispute between an A.F. of L. union and a C.I.O. union of which Bridges was an officer, he either caused to be published or acquiesced in the publication of a telegram which he had sent to the Secretary of Labor. The telegram referred to the judge's decision as "outrageous"; said that attempted enforcement of it would tie up the port of Los Angeles and involve the entire Pacific Coast; and concluded with the announcement that the C.I.O. union, representing some twelve thousand members, did "not intend to allow state courts to override the majority vote of members in choosing its officers and representatives and to override the National Labor Relations Board."

* * *

It must be recognized that Bridges was a prominent labor leader speaking at a time when public interest in the particular labor controversy was at its height. The observations we have previously made here upon the timeliness and importance of utterances as emphasizing rather than diminishing the value of constitutional protection, and upon the breadth and seriousness of the censorial effects of punishing publications in the manner followed below, are certainly no less applicable to a leading spokesman for labor than to a powerful newspaper taking another point of view.

In looking at the reason advanced in support of the judgment of contempt, we find that here, too, the possibility of causing unfair disposition of a pending case is the major justification asserted. And here again the gist of the offense, according to the court below, is intimidation.

Let us assume that the telegram could be construed as an announcement of Bridges' intention to call a strike, something which, it is admitted, neither the general law of California nor the court's decree prohibited. With an eye on the realities of the situation, we cannot assume that Judge Schmidt was unaware of the possibility of a strike as a consequence of his decision. If he was intimidated by the facts themselves, we do not believe that the most explicit statement of them could have sidetracked the course of justice. Again, we find exaggeration in the conclusion that the utterance even "tended" to interfere with justice. If there was electricity in the atmosphere, it was generated by the facts; the charge added by the Bridges telegram can be dismissed as negligible. The words of Mr. Justice Holmes, spoken in reference to very different facts, seem entirely applicable here: "I confess that I cannot find in all this or in the evidence in the case anything that would have affected a mind of reasonable fortitude, and still less can I find there anything that obstructed the administration of justice in any sense that I possibly can give to those words." Toledo Newspaper Co. v. United States, supra, 247 U.S. at 425.

Reversed.

MR. JUSTICE FRANKFURTER, with whom concurred the CHIEF JUSTICE, MR. JUSTICE ROBERTS and MR. JUSTICE BYRNES, dissenting.

Our whole history repels the view that it is an exercise of one of the civil liberties secured by the Bill of Rights for a leader of a large following or for a powerful metropolitan newspaper to attempt to overawe a judge in a matter immediately pending before him. The view of the majority deprives California of means for securing to its citizens justice according to law—means which, since the Union was founded, have been the possession, hitherto unchallenged, of all the states. This sudden break with the uninterrupted course of constitutional history has no constitutional warrant. To find justification for such deprivation of the historic powers of the states is to misconceive the idea of freedom of thought and speech as guaranteed by the Constitution.

Deeming it more important than ever before to enforce civil liberties with a generous outlook, but deeming it no less essential for the assurance of civil liberties that the federal system founded upon the Constitution be maintained, we believe that the careful ambiguities and silences of the majority opinion call for a full exposition of the issues in these cases.

While the immediate question is that of determining the power of the courts of California to deal with attempts to coerce their judgments in litigation immediately before them, the consequence of the Court's ruling today is a denial to the people of the forty-eight states of a right which they have always regarded as essential for the effective exercise of the judicial process, as well as a denial to the Congress of powers which were exercised from the very beginning even by the framers of the Constitution themselves. To be sure, the majority do not in so many words hold that trial by newspapers has constitutional sanctity. But the atmosphere of their opinion and several of its phrases mean that or they mean nothing. Certainly, the opinion is devoid of any frank recognition of the right of courts to deal with utterances calculated to intimidate the fair course of justice—a right which hitherto all the states have from time to time seen fit to confer upon their courts and which Congress conferred upon the federal courts in the Judiciary Act of 1789. If all that is decided today is that the majority deem the specific interferences with the administration of justice in California so tenuously related to the right of California to keep its courts free from coercion as to constitute a check upon free speech rather than upon impartial justice, it would be well to say so. Matters that involve so deeply the powers of the states, and that put to the test the professions by this Court of self-restraint in nullifying the political powers of state and nation, should not be left clouded.

We are not even vouchsafed reference to the specific provision of the Constitution which renders states powerless to insist upon trial by courts rather than trial by newspapers. So far as the Congress of the United States is concerned, we are referred to the First Amendment. That is specific. But we are here dealing with limitations upon California—with restraints upon the states. To say that the protection of freedom of speech of the First Amendment is absorbed by the Fourteenth does not say enough. Which one of the various limitations upon state power introduced by the Fourteenth Amendment absorbs the First? Some provisions of the Fourteenth Amendment apply only to citizens and one of the petitioners here is an alien; some of its provisions apply only to natural persons, and another petitioner here is a corporation. *See* Hague v. C.I.O., 307 U.S. 496, 514, and cases cited. Only the Due Process Clause assures constitutional protection of civil liberties to aliens and corporations. Corporations cannot claim for themselves the "liberty" which the Due Process Clause guarantees. That clause protects only their property. Pierce v. Society of Sisters, 268 U.S. 510, 535. The majority opinion is strangely silent in failing to avow the specific constitutional provision upon which its decision rests.

* * *

The administration of justice by an impartial judiciary has been basic to our conception of freedom ever since Magna Carta. It is the concern not merely of the immediate litigants. Its assurance is everyone's concern, and it is protected by the liberty guaranteed by the Fourteenth Amendment. That is why this Court has outlawed mob domination of a courtroom, Moore v. Dempsey, 261 U.S. 86, mental coercion of a defendant, Chambers v. Florida, 309 U.S. 227, a judicial system which does not provide disinterested judges, Tumey v. Ohio, 273 U.S. 510, and discriminatory selection of jurors, Pierre v. Louisiana, 306 U.S. 354; Smith v. Texas, 311 U.S. 128.

A trial is not a "free trade in ideas," nor is the best test of truth in a courtroom "the power of the thought to get itself accepted in the competition of the market." Compare Mr. Justice Holmes in Abrams v. United States, 250 U.S. 616, 630. A court is a forum with strictly defined limits for discussion. It is circumscribed in the range of its inquiry and in its methods by the Constitution, by laws, and by age-old traditions. Its judges are restrained in their freedom of expression by historic compulsions resting on no other officials of government. They are so circumscribed precisely because judges have in their keeping the enforcement of rights and the protection of liberties which, according to the wisdom of the ages, can only be enforced and protected by observing such methods and traditions.

* * *

Of course freedom of speech and of the press are essential to the enlightenment of a free people and in restraining those who wield power. Particularly should this freedom be employed in comment upon the work of courts, who are without many influences ordinarily making for humor and humility, twin antidotes to the corrosion of power. But the Bill of Rights is not self-destructive. Freedom of expression can hardly carry implications that nullify the guarantees of impartial trials. And since courts are the ultimate resorts for vindicating the Bill of Rights, a state may surely authorize appropriate historic means to assure that the process for such vindication be not wrenched from its rational tracks into the more primitive mêlée of passion and pressure. The need is great that courts be criticized, but just as great that they be allowed to do their duty.

* * *

* * * [T]he Constitution does not bar a state from acting on the theory of our system of justice, that the "conclusions to be reached in a case will be induced only by evidence and argument in open court, and not by any outside influence, whether of private talk or public print." Patterson v. Colorado, 205 U.S. 454, 462. The theory of our system of justice as thus stated for the Court by Mr. Justice Holmes has never been questioned by any member of the Court.

* * *

Comment however forthright is one thing. Intimidation with respect to specific matters still in judicial suspense, quite another. See Laski, Procedure for Constructive Contempt in England, 41 Harv.L.Rev. 1031, 1034; Goodhart, Newspapers and Contempt in English Law, 48 Harv.L.Rev. 885. A publication intended to teach the judge a lesson, or to vent spleen, or to discredit him, or to influence him in his future conduct, would not justify exercise of the contempt power. Compare Judge Learned Hand in Ex parte Craig, 282 F. 138, 160–61. It must refer to a matter under consideration and constitute in effect a threat to its impartial disposition. It must be calculated to create an atmospheric pressure incompatible with rational, impartial adjudication. But to interfere with justice it need not succeed. As with other offenses, the state should be able to proscribe attempts that fail because of the danger that attempts may succeed. The purpose, it will do no harm to repeat, is not to protect the court as a mystical entity or the judges as individuals or as anointed priests set apart from the community and spared the criticism to which in a democracy other public servants are exposed. The purpose is to protect immediate litigants and the public from the mischievous danger of an unfree or coerced tribunal.

* * *

The rule of law applied in these cases by the California court forbade publications having "a reasonable tendency to interfere with the orderly administration of justice in pending actions." To deny that this age-old formulation of the prohibition against interference with dispassionate adjudication is properly confined to the substantive evil is not only to turn one's back on history but also to indulge in an idle play on words, unworthy of constitutional adjudication. It was urged before us that the words "reasonable tendency" had a fatal pervasiveness, and that their replacement by "clear and present danger" was required to state a constitutionally permissible rule of law. The Constitution, as we have recently had occasion to remark, is not a formulary. * * * Nor does it require displacement of an historic test by a phrase which first gained currency on March 3, 1919. Schenck v. United States, 249 U.S. 47. Our duty is not ended with the recitation of phrases that are the short-hand of a complicated historic process. The phrase "clear and present danger" is merely a justification for curbing utterance where that is warranted by the substantive evil to be prevented. The phrase itself is an expression of tendency and not of accomplishment, and the literary difference between it and "reasonable tendency" is not of constitutional dimension.

* * *

No objections were made before us to the procedure by which the charges of contempt were tried. But it is proper to point out that neither case was tried by a judge who had participated in the trials to which the publications referred. Compare Cooke v. United States, 267 U.S. 517, 539. So it is clear that a disinterested tribunal was furnished, and since the Constitution does not require a state to furnish jury trials, Maxwell v. Dow, 176 U.S. 581; Palko v. Connecticut, 302 U.S. 319, 324, and states have discretion in fashioning criminal remedies, Tigner v. Texas, 310 U.S. 141, the situation here is the same as though a state had made it a crime to publish utterance having a "reasonable tendency to interfere with the orderly administration of justice in pending actions," and not dissimilar from what the United States has done in § 135 of the Criminal Code.

A BRIEF SUMMARY NOTE ON *BRIDGES v. CALIFORNIA*

Bridges v. California marks a suitable point for pause. Note it is the first case since *Patterson v. Colorado* that actually concerns the same problem dealt with in *Patterson,* i.e. newspaper contempt of court, alleged threat to fair trial, libel of judges, intimidation of judicial process, etc. "versus" freedom of the press, and in that respect draws a neat circle around the changes in first amendment doctrine, since the decision in *Patterson,* in 1907. It may warrant a convenient comparison, therefore, with *Patterson,* in marking the course of modern first amendment doctrine.[46] Second, *Bridges* is also a case that applies, through the majority opinion, the rigorized Holmes–Brandeis standard of substantive judicial review derived from the cases we have previously examined (e.g., *Abrams, Gitlow, Whitney*), but in which that standard appeared principally only in dissents. For that reason as well, it provides a convenient way of comparing a newer sort of first amendment "figure" graphically with the two originally introduced in these materials: the "absolute" view first suggested in the Introduction (sometimes identified to Justice Hugo Black), and the [mere] "no licensing" view, identified with Blackstone, and with Holmes in 1907.

Beginning with *Schenck,* Holmes repudiated the mere bad tendency test at least in cases involving political advocacy and criticism, substituting a case-specific, judicially reviewable, "clear and present danger" proof. Beginning with *Gitlow,* Brandeis advanced the stronger position (in which Holmes concurred), that even the actual eventuality of certain "harms" as a foreseen effect of social advocacy speech must be borne by the polity, as a necessary social cost of protecting social advocacy speech. In this sense, as we saw, the Holmes–Brandeis view is that the strong form of the first amendment disallows the internalizing of some negative free speech effects by holding the speaker responsible for them (namely, minor harms, moderate inconveniences, etc.,) though they are harms otherwise within the police power of the state to avoid, but not when they are the inevitable byproduct of highly protected freedoms of social advocacy or criticism. In a manner of speaking, in Brandeis' view, the first amendment disallows government from putting a higher premium on the avoidance of certain minor harms than on freedom of speech.

Roughly speaking, the comparisons yield four figures, the last three being the practically significant ones: the second (Blackstone) reflecting a very small area of first amendment operative force, the fourth, represented in the analysis and holding of *Bridges,* extending the field of first amendment preemption in two additional ways:

---

46. The next several assigned cases are meant principally to furnish a coherent, brief review of "free press-prior restraint" cases, in related settings, with no basic doctrinal changes but, rather, with a few refinements on the analysis provided in the *Bridges* case.

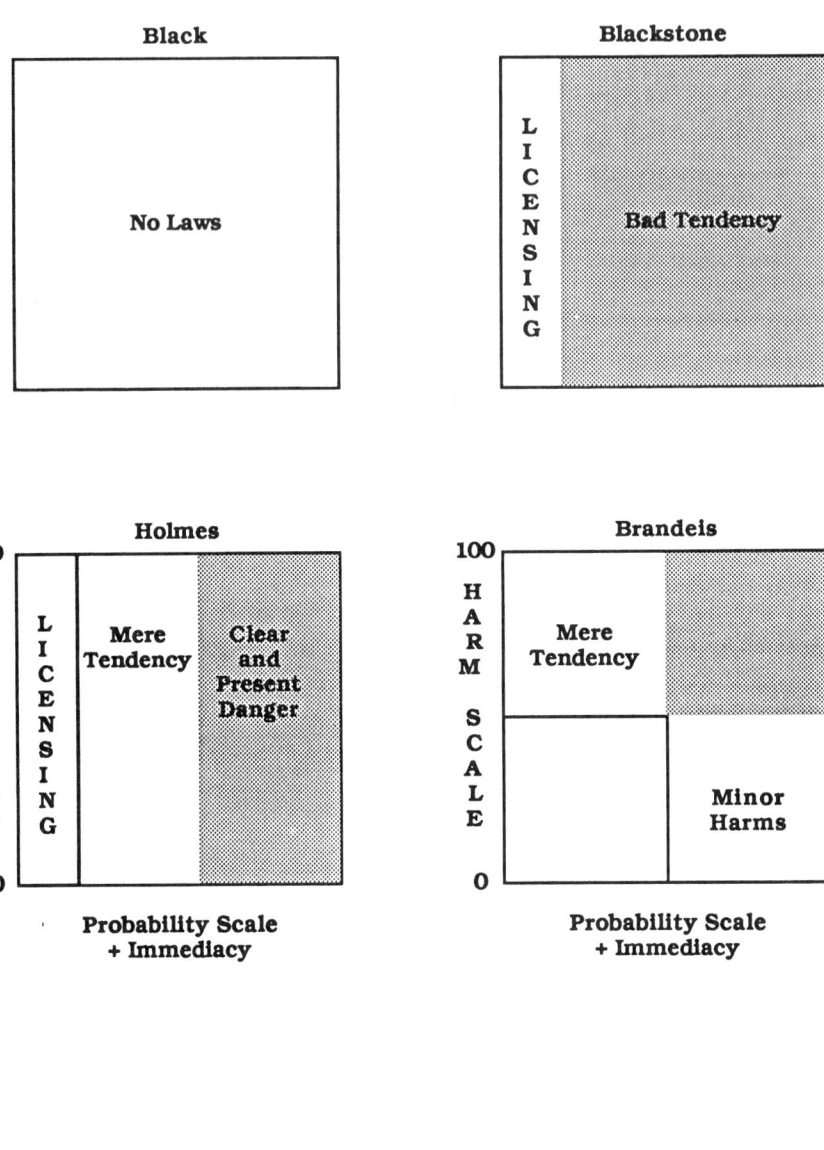

SHEPPARD v. MAXWELL
Supreme Court of the United States, 1966.
384 U.S. 333, 86 S.Ct. 1507, 16 L.Ed.2d 600.

MR. JUSTICE CLARK delivered the opinion of the Court.

This federal habeas corpus application involves the question whether Sheppard was deprived of a fair trial in his state conviction for the second-degree murder of his wife because of the trial judge's failure to protect Sheppard sufficiently from the massive, pervasive and prejudicial publicity that attended his prosecution. * * * We have concluded that Sheppard did not receive a fair trial consistent with the Due Process Clause of the Fourteenth Amendment and, therefore, reverse the judgment.

I.

Marilyn Sheppard, petitioner's pregnant wife, was bludgeoned to death in the upstairs bedroom of their lakeshore home in Bay Village, Ohio, a suburb of Cleveland. * * *

From the outset officials focused suspicion on Sheppard. After a search of the house and the premises on the morning of the tragedy, Dr. Gerber, the Coroner, is reported—and it is undenied—to have told his men, "Well, it is evident the doctor did this, so let's go get the confession out of him." He proceeded to interrogate and examine Sheppard while the latter was under sedation in his hospital room. On the same occasion, the Coroner was given the clothes Sheppard wore at the time of the tragedy together with the personal items in them. Later that afternoon Chief Eaton and two Cleveland police officers interrogated Sheppard at some length, confronting him with evidence and demanding explanations. Asked by Officer Shotke to take a lie detector test, Sheppard said he would if it were reliable. Shotke replied that it was "infallible" and "you might as well tell us all about it now." At the end of the interrogation Shotke told Sheppard: "I think you killed your wife." Still later in the same afternoon a physician sent by the Coroner was permitted to make a detailed examination of Sheppard. Until the Coroner's inquest on July 22, at which time he was subpoenaed, Sheppard made himself available for frequent and extended questioning.

* * *

Throughout this period the newspapers emphasized evidence that tended to incriminate Sheppard and pointed out discrepancies in his statements to authorities. * * * The newspapers also delved into Sheppard's personal life. Articles stressed his extramarital love affairs as a motive for the crime. The newspapers portrayed Sheppard as a Lothario, fully explored his relationship with Susan Hayes, and named a number of other women who were allegedly involved with him. The testimony at trial never showed that Sheppard had any illicit relationships besides the one with Susan Hayes.

On July 28, an editorial entitled "Why Don't Police Quiz Top Suspect" demanded that Sheppard be taken to police headquarters. It described him in the following language:

> "Now proved under oath to be a liar, still free to go about his business, shielded by his family, protected by a smart lawyer who has made monkeys of the police and authorities, carrying a gun part of the time, left free to do whatever he pleases. * * *"

A front-page editorial on July 30 asked: "Why Isn't Sam Sheppard in Jail?" It was later titled "Quit Stalling—Bring Him In." After calling Sheppard "the most unusual murder suspect ever seen around these parts" the article said that "[e]xcept for some superficial questioning during Coroner Sam Gerber's inquest he has been scot-free of any official grilling. * * *" It asserted that he was "surrounded by an iron curtain of protection [and] concealment."

* * *

* * * We do not detail the coverage further. There are five volumes filled with similar clippings from each of the three Cleveland newspapers covering the period from the murder until Sheppard's conviction in December 1954. The record includes no excerpts from newscasts on radio and television but since space was reserved in the courtroom for these media we assume that their coverage was equally large.

II.

With this background the case came on for trial two weeks before the November general election at which the chief prosecutor was a candidate for common pleas judge and the trial judge, Judge Blythin, was a candidate to succeed himself. Twenty-five days before the case was set, 75 veniremen were called as prospective jurors. All three Cleveland newspapers published the names and addresses of the veniremen. As a consequence, anonymous letters and telephone calls, as well as calls from friends, regarding the impending prosecution were received by all of the prospective jurors. The selection of the jury began on October 18, 1954.

* * * Private telephone lines and telegraphic equipment were installed * * * so that reports from the trial could be speeded to the papers. Station WSRS was permitted to set up broadcasting facilities on the third floor of the courthouse next door to the jury room, where the jury rested during recesses in the trial and deliberated. Newscasts were made from this room throughout the trial, and while the jury reached its verdict.

On the sidewalk and steps in front of the courthouse, television and newsreel cameras were occasionally used to take motion pictures of the participants in the trial, including the jury and the judge. Indeed, one television broadcast carried a staged interview of the judge as he entered the courthouse. In the corridors outside the courtroom there was a host of photographers and television personnel with flash cameras, portable lights and motion picture cameras. This group photographed the prospective jurors during selection of the jury. After the trial opened, the witnesses, counsel, and jurors were photographed and televised whenever they entered or left the courtroom. Sheppard was brought to the courtroom about 10 minutes before each session began; he was surrounded by reporters and extensively photographed for the newspapers and television. A rule of court prohibited picture-taking in the courtroom during the actual sessions of the court, but no restraints were put on photographers during recesses, which were taken once each morning and afternoon, with a longer period for lunch.

All of these arrangements with the news media and their massive coverage of the trial continued during the entire nine weeks of the trial.
* * *

* * *

The jurors themselves were constantly exposed to the news media. Every juror, except one, testified at voir dire to reading about the case in the Cleveland papers or to having heard broadcasts about it. Seven of the 12 jurors who rendered the verdict had one or more Cleveland papers delivered in their home; the remaining jurors were not interrogated on the point. Nor were there questions as to radios or television sets in the jurors' homes, but we must assume that most of them owned such conveniences. As the selection of the jury progressed, individual pictures of prospective members appeared daily. During the trial, pictures of the jury appeared over 40 times in the Cleveland papers alone. The court permitted photographers to take pictures of the jury in the box, and individual pictures of the members in the jury room. One newspaper ran pictures of the jurors at the Sheppard home when they went there to view the scene of the murder. The day before the verdict was rendered—while the jurors were at lunch and sequestered by two bailiffs—the jury was separated into two groups to pose for photographs which appeared in the newspaper.

* * *

3. While the jury was being selected, a two-inch headline asked: "But Who Will Speak for Marilyn?" The front-page story spoke of the "perfect face" of the accused. "Study that face as long as you want. Never will you get from it a hint of what might be the answer. * * * " The two brothers of the accused were described as "Prosperous, poised. His two sisters-in-law. Smart, chic, well-groomed. His elderly father. Courtly, reserved. A perfect type for the patriarch of a staunch clan." The author then noted Marilyn Sheppard was "still off stage," and that she was an only child whose mother died when she was very young and whose father had no interest in the case. But the author—through quotes from detective Chief James McArthur—assured readers that the prosecution's exhibits would speak for Marilyn. "Her story," McArthur stated, "will come into this courtroom through our witnesses." The article ends:

"Then you realize how what and who is missing from the perfect setting will be supplied.

"How in the Big Case justice will be done.

"Justice to Sam Sheppard.

"And to Marilyn Sheppard."

4. As has been mentioned, the jury viewed the scene of the murder on the first day of the trial. Hundreds of reporters, cameramen and onlookers were there, and one representative of the news media was permitted to accompany the jury while it inspected the Sheppard home. The time of the jury's visit was revealed so far in advance that one of the newspapers was able to rent a helicopter and fly over the house taking pictures of the jurors on their tour.

5. On November 19, a Cleveland police officer gave testimony that tended to contradict details in the written statement Sheppard made to the Cleveland police. Two days later, in a broadcast heard over Station WHK in Cleveland, Robert Considine likened Sheppard to a perjurer and compared the episode to Alger Hiss' confrontation with Whittaker Chambers. Though defense counsel asked the judge to question the jury to ascertain how many heard the broadcast, the court refused to do so. The judge also overruled the motion for continuance based on the same ground, saying:

> "Well, I don't know, we can't stop people, in any event, listening to it. It is a matter of free speech, and the court can't control everybody. * * * We are not going to harass the jury every morning. * * * It is getting to the point where if we do it every morning, we are suspecting the jury. I have confidence in this jury. * * * "

6. On November 24, a story appeared under an eight-column headline: "Sam Called A 'Jekyll–Hyde' By Marilyn, Cousin To Testify." It was related that Marilyn had recently told friends that Sheppard was a "Dr. Jekyll and Mr. Hyde" character. No such testimony was ever produced at the trial. The story went on to announce: "The prosecution has a 'bombshell witness' on tap who will testify to Dr. Sam's display of fiery temper—countering the defense claim that the defendant is a gentle physician with an even disposition." Defense counsel made motions for change of venue, continuance and mistrial, but they were denied. No action was taken by the court.

* * *

The principle that justice cannot survive behind walls of silence has long been reflected in the "Anglo–American distrust for secret trials." In re Oliver, 333 U.S. 257, 268 (1948). A responsible press has always been regarded as the handmaiden of effective judicial administration, especially in the criminal field. Its function in this regard is documented by an impressive record of service over several centuries. The press does not simply publish information about trials but guards against the miscarriage of justice by subjecting the police, prosecutors, and judicial processes to extensive public scrutiny and criticism. This Court has, therefore, been unwilling to place any direct limitations on the freedom traditionally exercised by the news media for "[w]hat transpires in the court room is public property." Craig v. Harney, 331 U.S. 367, 374 (1947). The "unqualified prohibitions laid down by the framers were intended to give to liberty of the press * * * the broadest scope that could be countenanced in an orderly society." Bridges v. California, 314 U.S. 252, 265 (1941). And where there was "no threat or menace to the integrity of the trial," Craig v. Harney, *supra,* at 377, we have consistently required that the press have a free hand, even though we sometimes deplored its sensationalism.

But the Court has also pointed out that "[l]egal trials are not like elections, to be won through the use of the meeting-hall, the radio, and the newspaper." Bridges v. California, *supra,* at 271. And the Court has insisted that no one be punished for a crime without "a charge fairly made and fairly tried in a public tribunal free of prejudice, passion, excitement, and tyrannical power." Chambers v. Florida, 309 U.S. 227, 236–237 (1940). "Freedom of discussion should be given the widest range compatible with the essential requirement of the fair and orderly administration of justice." * * *

The undeviating rule of this Court was expressed by Mr. Justice Holmes over half a century ago in Patterson v. Colorado, 205 U.S. 454, 462 (1907):

> "The theory of our system is that the conclusions to be reached in a case will be induced only by evidence and argument in open court, and not by any outside influence, whether of private talk or public print."

* * * [T]he judge never considered other means that are often utilized to reduce the appearance of prejudicial material and to protect the jury from outside influence. We conclude that these procedures would have been sufficient to guarantee Sheppard a fair trial and so do not consider what sanctions might be available against a recalcitrant press nor the charges of bias now made against the state trial judge.

The carnival atmosphere at trial could easily have been avoided since the courtroom and courthouse premises are subject to the control of the court. As we stressed in *Estes,* the presence of the press at judicial proceedings must be limited when it is apparent that the accused might otherwise be prejudiced or disadvantaged.[12] Bearing in mind the massive pretrial publicity, the judge should have adopted stricter rules governing the use of the courtroom by newsmen, as Sheppard's counsel requested. * * *

* * *

* * * And it is obvious that the judge should have further sought to alleviate this problem by imposing control over the statements made to the news media by counsel, witnesses, and especially the Coroner and police officers. The prosecution repeatedly made evidence available to the news media which was never offered in the trial. Much of the

---

12. The judge's awareness of his power in this respect is manifest from his assignment of seats to the press.

"evidence" disseminated in this fashion was clearly inadmissible. The exclusion of such evidence in court is rendered meaningless when news media make it available to the public. * * *

* * * Effective control of these sources—concededly within the court's power—might well have prevented the divulgence of inaccurate information, rumors, accusations that made up much of the inflammatory publicity, at least after Sheppard's indictment.

More specifically, the trial court might well have proscribed extrajudicial statements by any lawyer, party, witness, or court official which divulged prejudicial matters, such as the refusal of Sheppard to submit to interrogation or take any lie detector tests; any statement made by Sheppard to officials; the identity of prospective witnesses or their probable testimony; any belief in guilt or innocence; or like statements concerning the merits of the case. * * *

From the cases coming here we note that unfair and prejudicial news comment on pending trials has become increasingly prevalent. Due process requires that the accused receive a trial by an impartial jury free from outside influences. Given the pervasiveness of modern communications and the difficulty of effacing prejudicial publicity from the minds of the jurors, the trial courts must take strong measures to ensure that the balance is never weighed against the accused. And appellate tribunals have the duty to make an independent evaluation of the circumstances. Of course, there is nothing that proscribes the press from reporting events that transpire in the courtroom. But where there is a reasonable likelihood that prejudicial news prior to trial will prevent a fair trial, the judge should continue the case until the threat abates, or transfer it to another county not so permeated with publicity. In addition, sequestration of the jury was something the judge should have raised *sua sponte* with counsel. If publicity during the proceedings threatens the fairness of the trial, a new trial should be ordered. But we must remember that reversals are but palliatives; the cure lies in those remedial measures that will prevent the prejudice at its inception. The courts must take such steps by rule and regulation that will protect their processes from prejudicial outside interferences. * * *

Since the state trial judge did not fulfill his duty to protect Sheppard from the inherently prejudicial publicity which saturated the community and to control disruptive influences in the courtroom, we must reverse the denial of the habeas petition. The case is remanded to the District Court with instructions to issue the writ and order that Sheppard be released from custody unless the State puts him to its charges again within a reasonable time.

It is so ordered.

MR. JUSTICE BLACK dissents.

WOOD v. GEORGIA
Supreme Court of the United States, 1962.
370 U.S. 375, 82 S.Ct. 1364, 8 L.Ed.2d 569.

MR. CHIEF JUSTICE WARREN delivered the opinion of the Court.

We granted certiorari to consider the scope of the constitutional protection to be enjoyed by persons when the publication of their thoughts and opinions is alleged to be in conflict with the fair administration of justice in state courts. The petitioner, an elected sheriff in Bibb County, Georgia, contends that the Georgia courts, in holding him in contempt of court for expressing his personal ideas on a matter that was presently before the grand jury for its consideration, have bridged his liberty of free speech as protected by the First Amendment and the Due Process Clause of the Fourteenth Amendment to the Federal Constitution.

On June 6, 1960, a judge of the Bibb Superior Court issued a charge to a regularly impaneled grand jury, giving it special instructions to conduct an investigation into a political situation which had allegedly arisen in the county. The jury was advised that there appeared to be "an inane and inexplicable pattern of Negro bloc voting" in Bibb county, and that "rumors and accusations" had been made which indicated candidates for public office had paid large sums of money in an effort to gain favor and to obtain the Negro vote. The charge explained that certain Negro leaders, after having met and endorsed a candidate, had switched their support to an opposing candidate who put up a large sum of money, and that this "create[d] an unhealthy, dangerous, and unlawful situation [which] tend[ed] to corrupt public office holders and some candidates for public office." The charge continued by indicating the violations of law which would be involved should the grand jury find the charges to be founded in truth. * * *

The following day, while the grand jury was in session investigating the matters set forth in the instructions delivered by the court, the petitioner issued to the local press a written statement in which he criticized the judges' action and in which he urged the citizenry to take notice when their highest judicial officers threatened political intimidation and persecution of voters in the county under the guise of law enforcement. This news release, which was published and disseminated to the general public, stated:

> "Whatever the Judges' intention, the action * * * ordering [the grand jury] * * * to investigate 'negro block voting' will be considered one of the most deplorable examples of race agitation to come out of Middle Georgia in recent years.
>
> "At a time, when all thinking people want to preserve the good will and cooperation between the races in Bibb County, this action appears either as a crude attempt at judicial intimidation of negro voters and leaders, or, at best, as agitation for a 'negro vote' issue in local politics. * * * *"

The following day, the petitioner delivered to the bailiff of the court, stationed at the entrance to the grand jury room, "An Open

Letter to the Bibb County Grand Jury," which was made available to the the grand jury at petitioner's request. This letter, implying that the court's charge was false, asserted that in the petitioner's opinion, the Bibb County Democratic Executive Committee was the organization responsible for corruption in the purchasing of votes, and that the grand jury would be well-advised also to investigate that organization.

A month later, on July 7, 1960, the petitioner was cited in two counts of contempt based on the above statements. The citation charged that the language used by the petitioner was designed and calculated to be contemptuous of the court, to ridicule the investigation ordered by the charge, and "to hamper, hinder, interfere with and obstruct" the grand jury in its investigation. It also alleged that the news release was issued from the Bibb County Sheriff's Office, located in the courthouse in which the grand jury had been charged and where it was deliberating, and that the language imputed lack of judicial integrity to the three judges of the court responsible for the charge. An amendment to the citation alleged that the statements "in and of [themselves] created * * * a clear, present and imminent danger to the investigation being conducted * * * and * * * to the proper administration of justice in Bibb Superior Court."

* * *

We start with the premise that the right of courts to conduct their business in an untrammeled way lies at the foundation of our system of government and that courts necessarily must possess the means of punishing for contempt when conduct tends directly to prevent the discharge of their functions. While courts have continuously had the authority and power to maintain order in their courtrooms and to assure litigants a fair trial, the exercise of that bare contempt power is not what is questioned in this case. Here it is asserted that the exercise of the contempt power, to commit a person to jail for an utterance out of the presence of the court, has abridged the accused's liberty of free expression. In this situation the burden upon this Court is to define the limitations upon the contempt power according to the terms of the Federal Constitution.

In Bridges v. California, 314 U.S. 252, this Court for the first time had occasion to review a State's exercise of the contempt power utilized to punish the publisher of an out-of-court statement. The accused contended that the exercise abridged his right of free speech guaranteed against state infringement by the Fourteenth Amendment. To determine the scope of this constitutional protection, the Court reviewed the history of the contempt power, both in England and in this country. It held that "the only conclusion supported by [that] history is that the unqualified prohibitions laid down by the framers were intended to give to liberty of the press, as to the other liberties, the broadest scope that could be countenanced in an orderly society." Id., at 265.[5]

5. Specifically, the Court, after a thorough review of the history behind both the exercise of the contempt power and the adoption of the First Amendment, rejected the idea that the interests were to be accommodated by applying the common law of England at the time the Constitution was adopted. Bridges v. California, 314

Thus clarifying the exercise of this judicial power in the context of the protections assured by the First Amendment, the Court held that out-of-court publications were to be governed by the clear and present danger standard, described as "a working principle that the substantive evil must be extremely serious and the degree of imminence extremely high before utterances can be punished." *Id.*, at 263.[6] * * *

* * *

The respondent attempts to distinguish this case from *Bridges* by offering, as support for the Georgia court's conclusion that the petitioner's conduct presented a clear and present danger to the administration of justice, the fact that here there was an alleged interference with a grand jury and not an attempt to influence or coerce a judge. In the circumstances of this case, we find this argument unpersuasive.

First, it is important to emphasize that this case does not represent a situation where an individual is on trial; there was no "judicial proceeding pending" in the sense that prejudice might result to one litigant or the other by ill-considered misconduct aimed at influencing the outcome of a trial or a grand jury proceeding. * * * Rather, the grand jury here was conducting a general investigation into a matter touching each member of the community.

Historically, this body has been regarded as a primary security to the innocent against hasty, malicious and oppressive persecution; it serves the invaluable function in our society of standing between the accuser and the accused, whether the latter be an individual, minority group, or other, to determine whether a charge is founded upon reason or was dictated by an intimidating power or by malice and personal ill will. * * * [H]ere a panel of judges, themselves elected officers and charged under state law with the responsibility of instructing a grand jury to investigate political corruption, have exercised the contempt power to hold in contempt another elected representative of the people for publishing views honestly held and contrary to those contained in the charge. And, an effort by the petitioner to prove the truth of his allegations was rejected, the court holding irrelevant the truth or falsity of the facts and opinions expressed in the publications. * * *

* * *

* * * When the grand jury is performing its investigatory function into a general problem area, without specific regard to indicting a particular individual, society's interest is best served by a thorough and extensive investigation, and a greater degree of disinterestedness and impartiality is assured by allowing free expression of contemporary

U.S. 252, 263–268. For source materials on this subject, see Chafee, Free Speech in the United States (1941), c. 1; Fox, The History of Contempt of Court (1927), *passim*; Stansbury, Trial of James H. Peck (1833), *passim;* Thayer, Legal Control of the Press (3d ed. 1956), 483 *et seq.* See also Deutsch, Liberty of Expression and Contempt of Court, 27 Minn.L.Rev. 296 (1943); Nelles and King, Contempt by Publication in the United States, 28 Col.L.Rev. 401, 525 (1928).

6. The Court went on to say that the clear and present danger standard does not "purport to mark the furthermost constitutional boundaries of protected expression * * * [and that it does] no more than recognize a minimum compulsion of the Bill of Rights." Bridges v. California, *supra*, at 263.

opinion. Consistent suppression of discussion likely to affect pending investigations would mean that some continuing public grievances could never be discussed at all, or at least not at the moment when public discussion is most needed. The conviction here produces its "restrictive results at the precise time when public interest in the matters discussed would naturally be at its height," and "[n]o suggestion can be found in the Constitution that the freedom there guaranteed for speech and the press bears an inverse ratio to the timeliness and importance of the ideas seeking expression." Bridges v. California, *supra*, at 268, 269. Thus, in the absence of any showing of an actual interference with the undertakings of the grand jury, this record lacks persuasion in illustrating the serious degree of harm to the administration of law necessary to justify exercise of the contempt power. * * *

* * *

* * * [A]ssuming that the Court of Appeals did consider to be significant the fact that petitioner was a sheriff, we do not believe this fact provides any basis for curtailing his right of free speech. There is no evidence that the publications interfered with the performance of his duties as sheriff or with his duties, if any he had, in connection with the grand jury's investigation. We are not dealing with a situation where a sheriff refuses to issue summonses or to maintain order in the court building; nor, so far as the record shows, did the petitioner do any act which might present a substantive harm to the jury's solution of the problem placed before it. We are dealing here only with public expression.

The petitioner was an elected official and had the right to enter the field of political controversy, particularly where his political life was at stake. * * * The role that elected officials play in our society makes it all the more imperative that they be allowed freely to express themselves on matters of current public importance.

Our examination of the content of petitioner's statements and the circumstances under which they were published leads us to conclude that they did not present a danger to the administration of justice that should vitiate his freedom to express his opinions in the manner chosen.

The judgment is reversed.

Mr. Justice Frankfurter took no part in the decision of this case.

Mr. Justice White took no part in the decision of this case.

Mr. Justice Harlan, whom Mr. Justice Clark joins, dissenting.

Whether or not the clear and present danger doctrine of Bridges v. California, 314 U.S. 252, 260–263, 271, should be deemed to limit a state or federal court's use of the contempt power when employed against a member of its official entourage who has scandalized the conduct of the court in relation to and during the course of a pending judicial proceeding is a question which I need not reach in this case. For even under the most expansive view of *Bridges* and its offshoots the contempt judgment against this sheriff should be upheld.

* * *

* * * Congress has recognized the need for safeguarding the deliberations of federal grand juries by making it a crime to attempt to influence a federal grand juror by extrajudicial communication.[47] Even assuming that a State may constitutionally permit a grand jury, unlike a petit jury, to be influenced by extrajudicial statements, a question explicitly left open in Beck v. Washington, 369 U.S. 541, 546, it certainly does not compel them to that course.

The Court does not dispute this. But, says the Court, no individual is on trial here; and "When the grand jury is performing its investigatory function into a general problem area, without specific regard to indicting a particular individual, society's interest is best served by a thorough and extensive investigation, and a greater degree of disinterestedness and impartiality is assured by allowing free expression of contrary opinion." * * * This, however, is surely a policy decision with respect to which a State may legitimately take a different view. The Court does not suggest that Georgia was attempting to use the mantle of judicial proceedings in order to insulate the transaction of nonjudicial business from criticism; investigation is a traditional function of the grand jury. I see no reason why the State cannot determine for itself what shall and what shall not be considered by grand jurors in conducting any of their traditional tasks. Moreover, it is not the fact that individual rights were not at stake in this proceeding. The judge charged the jury:

> "if there is sufficient evidence of unlawful acts, then all parties participating, white and colored, candidates or non-candidates should be indicted by this Grand Jury so that the guilty parties, if there are any, may be brought to trial."

* * *

Accepting as I do for present purposes the *Bridges* test, this conviction must be upheld if the record supports the inference of clear and present danger.

II.

That test is amply met here. Petitioner, a public official connected with the court, accused, from his office in the courthouse, the Superior Court judges of fomenting race hatred; of misusing the criminal law to persecute and to intimidate political and racial minorities; of political naiveté, racial prejudice, and hypocrisy. He compared the calling of the grand jury to the activities of the Ku Klux Klan. He made an undisguised effort to influence the outcome of the investigation by declaring that only the politically naive could believe Bibb County

---

47. "Whoever attempts to influence the action or decision of any grand or petit juror of any court of the United States upon any issue or matter pending before such juror, or before the jury of which he is a member, or pertaining to his duties, by writing or sending to him any written communication, in relation to such issue or matter, shall be fined not more than $1,000 or imprisoned not more than six months, or both.

"Nothing in this section shall be construed to prohibit the communication of a request to appear before the grand jury." 18 U.S.C. § 1504.

Negroes might be guilty of selling votes. It was stipulated that both of petitioner's formal statements were read by the grand jurors during the course of their investigation.

The Court considers this evidence insufficient because there was no showing of "an actual interference with the undertakings of the jury," that the jurors "felt unable or unwilling to complete their assigned task because petitioner 'interfered' with its completion," that "the investigation was not ultimately successful or, if it was not, that the petitioner's conduct was responsible for its failure." * * * Surely the Court cannot mean that attempts to influence judicial proceedings are punishable only if they are successful. Speech creating sufficient danger of an evil which the State may prevent may certainly be punished regardless of whether that evil materializes. * * *

* * * In this instance that likelihood was increased by two factors which were not present in *Bridges, Pennekamp,* or *Craig,* in which the Court held the evidence insufficient to show clear and present danger. None of those cases involved statements by officers of the court; and all concerned statements whose alleged interference was with the deliberations of a judge rather than a jury. Georgia law requires the sheriff to execute and return court processes and orders and to preserve order during sessions of the courts. Ga.Code Ann., 1959, § 24–2813. Petitioner was thus a law-enforcement officer, whose office was in the very courthouse where the grand jury was sitting. Whether or not he issued the statements "in his capacity as sheriff," and whether or not the contempt citation alleged it, his words assumed an overtone of official quality and authority that lent them weight beyond those of an ordinary citizen.

Of equal if not greater importance is the fact that petitioner's statements were calculated to influence, not a judge chosen because of his independence, integrity, and courage and trained by experience and the discipline of law to deal only with evidence properly before him, but a grand jury of laymen chosen to serve for a limited term from the general population of Bibb County. It cannot be assumed with grand jurors, as it has been with judges, Craig v. Harney, *supra,* 331 U.S., at 376, that they are all "men of fortitude, able to thrive in a hardy climate." What may not seriously endanger the independent deliberations of a judge may well jeopardize those of a grand or petit jury. * * *

* * *

Finally, petitioner's case is not saved by the fact that both he and the judges he attacked are elected officials, or by the fact that the statement concerned an issue of some political moment. There was ample opportunity to bring the judges' performance to the voters after the investigation was closed. "Political interest" cannot be used as an excuse for affecting the result of a judicial inquiry.

I would affirm.

NEBRASKA PRESS ASSOCIATION v. STUART
Supreme Court of the United States, 1976.
427 U.S. 539, 96 S.Ct. 2791, 49 L.Ed.2d 683.

MR. CHIEF JUSTICE BURGER delivered the opinion of the Court.

The respondent State District Judge entered an order restraining the petitioners from publishing or broadcasting accounts of confessions or admissions made by the accused or facts "strongly implicative" of the accused in a widely reported murder of six persons. We granted certiorari to decide whether the entry of such an order on the showing made before the state court violated the constitutional guarantee of freedom of the press.

I

On the evening of October 18, 1975, local police found the six members of the Henry Kellie family murdered in their home in Sutherland, Neb., a town of about 850 people. Police released the description of a suspect, Erwin Charles Simants, to the reporters who had hastened to the scene of the crime. Simants was arrested and arraigned in Lincoln County Court the following morning, ending a tense night for this small rural community.

The crime immediately attracted widespread news coverage, by local, regional, and national newspapers, radio and television stations. Three days after the crime, the County Attorney and Simants' attorney joined in asking the County Court to enter a restrictive order relating to "matters that may or may not be publicly reported or disclosed to the public," because of the "mass coverage by news media" and the "reasonable likelihood of prejudicial news which would make difficult, if not impossible, the impaneling of an impartial jury and tend to prevent a fair trial." The County Court heard oral argument but took no evidence; no attorney for members of the press appeared at this stage. The County Court granted the prosecutor's motion for a restrictive order and entered it the next day, October 22. The order prohibited everyone in attendance from "releas[ing] or authoriz[ing] the release for public dissemination in any form or manner whatsoever any testimony given or evidence adduced"; the order also required members of the press to observe the Nebraska Bar–Press Guidelines.[1]

Simants' preliminary hearing was held the same day, open to the public but subject to the order. The County Court bound over the defendant for trial to the State District Court. The charges, as amend-

---

1. These Guidelines are voluntary standards adopted by members of the state bar and news media to deal with the reporting of crimes and criminal trials. They outline the matters of fact that may appropriately be reported, and also list what items are not generally appropriate for reporting, including confessions, opinions on guilt or innocence, statements that would influence the outcome of a trial, the results of tests or examinations, comments on the credibility of witnesses, and evidence presented in the jury's absence. The publication of an accused's criminal record should, under the Guidelines, be "considered very carefully." The Guidelines also set out standards for taking and publishing photographs, and set up a joint bar-press committee to foster cooperation in resolving particular problems that emerge.

ed to reflect the autopsy findings, were that Simants had committed the murders in the course of a sexual assault.

Petitioners—several press and broadcast associations, publishers, and individual reporters—moved on October 23 for leave to intervene in the District Court, asking that the restrictive order imposed by the County Court be vacated. The District Court conducted a hearing, at which the County Judge testified and newspaper articles about the *Simants* case were admitted in evidence. The District Judge granted petitioners' motion to intervene and, on October 27, entered his own restrictive order. The judge found "because of the nature of the crimes charged in the complaint that there is a clear and present danger that pre-trial publicity could impinge upon the defendant's right to a fair trial." The order applied only until the jury was impaneled, and specifically prohibited petitioners from reporting five subjects: (1) the existence or contents of a confession Simants had made to law enforcement officers, which had been introduced in open court at the arraignment; (2) the fact or nature of statements Simants had made to other persons; (3) the contents of a note he had written the night of the crime; (4) certain aspects of the medical testimony at the preliminary hearing; and (5) the identity of the victims of the alleged sexual assault and the nature of the assault. It also prohibited reporting the exact nature of the restrictive order itself. Like the County Court's order, this order incorporated the Nebraska Bar–Press Guidelines. Finally, the order set out a plan for attendance, seating, and courthouse traffic control during the trial.

* * *

The Nebraska Supreme Court balanced the "heavy presumption against * * * constitutional validity" that an order restraining publication bears, New York Times Co. v. United States, 403 U.S. 713, 714 (1971), against the importance of the defendant's right to trial by an impartial jury. Both society and the individual defendant, the court held, had a vital interest in assuring that Simants be tried by an impartial jury. Because of the publicity surrounding the crime, the court determined that this right was in jeopardy. The court noted that Nebraska statutes required the District Court to try Simants within six months of his arrest, and that a change of venue could move the trial only to adjoining counties, which had been subject to essentially the same publicity as Lincoln County. The Nebraska Supreme Court held that "[u]nless the absolutist position of the relators was constitutionally correct, it would appear that the District Court acted properly." 194 Neb., at 797, 236 N.W.2d, at 803.

The Nebraska Supreme Court rejected that "absolutist position," but modified the District Court's order to accommodate the defendant's right to a fair trial and the petitioners' interest in reporting pretrial events. The order as modified prohibited reporting of only three matters: (a) the existence and nature of any confessions or admissions made by the defendant to law enforcement officers, (b) any confessions or admissions made to any third parties, except members of the press, and (c) other facts "strongly implicative" of the accused. The Nebraska

Supreme Court did not rely on the Nebraska Bar–Press Guidelines. See n. 1, *supra*. After construing Nebraska law to permit closure in certain circumstances, the court remanded the case to the District Judge for reconsideration of the issue whether pretrial hearings should be closed to the press and public.

We granted certiorari to address the important issues raised by the District Court order as modified by the Nebraska Supreme Court, but we denied the motion to expedite review or to stay entirely the order of the State District Court pending Simants' trial. 423 U.S. 1027 (1975). We are informed by the parties that since we granted certiorari, Simants has been convicted of murder and sentenced to death. His appeal is pending in the Nebraska Supreme Court.

* * *

The problems presented by this case are almost as old as the Republic. Neither in the Constitution nor in contemporaneous writings do we find that the conflict between these two important rights was anticipated, yet it is inconceivable that the authors of the Constitution were unaware of the potential conflicts between the right to an unbiased jury and the guarantee of freedom of the press. * * *

* * *

The speed of communication and the pervasiveness of the modern news media have exacerbated these problems, however, as numerous appeals demonstrate. The trial of Bruno Hauptmann in a small New Jersey community for the abduction and murder of the Charles Lindberghs' infant child probably was the most widely covered trial up to that time, and the nature of the coverage produced widespread public reaction. Criticism was directed at the "carnival" atmosphere that pervaded the community and the courtroom itself. Responsible leaders of the press and the legal profession—including other judges—pointed out that much of this sorry performance could have been controlled by a vigilant trial judge and by other public officers subject to the control of the court. See generally Hudon, Freedom of the Press Versus Fair Trial: The Remedy Lies With the Courts, 1 Val.U.L.Rev. 8, 12–14 (1966); Hallam, Some Object Lessons on Publicity in Criminal Trials, 24 Minn.L.Rev. 453 (1940); Lippmann, The Lindbergh Case in Its Relation to American Newspapers, in Problems of Journalism 154–156 (1936).

* * *

The Sixth Amendment in terms guarantees "trial, by an impartial jury * * * " in federal criminal prosecutions. Because "trial by jury in criminal cases is fundamental to the American scheme of justice," the Due Process Clause of the Fourteenth Amendment guarantees the same right in state criminal prosecutions. Duncan v. Louisiana, 391 U.S. 145, 149 (1968). * * *

In the overwhelming majority of criminal trials, pre-trial publicity presents few unmanageable threats to this important right. But when the case is a "sensational" one tensions develop between the right of the accused to trial by an impartial jury and the rights guaranteed others by the First Amendment. The relevant decisions of this Court, even if not dispositive, are instructive by way of background.

* * *

The costs of failure to afford a fair trial are high. In the most extreme cases, like *Sheppard* and *Estes,* the risk of injustice was avoided when the convictions were reversed. But a reversal means that justice has been delayed for both the defendant and the State; in some cases, because of lapse of time retrial is impossible or further prosecution is gravely handicapped. Moreover, in borderline cases in which the conviction is not reversed, there is some possibility of an injustice unredressed. The "strong measures" outlined in *Sheppard v. Maxwell* are means by which a trial judge can try to avoid exacting these costs from society or from the accused.

The state trial judge in the case before us acted responsibly, out of a legitimate concern, in an effort to protect the defendant's right to a fair trial.[4] What we must decide is not simply whether the Nebraska courts erred in seeing the possibility of real danger to the defendant's rights, but whether in the circumstances of this case the means employed were foreclosed by another provision of the Constitution.

V

The First Amendment provides that "Congress shall make no law * * * abridging the freedom * * * of the press," and it is "no longer open to doubt that the liberty of the press, and of speech, is within the liberty safeguarded by the due process clause of the Fourteenth Amendment from invasion by state action." Near v. Minnesota ex rel. Olson, 283 U.S. 697, 707 (1931). See also Grosjean v. American Press Co., 297 U.S. 233, 244 (1936). The Court has interpreted these guarantees to afford special protection against orders that prohibit the publication or broadcast of particular information or commentary—orders that impose a "previous" or "prior" restraint on speech. None of our decided cases on prior restraints involved restrictive orders entered to protect a defendant's right to a fair and impartial jury, but the opinions on prior restraint have a common thread relevant to this case.

* * *

More recently in New York Times Co. v. United States, 403 U.S. 713 (1971), the Government sought to enjoin the publication of excerpts from a massive, classified study of this Nation's involvement in the Vietnam conflict, going back to the end of the Second World War. The dispositive opinion of the Court simply concluded that the Government had not met its heavy burden of showing justification for the prior restraint. Each of the six concurring Justices and the three dissenting Justices expressed his views separately, but "every member of the

---

4. The record also reveals that counsel for both sides acted responsibly in this case, and there is no suggestion that either sought to use pretrial news coverage for partisan advantage. A few days after the crime, newspaper accounts indicated that the prosecutor had announced the existence of a confession; we learned at oral argument that these accounts were false, although in fact a confession had been made. Tr. of Oral Arg. 36–37, 59.

Court, tacitly or explicitly, accepted the *Near* and *Keefe* condemnation of prior restraint as presumptively unconstitutional." * * *

The thread running through all these cases is that prior restraints on speech and publication are the most serious and the least tolerable infringement on First Amendment rights. A criminal penalty or a judgment in a defamation case is subject to the whole panoply of protections afforded by deferring the impact of the judgment until all avenues of appellate review have been exhausted. Only after judgment has become final, correct or otherwise, does the law's sanction become fully operative.

A prior restraint, by contrast and definition, has an immediate and irreversible sanction. If it can be said that a threat of criminal or civil sanctions after publication "chills" speech, prior restraint "freezes" it at least for the time.

* * *

We turn now to the record in this case to determine whether, as Learned Hand put it, "the gravity of the 'evil,' discounted by its probability, justifies such invasion of free speech as is necessary to avoid the danger." United States v. Dennis, 183 F.2d 201, 212 (CA2 1950), aff'd, 341 U.S. 494 (1951); see also L. Hand, The Bill of Rights 58–61 (1958). To do so, we must examine the evidence before the trial judge when the order was entered to determine (a) the nature and extent of pretrial news coverage; (b) whether other measures would be likely to mitigate the effects of unrestrained pretrial publicity; and (c) how effectively a restraining order would operate to prevent the threatened danger. The precise terms of the restraining order are also important. We must then consider whether the record supports the entry of a prior restraint on publication, one of the most extraordinary remedies known to our jurisprudence.

A

In assessing the probable extent of publicity, the trial judge had before him newspapers demonstrating that the crime had already drawn intensive news coverage, and the testimony of the County Judge, who had entered the initial restraining order based on the local and national attention the case had attracted. The District Judge was required to assess the probable publicity that would be given these shocking crimes prior to the time a jury was selected and sequestered. He then had to examine the probable nature of the publicity and determine how it would affect prospective jurors.

Our review of the pretrial record persuades us that the trial judge was justified in concluding that there would be intense and pervasive pretrial publicity concerning this case. He could also reasonably conclude, based on common human experience, that publicity might impair the defendant's right to a fair trial. He did not purport to say more, for he found only "a clear and present danger that pre-trial publicity *could* impinge upon the defendant's right to a fair trial." (Emphasis added.) His conclusion as to the impact of such publicity on prospective jurors was of necessity speculative, dealing as he was with factors unknown and unknowable.

B

We find little in the record that goes to another aspect of our task, determining whether measures short of an order restraining all publication would have insured the defendant a fair trial. * * *

Most of the alternatives to prior restraint of publication in these circumstances were discussed with obvious approval in Sheppard v. Maxwell, 384 U.S., at 357–362: (a) the change of trial venue to a place less exposed to the intense publicity that seemed imminent in Lincoln County;[7] (b) postponement of the trial to allow public attention to subside; (c) searching questioning of prospective jurors, as Mr. Chief Justice Marshall used in the *Burr* case, to screen out those with fixed opinions as to guilt or innocence; (d) the use of emphatic and clear instructions on the sworn duty of each juror to decide the issues only on evidence presented in open court. Sequestration of jurors is, of course, always available. Although that measure insulates jurors only after they are sworn, it also enhances the likelihood of dissipating the impact of pretrial publicity and emphasizes the elements of the jurors' oaths.

This Court has outlined other measures short of prior restraints on publication tending to blunt the impact of pretrial publicity. See Sheppard v. Maxwell, *supra*, at 361–362. * * *

* * * There is no finding that alternative measures would not have protected Simants' rights, and the Nebraska Supreme Court did no more than imply that such measures might not be adequate. Moreover, the record is lacking in evidence to support such a finding.

* * *

Finally, another feature of this case leads us to conclude that the restrictive order entered here is not supportable. At the outset the County Court entered a very broad restrictive order, the terms of which are not before us; it then held a preliminary hearing open to the public and the press. There was testimony concerning at least two incriminating statements made by Simants to private persons; the statement—evidently a confession—that he gave to law enforcement officials was also introduced. The State District Court's later order was entered after this public hearing and, as modified by the Nebraska Supreme Court, enjoined reporting of (1) "[c]onfessions or admissions against interest made by the accused to law enforcement officials"; (2) "[c]onfessions or admissions against interest, oral or written, if any, made by the accused to third parties, excepting any statements, if any, made by the accused to representatives of the news media"; and (3) all "[o]ther

---

7. The respondent and intervenors argue here that a change of venue would not have helped, since Nebraska law permits a change only to adjacent counties, which had been as exposed to pretrial publicity in this case as Lincoln County. We have held that state laws restricting venue must on occasion yield to the constitutional requirement that the State afford a fair trial. Groppi v. Wisconsin, 400 U.S. 505 (1971). We note also that the combined population of Lincoln County and the adjacent counties is over 80,000 providing a substantial pool of prospective jurors.

information strongly implicative of the accused as the perpetrator of the slayings." 194 Neb., at 801 236 N.W.2d, at 805.

To the extent that this order prohibited the reporting of evidence adduced at the open preliminary hearing, it plainly violated settled principles: "[T]here is nothing that proscribes the press from reporting events that transpire in the courtroom." Sheppard v. Maxwell, 384 U.S., at 362–363. See also Cox Broadcasting Corp. v. Cohn, 420 U.S. 469 (1975); Craig v. Harney, 331 U.S. 367 (1947). The County Court could not know that closure of the preliminary hearing was an alternative open to it until the Nebraska Supreme Court so construed state law; but once a public hearing had been held, what transpired there could not be subject to prior restraint.

The third prohibition of the order was defective in another respect as well. As part of a final order, entered after plenary review, this prohibition regarding "implicative" information is too vague and too broad to survive the scrutiny we have given to restraints on First Amendment rights. See, *e.g.,* Hynes v. Mayor of Oradell, 425 U.S. 610 (1976); Buckley v. Valeo, 424 U.S. 1, 76–82 (1976); NAACP v. Button, 371 U.S. 415 (1963). The third phase of the order entered falls outside permissible limits.

* * *

Reversed.

Mr. Justice Powell, concurring.

Although I join the opinion of the Court, in view of the importance of the case I write to emphasize the unique burden that rests upon the party, whether it be the State or a defendant, who undertakes to show the necessity for prior restraint on pretrial publicity.*

In my judgment a prior restraint properly may issue only when it is shown to be necessary to prevent the dissemination of prejudicial publicity that otherwise poses a high likelihood of preventing, directly and irreparably, the impaneling of a jury meeting the Sixth Amendment requirement of impartiality. This requires a showing that (i) there is a clear threat to the fairness of trial, (ii) such a threat is posed by the actual publicity to be restrained and (iii) no less restrictive alternatives are available. Notwithstanding such a showing, a restraint may not issue unless it also is shown that previous publicity or publicity from unrestrained sources will not render the restraint inefficacious. The threat to the fairness of the trial is to be evaluated in the context of Sixth Amendment law on impartiality, and any restraint must comply with the standards of specificity always required in the First Amendment context.

I believe these factors are sufficiently addressed in the Court's opinion to demonstrate beyond question that the prior restraint here was impermissible.

---

* In Times–Picayune Pub. Corp. v. Schulingkamp, 419 U.S. 1301, 1307 (1974), an in-chambers opinion, I noted that there is a heavy presumption against the constitutional validity of a court order restraining pretrial publicity.

MR. JUSTICE BRENNAN, with whom MR. JUSTICE STEWART and MR. JUSTICE MARSHALL join, concurring in the judgment.

The question presented in this case is whether, consistently with the First Amendment, a court may enjoin the press, in advance of publication,[1] from reporting or commenting on information acquired from public court proceedings, public court records, or other sources about pending judicial proceedings. The Nebraska Supreme Court upheld such a direct prior restraint on the press, issued by the judge presiding over a sensational state murder trial, on the ground that there existed a "clear and present danger that pretrial publicity could substantially impair the right of the defendant [in the murder trial] to a trial by an impartial jury unless restraints were imposed." State v. Simants, 194 Neb. 783, 794, 236 N.W.2d 794, 802 (1975). The right to a fair trial by a jury of one's peers is unquestionably one of the most precious and sacred safeguards enshrined in the Bill of Rights. I would hold, however, that resort to prior restraints on the freedom of the press is a constitutionally impermissible method for enforcing that right; judges have at their disposal a broad spectrum of devices for ensuring that fundamental fairness is accorded the accused without necessitating so drastic an incursion on the equally fundamental and salutary constitutional mandate that discussion of public affairs in a free society cannot depend on the preliminary grace of judicial censors.

SEATTLE TIMES COMPANY v. RHINEHART

Supreme Court of the United States, 1984.
467 U.S. 20, 104 S.Ct. 2199, 81 L.Ed.2d 17.

JUSTICE POWELL delivered the opinion of the Court.

This case presents the issue whether parties to civil litigation have a First Amendment right to disseminate, in advance of trial, information gained through the pretrial discovery process.

I

Respondent Rhinehart is the spiritual leader of a religious group, the Aquarian Foundation. The Foundation has fewer than 1,000 members, most of whom live in the State of Washington. Aquarian beliefs include life after death and the ability to communicate with the dead through a medium. Rhinehart is the primary Aquarian medium.

In recent years, the Seattle Times and the Walla Walla Union–Bulletin have published stories about Rhinehart and the Foundation. Altogether 11 articles appeared in the newspapers during the years 1973, 1978, and 1979. The five articles that appeared in 1973 focused on Rhinehart and the manner in which he operated the Foundation. They described seances conducted by Rhinehart in which people paid

---

1. In referring to the "press" and to "publication" in this opinion, I of course use those words as terms of art that encompass broadcasting by the electronic media as well.

him to put them in touch with deceased relatives and friends. The articles also stated that Rhinehart had sold magical "stones" that had been "expelled" from his body. One article referred to Rhinehart's conviction, later vacated, for sodomy. * * *

II

Rhinehart brought this action in the Washington Superior Court on behalf of himself and the Foundation against the Seattle Times, the Walla Walla Union–Bulletin, the authors of the articles, and the spouses of the authors. * * * The complaint alleges that the articles contained statements that were "fictional and untrue," and that the defendants—petitioners here—knew, or should have known, they were false. * * *

Petitioners filed an answer, denying many of the allegations of the complaint and asserting affirmative defenses.[3] Petitioners promptly initiated extensive discovery. They deposed Rhinehart, requested production of documents pertaining to the financial affairs of Rhinehart and the Foundation, and served extensive interrogatories on Rhinehart and the other respondents. Respondents turned over a number of financial documents, including several of Rhinehart's income tax returns. Respondents refused, however, to disclose certain financial information, the identity of the Foundation's donors during the preceding 10 years, and a list of its members during that period.

Petitioners filed a motion under the State's Civil Rule 37 requesting an order compelling discovery. * * * Respondents opposed the motion, arguing in particular that compelled production of the identities of the Foundation's donors and members would violate the First Amendment rights of members and donors to privacy, freedom of religion, and freedom of association. Respondents also moved for a protective order preventing petitioners from disseminating any information gained through discovery. Respondents noted that petitioners had stated their intention to continue publishing articles about respondents and this litigation, and their intent to use information gained through discovery in future articles.

In a lengthy ruling, the trial court initially granted the motion to compel and ordered respondents to identify all donors who made contributions during the five years preceding the date of the complaint, along with the amounts donated. The court also required respondents to divulge enough membership information to substantiate any claims of diminished membership. * * *

* * * [T]he trial court issued a protective order covering all information obtained through the discovery process that pertained to "the financial affairs of the various plaintiffs, the names and addresses of Aquarian Foundation members, contributors, or clients, and the names

---

3. Affirmative defenses included contentions that the articles were substantially true and accurate, that they were privileged under the First and Fourteenth Amendments, that the statute of limitations had run as to the 1973 articles, that the individual respondents had consented to any invasions of privacy, and that respondents had no reasonable expectation of privacy when performing before 1,100 prisoners.

and addresses of those who have been contributors, clients, or donors to any of the various plaintiffs." App. 65a. The order prohibited petitioners from publishing, disseminating, or using the information in any way except where necessary to prepare for and try the case. By its terms, the order did not apply to information gained by means other than the discovery process. * * *

Respondents appealed from the trial court's production order, and petitioner appealed from the protective order. The Supreme Court of Washington affirmed both. * * *

* * * We affirm.

III

Most States, including Washington, have adopted discovery provisions modeled on Rules 26 through 37 of the Federal Rules of Civil Procedure. * * * Rule 26(b)(1) provides that a party "may obtain discovery regarding any matter, not privileged, which is relevant to the subject matter involved in the pending action." It further provides that discovery is not limited to matters that will be admissible at trial so long as the information sought "appears reasonably calculated to lead to the discovery of admissible evidence." * * *

The Rules do not differentiate between information that is private or intimate and that to which no privacy interests attach. Under the Rules, the only express limitations are that the information sought is not privileged, and is relevant to the subject matter of the pending action. Thus, the Rules often allow extensive intrusion into the affairs of both litigants and third parties. If a litigant fails to comply with a request for discovery, the court may issue an order directing compliance that is enforceable by the court's contempt powers. * * *

Petitioners argue that the First Amendment imposes strict limits on the availability of any judicial order that has the effect of restricting expression. They contend that civil discovery is not different from other sources of information, and that therefore the information is "protected speech" for First Amendment purposes. Petitioners assert the right in this case to disseminate any information gained through discovery. They do recognize that in limited circumstances, not thought to be present here, some information may be restrained. They submit, however:

> "When a protective order seeks to limit expression, it may do so only if the proponent shows a compelling governmental interest. Mere speculation and conjecture are insufficient. Any restraining order, moreover, must be narrowly drawn and precise. Finally, before issuing such an order a court must determine that there are no alternatives which intrude less directly on expression." Brief for Petitioners 10.

We think the rule urged by petitioner would impose an unwarranted restriction on the duty and discretion of a trial court to oversee the discovery process.

IV

* * *

A

At the outset, it is important to recognize the extent of the impairment of First Amendment rights that a protective order, such as the one at issue here, may cause. As in all civil litigation, petitioners gained the information they wish to disseminate only by virtue of the trial court's discovery processes. As the Rules authorizing discovery were adopted by the state legislature, the processes thereunder are a matter of legislative grace. A litigant has no First Amendment right of access to information made available only for purposes of trying his suit. * * *

Moreover, pretrial depositions and interrogatories are not public components of a civil trial. Such proceedings were not open to the public at common law, Gannett Co. v. DePasquale, 443 U.S. 368, 389 (1979), and, in general, they are conducted in private as a matter of modern practice. See *id.*, at 396 (BURGER, C.J., concurring); Marcus, Myth and Reality in Protective Order Litigation, 69 Cornell L.Rev. 1 (1983). Much of the information that surfaces during pretrial discovery may be unrelated, or only tangentially related, to the underlying cause of action. Therefore, restraints placed on discovered, but not yet admitted, information are not a restriction on a traditionally public source of information.

Finally, it is significant to note that an order prohibiting dissemination of discovered information before trial is not the kind of classic prior restraint that requires exacting First Amendment scrutiny. See *Gannett Co. v. DePasquale, supra,* at 399 (POWELL, J., concurring). As in this case, such a protective order prevents a party from disseminating only that information obtained through use of the discovery process. Thus, the party may disseminate the identical information covered by the protective order as long as the information is gained through means independent of the court's processes. In sum, judicial limitations on a party's ability to disseminate information discovered in advance of trial implicates the First Amendment rights of the restricted party to a far lesser extent than would restraints on dissemination of information in a different context. * * *

B

Rule 26(c) furthers a substantial governmental interest unrelated to the suppression of expression. * * * The Washington Civil Rules enable parties to litigation to obtain information "relevant to the subject matter involved" that they believe will be helpful in the preparation and trial of the case. Rule 26, however, must be viewed in its entirety. Liberal discovery is provided for the sole purpose of assisting in the preparation and trial, or the settlement, of litigated disputes. Because of the liberality of pretrial discovery permitted by Rule 26(b)(1), it is necessary for the trial court to have the authority to issue protective orders conferred by Rule 26(c). It is clear from experience that pretrial discovery by depositions and interrogatories has a significant potential for abuse.[20] This abuse is not limited to matters of delay and expense; discovery also may seriously implicate privacy interests of litigants and third parties.[21] The Rules do not distinguish between public and private information. Nor do they apply only to parties to the litigation, as relevant information in the hands of third parties may be subject to discovery.

There is an opportunity, therefore, for litigants to obtain—incidentally or purposefully—information that not only is irrelevant but if publicly released could be damaging to reputation and privacy. * * *

C

We also find that the provision for protective orders in the Washington Rules requires, in itself, no heightened First Amendment scrutiny. To be sure, Rule 26(c) confers broad discretion on the trial court to decide when a protective order is appropriate and what degree of protection is required. The Legislature of the State of Washington, following the example of the Congress in its approval of the Federal Rules of Civil Procedure, has determined that such discretion is necessary, and we find no reason to disagree. The trial court is in the best position to weigh fairly the competing needs and interests of parties affected by discovery.[23] The unique character of the discovery process requires that the trial court have substantial latitude to fashion protective orders.

V

* * * We therefore hold that where, as in this case, a protective order is entered on a showing of good cause as required by Rule 26(c), is limited to the context of pretrial civil discovery, and does not restrict the dissemination of the information if gained from other sources, it does not offend the First Amendment.

The judgment accordingly is

Affirmed.

---

20. See Comments of the Advisory Committee on the 1983 Amendments to Fed. Rule Civ.Proc. 26 U.S.C. App., pp. 729–730 (1982 ed., Supp. I). In Herbert v. Lando, 441 U.S. 153 (1979), the Court observed: "There have been repeated expressions of concern about undue and uncontrolled discovery, and voices from this Court have joined the chorus. But until and unless there are major changes in the present Rules of Civil Procedure, reliance must be had on what in fact and in law are ample powers of the district judge to prevent abuse." Id., at 176–177 (footnote omitted); see also id., at 179 (Powell, J., concurring). But abuses of the Rules by litigants, and sometimes the inadequate oversight of discovery by trial courts, do not in any respect lessen the importance of discovery in civil litigation and the government's substantial interest in protecting the integrity of the discovery process.

21. Cf. Whalen v. Roe, 429 U.S. 589, 599 (1977); Cox Broadcasting Corp. v. Cohn, 420 U.S. 469, 488–491 (1975). Rule 26(c) includes among its express purposes the protection of a "party or person from annoyance, embarrassment, oppression or undue burden or expense." Although the Rule contains no specific reference to privacy or to other rights or interests that may be implicated, such matters are implicit in the broad purpose and language of the Rule.

23. In addition, heightened First Amendment scrutiny of each request for a protective order would necessitate burdensome evidentiary findings and could lead to time-consuming interlocutory appeals, as this case illustrates. See, e.g., Zenith Radio Corp. v. Matsushita Electric Industrial Co., 529 F.Supp. 866 (E.D.Pa.1981).

JUSTICE BRENNAN, with whom JUSTICE MARSHALL joins, concurring.

The Court today recognizes that pretrial protective orders, designed to limit the dissemination of information gained through the civil discovery process, are subject to scrutiny under the First Amendment. As the Court acknowledges, before approving such protective orders, "it is necessary to consider whether the 'practice in question [furthers] an important or substantial governmental interest unrelated to the suppression of expression' and whether 'the limitation of First Amendment freedoms [is] no greater than is necessary or essential to the protection of the particular governmental interest involved.'" * * *

* * * I agree that the respondents' interests in privacy and religious freedom are sufficient to justify this protective order and to overcome the protections afforded free expression by the First Amendment. I therefore join the Court's opinion.

NEW YORK TIMES COMPANY v. UNITED STATES

Supreme Court of the United States, 1971.
403 U.S. 713, 91 S.Ct. 2140, 29 L.Ed.2d 822.

PER CURIAM.

We granted certiorari in these cases in which the United States seeks to enjoin the New York Times and the Washington Post from publishing the contents of a classified study entitled "History of U.S. Decision–Making Process on Viet Nam Policy." * * *

"Any system of prior restraints of expression comes to this Court bearing a heavy presumption against its constitutional validity." Bantam Books, Inc. v. Sullivan, 372 U.S. 58, 70 (1963); see also Near v. Minnesota, 283 U.S. 697 (1931). The Government "thus carries a heavy burden of showing justification for the imposition of such a restraint." Organization for a Better Austin v. Keefe, 402 U.S. 415, 419 (1971). The District Court for the Southern District of New York in the *New York Times* case and the District Court for the District of Columbia Circuit in the *Washington Post* case held that the Government had not met that burden. We agree.

The judgment of the Court of Appeals for the District of Columbia Circuit is therefore affirmed. The order of the Court of Appeals for the Second Circuit is reversed and the case is remanded with directions to enter a judgment affirming the judgment of the District Court for the Southern District of New York. The stays entered June 25, 1971, by the Court are vacated. The judgments shall issue forthwith.

So ordered.

MR. JUSTICE BLACK, with whom MR. JUSTICE DOUGLAS joins, concurring.

I adhere to the view that the Government's case against the Washington Post should have been dismissed and that the injunction against the New York Times should have been vacated without oral argument when the cases were first presented to this Court. I believe that every moment's continuance of the injunctions against these newspapers amounts to a flagrant, indefensible, and continuing violation of the First Amendment. Furthermore, after oral argument, I agree completely that we must affirm the judgment of the Court of Appeals for the District of Columbia Circuit and reverse the judgment of the Court of Appeals for the Second Circuit for the reasons stated by my Brothers Douglas and Brennan. In my view it is unfortunate that some of my Brethren are apparently willing to hold that the publication of news may sometimes be enjoined. Such a holding would make a shambles of the First Amendment.

* * *

* * * Both the history and language of the First Amendment support the view that the press must be left free to publish news, whatever the source without censorship, injunctions, or prior restraints.

In the First Amendment the Founding Fathers gave the free press the protection it must have to fulfill its essential role in our democracy. The press was to serve the governed, not the governors. The Government's power to censor the press was abolished so that the press would remain forever free to censure the Government. The press was protected so that it could bare the secrets of government and inform the people. Only a free and unrestrained press can effectively expose deception in government. * * *

The Government's case here is based on premises entirely different from those that guided the Framers of the First Amendment. The Solicitor General has carefully and emphatically stated:

> "Now, Mr. Justice [Black], your construction of * * * [the First Amendment] is well known, and I certainly respect it. You say that no law means no law, and that should be obvious. I can only say, Mr. Justice, that to me it is equally obvious that 'no law' does not mean 'no law', and I would seek to persuade the Court that that is true. * * * [T]here are other parts of the Constitution that grant powers and responsibilities to the executive, and * * * the First Amendment was not intended to make it impossible for the Executive to function or to protect the security of the United States."[3]

And the Government argues in its brief that in spite of the First Amendment, "[t]he authority of the Executive Department to protect the nation against publication of information whose disclosure would endanger the national security stems from two interrelated sources: the constitutional power of the President over the conduct of foreign affairs and his authority as Commander-in-Chief."

In other words, we are asked to hold that despite the First Amendment's emphatic command, the Executive Branch, the Congress, and the Judiciary can make laws enjoining publication of current news and abridging freedom of the press in the name of "national security." The Government does not even attempt to rely on any act of Congress.

---

3. Tr. of Oral Arg. 76.

Instead it makes the bold and dangerously far-reaching contention that the courts should take it upon themselves to "make" a law abridging freedom of the press in the name of equity, presidential power, and national security, even when the representatives of the people in Congress have adhered to the command of the First Amendment and refused to make such a law. See concurring opinion of Mr. Justice Douglas, * * *. To find that the President has "inherent powers" to halt the publication of news by resort to the courts would wipe out the First Amendment and destroy the fundamental liberty and security of the very people the Government hopes to make "secure." No one can read the history of the adoption of the First Amendment without being convinced beyond any doubt that it was injunctions like those sought here that Madison and his collaborators intended to outlaw in this Nation for all time.

The word "security" is a broad, vague generality whose contours should not be invoked to abrogate the fundamental law embodied in the First Amendment. The guarding of military and diplomatic secrets at the expense of informed representative government provides no real security for our Republic. The Framers of the First Amendment, fully aware of both the need to defend a new nation and the abuses of the English and Colonial Governments, sought to give this new society strength and security by providing that freedom of speech, press, religion, and assembly should not be abridged. This thought was eloquently expressed in 1937 by Mr. Chief Justice Hughes—great man and great Chief Justice that he was—when the Court held a man could not be punished for attending a meeting run by Communists.

> "The greater the importance of safeguarding the community from incitements to the overthrow of our institutions by force and violence, the more imperative is the need to preserve inviolate the constitutional rights of free speech, free press and free assembly in order to maintain the opportunity for free political discussion, to the end that government may be responsive to the will of the people and that changes, if desired, may be obtained by peaceful means. Therein lies the security of the Republic, the very foundation of constitutional government."

MR. JUSTICE DOUGLAS, with whom MR. JUSTICE BLACK joins, concurring.

While I join the opinion of the Court I believe it necessary to express my views more fully.

It should be noted at the outset that the First Amendment provides that "Congress shall make no law * * * abridging the freedom of speech, or of the press." That leaves, in my view no room for governmental restraint on the press.[1]

---

1. See Beauharnais v. Illinois, 343 U.S. 250, 267 (dissenting opinion of Mr. Justice Black), 284 (my dissenting opinion); Roth v. United States, 354 U.S. 476, 508 (my dissenting opinion which Mr. Justice Black joined); Yates v. United States, 354 U.S. 298, 339 (separate opinion of Mr. Justice Black which I joined); New York Times Co. v. Sullivan, 376 U.S. 254, 293 (concurring opinion of Mr. Justice Black which I

There is, moreover, no statute barring the publication by the press of the material which the Times and the Post seek to use. Title 18 U.S.C. § 793(e) provides that "[w]hoever having unauthorized possession of, access to, or control over any document, writing * * * or information relating to the national defense which information the possessor has reason to believe could be used to the injury of the United States or to the advantage of any foreign nation, willfully communicates * * * the same to any person not entitled to receive it * * * [s]hall be fined not more than $10,000 or imprisoned not more than ten years, or both."

The Government suggests that the word "communicates" is broad enough to encompass publication.

There are eight sections in the chapter on espionage and censorship, §§ 792–799. In three of those eight "publish" is specifically mentioned: § 794(b) applies to "Whoever, in time of war, with intent that the same shall be communicated to the enemy, collects, records, *publishes,* or communicates * * * [the disposition of armed forces]."

Section 797 applies to whoever "reproduces, *publishes,* sells, or gives away" photographs of defense installations.

Section 798 relating to cryptography applies to whoever: "communicates, furnishes, transmits, or otherwise makes available * * * or *publishes*" the described material.[2] (Emphasis added.)

Thus it is apparent that Congress was capable of and did distinguish between publishing and communication in the various sections of the Espionage Act.

The other evidence that § 793 does not apply to the press is a rejected version of § 793. That version read: "During any national emergency resulting from a war to which the United States is a party, or from threat of such a war, the President may, by proclamation, declare the existence of such emergency and, by proclamation, prohibit the publishing or communicating of, or the attempting to publish or communicate any information relating to the national defense which in his judgment, is of such character that it is or might be useful to the enemy." 55 Cong.Rec. 1763. During the debates in the Senate the First Amendment was specifically cited and that provision defeated. 55 Cong.Rec. 2167.

Judge Gurfein's holding in the *Times* case that this act does not apply to this case was therefore preeminently sound. Moreover, the Act of September 23, 1950, in amending 18 U.S.C. § 793 states in § 1(b) that:

> "Nothing in this Act shall be construed to authorize, require, or establish military or civilian censorship or in any way to limit or infringe upon freedom of the press or of speech

---

joined); Garrison v. Louisiana, 379 U.S. 64, 80 (my concurring opinion which Mr. Justice Black joined).

2. These documents contain data concerning the communications system of the United States, the publication of which is made a crime. But the criminal sanction is not urged by the United States as the basis of equity power.

as guaranteed by the Constitution of the United States and no regulation shall be promulgated hereunder having that effect." 64 Stat. 987.

Thus Congress has been faithful to the command of the First Amendment in this area.

So any power that the Government possesses must come from its "inherent power."

The power to wage war is "the power to wage war successfully." See Hirabayashi v. United States, 320 U.S. 81, 93. But the war power stems from a declaration of war. The Constitution by Art. I, § 8, gives Congress, not the President, power "[t]o declare War." Nowhere are presidential wars authorized. We need not decide therefore what leveling effect the war power of Congress might have.

These disclosures [1] may have a serious impact. But that is no basis for sanctioning a previous restraint on the press. * * *

* * *

MR. JUSTICE BRENNAN, concurring.

I

I write separately in these cases only to emphasize what should be apparent: that our judgments in the present cases may not be taken to indicate the propriety, in the future, of issuing temporary stays and restraining orders to block the publication of material sought to be suppressed by the Government. So far as I can determine, never before has the United States sought to enjoin a newspaper from publishing information in its possession. The relative novelty of the questions presented, the necessary haste with which decisions were reached, the magnitude of the interests asserted, and the fact that all the parties have concentrated their arguments upon the question whether permanent restraints were proper may have justified at least some of the restraints heretofore imposed in these cases. Certainly it is difficult to fault the several courts below for seeking to assure that the issues here involved were preserved for ultimate review by this Court. But even if it be assumed that some of the interim restraints were proper in the two cases before us, that assumption has no bearing upon the propriety of similar judicial action in the future. To begin with, there has now been ample time for reflection and judgment; whatever values there may be in the preservation of novel questions for appellate review may not support any restraints in the future. More important, the First Amendment stands as an absolute bar to the imposition of judicial restraints in circumstances of the kind presented by these cases.

1. There are numerous sets of this material in existence and they apparently are not under any controlled custody. Moreover, the President has sent a set to the Congress. We start then with a case where there already is rather wide distribution of the material that is destined for publicity, not secrecy. I have gone over the material listed *in camera* brief of the United States. It is all history, not future events. None of it is more recent than 1968.

II

The error that has pervaded these cases from the outset was the granting of any injunctive relief whatsoever, interim or otherwise. The entire thrust of the Government's claim throughout these cases has been that publication of the material sought to be enjoined "could," or "might," or "may" prejudice the national interest in various ways. But the First Amendment tolerates absolutely no prior judicial restraints of the press predicated upon surmise or conjecture that untoward consequences may result. Our cases, it is true, have indicated that there is a single, extremely narrow class of cases in which the First Amendment's ban on prior judicial restraint may be overridden. Our cases have thus far indicated that such cases may arise only when the Nation "is at war," Schenck v. United States, 249 U.S. 47, 52 (1919), during which times "[n]o one would question that a government might prevent actual obstruction to its recruiting service or the publication of the sailing dates of transports or the number and locations of troops." Near v. Minnesota, 283 U.S. 697, 716 (1931). Even if the present world situation were assumed to be tantamount to a time of war, or if the power of presently available armaments would justify even in peacetime the suppression of information that would set in motion a nuclear holocaust, in neither of these actions has the Government presented or even alleged that publication of items from or based upon the material at issue would cause the happening of any event of that nature. * * * [O]nly governmental allegation and proof that publication must inevitably, directly, and immediately cause the occurrence of an event kindred to imperiling the safety of a transport already at sea can support even the issuance of an interim restraining order. In no event may mere conclusions be sufficient: for if the Executive Branch seeks judicial aid in preventing publication, it must inevitably submit the basis upon which that aid is sought to scrutiny by the judiciary. And therefore, every restraint issued in this case, whatever its form, has violated the First Amendment—and not less so because that restraint was justified as necessary to afford the courts an opportunity to examine the claim more thoroughly. Unless and until the Government has clearly made out its case, the First Amendment commands that no injunction may issue.

MR. JUSTICE STEWART, with whom MR. JUSTICE WHITE joins, concurring.

In the governmental structure created by our Constitution, the Executive is endowed with enormous power in the two related areas of national defense and international relations. This power, largely unchecked by the Legislative and Judicial branches, has been pressed to the very hilt since the advent of the nuclear missile age. For better or for worse, the simple fact is that a President of the United States possesses vastly greater constitutional independence in these two vital areas of power than does, say, a prime minister of a country with a parliamentary form of government.

In the absence of the governmental checks and balances present in other areas of our national life, the only effective restraint upon executive policy and power in the areas of national defense and international affairs may lie in an enlightened citizenry—in an informed and critical public opinion which alone can here protect the values of democratic government. For this reason, it is perhaps here that a press that is alert, aware, and free most vitally serves the basic purpose of the First Amendment. For without an informed and free press there cannot be an enlightened people.

Yet it is elementary that the successful conduct of international diplomacy and the maintenance of an effective national defense require both confidentiality and secrecy. Other nations can hardly deal with this Nation in an atmosphere of mutual trust unless they can be assured that their confidences will be kept. And within our own executive departments, the development of considered and intelligent international policies would be impossible if those charged with their formulation could not communicate with each other freely, frankly, and in confidence. In the area of basic national defense the frequent need for absolute secrecy is, of course, self-evident.

I think there can be but one answer to this dilemma, if dilemma it be. The responsibility must be where the power is. If the Constitution gives the Executive a large degree of unshared power in the conduct of foreign affairs and the maintenance of our national defense, then under the Constitution the Executive must have the largely unshared duty to determine and preserve the degree of internal security necessary to exercise that power successfully. It is an awesome responsibility, requiring judgment and wisdom of a high order. I should suppose that moral, political, and practical considerations would dictate that a very first principle of that wisdom would be an insistence upon avoiding secrecy for its own sake. For when everything is classified, then nothing is classified, and the system becomes one to be disregarded by the cynical or the careless, and to be manipulated by those intent on self-protection or self-promotion. I should suppose, in short, that the hallmark of a truly effective internal security system would be the maximum possible disclosure, recognizing that secrecy can best be preserved only when credibility is truly maintained. But be that as it may, it is clear to me that it is the constitutional duty of the Executive—as a matter of sovereign prerogative and not as a matter of law as the courts know law—through the promulgation and enforcement of executive regulations, to protect the confidentiality necessary to carry out its responsibilities in the fields of international relations and national defense.

This is not to say that Congress and the courts have no role to play. Undoubtedly Congress has the power to enact specific and appropriate criminal laws to protect government property and preserve government secrets. Congress has passed such laws, and several of them are of very colorable relevance to the apparent circumstances of these cases. And if a criminal prosecution is instituted, it will be the responsibility of the courts to decide the applicability of the criminal law under which the charge is brought. Moreover, if Congress should pass a specific law authorizing civil proceedings in this field, the courts would likewise have the duty to decide the constitutionality of such a law as well as its applicability to the facts proved.

But in the cases before us we are asked neither to construe specific regulations nor to apply specific laws. We are asked, instead, to perform a function that the Constitution gave to the Executive, not the Judiciary. We are asked, quite simply, to prevent the publication by two newspapers of material that the Executive Branch insists should not, in the national interest, be published. I am convinced that the Executive is correct with respect to some of the documents involved. But I cannot say that disclosure of any of them will surely result in direct, immediate, and irreparable damage to our Nation or its people. That being so, there can under the First Amendment be but one judicial resolution of the issues before us. I join the judgments of the Court.

Mr. Justice White, with whom Mr. Justice Stewart joins, concurring.

I concur in today's judgments, but only because of the concededly extraordinary protection against prior restraints enjoyed by the press under our constitutional system. I do not say that in no circumstances would the First Amendment permit an injunction against publishing information about government plans or operations. Nor, after examining the materials the Government characterizes as the most sensitive and destructive, can I deny that revelation of these documents will do substantial damage to public interests. Indeed, I am confident that their disclosure will have that result. But I nevertheless agree that the United States has not satisfied the very heavy burden that it must meet to warrant an injunction against publication in these cases, at least in the absence of express and appropriately limited congressional authorization for prior restraints in circumstances such as these.

* * *

The Criminal Code contains numerous provisions potentially relevant to these cases. Section 797 makes it a crime to publish certain photographs or drawings of military installations. Section 798, also in precise language, proscribes knowing and willful publication of any classified information concerning the cryptographic systems or communication intelligence activities of the United States as well as any information obtained from communication intelligence operations. If any of the material here at issue is of this nature, the newspapers are presumably now on full notice of the position of the United States and must face the consequences if they publish. I would have no difficulty in sustaining convictions under these sections on facts that would not justify the intervention of equity and the imposition of a prior restraint.

* * *

Mr. Chief Justice Burger, dissenting.

So clear are the constitutional limitations on prior restraint against expression, that from the time of Near v. Minnesota, 283 U.S. 697 (1931), until recently in Organization for a Better Austin v. Keefe, 402 U.S. 415 (1971), we have had little occasion to be concerned with cases involving prior restraints against news reporting on matters of public interest. There is, therefore, little variation among the members of the Court in terms of resistance to prior restraints against publication. Adherence to this basic constitutional principle, however, does not make these cases simple. In these cases, the imperative of free and unfettered press comes into collision with another imperative, the effective functioning of a complex modern government and specifically the effective exercise of certain constitutional powers of the Executive. Only those who view the First Amendment as an absolute in all circumstances—a view I respect, but reject—can find such cases as these to be simple or easy.

These cases are not simple for another and more immediate reason. We do not know the facts of the cases. No District Judge knew all the facts. No Court of Appeals judge knew all the facts. No member of this Court knows all the facts.

Why are we in this posture, in which only those judges to whom the First Amendment is absolute and permits of no restraint in any circumstances or for any reason, are really in a position to act?

I suggest we are in this posture because these cases have been conducted in unseemly haste. Mr. Justice Harlan covers the chronology of events demonstrating the hectic pressures under which these cases have been processed and I need not restate them. The prompt setting of these cases reflects our universal abhorrence of prior restraint. But prompt judicial action does not mean unjudicial haste.

Here, moreover, the frenetic haste is due in large part to the manner in which the Times proceeded from the date it obtained the purloined documents. It seems reasonably clear now that the haste precluded reasonable and deliberate judicial treatment of these cases and was not warranted. The precipitate action of this Court abridging trials not yet completed is not the kind of judicial conduct that ought to attend the disposition of a great issue.

The newspapers make a derivative claim under the First Amendment; they denominate this right as the public "right to know"; by implication the Times asserts a sole trusteeship of that right by virtue of its journalistic "scoop." The right is asserted as an absolute. Of course, the First Amendment right itself is not an absolute, as Justice Holmes so long ago pointed out in his aphorism concerning the right to shout "fire" in a crowded theater if there was no fire. There are other exceptions, some of which Chief Justice Hughes mentioned by way of example in *Near v. Minnesota*. There are no doubt other exceptions no one has had occasion to describe or discuss. Conceivably such exceptions may be lurking in these cases and would have been flushed had they been properly considered in the trial courts, free from unwarranted deadlines and frenetic pressures. An issue of this importance should be tried and heard in a judicial atmosphere conducive to thoughtful, reflective deliberation, especially when haste, in terms of hours, is unwarranted in light of the long period the Times, by its own choice, deferred publication.[1]

It is not disputed that the Times has had unauthorized possession of the documents for three to four months, during which it has had its expert analysts studying them, presumably digesting them and preparing the material for publication. During all of this time, the Times, presumably in its capacity as trustee of the public's "right to know," has held up publication for purposes it considered proper and thus public knowledge was delayed. No doubt this was a good reason; the analysis of 7,000 pages of complex material drawn from a vastly greater volume of material would inevitably take time and the writing of good news stories takes time. But why should the United States Government, from whom this information was illegally acquired by someone, along with all the counsel, trial judges, and appellate judges be placed under needless pressure? After these months of deferral, the alleged "right to know" has somehow and suddenly become a right that must be vindicated instanter.

* * *

The consequence of all this melancholy series of events is that we literally do not know what we are acting on. As I see it, we have been forced to deal with litigation concerning rights of great magnitude without an adequate record, and surely without time for adequate treatment either in the prior proceedings or in this Court. It is interesting to note that counsel on both sides, in oral argument before this Court, were frequently unable to respond to questions on factual points. Not surprisingly they pointed out that they had been working literally "around the clock" and simply were unable to review the documents that give rise to these cases and were not familiar with them. This Court is in no better posture. I agree generally with Mr. Justice Harlan and Mr. Justice Blackmun but I am not prepared to reach the merits.[3]

I would affirm the Court of Appeals for the Second Circuit and allow the District Court to complete the trial aborted by our grant of certiorari, meanwhile preserving the status quo in the *Post* case. I would direct that the District Court on remand give priority to the Times case to the exclusion of all other business of that court but I would not set arbitrary deadlines.

---

1. As noted elsewhere the Times conducted its analysis of the 47 volumes of Government documents over a period of several months and did so with a degree of security that a government might envy. Such security was essential, of course, to protect the enterprise from others. Meanwhile the Times has copyrighted its material and there were strong intimations in the oral argument that the Times contemplated enjoining its use by any other publisher in violation of its copyright. Paradoxically this would afford it a protection, analogous to prior restraint, against all others—a protection the Times denies the Government of the United States.

3. With respect to the question of inherent power of the executive to classify papers, records, and documents a secret, or otherwise unavailable for public exposure, and to secure aid of the courts for enforcement, there may be an analogy with respect to this Court. No statute gives this Court express power to establish and enforce the utmost security measures for the secrecy of our deliberations and records. Yet I have little doubt as to the inherent power of the Court to protect the confidentiality of its internal operations by whatever judicial measures may be required.

I should add that I am in general agreement with much of what Mr. Justice White has expressed with respect to penal sanctions concerning communication or retention of documents or information relating to the national defense.

We all crave speedier judicial processes but when judges are pressured as in these cases the result is a parody of the judicial function.

MR. JUSTICE HARLAN, with whom THE CHIEF JUSTICE and MR. JUSTICE BLACKMUN join, dissenting.

These cases forcefully call to mind the wise admonition of Mr. Justice Holmes, dissenting in Northern Securities Co. v. United States, 193 U.S. 197, 400–401 (1904):

> "Great cases like hard cases make bad law. For great cases are called great, not by reason of their real importance in shaping the law of the future, but because of some accident of immediate overwhelming interest which appeals to the feelings and distorts the judgment. These immediate interests exercise a kind of hydraulic pressure which makes what previously was clear seem doubtful, and before which even well settled principles of law will bend."

With all respect, I consider that the Court has been almost irresponsibly feverish in dealing with these cases.

* * *

These are difficult questions of fact, of law, and of judgment; the potential consequences of erroneous decision are enormous. The time which has been available to us, to the lower courts, and to the parties has been wholly inadequate for giving these cases the kind of consideration they deserve. It is a reflection on the stability of the judicial process that these great issues—as important as any that have arisen during my time on the Court—should have been decided under the pressures engendered by the torrent of publicity that has attended these litigations from their inception.

Forced as I am to reach the merits of these cases, I dissent from the opinion and judgments of the Court. Within the severe limitations imposed by the time constraints under which I have been required to operate, I can only state my reasons in telescoped form, even though in different circumstances I would have felt constrained to deal with the cases in the fuller sweep indicated above.

It is a sufficient basis for affirming the Court of Appeals of the Second Circuit in the *Times* litigation to observe that its order must rest on the conclusion that because of the time elements the Government had not been given an adequate opportunity to present its case to the District Court. At the least this conclusion was not an abuse of discretion.

NOTE

The preceding five cases (*Sheppard* through *The Pentagon Papers Case*) principally traced the working standards of first amendment prior restraint law as applied to the press. They are doctrinal derivatives from *Bridges v. California* itself, tracking that case (so to speak) and its general principles, to illustrate the Supreme Court's application of those principles in several ways, even to the current time. In proceeding in this fashion, however, we have in some measure departed from the previous main theme of our work, namely, the more general first amendment problem of social and political advocacy speech as such.

This central issue of first amendment controversy did not suddenly cease with cases of the sort we were last concerned with, such as *Gitlow v. New York* and *Whitney v. California*. To the contrary. *Dennis v. United States*, the next principal case, resumes virtually where we left off with the supposition—unsupported by example—that the rigorized Holmes–Brandeis standard (as reflected in *Bridges*) would control. Does it? And if it does, in what manner and degree? Just how is it to be applied?

DENNIS v. UNITED STATES

Supreme Court of the United States, 1951.
341 U.S. 494, 71 S.Ct. 857, 95 L.Ed. 1137.

MR. CHIEF JUSTICE VINSON announced the judgment of the Court and an opinion in which MR. JUSTICE REED, MR. JUSTICE BURTON and MR. JUSTICE MINTON join.

Petitioners were indicted July, 1948, for violation of the conspiracy provisions of the Smith Act, * * * during the period of April, 1945 to July, 1948. The pretrial motion to quash the indictment on the grounds *inter alia*, that the statute was unconstitutional was denied * * * and the case was set for trial on January 17, 1949. A verdict of guilty as to all the petitioners was returned by the jury on October 14, 1949. The Court of Appeals affirmed the convictions. 183 F.2d 201. We granted certiorari * * * limited to the following two questions: (1) Whether either § 2 or § 3 of the Smith Act, inherently or as construed and applied in the instant case, violates the First Amendment and other provisions of the Bill of Rights; (2) whether either § 2 or § 3 of the Act, inherently or as construed and applied in the instant case, violates the First and Fifth Amendments because of indefiniteness.

Sections 2 and 3 of the Smith Act * * * provide as follows:

"SEC. 2. (a) It shall be unlawful for any person—

"(1) to knowingly or willfully advocate, abet, advise, or teach the duty, necessity, desirability, or propriety of overthrowing or destroying any government in the United States by force or violence, or by the assassination of any officer of any such government;

"(2) with intent to cause the overthrow or destruction of any government in the United States, to print, publish, edit, issue, circulate, sell, distribute, or publicly display any written or printed matter advocating, advising, or teaching the duty, necessity, desirability, or propriety of overthrowing or destroying any government in the United States by force or violence;

"(3) to organize or help to organize any society, group, or assembly of persons who teach, advocate, or encourage the overthrow or destruction of any government in the United States by force or violence; or to be or become a member of, or affiliate with, any such society, group, or assembly of persons, knowing the purposes thereof.

"(b) For the purposes of this section, the term 'government in the United States' means the Government of the United States, the government of any State, Territory, or possession of the United States, the government of the District of Columbia, or the government of any political subdivision of any of them.

"SEC. 3. It shall be unlawful for any person to attempt to commit, or to conspire to commit, any of the acts prohibited by the provisions of this title."

The indictment charged the petitioners with wilfully and knowingly conspiring (1) to organize as the Communist Party of the United States of America a society, group and assembly of persons who teach and advocate the overthrow and destruction of the Government of the United States by force and violence, and (2) knowingly and wilfully to advocate and teach the duty and necessity of overthrowing and destroying the Government of the United States by force and violence. The indictment further alleged that § 2 of the Smith Act proscribes these acts and that any conspiracy to take such action is a violation of § 3 of the Act.

The trial of the case extended over nine months, six of which were devoted to the taking of evidence, resulting in a record of 16,000 pages. * * * [T]he Court of Appeals held that the record supports the following broad conclusions: By virtue of their control over the political apparatus of the Communist Political Association,[1] petitioners were able to transform that organization into the Communist Party; that the policies of the Association were changed from peaceful cooperation with the United States and its economic and political structure to a policy which had existed before the United States and the Soviet Union were fighting a common enemy, namely, a policy which worked for the overthrow of the Government by force and violence; that the Communist Party is a highly disciplined organization, adept at infiltration into

---

1. Following the dissolution of the Communist International in 1943, the Communist Party of the United States dissolved and was reconstituted as the Communist Political Association. The program of this Association was one of cooperation between labor and management, and, in general, one designed to achieve national unity and peace and prosperity in the postwar period.

strategic positions, use of aliases, and double-meaning language; that the Party is rigidly controlled; that Communists, unlike other political parties, tolerate no dissension from the policy laid down by the guiding forces, but that the approved program is slavishly followed by the members of the Party; that the literature of the Party and the statement and activities of its leaders, petitioners here, advocate, and the general goal of the Party was, during the period in question, to achieve a successful overthrow of the existing order by force and violence.

* * *

II.

The obvious purpose of the statute is to protect existing Government, not from change by peaceable, lawful and constitutional means, but, from change by violence, revolution and terrorism. That it is within the *power* of the Congress to protect the Government of the United States from armed rebellion is a proposition which requires little discussion. Whatever theoretical merit there may be to the argument that there is a "right" to rebellion against dictatorial governments is without force where the existing structure of the government provides for peaceful and orderly change. We reject any principle of governmental helplessness in the face of preparation for revolution, which principle, carried to its logical conclusion, must lead to anarchy. No one could conceive that it is not within the power of Congress to prohibit acts intended to overthrow the Government by force and violence. The question with which we are concerned here is not whether Congress has such *power*, but whether the *means* which it has employed conflict with the First and Fifth Amendments to the Constitution.

One of the bases for the contention that the means which Congress has employed are invalid takes the form of an attack on the face of the statute on the grounds that by its terms it prohibits academic discussion of the merits of Marxism–Leninism, that it stifles ideas and is contrary to all concepts of a free speech and a free press. Although we do not agree that the language itself has that significance, we must bear in mind that it is the duty of the federal courts to interpret federal legislation in a manner not inconsistent with the demands of the Constitution. * * * We are not here confronted with cases similar to * * * De Jonge v. Oregon, 299 U.S. 353 (1937), where a state court had given a meaning to a state statute which was inconsistent with the Federal Constitution. This is a federal statute which we must interpret as well as judge. Herein lies the fallacy of reliance upon the manner in which this Court has treated judgments of state courts. Where the statute as construed by the state court transgressed the First Amendment, we could not but invalidate the judgments of conviction.

The very language of the Smith Act negates the interpretation which petitioners would have us impose on that Act. It is directed at advocacy, not discussion. Thus, the trial judge properly charged the jury that they could not convict if they found that petitioners did "no more than pursue peaceful studies and discussions or teaching and advocacy in the realm of ideas." He further charged that it was not unlawful "to conduct in an American college or university a course explaining the philosophical theories set forth in the books which have been placed in evidence." Such a charge is in strict accord with the statutory language, and illustrates the meaning to be placed on those words. Congress did not intend to eradicate the free discussion of political theories, to destroy the traditional rights of Americans to discuss and evaluate ideas without fear of governmental sanction. Rather Congress was concerned with the very kind of activity in which the evidence showed these petitioners engaged.

III.
* * *

Although no case subsequent to *Whitney* and *Gitlow* has expressly overruled the majority opinions in those cases, there is little doubt that subsequent opinions have inclined toward the Holmes–Brandeis rationale. And in *American Communications Assn. v. Douds,* * * * we suggested that the Holmes–Brandeis philosophy insisted that where there was a direct restriction upon speech, a "clear and present danger" that the substantive evil would be caused was necessary before the statute in question could be constitutionally applied. And we stated, "[The First] Amendment requires that one be permitted to believe what he will. It requires that one be permitted to advocate what he will unless there is a clear and present danger that a substantial public evil will result therefrom." 339 U.S. at 412. But we further suggested that neither Justice Holmes nor Justice Brandeis ever envisioned that a shorthand phrase should be crystallized into a rigid rule to be applied inflexibly without regard to the circumstances of each case. Speech is not an absolute, above and beyond control by the legislature when its judgment, subject to review here, is that certain kinds of speech are so undesirable as to warrant criminal sanction. Nothing is more certain in modern society than the principle that there are no absolutes, that a name, a phrase, a standard has meaning only when associated with the considerations which gave birth to the nomenclature. See American Communications Assn. v. Douds, 339 U.S. at 397. To those who would paralyze our Government in the face of impending threat by encasing it in a semantic straitjacket we must reply that all concepts are relative.

In this case we are squarely presented with the application of the "clear and present danger" test, and must decide what that phrase imports. We first note that many of the cases in which this Court has reversed convictions by use of this or similar tests have been based on the fact that the interest which the State was attempting to protect was itself too insubstantial to warrant restriction of speech. * * *

Overthrow of the Government by force and violence is certainly a substantial enough interest for the Government to limit speech. Indeed, this is the ultimate value of any society, for if a society cannot protect its very structure from armed internal attack, it must follow that no subordinate value can be protected. If, then, this interest may be protected, the literal problem which is presented is what has been meant by the use of the phrase "clear and present danger" of the utterances bringing about the evil within the power of Congress to punish.

Obviously, the words cannot mean that before the Government may act, it must wait until the *putsch* is about to be executed, the plans have been laid and the signal is awaited. If Government is aware that a group aiming at its overthrow is attempting to indoctrinate its members to commit them to a course whereby they will strike when the leaders feel the circumstances permit, action by the Government is required. The argument that there is no need for Government to concern itself, for Government is strong, it possesses ample powers to put down a rebellion, it may defeat the revolution with ease needs no answer. For that is not the question. Certainly an attempt to overthrow the Government by force, even though doomed from the outset because of inadequate numbers or power of the revolutionists, is a sufficient evil for Congress to prevent. The damage which such attempts create both physically and politically to a nation makes it impossible to measure the validity in terms of the probability of success, or the immediacy of a successful attempt. In the instant case the trial judge charged the jury that they could not convict unless they found that petitioners intended to overthrow the Government as "speedily as circumstances would permit." This does not mean, and could not properly mean, that they would not strike until there was certainty of success. What was meant was that the revolutionists would strike when they thought the time was ripe. We must therefore reject the contention that success or probability of success is the criterion.

The situation with which Justices Holmes and Brandeis were concerned in *Gitlow* was a comparatively isolated event, bearing little relation in their minds to any substantial threat to the safety of the community. Such also is true of cases like Fiske v. Kansas, 274 U.S. 380 (1927), and De Jonge v. Oregon, 299 U.S. 353 (1937); but cf. Lazar v. Pennsylvania, 286 U.S. 532 (1932). They were not confronted with any situation comparable to the instant one—the development of an apparatus designed and dedicated to the overthrow of the Government, in the context of world crisis after crisis.

Chief Judge Learned Hand, writing for the majority below, interpreted the phrase as follows: "In each case [courts] must ask whether the gravity of the 'evil,' discounted by its improbability, justifies such invasion of free speech as is necessary to avoid the danger." 183 F.2d 212. We adopt this statement of the rule. As articulated by Chief Judge Hand, it is as succinct and inclusive as any other we might devise at this time. It takes into consideration those factors which we deem relevant, and relates their significances. More we cannot expect from words.

Likewise, we are in accord with the court below, which affirmed the trial court's finding that the requisite danger existed. The mere fact that from the period 1945 to 1948 petitioners' activities did not result in an attempt to overthrow the Government by force and violence is of course no answer to the fact that there was a group that was ready to make the attempt. The formation by petitioners of such a highly organized conspiracy, with rigidly disciplined members subject to call when the leaders, these petitioners, felt that the time had come for action, coupled with the inflammable nature of world conditions, similar uprisings in other countries, and the touch-and-go nature of our relations with countries with whom petitioners were in the very least ideologically attuned, convince us that their convictions were justified on this score. And this analysis disposes of the contention that a conspiracy to advocate, as distinguished from the advocacy itself, cannot be constitutionally restrained, because it comprises only the preparation. It is the existence of the conspiracy which creates the danger. Cf. Pinkerton v. United States, 328 U.S. 640 (1946); Goldman v. United States, 245 U.S. 474 (1918); United States v. Rabinowich, 238 U.S. 78 (1915). If the ingredients of the reaction are present, we cannot bind the Government to wait until the catalyst is added.

IV.

Although we have concluded that the finding that there was a sufficient danger to warrant the application of the statute was justified on the merits, there remains the problem of whether the trial judge's treatment of the issue was correct. He charged the jury, in relevant part, as follows:

> "In further construction and interpretation of the statute I charge you that it is not the abstract doctrine of overthrowing or destroying organized government by unlawful means which is denounced by this law but the teaching and advocacy of action for the accomplishment of that purpose, by language reasonably and ordinarily calculated to incite persons to such action. Accordingly, you cannot find the defendants or any of them guilty of the crime charged unless you are satisfied beyond a reasonable doubt that they conspired to organize a society, group and assembly of persons who teach and advocate the overthrow or destruction of the Government of the United States by force and violence and to advocate and teach the duty and necessity of overthrowing or destroying the Government of the United States by force and violence, with the intent that such teaching and advocacy be of a rule or principle of action and by language reasonably and ordinarily calculated to incite persons to such action, all with the intent to cause the overthrow or destruction of the Government of the United States by force and violence as speedily as circumstances would permit.

* * *

> "If you are satisfied that the evidence establishes beyond a reasonable doubt that the defendants, or any of them, are guilty of a violation of the statute, as I have interpreted it to you, I find as matter of law that there is sufficient danger of a substantive evil that the Congress has a right to prevent to justify the application of the statute under the First Amendment of the Constitution.

"This is a matter of law about which you have no concern. It is a finding on a matter of law which I deem essential to support my ruling that the case should be submitted to you to pass upon the guilt or innocence of the defendants. * * * "

It is thus clear that he reserved the question of the existence of the danger for his own determination, and the question becomes whether the issue is of such a nature that it should have been submitted to the jury.

* * * The argument that the action of the trial court is erroneous, in declaring as a matter of law that such violation shows sufficient danger to justify the punishment despite the First Amendment, rests on the theory that a jury must decide a question of the application of the First Amendment. We do not agree.

When facts are found that establish the violation of a statute, the protection against conviction afforded by the First Amendment is a matter of law. The doctrine that there must be a clear and present danger of a substantive evil that Congress has a right to prevent is a judicial rule to be applied as a matter of law by the courts. The guilt is established by proof of facts. Whether the First Amendment protects the activity which constitutes the violation of the statute must depend upon a judicial determination of the scope of the First Amendment applied to the circumstances of the case.

Petitioners' reliance upon Justice Brandeis' language in his concurrence in *Whitney, supra,* is misplaced. In that case Justice Brandeis pointed out that the defendant could have made the existence of the requisite danger the important issue at her trial, but that she had not done so. In discussing this failure, he stated that the defendant could have had the issue determined by the court *or* the jury.[6] No realistic construction of this disjunctive language could arrive at the conclusion that he intended to state that the question was *only* determinable by a jury. * * * Indeed, in the very case in which the phrase was born, *Schenck,* this Court itself examined the record to find whether the requisite danger appeared, and the issue was not submitted to a jury. And in every later case in which the Court has measured the validity of a statute by the "clear and present danger" test, that determination has been by the court, the question of the danger has not been submitted to the jury.

The question in this case is whether the statute which the legislature has enacted may be constitutionally applied. In other words, the Court must examine judicially the application of the statute to the particular situation, to ascertain if the Constitution prohibits the con-

---

6. "Whether in 1919, when Miss Whitney did the things complained of, there was in California such clear and present danger of serious evil, might have been made the important issue in the case. She might have required that the issue be determined either by the *court or the jury.* She claimed below that the statute as applied to her violated the Federal Constitution; but she did not claim that it was void because there was no clear and present danger of serious evil, nor did she request that the existence of these conditions of a valid measure thus restricting the rights of free speech and assembly be passed upon by *the court or a jury.* On the other hand, there was evidence which *the court or jury* might have found that such danger existed." (Emphasis added.) 274 U.S. at 379.

viction. We hold that the statute may be applied where there is a "clear and present danger" of the substantive evil which the legislature had the right to prevent. Bearing, as it does, the marks of a "question of law," the issue is properly one for the judge to decide.

* * *

We hold that §§ 2(a)(1), 2(a)(3) and 3 of the Smith Act do not inherently, or as construed or applied in the instant case, violate the First Amendment and other provisions of the Bill of Rights, or the First and Fifth Amendments because of indefiniteness. Petitioners intended to overthrow the Government of the United States as speedily as the circumstances would permit. Their conspiracy to organize the Communist Party and to teach and advocate the overthrow of the Government of the United States by force and violence created a "clear and present danger" of an attempt to overthrow the Government by force and violence. They were properly and constitutionally convicted for violation of the Smith Act. The judgments of the conviction are

Affirmed.

MR. JUSTICE CLARK took no part in the consideration or decision of this case.

MR. JUSTICE FRANKFURTER, concurring in affirmance of the judgment.

* * *

* * * The First Amendment categorically demands that "Congress shall make no law respecting an establishment of religion, or prohibiting the free exercise thereof; or abridging the freedom of speech, or of the press; or the right of the people peaceably to assemble, and to petition the Government for a redress of grievances." The right of a man to think what he pleases, to write what he thinks, and to have his thoughts made available for others to hear or read has an engaging ring of universality. The Smith Act and this conviction under it no doubt restrict the exercise of free speech and assembly. Does that, without more, dispose of the matter?

* * *

* * * Absolute rules would inevitably lead to absolute exceptions, and such exceptions would eventually corrode the rules.[5] The demands of free speech in a democratic society as well as the interest in national security are better served by candid and informed weighing of the competing interests, within the confines of the judicial process, than by

---

5. Professor Alexander Meiklejohn is a leading exponent of the absolutist interpretation of the First Amendment. Recognizing that certain forms of speech require regulation, he excludes those forms of expression entirely from the protection accorded by the Amendment. "The constitutional status of a merchant advertising his wares, of a paid lobbyist fighting for the advantage of his client, is utterly different from that of a citizen who is planning for the general welfare." Meiklejohn, Free Speech, 39. "The radio as it now operates among us is not free. Nor is it entitled to the protection of the First Amendment. It is not engaged in the task of enlarging and enriching human communication. It is engaged in making money. Id. at 104. Professor Meiklejohn even suggests that scholarship may now require such subvention and control that it no longer is entitled to protection by the First Amendment. See id. at 99–100. Professor Chafee in his review of the Meiklejohn book, 62 Harv.L. Rev. 894, has subjected this position to trenchant comment.

announcing dogmas too inflexible for the non-Euclidian problems to be solved.

But how are competing interests to be assumed? Since they are not subject to quantitative ascertainment, the issue necessarily resolves itself into asking, who is to make the adjustment?—who is to balance the relevant factors and ascertain which interest is in the circumstances to prevail? Full responsibility for the choice cannot be given to the courts. Courts are not representative bodies. They are not designed to be a good reflex of a democratic society. Their judgment is best informed, and therefore most dependable, within narrow limits. Their essential quality is detachment, founded on independence. History teaches that the independence of the judiciary is jeopardized when courts become embroiled in the passions of the day and assume primary responsibility in choosing between competing political, economic and social pressures.

Primary responsibility for adjusting the interests which compete in the situation before us of necessity belongs to the Congress. The nature of the power to be exercised by this Court has been delineated in decisions not charged with the emotional appeal of situations such as that now before us. We are to set aside the judgment of those whose duty it is to legislate only if there is no reasonable basis for it. * * *

* * * Some members of the Court—and at times a majority—have done more. They have suggested that our function in reviewing statutes restricting freedom of expression differs sharply from our normal duty in sitting in judgment on legislation. It has been said that such statutes "must be justified by clear public interest, threatened not doubtfully or remotely, but by clear and present danger. The rational connection between the remedy provided and the evil to be curbed, which in other contexts might support legislation against attack on due process grounds, will not suffice." Thomas v. Collins, 323 U.S. 516, 530. It has been suggested, with the casualness of a footnote, that such legislation is not presumptively valid, see United States v. Carolene Products Co., 304 U.S. 144, 152, n. 4, and it has been weightily reiterated that freedom of speech has a "preferred position" among constitutional safeguards. Kovacs v. Cooper, 336 U.S. 77, 88.

The precise meaning intended to be conveyed by these phrases need not now be pursued. It is enough to note that they have recurred in the Court's opinions, and their cumulative force has, not without justification, engendered belief that there is a constitutional principle, expressed by those attractive but imprecise words, prohibiting restriction upon utterance unless it creates a situation of "imminent" peril against which legislation may guard. It is on this body of the Court's pronouncements that the defendants' argument here is based.

In all fairness, the argument cannot be met by reinterpreting the Court's frequent use of "clear" and "present" to mean an entertainable "probability." In giving this meaning to the phrase "clear and present danger," the Court of Appeals was fastidiously confining the rhetoric of opinions to the exact scope of what was decided by them. We have greater responsibility for having given constitutional support, over repeated protests, to uncritical libertarian generalities.

* * *

We have recognized and resolved conflicts between speech and competing interests in six different types of cases.

* * *

I must leave to others the ungrateful task of trying to reconcile all these decisions. In some instances we have too readily permitted juries to infer deception from error, or intention from argumentative or critical statements. *Abrams v. United States,* * * * In other instances we weighted the interest in free speech so heavily that we permitted essential conflicting values to be destroyed. *Bridges v. California, supra,* * * * Viewed as a whole, however, the decisions express an attitude toward the judicial function and a standard of values which for me are decisive of the case before us.

First.—Free-speech cases are not an exception to the principle that we are not legislators, that direct policy-making is not our province. How best to reconcile competing interests is the business of legislatures, and the balance they strike is a judgment not to be displaced by ours, but to be respected unless outside the pale of fair judgment.

On occasion we have strained to interpret legislation in order to limit its effect on interests protected by the First Amendment. *Schneiderman v. United States, supra; Bridges v. Wixon, supra.* In some instances we have denied to States the deference to which I think they are entitled. *Bridges v. California, supra; Craig v. Harney, supra.* Once in this recent course of decisions the Court refused to permit a jury to draw inferences which seemed to me to be obviously reasonable. *Hartzel v. United States, supra.*

But in no case has a majority of this Court held that a legislative judgment, even as to freedom of utterance, may be overturned merely because the Court would have made a different choice between the competing interests had the initial legislative judgment been for it to make. * * *

* * *

One of the judges below rested his affirmance on the *Gitlow* decision, and the defendants do not attempt to distinguish the case. They place their argument squarely on the ground that the case has been overruled by subsequent decisions. It has not been explicitly overruled. But it would be disingenuous to deny that the dissent in *Gitlow* has been treated with the respect usually accorded to a decision.

The result of the *Gitlow* decision was to send a left-wing Socialist to jail for publishing a Manifesto expressing Marxist exhortations. It requires excessive tolerance of the legislative judgment to suppose that the *Gitlow* publication in the circumstances could justify serious concern.

In contrast, there is ample justification for a legislative judgment that the conspiracy now before us is a substantial threat to national order and security. If the Smith Act is justified at all, it is justified precisely because it may serve to prohibit the type of conspiracy for which these defendants were convicted. The court below properly held that as a matter of separability the Smith Act may be limited to those situations to which it can constitutionally be applied. See 183 F.2d at 214–215. Our decision today certainly does not mean that the Smith Act can constitutionally be applied to facts like those in *Gitlow v. New York.* While reliance may properly be placed on the attitude of judicial self-restraint which the *Gitlow* decision reflects, it is not necessary to depend on the facts or the full extent of the theory of that case in order to find that the judgment of Congress, as applied to the facts of the case now before us, is not in conflict with the First Amendment.

* * *

Bearing in mind that Mr. Justice Holmes regarded questions under the First Amendment as questions of "proximity and degree," Schenck v. United States, 249 U.S. at 52, it would be a distortion, indeed a mockery, of his reasoning to compare the "puny anonymities," 250 U.S. at 629, to which he was addressing himself in the *Abrams* case in 1919 or the publication that was "futile and too remote from possible consequences," 268 U.S. at 673, in the *Gitlow* case in 1925 with the setting of events in this case in 1950.

* * *

Throughout our decisions there has recurred a distinction between the statement of an idea which may prompt its hearers to take unlawful action, and advocacy that such action be taken. * * *

It is true that there is no divining rod by which we may locate "advocacy." Exposition of ideas readily merges into advocacy. The same Justice who gave currency to application of the incitement doctrine in this field dissented four times from what he thought was its misapplication. As he said in the *Gitlow* dissent, "Every idea is an incitement." 268 U.S. at 673. Even though advocacy of overthrow deserves little protection, we should hesitate to prohibit it if we thereby inhibit the interchange of rational ideas so essential to representative government and free society.

But there is underlying validity in the distinction between advocacy and the interchange of ideas, and we do not discard a useful tool because it may be misused. That such a distinction could be used unreasonably by those in power against hostile or unorthodox views does not negate the fact that it may be used reasonably against an organization wielding the power of the centrally controlled international Communist movement. The object of the conspiracy before us is so clear that the chance of error in saying that the defendants conspired to advocate rather than to express ideas is slight. Mr. Justice Douglas quite properly points out that the conspiracy before us is not a conspiracy to overthrow the Government. But it would be equally wrong to treat it as a seminar in political theory.

III.

These general considerations underlie decision of the case before us.

On the one hand is the interest in security. * * *

* * *

On the other hand is the interest in free speech. * * *

Of course no government can recognize a "right" of revolution, or a "right" to incite revolution if the incitement has no other purpose or effect. But speech is seldom restricted to a single purpose, and its effects may be manifold. A public interest is not wanting in granting freedom to speak their minds even to those who advocate the overthrow of the Government by force. For, as the evidence in this case abundantly illustrates, coupled with such advocacy is criticism of defects in our society. * * * It is a commonplace that there may be a grain of truth in the most uncouth doctrine, however false and repellent the balance may be. Suppressing advocates of overthrow inevitably will also silence critics who do not advocate overthrow but fear that their criticism may be so construed. No matter how clear we may be that the defendants now before us are preparing to overthrow our Government at the propitious moment, it is self-delusion to think that we can punish them for their advocacy without adding to the risks run by loyal citizens who honestly believe in some of the reforms these defendants advance. It is a sobering fact that in sustaining the convictions before us we can hardly escape restriction on the interchange of ideas.

* * *

It is not for us to decide how we would adjust the clash of interests which this case presents were the primary responsibility for reconciling it ours. Congress has determined that the danger created by advocacy of overthrow justifies the ensuing restriction on freedom of speech. The determination was made after due deliberation, and the seriousness of the congressional purpose is attested by the volume of legislation passed to effectuate the same ends.

Can we then say that the judgment Congress exercised was denied it by the Constitution? Can we establish a constitutional doctrine which forbids the elected representatives of the people to make this choice? Can we hold that the First Amendment deprives Congress of what it deemed necessary for the Government's protection?

To make validity of legislation depend on judicial reading of events still in the womb of time—a forecast, that is, of the outcome of forces at best appreciated only with knowledge of the topmost secrets of nations—is to charge the judiciary with duties beyond its equipment.
* * *

* * *

* * * All the Court says is that congress was not forbidden by the Constitution to pass this enactment and that a prosecution under it may be brought against a conspiracy such as the one before us.

* * *

MR. JUSTICE JACKSON, concurring.

This prosecution is the latest of never-ending, because never successful, quests for some legal formula that will secure an existing order against revolutionary radicalism. It requires us to reappraise, in the light of our own times and conditions, constitutional doctrines devised under other circumstances to strike a balance between authority and liberty.

Activity here charged to be criminal is conspiracy—that defendants conspired to teach and advocate, and to organize the Communist Party to teach and advocate, overthrow and destruction of the Government by force and violence. There is no charge of actual violence or attempt at overthrow.

* * *

The "clear and present danger" test was an innovation by Mr. Justice Holmes in the *Schenck* case, reiterated and refined by him and Mr. Justice Brandeis in later cases, all arising before the era of World War II revealed the subtlety and efficacy of modernized revolutionary techniques used by totalitarian parties. * * *

I would save it, unmodified, for application as a "rule of reason" in the kind of case for which it was devised. When the issue is criminality of a hot-headed speech on a street corner, or circulation of a few incendiary pamphlets, or parading by some zealots behind a red flag, or refusal of a handful of school children to salute our flag, it is not beyond the capacity of the judicial process to gather, comprehend, and weigh the necessary materials for decision whether it is a clear and present danger of substantive evil or a harmless letting off of steam. It is not a prophecy, for the danger in such cases has matured by the time of trial or it was never present. The test applies and has meaning where a conviction is sought to be based on a speech or writing which does not directly or explicitly advocate a crime but to which such tendency is sought to be attributed by construction or by implication from external circumstances. * * *

* * *

The authors of the clear and present danger test never applied it to a case like this, nor would I. If applied as it is proposed here, it means that the Communist plotting is protected during its period of incubation; its preliminary stages of organization and preparation are immune from the law; the Government can move only after imminent action is manifest, when it would, of course, be too late.

III.

The highest degree of constitutional protection is due to the individual acting without conspiracy. * * *

* * *

* * * With due respect to my colleagues, they seem to me to discuss anything under the sun except the law of conspiracy. * * *

* * *

I do not suggest that Congress could punish conspiracy to advocate something, the doing of which it may not punish. Advocacy or exposition of the doctrine of communal property ownership, or any political philosophy unassociated with advocacy of its imposition by force or seizure of government by unlawful means could not be reached through conspiracy prosecution. But it is not forbidden to put down force or violence, it is not forbidden to punish its teaching or advocacy, and the end being punishable, there is no doubt of the power to punish conspiracy for the purpose.

* * *

When our constitutional provisions were written, the chief forces recognized as antagonists in the struggle between authority and liberty were the Government on the one hand and the individual citizen on the other. It was thought that if the state could be kept in its place the individual could take care of himself.

In more recent times these problems have been complicated by the intervention between the state and the citizen of permanently organized, well-financed, semisecret and highly disciplined political organizations. Totalitarian groups here and abroad perfected the technique of creating private paramilitary organizations to coerce both the public government and its citizens. These organizations assert as against our Government all of the constitutional rights and immunities of individuals and at the same time exercise over their followers much of the authority which they deny to the Government. The Communist Party realistically is a state within a state, an authoritarian dictatorship within a republic. It demands these freedoms, not for its members, but for the organized party. It denies to its own members at the same time the freedom to dissent, to debate, to deviate from the party line, and enforces its authoritarian rule by crude purges, if nothing more violent.

The law of conspiracy has been the chief means at the Government's disposal to deal with the growing problems created by such organizations. I happen to think it is an awkward and inept remedy, but I find no constitutional authority for taking this weapon from the Government. There is no constitutional right to "gang up" on the Government.

While I think there was power in Congress to enact this statute and that, as applied in this case, it cannot be held unconstitutional,[15] I add that I have little faith in the long-range effectiveness of this conviction to stop the rise of the Communist movement. * * *

Mr. Justice Black, dissenting.

* * *

At the outset I want to emphasize what the crime involved in this case is, and what it is not. These petitioners were not charged with an

---

15. The defendants have had the benefit so far in this case of all the doubts and confusions afforded by attempts to apply the "clear and present danger" doctrine. While I think it has no proper application to the case, these efforts have been in response to their own contentions and favored rather than prejudiced them. There is no call for reversal on account of it.

attempt to overthrow the Government. They were not charged with overt acts of any kind designed to overthrow the Government. They were not even charged with saying anything or writing anything designed to overthrow the Government. The charge was that they agreed to assemble to talk and publish certain ideas at a later date: The indictment is that they conspired to organize the Communist Party and to use speech or newspapers and other publications in the future to teach and advocate the forcible overthrow of the Government. No matter how it is worded, this is a virulent form of prior censorship of speech and press, which I believe the First Amendment forbids. I would hold § 3 of the Smith Act authorizing this prior restraint unconstitutional on its face and as applied.

But let us assume, contrary to all constitutional ideas of fair criminal procedure, that petitioners although not indicted for the crime of actual advocacy, may be punished for it. Even on this radical assumption, the other opinions in this case show that the only way to affirm these convictions is to repudiate directly or indirectly the established "clear and present danger" rule. This the Court does in a way which greatly restricts the protections afforded by the First Amendment. The opinions for affirmance indicate that the chief reason for jettisoning the rule is the expressed fear that advocacy of Communist doctrine endangers the safety of the Republic. Undoubtedly, a governmental policy of unfettered communication of ideas does entail dangers. To the Founders of this Nation, however, the benefits derived from free expression were worth the risk. They embodied this philosophy in the First Amendment's command that "Congress shall make no law * * * abridging the freedom of speech, or of the press. * * * " I have always believed that the First Amendment is the keystone of our Government, that the freedoms it guarantees provide the best insurance against destruction of all freedom. At least as to speech in the realm of public matters, I believe that the "clear and present danger" test does not "mark the furthermost constitutional boundaries of protected expression" but does "no more than recognize a minimum compulsion of the Bill of Rights." Bridges v. California, 314 U.S. 252, 263.

* * *

Public opinion being what it now is, few will protest the conviction of these Communist petitioners. There is hope, however, that in calmer times, when present pressures, passions and fears subside, this or some later Court will restore the First Amendment liberties to the high preferred place where they belong in a free society.

Mr. Justice Douglas, dissenting.

If this were a case where those who claimed protection under the First Amendment were teaching the techniques of sabotage, the assassination of the President, the filching of documents from public files, the planting of bombs, the art of street warfare, and the like, I would have no doubts. The freedom to speak is not absolute; the teaching of methods of terror and other seditious conduct should be beyond the pale along with obscenity and immorality. This case was argued as if those were the facts. The argument imported much seditious conduct into the record. That is easy and it has popular appeal for the activities of Communists in plotting and scheming against the free world are common knowledge. But the fact is that no such evidence was introduced at the trial. * * * It may well be that indoctrination in the techniques of terror to destroy the Government would be indictable under either statute. But the teaching which is condemned here is of a different character.

So far as the present record is concerned, what petitioners did was to organize people to teach and themselves teach the Marxist–Leninist doctrine contained chiefly in four books.[3] Stalin, Foundations of Leninism (1924); Marx and Engels, Manifesto of the Communist Party (1848); Lenin, The State and Revolution (1917); History of the Communist Party of the Soviet Union (B.) (1939).

Those books are to Soviet Communism what Mein Kampf was to Nazism. If they are understood, the ugliness of Communism is revealed, its deceit and cunning are exposed, the nature of its activities becomes apparent, and the chances of its success less likely. That is not, of course, the reason why petitioners chose these books for their classrooms. They are fervent Communists to whom these volumes are gospel. They preached the creed with the hope that some day it would be acted upon.

The opinion of the Court does not outlaw these texts nor condemn them to the fire, as the Communists do literature offensive to their creed. But if the books themselves are not outlawed, if they can lawfully remain on library shelves, by what reasoning does their use in a classroom become a crime? It would not be a crime under the Act to introduce these books to a class, though that would be teaching what the creed of violent overthrow of the Government is. The Act, as construed, requires the element of intent—that those who teach the creed believe in it. The crime then depends not on what is taught but on who the teacher is. That is to make freedom of speech turn not on *what is said,* but on the *intent* with which it is said. Once we start down that road we enter territory dangerous to the liberties of every citizen.

There was a time in England when the concept of constructive treason flourished. Men were punished not for raising a hand against the king but for thinking murderous thoughts about him. The Framers of the Constitution were alive to that abuse and took steps to see that the practice would not flourish here. Treason was defined to require overt acts—the evolution of a plot against the country into an actual project. The present case is not one of treason. But the analogy is close when the illegality is made to turn on intent, not on the nature of the act. * * *

* * *

---

3. Other books taught were Stalin, Problems of Leninism, Strategy and Facts of World Communism (H.R.Doc. No. 619, 80th Cong., 2d Sess.), and Program of the Communist International.

* * * I repeat that we deal here with speech alone, not with speech plus acts of sabotage or unlawful conduct. Not a single seditious act is charged in the indictment. To make a lawful speech unlawful because two men conceive it is to raise the law of conspiracy to appalling proportions. That course is to make a radical break with the past and to violate one of the cardinal principles of our constitutional scheme.

* * *

There comes a time when even speech loses its constitutional immunity. Speech innocuous one year may at another time fan such destructive flames that it must be halted in the interests of the safety of the Republic. That is the meaning of the clear and present danger test. When conditions are so critical that there will be no time to avoid the evil that the speech threatens, it is time to call a halt. Otherwise, free speech which is the strength of the Nation will be the cause of its destruction.

* * *

I had assumed that the question of the clear and present danger, being so critical an issue in the case, would be a matter for submission to the jury. It was squarely held in Pierce v. United States, 252 U.S. 239, 244, to be a jury question. Mr. Justice Pitney, speaking for the Court, said: "Whether the statement contained in the pamphlet had a natural tendency to produce the forbidden consequences, as alleged, was a question to be determined not upon demurrer but by the jury at the trial." That is the only time the Court has passed on the issue. None of our other decisions is contrary. Nothing said in any of the nonjury cases has detracted from that ruling. The statement in *Pierce v. United States, supra,* states the law as it has been and as it should be. The Court, I think, errs when it treats the question as one of law.

Yet whether the question is one for the Court or the jury, there should be evidence of record on the issue. This record, however, contains no evidence whatsoever showing that the acts charged, *viz.,* the teaching of the Soviet theory of revolution with the hope that it will be realized, have created any clear and present danger to the Nation. The Court, however, rules to the contrary. It says, "The formation by petitioners of such a highly organized conspiracy, with rigidly disciplined members subject to call when the leaders, these petitioners, felt that the time had come for action, coupled with the inflammable nature of world conditions, similar uprisings in other countries, and the touch-and-go nature of our relations with countries with whom petitioners were in the very least ideologically attuned, convince us that their convictions were justified on this score."

That ruling is in my view not responsive to the issue in the case. We might as well say that the speech of petitioners is outlawed because Soviet Russia and her Red Army are a threat to world peace.

The nature of Communism as a force on the world scene would, of course, be relevant to the issue of clear and present danger of petitioners' advocacy within the United States. But the primary consideration is the strength and tactical position of petitioners and their converts in this country. On that there is no evidence in the record. If we are to take judicial notice of the threat of Communists within the nation, it should not be difficult to conclude that *as a political party* they are of little consequence. Communists in this country have never made a respectable or serious showing in any election. I would doubt that there is a village, let alone a city or county or state, which the Communists could carry. Communism in the world scene is no bogeyman; but Communism as a political faction or party in this country plainly is. Communism has been so thoroughly exposed in this country that it has been crippled as a political force. Free speech has destroyed it as an effective political party. It is inconceivable that those who went up and down this country preaching the doctrine of revolution which petitioners espouse would have any success. In days of trouble and confusion, when bread lines were long, when the unemployed walked the streets, when people were starving, the advocates of a shortcut by revolution might have a chance to gain adherents. But today there are no such conditions. But today there are no such conditions. The country is not in despair; the people know Soviet Communism; the doctrine of Soviet revolution is exposed in all of its ugliness and the American people want none of it.

How it can be said that there is a clear and present danger that this advocacy will succeed is, therefore, a mystery. * * *

* * *

* * * Free speech—the glory of our system of government—should not be sacrificed on anything less than plain and objective proof of danger that the evil advocated is imminent. On this record no one can say that petitioners and their converts are in such a strategic position as to have even the slightest chance of achieving their aims.

* * *

Vishinsky wrote in 1938 in The Law of the Soviet State, "In our state, naturally, there is and can be no place for freedom of speech, press, and so on for the foes of socialism."

Our concern should be that we accept no such standard for the United States. Our faith should be that our people will never give support to these advocates of revolution, so long as we remain loyal to the purposes for which our Nation was founded.

A BRIEF NOTE ON THE *DENNIS* CASE

Dennis v. United States marked the return of serious "sedition" cases to the Supreme Court.[47] The formula for first amendment judicial review, adopted and utilized in the majority opinion, obviously reflects some modification in the "clear and present" danger test as previously understood and applied in a variety of different factual settings during the previous decade-and-a-half, e.g., in *Bridges v. California*. There are, moreover, additional features of the opinion well worth some separate attention and discussion.[48]

The recast form of the first amendment standard against which courts are to test the constitutional permissibility of the prosecution was supplied by Judge Learned Hand, in the court of appeals. It is this recast form that Chief Justice Vinson accepts in the Supreme Court, namely, that in each case the question [49] is

> **Whether the gravity of the evil, discounted by its improbability, justifies such invasion of free speech as is necessary to avoid the danger.**

This would appear to suggest a revised figure of first amendment review, perhaps of the following sort:

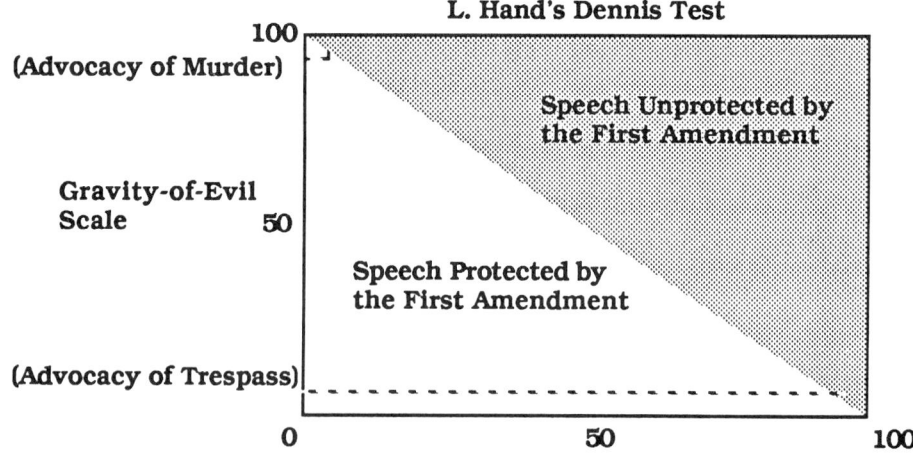

[G1749]

47. And correspondingly yielded a very wide range of critical academic reflections at the time. See, e.g., Gorfinkel & Mack, Dennis v. United States and the Clear and Present Danger Rule, 39 Calif.L.Rev. 475 (1951); Jaffe, Foreword, 65 Harv.L.Rev. 107 (1951); Nathanson, The Communist Trial and the Clear-and-Present-Danger Test, 63 Harv.L.Rev. 1167 (1950). The Smith Act provisions involved in *Dennis* were substantially narrowed, by statutory interpretation, in Yates v. United States, 354 U.S. 298, 77 S.Ct. 1064, 1 L.Ed.2d 1356 (1957). (Cf. Scales v. United States, 367 U.S. 203, 81 S.Ct. 1469, 6 L.Ed.2d 782 (1961); Noto v. United States, 367 U.S. 290, 81 S.Ct. 1517, 6 L.Ed.2d 836 (1961).

48. E.g., the extent to which the Court deferred to congressional "findings" respecting the extent of the threat to national security posed by militant international communism, the linkage between the American Communist Party with external communist movements, the nexus between its program of domestic advocacy and making ready for violent action pursuant to Soviet direction, etc., within which context the domestic advocacy program of the Party might be differently assessed than were these connections not assumed or not deemed relevant in light of the specific charges actually brought under the Smith Act (cf. the opinion of Justice Douglas).

49. For whom?—i.e. is "the question" principally or solely for *the legislature* that enacted the applicable criminal statute (to take the measure of the gravity of the harm felt sufficient to warrant the restriction on speech as the resulting statute does) or for *the trial judge* independently to determine (as an incident of the particular prosecution)? Or is it, rather, principally *a jury* question, to be determined by them in response to an instruction by the trial judge (re what the prosecution must prove to the jury's satisfaction beyond reasonable doubt, such that if the jury does not find the evidence in the case sufficient, it is to acquit)? Or is it, rather, a first amendment requirement-of-law (constitutional law), determinable de novo such that unless the record on the appeal clearly proves the elements of the test, the court of appeals is to reverse?

Social advocacy speech urging others to disregard trespass restrictions the speaker believes to be unfair and unworthy of respect, threaten only a relatively commonplace and, at that, a not very weighty social harm. Such specific advocacy of law violation may be subject to successful prosecution, but only if it actually induced such action or, at the least, was imminently likely to have done so at the moment of the speaker's arrest. Otherwise, the speech is protected by the first amendment, whether or not it involved the advocacy of an illegal act.[50] Such, at any rate, appears to be Judge Hand's suggestion,[51] applying his formula to this kind of case.

Advocacy speech urging others to take violent measures (e.g., arson, killing), on the other hand, is virtually always beyond the pale of protected speech, according to the figure seemingly implicit in the Hand, *Dennis* test. Thus, only in the instance where the advocacy was highly unlikely to be acted upon, considering all of the relevant circumstances, would it be protected under the first amendment proper-

50. Notice this change from the earlier Hand formulation, in *The Masses* case.

51. At least this is how it is generally understood, i.e. as a "sliding scale" balancing, trading off a greater latitude of constitutionally protected speech as against risks of bearable harms, while permitting more stringent measures against speech that threatens greater harms, the avoidance of which justifies interventions much more in advance of the threatened putsch. Yet, Hand's test may not be quite this simple. Note that the test is posed in the form of a *question* (i.e. the question in each case is *whether* the gravity of the evil, discounted by its improbability, justifies such invasion of free speech as is necessary to avoid the danger). It leaves open the possibility that in some instances, the answer is "no," perhaps because the kind or degree of harm sought to be avoided does not justify such invasion of free speech as concededly may be necessary to avoid the danger, given the kind of speech at stake. In the protection of social advocacy or political speech, in other words, some kinds or some degree of "harm" may have to be accepted as the price of freedom of speech—a price the first amendment exacts. (See, e.g., Cohen v. California, 403 U.S. 15, 91 S.Ct. 1780, 29 L.Ed.2d 284 (1971); Texas v. Johnson, 491 U.S. 397, 109 S.Ct. 2533, 105 L.Ed.2d 342 (1989); see also Brandeis' statements in Whitney v. California, 274 U.S. 357, 47 S.Ct. 641, 71 L.Ed. 1095 (1927)). Cf. Posner, Free Speech in an Economic Perspective, 20 Suffolk L.Rev. 1, 8–9, 36–37 (1986).

ly applied. Such, too, appears to be Judge Hand's suggestion, explaining why he concurred in sustaining the Smith Act convictions of the accused—for organizing to plan for and to advocate violence, to overthrow the government by force, despite the lack of evidence that there was imminent danger of either.

Judge Hand's test is reminiscent of his approach in the field of torts. Here, the trade off is between the gravity of the evil to be avoided, discounted by its improbability despite the speaker's advocacy aimed at bringing it to pass. *Where the harm to be feared is bearable,* even though punishable when actually committed (e.g., the acts of trespass themselves), only when speech is shown to be causatively responsible for having induced it (or at least to have made it virtually inevitable had the speaker not been restrained by force of law in the course of his efforts to bring it about), will the first amendment defense be denied. *Where the harm to be feared is extreme,* on the other hand, any first amendment defense is deemed to be dubious, within the formula thus laid down.[52] Absent any real reason to believe the advocacy of such extreme action was or would have been impotent under the circumstances, the first amendment does not protect it from punishment or from restraint.

In what respect(s) does this differ from the Holmes–Brandeis formulation? What would you say are the comparative strengths of weaknesses, as between the two? What other sorts of questions might one want to have answered, in deciding these matters? What is your view of the decision in *Dennis* itself?

BRANDENBURG v. OHIO

Supreme Court of the United States, 1969.
395 U.S. 444, 89 S.Ct. 1827, 23 L.Ed.2d 430.

PER CURIAM.

The appellant, a leader of a Ku Klux Klan group, was convicted under the Ohio Criminal Syndicalism statute for "advocat[ing] * * * the duty, necessity, or propriety of crime, sabotage, violence, or unlaw-

---

52. So, on the graphic diagram, even the direct advocacy of trespass remains protected by the first amendment except in the instance where, locating the particular case on the horizontal probability axis, the advocacy will almost certainly produce the law violation (rather than merely "have a tendency" or even have been "reasonably likely to have done so"), such that it falls into the grey (unprotected) zone rather than the white (protected) zone under the circumstances (e.g., it appears roughly at the "97%" point on the probability scale). Oppositely, the direct advocacy of someone's murder (or some group's killing) is validly subject to prosecution though there were but a bare possibility of action (e.g., a "3%" chance on the probability axis is enough to clear any first amendment defense), even fully assuming the advocacy is also part of a political movement or protest. Correspondingly, intermediately scaled kinds and degrees of "harm" are located appropriately on the vertical 0 to 100 (least to greatest) "gravity of evil" scale, with the first amendment defense failing at the point where, on the horizontal probability axis, the facts of the particular case would place the case in the grey (unprotected) area rather than the white (protected) area.

ful methods of terrorism as a means of accomplishing industrial or political reform" and for "voluntarily assembl[ing] with any society, group, or assemblage of persons formed to teach or advocate the doctrines of criminal syndicalism." Ohio Rev.Code Ann. § 2923.23. He was fined $1,000 and sentenced to one to 10 years' imprisonment. The appellant challenged the constitutionality of the criminal syndicalism statute under the First and Fourteenth Amendments to the United States Constitution, but the intermediate appellate court of Ohio affirmed his conviction without opinion. The Supreme Court of Ohio dismissed his appeal, *sua sponte,* "for the reason that no substantial constitutional question exists herein." It did not file an opinion or explain its conclusions. Appeal was taken to this Court, and we noted probable jurisdiction. 393 U.S. 948 (1968). We reverse.

The record shows that a man identified at trial as the appellant, telephoned an announcer-reporter on the staff of a Cincinnati television station and invited him to come to a Ku Klux Klan "rally" to be held at a farm in Hamilton County. With the cooperation of the organizers, the reporter and a cameraman attended the meeting and filmed the events. Portions of the films were later broadcast on the local station and on a national network.

The prosecution's case rested on the films and on testimony identifying the appellant as the person who communicated with the reporter and who spoke at the rally. The State also introduced into evidence several articles appearing in the film, including a pistol, a rifle, a shotgun, ammunition, a Bible, and a red hood worn by the speaker in the films.

One film showed 12 hooded figures, some of whom carried firearms. They gathered around a large wooden cross, which they burned. No one was present other than the participants and the newsmen who made the film. Most of the words uttered during the scene were incomprehensible when the film was projected, but scattered phrases could be understood that were derogatory of Negroes and, in one instance, of Jews. Another scene on the same film showed the appellant, in Klan regalia, making a speech. The speech, in full, was as follows:

> "This is an organizers' meeting. We have had quite a few members here today which are—we have hundreds, hundreds of members throughout the State of Ohio. I can quote from a newspaper clipping from the Columbus, Ohio Dispatch, five weeks ago Sunday morning. The Klan has more members in the State of Ohio than does any other organization. We're not a revengent organization, but if our President, our Congress, our Supreme Court, continues to suppress the white, Caucasian race, it's possible that there might have to be some revengeance taken.
>
> "We are marching on Congress July the Fourth, four hundred thousand strong. From there we are dividing into two groups, one group to march on St. Augustine, Florida, the other group to march into Mississippi. Thank you."

The second film showed six hooded figures one of whom, later identified as the appellant, repeated a speech very similar to that recorded on the first film. The reference to the possibility of "revengeance" was omitted, and one sentence was added: "Personally, I believe the nigger should be returned to Africa, the Jew returned to Israel." Though some of the figures in the films carried weapons, the speaker did not.

The Ohio Criminal Syndicalism Statute was enacted in 1919. From 1917 to 1920, identical or similar laws were adopted by 20 States and two territories. E. Dowell, A History of Criminal Syndicalism Legislation in the United States 21 (1939). In 1927, this Court sustained the constitutionality of California's Criminal Syndicalism Act, * * * the text of which is quite similar to that of the laws of Ohio. Whitney v. California, 274 U.S. 357 (1927). The Court upheld the statute on the ground that, without more, "advocating" violent means to effect political and economic change involves such danger to the security of the State that the State may outlaw it. * * * But *Whitney* has been thoroughly discredited by later decisions. See Dennis v. United States, 341 U.S. 494, at 507 (1951). These later decisions have fashioned the principle that the constitutional guarantees of free speech and free press do not permit a State to forbid or proscribe advocacy of the use of force or of law violation except where such advocacy is directed to inciting or producing imminent lawless action and is likely to incite or produce such action.[2] As we said in Noto v. United States, 367 U.S. 290, 297–298 (1961), "the mere abstract teaching * * * of the moral propriety or even moral necessity for a resort to force and violence, is not the same as preparing a group for violent action and steeling it to such action." See also Herndon v. Lowry, 301 U.S. 242, 259–261 (1937); Bond v. Floyd, 385 U.S. 116, 134 (1966). A statute which fails to draw this distinction impermissibly intrudes upon the freedoms guaranteed by the First and Fourteenth Amendments. It sweeps within its condemnation speech which our Constitution has immunized from governmental control. Cf. Yates v. United States, 354 U.S. 298 (1957); De Jonge v. Oregon, 299 U.S. 353 (1937); Stromberg v. California, 283 U.S. 359 (1931). See also United States v. Robel, 389 U.S. 258 (1967); Keyishian v. Board of Regents, 385 U.S. 589 (1967); Elfbrandt v. Russell, 384 U.S. 11 (1966); Aptheker v. Secretary of State, 378 U.S. 500 (1964); Baggett v. Bullitt, 377 U.S. 360 (1964).

Measured by this test, Ohio's Criminal Syndicalism Act cannot be sustained. The Act punishes persons who "advocate or teach the duty, necessity, or propriety" of violence "as a means of accomplishing industrial or political reform"; or who publish or circulate or display any book or paper containing such advocacy; or who "justify" the

---

2. It was on the theory that the Smith Act, 54 Stat. 670, 18 U.S.C. § 2385, embodied such a principle and that it had been applied only in conformity with it that this Court sustained the Act's constitutionality. Dennis v. United States, 341 U.S. 494 (1951). That this was the basis for *Dennis* was emphasized in Yates v. United States, 354 U.S. 298, 320–324 (1957), in which the Court overturned convictions for advocacy of the forcible overthrow of the Government under the Smith Act, because the trial judge's instructions had allowed conviction for mere advocacy, unrelated to its tendency to produce forcible action.

commission of violent acts "with intent to exemplify, spread or advocate the propriety of the doctrines of criminal syndicalism" or who "voluntarily assemble" with a group formed "to teach or advocate the doctrines of criminal syndicalism." Neither the indictment nor the trial judge's instructions to the jury in any way refined the statute's bald definition of the crime in terms of mere advocacy not distinguished from incitement to imminent lawless action.

Accordingly, we are here confronted with a statute which, by its own words and as applied, purports to punish mere advocacy and to forbid, on pain of criminal punishment, assembly with others merely to advocate the described type of action. Such a statute falls within the condemnation of the First and Fourteenth Amendments. The contrary teaching of *Whitney v. California, supra,* cannot be supported, and that decision is therefore overruled.

Reversed.

MR. JUSTICE BLACK, concurring.

I agree with the views expressed by Mr. Justice Douglas in his concurring opinion in this case that the "clear and present danger" doctrine should have no place in the interpretation of the First Amendment. I join the Court's opinion, which, as I understand it, simply cites Dennis v. United States, 341 U.S. 494 (1951), but does not indicate any agreement on the Court's part with the "clear and present danger" doctrine on which *Dennis* purported to rely.

MR. JUSTICE DOUGLAS, concurring.

While I join the opinion of the Court, I desire to enter a *caveat.*

The "clear and present danger" test was adumbrated by Mr. Justice Holmes in a case arising during World War I—a war "declared" by the Congress, not by the Chief Executive. * * *

* * *

* * * The dissents in *Abrams, Schaefer,* and *Pierce* show how easily "clear and present danger" is manipulated to crush what Brandeis called "[t]he fundamental right of free men to strive for better conditions through new legislation and new institutions" by argument and discourse (Pierce v. United States, *supra,* at 273) even in time of war. Though I doubt if the "clear and present danger" test is congenial to the First Amendment in time of a declared war, I am certain it is not reconcilable with the First Amendment in days of peace.

* * *

The Court in Herndon v. Lowry, 301 U.S. 242, overturned a conviction for exercising First Amendment rights to incite insurrection because of lack of evidence of incitement. Id., at 259–261. And see Hartzel v. United States, 322 U.S. 680. In Bridges v. California, 314 U.S. 252, 261–263, we approved the "clear and present danger" test in an elaborate dictum that tightened it and confined it to a narrow category. But in Dennis v. United States, 341 U.S. 494, we opened wide the door, distorting the "clear and present danger" test beyond recognition.

In that case the prosecution dubbed an agreement to teach the Marxist creed a "conspiracy." The case was submitted to a jury on a charge that the jury could not convict unless it found that the defendants "intended to overthrow the Government 'as speedily as circumstances would permit.'" * * * The Court sustained convictions under that charge, construing it to mean a determination of "'whether the gravity of the "evil," discounted by its improbability, justifies such invasion of free speech as is necessary to avoid the danger.'" *Id.*, at 510, quoting from United States v. Dennis, 183 F.2d 201, 212.

Out of the "clear and present danger" test came other offspring. Advocacy and teaching of forcible overthrow of government as an abstract principle is immune from prosecution. Yates v. United States, 354 U.S. 298, 318. But an "active" member, who has a guilty knowledge and intent of the aim to overthrow the Government by violence, Noto v. United States, 367 U.S. 290, may be prosecuted. Scales v. United States, 367 U.S. 203, 228.

Judge Learned Hand, who wrote for the Court of Appeals in affirming the judgment in *Dennis,* coined the "not improbable" test, 183 F.2d 201, 214, which this Court adopted and which Judge Hand preferred over the "clear and present danger" test. Indeed, in his book, The Bill of Rights 59 (1958), in referring to Holmes' creation of the "clear and present danger" test, he said, "I cannot help thinking that for once Homer nodded."

My own view is quite different. I see no place in the regime of the First Amendment for any "clear and present danger" test, whether strict and tight as some would make it, or free-wheeling as the Court in *Dennis* rephrased it.

When one reads the opinions closely and sees when and how the "clear and present danger" test has been applied, great misgivings are aroused. First, the threats were often loud but always puny and made serious only by judges so wedded to the status quo that critical analysis made them nervous. Second, the test was so twisted and perverted in *Dennis* as to make the trial of those teachers of Marxism an all-out political trial which was part and parcel of the cold war that has eroded substantial parts of the First Amendment.

* * *

The line between what is permissible and not subject to control and what may be made impermissible and subject to regulation is the line between ideas and overt acts.

The example usually given by those who would punish speech is the case of one who falsely shouts fire in a crowded theatre.

This is, however, a classic case where speech is brigaded with action. See Speiser v. Randall, 357 U.S. 513, 536–537 (DOUGLAS, J., concurring). They are indeed inseparable and a prosecution can be launched for the overt acts actually caused. Apart from rare instances of that kind, speech is, I think, immune from prosecution.

HESS v. INDIANA

Supreme Court of the United States, 1973.
414 U.S. 105, 94 S.Ct. 326, 38 L.Ed.2d 303.

PER CURIAM.

Gregory Hess appeals from his conviction in the Indiana courts for violating the State's disorderly conduct statute.[1] * * *

The events leading to Hess' conviction began with an antiwar demonstration on the campus of Indiana University. In the course of the demonstration, approximately 100 to 150 of the demonstrators moved into a public street and blocked the passage of vehicles. When the demonstrators did not respond to verbal directions from the sheriff to clear the street, the sheriff and his deputies began walking up the street, and the demonstrators in their path moved to the curbs on either side, joining a large number of spectators who had gathered. Hess was standing off the street as the sheriff passed him. The sheriff heard Hess utter the word "fuck" in what he later described as a loud voice and immediately arrested him on the disorderly conduct charge. It was later stipulated that what appellant had said was "We'll take the fucking street later," or "We'll take the fucking street again." Two witnesses who were in the immediate vicinity testified, apparently without contradiction, that they heard Hess' words and witnessed his arrest. They indicated that Hess did not appear to be exhorting the crowd to go back into the street, that he was facing the crowd and not the street when he uttered the statement, that his statement did not appear to be addressed to any particular person or group, and that his tone, although loud, was no louder than that of the other people in the area.

Indiana's disorderly conduct statute was applied in this case to punish only spoken words. It hardly needs repeating that "[t]he constitutional guarantees of freedom of speech forbid the States to punish the use of words or language not within 'narrowly limited classes of speech.'" Gooding v. Wilson, [405 U.S. 518,] 521–522 [(1972)]. The words here did not fall within any of these "limited classes." In the first place, it is clear that the Indiana courts specifically abjured any suggestion that Hess' words could be punished as obscene under Roth v. United States, 354 U.S. 476 (1957), and its progeny. Indeed, after Cohen v. California, 403 U.S. 15 (1971), such a contention with regard to the language at issue would not be tenable. By the same token, any suggestion that Hess' speech amounted to "fighting words," Chaplinsky v. New Hampshire, 315 U.S. 568 (1942), could not withstand scrutiny. Even if under other circumstances this language could be regarded as a personal insult, the evidence is undisputed that Hess' statement was not directed to any person or group in particular. Although the sheriff testified that he was offended by the

---

1. "Whoever shall act in a loud, boisterous or disorderly manner so as to disturb the peace and quiet of any neighborhood or family, by loud or unusual noise, or by tumultuous or offensive behavior, threatening, traducing, quarreling, challenging to fight or fighting, shall be deemed guilty of disorderly conduct, and upon conviction, shall be fined in any sum not exceeding five hundred dollars [$500] to which may be added imprisonment for not to exceed one hundred eighty [180] days."

language, he also stated that he did not interpret the expression as being directed personally at him, and the evidence is clear that appellant had his back to the sheriff at the time. Thus, under our decisions, the State could not punish this speech as "fighting words." Cantwell v. Connecticut, 310 U.S. 296, 309 (1940); *Cohen v. California, supra,* at 20.

In addition, there was no evidence to indicate that Hess' speech amounted to a public nuisance in that privacy interests were being invaded. "The ability of government, consonant with the Constitution, to shut off discourse solely to protect others from hearing it is * * * dependent upon a showing that substantial privacy interests are being invaded in an essentially intolerable manner." *Cohen v. California, supra,* at 21. The prosecution made no such showing in this case.

The Indiana Supreme Court placed primary reliance on the trial court's finding that Hess' statement "was intended to incite further lawless action on the part of the crowd in the vicinity of appellant and was likely to produce such action." * * * At best, however, the statement could be taken as counsel for present moderation; at worst, it amounted to nothing more than advocacy of illegal action at some indefinite future time. This is not sufficient to permit the State to punish Hess' speech. Under our decisions, "the constitutional guarantees of free speech and free press do not permit a State to forbid or proscribe advocacy of the use of force or of law violation except where such advocacy is directed to inciting or producing *imminent* lawless action and is likely to incite or produce such action." Brandenburg v. Ohio, 395 U.S. 444, 447 (1969). (Emphasis added.) * * * Since the uncontroverted evidence showed that Hess' statement was not directed to any person or group of persons, it cannot be said that he was advocating, in the normal sense, any action. And since there was no evidence, or rational inference from the import of the language, that his words were intended to produce, and likely to produce, *imminent* disorder, those words could not be punished by the State on the ground that they had "a 'tendency to lead to violence.'" * * *

Accordingly, the motion to proceed *in forma pauperis* is granted and the judgment of the Supreme Court of Indiana is reversed.

Mr. Justice Rehnquist, with whom The Chief Justice and Mr. Justice Blackmun join, dissenting.

* * *

The simple explanation for the result in this case is that the majority has interpreted the evidence differently from the courts below. In doing so, however, I believe the Court has exceeded the proper scope of our review. Rather than considering the "evidence" in the light most favorable to the appellee and resolving credibility questions against the appellant, as many of our cases have required, the Court has instead fashioned its own version of events from a paper record, some "uncontroverted evidence," and a large measure of conjecture. Since this is not the traditional function of any appellate court, and is surely not a wise or proper use of the authority of this Court, I dissent.

COHEN v. CALIFORNIA

Supreme Court of the United States, 1971.
403 U.S. 15, 91 S.Ct. 1780, 29 L.Ed.2d 284.

MR. JUSTICE HARLAN delivered the opinion of the Court.

This case may seem at first blush too inconsequential to find its way into our books, but the issue it presents is of no small constitutional significance.

Appellant Paul Robert Cohen was convicted in the Los Angeles Municipal Court of violating that part of California Penal Code § 415 which prohibits "maliciously and willfully disturb[ing] the peace or quiet of any neighborhood or person * * * by * * * offensive conduct * * *". He was given 30 days' imprisonment. The facts upon which his conviction rests are detailed in the opinion of the Court of Appeal of California, Second Appellate District, as follows:

> "On April 26, 1968, the defendant was observed in the Los Angeles County Courthouse in the corridor outside of division 20 of the municipal court wearing a jacket bearing the words 'Fuck the Draft' which were plainly visible. There were women and children present in the corridor. The defendant was arrested. The defendant testified that he wore the jacket knowing that the words were on the jacket as a means of informing the public of the depth of his feelings against the Vietnam War and the draft.
>
> "The defendant did not engage in, nor threaten to engage in, nor did anyone as the result of his conduct in fact commit or threaten to commit any act of violence. The defendant did not make any loud or unusual noise, nor was there any evidence that he uttered any sound prior to his arrest." * * *

In affirming the conviction the Court of Appeal held that "offensive conduct" means "behavior which has a tendency to provoke *others* to acts of violence or to in turn disturb the peace," and that the State had proved this element because, on the facts of this case, "[i]t was certainly reasonably foreseeable that such conduct might cause others to rise up to commit a violent act against the person of the defendant or attempt to forcibly remove his jacket." * * * The California Supreme Court declined review by a divided vote. * * * We now reverse.

* * *

I

In order to lay hands on the precise issue which this case involves, it is useful first to canvass various matters which this record does *not* present.

The conviction quite clearly rests upon the asserted offensiveness of the *words* Cohen used to convey his message to the public. The only "conduct" which the State sought to punish is the fact of communication. Thus, we deal here with a conviction resting solely upon "speech," cf. Stromberg v. California, 283 U.S. 359 (1931), not upon any separately identifiable conduct which allegedly was intended by Cohen to be perceived by others as expressive of particular views but which, on its face, does not necessarily convey any message and hence arguably could be regulated without effectively repressing Cohen's ability to express himself. Cf. United States v. O'Brien, 391 U.S. 367 (1968). Further, the State certainly lacks power to punish Cohen for the underlying content of the message the inscription conveyed. At least so long as there is no showing of an intent to incite disobedience to or disruption of the draft, Cohen could not, consistently with the First and Fourteenth Amendments, be punished for asserting the evident position on the inutility or immorality of the draft his jacket reflected. Yates v. United States, 354 U.S. 298 (1957).

Appellant's conviction, then, rests squarely upon his exercise of the "freedom of speech" protected from arbitrary governmental interference by the Constitution and can be justified, if at all, only as a valid regulation of the manner in which he exercised that freedom, not as a permissible prohibition on the substantive message it conveys. This does not end the inquiry, of course, for the First and Fourteenth Amendments have never been thought to give absolute protection to every individual to speak whenever or wherever he pleases or to use any form of address in any circumstances that he chooses. In this vein, too, however, we think it important to note that several issues typically associated with such problems are not presented here.

In the first place, Cohen was tried under a statute applicable throughout the entire State. Any attempt to support this conviction on the ground that the statute seeks to preserve an appropriately decorous atmosphere in the courthouse where Cohen was arrested must fail in the absence of any language in the statute that would have put appellant on notice that certain kinds of otherwise permissible speech or conduct would nevertheless, under California law, not be tolerated in certain places. * * *

In the second place, as it comes to us, this case cannot be said to fall within those relatively few categories of instances where prior decisions have established the power of government to deal more comprehensively with certain forms of individual expression simply upon a showing that such a form was employed. This is not, for example, an obscenity case. Whatever else may be necessary to give rise to the States' broader power to prohibit obscene expression, such expression must be, in some significant way, erotic. Roth v. United States, 354 U.S. 476 (1957). It cannot plausibly be maintained that this vulgar allusion to the Selective Service System would conjure up such psychic stimulation in anyone likely to be confronted with Cohen's crudely defaced jacket.

This Court has also held that the States are free to ban the simple use, without a demonstration of additional justifying circumstances, of so-called "fighting words," those personally abusive epithets which, when addressed to the ordinary citizen, are, as a matter of common knowledge, inherently likely to provoke violent reaction. Chaplinsky v. New Hampshire, 315 U.S. 568 (1942). While the four-letter word displayed by Cohen in relation to the draft is not uncommonly employed in a personally provocative fashion, in this instance it was clearly not "directed to the person of the hearer." Cantwell v. Connecticut, 310 U.S. 296, 309 (1940). No individual actually or likely to be present could reasonably have regarded the words on appellant's jacket as a direct personal insult. Nor do we have here an instance of the exercise of the State's police power to prevent a speaker from intentionally provoking a given group to hostile reaction. Cf. Feiner v. New York, 340 U.S. 315 (1951); Terminiello v. Chicago, 337 U.S. 1 (1949). There is, as noted above, no showing that anyone who saw Cohen was in fact violently aroused or that appellant intended such a result.

Finally, in arguments before this Court, much has been made of the claim that Cohen's distasteful mode of expression was thrust upon unwilling or unsuspecting viewers, and that the State might therefore legitimately act as it did in order to protect the sensitive from otherwise unavoidable exposure to appellant's crude form of protest. Of course, the mere presumed presence of unwitting listeners or viewers does not serve automatically to justify curtailing all speech capable of giving offense. See, e.g., Organization for a Better Austin v. Keefe, 402 U.S. 415 (1971). While this Court has recognized that government may properly act in many situations to prohibit intrusion into the privacy of the home of unwelcome views and ideas which cannot be totally banned from the public dialogue, e.g., Rowan v. United States Post Office Dept., 397 U.S. 728 (1970), we have at the same time consistently stressed that "we are often 'captives' outside the sanctuary of the home and subject to objectionable speech." Id., at 738. The ability of government, consonant with the Constitution, to shut off discourse solely to protect others from hearing it is, in other words, dependent upon a showing that substantial privacy interests are being invaded in an essentially intolerable manner. Any broader view of this authority would effectively empower a majority to silence dissidents simply as a matter of personal predilections.

In this regard, persons confronted with Cohen's jacket were in a quite different posture than, say, those subjected to the raucous emissions of sound trucks blaring outside their residences. Those in the Los Angeles courthouse could effectively avoid further bombardment of their sensibilities simply by averting their eyes. And while it may be that one has a more substantial claim to a recognizable privacy interest when walking through a courthouse corridor than, for example, strolling through Central Park, surely it is nothing like the interest in being free from unwanted expression in the confines of one's own home. Cf. *Keefe, supra.* Given the subtlety and complexity of the factors involved, if Cohen's "speech" was otherwise entitled to constitutional protection, we do not think the fact that some unwilling "listeners" in a public building may have been briefly exposed to it can serve to justify this breach of the peace conviction where, as here, there was no evidence that persons powerless to avoid appellant's conduct did in fact object to it, and where that portion of the statute upon which Cohen's conviction rests evinces no concern, either on its face or as construed by the California courts, with the special plight of the captive auditor, but, instead, indiscriminately sweeps within its prohibitions all "offensive conduct" that disturbs "any neighborhood or person." Cf. *Edwards v. South Carolina, supra.*

II

Against this background, the issue flushed by this case stands out in bold relief. It is whether California can exercise, as "offensive conduct," one particular scurrilous epithet from the public discourse, either upon the theory of the court below that its use is inherently likely to cause violent reaction or upon a more general assertion that the States, acting as guardians of public morality, may properly remove this offensive word from the public vocabulary.

The rationale of the California court is plainly untenable. At most it reflects an "undifferentiated fear or apprehension of disturbance [which] is not enough to overcome the right to freedom of expression." Tinker v. Des Moines Indep. Community School Dist., 393 U.S. 503, 508 (1969). We have been shown no evidence that substantial numbers of citizens are standing ready to strike out physically at whoever may assault their sensibilities with execrations like that uttered by Cohen. There may be some persons about with such lawless and violent proclivities, but that is an insufficient base upon which to erect, consistently with constitutional values, a governmental power to force persons who wish to ventilate their dissident views into avoiding particular forms of expression. The argument amounts to little more than the self-defeating proposition that to avoid physical censorship of one who has not sought to provoke such a response by a hypothetical coterie of the violent and lawless, the States may more appropriately effectuate that censorship themselves. * * *

Admittedly, it is not so obvious that the First and Fourteenth Amendments must be taken to disable the States from punishing public utterance of this unseemly expletive in order to maintain what they regard as a suitable level of discourse within the body politic.[5] We think, however, that examination and reflection will reveal the shortcomings of a contrary viewpoint.

---

5. The *amicus* urges, with some force, that this issue is not properly before us since the statute, as construed, punishes only conduct that might cause others to react violently. However, because the opinion below appears to erect a virtually irrebuttable presumption that use of this word will produce such results, the statute as thus construed appears to impose, in effect, a flat ban on the public utterance of this word. With the case in this posture, it does not seem inappropriate to inquire whether any other rationale might properly support this result. While we think it clear, for the reasons expressed above, that no statute which merely proscribes "offensive conduct" and has been construed as broadly as this one was below can subsequently be justified in this Court as discriminating between conduct that occurs in different places or that offends only certain persons, it is not so unreasonable to seek to justify its full broad sweep on an alternate rationale such as this. Because it is not so patently clear that acceptance of the justification presently under consideration would render the statute overbroad or unconstitutionally vague, and because the answer to appellee's argument seems quite clear, we do not pass on the contention that this claim is not presented on this record.

At the outset, we cannot overemphasize that, in our judgment, most situations where the State has a justifiable interest in regulating speech will fall within one or more of the various established exceptions, discussed above but not applicable here, to the usual rule that governmental bodies may not prescribe the form or content of individual expression. Equally important to our conclusion is the constitutional backdrop against which our decision must be made. The constitutional right of free expression is powerful medicine in a society as diverse and populous as ours. It is designed and intended to remove governmental restraints from the arena of public discussion, putting the decision as to what views shall be voiced largely into the hands of each of us, in the hope that use of such freedom will ultimately produce a more capable citizenry and more perfect polity and in the belief that no other approach would comport with the premise of individual dignity and choice upon which our political system rests. See Whitney v. California, 274 U.S. 357, 375–377 (1927) (Brandeis, J., concurring).

To many, the immediate consequence of this freedom may often appear to be only verbal tumult, discord, and even offensive utterance. These are, however, within established limits, in truth necessary side effects of the broader enduring values which the process of open debate permits us to achieve. That the air may at time seem filled with verbal cacophony is, in this sense not a sign of weakness but of strength. We cannot lose sight of the fact that, in what otherwise might seem a trifling and annoying instance of individual distasteful abuse of a privilege, these fundamental societal values are truly implicated. That is why "[w]holly neutral futilities * * * come under the protection of free speech as fully as do Keats' poems or Donne's sermons," Winters v. New York, 333 U.S. 507 (1948) (Frankfurter, J., dissenting), and why "so long as the means are peaceful, the communication need not meet standards of acceptability." Organization for a Better Austin v. Keefe, 402 U.S. 415 (1971).

Against this perception of the constitutional policies involved, we discern certain more particularized considerations that peculiarly call for reversal of this conviction. First, the principle contended for by the State seems inherently boundless. How is one to distinguish this from any other offensive word? * * * For, while the particular four-letter word being litigated here is perhaps more distasteful than most others of its genre, it is nevertheless often true that one man's vulgarity is another's lyric. Indeed, we think it is largely because governmental officials cannot make principled distinctions in this area that the Constitution leaves matters of taste and style so largely to the individual.

Additionally, we cannot overlook the fact, because it is well illustrated by the episode involved here, that much linguistic expression serves a dual communicative function: it conveys not only ideas capable of relatively precise, detached explication, but otherwise inexpressible emotions as well. In fact, words are often chosen as much for their emotive as their cognitive force. We cannot sanction the view that the Constitution, while solicitous of the cognitive content of individual speech has little or no regard for that emotive function which practically speaking, may often be the more important element of the overall message sought to be communicated. Indeed, as Mr. Justice Frankfurter has said, "[o]ne of the prerogatives of American citizenship is the right to criticize public men and measures—and that means not only informed and responsible criticism but the freedom to speak foolishly and without moderation." Baumgartner v. United States, 322 U.S. 665, 673–674 (1944).

Finally, and in the same vein, we cannot indulge the facile assumption that one can forbid particular words without also running a substantial risk of suppressing ideas in the process. Indeed, governments might soon seize upon the censorship of particular words as a convenient guise for banning the expression of unpopular views. We have been able, as noted above, to discern little social benefit that might result from running the risk of opening the door to such grave results.

It is, in sum, our judgment that, absent a more particularized and compelling reason for its actions, the State may not, consistently with the First and Fourteenth Amendments, make the simple public display here involved of this single four-letter expletive a criminal offense. Because that is the only arguably sustainable rationale for the conviction here at issue, the judgment below must be reversed.

Reversed.

MR. JUSTICE BLACKMUN, with whom THE CHIEF JUSTICE and MR. JUSTICE BLACK join.

I dissent, and I do so for two reasons:

1. Cohen's absurd and immature antic, in my view, was mainly conduct and little speech. * * * The California Court of Appeal appears so to have described it, 1 Cal.App.3d 94, 100, 81 Cal.Rptr. 503, 507, and I cannot characterize it otherwise. Further, the case appears to me to be well within the sphere of Chaplinsky v. New Hampshire, 315 U.S. 568 (1942), where Mr. Justice Murphy, a known champion of First Amendment freedoms, wrote for a unanimous bench. As a consequence, this Court's agonizing over First Amendment values seem misplaced and unnecessary.

2. I am not at all certain that the California Court of Appeal's construction of § 415 is now the authoritative California construction. The Court of Appeal filed its opinion on October 22, 1969. The Supreme Court of California declined review by a four-to-three vote on December 17. See 1 Cal.App.3d at 104, 81 Cal.Rptr., at 503. A month later on January 27, 1970, the State Supreme Court in another case construed § 415, evidently for the first time. In re Bushman, 1 Cal.3d 767, 83 Cal.Rptr. 375, 463 P.2d 727. * * * Inasmuch as this Court does not dismiss this case, it ought to be remanded to the California Court of Appeal for reconsideration in the light of the subsequently rendered decision by the State's highest tribunal in *Bushman.*

MR. JUSTICE WHITE concurs in Paragraph 2 of MR. JUSTICE BLACKMUN's dissenting opinion.

B. POLITICS, PRIVACY, LIBEL,[53] AND TORT LAW

First amendment revisions of the common law and a comparison of the complexity of modern views.

> "The concept of seditious libel strikes at the very heart of democracy. Political freedom ends when government can use its powers and its courts to silence its critics. My point is not the tepid one that there should be leeway for criticism of the government. It is rather that defamation of the government is an impossible notion for a democracy. In brief, I suggest, that the presence or absence in the law of the concept of seditious libel defines the society. A society may or may not treat obscenity or contempt by publication as legal offenses without altering its basic nature. If, however, it makes seditious libel an offense, it is not a free society no matter what its other characteristics." [54]

The figure of the first amendment we have been examining in the development of free speech-free press doctrine is one of concentric circles. At its core—where the greatest protection is provided—is "political process" speech: criticism of government policy; dissent from the political status quo; direct social advocacy of alternative policies; sharply offensive attacks on prevailing conventions; denunciations of the law itself.

In the general realm of social or political advocacy, we have seen several case examples that the modern first amendment is given

---

53. "Libel" is from Latin, "libellus," the diminutive of "liber"—meaning "a book" (as in "library"—a place for books.) Generally, it is anything in print or pictures that disparages a readily identifiable person or group of persons, tending to subject them to obloquy in the community at large, or diminishing their personal standing and reputation, or subjecting them to ridicule,—anything likely to cause third parties to think ill of them and on that account to draw away. Libel is the cousin of slander, from Old French "esclandre," a variant of "escandle," from Latin "scandalum," meaning scandal. (To slander a person is thus to utter something scandalous about them.) Together libel and slander comprise the core of the private law of defamation. See, e.g., cases and discussion in G. Christie, Cases and Materials on Torts 966–1032 (1989); R. Epstein, H. Kalven, C. Gregory, Cases and Materials on Torts 1085–1176 (1984). See also Shakespeare (Othello, act III, sc. III (London 1622)):

> Who steals my purse steals trash; 'tis something, nothing;
> 'Twas mine, 'tis his, and has been slave to thousands;
> But he that filches from me my good name
> Robs me of that which not enriches him,
> And makes me poor indeed.

54. Kalven, The New York Times Case: A Note on "The Central Meaning" of the First Amendment, 1964 Sup.Ct.Rev. 191, 205. See also H. Kalven, A Worthy Tradition (1988); A. Meiklejohn, Free Speech and Its Relation to Self–Government (1948); Blasi, The Pathological Perspective and the First Amendment, 85 Colum.L.Rev. 449 (1985); Blasi, The Checking Value in First Amendment Theory, 1977 Am.B. Found.Res.J. 521; Meiklejohn, The First Amendment Is an Absolute, 1961 Sup.Ct.Rev. 245.

considerable force. The nature of the public interest must be highly substantial to trench upon such speech by means of prior restraints or criminal prosecutions brought by government. A certain amount of public disturbance and of unwelcome affront in public places may have to be endured (e.g., *Cohen*). A certain level of public anxiety and of possible real danger will have to be accepted as well. A wide range of ideological expression, exhortation and of advocacy—even advocacy of law-breaking and of violence—may be protected (e.g., under the *Brandenburg* test).[55] Consider Holmes' strong proposition still again:

> Only the emergency that makes it immediately dangerous to leave the correction of evil counsel to time warrants making any exception to the sweeping command, "Congress shall make no law * * * abridging the freedom of speech." * * * That at any rate is the theory of our Constitution. It is an experiment, as all life is an experiment. Every year if not every day we have to wager our salvation upon some prophecy based upon imperfect knowledge. While that experiment is part of our system I think that we should be eternally vigilant against attempts to check the expression of opinions that we loathe and believe to be fraught with death, unless they so imminently threaten immediate interference with the lawful and pressing purposes of the law that an immediate check is required to save the country.[56]

In synthesizing these twentieth century case law developments, a keen student of the first amendment also saw them in a larger sense as a synecdoche for the repudiation of "seditious libel" as a possible public offense. Liability for defamation of government (i.e. preserving confidence in government by the punishment of defamatory attacks on government) is an "impossible notion" in a democratic country. It cannot serve as a trigger of liability for political speech, Harry Kalven suggested. It is irreconcilable with a strong view of the first amendment itself. Thus the quotation *supra,* with which this subsection begins.[57]

---

55. For endorsing reviews of *Brandenburg* (as framing a strong general standard combining the case specific, judicially reviewable, clear-and-present danger requirement of Holmes–Brandeis plus the direct advocacy requirement of Hand in *The Masses*), see BeVier, The First Amendment and Political Speech: An Inquiry into the Substance and Limit of Principle, 30 Stan.L. Rev. 299 (1978); Gunther, Learned Hand and the Origins of Modern First Amendment Doctrine: Some Fragments of History, 27 Stan.L.Rev. 719 (1975); Strong, Fifty Years of "Clear and Present Danger": From *Schenck* to *Brandenburg*—and Beyond, 1969 Sup.Ct.Rev. 41; Comment, *Brandenburg v. Ohio*: A Speech Test for All Seasons?, 43 U.Chi.L.Rev. 151 (1975). For criticisms, see Emerson, First Amendment Doctrine and the Burger Court, 68 Calif.L.Rev. 422 (1980); Linde, "Clear and Present Danger" Reexamined: Dissonance in the *Brandenburg* Concerto, 22 Stan.L. Rev. 1163 (1970).

56. The familiar quotation is from his dissent in *Abrams*. (And recall the Brandeis dictum, in *Whitney v. California,* that even "[t]he fact that speech is likely to result in some violence or in destruction of property is not enough to justify its suppression. There must be the probability of serious injury to the State. Among free men, the deterrents ordinarily to be applied to prevent crime are education and punishment for violation of the law, not abridgement of the rights of free speech and assembly.")

57. Again, the origin of the idea is in *Abrams,* where Holmes broke from his previous views in this regard. ("I wholly disagree with the argument that the First

At some general level of suitable abstraction, it is likely that nearly everyone will agree with this view—if merely because the point is kept quite abstract. The difficulty comes in the usual way, in trying to get more down to earth. We have seen this strong view of the first amendment at work in specific cases involving prior restraints and criminal statutes in a broad range of settings, to be sure, but just how far does this general notion repudiating "seditious libel" extend?—Does it extend not just to the complete protection of defaming characterizations of government incidental to political and politicized speech, and not just to the expression of polemics that may—in the opinion of many—flagrantly mischaracterize government policy or totally misstate the reasons for that policy, but also to defamatory falsehoods of those involved in public service as part of government? Are all those who give up their privacy to seek public service to be made to pay a bitter price? Is one who steps into, or is drawn into, public controversy inviting their own destruction as some sort of constitutional price-to-be-paid?

Anticipating such questions as these even in his dissent in *Abrams*, Justice Holmes drew a cautionary distinction between "seditious libel," —statements about government that may not only be critical but also false-in-fact and yet cannot on that account be made the object of prosecution [58]—and cases in which "private rights" seek more ordinary civil protection through legal process. May the more ordinary, civil tort law of libel and of slander re-enter the picture at this point? [59]

To what extent, then, may the civil law of defamation and of privacy survive the first (and fourteenth) amendment intact? [60] The following cases—opening with *New York Times Company v. Sullivan*—provide some rough guide to the Supreme Court's uneven response. The tort law of defamation has become extremely complex.[61]

Amendment left the common law of seditious libel in force. History seems to me against the notion. I had conceived that the United States through many years had shown its repentance for the Sedition Act of 1798, by repaying fines it imposed.")

58. (Only *false* defamatory statements about government were punishable under the Sedition Act of 1789, yet Holmes suggested that the history—of repaying fines levied under the Act—had repudiated the Sedition Act as being inconsistent with the first amendment.)

59. Zachariah Chafee, whose work strongly supported the Holmes-Brandeis view (that the First Amendment did not leave "the common law as to *seditious* libel in force"), also suggested that the first amendment left the general tort law of *personal civil* libel actions unimpaired: "We can all agree that the free speech clauses do not wipe out the common law as to * * * defamation of individuals." Z. Chafee, Free Speech in the United States 150 (1942).

60. Or, more generally, as Kalven put the question sharply: "At what point does the First Amendment no longer permit the states to afford *tort* remedies for harms [actually] caused by speech?" Kalven, The Reasonable Man and the First Amendment: Hill, Butts, and Walker, 1967 Sup. Ct.Rev. 267, 278. (Emphasis added.)

61. See generally, R. Smolla, Law of Defamation (1989), and chart at § 3.05; Smolla, Let the Author Beware: The Rejuvenation of the American Law of Libel, 132 U.Pa.L.Rev. 1 (1983). For a good overall review of the complexities through 1975, see Eaton, The American Law of Defamation Through Gertz v. Robert Welch, Inc. and Beyond: An Analytical Primer, 61 Va.L.Rev. 1349 (1975).

NEW YORK TIMES COMPANY v. SULLIVAN

Supreme Court of the United States, 1964.
376 U.S. 254, 84 S.Ct. 710, 11 L.Ed.2d 686.

Mr. Justice Brennan delivered the opinion of the Court.

We are required in this case to determine for the first time the extent to which the constitutional protections for speech and press limit a State's power to award damages in a libel action brought by a public official against critics of his official conduct.

Respondent L.B. Sullivan is one of the three elected Commissioners of the City of Montgomery, Alabama. He testified that he was "Commissioner of Public Affairs and the duties are supervision of the Police Department, Fire Department, Department of Cemetery and Department of Scales." He brought this civil libel action against the four individual petitioners, who are Negroes and Alabama clergymen, and against petitioner the New York Times Company, a New York corporation which publishes the New York Times, a daily newspaper. A jury in the Circuit Court of Montgomery County awarded him damages of $500,000, the full amount claimed, against all the petitioners, and the Supreme Court of Alabama affirmed. * * *

Respondent's complaint alleged that he had been libeled by statements in a full-page advertisement that was carried in the New York Times on March 29, 1960. Entitled "Heed Their Rising Voices," the advertisement began by stating that "As the whole world knows by now, thousands of Southern Negro students are engaged in widespread non-violent demonstrations in positive affirmation of the right to live in human dignity as guaranteed by the U.S. Constitution and the Bill of Rights." It went on to charge that "in their efforts to uphold these guarantees, they are being met by an unprecedented wave of terror by those who would deny and negate that document which the whole world looks upon as setting the pattern for modern freedom. * * *" Succeeding paragraphs purported to illustrate the "wave of terror" by describing certain alleged events. The text concluded with an appeal for funds for three purposes: support of the student movement, "the struggle for the right-to-vote," and the legal defense of Dr. Martin Luther King, Jr., leader of the movement, against a perjury indictment then pending in Montgomery.

The text appeared over the names of 64 persons, many widely known for their activities in public affairs, religion, trade unions, and the performing arts. Below these names, and under a line reading "we in the south who are struggling daily for dignity and freedom warmly endorse this appeal," appeared the names of the four individual petitioners and 16 other persons, all but two of whom were identified as clergymen in various Southern cities. The advertisement was signed at the bottom of the page by a "Committee to Defend Martin Luther King and the Struggle for Freedom in the South," and the officers of the Committee were listed.

Of the 10 paragraphs of text in the advertisement, the third and a portion of the sixth were the basis of respondent's claim of libel. They read as follows:

Third paragraph:

"In Montgomery, Alabama, after students sang 'My Country, 'Tis of Thee' on the State Capitol steps, their leaders were expelled from school, and truckloads of police armed with shotguns and tear-gas ringed the Alabama State College Campus. When the entire student body protested to state authorities by refusing to re-register, their dining hall was padlocked in an attempt to starve them into submission."

Sixth paragraph:

"Again and again the Southern violators have answered Dr. King's peaceful protests with intimidation and violence. They have bombed his home almost killing his wife and child. They have assaulted his person. They have arrested him seven times—for 'speeding,' 'loitering' and similar 'offenses.' And now they have charged him with 'perjury'—a *felony* under which they could imprison him for *ten years*. * * *"

Although neither of these statements mentions respondent by name, he contended that the word "police" in the third paragraph referred to him as the Montgomery Commissioner who supervised the Police Department, so that he was being accused of "ringing" the campus with police. He further claimed that the paragraph would be read as imputing to the police, and hence to him, the padlocking of the dining hall in order to starve the students into submission. As to the sixth paragraph, he contended that since arrests are ordinarily made by the police, the statement "They have arrested [Dr. King] seven times" would read as referring to him; he further contended that the "They" who did the arresting would be equated with the "They" who committed the other described acts and with the "Southern violators." Thus, he argued, the paragraph would be read as accusing the Montgomery police, and hence him, of answering Dr. King's protests with "intimidation and violence," bombing his home, assaulting his person, and charging him with perjury. Respondent and six other Montgomery residents testified that they read some or all of the statements as referring to him in his capacity as Commissioner.

It is uncontroverted that some of the statements contained in the two paragraphs were not accurate descriptions of events which occurred in Montgomery. * * * The campus dining hall was not padlocked on any occasion, and the only students who may have been barred from eating there were the few who had neither signed a preregistration application nor requested temporary meal tickets. Although the police were deployed near the campus in large numbers on three occasions, they did not at any time "ring" the campus, and they were not called to the campus in connection with the demonstration on the State Capitol steps, as the third paragraph implied. Dr. King had not been arrested seven times, but only four; and although he claimed to have been assaulted some years earlier in connection with his arrest for loitering outside a courtroom, one of the officers who made the arrest denied that there was such an assault.

On the premise that the charges in the sixth paragraph could be read as referring to him, respondent was allowed to prove that he had not participated in the events described. * * *

Respondent made no effort to prove that he suffered actual pecuniary loss as a result of the alleged libel.[3] One of his witnesses, a former employer, testified that if he had believed the statements, he doubted whether he "would want to be associated with anybody who would be a party to such things that are stated in that ad," and that he would not re-employ respondent if he believed "that he allowed the Police Department to do the things that the paper say he did." But neither this witness nor any of the others testified that he had actually believed the statements in their supposed reference to respondent.

The cost of the advertisement was approximately $4800, and it was published by the Times upon an order from a New York advertising agency acting for the signatory Committee. The agency submitted the advertisement with a letter from A. Philip Randolph, Chairman of the Committee, certifying that the persons whose names appeared on the advertisement had given their permission. Mr. Randolph was known to the Times' Advertising Acceptability Department as a responsible person, and in accepting the letter as sufficient proof of authorization it followed its established practice. There was testimony that the copy of the advertisement which accompanied the letter listed only the 64 names appearing under the text, and that the statement, "We in the south * * * warmly endorse this appeal," and the list of names thereunder, which included those of the individual petitioners, were subsequently added when the first proof of the advertisement was received. Each of the individual petitioners testified that he had not authorized use of his name, and that he had been unaware of its use until receipt of respondent's demand for a retraction. The manager of the Advertising Acceptability Department testified that he had approved the advertisement for publication because he knew nothing to cause him to believe that anything in it was false, and because it bore the endorsement of "a number of people who are well known and whose reputation" he "had no reason to question." Neither he nor anyone else at the Times made an effort to confirm the accuracy of the advertisement, either by checking it against recent Times news stories relating to some of the described events or by any other means.

Alabama law denies a public officer recovery of punitive damages in a libel action brought on account of a publication concerning his official conduct unless he first makes a written demand for a public retraction and the defendant fails or refuses to comply. Alabama Code, Tit. 7, § 914. Respondent served such a demand upon each of the petitioners. None of the individual petitioners responded to the de-

---

3. Approximately 394 copies of the edition of the Times containing the advertisement were circulated in Alabama. Of these, about 35 copies were distributed in Montgomery County. The total circulation of the Times for that day was approximately 650,000 copies.

mand, primarily because each took the position that he had not authorized the use of his name on the advertisement and therefore had not published the statements that respondent alleged had libeled him. The Times did not publish a retraction in response to the demand, but wrote respondent a letter stating, among other things, that "we * * * are somewhat puzzled as to how you think the statements in any way reflect on you" and "you might, if you desire, let us know in what respect you claim that the statements in the advertisement reflect on you." Respondent filed this suit a few days later without answering the letter. The Times did, however, subsequently publish a retraction of the advertisement upon the demand of Governor John Patterson of Alabama, who asserted that the publication charged him with "grave misconduct and * * * improper actions and omissions as Governor of Alabama and Ex–Officio Chairman of the State Board of Education of Alabama." When asked to explain why there had been a retraction for the Governor but not for respondent, the Secretary of the Times testified: "We did that because we didn't want anything that was published by the Times to be a reflection on the State of Alabama and the Governor was, as far as we could see, the embodiment of the State of Alabama and the proper representative of the State and, furthermore, we had by that time learned more of the actual facts which the ad purported to recite and, finally, the ad did refer to the action of the State authorities and the Board of Education presumably of which the Governor is the ex-officio chairman. * * *" On the other hand, he testified that he did not think that "any of the language in there referred to Mr. Sullivan."

The trial judge submitted the case to the jury under instructions that the statements in the advertisement were "libelous per se" and were not privileged, so that petitioners might be held liable if the jury found that they had published the advertisement and that the statements were made "of and concerning" respondent. The jury was instructed that, because the statements were libelous *per se,* "the law * * * implies legal injury from the bare fact of publication itself," "falsity and malice are presumed," "general damages need not be alleged or proved but are presumed," and "punitive damages may be awarded by the jury even though the amount of actual damages is neither found nor shown." An award of punitive damages—as distinguished from "general" damages, which are compensatory in nature—apparently requires proof of actual malice under Alabama law, and the judge charged that "mere negligence or carelessness is not evidence of actual malice or malice in fact, and does not justify an award of exemplary or punitive damages." He refused to charge, however, that the jury must be "convinced" of malice, in the sense of "actual intent" to harm or "gross negligence and recklessness," to make such an award, and he also refused to require that a verdict for respondent differentiate between compensatory and punitive damages. The judge rejected petitioners' contention that his rulings abridged the freedoms of speech and of the press that are guaranteed by the First and Fourteenth Amendments.

In affirming the judgment, the Supreme Court of Alabama sustained the trial judge's rulings and instructions in all respects. * * *

* * * We reverse the judgment. We hold that the rule of law applied by the Alabama courts is constitutionally deficient for failure to provide the safeguards for freedom of speech and of the press that are required by the First and Fourteenth Amendments in a libel action brought by a public official against critics of his conduct.[4] We further hold that under the proper safeguards the evidence presented in this case is constitutionally insufficient to support the judgment for respondent.

I.

We may dispose at the outset of two grounds asserted to insulate the judgment of the Alabama courts from constitutional scrutiny. The first is the proposition relied on by the State Supreme Court—that "The Fourteenth Amendment is directed against State action and not private action." That proposition has no application to this case. Although this is a civil lawsuit between private parties, the Alabama courts have applied a state rule of law which petitioners claim to impose invalid restrictions on their constitutional freedoms of speech and press. It matters not that the law has been applied in a civil action and that it is common law only, though supplemented by statute. * * *

The second contention is that the constitutional guarantees of freedom of speech and of the press are inapplicable here, at least so far as the Times is concerned, because the allegedly libelous statements were published as part of a paid, "commercial" advertisement. The argument relies on Valentine v. Chrestensen, 316 U.S. 52, where the Court held that a city ordinance forbidding street distribution of commercial and business advertising matter did not abridge the First Amendment freedoms, even as applied to a handbill having a commercial message on one side but a protest against certain official action on the other. The reliance is wholly misplaced. The Court in *Chrestensen* reaffirmed the constitutional protection for "the freedom of communicating information and disseminating opinion"; its holding was based upon the factual conclusions that the handbill was "purely commercial advertising" and that the protest against official action had been added only to evade the ordinance.

---

4. Since we sustain the contentions of all the petitioners under the First Amendment's guarantees of freedom of speech and of the press as applied to the States by the Fourteenth Amendment, we do not decide the questions presented by the other claims of violation of the Fourteenth Amendment. The individual petitioners contend that the judgment against them offends the Due Process Clause because there was no evidence to show that they had published or authorized the publication of the alleged libel, and that the Due Process and Equal Protection Clauses were violated by racial segregation and racial bias in the courtroom. The Times contends that the assumption of jurisdiction over its corporate person by the Alabama courts overreaches the territorial limits of the Due Process Clause. The latter claim is foreclosed from our review by the ruling of the Alabama courts that the Times entered a general appearance in the action and thus waived its jurisdictional objection; we cannot say that this ruling lacks "fair or substantial support" in prior Alabama decisions. See *Thompson v. Wilson*, 224 Ala. 299, 140 So. 439; compare *N.A.A.C.P. v. Alabama*, 357 U.S. 449, 454–458.

The publication here was not a "commercial" advertisement in the sense in which the word was used in *Chrestensen*. It communicated information, expressed opinion, recited grievances, protested claimed abuses, and sought financial support on behalf of a movement whose existence and objectives are matters of the highest public interest and concern. * * * That the Times was paid for publishing the advertisement is as immaterial in this connection as is the fact that newspapers and books are sold. * * * [W]e hold that if the allegedly libelous statements otherwise be constitutionally protected from the present judgment, they do not forfeit that protection because they were published in the form of a paid advertisement.

II.

Under Alabama law as applied in this case, a publication is "libelous per se" if the words "tend to injure a person * * * in his reputation" or to "bring [him] into public contempt"; the trial court stated that the standard was met if the words are such as to "injure him in his public office, or impute misconduct to him in his office or want of official integrity, or want of fidelity to a public trust. * * *" The jury must find that the words were published "of and concerning" the plaintiff, but where the plaintiff is a public official his place in the governmental hierarchy is sufficient evidence to support a finding that his reputation has been affected by statements that reflect upon the agency of which he is in charge. Once "libel per se" has been established, the defendant has no defense as to stated facts unless he can persuade the jury that they were true in all their particulars. * * *

The question before us is whether this rule of liability, as applied to an action brought by a public official against critics of his official conduct, abridges the freedom of speech and of the press that is guaranteed by the First and Fourteenth Amendments.

Respondent relies heavily, as did the Alabama courts, on statements of this Court to the effect that the Constitution does not protect libelous publications. Those statements do not foreclose our inquiry here. None of the cases sustained the use of libel laws to impose sanctions upon expression critical of the official conduct of public officials. The dictum of Pennekamp v. Florida, 328 U.S. 331, 348–349, that "when the statements amount to defamation, a judge has such remedy, in damages for libel as do other public servants," implied no view as to what remedy might constitutionally be afforded to public officials. * * * [L]ibel can claim no talismanic immunity from constitutional limitations. It must be measured by standards that satisfy the First Amendment. * * *

* * * [W]e consider this case against the background of a profound national commitment to the principle that debate on public issues should be uninhibited, robust, and wide-open, and that it may well include vehement, caustic and sometimes unpleasantly sharp attacks on government and public officials. * * * The present advertisement, as an expression of grievance and protest on one of the major public issues of our time, would seem clearly to qualify for the constitutional protection. The question is whether it forfeits that protection by the

falsity of some of its factual statements and by its alleged defamation of respondent.

Authoritative interpretations of the First Amendment guarantees have consistently refused to recognize an exception for any test of truth—whether administered by judges, juries, or administrative officials—and especially one that puts the burden of proving truth on the speaker. * * * As Madison said, "Some degree of abuse is inseparable from the proper use of every thing; and in no instance is this more true than in that of the press." 4 Elliot's Debates on the Federal Constitution (1876), p. 571. In Cantwell v. Connecticut, 310 U.S. 296, 310, the Court declared:

> "In the realm of religious faith, and in that of political belief, sharp differences arise. In both fields the tents of one man may seem the rankest error to his neighbor. To persuade others to his own point of view, the pleader, as we know, at times, resorts to exaggeration, to vilification of men who have been, or are, prominent in church or state, and even to false statement. But the people of this nation have ordained in the light of history, that, in spite of the probability of excesses and abuses, these liberties are, in the long view, essential to enlightened opinion and right conduct on the part of the citizens of a democracy."

That erroneous statement is inevitable in free debate, and that it must be protected if the freedoms of expression are to have the "breathing space" that they "need * * * to survive," N.A.A.C.P. v. Button, 371 U.S. 415, 433, was also recognized by the Court of Appeals for the District of Columbia Circuit in Sweeney v. Patterson, 128 F.2d 457, 458 (1942), cert. denied, 317 U.S. 678. Judge Edgerton spoke for a unanimous court which affirmed the dismissal of a Congressman's libel suit based upon a newspaper article charging him with anti-Semitism in opposing a judicial appointment. * * *

Injury to official reputation affords no more warrant for repressing speech that would otherwise be free than does factual error. Where judicial officers are involved, this Court has held that concern for the dignity and reputation of the courts does not justify the punishment as criminal contempt of criticism of the judge or his decision. Bridges v. California, 314 U.S. 252. This is true even though the utterance contains "half-truths" and "misinformation." * * * Such repression can be justified if at all, only by a clear and present danger of the obstruction of justice. * * *

If neither factual error nor defamatory content suffices to remove the constitutional shield from criticism of official conduct, the combination of the two elements is no less inadequate. This is the lesson to be drawn from the great controversy over the Sedition Act of 1798, 1 Stat. 596, which first crystallized a national awareness of the central meaning of the First Amendment. * * * The Act allowed the defendant the defense of truth, and provided that the jury were to be judges both of the law and the facts. Despite these qualifications, the Act was vigorously condemned as unconstitutional in an attack joined in by Jefferson and Madison. * * *

Although the Sedition Act was never tested in this Court, the attack upon its validity has carried the day in the court of history. Fines levied in its prosecution were repaid by Act of Congress on the ground that it was unconstitutional. * * * Jefferson, as President, pardoned those who had been convicted and sentenced under the Act and remitted their fines, stating: "I discharged every person under punishment or prosecution under the sedition law, because I considered, and now consider, that law to be a nullity, as absolute and as palpable as if Congress had ordered us to fall down and worship a golden image." * * *

There is no force in respondent's argument that the constitutional limitations implicit in the history of the Sedition Act apply only to Congress and not to the States. It is true that the First Amendment was originally addressed only to action by the Federal Government, and that Jefferson, for one, while denying the power of Congress "to controul the freedom of the press," recognized such a power in the States. See the 1804 Letter to Abigail Adams quoted in Dennis v. United States, 341 U.S. 494, 522, n. 4 (concurring opinion). But this distinction was eliminated with the adoption of the Fourteenth Amendment and the application to the States of the First Amendment's restrictions. See, e.g., Gitlow v. New York, 268 U.S. 652, 666; Schneider v. State, 308 U.S. 147, 160; Bridges v. California, 314 U.S. 252, 268; Edwards v. South Carolina, 372 U.S. 229, 235.

What a State may not constitutionally bring about by means of a criminal statute is likewise beyond the reach of its civil law of libel. The fear of damage awards under a rule such as that invoked by the Alabama courts here may be markedly more inhibiting than the fear of prosecution under a criminal statute. * * * The judgment awarded in this case—without the need for any proof of actual pecuniary loss—was one thousand times greater than the maximum fine provided by the Alabama criminal statute, and one hundred times greater than that provided by the Sedition Act. And since there is no double-jeopardy limitation applicable to civil lawsuits, this is not the only judgment that may be awarded against petitioners for the same publication. Whether or not a newspaper can survive a succession of such judgments, the pall of fear and timidity imposed upon those who would give voice to public criticism is an atmosphere in which the First Amendment freedoms cannot survive. * * *

The state rule of law is not saved by its allowance of the defense of truth. * * * A rule compelling the critic of official conduct to guarantee the truth of all his factual assertions—and to do so on pain of libel judgments virtually unlimited in amount—leads to a comparable "self-censorship." Allowance of the defense of truth, with the burden of proving it on the defendant, does not mean that only false speech will be deterred.[19] * * * Under such a rule, would-be critics of official

---

19. Even a false statement may be deemed to make a valuable contribution to

conduct may be deterred from voicing their criticism, even though it is believed to be true and even though it is in fact true, because of doubt whether it can be proved in court or fear of the expense of having to do so. They tend to make only statements which "steer far wider of the unlawful zone." * * * The rule thus dampens the vigor and limits the variety of public debate. It is inconsistent with the First and Fourteenth Amendments.

The constitutional guarantees require, we think, a federal rule that prohibits a public official from recovering damages for a defamatory falsehood relating to his official conduct unless he proves that the statement was made with "actual malice"—that is, with knowledge that it was false or with reckless disregard of whether it was false or not. * * *

Such a privilege for criticism of official conduct is appropriately analogous to the protection accorded a public official when *he* is sued for libel by a private citizen. In *Barr v. Mateo,* 360 U.S. 564, 575, this Court held the utterance of a federal official to be absolutely privileged if made "within the outer perimeter" of his duties. * * * It would give public servants an unjustified preference over the public they serve, if critics of official conduct did not have a fair equivalent of the immunity granted to the officials themselves.

We conclude that such a privilege is required by the First and Fourteenth Amendments.

III.

We hold today that the Constitution delimits a State's power to award damages for libel in actions brought by public officials against critics of their official conduct. Since this is such an action, the rule requiring proof of actual malice is applicable. While Alabama law apparently requires proof of actual malice for an award of punitive damages, where general damages are concerned malice is "presumed." Such a presumption is inconsistent with federal rule. * * * Since the trial judge did not instruct the jury to differentiate between general and punitive damages, it may be that the verdict was wholly an award of one or the other. But it is impossible to know, in view of the general verdict returned. Because of this uncertainty, the judgment must be reversed and the case remanded. * * *

Since respondent may seek a new trial, we deem that considerations of effective judicial administration require us to review the evidence in the present record to determine whether it could constitutionally support a judgment for respondent. * * *

Applying these standards, we consider that the proof presented to show actual malice lacks the convincing clarity which the constitutional standard demands, and hence that it would not constitutionally sustain the judgment for respondent under the proper rule of law. The case of the individual petitioners requires little discussion. * * *

---

public debate, since it brings about "the clearer perception and livelier impression of truth, produced by its collision with error." Mill, On Liberty (Oxford: Blackwell, 1947), at 15; see also Milton, Aeropagitica, in Prose Works (Yale, 1959, Vol. II, at 561).

As to the Times, we similarly conclude that the facts do not support a finding of malice. The statement by the Times' Secretary that, apart from the padlocking allegation, he thought the advertisement was "substantially correct," affords no constitutional warrant for the Alabama Supreme Court's conclusion that it was a "cavalier ignoring of the falsity of the advertisement [from which] the jury could not have but been impressed with the bad faith of The Times, and its maliciousness inferable therefrom." The statement does not indicate malice at the time of the publication; even if the advertisement was not "substantially correct"—although respondent's own proofs tend to show that it was—that opinion was at least a reasonable one, and there was no evidence to impeach the witness' good faith in holding it. The Times' failure to retract upon respondent's demand, although it later retracted upon the demand of Governor Patterson, is likewise not adequate evidence of malice for constitutional purposes. Whether or not a failure to retract may ever constitute such evidence, there are two reasons why it does not here. *First,* the letter written by the Times reflected a reasonable doubt on its part as to whether the advertisement could reasonably be taken to refer to respondent at all. *Second,* it was not a final refusal, since it asked for an explanation on this point—a request that respondent chose to ignore. Nor does the retraction upon the demand of the Governor supply the necessary proof. It may be doubted that a failure to retract which is not itself evidence of malice can retroactively become such by virtue of a retraction subsequently made to another party. But in any event that did not happen here, since the explanation given by the Times' Secretary for the distinction drawn between respondent and the Governor was a reasonable one, the good faith of which was not impeached.

Finally, there is evidence that the Times published the advertisement without checking its accuracy against the news stories in the Times' own files. The mere presence of the stories in the files does not, of course, establish that the Times "knew" the advertisement was false, since the state of mind required for actual malice would have to be brought home to the persons in the Times' organization having responsibility for the publication of the advertisement. With respect to the failure of those persons to make the check, the record shows that they relied upon their knowledge of the good reputation of many of whose names were listed as sponsors of the advertisement, and upon the letter from A. Philip Randolph, known to them as a responsible individual, certifying that the use of the names was authorized. There was testimony that the persons handling the advertisement saw nothing in it that would render it unacceptable under the Times' policy of rejecting advertisements containing "attacks of a personal character"; their failure to reject it on this ground was not unreasonable. We think the evidence against the Times supports at most a finding of negligence in failing to discover the misstatements, and is constitutionally insufficient to show the recklessness that is required for a finding of actual malice. * * *

We also think the evidence was constitutionally defective in another respect: it was incapable of supporting the jury's finding that the allegedly libelous statements were made "of and concerning" respondent. * * * There was no reference to respondent in the advertisement, either by name or official position. A number of the allegedly libelous statements—the charges that the dining hall was padlocked and that Dr. King's home was bombed, his person assaulted, and a perjury prosecution instituted against him—did not even concern the police; despite the ingenuity of the arguments which would attach this significance to the word "They," it is plain that these statements could not reasonably be read as accusing respondent of personal involvement in the acts in question. The statements upon which respondent principally relies as referring to him are the two allegations that did concern the police or police functions: that "truckloads of police * * * ringed the Alabama State College Campus" after the demonstration on the State Capitol steps, and that Dr. King had been "arrested * * * seven times." These statements were false only in that the police had been "deployed near" the campus but had not actually "ringed" it and had not gone there in connection with the State Capitol demonstration, and in that Dr. King had been arrested only four times. The ruling that these discrepancies between what was true and what was asserted were sufficient to injure respondent's reputation may itself raise constitutional problems, but we need not consider them here. Although the statements may be taken as referring to the police, they did not on their face make even an oblique reference to respondent as an individual. Support for the asserted reference must, therefore, be sought in the testimony of respondent's witnesses. But none of them suggested any basis for the belief that respondent himself was attacked in the advertisement beyond the bare fact that he was in overall charge of the Police Department and thus bore official responsibility for police conduct; to the extent that some of the witnesses thought respondent to have been charged with ordering or approving the conduct or otherwise being personally involved in it, they based this notion not on any statements in the advertisement, and not on any evidence that he had in fact been so involved, but solely on the unsupported assumption that, because of his official position, he must have been. * * * We hold that such a proposition may not constitutionally be utilized to establish that an otherwise impersonal attack on governmental operations was a libel of an official responsible for those operations. Since it was relied on exclusively here, and there was no other evidence to connect the statements with respondent, the evidence was constitutionally insufficient to support a finding that the statements referred to respondent.

The judgment of the Supreme Court of Alabama is reversed and the case is remanded to that court for further proceedings not inconsistent with this opinion.

Reversed and remanded.

MR. JUSTICE BLACK, with whom MR. JUSTICE DOUGLAS joins, concurring.

I concur in reversing this half-million-dollar judgment against the New York Times Company and the four individual defendants. In reversing the Court holds that "the Constitution delimits a State's power to award damages for libel in actions brought by public officials against critics of their official conduct." * * * I base my vote to reverse on the belief that the First and Fourteenth Amendments not merely "delimit" a State's power to award damages to "public officials against critics of their official conduct" but completely prohibit a State from exercising such a power. The Court goes on to hold that a State can subject such critics to damages if "actual malice" can be proved against them. "Malice," even as defined by the Court, is an elusive, abstract concept, hard to prove and hard to disprove. The requirement that malice be proved provides at best an evanescent protection for the right critically to discuss public affairs and certainly does not measure up to the sturdy safeguard embodied in the First Amendment. Unlike the Court, therefore, I vote to reverse exclusively on the ground that the Times and the individual defendants had an absolute, unconditional constitutional right to publish in the Times advertisement their criticisms of the Montgomery agencies and officials. I do not base my vote to reverse on any failure to prove that these individual defendants signed the advertisement or that their criticism of the Police Department was aimed at the plaintiff Sullivan, who was then the Montgomery City Commissioner having supervision of the city's police; for present purposes I assume these things were proved. Nor is my reason for reversal the size of the half-million-dollar judgment, large as it is. If Alabama has constitutional power to use its civil libel law to impose damages on the press for criticizing the way public officials perform or fail to perform their duties, I know of no provision in the Federal Constitution which either expressly or impliedly bars the State from fixing the amount of damages.

The half-million-dollar verdict does give dramatic proof, however, that state libel laws threaten the very existence of an American press virile enough to publish unpopular views on public affairs and bold enough to criticize the conduct of public officials. * * *

In my opinion the Federal Constitution has dealt with this deadly danger to the press in the only way possible without leaving the press open to destruction—by granting the press an absolute immunity for criticism of the way public officials do their public duty. * * *

* * *

We would, I think, more faithfully interpret the First Amendment by holding that at the very least it leaves the people and the press free to criticize officials and discuss public affairs with impunity. * * * An unconditional right to say what one pleases about public affairs is what I consider to be the minimum guarantee of the First Amendment.[6]

I regret that the Court has stopped short of this holding indispensable to preserve our free press from destruction.

MR. JUSTICE GOLDBERG, with whom MR. JUSTICE DOUGLAS joins, concurring in the result.

The Court today announces a constitutional standard which prohibits "a public official from recovering damages for a defamatory false-

---

6. Cf. Meiklejohn, Free Speech and Its Relation to Self–Government (1948).

hood relating to his official conduct unless he proves that the statement was made with 'actual malice'—that is, with knowledge that it was false or with reckless disregard of whether it was false or not." * * * The Court thus rules that the Constitution gives citizens and newspapers a "conditional privilege" immunizing nonmalicious misstatements of fact regarding the official conduct of a government officer. The impressive array of history and precedent marshaled by the Court, however, confirms my belief that the Constitution affords greater protection than that provided by the Court's standard to citizen and press in exercising the right of public criticism.

In my view, the First and Fourteenth Amendments to the Constitution afford to the citizen and to the press an absolute, unconditional privilege to criticize official conduct despite the harm which may flow from excesses and abuses. The prized American right "to speak one's mind," cf. Bridges v. California, 314 U.S. 252, 270, about public officials and affairs needs "breathing space to survive," N.A.A.C.P. v. Button, 371 U.S. 415, 433. The right should not depend upon a probing by the jury of the motivation [2] of the citizen or press. The theory of our Constitution is that every citizen may speak his mind and every newspaper express its view on matters of public concern and may not be barred from speaking or publishing because those in control of government think that what is said or written is unwise, unfair, false, or malicious. In a democratic society, one who assumes to act for the citizens in an executive, legislative, or judicial capacity must expect that his official acts will be commented upon and criticized. Such criticism cannot, in my opinion, be muzzled or deterred by the courts at the instance of public officials under the label of libel.

* * *

* * * It may be urged that deliberately and maliciously false statements have no conceivable value as free speech. That argument, however is not responsive to the real issue presented by this case, which is whether that freedom of speech which all agree is constitutionally protected can be effectively safeguarded by a rule allowing the imposition of liability upon a jury's evaluation of the speaker's state of mind. If individual citizens may be held liable in damages for strong words, which a jury finds false and maliciously motivated, there can be little doubt that public debate and advocacy will be constrained. And if newspapers, publishing advertisements dealing with public issues, thereby risk liability, there can also be little doubt that the ability of minority groups to secure publication of their views on public affairs and to seek support for their causes will be greatly diminished. * * *

2. The requirement of proving actual malice or reckless disregard may, in the mind of the jury, add little to the requirement of proving falsity, a requirement which the Court recognizes not to be an adequate safeguard. The thought suggested by Mr. Justice Jackson in United States v. Ballard, 322 U.S. 78, 92–93, is relevant here: "[A]s a matter of either practice or philosophy I do not see how we can separate an issue as to what is believed from considerations as to what is believable. The most convincing proof that one believes his statements is to show that they have been true in his experience. Likewise, that one knowingly falsified is best proved by showing that what he said happened never did happen." See note 4, *infra*.

This is not to say that the Constitution protects defamatory statements directed against the private conduct of a public official or private citizen. Freedom of press and of speech insures that government will respond to the will of the people and that changes may be obtained by peaceful means. Purely private defamation has little to do with the political ends of a self-governing society. The imposition of liability for private defamation does not abridge the freedom of public speech or any other freedom protected by the First Amendment.[4] This, of course, cannot be said "where public officials are concerned or where public matters are involved. * * * [O]ne main function of the First Amendment is to ensure ample opportunity for the people to determine and resolve public issues. Where public matters are involved, the doubts should be resolved in favor of freedom of expression rather than against it." * * *

* * *

The conclusion that the Constitution affords the citizen and the press an absolute privilege for criticism of official conduct does not leave the public official without defenses against unsubstantiated opinions or deliberate misstatements. * * * The public official certainly has equal if not greater access than most private citizens to media of communication. In any event, despite the possibility that some excesses and abuses may go unremedied, we must recognize that "the people of this nation have ordained in the light of history, that, in spite of the probability of excesses and abuses, [certain] liberties are, in the long view, essential to enlightened opinion and right conduct on the part of the citizens of a democracy." *Cantwell v. Connecticut,* 310 U.S. 296, 310. As Mr. Justice Brandeis correctly observed, "sunlight is the most powerful of all disinfectants." [7]

For these reasons, I strongly believe that the Constitution accords citizens and press an unconditional freedom to criticize official conduct. It necessarily follows that in a case such as this, where all agree that the allegedly defamatory statements related to official conduct, the judgments for libel cannot constitutionally be sustained.

NOTE

In *New York Times v. Sullivan,*[62] doubtless the noteworthy point is the direct comparison the Court drew between a particular category of

---

4. In most cases, as in the case at bar, there will be little difficulty in distinguishing defamatory speech relating to private conduct from that relating to official conduct. I recognize, of course, that there will be a gray area. The difficulties of applying a public-private standard are, however, certainly a different genre from those attending the differentiation between a malicious and nonmalicious state of mind. If the constitutional standard is to be shaped by a concept of malice, the speaker takes the risk not only that the jury will inaccurately determine his state of mind but also that the jury will fail properly to apply the constitutional standard set by the elusive concept of malice. * * *

7. See Freund, The Supreme Court of the United States (1949), p. 61.

62. See also Garrison v. Louisiana, 379 U.S. 64, 85 S.Ct. 209, 13 L.Ed.2d 125 (1964) (defamation of state court judges by local prosecutor protected by *Sullivan* from criminal defamation prosecution absent "malice" as defined in *Sullivan*).

civil libel actions and the general category of classic seditious libel actions, such that the two should be treated alike. A particular private libel action—one "brought by public officials against critics of their official conduct," carries with it virtually all the dampening effects historically associated with criminal seditious libel prosecutions—prosecutions also based on charges of false claims, albeit false claims about the government itself. The chilling prospect of having to answer in damages to the first kind of case (albeit a case privately brought in a civil proceeding by a public official at his or her own expense) is, by the Court, likened to the chilling prospect of having to answer to a seditious libel prosecution similarly based on a claim of false facts. Accordingly, if nonreckless factual inaccuracy would not sustain a successful prosecution of the latter sort despite the public damage such as it may be from the broadcast of the false statements thus made, then such nonreckless factual inaccuracy cannot be an occasion to be made to answer in a private civil action brought by the public official, albeit an action brought separately as a private, civil action for libel, for damages, in tort. The correction of error in each instance must rest with such resources of countervailing speech as the government (in the one case) and the public official (in the other case) can command, absent "malice." [63]—Insofar as that effort may not succeed in correcting the error, the residue of loss is to be treated by the courts as *damnum absque injuria*. The imperatives of the first amendment are said to require no less.[64]

63. "Malice" is defined specially as a minimum level of scienter: proof by evidence of convincing clarity that the statements were not merely false in fact but made under circumstances demonstrating a reckless disregard and indifference to truth or falsity,—"that the defendant in fact entertained serious doubts as to the truth of his publication," St. Amant v. Thompson, 390 U.S. 727, 731, 88 S.Ct. 1323, 1325–26, 20 L.Ed.2d 262, 267 (1968). It does not go to motive such as profit or self-interest in office seeking, etc.,—this does not satisfy the *Sullivan* standard. (See also Hustler Magazine v. Falwell, 485 U.S. 46, 108 S.Ct. 876, 99 L.Ed.2d 41 (1988); Beckley Newspapers Corp. v. Hanks, 389 U.S. 81, 82, 88 S.Ct. 197, 198–99, 19 L.Ed.2d 248, 250 (1967)).

64. Is it arguable, however, that the first amendment should not be interpreted in this manner, at least not insofar as the plaintiff may not seek damages but only correction or retraction of the false statements? Cf. a modified libel remedy furnished by state law that (a) does not require proof of "malice" to compel a published retraction but (b) disallows money damages absent proof of malice. Wherein is the undue "chilling effect" on the publisher obliged simply to correct the original error by court order, after a full adversary hearing in which the plaintiff has shown the statements made were untrue?—Even supposing the "government" as such might not be deemed entitled to any such remedy, why not the injured person, pursuant to a personal civil suit, recovering merely their costs and attorneys' fees? Cf. F. Haiman, Speech and Law in a Free Society 48–51 (1981); Franklin, Good Names and Bad Law: A Critique of Libel Law and a Proposal, 18 U.S.F.L.Rev. 1, 10 (1983); Ingber, Defamation: A Conflict Between Reason and Decency, 65 Va.L.Rev. 7815 (1979); Note, Vindication of the Reputation of a Public Official, 80 Harv.L.Rev. 1730 (1967). Aside from defense fees with which publishers might still be concerned when defending against such suits—a matter that might be addressed through fee-shifting provisions—is there a possible additional problem for publishers who might find themselves sued in a hostile forum?—Note, for example, where the N.Y. Times was sued, in the *Sullivan* case. Also consider this problem in light of Keeton v. Hustler Magazine, Inc., 465 U.S. 770, 104 S.Ct. 1473, 79 L.Ed.2d 790 (1984) (personal jurisdiction over defendant publisher under state long arm statute sustained in private libel action; *held*, the first amendment requires no special contacts to secure personal jurisdiction over libel defendant, i.e. publisher is suable in any place in which plaintiff can meet minimum fourteenth amendment ordinary due process stan-

On the other hand, the more removed a private party may be from having any effective means at their disposal to counter what has been falsely said of them, the less effective the Court's suggestion may seem to be. In that circumstance perhaps the first amendment ought not be regarded as erecting so severe a barrier to an ordinary tort action in defamation. And accordingly one might suppose that the first amendment ratio decidendi of *New York Times v. Sullivan* will not erect the same barriers against more ordinary defamation suits, i.e. those not involving public officials or their official conduct.[65] Perhaps the suggestion of concentric circles may itself be serviceable still again in describing these sorts of distinctions—of different first amendment standards in respect to different kinds of libel cases—depending upon who has brought the particular tort action, the subject of the claim, and the nature of the defendant as well. The case law refinements since *New York Times v. Sullivan* represent three decades of drawing the lines.

TIME, INC. v. HILL

Supreme Court of the United States, 1967.
385 U.S. 374, 87 S.Ct. 534, 17 L.Ed.2d 456.

MR. JUSTICE BRENNAN delivered the opinion of the Court.

The question in this case is whether appellant, publisher of Life Magazine, was denied constitutional protections of speech and press by the application by the New York courts of §§ 50–51 of the New York Civil Rights Law to award appellee damages on allegations that Life falsely reported that a new play portrayed an experience suffered by appellee and his family.

The article appeared in Life in February 1955. It was entitled "True Crime Inspires Tense Play," with the subtitle, "The ordeal of a family trapped by convicts gives Broadway a new thriller, 'The Desperate Hours.'" The text of the article reads as follows:

> "Three years ago Americans all over the country read about the desperate ordeal of the James Hill family, who were held prisoners in their home outside Philadelphia by three escaped convicts. Later they read about it in Joseph Hayes's novel, *The Desperate Hours*, inspired by the family's experience. Now they can see the story re-enacted in Hayes's Broadway play based on the book, and next year will see it in his

---

dards). Cf. also Miami Herald Pub. Co. v. Tornillo, 418 U.S. 241, 94 S.Ct. 2831, 41 L.Ed.2d 730 (1974).

65. So the majority reads the first amendment requirement of proof of "malice" in a libel action only in respect to "a State's power to award damages for libel in actions brought by public officials against critics of their official conduct." Even the Black–Goldberg–Douglas position that would furnish an absolute immunity for defamation "related to official conduct" offers no such immunity unless the defamation does relate to "official conduct." And, they insist, the line will not be difficult to draw. ("In most cases * * * there will be little difficulty in distinguishing defamatory speech relating to private conduct from that relating to official conduct.").

movie, which has been filmed but is being held up until the play has a chance to pay off.

"The play, directed by Robert Montgomery and expertly acted, is a heart-stopping account of how a family rose to heroism in a crisis. LIFE photographed the play during its Philadelphia tryout, transported some of the actors to the actual house where the Hills were besieged. On the next page scenes from the play are re-enacted on the site of the crime."

The pictures on the ensuing two pages included an enactment of the son being "roughed up" by one of the convicts, entitled "brutish convict," a picture of the daughter biting the hand of a convict to make him drop a gun, entitled "daring daughter," and one of the father throwing his gun through the door after a "brave try" to save his family is foiled.

The James Hill referred to in the article is the appellee. He and his wife and five children involuntarily became the subjects of a front-page news story after being held hostage by three escaped convicts in their suburban, Whitemarsh, Pennsylvania, home for 19 hours on September 11–12, 1952. The family was released unharmed. In an interview with newsmen after the convicts departed, appellee stressed that the convicts had treated the family courteously, had not molested them, and had not been at all violent. The convicts were thereafter apprehended in a widely publicized encounter with the police which resulted in the killing of two of the convicts. Shortly thereafter the family moved to Connecticut. The appellee discouraged all efforts to keep them in the public spotlight through magazine articles or appearances on television.

In the spring of 1953, Joseph Hayes' novel, The Desperate Hours, was published. The story depicted the experience of a family of four held hostage by three escaped convicts in the family's suburban home. But, unlike Hill's experience, the family of the story suffer violence at the hands of the convicts; the father and son are beaten and the daughter subjected to a verbal sexual insult. The book was made into a play, also entitled The Desperate Hours, and it is Life's article about the play which is the subject of appellee's action. The complaint sought damages under §§ 50–51 on allegations that the Life article was intended to, and did, give the impression that the play mirrored the Hill family's experience, which, to the knowledge of defendant " * * * was false and untrue." Appellant's defense was that the article was "a subject of legitimate news interest," "a subject of general interest and of value and concern to the public" at the time of publication, and that it was "published in good faith without any malice whatsoever * * * " A motion to dismiss the complaint for substantially these reasons was made at the close of the case and was denied by the trial judge on the ground that the proofs presented a jury question as to the truth of the article.

The jury awarded appellee $50,000 compensatory and $25,000 punitive damages. On appeal the Appellate Division of the Supreme Court ordered a new trial as to damages but sustained the jury verdict of liability. The court said as to liability:

> "Although the play was fictionalized, Life's article portrayed it as a re-enactment of the Hills' experience. It is an inescapable conclusion that this was done to advertise and attract further attention to the play, and to increase present and future magazine circulation as well. It is evident that the article cannot be characterized as a mere dissemination of news, nor even an effort to supply legitimate newsworthy information in which the public had, or might have a proper interest." 18 App.Div.2d 485, 489, 240 N.Y.S.2d 286, 290.

At the new trial on damages, a jury was waived and the court awarded $30,000 compensatory damages without punitive damages.[2]

The New York Court of Appeals affirmed the Appellate Division "on the majority and concurring opinions at the Appellate Division," two judges dissenting. 15 N.Y.2d 986, 207 N.E.2d 604. We noted probable jurisdiction of the appeal to consider the important constitutional questions of freedom of speech and press involved. * * * We reverse and remand the case to the Court of Appeals for further proceedings not inconsistent with this opinion.

I.

Since the reargument, we have had the advantage of an opinion of the Court of Appeals of New York which has materially aided us in our understanding of that court's construction of the statute. It is the opinion of Judge Keating for the court in Spahn v. Julian Messner, Inc., 18 N.Y.2d 324, 221 N.E.2d 543 (1966). The statute was enacted in 1903 following the decision of the Court of Appeals in 1902 in Roberson v. Rochester Folding Box Co., 171 N.Y. 538, 64 N.E. 442. *Roberson* was an action against defendants for adorning their flour bags with plaintiff's picture without her consent. It was grounded upon an alleged invasion of a "right of privacy," defined by the Court of Appeals to be "the claim that a man has the right to pass through this world, if he wills, without having his picture published ... or his eccentricities commented upon either in handbills, circulars, catalogues, periodicals or newspapers * * *" 171 N.Y., at 544, 64 N.E., at 443. The Court of Appeals traced the theory to the celebrated article of Warren and Brandeis, entitled The Right to Privacy, published in 1890. 4 Harv.L.Rev. 193. The Court of Appeals, however, denied the existence of such a right at common law but observed that "[the] legislative body could very well interfere and arbitrarily provide that no one should be permitted for his own selfish purpose to use the picture or the name of another for advertising purposes without his consent." * * * The legislature enacted §§ 50–51 in response to that observation.

---

2. Initially, appellee's wife was joined in the action, and was awarded $75,000 compensatory and $25,000 punitive damages by the jury. However, her action was apparently dismissed by stipulation prior to remand, because the action has since proceeded solely upon appellee's judgment.

Although "Right of Privacy" is the caption of §§ 50–51, the term nowhere appears in the text of the statute itself. The text of the statute appears to proscribe only conduct of the kind involved in *Roberson,* that is, the appropriation and use in advertising or to promote the sale of goods, of another's name, portrait or picture without his consent. An application of that limited scope would present different questions of violation of the constitutional protections for speech and press. * * *

The New York courts have, however, construed the statute to operate much more broadly. In *Spahn* the Court of Appeals stated that "Over the years since the statute's enactment in 1903, its social desirability and remedial nature have led to its being given a liberal construction consonant with its over-all purpose * * * " 18 N.Y.2d, at 327, 221 N.E.2d, at 544. Specifically, it has been held in some circumstances to authorize a remedy against the press and other communications media which publish the names, pictures, or portraits of people without their consent. Reflecting the fact, however, that such applications may raise serious questions of conflict with the constitutional protections for speech and press, decisions under the statute have tended to limit the statute's application. * * *

[I]t is particularly relevant that the Court of Appeals made crystal clear in the *Spahn* opinion that truth is a complete defense in actions under the statute based upon reports of newsworthy people or events. * * * Constitutional questions which might arise if truth were not a defense are therefore of no concern. Cf. Garrison v. Louisiana, 379 U.S. 64, 72–75.

But although the New York statute affords "little protection" to the "privacy" of a newsworthy person, "whether he be such by choice or involuntarily" the statute gives him a right of action when his name, picture, or portrait is the subject of a "fictitious" report or article. *Spahn* points up the distinction. *Spahn* was an action under the statute brought by the well-known professional baseball pitcher, Warren Spahn. He sought an injunction and damages against the unauthorized publication of what purported to be a biography of his life. The trial judge had found that "the record unequivocally establishes that the book publicizes areas of Warren Spahn's personal and private life, albeit inaccurate and distorted, and consists of a host, a preponderant percentage, of factual errors, distortions and fanciful passages. * * * "
* * * The Court of Appeals sustained the holding that in these circumstances the publication was proscribed by § 51 of the Civil Rights Law and was not within the exceptions and restrictions for newsworthy events engrafted onto the statute. * * *

* * *

If this is meant to imply that proof of knowing or reckless falsity is not essential to a constitutional application of the statute in these cases, we disagree with the Court of Appeals. We hold that the constitutional protections for speech and press preclude the application of the New York statute to redress false reports of matters of public interest in the absence of proof that the defendant published the report with knowledge of its falsity or in reckless disregard of the truth.

The guarantees for speech and press are not the preserve of political expression or comment upon public affairs, essential as those are to healthy government. * * * We have no doubt that the subject of the Life article, the opening of a new play linked to an actual incident, is a matter of public interest. "The line between the informing and the entertaining is too elusive for the protection of * * * [freedom of the press]." Winters v. New York, 333 U.S. 507, 510. Erroneous statement is no less inevitable in such a case than in the case of comment upon public affairs, and in both, if innocent or merely negligent, " * * * it must be protected if the freedoms of expression are to have the 'breathing space' that they 'need * * * to survive' * * *" *New York Times Co. v. Sullivan, supra,* at 271–272. * * *

In this context, sanctions against either innocent or negligent misstatement would present a grave hazard of discouraging the press from exercising the constitutional guarantees. Those guarantees are not for the benefit of the press so much as for the benefit of all of us. A broadly defined freedom of the press assures the maintenance of our political system and an open society. Fear of large verdicts in damage suits for innocent or merely negligent misstatement, even fear of the expense involved in their defense, must inevitably cause publishers to "steer * * * wider of the unlawful zone," New York Times Co. v. Sullivan, 376 U.S., at 279; * * *

* * *

We find applicable here the standard of knowing or reckless falsehood, not through blind application of *New York Times Co. v. Sullivan,* relating solely to libel actions by public officials, but only upon consideration of the factors which arise in the particular context of the application of the New York statute in cases involving private individuals. This is neither a libel action by a private individual nor a statutory action by a public official. Therefore, although the First Amendment principles pronounced in *New York Times* guide our conclusion, we reach that conclusion only by applying these principles in this discrete context. It therefore serves no purpose to distinguish the facts here from those in *New York Times.* Were this a libel action, the distinction which has been suggested between the relative opportunities of the public official and the private individual to rebut defamatory charges might be germane. And the additional state interest in the protection of the individual against damage to his reputation would be involved. Cf. Rosenblatt v. Baer, 383 U.S. 75, 91 (STEWART, J., concurring). Moreover, a different test might be required in a statutory action by a public official, as opposed to a libel action by a public official or a statutory action by a private individual. Different considerations might arise concerning the degree of "waiver" of the protection the State might afford. But the question whether the same standard should be applicable both to persons voluntarily and involuntarily thrust into the public limelight is not here before us.

II.

Turning to the facts of the present case, the proofs reasonably would support either a jury finding of innocent or merely negligent misstatement by Life, or a finding that Life portrayed the play as a re-enactment of the Hill family's experience reckless of the truth or with actual knowledge that the portrayal was false. * * *

* * *

III.

We do not think, however, that the instructions confined the jury to a verdict of liability based on a finding that the statements in the article were made with knowledge of their falsity or in reckless disregard of the truth. * * *

* * *

* * * Finally, nothing in the New York cases decided at the time of trial limited liability to cases of knowing or reckless falsity and *Spahn*, decided since, has left the question in doubt.

The requirement that the jury also find that the article was published "for trade purposes," as defined in the charge, cannot save the charge from constitutional infirmity. "That books, newspapers, and magazines are published and sold for profit does not prevent them from being a form of expression whose liberty is safeguarded by the First Amendment." Joseph Burstyn, Inc. v. Wilson, 343 U.S. 495, 501–502; * * *

IV.

* * *

The judgment of the Court of Appeals is set aside and the case is remanded for further proceedings not inconsistent with this opinion.

It is so ordered.

MR. JUSTICE BLACK, with whom MR. JUSTICE DOUGLAS joins, concurring. [Omitted.]

MR. JUSTICE DOUGLAS, concurring. [Omitted.]

MR. JUSTICE HARLAN, concurring in part and dissenting in part.

While I find much with which I agree in the opinion of the Court, I am constrained to express my disagreement with its view of the proper standard of liability to be applied on remand. Were the jury on retrial to find negligent rather than, as the Court requires, reckless or knowing "fictionalization," I think that federal constitutional requirements would be met.

* * *

* * * [T]here is a vast difference in the state interest in protecting individuals like Mr. Hill from irresponsibly prepared publicity and the state interest in similar protection for a public official. In *New York Times* we acknowledged public officials to be a breed from whom hardiness to exposure to charges, innuendoes, and criticisms might be

demanded and who voluntarily assumed the risk of such things by entry into the public arena. 376 U.S., at 273. But Mr. Hill came to public attention through an unfortunate circumstance not of his making rather than his voluntary actions and he can in no sense be considered to have "waived" any protection the State might justifiably afford him from irresponsible publicity. Not being inured to the vicissitudes of journalistic scrutiny such an individual is more easily injured and his means of self-defense are more limited. The public is less likely to view with normal skepticism what is written about him because it is not accustomed to seeing his name in the press and expects only a disinterested report.

The coincidence of these factors in this situation leads me to the view that a State should be free to hold the press to a duty of making a reasonable investigation of the underlying facts and limiting itself to "fair comment"[6] on the materials so gathered. Theoretically, of course, such a rule might slightly limit press discussion of matters touching individuals like Mr. Hill. But, from a pragmatic standpoint, until now the press, at least in New York, labored under the more exacting handicap of the existing New York privacy law and has certainly remained robust. * * *

* * *

MR. JUSTICE FORTAS, with whom THE CHIEF JUSTICE and MR. JUSTICE CLARK join, dissenting.

* * *

The Court today does not repeat the ringing words of so many of its members on so many occasions in exaltation of the right of privacy. Instead, it reverses a decision under the New York "Right of Privacy" statute because of the "failure of the trial judge to instruct the jury that a verdict of liability could be predicated only on a finding of knowing or reckless falsity in the publication of the Life article." In my opinion, the jury instructions, although they were not a textbook model, satisfied this standard.

* * *

NOTE

I. The Hill family, unlike Sullivan, were assuredly not public officials. Nor were they seeking public influence or office.[66] Nor was

---

6. A negligence standard has been applied in libel actions both where the underlying facts are alleged to be libelous, Layne v. Tribune Co., 108 Fla. 177, 146 So. 234, and where comment is the subject of the action, Clancy v. Daily News Corp., 202 Minn. 1, 277 N.W. 264. Similarly the press should not be constitutionally insulated from privacy actions brought by parties in the position of Mr. Hill when reasonable care has not been taken in ascertaining or communicating the underlying facts or where the publisher has not kept within the traditional boundaries of "fair comment" with relation to underlying facts and honest opinion. * * *

66. Cf., e.g., Monitor Patriot Co. v. Roy, 401 U.S. 265, 91 S.Ct. 621, 28 L.Ed.2d 35 (1971) (*Sullivan* applied to protect newspaper charge against senatorial candidate defaming him (as having a bootlegging back-the exaggerated portrayal of their experience in any sense part of any claim about official conduct, the actions of government, or the like. Accordingly, their case may seem to be quite far removed from seditious libel and justified concerns regarding inhibitions on reportage of alleged government wrongdoing or alleged abuses by public figures or of large, well-financed private organizations wielding influence, power, or authority. Why, then, the extension of the *Sullivan* "malice" standard to this kind of case, i.e. why did the Court make it as difficult in this case, as in *Sullivan,* to recover any damages at all?

II. In *Hill,* on the other hand, what was the harm for which the Hill family sought redress for *Life* magazine's larger-than-life references to their circumstances and actions during the time they were visited by the three convicts on the run? a) Injury to their standing in the community (i.e. reputation)?[67] b) The simple right not to be known *falsely* albeit not necessarily defamingly?[68] c) The right "to be left alone?"[69] d) The right to bury the past?[70] A combination of b), c) and d)? Granted that none of these need be dismissed as frivolous interests, nonetheless some tension remains: how substantially can they weigh against a freedom of the press generally to report on various events in public or in private life? More fundamentally, to what extent can one frame a suitable set of highly particularized liability rules that do not

---

ground), *held,* "a charge of criminal conduct, no matter how remote in time or place, can never be irrelevant to an official's or a candidate's fitness for office for purposes of the 'knowing falsehood or reckless disregard' rule of *New York Times v. Sullivan.*").

67. Consider the Court's following statements: "This is [not] a libel action brought by a private individual. * * * Were this a libel action, the distinction which has been suggested between the relative opportunities of the public official and the private individual to rebut defamatory charges might be germane. And the additional state interest in the protection of the individual against damage to his reputation would be involved." (Had the story been regarded as "defamatory," i.e. as damaging to Hill's reputation, the Court thus implies that they might have recovered damages (inclusive of damages for mental suffering), without need to prove "malice in fact."). Cf. *Gertz v. Robert Welch, Inc.,* 418 U.S. 323, 94 S.Ct. 2997, 41 L.Ed.2d 789 (1974).

68. Cf. *Cantrell v. Forest City Pub. Co.,* 419 U.S. 145, 95 S.Ct. 465, 42 L.Ed.2d 419 (1974) (reinstating jury award of compensatory damages for false light privacy claim for factual exaggerations by newspaper of wife's circumstances following husband's death from a collapsed highway bridge, the follow-up human interest story presenting her circumstances as more pitiful than the reporter knew to be true).—As illustrated by *Cantrell* and by *Hill,* while false light privacy claims may be distinguishable from ordinary libel claims—the "libellous" misportrayal causes (or is presumed to cause) shunning and disapproval rather than pity, sympathy, or adulation—they have the strong common feature of misrepresentations of persons as such. Not every jurisdiction permits recovery for false light claims, however, even assuming the *Sullivan* standard can be met. See, e.g., *Renwick v. News and Observer Pub. Co.,* 310 N.C. 312, 312 S.E.2d 405 (1984). See also Kalven, Privacy in Tort Law—Were Warren and Brandeis Wrong?, 31 Law & Contemp. Probs. 326 (1966); Zuckman, Invasion of Privacy—Some Communicative Torts Whose Time Has Gone, 47 Wash. & Lee L.Rev. (1990).

69. See Warren & Brandeis, The Right to Privacy, 4 Harv.L.Rev. 193 (1890).

70. Cf. *Briscoe v. Reader's Digest Ass'n,* 4 Cal.3d 529, 93 Cal.Rptr. 866, 483 P.2d 34 (1971) (Eleven years after the event, plaintiff was mentioned by name in a Reader's Digest review of truck hijackings; meantime he had become an exemplary citizen in a community unaware of his past. Publication brought the matter to light and to local attention—including his eleven-year-old daughter whom he had never told. Held, on demurrer, that the first amendment would not bar the action for publishing in alleged reckless disregard of personal privacy, though the report was unchallenged for accuracy. The Court distinguished *Time, Inc. v. Hill.* But query whether one would agree.)

also merely serve to entrench the status quo as to what shall be deemed fit to print?

Suppose, as a test of that problem, that New York law protected privacy very generally, even as Warren and Brandeis implied might be done; i.e. that absent demonstrable newsworthy interest and public information value in the disclosure of any person's particular activities, name, or personal address, no commercial publication may publish such information without first securing their consent. The exemption would of course cover a wide swath of ordinary political coverage easily inclusive of allegations of misconduct by public officials or by many private parties, including all those who are public figures with an admitted impact on public affairs. On the other hand, consider in light of such a possible law the practice of a newspaper to include the identification of crime victims (e.g., of murder, or burglary, or rape) as part of its general reporting, without securing their consent. Must the newspaper be prepared to demonstrate the "newsworthy interest" and "public information value" of each mention, in each case, or face damages for failure to censor its own reports? (Who is to say that there is no such value in information of this sort? [71])

71. See, e.g., Post, The Constitutional Concept of Public Discourse: Outrageous Opinion, Democratic Deliberation, and Hustler Magazine v. Falwell, 103 Harv.L. Rev. 601, 681 (1990) ("all speech is potentially relevant to democratic self-governance * * * "). See also Florida Star v. B.J.F., 491 U.S. 524, 109 S.Ct. 2603, 105 L.Ed.2d 443 (1989); Cox Broadcasting Corp. v. Cohn, 420 U.S. 469, 95 S.Ct. 1029, 43 L.Ed.2d 328 (1975) (report of rape victim's name secured from public record, suit for damages by the named person under state statute forbidding such practice). (It is strongly argued that publication of a rape victim's name gratuitously adds to the victim's anguish, that it may further discourage what is already regarded to be an underreported crime, and that it puts the victim at further risk of harassment and humiliation, e.g., by obscene telephone calls. It is also argued, however, that the fact of singling out rape for mandatory press censorship is itself a disservice that contributes to the status quo attitude toward rape—that it is somehow not the same as assault, attempted murder, or any other serious crime, and that state laws and press custom prohibiting its full and frank reporting are part of the problem and not any part of the answer. Suppose, moreover, a given newspaper strongly agrees with this latter view.—So, consistent with the first amendment, who is to decide?)

At the same time, and under just such a general statute as posited in the text, consider newspaper accurate identification of crime arrestees, i.e. the names of persons arrested for and charged with—but not yet either tried or convicted of crimes. How should one feel about this?—Is the one (publication of alleged crime victims' names) prohibitable? Is the other (publication of the accused person's name) nonetheless all right? Why?—Because there is a more legitimate public interest in knowing the one rather than the other? How so? Because the resulting harm or prejudice or anguish is manifestly greater in the one instance than in the other instance? Who says? What, then, is the difference to be, if any, in saying which may be forbidden and which not? (Cf. the Supreme Court's defense of editorial choice in Miami Herald Pub. Co. v. Tornillo, 418 U.S. 241, 94 S.Ct. 2831, 41 L.Ed.2d 730 (1974).)

Suppose there were no statutory restriction on the full and accurate reporting of crimes, and a newspaper accurately reports a particular crime. Suppose, however, the crime victim subsequently sues the newspaper for damages after being terrorized by the culprit who learned of her name and address from reading the local newspaper. May the victim recover on a theory of negligence, i.e. that the newspaper knew or ought to have known of the risk their publication thus engendered? Will the first amendment provide an adequate defense? Some courts believe it does not. See, e.g., Hyde v. City of Columbia, 637 S.W.2d 251 (Mo.App.1982), cert. denied sub nom. Tribune Publishing Company v. Hyde, 459 U.S. 1226, 103 S.Ct. 1233, 75 L.Ed.2d 467 (1983). For comments, see Linder, When Names Are Not News, They're Negligence: Media Liability for Personal Injuries Resulting from the Publication of Accurate Information, 52 UMKC

Alternatively, suppose (contrary to the actual facts of course), that the Hill family had been negotiating with *Look* magazine, pursuant to a proposed agreement that *Look* would have exclusive rights to publish a photo-journalism story of their adventure in exchange for $10,000—an arrangement that collapsed once *Life* published its own coverage as they did. On what legal theory might the Hill family attempt to recover $10,000 from *Life*?[72]—And why, on perfectly straightforward first amendment grounds, might the action nonetheless fail?

The issues raised in these variations on *Hill* (i.e. torts other than defamation and persons other than public officials or political figures) have momentarily taken us out of the post-*Sullivan* refinements on defamation as such. To gain some surer grasp on that particular subject, however, it may be well to turn to some further defamation cases again.

GERTZ v. ROBERT WELCH, INC.
Supreme Court of the United States, 1974.
418 U.S. 323, 94 S.Ct. 2997, 41 L.Ed.2d 789.

MR. JUSTICE POWELL delivered the opinion of the Court.

This court has struggled for nearly a decade to define the proper accommodation between the law of defamation and the freedoms of speech and press protected by the First Amendment. With this decision we return to that effort. We granted certiorari to reconsider the extent of a publisher's constitutional privilege against liability for defamation of a private citizen. 410 U.S. 925 (1973).

I

In 1968 a Chicago policeman named Nuccio shot and killed a youth named Nelson. The state authorities prosecuted Nuccio for the homicide and ultimately obtained a conviction for murder in the second

---

L.Rev. 4212 (1984); Note, Liability for Non-libelous Negligent Statements: First Amendment Considerations, 93 Yale L.J. 744 (1984).

—Had there been no Broadway play production to which the Life magazine photo-journalism story was deemed sufficiently pertinent at the time of its publication (to render it appropriately newsworthy as part of the play's actual origin and background), *then* should the civil action in *Hill* have prevailed? Even if (changing the facts still again) it were an accurate and not a "false light" sensationalized account? Why?— Because even as a wholly accurate account of what had occurred in fact, its reporting is too peripheral to any "political process" values of free speech to warrant any significant constitutional protection (such as the negligent and false reporting of misconduct by public figures receives under *New York Times v. Sullivan*)? Who decides whether that is so?

72. Cf. Zacchini v. Scripps–Howard Pub. Co., 433 U.S. 562, 97 S.Ct. 2849, 53 L.Ed.2d 965 (1977) (freelance reporter for Scripps–Howard Broadcasting Co. videotaped 15 second human cannonball act by defendant at commercial performance, despite request not to do so, and tape was shown with favorable comment on nightly news; held, five-to-four per opinion by Rehnquist for the Court, where no injunction was sought, but damages were sought for appropriation of commercial value, first amendment does not bar the action for "unlawful appropriation of plaintiff's professional property.")

degree. The Nelson family retained petitioner Elmer Gertz, a reputable attorney, to represent them in civil litigation against Nuccio.

Respondent published American Opinion, a monthly outlet for the views of the John Birch Society. Early in the 1960's the magazine began to warn of a nationwide conspiracy to discredit local law enforcement agencies and create in their stead a national police force capable of supporting a Communist dictatorship. As part of the continuing effort to alert the public to this assumed danger, the managing editor of American Opinion commissioned an article on the murder trial of Officer Nuccio. For this purpose he engaged a regular contributor to the magazine. In March 1969 respondent published the resulting article under the title "FRAME–UP: Richard Nuccio And The War On Police." The article purports to demonstrate that the testimony against Nuccio at his criminal trial was false and that his prosecution was part of the Communist campaign against the police.

In his capacity as counsel for the Nelson family in the civil litigation, petitioner attended the coroner's inquest into the boy's death and initiated actions for damages, but he neither discussed Officer Nuccio with the press nor played any part in the criminal proceeding. Notwithstanding petitioner's remote connection with the prosecution of Nuccio, respondent's magazine portrayed him as an architect of the "*frame*-up." According to the article, the police file on petitioner took "a big, Irish cop to lift." The article stated that petitioner had been an official of the "Marxist League for Industrial Democracy, originally known as the Intercollegiate Socialist Society, which has advocated the violent seizure of our government." It labeled Gertz a "Leninist" and a "Communist-fronter." It also stated that Gertz had been an officer of the National Lawyers Guild, described as a Communist organization that "probably did more than any other outfit to plan the Communist attack on the Chicago police during the 1968 Democratic Convention."

These statements contained serious inaccuracies. The implication that petitioner had a criminal record was false. Petitioner had been a member and officer of the National Lawyers Guild some 15 years earlier, but there was no evidence that he or that organization had taken any part in planning the 1968 demonstrations in Chicago. There was also no basis for the charge that petitioner was a "Leninist" or a "Communist-fronter." And he had never been a member of the "Marxist League for Industrial Democracy" or the "Intercollegiate Socialist Society."

The managing editor of American Opinion made no effort to verify or substantiate the charges against petitioner. Instead, he appended an editorial introduction stating that the author had "conducted extensive research into the Richard Nuccio Case." And he included in the article a photograph of petitioner and wrote the caption that appeared under it: "Elmer Gertz of Red Guild harasses Nuccio." Respondent placed the issue of American Opinion containing the article on sale at newsstands throughout the country and distributed reprints of the article on the streets of Chicago.

Petitioner filed a diversity action for libel in the United States District Court for the Northern District of Illinois. He claimed that the falsehoods published by respondent injured his reputation as a lawyer and a citizen. Before filing an answer, respondent moved to dismiss the complaint for failure to state a claim upon which relief could be granted, apparently on the ground that petitioner failed to allege special damages. But the court ruled that statements contained in the article constituted libel *per se* under Illinois law and that consequently petitioner need not plead special damages. 306 F.Supp. 310 (1969).

After answering the complaint, respondent filed a pretrial motion for summary judgment, claiming a constitutional privilege against liability for defamation.[1] It asserted that the article concerned an issue of public interest and concern. For those reasons, respondent argued, it was entitled to invoke the privilege enunicated in New York Times Co. v. Sullivan, 376 U.S. 254 (1964). Under this rule respondent would escape liability unless petitioner could prove publication of defamatory falsehood "with 'actual malice'—that is, with knowledge that it was false or with reckless disregard of whether it was false or not." *Id.,* at 280. Respondent claimed that petitioner could not make such a showing and submitted a supporting affidavit by the magazine's managing editor. The editor denied any knowledge of the falsity of the statements concerning petitioner and stated that he had relied on the author's reputation and on his prior experience with the accuracy and authenticity of the author's contributions to American Opinion.

The District Court denied respondent's motion for summary judgment in a memorandum opinion of September 16, 1970. The court did not dispute respondent's claim to the protection of the *New York Times* standard. Rather, it concluded that petitioner might overcome the constitutional privilege by making a factual showing sufficient to prove publication of defamatory falsehood in reckless disregard of the truth. During the course of the trial, however, it became clear that the trial court had not accepted all of respondent's asserted grounds for applying the *New York Times* rule to this case. It thought that respondent's claim to the protection of the constitutional privilege depended on the contention that petitioner was either a public official under the *New York Times* decision or a public figure under Curtis Publishing Co. v. Butts, 388 U.S. 130 (1967), apparently discounting the argument that a privilege would arise from the presence of a public issue. After all the evidence had been presented but before submission of the case to the jury, the court ruled in effect that petitioner was neither a public official nor a public figure. It added that, if he were, the resulting application of the *New York Times* standard would require a directed verdict for respondent. Because some statements in the article constituted libel *per se* under Illinois law, the court submitted the case to the jury under instructions that withdrew from its consideration all issues save the measure of damages. The jury awarded $50,000 to the petitioner.

---

1. Petitioner filed a cross-motion for summary judgment on grounds not specified in the record. The court denied petitioner's cross-motion without discussion in a memorandum opinion of September 16, 1970.

Following the jury verdict and on further reflection, the District Court concluded that the *New York Times* standard should govern this case even though petitioner was not a public official or public figure. It accepted respondent's contention that that privilege protected discussion of any public issue without regard to the status of a person defamed therein. Accordingly, the court entered judgment for respondent notwithstanding the jury's verdict. This conclusion anticipated the reasoning of a plurality of this Court in Rosenbloom v. Metromedia, Inc., 403 U.S. 29 (1971).

Petitioner appealed to contest the applicability of the *New York Times* standard to this case. Although the Court of Appeals for the Seventh Circuit doubted the correctness of the District Court's determination that petitioner was not a public figure, it did not overturn that finding.[3] It agreed with the District Court that respondent could assert the constitutional privilege because the article concerned a matter of public interest, citing this Court's intervening decision in *Rosenbloom v. Metromedia, Inc., supra.* The Court of Appeals read *Rosenbloom* to require application of the *New York Times* standard to any publication or broadcast about an issue of significant public interest, without regard to the position, fame, or anonymity of the person defamed, and it concluded that respondent's statements concerned such an issue. After reviewing the record, the Court of Appeals endorsed the District Court's conclusion that petitioner had failed to show by clear and convincing evidence that respondent had acted with "actual malice" as defined by *New York Times*. There was no evidence that the managing editor of American Opinion knew of the falsity of the accusations made in the article. In fact, he knew nothing about petitioner except what he learned from the article. The court correctly noted that mere proof of failure to investigate, without more, cannot establish reckless disregard for the truth. Rather, the publisher must act with a " 'high degree of awareness of * * * probable falsity.' " St. Amant v. Thompson, 390 U.S. 727, 731 (1968); * * * The evidence in this case did not reveal that respondent had cause for such an awareness. The Court of Appeals therefore affirmed, 471 F.2d 801 (1972). For the reasons stated below, we reverse.

II

The principal issue in this case is whether a newspaper or broadcaster that publishes defamatory falsehoods about an individual who is neither a public official nor a public figure may claim a constitutional privilege against liability for the injury inflicted by those statements. The Court considered this question on the rather different set of facts presented in Rosenbloom v. Metromedia, Inc., 403 U.S. 29 (1971). Rosenbloom, a distributor of nudist magazines, was arrested for selling obscene material while making a delivery to a retail dealer. The police

---

3. The court stated:

"[Petitioner's] considerable stature as a lawyer, author, lecturer, and participant in matters of public import undermine[s] the validity of the assumption that he is not a 'public figure' as that term has been used by the progeny of *New York Times*. Nevertheless, for purposes of decision we make that assumption and test the availability of the claim of privilege by the subject matter of the article." *Id.*, at 805.

obtained a warrant and seized his entire inventory of 3,000 books and magazines. He sought and obtained an injunction prohibiting further police interference in his business. He then sued a local radio station for failing to note in two of its newscasts that the 3,000 items seized were only "reportedly" or "allegedly" obscene and for broadcasting references to "the smut literature racket" and to "girlie-book peddlers" in its coverage of the court proceeding for injunctive relief. He obtained a judgment against the radio station, but the Court of Appeals for the Third Circuit held the *New York Times* privilege applicable to the broadcast and reversed. 415 F.2d 892 (1969).

This Court affirmed the decision below, but no majority could agree on a controlling rationale. The eight Justices [5] who participated in *Rosenbloom* announced their views in five separate opinions, none of which commanded more than three votes. The several statements not only reveal disagreement about the appropriate result in that case, they also reflect divergent traditions of thought about the general problem of reconciling the law of defamation with the First Amendment. One approach has been to extend the *New York Times* test to an expanding variety of situations. Another has been to vary the level of constitutional privilege for defamatory falsehood with the status of the person defamed. And a third view would grant to the press and broadcast media absolute immunity from liability for defamation. * * *

* * *

We begin with the common ground. Under the First Amendment there is no such thing as a false idea. However pernicious an opinion may seem, we depend for its correction not on the conscience of judges and juries but on competition of other ideas.[8] But there is no constitutional value in false statements of fact. Neither the intentional lie nor the careless error materially advances society's interest in "uninhibited, robust, and wide-open" debate on public issues. New York Times v. Sullivan, 376 U.S., at 270. They belong to that category of utterances which "are no essential part of any exposition of ideas, and are of such slight social value as a step to truth that any benefit that may be derived from them is clearly outweighed by the social interest in order and morality." Chaplinsky v. New Hampshire, 315 U.S. 568, 572 (1942).

Although the erroneous statement of fact is not worthy of constitutional protection, it is nevertheless inevitable in free debate. As James Madison pointed out in the Report on the Virginia Resolutions of 1798: "Some degree of abuse is inseparable from the proper use of every thing; and in no instance is this more true than in that of the press." 4 J. Elliot, Debates on the Federal Constitution of 1787, p. 571 (1876). And punishment of error runs the risk of inducing a cautious and restrictive exercise of the constitutionally guaranteed freedoms of

---

5. Mr. Justice Douglas did not participate in the consideration or the decision of *Rosenbloom*.

8. As Thomas Jefferson made the point in his first Inaugural Address: "If there be any among us who would wish to dissolve this Union or change its republican form, let them stand undisturbed as monuments of the safety with which error of opinion may be tolerated where reason is left free to combat it."

speech and press. Our decisions recognize that a rule of strict liability that compels a publisher or broadcaster to guarantee the accuracy of his factual assertions may lead to intolerable self-censorship. Allowing the media to avoid liability only by proving the truth of all injurious statements does not accord adequate protection to First Amendment liberties. As the Court states in *New York Times Co. v. Sullivan, supra,* at 279: "Allowance of the defense of truth with the burden of proving it on the defendant does not mean that only false speech will be deterred." The First Amendment requires that we protect some falsehood in order to protect speech that matters.

The need to avoid self-censorship by the news media is, however, not the only societal value at issue. If it were, this Court would have embraced long ago the view that publishers and broadcasters enjoy an unconditional and indefeasible immunity from liability for defamation. * * * Such a rule would, indeed, obviate the fear that the prospect of civil liability for injurious falsehood might dissuade a timorous press from the effective exercise of First Amendment freedoms. Yet absolute protection for the communications media requires a total sacrifice of the competing value served by the law of defamation.

The legitimate state interest underlying the law of libel is the compensation of individuals for the harm inflicted on them by defamatory falsehood. We would not lightly require the State to abandon this purpose, for, as Mr. Justice Stewart has reminded us, the individual's right to the protection of his own good name

> "reflects no more than our basic concept of the essential dignity and worth of every human being—a concept at the root of any decent system of ordered liberty. The protection of private personality, like the protection of life itself, is left primarily to the individual States under the Ninth and Tenth Amendments. But this does not mean that the right is entitled to any less recognition by this Court as a basic of our constitutional system." Rosenblatt v. Baer, 383 U.S. 75, 92 (1966) (concurring opinion).

Some tension necessarily exists between the need for a vigorous and uninhibited press and the legitimate interest in redressing wrongful injury. As Mr. Justice Harlan stated, "some antithesis between freedom of speech and press and libel actions persists, for libel remains premised on the content of speech and limits the freedom of the publisher to express certain sentiments, at least without guaranteeing legal proof of their substantial accuracy." *Curtis Publishing Co. v. Butts, supra,* at 152. In our continuing effort to define the proper accommodation between these competing concerns, we have been especially anxious to assure to the freedoms of speech and press that "breathing space" essential to their fruitful exercise. NAACP v. Button, 371 U.S. 415, 433 (1963). To that end this Court has extended a measure of strategic protection to defamatory falsehood.

The *New York Times* standard defines the level of constitutional protection appropriate to the context of defamation of a public person. Those who, by reason of the notoriety of their achievements or the vigor and success with which they seek the public's attention, are properly classed as public figures and those who hold governmental office may recover for injury to reputation only on clear and convincing proof that the defamatory falsehood was made with knowledge of its falsity or with reckless disregard for the truth. This standard administers an extremely powerful antidote to the inducement to media self-censorship of the common-law rule of strict liability for libel and slander. And it exacts a correspondingly high price from the victims of defamatory falsehood. Plainly many deserving plaintiffs, including some intentionally subjected to injury, will be unable to surmount the barrier of the *New York Times* test. Despite this substantial abridgement of the state law right to compensation for wrongful hurt to one's reputation, the Court has concluded that the protection of the *New York Times* privilege should be available to publishers and broadcasters of defamatory falsehood concerning public officials and public figures. *New York Times Co. v. Sullivan, supra; Curtis Publishing Co. v. Butts, supra.* We think that these decisions are correct, but we do not find their holding justified solely by reference to the interest of the press and broadcast media in immunity from liability. Rather, we believe that the *New York Times* rule states an accommodation between this concern and the limited state interest present in the context of libel actions brought by public persons. For the reasons stated below, we conclude that the state interest in compensating injury to the reputation of private individuals requires that a different rule obtain with respect to them.

Theoretically, of course, the balance between the needs of the press and the individual's claim to compensation for wrongful injury might be struck on a case-by-case basis. As Mr. Justice Harlan hypothesized, "it might seem, purely as an abstract matter, that the most utilitarian approach would be to scrutinize carefully every jury verdict in every libel case, in order to ascertain whether the final judgment leaves fully protected whatever First Amendment values transcend the legitimate state interest in protecting the particular plaintiff who prevailed." Rosenbloom v. Metromedia, Inc., 403 U.S., at 63 (footnote omitted). But this approach would lead to unpredictable results and uncertain expectations, and it could render our duty to supervise the lower courts unmanageable. Because an *ad hoc* resolution of the competing interest at stake in each particular case is not defeasible, we must lay down broad rules of general application. Such rules necessarily treat alike various cases involving differences as well as similarities. Thus it is often true that not all of the considerations which justify adoption of a given rule will obtain in each particular case decided under its authority.

With that caveat we have no difficulty in distinguishing among defamation plaintiffs. The first remedy of any victim of defamation is self-help—using available opportunities to contradict the lie or correct the error and thereby to minimize its adverse impact on reputation. Public officials and public figures usually enjoy significantly greater access to the channels of effective communication and hence have a more realistic opportunity to counteract false statements than private individuals normally enjoy.[9] Private individuals are therefore more vulnerable to injury, and the state interest in protecting them is correspondingly greater.

More important than the likelihood that private individuals will lack effective opportunities for rebuttal, there is a compelling normative consideration underlying the distinction between public and private defamation plaintiffs. An individual who decides to seek governmental office must accept certain necessary consequences of that involvement in public affairs. He runs the risk of closer public scrutiny than might otherwise be the case. And society's interest in the officers of government is not strictly limited to the formal discharge of official duties. As the Court pointed out in Garrison v. Louisiana, 379 U.S., at 77, the public's interest extends to "anything which might touch on an official's fitness for office. * * * Few personal attributes are more germane to fitness for office than dishonesty, malfeasance, or improper motivation, even though these characteristics may also affect the official's private character."

Those classed as public figures stand in a similar position. Hypothetically, it may be possible for someone to become a public figure through no purposeful action of his own, but the instances of truly involuntary public figures must be exceedingly rare. For the most part those who attain this status have assumed roles of especial prominence in the affairs of society. Some occupy positions of such persuasive power and influence that they are deemed public figures for all purposes. More commonly, those classed as public figures have thrust themselves to the forefront of particular public controversies in order to influence the resolution of the issues involved. In either event, they invite attention and comment.

Even if the foregoing generalities do not obtain in every instance, the communications media are entitled to act on the assumption that public officials and public figures have voluntarily exposed themselves to increased risk of injury from defamatory falsehood concerning them. No such assumption is justified with respect to a private individual. He has not accepted public office or assumed an "influential role in ordering society." Curtis Publishing Co. v. Butts, 388 U.S., at 164 (Warren, C.J., concurring in result). He has relinquished no part of his interest in the protection of his own good name, and consequently he has a more compelling call on the courts for redress of injury inflicted by defamatory falsehood. Thus, private individuals are not only more vulnerable to injury than public officials and public figures; they are also more deserving of recovery.

For those reasons we conclude that the States should retain substantial latitude in their efforts to enforce a legal remedy for defamatory falsehood injurious to the reputation of a private individual. The extension of the *New York Times* test proposed by the *Rosenbloom*

---

9. Of course, an opportunity for rebuttal seldom suffices to undo harm of defamatory falsehood. Indeed, the law of defamation is rooted in our experience that the truth rarely catches up with a lie. But the fact that the self-help remedy of rebuttal, standing alone, is inadequate to its task does not mean that it is irrelevant to our inquiry.

plurality would abridge this legitimate state interest to a degree that we find unacceptable. * * *

We hold that, so long as they do not impose liability without fault, the States may define for themselves the appropriate standard of liability for a publisher or broadcaster of defamatory falsehood injurious to a private individual. This approach provides a more equitable boundary between the competing concerns involved here. It recognizes the strength of the legitimate state interest in compensating private individuals for wrongful injury to reputation, yet shields the press and broadcast media from the rigors of strict liability for defamation. At least this conclusion obtains where as here, the substance of the defamatory statement "makes substantial danger to reputation apparent." This phrase places in perspective the conclusion we announce today. Our inquiry would involve considerations somewhat different from those discussed above if a State purported to condition civil liability on a factual misstatement whose content did not warn a reasonably prudent editor or broadcaster of its defamatory potential. Cf. Time, Inc. v. Hill, 385 U.S. 374 (1967). Such a case is not now before us, and we intimate no view as to its proper resolution.

IV

Our accommodation of the competing values at stake in defamation suits by private individuals allows the States to impose liability on the publisher or broadcaster of defamatory falsehood on a less demanding showing than that required by *New York Times*. This conclusion is not based on a belief that the considerations which prompted the adoption of the *New York Times* privilege for defamation of public officials and its extension to public figures are wholly inapplicable to the context of private individuals. Rather, we endorse this approach in recognition of the strong and legitimate state interest in compensating private individuals for injury to reputation. But this countervailing state interest extends no further than compensation for actual injury. For the reasons stated below, we hold that the States may not permit recovery of presumed or punitive damages, at least when liability is not based on a showing of knowledge of falsity or reckless disregard for the truth.

The common law of defamation is an oddity of tort law, for it allows recovery of purportedly compensatory damages without evidence of actual loss. Under the traditional rules pertaining to actions for libel, the existence of injury is presumed from the fact of publication. Juries may award substantial sums as compensation for supposed damage to reputation without any proof that such harm actually occurred. The largely uncontrolled discretion of juries to award damages where there is no loss unnecessarily compounds the potential of any system of liability for defamatory falsehood to inhibit the vigorous exercise of First Amendment freedoms. Additionally, the doctrine of presumed damages invites juries to punish unpopular opinion rather than to compensate individuals for injury sustained by the publication of a false fact. More to the point, the States have no substantial interest in securing for plaintiffs such as this petitioner gratuitous awards of money damages far in excess of any actual injury.

We would not, of course, invalidate state law simply because we doubt its wisdom, but here we are attempting to reconcile state law with a competing interest grounded in the constitutional command of the First Amendment. It is therefore appropriate to require that state remedies for defamatory falsehood reach no farther than is necessary to protect the legitimate interest involved. It is necessary to restrict defamation plaintiffs who do not prove knowledge of falsity or reckless disregard for the truth to compensation for actual injury. We need not define "actual injury," as trial courts have wide expression in framing appropriate jury instructions in tort actions. Suffice it to say that actual injury is not limited to out-of-pocket loss. Indeed, the more customary types of actual harm inflicted by defamatory falsehood include impairment of reputation and standing in the community, personal humiliation, and mental anguish and suffering. Of course, juries must be limited by appropriate instructions, and all awards must be supported by competent evidence concerning the injury, although there need be no evidence which assigns an actual dollar value to the injury.

We also find no justification for allowing awards of punitive damages against publishers and broadcasters held liable under state-defined standards of liability for defamation. In most jurisdictions jury discretion over the amounts awarded is limited only by the gentle rule that they not be excessive. Consequently, juries assess punitive damages in wholly unpredictable amounts bearing no necessary relation to the actual harm caused. And they remain free to use their discretion selectively to punish expressions of unpopular views. Like the doctrine of presumed damages, jury discretion to award punitive damages unnecessarily exacerbates the danger of media self-censorship, but, unlike the former rule, punitive damages are wholly irrelevant to the state interest that justifies a negligence standard for private defamation actions. They are not compensation for injury. Instead, they are private fines levied by civil juries to punish reprehensible conduct and to deter its future occurrence. In short, the private defamation plaintiff who establishes liability under a less demanding standard than that stated by *New York Times* may recover only such damages as are sufficient to compensate him for actual injury.

V

Notwithstanding our refusal to extend the *New York Times* privilege to defamation of private individuals, respondent contends that we should affirm the judgment below on the ground that petitioner is either a public official or a public figure. There is little basis for the former assertion. Several years prior to the present incident, petitioner had served briefly on housing committees appointed by the mayor of Chicago, but at the time of publication he had never held any remunerative governmental position. Respondent admits this but argues that petitioner's appearance at the coroner's inquest rendered him a "de facto public official." Our cases recognize no such concept. Respondent's suggestion would sweep all lawyers under the *New York Times* rule as officers of the court and distort the plain meaning of the "public official" category beyond all recognition. We decline to follow it.

Respondent's characterization of petitioner as a public figure raises a different question. That designation may rest on either of two alternative bases. In some instances an individual may achieve such pervasive fame or notoriety that he becomes a public figure for all purposes and in all contexts. More commonly, an individual voluntarily injects himself or is drawn into a particular public controversy and thereby becomes a public figure for a limited range of issues. In either case such persons assume special prominence in the resolution of public questions.

Petitioner has long been active in community and professional affairs. He has served as an officer of local civic groups and of various professional organizations, and he has published several books and articles on legal subjects. Although petitioner was consequently well known in some circles, he had achieved no general fame or notoriety in the community. None of the prospective jurors called at the trial had ever heard of petitioner prior to this litigation, and respondent offered no proof that this response was atypical of the local population. We would not lightly assume that a citizen's participation in community and professional affairs rendered him a public figure for all purposes. Absent clear evidence of general fame or notoriety in the community, and pervasive involvement in the affairs of society, an individual should not be deemed a public personality for all aspects of his life. It is preferable to reduce the public-figure question to a more meaningful context by looking to the nature and extent of an individual's participation in the particular controversy giving rise to the defamation.

In this context it is plain that petitioner was not a public figure. He played a minimal role at the coroner's inquest, and his participation related solely to his representation of a private client. He took no part in the criminal prosecution of Officer Nuccio. Moreover, he never discussed either the criminal or civil litigation with the press and was never quoted as having done so. He plainly did not thrust himself into the vortex of this public issue, nor did he engage the public's attention in an attempt to influence its outcome. We are persuaded that the trial court did not err in refusing to characterize petitioner as a public figure for the purpose of this litigation.

We therefore conclude that the *New York Times* standard is inapplicable to this case and that the trial court erred in entering judgment for respondent. Because the jury was allowed to impose liability without fault and was permitted to presume damages without proof of injury, a new trial is necessary. We reverse and remand for further proceedings in accord with this opinion.

It is so ordered.

Mr. Chief Justice Burger, dissenting.

* * *

* * * In today's opinion the Court abandons the traditional thread so far as the ordinary private citizen is concerned and introduces the concept that the media will be liable for negligence in publishing defamatory statements with respect to such persons. Although I agree with much of what Mr. Justice White states, I do not read the Court's new doctrinal approach in quite the way he does. I am frank to say I do not know the parameters of a "negligence" doctrine as applied to the news media. Conceivably this new doctrine could inhibit some editors, as the dissents of Mr. Justice Douglas and Mr. Justice Brennan suggest. But I would prefer to allow this area of law to continue to evolve as it has up to now with respect to private citizens rather than embark on a new doctrinal theory which has no jurisprudential ancestry.

The petitioner here was performing a professional representative role as an advocate in the highest tradition of the law, and under that tradition the advocate is not to be invidiously identified with his client. The important public policy which underlies this tradition—the right to counsel—would be gravely jeopardized if every lawyer who takes an "unpopular" case, civil or criminal, would automatically become fair game for irresponsible reporters and editors who might, for example, describe the lawyer as a "mob mouthpiece" for representing a client with a serious prior criminal record, or as an "ambulance chaser" for representing a claimant in a personal injury action.

I would reverse the judgment of the Court of Appeals and remand for reinstatement of the verdict of the jury and the entry of an appropriate judgment on that verdict.

MR. JUSTICE DOUGLAS, dissenting.

* * *

* * * I have stated before my view that the First Amendment would bar Congress from passing any libel law. This was the view held by Thomas Jefferson [2] and it is one Congress has never challenged through enactment of a civil libel statute. * * *

* * *

Continued recognition of the possibility of state libel suits for public discussion of public issues leaves the freedom of speech honored by the Fourteenth Amendment a diluted version of First Amendment protection. This view is only possible if one accepts the position that the First Amendment is applicable to the States only through the Due Process Clause of the Fourteenth, due process freedom of speech being only that freedom which this Court might deem to be "implicit in the concept of ordered liberty." But the Court frequently has rested state free speech and free press decisions on the Fourteenth Amendment generally rather than on the Due Process Clause alone. The Fourteenth Amendment speaks not only of due process but also of "privileges and immunities" of United States citizenship. I can conceive of

---

2. In 1798 Jefferson stated:

"[The First Amendment] thereby guard[s] in the same sentence, and under the same words, the freedom of religion, of speech, and of the press: insomuch, that whatever violates either, throws down the sanctuary which covers the others, *and that libels, falsehood, and defamation, equally with heresy and false religion, are withheld from the cognizance of federal tribunals.* * * *" 8 The Works of Thomas Jefferson 464–465 (Ford ed. 1904) (emphasis added).

no privilege or immunity with a higher claim to recognition against state abridgement than the freedoms of speech and of the press. In our federal system we are subject to two governmental regimes, and freedoms of speech and of the press protected against the infringement of only one are quite illusory. The identity of the oppressor is, I would think, a matter of relative indifference to the oppressed.

There can be no doubt that a State impinges upon free and open discussion when it sanctions the imposition of damages for such discussion through its civil libel laws. Discussion of public affairs is often marked by highly charged emotions, and jurymen, not unlike us all, are subject to those emotions. It is indeed this very type of speech which is the reason for the First Amendment since speech which arouses little emotion is little in need of protection. The vehicle for publication in this case was the American Opinion, a most controversial periodical which disseminates the views of the John Birch Society, an organization which many deem to be quite offensive. The subject matter involved "Communist plots," "conspiracies against law enforcement agencies," and the killing of a private citizen by the police. With any such amalgam of controversial elements pressing upon the jury, a jury determination, unpredictable in the most neutral circumstances, becomes for those who venture to discuss heated issues, a virtual roll of the dice separating them from liability for often massive claims of damage.

It is only the hardy publisher who will engage in discussion in the face of such risk, and the Court's preoccupation with proliferating standards in the area of libel increases the risks. It matters little whether the standard be articulated as "malice" or "reckless disregard of the truth" or "negligence," for the jury determinations by any of those criteria are virtually unreviewable. This Court, in its continuing delineation of variegated mantles of First Amendment protection, is, like the potential publisher, left with only speculation on how jury findings were influenced by the effect the subject matter of the publication had upon the minds and viscera of the jury. The standard announced today leaves the States free to "define for themselves the appropriate standard of liability for a publisher or broadcaster: in the circumstances of this case. This of course leaves the simple negligence standard as an option, with the jury free to impose damages upon a finding that the publisher failed to act as "a reasonable man." With such continued erosion of First Amendment protection, I fear that it may well be the reasonable man who refrains from speaking.

Since in my view the First and Fourteenth Amendments prohibit the imposition of damages upon respondent for this discussion of public affairs, I would affirm the judgment below.

MR. JUSTICE BRENNAN, dissenting.

* * * I adhere to my view expressed in *Rosenbloom v. Metromedia, Inc, supra,* that we strike the proper accommodation between avoidance of media self-censorship and protection of individual reputations only when we require States to apply the New York Times Co. v. Sullivan, 376 U.S. 254 (1964), knowing-or-reckless-falsity standard in civil libel actions concerning media reports of the involvement of private individuals in events of public or general interest.

* * *

MR. JUSTICE WHITE, dissenting.

* * *

II

The Court does not contend, and it could hardly do so, that those who wrote the First Amendment intended to prohibit the Federal Government, within its sphere of influence in the Territories and the District of Columbia, from providing the private citizen a peaceful remedy for damaging falsehood. At the time of the adoption of the First Amendment, many of the consequences of libel law already described had developed, particularly the rule that libels and some slanders were so inherently injurious that they were actionable without special proof of damages to reputation. As the Court pointed out in Roth v. United States, 354 U.S. 476, 482 (1957), 10 of the 14 States that had ratified the Constitution by 1792 had themselves provided constitutional guarantees for free expression, and 13 of the 14 nevertheless provided for the prosecution of libels. Prior to the Revolution, the American Colonies had adopted the common law of libel. Contrary to some popular notions, freedom of the press was sharply curtailed in colonial America. Seditious libel was punished as a contempt by the colonial legislatures and as a criminal offense in the criminal courts.

Scant, if any, evidence exists that the First Amendment was intended to abolish the common law of libel, at least to the extent of depriving ordinary citizens of meaningful redress against their defamers. * * *

* * *

The Court concedes that the dangers of self-censorship are insufficient to override the state interest in protecting the reputation of private individuals who are both more helpless and more deserving of state concern than public persons with more access to the media to defend themselves. It therefore refuses to condition the private plaintiff's recovery on a showing of intentional or reckless falsehood as required by *New York Times*. But the Court nevertheless extends the reach of the First Amendment to all defamation actions by requiring that the ordinary citizen, when libeled by a publication defamatory on its face, must prove some degree of culpability on the part of the publisher beyond the circulation to the public of a damaging falsehood. A rule at least as strict would be called for where the defamatory character of the publication is not apparent from its face. * * * [27] Furthermore, if this major hurdle to establish liability is surmounted, the Court requires proof of actual injury to reputation before any damages for such injury may be awarded.

---

27. If I read the Court correctly, it clearly implies that for those publications that do not make "substantial danger to reputation apparent," the *New York Times* actual-malice standard will apply. Apparently, this would be true even where the imputation concerned conduct or a condition that would be *per se* slander.

* * *

The Court evinces a deep-seated antipathy to "liability without fault." But this catch-phrase has no talismanic significance and is almost meaningless in this context where the Court appears to be addressing those libels and slanders that are defamatory on their face and where the publisher is no doubt aware from the nature of the material that it would be inherently damaging to reputation. He publishes notwithstanding, knowing that he will inflict injury. With this knowledge, he must intend to inflict that injury, his excuse being that he is privileged to do so—that he has published the truth. But as it turns out, what he has circulated to the public is a very damaging falsehood. Is he nevertheless "faultless"? Perhaps it can be said that the mistake about his defense was made in good faith, but the fact remains that it is he who launched the publication knowing that it could ruin a reputation.

In these circumstances, the law has heretofore put the risk of falsehood on the publisher where the victim is a private citizen and no grounds of special privilege are invoked. The Court would now shift this risk to the victim, even though he has done nothing to invite the calumny, is wholly innocent of fault, and is helpless to avoid his injury. I doubt that jurisprudential resistance to liability without fault is sufficient ground for employing the First Amendment to revolutionize the law of libel, and in my view, that body of legal rules poses no realistic threat to the press and its service to the public. The press today is vigorous and robust. To me, it is quite incredible to suggest that threats of libel suits from private citizens are causing the press to refrain from publishing the truth. I know of no hard facts to support that proposition and the Court furnishes none.

The communications industry has increasingly become concentrated in a few powerful hands operating very lucrative businesses reaching across the Nation and into almost every home. Neither the industry as a whole nor its individual components are easily intimidated, and we are fortunate that they are not. Requiring them to pay for the occasional damage they do to private reputation will play no substantial part in their future performance or their existence.

In any event, if the Court's principal concern is to protect the communications industry from large libel judgments, it would appear that its new requirements with respect to general and punitive damages would be ample protection. Why it also feels compelled to escalate the threshold standard of liability I cannot fathom, particularly when this will eliminate in many instances the plaintiff's responsibility of securing a judicial determination that the damaging publication was indeed false, whether or not he is entitled to recover money damages. Under the Court's new rules, the plaintiff must prove not only the defamatory statement but also some degree of fault accompanying it. The publication may be wholly false and the wrong to him unjustified, but his case will nevertheless be dismissed for failure to prove negligence or other fault on the part of the publisher. I find it unacceptable to distribute the risk in this manner and force the wholly innocent victim to bear the injury; for, as between the two, the defamer is the only culpable party. It is he who circulated a falsehood that he was not required to publish.

It is difficult for me to understand why the ordinary citizen should himself carry the risk of damage and suffer the injury in order to vindicate First Amendment values by protecting the press and others from liability for circulating false information. This is particularly true because such statements serve no purpose whatsoever in furthering the public interest or the search for truth but, on the contrary, may frustrate that search and at the same time inflict great injury on the defenseless individual. The owners of the press and the stockholders of the communications enterprises can much better bear the burden. And if they cannot, the public at large should somehow pay for what is essentially a public benefit derived at private expense.

DUN & BRADSTREET, INC. v. GREENMOSS BUILDERS, INC.

Supreme Court of the United States, 1985.
472 U.S. 749, 105 S.Ct. 2939, 86 L.Ed.2d 593.

JUSTICE POWELL announced the judgment of the Court and delivered an opinion, in which JUSTICE REHNQUIST and JUSTICE O'CONNOR joined.

In Gertz v. Robert Welch, Inc., 418 U.S. 323 (1974), we held that the First Amendment restricted the damages that a private individual could obtain from a publisher for a libel that involved a matter of public concern. More specifically, we held that in these circumstances the First Amendment prohibited awards of presumed and punitive damages for false and defamatory statements unless the plaintiff shows "actual malice," that is, knowledge of falsity or reckless disregard for the truth. The question presented in this case is whether this rule of *Gertz* applies when the false and defamatory statements do not involve matters of public concern.

I

Petitioner Dun & Bradstreet, a credit reporting agency, provides subscribers with financial and related information about businesses. All the information is confidential; under the terms of the subscription agreement the subscribers may not reveal it to anyone else. On July 26, 1976, petitioner sent a report to five subscribers indicating that respondent, a construction contractor, had filed a voluntary petition for bankruptcy. This report was false and grossly misrepresented respondent's assets and liabilities. That same day, while discussing the possibility of future financing with its bank, respondent's president was told that the bank had received the defamatory report. He immediately called petitioner's regional office, explained the error, and asked for a correction. In addition, he requested the names of the firms that had received the false report in order to assure them that the company was solvent. Petitioner promised to look into the matter but refused to divulge the names of those who had received the report.

After determining that its report was indeed false, petitioner issued a corrective notice on or about August 3, 1976, to the five subscribers who had received the initial report. The notice stated that one of respondent's former employees, not respondent itself, had filed for bankruptcy and that respondent "continued in business as usual." Respondent told petitioner that it was dissatisfied with the notice, and it again asked for a list of subscribers who had seen the initial report. Again petitioner refused to divulge their names.

Respondent then brought this defamation action in Vermont state court. It alleged that the false report had injured its reputation and sought both compensatory and punitive damages. The trial established that the error in petitioner's report had been caused when one of its employees, a 17-year-old high school student paid to review Vermont bankruptcy pleadings, had inadvertently attributed to respondent a bankruptcy petition filed by one of respondent's former employees. Although petitioner's representative testified that it was routine practice to check the accuracy of such reports with the businesses themselves, it did not try to verify the information about respondent before reporting it.

After trial, the jury returned a verdict in favor of respondent and awarded $50,000 in compensatory or presumed damages and $300,000 in punitive damages. Petitioner moved for a new trial. It argued that in *Gertz v. Robert Welch, Inc., supra,* at 349, this Court had ruled broadly that "the States may not permit recovery of presumed or punitive damages, at least when liability is not based on a showing of knowledge of falsity or reckless disregard for the truth," and it argued that the judge's instructions in this case permitted the jury to award such damages on a lesser showing. The trial court indicated some doubt as to whether *Gertz* applied to "non-media cases," but granted a new trial "[b]ecause of * * * dissatisfaction with its charge and * * * conviction that the interests of justice require[d]" it. App. 26.

The Vermont Supreme Court reversed. 143 Vt. 66, 461 A.2d 414 (1983). Although recognizing that "in certain instances the distinction between media and nonmedia defendants may be difficult to draw," the court stated that "no such difficulty is presented with credit reporting agencies, which are in the business of selling financial information to a limited number of subscribers who have paid substantial fees for their services." *Id.,* at 73, 461 A.2d, at 417. Relying on this distinguishing characteristic of credit reporting firms, the court concluded that such firms are not "the type of media worthy of First Amendment protection as contemplated by *New York Times* [Co. v. Sullivan, 376 U.S. 254 (1964),] and its progeny." *Id.,* at 73–74, 461 A.2d, at 417–418. It held that the balance between a private plaintiff's right to recover presumed and punitive damages without a showing of special fault and the First Amendment rights of "nonmedia" speakers "must be struck in favor of the private plaintiff defamed by a nonmedia defendant." *Id.,* at 75, 461 A.2d, at 418. Accordingly, the court held "that as a matter of federal constitutional law, the media protections outlined in *Gertz* are inapplicable to nonmedia defamation actions." *Ibid.*

Recognizing disagreement among the lower courts about when the protections of *Gertz* apply, we granted certiorari. 464 U.S. 959 (1983). We now affirm, although for reasons different from those relied upon by the Vermont Supreme Court.

* * *

In Gertz v. Robert Welch, Inc., 418 U.S. 323 (1974), we held that the protections of *New York Times* did not extend as far as *Rosenbloom* suggested. *Gertz* concerned a libelous article appearing in a magazine called American Opinion, the monthly outlet of the John Birch Society. The article in question discussed whether the prosecution of a policeman in Chicago was part of a Communist campaign to discredit local law enforcement agencies. The plaintiff, Gertz, neither a public official nor a public figure, was a lawyer tangentially involved in the prosecution. The magazine alleged that he was the chief architect of the "frame-up" of the police officer and linked him to Communist activity. Like every other case in which this Court has found constitutional limits to state defamation laws, *Gertz* involved expression on a matter of undoubted public concern.

* * *

IV

We have never considered whether the *Gertz* balance obtains when the defamatory statements involve no issue of public concern. To make this determination, we must employ the approach approved in *Gertz* and balance the State's interest in compensating private individuals for injury to their reputation against the First Amendment interest in protecting this type of expression. This state interest is identical to the one weighed in *Gertz.* * * *

The First Amendment interest, on the other hand, is less important than the one weighed in *Gertz.* We have long recognized that not all speech is of equal First Amendment importance. It is speech on " 'matters of public concern' " that is "at the heart of the First Amendment's protection." * * * In contrast, speech on matters of purely private concern is of less First Amendment concern. * * * As a number of state courts, including the court below, have recognized, the role of the Constitution in regulating state libel law is far more limited when the concerns that activated *New York Times* and *Gertz* are absent. In such a case,

> "[t]here is no threat to the free and robust debate of public issues; there is no potential interference with a meaningful dialogue of ideas concerning self-government; and there is no threat of liability causing a reaction of self-censorship by the press. The facts of the present case are wholly without the First Amendment concerns with which the Supreme Court of the United States has been struggling." Harley–Davidson Motorsports, Inc. v. Markley, 279 Or. 361, 366, 568 P.2d 1359, 1363 (1977).

* * *

* * * In *Gertz,* we found that the state interest in awarding presumed and punitive damages was not "substantial" in view of their effect on speech at the core of First Amendment concern. 418 U.S., at 349. This interest, however, *is* "substantial" relative to the incidental effect these remedies may have on speech of significantly less constitutional interest. The rationale of the common-law rules has been the experience and judgment of history that "proof of actual damage will be impossible in a great many cases where, from the character of the defamatory words and the circumstances of publication, it is all but certain that serious harm has resulted in fact." W. Prosser, Law of Torts § 112, p. 765 (4th ed. 1971); accord, *Rowe v. Metz, supra,* at 425–426, 579 P.2d, at 84; Note, Developments in Law—Defamation, 69 Harv.L.Rev. 875, 891–892 (1956). As a result, courts for centuries have allowed juries to presume that some damage occurred from many defamatory utterances and publications. Restatement of Torts § 568, Comment *b,* p. 162 (1938) (noting that Hale announced that damages were to be presumed for libel as early as 1670). This rule furthers the state interest in providing remedies for defamation by ensuring that those remedies are effective. In light of the reduced constitutional value of speech involving no matters of public concern, we hold that the state interest adequately supports awards of presumed and punitive damages—even absent a showing of "actual malice." [7]

V

The only remaining issue is whether petitioner's credit report involved a matter of public concern. In a related context, we have held that "[w]hether * * * speech addresses a matter of public concern must be determined by [the expression's] content, form, and context * * * as revealed by the whole record." *Connick v. Myers, supra,* at 147–148. These factors indicate that petitioner's credit report concerns no public issue.[8] It was speech solely in the individual interest of the speaker and its specific business audience. * * *

---

7. The dissent, purporting to apply the same balancing test that we do today, concludes that even speech on purely private matters is entitled to the protections of *Gertz.* * * * Its "balance," however, rests on a misinterpretation. In particular, the dissent finds language in *Gertz* that, it believes, shows the State's interest to be "irrelevant." * * *. It is then an easy step for the dissent to say that the State's interest is outweighed by even the reduced First Amendment interest in private speech. *Gertz,* however, did not say that the state interest was "irrelevant" in absolute terms. Indeed, such a statement is belied by *Gertz* itself, for it held that presumed and punitive damages were available under some circumstances. 418 U.S., at 349. Rather, what the *Gertz* language indicates is that the State's interest is not substantial relative to the First Amendment interest in *public speech.* This language is thus irrelevant to today's decision.

The dissent's "balance," moreover, would lead to the protection of all libels—no matter how attenuated their constitutional interest. If the dissent were the law, a woman of impeccable character who was branded a "whore" by a jealous neighbor would have no effective recourse unless she could prove "actual malice" by clear and convincing evidence. This is not malice in the ordinary sense, but in the more demanding sense of *New York Times.* The dissent would, in effect, constitutionalize the entire common law of libel.

8. The dissent suggests that our holding today leaves all credit reporting subject to reduced First Amendment protection. This is incorrect. The protection to be accorded a particular credit report depends on whether the report's "content, form, and context" indicate that it concerns a public matter. * * *

* * *

VI

We conclude that permitting recovery of presumed and punitive damages in defamation cases absent a showing of "actual malice" does not violate the First Amendment when the defamatory statements do not involve matters of public concern. Accordingly, we affirm the judgment of the Vermont Supreme Court.

It is so ordered.

CHIEF JUSTICE BURGER, concurring in the judgment.

In Gertz v. Robert Welch, Inc., 418 U.S. 323 (1974), contrary to well-established common law prevailing in the states, a divided Court held that a private plaintiff in a defamation action cannot recover for a published falsehood unless he proves that the defendant was at least negligent in publishing the falsehood. The Court further held that there can be no "presumed" damages in such an action and that the private plaintiff cannot receive "punitive" damages unless it is established that the publication was made with "actual malice," as defined in New York Times Co. v. Sullivan, 376 U.S. 254 (1964).

I dissented in *Gertz* because I believed that, insofar as the "ordinary private citizen" was concerned, 418 U.S., at 355, the Court's opinion "abandon[ed] the traditional thread," *id.*, at 354–355, that had been the theme of the law in this country up to that time. I preferred to "allow this area of law to continue to evolve as it [had] up to [then] with respect to private citizens rather than embark on a new doctrinal theory which [had] no jurisprudential ancestry." *Ibid.* *Gertz*, however, is now the law of the land, and until it is overruled, it must, under the principle of *stare decisis,* be applied by this Court.

The single question before the Court today is whether *Gertz* applies to this case. The plurality holds that *Gertz* does not apply because, unlike the challenged expression in *Gertz,* the alleged defamatory expression in this case does not relate to a matter of public concern. I agree that *Gertz* is limited to circumstances in which the alleged defamatory expression concerns a matter of general public importance, and that the expression in question here relates to a matter of essentially private concern. I therefore agree with the plurality opinion to the extent that it holds that *Gertz* is inapplicable in this case for the two reasons indicated. No more is needed to dispose of the present case.

I continue to believe, however, that *Gertz* was ill-conceived, and therefore agree with Justice White that *Gertz* should be overruled. I also agree generally with Justice White's observations concerning *New York Times Co. v. Sullivan.* *New York Times,* however, equates "reckless disregard of the truth" with malice; this should permit a jury instruction that malice may be found if the defendant is shown to have published defamatory material which, in the exercise of reasonable care, would have been revealed as untrue. But since the Court has not applied the literal language of *New York Times* in this way, I agree with Justice White that it should be reexamined. The great rights guaranteed by the First Amendment carry with them certain responsibilities as well.

Consideration of these issues inevitably recalls an aphorism of journalism that "too much checking on the facts has ruined many a good news story."

JUSTICE WHITE, concurring in the judgment.

* * *

I joined the judgment and opinion in *New York Times.* I also joined later decisions extending the *New York Times* standard to other situations. But I came to have increasing doubts about the soundness of the Court's approach and about some of the assumptions underlying it. I could not join the plurality opinion in *Rosenbloom,* and I dissented in *Gertz,* asserting that the common-law remedies should be retained for private plaintiffs. I remain convinced that *Gertz* was erroneously decided. I have also become convinced that the Court struck an improvident balance in the *New York Times* case between the public's interest in being fully informed about public officials and public affairs and the competing interest of those who have been defamed in vindicating their reputation.

In a country like ours, where the people purport to be able to govern themselves through their elected representatives, adequate information about their government is of transcendent importance. That flow of intelligence deserves full First Amendment protection. Criticism and assessment of the performance of public officials and of government in general are not subject to penalties imposed by law. But these First Amendment values are not at all served by circulating false statements of fact about public officials. On the contrary, erroneous information frustrates these values. They are even more disserved when the statements falsely impugn the honesty of those men and women and hence lessen the confidence in government. As the Court said in *Gertz:* "[T]here is no constitutional value in false statements of fact. Neither the intentional lie nor the careless error materially advances society's interest in 'uninhibited, robust, and wide-open' debate on public issues." 418 U.S., at 340. Yet in *New York Times* cases, the public official's complaint will be dismissed unless he alleges and makes out a jury case of a knowing or reckless falsehood. Absent such proof, there will be no jury verdict or judgment of any kind in his favor, even if the challenged publication is admittedly false. The lie will stand, and the public continue to be misinformed about public matters. This will recurringly happen because the putative plaintiff's burden is so exceedingly difficult to satisfy and can be discharged only by expensive litigation. Even if the plaintiff sues, he frequently loses on summary judgment or never gets to the jury because of insufficient proof of malice. If he wins before the jury, verdicts are often overturned by appellate courts for failure to prove malice. Furthermore, when the plaintiff loses, the jury will likely return a general verdict and there will be no judgment that the publication was false, even though it was without foundation in reality.² The public is left to conclude that the challenged statement was true after all. Their only chance of being accurately informed is measured by the public official's ability himself to counter the lie, unaided by the courts. That is a decidedly weak need to depend on for the vindication of First Amendment interests—"it is the rare case where the denial overtakes the original charge. Denials, retractions, and corrections are not 'hot' news, and rarely receive the prominence of the original story." *Rosenbloom,* 403 U.S., at 46–47 (opinion of BRENNAN, J.); *Gertz, supra,* at 363–364 (BRENNAN, J., dissenting).

* * *

The *New York Times* rule thus countenances two evils: first, the stream of information about public officials and public affairs is polluted and often remains polluted by false information; and second, the reputation and professional life of the defeated plaintiff may be destroyed by falsehoods that might have been avoided with a reasonable effort to investigate the facts. In terms of the First Amendment and reputational interests at stake, these seem grossly perverse results.

* * *

In *New York Times,* instead of escalating the plaintiff's burden of proof to an almost impossible level, we could have achieved our stated goal by limiting the recoverable damages to a level that would not unduly threaten the press. Punitive damages might have been scrutinized as Justice Harlan suggested in *Rosenbloom, supra,* at 77, or perhaps even entirely forbidden. Presumed damages to reputation might have been prohibited, or limited, as in *Gertz*. Had that course been taken and the common-law standard of liability been retained, the defamed public official, upon proving falsity, could at least have had a judgment to that effect. His reputation would then be vindicated; and to the extent possible, the misinformation circulated would have been countered. He might have also recovered a modest amount, enough perhaps to pay his litigation expenses. At the very least, the public official should not have been required to satisfy the actual malice standard where he sought no damages but only to clear his name. In

---

2. If the plaintiff succeeds in proving a jury case of malice, it may be that the jury will be asked to bring in separate verdicts on falsity and malice. In that event, there could be a verdict in favor of the plaintiff on falsity, but against him on malice. There would be no judgment in his favor, but the verdict on falsity would be a public one and would tend to set the record right and clear the plaintiff's name.

It might be suggested that courts, as organs of the government, cannot be trusted to discern what the truth is. But the logical consequence of that view is that the First Amendment forbids all libel and slander suits, for in each such suit, there will be no recovery unless the court finds the publication at issue to be factually false. Of course, no forum is perfect, but that is not a justification for leaving whole classes of defamed individuals without redress or a realistic opportunity to clear their names. We entrust to juries and the courts the responsibility of decisions affecting the life and liberty of persons. It is perverse indeed to say that these bodies are incompetent to inquire into the truth of a statement of fact in a defamation case. I can therefore discern nothing in the constitution which forbids a plaintiff to obtain a judicial decree that a statement is false—a decree he can then use in the community to clear his name and to prevent further damage from a defamation already published.

this way, both First Amendment and reputational interests would have been far better served.

We are not talking in these cases about mere criticism or opinion, but about misstatements of fact that seriously harm the reputation of another, by lowering him in the estimation of the community or to deter third persons from associating or dealing with him. Restatement of Torts § 559 (1938). The necessary breathing room for speakers can be ensured by limitations on recoverable damages; it does not also require depriving many public figures of any room to vindicate their reputations sullied by false statements of fact. It could be suggested that even without the threat of large presumed and punitive damages awards, press defendants' communication will be unduly chilled by having to pay for the actual damages caused to those they defame. But other commercial enterprises in this country not in the business of disseminating information must pay for the damage they cause as a cost of doing business, and it is difficult to argue that the United States did not have a free and vigorous press before the rule in *New York Times* was announced. In any event, the *New York Times* standard was formulated to protect the press from the chilling danger of numerous large damages awards. Nothing in the central rationale behind *New York Times* demands an absolute immunity from suits to establish the falsity of a defamatory misstatement about a public figure where the plaintiff cannot make out a jury case of actual malice.

* * *

The question before us is whether *Gertz* is to be applied in this case. For either of two reasons, I believe that it should not. First, I am unreconciled to the *Gertz* holding and believe that it should be overruled. Second, as Justice Powell indicates, the defamatory publication in this case does not deal with a matter of public importance. Consequently, I concur in the Court's judgment.

JUSTICE BRENNAN, with whom JUSTICE MARSHALL, JUSTICE BLACKMUN, and JUSTICE STEVENS join, dissenting.

This case involves a difficult question of the proper application of Gertz v. Robert Welch, Inc., 418 U.S. 323 (1974), to credit reporting—a type of speech at some remove from that which first gave rise to explicit First Amendment restrictions on state defamation law—and has produced a diversity of considered opinions, none of which speaks for the Court. * * *

* * *

II

The question presented here is narrow. Neither the parties nor the courts below have suggested that respondent Greenmoss Builders should be required to show actual malice to obtain a judgment and actual compensatory damages. Nor do the parties question the requirement of *Gertz* that respondent must show fault to obtain a judgment and actual damages. The only question presented is whether a jury award of presumed and punitive damages based on less than a showing of actual malice is constitutionally permissible. *Gertz* provides a forthright negative answer. To preserve the jury verdict in this case, therefore, the opinions of Justice Powell and Justice White have cut away the protective mantle of *Gertz.*

* * *

Even if not at "the essence of self-government," *Garrison v. Louisiana,* 379 U.S. 64, 74–75 (1964), the expression at issue in this case is important to both our public discourse and our private welfare. That its motivation might be the economic interest of the speaker or listeners does not diminish its First Amendment value. See Consolidated Edison Co. v. Public Service Comm'n of New York, 447 U.S. 530 (1980). Whether or not such speech is sufficiently central to First Amendment values to require actual malice as a standard of liability, this speech certainly falls within the range of speech that *Gertz* sought to protect from the chill of unrestrained presumed and punitive damages awards.

* * * The special harms caused by inaccurate credit reports, the lack of public sophistication about or access to such reports, and the fact that such reports by and large contain statements that are fairly readily susceptible of verification, all may justify appropriate regulation designed to prevent the social losses caused by false credit reports. And in the libel context, the States' regulatory interest in protecting reputation is served by rules permitting recovery for actual compensatory damages upon a showing of fault. Any further interest in deterring potential defamation through case-by-case judicial imposition of presumed and punitive damages awards on less than a showing of actual malice simply exacts too high a toll on First Amendment values. Accordingly, Greenmoss Builders should be permitted to recover for any actual damage it can show resulted from Dun & Bradstreet's negligently false credit report, but should be required to show actual malice to receive presumed or punitive damages. Because the jury was not instructed in accordance with these principles, we would reverse and remand for further proceedings not inconsistent with this opinion.

MIAMI HERALD PUBLISHING COMPANY v. TORNILLO

Supreme Court of the United States, 1974.
418 U.S. 241, 94 S.Ct. 2831, 41 L.Ed.2d 730.

MR. CHIEF JUSTICE BURGER delivered the opinion of the Court.

The issue in this case is whether a state statute granting a political candidate a right to equal space to reply to criticism and attacks on his record by a newspaper violates the guarantees of a free press.

I

In the fall of 1972, appellee, Executive Director of the Classroom Teachers Association, apparently a teachers' collective-bargaining agent, was a candidate for the Florida House of Representatives. On September 20, 1972, and again on September 29, 1972, appellant printed editorials critical of appellee's candidacy. In response to these editorials appellee demanded that appellant print verbatim his replies, defending the role of the Classroom Teachers Association and the organization's accomplishments for the citizens of Dade County. Appellant declined to print the appellee's replies, and appellee brought suit in Circuit Court, Dade County, seeking declaratory and injunctive relief and actual and punitive damages in excess of $5,000. The action was premised on Florida Statute § 104.38 (1973), a "right of reply" statute which provides that if a candidate for nomination or election is assailed regarding his personal character or official record by any newspaper, the candidate has the right to demand that the newspaper print, free of cost to the candidate, any reply the candidate may make to the newspaper's charges. The reply must appear in as conspicuous a place and in the same kind of type as the charges which prompted the reply, provided it does not take up more space than the charges. Failure to comply with the statute constitutes a first-degree misdemeanor.

Appellant sought a declaration that § 104.38 was unconstitutional. After an emergency hearing requested by appellee, the Circuit Court * * * held that § 104.38 was unconstitutional as an infringement on the freedom of the press under the First and Fourteenth Amendments to the Constitution. * * *

On direct appeal, the Florida Supreme Court reversed, holding that § 104.38 did not violate constitutional guarantees. * * * It held that free speech was enhanced and not abridged by the Florida right-of-reply statute, which in that court's view, furthered the "broad social interest in the free flow of information to the public." * * * It also held that the statute is not impermissibly vague; the statute informs "those who are subject to it as to what conduct on their part will render them liable to its penalties." *Id.*, at 85.[4] Civil remedies, including damages, were held to be available under this statute; the case was remanded to the trial court for further proceedings not inconsistent with the Florida Supreme Court's opinion.

* * *

The appellee and supporting advocates of an enforceable right of access to the press vigorously argue that government has an obligation to ensure that a wide variety of views reach the public. The contentions of access proponents will be set out in some detail. It is urged that at the time the First Amendment to the Constitution was ratified in 1791 as part of our Bill of Rights the press was broadly representative of the people it was serving. While many of the newspapers were intensely partisan and narrow in their views, the press collectively presented a broad range of opinions to readers. Entry into publishing was inexpensive; pamphlets and books provided meaningful alternatives to the organized press for the expression of unpopular ideas and often treated events and expressed views not covered by conventional

---

4. The Supreme Court placed the following limiting construction on the statute:

"[W]e hold that the mandate of the statute refers to 'any reply' which is wholly responsive to the charge made in the editorial or other article in a newspaper being replied to and further that such reply will be neither libelous nor slanderous of the publication not anyone else, nor vulgar nor profane." *Id.*, at 86.

newspapers. A true marketplace of ideas existed in which there was relatively easy access to the channels of communication.

Access advocates submit that although newspapers of the present are superficially similar to those of 1791 the press of today is in reality very different from that known in the early years of our national existence. In the past half century a communications revolution has seen the introduction of radio and television into our lives, the promise of a global community through the use of communications satellites, and the specter of a "wired" nation by means of an expanding cable television network with two-way capabilities. The printed press, it is said, has not escaped the effects of this revolution. Newspapers have become big business and there are far fewer of them to serve a larger literate population. Chains of newspapers, national newspapers, national wire and news services, and one-newspaper towns, are the dominant features of a press that has become noncompetitive and enormously powerful and influential in its capacity to manipulate popular opinion and change the course of events. * * *

* * *

The obvious solution, which was available to dissidents at an earlier time when entry into publishing was relatively inexpensive, today would be to have additional newspapers. But the same economic factors which have caused the disappearance of vast numbers of metropolitan newspapers, have made entry into the marketplace of ideas served by the print media almost impossible. It is urged that the claim of newspapers to be "surrogates for the public" carries with it a concomitant fiduciary obligation to account for that stewardship. From this premise it is reasoned that the only effective way to insure fairness and accuracy and to provide for some accountability is for government to take affirmative action. The First Amendment interest of the public in being informed is said to be in peril because the "marketplace of ideas" is today a monopoly controlled by the owners of the market.

* * *

IV

However much validity may be found in these arguments, at each point the implementation of a remedy such as an enforceable right of access necessarily calls for some mechanism, either governmental or consensual. If it is governmental coercion, this at once brings about a confrontation with the express provisions of the First Amendment and the judicial gloss on that Amendment developed over the years.

* * * In Columbia Broadcasting System, Inc. v. Democratic National Committee, 412 U.S. 94, 117 (1973), the plurality opinion as to Part III noted:

> "The power of a privately owned newspaper to advance its own political, social, and economic views is bounded by only two factors: first, the acceptance of a sufficient number of readers—and hence advertisers—to assure financial success; and, second, the journalistic integrity of its editors and publishers."

An attitude strongly adverse to any attempt to extend a right of access to newspapers was echoed by other Members of this Court in their separate opinions in that case. *Id.,* at 145 (STEWART, J., concurring); id., at 182 n. 12 (BRENNAN, J., joined by MARSHALL, J., dissenting). Recently, while approving a bar against employment advertising specifying "male" or "female" preference, the Court's opinion in Pittsburgh Press Co. v. Human Relations Comm'n, 413 U.S. 376, 391 (1973), took pains to limit its holding within narrow bounds * * *

* * *

Appellee's argument that the Florida statute does not amount to a restriction of appellant's right to speak because "the statute in question here has not prevented the Miami Herald from saying anything it wished" begs the core question. Compelling editors or publishers to publish that which "'reason' tells them should not be published" is what is at issue in this case. The Florida statute operates as a command in the same sense as a statute or regulation forbidding appellant to publish specified matter. Governmental restraint on publishing need not fall into familiar or traditional patterns to be subject to constitutional limitations on governmental powers. Grosjean v. American Press Co., 297 U.S. 233, 244–245 (1936). The Florida statute exacts a penalty on the basis of the content of a newspaper. The first phase of the penalty resulting from the compelled printing of a reply is exacted in terms of the cost in printing and composing time and materials and in taking up space that could be devoted to other material the newspaper may have preferred to print. * * *

Faced with the penalties that would accrue to any newspaper that published news or commentary arguably within the reach of the right-of-access statute, editors might well conclude that the safe course is to avoid controversy. Therefore, under the operation of the Florida statute, political and electoral coverage would be blunted or reduced. Government-enforced right of access inescapably "dampens the vigor and limits the variety of public debate," New York Times Co. v. Sullivan, 376 U.S., at 279. * * *

Even if a newspaper would face no additional costs to comply with a compulsory access law and would not be forced to forego publication of news or opinion by the inclusion of a reply, the Florida statute fails to clear the barriers of the First Amendment because of its intrusion into the function of editors. A newspaper is more than a passive receptacle or conduit for news, comment, and advertising. The choice of material to go into a newspaper, and the decisions made as to limitations on the size and content of the paper, and treatment of public issues and public officials—whether fair or unfair—constitute the exercise of editorial control and judgment. It has yet to be demonstrated how governmental regulation of this crucial process can be exercised consistent with the First Amendment guarantees of a free press as they have evolved to this time. Accordingly, the judgment of the Supreme Court of Florida is reversed.

It is so ordered.

Mr. Justice Brennan, with whom Mr. Justice Rehnquist joins, concurring.

I join the Court's opinion which, as I understand it, addresses only "right of reply" statutes and implies no view upon the constitutionality of "retraction" statutes affording plaintiffs able to prove defamatory falsehoods a statutory action to require publication of a retraction.
* * *

HUSTLER MAGAZINE v. FALWELL
Supreme Court of the United States, 1988.
485 U.S. 46, 108 S.Ct. 876, 99 L.Ed.2d 41.

Mr. Chief Justice Rehnquist delivered the opinion of the Court.

Petitioner Hustler Magazine, Inc., is a magazine of nationwide circulation. Respondent Jerry Falwell, a nationally known minister who has been active as a commentator on politics and public affairs, sued petitioner and its publisher, petitioner Larry Flynt, to recover damages for invasion of privacy, libel, and intentional infliction of emotional distress. The District Court directed a verdict against respondent on the privacy claim, and submitted the other two claims to a jury. The jury found for petitioners on the defamation count, but found for respondent on the claim for intentional infliction of emotional distress and awarded damages. We now consider whether this award is consistent with the First and Fourteenth Amendments of the United States Constitution.

The inside front cover of the November 1983 issue of Hustler Magazine featured a "parody" of an advertisement for Campari Liqueur that contained the name and picture of respondent and was entitled, "Jerry Falwell talks about his first time." This parody was modeled after actual Campari ads that included interviews with various celebrities about their "first times." Although it was apparent by the end of each interview that this meant the first time they sampled Campari, the ads clearly played on the sexual double entendre of the general subject of "first times." Copying the form and layout of these Campari ads, Hustler's editors chose respondent as the featured celebrity and drafted an alleged "interview" with him in which he stated that his "first time" was during a drunken incestuous rendezvous with his mother in an outhouse. The Hustler parody portrays respondent and his mother as drunk and immoral, and suggests that respondent is a hypocrite who preaches only when he is drunk. In small print at the bottom of the page, the ad contains the disclaimer, "ad parody—not to be taken seriously." The magazine's table of contents also lists the ad as "Fiction; Ad and Personality Parody."

Soon after the November issue of Hustler became available to the public, respondent brought this diversity action in the United States District Court for the Western District of Virginia against Hustler Magazine, Inc., Larry C. Flynt, and Flynt Distributing Co. Respondent stated in his complaint that publication of the ad parody in Hustler entitled him to recover damages for libel, invasion of privacy, and intentional infliction of emotional distress. The case proceeded to trial.[1] At the close of the evidence, the District Court granted a directed verdict for petitioners on the invasion of privacy claim. The jury then found against respondent on the libel claim, specifically finding that the ad parody could not "reasonably be understood as describing actual facts about [respondent] or actual events in which [he] participated." App. to Pet. for Cert. C1. The jury ruled for respondent on the intentional infliction of emotional distress claim, however, and stated that he should be awarded $100,000 in compensatory damages, as well as $50,000 each in punitive damages from petitioners.[2] Petitioners' motion for judgment notwithstanding the verdict was denied.

On appeal, the United States Court of Appeals for the Fourth Circuit affirmed the judgment against petitioners. Falwell v. Flynt, 797 F.2d 1270 (CA4 1986). The court rejected petitioners' argument that the "actual malice" standard of New York Times Co. v. Sullivan, 376 U.S. 254 (1964), must be met before respondent can recover for emotional distress. The court agreed that because respondent is concededly a public figure, petitioners are "entitled to the same level of first amendment protection in the claim for intentional infliction of emotional distress that they received in [respondent's] claim for libel." 797 F.2d, at 1274. But this does not mean that a literal application of the actual malice rule is appropriate in the context of an emotional distress claim. In the court's view, the *New York Times* decision emphasized the constitutional importance not of the statement or the defendant's disregard for the truth, but of the heightened level of culpability embodied in the requirement of "knowing * * * or reckless" conduct. Here, the *New York Times* standard is satisfied by the state-law requirement, and the jury's finding, that the defendants have acted intentionally or recklessly.[3] The Court of Appeals then went on to reject the contention that because the jury found that the ad parody did not describe actual facts about respondent, the ad was an opinion that is protected by the First Amendment. As the court put it, this was "irrelevant," as the issue is "whether [the ad's] publication was sufficiently outrageous to constitute intentional infliction of emotional distress." *Id.*, at 1276.[4] Petitioners then filed a petition for rehearing en banc, but this was denied by a divided court. Given the importance of the constitutional issues involved, we granted certiorari.

This case presents us with a novel question involving First Amendment limitations upon a State's authority to protect its citizens from

---

1. While this case was pending, the ad parody was published in Hustler magazine a second time.

2. The jury found no liability on the part of Flynt Distributing Co., Inc. It is consequently not a party to this appeal.

3. Under Virginia law, in an action for intentional infliction of emotional distress a plaintiff must show that the defendant's conduct (1) is intentional or reckless; (2) offends generally accepted standards of decency or morality; (3) is causally connected with the plaintiff's emotional distress; and (4) caused emotional distress that was severe. 797 F.2d at 1275, n. 4 (citing Womack v. Eldridge, 215 Va. 338, 210 S.E.2d 145 (1974)).

4. The court below also rejected several other contentions that petitioners do not raise in this appeal.

the intentional infliction of emotional distress. We must decide whether a public figure may recover damages for emotional harm caused by the publication of an ad parody offensive to him, and doubtless gross and repugnant in the eyes of most. Respondent would have us find that a State's interest in protecting public figures from emotional distress is sufficient to deny First Amendment protection to speech that is patently offensive and is intended to inflict emotional injury, even when that speech could not reasonably have been interpreted as stating actual facts about the public figure involved. This we decline to do.

At the heart of the First Amendment is the recognition of the fundamental importance of the free flow of ideas and opinions on matters of public interest and concern. "[T]he freedom to speak one's mind is not only an aspect of individual liberty—and thus a good unto itself—but also is essential to the common quest for truth and the vitality of society as a whole." Bose Corp. v. Consumers Union of United States, Inc., 466 U.S. 485, 503–504 (1984). We have therefore been particularly vigilant to ensure that individual expressions of ideas remain freed from governmentally imposed sanctions. The First Amendment recognizes no such thing as a "false" idea. Gertz v. Robert Welch, Inc., 418 U.S. 323, 339 (1974). As Justice Holmes wrote, "[W]hen men have realized that time has upset many fighting faiths, they may come to believe even more than they believe the very foundations of their own conduct that the ultimate good desired is better reached by free trade in ideas—that the best test of truth is the power of the thought to get itself accepted in the competition of the market. * * *" Abrams v. United States, 250 U.S. 616, 630 (1919) (dissenting opinion).

The sort of robust political debate encouraged by the First Amendment is bound to produce speech that is critical of those who hold public office or those public figures who are "intimately involved in the resolution of important public questions or, by reason of their fame, shape events in areas of concern to society at large." *Associated Press v. Walker,* decided with Curtis Publishing Co. v. Butts, 388 U.S. 130, 164 (1967) (Warren, C.J., concurring in result). Justice Frankfurter put it succinctly in Baumgartner v. United States, 322 U.S. 665, 673–674 (1944), when he said that "[o]ne of the prerogatives of American citizenship is the right to criticize public men and measures." Such criticism, inevitably, will not always be reasoned or moderate; public figures as well as public officials will be subject to "vehement, caustic, and sometimes unpleasantly sharp attacks," *New York Times, supra,* 376 U.S., at 270. "[T]he candidate who vaunts his spotless record and sterling integrity cannot convincingly cry 'Foul!' when an opponent or an industrious reporter attempts to demonstrate the contrary." Monitor Patriot Co. v. Roy, 401 U.S. 265, 274 (1971).

Of course, this does not mean that *any* speech about a public figure is immune from sanction in the form of damages. Since *New York Times Co. v. Sullivan, supra,* we have consistently ruled that a public figure may hold a speaker liable for the damage to reputation caused by publication of a defamatory falsehood, but only if the statement was made "with knowledge that it was false or with reckless disregard of whether it was false or not." *Id.,* 376 U.S., at 279–280. False statements of fact are particularly valueless; they interfere with the truth seeking function of the marketplace of ideas, and they cause damage to individual's reputation that cannot easily be repaired by counterspeech, however, persuasive or effective. See *Gertz,* 418 U.S. at 340, 344. But even though falsehoods have little value in and of themselves, they are "nevertheless inevitable in free debate," *id.,* at 340, and a rule that would impose strict liability on a publisher for false factual assertions would have an undoubted "chilling" effect on speech relating to public figures that does have constitutional value. "Freedoms of expression require 'breathing space'." Philadelphia Newspapers, Inc. v. Hepps, 475 U.S. 767, 772 (1986) (quoting *New York Times,* 376 U.S., at 272). This breathing space is provided by a constitutional rule that allows public figures to recover for libel or defamation only when they can prove *both* that the statement was false and that the statement was made with the requisite level of culpability.

Respondent argues, however, that a different standard should apply in this case because here the State seeks to prevent not reputational damage, but the severe emotional distress suffered by the person who is the subject of an offensive publication. Cf. Zacchini v. Scripps–Howard Broadcasting Co., 433 U.S. 562 (1977) (ruling that the "actual malice" standard does not apply to the tort of appropriation of a right of publicity). In respondent's view, and in the view of the Court of Appeals, so long as the utterance was intended to inflict emotional distress, was outrageous, and did in fact inflict serious emotional distress, it is of no constitutional import whether the statement was a fact or an opinion, or whether it was true or false. It is the intent to cause injury that is the gravamen of the tort, and the State's interest in preventing emotional harm simply outweighs whatever interest a speaker may have in speech of this type.

Generally speaking the law does not regard the intent to inflict emotional distress as one which should receive much solicitude, and it is quite understandable that most if not all jurisdictions have chosen to make it civilly culpable where the conduct in question is sufficiently "outrageous." But in the world of debate about public affairs, many things done with motives that are less than admirable are protected by the First Amendment. In Garrison v. Louisiana, 379 U.S. 64 (1964), we held that even when a speaker or writer is motivated by hatred or ill-will his expression was protected by the First Amendment:

> "Debate on public issues will not be uninhibited if the speaker must run the risk that it will be proved in court that he spoke out of hatred; even if he did speak out of hatred, utterances honestly believed contribute to the free interchange." *Id.,* at 73.

Thus while such a bad motive may be deemed controlling for purposes of tort liability in other areas of the law, we think the First Amendment prohibits such a result in the area of public debate about public figures.

Were we to hold otherwise, there can be little doubt that political cartoonists and satirists would be subjected to damages awards without any showing that their work falsely defamed its subject. Webster's defines a caricature as "the deliberately distorted picturing or imitating of a person, literary style, etc. by exaggerating features or mannerisms for satirical effect." Webster's New Unabridged Twentieth Century Dictionary of the English Language 275 (2d ed. 1979). The appeal of the political cartoon or caricature is often based on exploration of unfortunate physical traits or politically embarrassing events—an exploration often calculated to injure the feelings of the subject of the portrayal. The art of the cartoonist is often not reasoned or evenhanded, but slashing and one-sided. One cartoonist expressed the nature of the art in these words:

> "The political cartoon is a weapon of attack, of scorn and ridicule and satire; it is least effective when it tries to pat some politician on the back. It is usually as welcome as a bee sting and is always controversial in some quarters." Long, The Political Cartoon: Journalism's Strongest Weapon, The Quill, 56, 67 (Nov. 1962).

Several famous examples of this type of intentionally injurious speech were drawn by Thomas Nast, probably the greatest American cartoonist to date, who was associated for many years during the post-Civil War era with Harper's Weekly. In the pages of that publication Nast conducted a graphic vendetta against William M. "Boss" Tweed and his corrupt associates in New York City's "Tweed Ring." It has been described by one historian of the subject as "a sustained attack which in its passion and effectiveness stands alone in the history of American graphic art." M. Keller, The Art and Politics of Thomas Nast 177 (1968). Another writer explains that the success of the Nast cartoon was achieved "because of the emotional impact of its presentation. It continuously goes beyond the bounds of good taste and conventional matters." C. Press, The Political Cartoon 251 (1981).

Despite their sometimes caustic nature, from the early cartoon portraying George Washington as an ass down to the present day, graphic depictions and satirical cartoons have played a prominent role in public and political debate. Nast's castigation of the Tweed Ring, Walt McDougall's characterization of presidential candidate James G. Blaine's banquet with the millionaires at Delmonico's as "The Royal Feast of Belshazzar," and numerous other efforts have undoubtedly had an effect on the course and outcome of contemporaneous debate. Lincoln's tall, gangling posture, Teddy Roosevelt's glasses and teeth, and Franklin D. Roosevelt's jutting jaw and cigarette holder have been memorialized by political cartoons with an effect that could not have been obtained by the photographer or the portrait artist. From the viewpoint of history it is clear that our political discourse would have been considerably poorer without them.

Respondent contends, however, that the caricature in question here was so "outrageous" as to distinguish it from more traditional political cartoons. There is no doubt that the caricature of respondent and his mother published in Hustler is at best a distant cousin of the political cartoons described above, and a rather poor relation at that. If it were possible by laying down a principled standard to separate the one from the other, public discourse would probably suffer little or no harm. But we doubt that there is any such standard, and we are quite sure that the pejorative description "outrageous" does not supply one. "Outrageousness" in the area of political and social discourse has an inherent subjectiveness about it which would allow a jury to impose liability on the basis of the jurors' tastes or views, or perhaps on the basis of their dislike of a particular expression. An "outrageousness" standard thus runs afoul of our longstanding refusal to allow damages to be awarded because the speech in question may have an adverse emotional impact on the audience. See NAACP v. Claiborne Hardware Co., 458 U.S. 886, 910 (1982) ("Speech does not lose its protected character * * * simply because it may embarrass others or coerce them into action." And, as we stated in FCC v. Pacifica Foundation, 438 U.S. 726 (1978):

> "[T]he fact that society may find speech offensive is not a sufficient reason for suppressing it. Indeed, if it is the speaker's opinion that gives offense, that consequence is a reason for according it constitutional protection. For it is a central tenet of the First Amendment that the government must remain neutral in the marketplace of ideas." Id., at 745–746.

See also Street v. New York, 394 U.S. 576, 592 (1969) ("It is firmly settled that * * * the public expression of ideas may not be prohibited merely because the ideas are themselves offensive to some of their hearers").

Admittedly, these oft-repeated First Amendment principles, like other principles, are subject to limitations. We recognize in *Pacifica Foundation*, that speech that is "'vulgar,' 'offensive,' and 'shocking'" is "not entitled to absolute constitutional protection under all circumstances." 438 U.S., at 747. In Chaplinsky v. New Hampshire, 315 U.S. 568 (1942), we held that a state could lawfully punish an individual for the use of insulting "'fighting' words—those which by their very utterance inflict injury or tend to incite an immediate breach of the peace." Id., at 571–572. These limitations are but recognition of the observation in Dun & Bradstreet, Inc. v. Greenmoss Builders, Inc., 472 U.S. 749, 758 (1985), that this Court has "long recognized that not all speech is of equal First Amendment importance." But the sort of expression involved in this case does not seem to us to be governed by any exception to the general First Amendment principles stated above.

We conclude that public figures and public officials may not recover for the tort of intentional infliction of emotional distress by reason of publications such as the one here at issue without showing in addition that the publication contains a false statement of fact which was made with "actual malice," *i.e.* with knowledge that the statement was false or with reckless disregard as to whether or not it was true. This is not merely a "blind application," of the *New York Times* standard, see Time, Inc. v. Hill, 385 U.S. 374, 390 (1967), it reflects our considered judgment that such a standard is necessary to give adequate "breathing space" to the freedoms protected by the First Amendment.

Here it is clear that respondent Falwell is a "public figure" for purposes of First Amendment law.[5] The jury found against respondent on his libel claim when it decided that the Hustler ad parody could not "reasonably be understood as describing actual facts about [respondent] or actual events in which [he] participated." App. to Pet. for Cert. C1. The Court of Appeals interpreted the jury's finding to be that the ad parody "was not reasonably believable," 797 F.2d, at 1278, and in accordance with our custom we accept this finding. Respondent is thus relegated to his claim for damages awarded by the jury for the intentional infliction of emotional distress by "outrageous" conduct. But for reasons heretofore stated this claim cannot, consistently with the First Amendment, form a basis for the award of damages when the conduct in question is the publication of a caricature such as the ad parody involved here. The judgment of the Court of Appeals is accordingly

Reversed.

Mr. Justice Kennedy took no part in the consideration or decision of this case.

Mr. Justice White, concurring in the judgment.

As I see it, the decision in New York Times Co. v. Sullivan, 376 U.S. 254 (1964), has little to do with this case, for here the jury found that the ad contained no assertion of fact. But I agree with the Court that the judgment below, which penalized the publication of the parody, cannot be squared with the First Amendment.

NOTE

I. The lower court opinion [73] reproduced a portion of the deposition of Larry Flynt, including the following:

Q. Did you want to upset Reverend Falwell?

A. Yes * * *

Q. Do you recognize that in having published what you did in this ad, you were attempting to convey to the people who read it that Reverend Falwell was just as you characterized him, a liar?

A. Yeah. He's a liar, too.

Q. How about a hypocrite?

A. Yeah.

Q. That's what you wanted to convey?

---

5. Neither party disputes this conclusion. Respondent is the host of a nationally syndicated television show and was the founder and president of a political organization formerly known as the Moral Majority. He is also the founder of Liberty University in Lynchburg, Virginia, and is the author of several books and publications. Who's Who in America 849 (44th ed. 1986–1987).

73. Falwell v. Flynt, 797 F.2d 1270, 1273 (4th Cir.1986).

A. Yeah.

Q. Did you appreciate, at the time that you wrote "okay" or approved this publication, that for Reverend Falwell to function in his livelihood, and in his commitment and career, he has to have an integrity that people believe in? Did you not appreciate that?

A. Yeah.

Q. And wasn't one of your objectives to destroy that integrity, or harm it, if you could?

A. To assassinate it.

II. The immediate depiction of Falwell in the *Hustler* feature,—a feature in turn parodying advertisements for Campari, was, as the Court notes, not presented as an actual interview. On that basis, the action for libel was deemed to be lost. Because the jury found that the ad content could not "reasonably be understood as describing [any] actual facts," the libel branch of the plaintiff's cause of action was deemed to self-destruct.

But even assuming that an action in libel requires evidence that defendant published some assertion of a defamatory character in clear reference to the plaintiff—which assertion the plaintiff must prove to be false in fact,[74] in light of the deposition transcript might one not argue that Falwell could still meet (i.e. overcome) this minimum test? Why ought he not be allowed to establish by evidence of convincing clarity to the satisfaction of a jury that in fact he has been viciously maligned, i.e. that he is none of the kinds of person he is depicted to be—that he is not in fact anything like the kind of person he has been depicted as being[75]—and that he has plainly, therefore, been libeled by *Hustler?* What is it that bars him from recovering for defamation, even if he cannot recover for the intentional infliction of emotional distress?

Suppose Flynt had not libeled Falwell in the manner he employed but simply more directly, i.e. by simple assertion such as this: "This man Falwell is a liar and a hypocrite." Assuming Falwell can establish that he is neither (i.e. neither a liar nor a hypocrite), may he now be able to recover defamation damages from Flynt? If he could, at least if he could also meet the *Sullivan* requirement, could he recover not only for a statement published by Flynt of exactly that sort, but possibly even for this one as well: "In my opinion, Falwell is a liar and a hypocrite?"[76]

---

74. Cf. Burton v. Crowell Pub. Co., 82 F.2d 154 (2d Cir.1936) (recovery in libel allowed for damage to reputation consequential to publication of unretouched, not false-in-fact photograph, Opinion by Learned Hand).

75. Namely, as prurient and lecherous, a sensualist and hypocrite, etc.

76. For a recent significant case holding that the recasting of a given statement into the form of an opinion does not automatically convert it from actionable to inactionable, see Miklovich v. Lorain Journal Co., 497 U.S. ___, 110 S.Ct. 2695, 111 L.Ed.2d 1 (1990). (Where the published opinion implies to the reader the existence of facts as presumably known to the publisher and not furnished in the story, recovery may be based on the opinion's implicit claim of actual facts.)

III. —The case assuredly seems to leave open the possibility that in either of these other kinds of cases, some sort of action for libel might be brought. Perhaps nothing in the material we have already reviewed precludes such an action. Yet, surely the calculated harm arising from either of these forms of defamation may be no greater in fact (and may in some ways be considerably less, may it not?) than the calculated harm inflicted by the device Flynt actually chose. And the degree of real falsehood may be no greater, as well, may it not? Why, then, should the first amendment be deemed to bar one but allow the other, i.e. to make actionability depend upon the mere form in which the libel appears?

IV. Both the purpose and effect of allowing redress in defamation actions may appear to be quite consistent with characteristics of one genre of personal or of group libel—a genre one might call "libel by vicious fiction." Vicious fiction may—and arguably did in this instance—describe the *Hustler* technique.[77] More generally, one might describe "vicious fiction" as material willfully contrived to induce false, deeply negative, repugnant impressions of the person or the group who are thus made the object of the maligner's art. If such material is nonetheless to be deemed protected by the first amendment from actions in defamation (and *Hustler Magazine v. Falwell* provides a very strong example that it will be—at least in respect to public figures and political events [78]), it ought to be fairly easy to say why. What does the Court say, in *Hustler Magazine, Inc. v. Falwell?*[79]

This issue is joined strongly still again, in the following case—on "false" statements and civil rights claims in a newer setting: a case of the first amendment and the feminist critique. Although it is but a court of appeals decision (summarily affirmed by the Supreme Court), it is a useful bookend on the immediate subject of our review. It also

77. For an additional example—that makes the treatment of Falwell seem pale in comparison, see Dworkin v. Hustler Magazine Inc., 867 F.2d 1188 (9th Cir. 1989).

78. Indeed, *Hustler Magazine* would appear to limit one's hope for redress to that which can be gotten solely by one's efforts to falsify the critical perspective created by the defaming fiction,—to do so by the way one actually lives one's life and actually conducts oneself (thereby falsifying the defaming stereotype the vicious fiction summoned forth).

79. Consider the following conundrum: If (a) something is meant to and does defame; if (b) it also contains no "true" statement (but only a "false" statement insofar as it contains any statement at all); then (c) of what social good can it be such that it should nonetheless be protected by the first amendment? —Or is this a "conundrum" that would, if it were taken seriously, threaten a great deal of fiction indeed, e.g., from Shakespeare through Dickens, Mark Twain, Joseph Heller, and Tom Wolfe, and from Hogarth and Daumier through Nast, Herblock, Oliphant and Larry Flynt. (Moreover,—quite depending on your own point of view, might it also potentially threaten an uncertain number of other works as well, e.g., *Das Kapital* or *Mein Kampf* or, for that matter, portions of the *New* or *Old Testament* or the *Koran*.)

For a thoughtful review of *Hustler Magazine v. Falwell* in probing such matters more generally, see Post, The Constitutional Concept of Public Discourse: Outrageous Opinion, Democratic Deliberation, and Hustler Magazine v. Falwell, 103 Harv.L. Rev. 601 (1990). For an attempt to suggest that "[t]he advertisement [in *Hustler Magazine, Inc. v. Falwell*] was no more worthy of legal protection than a spite fence constructed to inflict harm for its own sake," however, see Fein, Hustler Magazine v. Falwell: A Mislitigated and Misreasoned Case, 30 Wm. & Mary L.Rev. 905 (1989) (reviewing R. Smolla, Jerry Falwell v. Larry Flynt: The First Amendment on Trial (1988)).

AMERICAN BOOKSELLERS ASSOCIATION, INC. v. HUDNUT

United States Court of Appeals for the Seventh Circuit, 1985.
771 F.2d 323 (7th Cir.1985), summarily aff'd, 475 U.S. 1001, 106 S.Ct. 1172, 89 L.Ed.2d 291 (1986).

EASTERBROOK, CIRCUIT JUDGE.

Indianapolis enacted an ordinance defining "pornography" as a practice that discriminates against women. "Pornography" is to be redressed through the administrative and judicial methods used for other discrimination. * * *

* * *

"Pornography" under the ordinance is "the graphic sexually explicit subordination of women, whether in pictures or in words, that also includes one or more of the following:

> (1) Women are presented as sexual objects who enjoy pain or humiliation; or
>
> (2) Women are presented as sexual objects who experience sexual pleasure in being raped; or
>
> * * *
>
> (6) Women are presented as sexual objects for domination, conquest, violation, exploitation, possession, or use, or through postures or positions of servility or submission or display."

* * *

The Indianapolis ordinance does not refer to the prurient interest, to offensiveness, or to the standards of the community. It demands attention to particular depictions, not to the work judged as a whole. It is irrelevant under the ordinance whether the work has literary, artistic, political, or scientific value. The City and many amici point to these omissions as virtues. They maintain that pornography influences attitudes, and the statute is a way to alter the socialization of men and women rather than to vindicate community standards of offensiveness. And as one of the principal drafters of the ordinance has asserted, "if a woman is subjected, why should it matter that the work has other value?" Catharine A. MacKinnon, Pornography, Civil Rights, and Speech, 20 Harv.Civ.Rts.—Civ.Lib.L.Rev. 1, 21 (1985).

Civil rights groups and feminists have entered this case as amici on both sides. Those supporting the ordinance say that it will play an important role in reducing the tendency of men to view women as sexual objects, a tendency that leads to both unacceptable attitudes and discrimination in the workplace and violence away from it. Those opposing the ordinance point out that much radical feminist literature is explicit and depicts women in ways forbidden by the ordinance and that the ordinance would reopen old battles. It is unclear how Indianapolis would treat works from James Joyce's *Ulysses* to Homer's *Iliad;* both depict women as submissive objects for conquest and domination.

We do not try to balance the arguments for and against an ordinance such as this. The ordinance discriminates on the ground of the content of the speech. Speech treating women in the approved way—in sexual encounters "premised on equality" (MacKinnon, *supra*, at 22)—is lawful no matter how sexually explicit. Speech treating women in the disapproved way—as submissive in matters sexual or as enjoying humiliation—is unlawful no matter how significant the literary, artistic, or political qualities of the work taken as a whole. The state may not ordain preferred viewpoints in this way. The Constitution forbids the state to declare one perspective right and silence opponents.

I

* * *

Trafficking is defined in § 16–3(g)(4) as the "production, sale, exhibition, or distribution of pornography." The offense excludes exhibition in a public or educational library, but a "special display" in a library may be sex discrimination. Section 16–3(g)(4)(C) provides that the trafficking paragraph "shall not be construed to make isolated passages or isolated parts actionable."

* * *

A woman aggrieved by trafficking in pornography may file a complaint "as a woman acting against the subordination of women" with the office of equal opportunity. * * *

The office investigates and within 30 days makes a recommendation to a panel of the equal opportunity advisory board. The panel then decides whether there is reasonable cause to proceed (§ 16–24(2)) and may refer the dispute to a conciliation conference or to a complaint adjudication committee for a hearing (§§ 16–24(3), 16–26(a)). The committee uses the same procedures ordinarily associated with civil rights litigation. It may make findings and enter orders, including both orders to cease and desist to "take further affirmative action * * * including but not limited to the power to restore complainant's losses. * * *" Section 16–26(d). Either party may appeal the committee's decision to the board, which reviews the record before the committee and may modify its decision.

* * *

II

The plaintiffs are a congeries of distributors and readers of books, magazines, and films. The American Booksellers Association comprises about 5,200 bookstores and chains. The Association for American Publishers includes most of the country's publishers. Video Shack, Inc., sells and rents video cassettes in Indianapolis. Kelly Bentley, a resident of Indianapolis, reads books and watches films. There are many more plaintiffs. Collectively the plaintiffs (or their members, whose interests they represent) make, sell, or read just about every kind of material that could be affected by the ordinance, from hard-core films to W.B. Yeats's poem "Leda and the Swan" (from the myth of Zeus in the form of a swan impregnating an apparently subordinate Leda) to the collected works of James Joyce, D.H. Lawrence and John Cleland.

* * *

The district court prevented the ordinance from taking effect. * * * [* * * The court concluded that the ordinance regulates speech rather than the conduct involved in making pornography. The regulation of speech could be justified, the court thought, only by a compelling interest in reducing sex discrimination, an interest Indianapolis had not established. The ordinance is also vague and overbroad, the court believed, and establishes a prior restraint of speech.]

* * *

III

"If there is any fixed star in our constitutional constellation, it is that no official, high or petty, can prescribe what shall be orthodox in politics, nationalism, religion, or other matters of opinion or force citizens to confess by word or act their faith therein." West Virginia State Board of Education v. Barnette, 319 U.S. 624, 642 (1943). Under the First Amendment the government must leave to the people the evaluation of ideas. Bald or subtle, an idea is as powerful as the audience allows it to be. A belief may be pernicious—the beliefs of Nazis led to the death of millions, those of the Klan to the repression of millions. A pernicious belief may prevail. Totalitarian governments today rule much of the planet, practicing suppression of billions and spreading dogma that may enslave others. One of the things that separates our society from theirs is our absolute right to propagate opinions that the government finds wrong or even hateful.

The ideas of the Klan may be propagated. Brandenburg v. Ohio, 395 U.S. 444 (1969). Communists may speak freely and run for office. De Jonge v. Oregon, 299 U.S. 353 (1937). The Nazi Party may march through a city with a large Jewish population. Collin v. Smith, 578 F.2d 1197 (7th Cir.), cert. denied, 439 U.S. 916 (1978). People may criticize the President by misrepresenting his positions, and they have a right to post their misrepresentations on public property. Lebron v. Washington Metropolitan Transit Authority, 749 F.2d 893 (D.C.Cir. 1984) (Bork, J.). People may teach religions that others despise. People may seek to repeal laws guaranteeing equal opportunity in employment or to revoke the constitutional amendments granting the vote to blacks and women. They may do this because "above all else, the First Amendment means that government has no power to restrict expression because of its message [or] its ideas. * * *" Police Department v. Mosley, 408 U.S. 92, 95 (1972). * * *

Under the ordinance graphic sexually explicit speech is "pornography" or not depending on the perspective the author adopts. Speech that "subordinates" women and also, for example, presents women as enjoying pain, humiliation, or rape, or even simply presents women in "positions of servility or submission or display" is forbidden, no matter how great the literary or political value of the work taken as a whole. Speech that portrays women in positions of equality is lawful, no matter how graphic the sexual content. This is thought control. It establishes an "approved" view of women, of how they may react to sexual encounters, of how the sexes may relate to each other. Those who espouse the approved view may use sexual images; those who do not, may not.

Indianapolis justifies the ordinance on the ground that pornography affects thoughts. Men who see women depicted as subordinate are more likely to treat them so. Pornography is an aspect of dominance. It does not persuade people so much as change them. It works by socializing, by establishing the expected and the permissible. In this view pornography is not an idea; pornography is the injury.

There is much to this perspective. Beliefs are also facts. People often act in accordance with the images and patterns they find around them. People raised in a religion tend to accept the tenets of that religion, often without independent examination. People taught from birth that black people are fit only for slavery rarely rebelled against that creed; beliefs coupled with the self-interest of the masters established a social structure that inflicted great harm while enduring for centuries. Words and images act at the level of the subconscious before they persuade at the level of the conscious. Even the truth has little chance unless a statement fits within the framework of beliefs that may never have been subjected to rational study.

Therefore we accept the premises of this legislation. * * *

Yet this simply demonstrates the power of pornography as speech. All of these unhappy effects depend on mental intermediation. Pornography affects how people see the world, their fellows, and social relations. If pornography is what pornography does, so is other speech. Hitler's orations affected how some Germans saw Jews. Communism is a world view, not simply a *Manifesto* by Marx and Engels or a set of speeches. Efforts to suppress communist speech in the United States were based on the belief that the public acceptability of such ideas would increase the likelihood of totalitarian government. Religions affect socialization in the most pervasive way. The opinion in Wisconsin v. Yoder, 406 U.S. 205 (1972), shows how a religion can dominate an entire approach to life, governing much more than the relation between the sexes. Many people believe that the existence of television, apart from the content of specific programs, leads to intellectual laziness, to a penchant for violence, to many other ills. The Alien and Sedition Acts passed during the administration of John Adams rested on a sincerely held belief that disrespect for the government leads to social collapse and revolution—a belief with support in the history of many nations. Most governments of the world act on this empirical regularity, suppressing critical speech. In the United States, however, the strength of the support for this belief is irrelevant. * * *

Racial bigotry, anti-semitism, violence on television, reporters' biases—these and many more influence the culture and shape our socialization. None is directly answerable by more speech, unless that speech too finds its place in the popular culture. Yet all is protected as speech, however insidious. Any other answer leaves the government in control of all of the institutions of culture, the great censor and director of which thoughts are good for us.

Sexual responses often are unthinking responses, and the association of sexual arousal with the subordination of women therefore may have a substantial effect. But almost all cultural stimuli provoke unconscious responses. Religious ceremonies condition their participants. Teachers convey messages by selecting what not to cover; the implicit message about what is off limits or unthinkable may be more powerful than the messages for which they present rational argument. Television scripts contain unarticulated assumptions. People may be conditioned in subtle ways. If the fact that speech plays a role in a process of conditioning were enough to permit governmental regulation, that would be the end of freedom of speech.

* * *

Much of Indianapolis's argument rests on the belief that when speech is "unanswerable," and the metaphor that there is a "marketplace of ideas" does not apply, the First Amendment does not apply either. The metaphor is honored; Milton's *Aeropagitica* and John Stewart [sic] Mill's *On Liberty* defend freedom of speech on the ground that the truth will prevail and many of the most important cases under the First Amendment recite this position. The Framers undoubtedly believed it. As a general matter it is true. But the Constitution does not make the dominance of truth a necessary condition of freedom of speech. To say that it does would be to confuse an outcome of free speech with a necessary condition for the application of the amendment.

A power to limit speech on the ground that truth has not yet prevailed and is not likely to prevail implies the power to declare truth. At some point the government must be able to say (as Indianapolis has said): "We know what the truth is, yet a free exchange of speech has not driven out falsity, so that we must now prohibit falsity." If the government may declare the truth, why wait for the failure of speech? Under the First Amendment, however, there is no such thing as a false idea, Gertz v. Robert Welch, Inc., 418 U.S. 323, 339 (1974), so the government may not restrict speech on the ground that in a free exchange truth is not yet dominant.

At any time, some speech is ahead in the game; the more numerous speakers prevail. Supporters of minority candidates may be forever "excluded" from the political process because their candidates never win, because few people believe their positions. This does not mean that freedom of speech has failed.

* * *

We come finally to the argument that pornography is "low value" speech, that it is enough like obscenity that Indianapolis may prohibit it. Some cases hold that speech far removed from politics and other subjects at the core of the Framers' concerns may be subjected to special regulation. * * *

At all events, "pornography" is not low value speech within the meaning of these cases. Indianapolis seeks to prohibit certain speech because it believes this speech influences social relations and politics on a grand scale, that it controls attitudes at home and in the legislature. This precludes a characterization of the speech as low value. True, pornography and obscenity have sex in common. But Indianapolis left out of its definition any reference to literary, artistic, political or scientific value. The ordinance applies to graphic sexually explicit subordination in works great and small.[3] The Court sometimes balances the value of speech against the costs of its restriction, but it does this by category of speech and not by the content of particular works. * * * Indianapolis has created an approved point of view and so loses the support of these cases.

Any rationale we could imagine in support of this ordinance could not be limited to sex discrimination. Free speech has been on balance an ally of those seeking change. Governments that want stasis start by restricting speech. Culture is a powerful force of continuity; Indianapolis paints pornography as part of the culture of power. Change in any complex system ultimately depends on the ability of outsiders to challenge accepted views and the reigning institutions. Without a strong guarantee of freedom of speech, there is no effective right to challenge what is.

IV

The definition of "pornography" is unconstitutional. No construction or excision of particular terms could save it. The offense of trafficking in pornography necessarily falls with the definition. We express no view on the district court's conclusions that the ordinance is vague and that it establishes a prior restraint. Neither is necessary to our judgment. We also express no view on the argument presented by several amici that the ordinance is itself a form of discrimination on account of sex.

* * *

---

3. Indianapolis briefly argues that Beauharnais v. Illinois, 343 U.S. 250 (1952), which allowed a state to penalize "group libel," supports the ordinance. In Collin v. Smith, *supra*, 578 F.2d at 1205, we concluded that cases such as *New York Times v. Sullivan* had so washed away the foundations of *Beauharnais* that it could not be considered authoritative. If we are wrong in this, however, the case still does not support the ordinance. It is not clear that depicting women as subordinate in sexually explicit ways, even combined with a depiction of pleasure in rape, would fit within the definition of a group libel. The well received film *Swept Away* used explicit sex, plus taking pleasure in rape, to make a political statement, not to defame. Work must be an insult or slur for its own sake to come within the ambit of *Beauharnais*, and a work need not be scurrilous at all to be "pornography" under the ordinance.

No amount of struggle with particular words and phrases in this ordinance can leave anything in effect. The district court came to the same conclusion. Its judgment is therefore

Affirmed.

SWYGERT, SENIOR CIRCUIT JUDGE, concurring.

* * *

I * * * believe that the majority's questionable and broad assertions regarding how human behavior can be conditioned by certain teachings and beliefs * * * are unnecessary. For even if this court accepts the City of Indianapolis' basic contention that pornography does condition unfavorable responses to women, the ordinance is still unconstitutional.

* * *

C. POLITICS AND "SYMBOLIC" DISSENT

The putative distinction between standard first amendment review and the different applications under *United States v. O'Brien*.

TINKER v. DES MOINES INDEPENDENT COMMUNITY SCHOOL DISTRICT

Supreme Court of the United States, 1969.
393 U.S. 503, 89 S.Ct. 733, 21 L.Ed.2d 731.

MR. JUSTICE FORTAS delivered the opinion of the Court.

Petitioner John F. Tinker, 15 years old, and petitioner Christopher Eckhardt, 16 years old, attended high schools in Des Moines, Iowa. Petitioner Mary Beth Tinker, John's sister, was a 13-year-old student in junior high school.

In December 1965, a group of adults and students in Des Moines held a meeting at the Eckhardt home. The group determined to publicize their objections to the hostilities in Vietnam and their support for a truce by wearing black armbands during the holiday season and by fasting on December 16 and New Year's Eve. Petitioners and their parents had previously engaged in similar activities, and they decided to participate in the program.

The principals of the Des Moines schools became aware of the plan to wear armbands. On December 14, 1965, they met and adopted a policy that any student wearing an armband to school would be asked to remove it, and if he refused he would be suspended until he returned without the armband. Petitioners were aware of the regulation that the school authorities adopted.

On December 16, Mary Beth and Christopher wore black armbands to their schools. John Tinker wore his armband the next day. They were all sent home and suspended from school until they would come back without their armbands. They did not return to school until after the planned period for wearing armbands had expired—that is, until after New Year's Day.

This complaint was filed in the United States District Court by petitioners, through their fathers, under § 1983 of Title 42 of the United States Code. It prayed for an injunction restraining the respondent school officials and the respondent members of the board of directors of the school district from disciplining the petitioners, and it sought nominal damages. After an evidentiary hearing the District Court dismissed the complaint. It upheld the constitutionality of the school authorities' action on the ground that it was reasonable in order to prevent disturbance of school discipline. 258 F.Supp. 971 (1966). The court referred to but expressly declined to follow the Fifth Circuit's holding in a similar case that the wearing of symbols like the armbands cannot be prohibited unless it "materially and substantially interfere[s] with the requirements of appropriate discipline in the operation of the school." Burnside v. Byars, 363 F.2d 744, 749 (1966).[1]

On appeal, the Court of Appeals for the Eighth Circuit considered the case *en banc*. The court was equally divided, and the District Court's decision was accordingly affirmed, without opinion. 383 F.2d 988 (1967). We granted certiorari. 390 U.S. 942 (1968).

I.

The District Court recognized that the wearing of an armband for the purpose of expressing certain views is the type of symbolic act that is within the Free Speech Clause of the First Amendment. See West Virginia v. Barnette, 319 U.S. 624 (1943); Stromberg v. California, 283 U.S. 359 (1931). Cf. Thornhill v. Alabama, 310 U.S. 88 (1940); Edwards v. South Carolina, 372 U.S. 229 (1963); Brown v. Louisiana, 383 U.S. 131 (1966). As we shall discuss, the wearing of armbands in the circumstances of this case was entirely divorced from actually or potentially disruptive conduct by those participating in it. It was closely akin to "pure speech" which, we have repeatedly held, is entitled to comprehensive protection under the First Amendment. Cf. Cox v. Louisiana, 379 U.S. 536, 555 (1965); Adderley v. Florida, 385 U.S. 39 (1966).

First Amendment rights, applied in light of the special characteristics of the school environment, are available to teachers and students. It can hardly be argued that either students or teachers shed their constitutional rights to freedom of speech or expression at the schoolhouse gate. This has been the unmistakable holding of this Court for almost 50 years. * * *

---

1. In *Burnside*, the Fifth Circuit ordered that high school authorities be enjoined from enforcing a regulation forbidding students to wear "freedom buttons." It is instructive that in Blackwell v. Issaquena County Board of Education, 363 F.2d 749 (1966), the same panel on the same day reached the opposite result on different facts. It declined to enjoin enforcement of such a regulation in another high school where the students wearing freedom buttons harassed students who did not wear them and created much disturbance.

* * *

II.

The problem posed by the present case does not relate to regulation of the length of skirts or the type of clothing, to hair style or deportment. * * * It does not concern aggressive, disruptive action or even group demonstrations. Our problem involves direct, primary First Amendment rights akin to "pure speech."

The school officials banned and sought to punish petitioners for a silent, passive, expression of opinion, unaccompanied by any disorder or disturbance on the part of petitioners. There is here no evidence whatever of petitioners' interference, actual or nascent, with the school's work or of collision with the rights of other students to be secure and to be let alone. Accordingly, this case does not concern speech or action that intrudes upon the work of the school or the rights of other students.

Only a few of the 18,000 students in the school system wore the black armbands. Only five students were suspended for wearing them. There is no indication that the work of the school or any class was disrupted. Outside the classrooms, a few students made hostile remarks to the children wearing armbands, but there were no threats or acts of violence on school premises.

The District Court concluded that the action of the school authorities was reasonable because it was based upon their fear of a disturbance from the wearing of the armbands. But, in our system, undifferentiated fear or apprehension of disturbance [the District Court's basis for sustaining the school authorities' action] is not enough to overcome the right to freedom of expression. Any departure from absolute regimentation may cause trouble. Any variation from the majority's opinion may inspire fear. Any words spoken in class, in the lunchroom or on the campus, that deviates from the views of another person, may start an argument or cause a disturbance. But our Constitution says we must take this risk, Terminiello v. Chicago, 337 U.S. 1 (1949); and our history says that it is this sort of freedom—this kind of openness— that is the basis of our national strength and of the independence and vigor of Americans who grow up and live in this relatively permissive, often disputatious society.

In order for the State in the person of school officials to justify prohibition of a particular expression of opinion, it must be able to show that its action was caused by something more than a mere desire to avoid the discomfort and unpleasantness that always accompany an unpopular viewpoint. Certainly where there is no finding and no showing that the exercise of the forbidden right would "materially and substantially interfere with the requirements of appropriate discipline in the operation of the school," the prohibition cannot be suspended. *Burnside v. Byars, supra,* at 749.

In the present case, the District Court made no such finding, and our independent examination of the record fails to yield evidence that the school authorities had reason to anticipate that the wearing of the armbands would substantially interfere with the work of the school or impinge upon the rights of other students. Even an official memorandum prepared after the suspension that listed the reasons for the ban on wearing the armbands made no reference to the anticipation of such disruption.[3]

On the contrary, the action of the school authorities appears to have been based upon an urgent wish to avoid the controversy which might result from the expression, even by the silent symbol of armbands, of opposition to this Nation's part in the conflagration in Vietnam.[4] It is revealing, in this respect, that the meeting at which the school principals decided to issue the contested regulation was called in response to a student's statement to the journalism teacher in one of the schools that he wanted to write an article on Vietnam and have it published in the school paper. (The student was dissuaded.)[5]

It is also relevant that the school authorities did not purport to prohibit the wearing of all symbols of political or controversial significance. The record shows that students in some of the schools wore buttons relating to national political campaigns, and some even wore the Iron Cross, traditionally a symbol of nazism. The order prohibiting the wearing of armbands did not extend to these. Instead, a particular symbol—black armbands worn to exhibit opposition to this Nation's involvement in Vietnam—was singled out for prohibition. Clearly, the prohibition of expression of one particular opinion, at least without evidence that it is necessary to avoid material and substantial interference with school work or discipline, is not constitutionally permissible.

In our system, state-operated schools may not be enclaves of totalitarianism. School officials do not possess absolute authority over their students. Students in school as well as out of school are "persons"

---

3. The only suggestions of fear of disorder in the report are these:

"A former student of one of our high schools was killed in Viet Nam. Some of his friends are still in school and it was felt that if any kind of a demonstration existed, it might evolve into something which would be difficult to control."

"Students at one of the high schools were heard to say they would wear armbands of other colors if the black bands prevailed."

Moreover, the testimony of school authorities at trial indicates that it was not fear of disruption that motivated the regulation prohibiting the armbands; the regulation was directed against "the principle of the demonstration" itself. School authorities simply felt that "the schools are no place for demonstrations," and if the students "didn't like the way our elected officials were handling things, it should be handled with the ballot box and not in the halls of our public schools."

4. The District Court found that the school authorities, in prohibiting black armbands, were influenced by the fact that "[t]he Viet Nam war and the involvement of the United States therein has been the subject of a major controversy for some time. When the armband regulation involved herein was promulgated, debate over the Viet Nam war had become vehement in many localities. A protest march against the war had been recently held in Washington, D.C. A wave of draft card burning incidents protesting the war swept the country. At that time two highly publicized draft card burning cases were pending in this Court. Both individuals supporting the war and those opposing it were quite vocal in expressing their views." 258 F.Supp., at 972–973.

5. After the principals' meeting, the director of secondary education and the principal of the high school informed the student that the principals were opposed to publication of his article. They reported that "we felt that it was a very friendly conversation, although we did not feel that we had convinced the student that our decision was a just one."

under our Constitution. They are possessed of fundamental rights which the State must respect, just as they themselves must respect their obligations to the State. In our system, students may not be regarded as closed circuit recipients of only that which the state chooses to communicate. They may not be confined to the expression of those sentiments that are officially approved. In the absence of a specific showing of constitutionally valid reasons to regulate their speech, students are entitled to freedom of expression of their views.
* * *

* * *

The principle of these cases is not confined to the supervised and ordained discussion which takes place in the classroom. The principal use to which the schools are dedicated is to accommodate students during prescribed hours for the purpose of certain types of activities. Among those activities is personal intercommunication among the students.[6] This is not only an inevitable part of the process of attending school; it is also an important part of the educational process. A student's rights therefore, do not embrace merely the classroom hours. When he is in the cafeteria, or on the playing field, or on the campus during the authorized hours, he may express his opinions, even on controversial subjects like the conflict in Vietnam, if he does so without "materially and substantially interfer[ing] with appropriate discipline in the operation of the school" and without colliding with the rights of others. *Burnside v. Byars, supra,* at 749. But conduct by the student, in class or out of it, which for any reason—whether it stems from time, place, or type of behavior—materially disrupts classwork or involves substantial disorder or invasion of the rights of others is, of course, not immunized by the constitutional guarantee of freedom of speech. Cf. Blackwell v. Issaquena County Board of Education, 363 F.2d 749 (C.A. 5th Cir.1966).

Under our Constitution, free speech is not a right that is given only to be so circumscribed that it exists in principle but not in fact. Freedom of expression would not truly exist if the right could be exercised only in an area that a benevolent government was provided as a safe haven for crackpots. The Constitution says that Congress (and the States) may not abridge the right to free speech. This provision means what it says. We properly read it to permit reasonable regulation of speech-connected activities in carefully restricted circumstances. But we do not confine the permissible exercise of First Amendment rights to a telephone booth or the four corners of a pamphlet, or to supervised and ordained discussion in a school classroom.

6. In Hammond v. South Carolina State College, 272 F.Supp. 947 (D.C.S.C.1957), District Judge Hemphill had before him a case involving a meeting on campus of 300 students to express their views on school practices. He pointed out that a school is not like a hospital or a jail enclosure. Cf. Cox v. Louisiana, 379 U.S. 536 (1965); Adderley v. Florida, 385 U.S. 39 (1966). It is a public place, and its dedication to specific uses does not imply that the constitutional rights of persons entitled to be there are to be gauged as if the premises were purely private property. Cf. Edwards v. South Carolina, 372 U.S. 229 (1963); Brown v. Louisiana, 383 U.S. 131 (1966).

If a regulation were adopted by school officials forbidding discussion of the Vietnam conflict, or the expression by any student of opposition to it anywhere on school property except as part of a prescribed classroom exercise, it would be obvious that the regulation would violate the constitutional rights of students, at least if it could not be justified by a showing that the students' activities would materially and substantially disrupt the work and discipline of the school. Cf. Hammond v. South Carolina State College, 272 F.Supp. 947 (D.C.S.C. 1967) (orderly protest meeting on state college campus); Dickey v. Alabama State Board of Education, 273 F.Supp. 613 (D.C.M.D.Ala.1967) (expulsion of student editor of college newspaper). In the circumstances of the present case, the prohibition of the silent, passive "witness of the armbands," as one of the children called it, is no less offensive to the Constitution's guarantees.

As we have discussed, the record does not demonstrate any facts which might reasonably have led school authorities to forecast substantial disruption of or material interference with school activities, and no disturbances or disorders on the school premises in fact occurred. These petitioners merely went about their ordained rounds in school. Their deviation consisted only in wearing on their sleeve a band of black cloth, not more than two inches wide. They wore it to exhibit their disapproval of the Vietnam hostilities and their advocacy of a truce, to make their views known, and, by their example, to influence others to adopt them. They neither interrupted school activities nor sought to intrude in the school affairs or the lives of others. They caused discussion outside of the classrooms, but no interference with work and no disorder. In the circumstances, our Constitution does not permit officials of the State to deny their form of expression.

We express no opinion as to the form of relief which should be granted, this being a matter for the lower courts to determine. We reverse and remand for further proceedings consistent with this opinion.

Reversed and remanded.

Mr. Justice Stewart, concurring.

Although I agree with much of what is said in the Court's opinion, and with its judgment in this case, I cannot share the Court's uncritical assumption that, school discipline aside, the First Amendment rights of children are co-extensive with those of adults. Indeed, I had thought the Court decided otherwise just last Term in Ginsberg v. New York, 390 U.S. 629. I continue to hold the view I expressed in that case: "[A] State may permissibly determine that, at least in some precisely delineated areas, a child—like someone in a captive audience—is not possessed of that full capacity for individual choice which is the presupposition of First Amendment guarantees." *Id.*, at 649–650 (concurring in result). Cf. Prince v. Massachusetts, 321 U.S. 158 (1944).

Mr. Justice White, concurring.

While I join the Court's opinion, I deem it appropriate to note, first, that the Court continues to recognize a distinction between communicating by words and communicating by acts or conduct which sufficiently impinges on some valid state interest; and, second, that I do not subscribe to everything the Court of Appeals said about free speech in its opinion in Burnside v. Byars, 363 F.2d 744, 748 (C.A.5th Cir.1966), a case relied upon by the Court in the matter now before us.

MR. JUSTICE BLACK, dissenting.

The Court's holding in this case ushers in what I deem to be an entirely new era in which the power to control pupils by the elected "officials of state supported public schools * * *" in the United States is in ultimate effect transferred to the Supreme Court.[1] The Court brought this particular case here on a petition for certiorari urging that the First and Fourteenth Amendments protect the right of school pupils to express their political views all the way "from kindergarten through high school." Here the constitutional right to "political expression" asserted was a right to wear black armbands during school hours and at classes in order to demonstrate to the other students that petitioners were mourning because of the death of United States soldiers in Vietnam and to protest that war which they were against. Ordered to refrain from wearing the armbands in school by the elected school officials and teachers vested with state authority to do so, apparently only seven out of the school system's 18,000 pupils deliberately refused to obey the order. One defying pupil was Paul Tinker, 8 years old, who was in the second grade; another, Hope Tinker, was 11 years old and in the fifth grade; a third member of the Tinker family was 13, in the eighth grade; and a fourth member of the same family was John Tinker, 15 years old, an 11th grade high school pupil. Their father, a Methodist minister without a church, is paid a salary by the American Friends Service Committee. Another student who defied the school order and insisted on wearing an armband in the school was Christopher Eckhardt, an 11th grade pupil and a petitioner in this case. His mother is an official in the Women's International League for Peace and Freedom.

As I read the Court's opinion it relies upon the following grounds for holding unconstitutional the judgment of the Des Moines school officials and the two courts below. First, the Court concludes that the wearing of armbands is "symbolic speech" which is "akin to 'pure speech'" and therefore protected by the First and Fourteenth Amendments. Secondly, the Court decides that the public schools are an appropriate place to exercise "symbolic speech" as long as normal school functions are not "unreasonably" disrupted. Finally, the Court arrogates to itself, rather than to the State's elected officials charged with running the schools, the decision as to which school disciplinary regulations are "reasonable."

* * *

---

1. The petition for certiorari here presented this single question:

"Whether the First and Fourteenth Amendments permit officials of state supported public schools to prohibit students from wearing symbols of political views within school premises where the symbols are not disruptive of school discipline or decorum."

While the record does not show that any of these armband students shouted, used profane language, or were violent in any manner, detailed testimony by some of them shows their armbands caused comments, warnings by other students, the poking of fun at them, and a warning by an older football player that other, nonprotesting students had better let them alone. There is also evidence that a teacher of mathematics had his lesson period practically "wrecked" chiefly by disputes with Mary Beth Tinker, who wore her armband for her "demonstration." Even a casual reading of the record shows that this armband did divert students' minds from their regular lessons, and that talk, comments, etc., made John Tinker "self-conscious" in attending school with his armband. While the absence of obscene remarks or boisterous and loud disorder perhaps justifies the Court's statement that the few armband students did not actually "disrupt" the classwork, I think the record overwhelmingly shows that the armbands did exactly what the elected school officials and principals foresaw they would, that is, took the students' minds off their classwork and diverted them to thoughts about the highly emotional subject of the Vietnam war. And I repeat that if the time has come when pupils of state-supported schools, kindergartens, grammar schools, or high schools, can defy and flout orders of school officials to keep their minds on their own schoolwork, it is the beginning of a new revolutionary era of permissiveness in this country fostered by the judiciary. The next logical step, it appears to me, would be to hold unconstitutional laws that bar pupils under 21 or 18 from voting, or from being elected members of the boards of education.

* * *

The true principles on this whole subject were in my judgment spoken by Mr. Justice McKenna for the Court in Waugh v. Mississippi University in 237 U.S. 589, 596–597 (1915). The State had there passed a law barring students from peaceably assembling in Greek letter fraternities and providing that students who joined them could be expelled from school. This law would appear on the surface to run afoul of the First Amendment's freedom of assembly clause. The law was attacked as violative of due process and of the privileges and immunities clause and as a deprivation of property and of liberty, under the Fourteenth Amendment. It was argued that the fraternity made its members more moral, taught discipline, and inspired its members to study harder and to obey better the rules of discipline and order. This Court rejected all the "fervid" pleas of the fraternities' advocates and decided unanimously against these Fourteenth Amendment arguments. The Court in its next to last paragraph made this statement which has complete relevance for us today:

> "It is said that the fraternity to which complainant belongs is a moral and of itself a disciplinary force. This need not be denied. But whether such membership makes against discipline was for the State of Mississippi to determine. It is to be remembered that the University was established by the State and is under the control of the State, and the enactment of the statute may have been induced by the opinion that

> *membership in the prohibited societies divided the attention of the students and distracted from that singleness of purpose which the State desired to exist in its public educational institutions.* It is not for us to entertain conjectures in opposition to the views of the State and annul its regulations upon disputable considerations of their wisdom or necessity." (Emphasis supplied.)

It is on the foregoing argument that this Court sustained the power of Mississippi to curtail the First Amendment's right of peaceable assembly. And the same reasons are equally applicable to curtailing in the States' public schools the right to complete freedom of expression. Iowa's public schools, like Mississippi's university, are operated to give students an opportunity to learn, not to talk politics by actual speech, or by "symbolic" speech. And, as I have pointed out before, the record amply shows that public protest in the school classes against the Vietnam war "distracted from that singleness of purpose which the State [here Iowa] desired to exist in its public educational institutions." Here the Court should accord Iowa educational institutions the same right to determine for themselves to what extent free expression should be allowed in its schools as it accorded Mississippi with reference to freedom of assembly. * * * One does not need to be a prophet or the son of a prophet to know that after the Court's holding today some students in Iowa schools and indeed in all schools will be ready, able, and willing to defy their teachers on practically all orders. * * * It is no answer to say that the particular students here have not yet reached such high points in their demands to attend classes in order to exercise their political pressures. Turned loose with lawsuits for damages and injunctions against their teachers as they are here, it is nothing but wishful thinking to imagine that young, immature students will not soon believe it is their right to control the schools rather than the right of the States that collect taxes to hire teachers for the benefit of the pupils. This case, therefore, wholly without constitutional reasons in my judgment, subjects all the public schools in the country to the whims and caprices of their loudest-mouthed, but maybe not their brightest, students. * * * I dissent.

MR. JUSTICE HARLAN, dissenting.

I certainly agree that state public school authorities in the discharge of their responsibilities are not wholly exempt from the requirements of the Fourteenth Amendment respecting the freedoms of expression and association. At the same time I am reluctant to believe that there is any disagreement between the majority and myself on the proposition that school officials should be accorded the widest authority in maintaining discipline and good order in their institutions. To translate that proposition into a workable constitutional rule, I would, in cases like this, cast upon those complaining the burden of showing that a particular school measure was motivated by other than legitimate school concerns—for example, a desire to prohibit the expression of an unpopular point of view, while permitting expression of the dominant opinion.

Finding nothing in this record which impugns the good faith of respondents in promulgating the armband regulation, I would affirm the judgement below.

UNITED STATES v. O'BRIEN

Supreme Court of the United States, 1968.
391 U.S. 367, 88 S.Ct. 1673, 20 L.Ed.2d 672.

MR. CHIEF JUSTICE WARREN delivered the opinion of the Court.

On the morning of March 31, 1966, David Paul O'Brien and three companions burned their Selective Service registration certificates on the steps of the South Boston Courthouse. A sizable crowd, including several agents of the Federal Bureau of Investigation, witnessed the event.[1] Immediately after the burning, members of the crowd began attacking O'Brien and his companions. An FBI agent ushered O'Brien to safety inside the courthouse. After he was advised of his right to counsel and to silence, O'Brien stated to FBI agents that he had burned his registration certificate because of his beliefs, knowing that he was violating federal law. He produced the charred remains of the certificate, which, with his consent, were photographed.

For this act, O'Brien was indicted, tried, convicted, and sentenced in the United States District Court for the District of Massachusetts.[2] He did not contest the fact that he had burned the certificate. He stated in argument to the jury that he burned the certificate publicly to influence others to adopt his antiwar beliefs, as he put it, "so that other people would reevaluate their positions with Selective Service, with the armed forces, and reevaluate their place in the culture of today, to hopefully consider my position."

The indictment upon which he was tried charged that he "willfully and knowingly did mutilate, destroy, and change by burning * * * [his] Registration Certificate * * *; in violation of Title 50, App., United States Code, Section 462(b)." Section 462(b) is part of the Universal Military Training and Service Act of 1948. Section 462(b)(3), one of six numbered subdivisions of § 462(b), was amended by Congress in 1965, 79 Stat. 586 (adding the words italicized below), so that at the time O'Brien burned his certificate an offense was committed by any person,

> "who forges, alters, *knowingly destroys, knowingly mutilates,* or in any manner changes any such certificate * * *." (Italics supplied.)

In the District Court, O'Brien argued that the 1965 Amendment prohibiting the knowing destruction or mutilation of certificates was unconsti-

---

[1]. At the time of the burning, the agents knew only that O'Brien and his three companions had burned small white cards. They later discovered that the card O'Brien had burned was his registration certificate, and the undisputed assumption is that the same is true of his companions.

[2]. He was sentenced under the Youth Corrections Act, 18 U.S.C. § 5010(b), to the custody of the Attorney General for a maximum period of six years for supervision and treatment.

tutional because it was enacted to abridge free speech, and because it served no legitimate legislative purpose. The District Court rejected these arguments, holding that the statute on its face did not abridge First Amendment rights, that the court was not competent to inquire into the motives of Congress in enacting the 1965 Amendment, and that the Amendment was a reasonable exercise of the power of Congress to raise armies.

On appeal, the Court of Appeals for the First Circuit held the 1965 Amendment unconstitutional as a law abridging freedom of speech.[4] At the time the Amendment was enacted, a regulation of the Selective Service System required registrants to keep their registration certificates in their "personal possession at all times." 32 CFR § 1617.1 (1962).[5] Wilful violations of regulations promulgated pursuant to the Universal Military Training and Service Act were made criminal by statute. 50 U.S.C.App. § 462(b)(6). The Court of Appeals, therefore, was of the opinion that conduct punishable under the 1965 Amendment was already punishable under the nonpossession regulation, and consequently that the Amendment served no valid purpose; further, that in light of the prior regulation, the Amendment must have been "directed at public as distinguished from private destruction." On this basis, the court concluded that the 1965 Amendment ran afoul of the First Amendment by singling out persons engaged in protests for special treatment. * * *

* * * We granted the Government's petition to resolve the conflict in the circuits, and we also granted O'Brien's cross-petition. We hold that the 1965 Amendment is constitutional both as enacted and as applied we therefore vacate the judgment of the Court of Appeals and reinstate the judgment and sentence of the District Court * * *.

I.

* * *

* * * We note at the outset that the 1965 Amendment plainly does not abridge free speech on its face, and we do not understand O'Brien to argue otherwise. Amended § 12(b)(3) on its face deals with conduct having no connection with speech. It prohibits the knowing destruction of certificates issued by the Selective Service System, and there is nothing necessarily expressive about such conduct. The Amendment does not distinguish between public and private destruction, and it does not punish only destruction engaged in for the purpose of expressing views. Compare Stromberg v. People of State of California, 283 U.S. 359 (1931). A law prohibiting destruction of Selective Service certificates no more abridges free speech on its face than a motor vehicle law prohibiting the destruction of drivers' licenses, or a tax law prohibiting the destruction of books and records.

---

4. O'Brien v. United States, 376 F.2d 538 (C.A. 1st Cir.1967).

5. The portion of 32 CFR relevant to the instant case was revised as of January 1, 1967. Citations in this opinion are to the 1962 edition which was in effect when O'Brien committed the crime, and when Congress enacted the 1965 Amendment.

O'Brien nonetheless argues that the 1965 Amendment is unconstitutional in its application to him, and is unconstitutional as enacted because what he calls the "purpose" of Congress was "to suppress freedom of speech." We consider these arguments separately.

II.

O'Brien first argues that the 1965 Amendment is unconstitutional as applied to him because his act of burning his registration certificate was protected "symbolic speech" within the First Amendment. His argument is that the freedom of expression which the First Amendment guarantees includes all modes of "communication of ideas by conduct," and that his conduct is within this definition because he did it in "demonstration against the war and against the draft."

We cannot accept the view that an apparently limitless variety of conduct can be labeled "speech" whenever the person engaging in the conduct intends thereby to express an idea. However, even on the assumption that the alleged communicative element in O'Brien's conduct is sufficient to bring into play the First Amendment, it does not necessarily follow that the destruction of a registration certificate is constitutionally protected activity. This Court has held that when "speech" and "nonspeech" elements are combined in the same course of conduct, a sufficiently important governmental interest in regulating the nonspeech element can justify incidental limitations on First Amendment freedoms. To characterize the quality of the governmental interest which must appear, the Court has employed a variety of descriptive terms: compelling; substantial; subordinating; paramount; cogent; strong. Whatever imprecision inheres in these terms, we think it clear that a government regulation is sufficiently justified if it is within the constitutional power of the Government; if it furthers an important or substantial governmental interest; if the governmental interest is unrelated to the suppression of free expression; and if the incidental restriction on alleged First Amendment freedoms is no greater than is essential to the furtherance of that interest. We find that the 1965 Amendment to § 12(b)(3) of the Universal Military Training and Service Act meets all of these requirements, and consequently that O'Brien can be constitutionally convicted for violating it.

The constitutional power of Congress to raise and support armies and to make all laws necessary and proper to that end is broad and sweeping. Lichter v. United States, 334 U.S. 742, 755–758 (1948); Selective Draft Law Cases, 245 U.S. 366 (1918); see also Ex parte Quirin, 317 U.S. 1, 25–26 (1942). The power of Congress to classify and conscript manpower for military service is "beyond question." Lichter v. United States, 334 U.S. at 756; *Selective Draft Law Cases, supra.* Pursuant to this power, Congress may establish a system of registration for individuals liable for training and service, and may require such individuals within reason to cooperate in the registration system. The issuance of certificates indicating the registration and eligibility classification of individuals is a legitimate and substantial administrative aid in the functioning of this system. And legislation to insure the continuing availability of issued certificates serves a legitimate and substantial purpose in the system's administration.

* * * Many of these purposes would be defeated by the certificates' destruction or mutilation. Among these are:

1. The registration certificate serves as proof that the individual described thereon has registered for the draft. The classification certificate shows the eligibility classification of a named but undescribed individual. * * * Correspondingly, the availability of the certificates for such display relieves the Selective Service System of the administrative burden it would otherwise have in verifying the registration and classification of all suspected delinquents. Further, since both certificates are in the nature of "receipts" attesting that the registrant has done what the law requires, it is in the interest of the just and efficient administration of the system that they be continually available, in the event, for example, of a mix-up in the registrant's file. Additionally, in a time of national crisis, reasonable availability of each registrant of the two small cards assures a rapid and uncomplicated means for determining his fitness for immediate induction, no matter how distant in our mobile society he may be from his local board.

2. The information supplied on the certificates facilitates communication between registrants and local boards, simplifying the system and benefiting all concerned. To begin with, each certificate bears the address of the registrant's local board, an item unlikely to be committed to memory. Further, each card bears the registrant's Selective Service number, and a registrant who has his number readily available so that he can communicate it to his local board when he supplies or requests information can make simpler the board's task in locating his file. Finally, a registrant's inquiry, particularly through a local board other than his own, concerning his eligibility status is frequently answerable simply on the basis of his classification certificate; whereas, if the certificate were not reasonably available and the registrant were uncertain of his classification, the task of answering his questions would be considerably complicated.

3. Both certificates carry continual reminders that the registrant must notify his local board of any change of address, and other specified changes in his status. The smooth functioning of the system requires that local boards be continually aware of the status and whereabouts of registrants, and the destruction of certificates deprives the system of a potentially useful notice device.

* * *

We think it apparent that the continuing availability to each registrant of his Selective Service certificates substantially furthers the smooth and proper functioning of the system that Congress has established to raise armies. We think it also apparent that the nation has a vital interest in having a system for raising armies that functions with maximum efficiency and is capable of easily and quickly responding to continually changing circumstances. For these reasons, the Government has a substantial interest in assuring the continuing availability of issued Selective Service certificates.

It is equally clear that the 1965 Amendment specifically protects this substantial governmental interest. We perceive no alternative means that would more precisely and narrowly assure the continuing availability of issued Selective Service certificates than a law which prohibits their wilful mutilation or destruction. * * * The 1965 Amendment prohibits such conduct and does nothing more. In other words, both the governmental interest and the operation of the 1965 Amendment are limited to the noncommunicative aspect of O'Brien's conduct. The governmental interest and the scope of the 1965 Amendment are limited to preventing harm to the smooth and efficient functioning of the Selective Service System. When O'Brien deliberately rendered unavailable his registration certificate, he wilfully frustrated this governmental interest. For this noncommunicative impact of his conduct, and for nothing else, he was convicted.

The case at bar is therefore unlike one where the alleged governmental interest in regulating conduct arises in some measure because the communication allegedly integral to the conduct is itself thought to be harmful. In Stromberg v. People of State of California, 283 U.S. 359 (1931), for example, this Court struck down a statutory phrase which punished people who expressed their "opposition to organized government" by displaying "any flag, badge, banner, or device." Since the statute there was aimed at suppressing communication it could not be sustained as a regulation of noncommunicative conduct. See also, NLRB v. Fruit & Vegetable Packers Union, 377 U.S. 58, 79 (1964) (concurring opinion).

In conclusion, we find that because of the Government's substantial interest in assuring the continuing availability of issued Selective Service certificates, because amended § 462(b) is an appropriately narrow means of protecting this interest and condemns only the independent noncommunicative impact of conduct within its reach, and because the noncommunicative impact of O'Brien's act of burning his registration certificate frustrated the Government's interest, a sufficient governmental interest has been shown to justify O'Brien's conviction.

III.

O'Brien finally argues that the 1965 Amendment is unconstitutional as enacted because what he calls the "purpose" of Congress was "to suppress freedom of speech." We reject this argument because under settled principles the purpose of Congress, as O'Brien uses that term, is not a basis for declaring this legislation unconstitutional.

It is a familiar principle of constitutional law that this Court will not strike down an otherwise constitutional statute on the basis of an alleged illicit legislative motive. As the Court long ago stated:

> "The decisions of this court from the beginning lend no support whatever to the assumption that the judiciary may restrain the exercise of lawful power on the assumption that a wrongful purpose or motive has caused the power to be exerted." McCray v. United States, 195 U.S. 27, 56 (1904).

* * *

Inquiries into congressional motives or purposes are a hazardous matter. When the issue is simply the interpretation of legislation, the Court will look to statements by legislators for guidance as to the purpose of the legislature,[30] because the benefit to sound decision making in this circumstance is thought sufficient to risk the possibility of misreading Congress' purpose. It is entirely a different matter when we are asked to void a statute that is, under well-settled criteria, constitutional on its face, on the basis of what fewer than a handful of Congressmen said about it. What motivates one legislator to make a speech about a statute is not necessarily what motivates scores of others to enact it, and the stakes are sufficiently high for us to eschew guesswork. We decline to void essentially on the ground that it is unwise legislation which Congress had the undoubted power to enact and which could be reenacted in its exact form if the same or another legislator made a "wiser" speech about it.

* * *

We think it not amiss, in passing, to comment upon O'Brien's legislative-purpose argument. There was little floor debate on this legislation in either House. Only Senator Thurmond commented on its substantive features in the Senate. 111 Cong.Rec. 19746, 20433. After his brief statement, and without any additional substantive comments, the bill, H.R. 10306, passed the Senate. 111 Cong.Rec. 20434. In the House debate only two Congressmen addressed themselves to the Amendment—Congressmen Rivers and Bray. 111 Cong.Rec. 19871, 19872. The bill was passed after their statements without any further debate by a vote of 393 to 1. It is principally on the basis of the statements by these three Congressmen that O'Brien makes his congressional-"purpose" argument. We note that if we were to examine legislative purpose in the instant case, we would be obliged to consider not only these statements but also the more authoritative reports of the Senate and House Armed Services Committees. The portions of those reports explaining the purpose of the Amendment are reproduced in

---

30. The Court may make the same assumption in a very limited and well-defined class of cases where the very nature of the constitutional question requires an inquiry into legislative purpose. The principal class of cases is readily apparent—those in which statutes have been challenged as bills of attainder. This Court's decisions have defined a bill of attainder as a legislative Act which inflicts punishment on named individuals or members of an easily ascertainable group without a judicial trial. In determining whether a particular statute is a bill of attainder, the analysis necessarily requires an inquiry into whether the three definitional elements—specificity in identification, punishment, and lack of a judicial trial—are contained in the statute. The inquiry into whether the challenged statute contains the necessary element of punishment has on occasion led the Court to examine the legislative motive in enacting the statute. See, e.g., United States v. Lovett, 328 U.S. 303 (1946). Two other decisions not involving a bill of attainder analysis contain an inquiry into legislative purpose or motive of the type that O'Brien suggests we engage in in this case. Kennedy v. Mendoza-Martinez, 372 U.S. 144, 169–184 (1963); Trop v. Dulles, 356 U.S. 86, 79–97 (1958). The inquiry into legislative purpose or motive in *Kennedy* and *Trop*, however, was for the same limited purpose as in the bill of attainder decisions—i.e. to determine whether the statutes under review were punitive in nature. We face no such inquiry in this case. The 1965 Amendment to § 462(b) was clearly penal in nature, designed to impose criminal punishment for designated acts.

the Appendix in their entirety. While both reports make clear a concern with the "defiant" destruction of so-called "draft cards" and with "open" encouragement to others to destroy their cards, both reports also indicate that this concern stemmed from an apprehension that unrestrained destruction of cards would disrupt the smooth functioning of the Selective Service System.

IV.

Since the 1965 Amendment to § 12(b)(3) of the Universal Military Training and Service Act is constitutional as enacted and as applied, the Court of Appeals should have affirmed the judgment of conviction entered by the District Court. Accordingly, we vacate the judgment of the Court of Appeals, and reinstate the judgment and sentence of the District Court. This disposition makes unnecessary consideration of O'Brien's claim that the Court of Appeals erred in affirming his conviction on the basis of the nonpossession regulation.[31]

It is so ordered.

MR. JUSTICE MARSHALL took no part in the consideration or decision of these cases.

* * *

MR. JUSTICE HARLAN, concurring.

The crux of the Court's opinion, which I join, is of course its general statement, ante, that:

> "a government regulation is sufficiently justified if it is within the constitutional power of the Government; if it furthers an important or substantial governmental interest; if the governmental interest is unrelated to the suppression of free expression; and if the incidental restriction on alleged First Amendment freedoms is no greater than is essential to the furtherance of that interest."

I wish to make explicit my understanding that this passage does not foreclose consideration of First Amendment claims in those rare instances when an "incidental" restriction upon expression, imposed by a regulation which furthers an "important or substantial" governmental interest and satisfies the Court's other criteria, in practice has the effect of entirely preventing a "speaker" from reaching a significant audience with whom he could not otherwise lawfully communicate. This is not such a case, since O'Brien manifestly could have conveyed his message in many ways other than by burning his draft card.

MR. JUSTICE DOUGLAS, dissenting.

The Court states that the constitutional power of Congress to raise and support armies is "broad and sweeping" and that Congress' power "to classify and conscript manpower for military service is 'beyond question.'" This is undoubtedly true in times when, by declaration of

---

31. The other issues briefed by O'Brien were not raised in the petition for certiorari in No. 232 or in the cross-petition in No. 233. Accordingly, those issues are not before this Court.

Congress, the Nation is in a state of war. The underlying and basic problem in this case, however, is whether conscription is permissible in the absence of a declaration of war. That question has not been briefed nor was it presented in oral argument; but it is, I submit, a question upon which the litigants and the country are entitled to a ruling. I have discussed in Holmes v. United States, 390 U.S. 936, the nature of the legal issue and it will be seen from my dissenting opinion in that case that this Court has never ruled on the question. It is time that we made a ruling. This case should be put down for reargument and heard with *Holmes v. United States* and with Hart v. United States, 390 U.S. 956, in which the Court today denies certiorari.

CLARK v. COMMUNITY FOR CREATIVE NON-VIOLENCE
Supreme Court of the United States, 1984.
468 U.S. 288, 104 S.Ct. 3065, 82 L.Ed.2d 221.

JUSTICE WHITE delivered the opinion of the Court.

The issue in this case is whether a National Park Service regulation prohibiting camping in certain parks violates the First Amendment when applied to prohibit demonstrators from sleeping in Lafayette Park and the Mall in connection with a demonstration to call attention to the plight of the homeless. We hold that it does not and reverse the contrary judgment of the Court of Appeals.

I

The Interior Department, through the National Park Service, is charged with responsibility for the management and maintenance of the National Parks and is authorized to promulgate rules and regulations for the use of the parks in accordance with the purposes for which they were established. 16 U.S.C. §§ 1, 1a–1, 3. The network of National Parks includes the National Memorial-core parks, Lafayette Park and the Mall, which are set in the heart of Washington, D.C., and which are unique resources that the Federal Government holds in trust for the American people. Lafayette Park is a roughly 7-acre square located across Pennsylvania Avenue from the White House. Although originally part of the White House grounds, President Jefferson set it aside as a park for the use of residents and visitors. It is a "garden park with a * * * formal landscaping of flowers and trees, with fountains, walks and benches." * * * The Mall is a stretch of land running westward from the Capitol to the Lincoln Memorial some two miles away. It includes the Washington Monument, a series of reflecting pools, trees, lawns, and other greenery. It is bordered by, *inter alia,* the Smithsonian Institution and the National Gallery of Art. Both the Park and the Mall were included in Major Pierre L'Enfant's original plan for the Capital. Both are visited by vast numbers of visitors from around the country, as well as by large numbers of residents of the Washington metropolitan area.

Under the regulations involved in this case, camping in National Parks is permitted only in campgrounds designated for that purpose. 36 CFR § 50.27(a) (1983). No such campgrounds have ever been designated in Lafayette Park or the Mall. * * * Demonstrations for the airing of views or grievances are permitted in the Memorial-core parks, but for the most part only by Park Service permits. * * * Temporary structures may be erected for demonstration purposes but may not be used for camping. 36 CFR § 50.19(e)(8) (1983).[2]

In 1982, the Park Service issued a renewable permit to respondent Community for Creative Non–Violence (CCNV) to conduct a wintertime demonstration in Lafayette Park and the Mall for the purpose of demonstrating the plight of the homeless. The permit authorized the erection of two symbolic tent cities: 20 tents in Lafayette Park that would accommodate 50 people and 40 tents in the Mall with a capacity of up to 100. The Park Service, however, relying on the above regulations, specifically denied CCNV's request that demonstrators be permitted to sleep in the symbolic tents.

* * * The District Court granted summary judgment in favor of the Park Service. The Court of Appeals, sitting *en banc*, reversed. * * *

II

We need not differ with the view of the Court of Appeals that overnight sleeping in connection with the demonstration is expressive conduct protected to some extent by the First Amendment.[5] We assume for present purposes, but do not decide, that such is the case, cf. United States v. O'Brien, 391 U.S. 367, 376 (1968), but this assumption only begins the inquiry. Expression, whether oral or written or symbolized by conduct, is subject to reasonable time, place, or manner restrictions. We have often noted that restrictions of this kind are valid provided that they are justified without reference to the content of the regulated speech, that they are narrowly tailored to serve a

---

2. Section 50.19(e)(8), as amended, prohibits the use of certain temporary structures:

"In connection with permitted demonstrations or special events, temporary structures may be erected for the purpose of symbolizing a message or meeting logistical needs such as first aid facilities, lost children areas or the provision of shelter for electrical and other sensitive equipment or displays. Temporary structures may not be used outside designated camping areas for living accommodation activities such as sleeping, or making preparations to sleep (including the laying down of bedding for the purpose of sleeping), or storing personal belongings, or making any fire, or doing any digging or earth breaking or carrying on cooking activities. The above-listed activities constitute camping when it reasonably appears, in light of all the circumstances, that the participants, in conducting these activities, are in fact using the area as a living accommodation regardless of the intent of the participants or the nature of any other activities in which they may also be engaging."

5. We reject the suggestion of the plurality below, however, that the burden on the demonstrators is limited to "the advancement of a plausible contention" that their conduct is expressive. *Id.*, at 26, n. 16, 703 F.2d, at 593, n. 16. Although it is common to place the burden upon the Government to justify impingements on First Amendment interests, it is the obligation of the person desiring to engage in assertedly expressive conduct to demonstrate that the First Amendment even applies. To hold otherwise would be to create a rule that all conduct is presumptively expressive. In the absence of a showing that such a rule is necessary to protect vital First Amendment interests, we decline to deviate from the general rule that one seeking relief bears the burden of demonstrating that he is entitled to it.

significant governmental interest, and that they leave open ample alternative channels for communication of the information. * * *

It is also true that a message may be delivered by conduct that is intended to be communicative and that, in context, would reasonably be understood by the viewer to be communicative. Spence v. Washington, 418 U.S. 405 (1974); Tinker v. Des Moines School District, 393 U.S. 503 (1969). Symbolic expression of this kind may be forbidden or regulated if the conduct itself may constitutionally be regulated, if the regulation is narrowly drawn to further a substantial governmental interest, and if the interest is unrelated to the suppression of free speech. *United States v. O'Brien, supra.*

Petitioners submit, as they did in the Court of Appeals, that the regulation forbidding sleeping is defensible either as a time, place, or manner restriction or as a regulation of symbolic conduct. We agree with that assessment. The permit that was issued authorized the demonstration but required compliance with 36 CFR § 50.19 (1983), which prohibits "camping" on park lands, that is, the use of park lands for living accommodations, such as sleeping, storing personal belongings, making fires, digging, or cooking. These provisions, including the ban on sleeping are clearly limitations on the manner in which the demonstration could be carried out. That sleeping like the symbolic tents themselves, may be expressive and part of the message delivered by the demonstration does not make the ban any less a limitation on the manner of demonstrating, for reasonable time, place, or manner regulations normally have the purpose and direct effect of limiting expression but are nevertheless valid. * * *

The requirement that the regulation be content-neutral is clearly satisfied. The courts below accepted that view, and it is not disputed here that the prohibition on camping, and on sleeping specifically, is content-neutral and is not being applied because of disagreement with the message presented. Neither was the regulation faulted, nor could it be, on the ground that without overnight sleeping the plight of the homeless could not be communicated in other ways. The regulation otherwise left the demonstration intact, with its symbolic city, signs, and the presence of those who were willing to take their turns in a day-and-night vigil. Respondents do not suggest that there was, or is, any barrier to delivering to the media, or to the public by other means, the intended message concerning the plight of the homeless.

It is also apparent to us that the regulation narrowly focuses on the Government's substantial interest in maintaining the parks in the heart of our Capital in an attractive and intact condition, readily available to the millions of people who wish to see and enjoy them by their presence. To permit camping—using these areas as living accommodations—would be totally inimical to these purposes, as would be readily understood by those who have frequented the National Parks across the country and observed the unfortunate consequences of the activities of those who refuse to confine their camping to designated areas.

It is urged by respondents, and the Court of Appeals was of this view, that if the symbolic city of tents was to be permitted and if the demonstrators did not intend to cook, dig, or engage in aspects of camping other than sleeping, the incremental benefit to the parks could not justify the ban on sleeping, which was here an expressive activity said to enhance the message concerning the plight of the poor and homeless. We cannot agree. In the first place, we seriously doubt that the First Amendment requires the Park Service to permit a demonstration in Lafayette Park and the Mall involving a 24-hour vigil and the erection of tents to accommodate 150 people. Furthermore, although we have assumed for present purposes that the sleeping banned in this case would have an expressive element, it is evident that its major value to this demonstration would be facilitative. Without a permit to sleep, it would be difficult to get the poor and homeless to participate or to be present at all. This much is apparent from the permit application filed by respondents: "Without the incentive of sleeping space or a hot meal, the homeless would not come to the site." App. 14. The sleeping ban, if enforced, would thus effectively limit the nature, extent, and duration of the demonstration and to that extent ease the pressure on the parks.

Beyond this, however, it is evident from our cases that the validity of this regulation need not be judged solely by reference to the demonstration at hand. Heffron v. International Society for Krishna Consciousness, Inc., 452 U.S., at 652–653. Absent the prohibition on sleeping, there would be other groups who would demand permission to deliver an asserted message by camping in Lafayette Park. Some of them would surely have as credible a claim in this regard as does CCNV, and the denial of permits to still others would present difficult problems for the Park Service. With the prohibition, however, as is evident in the case before us, at least some around-the-clock demonstrations lasting for days on end will not materialize, others will be limited in size and duration, and the purposes of the regulation would be more effectively and not clumsily achieved by preventing tents and 24-hour vigils entirely in the core areas. But the Park Service's decision to permit nonsleeping demonstrations does not, in our view, impugn the camping prohibition as a valuable, but perhaps imperfect, protection to the parks. If the Government has a legitimate interest in ensuring that the National Parks are adequately protected, which we think it has, and if the parks would be more exposed to harm without the sleeping prohibition than with it, the ban is safe from invalidation under the First Amendment as a reasonable regulation of the manner in which a demonstration may be carried out. As in *City Council of Los Angeles v. Taxpayers for Vincent,* the regulation "responds precisely to the substantive problems which legitimately concern the [Government]." 466 U.S., at 810.

We have difficulty, therefore, in understanding why the prohibition against camping, with its ban on sleeping overnight, is not a reasonable time, place, or manner regulation that withstands constitutional scrutiny. Surely the regulation is not unconstitutional on its face. None of its provisions appear unrelated to the ends that it was designed to serve. Nor is it any less valid when applied to prevent camping in Memorial-core parks by those who wish to demonstrate and deliver a message to the public and the central Government. Damage to the parks as well as their partial inaccessibility to other members of the public can as easily result from camping by demonstrators as by nondemonstrators. In neither case must the Government tolerate it. All those who would resort to the parks must abide by otherwise valid rules for their use, just as they must observe the traffic laws, sanitation regulations, and laws to preserve the public peace.[7] This is no more than a reaffirmation that reasonable time, place, or manner restrictions on expression are constitutionally acceptable.

Contrary to the conclusion of the Court of Appeals, the foregoing analysis demonstrates that the Park Service regulation is sustainable under the four-factor standard of United States v. O'Brien, 391 U.S. 367 (1968), for validating a regulation of expressive conduct, which, in the last analysis is little, if any, different from the standard applied to time, place, or manner restrictions.[8] No one contends that aside from its impact on speech a rule against camping or overnight sleeping in public parks is beyond the constitutional power of the Government to enforce. And for the reasons we have discussed above, there is a substantial Government interest in conserving park property, an interest that is plainly served by, and requires for its implementation, measures such as the proscription of sleeping that are designed to limit the wear and tear on park properties. That interest is unrelated to suppression of expression.

We are unmoved by the Court of Appeals' view that the challenged regulation is unnecessary, and hence invalid, because there are less speech-restrictive alternatives that could have satisfied the Government interest in preserving park lands. There is no gainsaying that preventing overnight sleeping will avoid a measure of actual or threatened damage to Lafayette Park and the Mall. The Court of Appeals' suggestions that the Park Service minimize the possible injury by reducing the size, duration, or frequency of demonstrations would still curtail the total allowable expression in which demonstrators could engage, whether by sleeping or otherwise, and these suggestions represent no more than a disagreement with the Park Service over how much protection the core parks require or how an acceptable level of preservation is to be attained. We do not believe, however, that either

---

7. When the Government seeks to regulate conduct that is ordinarily nonexpressive it may do so regardless of the situs of the application of the regulation. Thus, even against people who choose to violate Park Service regulations for expressive purposes, the Park Service may enforce regulations relating to grazing animals, 36 CFR § 50.13 (1983); flying model planes, § 50.16; gambling, § 50.17; hunting and fishing, § 50.18; setting off fireworks, § 50.25(g); and urination, § 50.26(b).

8. Reasonable time, place, or manner restrictions are valid even though they directly limit oral or written expression. It would be odd to insist on a higher standard for limitations aimed at regulable conduct and having only an incidental impact on speech. Thus, if the time, place, or manner restriction on expressive sleeping, if that is what is involved in this case, sufficiently and narrowly serves a substantial enough governmental interest to escape First Amendment concerns or that there is an inadequate nexus between the regulation and the interest sought to be served.
* * *

United States v. O'Brien or the time, place, or manner decisions assign to the judiciary the authority to replace the Park Service as the manager of the Nation's parks or endow the judiciary with the competence to judge how much protection of park lands is wise and how that level of conservation is to be attained.

Accordingly, the judgment of the Court of Appeals is

Reversed.

CHIEF JUSTICE BERGER, concurring.

* * *

JUSTICE MARSHALL with whom JUSTICE BRENNAN joins, dissenting.

* * *

* * * Missing from the majority's description is any inkling that Lafayette Park and the Mall have served as the sites for some of the most rousing political demonstrations in the Nation's history. It is interesting to learn, I suppose, that Lafayette Park and the Mall were both part of Major Pierre L'Enfant's original plan for the Capital. Far more pertinent, however, is that these areas constitute, in the Government's words, "a fitting and powerful forum for political expression and political protest." Brief for Petitioners 11.

The primary purpose for making *sleep* an integral part of the demonstration was "to re-enact the central reality of homelessness," Brief for Respondent 2, and to impress upon public consciousness, in as dramatic a way as possible, that homelessness is a widespread problem, often ignored, that confronts its victims with life-threatening deprivations. * * *

In a long line of cases, this Court has afforded First Amendment protection to expressive conduct that qualifies as symbolic speech. See, e.g., Tinker v. Des Moines School Dist., 393 U.S. 503 (1969) (black armband worn by students in public schools as protest against United States policy in Vietnam war); Brown v. Louisiana, 383 U.S. 131 (1966) (sit-in by Negro students in "whites only" library to protest segregation); Stromberg v. California, 283 U.S. 359 (1931) (flying red flag as gesture of support for communism). In light of the surrounding context, respondents' proposed activity meets the qualifications. The Court has previously acknowledged the importance of context in determining whether an act can properly be denominated as "speech" for First Amendment purposes and has provided guidance concerning the way in which courts should "read" a context in making this determination. The leading case is Spence v. Washington, 418 U.S. 405 (1974), where this Court held that displaying a United States flag with a peace symbol attached to it was conduct protected by the First Amendment. The Court looked first to the intent of the speaker—whether there was an "intent to convey a particularized message"—whether "the likelihood was great that the message would be understood by those who viewed it." * * *

Nor can there be any doubt that in the surrounding circumstances the likelihood was great that the political significance of sleeping in the parks would be understood by those who viewed it. Certainly the news media understood the significance of respondents' proposed activity; newspapers and magazines from around the nation reported their previous sleep-in and their planned display. Ordinary citizens, too, would likely understand the political message intended by respondents. This likelihood stems from the remarkably apt fit between the activity in which respondents seek to engage and the social problem they seek to highlight. By using sleep as an integral part of their mode of protest, respondents "can express with their bodies the poignancy of their plight. They can physically demonstrate the neglect from which they suffer with an articulateness even Dickens could not match." Community for Creative Non-Violence v. Watt, 227 U.S.App.D.C. 19, 34, 703 F.2d 586, 601 (1983) (Edwards, J. concurring).

* * *

The Government contends that a foreseeable difficulty of administration counsels against recognizing sleep as a mode of expression protected by the First Amendment. The predicament the Government envisions can be termed "the imposter problem": the problem of distinguishing bona fide protesters from imposters whose requests for permission to sleep in Lafayette Park or the Mall on First Amendment grounds would mask ulterior designs—the simple desire, for example, to avoid the expense of hotel lodgings. The Government maintains that such distinctions cannot be made without inquiring into the sincerity of demonstrators and that such an inquiry would itself pose dangers to First Amendment values because it would necessarily be content-sensitive. I find this argument unpersuasive. First, a variety of circumstances *already* require government agencies to engage in the delicate task of inquiring into the sincerity of claimants asserting First Amendment rights. See, *e.g.,* Wisconsin v. Yoder, 406 U.S. 205, 215–216 (1972) (exception of members of religious group from compulsory education statute justified by group's adherence to deep religious conviction rather than subjective secular values); Welsh v. United States, 398 U.S. 333, 343–344 (1970) (eligibility for exemption from military service as conscientious objector status justified by sincere religious beliefs). It is thus incorrect to imply that any scrutiny of the asserted purpose of persons seeking a permit to display sleeping as a form of symbolic speech would import something altogether new and disturbing into our First Amendment jurisprudence. Second, the administrative difficulty the Government envisions is now nothing more than a vague apprehension. If permitting sleep to be used as a form of protected First Amendment activity actually created the administrative problems the Government now envisions, there would emerge a clear factual basis upon which to establish the necessity for the limitation the Government advocates.

The Government's final argument against granting respondents' proposed activity any degree of First Amendment protection is that the contextual analysis upon which respondents rely is fatally flawed by overinclusiveness. The Government contends that the *Spence* approach is overinclusive because it accords First Amendment status to a wide variety of acts that, although expressive, are obviously subject to prohibition. As the Government notes, "[a]ctions such as assassination of political figures and the bombing of government buildings can fairly be characterized as intended to convey a message that is readily perceived by the public." Brief for Petitioners 24, n. 18. The Government's argument would pose a difficult problem were the determination whether an act constitutes "speech" the end of First Amendment analysis. But such a determination is not the end. If an act is defined as speech, it must still be balanced against countervailing government interests. The balancing which the First Amendment requires would doom any argument seeking to protect antisocial acts such as assassination or destruction of government property from government interference because compelling interests would outweigh the expressive value of such conduct.

II

Although sleep in the context of this case is symbolic speech protected by the First Amendment, it is nonetheless subject to reasonable time, place, and manner restrictions. I agree with the standard enunciated by the majority: "[R]estrictions of this kind are valid provided that they are justified without reference to the content of the regulated speech, that they are narrowly tailored to serve a significant governmental interest, and that they leave open ample alternative channels for communication of the information." *Ante,* (citations omitted).[6] I conclude, however, that the regulations at issue in this case, as applied to respondents, fail to satisfy this standard.

According to the majority, the significant Government interest advanced by denying respondents' request to engage in sleep-speech is the interest in "maintaining the parks in the heart of our Capital in an attractive and intact condition, readily available to the millions of people who wish to see and enjoy them by their presence." * * * That interest is indeed significant. However, neither the Government nor the majority adequately explains how prohibiting respondents' planned activity will substantially further that interest.

The majority's attempted explanation begins with the curious statement that it seriously doubts that the First Amendment requires the Park Service to permit a demonstration in Lafayette Park and the Mall involving a 24-hour vigil and the erection of tents to accommodate 150 people. * * * I cannot perceive why the Court should have "serious doubts" regarding this matter and it provides no explanation for its uncertainty. Furthermore, even if the majority's doubts were well founded, I cannot see how such doubts relate to the problem at hand. The issue posed by this case is not whether the Government is constitutionally compelled to permit the erection of tents and the staging of a continuous 24-hour vigil; rather, the issue is whether any substantial Government interest is served by banning sleep that is part of a political demonstration.

---

6. I also agree with the majority that no substantial difference distinguishes the test applicable to time, place, and manner restrictions and the test articulated in United States v. O'Brien, 391 U.S. 367 (1968). See *ante,* n. 8.

What the Court may be suggesting is that if the tents and the 24–hour vigil are permitted, but not constitutionally required to be permitted, then respondents have no constitutional right to engage in expressive conduct that supplements these activities. Put in arithmetical terms, the Court appears to contend that if X is permitted by grace rather than by constitutional compulsion, X + 1 can be denied without regard to the requirements the Government must normally satisfy in order to restrain protected activity. This notion, however, represents a misguided conception of the First Amendment. The First Amendment requires the Government to justify *every* instance of abridgment. * * * Moreover, the stringency of that requirement is not diminished simply because the activity the Government seeks to restrain is supplemental to other activity that the Government may have permitted out of grace but was not constitutionally compelled to allow. If the Government cannot adequately justify abridgment of protected expression, there is no reason why citizens should be prevented from exercising the *first* of the rights safeguarded by our Bill of Rights.

The majority's second argument is comprised of the suggestion that, although sleeping contains an element of expression, "its major value to [respondents'] demonstration would have been facilitative." * * * While this observation does provide a hint of the weight the Court attached to respondents' First Amendment claims, it is utterly irrelevant to whether the Government's ban on sleeping advances a substantial Government interest.

The majority's third argument is based upon two claims. The first is that the ban on sleeping relieves the Government of an administrative burden because, without the flat ban, the process of issuing and denying permits to other demonstrators asserting First Amendment rights to sleep in the parks "would present difficult problems for the Park Service." * * * The second is that the ban on sleeping will increase the probability that "some around-the-clock demonstrations for days on end will not materialize, [that] others will be limited in size and duration, and that the purpose of the regulation will thus be materially served," *ante,* that purpose being "to limit the wear and tear on park properties." * * *

The flaw in these two contentions is that neither is supported by a factual showing that evinces a real, as opposed to a merely speculative, problem. The majority fails to offer any evidence indicating that the absence of an absolute ban on sleeping would present administrative problems to the Park Service that are substantially more difficult than those it ordinarily confronts. A mere apprehension of difficulties should not be enough to overcome the right to free expression. See United States v. Grace, 461 U.S. 171, 182 (1983); Tinker v. Des Moines School Dist., 393 U.S., at 508. Moreover, if the Government's interest in avoiding administrative difficulties, were truly "substantial," one would expect the agency most involved in administering the parks at least to allude to such an interest. Here, however, the perceived difficulty of administering requests from other demonstrators seeking to convey messages through sleeping was not among the reasons underlying the Park Service regulations. Nor was it mentioned by the Park Service in its rejection of respondents' particular request.

The Court's erroneous application of the standard for ascertaining a reasonable time, place, and manner restriction is also revealed by the majority's conclusion that a substantial governmental interest is served by the sleeping ban because it will discourage "around-the-clock demonstrations for days" and thus further the regulation's purpose to "limit wear and tear on park properties." * * * The majority cites no evidence indicating that sleeping engaged in as symbolic speech will cause *substantial* wear and tear on park property. Furthermore, the Government's application of the sleeping ban in the circumstances of this case is strikingly underinclusive. The majority acknowledges that a proper time, place, and manner restriction must be "narrowly tailored." Here, however, the tailoring requirement is virtually forsaken inasmuch as the Government offers no justification for applying its absolute ban on sleeping yet is willing to allow respondents to engage in activities—such as feigned sleeping—that is no less burdensome.

In short, there are no substantial Government interests advanced by the Government's regulations as applied to respondents. All that the Court's decision advances are the prerogatives of a bureaucracy that over the years has shown an implacable hostility toward citizens' exercise of First Amendment rights.[10]

III

The disposition of this case impels me to make two additional observations. First, in this case, as in some others involving time, place, and manner restrictions,[11] the Court has dramatically lowered its scrutiny of governmental regulations once it has determined that such regulations are content-neutral. The result has been the creation of a two-tiered approach to First Amendment cases: while regulations that turn on the content of the expression are subjected to a strict form of judicial review, regulations that are aimed at matters other than expression receive only a minimal level of scrutiny. The minimal scrutiny prong of this two-tiered approach has led to an unfortunate diminution of First Amendment protection. By narrowly limiting its concern to whether a given regulation creates a content-based distinction, the Court has seemingly overlooked the fact that content-neutral

---

10. At oral argument, the Government suggested that the ban on sleeping should not be invalidated as applied to respondents simply because the Government is willing to allow respondents to engage in other nonverbal acts of expression that may also trench upon the Government interests served by the ban. Tr. of Oral Arg. 15, 23. The Government maintains that such a result makes the Government a victim of its own generosity. However, the Government's characterization of itself as an unstinting provider of opportunities for protected expression is thoroughly discredited by a long line of decisions *compelling* the National Park Service to allow the expressive conduct it now claims to permit as a matter of grace. See, e.g., Women Strike for Peace v. Morton, 153 U.S.App. D.C. 198, 472 F.2d 1273 (1972); A Quaker Action Group v. Morton, 170 U.S.App.D.C. 124, 516 F.2d 717 (1975); United States v. Abney, 175 U.S.App.D.C. 247, 534 F.2d 984 (1976).

11. See, e.g., City Council of Los Angeles v. Taxpayers for Vincent, 466 U.S. 789 (1984); Heffron v. International Society for Krishna Consciousness, Inc., 452 U.S. 640 (1981). But see United States v. Grace, 461 U.S. 171 (1983); Tinker v. Des Moines School Dist., 393 U.S. 503 (1969); Brown v. Louisiana, 383 U.S. 131 (1966).

restrictions are also capable of unnecessarily restricting protected expressive activity.[13] To be sure, the general prohibition against content-based regulations is an essential tool of First Amendment analysis. It helps to put into operation the well-established principle that "government may not grant the use of a forum to people whose views it finds acceptable, but deny use to those wishing to express less favored or more controversial views." Police Department of Chicago v. Mosley, 408 U.S. 92, 95–96 (1972). The Court, however, has transformed the ban against content distinctions from a floor that offers all persons at least equal liberty under the First Amendment into a ceiling that restricts persons to the protection of First Amendment equality—but nothing more.[14] The consistent imposition of silence upon all may fulfill the dictates of an evenhanded content-neutrality. But it offends our "profound national commitment to the principle that debate on public issues should be uninhibited, robust, and wide-open." New York Times Co. v. Sullivan, 376 U.S., at 270.

Second, the disposition of this case reveals a mistaken assumption regarding the motives and behavior of Government officials who create and administer content-neutral regulations. The Court's salutary skepticism of governmental decisionmaking in First Amendment matters suddenly dissipates once it determines that a restriction is not content-based. The Court evidently assumes that the balance struck by officials is deserving of deference so long as it does not appear to be tainted by content discrimination. What the Court fails to recognize is that public officials have strong incentives to overregulate even in the absence of an intent to censor particular views. This incentive stems from the fact that of the two groups whose interests officials must accommodate—on the one hand, the interests of the general public and, on the other, the interests of those who seek to use a particular forum

---

13. See Redish, The Content Distinction in First Amendment Analysis, 34 Stan.L. Rev. 113 (1981).

14. Furthermore, a content-neutral regulation does not necessarily fall with random or equal force upon different groups or different points of view. A content-neutral regulation that restricts an inexpensive mode of communication will fall most heavily upon relatively poor speakers and the points of view that such speakers typically espouse. See, e.g., City Council of Los Angeles v. Taxpayers for Vincent, supra, at 812–813, n. 30. This sort of latent inequality is very much in evidence in this case for respondents lack the financial means necessary to buy access to more conventional modes of persuasion.

A disquieting feature about the disposition of this case is that it lends credence to the charge that judicial administration of the First Amendment, in conjunction with a social order marked by large disparities in wealth and other sources of power, tends systematically to discriminate against efforts by the relatively disadvantaged to convey their political ideas. In the past, this Court has taken such considerations into account in adjudicating the First Amendment rights of those among us who are financially deprived. See, e.g., Martin v. Struthers, 319 U.S. 141, 146 (1943) (striking down ban on door-to-door distribution of circulars in part because this mode of distribution is "essential to the poorly financed causes of little people"); Marsh v. Alabama, 326 U.S. 501 (1946) (State cannot impose criminal sanction on person for distributing literature on sidewalk of town owned by private corporation). Such solicitude is noticeably absent from the majority's opinion, continuing a trend that has not escaped the attention of commentators. See, e.g., Dorsen & Gora, Free Speech, Property, and The Burger Court: Old Values, New Balances, 1982 S.Ct.Rev. 195; Van Alstyne, The Recrudescence of Property Rights as the Foremost Principle of Civil Liberties: The First Decade of the Burger Court, 43 Law & Contemp.Prob. 66 (summer 1980).

for First Amendment activity—the political power of the former is likely to be far greater than that of the latter.[16]

* * *

For the foregoing reasons, I respectfully dissent.

A NOTE ON "SYMBOLIC EXPRESSION" AND THE "*O'BRIEN* TEST"

Suppose an ordinary jaywalking ordinance, i.e. a city ordinance making it a misdemeanor to cross city streets "other than at intersections and otherwise as designated, within marked lines." Suppose that X and Y are each in turn arrested for jaywalking, albeit at different times. Suppose in respect to X (but not Y), that X's very act of jaywalking was itself an obvious part of his remonstrance in protest of the (un)wisdom of the ordinance itself.

> *Query:* Does X have any invokable first amendment claim against the jaywalking ordinance as applied?[80] If he does, what is that claim, and how will it work out, i.e. will his conviction nonetheless be sustained?[81]

Is the case suitable to analyze under "reasonable time, place, and manner" *speech*-regulating rules?[82] Perhaps, but one needs to do some explaining, if one thinks that it is. The ordinance does not regulate speech as such at all.[83] Compare, for contrast, the *Pacifica Foundation* case.[84] There, an FCC regulation forbidding the use of "vulgar" language over ordinary commercial radio frequencies, during daylight hours, was indubitably a regulation of speech.[85] To be sure, it went

---

16. See Goldberger, Judicial Scrutiny in Public Forum Cases: Misplaced Trust in the Judgment of Public Officials, 32 Buffalo L.Rev. 175, 208 (1983).

80. Y, of course, would have no first amendment standing to object to the jaywalking ordinance as applied to him since (by stipulation) Y was not expressing any message at all (rather, Y was merely taking a short cut to cross the street, nothing more).

81. If one concludes that X's conviction cannot be sustained (perhaps by application of the *O'Brien* test?), how does one reconcile that result with the different fate of Y?—Why should Y be subject to a fine or a day or two in jail, when he did no more than X did, in jaywalking, and in one sense Y even did less (i.e. Y was neither willfully defying the law as such nor showing some degree of contempt of the law, as X; *why should Y be subject to punishment if X is not likewise to be punished*)? (Why should X get off, *at all?*)

82. See cases and discussion *infra* at ___, II.B.2. Time, Place, and Manner Regulation.

83. Similarly, consider a municipal ordinance of an ordinary sort making it a misdemeanor "to burn anything on the public streets of the town," an ordinance enacted as a simple public safety measure. Would it not be incorrect to review the malicious mischief ordinance under the case law pertinent to "time, place, and manner *speech* regulations"? (The ordinance is not a regulation of "speech," rather, it is a regulation of fires; it regulates when and where fires may (or, rather, may not) take place. (Cf. Texas v. Johnson, 491 U.S. 397, 109 S.Ct. 2533, 105 L.Ed.2d 342 (1989), and see the notes and discussion following that case, infra.)

84. FCC v. Pacifica Foundation, 438 U.S. 726, 98 S.Ct. 3026, 57 L.Ed.2d 1073 (1978).

85. Similarly, compare City Council v. Taxpayers for Vincent, 466 U.S. 789, 104 S.Ct. 2118, 80 L.Ed.2d 772 (1984) (city ordinance forbidding any posting of notices from utility poles or utility lines in the city, defended as a neutral measure to improve city's appearance, attacked as applied to election posters as an unreason-

"merely" to the use of certain words (i.e. vulgar, offensive words) rather than to the content of the broadcaster's message, but even so it was plainly a regulation of speech. This jaywalking ordinance seems quite far removed from regulations of that sort. It was solely the illegality of X's walking (rather than talking) that—just as in Y's case—solely brings him afoul of this law. So cases such as *Pacifica Foundation* are prima facie inapplicable to the kind of case we have put.

I.

Beginning with the observation just offered, it would appear that a strong case can be made that X secures no first amendment purchase against the jaywalking charge, i.e. "jaywalking" is simply not "speech," and it is solely for jaywalking that X has been charged. That X committed the offense to dramatize some grievance ought not, perhaps, be held against him vis-a-vis the treatment Y receives in the courts, but even that is far from clear under some not unreasonable views.[86]

The case is different, moreover, not merely from cases such as the *Pacifica Foundation* case, but arguably distinguishable from cases such as *Tinker v. Des Moines School District*, as well. There, it was said, the wearing of an armband is "akin to pure speech," and, objectively, that may well be true of armbands in general, including (but not limited to) the sort of armband involved in the particular case.[87] Thus a regulation of when and where one may or may not wear an armband may be regarded as a regulation of speech, bringing the first amendment directly to bear. The case may also be different from *Street* and from *Spence,* two cases involving flag regulation laws, that lie immediately ahead in these materials; flags, especially the standard national flag, are typically communicative—they say something and usually are meant to communicate something. When, therefore, the regulation is one of "flag use," it may be quite right to regard the regulation as, in some measure, a regulation of speech. But, again, we seem to have nothing similar here.

The case is different also from Stromberg v. California,[88] as well, where the act (displaying a red flag) was forbidden as a means of expression (of opposition to established government)—it is the same point made by several other examples given in several of the cases noted—and distinguished—in *O'Brien* itself. To make the jaywalking case similar to *Stromberg* or to *Street,* would require one to redo the ordinance—to make jaywalking a crime when engaged in as a means of social protest, but not otherwise, thus discriminating between X and Y, which the ordinance does not do.

able restriction on candidate's committee to hang posters which city conceded provided no hazard to traffic or to public safety.)

86. See discussion, note 81 supra (suggesting the appropriateness of a higher fine justified by the deterrence of willful violators).

87. As noted in the Introduction (Part I) to these materials, a merely generous construction of the words of the first amendment might well include politically expressive insignia (such as armbands) as "speech." To do the same for "jaywalking," in contrast, might well seem to empty the amendment of any coherence at all.

88. 283 U.S. 359, 51 S.Ct. 532, 75 L.Ed. 1117 (1931).

Neither is the case one in which, though the ordinance is neutral on its face (i.e. in its non-speech concern and apparent ordinariness), there is nonetheless very strong evidence that in fact it was adopted as a means of suppressing a feared message or expression, and would not otherwise have been laid into place. Whatever the proper treatment of any law so conceived and adopted (e.g., in both *Tinker* and *O'Brien*), we have made no similar suggestion here.[89] In each (indeed, perhaps in all) of the above-mentioned distinguishing circumstances, the first amendment might well be deemed to apply. To be sure, that conclusion—that the first amendment applies—would not automatically mean that each involved litigant necessarily prevails, but it clearly will require some first amendment discussion to show why not. Here, in contrast, the cases may have an entirely different feel.[90]

II.

Nonetheless, note that both *O'Brien* and *Clark* actually suggest otherwise, i.e. they suggest that the first amendment can be invoked by X (although clearly not by Y). Just because O'Brien was trying to make a strong political point by publicly burning his draft card (and just because, likewise, the Community for Creative Non–Violence was trying to make a similar point of its own by maintaining its lived-in tents in Lafayette Park), they evidently did gain a degree of first amendment benefit that the ordinary draft card mutilator, or the ordinary camper, could not claim. Significantly, that is, the majority of the Supreme Court in each case seems to be satisfied this is so, even if in each case the majority also concluded that the regulation was valid as applied.

In this respect (if in no other), it is well worth one's time to note how the cases are something of a first amendment-*favoring* surprise. They treat sleeping out as "speech," and burning a piece of pasteboard as "speech." A priori, there was no reason to suppose that such a concession would necessarily be made, even under a presumption of generous construction of the first amendment as such.

So far as that concession has been made by the Supreme Court, moreover, presumably it is available in our jaywalking case as well. Looking at that case again, with the hindsight of these remarks, there seems to be no ground to exclude X's case from the advantage of this development (though it will not apply to Y). In some measure, then, it appears that X's case will be treated differently from Y's. And, according to the test now shown to be applicable to X's case (i.e. the test laid out in the *O'Brien* case by Chief Justice Warren), presumably X cannot be validly convicted unless, in addition to proving the usual

---

89. In short, the hypothetical case is not one appropriate for analysis pursuant to the "cellophane wrapper" doctrine— where the evidence is clear and convincing that the legislature was *trying to do one thing* (suppress dissent) *under the guise of doing another thing* (regulating traffic). Here, by hypothesis, the ordinance was bona fide in its valid police power concern.

90. Again, if one is inclined to think otherwise, pause for a moment to compare the treatment of Y—why should X get any advantage over Y under the circumstances, in being acquitted of the jaywalking offense? (Similarly, in the malicious mischief "burning" cases, compared in an earlier footnote *supra*.)

elements of the jaywalking offense as committed by X, the government can also prove the following things as well:

a) That not only was the jaywalking law well within the constitutional power of government (a standard requirement the government must satisfy in any case whether or not it involves the first amendment), but that the law in question "furthers an important or substantial governmental interest," and not merely one that might suffice if no first amendment interests were involved;

b) That the important or substantial governmental interest, moreover, is one that is itself "unrelated to the suppression of free expression"; and

c) That the restriction on free speech (incidental to the restriction as applied) "is (also) no greater than is essential to the furtherance of that (important or substantial) interest." All of this would clearly imply that the X case might come out differently from the Y case because, by stipulation, the government must meet some burdens (and will fail if it cannot carry those burdens) which it need not meet in the prosecution of Y.[91]

III.

Yet, before becoming unduly involved in this matter with high optimism, note the likelihood that in fact rarely will one expect the government to fail to meet the requirements of the *O'Brien* test as it appears to have been applied. Both *O'Brien* and *Clark* tend to show how that is so. Applied to our hypothetical jaywalking case, it is altogether likely that X will also fail.[92] To be sure, if one applies the last part of the *O'Brien* test by concentrating on X's particular arrest and prosecution, it might well appear that X should tend to prevail.[93] But judging the matter from the *O'Brien* and *Clark* cases themselves, the Supreme Court seems wholly disinclined to test these types of cases in any such (limited) case-specific, way. Rather, the issue is tested more from a generalized perspective, rather than from an ex post

---

91. To consider only the first step, for instance, presumably in some instances the government will not be able to show any "substantial" or "important" (as distinct from merely permissible) interest served by the regulation in question, even if, in our particular case, it may be able to do so—as it probably can. And so, too, with the requirement set forth in *O'Brien*, with respect to step c.

92. The governmental interest will surely be said to be important or substantial, (i.e. it will be identified to public safety itself). As to the second step of the test, moreover, we have already passed it (in that we have already stipulated that the jaywalking ordinance is admittedly unrelated to the suppression of free expression as such). And while one might dispute how essential the prohibition of jaywalking is to the furtherance of the substantial and important governmental interest (of safe street use), it is likely to be thought "essential" enough for the ordinance to be sustained as applied. Test it by your own review and comparison of *O'Brien* and *Clark*, and see whether you agree.

93. This would seem to be so, consistent with the last part of the *O'Brien* standards as set out by the Court, because being able to apply the ordinance to X in the particular circumstances seems quite inessential to the furtherance of the common substantial interest in public traffic safety. (Little, if any, actual traffic problem was caused by X.) And, accordingly, by offering this very observation, one might think that, therefore, X should prevail, given the standards said to be applicable to his case.

case-specific perspective, i.e. it is tested by viewing the potential class of first amendment violators overall as a class, though there is as yet no such real aggregation of violations at hand.[94]

In brief, under *O'Brien* and *Clark,* the question is not treated in terms of whether X as a person created such a traffic danger (or might have created such a danger) in such circumstances that as applied to him, sustaining the ordinance was essential to secure traffic safety at the time; rather, it is treated as whether, were all persons "like X" to be deemed exempt, then might the hazard to traffic safety become substantial? If the reasonable answer to that question is "yes," then X's conviction will, in turn, be sustained. Where treating like future cases, as one says one must treat this case, may lead to substantial frustration of important public interests, even if this case by itself does not do so, the issue will be treated by the expectation of what would lie ahead, rather than by that which has happened. By this standard, few *O'Brien*-type cases will come out favorably to the first amendment claim.[95]

IV.

Even so, note, finally, that the rather undemanding criteria (de facto) of the *O'Brien* approach may control only within its own quite narrowly stated field of regulation, i.e. those regulations which, on their face, do not limit anything one ordinarily would regard as either speech or (even) as "akin" to speech. So, just as a parting counterexample, i.e. an example of an ordinance not subject to the *O'Brien* test (but subject, rather, to more stringent first amendment review?),[96] any ordinance in any way presuming to restrict one's use of the streets as places of "public demonstration" or "protest," would presumably remain subject to more stringent first amendment review. Thus qualified, the *O'Brien* test may be limited, and useful, within its narrow area of fit.[97]

---

94. As a mnemonic aid, rock fans may recall a memorable line from a lyric by the Grateful Dead. ("Trouble ahead, trouble behind, and you know this notion just crossed my mind.") So, the Court concludes that were it to sustain the camping "right" of the Creative Non–Violence group on first amendment grounds, it would be bound to treat others equally so to sustain a similar camping right in them in any similar case, i.e. where camping was also part of a political demonstration designed to capture public attention in the same way. Yet, if each group wishing to make its point in this way could do so in the same manner and to the same extent as Creative Non–Violence, under claim of an equal first amendment right, then indeed the park's use as a park would be substantially (perhaps wholly) subverted, i.e. effectively destroyed for ordinary park use.

95. For a generalization and review of this approach to first amendment questions, see Easterbrook, The Supreme Court 1983 Term Forward: The Court and the Economic System, 98 Harv.L.Rev. 4 (1984).

96. Compare and determine whether the different "test" as framed by the Supreme Court in respect to "time, place, and manner" speech regulations (*infra*) is de facto more protective than the *O'Brien* test just reviewed.

97. The more serious difficulty *re O'Brien* has been, rather, that some Justices have treated it as a general first amendment test.

SCHACHT v. UNITED STATES
Supreme Court of the United States, 1970.
398 U.S. 58, 90 S.Ct. 1555, 26 L.Ed.2d 44.

MR. JUSTICE BLACK delivered the opinion of the Court.

The petitioner, Daniel Jay Schacht, was indicted in a United States District Court for violating 18 U.S.C. § 702, which makes it a crime for any person "without authority [to wear] the uniform or a distinctive part thereof * * * of any of the armed forces of the United States. * * * " He was tried and convicted by a jury, and on February 29, 1968, he was sentenced to pay a fine of $250 and to serve a six-month prison term, the maximum sentence allowable under 18 U.S.C. § 702. There is no doubt that Schacht did wear distinctive parts of the uniform of the United States Army[2] and that he was not a member of the Armed Forces. He has defended his conduct since the beginning, however, on the ground that he was authorized to wear the uniform by an Act of Congress, 10 U.S.C. § 772(f), which provides as follows:

"When wearing by persons not on active duty authorized.

* * *

"(f) While portraying a member of the Army, Navy, Air Force, or Marine Corps, an actor in a theatrical or motion-picture production may wear the uniform of that armed force *if the portrayal does not tend to discredit that armed force.*" (Emphasis added.)

Schacht argued in the trial court and in this Court that he wore the army uniform as an "actor" in a "theatrical production" performed several times between 6:30 and 8:30 a.m. on December 4, 1967, in front of the Armed Forces Induction Center at Houston, Texas. The street skit in which Schacht wore the army uniform as a costume was designed, in his view, to expose the evil of the American presence in Vietnam and was part of a larger, peaceful antiwar demonstration at the induction center that morning. * * *

* * *

"The skit was composed of three people. There was Schacht who was dressed in a uniform and cap. A second person was wearing 'military colored' coveralls. The third person was outfitted in typical Viet Cong apparel. The first two men carried water pistols. One of them would yell, 'Be an able American,' and then they would shoot the Viet Cong with their pistols. The pistols expelled a red liquid which, when it struck the victim, created the impression that he was bleeding. Once the victim fell down the other two would walk up to him and exclaim, 'My God, this is a pregnant woman.' Without

---

2. Schacht wore a blouse of the type currently authorized for Army enlisted men with a shoulder patch designating service in Europe. The buttons on his blouse were of the official Army design. On his head Schacht wore an outmoded military hat. Affixed to the hat in an inverted position was the eagle insignia currently worn on the hats of Army officers.

noticeable variation this skit was reenacted several times during the morning of the demonstration." 414 F.2d 630, 632.

Our previous cases would seem to make it clear that 18 U.S.C. § 702, making it an offense to wear our military uniforms without authority is, standing alone, a valid statute on its face. See, e.g., United States v. O'Brien, 391 U.S. 367 (1968). But the general prohibition of 18 U.S.C. § 702 cannot always stand alone in view of 10 U.S.C. § 772, which authorizes the wearing of military uniforms under certain conditions and circumstances including the circumstance of an actor portraying a member of the armed services in a "theatrical production." 10 U.S.C. § 772(f). The Government's argument in this case seems to imply that somehow what these amateur actors did in Houston should not be treated as a "theatrical production" within the meaning of § 772(f). We are unable to follow such a suggestion. Certainly theatrical productions need not always be performed in buildings or even on a defined area such as a conventional stage. Nor need they be performed by professional actors or be heavily financed or elaborately produced. Since time immemorial, outdoor theatrical performances, often performed by amateurs, have played an important part in the entertainment and the education of the people of the world. Here, the record shows without dispute the preparation and repeated presentation by amateur actors of a short play designed to create in the audience an understanding of and opposition to our participation in the Vietnam war. *Supra,* * * *. It may be that the performances were crude and amateurish and perhaps unappealing, but the same thing can be said about many theatrical performances. We cannot believe that when Congress wrote out a special exception for theatrical productions it intended to protect only a narrow and limited category of professionally produced plays. Of course, we need not decide here all the questions concerning what is and what is not within the scope of § 772(f). We need only find, as we emphatically do, that the street skit in which Schacht participated was a "theatrical production" within the meaning of that section.

This brings us to petitioner's complaint that giving force and effect to the last clause of § 772(f) would impose an unconstitutional restraint on his right of free speech. We agree. This clause on its face simply restricts § 772(f)'s authorization to those dramatic portrayals that do not "tend to discredit" the military, but, when this restriction is read together with 18 U.S.C. § 702, it becomes clear that Congress has in effect made it a crime for an actor wearing a military uniform to say things during his performance critical of the conduct or policies of the Armed Forces. An actor, like everyone else in our country, enjoys a constitutional right to freedom of speech, including the right openly to criticize the Government during a dramatic performance. The last clause of § 772(f) denies this constitutional right to an actor who is wearing a military uniform by making it a crime for him to say things that tend to bring the military into discredit and disrepute. In the present case Schacht was free to participate in any skit at the demonstration that praised the Army, but under the final clause of § 772(f) he could be convicted of a federal offense if his portrayal attacked the

Army instead of praising it. In light of our earlier finding that the skit in which Schacht participated was a "theatrical production" within the meaning of § 772(f), it follows that his conviction can be sustained only if he can be punished for speaking out against the role of our Army and our country in Vietnam. Clearly punishment for this reason would be an unconstitutional abridgment of freedom of speech. The final clause of § 772(f), which leaves Americans free to praise the war in Vietnam but can send persons like Schacht to prison for opposing it, cannot survive in a country which has the First Amendment. To preserve the constitutionality of § 772(f) that final clause must be stricken from the section.

* * *

Reversed.

MR. JUSTICE HARLAN, concurring.

* * *

MR. JUSTICE WHITE, with whom THE CHIEF JUSTICE and MR. JUSTICE STEWART join, concurring in the result.

I agree that Congress cannot constitutionally distinguish between those theatrical performances that do and those that do not "tend to discredit" the military, in authorizing persons not on active duty to wear a uniform. I do not agree, however, with the Court's conclusion that as a matter of law petitioner must be found to have been engaged in a "theatrical production" within the meaning of 10 U.S.C. § 772(f). That issue, it seems to me, is properly left to the determination of the jury.

* * * The critical question in deciding what is to count as a "theatrical production" ought to be whether or not, considering all the circumstances of the performance, an ordinary observer would have thought he was seeing a fictitious portrayal rather than a piece of reality. And, although the judge's instructions here did not precisely reflect this interpretation, this question seems eminently suited to resolution by the jury.

Under proper instructions, then, a jury could have concluded that no theatrical production was involved, in which case the verdict should be sustained. However, the judge's instructions also permitted conviction on a finding that petitioner was engaged in a theatrical production, but that the production tended to discredit the military. See App. 51–54. Since the general verdict does not disclose which of these findings—only one of which can constitutionally entail conviction—was the actual finding, the conviction must of course be reversed. Stromberg v. California, 283 U.S. 359 (1931). I thus join the judgment of reversal but find it neither necessary nor correct to hold that petitioner's "theatrics" perforce amounted to a "theatrical production."

SPENCE v. STATE OF WASHINGTON
Supreme Court of the United States, 1974.
418 U.S. 405, 94 S.Ct. 2727, 41 L.Ed.2d 842.

PER CURIAM.

Appellant displayed a United States flag, which he owned, out of the window of his apartment. Affixed to both surfaces of the flag was a large peace symbol fashioned of removable tape. Appellant was convicted under a Washington statute forbidding the exhibition of a United States flag to which is attached or superimposed figures, symbols, or other extraneous material. The Supreme Court of Washington affirmed appellant's conviction. * * * We reverse on the ground that as applied to appellant's activity the Washington statute impermissibly infringed protected expression.

I

On May 10, 1970, appellant, a college student, hung his United States flag from the window of his apartment on private property in Seattle, Washington. The flag was upside down, and attached to the front and back was a peace symbol (i.e., a circle enclosing a trident) made of removable black tape. The window was above the ground floor. The flag measured approximately three by five feet and was plainly visible to passersby. The peace symbol occupied roughly half of the surface of the flag.

Three Seattle police officers observed the flag and entered the apartment house. They were met at the main door by appellant who said: "I suppose you are here about the flag. I didn't know there was anything wrong with it. I will take it down." Appellant permitted the officers to enter his apartment, where they seized the flag and arrested him. Appellant cooperated with the officers. There was no disruption or altercation.

Appellant was not charged under Washington's flag-desecration statute. See Wash.Rev.Code § 9.86.030, as amended.[1] Rather, the State relied on the so-called "improper use" statute, Wash.Rev.Code § 9.86.020. This statute provides, in pertinent part:

"No person shall, in any manner, for exhibition or display:

"(1) Place or cause to be placed any word, figure, mark, picture, design, drawing or advertisement of any nature upon any flag, standard, color, ensign or shield of the United States or of this state * * * or

"(2) Expose to public view any such flag, standard, color, ensign or shield upon which shall have been printed, painted or otherwise produced, or to which shall have been attached,

---

1. This statute provides in part:
"No person shall knowingly cast contempt upon any flag, standard, color, ensign or shield * * * by publicly mutilating, defacing, burning, or trampling upon said flag, standard, color, ensign or shield."

appended, affixed or annexed any such word, figure, mark, picture, design, drawing or advertisement * * * "[2]

* * *

The State based its case on the flag itself and the testimony of the three arresting officers, who testified that they had observed the flag displayed from appellant's window and that on the flag was superimposed what they identified as a peace symbol. Appellant took the stand in his own defense. He testified that he put a peace symbol on the flag and displayed it to public view as a protest against the invasion of Cambodia and the killings at Kent State University, events which occurred a few days prior to his arrest. He said that his purpose was to associate the American flag with peace instead of war and violence:

> "I felt there had been so much killing and that this was not what America stood for. I felt that the flag stood for America and I wanted people to know that I thought America stood for peace."

Appellant further testified that he chose to fashion the peace symbol from tape so that it could be removed without damaging the flag. The State made no effort to controvert any of appellant's testimony.

The trial court instructed the jury in essence that the mere act of displaying the flag with the peace symbol attached, if proved beyond a reasonable doubt, was sufficient to convict. There was no requirement of specific intent to do anything more than display the flag in that manner. * * *

II

A number of factors are important in the instant case. First, this was a privately owned flag. In a technical property sense it was not the property of any government. We have no doubt that the State or National Governments constitutionally may forbid anyone from mishandling in any manner a flag that is public property. But this is a different case. Second, appellant displayed his flag on private property. He engaged in no trespass or disorderly conduct. Nor is this a case that might be analyzed in terms of reasonable time, place, or manner restraints on access to a public area. Third, the record is devoid of proof of any risk of breach of the peace. It was not appellant's purpose to incite violence or even stimulate a public demonstration. There is no evidence that any crowd gathered or that appellant made any effort to attract attention beyond hanging the flag out of his own window. Indeed, on the facts stipulated by the parties there is no evidence that anyone other than the three police officers observed the flag.

---

[2]. Washington Rev.Code § 9.86.010 defines the flags and other symbols protected by the desecration and improper-use statutes as follows:

"The words flag, standard, color, ensign or shield, as used in this chapter, shall include any flag, standard, color, ensign or shield, or copy, picture or representation thereof, made of any substance or represented or produced thereon, and of any size, evidently purporting to be such flag, standard, color, ensign or shield of the United States or of this state, or a copy, picture or representation thereof."

Fourth, the State concedes, as did the Washington Supreme Court that appellant engaged in a form of communication. Although the stipulated facts fail to show that any member of the general public viewed the flag, the State's concession is inevitable on this record. The undisputed facts are that appellant "wanted people to know that I thought America stood for peace." To be sure, appellant did not choose to articulate his views through printed or spoken words. It is therefore necessary to determine whether his activity was sufficiently imbued with elements of communication to fall within the scope of the First and Fourteenth Amendments, for as the Court noted in United States v. O'Brien, 391 U.S. 367, 376 (1968), "[w]e cannot accept the view that an apparently limitless variety of conduct can be labeled 'speech' whenever the person engaging in the conduct intends thereby to express an idea." But the nature of appellant's activity, combined with the factual context and environment in which it was undertaken, lead to the conclusion that he engaged in a form of protected expression.

The Court for decades has recognized the communicative connotations of the use of flags. * * * On this record there can be little doubt that appellant communicated through the use of symbols. The symbolism included not only the flag but also the superimposed peace symbol.

Moreover, the context in which a symbol is used for purposes of expression is important, for the context may give meaning to the symbol. See Tinker v. Des Moines Independent Community School District, 393 U.S. 503 (1969). In *Tinker* the wearing of black armbands in a school environment conveyed an unmistakable message about a contemporaneous issue of intense public concern—the Vietnam hostilities. *Id.*, at 505–514. In this case, appellant's activity was roughly simultaneous with and concededly triggered by the Cambodian incursion and the Kent State tragedy, also issues of great public moment. * * * A flag bearing a peace symbol and displayed upside down by a student today might be interpreted as nothing more than bizarre behavior, but it would have been difficult for the great majority of citizens to miss the drift of appellant's point at the time that he made it.

It may be noted, further, that this was not an act of mindless nihilism. Rather, it was a pointed expression of anguish by appellant about the then-current domestic and foreign affairs of his government. An intent to convey a particularized message was present, and in the surrounding circumstances the likelihood was great that the message would be understood by those who viewed it.

* * *

We are met at the outset with something of an enigma in the manner in which the case was presented to us. The Washington Supreme Court rejected any reliance on a breach-of-the-peace rationale. * * * It based its result primarily on the ground that "the nation and state both have a recognizable interest in preserving the flag as a symbol of the nation. * * * "[4] Yet counsel for the State declined to

---

4. * * * A subsidiary ground relied on by the Washington Supreme Court must be

support the highest state court's principal rationale in argument before us. He pursued instead the breach-of-the-peace theory discarded by the state court. Indeed, that was the only basis on which he chose to support the constitutionality of the state statute.

Despite counsel's approach, we think it appropriate to review briefly the range of various state interests that might be thought to support the challenged conviction, drawing upon the arguments before us, the opinions below, and the Court's opinion in Street v. New York, 394 U.S. 576, 590–594 (1969). The first interest at issue is prevention of breach of the peace. In our view, the Washington Supreme Court correctly rejected this notion. It is totally without support in the record.

We are also unable to affirm the judgment below on the ground that the State may have desired to protect the sensibilities of passersby. "It is firmly settled that under our Constitution the public expression of ideas may not be prohibited merely because the ideas are themselves offensive to some of their hearers." *Street v. New York, supra,* at 592. Moreover, appellant did not impose his ideas upon a captive audience. Anyone who might have been offended could easily have avoided the display. See Cohen v. California, 403 U.S. 15 (1971). Nor may appellant be punished for failing to show proper respect for our national emblem. Street v. New York, *supra,* 394 U.S., at 593; *West Virginia State Board of Education v. Barnette, supra.*[6]

We are brought, then, to the state court's thesis that Washington has an interest in preserving the national flag as an unalloyed symbol of our country. The court did not define this interest; it simply asserted it. * * * Mr. Justice Rehnquist's dissenting opinion today, * * * adopts essentially the same approach. Presumably, this interest might be seen as an effort to prevent the appropriation of a revered national symbol by an individual, interest group, or enterprise where there was a risk that association of the symbol with a particular product or viewpoint might be taken erroneously as evidence of governmental endorsement.[7] Alternatively, it might be argued that the interest asserted by the state court is based on the uniquely universal character of the national flag as a symbol. For the great majority of us, the flag is a symbol of patriotism, of pride in the history of our country, and of the service, sacrifice, and valor of the millions of

---

rejected summarily. It found the inhibition on appellant's freedom of expression "minuscule and trifling" because there are "thousands of other means available to [him] for the dissemination of his personal views. * * *" * * * As the Court noted in e.g., Schneider v. State of New Jersey, 308 U.S. 147 (1939), "one is not to have the exercise of his liberty of expression in appropriate places abridged on the plea that it may be exercised in some other place."

6. Counsel for the State conceded that promoting respect for the flag is not a legitimate state interest.

7. Undoubtedly such a concern underlies that portion of the improper-use statute forbidding the utilization of representations of the flag in a commercial context. * * * There is no occasion in this case to address the application of the challenged statute to commercial behavior. Cf. Halter v. Nebraska, 205 U.S. 34 (1907). Mr. Justice Rehnquist's dissent places major reliance on *Halter,* * * * despite the fact that *Halter* was decided nearly 20 years before the Court concluded that the First Amendment applies to the States by virtue of the Fourteenth Amendment. See Gitlow v. New York, 268 U.S. 652 (1925).

Americans who in peace and war have joined together to build and to defend a Nation in which self-government and personal liberty endure. It evidences both the unity and diversity which are America. For others the flag carries in varying degrees a different message. "A person gets from a symbol the meaning he puts into it, and what is one man's comfort and inspiration is another's jest and scorn." West Virginia State Board of Education v. Barnette, 319 U.S., at 632–633. It might be said that we all draw something from our national symbol, for it is capable of conveying simultaneously a spectrum of meanings. If it may be destroyed or permanently disfigured, it could be argued that it will lose its capability of mirroring the sentiments of all who view it.

But we need not decide in this case whether the interest advanced by the court below is valid.[8] We assume, *arguendo,* that it is. The statute is nonetheless unconstitutional as applied to appellant's activity.[9] There was no risk that appellant's acts would mislead viewers into assuming that the Government endorsed his viewpoint. To the contrary, he was plainly and peacefully[10] protesting the fact that it did not. Appellant was not charged under the desecration statute, * * * nor did he permanently disfigure the flag or destroy it. He displayed it as a flag of his country in a way closely analogous to the manner in which flags have always been used to convey ideas. Moreover, his message was direct, likely to be understood, and within the contours of the First Amendment. Given the protected character of his expression and in light of the fact that no interest the State may have in

8. If this interest is valid, we note that it is directly related to expression in the context of activity like that undertaken by appellant. For that reason and because no other governmental interest unrelated to expression has been advanced or can be supported on this record, the four-step analysis of United States v. O'Brien, 391 U.S. 367, 377 (1968), is inapplicable.

9. Because we agree with appellant's as-applied argument, we do not reach the more comprehensive overbreadth contention he also advances. But it is worth noting the nearly limitless sweep of the Washington improper-use flag statute. Read literally, it forbids a veteran's group from attaching, *e.g.,* battalion commendations to a United States flag. It proscribes photographs of war heroes standing in front of the flag. It outlaws newspaper mastheads composed of the national flag with superimposed print. Other examples could easily be listed.

Statutes of such sweep suggest problems of selective enforcement. We are, however, unable to agree with appellant's void-for-vagueness argument. The statute's application is quite mechanical, particularly when implemented with jury instructions like the ones given in this case. The law in Washington, simply put, is that *nothing* may be affixed to or superimposed on a United States flag or a representation thereof. Thus, if selective enforcement has occurred, it has been a result of prosecutorial discretion, not the language of the statute. Accordingly, this case is unlike Smith v. Goguen, 415 U.S. 566 (1974), where the words of the statute at issue ("publicly * * * treats contemptuously") were themselves sufficiently indefinite to prompt subjective treatment by prosecutorial authorities.

10. Appellant's activity occurred at a time of national turmoil over the introduction of United States forces into Cambodia and the deaths at Kent State University. It is difficult now, more than four years later, to recall vividly the depth of emotion that pervaded most colleges and universities at the time, and that was widely shared by young Americans everywhere. A spontaneous outpouring of feeling resulted in widespread action, not all of it rational when viewed in retrospect. This included the closing down of some schools, as well as other disruptions of many centers of education. It was against this highly inflamed background that appellant chose to express his own views in a manner that can fairly be described as gentle and restrained as compared to the actions undertaken by a number of his peers.

preserving the physical integrity of a privately owned flag was significantly impaired on these facts, the conviction must be invalidated.[11]

The judgment is reversed.

It is so ordered.

Judgment reversed.

MR. JUSTICE DOUGLAS, concurring.

I would reverse the judgment for substantially the same reasons given by the Iowa Supreme Court in State v. Kool, 212 N.W.2d 518 (1973). In that case the defendant hung a peace symbol made of cardboard and wrapped in tinfoil in the window of his home and hung a replica of the United States Flag behind the peace symbol but in an upside-down position. The state statute made it a crime to "cast contempt upon, satirize, deride or burlesque [the] flag," Iowa Code § 32.1.

The court held that defendant's conduct constituted "symbolic speech." The court, in reversing the conviction, said:

"Someone in Newton might be so intemperate as to disrupt the peace because of this display. But if absolute assurance of tranquility is required, we may as well forget about free speech. Under such a requirement, the only 'free' speech would consist of platitudes. That kind of speech does not need constitutional protection." 212 N.W.2d, at 521.

MR. CHIEF JUSTICE BURGER, dissenting.

If the constitutional role of this Court were to strike down unwise laws or restrict unwise application of some laws, I could agree with the result reached by the Court. That is not our function, however, and it should be left to each State and ultimately the common sense of its people to decide how the flag, as a symbol of national unity, should be protected.

MR. JUSTICE REHNQUIST, with whom THE CHIEF JUSTICE and MR. JUSTICE WHITE join, dissenting.

The Court holds that a Washington statute prohibiting persons from attaching material to the American flag was unconstitutionally applied to appellant. Although I agree with the Court that appellant's activity was a form of communication, I do not agree that the First Amendment prohibits the State from restricting this activity in furtherance of other important interests. And I believe the rationale by which the Court reaches its conclusion is unsound.

"[T]he right of free speech is not absolute at all times and under all circumstances." Chaplinsky v. New Hampshire, 315 U.S. 568, 571

11. The similarity of our holding to that of the Iowa Supreme Court in State v. Kool, 212 N.W.2d 518 (1973), merits note. In that case, the defendant displayed a replica of the United States flag upside down in his window, superimposing a peace symbol to create an effect identical to that achieved by Spence. Recognizing the communicative character of the defendant's activity, the Iowa Supreme Court reversed his conviction for flag misuse and held the statute unconstitutional as applied. The court eschewed an overbreadth analysis, and it rejected a number of the state interests we have found unavailing in the instant case.

(1942). This Court has long recognized, for example, that some forms of expression are not entitled to any protection at all under the First Amendment, despite the fact that they could reasonably be thought protected under its literal language. See Roth v. United States, 354 U.S. 476 (1957). The Court has further recognized that even protected speech may be subject to reasonable limitation when important countervailing interests are involved. Citizens are not completely free to commit perjury, to libel other citizens, to infringe copyrights, to incite riots, or to interfere unduly with passage through a public thoroughfare. The right of free speech, though precious, remains subject to reasonable accommodation to other valued interests.

Since a State concededly may impose some limitations on speech directly, it would seem to follow *a fortiori* that a State may legislate to protect important state interests even though an incidental limitation on free speech results. Virtually any law enacted by a State, when viewed with sufficient ingenuity, could be thought to interfere with some citizen's preferred means of expression. But no one would argue, I presume, that a State could not prevent the painting of public buildings simply because a particular class of protesters believed their message would best be conveyed through that medium. Had appellant here chosen to tape his peace symbol to a federal courthouse, I have little doubt that he could be prosecuted under a statute properly drawn to protect public property.

Yet the Court today holds that the State of Washington cannot limit use of the American flag, at least insofar as its statute prevents appellant from using a privately owned flag to convey his personal message. Expressing its willingness to assume, *arguendo,* that Washington has a valid interest in preserving the integrity of the flag, the Court nevertheless finds that interest to be insufficient in this case. To achieve this result the Court first devalues the State's interest under these circumstances, noting that "no interest the State may have in preserving the physical integrity of a privately owned flag was significantly impaired on these facts. * * * " The Court takes pains to point out that appellant did not "permanently disfigure the flag or destroy it," and emphasizes that the flag was displayed "in a way closely analogous to the manner in which flags have always been used to convey ideas." The Court then restates the notion that such state interests are secondary to messages which are "direct, likely to be understood, and within the contours of the First Amendment." * * * In my view the first premise demonstrates a total misunderstanding of the State's interest in the integrity of the American flag, and the second premise places the Court in the position either of ultimately favoring appellant's message because of its subject matter, a position about which almost all members of the majority have only recently expressed doubt, or, alternatively, of making the flag available for a limitless succession of political and commercial messages. I shall treat these issues in reverse order.

The statute under which appellant was convicted is no stranger to this Court, a virtually identical statute having been before the Court in Halter v. Nebraska, 205 U.S. 34 (1907). In that case the Court held that the State of Nebraska could enforce its statute to prevent use of a flag representation on beer bottles, stating flatly that "a State will be wanting in care for the well-being of its people if it ignores the fact that they regard the flag as a symbol of their country's power and prestige * * *." *Id.,* at 42. The Court then continued: "Such an use tends to degrade and cheapen the flag in the estimation of the people, as well as to defeat the object of maintaining it as an emblem of national power and national honor." *Ibid.*

The Court today finds *Halter* irrelevant to the present case, pointing out that it was decided almost 20 years before the First Amendment was applied to the States and further noting that it involved "commercial behavior," a form of expression the Court presumably will consider another day. Insofar as *Halter* assesses the State's interest, of course, the Court's argument is simply beside the point. But even as the argument relates to appellant's interest, I find it somewhat difficult to grasp. The Court may possibly be suggesting that political expression deserves greater protection than other forms of expression, but that suggestion would seem quite inconsistent with the position taken in Lehman v. Shaker Heights, 418 U.S. 298,[2] by nearly all Members of the majority in the instant case. Yet if the Court is suggesting that *Halter* would now be decided differently, and that the State's interest in the flag falls before any speech which is "direct, likely to be understood, and within the contours of the First Amendment," that view would mean the flag could be auctioned as a background to anyone willing and able to buy or copy one. I find it hard to believe the Court intends to presage that result.

Turning to the question of the State's interest in the flag, it seems to me that the Court's treatment lacks all substance. The suggestion that the State's interest somehow diminishes when the flag is decorated with *removable* tape trivializes something which is not trivial. The State of Washington is hardly seeking to protect the flag's resale value, and yet the Court's emphasis on the lack of actual damage to the flag suggests that this is a significant aspect of the State's interest. Surely the Court does not mean to imply that appellant *could* be prosecuted if he subsequently tore the flag in the process of trying to take the tape off. Unlike flag-desecration statutes, which the Court correctly notes are not at issue in this case, the Washington statute challenged here

---

2. The plurality opinion of Mr. Justice Blackmun took the position that a ban against political advertising on publicly owned buses was not unconstitutional since "[n]o First Amendment forum is here to be found." Mr. Justice Douglas, concurring in the judgment, stated that petitioner in that case had no "constitutional right to spread his message before this captive audience," but specifically noted:

"I do not view the content of the message as relevant either to petitioner's right to express it or to the commuters' right to be free from it. Commercial advertisements may be as offensive and intrusive to captive audiences as any political message."

Mr. Justice Brennan, with whom Mr. Justice Stewart, Mr. Justice Marshall, and Mr. Justice Powell joined, dissenting, stated: "There is some doubt concerning whether the 'commercial speech' distinction announced in Valentine v. Chrestensen, 316 U.S. 52 (1942), retains continuing validity." referring to Mr. Justice Douglas' concurring opinion in Camarano v. United States, 358 U.S. 498 (1959). The dissent further stated: "Once a public forum for communication has been established, both free speech and equal protection principles prohibit discrimination based *solely* upon subject matter or content." (Emphasis in original.)

seeks to prevent personal *use* of the flag, not simply particular forms of *abuse*. The State of Washington has chosen to set the flag apart for a special purpose, and has directed that it not be turned into a common background for an endless variety of superimposed messages. The physical condition of the flag itself is irrelevant to that purpose.

The true nature of the State's interest in this case is not only one of preserving "the physical integrity of the flag," but also one of preserving the flag as "an important symbol of nationhood and unity." Although the Court treats this important interest with a studied inattention, it is hardly one of recent invention and has previously been accorded considerable respect by this Court. In *Halter*, for example, the Court stated:

> "As the statute in question evidently had its origin in a purpose to cultivate a feeling of patriotism among the people of Nebraska, we are unwilling to adjudge that in legislation for that purpose the state erred in duty or has infringed the constitutional right of anyone. On the contrary, it may reasonably be affirmed that a duty rests upon each state in every legal way to encourage its people to love the Union with which the state is indissolubly connected." 205 U.S., at 43.

There was no question in *Halter* of physical impairment of a flag since no actual flag was even involved. And it certainly would have made no difference to the Court's discussion of the State's interest if the plaintiff in error in that case had chosen to advertise his product by decorating the flag with beer bottles fashioned from some removable substance.[5] It is the character, not the cloth, of the flag which the State seeks to protect.

The value of this interest has been emphasized in recent as well as distant times. Mr. Justice Fortas, for example, noted in Street v. New York, 394 U.S. 576, 616 (1969), that "the flag is a special kind of personalty, a form of property "burdened with peculiar obligations and restrictions." *Id.*, at 617 (dissenting opinion).[6] Mr. Justice White, has observed that "[t]he flag is a national property, and the nation may regulate those who would make, imitate, sell, possess, or use it." Smith v. Goguen, 415 U.S., at 587 (concurring in judgment). I agree. What appellant here seeks is simply license to use the flag however he pleases, so long as the activity can be tied to a concept of speech, regardless of any state interest in having the flag used only for more limited purposes. I find no reasoning in the Court's opinion which convinces me that the Constitution requires such license to be given.

The fact that the State has a valid interest in preserving the character of the flag does not mean, of course, that it can employ all

---

5. It should be noted that *Halter* makes no mention of the argument that allowing use of the flag for a personal or commercial purpose might suggest endorsement of that purpose by the government. While this might be an *additional* state interest in appropriate cases, it is by no means an indispensable element of the State's concern about the integrity of the flag.

6. The majority of the Court in *Street* stated: "We add that disrespect for our flag is to be deplored no less in these vexed times than in calmer periods of our history", 394 U.S., at 594, citing *Halter*.

conceivable means to enforce it. It certainly could not require all citizens to own the flag or compel citizens to salute one. West Virginia State Board of Education v. Barnette, 319 U.S. 624 (1943). It presumably cannot punish criticism of the flag, or the principles for which it stands, any more than it could punish criticism of this country's policies or ideas. But the statute in this case demands no such allegiance. Its operation does not depend upon whether the flag is used for communicative or noncommunicative purposes; upon whether a particular message is deemed commercial or political; upon whether the use of the flag is respectful or contemptuous; or upon whether any particular segment of the State's citizenry might applaud or oppose the intended message. It simply withdraws a unique national symbol from the roster of materials that may be used as a background for communications. Since I do not believe the Constitution prohibits Washington from making that decision, I dissent.

TEXAS v. JOHNSON

Supreme Court of the United States, 1989.
491 U.S. 397, 109 S.Ct. 2533, 105 L.Ed.2d 342.

MR. JUSTICE BRENNAN delivered the opinion of the Court.

After publicly burning an American flag as a means of political protest, Gregory Lee Johnson was convicted of desecrating a flag in violation of Texas law. This case presents the question whether his conviction is consistent with the First Amendment. We hold that it is not.

I

While the Republican National Convention was taking place in Dallas in 1984, respondent Johnson participated in a political demonstration dubbed the "Republican War Chest Tour." As explained in literature distributed by the demonstrators and in speeches made by them, the purpose of this event was to protest the policies of the Reagan administration and of certain Dallas-based corporations. The demonstrators marched through the Dallas streets, chanting political slogans and stopping at several corporate locations to stage "die-ins" intended to dramatize the consequences of nuclear war. On several occasions they spray-painted the walls of buildings and overturned potted plants, but Johnson himself took no part in such activities. He did, however, accept an American flag handed to him by a fellow protestor who had taken it from a flag pole outside one of the targeted buildings.

The demonstration ended in front of Dallas City Hall, where Johnson unfurled the American flag, doused it with kerosene, and set it on fire. While the flag burned, the protestors chanted, "America, the red, white, and blue, we spit on you." After the demonstrators dispersed, a witness to the flag-burning collected the flag's remains and buried them in his backyard. No one was physically injured or threatened with injury, though several witnesses testified that they had been seriously offended by the flag-burning.

Of the approximately 100 demonstrators, Johnson alone was charged with a crime. The only criminal offense with which he was charged was the desecration of a venerated object in violation of Tex.Penal Code Ann. § 42.09(a)(3) (1989).[1] After a trial, he was convicted, sentenced to one year in prison, and fined $2,000. The Court of Appeals for the Fifth District of Texas at Dallas affirmed Johnson's conviction. 706 S.W.2d 120 (1986), but the Texas Court of Criminal Appeals reversed, 755 S.W.2d 92 (1988), holding that the State could not, consistent with the First Amendment, punish Johnson for burning the flag in these circumstances.

* * *

Because it reversed Johnson's conviction on the ground that § 42.09 was unconstitutional as applied to him, the state court did not address Johnson's argument that the statute was, on its face, unconstitutionally vague and overbroad. We granted certiorari, * * *, and now affirm.

II

Johnson was convicted of flag desecration for burning the flag rather than for uttering insulting words. This fact somewhat complicates our consideration of his conviction under the First Amendment. We must first determine whether Johnson's burning of the flag constituted expressive conduct, permitting him to invoke the First Amendment in challenging his conviction. See, *e.g.,* Spence v. Washington, 418 U.S. 405, 409–411 (1974). If his conduct was expressive, we next decide whether the State's regulation is related to the suppression of free expression. See, *e.g.,* United States v. O'Brien, 391 U.S. 367, 377 (1968); *Spence, supra,* at 414, n. 8. If the State's regulation is not related to expression, then the less stringent standard we announced in *United States v. O'Brien* for regulations of noncommunicative conduct controls. See *O'Brien, supra,* at 377. If it is, then we are outside of *O'Brien*'s test, and we must ask whether this interest justifies Johnson's conviction under a more demanding standard.[3] See *Spence, supra,* at 411. * * *

---

1. Tex.Penal Code Ann. § 42.09 (1989) provides in full:

"§ 42.09. Desecration of Venerated Object

"(a) A person commits an offense if he intentionally or knowingly desecrates:

"(1) a public monument;

"(2) a place of worship or burial; or

"(3) a state or national flag.

"(b) For purposes of this section, 'desecrate' means deface, damage, or otherwise physically mistreat in a way that the actor knows will seriously offend one or more persons likely to observe or discover his action.

"(c) An offense under this section is a Class A misdemeanor."

3. Although Johnson has raised a facial challenge to Texas' flag-desecration statute, we choose to resolve this case on the basis of his claim that the statute as applied to him violates the First Amendment. Section 42.09 regulates only physical conduct with respect to the flag, not the written or spoken word, and although one violates the statute only if one "knows" that one's physical treatment of the flag "will seriously offend one or more persons likely to observe or discover his action," Tex.Penal Code Ann. § 42.09(b) (1989), this fact does not necessarily mean that the statute

The First Amendment literally forbids the abridgement only of "speech," but we have long recognized that its protection does not end at the spoken or written word. While we have rejected "the view that an apparently limitless variety of conduct can be labeled 'speech' whenever the person engaging in the conduct intends thereby to express an idea," *United States v. O'Brien, supra,* at 376, we have acknowledged that conduct may be "sufficiently imbued with elements of communication to fall within the scope of the First and Fourteenth Amendments." *Spence, supra,* at 49.

* * *

Especially pertinent to this case are our decisions recognizing the communicative nature of conduct relating to flags. Attaching a peace sign to the flag, *Spence, supra,* at 409–410; saluting the flag, *Barnette,* 319 U.S., at 632; and displaying a red flag, Stromberg v. California, 283 U.S. 359, 368–369 (1931), we have held, all may find shelter under the First Amendment. See also Smith v. Goguen, 415 U.S. 566, 588 (1974) (WHITE, J., concurring in judgment) (treating flag "contemptuously" by wearing pants with small flag sewn into their seat is expressive conduct). That we have had little difficulty identifying an expressive element in conduct relating to flags should not be surprising. The very purpose of a national flag is to serve as a symbol of our country; it is, one might say, "the one visible manifestation of two hundred years of nationhood." *Id.,* at 603 (REHNQUIST, J., dissenting). * * *

We have not automatically concluded, however, that any action taken with respect to our flag is expressive. Instead, in characterizing such action for First Amendment purposes, we have considered the context in which it occurred. In *Spence,* for example, we emphasized that Spence's taping of a peace sign to his flag was "roughly simultaneous with and concededly triggered by the Cambodian incursion and the Kent State tragedy." 418 U.S., at 410. The State of Washington had conceded, in fact, that Spence's conduct was a form of communication, and we stated that "the State's concession is inevitable on this record." *Id.,* at 409.

The State of Texas conceded for purposes of its oral argument in this case that Johnson's conduct was expressive conduct, Tr. of Oral Arg. 4, and this concession seems to us as prudent as was Washington's in *Spence.* Johnson burned an American flag as part—indeed, as the culmination—of a political demonstration that coincided with the convening of the Republican Party and its renomination of Ronald Reagan

applies only to *expressive* conduct protected by the First Amendment. *Cf.* Smith v. Goguen, 415 U.S. 566, 588 (1974) (White, J., concurring in judgment) (statute prohibiting "contemptuous" treatment of flag encompasses only expressive conduct). A tired person might, for example, drag a flag through the mud, knowing that this conduct is likely to offend others, and yet have no thought of expressing any idea; neither the language nor the Texas courts' interpretations of the statute precludes the possibility that such a person would be prosecuted for flag desecration. Because the prosecution of a person who had not engaged in expressive conduct would pose a different case and because we are capable of disposing of this case on narrower grounds, we address only Johnson's claim that § 42.09 as applied to political expression like his violates the First Amendment.

for President. The expressive, overtly political nature of this conduct was both intentional and overwhelmingly apparent. * * *

III

The Government generally has a freer hand in restricting expressive conduct than it has in restricting the written or spoken word. See *O'Brien*, 391 U.S., at 376–377; Clark v. Community for Creative Non–Violence, 468 U.S. 288, 293 (1984) * * * It may not, however, proscribe particular conduct *because* it has expressive elements. "[W]hat might be termed the more generalized guarantee of freedom of expression makes the communicative nature of conduct an inadequate *basis* for singling out that conduct for proscription. A law *directed at* the communicative nature of conduct must, like a law directed at speech itself, be justified by the substantial showing of need that the First Amendment requires." Community for Creative Non–Violence v. Watt, 703 F.2d 586, 622–623 (D.C.Cir.1983) (Scalia, J., dissenting) * * *

Thus, although we have recognized that where "'speech' and 'nonspeech' elements are combined in the same course of conduct, a sufficiently important governmental interest in regulating the nonspeech element can justify incidental limitations on First Amendment freedoms," *O'Brien, supra,* at 376, we have limited the applicability of *O'Brien*'s relatively lenient standard to those cases in which "the governmental interest is unrelated to the suppression of free expression." * * *

In order to decide whether *O'Brien*'s test applies here, therefore, we must decide whether Texas has asserted an interest in support of Johnson's conviction that is unrelated to the suppression of expression. If we find that an interest asserted by the State is simply not implicated on the facts before us, we need not ask whether *O'Brien*'s test applies. See *Spence, supra,* at 414, n. 8. The State offers two separate interests to justify this conviction: preventing breaches of the peace, and preserving the flag as a symbol of nationhood and national unity. We hold that the first interest is not implicated on this record and that the second is related to the suppression of expression.

A

Texas claims that its interest in preventing breaches of the peace justifies Johnson's conviction for flag desecration.[4] However, no disturbance of the peace actually occurred or threatened to occur because of

---

4. Relying on our decision in Boos v. Barry, 485 U.S. 312 (1988), Johnson argues that this state interest is related to the suppression of free expression within the meaning of United States v. O'Brien, 391 U.S. 367 (1968). He reasons that the violent reaction to flag-burnings feared by Texas would be the result of the message conveyed by them, and that this fact connects the State's interest to the suppression of expression. Brief for Respondent 12, n. 11. This view has found some favor in the lower courts. See Monroe v. State Court of Fulton County, 739 F.2d 568, 574–575 (CA11 1984). Johnson's theory may overread *Boos* insofar as it suggests that a desire to prevent a violent audience reaction is "related to expression" in the same way that a desire to prevent an audience from being offended is "related to expression." Because we find that the State's interest in preventing breaches of the peace is not implicated on these facts, however, we need not venture further into this area.

Johnson's burning of the flag. Although the State stresses the disruptive behavior of the protestors during their march toward City Hall, Brief for Petitioner 34–36, it admits that "no actual breach of the peace occurred at the time of the flagburning or in response to the flagburning." *Id.,* at 34. The State's emphasis on the protestors' disorderly actions prior to arriving at City Hall is not only somewhat surprising given that no charges were brought on the basis of this conduct, but it also fails to show that a disturbance of the peace was a likely reaction to Johnson's conduct. The only evidence offered by the State at trial to show the reaction to Johnson's actions was the testimony of several persons who had been seriously offended by the flag-burning. *Id.,* at 6–7.

The State's position, therefore, amounts to a claim that an audience that takes serious offense at particular expression is necessarily likely to disturb the peace and that the expression may be prohibited on this basis. Our precedents do not countenance such a presumption. On the contrary, they recognize that a principal "function of free speech under our system of government is to invite dispute. It may indeed best serve its high purpose when it induces a condition of unrest, creates dissatisfaction with conditions as they are, or even stirs people to anger." Terminiello v. Chicago, 337 U.S. 1, 4 (1949). See also * * * Hustler Magazine, Inc. v. Falwell, 485 U.S. 46, 55–56 (1988). * * *

Nor does Johnson's expressive conduct fall within that small class of "fighting words" that are "likely to provoke the average person to retaliation, and thereby cause a breach of peace." Chaplinsky v. New Hampshire, 315 U.S. 568, 574 (1942). No reasonable onlooker would have regarded Johnson's generalized expression of dissatisfaction with the policies of the Federal Government as a direct personal insult or an invitation to exchange fisticuffs. * * *

We thus conclude that the State's interest in maintaining order is not implicated on these facts. The State need not worry that our holding will disable it from preserving the peace. We do not suggest that the First Amendment forbids a State to prevent "imminent lawless action." *Brandenburg, supra,* at 447. And, in fact, Texas already has a statute specifically prohibiting breaches of the peace, Tex.Penal Code Ann. § 42.01 (1989), which tends to confirm that Texas need not punish this flag desecration in order to keep the peace. * * *

B

The State also asserts an interest in preserving the flag as a symbol of nationhood and national unity. In *Spence,* we acknowledged that the Government's interest in preserving the flag's special symbolic value "is directly related to expression in the context of activity" such as affixing a peace symbol to a flag. 418 U.S., at 414, n. 8. We are equally persuaded that this interest is related to expression in the case of Johnson's burning of the flag. The State, apparently, is concerned that such conduct will lead people to believe either that the flag does not stand for nationhood and national unity, but instead reflects other, less positive concepts, or that the concepts reflected in the flag do not in fact exist, that is, we do not enjoy unity as a Nation. These concerns blossom only when a person's treatment of the flag communicates some message, and thus are related "to the suppression of free expression" within the meaning of *O'Brien*'s test altogether.

IV

It remains to consider whether the State's interest in preserving the flag as a symbol of nationhood and national unity justifies Johnson's conviction.

As in *Spence*, "[w]e are confronted with a case of prosecution for the expression of an idea through activity," and "[a]ccordingly, we must examine with particular care the interests advanced by [petitioner] to support its prosecution." Johnson was not, we add, prosecuted for the expression of just any idea; he was prosecuted for his expression of dissatisfaction with the policies of this country, expression situated at the core of our First Amendment values. * * *

Moreover, Johnson was prosecuted because he knew that his politically charged expression would cause "serious offense." If he had burned the flag as a means of disposing of it because it was dirty or torn, he would not have been convicted of flag desecration under this Texas law: federal law designates burning as the preferred means of disposing of a flag "when it is in such condition that it is no longer a fitting emblem for display." 36 U.S.C. § 176(k), and Texas has no quarrel with this means of disposal. Brief for Petitioner 45. The Texas law is thus not aimed at protecting the physical integrity of the flag in all circumstances, but is designated instead to protect it only against impairments that would cause serious offense to others.[6] Texas concedes as much: "Section 42.09(b) reaches only those severe acts of physical abuse of the flag carried out in a way likely to be offensive. The statute mandates intentional or knowing abuse, that is, the kind of mistreatment that is not innocent, but rather is intentionally designed to seriously offend other individuals." *Id.*, at 44.

Whether Johnson's treatment of the flag violated Texas law thus depended on the likely communicative impact of his expressive conduct.[7] Our decision in *Boos v. Barry, supra*, tells us that this restriction

---

6. *Cf.* Smith v. Goguen, 415 U.S., at 590–591 (Blackmun, J., dissenting) (emphasizing that lower court appeared to have construed state statute so as to protect physical integrity of the flag in all circumstances); *id.*, at 597–598 (Rehnquist, J., dissenting) (same).

7. Texas suggests that Johnson's conviction did not depend on the onlookers' reaction to the flag-burning because § 42.09 is violated only when a person physically mistreats the flag in a way that he "*knows* will seriously offend one or more persons likely to observe or discover his action." Tex.Penal Code Ann. § 42.09(b) (1969) (emphasis added). "The 'serious offense' language of the statute," Texas argues, "refers to an individual's intent and to the manner in which the conduct is effectuated, not to the reaction of the crowd." Brief for Petitioner 44. If the statute were aimed only at the actor's intent and not at the communicative impact of his actions, however, there would be little reason for the law to be triggered only when an audience is "likely" to be present. At Johnson's trial, indeed, the State itself seems not to have seen the distinction between knowledge and actual communicative impact that it now stresses; it proved the element of knowledge by offering the testimony of persons who had in fact been seriously offended by Johnson's conduct. *Id.*, at 6–7. In any event, we find the distinction between Texas' statute and one dependent on actual audience reaction too precious to be of constitutional significance. Both kinds of statutes clearly

on Johnson's expression is content-based. In *Boos,* we considered the constitutionality of a law prohibiting "the display of any sign within 500 feet of a foreign embassy if that sign tends to bring that foreign government into 'public odium' or 'public disrepute.'" *Id.,* at 315. Rejecting the argument that the law was content-neutral because it was justified by "our international law obligation to shield diplomats from speech that offends their dignity," *id.,* at 320, we held that "[t]he emotive impact of speech on its audience is not a 'secondary effect'" unrelated to the content of the expression itself. * * *

According to the principles announced in *Boos,* Johnson's political expression was restricted because of the content of the message he conveyed. We must therefore subject the State's asserted interest in preserving the special symbolic character of the flag to "the most exacting scrutiny." * * * *[8]

Texas argues that its interest in preserving the flag as a symbol of nationhood and national unity survives this close analysis. Quoting extensively from the writings of this Court chronicling the flag's historic and symbolic role in our society, the State emphasizes the "'special place'" reserved for the flag in our Nation. Brief for Petitioner 22, quoting Smith v. Goguen, 415 U.S., at 601 (REHNQUIST, J., dissenting). The State's argument is not that it has an interest simply in maintaining the flag as a symbol of *something,* no matter what it symbolizes; indeed, if that were the State's position, it would be difficult to see how that interest is endangered by highly symbolic conduct such as Johnson's. Rather, the State's claim is that it has an interest in preserving the flag as a symbol of *nationhood* and *national unity,* a symbol with a determinate range of meanings. Brief for Petitioner 20–24. According to Texas, if one physically treats the flag in a way that would tend to cast doubt on either the idea that nationhood and national unity are the flag's referents or that national unity actually exists, the message conveyed thereby is a harmful one and therefore may be prohibited.[9]

If there is a bedrock principle underlying the First Amendment, it is that the Government may not prohibit the expression of an idea

are aimed at protecting onlookers from being offended by the ideas expressed by the prohibited activity.

8. Our inquiry is, of course, bounded by the particular facts of this case and by the statute under which Johnson was convicted. There was no evidence that Johnson himself stole the flag he burned, Tr. of Oral Arg. 17, nor did the prosecution or the arguments urged in support of it depend on the theory that the flag was stolen. *Ibid.* Thus, our analysis does not rely on the way in which the flag was acquired, and nothing in our opinion should be taken to suggest that one is free to steal a flag so long as one later uses it to communicate an idea. We also emphasize that Johnson was prosecuted *only* for flag desecration—not for trespass, disorderly conduct, or arson.

9. Texas claims that "Texas is not endorsing protecting, avowing or prohibiting any particular philosophy." Brief for Petitioner 29. If Texas means to suggest that its asserted interest does not prefer Democrats over Socialists, or Republicans over Democrats, for example, then it is beside the point, for Johnson does not rely on such an argument. He argues instead that the State's desire to maintain the flag as a symbol of nationhood and national unity assumes that there is only one proper view of the flag. Thus, if Texas means to argue that its interest does not prefer *any* viewpoint over another, it is mistaken; surely one's attitude towards the flag and its referents is a viewpoint.

simply because society finds the idea itself offensive or disagreeable. [Citations omitted.]

We have not recognized an exception to this principle even where our flag has been involved. In Street v. New York, 394 U.S. 576 (1969), we held that a State may not criminally punish a person for uttering words critical of the flag. Rejecting the argument that the conviction could be sustained on the ground that Street had "failed to show the respect for our national symbol which may properly be demanded of every citizen," we concluded that "the constitutionally guaranteed 'freedom to be intellectually * * * diverse or even contrary,' and the 'right to differ as to things that touch the heart of the existing order,' encompass the freedom to express publicly one's opinions about our flag, including those opinions which are defiant or contemptuous." *Id.*, at 593. * * *

* * *

In short, nothing in our precedents suggests that a State may foster its own view of the flag by prohibiting expressive conduct relating to it.[10] To bring its argument outside our precedents, Texas attempts to convince us that even if its interest in preserving the flag's symbolic role does not allow it to prohibit words or some expressive conduct critical of the flag, it does permit it to forbid the outright destruction of the flag. The State's argument cannot depend here on the distinction between written or spoken words and nonverbal conduct. That distinction, we have shown, is of no moment where the nonverbal conduct is expressive, as it is here, and where the regulation of that conduct is related to expression, as it is here. See *supra*. In addition, both *Barnette* and *Spence* involved expressive conduct, or only verbal communication, and both found that conduct protected.

Texas' focus on the precise nature of Johnson's expression, moreover, misses the point of our prior decisions: their enduring lesson, that the Government may not prohibit expression simply because it disagrees with its message, is not dependent on the particular mode in which one chooses to express an idea.[11] If we were to hold that a State

---

10. Our decision in Halter v. Nebraska, 205 U.S. 34 (1907), addressing the validity of a state law prohibiting certain commercial uses of the flag, is not to the contrary. That case was decided "nearly 20 years before the Court concluded that the First Amendment applies to the States by virtue of the Fourteenth Amendment." Spence v. Washington, 418 U.S. 405, 413, n. 7 (1974). More important, as we continually emphasized in *Halter* itself, that case involved purely commercial rather than political speech. 205 U.S., at 38, 41, 42, 45.

Nor does San Francisco Arts & Athletics v. Olympic Committee, 483 U.S. 522, 527 (1987), addressing the validity of Congress' decision to "authoriz[e] the United States Olympic Committee to prohibit certain commercial and promotional uses of the word 'Olympic,'" relied upon by the dissent, *post*, even begin to tell us whether the Government may criminally punish physical conduct towards the flag engaged in as a means of political protest.

11. The dissent appears to believe that Johnson's conduct may be prohibited and, indeed, criminally sanctioned, because "his act * * * conveyed nothing that could not have been conveyed and was not conveyed just as forcefully in a dozen different ways." * * * Not only does this assertion sit uneasily next to the dissent's quite correct reminder that the flag occupies a unique position in our society—which demonstrates that messages conveyed without use of the flag are not "just as forcefu[l]" as those conveyed with it—but it also ignores the fact that, in *Spence, supra*, we "rejected summarily" this very claim. See 418 U.S., at 411, n. 4.

may forbid flag-burning wherever it is likely to endanger the flag's symbolic role, but allow it wherever burning a flag promotes that role—as where, for example, a person ceremoniously burns a dirty flag—we would be saying that when it comes to impairing the flag's physical integrity, the flag itself may be used as a symbol—as a substitute for the written or spoken word or a "short cut from mind to mind"—only in one direction. We would be permitting a State to "prescribe what shall be orthodox" by saying that one may burn the flag to convey one's attitude toward it and its referents only if one does not endanger the flag's representation of nationhood and national unity.

We never before have held that the Government may ensure that a symbol be used to express only one view of that symbol or its referents. Indeed, in *Schacht v. United States,* we invalidated a federal statute permitting an actor portraying a member of one of our armed forces to " 'wear the uniform of that armed force if the portrayal does not tend to discredit that armed force.' " 398 U.S., at 60, quoting 10 U.S.C. § 772(f). This proviso, we held, "which leaves Americans free to praise the war in Vietnam but can send persons like Schacht to prison for opposing it, cannot survive in a country which has the First Amendment." *Id.,* at 63.

We perceive no basis on which to hold that the principle underlying our decision in *Schacht* does not apply to this case. To conclude that the Government may permit designated symbols to be used to communicate only a limited set of messages would be to enter territory having no discernible or defensible boundaries. Could the Government, on this theory, prohibit the burning of state flags? Of copies of the Presidential seal? Of the Constitution? In evaluating these choices under the First Amendment, how would we decide which symbols were sufficiently special to warrant this unique status? To do so, we would be forced to consult our own political preferences, and impose them on the citizenry, in the very way that the First Amendment forbids us to do. * * *

There is, moreover, no indication—either in the text of the Constitution or in our cases interpreting it—that a separate juridical category exists for the American flag alone. Indeed, we would not be surprised to learn that the persons who framed our Constitution and wrote the Amendment that we now construe were not known for their reverence for the Union Jack. The First Amendment does not guarantee that other concepts virtually sacred to our Nation as a whole—such as the principle that discrimination on the basis of race is odious and destructive—will go unquestioned in the marketplace of ideas. See Brandenburg v. Ohio, 395 U.S. 444 (1969). We decline, therefore, to create for the flag an exception to the joust of principles protected by the First Amendment.

It is not the State's ends, but its means, to which we object. It cannot be gainsaid that there is a special place reserved for the flag in this Nation, and thus we do not doubt that the Government has a legitimate interest in making efforts to "preserv[e] the national flag as an unalloyed symbol of our country." *Spence,* 418 U.S., at 412. We reject the suggestion, urged at oral argument by counsel for Johnson, that the Government lacks "any state interest whatsoever" in regulating the manner in which the flag may be displayed. Tr. of Oral Arg. 38. Congress has, for example, enacted precatory regulations describing the proper treatment of the flag, see 36 U.S.C. §§ 173–177, and we cast no doubt on the legitimacy of its interest in making such recommendations. To say that the Government has an interest in encouraging proper treatment of the flag, however, is not to say that it may criminally punish a person for burning a flag as a means of political protest. "National unity as an end which officials may foster by persuasion and example is not in question. The problem is whether under our Constitution compulsion as here employed is a permissible means for its achievement." *Barnette,* 319 U.S., at 640.

We are fortified in today's conclusion by our conviction that forbidding criminal punishment for conduct such as Johnson's will not endanger the special role played by our flag or the feelings it inspires.

* * *

We are tempted to say, in fact, that the flag's deservedly cherished place in our community will be strengthened, not weakened, by our holding today. Our decision is a reaffirmation of the principles of freedom and inclusiveness that the flag best reflects, and of the conviction that our toleration of criticism such as Johnson's is a sign and source of our strength. Indeed, one of the proudest images of our flag, the one immortalized in our own national anthem, is of the bombardment it survived at Fort McHenry. It is the nation's resilience, not its rigidity, that Texas sees reflected in the flag—and it is that resilience that we reassert today.

The way to preserve the flag's special role is not to punish those who feel differently about these matters. It is to persuade them that they are wrong.

> "To courageous, self-reliant men, with confidence in the power of free and fearless reasoning applied through the processes of popular government, no danger flowing from speech can be deemed clear and present, unless the incidence of the evil apprehended is so imminent that it may befall before there is opportunity for full discussion. If there be time to expose through discussion the falsehood and fallacies, to avert the evil by the processes of education, the remedy to be applied is more speech, not enforced silence." Whitney v. California, 274 U.S. 357, 377 (1927) (BRANDEIS, J., concurring).

And, precisely because it is our flag that is involved, one's response to the flag-burner may exploit the uniquely persuasive power of the flag itself. We can imagine no more appropriate response to burning a flag than waving one's own, no better way to counter a flag-burner's message then by saluting the flag that burns, no surer means of preserving the dignity even of the flag that burned than by—as one witness here did—according its remains a respectful burial. We do not consecrate the flag by punishing its desecration, for in doing so we dilute the freedom that this cherished emblem represents.

V

Johnson was convicted for engaging in expressive conduct. The State's interest in preventing breaches of the peace does not support his conviction because Johnson's conduct did not threaten to disturb the peace. Nor does the State's interest in preserving the flag as a symbol of nationhood and national unity justify his criminal conviction for engaging in political expression. The judgment of the Texas Court of Criminal Appeals is therefore

Affirmed.

JUSTICE KENNEDY, concurring.

I write not to qualify the words Justice Brennan chooses so well, for he says with power all that is necessary to explain our ruling. I join his opinion without reservation, but with a keen sense that this case, like others before us from time to time, exacts its personal toll. This prompts me to add to our pages these few remarks.

The case before us illustrates better than most that the judicial power is often difficult in its exercise. We cannot here ask another branch to share responsibility, as when the argument is made that a statute is flawed or incomplete. For we are presented with a clear and simple statute to be judged against a pure command of the Constitution. The outcome can be laid at no door but ours.

The hard fact is that sometimes we must make decisions we do not like. We make them because they are right, right in the sense that the law and the Constitution, as we see them, compel the result. And so great is our commitment to the process that, except in the rare case, we do not pause to express distaste for the result, perhaps for fear of undermining a valued principle that dictates the decision. This is one of those rare cases.

Our colleagues in dissent advance powerful arguments why respondent may be convicted for his expression, reminding us that among those who will be dismayed by our holding will be some who have had the singular honor of carrying the flag in battle. And I agree that the flag holds a lonely place of honor in an age when absolutes are distrusted and simple truths are burdened by unneeded apologetics.

With all respect to those views, I do not believe the Constitution gives us the right to rule as the dissenting members of the Court urge, however painful this judgment is to announce. Though symbols often are what we ourselves make of them, the flag is constant in expressing beliefs Americans share, beliefs in law and peace and that freedom which sustains the human spirit. The case here today forces recognition of the costs to which those beliefs commit us. It is poignant but fundamental that the flag protects those who hold it in contempt.

For all the record shows, this respondent was not a philosopher and perhaps did not even possess the ability to comprehend how repellent his statements must be to the Republic itself. But whether or not he could appreciate the enormity of the offense he gave, the fact remains that his acts were speech, in both the technical and the fundamental meaning of the Constitution. So I agree with the Court that he must go free.

CHIEF JUSTICE REHNQUIST, with whom JUSTICE WHITE and JUSTICE O'CONNOR join, dissenting.

In holding this Texas statute unconstitutional, the Court ignores Justice Holmes' familiar aphorism that "a page of history is worth a volume of logic." New York Trust Co. v. Eisner, 256 U.S. 345, 249 (1921). For more than 200 years, the American flag has occupied a unique position as the symbol of our Nation, a uniqueness that justifies a governmental prohibition against flag burning in the way respondent Johnson did here.

At the time of the American Revolution, the flag served to unify the Thirteen Colonies at home, while obtaining recognition of national sovereignty abroad. Ralph Waldo Emerson's Concord Hymn describes the first skirmishes of the Revolutionary War in these lines:

> "By the rude bridge that arched the flood
> Their flag to April's breeze unfurled,
> Here once the embattled farmers stood
> And fired the shot heard round the world."

During that time, there were many colonial and regimental flags, adorned with such symbols as pine trees, beavers, anchors, and rattle snakes, bearing slogans such as "Liberty or Death," "Hope," "An Appeal to Heaven," and "Don't Tread on Me." The first distinctive flag of the Colonies was the "Grand Union Flag"—with 13 stripes and a British flag in the left corner—which was flown for the first time on January 2, 1776, by troops of the Continental Army around Boston. By June 14, 1777, after we declared our independence from England, the Continental Congress resolved:

> "That the flag of the thirteen United States be thirteen stripes, alternate red and white: that the union be thirteen stars, white in a blue field, representing a new constellation." 8 Journal of the Continental Congress 1774–1789, p. 464 (Ford Ed.1907).

One immediate result of the flag's adoption was that American vessels harassing British shipping sailed under an authorized national flag. Without such a flag, the British could treat captured seamen as pirates and hang them summarily; with a national flag, such seamen were treated as prisoners of war.

During the War of 1812, British naval forces sailed up Chesapeake Bay and marched overland to sack and burn the city of Washington. They then sailed up the Patapsco River to invest the city of Baltimore, but to do so it was first necessary to reduce Fort McHenry in Baltimore Harbor. Francis Scott Key, a Washington lawyer, had been granted permission by the British to board one of their warships to negotiate the release of an American who had been taken prisoner. That night, waiting anxiously on the British ship, Key watched the British fleet firing on Fort McHenry. Finally, at daybreak, he saw the fort's American flag still flying; the British attack had failed. Intensely moved he began to scribble on the back of an envelope the poem that became our national anthem:

> "Oh! say can you see by the dawn's early light,
> What so proudly we hailed at the twilight's last gleaming?
> Whose broad stripes and bright stars, thro' the perilous fight,
> O'er the ramparts we watched were so gallantly streaming?
> And the rockets' red glare, the bombs bursting in air,
> Gave proof thro' the night that our flag was still there.
> Oh! say does that star-spangled banner yet wave
> O'er the land of the free and the home of the brave?"

* * *

The flag symbolizes the Nation in peace as well as in war. It signifies our national presence on battleships, airplanes, military installations, and public buildings from the United States Capitol to the thousands of county courthouses and city halls throughout the country. Two flags are prominently placed in our courtroom. Countless flags are placed by the graves of loved ones each year on what was first called Decoration Day, and is now called Memorial Day. The flag is traditionally placed on the casket of deceased members of the Armed Forces, and it is later given to the deceased's family. * * *

No other American symbol has been as universally honored as the flag. In 1931, Congress declared "The Star Spangled Banner" to be our national anthem. 36 U.S.C. § 170. In 1949, Congress declared June 14th to be Flag Day. § 157. In 1987, John Philip Sousa's "The Stars and Stripes Forever" was designated as the national march. Pub.L. 101–186, 101 Stat. 1286. Congress has also established "The Pledge of Allegiance to the Flag" and the manner of its deliverance. 36 U.S.C. § 172. The flag has appeared as the principal symbol of approximately 33 United States postal stamps and in the design of at least 43 more, more times than any other symbol. United States Postal Service, Definitive Mint Set 15 (1988).

* * * With the exception of Alaska and Wyoming, all of the States now have statutes prohibiting the burning of the flag. Most of the state statutes are patterned after the Uniform Flag Act of 1917, which in § 3 provides: "No person shall publicly mutilate, deface, defile, defy, trample upon, or by word or act cast contempt upon any such flag, standard, color, ensign or shield." Proceedings of National Conference of Commissioners on Uniform State Laws 323–324 (1917). * * *

The American flag, then, throughout more than 200 years of our history, has come to be the visible symbol embodying our Nation. It does not represent the views of any particular political party, and it does not represent any particular political philosophy. The flag is not simply another "idea" or "point of view" competing for recognition in the marketplace of ideas. Millions and millions of Americans regard it with an almost mystical reverence regardless of what sort of social, political, or philosophical beliefs they may have. I cannot agree that the First Amendment invalidates the Act of Congress, and the laws of 48 of 50 States, which make criminal the public burning of the flag.

More than 80 years ago in Halter v. Nebraska, 205 U.S. 34 (1907), this Court upheld the constitutionality of a Nebraska statute that forbade the use of representations of the American flag for advertising purposes upon articles of merchandise. The Court there said:

> "For that flag every true American has not simply an appreciation but a deep affection. * * * Hence, it has often occurred that insults to a flag have been the cause of war, and indignities put upon it, in the presence of those who revere it, have often been resented and sometimes punished on the spot." Id., at 41.

Only two Terms ago, in San Francisco Arts & Athletics, Inc. v. United States Olympic Committee, 483 U.S. 522 (1987), the Court held that Congress could grant exclusive use of the word "Olympic" to the United States Olympic Committee. The Court thought that this "restrictio[n] on expressive speech properly [was] characterized as incidental to the primary congressional purpose of encouraging and rewarding the USOC's activities." Id., at 536. As the Court stated, "when a word [or symbol] acquires value 'as the result of organization and the expenditure of labor, skill, and money' by an entity, that entity constitutionally may obtain a limited property right in the word [or symbol]." Id., at 532, quoting International News Service v. Associated Press, 248 U.S. 215, 239 (1918). Surely Congress or the States may recognize a similar interest in the flag.

But the Court insists that the Texas statute prohibiting the public burning of the American flag infringes on respondent Johnson's freedom of expression. Such freedom, of course, is not absolute. See Schenck v. United States, 249 U.S. 47 (1919). In Chaplinsky v. New Hampshire, 315 U.S. 568 (1942), a unanimous Court said:

> "Allowing the broadest scope to the language and purpose of the Fourteenth Amendment, it is well understood that the right of free speech is not absolute at all times and under all circumstances. There are certain well-defined and narrowly limited classes of speech, the prevention and punishment of which have never been thought to raise any Constitutional problem. These include the lewd and obscene, the profane, the libelous, and the insulting or 'fighting' words—those which by their very utterance inflict injury or tend to incite an immediate breach of the peace. It has been well observed that such utterances are no essential part of any exposition of ideas, and are of such slight social value as a step to truth that any benefit that may be derived from them is clearly outweighed by the social interest in order and morality." Id., at 571–572 (footnotes omitted).

The Court upheld Chaplinsky's conviction under a state statute that made it unlawful to "address any offensive, derisive or annoying word to any person who is lawfully in any street or other public place." Id., at 569. Chaplinsky had told a local Marshal, "You are a God damned racketeer" and a "damned Fascist and the whole government of Rochester are Fascists or agents of Fascists." *Ibid.*

Here it may equally well be said that the public burning of the American flag by Johnson was no essential part of any exposition of ideas, and at the same time it had a tendency to incite a breach of the peace. Johnson was free to make any verbal denunciation of the flag that he wished; indeed, he was free to burn the flag in private. He could publicly burn other symbols of the Government or effigies of political leaders. He did lead a march through the streets of Dallas, and conducted a rally in front of the Dallas City Hall. He engaged in a "die-in" to protest nuclear weapons. He shouted out various slogans during the march, including "Reagan, Mondale which will it be? Either one means World War III"; "Ronald Reagan, killer of the hour, Perfect example of U.S. power"; and "red, white and blue, we spit on you, you stand for plunder, you will go under." Brief for Respondent 3. For none of these acts was he arrested or prosecuted; it was only when he proceeded to burn publicly an American flag stolen from its rightful owner that he violated the Texas statute.

The Court could not, and did not, say that Chaplinsky's utterances were not expressive phrases—they clearly and succinctly conveyed an extremely low opinion of the addressee. The same may be said of Johnson's public burning of the flag in this case; it obviously did convey Johnson's bitter dislike of his country. But his act, like Chaplinsky's provocative words, conveyed nothing that could not have been conveyed and was not conveyed just as forcefully in a dozen different ways. As with "fighting words," so with flag burning, for purposes of the First Amendment: It is "no essential part of any exposition of ideas, and [is] of such slight social value as a step to truth that any benefit that may be derived from [it] is clearly outweighed" by the public interest in avoiding a probable breach of the peace. The highest courts of several States have upheld state statutes prohibiting the public burning of the flag on the grounds that it is so inherently inflammatory that it may cause a breach of public order. * * *

The result of the Texas statute is obviously to deny one in Johnson's frame of mind one of many means of "symbolic speech." Far from being a case of "one picture being worth a thousand words," flag burning is the equivalent of an inarticulate grunt or roar that, it seems fair to say, is most likely to be indulged in not to express any particular idea, but to antagonize others. * * * It was Johnson's use of this particular symbol, and not the idea that he sought to convey by it or by his many other expressions, for which he was punished.

Our prior cases dealing with flag desecration statutes have left open the question that the Court resolves today. In Street v. New York, 394 U.S. 576, 579 (1969), the defendant burned a flag in the street, shouting "We don't need no damned flag" and, "[i]f they let that happen to Meredith we don't need an American flag." The Court ruled that since the defendant might have been convicted solely on the basis of his words, the conviction could not stand, but it expressly reserved the question of whether a defendant could constitutionally be convicted for burning the flag. *Id.,* at 581.

Chief Justice Warren, in dissent, stated: "I believe that the States and Federal Government do have the power to protect the flag from acts of desecration and disgrace. * * * [I]t is difficult for me to imagine that, had the Court faced this issue, it would have concluded otherwise." *Id.,* at 605. Justices Black and Fortas also expressed their personal view that a prohibition on flag burning did not violate the Constitution. See *id.,* at 610 (Black, J., dissenting) ("It passes my belief that anything in the Federal Constitution bars a State from making the deliberate burning of the American Flag an offense"); *id.,* at 615–617 (Fortas, J., dissenting) ("[T]he States and the Federal Government have the power to protect the flag from acts of desecration committed in public. * * * [T]he flag is a special kind of personality. Its use is traditionally and universally subject to special rules and regulation. * * * A person may 'own' a flag, but ownership is subject to special burdens and responsibilities. A flag may be property, in a sense; but it is property burdened with peculiar obligations and restrictions. Certainly * * * these special conditions are not *per se* arbitrary or beyond governmental power under our Constitution").

* * *

But the Court today will have none of this. The uniquely deep awe and respect for our flag felt by virtually all of us are bundled off under the rubric of "designated symbols," *ante,* that the First Amendment prohibits the government from "establishing." But the government has not "established" this feeling; 200 years of history have done that. The government is simply recognizing as a fact the profound regard for the American flag created by that history when it enacts statutes prohibiting the disrespectful public burning of the flag.

The Court concludes its opinion with a regrettably patronizing civics lecture, presumably addressed to the Members of both Houses of Congress, the members of the 48 state legislatures that enacted prohibitions against flag burning, and the troops fighting under that flag in Vietnam who objected to its being burned: "The way to preserve the flag's special role is not to punish those who feel differently about these matters. It is to persuade them that they are wrong." * * * The Court's role as the final expositor of the Constitution is well established, but its role as a platonic guardian admonishing those responsible to public opinion as if they were truant school children has no similar place in our system of government. The cry of "no taxation without representation" animated those who revolted against the English Crown to found our Nation—the idea that those who submitted to government should have some say as to what kind of laws would be passed. Surely one of the high purposes of a democratic society is to legislate against conduct that is regarded as evil and profoundly offensive to the majority of people—whether it be murder, embezzlement, pollution, or flag burning.

* * * The Court decides that the American flag is just another symbol, about which not only must opinions pro and con be tolerated,

but for which the most minimal public respect may not be enjoined. The government may conscript men into the Armed Forces where they must fight and perhaps die for the flag, but the government may not prohibit the public burning of the banner under which they fight. I would uphold the Texas statute as applied in this case.

JUSTICE STEVENS, dissenting. [Omitted.]

NOTES ON PROTECTING THE FLAG OF THE UNITED STATES

1. Is there a distinction to be made in cases such as *Texas v. Johnson* between political uses of an intact flag, which uses may be highly offensive to passersby, and acts of burning or tearing or spitting on the same flag, as in *Texas v. Johnson,* itself? Consider the following:

a) A group self-styled as American Nazis, with swastika armbands, brown shirts, and black boots, conducts a parade, at the front of which an American flag is carried. Many whom they pass by on the parade route are affronted by what they regard as an obscene misappropriation of the flag by the (Nazi) marchers, even as the marchers had reason to expect that they would (and may in fact have wanted them to be);

b) The same group, far from carrying the flag out front, march with a crushed flag held in the fist of the lead marcher. At the parade's end, the leader gives a short speech decrying "mongrelization" of races in the United States. To lend emphasis to his (and the marchers') contempt for what they regard the United States as "representing," the leader sets fire to the crushed flag.

Does the first amendment apply to both instances alike? (May carrying the flag, intact, upright, on a standard, be more protected—because more closely akin to "pure speech—while burning the flag doesn't make it across the first amendment at all? May the latter be generally, or even specially, prohibited, even assuming the former cannot?)

2. Adopted by Congress in 1968, 18 U.S.C.A. § 700 (captioned "Desecration of the Flag of the United States")[98] provided as follows:

(a) Whoever knowingly casts contempt upon any flag of the United States by publicly mutilating, defacing, defiling, burning, or trampling upon it shall be fined not more than $1,000 or imprisoned for not more than one year, or both.

(b) The term "flag of the United States" as used in this section shall include any flag, standard colors, ensign, or any picture or representation of either, or of any part or parts of

---

98. Pub.L. 90–381, § 1, July 5, 1968, 82 Stat. 291.

either made of any substance or represented on any substance, of any size evidently purporting to be either of said flag, standard, color, or ensign of the United States of America, or a picture or representation of either, upon which shall be shown the colors, the stars and the stripes, in any number of either thereof, or of any part or parts of either, by which the average person seeing the same without deliberation may believe the same to represent the flag, standards, colors, or ensign of the United States of America.

(c) Nothing in this section shall be construed as indicating an intent on the part of Congress to deprive any State, territory, possession, or the Commonwealth of Puerto Rico of jurisdiction over any offense over which it would have jurisdiction in the absence of this section.

It is widely assumed that any prosecution brought against Johnson under this statute would fail, given the Supreme Court's decision in *Texas v. Johnson,* itself. Do you agree?

On October 12, 1989, three months after the decision in *Texas v. Johnson,* by vote of 371 to 343, the House of Representatives approved the following substitution for part (a) of this statute and the Senate speedily concurred (103 Stat. 777, 18 U.S.C.A. § 700):

Whoever knowingly mutilates, defaces, physically defiles, burns, maintains on the floor or ground, or tramples upon any flag of the United States shall be fined under this title or imprisoned for not more than one year or both.

Suppose a case identical to *Texas v. Johnson* were to be prosecuted under the federal statute in its revised form *supra.* Upon defense motion to dismiss the charge, on first amendment grounds, what result and why?[99]

---

3. The same day the House adopted the revised version of the federal statute already noted *supra,* Marlin Fitzwater, White House spokesman, expressed reservations about the sufficiency of the legislative change, in keeping with President Bush's support for a proposed amendment which would provide:

[Proposed 27th Amendment to the Constitution]

The Congress and the States Shall have Power to Prohibit the Physical Desecration of the Flag of the United States.

Suppose the proposed twenty-seventh amendment were adopted. What would be its effect?

a) E.g., would the display of a flag, upside down in one's street-facing front apartment window, but intact and unsullied, be subject to

---

[99]. See United States v. Eichman, 496 U.S. ___, 110 S.Ct. 2404, 110 L.Ed.2d 287 (1990).

legislation based on the power enumerated in the proposed amendment?[1]

b) If it were deemed subject to prohibition based on the provision of the proposed amendment, would it therefore not be subject to first amendment protection?[2]

---

4. During the spring of 1989, at the Chicago Art Institute, a controversial exhibit created a very strong protest calling for prosecution of the person who prepared it (and the exhibit was removed by the Institute). The exhibit, in a public gallery, was accompanied by a placard captioned as follows: "What is the proper way to display the flag?" On the wall, photographs were displayed in which the flag was featured in brutal scenes of American involvement in Vietnam and elsewhere. On the floor, a large American flag was stretched out, flat. In front of the flag was a projected shelf with a book laid open for persons to sign on a line of its open blank pages, if they chose to do so. To sign the book, one was likely to step on the laid-out flag. Consider:

a) Prosecution of the artist under (1) the 1968 version, or (2) the 1989 version, of the federal statute,[3] *supra*;

b) Prosecution instead, or additionally, of any visitor who walked on the flag or stood on one part of it, while signing the book;

c) A civil suit, brought by the artist, to enjoin the removal of the exhibit, i.e. a suit seeking to have the exhibit restored, brought against the Art Institute, a public body of the City of Chicago.[4]

---

1. Would a Raquel Welch bikini, fashioned from a stars and stripes motif, be subject to a law based on this proposed amendment?

2. I.e. note that the amendment does not provide that "the first amendment shall not be construed to extend to any legislation adopted pursuant to this amendment." (Neither does it provide that "legislation adopted pursuant to this amendment shall be immune from first amendment review.")

3. Under the new form of the act of Congress, incidentally, note that the exhibit would evidently be subject to the act whether or not anyone actually walked on the flag (i.e. even if a rope barrier were placed around the floor arrangement, and the shelf and sign-in book were removed or placed off to one side). Does this raise any separate or additional problem?

4. One may postpone additional consideration of this case for review *infra*, cases and materials on "forum" analysis, and/or time, place, and manner regulations of speech.

Chapter 3

THE FIRST AMENDMENT IN SPECIFIC ENVIRONMENTS

A. **The Government as employer, contractor, purchaser of services, and provider of benefits, and the extent to which the first amendment may limit its power to set conditions. Herein of the right-privilege doctrine and the unconstitutional conditions doctrine. The *Pickering–Connick* (balancing) test. Political affiliation and eligibility for public service; first amendment constraints on political litmus tests.**

The cases and materials we have thus far examined have concerned general laws of general application. These laws typically forbade conduct or utterances of a certain sort,[1] and they provided criminal or civil sanctions for such violations as might occur. Alternatively, they provided mechanisms for restraining or disallowing certain categories of utterances, i.e. they operated as a form of prior restraint.[2]

In contrast, the kinds of laws and regulations now to be considered do not limit what may be published or advocated by citizens or by people in general. Rather, they apply only to persons engaged in certain activities, usually under the control of the government, and they presume merely to regulate the terms of that activity and the freedom of speech of those engaged in that activity, and nothing more. In short, they are not general restrictions on freedom of speech at all. Often, moreover, the restrictions imposed as an incident of the regulated activity do not carry any threat of fine or imprisonment of the person who violates those restrictions. In fact, even provision for civil liability is rare. Rather, they typically provide merely for the severance of the offending party from the relationship he or she has had, in the event of breach of the conditions.[3]

---

1. E.g., obstructing the draft, advocating violating the law, urging the overthrow of the government, inciting to riot, advocating immoral behavior, portraying others as unworthy, advocating discrimination, etc.

2. E.g., permit requirements, licensing requirements, injunctions, restraining orders, arrest prior to speech or publication, etc.

3. Though this is not always true, i.e. a criminal sanction or civil sanction may sometimes also apply. See, e.g., Scopes v.

Moreover, in all of these cases, the regulated party was a free agent at the beginning, and typically became equally a free agent at the end. Not only is the field marked by an absence of duress in the usual sense—of the threatened use of fine or imprisonment for what one may say or write; rather, neither is there any duress originating with the government *compelling* one to enter into the relationship, from which one is also free to withdraw. While the affected party must take "the bitter with the sweet"[4] insofar as the terms offered for acceptance may be—and characteristically will be—nonnegotiable (e.g., fixed by statute), there is no duress applied by the government to compel one to enter the relationship in the first place.[5] In a practical view of the matter, one's continuing conformity to the limitations identified by government, and made applicable to the particular activity administered by government, is treated simply as a continuing condition precedent to one's eligibility, and usually nothing more.[6]

State, 154 Tenn. 105, 289 S.W. 363 (1927); Snepp v. United States, 444 U.S. 507, 100 S.Ct. 763, 62 L.Ed.2d 704 (1980), discussed *infra* (in *Scopes,* the offending teacher was criminally prosecuted; in *Snepp,* the offending ex-employee had a constructive trust imposed on his entire book royalties, as we shall see). Nonetheless, in each case the enforcement technique was otherwise consistent with the rationale of merely keeping the affected party to the terms of the arrangement that he was under no duress to have made, so both cases are entirely appropriate to review here.

4. The phrase is lifted from a notable opinion by Justice Rehnquist, in Arnett v. Kennedy, 416 U.S. 134, 40 S.Ct. 1633, 416 L.Ed.2d 134 (1974), dissenting from a holding that a nonprobationary federal civil service employee was entitled to some kind of due process hearing before being terminated for cause despite not having been promised any such hearing. In Justice Rehnquist's view, in dissent, the employee was entitled to as much due process as he was promised and nothing more: "[W]here the grant of a substantive right is inextricably intertwined with the limitations on the procedures which are to be employed in determining that right, a litigant [must] take the bitter with the sweet. [Here] the property interest which appellee had in his employment was itself conditioned by procedural limitations which had accompanied the grant of that interest." The employee got all the due process he was entitled to get; he was entitled to get nothing more. Cf. Cleveland Board of Educ. v. Loudermill, 470 U.S. 532, 105 S.Ct. 1487, 84 L.Ed.2d 494 (1985) (also rejecting Justice Rehnquist's view).

5. Of course, one's personal circumstances may affect one's freedom of choice as a practical matter, but no more so here, than in many other areas. Cf., e.g., Harris v. McRae, 448 U.S. 297, 100 S.Ct. 2671, 65 L.Ed.2d 784 (1980) (reimbursement of health care providers by government for women on restricted incomes who elect full term pregnancy and child birth, no reimbursement to health care provider if, instead, the same woman seeks an abortion). See generally, C. Reich, Individual Rights and Social Welfare, 74 Yale L.J. 1245 (1966); C. Reich, The New Property, 73 Yale L.J. 733 (1964).

6. Recall, for immediate comparison from Con. Law I, Massachusetts v. Mellon, 262 U.S. 447, 43 S.Ct. 597, 67 L.Ed. 1078 (1923). Congress enacted a measure (the Maternity Act) setting aside certain funds for which states could make application subject to making such reports and meeting such conditions as might be prescribed by a federal agency, the funds to be withheld insofar as it might be determined that they were not being expended in the manner the federal agency prescribed. Massachusetts filed suit in the Supreme Court against Mellon, the Secretary of the Treasury, seeking a declaratory judgment that the "act is invalid because it assumes powers not granted to Congress and usurps the local police power" of the states, due to the strings attached to the grants. The Supreme Court dismissed for lack of jurisdiction, not because the case was not within the Court's original jurisdiction (it was), but because, the Court said, the proceeding was itself "not of a justiciable character." Why not? Partly, perhaps, because the issue had not been sufficiently joined between the parties, i.e. Massachusetts had not even applied for any funds. But the Court also said: "Probably, it would be sufficient to point out that the powers of the State are not invaded, since the statute imposes no obligation *but simply extends an option which the State is free to accept or reject.* * * * In the last analysis, the

The restrictions, in short, are twice distinguishable from the general laws we have previously examined. (1) They apply only to those who, with full and reasonable notice of them, accept the relationship to which they are made applicable (usually, a relationship of special advantage, e.g., a government job, contract, grant, or some kind of largesse). (2) Continuing compliance itself is merely a continuing condition of sustaining that relationship, moreover, and typically nothing more. So, much as in any ordinary private commercial contract, at most one thus needs to adhere to "the bitter," only so long as one wants to continue to enjoy "the sweet."

How, if at all, or in what measure, and by what standards, does the first amendment apply in these circumstances? These are the questions we shall next address. The cases and materials chosen for the purpose are illustrative, rather than exhaustive. They should, however, provide a useful guide. Before we get into them, we may note the different ways the overall problem might be addressed.

Roughly, by way of introduction, there have been three quite different perspectives that the courts have brought to bear. Each of the first two of these perspectives is characterized by a particular deductive logic and each, within the limits of its perspective, seems to be compelling and inexorably correct. (As we shall notice, however, they are also 180 degrees apart.) The third manner of addressing the general question considered in this section may be considerably less clear,—but the assigned principal cases which follow in this collection of materials may be helpful in seeing how it works out in practice. Here are the three, broadly suggested, alternative approaches variously reflected in the general case law:

a. In cases that fit the general description provided *supra*, we treat the government and the individual as free agents, mutually competent to determine their own best interests and we measure the terms of the arrangement according to general principles of the common law of contracts, modified to such extent as statutory law may provide.[7]

b. To the contrary, in cases that fit the general description provided *supra*, the common law of contracts is essentially

---

complaint of the plaintiff State is brought to the naked contention that Congress has usurped the reserved powers of the several States by the mere enactment of the statute, though nothing has been done and *nothing is to be done without their consent;* and it is plain that that question, as it is thus presented, is political and not judicial in character, and therefore is not a matter which admits of the exercise of the judicial power." 262 U.S. at 480–83, 43 S.Ct. at 598–99, 67 L.Ed. at 1082–83. (Emphasis added.) See also South Dakota v. Dole, 483 U.S. 203, 107 S.Ct. 2793, 97 L.Ed.2d 171 (1987); Chas. C. Steward Machine Co. v. Davis, 301 U.S. 548, 57 S.Ct. 883, 81 L.Ed. 1279 (1937). But see United States v. Butler, 297 U.S. 1, 56 S.Ct. 312, 80 L.Ed. 477 (1936); McCoy & Friedman, Conditional Spending: Federalism's Trojan Horse, 1988 Supreme Ct.Rev. 85.

7. See, e.g., the discussion in note 6 *supra*, addressing the tenth amendment in a somewhat similar fashion. Cf. also cases condoning the waiver of constitutional rights from criminal procedure (e.g., "waivers" of constitutional rights in guilty plea bargains, or of one's right to counsel following a *Miranda* warning, or of one's right to counsel at trial).

irrelevant and cannot be invoked. Rather, the first amendment disallows government from imposing restrictions on free speech, as much so by contract as by any other device. The first amendment does not permit the buying up of free speech, whether from willing sellers or from unwilling, but necessitous, sellers. All such terms, conditions, regulations, or restrictions, insofar as they come from government, are constitutionally void.

c. In cases that fit the general description provided *supra*, the first amendment does apply, and it applies unexceptionally,[8] to be sure. Still, one must then struggle to sort out just what that means in each case. We have, for instance, already seen that a certain kind of restriction may be valid at certain times though not at other times, or in certain places and circumstances though it might not otherwise be sustainable. Unsurprisingly, the same will be just as true, here.

It is easier to state the position in *c supra*, than it is to grasp its actual workings in the Supreme Court. The principal cases immediately ahead of us, however, should be helpful in working it out. Like some comparable cases already behind us (e.g., the post-*New York Times v. Sullivan* libel cases refining first amendment libel law distinctions), moreover, some of these decisions have developed a number of line-drawing distinctions of their own, i.e. somewhat formal distinctions, peculiar to this field.[9] We shall see shortly how well they work here. These cases also all arise from a history in which the first two positions were each separately put forward, however, so it will pay us to understand their respective perspectives a little bit more.[10]

---

8. I.e. compare either the Learned Hand or the Holmes–Brandeis test, and apply either with due care, here.

9. The tendency toward formal complexity in subsets of first amendment law is a recurring tendency, just as it is in criminal procedure or other areas of constitutional review. In some measure, it arises from the inevitability of cases crowding the margin of constitutional uncertainty and from the felt need of the Supreme Court to provide clearer guidance to all with a need to know what "the rules" are, whether they are plaintiffs or defendants, prosecutors or those in danger of prosecution, administrative agencies, lower courts, or legislatures. In the natural life of these systems, however, it is also true that the complexity of "the rules" thus laid down tends inevitably to engender its own uncertainties. (The distinctions become so esoteric and tenuous and/or so debatable that eventually the whole system may crash under its own weight.) There is, moreover, a serious first amendment hazard at risk in these complex approaches. The risk is that one may lose sight of some organizing philosophy common to all first amendment cases in trying too hard to figure out which is the "right" set of rules that technically appear to govern one's immediate case, and thereby be misled into foregoing access to a far more powerful set of more general observations that might well be important to set matters right.

10. Moreover, each of these prior perspectives continues to be used at the margins of first amendment disputes in the Supreme Court by different Justices, e.g., Chief Justice Rehnquist not infrequently invokes the "right-privilege" distinction, while Justices Brennan, Marshall, and Blackmun often invoked the "unconstitutional conditions" doctrine instead.

B. A Return to the Early Holmes and the Right-Privilege Distinction of *McAuliffe v. Mayor of New Bedford*

In a famous Massachusetts case, in 1892, dismissing the appeal of a New Bedford policeman who was fired following some public remarks critical of how the police department was run, Justice Holmes dispatched the police officer's first amendment objection with the following epigrammatic response: [11]

> The petitioner may have a constitutional right to talk politics, but he has no constitutional right to be a policeman. There are few employments for hire in which the servant does not agree to *suspend his constitutional right of free speech,* as well as of idleness, by the implied terms of his contract. The servant cannot complain, *as he takes the employment on the terms which are offered him.*

This view of Holmes [12] became widely quoted and relied upon in many other courts, including the Supreme Court, between 1892 and 1954.[13] In 1927, for example, the *Scopes* ("Monkey Trial") case, on appeal to the Tennessee Supreme Court, followed the same approach as the McAuliffe case, under Holmes. Scopes, one may recall, was represented in this famous trial by Clarence Darrow. Scopes had been criminally prosecuted for violating a Tennessee law applicable to public school teachers, forbidding the teaching of "any theory that denies the story of the divine creation of man as taught in the Bible," such as Darwin's view respecting the "Origin of the Species."[14] Despite Darrow's defense efforts in his behalf, Scopes was convicted at trial by the jury. On his appeal on first and fourteenth amendment grounds to the state supreme court, this was the court's response: [15]

> He [Scopes] was under contract with the State to work in an institution of the State. He had no right or privilege to serve the State except upon such terms as the State prescribed. * * * The Statute before us is not an exercise of the police power of the State undertaking to regulate the conduct * * * of individuals [16] * * *. [I]t is an Act of the State as a corpora-

---

11. McAuliffe v. Mayor of New Bedford, 155 Mass. 216, 220, 29 N.E. 517, 518 (1892). (Emphasis added.)

12. Essentially, a view of the relationship as sounding in contract, with each party competent to determine the acceptability of the terms, is it not?

13. For a general review, see Van Alstyne, The Demise of the Right–Privilege Distinction in Constitutional Law, 83 Harv. L.Rev. 1429 (1968). For a more critical, modern, comprehensive review, see K. Sullivan, Unconstitutional Conditions, 102 Harv.L.Rev. 1415 (1989).

14. H.L. Mencken covered the trial proceedings. William Jennings Bryan, thrice Democratic nominee for the presidency, appeared as an expert witness for the state.

15. Scopes v. State, 154 Tenn. 105, 109–112, 289 S.W. 363, 364–65 (1927).

16. I.e. the statute did not regulate persons generally, and did not regulate teachers in private schools—schools not supported or administered by the state; it is in just this sense, the state supreme court says, that the police power of the state is not in any way involved in this case. Cf. Meyer v. Nebraska, 262 U.S. 390, 43 S.Ct. 625, 67 L.Ed. 1042 (1923) (state statute forbidding any instruction in any language other than English prior to the eighth grade, held unconstitutional under the fourteenth amendment, as applied to

tion, a proprietor, an employer. It is a declaration of a master as to the character of work the master's servant will, or rather shall not, perform. In dealing with its own employees engaged upon its own work, the State is not hampered by the limitations of * * * the Fourteenth Amendment to the Constitution of the United States.

Note, then, the dispositive proposition relied upon by the state supreme court in *Scopes v. State,* i.e. not that the speech restriction was all right under the fourteenth amendment, but, rather, that in dealing with its own employees employed upon its own work, the State is "not hampered" by the limitations of the fourteenth amendment. The same thought is inferable from Holmes' premises in the *McAuliffe* decision: the legal frame of reference is ordinary contract law (and even then as modified by the state statute fixing the terms) and not constitutional law.[17] One's agreement to suspend one's "constitutional right of free speech" is treated in just the same way as one's agreement to suspend one's constitutional right to loaf, i.e. as something for one to decide to do or not to do, neither more nor less, but binding insofar as one does. When, therefore, the state acts pursuant to its general police power to restrict what its citizens choose to say—whether about the police department, or about the Book of Genesis vs. Darwin, or anything else, it must answer to the first amendment. When the state acts differently, as an employer, on the other hand, it need answer merely as any employer need do: i.e. were the terms made clear? Did they come attached to the position with respect to which they were enforced? Did the employee expressly, or impliedly, agree?

The analogy to the Supreme Court's spending power, tenth amendment "states' rights" position in *Massachusetts v. Mellon* is quite striking.[18] There, in dicta, the state was described also as a free agent to decide for itself whether the changes in its laws that it might not otherwise choose to make were worthwhile making, and it was under no duty to make any changes it deemed inappropriate. Moreover, having made those changes (in order to become eligible for federal assistance), it could at any time change its mind, change its laws back again, and give up the relationship it had previously entered into. So, too, with the public employee, in *McAuliffe,* and the public school teacher, in *State v. Scopes.* All were free agents, but not more.

C. The Unconstitutional Conditions Doctrine

The use of the preceding approach to public sector free speech restrictions generally goes under the rubric of the "right-privilege"

teacher in private, Lutheran school, neither supported nor assisted in any way by the state).

17. ("The servant cannot complain, as he takes the employment *on the terms which are offered him.*")

18. See discussion and review in note 6 *supra.*

doctrine. As already indicated, it had a very substantial career in the courts. Yet, even as it continued to be applied,[19] it faced headwinds within the Supreme Court, headwinds blown by a counter doctrine as old as itself.

The most familiar statement of this counter doctrine is forcefully presented in a well known opinion by Justice Sutherland, writing for a majority of the Supreme Court in *Frost & Frost Trucking Co. v. Railroad Commission,* a commercial case (rather than a first amendment case) decided in 1926.[20] Sutherland's emphasis in the case was on the point that the government is *not* treated like a private party for constitutional purposes, i.e. it is bound by uniform constitutional constraints. It is government the first and fourteenth amendments are meant to constrain (and do constrain), regardless of the guise or capacity in which government acts.[21] That government seeks to limit one's speech by the terms of some leasehold, or by the terms of some contract, or by the terms of some permit (e.g., as a condition of using its streets), rather than by direct mandate, should gain it no ground. In Sutherland's oft quoted words: [22]

> It would be a palpable incongruity to strike down an act of state legislation which, by words of express divestment, seeks to strip the citizen of rights guaranteed by the federal Constitution, but to uphold an act by which the same result is accomplished under the guise of a surrender of a right in exchange for a valuable privilege the state threatens otherwise to withhold. * * * It is inconceivable that guarantees embedded in the Constitution of the United States may be thus manipulated out of existence.

The obvious basis for this view is the observation that government remains government regardless of the capacity in which it presumes to act. And what government cannot do to anyone directly (because barred by the first amendment), neither can it do indirectly by offering a trade, i.e. the "surrender of a right in exchange for a valuable privilege," such as a public job, a public contract, a rent-controlled apartment, or something else. If, then, the restriction would fail when

---

19. Among the last cases to apply the distinction were Bailey v. Richardson, 182 F.2d 46 (D.C.Cir.1950), aff'd by an equally divided Court, 341 U.S. 918, 71 S.Ct. 669, 95 L.Ed. 1352 (1951), and Adler v. Board of Educ. of City of New York, 341 U.S. 485, 72 S.Ct. 380, 96 L.Ed. 517 (1952). Cf. Keyishian v. Board of Regents, 385 U.S. 589, 607–06, 87 S.Ct. 675, 685–87, 17 L.Ed.2d 629, 643–44 (1967).

20. Interestingly, as an aside, note that it was Sutherland who nonetheless wrote the Court's opinion in *Massachusetts v. Mellon,* in which the dicta are more of a piece with the right-privilege distinction.

21. Whether the amendment(s) should have stopped with limiting government power alone may be arguable, i.e. perhaps they should also have restricted corporate power as well, but we need not pause to argue it here. For without arguing, much less presuming to settle, that proposition— about corporate power or other varieties of privately-held power, there is no doubt that at least the first amendment controls Congress, and the fourteenth amendment controls the states.

22. Frost & Frost Trucking Co. v. Railroad Com'n, 271 U.S. 583, 46 S.Ct. 605, 70 L.Ed. 1101 (1926). For earlier expressions to the same effect, see, e.g., Doyle v. Continental Ins. Co., 94 U.S. 535, 543, 24 L.Ed. 148, 152 (1876) ("Though a State may have the power * * * of prohibiting all foreign corporations from transacting business within its jurisdiction, it has no power to impose *unconstitutional conditions* upon their doing so.") (Emphasis added.)

proposed as a direct restriction on one's speech without reference to the carrot held out, it should fare no better as a term proposed in a contract, or as a term proposed in a lease, or as a term proposed in a permit of some kind. The first amendment makes an offending term substantively void. Accordingly, the result would seem to be the one proposed *b* supra.[23]

Now, compare with these sharply differing approaches [24] the cases assigned for this part, beginning with the *Pickering* case that is quite recent and that immediately follows. Which view, if either, does it support? How, if at all, does it differ from each?

PICKERING v. BOARD OF EDUCATION OF WILL COUNTY, ILLINOIS

Supreme Court of the United States, 1968.
391 U.S. 563, 88 S.Ct. 1731, 20 L.Ed.2d 811.

MR. JUSTICE MARSHALL delivered the opinion of the Court.

* * *

I.

In February of 1961, the appellee Board of Education asked the voters of the school district to approve a bond issue to raise $4,875,000 to erect two new schools. The proposal was defeated. Then, in December of 1961, the Board submitted another bond proposal to the voters which called for the raising of $5,500,000 to build two new schools. This second proposal passed and the schools were built with the money raised by the bond sales. In May of 1964 a proposed increase in the tax rate to be used for educational purposes was submitted to the voters by the Board and was defeated. Finally, on September 19, 1964, a second proposal to increase the tax rate was submitted by the Board and was likewise defeated. It was in connection with this last proposal of the School Board that appellant wrote the letter to the editor (which we reproduce in an Appendix to this opinion) that resulted in his dismissal.

---

23. Actually, there are at least two distinct versions of this doctrine of unconstitutional conditions, a stronger and weaker (but still potent) form. In its stronger form, the doctrine may imply that unless the state could forbid the class of activity or speech to citizens in general, it cannot forbid that class of activity or speech by contract or by regulation of others whom it seeks to control by making abstention from such activity or speech a condition of their eligibility for a public contract or public sector "privilege." In its lesser (but still potent) form, it means only this: that unless the state could forbid such activity or speech to equivalently situated persons in the *private* sector, it cannot forbid such activity or speech as a condition of eligibility in the *public* sector—the Constitution requires no less. For a discussion of this latter version see Linde, Justice Douglas on Freedom in the Welfare State: Constitutional Rights in the Public Sector, 39 Wash.L.Rev. 4 (1964), 40 Wash.L.Rev. 10 (1965). (But see Van Alstyne, A Comment on the Inappropriate Uses of an Old Analogy, 16 U.C.L.A.L.Rev. 751 (1969).)

24. [They are sharply different, are they not?]

Prior to the vote on the second tax increase proposal a variety of articles attributed to the District 205 Teachers' Organization appeared in the local paper. These articles urged passage of the tax increase and stated that failure to pass the increase would result in a decline in the quality of education afforded children in the district's schools. A letter from the superintendent of schools making the same point was published in the paper two days before the election and submitted to the voters in mimeographed form the following day. It was in response to the foregoing material, together with the failure of the tax increase to pass, that appellant submitted the letter in question to the editor of the local paper.

The letter constituted, basically, an attack on the School Board's handling of the 1961 bond issue proposals and its subsequent allocation of financial resources between the schools' educational and athletic programs. It also charged the superintendent of schools with attempting to prevent teachers in the district from opposing or criticizing the proposed bond issue.

The Board dismissed Pickering for writing and publishing the letter. Pursuant to Illinois law, the Board was then required to hold a hearing on the dismissal. At the hearing the Board charged that numerous statements in the letter were false and that the publication of the statements unjustifiably impugned the "motives, honesty, integrity, truthfulness, responsibility and competence" of both the Board and the school administration. The Board also charged that the false statements damaged the professional reputations of its members and of the school administrators, would be disruptive of faculty discipline, and would tend to foment "controversy, conflict and dissention" among teachers, administrators, the Board of Education, and the residents of the district. Testimony was introduced from a variety of witnesses on the truth or falsity of the particular statements in the letter with which the Board took issue. The Board found the statements to be false as charged. No evidence was introduced at any point in the proceedings as to the effect of the publication of the letter on the community as a whole or on the administration of the school system in particular, and no specific findings along these lines were made.

The Illinois courts reviewed the proceeding solely to determine whether the Board's findings were supported by substantial evidence and whether, on the facts as found, the Board could reasonably conclude that appellant's publication of the letter was "detrimental to the best interests of the schools." Pickering's claim that his letter was protected by the First Amendment was rejected on the ground that his acceptance of a teaching position in the public schools obliged him to refrain from making statements about the operation of the schools "which in the absence of such position he would have an undoubted right to engage in." It is not altogether clear whether the Illinois Supreme Court held that the First Amendment had no applicability to appellant's dismissal for writing the letter in question or whether it determined that the particular statements made in the letter were not entitled to First Amendment protection. In any event, it clearly rejected Pickering's claim that, on the facts of this case, he could not constitutionally be dismissed from his teaching position.

II.

To the extent that the Illinois Supreme Court's opinion may be read to suggest that teachers may constitutionally be compelled to relinquish the First Amendment rights they would otherwise enjoy as citizens to comment on matters of public interest in connection with the operation of the public schools in which they work, it proceeds on a premise that has been unequivocally rejected in numerous prior decisions of this Court. * * * "[T]he theory that public employment which may be denied altogether may be subjected to any conditions, regardless of how unreasonable, has been uniformly rejected." Keyishian v. Board of Regents, *supra*, 385 U.S. at 605–606. At the same time it cannot be gainsaid that the State has interests as an employer in regulating the speech of its employees that differ significantly from those it possesses in connection with regulation of the speech of the citizenry in general. The problem in any case is to arrive at a balance between the interests of the teacher, as a citizen, in commenting upon matters of public concern and the interest of the State, as an employer, in promoting the efficiency of the public services it performs through its employees.

III.

The Board contends that "the teacher by virtue of his public employment has a duty of loyalty to support his superiors in attaining the generally accepted goals of education and that, if he must speak out publicly, he should do so factually and accurately, commensurate with his education and experience." Appellant, on the other hand, argues that the test applicable to defamatory statements directed against public officials by persons having no occupational relationship with them, namely, that statements to be legally actionable must be made "with knowledge that [they were] * * * false or not," New York Times Co. v. Sullivan, 376 U.S. 254, 280 (1964), should also be applied to public statements made by teachers. Because of the enormous variety of fact situations in which critical statements by teachers and other public employees may be thought by their superiors, against whom the statements are directed to furnish grounds for dismissal, we do not deem it either appropriate or feasible to attempt to lay down a general standard against which all such statements may be judged. However, in the course of evaluating the conflicts of First Amendment protection and the need for orderly school administration in the context of this case, we shall indicate some of the general lines along which an analysis of the controlling interests should run.

An examination of the statements in appellant's letter objected to by the Board reveals that they, like the letter as a whole, consist essentially of criticism of the Board's allocation of school funds between educational and athletic programs, and of both the Board's and the superintendent's methods of informing, or preventing the informing of, the district's taxpayers of the real reasons why additional tax revenues were being sought for the schools. The statements are in no way directed towards any person with whom appellant would normally be in contact in the course of his daily work as a teacher. Thus no question of maintaining either discipline by immediate superiors or harmony among coworkers is presented here. Appellant's employment relationships with the Board and, to a somewhat lesser extent, with the superintendent are not the kind of close working relationships for which it can persuasively be claimed that personal loyalty and confidence are necessary to their proper functioning. Accordingly, to the extent that the Board's position here can be taken to suggest that even comments on matters of public concern that are substantially correct * * * may furnish grounds for dismissal if they are sufficiently critical in tone, we unequivocally reject it.[3]

We next consider the statements in appellant's letter which we agree to be false. The Board's original charges included allegations that the publication of the letter damaged the professional reputations of the Board and the superintendent and would foment controversy and conflict among the Board, teachers, administrators, and the residents of the district. However, no evidence to support these allegations was introduced at the hearing. So far as the record reveals, Pickering's letter was greeted by everyone but its main target, the Board, with massive apathy and total disbelief. The Board must, therefore, have decided, perhaps by analogy with the law of libel, that the statements were per se harmful to the operation of the schools.

However, the only way in which the Board could conclude, absent any evidence of the actual effect of the letter, that the statements contained therein were per se detrimental to the interest of the schools was to equate the Board members' own interests with that of the schools. Certainly an accusation that too much money is being spent on athletics by the administrators of the school system (which is precisely the import of that portion of appellant's letter containing the statements that we have found to be false, see Appendix, *infra*) cannot reasonably be regarded as per se detrimental to the district's schools. Such an accusation reflects rather a difference of opinion between Pickering and the Board as to the preferable manner of operating the school system, a difference of opinion that clearly concerns an issue of general public interest.

In addition, the fact that particular illustrations of the Board's claimed undesirable emphasis on athletic programs are false would not normally have any necessary impact on the actual operation of the schools, beyond its tendency to anger the Board. For example, Pickering's letter was written after the defeat at the polls of the second

---

3. It is possible to conceive of some positions in public employment in which the need for confidentiality is so great that even completely correct public statements might furnish a permissible ground for dismissal. Likewise, positions in public employment in which the relationship between superior and subordinate is of such a personal and intimate nature that certain forms of public criticism of the superior by the subordinate would seriously undermine the effectiveness of the working relationship between them can also be imagined. We intimate no views as to how we would resolve any specific instances of such situations, but merely note that significantly different considerations would be involved in such cases.

proposed tax increase. It could, therefore, have had no effect on the ability of the school district to raise necessary revenue, since there was no showing that there was any proposal to increase taxes pending when the letter was written.

More importantly, the question whether a school system requires additional funds is a matter of legitimate public concern on which the judgment of the school administration, including the School Board, cannot, in a society that leaves such questions to popular vote, be taken as conclusive. On such a question free and open debate is vital to informed decision-making by the electorate. Teachers are, as a class, the members of a community most likely to have informed and definite opinions as to how funds allotted to the operation of the schools should be spent. Accordingly, it is essential that they be able to speak out freely on such questions without fear of retaliatory dismissal.

In addition, the amounts expended on athletics which Pickering reported erroneously were matters of public record on which his position as a teacher in the district did not qualify him to speak with any greater authority than any other taxpayer. The Board could easily have rebutted appellant's errors by publishing the accurate figures itself, either via a letter to the same newspaper or otherwise. We are thus not presented with a situation in which a teacher has carelessly made false statements about matters so closely related to the day-to-day operations of the schools that any harmful impact on the public would be difficult to counter because of the teacher's presumed greater access to the real facts. Accordingly, we have no occasion to consider at this time whether under such circumstances a school board could reasonably require that a teacher make substantial efforts to verify the accuracy of his charges before publishing them.[4]

What we do have before us is a case in which a teacher has made erroneous public statements upon issues then currently the subject of public attention, which are critical of his ultimate employer but which are neither shown nor can be presumed to have in any way either impeded the teacher's proper performance of his daily duties in the classroom[5] or to have interfered with the regular operation of the schools generally. In these circumstances we conclude that the interest of the school administration in limiting teachers' opportunities to contribute to public debate is not significantly greater than its interest in limiting a similar contribution by any member of the general public.

IV.

The public interest in having free and unhindered debate on matters of public importance—the core value of the Free Speech Clause

---

4. There is likewise no occasion furnished by this case for consideration of the extent to which teachers can be required by narrowly drawn grievance procedures to submit complaints about the operation of the schools to their superiors for action thereon prior to bringing the complaints before the public.

5. We also note that this case does not present a situation in which a teacher's public statements are so without foundation as to call into question his fitness to perform his duties in the classroom. In such a case, of course, the statements would merely be evidence of the teacher's general competence, or lack thereof, and not an independent basis for dismissal.

of the First Amendment—is so great that it has been held that a State cannot authorize the recovery of damages by a public official for defamatory statements directed at him except when such statements are shown to have been made either with knowledge of their falsity or with reckless disregard for their truth or falsity. New York Times Co. v. Sullivan, 376 U.S. 254 (1964); St. Amant v. Thompson, 390 U.S. 727 (1968). Compare Linn v. United States Plant Guard Workers, 383 U.S. 53 (1966). The same test has been applied to suits for invasion of privacy based on false statements where a "matter of public interest" is involved. Time, Inc. v. Hill, 385 U.S. 374 (1967). It is therefore perfectly clear that, were appellant a member of the general public, the State's power to afford the appellee Board of Education or its members any legal right to sue him for writing the letter at issue here would be limited by the requirement that the letter be judged by the standard laid down in *New York Times*.

This Court has also indicated, in more general terms, that statements by public officials on matters of public concern must be accorded First Amendment protection despite the fact that the statements are directed at their nominal superiors. Garrison v. State of Louisiana, 379 U.S. 64 (1964); Wood v. Georgia, 370 U.S. 375 (1962). In *Garrison,* the *New York Times* test was specifically applied to a case involving a criminal defamation conviction stemming from statements made by a district attorney about the judges before whom he regularly appeared.

While criminal sanctions and damage awards have a somewhat different impact on the exercise of the right to freedom of speech from dismissal from employment, it is apparent that the threat of dismissal from public employment is nonetheless a potent means of inhibiting speech. We have already noted our disinclination to make an across-the-board equation of dismissal from public employment for remarks critical of superiors with awarding damages in a libel suit by a public official for similar criticism. However, in a case such as the present one, in which the fact of employment is only tangentially and insubstantially involved in the subject matter of the public communication made by a teacher, we conclude that it is necessary to regard the teacher as the member of the general public he seeks to be.

In sum, we hold that, in a case such as this, absent proof of false statements knowingly or recklessly made by him,[6] a teacher's exercise of his right to speak on issues of public importance may not furnish the basis for his dismissal from public employment. Since no such showing has been made in this case regarding appellant's letter, see Appendix, *infra,* his dismissal for writing it cannot be upheld and the judgment of the Illinois Supreme Court must, accordingly, be reversed and the case remanded for further proceedings not inconsistent with this opinion. It is so ordered.

Judgment reversed and case remanded with directions.

---

6. Because we conclude that appellant's statements were not knowingly or recklessly false, we have no occasion to pass upon the additional question whether a statement that was knowingly or recklessly false would, if it were neither shown nor could reasonably be presumed to have had any harmful effects, still be protected by the First Amendment. See also n. 5, *supra.*

* * *

MR. JUSTICE WHITE, concurring in part and dissenting in part.

The Court holds that truthful statements by a school teacher critical of the school board are within the ambit of the First Amendment. So also are false statements innocently or negligently made. The State may not fire the teacher for making either unless, as I gather it, there are special circumstances, not present in this case, demonstrating an overriding state interest, such as the need for confidentiality or the special obligations which a teacher in a particular position may owe to his superiors.[25] The core of today's decision is the holding that Pickering's discharge must be tested by the standard of New York Times Co. v. Sullivan, 376 U.S. 254 (1964). To this extent I am in agreement.

The Court goes on, however, to reopen a question I had thought settled by *New York Times* and the cases that followed it, particularly Garrison v. Louisiana, 379 U.S. 64 (1964). The Court devotes several pages to reexamining the facts in order to reject the determination below that Pickering's statements harmed the school system, *ante*, when the question of harm is clearly irrelevant given the Court's determination that Pickering's statements were neither knowingly nor recklessly false and its ruling that in such circumstances a teacher may not be fired even if the statements are injurious. The Court then gratuitously suggests that when statements are found to be knowingly or recklessly false, it is an open question whether the First Amendment still protects them unless they are shown or can be presumed to have caused harm. *Ante* n. 6. Deliberate or reckless falsehoods serve no First Amendment ends and deserve no protection under that Amendment. The Court unequivocally recognized this in *Garrison,* where after reargument the Court said that "the knowingly false statement and the false statement made with reckless disregard of the truth, do not enjoy constitutional protection." 379 U.S. at 75. The Court today neither explains nor justifies its withdrawal from the firm stand taken in *Garrison.* As I see it, a teacher may be fired without violation of the First Amendment for knowingly or recklessly making false statements regardless of their harmful impact on the schools. As the Court holds, however, in the absence of special circumstances he may not be fired if his statements were true or only negligently false, even if there is some harm to the school system. I therefore see no basis or necessity for the Court's foray into fact-finding with respect to whether the record supports a finding as to injury.[26] If Pickering's false statements were

25. See *ante*, at nn. 3, 4. The Court does not elaborate upon its suggestion that there may be situations in which, with reference to certain areas of public comment, a teacher may have special obligations to his superiors. It simply holds that in this case, with respect to the particular public comment made by Pickering, he is more like a member of the general public and, apparently, too remote from the school board to require placing him into any special category. Further, as I read the Court's opinion, it does not foreclose the possibility that under the First Amendment a school system may have an enforceable rule, applicable to teachers, that public statements about school business must first be submitted to the authorities to check for accuracy.

26. Even if consideration of harm were necessary in this case, I could not join the Court in concluding on this record that

either knowingly or recklessly made, injury to the school system becomes irrelevant, and the First Amendment would not prevent his discharge. For the State to be constitutionally precluded from terminating his employment, reliance on some other constitutional provision would be required.

Nor can I join the Court in its findings with regard to whether Pickering knowingly or recklessly published false statements. Neither the State in presenting its evidence nor the state tribunals in arriving at their findings and conclusions of law addressed themselves to the elements of the new standard which the Court holds the First Amendment to require in the circumstances of this case. Indeed, the state courts expressly rejected the applicability of both *New York Times* and *Garrison*. I find it wholly unsatisfactory for this Court to make the initial determination of knowing or reckless falsehood from the cold record now before us. It would be far more appropriate to remand this case to the state courts for further proceedings in light of the constitutional standard which the Court deems applicable to this case, once the relevant facts have been ascertained in appropriate proceedings.

UNITED STATES CIVIL SERVICE COMMISSION v. NATIONAL ASSOCIATION OF LETTER CARRIERS

Supreme Court of the United States, 1973.
413 U.S. 548, 93 S.Ct. 2880, 37 L.Ed.2d 796.

MR. JUSTICE WHITE delivered the opinion of the Court.

On December 11, 1972, we noted probable jurisdiction of this appeal, 409 U.S. 1058, based on a jurisdictional statement presenting the single question whether the prohibition in § 9(a) of the Hatch Act, now codified in 5 U.S.C. § 7324(a)(2), against federal employees taking "an active part in political management or in political campaigns," is unconstitutional on its face. Section 7324(a) provides:

> "An employee in an Executive agency or an individual employed by the government of the District of Columbia may not—
>
> "(1) use his official authority or influence for the purpose of interfering with or affecting the result of an election; or
>
> "(2) take an active part in political campaigns.
>
> "For the purpose of this subsection, the phrase 'an active part in political management or in political campaigns' means those acts of political management or political campaigning which were prohibited on the part of employees in the competitive service before July 19, 1940, by determinations of the Civil Service Commission under the rules prescribed by the Presi-

harm to the school administration was not proved and could not be presumed.

dent."[1]

A divided three-judge court sitting in the District of Columbia had held the section unconstitutional. 346 F.Supp. 578 (1972). We reverse the judgment of the District Court.

I

The case began when the National Association of Letter Carriers, six individual federal employees and certain local Democratic and Republican political committees filed a complaint, asserting on behalf of themselves and all federal employees that 5 U.S.C. § 7324(a)(2) was unconstitutional on its face and seeking an injunction against its enforcement.

Each of the plaintiffs alleged that the Civil Service Commission was enforcing, or threatening to enforce, the Hatch Act's prohibition against active participation in political management or political campaigns with respect to certain defined activity in which that plaintiff desired to engage.[3] The Union, for example, stated among other things that its members desired to campaign for candidates for public office. The Democratic and Republican Committees complained of not being able to get federal employees to run for state and local offices. Plaintiff Hummel stated that he was aware of the provision of the Hatch Act and that the activities he desired to engage in would violate that Act as, for example, his participating as a delegate in a party convention or holding office in a political club.

* * *

II

As the District Court recognized, the constitutionality of the Hatch Act's ban on taking an active part in political management or political campaigns has been here before. This very prohibition was attacked in the *Mitchell* case [1947] by a labor union and various federal employees as being violative of the First, Ninth, and Tenth Amendments and as contrary to the Fifth Amendment by being vague and indefinite, arbitrarily discriminatory, and a deprivation of liberty. The Court there first determined that with respect to all but one of the plaintiffs there was no case or controversy present within the meaning of Art. III because the Court could only speculate as to the type of political activity the appellants there desired to engage in or as to the contents of their proposed public statements or the circumstances of their

---

1. The Hatch Act is found in Titles 5 and 18 of the United States Code, both of which have been enacted into positive law. 80 Stat. 378, 62 Stat. 683. Section 7324(a)(2) of Title 5 is derived from two sections in the Act, with the prohibition against certain political activity being found in § 9(a), 53 Stat. 1148, while the portion defining the proscribed activity stems from § 15, 54 Stat. 771.

3. The Union alleged that its members were desirous of

"a. Running in local elections for such offices as school board member, city council member or mayor.

"b. Writing letters on political subjects to newspapers.

"c. Participating as a delegate in a political convention and running for office in a political party.

"d. Campaigning for candidates for political office." * * *

publication. As to the plaintiff Poole, however, the Court noted that "[h]e was a ward executive committeeman of a political party and was politically active on election day as a worker at the polls and a paymaster for the services of other party workers." * * *

The Government, the Court thought, was empowered to prevent federal employees from contributing energy as well as from collecting money for partisan political ends: "Congress and the President are responsible for an efficient public service. If, in their judgment, efficiency may be best obtained by prohibiting active participation by classified employees in politics as party officers or workers, we see no constitutional objection." *Id.*, at 99 (footnote omitted). Another Congress might determine otherwise, but "[t]he teaching of experience * * * evidently led Congress to enact the Hatch Act," *id.*, at 99, which the Court refused to invalidate and which it viewed as leaving "untouched full participation by employees in political decisions at the ballot box and forbids only the partisan activity of federal personnel deemed offensive to efficiency." *Ibid.* The Act did not interfere with a "wide range of public activities." *Id.*, at 100. It was "only partisan political activity that is interdicted. * * * [Only] active participation in political management and political campaigns [is proscribed]. Expressions, public or private, on public affairs, personalities and matters of public interest, not an object of party action, are unrestricted by law so long as the Government employee does not direct his activities toward party success." *Ibid.* The Court concluded that what Mr. Poole had done was within the power of Congress and the Executive to prevent.

We hesitatingly reaffirm the *Mitchell* holding that Congress had, and has, the power to prevent Mr. Poole and others like him from holding a party office, working at the polls, and acting as party paymaster for other party workers. An Act of Congress going no farther would in our view unquestionably be valid. So would it be if, in plain and understandable language, the statute forbade activities such as organizing a political party or club; actively participating in fund-raising activities for a partisan candidate or political party; becoming a partisan candidate for, or campaigning for, an elective public office; actively managing the campaign of a partisan candidate for public office; initiating or circulating a partisan nominating petition or soliciting votes for a partisan candidate for public office; or serving as a delegate, alternative or proxy to a political party convention. Our judgment is that neither the First Amendment nor any other provision of the Constitution invalidates a law barring this kind of partisan political conduct by federal employees.

* * *

[A]s the Court held in Pickering v. Board of Education, 391 U.S. 563, 568 (1968), the government has an interest in regulating the conduct and "the speech of its employees that differ[s] significantly from those it possesses in connection with regulation of speech of the citizenry in general. The problem in any case is to arrive at a balance between the interests of the [employee], as a citizen, in commenting upon matters of public concern and the interest of the [government], as an employer, in promoting the efficiency of the public services it performs through its employees." Although Congress is free to strike a different balance than it has, if it so chooses, we think the balance it has so far struck is sustainable by the obviously important interests sought to be served by the limitations on partisan political activities now contained in the Hatch Act.

* * *

III

But however constitutional the proscription of identifiable partisan conduct in understandable language may be, the District Court's judgment was that § 7324(a)(2) was both unconstitutionally vague and fatally overbroad. Appellees make the same contentions here, but we cannot agree that the section is unconstitutional on its face for either reason.

* * *

We take quite a different view of the statute. As we see it, our task is not to destroy the Act if we can, but to construe it, if consistent with the will of Congress, so as to comport with constitutional limitations. With this in mind and having examined with some care the proceedings surrounding the passage of the 1940 Act and adoption of the substitute for § 15, we think it appears plainly enough that Congress intended to deprive the Civil Service Commission of rulemaking power in the sense of exercising a subordinate legislative role in fashioning a more expansive definition of the kind of conduct that would violate the prohibition against taking an active part in political management or political campaigns. But it is equally plain, we think, that Congress accepted the fact that the Commission had been performing its investigative and adjudicative role under Civil Service Rule I since 1907 and that the Commission had, on a case-by-case basis, fleshed out the meaning of Rule I and so developed a body of law with respect to what partisan conduct by federal employees was forbidden by the rule. 86 Cong.Rec. 2342, 2353. It is also apparent, in our view, that the rules that had evolved over the years from repeated adjudications were subject to sufficiently clear and summary statement for the guidance of the classified service. * * *

* * *

Whatever might be the difficulty with a provision against taking "active part in political management or in political campaigns," the Act specifically provides that the employee retains the right to vote as he chooses and to express his opinion on political subjects and candidates. The Act exempts research and educational activities supported by the District of Columbia or by religious, philanthropic, or cultural organizations, 5 U.S.C. § 7324(c); and § 7326 exempts nonpartisan political activity: questions, that is, that are not identified with national or state political parties are not covered by the Act, including issues with respect to constitutional amendments, referendums, approval of municipal ordinances, and the like. Moreover, the plain import of the 1940 amendment to the Hatch Act is that the proscription against taking an active part in the proscribed activities is not open-ended but is limited to those rules and proscriptions that had been developed under Civil Service Rule I up to the date of the passage of the 1940 Act. Those rules, as refined by further adjudications within the outer limits of the 1940 rules, were restated by the Commission in 1970 in the form of regulations specifying the conduct that would be prohibited or permitted by § 7324 and its companion sections.

We have set out these regulations in the margin.[21] * * *

---

21. The pertinent regulations, appearing in 5 CFR pt. 733, provide:

"PERMISSIBLE ACTIVITIES

"§ 733.111 Permissible activities.

"(a) All employees are free to engage in political activity to the widest extent consistent with the restrictions imposed by law and this subpart. Each employee retains the right to—

"(1) Register and vote in any election;

"(2) Express his opinion as an individual privately and publicly on political subjects and candidates;

"(3) Display a political picture, sticker, badge, or button;

"(4) Participate in the nonpartisan activities of a civic, community, social, labor, or professional organization, or of a similar organization;

"(5) Be a member of a political party or other political organization and participate in its activities to the extent consistent with law;

"(6) Attend a political convention, rally, fund-raising function; or other political gathering;

"(7) Sign a political petition as an individual;

"(8) Make a financial contribution to a political party or organization;

"(9) Take an active part, as an independent candidate, or in support of an independent candidate, in a partisan election covered by § 733.124;

"(10) Take an active part, as a candidate or in support of a candidate, in a nonpartisan election;

"(11) Be politically active in connection with a question which is not specifically identified with a political party, such as a constitutional amendment, referendum, approval of a municipal ordinance or any other question or issue of a similar character;

"(12) Serve as an election judge or clerk, or in a similar position to perform nonpartisan duties as prescribed by State or local law; and

"(13) Otherwise participate fully in public affairs except as prohibited by law, in a manner which does not materially compromise his efficiency or integrity as an employee or the neutrality, efficiency, or integrity of his agency.

"(b) Paragraph (a) of this section does not authorize an employee to engage in political activity in violation of law, while on duty, or while in a uniform that identifies him as an employee. The head of an agency may prohibit or limit the participation of an employee or class of employees of his agency in an activity permitted by paragraph (a) of this section, if participation in the activity would interfere with the efficient performance of official duties, or create a conflict or apparent conflict of interests.

"PROHIBITED ACTIVITIES

"§ 733.121. Use of official authority; prohibition.

"An employee may not use his official authority or influence for the purpose of interfering with or affecting the result of an election.

"§ 733.122. Political management and political campaigning; prohibitions.

"(a) An employee may not take an active part in political management or in a political campaign, except as permitted by this subpart.

"(b) Activities prohibited by paragraph (a) of this section include but are not limited to—

"(1) Serving as an officer of a political party, a member of a National, State, or local committee of a political party, an officer or member of a committee of a partisan political club, or being a candidate for any of these positions;

"(2) Organizing or reorganizing a political party organization or political club;

"(3) Directly or indirectly soliciting, receiving, collecting, handling, disbursing, or accounting for assessments, contributions,

* * *

It is also important in this respect that the Commission has established a procedure by which an employee in doubt about the validity of a proposed course of conduct may seek and obtain advice from the Commission and thereby remove any doubt there may be as to the meaning of the law, at least insofar as the Commission itself is concerned.

Neither do we discern anything fatally overbroad about the statute when it is considered in connection with the Commission's construction of its terms represented by the 1970 regulations we now have before us. The major difficulties in this respect again relate to the prohibition in §§ 733.122(a)(10) and (12) on endorsements in advertisements, broadcasts, and literature and on speaking at political party meetings in support of partisan candidates for public or party office. But these restrictions are clearly stated, they are political acts normally performed only in the context of partisan campaigns by one taking an active role in them, and they are sustainable for the same reasons that the other acts of political campaigning are constitutionally proscribable. They do not, therefore, render the remainder of the statute vulnerable by reason of overbreadth.

Even if the provisions forbidding partisan campaign endorsements and speechmaking were to be considered in some respects unconstitutionally overbroad, we would not invalidate the entire statute as the District Court did. The remainder of the statute, as we have said, covers a whole range of easily identifiable and constitutionally proscribable partisan conduct on the part of federal employees, and the extent to which pure expression is impermissibly threatened, if at all, by §§ 733.122(a)(10) and (12), does not in our view make the statute substantially overbroad and so invalid on its face. Broadrick v. Oklahoma, 413 U.S. 601.

For the foregoing reasons, the judgment of the District Court is reversed.

So ordered.

or other funds for a partisan political purpose;

"(4) Organizing, selling tickets to, promoting, or actively participating in a fundraising activity of a partisan candidate, political party, or political club;

"(5) Taking an active part in managing the political campaign of a partisan candidate for public office or political party office;

"(6) Becoming a partisan candidate for, or campaigning for, an elective public office;

"(7) Soliciting votes in support of or in opposition to a partisan candidate for public office or political party office;

"(8) Acting as recorder, watcher, challenger, or similar officer at the polls on behalf of a political party or partisan candidate;

"(9) Driving voters to the polls on behalf of a political party or partisan candidate;

"(10) Endorsing or opposing a partisan candidate for public office or political party office in a political advertisement, a broadcast, campaign literature, or similar material;

"(11) Serving as a delegate, alternate, or proxy to a political party convention;

"(12) Addressing a convention, caucus, rally, or similar gathering of a political party in support of or in opposition to a partisan candidate for public office or political party office; and

"(13) Initiating or circulating a partisan nominating petition."

* * *

MR. JUSTICE DOUGLAS, with whom MR. JUSTICE BRENNAN and MR. JUSTICE MARSHALL concur, dissenting.

The Hatch Act by § 9(a) prohibits federal employees from taking "an active part in political management or in political campaigns." Some of the employees, whose union is speaking for them, want

"to run in state and local elections for the school board, for city council, for mayor";

"to write letters on political subjects to newspapers";

"to be a delegate in a political convention";

"to run for an office and hold office in a political party or political club";

"to campaign for candidates for political office";

"to work at polling places in behalf of a political party."

There is no definition of what "an active part * * * in political campaigns" means. The Act incorporates over 3,000 rulings of the Civil Service Commission between 1886 and 1940 and many hundreds of rulings since 1940. But even with that gloss on the Act, the critical phrases lack precision. In 1971 the Commission published a three-volume work entitled Political Activities Reporter which contains over 800 of its decisions since the enactment of the Hatch Act. One can learn from studying those volumes that it is not "political activity" to march in a band during a political parade or to wear political badges or to "participate fully in public affairs, except as prohibited by law, in a manner which does not materially compromise his efficiency or integrity as an employee or the neutrality, efficiency, or integrity of his agency." 5 CFR § 733.111(1)(13).

That is to say, some things, like marching in a band, are clear. Others are pregnant with ambiguity as "participate fully in public affairs, except as prohibited by law, in a manner which does not materially compromise, etc. Permission to "[t]ake an active part * * * in a non-partisan election," 5 CFR § 733.111(1)(10), also raises large questions of uncertainty because one may be partisan for a person, an issue, a candidate without feeling an identification with one political party or the other.

The District Court felt that the prohibitions in the Act are "worded in generalities that lack precision," 346 F.Supp., 578, 582, with the result that it is hazardous for an employee "if he ventures to speak on a political matter since he will not know when his words or acts relating to political subjects will offend." *Id.*, at 582–583.

The chilling effect of these vague and generalized prohibitions is so obvious as not to need elaboration. * * *

* * *

Mitchell is of a different vintage from the present case. Since its date, a host of decisions have illustrated the need for narrowly drawn statutes that touch First Amendment rights. * * *

* * *

A nursing assistant at a veterans' hospital put an ad in a newspaper reading:

> "To All My Many Friends of Poplar Bluff and Butler County I want to take this opportunity to ask your vote and support in the election, TUESDAY, AUGUST 7th. A very special person is seeking the Democratic nomination for Sheriff. I do not have to tell you of his qualifications, his past records stand.
>
> "This person is my dad, Lester (Less) Massingham.
>
> "THANK YOU
>
> "WALLACE (WALLY) MASSINGHAM"

He was held to have violated the Act. Massingham, 1 Political Activity Reporter 792, 793 (1959).

Is a letter a permissible "expression" of views or a prohibited "solicitation?" The Solicitor General says it is a "permissible" expression; but the Commission ruled otherwise. For an employee who does not have the Solicitor General as counsel great consequences flow from an innocent decision. He may lose his job. Therefore the most prudent thing is to do nothing. Thus is self-imposed censorship imposed on many nervous people who live on narrow economic margins.

I would strike this provision of the law down as unconstitutional so that a new start may be made on this old problem that confuses and restricts nearly five million federal, state, and local public employees today that live under the present Act.

MT. HEALTHY CITY SCHOOL DISTRICT BOARD OF EDUCATION v. DOYLE

Supreme Court of the United States, 1977.
429 U.S. 274, 97 S.Ct. 568, 50 L.Ed.2d 471.

MR. JUSTICE REHNQUIST delivered the opinion of the Court.

Respondent Doyle sued petitioner Mt. Healthy Board of Education in the United States District Court for the Southern District of Ohio. Doyle claimed that the Board's refusal to renew his contract in 1971 violated his rights under the First and Fourteenth Amendments to the United States Constitution. After a bench trial the District Court held that Doyle was entitled to reinstatement with backpay. The Court of Appeals for the Sixth Circuit affirmed the judgment, * * * and we granted the Board's petition for certiorari * * *.

* * *

Doyle was first employed by the Board in 1966. He worked under one-year contracts for the first three years, and under a two-year contract from 1969 to 1971. In 1969 he was elected president of the Teachers' Association, in which position he worked to expand the subjects of direct negotiation between the Association and the Board of Education. During Doyle's one-year term as president of the Association, and during the succeeding year when he served on its executive committee, there was apparently some tension in relations between the Board and the Association.

Beginning early in 1970, Doyle was involved in several incidents not directly connected with his role in the Teachers' Association. In one instance, he engaged in an argument with another teacher which culminated in the other teacher's slapping him. Doyle subsequently refused to accept an apology and insisted upon some punishment for the other teacher. His persistence in the matter resulted in the suspension of both teachers for one day, which was followed by a walkout by a number of other teachers, which in turn resulted in the lifting of the suspensions.

On other occasions, Doyle got into an argument with employees of the school cafeteria over the amount of spaghetti which had been served him; referred to students, in connection with a disciplinary complaint, as "sons of bitches"; and made an obscene gesture to two girls in connection with their failure to obey commands made in his capacity as cafeteria supervisor. Chronologically the last in the series of incidents which respondent was involved in during his employment by the Board was a telephone call by him to a local radio station. It was the Board's consideration of this incident which the court below found to be a violation of the First and Fourteenth Amendments.

In February 1971, the principal circulated to various teachers a memorandum relating to teacher dress and appearance, which was apparently prompted by the view of some in the administration that there was a relationship between teacher appearance and public support for bond issues. Doyle's response to the receipt of the memorandum—on a subject which he apparently understood was to be settled by joint teacher-administration action—was to convey the substance of the memorandum to a disc jockey at WSAI, a Cincinnati radio station, who promptly announced the adoption of the dress code as a news item. Doyle subsequently apologized to the principal, conceding that he should have made some prior communication of his criticism to the school administration.

Approximately one month later the superintendent made his customary annual recommendations to the Board as to the rehiring of nontenured teachers. He recommended that Doyle not be rehired. The same recommendation was made with respect to nine other teachers in the district, and in all instances, including Doyle's, the recommendation was adopted by the Board. Shortly after being notified of this decision, respondent requested a statement of reasons for the Board's actions. He received a statement citing "a notable lack of tact in handling professional matters which leaves much doubt as to your sincerity in establishing good school relationships." That general statement was followed by references to the radio station incident and to the obscene gesture incident.[1]

1. "I. You have shown a notable lack of tact in handling professional matters

The District Court found that all of these incidents had in fact occurred. It concluded that respondent Doyle's telephone call to the radio station was "clearly protected by the First Amendment," and that because it had played a "substantial part" in the decision of the Board not to renew Doyle's employment, he was entitled to reinstatement with backpay. App. to Pet. for Cert. 12–13a. The District Court did not expressly state what test it was applying in determining that the incident in question involved conduct protected by the First Amendment, but simply held that the communication to the radio station was such conduct. The Court of Appeals affirmed in a brief *per curiam* opinion. 529 F.2d 524.

* * *

* * * There is no suggestion by the Board that Doyle violated any established policy, or that its reaction to his communication to the radio station was anything more than an ad hoc response to Doyle's action in making the memorandum public. We therefore accept the District Court's finding that the communication was protected by the First and Fourteenth Amendments. We are not, however, entirely in agreement with that court's manner of reasoning from this finding to the conclusion that Doyle is entitled to reinstatement with backpay.

The District Court made the following "conclusions" on this aspect of the case:

> "1) If a non-permissible reason, e.g., exercise of First Amendment rights, played a substantial part in the decision not to renew—even in the face of other permissible grounds— the decision may not stand (citations omitted).
>
> "2) A non-permissible reason did play a substantial part. That is clear from the letter of the Superintendent immediately following the Board's decision, which stated two reasons— the one, the conversation with the radio station clearly protected by the First Amendment. * * *

At the same time, though, it stated that

"[i]n fact, as this Court sees it and finds, both the Board and the Superintendent were faced with a situation in which there did exist in fact reason * * * independent of any First Amendment rights or exercise thereof, to not extend tenure." *Id.*, at 12a.

Since respondent Doyle had no tenure, and there was therefore not even a state-law requirement of "cause" or "reason" before a decision

---

which leaves much doubt as to your sincerity in establishing good school relationships.

"A. You assumed the responsibility to notify W.S.A.I. Radio Station in regards to the suggestion of the Board of Education that teachers establish an appropriate dress code for professional people. This raised much concern not only within this community, but also in neighboring communities.

"B. You used obscene gestures to correct students in a situation in the cafeteria causing considerable concern among those students present.

"Sincerely yours,
"Rex Ralph
"Superintendent"

could be made not to renew his employment, it is not clear what the District Court meant by this latter statement. * * *

* * * The difficulty with the rule enunciated by the District Court is that it would require reinstatement in cases where a dramatic and perhaps abrasive incident is inevitably on the minds of those responsible for the decision to rehire, and does indeed play a part in that decision—even if the same decision would have been reached had the incident not occurred. The constitutional principle at stake is sufficiently vindicated if such an employee is placed in no worse a position than if he had not engaged in the conduct. A borderline or marginal candidate should not have the employment question resolved against him because of constitutionally protected conduct. But that same candidate ought not to be able, by engaging in such conduct, to prevent his employer from assessing his performance record and reaching a decision not to rehire on the basis of that record, simply because the protected conduct makes the employer more certain of the correctness of its decision.

* * *

Initially, in this case, the burden was properly placed upon respondent to show that his conduct was constitutionally protected, and that this conduct was a "substantial factor"—or, to put in it other words, that it was a "motivating factor" in the Board's decision not to rehire him. Respondent having carried that burden, however, the District Court should have gone on to determine whether the Board had shown by a preponderance of the evidence that it would have reached the same decision as to respondent's reemployment even in the absence of the protected conduct.

We cannot tell from the District Court opinion and conclusions, nor from the opinion of the Court of Appeals affirming the judgment of the District Court, what conclusion those courts would have reached had they applied this test. The judgment of the Court of Appeals is therefore vacated, and the case remanded for further proceedings consistent with this opinion.

So ordered.

GIVHAN v. WESTERN LINE CONSOLIDATED SCHOOL DISTRICT

Supreme Court of the United States, 1979.
439 U.S. 410, 99 S.Ct. 693, 58 L.Ed.2d 619.

Mr. Justice Rehnquist delivered the opinion of the Court.

Petitioner Bessie Givhan was dismissed from her employment as a junior high English teacher at the end of the 1970–71 school year.[1] At

1. In a letter to petitioner, dated July 28, 1971, District Superintendent C.L. Morris gave the following reasons for the decision not to renew her contract:

the time of petitioner's termination, respondent Western Line Consolidated School District was the subject of a desegregation order entered by the United States District Court for the Northern District of Mississippi. Petitioner filed a complaint * * * seeking reinstatement on the dual grounds that nonrenewal of her contract * * * infringed her right of free speech secured by the First and Fourteenth Amendments of the United States Constitution. In an effort to show that its decision was justified, respondent School District introduced evidence of, among other things, a series of private encounters between petitioner and the school principal in which petitioner allegedly made "petty and unreasonable demands" in a manner variously described by the principal as "insulting," "hostile," "loud," and "arrogant." After a two-day bench trial, the District Court held that petitioner's termination had violated the First Amendment. Finding that petitioner had made "demands" on but two occasions and that those demands "were neither 'petty' nor 'unreasonable,' insomuch as all the complaints in question involved employment policies and practices at [the] school which [petitioner] conceived to be racially discriminatory in purpose or effect," the District Court concluded that "the primary reason was the school district's failure to renew [petitioner's] contract was her criticism of the policies and the practices of the school district, especially the school to which she was assigned to teach." * * * Accordingly, the District Court held that the dismissal violated petitioner's First Amendment rights, as enunciated in Perry v. Sindermann, 408 U.S. 593 (1972), and Pickering v. Board of Education, 391 U.S. 563 (1968), and ordered her reinstatement.

The Court of Appeals for the Fifth Circuit reversed. * * * Although it found the District Court's findings not clearly erroneous, the Court of Appeals concluded that because petitioner had privately expressed her complaints and opinions to the principal, her expression was not protected under the First Amendment. * * * We are unable to agree that private expression of one's views is beyond constitutional protection, and therefore reverse the Court of Appeals' judgment and remand the case so that it may consider the contentions of the parties freed from this erroneous view of the First Amendment.

This Court's decisions in *Pickering, Perry,* and *Mt. Healthy* do not support the conclusion that a public employee forfeits his protection against governmental abridgment of freedom of speech if he decides to express his views privately rather than publicly. While those cases each arose in the context of a public employee's public expression, the rule to be derived from them is not dependent on that largely coincidental fact.

* * *

The First Amendment forbids abridgment of the "freedom of speech." Neither the Amendment itself nor our decisions indicate that

"(1) [A] flat refusal to administer standardized national tests to the pupils in your charge; (2) an announced intention not to co-operate with the administration of the Glen Allan Attendance Center; (3) and an antagonistic and hostile attitude to the administration of the Glen Allan Attendance Center demonstrated throughout the school year."

this freedom is lost to the public employee who arranges to communicate privately with his employer rather than to spread his views before the public. We decline to adopt such a view of the First Amendment.

* * *

* * * Since this case was tried before *Mt. Healthy* was decided, it is not surprising that respondents did not attempt to prove in the District Court that the decision not to rehire petitioner would have been made even absent consideration of her "demands." * * *

Accordingly, the judgment of the Court of Appeals is vacated insofar as it relates to petitioner, and the case is remanded for further proceedings consistent with this opinion.

So ordered.

MR. JUSTICE STEVENS, concurring.

Because this Court's opinion in Mt. Healthy City Bd. of Ed. v. Doyle, 429 U.S. 274, had not been announced when the District Court decided this case, it did not expressly find that respondents would have rehired petitioner if she had not engaged in constitutionally protected conduct. The District Court did find, however, that petitioner's protected conduct was the "primary" reason for respondents' decision.* The Court of Appeals regarded that finding as foreclosing respondents' *Mt. Healthy* claim. In essence, the Court of Appeals concluded that the District Court would have made an appropriate finding in the issue if it had had access to our *Mt. Healthy* opinion.

My understanding of the District Court's finding is the same as the Court of Appeals'. Nevertheless, I agree that the District Court should have the opportunity to decide whether there is any need for further proceedings on the issue. If that court regards the present record as adequate to enable it to supplement its original findings without taking additional evidence, it is free to do so. On that understanding, I join the Court's opinion.

CONNICK v. MYERS

Supreme Court of the United States, 1983.
461 U.S. 138, 103 S.Ct. 1684, 75 L.Ed.2d 708.

JUSTICE WHITE delivered the opinion of the Court.

I

The respondent, Sheila Myers, was employed as an assistant District Attorney in New Orleans for five and a half years. She served at the pleasure of petitioner Harry Connick, the District Attorney for Orleans Parish. During this period Myers competently performed her responsibilities of trying criminal cases.

---

* App. to Pet. for cert. 35a. See also *id.*, at 36a, where the District Court stated that petitioner's protected activity was "almost entirely" responsible for her termination.

In the early part of October 1980, Myers was informed that she would be transferred to prosecute cases in a different section of the criminal court. Myers was strongly opposed to the proposed transfer [1] and expressed her view to several of her supervisors, including Connick. Despite her objections, on October 6 Myers was notified that she was being transferred. Myers again spoke with Dennis Waldron, one of the First Assistant District Attorneys, expressing her reluctance to accept the transfer. A number of other office matters were discussed and Myers later testified that, in response to Waldron's suggestion that her concerns were not shared by others in the office, she informed him that she would do some research on the matter.

That night Myers prepared a questionnaire soliciting the views of her fellow staff members concerning office transfer policy, office morale, the need for a grievance committee, the level of confidence in supervisors, and whether employees felt pressured to work in political campaigns. Early the following morning, Myers typed and copied the questionnaire. She also met with Connick who urged her to accept the transfer. She said she would "consider" it. Connick then left the office. Myers then distributed the questionnaire to 15 Assistant District Attorneys. Shortly after noon, Dennis Waldron learned that Myers was distributing the survey. He immediately phoned Connick and informed him that Myers was creating a "mini-insurrection" within the office. Connick returned to the office and told Myers that she was being terminated because of her refusal to accept the transfer. She was also told that her distribution of the questionnaire was considered an act of insubordination. Connick particularly objected to the question which inquired whether employees "had confidence in and would rely on the word" of various superiors in the office, and to a question concerning pressure to work in political campaigns which he felt would be damaging if discovered by the press.

Myers filed suit under 42 U.S.C. § 1983 (1976 ed., Supp. V), contending that her employment was wrongfully terminated because she had exercised her constitutionally protected right of free speech. The District Court agreed, ordered Myers reinstated, and awarded backpay, damages, and attorney's fees. 507 F.Supp. 752 (ED La.1981).[3] The District Court found that although Connick informed Myers that she was being fired because of her refusal to accept a transfer, the facts showed that the questionnaire was the real reason for her termination. The court then proceeded to hold that Myers' questionnaire involved matters of public concern and that the State had not "clearly demonstrated" that the survey "substantially interfered" with the operations of the District Attorney's office.

---

1. Myers' opposition was at least partially attributable to her concern that a conflict of interest would have been created by the transfer because of her participation in a counseling program for convicted defendants released on probation in the section of the criminal court to which she was to be assigned.

3. Petitioner has also objected to the assessment of damages as being in violation of the Eleventh Amendment, and to the award of attorney's fees. Because of our disposition of the case, we do not reach these questions.

Connick appealed to the United States Court of Appeals for the Fifth Circuit, which affirmed on the basis of the District Court's opinion. * * *

II

* * *

A

The District Court got off on the wrong foot in this case by initially finding that, "[t]aken as a whole, the issues presented in the questionnaire relate to the effective functioning of the District Attorney's Office and are matters of public importance and concern." 507 F.Supp., at 758. Connick contends at the outset that no balancing of interests is required in this case because Myers' questionnaire concerned only internal office matters and that such speech is not upon a matter of "public concern," as the term was used in *Pickering*. Although we do not agree that Myers' communication in this case was wholly without First Amendment protection, there is much force to Connick's submission. The repeated emphasis in *Pickering* on the right of a public employee "as a citizen, in commenting upon matters of public concern," was not accidental. This language reiterated in all of *Pickering*'s progeny, reflects both the historical evolvement of the rights of public employees, and the common-sense realization that government offices could not function if every employment decision became a constitutional matter.

* * *

Pickering, its antecedents, and its progeny lead us to conclude that if Myers' questionnaire cannot be fairly characterized as constituting speech on a matter of public concern, it is unnecessary for us to scrutinize the reasons for her discharge. When employee expression cannot be fairly considered as relating to any matter of political, social, or other concern to the community, government officials should enjoy wide latitude in managing their offices, without intrusive oversight by the judiciary in the name of the First Amendment. Perhaps the government employer's dismissal of the worker may not be fair, but ordinary dismissals from government service which violate no fixed tenure or applicable statute or regulation are not subject to judicial review even if the reasons for the dismissal are alleged to be mistaken or unreasonable. * * *

We do not suggest, however, that Myers' speech, even if not touching upon a matter of public concern, is totally beyond the protection of the First Amendment. * * * For example, an employee's false criticism of his employer on grounds not of public concern may be cause for his discharge but would be entitled to the same protection in a libel action accorded an identical statement made by a man on the street. We hold only that when a public employee speaks not as a citizen upon matters of public concern, but instead as an employee upon matters only of personal interest, absent the most unusual circumstances, a federal court is not the appropriate forum in which to review the wisdom of a personnel decision taken by a public agency allegedly in reaction to the employee's behavior. * * * Our responsibility is to ensure that citizens are not deprived of fundamental rights by virtue of working for the government; this does not require a grant of immunity for employee grievances not afforded by the First Amendment to those who do not work for the State.

Whether an employee's speech addresses a matter of public concern must be determined by the content, form, and context of a given statement, as revealed by the whole record.[7] In this case, with but one exception, the questions posed by Myers to her co-workers do not fall under the rubric matters of "public concern." We view the questions pertaining to the confidence and trust that Myers' co-workers possess in various supervisors, the level of office morale, and the need for a grievance committee as mere extensions of Myers' dispute over her transfer to another section of the criminal court. Unlike the dissent, * * *, we do not believe these questions are of public import in evaluating the performance of the District Attorney as an elected official. Myers did not seek to inform the public that the District Attorney's Office was not discharging its governmental responsibilities in the investigation and prosecution of criminal cases. Nor did Myers seek to bring to light actual or potential wrongdoing or breach of public trust on the part of Connick and others. Indeed, the questionnaire, if released to the public, would convey no information at all other than the fact that a single employee is upset with the status quo. While discipline and morale in the workplace are related to an agency's efficient performance of its duties, the focus of Myers' questions is not to evaluate the performance of the office but rather to gather ammunition for another round of controversy with her superiors. These questions reflect one employee's dissatisfaction with a transfer and an attempt to turn that displeasure into a cause célèbre.[8]

* * *

One question in Myers' questionnaire, however, does touch upon a matter of public concern. Question 11 inquires if assistant district attorneys "ever feel pressured to work in political campaigns on behalf of office supported candidates." * * *

B

Because one of the questions in Myers' survey touched upon a matter of public concern and contributed to her discharge, we must determine whether Connick was justified in discharging Myers. Here

---

7. The inquiry into the protected status of speech is one of law, not fact. * * *

8. This is not a case like *Givhan*, where an employee speaks out as a citizen on a matter of general concern, not tied to a personal employment dispute, but arranges to do so privately. Mrs. Givhan's right to protest racial discrimination—a matter inherently of public concern—is not forfeited by her choice of a private forum. 439 U.S., at 415–416. Here, however, a questionnaire not otherwise of public concern does not attain that status because its subject matter could, in different circumstances, have been the topic of communication to the public that might be of general interest. The dissent's analysis of whether discussions of office morale and discipline could be matters of public concern is beside the point—it does not answer whether *this* questionnaire is such speech.

the District Court erred in imposing an unduly onerous burden on the State to justify Myers' discharge. * * *

C

* * *

We agree with the District Court that there is no demonstration here that the questionnaire impeded Myers' ability to perform her responsibilities. The District Court was also correct to recognize that "it is important to the efficient and successful operation of the District Attorney's office for Assistants to maintain close working relationships with their superiors." 507 F.Supp., at 759. Connick's judgment, and apparently also that of his first assistant Dennis Waldron, who characterized Myers' actions as causing a "mini-insurrection," was that Myers' questionnaire was an act of insubordination which interfered with working relationships.[11] When close working relationships are essential to fulfilling public responsibilities, a wide degree of deference to the employer's judgment is appropriate. Furthermore, we do not see the necessity for an employer to allow events to unfold to the extent that the disruption of the office and the destruction of working relationships is manifest before taking action. We caution that a stronger showing may be necessary if the employee's speech more substantially involved matters of public concern.

* * *

Also relevant is the manner, time, and place in which the questionnaire was distributed. * * * Although some latitude in when official work is performed is to be allowed when professional employees are involved, and Myers did not violate announced office policy,[14] the fact that Myers, unlike Pickering, exercised her rights to speech at the office supports Connick's fears that the functioning of his office was endangered.

Finally, the context in which the dispute arose is also significant. This is not a case where an employee, out of purely academic interest, circulated a questionnaire so as to obtain useful research. Myers acknowledges that it is no coincidence that the questionnaire followed upon the heels of the transfer notice. When employee speech concerning office policy arises from an employment dispute concerning the very application of that policy to the speaker, additional weight must be given to the supervisor's view that the employee has threatened the authority of the employer to run the office. * * *

---

11. Waldron testified that from what he had learned of the events on October 7, Myers "was trying to stir up other people not to accept the changes [transfers] that had been made on the memorandum and that were to be implemented." App. 167. In his view, the questionnaire was a "final act of defiance" and that, as a result of Myers' action, "there were going to be some severe problems about the changes." *Ibid.* Connick testified that he reached a similar conclusion after conducting his own investigation. "After I satisfied myself that not only wasn't she accepting the transfer, but that she was affirmatively opposing it and disrupting the routine of the office by this questionnaire. I called her in * * * [and dismissed her]." *Id.,* at 130.

14. The violation of such a rule would strengthen Connick's position. See Mt. Healthy City Board of Ed. v. Doyle, 429 U.S., at 284.

III

Myers' questionnaire touched upon matters of public concern in only a most limited sense; her survey, in our view, is most accurately characterized as an employee grievance concerning internal office policy. The limited First Amendment interest involved here does not require that Connick tolerate action which he reasonably believed would disrupt the office, undermine his authority, and destroy close working relationships. Myers' discharge therefore did not offend the First Amendment. We reiterate, however, the caveat we expressed in *Pickering*, 391 U.S., at 569; "Because of the enormous variety of fact situations in which critical statements by * * * public employees may be thought by their superiors * * * to furnish grounds for dismissal, we do not deem it either appropriate or feasible to attempt to lay down a standard against which all such statements may be judged."

* * * The judgment of the Court of Appeals is

Reversed.

JUSTICE BRENNAN, with whom JUSTICE MARSHALL, JUSTICE BLACKMUN, and JUSTICE STEVENS join, dissenting.

Shelia Myers was discharged for circulating a questionnaire to her fellow Assistant District Attorneys seeking information about the effect of petitioner's personnel policies on employee morale and the overall work performance of the District Attorney's Office. The Court concludes that her dismissal does not violate the First Amendment, primarily because the questionnaire addresses matters that, in the Court's view, are not of public concern. It is hornbook law, however, that speech about "the manner in which government is operated or should be operated" is an essential part of the communications necessary for self-governance the protection of which was a central purpose of the First Amendment. Mills v. Alabama, 384 U.S. 214, 218 (1966). Because the questionnaire addressed such matters and its distribution did not adversely affect the operations of the District Attorney's Office or interfere with Myers' working relationship with her fellow employees, I dissent.

I

* * *

In *Pickering* we held that the First Amendment affords similar protection to critical statements by a public school teacher directed at the Board of Education for whom he worked. 391 U.S., at 574. In so doing, we recognized that "free and open debate" about the operation of public schools "is vital to informed decision-making by the electorate." *Id.*, at 571–572. We also acknowledged the importance of allowing teachers to speak out on school matters.

> "Teachers are, as a class, the members of a community most likely to have informed and definite opinions as to how funds allotted to the operation of the schools should be spent. Accordingly, it is essential that they be able to speak out freely on

such questions without fear of retaliatory dismissal." *Id.,* at 572.

See also *Arnett v. Kennedy,* 416 U.S. 134, 228 (1974) (MARSHALL, J., dissenting) (describing "[t]he importance of Government employees' being assured of their right to freely comment on the conduct of Government, to inform the public of abuses of power and of the misconduct of their superiors * * * ").

Applying these principles, I would hold that Myers' questionnaire addressed matters of public concern because it discussed subjects that could reasonably be expected to be of interest to persons seeking to develop informed opinions about the manner in which the Orleans Parish District Attorney, an elected official charged with managing a vital governmental agency, discharges his responsibilities. The questionnaire sought primarily to obtain information about the impact of the recent transfers on morale in the District Attorney's Office. It is beyond doubt that personnel decisions that adversely affect discipline and morale may ultimately impair an agency's efficient performance of its duties. See *Arnett v. Kennedy, supra,* at 168 (opinion of POWELL, J.). Because I believe the First Amendment protects the right of public employees to discuss such matters so that the public may be better informed about how their elected officials fulfill their responsibilities, I would affirm the District Court's conclusion that the questionnaire related to matters of public importance and concern.

* * *

* * * The proper means to ensure that the courts are not swamped with routine employee grievances mischaracterized as First Amendment cases is not to restrict artificially the concept of "public concern," but to require that adequate weight be given to the public's important interests in the efficient performance of governmental functions and in preserving employee discipline and harmony sufficient to achieve that end. * * *

III

Although the Court finds most of Myers' questionnaire unrelated to matters of public interest, it does hold that one question—asking whether Assistants felt pressured to work in political campaigns on behalf of office-supported candidates—addressed a matter of public importance and concern. The court also recognizes that this determination of public interest must weigh heavily in the balancing of competing interests required by *Pickering.* Having gone that far, however, the Court misapplies the *Pickering* test and holds—against our previous authorities—that a public employer's mere apprehension that speech will be disruptive justifies suppression of that speech when all the objective evidence suggests that those fears are essentially unfounded.

* * *

The District Court weighed all of the relevant factors identified by our cases. It found that petitioner failed to establish that Myers violated either a duty of confidentiality or an office policy. * * *

Noting that most of the copies of the questionnaire were distributed during lunch, it rejected the contention that the distribution of the questionnaire impeded Myers' performance of her duties, and it concluded that "Connick has not shown *any* evidence to indicate that the plaintiff's work performance was adversely affected by her expression."

* * *

The Court accepts all of these findings. See *ante.* It concludes, however, that the District Court failed to give adequate weight to the context in which the questionnaire was distributed and to the need to maintain close working relationships in the District Attorney's Office. In particular, the Court suggests the District Court failed to give sufficient weight to the disruptive potential of Question 10, which asked whether the Assistants had confidence in the word of five named supervisors. *Ante.* The District Court, however, explicitly recognized that this was petitioner's "most forceful argument"; but after hearing the testimony of four of the five supervisors named in the question, it found that the question had no adverse effect on Myers' relationship with her superiors. 507 F.Supp., at 759.

* * *

In this regard, our decision in Tinker v. Des Moines Independent Community School District, 393 U.S. 503 (1969), is controlling. *Tinker* arose in a public school, a context similar to the one in which the present case arose in that the determination of the scope of the Constitution's guarantee of freedom of speech required consideration of the "special characteristics of the * * * environment: in which the expression took place. See *id.,* at 506. At issue was whether public high school students could constitutionally be prohibited from wearing black armbands in school to express their opposition to the Vietnam conflict. The District Court had ruled that such a ban "was reasonable because it was based upon [school officials'] fear of a disturbance from the wearing of armbands." *Id.,* at 508. We found that justification inadequate, because "in our system, undifferentiated fear or apprehension of disturbance is not enough to overcome the right to freedom of expression." *Ibid.* We concluded:

> "In order for the State * * * to justify prohibition of a particular expression of opinion, it must be able to show that its action was caused by something more than a mere desire to avoid the discomfort and unpleasantness that always accompany an unpopular viewpoint. *Certainly where there is no finding and no showing that engaging in the forbidden conduct would 'materially and substantially interfere with the requirements of appropriate discipline in the operation of the school,' the prohibition cannot be sustained."* *Id.,* at 509 (emphasis supplied) (quoting Burnside v. Byars, 363 F.2d 744, 749 (CA5 1966)).

Because the speech at issue addressed matters of public importance, a similar standard should be applied here. * * *

IV

The Court's decision today inevitably will deter public employees from making critical statements about the manner in which government agencies are operated for fear that doing so will provoke their dismissal. As a result, the public will be deprived of valuable information with which to evaluate the performance of elected officials. Because protecting the dissemination of such information is an essential function of the First Amendment, I dissent.

RANKIN v. McPHERSON
Supreme Court of the United States, 1987.
483 U.S. 378, 107 S.Ct. 2891, 97 L.Ed.2d 315.

JUSTICE MARSHALL delivered the opinion of the Court.

The issue in this case is whether a clerical employee in a county Constable's office was properly discharged for remarking, after hearing of an attempt on the life of the President, "If they go for him again, I hope they get him."

I

On January 12, 1981, respondent Ardith McPherson was appointed a deputy in the office of the Constable of Harris County, Texas. The Constable is an elected official who functions as a law enforcement officer. At the time of her appointment, McPherson, a black woman, was 19 years old and had attended college for a year, studying secretarial science. Her appointment was conditional for a 90-day probationary period.

Although McPherson's title was "deputy constable," this was the case only because all employees of the Constable's office, regardless of job function, were deputy constables. * * * She was not a commissioned peace officer, did not wear a uniform, and was not authorized to make arrests or permitted to carry a gun.[2] McPherson's duties were purely clerical. Her work station was a desk at which there was no telephone, in a room to which the public did not have ready access. Her job was to type data from court papers into a computer that maintained an automated record of the status of civil process in the county. Her training consisted of two days of instruction in the operation of her computer terminal.

On March 30, 1981, McPherson and some fellow employees heard on an office radio that there had been an attempt to assassinate the President of the United States. Upon hearing that report, McPherson

---

[2]. In order to serve as a commissioned peace officer, as the Court of Appeals noted, a deputy would have to undergo a background check, a psychological examination, and over 300 hours of training in law enforcement. 786 F.2d 1233, 1237 (CA5 1986). Constable Rankin testified that while his office had on occasion been asked to guard various dignitaries visiting Houston, Tr. 24, a deputy who was not a commissioned peace officer would never be assigned to such duty, id., at 30. Nor would such a deputy even be assigned to serve process. Id., at 32.

engaged a co-worker, Lawrence Jackson, who was apparently her boyfriend, in a brief conversation, which according to McPherson's uncontroverted testimony went as follows:

"Q: What did you say?

"A: I said I felt that that would happen sooner or later.

"Q: Okay. And what did Lawrence say?

"A: Lawrence said, yeah, agreeing with me.

"Q: Okay. Now when you—after Lawrence spoke, then what was your next comment?

"A: Well, we were talking—it's a wonder why they did that. I felt like it would be a black person that did that, because I feel like most of my kind is on welfare and CETA, and they use medicaid, and at the time, I was thinking that's what it was.

" * * * But then after I said that, and then Lawrence said, yeah, he's cutting back medicaid and food stamps. And I said, yeah, welfare and CETA. I said, shoot, if they go for him again, I hope they get him."

McPherson's last remark was overheard by another deputy constable, who, unbeknownst to McPherson was in the room at the time. The remark was reported to Constable Rankin, who summoned McPherson. McPherson readily admitted that she had made the statement, but testified that she told Rankin, upon being asked if she made the statement, "Yes, but I didn't mean anything by it." * * * After their discussion, Rankin fired McPherson.

* * *

II

It is clearly established that a State may not discharge an employee on a basis that infringes that employee's constitutionally protected interest in freedom of speech. * * *

The determination whether a public employer has properly discharged an employee for engaging in speech requires "a balance between the interests of the [employee], as a citizen, in commenting upon matters of public concern and the interest of the State, as an employer, in promoting the efficiency of the public services it performs through its employees." Pickering v. Board of Education, 391 U.S. 563, 568 (1968); Connick v. Myers, 461 U.S. 138, 140 (1983). This balancing is necessary in order to accommodate the dual role of the public employer as a provider of public services and as a government entity operating under the constraints of the First Amendment. On the one hand, public employers are *employers,* concerned with the efficient function of their operations; review of every personnel decision made by a public employer could in the long run, hamper the performance of public functions. On the other hand, "the threat of dismissal from public employment is * * * a potent means of inhibiting speech." *Pickering,* 391 U.S., at 574. Vigilance is necessary to ensure that public employers do not use authority over employees to silence discourse, not because it hampers public functions but simply because superiors disagree with the content of employees' speech.

A

The threshold question in applying this balancing test is whether McPherson's speech may be "fairly characterized as constituting speech on a matter of public concern." *Connick*, 461 U.S., at 146.[7] * * *

Considering the statement in context, as *Connick* requires, discloses that it plainly dealt with a matter of public concern. The statement was made in the course of a conversation addressing the policies of the President's administration.[10] It came on the heels of a news bulletin regarding what is certainly a matter of heightened public attention: an attempt on the life of the President.[11] * * *

B

Because McPherson's statement addressed a matter of public concern, *Pickering* next requires that we balance McPherson's interest in making her statement against "the interest of the State, as an employer, in promoting the efficiency of the public services it performs through its employees." 391 U.S., at 568.[13] The State bears a burden of justifying the discharge on legitimate grounds. *Connick*, 461 U.S., at 150.

In performing the balancing, the statement will not be considered in a vacuum; the manner, time, and place of the employee's expression are relevant, as is the context in which the dispute arose. See id., at 152–153; Givhan v. Western Line Consolidated School Dist., 439 U.S. 410, 415, n. 4 (1979). We have previously recognized as pertinent

---

7. Even where a public employee's speech does not touch upon a matter of public concern, that speech is not "totally beyond the protection of the First Amendment," Connick v. Myers, 461 U.S., at 147, but "absent the most unusual circumstances a federal court is not the appropriate forum in which to review the wisdom of a personnel decision taken by a public agency allegedly in reaction to the employee's behavior." *Ibid.*

10. McPherson actually made the statement at issue not once, but twice, and only in the first instance did she make the statement in the context of a discussion of the President's policies. McPherson repeated the statement to Constable Rankin at his request. We do not consider the second statement independently of the first, however. Having been required by the Constable to repeat her statement, McPherson might well have been deemed insubordinate had she refused. A public employer may not divorce a statement made by an employee from its context by requiring the employee to repeat the statement, and use that statement standing alone as the basis for discharge. Such a tactic could in some cases merely give the employee the choice of being fired for failing to follow orders or for making a statement which, may not warrant the same level of First Amendment protection it merited when originally made.

11. The private nature of the statement does not, contrary to the suggestion of the United States, Brief for United States as *Amicus Curiae* 18, vitiate the status of the statement as addressing a matter of public concern. See Givhan v. Western Line Consolidated School Dist., 439 U.S. 410, 414–416 (1979).

13. We agree with Justice Powell that a purely private statement on a matter of public concern will rarely, if ever, justify discharge of a public employee. * * * To the extent petitioner's claim that McPherson's speech rendered her an unsuitable employee for a law enforcement agency implicates a serious state interest and necessitates the application of the balancing element of the *Pickering* analysis, we proceed at that task.

considerations whether the statement impairs discipline by superiors or harmony among co-workers, has a detrimental impact on close working relationships for which personal loyalty and confidence are necessary, or impedes the performance of the speaker's duties or interferes with the regular operation of the enterprise. Pickering, 391 U.S., at 570–573.

These considerations, and indeed the very nature of the balancing test, make apparent that the state interest element of the test focuses on the effective functioning of the public employer's enterprise. Interference with work, personnel relationships, or the speaker's job performance can detract from the public employer's function; avoiding such interference can be a strong state interest. From this perspective, however, petitioners fail to demonstrate a state interest that outweighs McPherson's First Amendment rights. While McPherson's statement was made at the workplace, there is no evidence that it interfered with the efficient functioning of the office. The Constable was evidently not afraid that McPherson had disturbed or interrupted other employees— he did not inquire to whom respondent had made the remark and testified that he "was not concerned who she had made it to," * * *. In fact, Constable Rankin testified that the possibility of interference with the functions of the Constable's office had not been a consideration in his discharge of respondent and that he did not even inquire whether the remark had disrupted the work of the office.[14]

Nor was there any danger that McPherson had discredited the office by making her statement public. McPherson's speech took place in an area to which there was ordinarily no public access; her remark was evidently made in a private conversation with another employee. There is no suggestion that any member of the general public was present or heard McPherson's statement. Nor is there any evidence that employees other than Jackson who worked in the room even heard the remark. * * *

While the facts underlying Rankin's discharge of McPherson are, despite extensive proceedings in the District Court, still somewhat unclear, it is undisputed that he fired McPherson based on the content of her speech. Evidently because McPherson had made the statement, and because the Constable believed that she "meant it," he decided that she was not a suitable employee to have in a law enforcement agency. But in weighing the State's interest in discharging an employee based on any claim that the content of a statement made by the employee somehow undermines the mission of the public employer, some attention must be paid to the responsibilities of the employee within the agency. The burden of caution employees bear with respect to the words they speak will vary with the extent of authority and public accountability the employee's role entails. Where, as here, an employee serves no confidential, policymaking, or public contact role, the danger to the agency's successful functioning from that employee's private speech is minimal. We cannot believe that every employee in

---

14. He testified: "I did not base my action on whether the work was interrupted or not. I based my action on a statement that was made to me direct." Tr. 45.

Constable Rankin's office, whether computer operator, electrician, or file clerk, is equally required, on pain of discharge, to avoid any statement susceptible of being interpreted by the Constable as an indication that the employee may be unworthy of employment in his law enforcement agency. At some point, such concerns are so removed from the effective functioning of the public employer that they cannot prevail over the free speech rights of the public employee.[18]

This is such a case. McPherson's employment-related interaction with the Constable was apparently negligible. Her duties were purely clerical and were limited solely to the civil process function of the Constable's office. There is no indication that she would ever be in a position to further—or indeed to have any involvement with—the minimal law enforcement activity engaged in by the Constable's office. Given the function of the agency, McPherson's position in the office, and the nature of her statement, we are not persuaded that Rankin's interest in discharging her outweighed her rights under the First Amendment.

Because we agree with the Court of Appeals that McPherson's discharge was improper, the judgment of the Court of Appeals is

Affirmed.

JUSTICE POWELL, concurring.

* * *

There is no dispute that McPherson's comment was made during a private conversation with a co-worker who happened also to be her boyfriend. She had no intention or expectation that it would be overheard or acted on by others. Given this, I think it is unnecessary to engage in the extensive analysis normally required by Connick v. Myers, 461 U.S. 138 (1983), and Pickering v. Board of Education, 391 U.S. 563 (1968). If a statement is on a matter of public concern, as it was here, it will be an unusual case where the employer's legitimate interests will be so great as to justify punishing an employee for this type of private speech that routinely takes place at all levels in the workplace. The risk that a single, offhand comment directed to only one other worker will lower morale, disrupt the work force, or otherwise undermine the mission of the office borders on the fanciful. To the extent that the full constitutional analysis of the competing interests is required, I generally agree with the Court's opinion.

* * *

JUSTICE SCALIA, with whom THE CHIEF JUSTICE, JUSTICE WHITE, and JUSTICE O'CONNOR join, dissenting.

I agree with the proposition, felicitously put by Constable Rankin's counsel, that no law enforcement agency is required by the First

---

18. This is not to say that clerical employees are insulated from discharge where their speech, taking the acknowledged factors into account, truly injures the public interest in the effective functioning of the public employer. Compare McMullen v. Carson, 754 F.2d 936 (CA11 1985) (clerical employee in sheriff's office properly discharged for stating on television news that he was an employee for the sheriff's office and a recruiter for the Ku Klux Klan).

Amendment to permit one of its employees to "ride with the cops and cheer for the robbers." App. 94. The issue in this case is whether Constable Rankin, a law enforcement official, is prohibited by the First Amendment from preventing his employees from saying of the attempted assassination of President Reagan—on the job and within hearing of other employees—"If they go for him again, I hope they get him." The Court, applying the two-prong analysis of Connick v. Myers, 461 U.S. 138 (1983), holds that McPherson's statement was protected by the First Amendment because (1) it "addressed a matter of public concern," and (2) McPherson's interest in making the statement outweighs Rankin's interest in suppressing it. In so doing, the Court significantly and irrationally expands the definition of "public concern"; it also carves out a new and very large class of employees—*i.e.* those in "nonpolicymaking" positions—who, if today's decision is to be believed, can never be disciplined for statements that fall within the Court's expanded definition. Because I believe the Court's conclusions rest upon a distortion of both the record and the Court's prior decisions, I dissent.

I

To appreciate fully why the majority errs in reaching its first conclusion, it is necessary to recall the origins and purposes of *Connick*'s "public concern" requirement. The Court long ago rejected Justice Holmes' approach to the free speech rights of public employees, that "[a policeman] may have a constitutional right to talk politics, but he has no constitutional right to be a policeman," McAuliffe v. Mayor of New Bedford, 155 Mass. 216, 220, 29 N.E. 517 (1892). We have, however, recognized that the government's power as an employer to make hiring and firing decisions on the basis of what its employees and prospective employees say has a much greater scope than its power to regulate expression by the general public. See, *e.g.*, Pickering v. Board of Education, 391 U.S. 563, 568 (1968).

Specifically, we have held that the First Amendment's protection against adverse personnel decisions extends only to speech on matters of "public concern," Connick, supra, at 147–149, which we have variously described as those matters dealing in some way with "the essence of self-government," Garrison v. Louisiana, 379 U.S. 64, 74–75 (1964), matters as to which "free and open debate is vital to informed decisionmaking by the electorate," Pickering, *supra,* at 571–572, and matters as to which "debate * * * [must] be uninhibited, robust, and wide-open,' " Dun & Bradstreet, Inc. v. Greenmoss Builders, Inc., 472 U.S. 749, 755 (1985) (plurality opinion) (quoting New York Times Co. v. Sullivan, 376 U.S. 254, 270 (1964)). In short, speech on matters of public concern is that speech which lies "at the heart of the First Amendment's protection," First Nat'l Bank v. Bellotti, 435 U.S. 765, 776 (1978). If, but only if, an employee's speech falls within this category, a public employer seeking to abridge or punish it must show that the employee's interest is outweighed by the government's interest, "as an employer, in promoting the efficiency of the public services it performs through its employees." Pickering, supra, at 568.

McPherson fails this threshold requirement. * * *

* * *

That McPherson's statement does not constitute speech on a matter of "public concern" is demonstrated by comparing it with statements that have been found to fit that description in prior decisions involving public employees. McPherson's statement is a far cry from the question by the assistant district attorney in *Connick* whether her co-workers "ever [felt] pressured to work in political campaigns," *Connick,* 461 U.S., at 149; from the letter written by the public school teacher in *Pickering* criticizing the board of education's proposals for financing school construction, *Pickering, supra,* at 566; from the legislative testimony of a state college teacher in Perry v. Sindermann, 408 U.S. 593, 595 (1972), advocating that a particular college be elevated to 4–year status; from the memorandum given by a teacher to a radio station in Mt. Healthy City Board of Ed. v. Doyle, 429 U.S. 274, 282 (1977), dealing with teacher dress and appearance; and from the complaints about school board policies and practices at issue in Givhan v. Western Line Consolidated School Dist., 439 U.S. 410, 413 (1979). See *Connick, supra,* at 145–146.

* * *

II

Even if I agreed that McPherson's statement was speech on a matter of "public concern," I would still find it unprotected. It is important to be clear on what the issue is in this part of the case. It is not, as the Court suggests, whether "Rankin's interest in *discharging* [McPherson] outweighed her rights under the First Amendment." * * * (emphasis added). Rather, it is whether his interest *in preventing the expression of such statements in his agency* outweighed her First Amendment interest in making the statement. We are not deliberating, in other words, (or at least should not be) about whether the sanction of dismissal was, as the concurrence puts it, "an * * * intemperat[e] employment decision." It may well have been—and personally I think it was. But we are not sitting as a panel to develop sound principles of proportionality for adverse actions in the state civil service. We are asked to determine whether, given the interests of this law enforcement office, McPherson had a *right* to say what she did—so that she could not only not be fired for it, but could not be formally reprimanded for it, or even prevented from repeating it endlessly into the future. It boggles the mind to think that she has such a right.

* * *

Because the statement at issue here did not address a matter of public concern, and because, even if it did, a law enforcement agency has adequate reason not to permit such expression, I would reverse the judgment of the court below.

D. A Reprise on the Problem: Applying the "*Connick*" Test

It is surely clear from *Pickering, et al.* that the first amendment does apply even though it is "merely" one's government-linked status that is put at risk by offending a rule or agreement disallowing one to speak. At the same time, it is also clear from the same cases that the analysis will not run according to a simple model of "unconstitutional condition," insofar as it appears to be the case that some restrictions may be sustained though the state could take no action at all if the same things had all been said by someone else, i.e. someone not linked with the government in the manner as the person against whom some adverse action has been taken or proposed. Evidently, some sort of context-specific analysis not wholly dissimilar from Hand's sliding scale, "gravity-of-the evil" formulation is being applied here, adjusted and fine-tuned by elements taken from *Times v. Sullivan,* as well. The exact manner in which that calculus has currently worked out is by no means self-evident, however, even as the *Connick* and *Rankin* decisions attest. (Note also all the disclaiming dicta, even in *Pickering* itself.) [25]

The sheer frequency with which public employment "free speech" claims arise with respect to whether what an employee said about one thing or another is or is not protected by the first amendment in some manner, exerts unusual pressure on the Supreme Court to announce a stylized (i.e. somewhat mechanical) way of going about these questions, principally for the guidance of lower courts. One good way of seeing whether one thinks one has grasped these rather stylized guidelines may be to see whether one can apply them with a certain firm sense of confidence, say, in the following sort of case. So, let's see how you think it ought to proceed.

An untenured assistant professor of psychiatry at UNC Medical School made an appointment with the dean. At that time, in the dean's office, he complained to the dean that a senior professor commonly used his assigned parking place in the faculty lot, and requested the dean to intervene without mentioning how the matter came to the dean's attention. He

---

25. E.g., that had Pickering been employed *by the board itself,* or had there been evidence that his published letter actually affected any bond issue adversely (*and* had the margin of falsehood been more substantial than it was), *or* had any of the falsehoods been known by Pickering to be false, *or* were there some evidence that his letter produced friction within the school where he worked, *or* had there been a limited school rule requiring submission of any letter bearing on the operation of the school to be processed internally for the limited purpose of bringing possible factual error to Pickering's attention before he went public (*and* had he failed to go through that process), *then* his dismissal might have been sustained, despite all the Court says about *Sullivan,* etc. And does not *Connick* appear clearly to imply that if one makes complaint to a superior as a public employee (and does not go to the newspapers with the complaint), still [s]he may be fired though the complaint is well taken and quite courteously expressed, if it is "merely" a workplace grievance not deemed by the Court to raise any issue of general public policy? Note also the scope of the political activity ban sustained in the *Letter Carriers* case. On balance, how strongly in fact does the first amendment seem to operate in these several cases? See S. Shiffrin, The First Amendment, Democracy, and Romance 72–80, 106–09 (1990).

also complained to the dean that the same senior professor was, in his view, overprescribing barbituates for his clinical patients at the UNC Medical Center and was having sex in his clinic office with two or three of the patients. The dean assured him he would look into both matters promptly. In the meantime, for the best interests of all concerned, he directed the assistant professor not to speak to anyone else.

Three weeks later, the senior departmental faculty met to review junior faculty members for tenure. On a closely divided vote, tenure was not recommended for the assistant professor to whom we have just referred. The dean voted with the majority; so did the senior professor to whom the dean had spoken about the parking matter (in the course of which he identified the assistant professor who brought the matter to his attention). The dean had said less to the senior professor on the handling of clinical patients because, in his view, the assistant professor had simply not been in a suitable position to know and, in the dean's view, was almost surely mistaken in his perception of the other professor's professional practices. He did, however, ask whether the other man's clinical practice was free of any problems; he assumed that his question was pointed enough such that were there something improper going on, doubtless the other man would get the point—that the dean had evidently heard something—and would quickly desist from anything he may have been doing wrong. As to the parking matter, incidentally, the assistant professor was mistaken; his parking place had been frequently usurped by another staff member, but it was someone other than the senior professor whom he had identified to the dean.

The adverse tenure recommendation was to be forwarded to the Board of Trustees for final action. Under the university's rules, it was not final until the trustees voted, although rarely had the Board reached an outcome at odds with the recommendation they received. In the meantime, the assistant professor, frustrated that the dean had not contacted him again to say what steps had been taken on the matters he had brought to the dean's attention, and discouraged by the adverse vote on his tenure (which, if it were not overturned by the trustees, would mean that he would not be continued in his position beyond the end of the year), felt he could wait no longer—and spoke to a friend on the staff of the *Daily Tarheel* about the likelihood of overprescription of barbituates at the clinic and possible sexual misconduct with clinic patients as well.

The day following publication of the story in the *Daily Tarheel,* the trustees met in regular session and, among other things, voted unanimously to deny the assistant professor tenure. The same day, the dean so advised the assistant professor and also asked him directly whether he was the source of the *Tarheel* story. When the assistant professor replied that, yes, he was the source, the dean suspended him for the balance of the term altogether. (Coupled with the denial of tenure, this meant that the assistant professor was finished, at once.)

Supposing the assistant professor were at once to bring suit on grounds that he had been punished for his good faith efforts to speak without fear of retribution, consistent with the first amendment, what likely result and why? More particularly, according to the *Pickering–Givhan–Mt. Healthy–Connick* and *Rankin* profile of standards and burdens of proof and procedures applicable to the case, how will it proceed, step by step, and what relief, if any, is the plaintiff entitled to receive?

After you have run through the preceding problem, consider the following reprise as well. A principal case, featured in the introductory materials, was the famous *Scopes* case. It differed from the preceding problem in that Scopes wished to teach materials other than those the state itself specifically prescribed solely for use in its own schools and its own classrooms—but the state law did not restrict what Scopes might say elsewhere (the original doctrine of "unconstitutional conditions" itself thus does not appear to be involved at all); it did not restrict Scopes from writing critical letters publicly complaining of the curricular restriction, criticizing the law, etc., as stridently as much as he might feel inclined. It did not forbid him to go public with anything he might find wrong with the schools or the manner in which they were operated, either. On what basis, on the strength of the materials you have thus far covered, could a modern Scopes presume to invoke the free speech clause to depart from the school board's (or state law) prescribed materials he is solely to use in class, and defend against being dismissed for insubordination?[26] (Is there any foundation for

---

26. The difficulty and distinction is evident in considering the original logic of the doctrine of unconstitutional conditions itself. Justice Sutherland's quotation *supra* from the *Frost* case spoke of the government requiring "a surrender of a right in exchange for a valuable privilege the state threatens otherwise to withhold." So, the doctrine begins with the observation that one has a right of some sort (e.g., to write letters to the editor of the local newspaper, criticizing the local school board, as in *Pickering,* or the local police department, as in *McAuliffe*) which one must put aside if, and as long as, one accepts the valuable privilege the state threatens otherwise to withhold. In cases such as *Scopes,* however, the logic does not work, does it? I.e. Scopes never had a first amendment "right" to commandeer a public school classroom—access to the classroom is itself part of the "valuable privilege" *he gets,* rather than such access being a part of some pre-existing right he is made to give up. Moreover, in "exchange" for conducting himself in the classroom as the state-employer dictates, neither is Scopes asked nor is he required to abstain from any pre-existing right he holds (except in the sense Holmes mentioned in passing in *McAuliffe,* i.e. while performing his duties at the appointed time in the classroom, to that extent he does lay aside such "constitutional right" as he might otherwise have used just to loaf). In the *Letter Carriers* case, the postal employees are made to forego off-the-job political activities they were otherwise constitutionally entitled to engage in so it is logical to talk about the Civil Service restrictions as challengeable under the doctrine of unconstitutional conditions. But what if the restrictions were (merely) that, as lettermen, delivering mail, the postal employee is not to seize the advantage of using that role to ring the doorbell and engage the homeowner in his solicitation of some candidate or political cause he holds dear? Is there any problem

what is elsewhere sometimes called "academic freedom," or would it make any difference whether the claim arises at the state university level rather than the state public school level? If you think so, why, and on what grounds? [27]

Consider the following news item from the *New York Times*.

Book Ban in California School Strikes Down Familiar Target [28]

BORON, Calif., Aug. 30—If a group of local parents had let her speak to them before "The Catcher in the Rye" was banned from her high school, Shelley Keller–Gage says she would have told them she believes it is a highly moral book that deals with the kinds of difficulties their own children are facing.

But Mrs. Keller–Gage, an English teacher, was asked not to speak, and a small group of people led by a woman who says she has not read—and never would read—such a book, persuaded the school board to ban it this month from the Boron High School supplementary reading list.

The school board's 4–to–1 vote has aroused this small sunbaked town of 4,000 at the edge of the Mojave Desert. * * * Ed Roberts, a school board member who works for a transportation company, carries a copy in the front seat of his pickup truck. He has shown one passage to people so often that the book frequently falls open to that section, whose profanity he finds objectionable.

Jim Sommers, the head of the school board, who operates Jim's Mobil Service, says he is halfway through the book, though he is having a hard time keeping up his interest. * * *

Vickie Swindler, the parent who raised the first objections when her 14–year–old daughter, Brook, showed her the book, has been calling her friends, reading passages from it, mostly the one on page 32 with three goddamns in it.

---

with a local rule forbidding one employed as a jailer inside the city jail not to solicit for political causes among the inmates—when no one else is permitted (i.e. "has a right") to enter the cellblocks and solicit for their causes?

27. As a matter of historical fact, the Tennessee statute involved in *Scopes* applied to *all* state supported *universities* and colleges as well. For a recent review of academic freedom in the Supreme Court, see Van Alstyne, The First Amendment and the Usages of Academic Freedom in the Supreme Court of the United States: An Unhurried Historical Review, 53 Law & Contemp.Prob. ___ (1990).

28. N.Y. Times, Sept. 4, 1989, § 1, p. 1, col. 5. In addition to the following principal case, see Parducci v. Rutland, 316 F.Supp. 352 (M.D.Ala.1970) (high school English teacher reinstated on first amendment grounds by federal court following dismissal for refusal of principal's demand to discontinue reading assignment to Kurt Vonnegut's Slaughterhouse Five); Hazelwood School Dist. v. Kuhlmeier, 484 U.S. 260, 108 S.Ct. 562, 98 L.Ed.2d 592 (1988) (6–3, high school principal's censorship of school financed student newspaper sustained); Bethel School Dist. No. 403 v. Fraser, 478 U.S. 675, 106 S.Ct. 3159, 92 L.Ed.2d 549 (1986) (suspension of student using sexual reference in student assembly address supporting another student for elective office, sustained). Cf. Papish v. Board of Curators of Univ. of Missouri, 410 U.S. 667, 93 S.Ct. 1197, 35 L.Ed.2d 618 (1973) (graduate student reinstated on first amendment grounds following expulsion for on campus distribution of student newspaper not financially subsidized by the state university, containing sexually explicit political cartoon and "M* * * F* * *" word).

When she found out about the language in it, Mrs. Swindler said, "I called the school, and I said, 'How the hell did this teacher get this book?'"

"Yes, there's harshness and profanity in society," said F.O. Roe, a school board member who runs a furniture and flower shop, responding to the argument that the book's contents are no longer as shocking as they once were. "But we don't have to accept them, just the same as we don't have to accept the narcotics that are in the streets and the murders that are happening all over the country. We live in harmony in this little town."

Mrs. Keller–Gage said the Salinger book might carry a particular message for people like these.

"These people are being just like Holden, the ones who are trying to censor the book," she said. "They are trying to be catchers in the rye." The book derives its title from a passage in which Holden Caulfield describes his vision of himself as a protector of innocence. * * *

When she assigned the book to her English classes, Mrs. Keller–Gage said, she told her students, "if you're looking for titillation, go home and turn on HBO, because you're not going to get it from this book."

For those whose parents objected to "The Catcher in the Rye," she offered an alternate text, Ray Bradbury's "Dandelion Wine," which she said was "the most innocent book I could think of that would still be at their reading level."

As the school year began this week, Mrs. Keller–Gage's three dozen copies of "The Catcher in the Rye" were on a top shelf of her classroom closet, inside a tightly taped cardboard box.

In their place, she said, she would be assigning "Farenheit 451," by Ray Bradbury, a novel about book burning.

If Ms. Keller–Gage untaped the cardboard box, returned "The Catcher in the Rye," to her high school English class supplementary list, and then promptly was dismissed (for insubordination) for having done so, under the circumstances, what result in court if the dismissal were challenged on first amendment ground? In the following case, what difference would there be, if any, had the school board forbidden acquisition (rather than directed removal) of the named books?

BOARD OF EDUCATION v. PICO

Supreme Court of the United States, 1982.
457 U.S. 853, 102 S.Ct. 2799, 73 L.Ed.2d 435.

JUSTICE BRENNAN announced the judgment of the Court and delivered an opinion, in which JUSTICE MARSHALL and JUSTICE STEVENS joined, and in which JUSTICE BLACKMUN joined except for Part II–A–(1).

The principal question presented is whether the First Amendment imposes limitations upon the exercise by a local school board of its discretion to remove library books from high school and junior high school libraries.

I

Petitioners are the Board of Education of the Island Trees Union Free School District No. 26, in New York, and Richard Ahrens, Frank Martin, Christina Fasulo, Patrick Hughes, Richard Melchers, Richard Michaels, and Louis Nessim. When this suit was brought, Ahrens was the President of the Board, Martin was the Vice President, and the remaining petitioners were Board members. * * * Respondents are Steven Pico, Jacqueline Gold, Glenn Yarris, Russell Rieger, and Paul Sochinski. When this suit was brought, Pico, Gold, Yarris, and Rieger were students at the High School, and Sochinski was a student at the Junior High School.

In September 1975, petitioners Ahrens, Martin, and Hughes attended a conference sponsored by Parents of New York United (PONYU), a politically conservative organization of parents concerned about education legislation in the State of New York. At the conference these petitioners obtained lists of books described by Ahrens as "objectionable," * * * and by Martin as "improper fare for school students," * * *. It was later determined that the High School library contained nine of the listed books, and that another listed book was in the Junior High School library.[3] In February 1976, at a meeting with the Superintendent of Schools and the Principals of the High School and Junior High School, the Board gave an "unofficial direction" that the listed books be removed from the library shelves and delivered to the Board's offices, so that Board members could read them. When this directive was carried out, it became publicized, and the Board issued a press release justifying its action. It characterized the removed books as "anti-American, anti-Christian, anti-Sem[i]tic, and just plain filthy," and concluded that "[i]t is our duty, our moral obligation, to protect the children in our schools from this moral danger as surely as from physical and medical dangers." * * *

---

3. The nine books in the High School library were: Slaughter House Five, by Kurt Vonnegut, Jr.; The Naked Ape, by Desmond Morris; Down These Mean Streets, by Piri Thomas; Best Short Stories of Negro Writers, edited by Langston Hughes; Go Ask Alice, of anonymous authorship; Laughing Boy, by Oliver La-Farge; Black Boy, by Richard Wright; A Hero Ain't Nothin' But A Sandwich, by Alice Childress; and Soul On Ice, by Eldridge Cleaver. The book in the Junior High School library was A Reader for Writers, edited by Jerome Archer. Still another listed book, The Fixer, by Bernard Malamud, was found to be included in the curriculum of a 12th grade literature course. * * *

A short time later, the Board appointed a "Book Review Committee," consisting of four Island Trees parents and four members of the Island Trees schools staff, to read the listed books and to recommend to the Board whether the books should be retained, taking into account the books "educational suitability," "good taste," "relevance," and "appropriateness to age and grade level." In July, the Committee made its final report to the Board, recommending that five of the listed books be retained and that two others be removed from the school libraries. As for the remaining four books, the Committee could not agree on two, took no position on one, and recommended that the last book be made available to students only with parental approval. The Board substantially rejected the Committee's report later that month, deciding that only one book should be returned to the High School library without restriction [10] that another should be made available subject to parental approval,[11] but that the remaining nine books should "be removed from elementary and secondary libraries and [from] use in the curriculum." * * *[12] The Board gave no reasons for rejecting the recommendations of the Committee that it had appointed.

Respondents reacted to the Board's decision by bringing the present action under 42 U.S.C. § 1983 in the United States District Court for the Eastern District of New York. They alleged that petitioners had

> "ordered the removal of the books from school libraries and proscribed their use in the curriculum because particular passages in the books offended their social, political and moral tastes and not because the books, taken as a whole, were lacking in educational value." * * *

Respondents claimed that the Board's actions denied them their rights under the First Amendment. They asked the court for a declaration that the Board's actions were unconstitutional, and for preliminary and permanent injunctive relief ordering the Board to return the nine books to the school libraries and to refrain from interfering with the use of those books in the schools' curricula. * * *

The District Court granted summary judgment in favor of petitioners. * * * In the court's view, "the parties substantially agree[d] about the motivation behind the board's actions," * * *—namely, that

> "the board acted not on religious principles but on its conservative educational philosophy, and on its belief that the nine books removed from the school library and curriculum were irrelevant, vulgar, immoral, and in bad taste, making them educationally unsuitable for the district's junior and senior high school students." *Id.,* at 392.

10. Laughing Boy. 474 F.Supp., at 391, n. 12.

11. Black Boy. 474 F.Supp., at 391, n. 13.

12. As a result, the nine removed books could not be assigned or suggested to students in connection with school work. *Id.,* at 391. However, teachers were not instructed to refrain from discussing the removed books or the ideas and positions expressed in them. App. 131.

With this factual premise as its background, the court rejected respondents' contention that their First Amendment rights had been infringed by the Board's actions. * * *

A three-judge panel of the United States Court of Appeals for the Second Circuit reversed the judgment of the District Court, and remanded the action for a trial on respondents' allegations. * * *

II

We emphasize at the outset the limited nature of the substantive question presented by the case before us. * * *

Of course, courts should not "intervene in the resolution of conflicts which arise in the daily operation of school systems" unless "basic constitutional values" are "directly and sharply implicate[d]" in those conflicts. Epperson v. Arkansas, 393 U.S., at 104. But we think that the First Amendment rights of students may be directly and sharply implicated by the removal of books from the shelves of a school library. Our precedents have focused "not only on the role of the First Amendment in fostering individual self-expression but also on its role in affording the public access to discussion, debate, and the dissemination of information and ideas." First National Bank of Boston v. Bellotti, 435 U.S. 765, 783 (1978). And we have recognized that "the State may not, consistently with the spirit of the First Amendment, contract the spectrum of available knowledge." Griswold v. Connecticut, 381 U.S. 479, 482 (1965). In keeping with this principle, we have held that in a variety of contexts "the Constitution protects the right to receive information and ideas." Stanley v. Georgia, 394 U.S. 557, 564 (1969); see Kleindienst v. Mandel, 408 U.S. 753, 762–763 (1972) (citing cases). This right is an inherent corollary of the rights of free speech and press that are explicitly guaranteed by the Constitution, in two senses. First, the right to receive ideas follows ineluctably from the sender's First Amendment right to send them: "The right of freedom of speech and press * * * embraces the right to distribute literature, and necessarily protects the right to receive it." Martin v. Struthers, 319 U.S. 141, 143 (1943) (citation omitted). "The dissemination of ideas can accomplish nothing if otherwise willing addressees are not free to receive and consider them. It would be a barren marketplace of ideas that had only sellers and no buyers." Lamont v. Postmaster General, 381 U.S. 301, 308 (1965) (BRENNAN, J., concurring).

More importantly, the right to receive ideas is a necessary predicate to the recipient's meaningful exercise of his own rights of speech, press, and political freedom. Madison admonished us:

> "A popular Government, without popular information, or the means of acquiring it, is but a Prologue to a Farce or a Tragedy; or, perhaps both. Knowledge will forever govern ignorance: And a people who mean to be their own Governors, must arm themselves with the power which knowledge gives."
> 9 Writings of James Madison 103 (G. Hunt ed. 1910).

* * *

* * * Petitioners emphasize the inculcative function of secondary education, and argue that they must be allowed *unfettered* discretion to "transmit community values" through the Island Trees schools. But that sweeping claim overlooks the unique role of the school library. It appears from the record that use of the Island Trees school libraries is completely voluntary on the part of students. Their selection of books from these libraries is entirely a matter of free choice; the libraries afford them an opportunity at self-education and individual enrichment that is wholly optional. Petitioner might well defend their claim of absolute discretion in matters of *curriculum* by reliance upon their duty to inculcate community values. But we think that petitioners' reliance upon that duty is misplaced where, as here, they attempt to extend their claim of absolute discretion beyond the compulsory environment of the classroom, into the school library and the regime of voluntary inquiry that there holds sway.

(2)

In rejecting petitioners' claim of absolute discretion to remove books from their school libraries, we do not deny that local school boards have a substantial legitimate role to play in the determination of school library content. We thus must turn to the question of the extent to which the First Amendment places limitations upon the discretion of petitioners to remove books from their libraries. In this inquiry we enjoy the guidance of several precedents. *West Virginia Board of Education v. Barnette* stated:

> "If there is any fixed star in our constitutional constellation, it is that no official, high or petty, can prescribe what shall be orthodox in politics, nationalism, religion, or other matters of opinion * * *. If there are any circumstances which permit an exception, they do not now occur to us." 319 U.S., at 642.

This doctrine has been reaffirmed in later cases involving education. For example, *Keyishian v. Board of Regents, supra,* at 603, noted that "the First Amendment * * * does not tolerate laws that cast a pall of orthodoxy over the classroom;" see also Epperson v. Arkansas, 393 U.S., at 104–105. And Mt. Healthy City Board of Ed. v. Doyle, 429 U.S. 274 (1977), recognized First Amendment limitations upon the discretion of a local school board to refuse to rehire a non-tenured teacher. * * *

With respect to the present case, the message of these precedents is clear. Petitioners rightly possess significant discretion to determine the content of their school libraries. But that discretion may not be exercised in a narrowly partisan or political manner. If a Democratic school board, motivated by party affiliation, ordered the removal of all books written by or in favor of Republicans, few would doubt that the order violated the constitutional rights of the students denied access to those books. The same conclusion would surely apply if an all-white school board, motivated by racial animus, decided to remove all books authored by blacks or advocating racial equality and integration. Our Constitution does not permit the official suppression of *ideas.* Thus whether petitioners' removal of books from their school libraries denied respondents their First Amendment rights depends upon the motivation behind petitioners' actions. If petitioners *intended* by their removal decision to deny respondents access to ideas with which petitioners disagreed, and if this intent was the decisive factor in petitioners' decision,[22] then petitioners have exercised their discretion in violation of the Constitution. To permit such intentions to control official actions would be to encourage the precise sort of officially prescribed orthodoxy unequivocally condemned in *Barnette*. On the other hand, respondents implicitly concede that an unconstitutional motivation would *not* be demonstrated if it were shown that petitioners had decided to remove the books at issue because those books were pervasively vulgar. * * * And again, respondents concede that if it were demonstrated that the removal decision was based solely upon the "educational suitability" of the books in question, then their removal would be "perfectly permissible." * * * In other words, in respondents' view such motivations, if decisive of petitioners' actions, would not carry the danger of an official suppression of ideas, and thus would not violate respondents' First Amendment rights.

As noted earlier, nothing in our decision today affects in any way the discretion of a local school board to choose books to *add* to the libraries of their schools. Because we are concerned in this case with the suppression of ideas, our holding today affects only the discretion to *remove* books. In brief, we hold that local school boards may not remove books from school library shelves simply because they dislike the ideas contained in those books and seek by their removal to "prescribe what shall be orthodox in politics, nationalism, religion, or other matters of opinion." West Virginia Board of Education v. Barnette, 319 U.S., at 642. Such purposes stand inescapably condemned by our precedents.

B

We now turn to the remaining question presented by this case: Do the evidentiary materials that were before the District Court, when construed most favorably to respondents, raise a genuine issue of material fact whether petitioners exceeded constitutional limitations in exercising their discretion to remove the books from the school libraries? We conclude that the materials do raise such a question, which forecloses summary judgment in favor of petitioners.

* * *

Construing these claims, affidavit statements, and other evidentiary materials in a manner favorable to respondents, we cannot conclude that petitioners were "entitled to a judgment as a matter of law." The evidence plainly does not foreclose the possibility that petitioners' decision to remove the books rested decisively upon disagreement with constitutionally protected ideas in those books, or upon a desire on petitioners' part to impose upon the students of the Island Trees High

---

22. By "decisive factor" we mean a "substantial factor" in the absence of which the opposite decision would have been reached. See Mt. Healthy City Board of Ed. v. Doyle, 429 U.S. 274, 287 (1977).

School and Junior High School a political orthodoxy to which petitioners and their constituents adhered. Of course, some of the evidence before the District Court might lead a finder of fact to accept petitioners' claim that their removal decision was based upon constitutionally valid concerns. But that evidence at most creates a genuine issue of material fact on the critical question of the credibility of petitioners' justifications for their decision: On that issue, it simply cannot be said that there is no genuine issue as to any material fact.

The mandate shall issue forthwith.

Affirmed.

JUSTICE BLACKMUN, concurring in part and concurring in the judgment.

While I agree with much in today's plurality opinion, and while I accept the standard laid down by the plurality to guide proceedings on remand, I write separately because I have a somewhat different perspective on the nature of the First Amendment right involved.

* * *

In my view, then, the principle involved here is both narrower and more basic than the "right to receive information" identified by the plurality. I do not suggest that the State has any affirmative obligation to provide students with information or ideas, something that may well be associated with a "right to receive." * * * And I do not believe, as the plurality suggests, that the right at issue here is somehow associated with the peculiar nature of the school library, * * *; if schools may be used to inculcate ideas, surely libraries may play a role in that process. Instead, I suggest that certain forms of state discrimination *between* ideas are improper. In particular, our precedents command the conclusion that the State may not act to deny access to an idea simply because state officials disapprove of that idea for partisan or political reasons.[2]

* * *

II

In my view, we strike a proper balance here by holding that school officials may not remove books for the *purpose* of restricting access to the political ideas or social perspectives discussed in them, when that action is motivated simply by the officials' disapproval of the ideas involved. * * *

* * *

* * * And I believe that tying the First Amendment right to the *purposeful* suppression of ideas makes the concept more manageable than Justice Rehnquist acknowledges. Most people would recognize that refusing to allow discussion of current events in Latin class is a policy designed to "inculcate" Latin, not to suppress ideas. Similarly, removing a learned treatise criticizing American foreign policy from an

---

2. In effect, my view presents the obverse of the plurality's analysis: while the plurality focuses on the failure to provide information, I find crucial the State's decision to single out an idea for disapproval and then deny access to it.

elementary school library because the students would not understand it is an action unrelated to the *purpose* of suppressing ideas. In my view, however, removing the same treatise because it is "anti-American" raises a far more difficult issue.

* * * And while it is not clear to me from Justice Rehnquist's discussion whether a State operates its public libraries in its "role as sovereign," surely difficult constitutional problems would arise if a State chose to exclude "anti-American" books from its public libraries—even if those books remained available at local bookstores.

* * * Arguing that the majority in the community rejects the ideas involved, * * * (BURGER, C.J., dissenting), does not refute this principle: "The very purpose of a Bill of Rights was to withdraw certain subjects from the vicissitudes of political controversy, to place them beyond the reach of majorities and officials * * *." *Barnette,* 319 U.S., at 639.

* * *

Because I believe that the plurality has derived a standard similar to the one compelled by my analysis, I join all but Part II–A(1) of the plurality opinion.

JUSTICE WHITE, concurring in the judgment.

The District Court found that the books were removed from the school library because the school board believed them "to be, in essence, vulgar." 474 F.Supp. 387, 397 (EDNY 1979). Both Court of Appeals judges in the majority concluded, however, that there was a material issue of fact that precluded summary judgment sought by petitioners. The unresolved factual issue, as I understand it, is the reason or reasons underlying the school board's removal of the books. I am not inclined to disagree with the Court of Appeals on such a fact-bound issue and hence concur in the judgment of affirmance. Presumably this will result in a trial and the making of a full record and findings on the critical issues.

* * *

CHIEF JUSTICE BURGER, with whom JUSTICE POWELL, JUSTICE REHNQUIST, and JUSTICE O'CONNOR join, dissenting.

The First Amendment, as with other parts of the Constitution, must deal with new problems in a changing world. In an attempt to deal with a problem in an area traditionally left to the states, a plurality of the Court, in a lavish expansion going beyond any prior holding under the First Amendment, expresses its view that a school board's decision concerning what books are to be in the school library is subject to federal-court review. Were this to become the law, this Court would come perilously close to becoming a "super censor" of school board library decisions. Stripped to its essentials, the issue comes down to two important propositions: *first,* whether local schools are to be administered by elected school boards, or by federal judges and teenage pupils; and *second,* whether the values of morality, good taste, and relevance to education are valid reasons for school board decisions concerning the contents of a school library. In an attempt to place this case within the protection of the First Amendment, the plurality suggests a new "right" that, when shorn of the plurality's rhetoric, allows this Court to impose its own views about what books must be made available to students.

I

A

I agree with the fundamental proposition that "students do not 'shed their constitutional rights to freedom of speech or expression at the schoolhouse gate.'" * * * Here, however, no restraints of any kind are placed on the students. They are free to read the books in question, which are available at public libraries and bookstores; they are free to discuss them in the classroom or elsewhere. Despite this absence of any direct external control on the students' ability to express themselves, the plurality suggests that there is a new First Amendment "entitlement" to have access to particular books in a school library.

* * *

The plurality also cites *Tinker, supra*, to establish that the recipient's right to free speech encompasses a right to have particular books retained on the school library shelf. * * * But the cited passage of *Tinker* notes only that school officials may not *prohibit* a student from expressing his or her view on a subject unless that expression interferes with the legitimate operations of the school. The government does not "contract the spectrum of available knowledge." Griswold v. Connecticut, 381 U.S. 479, 482 (1965), * * *, by choosing not to retain certain books on the school library shelf; it simply chooses not to be the conduit for that particular information. In short, even assuming the desirability of the policy expressed by the plurality, there is not a hint in the First Amendment, or in any holding of this Court, of a "right" to have the government provide continuing access to certain books.

B

Whatever role the government might play as a conduit of information, schools in particular ought not be made a slavish courier of the material of third parties. The plurality pays homage to the ancient verity that in the administration of the public schools "'there is a legitimate and substantial community interest in promoting respect for authority and traditional values be they social, moral, or political.'" * * * If, as we have held, schools may legitimately be used as vehicles for "inculcating fundamental values necessary to the maintenance of a democratic political system," Ambach v. Norwick, 441 U.S. 68, 77 (1979), school authorities must have broad discretion to fulfill that obligation. Presumably all activity within a primary or secondary school involves the conveyance of information and at least an implied approval of the worth of that information. How are "fundamental values" to be inculcated except by having school boards make content-based decisions about the appropriateness of retaining materials in the school library and curriculum. In order to fulfill its function, an elected school board *must* express its views on the subjects which are taught to its students. In doing so those elected officials express the views of their community; they may err, of course, and the voters may remove them. It is a startling erosion of the very idea of democratic government to have this Court arrogate to itself the power the plurality asserts today.

The plurality concludes that under the Constitution school boards cannot choose to retain or dispense with books if their discretion is exercised in a "narrowly partisan or political manner." * * * The plurality concedes that permissible factors are whether the books are "pervasively vulgar," * * * or educationally unsuitable. * * * "Educational suitability," however, is a standardless phrase. This conclusion will undoubtedly be drawn in many—if not most—instances because of the decisionmaker's content-based judgment that the ideas contained in the book or the idea expressed from the author's method of communication are inappropriate for teenage pupils.

The plurality also tells us that a book may be removed from a school library if it is "pervasively vulgar." But why must the vulgarity be "pervasive" to be offensive? Vulgarity might be concentrated in a single poem or a single chapter or a single page, yet still be inappropriate. Or a school board might reasonably conclude that even "random" vulgarity is inappropriate for teenage school students. A school board might also reasonably conclude that the school board's retention of such books gives those volumes an implicit endorsement. * * *

* * *

* * * Books may be acquired from bookstores, public libraries, or other alternative sources unconnected with the unique environment of the local public schools.

II

No amount of "limiting" language could rein in the sweeping "right" the plurality would create. The plurality distinguishes library books from textbooks because library books "by their nature are optional rather than required reading." * * * It is not clear, however, why this distinction requires *greater* scrutiny before "optional" reading materials may be removed. It would appear that required reading and textbooks have a greater likelihood of imposing a " 'pall of orthodoxy' " over the educational process than do [sic] optional reading. * * * In essence, the plurality's view transforms the availability of this "optional" reading into a "right" to have this "optional" reading maintained at the demand of teenagers.

* * *

III

Through the use of bits and pieces of prior opinions unrelated to the issue of this case, the plurality demeans our function of constitutional adjudication. Today the plurality suggests that the *Constitution* distinguishes between school libraries and school classrooms, between *removing* unwanted books and *acquiring* books. Even more extreme, the plurality concludes that the Constitution *requires* school boards to justify to its teenage pupils the decision to remove a particular book from a school library. I categorically reject this notion that the

Constitution dictates that judges, rather than parents, teachers, and local school boards, must determine how the standards of morality and vulgarity are to be treated in the classroom.

JUSTICE POWELL, dissenting.

The plurality opinion today rejects a basic concept of public school education in our country: that the States and locally elected school boards should have the responsibility for determining the educational policy of the public schools. After today's decision any junior high school student, by instituting a suit against a school board or teacher, may invite a judge to overrule an educational decision by the official body designated by the people to operate the schools.

* * *

As Justice Rehnquist tellingly observes, how does one limit—on a principled basis—today's new constitutional right? If a 14-year-old child may challenge a school board's decision to remove a book from the library, upon what theory is a court to prevent a like challenge to a school board's decision not to purchase that identical book? And at the even more "sensitive" level of "receiving ideas," does today's decision entitle student oversight of which courses may be added or removed from the curriculum, or even of what a particular teacher elects to teach or not teach in the classroom? Is not the "right to receive ideas" as much—or indeed even more—implicated in these educational questions?[2]

* * *

APPENDIX TO OPINION OF POWELL, J., DISSENTING

"The excerpts which led the Board to look into the educational suitability of the books in question are set out (with minor corrections after comparison with the text of the books themselves) below. The pagination and the underlinings are retained from the original report used by the board. In new editions of some of the books, the quotes appear at different pages.

"1) *SOUL ON ICE* by Eldridge Cleaver

PAGE QUOTE

157–158 '* * * There are white men who will pay you to fuck their wives. They approach you and say, "How would you like to fuck a white woman?" "What is this?" you ask. "On the up-and-up," he assures you. "It's all right. She's my wife. She needs black rod, is all. She has to have it. I'll pay you. It's all on the level, no trick involved. Interested?" * * *

---

2. The plurality suggests that the books in a school library derive special protection under the Constitution because the school library is a place in which students exercise unlimited choice. * * * This suggestion is without support in law or fact. It is contradicted by this very case. The school board in this case does not view the school library as a place in which students pick from an unlimited range of books—some of which may be inappropriate for young people. Rather, the school library is analogous to an assigned reading list within which students may exercise a degree of choice.

* * *

"4) *GO ASK ALICE* by Anonymous

PAGE QUOTE

31 'I wonder if sex without acid could be so exciting, so wonderful, so indescribable. I always thought it just took a minute, or that it would be like dogs mating.'

47 'Chris and I walked into Richie and Ted's apartment to find the bastards stoned and making love to each other * * * low class queer.'

81 'shitty, goddamned, pissing, ass, goddamned beJesus, screwing life's, ass, shit. Doris was ten and had *humped* with who knows how many men in between * * * her current stepfather started having sex with her but good * * * *sonofabitch balling her*'

* * *

"7) *BLACK BOY* by Richard Wright

PAGE QUOTE

70–71 'We black children—seven or eight or nine years of age—used to run to the Jew's store and shout:

* * * Bloody Christ Killers

Never trust a Jew

Bloody Christ Killers

What won't a Jew do * * *

Red, white and blue

Your pa was a Jew

Your ma a dirty dago

What the hell is you?'

265 'Crush that nigger's nuts, nigger!' 'Hit that nigger!' 'Aw, fight you goddam niggers!' 'Sock 'im, in his f-k-g-piece!' 'Make 'im bleed!' "

* * *

JUSTICE REHNQUIST, with whom THE CHIEF JUSTICE and JUSTICE POWELL join, dissenting.

* * *

* * * Though for reasons stated in Part II of this opinion I entirely disagree with Justice Brennan's treatment of the constitutional issue, I also disagree with his opinion for the entirely separate reason that it is not remotely tailored to the facts presented by this case.

In the course of his discussion, Justice Brennan states:

"Petitioners rightly possess significant discretion to determine the content of their school libraries. But that discretion may not be exercised in a narrowly partisan or political manner. If a Democratic school board, motivated by party affiliation, ordered the removal of all books written by or in favor of Republicans, few would doubt that the order violated the constitutional rights of the students. * * * The same conclusion would surely apply if an all-white school board, motivated by racial animus, decided to remove all books authored by blacks or advocating racial equality and integration. Our Constitution does not permit the official suppression of *ideas*." * * * (emphasis in original).

I can cheerfully concede all of this, but as in so many other cases the extreme examples are seldom the ones that arise in the real world of constitutional litigation. In *this case* the facts taken most favorably to respondents suggest that nothing of this sort happened. The nine books removed undoubtedly can contain "ideas," but in the light of the excerpts from them found in the dissenting opinion of Judge Mansfield in the Court of Appeals, it is apparent that eight of them contained demonstrable amounts of vulgarity and profanity, see 638 F.2d 404, 419–422, n. 1 (CA2 1980), and the ninth contained nothing that could be considered partisan or political, see *id.*, at 428, n. 6. As already demonstrated, respondents admitted as much. Petitioners did not, for the reasons stated hereafter, run afoul of the First and Fourteenth Amendments by removing these particular books from the library in the manner in which they did. I would save for another day—feeling quite confident that that day will not arrive—the extreme examples posed in Justice Brennan's opinion.

B

Considerable light is shed on the correct resolution of the constitutional question in this case by examining the role played by petitioners. Had petitioners been the members of a town council, I suppose all would agree that, absent a good deal more than is present in this record, they could not have prohibited the sale of these books by private booksellers within the municipality. But we have also recognized that the government may act in other capacities than as sovereign, and when it does the First Amendment may speak with a different voice:

> "[I]t cannot be gainsaid that the State has interests as an employer in regulating the speech of its employees that differ significantly from those it possesses in connection with regulation of the speech of the citizenry in general. The problem in any case is to arrive at a balance between the interests of the teacher, as a citizen, in commenting upon matters of concern and the interest of the State, as an employer, in promoting the efficiency of the public services it performs through its employees." Pickering v. Board of Education, 391 U.S. 563, 568 (1968).

By the same token, expressive conduct which may not be prohibited by the State as sovereign may be proscribed by the State as property owner: "The State, no less than a private owner of property, has power to preserve the property under its control for the use to which it is lawfully dedicated." Adderley v. Florida, 385 U.S. 39, 47 (1966) (upholding state prohibition of expressive conduct on certain state property).

With these differential roles of government in mind, it is helpful to assess the role of government as educator, as compared with the role of government as sovereign. When it acts as an educator, at least at the elementary and secondary school level, the government is engaged in inculcating social values and knowledge in relatively impressionable young people. Obviously there are innumerable decisions to be made as to what courses should be taught, what books should be purchased, or what teachers should be employed. In every one of these areas the members of a school board will act on the basis of their own personal or moral values, will attempt to mirror those of the community, or will abdicate the making of such decisions to so-called "experts."[5] In this connection I find myself entirely in agreement with the observation of the Court of Appeals for the Seventh Circuit in Zykan v. Warsaw Community School Corp., 631 F.2d 1300, 1305 (1980), that it is "permissible and appropriate for local boards to make educational decisions based upon their personal social, political and moral views." * * *

II

Justice Brennan would hold that the First Amendment gives high school and junior high school students a "right to receive ideas" in the school. * * * This right is a curious entitlement. It exists only in the library of the school, and only if the idea previously has been acquired by the school in book form. It provides no protection against a school board's decision not to acquire a particular book, even though that decision denies access to ideas as fully as removal of the book from the library, and it prohibits removal of previously acquired books only if the remover "dislike[s] the ideas contained in those books," even though removal for any other reason also denies the students access to the books. * * *

But it is not the limitations which Justice Brennan places on the right with which I disagree; they simply demonstrate his discomfort with the new doctrine which he fashions out of whole cloth. It is the very existence of a right to receive information, in the junior high school and high school setting, which I find wholly unsupported by our past decisions and inconsistent with the necessarily selective process of elementary and secondary education.

* * *

B

There are even greater reasons for rejecting Justice Brennan's analysis, however, than the significant fact that we have never adopted it in the past. "The importance of public schools in the preparation of individuals for participation as citizens, and in the preservation of the

---

5. There are intimations in Justice Brennan's opinion that if petitioners had only consulted literary experts, librarians, and teachers their decision might better withstand First Amendment attack. * * * These observations seem to me wholly fatuous; surely ideas are no more accessible or no less suppressed if the school board merely ratifies the opinion of some group rather than following its own opinion.

values on which our society rests, has long been recognized by our decisions." Ambach v. Norwick, 441 U.S. 68, 76 (1979). Public schools fulfill the vital role of teaching students the basic skills necessary to function in our society, and of "inculcating fundamental values necessary to the maintenance of a democratic political system." * * * The idea that such students have a right of access, *in the school,* to information other than that thought by their educators to be necessary is contrary to the very nature of an inculcative education.

* * *

As already mentioned, elementary and secondary schools are inculcative in nature. The libraries of such schools serve as supplements to this inculcative role. Unlike university or public libraries, elementary and secondary school libraries are not designed for freewheeling inquiry; they are tailored, as the public school curriculum is tailored, to the teaching of basic skills and ideas. Thus, Justice Brennan cannot rely upon the nature of school libraries to escape the fact that the First Amendment right to receive information simply has no application to the one public institution which, by its very nature, is a place for the selective conveyance of ideas.

After all else is said, however, the most obvious reason that petitioners' removal of the books did not violate respondents' right to receive information is the ready availability of the books elsewhere. Students are not denied books by their removal from a school library. The books may be borrowed from a public library, read at a university library, purchased at a bookstore, or loaned by a friend. The government as educator does not seek to reach beyond the confines of the school. Indeed, following the removal from the school library of the books at issue in this case, the local public library put all nine books on display for public inspection. Their contents were fully accessible to any inquisitive student.

* * *

D

Intertwined as a basis for Justice Brennan's opinion, along with the "right to receive information," is the statement that "[o]ur Constitution does not permit the official suppression of *ideas.*" * * * (emphasis in original). There would be few champions, I suppose, of the idea that our Constitution *does* permit the official suppression of ideas; my difficulty is not with the admittedly appealing catchiness of the phrase, but with my doubt that it is really a useful analytical tool in solving difficult First Amendment problems. Since the phrase appears in the opinion "out of the blue," without any reference to previous First Amendment decisions of this Court, it would appear that the Court for years has managed to decide First Amendment cases without it.

I would think that prior cases decided under established First Amendment doctrine afford adequate guides in this area without resorting to a phrase which seeks to express "a complicated process of constitutional adjudication by a deceptive formula." Kovacs v. Cooper, 336 U.S. 77, 96 (1949) (Frankfurter, J., concurring). A school board which publicly adopts a policy forbidding the criticism of United States foreign policy by any student, any teacher, or any book on the library shelves is indulging in one kind of "suppression of ideas." A school board which adopts a policy that there shall be no discussion of current events in a class for high school sophomores devoted to second-year Latin "suppresses ideas" in quite a different context. * * *

I think a far more satisfactory basis for addressing these kinds of questions is found in the Court's language in *Tinker v. Des Moines School District*, where noted:

> "[A] particular symbol—black armbands worn to exhibit opposition to this Nation's involvement in Vietnam—was singled out for prohibition. Clearly, the prohibition of expression of one particular opinion, at least without evidence that it is necessary to avoid material and substantial interference with schoolwork or discipline, is not constitutionally permissible." 393 U.S., at 510–511.

In the case before us the petitioners may in one sense be said to have "suppressed" the "ideas" of vulgarity and profanity, but that is hardly an apt description of what was done. They ordered the removal of books containing vulgarity and profanity, but they did not attempt to preclude discussion about the themes of the books or the books themselves. App. 140. Such a decision, on respondents' version of the facts in this case, is sufficiently related to "educational suitability" to pass muster under the First Amendment.

E

* * *

I think the Court will far better serve the cause of First Amendment jurisprudence by candidly recognizing that the role of government as sovereign is subject to more stringent limitations than is the role of government as employer, property owner, or educator. It must also be recognized that the government as educator is subject to fewer strictures when operating an elementary and secondary school system than when operating an institution of higher learning. Cf. Tilton v. Richardson, 403 U.S. 672, 685–686 (1971) (opinion of JUSTICE BURGER, C.J.).
* * *

* * *

JUSTICE O'CONNOR, dissenting.

If the school board can set the curriculum, select teachers, and determine initially what books to purchase for the school library, it surely can decide which books to discontinue or remove from the school library so long as it does not also interfere with the right of students to read the material and to discuss it. As Justice Rehnquist persuasively argues, the plurality's analysis overlooks the fact that in this case the government is acting in its special role as educator.

I do not personally agree with the Board's action with respect to some of the books in question here, but it is not the function of the courts to make the decisions that have been properly relegated to the elected members of school boards. It is the school board that must determine educational suitability, and it has done so in this case. I therefore join The Chief Justice's dissent.

SNEPP v. UNITED STATES
Supreme Court of the United States, 1980.
444 U.S. 507, 100 S.Ct. 763, 62 L.Ed.2d 704.

* * *

PER CURIAM.

In No. 78–1871, Frank W. Snepp III seeks review of a judgment enforcing an agreement that he signed when he accepted employment with the Central Intelligence Agency (CIA). He also contends that punitive damages are an inappropriate remedy for the breach of his promise to submit all writings about the Agency for prepublication review. In No. 79–265, the United States conditionally cross petitions from a judgment refusing to find that profits attributable to Snepp's breach are impressed with a constructive trust. We grant the petitions for certiorari in order to correct the judgment from which both parties seek relief.

I

Based on his experiences as a CIA agent, Snepp published a book about certain CIA activities in South Vietnam. Snepp published the account without submitting it to the Agency for prepublication review. As an express condition of his employment with the CIA in 1968, Snepp had executed an agreement promising that he would "not * * * publish * * * any information or material relating to the Agency, its activities or intelligence activities generally, either during or after the term of [his] employment * * * without specific prior approval by the Agency." App. to Pet. for Cert. in No. 78–1871, p. 59a. The promise was an integral part of Snepp's concurrent undertaking "not to disclose any classified information relating to the Agency without proper authorization." *Id.*, at 58a. Thus, Snepp had pledged not to divulge *classified* information and not to publish *any* information without prepublication clearance. The Government brought this suit to enforce Snepp's agreement. It sought a declaration that Snepp had breached the contract, an injunction requiring Snepp to submit future writings for prepublication review, and an order imposing a constructive trust for the Government's benefit on all profits that Snepp might earn from publishing the book in violation of his fiduciary obligations to the Agency.

The District Court found that Snepp had "willfully, deliberately and surreptitiously breached his position of trust with the CIA and the [1968] secrecy agreement" by publishing his book without submitting it for prepublication review. 456 F.Supp. 176, 179 (ED Va.1978). The court also found that Snepp deliberately misled CIA officials into believing that he would submit the book for prepublication clearance. Finally, the court determined as a fact that publication of the book had "caused the United States irreparable harm and loss." *Id.*, at 180. The District Court therefore enjoined future breaches of Snepp's agreement and imposed a constructive trust on Snepp's profits.

The Court of Appeals accepted the findings of the District Court and agreed that Snepp had breached a valid contract. It specifically affirmed the finding that Snepp's failure to submit his manuscript for prepublication review had inflicted "irreparable harm" on intelligence activities vital to our national security. 595 F.2d 926, 935 (CA4 1979). Thus, the court upheld the injunction against future violations of Snepp's prepublication obligation. The court, however, concluded that the record did not support imposition of a constructive trust. The conclusion rested on the court's perception that Snepp had a First Amendment right to publish unclassified information and the Government's concession—for the purposes of this litigation—that Snepp's book divulged no classified intelligence. *Id.*, at 935–936. In other words, the court thought that Snepp's fiduciary obligation extended only to reserving the confidentiality of classified material. It therefore limited recovery to nominal damages and to the possibility of punitive damages if the Government—in a jury trial—could prove tortious conduct.

* * *

II

Snepp's employment with the CIA involved an extremely high degree of trust. In the opening sentence of the agreement that he signed, Snepp explicitly recognized that he was entering a trust relationship. The trust agreement specifically imposed the obligation not to publish *any* information relating to the Agency without submitting the information for clearance. Snepp stipulated at trial that—after undertaking this obligation—he had been "assigned to various positions of trust" and that he had been granted "frequent access to classified information, including information regarding intelligence sources and methods." 456 F.Supp., at 178. Snepp published his book about CIA activities on the basis of this background and exposure. He deliberately and surreptitiously violated his obligation to submit all material for prepublication review. Thus, he exposed the classified information with which he had been entrusted to the risk of disclosure.

Whether Snepp violated his trust does not depend upon whether his book actually contained classified information. The Government does not deny—as a general principle—Snepp's right to publish unclassified information. Nor does it contend—at this stage of the litigation—that Snepp's book contains classified material. The Government simply claims that, in light of the special trust reposed in him and the agreement that he signed, Snepp should have given the CIA an opportunity to determine whether the material he proposed to publish would compromise classified information or sources. Neither of the Government's concessions undercuts its claim that Snepp's failure to submit to prepublication review was a breach of his trust.

Both the District Court and the Court of Appeals found that a former intelligence agent's publication of unreviewed material relating to intelligence activities can be detrimental to vital national interests even if the published information is unclassified. When a former agent relies on his own judgment about what information is detrimental, he may reveal information that the CIA—with its broader understanding of what may expose classified information and confidential sources—could have identified as harmful. In addition to receiving intelligence from domestically based or controlled sources, the CIA obtains information from the intelligence services of friendly nations and from agents operating in foreign countries. The continued availability of these foreign sources depends upon the CIA's ability to guarantee the security of information that might compromise them and even endanger the personal safety of foreign agents.

* * *

III

The decision of the Court of Appeals denies the Government the most appropriate remedy for Snepp's acknowledged wrong. Indeed, as a practical matter, the decision may well leave the Government with no reliable deterrent against similar breaches of security. No one disputes that the actual damages attributable to a publication such as Snepp's generally are unquantifiable. Nominal damages are a hollow alternative, certain to deter no one. The punitive damages recoverable after a jury trial are speculative and unusual. Even if recovered, they may bear no relation to either the Government's irreparable loss or Snepp's unjust gain.

The Government could not pursue the only remedy that the Court of Appeals left it without losing the benefit of the bargain it seeks to enforce. Proof of tortious conduct necessary to sustain an award of punitive damages might force the Government to disclose some of the very confidences that Snepp promised to protect. The trial of such a suit, before a jury if the defendant so elects, would subject the CIA and its officials to probing discovery into the Agency's highly confidential affairs. Rarely would the Government run this risk. In a letter introduced at Snepp's trial, former CIA Director Colby noted the analogous problem in criminal cases. Existing law, he stated, "requires the revelation in open court of confirming or additional information of such a nature that the potential damage to the national security precludes prosecution." App. to Pet. for Cert. in No. 78–1871, p. 68a. When the Government cannot secure its remedy without unacceptable risks, it has no remedy at all.

A constructive trust, on the other hand, protects both the Government and the former agent from unwarranted risks. This remedy is the natural and customary consequence of a breach of trust. It deals fairly with both parties by conforming relief to the dimensions of the wrong. If the agent secures prepublication clearance, he can publish with no fear of liability. If the agent publishes unreviewed material in violation of his fiduciary and contractual obligation, the trust remedy simply requires him to disgorge the benefits of his faithlessness. Since the remedy is swift and sure, it is tailored to deter those who would place sensitive information at risk. And since the remedy reaches only funds attributable to the breach, it cannot saddle the former agent with exemplary damages out of all proportion to his gain. The decision of the Court of Appeals would deprive the Government of this equitable and effective means of protecting intelligence that may contribute to national security. We therefore reverse the judgment of the Court of Appeals insofar as it refused to impose a constructive trust of Snepp's profits, and we remand the cases to the Court of Appeals for reinstatement of the full judgment of the District Court.

So ordered.

Mr. Justice Stevens, with whom Mr. Justice Brennan and Mr. Justice Marshall join, dissenting.

* * *

In this case Snepp admittedly breached his duty to submit the manuscript of his book, Decent Interval, to the CIA for prepublication review. However, the Government has conceded that the book contains no classified, nonpublic material. Thus, by definition, the interest in confidentiality that Snepp's contract was designed to protect has not been compromised. Nevertheless, the Court today grants the Government unprecedented and drastic relief in the form of a constructive trust over the profits derived by Snepp from the sale of the book. Because that remedy is not authorized by any applicable law and because it is most inappropriate for the Court to dispose of this novel issue summarily on the Government's conditional cross-petition for certiorari, I respectfully dissent.

I

The rule of law the Court announces today is not supported by statute, by the contract, or by the common law. Although Congress has enacted a number of criminal statutes punishing the unauthorized dissemination of certain types of classified information, it has not seen fit to authorize the constructive trust remedy the Court creates today. Nor does either of the contracts Snepp signed with the Agency provide for any such remedy in the event of a breach. The Court's *per curiam* opinion seems to suggest that its result is supported by a blend of the law of trusts and the law of contracts. But neither of these branches of the common law supports the imposition of a constructive trust under the circumstances of this case.

Plainly this is not a typical trust situation in which a settlor has conveyed legal title to certain assets to a trustee for the use and benefit of designated beneficiaries. Rather, it is an employment relationship in which the employee possesses fiduciary obligations arising out of his duty of loyalty to his employer. One of those obligations, long recognized by the common law even in the absence of a written employment agreement, is the duty to protect confidential or "classified" information. If Snepp had breached that obligation, the common law would support the implication of a constructive trust upon the benefits derived from his misuse of confidential information.

But Snepp did not breach his duty to protect confidential information. Rather, he breached a contractual duty, imposed in aid of the basic duty to maintain confidentiality, to obtain prepublication clearance. In order to justify the imposition of a constructive trust, the majority attempts to equate this contractual duty with Snepp's duty not to disclose, labeling them both as "fiduciary." I find nothing in the common law to support such an approach.

Employment agreements often contain covenants designed to ensure in various ways that an employee fully complies with his duty not to disclose or misuse confidential information. One of the most common is a covenant not to compete. Contrary to the majority's approach in this case, the courts have not construed such covenants broadly simply because they support a basic fiduciary duty; nor have they granted sweeping remedies to enforce them. On the contrary, because such covenants are agreements in restraint of an individual's freedom of trade, they are enforceable only if they can survive scrutiny under the "rule of reason." That rule, originally laid down in the seminal case of Mitchel v. Reynolds, 1 P.Wms. 181, 24 Eng.Rep. 347 (1711), requires that the covenant be reasonably necessary to protect a legitimate interest of the employer (such as an interest in confidentiality), that the employer's interest not be outweighed by the public interest, and that the covenant not be of any longer duration or wider geographical scope than necessary to protect the employer's interest.

The Court has not persuaded me that a rule of reason analysis should not be applied to Snepp's covenant to submit to prepublication review. Like an ordinary employer, the CIA has a vital interest in protecting certain types of information; at the same time, the CIA employee has a countervailing interest in preserving a wide range of work opportunities (including work as an author) and in protecting his First Amendment rights. The public interest lies in a proper accommodation that will preserve the intelligence mission of the Agency while not abridging the free flow of unclassified information. When the Government seeks to enforce a harsh restriction on the employee's freedom, despite its admission that the interest the agreement was designed to protect—the confidentiality of classified information—has not been compromised, an equity court might well be persuaded that the case is not one in which the covenant should be enforced.

But even assuming that Snepp's covenant to submit to prepublication review should be enforced, the constructive trust imposed by the Court is not an appropriate remedy. If an employee has used his employer's confidential information for his own personal profit, a constructive trust over those profits is obviously an appropriate remedy because the profits are the direct result of the breach. But Snepp admittedly did not use confidential information in his book; nor were the profits from his book in any sense a product of his failure to submit the book for prepublication review. For, even if Snepp had submitted the book to the Agency for prepublication review, the Government's censorship authority would surely have been limited to the excision of classified material. In this case, then, it would have been obliged to clear the book for publication in precisely the same form as it now stands. Thus, Snepp has not gained any profits as a result of his breach; the Government, rather than Snepp, will be unjustly enriched if he is required to disgorge profits attributable entirely to his own legitimate activity.

Despite the fact that Snepp has not caused the Government the type of harm that would ordinarily be remedied by the imposition of a constructive trust, the Court attempts to justify a constructive trust remedy on the ground that the Government has suffered *some* harm. The Court states that publication of "unreviewed material" by a former CIA agent "can be detrimental to vital national interests even if the published information is unclassified." * * * It then seems to suggest that the injury in such cases stems from the Agency's inability to catch "harmful" but unclassified information before it is published. I do not believe, however, that the Agency has any authority to censor its employees' publication of unclassified information on the basis of its opinion that publication may be "detrimental to vital national interests" or otherwise "identified as harmful." *Ibid.* The CIA never attempted to assert such power over Snepp in either of the contracts he signed; rather, the Agency itself limited its censorship power to preventing the disclosure of "classified" information. Moreover, even if such a wide-ranging prior restraint would be good national security policy, I would have great difficulty reconciling it with the demands of the First Amendment.

* * *

III

The uninhibited character of today's exercise in lawmaking is highlighted by the Court's disregard of two venerable principles that favor a more conservative approach to this case.

First, for centuries the English-speaking judiciary refused to grant equitable relief unless the plaintiff could show that his remedy at law was inadequate. Without waiting for an opportunity to appraise the adequacy of the punitive damages remedy in this case, the Court has jumped to the conclusion that equitable relief is necessary.

Second, and of greater importance, the Court seems unaware of the fact that its drastic new remedy has been fashioned to enforce a species of prior restraint on citizen's right to criticize his government. Inherent in this prior restraint is the risk that the reviewing agency will misuse its authority to delay the publication of a critical work or to persuade an author to modify the contents of his work beyond the demands of secrecy. The character of the covenant as a prior restraint on free speech surely imposes an especially heavy burden on the censor to justify the remedy it seeks. It would take more than the Court has written to persuade me that that burden has been met.

I respectfully dissent.

UNITED STATES v. ROBEL

Supreme Court of the United States, 1967.
389 U.S. 258, 88 S.Ct. 419, 19 L.Ed.2d 508.

MR. CHIEF JUSTICE WARREN delivered the opinion of the Court.

This appeal draws into question the constitutionality of § 5(a)(1)(D) of the Subversive Activities Control Act of 1950, 64 Stat. 992, 50 U.S.C. § 784(a)(1)(D), which provides that when a Communist-action organization[2] is under a final order to register, it shall be unlawful for any member of the organization "to engage in any employment in any defense facility." In Communist Party v. Subversive Activities Control Board, 367 U.S. 1 (1961), this Court sustained an order of the SACB requiring the Communist Party of the United States to register as a Communist-action organization under the Act. The Board's order became final on October 20, 1961. At that time appellee, a member of the Communist Party, was employed as a machinist at the Seattle, Washington, shipyard of Todd Shipyards Corporation. On August 20, 1962, the Secretary of Defense, acting under authority delegated by § 5(b) of the Act, designated that shipyard a "defense facility." Appellee's continued employment at the shipyard after that date subjected him to prosecution under § 5(a)(1)(D), and on May 21, 1963, an indictment was filed charging him with a violation of that section. The indictment alleged in substance that appellee had "unlawfully and willfully engage[d] in employment" at the shipyard with knowledge of the outstanding order against the Party and with knowledge and notice of the shipyard's designation as a defense facility by the Secretary of Defense. The United States District Court for the Western District of Washington granted appellee's motion to dismiss the indictment as a "likely constitutional infirmity" in § 5(a)(1)(D), the District Court read into that section "the requirements of active membership and specific intent." Because the indictment failed to allege that appellee's Communist Party membership was of that quality, the indictment was dismissed. The Government, unwilling to accept that narrow construction of § 5(a)(1)(D) and insisting on the broadest possible application of the statute,[3] initially took its appeal to the Court of Appeals for the Ninth Circuit. * * * We affirm the judgment of the District Court, but on the ground that § 5(a)(1)(D) is an unconstitutional abridgment of the right of association protected by the First Amendment. * * *

When Congress' exercise of one of its enumerated powers clashes with those individual liberties protected by the Bill of Rights, it is our "delicate and difficult task" to determine whether the resulting restriction on freedom can be tolerated. See Schneider v. State, 308 U.S. 147, 161 (1939). The Government emphasizes that the purpose of

---

2. Section 3(3)(a) of the Act, 50 U.S.C. § 784(3)(a), defines a "Communist-action organization" as: "any organization in the United States (other than a diplomatic representative or mission of a foreign government accredited as such by the State Department) which (i) is substantially directed, dominated, or controlled by the foreign government or foreign organization controlling the world Communist movement * * * and (ii) operates primarily to advance the objectives of such world Communist movement. * * *"

3. The Government has persisted in this view in its arguments to this Court. Brief for the Government 48–56.

§ 5(a)(1)(D) is to reduce the threat of sabotage and espionage in the Nation's defense plants. The Government's interest in such a prophylactic measure is not insubstantial. But it cannot be doubted that the means chosen to implement that governmental purpose in this instance cut deeply into the right of association. Section 5(a)(1)(D) put appellee to the choice of surrendering his organizational affiliation, regardless of whether his membership threatened the security of a defense facility,[10] or giving up his job.[11] When appellee refused to make that choice, he became subject to a possible criminal penalty of five years' imprisonment and a $10,000 fine. The statute quite literally establishes guilt by association alone, without any need to establish that an individual's association poses the threat feared by the Government in proscribing it. The inhibiting effect on the exercise of First Amendment rights is clear.

* * * It is made irrelevant to the statute's operation that an individual may be a passive or inactive member of a designated organization, that he may be unaware of the organization's unlawful aims, or that he may disagree with those unlawful aims.[16] It is also made irrelevant that an individual who is subject to the penalties of § 5(a)(1)(D) may occupy a nonsensitive position in a defense facility. Thus, § 5(a)(1)(D) contains the fatal defect of overbreadth because it seeks to bar employment both for association which may be proscribed and for association which may not be proscribed consistently with First Amendment rights. * * *

We are not unmindful of the congressional concern over the danger of sabotage and espionage in national defense industries, and nothing we hold today should be read to deny Congress the power under narrowly drawn legislation to keep from sensitive positions in defense facilities those who would use their positions to disrupt the Nation's production facilities. * * * The task of writing legislation which will stay within those bounds has been committed to Congress. Our decision today simply recognizes that, when legitimate legislative concerns are expressed in a statute which imposes a substantial burden on protected First Amendment activities, Congress must achieve its goal by means which have a "less drastic" impact on the continued vitality of First Amendment freedoms. *Shelton v. Tucker, supra;* cf. United States v. Brown, 381 U.S. 437, 461 (1965). The Constitution and the

---

10. The appellee has worked at the shipyard, apparently without incident and apparently without concealing his Communist Party membership, for more than 10 years. And we are told that, following appellee's indictment and arrest, "he was released on his own recognizance, and immediately returned to his job as a machinist at the Todd Shipyards, where he has worked ever since." Brief for Appellee 6, n. 8. As far as we can determine, appellee is the only individual the Government has attempted to prosecute under § 5(a)(1)(D).

11. We recognized in Green v. McElroy, 360 U.S., at 492, that "the right to hold specific private employment and to follow a chosen profession free from unreasonable governmental interference comes within the 'liberty' and 'property' concepts of the Fifth Amendment."

16. A number of complex motivations may impel an individual to align himself with a particular organization. See Gibson v. Florida Legislative Investigation Committee, 372 U.S. 539, 562–565 (1963) (concurring opinion). It is for that reason that the mere presence of an individual's name on an organization's membership rolls is insufficient to impute to him the organization's illegal goals.

basic position of First Amendment rights in our democratic fabric demand nothing less.

Affirmed.

MR. JUSTICE MARSHALL took no part in the consideration of this case.

MR. JUSTICE BRENNAN, concurring in the result.

I too agree that the judgment of the District Court should be affirmed but I reach that result for different reasons.

* * *

* * * Even if the statute is not overbroad on its face—because there may be "defense facilities" so essential to our national security that Congress could constitutionally exclude all Party members from employment in them—the congressional delegation of authority to the Secretary of Defense to designate "defense facilities" creates the danger of overbroad, unauthorized, and arbitrary application of criminal sanctions in an area of protected freedoms and therefore, in my view, renders this statute invalid. Because the statute contains no meaningful standard by which the Secretary is to govern his designations, and no procedures to contest or review his designations, the "defense facility" formulation is constitutionally insufficient to mark "the field within which the [Secretary] is to act so that it may be known whether he has kept within it in compliance with the legislative will." Yakus v. United States, 321 U.S. 414, 425 (1944).

* * *

This is persuasive evidence that the matter of the designation of "defense facilities" was purposely committed by Congress entirely to the discretionary judgment of the Secretary. Unlike the opportunities for hearing and judicial review afforded the Party itself, the Party member was not to be heard by the Secretary to protest the designation of his place of employment as a "defense facility," nor was the member to have recourse to the courts. This pointed distinction, as in the case of the statute before the Court in Schilling v. Rogers, 363 U.S. 666, 674, is compelling evidence "that in this Act Congress was advertent to the role of courts, and an absence in any specific area of any kind of provision for judicial participation strongly indicates a legislative purpose that there be no such participation." This clear indication of the congressional plan, coupled with a flexibility—as regards the boundaries of the Secretary's discretion—so unguided as to be entirely unguiding, must also mean that Congress contemplated that an affected Party member was not to be heard to contend even at his criminal trial that the Secretary acted beyond the scope of his powers, or that the designation of the particular facility was arbitrary and capricious.
* * *

The legislative history of the section confirms this conclusion.
* * *

* * *

MR. JUSTICE WHITE, with whom MR. HARLAN joins, dissenting.
* * *

The constitutional right found to override the public interest in national security defined by Congress is the right of association, here the right of appellee Robel to remain a member of the Communist Party after being notified of its adjudication as a Communist-action organization. Nothing in the Constitution requires this result. The right of association is not mentioned in the Constitution. It is a judicial construct appended to the First Amendment rights to speak freely, to assemble, and to petition for redress of grievances. While the right of association has deep roots in history and is supported by the inescapable necessity for group action in a republic as large and complex as ours, it has only recently blossomed as the controlling factor in constitutional litigation; its contours as yet lack delineation. Although official interference with First Amendment rights has drawn close scrutiny, it is now apparent that the right of association is not absolute and is subject to significant regulation by the State. The law of criminal conspiracy restricts the purposes for which men may associate and the means they may use to implement their plans. Labor unions, and membership in them, are intricately controlled by statutes, both federal and state, as are political parties and corporations.

* * *

The national interest asserted by the Congress is real and substantial. After years of study, Congress prefaced the Subversive Activities Control Act of 1950, 64 Stat. 987, 50 U.S.C. §§ 781–798, with its findings that there exists an international Communist movement which by treachery, deceit, espionage, and sabotage seeks to overthrow existing governments; that the movement operates in this country through Communist-action organizations which are under foreign domination and control and which seek to overthrow the Government by any necessary means, including force and violence; that the communist movement in the United States is made up of thousands of adherents, rigidly disciplined, operating in secrecy, and employing espionage and sabotage tactics in form and manner evasive of existing laws. Congress therefore, among other things, defined the characteristics of Communist-action organizations, provided for their adjudication by the SACB, and decided that the security of the United States required the exclusion of Communist-action organization members from employment in certain defense facilities. After long and complex litigation, the SACB found the Communist Party to be a Communist-action organization within the meaning of the Act. That conclusion was affirmed both by the Court of Appeals, Communist Party v. Subversive Activities Control Board, 277 F.2d 78 (D.C.Cir.1959), and this Court, 367 U.S. 1 (1961).
* * *

* * *

The statute does not prohibit membership in the Communist Party. Nor are appellee and other Communists excluded from all employment in the United States, or even from all defense plants. The touchstones for exclusion are the requirements of national security, and the facilities designated under this standard amount to only about one percent of all the industrial establishments in the United States.

* * *

The Court says that mere membership in an association with knowledge that the association pursues unlawful aims cannot be the basis for criminal prosecution, Scales v. United States, 367 U.S. 203 (1961), or for denial of a passport, Aptheker v. Secretary of State, 378 U.S. 500 (1964). But denying the opportunity to be employed in some defense plants is a much smaller deterrent to the exercise of associational rights than denial of a passport or a criminal penalty attached solely to membership, and the Government's interest in keeping potential spies and saboteurs from defense plants is much greater than its interest in keeping disloyal Americans from traveling abroad or in committing all Party members to prison. * * *

* * *

ELROD v. BURNS

Supreme Court of the United States, 1976.
427 U.S. 347, 96 S.Ct. 2673, 49 L.Ed.2d 547.

MR. JUSTICE BRENNAN announced the judgment of the Court and delivered an opinion in which MR. JUSTICE WHITE and MR. JUSTICE MARSHALL joined.

This case presents the question whether public employees who allege that they were discharged or threatened with discharge solely because of their partisan political affiliation or nonaffiliation state a claim for deprivation of constitutional rights secured by the First and Fourteenth Amendments.

* * *

II

In December 1970, the Sheriff of Cook County, a Republican, was replaced by Richard Elrod, a Democrat. At that time, respondents, all Republicans, were employees of the Cook County Sheriff's Office. They were non-civil-service employees and, therefore, not covered by any statute, ordinance, or regulation protecting them from arbitrary discharge. One respondent, John Burns, was Chief Deputy of the Process Division and supervised all departments of the Sheriff's Office working on the seventh floor of the building housing that office. Frank Vargas was a bailiff and security guard at the Juvenile Court of Cook County. Fred L. Buckley was employed as a process server in the office. Joseph Dennard was an employee in the office.

It has been the practice of the Sheriff of Cook County, when he assumes office from a Sheriff of a different political party, to replace non-civil-service employees of the Sheriff's Office with members of his own party when the existing employees lack or fail to obtain requisite support from, or fail to affiliate with, that party. Consequently, subsequent to Sheriff Elrod's assumption of office, respondents, with the exception of Buckley, were discharged from their employment solely because they did not support and were not members of the Democratic Party and had failed to obtain the sponsorship of one of its leaders. Buckley is in imminent danger of being discharged solely for the same reasons. * * *

* * *

IV

The Cook County Sheriff's practice of dismissing employees on a partisan basis is but one form of the general practice of political patronage. The practice also includes placing loyal supporters in government jobs that may or may not have been made available by political discharges. Nonofficeholders may be the beneficiaries of lucrative government contracts for highway construction, buildings, and supplies. Favored wards may receive improved public services. Members of the judiciary may even engage in the practice through the appointment of receiverships, trusteeships, and refereeships. Although political patronage comprises a broad range of activities, we are here concerned only with the constitutionality of dismissing public employees for partisan reasons.

Patronage practice is not new to American politics. It has existed at the federal level at least since the Presidency of Thomas Jefferson, although its popularization and legitimation primarily occurred later, in the Presidency of Andrew Jackson. The practice is not unique to American politics. It has been used in many European countries, and in darker times, it played a significant role in the Nazi rise to power in Germany and other totalitarian states. * * *

* * *

V

The cost of the practice of patronage is the restraint it places on freedoms of belief and association. In order to maintain their jobs, respondents were required to pledge their political allegiance to the Democratic Party, work for the election of other candidates of the Democratic Party, contribute a portion of their wages to the Party, or obtain the sponsorship of a member of the Party, usually at the price of one of the first three alternatives. Regardless of the incumbent party's identity, Democratic or otherwise, the consequences for association and belief are the same. An individual who is a member of the out-party maintains affiliation with his own party at the risk of losing his job. He works for the election of his party's candidates and espouses its policies at the same risk. The financial and campaign assistance that he is induced to provide to another party furthers the advancement of that party's policies to the detriment of his party's views and ultimately his own beliefs, and any assessment of his salary is tantamount to coerced belief. See Buckley v. Valeo, 424 U.S. 1, 19 (1976). Even a pledge of allegiance to another party, however ostensible, only serves to compromise the individual's true beliefs. Since the average public employee is hardly in the financial position to support his party and another, or to lend his time to two parties, the individual's ability to act according to his beliefs and to associate with others of his political persuasion is constrained, and support for his party is diminished.

* * *

Our concern with the impact of patronage on political belief and association does not occur in the abstract, for political belief and association constitute the core of those activities protected by the First Amendment.[10] Regardless of the nature of the inducement, whether it be by the denial of public employment or, as in Board of Education v. Barnette, 319 U.S. 624 (1943), by the influence of a teacher over students, "[i]f there is any fixed star in our constitutional constellation, it is that no official, high or petty, can prescribe what shall be orthodox in politics, nationalism, religion, or other matters of opinion or force citizens to confess by word or act with their faith therein." *Id.,* at 642. And, though freedom of belief is central, "[t]he First Amendment protects political association as well as political expression." *Buckley v. Valeo, supra,* at 15. "There can no longer be any doubt that freedom to associate with others for the common advancement of political beliefs and ideas is a form of 'orderly group activity' protected by the First and Fourteenth Amendments. NAACP v. Button, 371 U.S. 415, 430 (1963); Bates v. Little Rock, 361 U.S. 516, 522–523 (1960); NAACP v. Alabama, 357 U.S. 449, 460–461 (1958). The right to associate with the political party of one's choice is an integral part of this basic constitutional freedom." Kusper v. Pontikes, 414 U.S. 51, 56–57 (1973).

These protections reflect our "profound national commitment to the principle that debate on public issues should be uninhibited, robust, and wide-open," New York Times Co. v. Sullivan, 376 U.S. 254, 270 (1964), a principle itself reflective of the fundamental understanding that "[c]ompetition in ideas and governmental policies is at the core of our electoral process. * * *" Williams v. Rhodes, 393 U.S., at 32. Patronage, therefore, to the extent it compels or restrains belief and association, is inimical to the process which undergirds our system of government and is "at war with the deeper traditions of democracy embodied in the First Amendment." Illinois State Employees Union v. Lewis, 473 F.2d, at 576. As such, the practice unavoidably confronts decisions by this Court either invalidating or recognizing as invalid government action that inhibits belief and association through the conditioning of public employment on political faith.

The Court recognized in United Public Workers v. Mitchell, 330 U.S. 75, 100 (1947), that "Congress may not 'enact a regulation providing that no Republican, Jew or Negro shall be appointed to federal office. * * *'" This principle was reaffirmed in Wieman v. Updegraff, 344 U.S. 183 (1952), which held that a State could not require its employees to establish their loyalty by extracting an oath denying past affiliation with Communists. And in Cafeteria Workers v. McElroy, 367 U.S. 886, 898 (1961), the Court recognized again that the govern-

---

10. "It is important to note that while it is the Fourteenth Amendment which bears directly upon the State it is the more specific limiting principles of the First Amendment that finally govern this case." Board of Education v. Barnette, 319 U.S. 624, 639 (1943).

ment could not deny employment because of previous membership in a particular party.[11]

Particularly pertinent to the constitutionality of the practice of patronage dismissals are Keyishian v. Board of Regents, 385 U.S. 589 (1967), and Perry v. Sindermann, 408 U.S. 593 (1972). In *Keyishian,* the Court invalidated New York statutes barring employment merely on the basis of membership in "subversive" organizations. *Keyishian* squarely held that political association alone could not, consistently with the First Amendment, constitute an adequate ground for denying public employment.[12] In *Perry,* the Court broadly rejected the validity of limitations on First Amendment rights as a condition to the receipt of a governmental benefit, to a person on a basis that infringes his constitutionally protected interests—especially, his interest in freedom of speech. For if the government could deny a benefit to a person because of his constitutionally protected speech or associations, his exercise of those freedoms would in effect be penalized and inhibited. This would allow the government to 'produce a result which [it] could not command directly.' Speiser v. Randall, 357 U.S. 513, 526 (1958). Such interference with constitutional rights is impermissible." 408 U.S., at 597.

Patronage practice falls squarely within the prohibitions of *Keyishian* and *Perry*. Under that practice, public employees hold their jobs on the condition that they provide, in some acceptable manner, support for the favored political party. * * *

VI

Although the practice of patronage dismissals clearly infringes First Amendment interests, our inquiry is not at an end, for the prohibition on encroachment of First Amendment protections is not an absolute. Restraints are permitted for appropriate reasons. *Keyishian* and *Perry,* however, not only serve to establish a presumptive prohibition on infringement, but also serve to dispose of one suggested by petitioners' reference to this Court's affirmance by an equally divided court in Bailey v. Richardson, 341 U.S. 918 (1951), aff'g 182 F.2d 46 (D.C.Cir.1950). That is the notion that because there is no right to a governmental benefit, such as public employment, the benefit may be denied for any reason. *Perry,* however, emphasized that "[f]or at least a quarter-century, this Court has made clear that even though a person has no 'right' to a valuable governmental benefit and even though the government may deny him the benefit for any number of reasons, there are some reasons upon which the government may not rely." 408 U.S., at 597. *Perry* and *Keyishian* properly recognize one such impermissible reason: The denial of a public benefit for the purpose of creating an

---

11. Protection of First Amendment interests has not been limited to invalidation of conditions on government employment requiring allegiance to a particular political party. This Court's decisions have prohibited conditions on public benefits, in the form of jobs or otherwise, which dampen the exercise generally of First Amendment rights, however slight the inducement to the individual to forsake those rights.

12. Thereafter, United States v. Robel, 389 U.S. 258 (1967), similarly held that mere membership in the Communist Party could not bar a person from employment in private defense establishments important to national security.

incentive enabling it to achieve what it may not command directly. "[T]he theory that public employment which may be denied altogether may be subjected to any conditions, regardless of how unreasonable, has been uniformly rejected." Keyishian v. Board of Regents, 385 U.S., at 605–606. "It is too late in the day to doubt that the liberties of religion and expression may be infringed by the denial of or placing of conditions upon a benefit or privilege." * * *

While the right-privilege distinction furnishes no ground on which to justify patronage, petitioners raise several other justifications requiring consideration. Before examining those justifications, however, it is necessary to have in mind the standards according to which their sufficiency is to be measured. It is firmly established that a significant impairment of First Amendment rights must survive exacting scrutiny. Buckley v. Valeo, 424 U.S., at 64–65; NAACP v. Alabama, 357 U.S. 449, 460–461 (1958). "This type of scrutiny is necessary even if any deterrent effect on the exercise of First Amendment rights arises, not through direct government action, but indirectly as an unintended but inevitable result of the government's conduct. * * *" *Buckley v. Valeo, supra,* at 65. Thus encroachment "cannot be justified upon a mere showing of a legitimate state interest." Kusper v. Pontikes, 414 U.S., at 58. The interest advanced must be paramount, one of vital importance, and the burden is on the government to show the existence of such an interest. * * * [I]f conditioning the retention of public employment on the employee's support of the in-party is to survive constitutional challenge, it must further some vital government end by a means that is least restrictive of freedom of belief and association in achieving that end, and the benefit gained must outweigh the loss of constitutionally protected rights.[17]

One interest which has been offered in justification of patronage is the need to insure effective government and the efficiency of public employees. It is argued that employees of political persuasions not the same as that of the party in control of public office will not have the incentive to work effectively and may even be motivated to subvert the incumbent administration's efforts to govern effectively. We are not persuaded. The inefficiency resulting from the wholesale replacement of large numbers of public employees every time political office changes hands belies this justification. And the prospect of dismissal after an election in which the incumbent party has lost is only a disincentive to good work.[18] Further, it is not clear that dismissal in order to make

17. The Court's decision in United States v. O'Brien, 391 U.S. 367 (1968), does not support petitioners. *O'Brien* dealt with the constitutionality of laws regulating the "nonspeech" elements of expressive conduct. No such regulation is involved here, for it is association and belief per se, not any particular form of conduct, which patronage seeks to control. * * *

18. It does not appear that efficiency and effective government were the concerns of elected officials in this case. Employees originally dismissed were reinstated after obtaining sponsorship letters, a practice hardly promotive of efficiency if the employee's work had been less than par or if the employee had previously behaved in an insubordinate manner. App. 14. Complaints by one supervisor that too many people were being discharged too fast, without adequately trained replacements, were met with the response that the number of dismissals was to be maintained because the job openings were needed for partisan appointments. *Id.,* at 15. Republican employee of the Sheriff's Office

room for a patronage appointment will result in replacement by a person more qualified to do the job since appointment often occurs in exchange for the delivery of votes, or other party service, not job capability. More fundamentally, however, the argument does not succeed because it is doubtful that the mere difference of political persuasion motivates poor performance; nor do we think it legitimately may be used as a basis for imputing such behavior. The Court has consistently recognized that mere political association is an inadequate basis for imputing disposition to ill-willed conduct. See Keyishian v. Board of Regents, 385 U.S., at 606–608; Elfbrandt v. Russell, 384 U.S. 11, 19 (1966); Wieman v. Updegraff, 344 U.S., at 190–191.[19] * * *

Even if the first argument that patronage serves effectiveness and efficiency be rejected, it still may be argued that patronage serves those interests by giving the employees of an incumbent party the incentive to perform well in order to insure their party's incumbency and thereby their jobs. Patronage, according to the argument, thus makes employees highly accountable to the public. But the ability of officials more directly accountable to the electorate to discharge employees for cause and the availability of merit systems, growth in the use of which has been quite significant, convince us that means less intrusive than patronage still exist for achieving accountability in the public work force and, thereby, effective and efficient government. The greater effectiveness of patronage over these less drastic means, if any, is at best marginal, a gain outweighed by the absence of intrusion on protected interests under the alternatives.

The lack of any justification for patronage dismissals as a means of furthering government effectiveness and efficiency distinguishes this case from CSC v. Letter Carriers, 413 U.S. 548 (1973), and United Public Workers v. Mitchell, 330 U.S. 75 (1949). In both of those cases, legislative restraints on political management and campaigning, by public employees were upheld despite their encroachment on First Amendment rights because, *inter alia,* they did serve in a necessary

---

was told that his dismissal had nothing to do with the quality of his work, but that his position was needed for a Democratic replacement. *Id.,* at 22.

19. In this regard, petitioners' reliance on American Communications Assn. v. Douds, 339 U.S. 382 (1950), is misplaced. To be sure, that decision upheld a section of the National Labor Relations Act denying certain benefits of the Act to labor organizations which had not filed with the National Labor Relations Board affidavits that their leaders were not members of the Communist Party. The Court there deferred to a legislative determination that, with respect to labor relations, the Communist Party was unlike other parties in its use of union leadership to bring about strikes and other obstructions to commerce. The Court was careful to note in *Douds,* however, that the precise holding in that case would not serve as a departure point for interferences of ill conduct grounded merely on political association. *Id.,* at 410. Indeed, the Court in *Douds* also carefully observed that political affiliations and beliefs "are circumstances ordinarily irrelevant to permissible subjects of government action." *Id.,* at 391.

Those caveats were well stated. With but three exceptions shortly after *Douds,* Adler v. Board of Education, 342 U.S. 485 (1952); Garnder v. Los Angeles Board, 341 U.S. 716 (1951); and Gerende v. Board of Supervisors, 341 U.S. 56 (1951), the Court's decisions have consistently rejected all inferences based merely on belief and association, and we do so today. See, e.g., Keyishian v. Board of Regents, 385 U.S., at 606–608; Wieman v. Updegraff, 344 U.S., at 188–190.

manner to foster and protect efficient and effective government.[20] Interestingly, the activities that were restrained by the legislation involved in those cases are characteristic of patronage practices. As the Court observed in *Mitchell:* "The conviction that an actively partisan governmental personnel threatens good administration has deepened since [1882]. Congress recognizes danger to the service in that political rather than official effort may earn advancement and to the public in that governmental favor may be channeled through political connections." 330 U.S., at 97–98.

A second interest advanced in support of patronage is the need for political loyalty of employees, not to the end that effectiveness and efficiency be insured, but to the end that representative government not be undercut by tactics obstructing the implementation of policies of the new administration, policies presumably sanctioned by the electorate. The justification is not without force, but is nevertheless inadequate to validate patronage wholesale. Limiting patronage dismissals to policymaking positions is sufficient to achieve this governmental end. Nonpolicy making individuals usually have only limited responsibility and are therefore not in a position to thwart the goals of the in-party.

No clear line can be drawn between policymaking and nonpolicymaking positions. While nonpolicymaking individuals usually have limited responsibility, that is not to say that one with a number of responsibilities is necessarily in a policymaking position. The nature of the responsibilities is critical. Employee supervisors, for example, may have many responsibilities, but those responsibilities may have only limited and well-defined objectives. An employee with responsibilities that are not well defined or are of broad scope more likely functions in a policymaking position. In determining whether an employee occupies a policymaking position, consideration should also be given to whether the employee acts as an adviser or formulates plans for the implementation of broad goals. Thus, the political loyalty "justification is a matter of proof, or at least argument, directed at particular kinds of jobs." Illinois State Employees Union v. Lewis, 472 F.2d, at 574. Since, as we have noted, it is the government's burden to demonstrate an overriding interest in order to validate an encroachment on protected interests, the burden of establishing this justification as to any particular respondent will rest on the petitioners on remand, cases of doubt being resolved in favor of the particular respondent.

It is argued that a third interest supporting patronage dismissals is the preservation of the democratic process. According to petitioners, " 'we have contrived no system for the support of party that does not place considerable reliance on patronage. The party organization makes a democratic government work and charges a price for its

---

20. Legislative restraints on political management and campaigning were also upheld in *Letter Carrier* and *Mitchell* because they served to protect individual belief and association and, thereby, the political process. The distinction between this case and those cases in that respect is treated *infra,* this page and at 368–371.

services.'"[21] The argument is thus premised on the centrality of partisan politics to the democratic process.

Preservation of the democratic process is certainly an interest protection of which may in some instances justify limitations on First Amendment freedoms. See Buckley v. Valeo, 424 U.S. 1 (1976); *CSC v. Letter Carriers, supra;* Williams v. Rhodes, 393 U.S. 23 (1968); *United Public Workers v. Mitchell, supra.* But however important preservation of the two party system or any system involving a fixed number of parties may or may not be,[22] *Williams v. Rhodes, supra,* at 32, we are not persuaded that the elimination of patronage practice or, as is specifically involved here, the interdiction of patronage dismissals, will bring about the demise of party politics. Political parties existed in the absence of active patronage practice prior to the administration of Andrew Jackson, and they have survived substantial reduction in their patronage power through the establishment of merit systems.

Patronage dismissals thus are not the least restrictive alternative to achieving the contribution they may make to the democratic process. The process functions as well without the practice, perhaps even better, for patronage dismissals clearly also retard that process. Patronage can result in the entrenchment of one or a few parties to the exclusion of others. And most indisputably, as we recognized at the outset, patronage is a very effective impediment to the associational and speech freedoms which are essential to a meaningful system of democratic government. Thus, if patronage contributes at all to the elective process, that contribution is diminished by the practice's impairment of the same.

To be sure, *Letter Carriers* and *Mitchell* upheld Hatch Act restraints sacrificing political campaigning and management activities themselves protected by the First Amendment. But in those cases it was the Court's judgment that congressional subordination of those activities was permissible to safeguard the core interests of individual belief and association.[26] Subordination of some First Amendment activity was permissible to protect other such activity. Today, we hold that subordination of other First Amendment activity, that is, patronage dismissals, not only is permissible, but also is mandated by the First Amendment. And since patronage dismissals fall within the category

---

21. Brief for Petitioners 43, quoting V. Key, Politics, Parties and Pressure Groups 369 (95th ed. 1964).

22. Partisan politics bears the imprimature only of tradition, not the Constitution. "It may be correct that the patronage system has been followed for 'almost two hundred years' and therefore was in existence when the Constitution was adopted. However, the notoriety of the practice in the administration of Andrew Jackson in 1828 implies that it was not prevalent theretofore; we are not aware of any discussion of the practice during the drafting of the Constitution or the First Amendment. In any event, if the age of a pernicious practice were a sufficient reason for its continued acceptance, the constitutional attack on racial discrimination would, of course, have been doomed to failure." Illinois State Employees Union v. Lewis, 473 F.2d 561, 568 n. 14 (CA7 1972).

26. "To declare that the present supposed evils of political activity are beyond the power of Congress to redress would leave the nation impotent to deal with what many sincere men believe is a material threat to the democratic system." United Public Workers v. Mitchell, 330 U.S., at 99. "Congress may reasonably desire to limit party activity of federal employees so as to avoid a tendency toward a one-party system." *Id.,* at 100.

of political campaigning and management, this conclusion irresistibly flows from *Mitchell* and *Letter Carriers*. For if the First Amendment did not place individual belief and association above political campaigning and management, at least in the setting of public employment, the restraints on those latter activities could not have been judged permissible in *Mitchell* and *Letter Carriers*.[27]

* * *

In summary, patronage dismissals severely restrict political belief and association. Though there is a vital need for government efficiency and effectiveness, such dismissals are on balance not the least restrictive means for fostering that end. There is also a need to insure that policies which the electorate has sanctioned are effectively implemented. That interest can be fully satisfied by limiting patronage dismissals to policymaking positions. Finally, patronage dismissals cannot be justified by their contribution to the proper functioning of our democratic process through their assistance to partisan politics since political parties are nurtured by other, less intrusive and equally effective methods. More fundamentally, however, any contribution of patronage dismissals to the democratic process does not suffice to override their severe encroachment on First Amendment freedoms. We hold, therefore, that the practice of patronage dismissals is unconstitutional under the First and Fourteenth Amendments, and that respondents thus stated a valid claim for relief.

VII

There remains the question whether the issuance of a preliminary injunction was properly directed by the Court of Appeals. The District Court predicated its denial of respondent's motion for a preliminary injunction on its finding that the allegations in their complaints and affidavits did not constitute a sufficient showing of irreparable injury and that respondents had an adequate remedy at law. The Court of Appeals held, however: "Inasmuch as this case involves First Amendment rights of association which must be carefully guarded against infringement by public office holders, we judge that injunctive relief is clearly appropriate in these cases." 509 F.2d, at 1136. We agree.

At the time a preliminary injunction was sought in the District Court, one of the respondents was only threatened with discharge. In addition, many of the members of the class respondents were seeking to have certified prior to the dismissal of their complaint were threatened with discharge or had agreed to provide support for the Democratic Party in order to avoid discharge. It is clear therefore that First Amendment interests were either threatened or in fact being impaired at the time relief was sought. The loss of First Amendment freedoms, for even minimal periods of time unquestionably constitutes irreparable

---

27. The judgment that the First Amendment interests in political campaigning and management must, in the setting of public employment, give way to the First Amendment interests in individual belief and association does not necessarily extend to other contexts. Restraining political campaigning and management in the area of public employment leaves it free to continue in other settings. The consequence of no such restraint, however, is the complete restriction of individual belief and association for each public employee affected.

injury. See New York Times Co. v. United States, 403 U.S. 713 (1971). Since such injury was both threatened and occurring at the time of respondents' motion and since respondents sufficiently demonstrated a probability of success on the merits, the Court of Appeals might properly have held that the District Court abused its discretion in denying preliminary injunctive relief. See Bantam Books, Inc. v. Sullivan, 372 U.S. 58, 67 (1963).

The judgment of the Court of Appeals is

Affirmed.

MR. JUSTICE STEVENS did not participate in the consideration of this case.

MR. JUSTICE STEWART, with whom MR. JUSTICE BLACKMUN joins, concurring in the judgment.

Although I cannot join the plurality's wide-ranging opinion, I can and do concur in its judgment.

This case does not require us to consider the broad contours of the so-called patronage system, with all its variations and permutations. In particular, it does not require us to consider the constitutional validity of a system that confines the hiring of some governmental employees to those of a particular political party, and I would intimate no views whatever on that question.*

The single substantive question involved in this case is whether a nonpolicymaking, nonconfidential government employee can be discharged or threatened with discharge from a job that he is satisfactorily performing upon the sole ground of his political beliefs. I agree with the plurality that he cannot. See Perry v. Sindermann, 408 U.S. 593, 597–598 (1972).

MR. CHIEF JUSTICE BERGER, dissenting.

The Court's decision today represents a significant intrusion into the area of legislative and policy concerns—the sort of intrusion Mr. Justice Brennan has recently protested in other contexts. I therefore join Mr. Justice Powell's dissenting opinion, and add a few words simply to emphasize an aspect that seems particularly important to me.

The Illinois Legislature has pointedly decided that roughly half of the Sheriff's staff shall be made up of tenured career personnel and the balance left exclusively to the choice of the elected head of the department. The Court strains the rational bounds of First Amendment doctrine and runs counter to longstanding practices that are part of the fabric of our democratic system to hold that the Constitution *commands* something it has not been thought to require for 185 years. For all that time our system has wisely left these matters to the States and, on the federal level, to the Congress. The Court's action is a classic example of trivializing constitutional adjudication—a function of the highest importance in our system.

*[Ed. Note. In 1990, the Court extended *Elrod* to apply equally to hiring, rehiring, promotions, and transfers. *See* Rutan v. Republican Party of Illinois, 497 U.S. ——, 110 S.Ct. 2729, 111 L.Ed.2d 52 (1990).]

* * *

Mr. Justice Powell, with whom The Chief Justice and Mr. Justice Rhenquist join, dissenting.

The Court holds unconstitutional a practice as old as the Republic, a practice which has contributed significantly to the democratization of American politics. This decision is urged on us in the name of First Amendment rights, but in my view the judgment neither is constitutionally required nor serves the interest of a representative democracy. It also may well deserve—rather than promote—core values of the First Amendment. I therefore dissent.

* * *

III

It might well be possible to dispose of this case on the ground that it implicates no First Amendment right of the respondents, and therefore that they have failed to state a cause of action. They are employees seeking to avoid discharge—not citizens desiring an opportunity to be hired by the county without regard to their political affiliation or loyalty. Respondents' complaint acknowledges the longstanding existence of the patronage system they now challenge:

> "For many years past and continuing to this time it has been the practice of the elected Sheriff of Cook County, when he assumes office from a Sheriff of a different political party, to replace all or substantially all of the non-civil service employees of the Sheriff's office who did not (a) Pledge their political allegiance to the political party of the incoming Sheriff; [and/or meet other specified political requirements]. * * *"
> App. 3.

We thus have complaining employees who apparently accepted patronage jobs knowingly and willingly, while fully familiar with the "tenure" practices long prevailing in the Sheriff's Office. Such employees have *benefited* from their political beliefs and activities; they have not been penalized for them. In these circumstances, I am inclined to agree with the holding of the Supreme Court of Pennsylvania in American Federation of State Employees v. Shapp, 443 Pa. 527, 280 A.2d 375 (1971), that beneficiaries of a patronage system may not be heard to challenge it when it comes their turn to be replaced. See also Nunnery v. Barber, 503 F.2d 1349 (CA4 1974).

* * *

IV

The question is whether it is consistent with the First and Fourteenth Amendments for a State to offer some employment conditioned, explicitly or implicitly, on partisan political affiliation and on the political fortunes of the incumbent officeholder. This is to be determined, as the plurality opinion agrees, by whether patronage hiring practices sufficiently advance important state interests to justify the consequent burdening of First Amendment interests. Buckley v. Valeo, 424 U.S. 1, 25 (1976); * * *. It is difficult to disagree with the view, as an abstract proposition, that government employment ordinarily should not be conditioned upon one's political beliefs or activities. But we deal here with a highly practical and rather fundamental element of our political system, not the theoretical abstractions of a political science seminar. In concluding that patronage hiring practices are unconstitutional, the plurality seriously underestimates the strength of the government interest—especially at the local level—in allowing some patronage hiring practices, and it exaggerates the perceived burden on First Amendment rights.

A

As indicated above, patronage hiring practices have contributed to American democracy by stimulating political activity and by strengthening parties, thereby helping to make government accountable.[6] It cannot be questioned seriously that these contributions promote important state interests. * * *

* * *

The complaining parties are or were employees of the Sheriff. In many communities, the sheriff's duties are as routine as process serving, and his election attracts little or no general public interest. In the States, and especially in the thousands of local communities, there are large numbers of elective offices, and many are as relatively obscure as that of the local sheriff or constable. Despite the importance of elective offices to the ongoing work of local governments, election campaigns for lesser offices in particular usually attract little attention from the media, with consequent disinterest and absence of intelligent participation on the part of the public. Unless the candidates for these offices are able to dispense the traditional patronage that has accrued to the offices, they also are unlikely to attract donations of time or money from voluntary groups. In short, the resource pools that fuel the intensity of political interest and debate in "important" elections frequently "could care less" about who fills the office deemed to be relatively unimportant. Long experience teaches that at this local level traditional patronage practices contribute significantly to the democratic process. The candidates for these offices derive their support at the precinct level, and their modest funding for publicity, from cadres of friends and political associates who hope to benefit if their "man" is elected.[8] The activities of the latter are often the principal

---

6. Some commentators have believed that patronage hiring practices promote other social interests as well:

"Patronage is peculiarly important for minority groups, involving much more than the mere spoils of office. Each first appointment given a member of any underdog element is a boost in that element's struggle for social acceptance. It means that another barrier to their advance has been lifted, another shut door has swung open." S. Lubell, The Future of American Politics 76–77 (1952).

8. Former Senator Paul H. Douglas (D.Ill.) said of patronage hiring practices:

"In short, I am for civil service but not for having civil service dominate public employment 100 percent. That would give us the bureaucracy of Germany and France which I do not regard as ideal.

* * *

"But I would like to have you consider just how long most liberals would be able to last in Congress if you stripped us of all patronage, as you desire. We who try to defend the interests of the people, the con-source of political information for the voting public. The "robust" political discourse that the plurality opinion properly emphasizes is furthered—not restricted—by the time-honored system.

Patronage hiring practices also enable party organizations to persist and function at the local level. Such organizations become visible to the electorate at large only at election time, but the dull periods between elections require ongoing activities: precinct organizations must be maintained; new voters registered; and minor political "chores" performed for citizens who otherwise may have no practical means of access to officeholders. In some communities party organizations and clubs also render helpful social services.

It is naive to think that these types of political activities are motivated at these levels by some academic interest in "democracy" or other public service impulse. For the most part, as every politician knows, the hope of some reward generates a major portion of the local political activity supporting parties. It is difficult to overestimate the contributions to our system by the major political parties, fortunately limited in number compared to the fractionalization that has made the continued existence of democratic government doubtful in some other countries. Parties generally are stable, high-profile, and permanent institutions. When the names on a long ballot are meaningless to the average voter, party affiliation affords a guidepost by which voters may rationalize a myriad of political choices. Cf. Buckley v. Valeo, 424 U.S., at 66–68. Voters can and do hold parties to long-term accountability, and it is not too much to say that, in their absence, responsive and responsible performance in low-profile offices, particularly, is difficult to maintain.

It is against decades of experience to the contrary, then, that the plurality opinion concludes that patronage hiring practices interfere with the "free functioning of the electoral process." *Ante*. This *ad hoc* judicial judgment runs counter to the judgments of the representatives of the people in state and local governments, representatives who have chosen, in most instances, to retain some patronage practices in combination with a merit-oriented civil service. * * *

B

I thus conclude that patronage hiring practices sufficiently serve important state interests, including some interest sought to be advanced by the First Amendment, to justify a tolerable intrusion on the First Amendment interests of employees or potential employees.

The plurality opinion asserts that patronage hiring practices contravene the fundamental principle that " 'no official, high or petty, can prescribe what shall be orthodox in politics, nationalism, religion, or other matters of opinion. * * *' " *Ante,* quoting Board of Education v. Barnette, 319 U.S. 624, 642 (1943). But such practices simply cannot be

sumers and the taxpayers commonly face the powerful opposition of the special-interest groups which will spend enormous sums of money to defeat us. * * * If we are to survive we need some support rooted in gratitude for material favors which at the same time do not injure the general public." Letter to New Republic, July 14, 1952, p. 2.

so construed. This case differs materially from previous cases involving the imposition of political conditions on employment, see, e.g., Garner v. Los Angeles Board, 341 U.S. 716 (1951), cases where there was an attempt to exclude "a minority group odious to the majority." *Id.,* at 725 (Frankfurter, J., concurring in part and dissenting in part). In that context there was a danger that governmental action was directed toward the elimination of political beliefs by penalizing adherents to them. But patronage hiring practices have been consistent historically with vigorous ideological competition in the political "marketplace." And even after one becomes a beneficiary, the system leaves significant room for individual political expression. Employees, regardless of affiliation, may vote freely [11] and express themselves on some political issues. See Perry v. Sindermann, 408 U.S. 593 (1972); Pickering v. Board of Education, 391 U.S. 563 (1968). The principal intrusion of patronage hiring practices on First Amendment interests thus arises from the coercion of associational choices that may be created by one's desire initially to obtain employment. This intrusion, while not insignificant, must be measured in light of the limited role of patronage hiring in most government employment. The pressure to abandon one's beliefs and associations to obtain government employment—especially employment of such uncertain duration—does not seem to me to assume impermissible proportions in light of the interests to be served.

BRANTI v. FINKEL

Supreme Court of the United States, 1980.
445 U.S. 507, 100 S.Ct. 1287, 63 L.Ed.2d 574.

Mr. Justice Stevens delivered the opinion of the Court.

The question presented is whether the First and Fourteenth Amendments to the Constitution protect an assistant public defender who is satisfactorily performing his job from discharge solely because of his political beliefs.

* * *

The critical facts can be summarized briefly. The Rockland County Public Defender is appointed by the County Legislature for a term of six years. He in turn appoints nine assistants who serve at his pleasure. The two respondents have served as assistants since their respective appointments in March 1971 and September 1975; they are both Republicans.[4]

---

11. It appears that before the adoption of the Australian ballot, one's access to or retention of a government job sometimes could depend on voting "correctly." D. Rosenblum, *supra,* n. 2, at 61. Today this ultimate core of political expression is beyond the reach of any coercive effects of the patronage system.

4. The District Court noted that Finkel had changed his party registration from Republican to Democrat in 1977 in the apparent hope that such action would enhance his chances of being reappointed as an assistant when a new, Democratic public defender was appointed. The court concluded that, despite Finkel's formal change of party registration, the parties had re-

Petitioner Branti's predecessor, a Republican, was appointed in 1972 by a Republican-dominated County Legislature. By 1977, control of the legislature had shifted to the Democrats and petitioner, also a Democrat, was appointed to replace the incumbent when his term expired. As soon as petitioner was formally appointed on January 3, 1978, he began executing termination notices for six of the nine assistants then in office. Respondents were among those who were to be terminated. With one possible exception, the nine who were to be appointed or retained were all Democrats and were all selected by Democratic legislators or Democratic town chairmen on a basis that had been determined by the Democratic caucus.

The District Court found that Finkel and Tabakman had been selected for termination solely because they were Republicans and thus did not have the necessary Democratic sponsors:

> "The sole grounds for the attempted removal of plaintiffs were the facts that plaintiffs' political beliefs differed from those of the ruling Democratic majority in the County Legislature and that the Democratic majority had determined that Assistant Public Defender appointments were to be made on political bases." * * *

The court rejected petitioner's belated attempt to justify the dismissals on nonpolitical grounds. Noting that both Branti and his predecessor had described respondents as "competent attorneys," the District Court expressly found that both had been "satisfactorily performing their duties as Assistant Public Defenders." * * *

Having concluded that respondents had been discharged solely because of their political beliefs, the District Court held that those discharges would be permissible under this Court's decision in Elrod v. Burns, 427 U.S. 347 (1976), only if assistant public defenders are the type of policymaking, confidential employees who may be discharged solely on the basis of their political affiliations. The court concluded that respondents clearly did not fall within that category. Although recognizing that they had broad responsibilities with respect to particular cases that were assigned to them, the court found that respondents had "very limited, if any, responsibility" with respect to the overall operation of the public defender's office. They did not "act as advisors or formulate plans for the implementation of the broad goals of the office" and, although they made decisions in the context of specific cases, "they do not make decisions about the orientation and operation of the office in which they work." 457 F.Supp., at 1291.

The District Court also rejected the argument that the confidential character of respondents' work justified conditioning their employment on political grounds. The court found that they did not occupy any confidential relationship to the policymaking process, and did not have access to confidential documents that influenced policymaking deliberations. Rather, the only confidential information to which they had access was the product of their attorney-client relationship with the

garded him as a Republican at all relevant times. 457 F.Supp., at 1285, n. 2.

office's clients; to the extent that such information was shared with the public defender, it did not relate to the formulation of office policy.

In light of these factual findings, the District Court concluded that petitioner could not terminate respondents' employment as assistant public defenders consistent with the First and Fourteenth Amendments. On appeal, a panel of the Second Circuit affirmed, specifically holding that the District Court's findings of fact were adequately supported by the record. That court also expressed "no doubt" that the District Court "was correct in concluding that an assistant public defender was neither a policymaker nor a confidential employee." We granted certiorari * * * and now affirm.

Petitioner advances two principal arguments for reversal: First, that the holding in *Elrod v. Burns* is limited to situations in which government employees are coerced into pledging allegiance to a political party that they would not voluntarily support and does not apply to a simple requirement that an employee be sponsored by the party in power; and, second, that, even if party sponsorship is an unconstitutional condition of continued public employment for clerks, deputies, and janitors, it is an acceptable requirement for an assistant public defender.

I

In *Elrod v. Burns* the Court held that the newly elected Democratic Sheriff of Cook County, Ill., had violated the constitutional rights of certain non-civil-service employees by discharging them "because they did not support and were not members of the Democratic Party and had failed to obtain the sponsorship of one of its leaders." 427 U.S., at 351. That holding was supported by two separate opinions.

Writing for the plurality, Mr. Justice Brennan identified two separate but interrelated reasons supporting the conclusion that the discharges were prohibited by the First and Fourteenth Amendments. First, he analyzed the impact of a political patronage system [7] on freedom of belief and association. Noting that in order to retain their jobs, the Sheriff's employees were required to pledge their allegiance to the Democratic Party, work for or contribute to the party's candidates, or obtain a Democratic sponsor, he concluded that the inevitable tendency of such a system was to coerce employees into compromising their true beliefs.[8] That conclusion, in his opinion, brought the practice

---

7. Mr. Justice Brennan noted that many other practices are included within the definition of a patronage system, including placing supporters in government jobs not made available by political discharges, granting supporters lucrative government contracts, and giving favored wards improved public services. In that case, as in this, however, the only practice at issue was the dismissal of public employees for partisan reasons. 427 U.S., at 353; *id.*, at 374 (opinion of Stewart, J.). In light of the limited nature of the question presented, we have no occasion to address petitioner's argument that there is a compelling governmental interest in maintaining a political sponsorship system for filling vacancies in the public defender's office.

8. "An individual who is a member of the out-party maintains affiliation with his own party at the risk of losing his job. He works for the election of his party's candidates and espouses its policies at the same risk. The financial and campaign assistance that he is induced to provide to another party furthers the advancement of that

within the rule of cases like Board of Education v. Barnette, 319 U.S. 624 (1943), condemning the use of governmental power to prescribe what the citizenry must accept as orthodox opinion.[9]

Second, apart from the potential impact of patronage dismissals on the formation and expression of opinion, Mr. Justice Brennan also stated that the practice had the effect of imposing an unconstitutional condition on the receipt of a public benefit and therefore came within the rule of cases like Perry v. Sindermann, 408 U.S. 593 (1972). In support of the holding in *Perry* that even an employee with no contractual right to retain his job cannot be dismissed for engaging in constitutionally protected speech, the Court had stated:

> "For at least a quarter-century, this Court has made clear that even though a person has no 'right' to a valuable governmental benefit and even though the government may deny him the benefit for any number of reasons, there are some reasons upon which the government may not rely. It may not deny a benefit to a person on a basis that infringes his constitutionally protected interests—especially, his interest in freedom of speech. For if the government could deny a benefit to a person because of his constitutionally protected speech or associations, his exercise of those freedoms would in effect be penalized and inhibited. This would allow the government to 'produce a result which [it] could not command directly.' Speiser v. Randall, 357 U.S. 513, 526 (1958). Such interference with constitutional rights is impermissible."

* * *

If the First Amendment protects a public employee from discharge based on what he has said, it must also protect him from discharge based on what he believes.[10] Under this line of analysis, unless the

---

party's policies to the detriment of his party's views and ultimately his own beliefs, and any assessment of his salary is tantamount to coerced belief. See Buckley v. Valeo, 424 U.S. 1, 19 (1976). Even a pledge of allegiance to another party, however ostensible, only serves to compromise the individuals' true beliefs. Since the average public employee is hardly in the financial position to support his party and another, or to lend his time to two parties, the individual's ability to act according to his beliefs and to associate with others of his political persuasion is constrained, and support for his party is diminished." *Id.,* at 355–356.

Mr. Justice Brennan also indicated that a patronage system may affect freedom of belief more indirectly, by distorting the electoral process. Given the increasingly pervasive character of government employment, he concluded that the power to starve political opposition by commanding partisan support, financial and otherwise, may have a significant impact on the formation and expression of political beliefs.

9. "Regardless of the nature of the inducement, whether it be by the denial of public employment, or as in Board of Education v. Barnette, 319 U.S. 624 (1943), by the influence of a teacher over students, '[i]f there is any fixed star in our constitutional constellation, it is that no official high or petty, can prescribe what shall be orthodox in politics, nationalism, religion, or other matters of opinion or force citizens to confess by word or act their faith therein.' *Id.,* at 642." *Id.,* at 356.

10. "The Court recognized in United Public Workers v. Mitchell, 330 U.S. 75, 100 (1947), that 'Congress may not "enact a regulation providing that no Republican, Jew or Negro shall be appointed to federal office. * * * "' This principle was reaffirmed in Wieman v. Updegraff, 344 U.S. 183 (1952), which held that a State could not require its employees to establish their loyalty by extracting an oath denying past affiliation with Communists. And in Cafeteria Workers v. McElroy, 367 U.S. 886, 989 (1961), the Court recognized again that

government can demonstrate "an overriding interest," 427 U.S., at 368, "of vital importance," *id.*, at 362, requiring that a person's private beliefs conform to those of the hiring authority, his beliefs cannot be the sole basis for depriving him of continued public employment.

Mr. Justice Stewart's opinion concurring in the judgment avoided comment on the first branch of Mr. Justice Brennan's analysis, but expressly relied on the same passage from *Perry v. Sindermann* that is quoted above.

Petitioner argues that *Elrod v. Burns* should be read to prohibit only dismissals resulting from an employee's failure to capitulate to political coercion. Thus, he argues that, so long as an employee is not asked to change his political affiliation or to contribute to or work for the party's candidates, he may be dismissed with impunity—even though he would not have been dismissed if he had had the proper political sponsorship and even though the sole reason for dismissing him was to replace him with a person who did have such sponsorship. Such an interpretation would surely emasculate the principles set forth in *Elrod*. While it would perhaps eliminate the more blatant forms of coercion described in *Elrod*, it would not eliminate the coercion of belief that necessarily flows from the knowledge that one must have a sponsor in the dominant party in order to retain one's job.[11] More importantly, petitioner's interpretation would require the Court to repudiate entirely the conclusion of both Mr. Justice Brennan and Mr. Justice Stewart that the First Amendment prohibits the dismissal of a public employee solely because of his private political beliefs.

In sum, there is no requirement that dismissed employees prove that they, or other employees, have been coerced into changing, either actually or ostensibly, their political allegiance. To prevail in this type of an action, it was sufficient as *Elrod* holds, for respondents to prove that they were discharged "solely for the reason that they were not affiliated with or sponsored by the Democratic Party." 427 U.S., at 350.

II

Both opinions in *Elrod* recognize that party affiliation may be an acceptable requirement for some types of government employment. Thus, if an employee's private political beliefs would interfere with the discharge of his public duties, his First Amendment rights may be required to yield to the State's vital interest in maintaining governmental effectiveness and efficiency. *Id.*, at 366. In *Elrod*, it was clear that the duties of the employees—the chief deputy of the process division of

---

the government could not deny employment because of previous membership in a particular party." *Id.*, at 357–358.

11. As Mr. Justice Brennan pointed out in *Elrod*, political sponsorship is often purchased at the price of political contributions or campaign work in addition to a simple declaration of allegiance to the party. *Id.*, at 355. Thus, an employee's realization that he must obtain a sponsor in order to retain his job is very likely to lead to the same type of coercion as that described by the plurality in *Elrod*. While there was apparently no overt political pressure exerted on respondents in this case, the potentially coercive effect of requiring sponsorship was demonstrated by Mr. Finkel's change of party registration in a futile attempt to retain his position.

the sheriff's office, a process server and another employee in that office, and a bailiff and security guard at the Juvenile Court of Cook County—were not of that character, for they were, as Mr. Justice Stewart stated, "nonpolicymaking, nonconfidential employees. *Id.,* at 375.[12]

As Mr. Justice Brennan noted in *Elrod,* it is not always easy to determine whether a position is one in which political affiliation is a legitimate factor to be considered. *Id.,* at 367. Under some circumstances, a position may be appropriately considered political even though it is neither confidential nor policymaking in character. As one obvious example, if a State's election laws require that precincts be supervised by two election judges of different parties, a Republican judge could be legitimately discharged solely for changing his party registration. That conclusion would not depend on any finding that the job involved participation in policy decisions or access to confidential information. Rather, it would simply rest on the fact that party membership was essential to the discharge of the employee's governmental responsibilities.

It is equally clear that party affiliation is not necessarily relevant to every policymaking or confidential position. The coach of a state university's football team formulates policy, but no one could seriously claim that Republicans make better coaches than Democrats, or vice versa, no matter which party is in control of the state government. On the other hand, it is equally clear that the Governor of a State may appropriately believe that the official duties of various assistants who help him write speeches, explain his views to the press, or communicate with the legislature cannot be performed effectively unless those persons share his political beliefs and party commitments. In sum, the ultimate inquiry is not whether the label "policymaker" or "confidential" fits a particular position; rather, the question is whether the hiring authority can demonstrate that party affiliation is an appropriate requirement for the effective performance of the public office involved.

Having thus framed the issue, it is manifest that the continued employment of an assistant public defender cannot properly be conditioned upon his allegiance to the political party in control of the county government. The primary, if not the only, responsibility of an assistant public defender is to represent individual citizens in controversy with

---

12. The plurality emphasized that patronage dismissals could be justified only if they advanced a governmental, rather than a partisan, interest. 427 U.S., at 362. That standard clearly was not met to the extent that employees were expected to perform extracurricular activities for the party, or were being rewarded for past services to the party. Government funds, which are collected from taxpayers of all parties on a nonpolitical basis, cannot be expended for the benefit of one political party simply because that party has control of the government. The compensation of government employees, like the distribution of other public benefits, must be justified by a governmental purpose.

The Sheriff argued that his employees' political beliefs did have a bearing on the official duties they were required to perform because political loyalty was necessary to the continued efficiency of the office. But after noting the tenuous link between political loyalty and efficiency where process servers and clerks were concerned, the plurality held that any small gain in efficiency did not outweigh the employees' First Amendment rights. *Id.,* at 366.

the State.[13] As we recently observed in commenting on the duties of counsel appointed to represent indigent defendants in federal criminal proceedings:

> "[T]he primary office performed by appointed counsel parallels the office of privately retained counsel. Although it is true that appointed counsel serves pursuant to statutory authorization and in furtherance of the federal interest in insuring effective representation of criminal defendants, his duty is not to the public at large, except in that general way. His principal responsibility is to serve the undivided interests of his client. Indeed, an indispensable element of the effective performance of his responsibilities is the ability to act independently of the government and to oppose it in adversary litigation." Ferri v. Ackerman, 444 U.S. 193, 204 (1979).

Thus, whatever policymaking occurs in the public defender's office must relate to the needs of individual clients and not to any partisan political interests. Similarly, although an assistant is bound to obtain access to confidential information arising out of various attorney-client relationships, that information has no bearing whatsoever on partisan political concerns. Under these circumstances, it would undermine, rather than promote, the effective performance of an assistant public defender's office to make his tenure independent of his allegiance to the dominant political party.

Accordingly, the entry of an injunction against termination of respondents' employment on purely political grounds was appropriate and the judgment of the Court of Appeals is

Affirmed.

Mr. Justice Stewart, dissenting.

I joined the judgment of the Court in Elrod v. Burns, 427 U.S. 347 (1976), because it is my view that, under the First and Fourteenth Amendments, "a nonpolicymaking, nonconfidential government employee can[not] be discharged * * * from a job that he is satisfactorily performing upon the sole ground of his political beliefs." *Id.*, at 375. That judgment in my opinion does not control the present case for the simple reason that the respondents here clearly are not "nonconfidential" employees.

The respondents in the present case are lawyers, and the employment positions involved are those of assistants in the office of the Rockland County Public Defender. The analogy to a firm of lawyers in the private sector is a close one, and I can think of few occupational relationships more instinct with the necessity of mutual confidence and trust than that kind of professional association.

---

13. This is in contrast to the broader public responsibilities of an official such as a prosecutor. We express no opinion as to whether the deputy of such an official could be dismissed on grounds of political party affiliation or loyalty. Cf. Newcomb v. Brennan, 558 F.2d 825 (CA7 1977), cert. denied, 434 U.S. 968 (dismissal of deputy city attorney).

I believe that the petitioner, upon his appointment as Public Defender, was not constitutionally compelled to enter such a close professional and necessarily confidential association with the respondents if he did not wish to do so.*

Mr. Justice Powell, with whom Mr. Justice Rehnquist joins, and with whom Mr. Justice Stewart joins as to Part I, dissenting.

The Court today continues the evisceration of patronage practices begun in Elrod v. Burns, 427 U.S. 347 (1976). With scarcely a glance at almost 200 years of American political tradition, the Court further limits the relevance of political affiliation to the selection and retention of public employees. Many public positions previously filled on the basis of membership in national political parties now must be staffed in accordance with a constitutionalized civil service standard that will affect the employment practices of federal, state, and local governments. Governmental hiring practices long thought to be a matter of legislative and executive discretion now will be subjected to judicial oversight. Today's decision is an exercise of judicial lawmaking that, as The Chief Justice wrote in his *Elrod* dissent, "represents a significant intrusion into the area of legislative and policy concerns." *Id.*, at 375. I dissent.

I

The Court contends that its holding is compelled by the First Amendment. In reaching this conclusion, the Court largely ignores the substantial governmental interests served by patronage. Patronage is a long-accepted practice [1] that never has been eliminated totally by civil service laws and regulations. The flaw in the Court's opinion lies not only in its application of First Amendment principles, see Parts II–IV, *infra*, but also in its promulgation of a new, and substantially expanded, standard for determining which governmental employees may be retained or dismissed on the basis of political affiliation.[2]

---

* Contrary to repeated statements in the Court's opinion, the present case does not involve "private political beliefs," but public affiliation with a political party.

1. When Thomas Jefferson became the first Chief Executive to succeed a President of the opposing party, he made substantial use of appointment and removal powers. Andrew Jackson, the next President to follow an antagonistic administration, used patronage extensively when he took office. The use of patronage in the early days of our Republic played an important role in democratizing American politics. Elrod v. Burns, 427 U.S., at 378–379 (Powell, J., dissenting). President Lincoln's patronage practices and his reliance upon the newly formed Republican Party enabled him to build support for his national policies during the Civil War. See E. McKitrick, Party Politics and the Union and Confederate War Efforts, in the American Party System 117, 131–133 (W. Chambers & W. Burnham eds. 1967). Subsequent patronage reform efforts were "concerned primarily with the corruption and inefficiency that patronage was thought to induce in civil service and the power that patronage practices were thought to give the 'professional' politicians who relied on them." Elrod v. Burns, 427 U.S., at 379 (Powell, J., dissenting). As a result of these efforts, most federal and state civil service employment was placed on a nonpatronage basis. *Ibid.* A significant segment of public employment has remained, however, free from civil service constraints.

2. The Court purports to limit the issue in this case to the dismissal of public employees. * * * Yet the Court also states that "it is difficult to formulate any justification of tying either the selection or retention of an assistant public defender to his party affiliation." * * * If this latter statement is not a holding of the Court, it at least suggests that the Court perceives no constitutional distinction between selection and dismissal of public employees.

* * *

The standard articulated by the Court is framed in vague and sweeping language certain to create vast uncertainty. Elected and appointed officials at all levels who now receive guidance from civil service laws, no longer will know when political affiliation is an appropriate consideration in filling a position. Legislative bodies will not be certain whether they have the final authority to make the delicate line-drawing decisions embodied in the civil service laws. Prudent individuals requested to accept a public appointment must consider whether their predecessors will threaten to oust them through legal action.

One example at the national level illustrates the nature and magnitude of the problem created by today's holding. The President customarily has considered political affiliation in removing and appointing United States attorneys. Given the critical role that these key law enforcement officials play in the administration of the Department of Justice, both Democratic and Republican Attorneys General have concluded, not surprisingly, that they must have the confidence and support of the United States attorneys. And political affiliation has been used as one indicator of loyalty.

Yet, it would be difficult to say, under the Court's standard, that "partisan" concerns properly are relevant to the performance of the duties of a United States attorney. * * *

A constitutional standard that is both uncertain in its application and impervious to legislative change will now control selection and removal of key governmental personnel. Federal judges will now be the final arbiters as to who federal, state, and local governments may employ. In my view, the Court is not justified in removing decisions so essential to responsible and efficient governance from the discretion of legislative and executive officials.

II

The Court errs not only in its selection of a standard, but more fundamentally in its conclusion that the First Amendment prohibits the use of membership in a national political party as a criterion for the dismissal of public employees. In reaching this conclusion, the Court makes new law from inapplicable precedents. * * *

Both *Keyishian* and *Perry* involved faculty members who were dismissed from state educational institutions because of their political views.[7] In *Keyishian,* the Court reviewed a state statute that permitted dismissals of faculty members from state institutions for "treasonable or seditious" utterances or acts. The Court noted that academic freedom is "a special concern of the First Amendment, which does not tolerate laws that cast a pall of orthodoxy over the classroom." 385 U.S., at 603. Because of the ambiguity in the statutory language, the

---

7. * * * The Court also relies upon United Public Workers v. Mitchell, 330 U.S. 75 (1947). * * * In that case, the Court upheld limitations on the political conduct of public employees that far exceed any burden on First Amendment rights demonstrated in this case.

Court held that the law was unconstitutionally vague. The Court also held that membership in the Communist Party could not automatically disqualify a person from holding a faculty position in a state university. *Id.,* at 606. In *Perry,* the Court held that the Board of Regents of a state university system could not discharge a professor in retaliation for his exercise of free speech. 408 U.S., at 598. In neither case did the State suggest that the governmental positions traditionally had been regarded as patronage positions. Thus, the Court correctly held that no substantial state interest justified the infringement of free speech. This case presents a question quite different from that in *Keyishian* and *Perry.*

The constitutionality of appointing or dismissing public employees on the basis of political affiliation depends upon the governmental interests served by patronage. * * *

III

Patronage appointments help build stable political parties by offering rewards to persons who assume the tasks necessary to the continued functioning of political organizations. * * * The use of patronage to fill such positions builds party loyalty and avoids "splintered parties and unrestrained factionalism [that might] do significant damage to the fabric of government." Storer v. Brown, 415 U.S. 724, 736 (1974).

* * * Political parties, dependent in many ways upon patronage, serve a variety of substantial governmental interests. A party organization allows political candidates to muster donations of time and money necessary to capture the attention of the electorate. Particularly in a time of growing reliance upon expensive television advertisements, a candidate who is neither independently wealthy nor capable of attracting substantial contributions must rely upon party workers to bring his message to the voters.[9] In contests for less visible offices, a candidate may have no efficient method of appealing to the voters unless he enlists the efforts of persons who seek reward through the patronage system. Insofar as the Court's decision today limits the ability of candidates to present their views to the electorate, our democratic process surely is weakened.

Strong political parties also aid effective governance after election campaigns end. Elected officials depend upon appointees who hold similar views to carry out their policies and administer their programs. Patronage—the right to select key personnel and to reward the party "faithful"—serves the public interest by facilitating the implementation of policies endorsed by the electorate. The Court's opinion casts a shadow over this time-honored element of our system. It appears to recognize that the implementation of policy is a legitimate goal of the patronage system and that some, but not all, policymaking employees may be replaced on the basis of their political affiliation. But the Court does not recognize that the implementation of policy often

---

9. Television and radio enable well-financed candidates to go directly into the homes of voters far more effectively than even the most well-organized "political machine." See D. Broder, The Party's Over: The Failure of Politics in America 239–240 (1972).

depends upon the cooperation of public employees who do not hold policymaking posts. As one commentator has written: "What the Court forgets is that, if government is to work, policy implementation is just as important as policymaking. No matter how wise the chief, he has to have the right Indians to transform his ideas into action, to get the job done." [13] The growth of the civil service system already has limited the ability of elected politicians to effect political change. Public employees immune to public pressure "can resist changes in policy without suffering either the loss of their jobs or a cut in their salary." Such effects are proper when they follow from legislative or executive decisions to withhold some jobs from the patronage system. But the Court tips the balance between patronage and nonpatronage positions, and, in my view, imposes unnecessary constraints upon the ability of responsible officials to govern effectively and to carry out new policies.

The breakdown of party discipline that handicaps elected officials also limits the ability of the electorate to choose wisely among candidates. Voters with little information about individuals seeking office traditionally have relied upon party affiliation as a guide to choosing among candidates. With the decline in party stability, voters are less able to blame or credit a party for the performance of its elected officials. Our national party system is predicated upon the assumption that political parties sponsor, and are responsible for, the performance of the persons they nominate for office.[17]

In sum, the effect of the Court's decision will be to decrease the accountability and denigrate the role of our national political parties. This decision comes at a time when an increasing number of observers question whether our national political parties can continue to operate effectively. * * *

IV

The facts of this case also demonstrate that the Court's decision well may impair the right of local voters to structure their government. Consideration of the form of local government in Rockland County, N.Y., demonstrates the antidemocratic effect of the Court's decision.

The voters of the county elect a legislative body. Among the responsibilities that the voters give to the legislature is the selection of a county public defender. In 1972, when the county voters elected a Republican majority in the legislature a Republican was selected as Public Defender. The Public Defender retained one respondent and appointed the other as Assistant Public Defender. Not surprisingly, both respondents are Republican. In 1976, the voters elected a majority of Democrats to the legislature. The Democratic majority, in turn,

---

13. Peters, A Kind Word for the Spoils System, The Washington Monthly, Sept. 1976, p. 30.

17. In local elections, a candidate's party affiliation may be the most salient information communicated to voters. One study has indicated that affiliation remains the predominant influence on voter choice in low-visibility elections such as contests for positions in the state legislature. See Murray & Vedlitz, Party Voting in Lower-Level Electoral Contests, 59 Soc. Sci.Q. 752, 756 (1979).

selected a Democratic Public Defender who replaced both respondents with Assistant Public Defenders approved by the Democratic legislators. * * *, and n. 5.

The voters of Rockland County are free to elect their public defender and assistant public defenders instead of delegating their selection to elected and appointed officials. Certainly the Court's holding today would not preclude the voters, the ultimate "hiring authority," from choosing both public defenders and their assistants by party membership. The voters' choice of public officials on the basis of political affiliation is not yet viewed as an inhibition of speech; it is democracy. Nor may any incumbent contend seriously that the voters' decision not to re-elect him because of his political views is an impermissible infringement upon his right of free speech or affiliation. In other words, the operation of democratic government depends upon the selection of elected officials on precisely the basis rejected by the Court today.

Although the voters of Rockland County could have elected both the public defender and his assistants, they have given their legislators a representative proxy to appoint the public defender. And they have delegated to the public defender the power to choose his assistants. Presumably the voters have adopted this course in order to facilitate more effective representative government. Of course, the voters could have instituted a civil service system that would preclude the selection of either the public defender or his assistants on the basis of political affiliation. But the continuation of the present system reflects the electorate's decision to select certain public employees on the basis of political affiliation.

* * *

V

The benefits of political patronage and the freedom of voters to structure their representative government are substantial governmental interests that justify the selection of the assistant public defenders of Rockland County on the basis of political affiliation. The decision to place certain governmental positions within a civil service system is a sensitive political judgment that should be left to the voters and to elected representatives of the people. But the Court's constitutional holding today displaces political responsibility with judicial fiat. In my view, the First Amendment does not incorporate a national civil service system. I would reverse the judgment of the Court of Appeals.

E. The Government's Management of Public Property: First Amendment Rights of Access and Use

The movement of doctrine from *Davis v. Commonwealth* to *Hague v. CIO,* and subsequent general distinctions of "time, place, and manner," affecting first amendment rights of free speech. The emergence of "forum" analysis in lieu of time, place, and manner review. An inquiry into property rights and regulations of the airwaves—FCC broadcast regulation vis-a-vis the unregulated private press. A review of private property and first amendment easements of unwanted speech.

1. Government–Held Property and Free Speech Access and Use: Public Forum Doctrine and the First Amendment

To what extent may government restrict access and use of property under its own ownership or control? In the course of his dissent in Board of Education v. Pico,[29] Justice Rehnquist (now Chief Justice Rehnquist) said the following:[30]

> Had petitioners been the members of a town council, I suppose all would agree that, absent a good deal more than is present in this record, they could not have prohibited the sale of these books by private booksellers within the municipality. But we have also recognized that the government may act in other capacities than as sovereign, and when it does the First Amendment may speak with a different voice:
>
>> [I]t cannot be gainsaid that the State has interests as an employer in regulating the speech of its employees that differ significantly from those it possesses in connection with regulation of the speech of the citizenry in general * * *[31]
>
> By the same token, expressive conduct which may not be prohibited by the State as sovereign may be proscribed by the State *as property owner: "The State, no less than a private party, has power to preserve the property under its control for the use to which it is lawfully dedicated."*[32]

---

29. 457 U.S. 853, 102 S.Ct. 2799, 73 L.Ed.2d 435 (1982) (school board removal of certain objectionable books from public school library) (the case is reproduced *supra* at 333).

30. 457 U.S. at 908, 102 S.Ct. at 2829, 73 L.Ed.2d at 472–73.

31. (Quoting from *Pickering*).

32. (Quoting from the majority opinion in Adderly v. Florida, 385 U.S. 39, 47, 87 S.Ct. 242, 247, 17 L.Ed.2d 149, 155–56 (1966) (emphasis added) (five-to-four decision sustaining criminal trespass conviction of demonstrators within curtilage of a local jail, following request to leave the outside yard where the protestors had gathered to protest the arrest and confinement of others held in the jail, Opinion by Justice Black concluding that a total bar of persons from the immediate external premises was all right under the first amendment, despite focused nature of the demonstration and lack of requirement that there be any actual threat to jail security by the particular demonstration). See also Greer v. Spock, 424 U.S. 828, 96 S.Ct. 1211, 47 L.Ed.2d 505 (1976) (divided decision, total ban on handbill distribution even at open intersection of vast military base, sustained). Cf. Brown v. Louisiana, 383 U.S. 131, 86 S.Ct. 719, 15 L.Ed.2d 637 (1966) (breach of peace conviction for standing inside public library anteroom as form of mute protest reversed). See also Tinker v. Des Moines Indep. Community School Dist., 393 U.S. 503, 89 S.Ct. 733, 21 L.Ed.2d 731 (1969) (armbands worn on public school premises held to be protected by first amendment).

"No less than * * * a *private* party?" But a private party could close his or her property entirely, or admit to its use those whom it pleased themselves so to do, pretty much at will. To what extent may government restrict access and use of property under public ownership, consistent with the first amendment?[33] May it do so as much as a private party may do with such property as such private parties otherwise lawfully possess?

Presumably a municipality may be under no original constitutional obligation to acquire land for a park or to commit such land as it may already hold to any particular local use—such as to provide some sort of public park. For that matter, neither a city nor a state may be under any constitutional duty to acquire private property by eminent domain to provide for sidewalks or streets. May a city, a state (or, for that matter, the federal government itself), upon undertaking to provide for parks, thoroughfares, public buildings, schools, military bases, etc., enact enforceable regulations carefully restricting the lawful uses of each solely to the lawfully dedicated, exactly specified, function of each? May it do so "*no less than a private party has power*" equivalently to do, in respect to such property as they might likewise own, in respect to all such property as is lawfully theirs?[34]

In the case of providing for a public park, for instance, may the municipality decide to bear the ownership and maintenance responsibilities to provide such a park exclusively as a haven within the community—for residents to stroll the pathways, to view the garden, to picnic in quiet places, to read poetry, to reflect, and to relax: a sheltered place away from the hurly-burly of business, of noise, of electioneering, of the cacophony of vendors, leafleteers, petition-circulators, itinerant ministers, political demonstrators, and the like? May it not do so, and, if not, why not? If, moreover, the city council should decide that such speech presentations as might be conducted in moderate tones, on constructive subjects as in its view may be conducive to the general welfare of the local community, but not otherwise, may it not make

---

33. May the question be affected somewhat by the equal protection clause, apart from the first amendment? I.e. we know (from Con Law I) that though the state need not provide for public schools or public parks, and though admission to either may, in that original sense, be a "privilege" rather than a "right," still, once embarked on the venture, the state is then controlled by the equal protection clause in determining standards of admission and standards of treatment of those admitted. Will an equal protection analysis respond to all questions in this area? (E.g., if those who are Republicans or Democrats are permitted speech uses on public property, does equal protection require equal terms of use to those who are Nazis, Klan members, Communists, Pedophiles, militant Shiite Muslims, etc.?) If the issue is approached solely through the equal protection clause, uninformed by the first amendment, which standard of substantive judicial review will be applied ("strict scrutiny" or "mere rationality" review)? Suppose, moreover, the public property at issue is not authorized for speech uses by anyone else (i.e. there is no favored group, person, or point of view extended speaking privileges but, rather, no political speech uses are allowed at all), on what basis will one attempt to mount an equal protection claim in such a case? Equal protection jurisprudence usually requires the leverage of comparing one's less favored treatment with the more favored treatment of others, shifting the burden to the government to justify the disparity of treatment. *But if no one is favored, what then*?

34. E.g., Busch Gardens outside Williamsburg, Virginia, or Sarah P. Duke Gardens, inside Duke University, Durham, North Carolina, each being private property neither owned nor managed under government auspices.

provision solely for such presentations while declining to authorize any other speech presentations within the park?[35] What constitutional clause or principle can plausibly be interposed against such decisions? Such is the general question we shall be reviewing, through the general case law, here.

Likewise in the case of a proposed street, the felt local need for a street may be solely to facilitate the more efficient movement of pedestrian and vehicular traffic "from point A to point B," i.e. the facilitation of traffic and movement with more efficiency and with less congestion, inconvenience, and lost time occasioned by having to circumnavigate the area through which the proposed street is newly to be provided than when it was not furnished or maintained at public expense. No other uses are allowed. May stationary assembly therefore be prohibited? May lingering also be prohibited, at least when not strictly incidental to getting through from one end of the street to the other end, or not incidental solely to the completion of such errands as one may have with such businesses, public offices, or homes, as may happen to grow up on this street? In short, may all such uses other than those incidental to the use of the sidewalk and street as a passageway, whether through the area, or to-and-from public and private premises lawfully located along its way, be forbidden? Does the first amendment have anything to say about this?[36]

Another property the municipality may own might be a civic center auditorium. Alternatively, it may be a line of utility poles edging residential or city streets. In rationing the possible uses of each of these, is public authority also entitled to "no less" than the full

---

35. Recall from Con Law I, that in Maher v. Roe, 432 U.S. 464, 97 S.Ct. 2376, 53 L.Ed.2d 484 (1977), a majority of the Supreme Court sustained a state law providing Medicaid funds to reimburse low-income eligible women for the costs of childbirth, but not for the costs of low-income women electing nontherapeutic first trimester abortions. See also Harris v. McRae, 448 U.S. 297, 100 S.Ct. 2671, 65 L.Ed.2d 784 (1980) (similar case sustaining a similar, more strict federal limitation on federal funds available for state Medicaid reimbursement). The rationale was that the act placed "no affirmative obstacle" in the path "of a woman's exercise of her freedom of choice," in leaving the woman electing an abortion to such private resources as she might (or might not) possess to exercise that choice. Will a similar rationale apply here? I.e. may tax funds or public property be made available to assist those whose speech is deemed constructive and a positive good (like subsidizing low income persons who choose childbirth vis-a-vis abortion) and not otherwise? Cf. Board of Educ. v. Pico, 457 U.S. 853, 102 S.Ct. 2799, 73 L.Ed.2d 435 (1982) (the very function of public schools is, in part, to "inculcate" "community" values.)

36. May news vendors thus be forbidden to utilize the sidewalks and streets for hawking such newspapers as they seek to sell? May the sidewalks be kept clean by forbidding persons who neither have relevant errands nor an interest simply to pass through, to distribute political handbills or anything else, there? May fixed-in-place machines be forbidden from being installed (e.g., news vending machines)? (Cf. City of Lakewood v. Plain Dealer Pub. Co., 486 U.S. 750, 770–81, 108 S.Ct. 2138, 2156, 100 L.Ed.2d 771, 797–99 (1988) (dissenting opinion) ("The right to leaflet does not create a right to build a booth on city streets from which leafletting can be conducted.") If, on the other hand, to defray the expenses of putting in and maintaining the streets, the city decides to auction street corner machine-installation space, may it do so? May it seek a higher price than it otherwise might hope to secure, by offering an exclusive license to the highest bidder (as a private business might do in leasing equivalent space inside a shopping mall), if it so elects? See Goldberger, A Reconsideration of Cox v. New Hampshire: Can Demonstrators Be Required to Pay the Costs of Using America's Public Forums?, 62 Tex.L. Rev. 403 (1983).

power a private party may exercise in respect to their equivalent private property (e.g., a privately-owned auditorium, a private company's own utility poles),[37] so far as the first amendment is concerned? Recall, too, from the *Tornillo* case, that what a private newspaper owner decides as appropriate editorial policy is virtually conclusive of what goes into that newspaper, i.e. that neither the first amendment requires—nor can any state generally require—such a newspaper to carry material it does not see fit to print.[38] Is the same true of government when it operates not as regulator of private property uses (as Florida attempted to do in respect to the Miami Herald), but merely as owner of property itself? [39]

37. Consider, too, a common variation of a case of this sort, i.e. the utility poles along a public right of way may be owned by a private utility company, but the company is one that is also a state or local regulated service monopoly, subject to having its rates and business practices closely controlled by government agencies. To what extent: (a) may the private company be forbidden by government directive from using its own "property" (e.g., its utility poles) to post *its own* speech messages; or (b) to what extent may the private company be required by government to permit third-party speech use of its utility poles; or (c) to what extent may the private company be required to yield such third-party access rights—to post speech notices on its poles—by force of the first amendment itself, even if not so required by government directive? (When does private property become a first amendment public forum of some sort?)

38. Cf. Marsh v. Alabama, 326 U.S. 501, 66 S.Ct. 276, 90 L.Ed. 265 (1946) (trespass conviction of Jehovah's Witness arrested by deputy sheriff paid by Gulf Shipbuilding Company that owned the entirety of the Town of Chickasaw, following refusal by the Witness to desist from distributing religious pamphlets and leave the sidewalk of the town's business block as requested pursuant to the Company's policy, reversed; company-owned town treated in respect to its public areas as directly subject to fourteenth amendment free speech access and use rights of third parties as though it were an ordinary town despite fee simple title of the corporation, Supreme Court dividing five-to-three). But see Hudgens v. NLRB, 424 U.S. 507, 96 S.Ct. 1024, 47 L.Ed.2d 196 (1976) (overruling Amalgamated Food Employees Union Local 590 v. Logan Valley Plaza, 391 U.S. 398, 88 S.Ct. 1601, 20 L.Ed.2d 603 (1968), and holding that the fourteenth amendment creates no first amendment easement rights to claim access and picketing or leaflet rights within the property of a privately owned shopping center, even if nondisruptive, and even if such shopping plazas overall account for 40% of all retail sales in the United States and may de facto have significantly displaced downtown business areas and public plazas.) But a state constitutional free speech provision construed to forbid shopping center owners from forbidding nondisruptive petition activity or other political speech activity to take place within the shopping center may nonetheless be valid as against constitutional claims by the company (that such state-law imposed restriction deprives them of property without due process or constitutes a taking for public use without just compensation). PruneYard Shopping Center v. Robins, 447 U.S. 74, 100 S.Ct. 2035, 64 L.Ed.2d 741 (1980). Query, would *Marsh* enable labor organizers to go onto privately owned farms to contact migratory farm workers temporarily housed there, or would *Hudgens* sustain the validity of a trespass prosecution as brought on behalf of the owner who forbade such entry? (See Note, First Amendment and the Problem of Access to Migrant Labor Camps, 60 Cornell L.Rev. 560 (1976). Query, would *PruneYard* sustain a state constitutional provision as applied to a private university disallowing outsiders to leaflet on the campus without a university-issued permit? (See State v. Schmid, 84 N.J. 535, 423 A.2d 615 (1980), appeal dismissed sub nom. Princeton University v. Schmid, 455 U.S. 100, 102 S.Ct. 867, 70 L.Ed.2d 855 (1982).

39. May it lawfully dedicate certain public property solely to the end of communicating its own views, for instance, excluding all replies, rebuttals, and other communications? Why not? Suppose a city decides to acquire its own cablevision company. Having once acquired the company, may the city put on exactly what it sees fit (as presumably the Miami Herald may do with its own newspaper pages)? For a general (useful but inconclusive) review, see M. Yudof, When Government Speaks (1982); cf. Kamenshine, The First Amendment's Implied Political Establishment Clause, 67 Calif.L.Rev. 1104 (1979). See also Shiffrin, Government Speech, 27 U.C. L.A.L.Rev. 565 (1980).

As one can see simply from these few casual examples, the questions raised here are far from obviously self-answering. Perhaps that ought not be a surprise. For aside from such early examples as the Post Office, the assumption of ownership and management responsibility by the public sector for other kinds of property (housing, for instance) is a relatively recent phenomenon in a more general way. To what extent does the first amendment create—or not create—claims against government when it manages public property? Or, to frame the same question somewhat differently, to what extent may each kind of government managed property be some kind of "public forum" in fact? The answer, such as it is, tends to track a great deal of our earlier work.[40]

I.

The dictum by Justice Rehnquist (quoting from an earlier opinion by Justice Black) with which this Section began, harkens back to the perspective of the very first case to be reviewed in the Supreme Court on this subject, in 1897. That case was *Davis v. Commonwealth*.[41] The *Davis* case was altogether contemporary with *Patterson v. Colorado,* and with *McAuliffe v. Mayor of New Bedford,* the two turn-of-the-century decisions authored by Justice Holmes, prior to the later Opinions and dissents Holmes and Brandeis authored in the twenties, opinions and dissents that marked the first great movement in this country in the protection of freedom of speech. The *Davis* case treated restrictions on the speech-use of government-held property very much in the manner the Rehnquist dictum would suggest even now.

Davis, an itinerant minister, had been convicted of speaking in Boston Common without a permit as required by city ordinance.[42] Relying heavily on Justice Holmes's opinion in the Supreme Judicial Court of Massachusetts, affirming Davis's conviction, a unanimous Supreme Court gave Davis's appeal very short shrift. In the Supreme Judicial Court of Massachusetts, this had been Holmes's dispositive view: [43]

> For the Legislature absolutely or conditionally to forbid public speaking in a highway or public park is no more an infringement of the rights of a member of the public *than for the owner of a private house* to forbid it in his house. When no proprie-

---

40. For a recent comprehensive critical review of the general subject, see Werhan, The Supreme Court's Public Forum Doctrine and the Return of Formalism, 7 Cardozo L.Rev. 335 (1986). See also Cass, First Amendment Access to Government Facilities, 65 Va.L.Rev. 1287 (1979); Farber & Nowak, The Misleading Nature of Public Forum Analysis: Content and Context in First Amendment Adjudication, 70 Va.L. Rev. 1219 (1984); Hornung, The First Amendment Right to A Public Forum, 1969 Duke L.J. 931; Kalven, The Concept of the Public Forum: Cox v. Louisiana, 1965 Sup.Ct.Rev. 1; Stone, Fora Americana: Speech in Public Places, 1974 Sup.Ct. Rev. 233; Note, The Public Forum: Minimum Access, Equal Access, and the First Amendment, 28 Stan.L.Rev. 117 (1975).

41. 167 U.S. 43, 17 S.Ct. 731, 42 L.Ed. 71 (1897).

42. The ordinance (see 162 Mass. at 510, 39 N.E. at 113) provided: "No person shall, in or upon any of the public grounds, make any public address * * * except in accordance with a permit from the mayor."

43. Commonwealth v. Davis, 162 Mass. 510, 511, 39 N.E. 113, 113 (1895). (Emphasis added.)

tary right interferes, the Legislature may end the right of the public to enter upon the public place by putting an end to the dedication to public uses. *So it may take the lesser step of limiting the public use to certain purposes.*

Doing little more than to quote this portion of Justice Holmes's Opinion (the whole report of the case in the Supreme Court is barely three pages), the Supreme Court unanimously affirmed.[44]

In 1920 (shortly following the *Schenck* and *Abrams* cases from World War I and the Espionage Act), in contrast with *Davis,* Justice Holmes and Justice Brandeis dissented in a case involving the Postmaster General's revocation of second-class mailing privileges for a newspaper editorially promoting pro-German views, *The Milwaukee Leader.* The second-class rates denied the publisher—because of the content of his newspaper—were far lower than the third-class rates the *Leader*

---

44. The Court made no more of Davis's separate objection that, assuming public addresses might be altogether forbidden in Boston Common, the ordinance did not do so but, rather, held out the possibility of such a use pursuant to a permit that the mayor was authorized to grant or deny seemingly at will. ("The plaintiff in error cannot avail himself of the right granted by the state and yet obtain exemption from the lawful regulations to which this right on his part was subjected by law.") (167 U.S. at 48, 17 S.Ct. at 733, 42 L.Ed. at 72). Subsequent cases have abandoned this branch of the *Davis* case, i.e. permit systems, to be constitutional (as a form of prior restraint) must minimally have: (a) clear substantive standards limiting the administrator's discretion to (b) tightly confined, valid, grounds for disallowing the permit under specified circumstances, (c) a virtually costless opportunity for a party denied a permit to secure immediate review of any adverse administrative decision, in (d) a regular adversary proceeding before a neutral party (e.g., a regular judge, rather than an administrator), in which proceeding (e) the burden rests with the state to sustain the denial of the permit (rather than the burden resting with the private party to show why it should not be sustained). A permit system not complying with these standards need not be complied with and may, when a prosecution is brought for one's failure to have applied as required by the law, be attacked as void on its face. See, e.g., City of Lakewood v. Plain Dealer Pub. Co., 486 U.S. 750, 108 S.Ct. 2138, 100 L.Ed.2d 771 (1988); Southeastern Promotions, Ltd. v. Conrad, 420 U.S. 546, 95 S.Ct. 1239, 43 L.Ed.2d 448 (1975); Shuttlesworth v. Birmingham, 394 U.S. 147, 89 S.Ct. 935, 22 L.Ed.2d 162 (1969); Carroll v. President and Com'rs, 393 U.S. 175, 89 S.Ct. 347, 21 L.Ed.2d 325 (1968); Staub v. Baxley, 355 U.S. 313, 78 S.Ct. 277, 2 L.Ed.2d 302 (1958); Kunz v. New York, 340 U.S. 290, 71 S.Ct. 312, 95 L.Ed. 280 (1951); Niemotko v. Maryland, 340 U.S. 268, 71 S.Ct. 325, 95 L.Ed. 267 (1951); Saia v. New York, 334 U.S. 558, 68 S.Ct. 1148, 92 L.Ed. 1574 (1948). Thomas v. Collins, 323 U.S. 516, 65 S.Ct. 315, 89 L.Ed. 430 (1945); Lovell v. Griffin, 303 U.S. 444, 58 S.Ct. 666, 82 L.Ed. 949 (1938) ("[A]s the ordinance is void on its face, it was not necessary for appellant to seek a permit under it. She was entitled to contest its validity in answer to the charge against her.") The exceptional first amendment requirements of (prior restraint) administrative permit systems, where permission turns on administrative discretion by officials who are likely to err on the side of avoiding blame for a demonstration or an address that might be disruptive or offensive, was anticipated even in Blackstone's Commentaries (vol. iv, p. 150 (1769)) on press licensing, as we noted earlier. ("To subject the press to the restrictive power of a licenser, as was formerly done, * * * is to subject all freedom of sentiment to the prejudices of one man, and make him the arbitrary and infallible judge of all controverted points in learning, religion and government * * *.") See also Bantam Books, Inc. v. Sullivan, 372 U.S. 58, 83 S.Ct. 631, 9 L.Ed. 584 (1963) ("Any system of prior restraints of expression comes to this Court bearing a heavy presumption against its constitutional validity."); Freedman v. Maryland, 380 U.S. 51, 85 S.Ct. 734, 13 L.Ed.2d 649 (1965). But see other cases and discussion in Blasi, Prior Restraints on Demonstrations, 68 Mich.L. Rev. 1482 (1970). See also Blasi, Toward a Theory of Prior Restraint, 66 Minn.L.Rev. 11 (1981); Emerson, The Doctrine of Prior Restraint, 20 Law & Contemp. Probs. 648 (1955); Monaghan, First Amendment "Due Process," 83 Harv.L.Rev. 518 (1970); Redish, The Proper Role of the Prior Restraint Doctrine in First Amendment Theory, 70 Va.L.Rev. 53 (1984).

would have to pay were the revocation sustained. In fact, they were estimated to represent but one-sixth the Post Office's estimated actual cost of carrying the kind of mail thus favored by this rate, i.e. the rates provided a heavily tax-subsidized advantage to newspapers delivered by mail. A majority of the Supreme Court sustained the Postmaster General's decision. Brandeis and Holmes dissented, albeit, technically, on statutory grounds.[45] Even so, Justice Brandeis expressed doubts of the constitutionality of the Postmaster's actions along the following lines. Note the strong similarity of some of this passage to the development of the doctrine of unconstitutional conditions in the public status (employment) cases, reviewed in the previous section of these materials: [46]

> Congress may not through its postal police power put limitations upon the freedom of the press which if directly attempted would be unconstitutional. * * * Government might, of course, decline altogether to distribute newspapers; or it might decline to carry any at less than the cost of the service; and it would not thereby abridge the freedom of the press, since to all papers other means of transportation would be left open. But to carry newspapers generally at a sixth of the cost of the service and to deny that service to one paper of the same general character, because to the Postmaster General views therein expressed in the past seem illegal, would prove an

---

45. Recall that technically, in *Abrams v. United States,* the 1919 Espionage Act case in which Holmes wrote his principal dissent defending a robust standard of free speech protection under the first amendment, the dissent similarly first held that the acts for which Abrams was prosecuted were not, in his view, reached by the Espionage Act. The general rule of statutory interpretation, where constitutional issues of a substantial nature would be raised if one view of the statute were taken but are fairly avoided under a different view of the statute itself, has frequently been pressed into service in first amendment cases, sometimes even when it has seemed to strain the words of the Act in question at the time. See, e.g., Yates v. United States, 354 U.S. 298, 77 S.Ct. 1064, 1 L.Ed.2d 1356 (1957) (follow-up case to *Dennis v. United States,* narrowly construing Smith Act to reach only active incitement of violence to overthrow government, despite statutory language making the teaching of the desirability of such action a felony). On the other hand, once the Court appears to have confronted and settled the first amendment controlling standard in what it may deem to be a clear and substantial fashion, there is sometimes less disposition to "save" a statute by interpreting it to hold that it does not, as sparingly interpreted, violate that standard. An excellent example is United States v. Robel, 389 U.S. 258, 88 S.Ct. 419, 19 L.Ed.2d 508 (1967), included in the materials *supra.* For an excellent general discussion of the point, see Gunther, Reflections on Robel: It's Not What the Court Did But the Way It Did It, 20 Stan.L.Rev. 1140 (1968).

46. U.S. ex rel. Milwaukee Social Democratic Pub. Co. v. Burleson, 255 U.S. 407, 430–31, 41 S.Ct. 352, 360–61, 65 L.Ed. 704, 717 (1921). See also Hannegan v. Esquire, Inc., 327 U.S. 146, 66 S.Ct. 456, 90 L.Ed. 586 (1946) (finding no statutory discretion in Postmaster General to revoke second class mailing privilege for Esquire Magazine ("The Magazine for Men"), the advantage of the mail rate providing a stipulated $500,000 advantage or annual indirect subsidy. The Postmaster General acted under his view that the statute's second class mailing advantage was limited to such magazines as might "contribute to the public good and the public welfare," which, in his view, excluded Esquire, given Esquire's "dominant tone" ("smoking-room type of humor, featuring, in the main, sex," which some witnesses regarded as "highly objectionable, calling them salacious and indecent"). Statute construed narrowly because "grave constitutional questions are immediately raised once it is said that the uses of the mails is a privilege which may be extended or withheld on any grounds whatsoever," *id.* at 156, 66 S.Ct. at 461, 90 L.Ed. at 592, citing to Brandeis and Holmes in *Burleson.*

effective censorship and abridge seriously freedom of expression.

The dissent in *Burleson* is of a piece with the simultaneous emergence in the twenties of the stronger perspectives Brandeis and Holmes contributed to first amendment jurisprudence generally. It seems quite far from the view reflected in *Davis v. Commonwealth* in 1897. Moreover, a dictum added by Holmes in his concurrence to the Brandeis dissent in *Burleson*[47] went a step further. "The United States," Holmes suggested, "may give up the Post Office when it sees fit, *but while it carries it on the use of the mails is almost as much a part of free speech as the right to use our tongues * * *.*"

But if use of the mails were regarded as "almost as much a part of free speech as the right to use our tongues," as Holmes suggests that it may be for first amendment purposes, note the difference it would at once make in the relevant legal standard in measuring the terms of access and use of the mails. Presumably, restrictions on using the mails would have to satisfy first amendment standards not significantly different from those that apply to the right to use "our tongues."[48] In 1939, as the following case shows, this idea begins to take hold in a more general way.[49]

HAGUE v. COMMITTEE FOR INDUSTRIAL ORGANIZATION
Supreme Court of the United States, 1939.
307 U.S. 496, 59 S.Ct. 954, 83 L.Ed. 1423.

MR. JUSTICE ROBERTS delivered an opinion in which MR. JUSTICE BLACK concurred.

* * *

* * * The bill * * * alleges that respondents have repeatedly applied for permits to hold public meetings in the city for the stated purpose, as required by ordinance,[1] although they do not admit the

---

47. 255 U.S. at 437, 41 S.Ct. at 363, 65 L.Ed. at 720. (Emphasis added.)

48. Applied in Lamont v. Postmaster General, 381 U.S. 301, 85 S.Ct. 1493, 14 L.Ed.2d 398 (1965). Cf. Rowan v. United States Post Office Department, 397 U.S. 728, 90 S.Ct. 1484, 25 L.Ed.2d 736 (1970) (federal statute forbidding mailings to homeowners filing notice with Post Office of desire not to receive certain mail they, not the Post Office, deem undesirable, sustained).

49. For a comprehensive review, see Gibbons, Hague v. CIO: A Retrospective, 52 N.Y.U.L.Rev. 731 (1977).

1. "The Board of Commissioners of Jersey City Do Ordain:

"1. From and after the passage of this ordinance, no public parades or public assembly in or upon the public streets, highways, public parks or public buildings of Jersey City shall take place or be conducted until a permit shall be obtained from the Director of Public Safety.

"2. The Director of Public Safety is hereby authorized and empowered to grant permits for parades and public assembly, upon application made to him at least three days prior to the proposed parade or public assembly.

"3. The Director of Public Safety is hereby authorized to refuse to issue said permit when, after investigation of all of the facts and circumstances pertinent to said application, he believes it to be proper to refuse the issuance thereof; provided, however, that said permit shall only be refused for the purpose of preventing riots, disturbances or disorderly assemblage.

validity of the ordinance; but in execution of a common plan and purpose, the petitioners have consistently refused to issue any permits for meetings to be held by, or sponsored by, respondents, and have thus prevented the holding of such meetings; that the respondents did not, and do not, propose to advocate the destruction or overthrow of the government of the United States, or that of New Jersey, but that their sole purpose is to explain to workingmen the purposes of the National Labor Relations Act, the benefits to be derived from it, and the aid which the Committee for Industrial Organization would furnish workingmen to that end; * * *

* * *

The bill charges that the ordinances are unconstitutional and void, or are being enforced against respondents in an unconstitutional and discriminatory way; and that the petitioners, as officials of the city, purporting to act under the ordinances, have deprived respondents of the privileges of free speech and peaceable assembly secured to them, as citizens of the United States, by the Fourteenth Amendment, U.S.C. A.Const. It prays an injunction against continuance of petitioners' conduct.

* * *

The findings are that the petitioners, as officials, have adopted and enforced a deliberate policy of forbidding the respondents and their associates from communicating their views respecting the National Labor Relations Act to the citizens of Jersey City by holding meetings or assemblies in the open air and at public places; that there is no competent proof that the proposed speakers have ever spoken at an assembly where a breach of the peace occurred or at which any utterances were made which violated the canons of proper discussion or gave occasion for disorder consequent upon what was said; that there is no competent proof that the parks of Jersey City are dedicated to any general purpose other than the recreation of the public and that there is competent proof that the municipal authorities have granted permits to various persons other than the respondents to speak at meetings in the streets of the city.

* * *

The question now presented is whether freedom to disseminate information concerning the provisions of the National Labor Relations Act, to assemble peaceably for discussion of the Act, and of the opportunities and advantages offered by it, is a privilege or immunity of a citizen of the United States secured against State abridgment by Section 1 of the Fourteenth Amendment; and whether R.S. § 1979 and Section 24(14) of the Judicial Code afford redress in a federal court for such abridgment. This is the narrow question presented by the record, and we confine our decision to it, without consideration of broader issues which the parties urge. * * *

"4. Any person or persons violating any of the provisions of this ordinance shall upon conviction before a police magistrate of the City of Jersey City be punished by a fine not exceeding two hundred dollars or imprisonment in the Hudson County jail for a period not exceeding ninety days or both."

Although it has been held that the Fourteenth Amendment created no rights in citizens of the United States, but merely secured existing rights against state abridgment, it is clear that the right peaceably to assemble and to discuss these topics, and to communicate respecting them, whether orally or in writing, is a privilege inherent in citizenship of the United States which the Amendment protects.

In the *Slaughter–House Cases* it was said, 16 Wall. page 79: "The right to peaceably assemble and petition for redress of grievances, the privilege of the writ of habeas corpus, are rights of the citizen guaranteed by the Federal Constitution.

* * *

Natural persons, and they alone, are entitled to the privileges and immunities which Section 1 of the Fourteenth Amendment secures for "citizens of the United States." Only the individual respondents may, therefore, maintain this suit.

Second. What has been said demonstrates that, in the light of the facts found, privileges and immunities of the individual respondents as citizens of the United States, were infringed by the petitioners, by virtue of their official positions, under color of ordinances of Jersey City, unless, as petitioners contend, the city's ownership of streets and parks is as absolute as one's ownership of his home, with consequent power altogether to exclude citizens from the use thereof, or unless, though the city holds the streets in trust for public use, the absolute denial of their use to the respondents is a valid exercise of the police power.

The findings of fact negative the latter assumption. In support of the former the petitioners rely upon Davis v. Massachusetts, 167 U.S. 43. * * *

The decision seems to be grounded on the holding of the State court that the Common "was absolutely under the control of the legislature," and that it was thus "conclusively determined there was no right in the plaintiff in error to use the common except in such mode and subject to such regulations as the legislature, in its wisdom, may have deemed proper to prescribe." * * *

* * *

We have no occasion to determine whether, on the facts disclosed, the *Davis Case* was rightly decided, but we cannot agree that it rules the instant case. Wherever the title of streets and parks may rest, they have immemorially been held in trust for the use of the public and, time out of mind, have been used for purposes of assembly, communicating thoughts between citizens, and discussing public questions. Such use of the streets and public places has, from ancient times, been a part of the privileges, immunities, rights, and liberties of citizens. The privilege of a citizen of the United States to use the streets and parks for communication of views on national questions may be regulated in the interest of all; it is not absolute, but relative, and must be exercised in subordination to the general comfort and convenience, and in consonance with peace and good order; but it must not, in the guise of regulation, be abridged or denied.

We think the court below was right in holding the ordinance quoted in Note 1 void upon its face. It does not make comfort or convenience in the use of streets or parks the standard of official action. It enables the Director of Safety to refuse a permit on his mere opinion that such refusal will prevent "riots, disturbances or disorderly assemblage." It can thus, as the record discloses, be made the instrument of arbitrary suppression of free expression of views on national affairs for the prohibition of all speaking will undoubtedly "prevent" such eventualities. But uncontrolled official suppression of the privilege cannot be made a substitute for the duty to maintain order in connection with the exercise of the right.

* * *

Paragraph 4 has to do with public meetings. Although the court below held the ordinance void, the decree enjoins the petitioners as to the manner in which they shall administer it. There is an initial command that the petitioners shall not place "any previous restraint" upon the respondents in respect of holding meetings provided they apply for a permit as required by the ordinance. This is followed by an enumeration of the conditions under which a permit may be granted or denied. We think this is wrong. As the ordinance is void, the respondents are entitled to a decree so declaring and an injunction against its enforcement by the petitioners. They are free to hold meetings without a permit and without regard to the terms of the void ordinance. The courts cannot rewrite the ordinance, as the decree, in effect, does.

* * *

MR. JUSTICE STONE.

I do not doubt that the decree below, modified as has been proposed, is rightly affirmed, but I am unable to follow the path by which some of my brethren have attained that end, and I think the matter is of sufficient importance to merit discussion in some detail.

It has been explicitly and repeatedly affirmed by this Court, without a dissenting voice, that freedom of speech and of assembly for any lawful purpose are rights of personal liberty secured to all persons, without regard to citizenship, by the due process clause of the Fourteenth Amendment * * *.

* * *

Both courts below found, and the evidence supports the findings, that the purpose of respondents, other than the Civil Liberties Union, in holding meetings in Jersey City, was to organize labor unions in various industries in order to secure to workers the benefits of collective bargaining with respect to betterment of wages, hours of work and other terms and conditions of employment. Whether the proposed unions were to be organized in industries which might be subject to the National Labor Relations Act or the jurisdiction of the National Labor Relations Board does not appear. Neither court below has made any finding that the meetings were called to discuss, or that they ever did in fact discuss, the National Labor Relations Act. The findings do not support the conclusion that the proposed meetings involved any such relationship between the national government and respondents or any of them, assuming they are citizens of the United States, as to show that the asserted right or privilege was that of a citizen of the United States, and I cannot say that an adequate basis has been laid for supporting a theory—which respondents themselves evidently did not entertain—that any of their privileges as citizens of the United States, guaranteed by the Fourteenth Amendment, were abridged, as distinguished from the privileges guaranteed to all persons by the due process clause. * * *

No more grave and important issue can be brought to this Court than that of freedom of speech and assembly, which the due process clause guarantees to all persons regardless of their citizenship, but which the privileges and immunities clause secures only to citizens, and then only to the limited extent that their relationship to the national government is affected. I am unable to rest decision here on the assertion, which I think the record fails to support, that respondents must depend upon their limited privileges as citizens of the United States in order to sustain their cause, or upon so palpable an avoidance of the real issue in the case, which respondents have raised by their pleadings and sustained by their proof. * * * I think respondents' right to maintain it does not depend on their citizenship and cannot rightly be made to turn on the existence or non-existence of a purpose to disseminate information about the National Labor Relations Act. It is enough that petitioners have prevented respondents from holding meetings and disseminating information whether for the organization of labor unions or for any other lawful purpose.

* * *

SCHNEIDER v. STATE
Supreme Court of the United States, 1939.
308 U.S. 147, 60 S.Ct. 146, 84 L.Ed. 155.

MR. JUSTICE ROBERTS delivered the opinion of the Court.

Four cases are here, each of which presents the question whether regulations embodied in a municipal ordinance abridge the freedom of speech and of the press secured against state invasion by the Fourteenth Amendment of the Constitution.

No. 13

The Municipal Code of the City of Los Angeles, 1936, provides:
"Sec. 28.00. 'Hand–Bill' shall mean any hand-bill, dodger, commercial advertising circular, folder, booklet, letter, card, pamphlet, sheet, poster, sticker, banner, notice or other writ-

ten, printed or painted matter calculated to attract attention of the public."

"Sec. 28.01. No person shall distribute any hand-bill to or among pedestrians along or upon any street, sidewalk or park, or to passengers on any street car, or throw, place or attach any hand-bill in, to, or upon any automobile or other vehicle."

The appellant was charged in the Municipal Court with a violation of § 28.01. Upon his trial it was proved that he distributed handbills to pedestrians on a public sidewalk and had more than three hundred in his possession for that purpose. Judgment of conviction was entered and sentence imposed. The Superior Court of Los Angeles County affirmed the judgment. That court being the highest court in the State authorized to pass upon such a case, an appeal to this court was allowed.

The hand-bill which the appellant was distributing bore a notice of a meeting to be held under the auspices of "Friends of Lincoln Brigade" at which speakers would discuss the war in Spain.

The court below sustained the validity of the ordinance on the ground that experience shows littering of the streets results from the indiscriminate distribution of hand-bills.[3] It held that the right of free expression is not absolute but subject to reasonable regulation and that the ordinance does not transgress the bounds of reasonableness. Lovell v. City of Griffin, 303 U.S. 444, was distinguished on the ground that the ordinance there in question prohibited distribution anywhere within the city while the one involved forbids distribution in a very limited number of places.

No. 18

An ordinance of the City of Milwaukee, Wisconsin, provides: "It is hereby made unlawful for any person * * * to * * * throw * * * paper * * * or to circulate or distribute any circular, hand-bills, cards, posters, dodgers, or other printed or advertising matter * * * in or upon any sidewalk, street, alley, wharf, boat landing, dock or other public place, park or ground within the City of Milwaukee * * *"

The petitioner, who was acting as a picket, stood in the street in front of a meat market and distributed to passing pedestrians hand-bills which pertained to a labor dispute with the meat market, set forth the position of organized labor with respect to the market, and asked citizens to refrain from patronizing it. Some of the bills were thrown in the street by the persons to whom they were given and it resulted that many of the papers lay in the gutter and in the street. The police officers who arrested the petitioner and charged him with a violation of

---

3. On the hand-bill were the words "Admission 25¢ and 50¢." The Superior Court adverted to these and said: "Whatever traffic in ideas the Friends of Lincoln Brigade may have planned for the meeting, the cards themselves seem to fall within the classification of commercial advertising rather than the expression of one's views. But if this be so, our conclusion is not thereby changed."

the ordinance did not arrest any of those who received the bills and threw them away. The testimony was that the action of the officers accorded with a policy of the police department in enforcement of the ordinance to the effect that, when such distribution resulted in littering of the streets the one who was the cause of the littering, that is, he who passed out the bills, was arrested rather than those who received them and afterwards threw them away. The Milwaukee County court found the petitioner guilty and fined him. On appeal the judgment was affirmed by the Supreme Court.

The court held that the purpose of the ordinance was to prevent an unsightly, untidy, and offensive condition of the sidewalks. It distinguished *Lovell v. City of Griffin, supra,* on the ground that the ordinance there considered manifestly was not aimed at prevention of littering of the streets. The court approved the administrative construction of the ordinance by the police officials and felt that this construction sustained its validity. The court said: "Unless and until delivery of the hand-bills was shown to result in a littering of the streets their distribution was not interfered with."

No. 29

An ordinance of the City of Worcester, Massachusetts, provides: "No person shall distribute in, or place upon any street or way, any placard, handbill, flyer, poster, advertisement or paper of any description. * * * "

The appellants distributed in a street leaflets announcing a protest meeting in connection with the administration of state unemployment insurance. They did not throw any of the leaflets on the sidewalk or scatter them. Some of those to whom the leaflets were handed threw them on the sidewalk and the street, with the result that some thirty were lying about.

The appellants were arrested and charged with a violation of the ordinance. The Superior Court of Worcester County rendered a judgment of conviction and imposed sentence. The Supreme Judicial Court overruled exceptions. That court held the ordinance a valid regulation of the use of the streets and sought thus to distinguish it from the one involved in *Lovell v. City of Griffin, supra,* which the court said was not such a regulation. Referring to the ordinance the court said: "It interferes in no way with the publication of anything in the city of Worcester, except only that it excludes the public streets and ways from the places available for free distribution. It leaves open for such distribution all other places in the city, public and private."

* * *

This court has characterized the freedom of speech and that of the press as fundamental personal rights and liberties. The phrase is not an empty one and was not lightly used. It reflects the belief of the framers of the Constitution that exercise of the rights lies at the foundation of free government by free men. It stresses, as do many opinions of this court, the importance of preventing the restriction of enjoyment of these liberties.

In every case, therefore, where legislative abridgment of the rights is asserted, the courts should be astute to examine the effect of the challenged legislation. Mere legislative preferences or beliefs respecting matters of public convenience may well support regulation directed at other personal activities, but be insufficient to justify such as diminishes the exercise of rights so vital to the maintenance of democratic institutions. And so, cases arise, the delicate and difficult task falls upon the courts to weigh the circumstances and to appraise the substantiality of the reasons advanced in support of the regulation of the free enjoyment of the rights.

In *Lovell v. City of Griffin, supra,* this court held void an ordinance which forbade the distribution by hand or otherwise of literature of any kind without written permission from the city manager. The opinion pointed out that the ordinance was not limited to obscene and immoral literature or that which advocated unlawful conduct, placed no limit on the privilege of distribution in the interest of public order, was not aimed to prevent molestation of inhabitants or misuse or littering of streets, and was without limitation as to time or place of distribution. The court said that, whatever the motive, the ordinance was bad because it imposed penalties for the distribution of pamphlets, which had become historical weapons in the defense of liberty, by subjecting such distribution to license and censorship; and that the ordinance was void on its face, because it abridged the freedom of the press. Similarly in Hague v. C.I.O., 307 U.S. 496, an ordinance was held void on its face because it provided for previous administrative censorship of the exercise of the right of speech and assembly in appropriate public places.

The Los Angeles, the Milwaukee, and the Worcester ordinances under review do not purport to license distribution but all of them absolutely prohibit it in the streets and, one of them, in other public places as well.

The motive of the legislation under attack in Numbers 13, 18, and 29 is held by the courts below to be the prevention of littering of the streets and, although the alleged offenders were not charged with themselves scattering paper in the streets, their convictions were sustained upon the theory that distribution by them encouraged or resulted in such littering. We are of opinion that the purpose to keep the streets clean and of good appearance is insufficient to justify an ordinance which prohibits a person rightfully on a public street from handing literature to one willing to receive it. Any burden imposed upon the city authorities in cleaning and caring for the streets as an indirect consequence of such distribution results from the constitutional protection of the freedom of speech and press. This constitutional protection does not deprive a city of all power to prevent street littering. There are obvious methods of preventing littering. Amongst these is the punishment of those who actually throw papers on the street.

It is argued that the circumstance that in the actual enforcement of the Milwaukee ordinance the distributor is arrested only if those who receive the literature throw it in the streets, renders it valid. But, even as thus construed, the ordinance cannot be enforced without unconstitutionally abridging the liberty of free speech. As we have pointed out, the public convenience in respect of cleanliness of the streets does not justify an exertion of the police power which invades the free communication of information and opinion secured by the Constitution.

It is suggested that the Los Angeles and Worcester ordinances are valid because their operation is limited to streets and alleys and leaves persons free to distribute printed matter in other public places. But, as we have said, the streets are natural and proper places for the dissemination of information and opinion; and one is not to have the exercise of his liberty of expression in appropriate places abridged on the plea that it may be exercised in some other place.

* * *

The judgment in each case is reversed and the causes are remanded for further proceedings not inconsistent with this opinion.

Reversed.

MR. JUSTICE MCREYNOLDS is of opinion that the judgment in each case should be affirmed.

NOTE

Hague, Schneider, Lovell, and similar cases suggest that to some extent the first amendment creates a tentative free speech easement of access and use in certain kinds of publicly-owned property, at least for politically-related speech, and perhaps for some other kinds (e.g., religiously-impelled speech) as well. Beyond this important point, these cases likewise appear also to reject exclusionary rationales based on public interest claims to avoid certain costs, disruptions, and other minor harms as sufficient grounds to disallow certain kinds of proposed uses of publicly-held property. (E.g., the Court in *Schneider* concedes that punishing only those who throw leaflets into the streets may not be as efficient as forbidding the distribution of leaflets in the first place, in keeping the sidewalks and streets free of litter.) How far do these new kinds of first amendment protections extend? And if they extend in some measure to other sorts of publicly-held property, do they extend there with the same, rather full measure of protection as in streets, parks, and sidewalks, or are they subject to greater restriction the less "traditional" the nature of the "public forum" may chance to be? For those lacking extensive private property holdings, incidentally, note that these kinds of forums, such as they are, are sometimes all that some groups and individuals may have.[50] Is it arguable, moreover, that

---

50. See, e.g., Van Alstyne, The Recrudescence of Property Rights as the

whenever and *wherever* it is *public* property, the burden does not rest with the free speech user to show some legal entitlement other than the first amendment itself to use that property to communicate his or her message? That the burden, rather, is on government at all times to justify the kind of restriction it has presumed to impose, or else to step aside—a burden, moreover, (again as illustrated in the *Schneider* decision) with a bite?

As to what kind of restriction(s) may or may not be sustainable, the following several cases, decided together in the Supreme Court, may furnish some further clues.[51]

2. Time, Place, and Manner Regulation

NIEMOTKO v. MARYLAND
Supreme Court of the United States, 1951.
340 U.S. 268, 71 S.Ct. 325, 95 L.Ed. 267.

MR. CHIEF JUSTICE VINSON delivered the opinion of the Court.

Appellants are two members of the religious group known as Jehovah's Witnesses. At the invitation of local coreligionists, they scheduled Bible talks in the public park of the city of Havre de Grace, Maryland. Although there is no ordinance prohibiting or regulating the use of this park, it has been the custom for organizations and individuals desiring to use it for meetings and celebrations of various kinds to obtain permits from the Park Commissioner. In conformity with this practice, the group requested permission of the Park Commissioner for use of the park on four consecutive Sundays in June and July, 1949. This permission was refused.

Having been informed that an Elks' Flag Day ceremony was scheduled for the first Sunday, the applicants did not pursue their request for the use of the park for that particular day, but, instead, filed a written request with the City Council for the following three Sundays. This request was filed at the suggestion of the Mayor, it appearing that under the custom of the municipality there is a right of appeal to the City Council from the action of the Park Commissioner. The Council held a hearing at which the request was considered. At

---

Foremost Principle of Civil Liberties: The First Decade of the Burger Court, 43 Law & Contemp.Probs. 66, 73 (1980) ("In the not-distant past, not to have private property was quite frequently fatal to one's abstract freedoms. One may have had an abstract freedom of speech. To exercise it, however, he must stand in some place or speak over some medium. If he had no front porch of his own, he could not, on that account, commandeer his neighbor's. Neither could commandeer the state's.") See also Van Alstyne, Interpretations of The First Amendment 68–90 (1984) (Scarcity, Property, and Government Policy: The First Amendment as a Mobius Strip).

51. See also Cohen v. California, 403 U.S. 15, 91 S.Ct. 1780, 29 L.Ed.2d 284 (1971); Tinker v. Des Moines Indep. Community School Dist., 393 U.S. 503, 89 S.Ct. 733, 21 L.Ed.2d 731 (1969), each of which in several respects previewed the first amendment considerations once again at work here as well, and each of which postdates the following cases from the Supreme Court.

this hearing the applicants and their attorney appeared. The request was denied.

Because they were awaiting the decision of the Council on their application, the applicants took no further steps on the second Sunday, but, after the denial of the request, they proceeded to hold their meeting on the third Sunday. No sooner had appellant Niemotko opened the meeting and commenced delivering his discourse, then the police, who had been ordered to the park by the Mayor, arrested him. At the meeting held in the park on the fourth and following Sunday, appellant Kelley was arrested before he began his lecture.

Appellants were subsequently brought to trial before a jury on a charge of disorderly conduct under the Maryland disorderly conduct statute. Flack's Md.Ann.Code, 1939 (1947 Cum.Supp.), Art. 27, § 131. They were convicted and each fined $25 and costs. Under the rather unique Maryland procedure, the jury is the judge of the law as well as the facts. Md.Const., Art. XV, § 5; see opinion below, * * *, 71 A.2d 9, 11. This means that there is normally no appellate review of any question dependent on the sufficiency of the evidence. Relying on this Maryland rule, the Court of Appeals declined to review the case under its normal appellate power, and further declined to take the case on certiorari, stating that the issues were not "matters of public interest" which made it desirable to review. Being of opinion that the case presented substantial constitutional issues, we noted probable jurisdiction, the appeal being properly here under 28 U.S.C. § 1257(2).

In cases in which there is a claim of denial of rights under the Federal Constitution, this Court is not bound by the conclusions of lower courts, but will reexamine the evidentiary basis on which those conclusions are founded. See *Feiner v. New York,* decided this day, * * *. A brief recital of the facts as they were adduced at this trial will suffice to show why these convictions cannot stand. At the time of the arrest of each of these appellants, there was no evidence of disorder, threats of violence or riot. There was no indication that the appellants conducted themselves in a manner which could be considered as detrimental to the public peace or order. On the contrary, there was positive testimony by the police that each of the appellants had conducted himself in a manner beyond reproach. It is quite apparent that any disorderly conduct which the jury found must have been based on the fact that appellants were using the park without a permit, although, as we have indicated above, there is no statute or ordinance prohibiting or regulating the use of the park without a permit.

This Court has many times examined the licensing systems by which local bodies regulate the use of their parks and public places. See *Kunz v. New York,* decided this day, * * *. See also Saia v. New York, 334 U.S. 558 (1948); Hague v. C.I.O., 307 U.S. 496 (1939); Lovell v. Griffin, 303 U.S. 444 (1938). In those cases this Court condemned statutes and ordinances which required that permits be obtained from local officials as a prerequisite to the use of public places, on the grounds that a license requirement constituted a prior restraint on freedom of speech, press and religion, and, in the absence of narrowly drawn, reasonable and definite standards for the officials to follow, must be invalid. See *Kunz v. New York,* * * *. In the instant case we are met with no ordinance or statute regulating or prohibiting the use of the park; all that is here is an amorphous "practice," whereby all authority to grant permits for the use of the park is in the Park Commissioner and the City Council. No standards appear anywhere; no narrowly drawn limitations; no circumscribing of this absolute power; no substantial interest of the community to be served. It is clear that all that has been said about the invalidity of such limitless discretion must be equally applicable here.

This case points up with utmost clarity the wisdom of this doctrine. For the very possibility of abuse, which those earlier decisions feared, has occurred here. Indeed, rarely has any case been before this Court which shows so clearly an unwarranted discrimination in a refusal to issue such a license. It is true that the City Council held a hearing at which it considered the application. But we have searched the record in vain to discover any valid basis for the refusal. In fact, the Mayor testified that the permit would probably have been granted if, at the hearing, the applicants had not started to "berate" the Park Commissioner for his refusal to issue the permit. The only questions asked of the Witnesses at the hearing pertained to their alleged refusal to salute the flag, their views on the Bible, and other issues irrelevant to unencumbered use of the public parks. The conclusion is inescapable that the use of the park was denied because of the City Council's dislike for or disagreement with the Witnesses or their views. The right to equal protection of the laws, in the exercise of those freedoms of speech and religion protected by the First and Fourteenth Amendments, has a firmer foundation than the whims or personal opinions of a local governing body.

In this Court, it is argued that state and city officials should have the power to exclude religious groups, as such, from the use of the public parks. But that is not the case. For whatever force this contention could possibly have is lost in the light of the testimony of the Mayor at the trial that within his memory permits had always been issued for religious organizations and Sunday-school picnics. We might also point out that the attempt to designate the park as a sanctuary for peace and quiet not only does not defeat these appellants, whose own conduct created no disturbance, but this position is also more than slightly inconsistent, since, on the first Sunday here involved, the park was the situs for the Flag Day ceremony of the Order of Elks.

It thus becomes apparent that the lack of standards in the license-issuing "practice" renders that "practice" a prior restraint in contravention of the Fourteenth Amendment, and that the completely arbitrary and discriminatory refusal to grant the permits was a denial of equal protection. Inasmuch as the basis of the convictions was the lack of the permits, and that lack was, in turn, due to the unconstitutional defects discussed, the convictions must fall.

Reversed.

MR. JUSTICE BLACK concurs in the result.

MR. JUSTICE FRANKFURTER, concurring in the result.*

* * *

These cases present three variations upon a theme of great importance. Legislatures, local authorities, and the courts have for years grappled with claims of the right to disseminate ideas in public places as against claims of an effective power in government to keep the peace and to protect other interests of a civilized community. These cases are of special interest because they show the attempts of three communities to meet the problem in three different ways. It will, I believe, further analysis to use the three situations as cross-lights on one another.

* * *

The results in these multifarious cases have been expressed in language looking in two directions. While the Court has emphasized the importance of "free speech," it has recognized that "free speech" is not in itself a touchstone. The Constitution is not unmindful of other important interests, such as public order, if interference with free expression of ideas is not found to be the overbalancing consideration. More important than the phrasing of the opinions are the questions on which the decisions appear to have turned.

(1) What is the interest deemed to require the regulation of speech? The State cannot of course forbid public proselyting or religious argument merely because public officials disapprove the speaker's views. It must act in patent good faith to maintain the public peace, to assure the availability of the streets for their primary purposes of passenger and vehicular traffic, or for equally indispensable ends of modern community life.

(2) What is the method used to achieve such ends as a consequence of which public speech is constrained or barred? A licensing standard which gives an official authority to censor the content of a speech differs toto coelo from one limited by its terms, or by nondiscriminatory practice, to considerations of public safety and the like. Again, a sanction applied after the event assures consideration of the particular circumstances of a situation. The net of control must not be cast too broadly.

(3) What mode of speech is regulated? A sound truck may be found to affect the public peace as normal speech does not. A man who is calling names or using the kind of language which would reasonably stir another to violence does not have the same claim to protection as one whose speech is an appeal to reason.

(4) Where does the speaking which is regulated take place? Not only the general classifications—streets, parks, private buildings—are relevant. The location and size of a park; its customary use for the recreational, esthetic and contemplative needs of a community; the facilities, other than a park or street corner, readily available in a community for airing views, are all pertinent considerations in assess-

---

* [In this case, No. 50, *Kunz v. New York,* * * *.]
* * *, and No. 93, *Feiner v. New York,*

ing the limitations the Fourteenth Amendment puts on State power in a particular situation.

III.

Due regard for the interests that were adjusted in the decisions just canvassed affords guidance for deciding the cases before us.

1. In the *Niemotko* case, neither danger to the public peace, nor consideration of time and convenience to the public, appears to have entered into denial of the permit. Rumors that there would be violence by those opposed to the meeting appeared only after the Council made its decision, and in fact never materialized. The city allowed other religious groups to use the park. To allow expression of religious views by some and deny the same privilege to others merely because they or their views are unpopular, even deeply so, is a denial of equal protection of the law forbidden by the Fourteenth Amendment.

2. The *Kunz* case presents a very different situation. We must be mindful of the enormous difficulties confronting those charged with the task of enabling the polyglot millions in the City of New York to live in peace and tolerance. Street-preaching in Columbus Circle is done in a milieu quite different from preaching on a New England village green. Again, religious polemic does not touch the merely ratiocinative nature of man, and the ugly facts disclosed by the record of this case show that Kunz was not reluctant to offend the deepest religious feelings of frequenters of Columbus Circle. Especially in such situations, this Court should not substitute its abstract views for the informed judgment of local authorities confirmed by local courts.

* * *

In the present case, Kunz was not arrested for what he said on the night of arrest, nor because at that time he was disturbing the peace or interfering with traffic. He was arrested because he spoke without a license, and the license was refused because the police commissioner thought it likely on the basis of past performance that Kunz would outrage the religious sensibilities of others. If such had been the supportable finding on the basis of fair standards in safeguarding peace in one of the most populous centers of New York City, this Court would not be justified in upsetting it. It would not be censorship in advance. But here the standards are defined neither by language nor by settled construction to preclude discriminatory or arbitrary action by officials. The ordinance, as judicially construed, provides that anyone who, in the judgment of the licensing officials, would "ridicule" or "denounce" religion creates such a danger of public disturbance that he cannot speak in any park or street in the City of New York. Such a standard, considering the informal procedure under which it is applied, too readily permits censorship of religion by the licensing authorities. Cantwell v. Connecticut, 310 U.S. 296. The situation here disclosed is not, to reiterate, beyond control on the basis of regulation appropriately directed to the evil.

3. Feiner was convicted under New York Penal Law, § 722, which provides:

"Any person who with intent to provoke a breach of the peace, or whereby a breach of the peace may be occasioned, commits any of the following acts shall be deemed to have committed the offense of disorderly conduct:

* * *

"2. Acts in such a manner as to annoy, disturb, interfere with, obstruct, or be offensive to others; ...."

A State court cannot of course preclude review of due process questions merely by phrasing its opinion in terms of an ultimate standard which in itself satisfies due process. * * * But this Court * * * should not overturn a fair appraisal of facts made by State courts in the light of their knowledge of local conditions.

Here, Feiner forced pedestrians to walk in the street by collecting a crowd on the public sidewalk, he attracted additional attention by using sound amplifiers, he indulged in namecalling, he told part of his audience that it should rise up in arms. In the crowd of 75 to 80 persons, there was angry muttering and pushing. Under these circumstances, and in order to prevent a disturbance of the peace, an officer asked Feiner to stop speaking. When he had twice ignored the request, Feiner was arrested. The trial judge concluded that "the officers were fully justified in feeling that a situation was developing which could very, very easily result in a serious disorder." His view was sustained by an intermediate appellate court and by a unanimous decision of the New York Court of Appeals. 300 N.Y. 391, 91 N.E.2d 316. The estimate of a particular local situation thus comes here with the momentum of the weightiest judicial authority of New York.

* * *

* * * Here, there were two police officers present for 20 minutes. They interfered only when they apprehended imminence of violence. It is not a constitutional principle that, in acting to preserve order, the police must proceed against the crowd, whatever its size and temper, and not against the speaker.

It is true that breach-of-peace statutes, like most tools of government, may be misused. Enforcement of these statutes calls for public tolerance and intelligent police administration. These, in the long run, must give substance to whatever this Court may say about free speech. But the possibility of misuse is not alone a sufficient reason to deny New York the power here asserted or so limit it by constitutional construction as to deny its practical exercise.

KUNZ v. NEW YORK
Supreme Court of the United States, 1951.
340 U.S. 290, 71 S.Ct. 312, 95 L.Ed. 280.

Mr. Justice Vinson delivered the opinion of the Court.

New York City has adopted an ordinance which makes it unlawful to hold public worship meetings on the streets without first obtaining a permit from the city police commissioner. Appellant, Carl Jacob Kunz, was convicted and fined $10 for violating this ordinance by holding a religious meeting without a permit. The conviction was affirmed by the Appellate Part of the Court of Special Sessions, and by the New York Court of Appeals, three judges dissenting, 300 N.Y. 273, 90 N.E.2d 455 (1950). The case is here on appeal, it having been urged that the ordinance is invalid under the Fourteenth Amendment.

Appellant is an ordained Baptist minister who speaks under the auspices of the "Outdoor Gospel Work," of which he is the director. He has been preaching for about six years, and states that it is his conviction and duty to "go out on the highways and byways and preach the word of God." In 1946, he applied for and received a permit under the ordinance in question, there being no question that appellant comes within the classes of persons entitled to receive permits under the ordinance.[2] This permit, like all others, was good only for the calendar year in which issued. In November, 1946, his permit was revoked after a hearing by the police commissioner. The revocation was based on evidence that he had ridiculed and denounced other religious beliefs in his meetings. * * *

Although the penalties of the ordinance apply to anyone who "ridicules and denounces other religious beliefs," the ordinance does not specify this as a ground for permit revocation. Indeed, there is no mention in the ordinance of any power of revocation. However, appellant did not seek judicial or administrative review of the revocation proceedings, and any question as to the propriety of the revocation is not before us in this case. In any event, the revocation affected appellant's rights to speak in 1946 only. Appellant applied for another permit in 1947, and again in 1948, but was notified each time that his application was "disapproved," with no reason for the disapproval being given. On September 11, 1948, appellant was arrested for speaking at Columbus Circle in New York City without a permit. It is from the conviction which resulted that this appeal has been taken.

Appellant's conviction was thus based upon his failure to possess a permit for 1948. We are here concerned only with the propriety of the action of the police commissioner in refusing to issue that permit. Disapproval of the 1948 permit application by the police commissioner was justified by the New York courts on the ground that a permit had previously been revoked "for good reasons."[3] It is noteworthy that there is no mention in the ordinance of reasons for which such a permit application can be refused. This interpretation allows the police commissioner, an administrative official, to exercise discretion in denying subsequent permit applications on the basis of his interpretation, at that time, of what is deemed to be conduct condemned by the ordi-

---

2. The New York Court of Appeals has construed the ordinance to require that all initial requests for permits by eligible applicants must be granted. 300 N.Y. at 276, 90 N.E.2d at 456.

3. The New York Court of Appeals said: "The commissioner had no reason to assume, and no promise was made, that defendant wanted a new permit for any uses different from the disorderly ones he had been guilty of before." 300 N.Y. at 278, 90 N.E.2d at 457.

nance. We have here, then, an ordinance which gives an administrative official discretionary power to control in advance the right of citizens to speak on religious matters on the streets of New York. As such, the ordinance is clearly invalid as a prior restraint on the exercise of First Amendment rights.

* * *

* * * We do not express any opinion on the propriety of punitive remedies which the New York authorities may utilize. We are here concerned with suppression—not punishment. It is sufficient to say that New York cannot vest restraining control over the right to speak on religious subjects in an administrative official where there are no appropriate standards to guide his action.

Reversed.

MR. JUSTICE BLACK concurs in the result.

* * *

MR. JUSTICE JACKSON, dissenting.

* * *

I.

To know what we are doing, we must first locate the point at which rights asserted by Kunz conflict with powers asserted by the organized community. New York City has placed no limitation upon any speech Kunz may choose to make on private property, but it does require a permit to hold religious meetings in its streets. The ordinance, neither by its terms nor as it has been applied, prohibited Kunz,[1] even in street meetings, from preaching his own religion or making any temperate criticism or refutation of other religions; indeed, for the year 1946, he was given a general permit to do so. His meetings, however, brought "a flood of complaints" to city authorities that he was engaging in scurrilous attacks on Catholics and Jews. On notice, he was given a hearing at which eighteen complainants appeared. The Commissioner revoked his permit and applications for 1947 and 1948 were refused. For a time he went on holding meetings without a permit in Columbus Circle, where in September, 1948, he was arrested for violation of the ordinance. He was convicted and fined ten dollars.

At these meetings, Kunz preached, among many other things of like tenor, that "The Catholic Church makes merchandise out of souls," that Catholicism is "a religion of the devil," and that the Pope is "the anti-Christ." The Jews he denounced as "Christ-killers," and he said of them, "All the garbage that didn't believe in Christ should have been burnt in the incinerators. It's a shame they all weren't." These utterances, as one might expect, stirred strife and threatened violence. Testifying in his own behalf, Kunz stated that he "became acquainted with" one of the complaining witnesses, whom he thought to be a Jew,

---

1. Kunz is within the classifications of persons to whom such permits may issue. Hence, we have here no challenge based on its exclusions. If an excluded person made appropriate challenge on equal protection grounds, I should very much doubt if the ordinance could be sustained.

"when he happened to sock one of my Christian boys in the puss." Kunz himself complained to the authorities, charging a woman interrupter with disorderly conduct. He also testified that when an officer is not present at his meetings "I have trouble then," but "with an officer, no trouble."

* * *

II.

This Court today initiates the doctrine that language such as this, in the environment of the street meeting, is immune from prior municipal control. We would have a very different question if New York had presumed to say that Kunz could not speak his piece in his own pulpit or hall. But it has undertaken to restrain him only if he chooses to speak at street meetings. There is a world of difference. The street preacher takes advantage of people's presence on the streets to impose his message upon what, in a sense, is a captive audience. A meeting on private property is made up of an audience that has volunteered to listen. The question, therefore, is not whether New York could, if it tried, silence Kunz, but whether it must place its streets at his service to hurl insults at the passer-by.

* * *

These terse epithets come down to our generation weighted with hatreds accumulated through centuries of bloodshed. They are recognized words of art in the profession of defamation. They are not the kind of insult that men bandy and laugh off when the spirits are high and the flagons are low. They are not in that class of epithets whose literal sting will be drawn if the speaker smiles when he uses them. They are always, and in every context, insults which do not spring from reason and can be answered by none. Their historical associations with violence are well understood, both by those who hurl and those who are struck by these missiles. Jews, many of whose families perished in extermination furnaces of Dachau and Auschwitz, are more than tolerant if they pass off lightly the suggestion that unbelievers in Christ should all have been burned. Of course, people might pass this speaker by as a mental case, and so they might file out of a theatre in good order at the cry of "fire." But in both cases there is genuine likelihood that someone will get hurt.

* * *

A hostile reception of his subject certainly does not alone destroy one's right to speak. A temperate and reasoned criticism of Roman Catholicism or Judaism might, and probably would, cause some resentment and protest. But in a free society all sects and factions, as the price of their own freedom to preach their views, must suffer that freedom in others. Tolerance of unwelcome, unorthodox ideas or information is a constitutionally protected policy not to be defeated by persons who would break up meetings they do not relish.

III.

It is worthwhile to note that the judicial technique by which this Court strikes down the ordinance is very different from that employed by the New York Court of Appeals, which sustained it. The contrary results appear to be largely due to this dissimilarity.

The Court of Appeals did not treat the ordinance as existing in a vacuum but considered all the facts of the controversy. While it construed the ordinance "as requiring the commissioner to give an annual permit for street preaching, *to anyone* who, like defendant, is a minister of religion," 300 N.Y. 273, 276, 90 N.E.2d 455, 456 (1949) (emphasis supplied), it held on the facts that when, as here, the applicant "claims a constitutional right to incite riots, and a constitutional right to the services of policemen to quell those riots," then a permit need not be issued. *Id.* at 278, 90 N.E.2d at 457.

* * *

Of course, as to the press, there are the best of reasons against any licensing or prior restraint. Decisions such as *Near v. Minnesota, supra,* hold any licensing or prior restraint of the press unconstitutional, and I heartily agree. But precedents from that field cannot reasonably be transposed to the street-meeting field. The impact of publishing on public order has no similarity with that of a street meeting. Publishing does not make private use of public property. It reaches only those who choose to read, and, in that way, is analogous to a meeting held in a hall where those who come do so by choice. Written words are less apt to incite or provoke to mass action than spoken words, speech being the primitive and direct communication with the emotions. Few are the riots caused by publication alone, few are the mobs that have not had their immediate origin in harangue. The vulnerability of various forms of communication to community control must be proportioned to their impact upon other community interests.

It is suggested that a permit for a street meeting could be required if the ordinance would prescribe precise standards for its grant or denial. * * *

Of course, standards for administrative action are always desirable, and the more exact the better. But I do not see how this Court can condemn municipal ordinances for not setting forth comprehensive First Amendment standards. This Court never has announced what those standards must be, it does not now say what they are, and it is not clear that any majority could agree on them. In no field are there more numerous individual opinions among the Justices. The Court as an institution not infrequently disagrees with its former self or relies on distinctions that are not very substantial. * * * It seems hypercritical to strike down local laws on their faces for want of standards when we have no standards. And I do not find it required by existing authority. I think that where speech is outside of constitutional immunity the local community or the State is left a large measure of discretion as to the means for dealing with it.

V.

* * *

City officials stopped the meetings of both Feiner and Kunz. The process by which Feiner was stopped was the order of patrolmen, put into immediate effect without hearing. Feiner may have believed there would be no interference but Kunz was duly warned by refusal of a permit. He was advised of charges, given a hearing, confronted by witnesses, and afforded a chance to deny the charges or to confess them and offer to amend his ways. The decision of revocation was made by a detached and responsible administrative official and Kunz could have had the decision reviewed in court.

* * *

But if the Court conceives, as Feiner indicates, that upon uttering insulting, provocative or inciting words the policeman on the beat may stop the meeting, then its assurance of free speech in this decision is "a promise to the ear to be broken to the hope," if the patrolman on the beat happens to have prejudices of his own. Turning then to the permit system as applied by the Court of Appeals, whose construction binds us, we find that issuance the first time is required. Denial is warranted only in such unusual cases as where an applicant has had a permit which has been revoked for cause and he asserts the right to continue the conduct which was cause for revocation. If anything less than a reasonable certainty of disorder was shown, denial of a permit would be improper. The procedure by which that decision is reached commends itself to the orderly mind—complaints are filed, witnesses are heard, opportunity to cross-examine is given, and decision is reached by what we must assume to be an impartial and reasonable administrative officer, and, if he denies the permit, the applicant may carry his cause to the courts. He may thus have a civil test of his rights without the personal humiliation of being arrested as presenting a menace to public order. It seems to me that this procedure better protects freedom of speech than to let everyone speak without leave, but subject to surveillance and to being ordered to stop in the discretion of the police.

* * *

Of course, emergencies may arise either with or without the permit system. A speaker with a permit may go beyond bounds and incite violence, or a mob may undertake to break up an authorized and properly conducted meeting. In either case, the policeman on the spot must make the judgment as to what measures will most likely avoid violent disorders. But these emergencies seem less likely to occur with the permit system than if every man and his adversary take the law in their own hands.

* * *

Addressing himself to the subject, "Authority and the Individual," one of the keenest philosophers of our time observes: "The problem, like all those with which we are concerned, is one of balance; too little liberty brings stagnation, and too much brings chaos." Perhaps it is the fever of our times that inclines the Court today to favor chaos. My hope is that few will take advantage of the license granted by today's decision. But life teaches one to distinguish between hope and faith.

FEINER v. NEW YORK
Supreme Court of the United States, 1951.
340 U.S. 315, 71 S.Ct. 303, 95 L.Ed. 295.

Mr. Chief Justice Vinson delivered the opinion of the Court.

Petitioner was convicted of the offense of disorderly conduct, a misdemeanor under the New York penal laws, in the Court of Special Sessions of the City of Syracuse and was sentenced to thirty days in the county penitentiary. The conviction was affirmed by the Onondaga County Court and the New York Court of Appeals, 300 N.Y. 391, 91 N.E.2d 316 (1950). The case is here on certiorari, 339 U.S. 962 (1950), petitioner having claimed that the conviction is in violation of his right of free speech under the Fourteenth Amendment.

In the review of state decisions where First Amendment rights are drawn in question, we of course make an examination of the evidence to ascertain independently whether the right has been violated. Here, the trial judge, who heard the case without a jury, rendered an oral decision at the end of the trial, setting forth his determination of the facts upon which he found the petitioner guilty. His decision indicated generally that he believed the state's witnesses, and his summation of the testimony was used by the two New York courts on review in stating the facts. Our appraisal of the facts is, therefore, based upon the uncontroverted facts and, where controversy exists, upon that testimony which the trial judge did reasonably conclude to be true.

On the evening of March 8, 1949, petitioner Irving Feiner was addressing an open-air meeting at the corner of South McBride and Harrison Streets in the City of Syracuse. At approximately 6:30 p.m., the police received a telephone complaint concerning the meeting, and two officers were detailed to investigate. One of these officers went to the scene immediately, the other arriving some twelve minutes later. They found a crowd of about seventy-five or eighty people, both Negro and white, filling the sidewalk and spreading out into the street. Petitioner, standing on a large wooden box on the sidewalk, was addressing the crowd through a loudspeaker system attached to an automobile. Although the purpose of his speech was to urge his listeners to attend a meeting to be held that night in the Syracuse Hotel, in its course he was making derogatory remarks concerning President Truman, the American Legion, the Mayor of Syracuse, and other local political officials.

The police officers made no effort to interfere with petitioner's speech, but were first concerned with the effect of the crowd on both pedestrian and vehicular traffic. They observed the situation from the opposite side of the street, noting that some pedestrians were forced to walk in the street to avoid the crowd. Since traffic was passing at the time, the officers attempted to get the people listening to petitioner back on the sidewalk. The crowd was restless and there was some pushing, shoving and milling around. One of the officers telephoned the police station from a nearby store, and then both policemen crossed the street and mingled with the crowd without any intention of arresting the speaker.

At this time, petitioner was speaking in a "loud, high-pitched voice." He gave the impression that he was endeavoring to arouse the Negro people against the whites, urging that they rise up in arms and fight for equal rights. The statements before such a mixed audience "stirred up a little excitement." Some of the onlookers made remarks to the police about their inability to handle the crowd and at least one threatened violence if the police did not act. There were others who appeared to be favoring petitioner's arguments. Because of the feeling that existed in the crowd both for and against the speaker, the officers finally "stepped in to prevent it from resulting in a fight." One of the officers approached the petitioner, not for the purpose of arresting him, but to get him to break up the crowd. He asked petitioner to get down off the box, but the latter refused to accede to his request and continued talking. The officer waited for a minute and then demanded that he cease talking. Although the officer had thus twice requested petitioner to stop over the course of several minutes, petitioner not only ignored him but continued talking. During all this time, the crowd was pressing closer around petitioner and the officer. Finally, the officer told petitioner he was under arrest and ordered him to get down from the box, reaching up to grab him. Petitioner stepped down, announcing over the microphone that "the law has arrived, and I suppose they will take over now." In all, the officer had asked petitioner to get down off the box three times over a space of four or five minutes. Petitioner had been speaking for over a half hour.

On these facts, petitioner was specifically charged with violation of § 722 of the Penal Law of New York, the pertinent part of which is set out in the margin. The bill of particulars, demanded by petitioner and furnished by the State, gave in detail the facts upon which the prosecution relied to support the charge of disorderly conduct. Paragraph C is particularly pertinent here: "By ignoring and refusing to heed and obey reasonable police orders issued at the time and place mentioned in the Information to regulate and control said crowd and to prevent a breach or breaches of the peace and to prevent injury to pedestrians attempting to use said walk, and being forced into the highway adjacent to the place in question, and prevent injury to the public generally."

We are not faced here with blind condonation by a state court of arbitrary police action. Petitioner was accorded a full, fair trial. The trial judge heard testimony supporting and contradicting the judgment of the police officers that a clear danger of disorder was threatened. After weighing this contradictory evidence, the trial judge reached the conclusion that the police officers were justified in taking action to prevent a breach of the peace. The exercise of the police officers' proper discretionary power to prevent a breach of the peace was thus approved by the trial court and later by two courts on review.[2] The

2. The New York Court of Appeals said: "An imminent danger of a breach of the

courts below recognized petitioner's right to hold a street meeting at this locality, to make use of loud-speaking equipment in giving his speech, and to make derogatory remarks concerning public officials and the American Legion. They found that the officers in making the arrest were motivated solely by a proper concern for the preservation of order and protection of the general welfare, and that there was no evidence which could lend color to a claim that the acts of the police were a cover for suppression of petitioner's views and opinions. Petitioner was thus neither arrested nor convicted for the making or the content of his speech. Rather, it was the reaction which it actually engendered.

The language of Cantwell v. Connecticut, 310 U.S. 296 (1940), is appropriate here. "The offense known as breach of the peace embraces a great variety of conduct destroying or menacing public order and tranquility. It includes not only violent acts but acts and words likely to produce violence in others. No one would have the hardihood to suggest that the principle of freedom of speech sanctions incitement to riot or that religious liberty connotes the privilege to exhort others to physical attack upon those belonging to another sect. When clear and present danger of riot, disorder, interference with traffic upon the public streets, or other immediate threat to public safety, peace, or order, appears, the power of the State to prevent or punish is obvious." 310 U.S. at 308. The findings of the New York courts as to the condition of the crowd and the refusal of petitioner to obey the police requests, supported as they are by the record of this case, are persuasive that the conviction of petitioner for violation of public peace, order and authority does not exceed the bounds of proper state police action. This Court respects, as it must, the interest of the community in maintaining peace and order on its streets. Schneider v. State, 308 U.S. 147, 160 (1939); Kovacs v. Cooper, 336 U.S. 77, 82 (1949). We cannot say that the preservation of that interest here encroaches on the constitutional rights of this petitioner.

We are well aware that the ordinary murmurings and objections of a hostile audience cannot be allowed to silence a speaker, and are also mindful of the possible danger of giving overzealous police officials complete discretion to break up otherwise lawful public meetings. "A State may not unduly suppress free communication of views, religious or other, under the guise of conserving desirable conditions." *Cantwell v. Connecticut, supra,* at 308. But we are not faced here with such a situation. It is one thing to say that the police cannot be used as an instrument for the suppression of unpopular views, and another to say that, when as here the speaker passes the bounds of argument or

peace, of a disturbance of public order, perhaps even of riot, was threatened. ... The defendant, as indicated above, disrupted pedestrian and vehicular traffic on the sidewalk and street, and, with intent to provoke a breach of the peace and with knowledge of the consequences, so inflamed and agitated a mixed audience of sympathizers and opponents that, in the judgment of the police officers present, a clear danger of disorder and violence was threatened. Defendant then deliberately refused to accede to the reasonable request of the officer, made within the lawful scope of his authority, that the defendant desist in the interest of public welfare and safety." 300 N.Y. 391, 400, 402, 91 N.E.2d 316, 319, 321 (1950).

persuasion and undertakes incitement to riot, they are powerless to prevent a breach of the peace. Nor in this case can we condemn the considered judgment of three New York courts approving the means which the police, faced with a crisis, used in the exercise of their power and duty to preserve peace and order. The findings of the state courts as to the existing situation and the imminence of greater disorder coupled with petitioner's deliberate defiance of the police officers convince us that we should not reverse this conviction in the name of free speech.

Affirmed.

MR. JUSTICE BLACK, dissenting.

* * *

The record before us convinces me that petitioner, a young college student, has been sentenced to the penitentiary for the unpopular views he expressed on matters of public interest while lawfully making a street-corner speech in Syracuse, New York.[2] Today's decision, however, indicates that we must blind ourselves to this fact because the trial judge fully accepted the testimony of the prosecution witnesses on all important points. * * *

* * *

The Court's opinion apparently rests on this reasoning: The policeman, under the circumstances detailed, could reasonably conclude that serious fighting or even riot was imminent; therefore he could stop petitioner's speech to prevent a breach of peace; accordingly, it was "disorderly conduct" for petitioner to continue speaking in disobedience of the officer's request. As to the existence of a dangerous situation on the street corner, it seems far-fetched to suggest that the "facts" show any imminent threat of riot or uncontrollable disorder. It is neither unusual nor unexpected that some people at public street meetings mutter, mill about, push, shove, or disagree, even violently, with the speaker. Indeed, it is rare where controversial topics are discussed that an outdoor crowd does not do some or all of these things. Nor does one isolated threat to assault the speaker forebode disorder. Especially should the danger be discounted where, as here, the person threatening was a man whose wife and two small children accompanied him and who, so far as the record shows, was never close enough to petitioner to carry out the threat.

---

2. There was no charge that any city or state law prohibited such a meeting at the place or time it was held. Evidence showed that it was customary to hold public gatherings on that same corner every Friday night, and the trial judge who convicted petitioner admitted that he understood the meeting was a lawful one. Nor did the judge treat the lawful meeting as unlawful because a crowd congregated on the sidewalk. Consequently, any discussion of disrupted pedestrian and vehicular traffic, while suggestive coloration, is immaterial under the charge and conviction here. It is implied in a concurring opinion that the use of sound amplifiers in some way caused the meeting to become less lawful. This fact, however, had nothing to do with the conviction of petitioner. In sentencing him the trial court said: "You had a perfect right to appear there and to use that implement, the loud speaker. You had a right to have it in the street."
* * *

Moreover, assuming that the "facts" did indicate a critical situation, I reject the implication of the Court's opinion that the police had no obligation to protect petitioner's constitutional right to talk. The police of course have power to prevent breaches of the peace. But if, in the name of preserving order, they ever can interfere with a lawful public speaker, they first must make all reasonable efforts to protect him.[8] Here the policemen did not even pretend to try to protect petitioner. According to the officers' testimony, the crowd was restless but there is no showing of any attempt to quiet it; pedestrians were forced to walk into the street, but there was no effort to clear a path on the sidewalk; one person threatened to assault petitioner but the officers did nothing to discourage this when even a word might have sufficed. Their duty was to protect petitioner's right to talk, even to the extent of arresting the man who threatened to interfere. Instead, they shirked that duty and acted only to suppress the right to speak.[9]

* * *

In my judgment, today's holding means that as a practical matter, minority speakers can be silenced in any city. * * * This is true regardless of the fact that in two other cases decided this day, Kunz v. New York, 340 U.S. 290; Niemotko v. Maryland, 340 U.S. 268 (1951), a majority, in obedience to past decisions of this Court, provides a theoretical safeguard for freedom of speech. For whatever is thought to be guaranteed in *Kunz* and *Niemotko* is taken away by what is done here. The three cases read together mean that while previous restraints probably cannot be imposed on an unpopular speaker, the police have discretion to silence him as soon as the customary hostility to his views develops.

In this case I would reverse the conviction, thereby adhering to the great principles of the First and Fourteenth Amendments as announced for this Court in 1940 by Mr. Justice Roberts:

> "In the realm of religious faith, and in that of political belief, sharp differences arise. In both fields the tenets of one man may seem the rankest error to his neighbor. To persuade others to his own point of view, the pleader, as we know, at times, resorts to exaggeration, to vilification of men who have been, or are, prominent in church or state, and even to false

---

8. Cf. Hague v. C.I.O., 307 U.S. 496 (1939); Terminiello v. Chicago, 337 U.S. 1 (1949); Sellers v. Johnson, 163 F.2d 877 (1947); see also, Summary of Brief for Committee on the Bill of Rights of the American Bar Association as *amicus curiae, Hague v. C.I.O., supra,* reprinted at 307 U.S. at 678–682.

9. In Schneider v. State, 308 U.S. 147, we held that a purpose to prevent littering of the streets was insufficient to justify an ordinance which prohibited a person lawfully on the street from handing literature to one willing to receive it. We said at page 162, "There are obvious methods of preventing littering. Amongst these is the punishment of those who actually throw papers on the streets." In the present case as well, the threat of one person to assault a speaker does not justify suppression of the speech. There are obvious available alternative methods of preserving public order. One of these is to arrest the person who threatens an assault. Cf. Dean Milk Co. v. Madison, 340 U.S. 349 (1951), decided today, in which the Court invalidates a municipal health ordinance under the Commerce Clause because of a belief that the city could have accomplished its purposes by reasonably adequate alternatives. The Court certainly should not be less alert to protect freedom of speech than it is to protect freedom of trade.

statement. But the people of this nation have ordained in the light of history, that, in spite of the probability of excesses and abuses, these liberties are, in the long view, essential to enlightened opinion and right conduct on the part of the citizens of a democracy." Cantwell v. Connecticut, 310 U.S. 296, 310 (1940).

I regret my inability to persuade the Court not to retreat from this principle.

Mr. Justice Douglas, with whom Mr. Justice Minton concurs, dissenting. [Omitted.]

NOTE

The preceding cases illustrate and apply a general doctrine of "reasonable time, place, and manner" regulation of speech-related activities. Is this doctrine confined to regulations applicable only to public places (i.e. premises owned or managed under government auspices), or is it, rather, a more general doctrine (e.g., applicable just as well to noise-level controls regarding speech-activities on private property—like the common law of nuisance, permitting a home-owner to seek injunctive relief from excessive noise broadcast from the neighboring house)? In either case, what are the elements of this test? For example, to satisfy the first amendment, (a) must the regulation be drawn as the "least restrictive" means consistent with accomplishing its objectives, and (b) may it have to give way, even so, for the acceptance of at least some minor inconveniences, so to allow adequate breathing space for such speech uses as those who are otherwise lawfully present may wish to pursue? Consider these cases:

UNITED STATES v. GRACE
Supreme Court of the United States, 1983.
461 U.S. 171, 103 S.Ct. 1702, 75 L.Ed.2d 736.

Justice White delivered the opinion of the Court.

In this case we must determine whether 40 U.S.C. § 13k, which prohibits, among other things, the "display [of] any flag, banner, or device designed or adapted to bring into public notice any party, organization, or movement"[1] in the United States Supreme Court building and on its grounds, violates the First Amendment.

I

In May 1978 appellee Thaddeus Zywicki, standing on the sidewalk in front of the Supreme Court building, distributed leaflets to passers-

---

1. * * * In its entirety § 13k provides: "It shall be unlawful to parade, stand, or move in processions or assemblages in the Supreme Court Building or grounds, or to display therein any flag, banner, or device designed or adapted to bring into public notice any party, organization, or movement." 63 Stat. 617.

by. The leaflets were reprints of a letter to the editor of the Washington Post from a United States Senator concerning the removal of unfit judges from the bench. A Supreme Court police officer approached Zywicki and told him, accurately, that Title 40 of the United States Code prohibited the distribution of leaflets on the Supreme Court grounds, which includes the sidewalk.

In January 1980 Zywicki again visited the sidewalk in front of the Court to distribute pamphlets containing information about forthcoming meetings and events concerning "the oppressed peoples of Central America." Zywicki again was approached by a Court police officer and was informed that the distribution of the leaflets on the Court grounds was prohibited by law. The officer indicated that Zywicki would be arrested if the leafletting continued. Zywicki left.

* * *

Around noon on March 17, 1980, appellee Mary Grace entered upon the sidewalk in front of the Court and began to display a four foot by two and a half foot sign on which was inscribed the verbatim text of the First Amendment. A Court police officer approached Grace and informed her that she would have to go across the street if she wished to display the sign. Grace was informed that Title 40 of the United States Code prohibited her conduct and that if she did not cease she would be arrested. Grace left the grounds.

On May 13, 1980, Zywicki and Grace filed the present suit in the United States District Court for the District of Columbia. They sought an injunction against continued enforcement of 40 U.S.C. § 13k and a declaratory judgment that the statute was unconstitutional on its face.
* * *

The Court of Appeals determined that the District Court's dismissal for failure to exhaust administrative remedies was erroneous and went on to strike down § 13k on its face as an unconstitutional restriction on First Amendment rights in a public place. * * *

The Government appealed from the Court of Appeals' judgment. We noted probable jurisdiction, 457 U.S. 1131 (1982).

II

* * * We agree with the United States that the statute covers the particular conduct of Zywicki or Grace and that it is therefore proper to reach the constitutional question involved in this case.

The statutory ban is on the display of a "flag, banner, or device designed or adapted to bring into public notice any party, organization, or movement." 40 U.S.C. § 13k. It is undisputed that Grace's picket sign containing the text of the First Amendment falls within the description of a "flag, banner, or device." Although it is less obvious, it is equally uncontested that Zywicki's leaflets fall within the proscription as well.

* * *

III

The First Amendment provides that "Congress shall make no law * * * abridging the freedom of speech. * * *" There is no doubt that as a general matter peaceful picketing and leafletting are expressive activities involving "speech" protected by the First Amendment. * * *

It is also true that "public places" historically associated with the free exercise of expressive activities, such as streets, sidewalks, and parks, are considered, without more, to be "public forums." * * * In such places, the government's ability to permissibly restrict expressive conduct is limited: the government may enforce reasonable time, place, and manner regulations as long as the restrictions "are content-neutral, are narrowly tailored to serve a significant government interest, and leave open ample alternative channels of communication." * * *

* * *

IV

It is argued that the Supreme Court building and grounds fit neatly within the description of nonpublic forum property. Although the property is publicly owned, it has not been traditionally held open for the use of the public for expressive activities. As *Greer v. Spock, supra,* teaches, the property is not transformed into "public forum" property merely because the public is permitted to freely enter and leave the grounds at practically all times and the public is admitted to the building during specified hours.[7] Under this view it would be necessary only to determine that the restrictions imposed by § 13k are reasonable in light of the use to which the building and grounds are dedicated and that there is no discrimination on the basis of content. We need not make that judgment at this time, however, because § 13k covers the public sidewalks as well as the building and grounds inside the sidewalks. As will become evident, we hold that § 13k may not be applied to the public sidewalks.

The prohibitions imposed by § 13k technically cover the entire grounds of the Supreme Court as defined in 40 U.S.C. § 13p.[8] That section describes the Court grounds as extending to the curb of each of the four streets enclosing the block on which the building is located. Included within this small geographical area, therefore, are not only the building, the plaza and surrounding promenade, lawn area, and

---

7. The limitation on the hours during which the public is permitted in the Supreme Court building is the only regulation promulgated under 40 U.S.C. § 13l. The regulation provides:

"The Supreme Court Building at 1 First Street, N.E., Washington, D.C. 20543, is open to the public Monday through Friday, from 9 a.m. to 4:30 p.m., except on Federal holidays. The building is closed at all other times, although persons having legitimate business may be admitted at other times when so authorized by responsible officials."

8. Section 13p provides:

"For the purposes of sections 13f to 13p of this title the Supreme Court grounds shall be held to extend to the line of the face of the east curb of First Street Northeast, between Maryland Avenue Northeast and East Capitol Street; to the line of the face of the south curb of Maryland Avenue Northeast, between First Street Northeast and Second Street Northeast; to the line of the face of the west curb of Second Street Northeast, between Maryland Avenue Northeast and East Capitol Street; and to the line of the face of the north curb of East Capitol Street between First Street Northeast and Second Street Northeast."

steps, but also the sidewalks. The sidewalks comprising the outer boundaries of the Court grounds are indistinguishable from any other sidewalks in Washington, D.C., and we can discern no reason why they should be treated any differently.[9] Sidewalks, of course, are among those areas of public property that traditionally have been held open to the public for expressive activities and are clearly within those areas of public property that may be considered, generally without further inquiry, to be public forum property. In this respect, the present case differs from *Greer v. Spock, supra.* In *Greer,* the streets and sidewalks at issue were located within an enclosed military reservation, Fort Dix, N.J., and were thus separated from the streets and sidewalks of any municipality. That is not true of the sidewalks surrounding the Court. There is no separation, no fence, and no indication whatever persons stepping from the street to the curb and sidewalks that serve as the perimeter of the Court grounds that they have entered some special type of enclave. In United States Postal Service v. Greenburgh Civic Assns., 453 U.S. 114, 133 (1981), we stated that "Congress * * * may not by its own *ipse dixit* destroy the 'public forum' status of streets and parks which have historically been public forums. * * * " The inclusion of the public sidewalks within the scope of § 123's prohibition, however, results in the destruction of public forum status that is at least presumptively impermissible. Traditional public forum property occupies a special position in terms of First Amendment protection and will not lose its historically recognized character for the reason that it abuts government property that has been dedicated to a use other than as a forum for public expression. Nor may the government transform the character of the property by the expedient of including it within the statutory definition of what might be considered a nonpublic forum parcel of property. The public sidewalks forming the perimeter of the Supreme Court grounds, in our view, are public forums and should be treated as such for First Amendment purposes.

V

The Government submits that § 13k qualifies as a reasonable time, place, and manner restriction which may be imposed to restrict communicative activities on public forum property such as sidewalks. The argument is that the inquiry should not be confined to the Supreme Court grounds but should focus on "the vicinity of the Supreme Court" or "the public places of Washington, D.C." Brief for Appellants 16, n. 5. Viewed in this light, the Government contends that there are sufficient alternative areas within the relevant forum, such as the streets around the Court or the sidewalks across those streets to permit § 13k to be considered a reasonable "place" restriction having only a minimal impact on expressive activity. * * *

* * *

9. Because the prohibitions of § 13k are expressly made applicable to the entire grounds under § 13p, the statute cannot be construed to exclude the sidewalks. Thus we must consider Congress' extension of § 13k's prohibitions to the sidewalks to be a reasoned choice.

We do not denigrate the necessity to protect persons and property or to maintain proper order and decorum within the Supreme Court grounds, but we do question whether a total ban on carrying a flag, banner, or device on the public sidewalks substantially serves these purposes. There is no suggestion, for example, that appellees' activities in any way obstructed the sidewalks or access to the building, threatened injury to any person or property, or in any way interfered with the orderly administration of the building or other parts of the grounds. As we have said, the building's perimeter sidewalks are indistinguishable from other public sidewalks in the city that are normally open to the conduct that is at issue here and that § 13k forbids. A total ban on that conduct is no more necessary for the maintenance of peace and tranquility on the public sidewalks surrounding the building than on any other sidewalks in the city. Accordingly, § 13k cannot be justified on this basis.

The United States offers another justification for § 13k that deserves our attention. It is said that the federal courts represent an independent branch of the Government and that their decisionmaking processes are different from those of the other branches. Court decisions are made on the record before them and in accordance with the applicable law. The views of the parties and of others are to be presented by briefs and oral argument. Courts are not subject to lobbying, judges do not entertain visitors in their chambers for the purpose of urging that cases be resolved one way or another, and they do not and should not respond to parades, picketing, or pressure groups. Neither, the Government urges, should it *appear* to the public that the Supreme Court is subject to outside influence or that picketing or marching, singly or in groups, is an acceptable or proper way of appealing to or influencing the Supreme Court. Hence, we are asked to hold that Congress was quite justified in preventing the conduct in dispute here from occurring on the sidewalks at the edge of the Court grounds.

As was the case with the maintenance of law and order on the Court grounds, we do not discount the importance of this proffered purpose for § 13k. But, again, we are unconvinced that the prohibitions of § 13k that are at issue here sufficiently serve that purpose to sustain its validity insofar as the public sidewalks on the perimeter of the grounds are concerned. Those sidewalks are used by the public like other public sidewalks. There is nothing to indicate to the public that these sidewalks are part of the Supreme Court grounds or are in any way different from public sidewalks in the city. We seriously doubt that the public would draw a different inference from a lone picketer carrying a sign on the sidewalks around the building than it would from a similar picket on the sidewalks across the street.

We thus perceive insufficient justification for § 13k's prohibition of carrying signs, banners, or devices on the public sidewalks surrounding the building. We hold that under the First Amendment the section is unconstitutional as applied to those sidewalks. Of course, this is not to say that those sidewalks, like other sidewalks, are not subject to reasonable time, place, and manner restrictions, either by statute or by regulations issued pursuant to 40 U.S.C. § 131.

The judgment below is accordingly affirmed to the extent indicated by this opinion and is otherwise vacated.

So ordered.

JUSTICE MARSHALL, concurring in part and dissenting in part.

I would hold 40 U.S.C. § 13k unconstitutional on its face. The statute in no way distinguishes the sidewalks from the rest of the premises, and excising the sidewalks from its purview does not bring it into conformity with the First Amendment. Visitors to this Court do not lose their First Amendment rights at the edge of the sidewalks any more than "students or teachers shed their constitutional rights to freedom of speech or expression at the schoolhouse gate." Tinker v. Des Moines Independent Community School District, 393 U.S. 503, 506 (1969). Since the continuing existence of the statute will inevitably have a chilling effect on freedom of expression, there is no virtue in deciding its constitutionality on a piecemeal basis.

When a citizen is "in a place where [he] has every right to be," Brown v. Louisiana, 383 U.S. 131, 142 (1966) (opinion of Fortas, J., joined by Warren, C.J., and Douglas, J.), he cannot be denied the opportunity to express his views simply because the government has not chosen to designate the area as a forum for public discussion. While the right to conduct expressive activities in such areas as streets, parks, and sidewalks is reinforced by their traditional use for purposes of assembly, Hague v. CIO, 307 U.S. 496, 515 (1939) (opinion of Roberts, J., joined by Black, J.), that right ultimately rests on the principle that "one who is rightfully on a street which the state has left open to the public carries with him there *as elsewhere* the constitutional right to express his views in an orderly fashion." Jamison v. Texas, 318 U.S. 413, 416 (1943) (emphasis added). Every citizen lawfully present in a public place has a right to engage in peaceable and orderly expression that is not incompatible with the primary activity of the place in question, whether that place is a school, a library, a private lunch counter, the grounds of a statehouse, the grounds of the United States Capitol, a bus terminal, an airport, or a welfare center. As we stated in Grayned v. City of Rockford, 408 U.S. 104, 116 (1972), "[t]he crucial question is whether the manner of expression is basically incompatible with the normal activity of a particular place at a particular time." "[O]ne is not to have the exercise of his liberty of expression in appropriate places abridged on the plea that it may be exercised in some other place." Schneider v. State, 308 U.S. 147, 163 (1939).

I see no reason why the premises of this Court should be exempt from this basic principle. It would be ironic indeed if an exception to the Constitution were to be recognized for the very institution that has the chief responsibility for protecting constitutional rights. I would apply to the premises of this Court the same principle that this Court has applied to other public places.

* * *

JUSTICE STEVENS, concurring in part and dissenting in part.

On three occasions Zywicki distributed leaflets and handbills. I would not construe that activity as the "display" of any "flag, banner, or device." A typical passerby would not have learned Zywicki's message from the "display" of his literature. Only after the material left Zywicki's possession would his message have become intelligible.

On one occasion Grace carried a sign on which the text of the First Amendment was written. I agree that this was the "display" of a "device," but I do not agree that her device was "designed or adapted to bring into public notice any party, organization, or movement." A typical passerby could not, merely by observing her sign, confidently link her with any specific party, organization, or "movement" as that term was understood when this statute was drafted.

* * *

Because neither of the appellees has violated the statute, I would affirm the judgment of the Court of Appeals to the extent that it requires that appellants be restrained from causing appellees' arrest for engaging in the activities disclosed by this record.

CITY COUNCIL v. TAXPAYERS FOR VINCENT
Supreme Court of the United States, 1984.
466 U.S. 789, 104 S.Ct. 2118, 80 L.Ed.2d 772.

JUSTICE STEVENS delivered the opinion of the Court.

Section 28.04 of the Los Angeles Municipal Code prohibits the posting of signs on public property.[1] The question presented is whether that prohibition abridges appellees' freedom of speech within the meaning of the First Amendment.

In March 1979, Roland Vincent was a candidate for election to the Los Angeles City Council. A group of his supporters known as Taxpayers for Vincent (Taxpayers) entered into a contract with a political sign service company known as Candidates' Outdoor Graphics Service (COGS) to fabricate and post signs with Vincent's name on them. COGS produced 15- by 44-inch cardboard signs and attached them to utility poles at various locations by draping them over crosswires which support the poles and stapling the cardboard together at the bottom. The signs' message was: "Roland Vincent—City Council."

Acting under the authority of § 28.04 of the Municipal Code, employees of the city's Bureau of Street Maintenance routinely re-

---

1. The ordinance reads as follows:

"Sec. 28.04. Hand-bills, signs-public places and objects:

"(a) No person shall print, mark or write on, or post or otherwise affix, any hand-bill or sign to or upon any sidewalk, crosswalk, curb, curbstone, street lamp post, hydrant, tree, shrub, tree stake or guard, railroad trestle, electric light or power or telephone or telegraph or trolley wire pole, or wire appurtenance thereof or upon any fixture of the fire alarm or police telegraph system or upon any lighting system, public bridge, drinking fountain, life buoy, life preserver, life boat or other life saving equipment, street sign or traffic sign.

* * *

moved all posters attached to utility poles and similar objects covered by the ordinance, including the COGS signs. The weekly sign removal report covering the period March 1–March 7, 1979, indicated that among the 1,207 signs removed from public property during that week, 48 were identified as "Roland Vincent" signs. Most of the other signs identified in that report were apparently commercial in character.

* * *

* * * [T]he District Court concluded that the sign prohibition does not prevent taxpayers or COGS "from exercising their free speech rights on the public streets and in other public places; they remain free to picket and parade, to distribute handbills, to carry signs and to post their signs and handbills on their automobiles and on private property with the permission of the owners thereof."

In its conclusions of law the District Court characterized the esthetic and economic interests in improving the beauty of the City "by eliminating clutter and visual blight" as "legitimate and compelling." Those interests, together with the interest in protecting the safety of workmen who must scale utility poles and the interest in eliminating traffic hazards, adequately supported the sign prohibition as a reasonable regulation affecting the time, place, and manner of expression. The Court of Appeals did not question any of the District Court's findings of fact, but it rejected some of its conclusions of law. The Court of Appeals reasoned that the ordinance was presumptively unconstitutional because significant First Amendment interests were involved. It noted that the City had advanced three separate justifications for the ordinance, but concluded that none of them was sufficient. The Court of Appeals held that the City had failed to make a sufficient showing that its asserted interests in esthetics and preventing visual clutter were substantial because it had not offered to demonstrate that the City was engaged in a comprehensive effort to remove other contributions to an unattractive environment in commercial and industrial areas. The City's interest in minimizing traffic hazards was rejected because it was readily apparent that no substantial traffic problems would result from permitting the posting of certain kinds of signs on many of the publicly owned objects covered by the ordinance. Finally, while acknowledging that a flat prohibition against signs on certain objects such as fire hydrants and traffic signals would be a permissible method of preventing interference with the intended use of public property, and that regulation of the size, design, and construction of posters, or of the method of removing them, might be reasonable the Court of Appeals concluded that the City had not justified its total ban.

* * *

The ordinance prohibits appellees from communicating with the public in a certain manner, and presumably diminishes the total quantity of their communication in the City. The application of the ordinance to appellees' expressive activities surely raises the question whether the ordinance abridges their "freedom of speech" within the meaning of the First Amendment, and the appellees certainly have standing to challenge the application of the ordinance to their own expressive activities. "But to say the ordinance presents a First Amendment *issue* is not necessarily to say that it constitutes a First Amendment *violation.*" Metromedia, Inc. v. San Diego, 453 U.S., at 561 (BURGER, C.J., dissenting). It has been clear since this Court's earliest decisions concerning the freedom of speech that the state may sometimes curtail speech when necessary to advance a significant and legitimate state interest. Schenck v. United States, 249 U.S. 47, 52 (1919).

As *Stromberg* and *Lovell* demonstrate, there are some purported interests—such as a desire to suppress support for a minority party or an unpopular cause, or to exclude the expression of certain points of view from the marketplace of ideas—that are so plainly illegitimate that they would immediately invalidate the rule. The general principle that has emerged from this line of cases is that the First Amendment forbids the government to regulate speech in ways that favor some viewpoints or ideas at the expense of others. * * *

That general rule has no application to this case. For there is not even a hint of bias or censorship in the City's enactment or enforcement of this ordinance. There is no claim that the ordinance was designed to suppress certain ideas that the City finds distasteful or that it has been applied to appellees because of the views that they express. The text of the ordinance is neutral—indeed it is silent—concerning any speaker's point of view, and the District Court's findings indicate that it has been applied to appellees and others in an evenhanded manner.

In United States v. O'Brien, 391 U.S. 367 (1968), the Court set forth the appropriate framework for reviewing a viewpoint-neutral regulation of this kind:

> "[A] government regulation is sufficiently justified if it is within the constitutional power of the Government; if it furthers an important or substantial governmental interest; if the governmental interest is unrelated to the suppression of free expression; and if the incidental restriction on alleged First Amendment freedoms is no greater than is essential to the furtherance of that interest." *Id.,* at 377.

It is well settled that the state may legitimately exercise its police powers to advance esthetic values. Thus, in Berman v. Parker, 389 U.S. 26, 32–33 (1954), in referring to the power of the legislature to remove blighted housing, this Court observed that such housing may be "an ugly sore, a blight on the community which robs it of charm, which makes it a place from which men turn." *Ibid.* We concluded: "The concept of the public welfare is broad and inclusive. The values it represents are spiritual as well as physical, aesthetic as well as monetary." *Id.,* at 33 (citation omitted). * * *

* * *

III

In Kovacs v. Cooper, 336 U.S. 77 (1949), the Court rejected the notion that a city is powerless to protect its citizens from unwanted exposure to certain methods of expression which may legitimately be deemed a public nuisance. In upholding an ordinance that prohibited loud and raucous sound trucks, the Court held that the State had a substantial interest in protecting its citizens from unwelcome noise. In Lehman v. City of Shaker Heights, 418 U.S. 298 (1974), the Court upheld that city's prohibition of political advertising on its buses, stating that the city was entitled to protect unwilling viewers against intrusive advertising that may interfere with the city's goal of making its buses "rapid, convenient, pleasant, and inexpensive," *id.*, at 302–303 (plurality opinion). * * * These cases indicate that the municipalities have a weighty, essentially esthetic interest in proscribing intrusive and unpleasant formats for expression.

Metromedia, Inc. v. San Diego, supra, dealt with San Diego's prohibition of certain forms of outdoor billboards. There the Court considered the city's interest in avoiding visual clutter, and seven Justices explicitly concluded that this interest was sufficient to justify a prohibition of billboards, see *id.*, at 507–508 (opinion of WHITE, J., joined by STEWART, MARSHALL, and POWELL, JJ.); *id.*, at 552 (STEVENS, J. dissenting in part); *id.*, at 559–561 (BURGER, C.J., dissenting); *id.*, at 570 (REHNQUIST, J., dissenting). * * *

We reaffirm the conclusion of the majority in *Metromedia*. The problem addressed by this ordinance—the visual assault on the citizens of Los Angeles presented by an accumulation of signs posted on public property—constitutes a significant substantive evil within the City's power to prohibit. * * *

IV

We turn to the question whether the scope of the restriction on appellees' expressive activity is substantially broader than necessary to protect the City's interest in eliminating visual clutter. The incidental restriction on expression which results from the City's attempt to accomplish such a purpose is considered justified as a reasonable regulation of the time, place, or manner of expression if it is narrowly tailored to serve that interest. * * * The District Court found that the signs prohibited by the ordinance do constitute visual clutter and blight. By banning these signs, the City did no more than eliminate the exact source of the evil it sought to remedy. The plurality wrote in *Metromedia*: "It is not speculative to recognize that billboards by their very nature, wherever located and however constructed, can be perceived as an 'esthetic harm.'" 453 U.S., at 510. The same is true of posted signs.

It is true that the esthetic interest in preventing the kind of litter that may result from the distribution of leaflets on the public streets and sidewalks cannot support a prophylactic prohibition against the citizen's exercise of that method of expressing his views. In Schneider v. State, 308 U.S. 147 (1939), the Court held that ordinances that absolutely prohibited handbilling on the streets were invalid. The Court explained that cities could adequately protect the esthetic interest in avoiding litter without abridging protected expression merely by penalizing those who actually litter. See *id.,* at 162. Taxpayers contend that their interest in supporting Vincent's political campaign, which affords them a constitutional right to distribute brochures and leaflets on the public streets of Los Angeles, provides equal support for their asserted right to post temporary signs on objects adjacent to the streets and sidewalks. They argue that the mere fact that their temporary signs "add somewhat" to the city's visual clutter is entitled to no more weight than the temporary unsightliness of discarded handbills and the additional street-cleaning burden that were insufficient to justify the ordinances reviewed in *Schneider.*

The rationale of *Schneider* is inapposite in the context of the instant case. There, individual citizens were actively exercising their right to communicate directly with potential recipients of their message. The conduct continued only while the speakers or distributors remained on the scene. In this case, appellees posted dozens of temporary signs throughout an area where they would remain unattended until removed. * * * One who is rightfully on a street open to the public "carries with him there as elsewhere the constitutional right to express his views in an orderly fashion. This right extends to the communication of ideas by handbills and literature as well as by the spoken word." Jamison v. Texas, 318 U.S. 413, 416 (1943); * * *

With respect to signs posted by appellees, however, it is the tangible medium of expressing the message that has the adverse impact on the appearance of the landscape. In *Schneider,* an antilittering statute could have addressed the substantive evil without prohibiting expressive activity, whereas application of the prophylactic rule actually employed gratuitously infringed upon the right of an individual to communicate directly with a willing listener. Here, the substantive evil—visual blight—is not merely a possible byproduct of the activity, but is created by the medium of expression itself. In contrast to *Schneider,* therefore, the application of the ordinance in this case responds precisely to the substantive problem which legitimately concerns the City. The ordinance curtails no more speech than is necessary to accomplish its purpose.

V

The Court of Appeals accepted the argument that a prohibition against the use of unattractive signs cannot be justified on esthetic grounds if it fails to apply to all equally unattractive signs wherever they might be located. A comparable argument was categorically rejected in *Metromedia.* In that case it was argued that the city could not simultaneously permit billboards to be used for onsite advertising and also justify the prohibition against offsite advertising on esthetic grounds, since both types of advertising were equally unattractive. The Court held, however, that the city could reasonably conclude that the esthetic interest was outweighed by the countervailing interest in one kind of advertising even thought it was not outweighed by the other.

So here, the validity of the esthetic interest in the elimination of signs on public property is not compromised by failing to extend the ban to private property. The private citizen's interest in controlling the use of his own property justifies the disparate treatment. Moreover, by not extending the ban to all locations, a significant opportunity to communicate by means of temporary signs is preserved, and private property owners' esthetic concerns will keep the posting of signs on their property within reasonable bounds. Even if some visual blight remains, a partial, content-neutral ban may nevertheless enhance the City's appearance.

Furthermore, there is no finding that in any area where appellees seek to place signs, there are already so many signs posted on adjacent private property that the elimination of appellees' signs would have an inconsequential effect on the esthetic values with which the City is concerned. There is simply no predicate in the findings of the District Court for the conclusion that the prohibition against the posting of appellees' signs fails to advance the City's esthetic interest.

VI

While the First Amendment does not guarantee the right to employ every conceivable method of communication at all times and in all places, Heffron v. International Society for Krishna Consciousness, Inc., 452 U.S., at 647, a restriction on expressive activity may be invalid if the remaining modes of communication are inadequate. * * * The Los Angeles ordinance does not affect any individual's freedom to exercise the right to speak and to distribute literature in the same place where the posting of signs on public property is prohibited. To the extent that the posting of signs on public property has advantages over these forms of expression, see, e.g., Talley v. California, 362 U.S. 60, 64–65 (1960), there is no reason to believe that these same advantages cannot be obtained through other means. To the contrary, the findings of the District Court indicate that there are ample alternative modes of communication in Los Angeles. Notwithstanding appellee's general assertions in their brief concerning the utility of political posters, nothing in the findings indicates that the posting of political posters on public property is a uniquely valuable or important mode of communication, or that appellees' ability to communicate effectively is threatened by ever-increasing restrictions on expression.

VII

Appellees suggest that the public property covered by the ordinance either is itself a "public forum" for First Amendment purposes, or at least should be treated in the same respect as the "public forum" in which the property is located. "Traditional public forum property occupies a special position in terms of First Amendment protection" United States v. Grace, 461 U.S., at 180, and appellees maintain that their sign-posting activities are entitled to this protection.

* * *

Appellees' reliance on the public forum doctrine is misplaced. They fail to demonstrate the existence of a traditional right of access respecting such items as utility poles for purposes of their communication comparable to that recognized for public streets and parks, and it is clear that "the First Amendment does not guarantee access to government property simply because it is owned or controlled by the government." United States Postal Service v. Greenburgh Civic Assns., 453 U.S. 114, 129 (1981). Rather, the "existence of a right of access to public property and the standard by which limitations upon such a right must be evaluated differ depending on the character of the property at issue." Perry Educational Assn. v. Perry Local Educators' Assn., 460 U.S. 37, 44 (1983).

Lampposts can of course be used as signposts, but the mere fact that government property can be used as a vehicle for communication does not mean that the Constitution requires such uses to be permitted. Cf. United States Postal Service v. Greenburgh Civic Assns., 453 U.S., at 131.[31] Public property which is not by tradition or designation a forum for public communication may be reserved by the State "for its intended purposes, communicative or otherwise, as long as the regulation on speech is reasonable and not an effort to suppress expression merely because public officials oppose the speaker's view." Perry Education Assn. v. Perry Local Educators' Assn., 460 U.S., at 46. Given our analysis of the legitimate interest served by the ordinance, its viewpoint neutrality, and the availability of alternative channels of communication, the ordinance is certainly constitutional as applied to appellees under this standard.[32]

VIII

Finally, Taxpayers and COGS argue that Los Angeles could have written an ordinance that would have had a less severe effect on expressive activity such as theirs, by permitting the posting of any kind of sign at any time on some types of public property, or by making a variety of other more specific exceptions to the ordinance: for signs carrying certain types of messages (such as political campaign signs), for signs posted during specific time periods (perhaps during political

---

31. Any tangible property owned by the government could be used to communicate—bumper stickers may be placed on official automobiles—and yet appellees could not seriously claim the right to attach "Taxpayer for Vincent" bumper stickers to city-owned automobiles. At some point, the government's relationship to things under its dominion and control is virtually identical to a private owner's property interest in the same kinds of things, and in such circumstances, the State, "no less than a private owner of property, has power to preserve the property under its control for the use to which it is lawfully dedicated." Adderley v. Florida, 385 U.S. 39, 47 (1966).

32. Just as it is not dispositive to label the posting of signs on public property as a discrete medium of expression, it is also of limited utility in the context of this case to focus on whether the tangible property itself should be deemed a public forum. Generally an analysis of whether property is a public forum provides a workable analytical tool. However, "the analytical line between a regulation of the 'time, place, and manner' in which First Amendment rights may be exercised in a traditional public forum, and the question of whether a particular piece of personal or real property owned or controlled by the government is in fact a 'public forum' may blur at the edges," United States Postal Service v. Greenburgh Civic Assns., 453 U.S. 114, 132 (1981), and this is particularly true in cases falling between the paradigms of government property interests essentially mirroring analogous private interests and those clearly held in trust, either by tradition or recent convention, for the use of citizens at large.

campaigns), for particular locations (perhaps for areas already cluttered by an excessive number of signs on adjacent private property), or for signs meeting design specifications (such as size or color). Plausible public policy arguments might well be made in support of any such exception, but it by no means follows that it is therefore constitutionally mandated, cf. Singer v. United States, 380 U.S. 24, 34–35 (1965), nor is it clear that some of the suggested exceptions would even be constitutionally permissible. For example, even though political speech is entitled to the fullest possible measure of constitutional protection, there are a host of other communications that command the same respect. An assertion that "Jesus Saves," that "Abortion is Murder," that every woman has the "Right to Choose," or that "Alcohol Kills," may have a claim to a constitutional exemption from the ordinance that is just as strong as "Roland Vincent—City Council." * * *

Any constitutionally mandated exception to the City's total prohibition against temporary signs on public property would necessarily rest on a judicial determination that the City's traffic control and safety interests had little or no applicability within the excepted category, and that the City's interests in esthetics are not sufficiently important to justify the prohibition in that category. But the findings of the District Court provide no basis for questioning the substantiality of the esthetic interest at stake, or for believing that a uniquely important form of communication has been abridged for the categories of expression engaged in by Taxpayers and COGS. Therefore, we accept the City's position that it may decide that the esthetic interest in avoiding "visual clutter" justifies a removal of signs creating or increasing that clutter. The findings of the District Court that COGS signs add to the problems addressed by the ordinance and, if permitted to remain, would encourage others to post additional signs, are sufficient to justify application of the ordinance to these appellees.

* * *

The judgment of the Court of Appeals is reversed, and the case is remanded to that Court.

It is so ordered.

JUSTICE BRENNAN, with whom JUSTICE MARSHALL and JUSTICE BLACKMUN join, dissenting.

* * *

The Court finds that the City's "interest [in eliminating visual clutter] is sufficiently substantial to justify the effect of the ordinance on appellees' expression" and that the effect of the ordinance on speech is "no greater than necessary to accomplish the City's purpose." * * * These are the right questions to consider when analyzing the constitutionality of the challenged ordinance, * * * but the answers that the Court provides reflect a startling insensitivity to the principles embodied in the First Amendment. In my view, the City of Los Angeles has not shown that its interest in eliminating "visual clutter" justifies its restriction of appellees' ability to communicate with the local electorate.

I

* * *

In deciding this First Amendment question, the critical importance of the posting of signs as a means of communication must not be overlooked. Use of this medium of communication is particularly valuable in part because it entails a relatively small expense in reaching a wide audience, allows flexibility in accommodating various formats, typographies, and graphics and conveys its message in a manner that is easily read and understood by its reader or viewer. There may be alternative channels of communication, but the prevalence of a large number of signs in Los Angeles is a strong indication that, for many speakers, those alternatives are far less satisfactory. * * *

Nevertheless, the City of Los Angeles asserts that ample alternative avenues of communication are available. The City notes that, although the posting of signs on public property is prohibited, the posting of signs on private property and the distribution of handbills are not. Brief for Appellants 25–26. But there is no showing that either of these alternatives would serve appellees' needs nearly as well as would the posting of signs on public property. First, there is no proof that a sufficient number of private parties would allow the posting of signs on their property. Indeed, common sense suggests the contrary at least in some instances. A speaker with a message that is generally unpopular or simply unpopular among property owners is hardly likely to get his message across if forced to rely on this medium. It is difficult to believe, for example, that a group advocating an increase in the rate of a property tax would succeed in persuading private property owners to accept its signs.

Similarly, the adequacy of distributing handbills is dubious, despite certain advantages of handbills over signs. See Martin v. Struthers, 319 U.S. 141, 145–146 (1943). Particularly when the message to be carried is best expressed by a few words or a graphic image, a message on a sign will typically reach far more people than one on a handbill. The message on a posted sign remains to be seen by passersby as long as it is posted, while a handbill is typically read by a single reader and discarded. Thus, not only must handbills be printed in large quantity, but many hours must be spent distributing them. The average cost of communicating by handbill is therefore likely to be far higher than the average cost of communicating by poster. For that reason, signs posted on public property are doubtless "essential to the poorly financed causes of little people, *id.*, at 146, and their prohibition constitutes a total ban on an important medium of communication. Cf. Stone, Fora Americana: Speech in Public Places, 1974 S.Ct.Rev. 233, 257. Because the City has completely banned the use of this particular medium of communication, and because, given the circumstances, there are no equivalent alternative media that provide an adequate substitute, the Court must examine with particular care the justifications that the City proffers for its ban. * * *

* * *

Initially, a reviewing court faces substantial difficulties determining whether the actual objective is related to the suppression of speech. The asserted interest in aesthetics may be only a facade of content-based suppression. Of course, all would agree that the improvement and preservation of the aesthetic environment are important governmental functions, and that some restrictions on speech may be necessary to carry out these functions. *Metromedia, supra,* at 530. But a governmental interest in aesthetics cannot be regarded as sufficiently compelling to justify a restriction of speech based on an assertion that the content of the speech is, in itself, aesthetically displeasing. Cohen v. California, 403 U.S. 15 (1971). Because aesthetic judgments are so subjective, however, it is too easy for government to enact restrictions on speech for just such illegitimate reasons and to evade effective judicial review by asserting that the restriction is aimed at some displeasing aspect of the speech that is not solely communicative—for example, its sound, its appearance, or its location. An objective standard for evaluating claimed aesthetic judgments is therefore essential; for without one, courts have no reliable means of assessing the genuineness of such claims.

For example, in evaluating the ordinance before us in this case, the City might be pursuing either of two objectives, motivated by two very different judgments. One objective might be the elimination of "visual clutter," attributable in whole or in part to signs posted on public property. The aesthetic judgment underlying this objective would be that the clutter created by these signs offends the community's desire for an orderly, visually pleasing environment. A second objective might simply be the elimination of the messages typically carried by the signs. In that case, the aesthetic judgment would be that the signs' messages are themselves displeasing. The first objective is lawful, of course, but the second is not. Yet the City might easily mask the second objective by asserting the first and declaring that signs constitute visual clutter. In short, we must avoid the unquestioned acceptance of the City's bare declaration of an aesthetic objective lest we fail in our duty to prevent unlawful trespasses upon First Amendment protections.

B

A total ban on an important medium of communication may be upheld only if the government proves that the ban (1) furthers a substantial government objective, and (2) constitutes the least speech-restrictive means of achieving that objective. * * *

* * *

In cases like this, where a total ban is imposed on a particularly valuable method of communication, a court should require the government to provide tangible proof of the legitimacy and substantiality of its aesthetic objective. Justifications for such restrictions articulated by the government should be critically examined to determine whether the government has committed itself to addressing the identified aesthetic problem.

In my view, such statements of aesthetic objectives should be accepted as substantial and unrelated to the suppression of speech only if the government demonstrates that it is pursuing an identified objective seriously and comprehensively and in ways that are unrelated to the restriction of speech. *Metromedia,* 453 U.S., at 531 (BRENNAN, J., concurring in judgment). Without such a demonstration, I would invalidate the restriction as violative of the First Amendment. By requiring this type of showing, courts can ensure that governmental regulation of the aesthetic environment remains within the constraints established by the First Amendment. First, we would have a reasonably reliable indication that it is not the content or communicative aspect of speech that the government finds unaesthetic. Second, when a restriction of speech is part of a comprehensive and seriously pursued program to promote an aesthetic objective, we have a more reliable indication of the government's own assessment of the substantiality of its objective. * * *

This does not mean that a government must address all aesthetic problems at one time or that a government should hesitate to pursue aesthetic objectives. What it does mean, however, is that when such an objective is pursued, it may not be pursued solely at the expense of First Amendment freedoms, nor may it be pursued by arbitrarily discriminating against a form of speech that has the same aesthetic characteristics as other forms of speech that are also present in the community. * * *

* * * In this case, however, as the Court of Appeals found, there is no indication that the City has addressed its visual clutter problem in any way other than by prohibiting the posting of signs—throughout the City and without regard to the density of their presence. 682 F.2d 847, 852 (CA9 1982). Therefore, I would hold that the prohibition violates appellees' First Amendment rights.

* * *

In the absence of such a showing in this case, I believe that Los Angeles' total ban sweeps so broadly and trenches so completely on the appellees' use of an important medium of political expression that it must be struck down as violative of the First Amendment.[7]

I therefore dissent.

WARD v. ROCK AGAINST RACISM
Supreme Court of the United States, 1989.
491 U.S. 781, 109 S.Ct. 2746, 105 L.Ed.2d 661.

JUSTICE KENNEDY delivered the opinion of the Court.

---

[7]. Although the Court does not reach the question, appellants argue that the City's interest in traffic safety provides an independent and significant justification for its ban on signs. As the Court of Appeals concluded, however, "[t]he City has not offered to prove facts that raise any genuine issue regarding traffic safety hazards with respect to the posting of signs on many of the objects covered by the ordinance." 862 F.2d, at 852.

In the southeast portion of New York City's Central Park, about 10 blocks upward from the park's beginning point at 59th Street, there is an amphitheater and stage structure known as the Naumberg Acoustic Bandshell. The Bandshell faces west across the remaining width of the park. In close proximity to the Bandshell, and lying within the directional path of its sound, is a grassy open area called the Sheep Meadow. The city has designated the Sheep Meadow as a quiet area for passive recreations like reclining, walking, and reading. Just beyond the park, and also within the potential sound range of the Bandshell, are the apartments and residences of Central Park West.

This case arises from the city's attempt to regulate the volume of amplified music at the Bandshell so the performances are satisfactory to the audience without intruding upon those who use the Sheep Meadow or live on Central Park West and in its vicinity.

The city's regulation requires Bandshell performers to use sound-amplification equipment and a sound technician provided by the city. The challenge to this volume control technique comes from the sponsor of a rock concert. The trial court sustained the noise control measures, but the Court of Appeals for the Second Circuit reversed. We granted certiorari to resolve the importance of First Amendment issues presented by the case.

I

Rock Against Racism, respondent in this case, is an unincorporated association which, in its own words, is "dedicated to the espousal and promotion of antiracist views." App. to Pet. for Cert. 3. Each year from 1979 through 1986, RAR has sponsored a program of speeches and rock music at the Bandshell. RAR has furnished the sound equipment and sound technician used by the various performing groups at these annual events.

Over the years, the city received numerous complaints about excessive sound amplification at respondent's concerts from park users and residents of areas adjacent to the park. On some occasions RAR was less than cooperative when city officials asked that the volume be reduced; at one concert, police felt compelled to cut off the power to the sound system, an action that caused the audience to become unruly and hostile. App. 127–131, 140–141, 212–214, 345–347.

Before the 1984 concert, city officials met with RAR representative to discuss the problem of excessive noise. It was decided that the city would monitor sound levels at the edge of the concertground, and would revoke respondent's event permit if specific volume limits were exceeded. Sound levels at the concert did exceed acceptable levels for sustained periods of time, despite repeated warnings and requests that the volume be lowered. Two citations for excessive volume were issued to respondent during the concert. When the power was eventually shut off, the audience became abusive and disruptive.

* * *

The city considered various solutions to the sound amplification problem. The idea of a fixed decibel limit for all performers using the

Bandshell was rejected because the impact on listeners of a single decibel level is not constant, but varies in response to changes in air temperature, foliage, audience size, and like factors. * * * The city also rejected the possibility of employing a sound technician to operate the equipment provided by the various sponsors of Bandshell events, because the city's technician might have had difficulty satisfying the needs of sponsors while operating unfamiliar, and perhaps inadequate, sound equipment. * * * Instead, the city concluded that the most effective way to achieve adequate but not excessive sound amplification would be for the city to furnish high quality sound equipment and retain an independent, experienced sound technician for all performances at the Bandshell. After an extensive search the city hired a private sound company capable of meeting the needs of all the varied users of the Bandshell.

The Use Guidelines were promulgated on March 21, 1986. After learning that it would be expected to comply with the guidelines at its upcoming annual concert in May 1986, respondent returned to the District Court and filed a motion for an injunction against the enforcement of certain aspects of the guidelines. The District Court preliminarily enjoined enforcement of the sound-amplification rule on May 1, 1986. See Rock Against Racism v. Ward, 636 F.Supp. 178 (S.D.N.Y. 1986). Under the protection of the injunction, and alone among users of the Bandshell in the 1986 season, RAR was permitted to use its own sound equipment and technician, just as it had done in prior years. RAR's 1986 concert again generated complaints about excessive noise from park users and nearby residents. App. 127, 138.

After the concert, respondent amended its complaint to seek damages and a declaratory judgment striking down the guidelines as facially invalid. After hearing five days of testimony about various aspects of the guidelines, the District Court issued its decision upholding the sound-amplification guideline. * * *

* * * Applying this Court's three-part test for judging the constitutionality of government regulation of the time, place, or manner of protected speech, the court found the city's regulation valid.

The Court of Appeals reversed. 858 F.2d 367 (C.A.2 1988). After recognizing that "[c]ontent neutral time, place and manner regulations are permissible so long as they are narrowly tailored to serve a substantial government interest and do not unreasonably limit alternative avenues of expression," the court added the proviso that "the method and extent of such regulation must be reasonable, that is, it must be the least intrusive upon the freedom of expression as is reasonably necessary to achieve a legitimate purpose of regulation." * * *

* * * Because the Court of Appeals erred in requiring the city to prove that its regulation was the least intrusive means of furthering its legitimate governmental interests, and because the ordinance is valid on its face, we now reverse.

II

Music is one of the oldest forms of human expression. From Plato's discourse in the Republic to the totalitarian state in our own times, rulers have known its capacity to appeal to the intellect and to the emotions, and have censored musical compositions to serve the needs of the state. See 2 Dialogues of Plato, Republic, bk. III, pp. 231, 245–248 (B. Jowett trans., 4th ed. 1953) ("[o]ur poets must sing in another and a nobler strain"); Musical Freedom and Why Dictators Fear It, N.Y. Times, Aug. 23, 1981, section 2, p. 1, col. 5; Soviet Schizophrenia Toward Stravinsky, N.Y. Times, June 26, 1982, section 1, p. 25, col. 2; Symphonic Voice from China Is Heard Again, N.Y. Times, Oct. 11, 1987, section 2, p. 27, col. 1. The Constitution prohibits any like attempts in our own legal order. Music, as a form of expression and communication, is protected under the First Amendment. * * *

* * * Here the Bandshell was open, apparently, to all performers; and we decide the case as one in which the Bandshell is a public forum for performances in which the government's right to regulate expression is subject to the protections of the First Amendment. * * * Our cases make clear, however, that even in a public forum the government may impose reasonable restrictions on the time, place, or manner of protected speech, provided the restrictions "are justified without reference to the content of the regulated speech, that they are narrowly tailored to serve a significant governmental interest, and that they leave open ample alternative channels for communication of information." * * *

A

* * *

The principal justification for the sound-amplification for guideline is the city's desire to control noise levels at Bandshell events, in order to retain the character of the Sheep Meadow and its more sedate activities, and to avoid undue intrusion into residential areas and other areas of the park. This justification for the guideline "ha[s] nothing to do with content," *Boos v. Barry, supra,* at 320, and it satisfies the requirement that time, place, or manner regulations be content-neutral.

The only other justification offered below was the city's interest in "ensur[ing] the quality of sound at Bandshell events." 658 F.Supp., at 1352; see 848 F.2d, at 370, n. 3. Respondent urges that this justification is not content-neutral because it is based upon the quality, and thus the content, of the speech being regulated. In respondent's view, the city is seeking to assert artistic control over performers at the Bandshell by enforcing a bureaucratically determined, value-laden conception of good sound. That all performers who have used the city's sound equipment have been completely satisfied is of no moment, respondent argues, because "[t]he First Amendment does not permit and cannot tolerate state control of artistic expression merely because the State claims that [its] efforts will lead to 'top-quality' results." Brief for Respondent 19.

While respondent's arguments that the government may not interfere with artistic judgment may have much force in other contexts, they are inapplicable to the facts of this case. The city has disclaimed in express terms any interest in imposing its own view of appropriate sound mix on performers. To the contrary, as the District Court found, the city requires its sound technician to defer to the wishes of event sponsors concerning sound mix. 658 F.Supp., at 1352–1353. On this record, the city's concern with sound quality extends only to the clearly content-neutral goals of ensuring adequate sound amplification and avoiding the volume problems associated with inadequate sound mix. Any governmental attempt to serve purely aesthetic goals by imposing subjective standards of acceptable sound mix on performers would raise serious First Amendment concerns, but this case provides us with no opportunity to address those questions. As related above, the District Court found that the city's equipment and its sound technician could meet all of the standards requested by the performers, including RAR.

* * *

The city's regulation is also "narrowly tailored to serve a significant governmental interest." *Community for Creative Non–Violence*, 468 U.S., at 293. Despite respondent's protestations to the contrary, it can no longer be doubted that government "ha[s] a substantial interest in protecting its citizens from unwelcome noise." * * *

We think it also apparent that the city's interest in ensuring the sufficiency of sound amplification at Bandshell events is a substantial one. The record indicates that inadequate sound amplification has had an adverse affect on the ability of some audiences to hear and enjoy performances at the Bandshell. The city enjoys a substantial interest in ensuring the ability of its citizens to enjoy whatever benefits the city parks have to offer, from amplified music to silent meditation. See *Community for Non–Violence, supra,* at 296.

The Court of Appeals recognized the city's substantial interest in limiting the sound emanating from the Bandshell. See 848 F.2d, at 370. The court concluded, however, that the city's sound-amplification guideline was not narrowly tailored to further this interest, because "it has not [been] shown * * * that the requirement of the use of the city's sound system and technician was the *least intrusive means* of regulating the volume." *Id.,* at 371 (emphasis added). In the court's judgment, there were several alternative methods of achieving the desired end that would have been less restrictive of respondent's First Amendment rights.

The Court of Appeals erred in sifting through all the available or imagined alternative means of regulating sound volume in order to determine whether the city's solution was "the least intrusive means" of achieving the desired end. This "less-restrictive-alternative analysis * * * has never been a part of the inquiry into the validity of a time, place, and manner regulation." * * *

The Court of Appeals apparently drew its least-intrusive-means requirement from United States v. O'Brien, 391 U.S. 367, 377 (1968), the case in which we established the standard for judging the validity of restrictions on expressive conduct. See 848 F.2d, at 370. The court's reliance was misplaced, however, for we have held that the *O'Brien* test "in the last analysis is little, if any, different from the standard applied to time, place, or manner restrictions." *Community for Creative Non-Violence, supra,* 468 U.S., at 298. * * *

* * *

Lest any confusion on the point remain, we reaffirm today that a regulation of time, place, or manner of protected speech must be narrowly tailored to serve the government's legitimate content-neutral interests but that it need not be the least-restrictive or least-intrusive means of doing so. Rather, the requirement of narrow tailoring is satisfied "so long as the * * * regulation promotes a substantial government interest that would be achieved less effectively absent the regulation." * * * To be sure, this standard does not mean that a time, place, or manner regulation may burden substantially more speech than is necessary to further the government's legitimate interests. Government may not regulate expression in such a manner that a substantial portion of the burden on speech does not serve to advance its goals.[7]
* * *

It is undeniable that the city's substantial interest in limiting sound volume is served in a direct and effective way by the requirement that the city's sound technician control the mixing board during performances. Absent this requirement, the city's interest would have been served less well, as is evidenced by the complaints about excessive volume generated by respondent's past concerts. * * *

The city's second content-neutral justification for the guideline, that of ensuring "that the sound amplification [is] sufficient to reach all listeners within the defined concertground," 658 F.Supp., at 1352, also supports the city's choice of regulatory methods. By providing competent sound technicians and adequate amplification equipment, the city eliminated the problems of inexperienced technicians and insufficient sound volume that had plagued some Bandshell performers in the past. No doubt this concern is not applicable to respondent's concerts, which apparently were characterized by more-than-adequate sound amplification. But that fact is beside the point, for the validity of the regulation depends on the relation it bears to the overall problem the government seeks to correct, not on the extent to which it furthers the government's interests in an individual case. * * *

Respondent nonetheless argues that the sound-amplification guideline is not narrowly tailored because, by placing control of sound mix in

---

7. The dissent's attempt to analogize the sound-amplification guideline to a total ban on distribution of handbills is imaginative but misguided. * * * The guideline does not ban all concerts, or even all rock concerts, but instead focuses on the source of the evils the city seeks to eliminate—excessive and inadequate sound amplification—and eliminates them without at the same time banning or significantly restricting a substantial quantity of speech that does not create the same evils. This is the essence of narrow tailoring. A ban on handbilling, of course, would suppress a great quantity of speech that does not cause the evils that it seeks to eliminate, whether they be fraud, crime, litter, traffic congestion, or noise. See Martin v. Struthers, 319 U.S. 141, 145–146 (1943). For that reason a complete ban on handbilling would be substantially broader than necessary to achieve the interests justifying it.

the hands of the city's technician, the guideline sweeps far more broadly than is necessary to further the city's legitimate concern with sound volume. According to respondent, the guideline "targets * * * more than the exact source of the 'evil' it seeks to remedy." * * *

If the city's regulatory scheme had a substantial deleterious effect on the ability of Bandshell performers to achieve the quality of sound they desired, respondent's concerns would have considerable force. The District Court found, however, that pursuant to city policy, the city's sound technician "give[s] the sponsor autonomy with respect to the sound mix * * * [and] does all that he can to accommodate the sponsor's desires in those regards." 658 F.Supp., at 1352. The court squarely rejected respondent's claim that the city's "technician is not able properly to implement a sponsor's instructions as to sound quality or mix," finding that "[n]o evidence to that effect was offered at trial; as noted, the evidence is to the contrary." * * *

C

The final requirement, that the guideline leave open ample alternative channels of communication, is easily met. Indeed, in this respect the guideline is far less restrictive than regulations we have upheld in other cases, for it does not attempt to ban any particular manner or type of expression at a given place or time. * * * Rather, the guideline continues to permit expressive activity in the Bandshell, and has no effect on the quantity or content of that expression beyond regulating the extent of amplification. That the city's limitations on volume may reduce to some degree the potential audience for respondent's speech is of no consequence, for there has been no showing that the remaining avenues of communication are inadequate. * * *

III

* * * The judgment of the Court of Appeals is

Reversed.

Justice Blackmun concurs in the result.

Justice Marshall, with whom Justice Brennan and Justice Stevens join, dissenting.

No one can doubt that government has a substantial interest in regulating the barrage of excessive sound that can plague urban life. Unfortunately, the majority plays to our shared impatience with loud noise to obscure the damage that it does to our First Amendment rights. Until today, a key safeguard of free speech has been government's obligation to adopt the least intrusive restriction necessary to achieve its goals. By abandoning the requirement that time, place, and manner regulations must be narrowly tailored, the majority replaces constitutional scrutiny with mandatory deference. The majority's willingness to give government officials a free hand in achieving their policy ends extends so far as to permit, in this case, government control of speech in advance of its dissemination. Because New York City's Sound Amplification Guidelines (Guidelines) are not narrowly tailored to serve its interest in regulating loud noise, and because they constitute an impermissible prior restraint, I dissent.

I

The majority sets forth the appropriate standard for assessing the constitutionality of the Guidelines. A time, place, and manner regulation of expression must be content-neutral, serve a significant government interest, be narrowly tailored to serve that interest, and leave open ample alternative channels of communication. * * *

My complaint is with the majority's serious distortion of the narrow tailoring requirement. Our cases have not, as the majority asserts, "clearly" rejected a less restrictive alternative test. * * * While there is language in a few opinions which, taken out of context, supports the majority's position, in practice, the Court has interpreted the narrow tailoring requirement to mandate an examination of alternative methods of serving the asserted governmental interest and a determination whether the greater efficacy of the challenged regulation outweighs the increased burden it places on protected speech. * * * In *Schneider,* for example, the Court invalidated a ban on handbill distribution on public streets, notwithstanding that it was the most effective means of serving government's legitimate interest in minimizing litter, noise, and traffic congestion, and in preventing fraud. The Court concluded that punishing those who actually litter or perpetrate frauds was a much less intrusive, albeit not quite as effective, means to serve those significant interests. * * * [S]ee also *Martin, supra,* 319 U.S., at 148 (invalidating ban on door-to-door distribution of handbills because directly punishing fraudulent solicitation was a less intrusive yet still effective means of serving government's interest in preventing fraud).

The Court's past concern for the extent to which a regulation burdens speech more than would a satisfactory alternative is noticeably absent from today's decision. The majority requires only that government show that its interest cannot be served as effectively without the challenged restriction. * * * It will be enough, therefore, that the challenged regulation advances the government's interest only in the slightest, for any differential burden on speech that results does not enter the calculus. Despite its protestations to the contrary, the majority thus has abandoned the requirement that restrictions on speech be narrowly tailored in any ordinary use of the phrase. Indeed, after today's decision, a city could claim that bans on handbill distribution or on door-to-door solicitation are the most effective means of avoiding littering and fraud, or that a ban on loudspeakers and radios in a public park is the most effective means of avoiding loud noise. Logically extended, the majority's analysis would permit such far reaching restrictions on speech.

* * *

Had the majority not abandoned the narrow tailoring requirement, the Guidelines could not possibly survive constitutional scrutiny. Government's interest in avoiding loud sounds cannot justify giving government total control over sound equipment, any more than its interest in avoiding litter could justify a ban on handbill distribution. In both cases, government's legitimate goals can be effectively and less intrusively served by directly punishing the evil—the persons responsible for excessive sounds and the persons who litter. Indeed, the city concedes that it has an ordinance generally limiting noise but has chosen not to enforce it. See Tr. of Oral Arg. 5–6.[6]

* * *

II

The majority's conclusion that the city's exclusive control of sound equipment is constitutional is deeply troubling for another reason. It places the Court's imprimatur on a quintessential prior restraint, incompatible with fundamental First Amendment values. * * *

* * *

The majority concedes that the standards in the Guidelines are "undoubtedly flexible" and that "the officials implementing them will exercise considerable discretion." * * * Nevertheless, it concludes that "[b]y its own terms the city's sound-amplification guideline must be interpreted to forbid city officials purposefully to select inadequate sound systems or to vary the sound quality or volume based on the message being delivered by performers." * * * Although the majority wishes it were so, the language of the Guidelines simply does not support such a limitation on the city's discretion. Alternatively, the majority finds a limitation in the city's practice of deferring to the sponsor with respect to sound mix, and of conferring "with the sponsor if any questions of excessive sound arise, before taking any corrective action." 658 F.Supp. 1346, 1352 (S.D.N.Y.1987). A promise to consult, however, does not provide the detailed "neutral criteria" necessary to prevent future abuses of discretion any more than did the city's promise in *Lakewood* to deny permit applications only for reasons related to the health, safety, or welfare of Lakewood citizens. Indeed, a presumption that city officials will act in good faith and adhere to standards absent from a regulation's face is "the very presumption that the doctrine forbidding unbridled discretion disallows." *Lakewood,* 486 U.S., at ___, 108 S.Ct. at 2150.

Second, even if there were narrowly drawn guidelines limiting the city's discretion, the Guidelines would be fundamentally flawed. For the requirement that there be detailed standards is of value only so far as there is a judicial mechanism to enforce them. Here, that necessary safeguard is absent. The city's sound technician consults with the performers for several minutes before the performance and then decides how to present each song or piece of music. During the perform-

---

6. Because I conclude that the Guidelines are not narrowly tailored, there is no need to consider whether there are ample alternative channels for communication. I note only that the availability of alternative channels of communication outside a public park does not magically validate a government restriction on protected speech within it. See Southeastern Promotions, Ltd. v. Conrad, 420 U.S. 546, 556 (1975) ("'[O]ne is not to have the exercise of his liberty of expression in appropriate places abridged on the plea that it may be exercised in some other place,'" quoting Schneider v. State, 308 U.S. 147, 163 (1939).

ance itself, the technician makes hundreds of decisions affecting the mix and volume of sound. Tr. of Oral Arg. 13. The music is played immediately after each decision. There is, of course, no time for appeal in the middle of a song. As a result, no court ever determines that a particular restraint on speech is necessary. The city's admission that it does not impose sanctions on violations of its general sound ordinance because the necessary litigation is too costly and time-consuming only underscores its contempt for the need for judicial review of restrictions on speech. * * * With neither prompt judicial review nor detailed and neutral standards fettering the city's discretion to restrict protected speech, the Guidelines constitute a quintessential and unconstitutional, prior restraint.

III

Today's decision has significance far beyond the world of rock music. Government no longer need balance the effectiveness of regulation with the burdens on free speech. After today, government need only assert that it is most effective to control speech in advance of its expression. Because such a result eviscerates the First Amendment, I dissent.

3. Forum Analysis

SOUTHEASTERN PROMOTIONS, LTD. v. CONRAD

Supreme Court of the United States, 1975.
420 U.S. 546, 95 S.Ct. 1239, 43 L.Ed.2d 448.

Mr. Justice Blackmun delivered the opinion of the Court.

The issue in this case is whether First Amendment rights were abridged when respondents denied petitioner the use of a municipal facility in Chattanooga, Tenn., for the showing of the controversial rock musical "Hair." * * *

I

Petitioner, Southeastern Promotions, Ltd., is a New York corporation engaged in the business of promoting and presenting theatrical productions for profit. On October 29, 1971, it applied for the use of the Tivoli, a privately owned Chattanooga theater under long-term lease to the city, to present "Hair" there for six days beginning November 23. This was to be a road company showing of the musical that had played for three years on Broadway, and had appeared in over 140 cities in the United States.[1]

Respondents are the directors of the Chattanooga Memorial Auditorium, a municipal theater. Shortly after receiving Southeastern's

---

1. Twice previously, petitioner informally had asked permission to use the Tivoli, and had been refused. In other cities, it had encountered similar resistance and had successfully sought injunctions ordering local officials to permit use of municipal facilities. * * *

Ch. 3   *GOVT.'S MANAGEMENT OF PUBLIC PROPERTY*   441

application, the directors met, and, after a brief discussion, voted to reject it. None of them had seen the play or read the script, but they understood from outside reports that the musical, as produced elsewhere, involved nudity and obscenity on stage. Although no conflicting engagement was scheduled for the Tivoli, respondents determined that the production would not be "in the best interest of the community." Southeastern was so notified but no written statement of reasons was provided.

On November 1 petitioner, alleging that respondents' action abridged its First Amendment rights, sought a preliminary injunction from the United States District Court for the Eastern District of Tennessee. Respondents did not then file an answer to the complaint. A hearing was held on November 4. The District Court took evidence as to the play's content, and respondent Conrad gave the following account of the board's decision:

> "We use the general terminology in turning down the request for its use that we felt it was not in the best interest of the community and I can't speak beyond that. That was the board's determination.
>
> "Now, I would have to speak for myself, the policy to which I would refer, as I mentioned, basically indicates that we will, as a board, allow those productions which are clean and healthful and culturally uplifting, or words to that effect. They are quoted in the original dedication booklet of the Memorial Auditorium." App. 25.[4]

The court denied preliminary relief, concluding that petitioner had failed to show that it would be irreparably harmed pending a final judgment since scheduling was "purely a matter of financial loss or gain" and was compensable.

Southeastern some weeks later pressed for a permanent injunction permitting it to use the larger auditorium, rather than the Tivoli, on Sunday, April 9, 1972. The District Court held three days of hearings beginning April 3. On the issue of obscenity vel non, presented to an advisory jury, it took evidence consisting of the full script and libretto, with production notes and stage instructions, a recording of the musical numbers, a souvenir program, and the testimony of seven witnesses who had seen the production elsewhere. The jury returned a verdict that "Hair" was obscene. The District Court agreed. It concluded that conduct in the production—group nudity and simulated sex—would

---

4. The Memorial Auditorium, completed in 1924, was dedicated to the memory of Chattanooga citizens who had "offered their lives" in World War I. The booklet referred to is entitled Souvenir of Dedication of Soldiers & Sailors Auditorium Chattanooga, Tenn. It contains the following:

"It will be [the board's] endeavor to make [the auditorium] the community center of Chattanooga; where civic, educational, religious, patriotic and charitable organizations and associations may have a common meeting place to discuss and further the upbuilding and general welfare of the city and surrounding territory.

"It will not be operated for profit, and no effort to obtain financial returns above the actual operating expenses will be permitted. Instead its purpose will be devoted for cultural advancement, and for clean, healthful, entertainment which will make for the upbuilding of a better citizenship." Exhibit 2, p. 40.

violate city ordinances and state statutes making public nudity and obscene acts criminal offenses. This criminal conduct, the court reasoned, was neither speech nor symbolic speech, and was to be viewed separately from the musical's speech elements. Being pure conduct, comparable to rape or murder, it was not entitled to First Amendment protection. Accordingly, the court denied the injunction. 341 F.Supp. 465 (1972).

On appeal, the United States Court of Appeals for the Sixth Circuit, by a divided vote, affirmed. 486 F.2d 894 (1973). The majority relied primarily on the lower court's reasoning. Neither the judges of the Court of Appeals nor the District Court saw the musical performed. Because of the First Amendment overtones, we granted certiorari. 415 U.S. 912 (1974).

Petitioner urges reversal on the grounds that (1) respondents' action constituted an unlawful prior restraint, (2) the courts below applied an incorrect standard for the determination of the issue of obscenity vel non, and (3) the record does not support a finding that "Hair" is obscene. We do not reach the latter two contentions, for we agree with the first. We hold that respondents' rejection of petitioner's application to use this public forum accomplished a prior restraint under a system lacking in constitutionally required minimal procedural safeguards. Accordingly, on this narrow ground, we reverse.

II

Respondents' action here is indistinguishable in its censoring effect from the official actions consistently identified as prior restraints in a long line of this Court's decisions. * * *

* * *

Respondents' action was no less a prior restraint because the public facilities under their control happened to be municipal theaters. The Memorial Auditorium and the Tivoli were public forums designed for and dedicated to expressive activities. There was no question as to the usefulness of either facility for petitioner's production. There was no contention by the board that these facilities could not accommodate a production of this size. None of the circumstances qualifying as an established exception to the doctrine of prior restraint was present. Petitioner was not seeking to use a facility primarily serving a competing use. See, e.g., Cameron v. Johnson, 390 U.S. 611 (1968); Adderley v. Florida, 385 U.S. 39 (1966); Brown v. Louisiana, 383 U.S. 131 (1966). Nor was rejection of the application based on any regulation of time, place, or manner related to the nature of the facility or applications from other users. See Cox v. New Hampshire, 312 U.S. 569, 574 (1941); Poulos v. New Hampshire, 345 U.S. 395, 408 (1953). No rights of individuals in surrounding areas were violated by noise or any other aspect of the production. See Kovacs v. Cooper, 336 U.S. 77 (1949). There was no captive audience. See Lehman v. City of Shaker Heights, 418 U.S. 298, 304, 306–308 (1974); Public Utilities Comm'n v. Pollak, 343 U.S. 451, 467–468 (1952) (DOUGLAS, J., dissenting).

Whether petitioner might have used some other, privately owned, theater in the city for the production is of no consequence. There is reason to doubt on this record whether any other facility would have served as well as these, since none apparently had the seating capacity, acoustical features, stage equipment, and electrical service that the show required. Even if a privately owned forum had been available, that fact alone would not justify an otherwise impermissible prior restraint. "[O]ne is not to have the exercise of his liberty of expression in appropriate places abridged on the plea that it may be exercised in some other place." Schneider v. State, 308 U.S., at 163.

Thus, it does not matter for purposes of this case that the board's decision might not have had the effect of total suppression of the musical in the community. Denying use of the municipal facility under the circumstances present here constituted the prior restraint. That restraint was final. * * *

* * *

* * * In *Freedman* the Court struck down a state scheme for the licensing of motion pictures, holding "that, because only a judicial determination in an adversary proceeding ensures the necessary sensitivity to freedom of expression, only a procedure requiring a judicial determination suffices to impose a valid final restraint." 380 U.S., at 58. We held in *Freedman,* and we reaffirm here, that a system of prior restraint runs afoul of the First Amendment if it lacks certain safeguards: First, the burden of instituting judicial proceedings, and of proving that the material is unprotected, must rest on the censor. Second, any restraint prior to judicial review can be imposed only for a specified brief period and only for the purpose of preserving the status quo. Third, a prompt final judicial determination must be assured.

Although most of our cases have pertained to motion picture licensing or censorship, this Court has applied *Freedman* to the system by which federal customs agents seize imported materials, *United States v. Thirty-seven Photographs, supra,* and to that by which postal officials restrict use of the mails, *Blount v. Rizzi, supra.* In *Blount* we held unconstitutional provisions of the postal laws designed to control use of the mails for commerce in obscene materials. The provisions enabled the Postmaster General to halt delivery of mail to an individual and prevent payment of money orders to him. The administrative order became effective without judicial approval, and the burden of obtaining judicial review was placed upon the user.

If a scheme that restricts access to the mails must furnish the procedural safeguards set forth in *Freedman,* no less must be expected of a system that regulates use of a public forum. Respondents here had the same powers of licensing and censorship exercised by postal officials in *Blount,* and by boards and officials in other cases.

The theory underlying the requirement of safeguards is applicable here with equal if not greater force. An administrative board assigned to screening stage productions—and keeping off stage anything not deemed culturally uplifting or healthful—may well be less responsive than a court, an independent branch of government, to constitutionally protected interests in free expression. * * *

* * *

Procedural safeguards were lacking here in several respects. The board's system did not provide a procedure for prompt judicial review. Although the District Court commendably held a hearing on petitioner's motion for a preliminary injunction within a few days of the board's decision, it did not review the merits of the decision at that time. The question at the hearing was whether petitioner should receive *preliminary* relief, i.e., whether there was likelihood of success on the merits and whether petitioner would suffer irreparable injury pending full review. Effective review on the merits was not obtained until more than five months later. Throughout, it was petitioner, not the board, that bore the burden of obtaining judicial review. It was petitioner that had the burden of persuasion at the preliminary hearing if not at the later stages of the litigation. Respondents did not file a formal answer to the complaint for five months after petitioner sought review. During the time prior to judicial determination, the restraint altered the status quo. Petitioner was forced to forgo the initial dates planned for the engagement and to seek to schedule the performance at a later date. The delay and uncertainty inevitably discouraged use of the forum.

The procedural shortcomings that form the basis for our decision are unrelated to the standard that the board applied. Whatever the reasons may have been for the board's exclusion of the musical, it could not escape the obligation to afford appropriate procedural safeguards. We need not decide whether the standard of obscenity applied by respondents or the courts below was sufficiently precise or substantively correct, or whether the production is in fact obscene. * * * The standard, whatever it may be, must be implemented under a system that assures prompt judicial review with a minimal restriction of First Amendment rights necessary under the circumstances.

Reversed.

Mr. Justice Douglas, dissenting in part and concurring in the result in part.

* * *

A municipal theater is no less a forum for the expression of ideas than is a public park, or a sidewalk; the forms of expression adopted in such a forum may be more expensive and more structured than those typically seen in our parks and streets, but they are surely no less entitled to the shelter of the First Amendment. As soon as municipal officials are permitted to pick and choose, as they are in all existing socialist regimes, between those productions which are "clean and healthful and culturally uplifting" in content and those which are not, the path is cleared for a regime of censorship under which full voice can be given only to those views which meet with the approval of the powers that be.

There was much testimony in the District Court concerning the pungent social and political commentary which the musical "Hair" levels against various sacred cows of our society: the Vietnam war, the draft, and the puritanical conventions of the Establishment. This commentary is undoubtedly offensive to some, but its contribution to social consciousness and intellectual ferment is a positive one. In this respect, the musical's often ribald humor and trenchant social satire may someday merit comparison to the most highly regarded works of Aristophanes, a fellow debunker of established tastes and received wisdom, yet one whose offerings would doubtless meet with a similarly cold reception at the hands of Establishment censors. No matter how many procedural safeguards may be imposed, any system which permits governmental officials to inhibit or control the flow of disturbing and unwelcome ideas to the public threatens serious diminution of the breadth and richness of our cultural offerings.

Mr. Justice White, with whom The Chief Justice joins, dissenting. [Omitted.]

Mr. Justice Rehnquist, dissenting.

The Court treats this case as if it were on all fours with Freedman v. Maryland, 380 U.S. 51 (1965), which it is not. *Freedman* dealt with the efforts of the State of Maryland to prohibit the petitioner in that case from showing a film "at his Baltimore theater," *id.*, at 52. Petitioner here did not seek to show the musical production "Hair" at its Chattanooga theater, but rather at a Chattanooga theater owned by the city of Chattanooga.

The Court glosses over this distinction by treating a community-owned theater as if it were the same as a city park or city street, which it is not. The Court's decisions have recognized that city streets and parks are traditionally open to the public, and that permits or licenses to use them are not ordinarily required. "[O]ne who is rightfully on a street which the state has left open to the public carries with him there as elsewhere the constitutional right to express his views in an orderly fashion. This right extends to the communication of ideas by handbills and literature as well as by the spoken word." Jamison v. Texas, 318 U.S. 413, 416 (1943). The Court has therefore held that where municipal authorities seek to exact a license or permit for those who wish to use parks or streets for the purpose of exercising their right of free speech, the standards governing the licensing authority must be objective, definite, and nondiscriminatory. Shuttlesworth v. City of Birmingham, 394 U.S. 147 (1969). But until this case the Court has not equated a public auditorium, which must of necessity schedule performances by a process of inclusion and exclusion, with public streets and parks.

* * *

* * * In Adderley v. Florida, 385 U.S. 39, 47–48 (1966), the Court said:

"The State, no less than a private owner of property, has power to preserve the property under its control for the use to which it is lawfully dedicated. For this reason there is no merit to the petitioners' argument that they had a constitutional right to stay on the property. * * * The United States Constitution does not forbid a State to control the use of its own property for its own lawful nondiscriminatory purpose."

The Court avoids the impact of cases such as *Adderley* by insisting that the municipal auditorium and the theater were "public forums designed for and dedicated to expressive activities," * * *, and that the rejection of petitioner's application was not based on "any regulation of time, place, or manner related to the nature of the facility or applications from other users." *Ibid.* But the apparent effect of the Court's decision is to tell the managers of municipal auditoriums that they may exercise no selective role whatsoever in deciding what performances may be booked. The auditoriums in question here have historically been devoted to "clean, healthful entertainment"; they have accepted only productions not inappropriate for viewing by children so that the facilities might serve as a place for entertaining the whole family. Viewed apart from any constitutional limitations, such a policy would undoubtedly rule out much worthwhile adult entertainment. But if it is the desire of the citizens of Chattanooga, who presumably have paid for and own the facilities, that the attractions to be shown there should not be of the kind which would offend any substantial number of potential theatergoers, I do not think the policy can be described as arbitrary or unreasonable.[2] Whether or not the production of the version of "Hair" here under consideration is obscene, the findings of fact made by the District Court and affirmed on appeal do indicate that it is not entertainment designed for the whole family.

* * *

A municipal theater may not be run by municipal authorities as if it were a private theater, free to judge on a content basis alone which plays it wishes to have performed and which it does not. But, just as surely, that element of it which is "theater" ought to be accorded some constitutional recognition along with that element of it which is "municipal." I do not believe fidelity to the First Amendment requires the exaggerated and rigid procedural safeguards which the Court insists upon in this case. I think that the findings of the District Court and the Court of Appeals support the conclusion that petitioner was denied a lease for constitutionally adequate and nondiscriminatory reasons. I would therefore affirm the judgment of the Court of Appeals.

---

2. Limitations on the use of municipal auditoriums by government must be sufficiently reasonable to satisfy the Due Process Clause and cannot unfairly discriminate in violation of the Equal Protection Clause. A municipal auditorium which opened itself to Republicans while closing itself to Democrats would run afoul of the Fourteenth Amendment. There is no allegation in the instant case that the auditoriums accepted equally graphic productions while unfairly discriminating against "Hair" because of its expressions of political and social belief.

PERRY EDUCATION ASSOCIATION v. PERRY LOCAL EDUCATORS' ASSOCIATION

Supreme Court of the United States, 1983.
460 U.S. 37, 103 S.Ct. 948, 74 L.Ed.2d 794.

JUSTICE WHITE delivered the opinion of the Court.

Perry Education Association is the duly elected exclusive bargaining representative for the teachers of the Metropolitan School District of Perry Township, Ind. A collective-bargaining agreement with the Board of Education provided that Perry Education Association, but no other union, would have access to the interschool mail system and teacher mailboxes in the Perry Township schools. The issue in this case is whether the denial of similar access to the Perry Local Educators' Association, a rival teacher group, violates the First and Fourteenth Amendments.

I

The Metropolitan School District of Perry Township, Ind., operates a public school system of 13 separate schools. Each school building contains a set of mailboxes for the teachers. Interschool delivery by school employees permits messages to be delivered rapidly to teachers in the District.[1] The primary function of this internal mail system is to transmit official messages among the teachers and between the teachers and the school administration. In addition, teachers use the system to send personal messages, and individual school building principals have allowed delivery of messages from various private organizations.[2]

Prior to 1977, both the Perry Education Association (PEA) and the Perry Local Educators' Association (PLEA) represented teachers in the School District and apparently had equal access to the interschool mail system. In 1977, PLEA challenged PEA's status as *de facto* bargaining representative for the Perry Township teachers by filing an election petition with the Indiana Education Employment Relations Board (Board). PEA won the election and was certified as the exclusive representative, as provided by Indiana law. * * *

The Board permits a school district to provide access to communication facilities to the union selected for the discharge of the exclusive representative duties of representing the bargaining unit and its individual members without having to provide equal access to rival unions. Following the election, PEA and the School District negotiated a labor contract in which the School Board gave PEA "access to teachers'

---

1. The United States Postal Service, in a submission as *amicus curiae,* suggests that the interschool delivery of material to teachers at various schools in the District violates the Private Express statutes, 18 U.S.C. §§ 1693–1699 and 39 U.S.C. §§ 601–606, which generally prohibit the carriage of letters over postal routes without payment of postage. We agree with the Postal Service that this question does not directly bear on the issues before the Court in this case. Accordingly, we express no opinion on whether the mail delivery practices involved here comply with the Private Express statutes or other Postal Service regulations.

2. Local parochial schools, church groups, YMCA's, and Cub Scout units have used the system. The record does not indicate whether any requests for use have been denied, nor does it reveal whether permission must separately be sought for every message that a group wishes delivered to the teachers.

mailboxes in which to insert material" and the right to use the interschool mail delivery system to the extent that the School District incurred no extra expense by such use. The labor agreement noted that these access rights were being accorded to PEA "acting as the representative of the teachers" and went on to stipulate that these access rights shall not be granted to any other "school employee organization"—a term of art defined by Indiana law to mean "any organization which has school employees as members and one of whose primary purposes is representing school employees in dealing with their school employer." The PEA contract with these provisions was renewed in 1980 and is presently in force.

The exclusive-access policy applies only to use of the mailboxes and school mail system. PLEA is not prevented from using other school facilities to communicate with teachers. PLEA may post notices on school bulletin boards; may hold meetings on school property after school hours; and may, with approval of the building principals, make announcements on the public address system. Of course, PLEA also may communicate with teachers by word of mouth, telephone, or the United States mail. Moreover, under Indiana law, the preferential access of the bargaining agent may continue only while its status as exclusive representative is insulated from challenge. * * * While a representation contest is in progress, unions must be afforded equal access to such communication facilities.

PLEA and two of its members filed this action under 42 U.S.C. § 1983 against PEA and individual members of the Perry Township School Board. Plaintiffs contended that PEA's preferential access to the internal mail system violates the First Amendment and the Equal Protection Clause of the Fourteenth Amendment. They sought injunctive and declaratory relief and damages. Upon cross-motions for summary judgment, the District Court entered judgment for the defendants. * * *

The Court of Appeals for the Seventh Circuit reversed. Perry Local Educators' Assn. v. Hohlt, 652 F.2d 1286 (1981). The court held that once the School District "opens its internal mail system to PEA but denies it to PLEA, it violates both the Equal Protection Clause and the First Amendment." * * * It acknowledged that PEA had "legal duties to the teachers that PLEA does not have" but reasoned that "[w]ithout an independent reason why equal access for other labor groups and individual teachers is undesirable, the special duties of the incumbent do not justify opening the system to the incumbent alone." * * *

PEA now seeks review of this judgment by way of appeal.

* * *

III

The primary question presented is whether the First Amendment, applicable to the States by virtue of the Fourteenth Amendment, is violated when a union that has been elected by public school teachers as their exclusive bargaining representative is granted access to certain means of communication, while such access is denied to a rival union. There is no question that constitutional interests are implicated by denying PLEA use of the interschool mail system. "It can hardly be argued that either students or teachers shed their constitutional rights to freedom of speech or expression at the schoolhouse gate." Tinker v. Des Moines School District, 393 U.S. 503, 506 (1969); Healy v. James, 408 U.S. 169 (1972). The First Amendment's guarantee of free speech applies to teachers' mailboxes as surely as it does elsewhere within the school, *Tinker v. Des Moines School District, supra,* and on sidewalks outside, Police Department of Chicago v. Mosley, 408 U.S. 92 (1972). But this is not to say that the First Amendment requires equivalent access to all parts of a school building in which some form of communicative activity occurs. "[N]owhere [have we] suggested that students, teachers, or anyone else has an absolute constitutional right to use all parts of a school building or its immediate environs for * * * unlimited expressive purposes." Grayned v. City of Rockford, 408 U.S. 104, 117–118 (1972). The existence of a right of access to public property and the standard by which limitations upon such a right must be evaluated differ depending on the character of the property at issue.

A

In places which by long tradition or by government fiat have been devoted to assembly and debate, the rights of the State to limit expressive activity are sharply circumscribed. At one end of the spectrum are streets and parks which "have immemorially been held in trust for the use of the public and, time out of mind, have been used for purposes of assembly, communicating thoughts between citizens, and discussing public questions." Hague v. CIO, 307 U.S. 496, 515 (1939). In these quintessential public forums, the government may not prohibit all communicative activity. For the State to enforce a content-based exclusion it must show that its regulation is necessary to serve a compelling state interest and that it is narrowly drawn to achieve that end. * * * The State may also enforce regulations of the time, place, and manner of expression which are content-neutral, are narrowly tailored to serve a significant government interest, and leave open ample alternative channels of communication. * * *

A second category consists of public property which the State has opened for use by the public as a place for expressive activity. The Constitution forbids a State to enforce certain exclusions from a forum generally open to the public even if it was not required to create the forum in the first place. City of Madison Joint School District v. Wisconsin Employment Relations Comm'n, 429 U.S. 167 (1976) (school board meeting); Southeastern Promotions, Ltd. v. Conrad, 420 U.S. 546 (1975) (municipal theater).[7] Although a State is not required to indefinitely retain the open character of the facility, as long as it does so it is bound by the same standards as apply in a traditional public forum.

---

7. A public forum may be created for a limited purpose such as use by certain groups, e.g., *Widmar v. Vincent* (student groups), or for the discussion of certain subjects, e.g., *City of Madison Joint School District v. Wisconsin Public Employment Relations Comm'n* (school board business).

Reasonable time, place, and manner regulations are permissible, and a content-based prohibition must be narrowly drawn to effectuate a compelling state interest. *Widmar v. Vincent, supra,* at 269–270.

Public property which is not by tradition or designation a forum for public communication is governed by different standards. We have recognized that the "First Amendment does not guarantee access to property simply because it is owned or controlled by the government." *United States Postal Service v. Council of Greenburgh Civic Assns., supra,* at 129. In addition to time, place, and manner regulations, the State may reserve the forum for its intended purposes, communicative or otherwise, as long as the regulation on speech is reasonable and not an effort to suppress expression merely because public officials oppose the speaker's view. 453 U.S., at 131, n. 7. As we have stated on several occasions, " ' "[t]he State, no less than a private owner of property, has power to preserve the property under its control for the use to which it is lawfully dedicated." ' " *Id.,* at 129–130, quoting Greer v. Spock, 424 U.S. 828, 836 (1976), in turn quoting Adderley v. Florida, 385 U.S. 39, 47 (1966).

The school mail facilities at issue here fall within this third category. The Court of Appeals recognized that Perry School District's interschool mail system is not a traditional public forum: "We do not hold that a school's internal mail system is a public forum in the sense that a school board may not close it to all but official business if it chooses." 652 F.2d, at 1301. On this point the parties agree. Nor do the parties dispute that, as the District Court observed, the "normal and intended function [of the school mail facilities] is to facilitate internal communication of school-related matters to the teachers." Perry Local Educators' Assn. v. Hohlt, IP 79–189–C (SD Ind., Feb. 25, 1980), p. 4. The internal mail system, at least by policy, is not held open to the general public. It is instead PLEA's position that the school mail facilities have become a "limited public forum" from which it may not be excluded because of the periodic use of the system by private non-school-connected groups, and PLEA's own unrestricted access to the system prior to PEA's certification as exclusive representative.

Neither of these arguments is persuasive. The use of the internal school mail by groups not affiliated with the schools is no doubt a relevant consideration. If by policy or by practice the Perry School District has opened its mail system for indiscriminate use by the general public, then PLEA could justifiably argue a public forum has been created. This, however, is not the case. As the case comes before us, there is no indication in the record that the school mailboxes and interschool delivery system are open for use by the general public. Permission to use the system to communicate with teachers must be secured from the individual building principal. There is no court finding or evidence in the record which demonstrates that this permission has been granted as a matter of course to all who seek to distribute material. We can only conclude that the schools do allow some outside organizations such as the YMCA, Cub Scouts, and other civic and church organizations to use the facilities. This type of selective access does not transform government property into a public forum. In *Greer v. Spock, supra,* at 838, n. 10, the fact that other civilian speakers and entertainers had sometimes been invited to appear at Fort Dix did not convert the military base into a public forum. And in Lehman v. City of Shaker Heights, 418 U.S. 298 (1974) (opinion of BLACKMUN, J.), a plurality of the Court concluded that a city transit system's rental of space in its vehicles for commercial advertising did not require it to accept partisan political advertising.

Moreover, even if we assume that by granting access to the Cub Scouts, YMCA's, and parochial schools, the School District has created a "limited" public forum, the constitutional right of access would in any event extend only to other entities of similar character. While the school mail facilities thus might be a forum generally open for use by the Girl Scouts, the local boys' club, and other organizations that engage in activities of interest and educational relevance to students, they would not as a consequence be open to an organization such as PLEA, which is concerned with the terms and conditions of teacher employment.

PLEA also points to its ability to use school mailboxes and delivery system on an equal footing with PEA prior to the collective-bargaining agreement signed in 1978. Its argument appears to be that the access policy in effect at that time converted the school mail facilities into a limited public forum generally open for use by employee organizations, and that once this occurred, exclusions of employee organizations thereafter must be judged by the constitutional standard applicable to public forums. The fallacy in the argument is that it is not the forum, but PLEA itself, which has changed. Prior to 1977, there was no exclusive representative for the Perry School District teachers. PEA and PLEA each represented its own members. Therefore the School District's policy of allowing both organizations to use the school mail facilities simply reflected the fact that both unions represented the teachers and had legitimate reasons for use of the system. PLEA's previous access was consistent with the School District's preservation of the facilities for school-related business, and did not constitute creation of a public forum in any broader sense.

* * * In the Court of Appeals' view, however, the access policy adopted by the Perry schools favors a particular viewpoint, that of PEA, on labor relations, and consequently must be strictly scrutinized regardless of whether a public forum is involved. There is, however, no indication that the School Board intended to discourage one viewpoint and advance another. We believe it is more accurate to characterize the access policy as based on the *status* of the respective unions rather than their views. Implicit in the concept of the nonpublic forum is the right to make distinctions in access on the basis of subject matter and speaker identity. These distinctions may be impermissible in a public forum but are inherent and inescapable in the process of limiting a nonpublic forum to activities compatible with the intended purpose of the property. The touchstone for evaluating these distinctions is whether they are reasonable in light of the purpose which the forum at issue serves.

B

The differential access provided PEA and PLEA is reasonable because it is wholly consistent with the District's legitimate interest in "'preserv[ing] the property * * * for the use to which it is lawfully dedicated.'" *United States Postal Service,* 453 U.S., at 129–130. Use of school mail facilities enables PEA to perform effectively its obligations as exclusive representative of *all* Perry Township teachers. Conversely, PLEA does not have any official responsibility in connection with the School District and need not be entitled to the same rights of access to school mailboxes. We observe that providing exclusive access to recognized bargaining representatives is a permissible labor practice in the public sector. * * *

The Court of Appeals accorded little or no weight to PEA's special responsibilities. In its view these responsibilities, while justifying PEA's access, did not justify denying equal access to PLEA. The Court of Appeals would have been correct if a public forum were involved here but the internal mail system is not a public forum. As we have already stressed, when government property is not dedicated to open communication the government may—without further justification—restrict use to those who participate in the forum's official business.[13]

Finally, the reasonableness of the limitations of PLEA's access to the school mail system is also supported by the substantial alternative channels that remain open for union-teacher communication to take place. These means range from bulletin boards to meeting facilities to the United States mail. During election periods, PLEA is assured of equal access to all modes of communication. There is no showing here that PLEA's ability to communicate with teachers is seriously impinged by the restricted access to the internal mail system. * * *

IV

The Court of Appeals also held that the differential access provided the rival unions constituted impermissible content discrimination in violation of the Equal Protection Clause of the Fourteenth Amendment. We have rejected this contention when cast as a First Amendment argument, and it fares no better in equal protection garb. As we have explained above, PLEA did not have a First Amendment or other right of access to the interschool mail system. The grant of such access to

---

13. The Court of Appeals was also mistaken in finding that the exclusive-access policy was not closely tailored to the official responsibilities of PEA. The Court of Appeals thought the policy overinclusive—because the collective-bargaining agreement does not limit PEA's use of the mail system to messages related to its special legal duties. The record, however, does not establish that PEA enjoyed or claimed unlimited access by usage or otherwise; indeed, the collective-bargaining agreement indicates that the right of access was accorded to PEA "acting as the representative of the teachers." In these circumstances, we do not find it necessary to decide the reasonableness of a grant of access for unlimited purposes.

The Court of Appeals also indicated that the access policy was underinclusive because the School District permits outside organizations with no special duties to teachers to use the system. As we have already noted in text, see *supra,* * * *, there was no District policy of open access for private groups and, in any event, the provision of access to these private groups does not undermine the reasons for not allowing similar access by a rival labor union. * * *

PEA, therefore, does not burden a fundamental right of PLEA. Thus, the decision to grant such privileges to PEA need not be tested by the strict scrutiny applied when government action impinges upon a fundamental right protected by the Constitution. See San Antonio Independent School District v. Rodriguez, 411 U.S. 1, 17 (1973). The School District's policy need only rationally further a legitimate state purpose. That purpose is clearly found in the special responsibilities of an exclusive bargaining representative. See *supra,* at 51–52.

The Seventh Circuit and PLEA rely on Police Department of Chicago v. Mosley, 408 U.S. 92 (1972), and Carey v. Brown, 447 U.S. 455 (1980). In *Mosley* and *Carey,* we struck down prohibitions on peaceful picketing in a public forum. In *Mosley,* the city of Chicago permitted peaceful picketing on the subject of a school's labor-management dispute, but prohibited other picketing in the immediate vicinity of the school. In *Carey,* the challenged state statute barred all picketing of residences and dwellings except the peaceful picketing of a place of employment involved in a labor dispute. In both cases, we found the distinction between classes of speech violative of the Equal Protection Clause. The key to those decisions, however, was the presence of a public forum. In a public forum, by definition, all parties have a constitutional right of access and the State must demonstrate compelling reasons for restricting access to a single class of speakers, a single viewpoint, or a single subject.

When speakers and subjects are similarly situated, the State may not pick and choose. Conversely on government property that has not been made a public forum, not all speech is equally situated, and the State may draw distinctions which relate to the special purpose for which the property is used. As we have explained above, for a school mail facility, the difference in status between the exclusive bargaining representative and its rival is such a distinction.

* * *

* * * The judgment of the Court of Appeals is

Reversed.

JUSTICE BRENNAN, with whom JUSTICE MARSHALL, JUSTICE POWELL, and JUSTICE STEVENS join, dissenting.

The Court today holds that an incumbent teachers' union may negotiate a collective-bargaining agreement with a school board that grants the incumbent access to teachers' mailboxes and to the interschool mail system and denies such access to a rival union. Because the exclusive-access provision in the collective-bargaining agreement amounts to viewpoint discrimination that infringes the respondents' First Amendment rights and fails to advance any substantial state interest, I dissent.

I

The Court properly acknowledges that teachers have protected First Amendment rights within the school context. See Tinker v. Des Moines School District, 393 U.S. 503, 506 (1969). In particular, we have held that teachers may not be "compelled to relinquish the First Amendment rights they would otherwise enjoy as citizens to comment on matters of public interest in connection with the operation of the public schools in which they work." Pickering v. Board of Education, 391 U.S. 563, 568 (1968). See also Mt. Healthy City Board of Education v. Doyle, 429 U.S. 274, 284 (1977). We also have recognized in the school context the First Amendment right of "individuals to associate to further their personal beliefs," Healy v. James, 408 U.S. 169, 181 (1972), and have acknowledged the First Amendment rights of dissident teachers in matters involving labor relations. City of Madison Joint School District v. Wisconsin Employment Relations Comm'n, 429 U.S. 167, 176, n. 10 (1976). Against this background it is clear that the exclusive-access policy in this case implicated the respondents' First Amendment rights by restricting their freedom of expression in issues important to the operation of the school system. As the Court of Appeals suggested, this speech is "if not at the very apex of any hierarchy of protected speech, at least not far below it." * * *

* * *

The Court fundamentally misperceives the essence of the respondents' claims and misunderstands the thrust of the Court of Appeals' well-reasoned opinion. This case does not involve an "absolute access" claim. It involves an "equal access" claim. As such it does not turn on whether the internal school mail system is a "public forum." In focusing on the public forum issue, the Court disregards the First Amendment's central proscription against censorship, in the form of viewpoint discrimination, in any forum, public or nonpublic.

A

The First Amendment's prohibition against government discrimination among viewpoints on particular issues falling within the realm of protected speech has been noted extensively in the opinions of this Court. In Niemotko v. Maryland, 340 U.S. 268 (1951), two Jehovah's Witnesses were denied access to a public park to give Bible talks. Members of other religious groups had been granted access to the park for purposes related to religion. The Court found that the denial of access was based on public officials' disagreement with the Jehovah's Witnesses views, *id.,* at 272, and held it invalid. During the course of its opinion, the Court stated: "The right to equal protection of the laws, in the exercise of those freedoms of speech and religion protected by the First and Fourteenth Amendments, has a firmer foundation than the whims or personal opinions of a local governing body." *Ibid.* In an opinion concurring in the result, Justice Frankfurter stated that "[t]o allow expression of religious views by some and deny the same privilege to others merely because they or their views are unpopular, even deeply so, is a denial of equal protection of the law forbidden by the Fourteenth Amendment." * * *

* * *

There is another line of cases, closely related to those implicating the prohibition against viewpoint discrimination, that have addressed the First Amendment principle of subject-matter, or content neutrality. Generally, the concept of content neutrality prohibits the government from choosing the subjects that are appropriate for public discussion. The content-neutrality cases frequently refer to the prohibition against viewpoint discrimination and both concepts have their roots in the First Amendment's bar against censorship. But unlike the viewpoint-discrimination concept, which is used to strike down government restrictions on speech by particular speakers, the content-neutrality principle is invoked when the government has imposed restrictions on speech related to an entire subject area. The content-neutrality principle can be seen as an outgrowth of the core First Amendment prohibition against viewpoint discrimination. See generally Stone, Restrictions of Speech Because of its Content: The Peculiar Case of Subject–Matter Restrictions, 46 U.Chi.L.Rev. 81 (1978).

* * *

Once the government permits discussion of certain subject matter, it may not impose restrictions that discriminate among viewpoints on those subjects whether a nonpublic forum is involved or not. * * * We have never held that government may allow discussion of a subject then discriminate among viewpoints on that particular topic, even if the government for certain reasons may entirely exclude discussion of the subject from the forum. In this context, the greater power does not include the lesser because for First Amendment purposes exercise of the lesser power is more threatening to core values. Viewpoint discrimination is censorship in its purest form and government regulation that discriminates among viewpoints threatens the continued vitality of "free speech."

B

* * * This case does not involve a claim of an absolute right of access to the forum to discuss any subject matter. If it did, public forum analysis might be relevant. This case involves a claim of equal access to discuss a subject that the Board has approved for discussion in the forum. In essence, the respondents are not asserting a right of access at all; they are asserting a right to be free from discrimination. The critical inquiry, therefore, is whether the Board's grant of exclusive access to the petitioner amounts to prohibited viewpoint discrimination.

II

The Court addresses only briefly the respondents' claim that the exclusive-access provision amounts to viewpoint discrimination. In rejecting this claim, the Court starts from the premise that the school mail system is not a public forum and that, as a result, the Board has no obligation to grant access to the respondents. The Court then suggests that there is no indication that the Board intended to discourage one viewpoint and to advance another. In the Court's view, the exclusive-access policy is based on the status of the respective parties rather than on their views. * * *

* * *

Addressing the question of viewpoint discrimination directly, free of the Court's irrelevant public forum analysis, it is clear that the exclusive-access policy discriminates on the basis of viewpoint. The Court of Appeals found that "[t]he access policy adopted by the Perry schools, in form a speaker restriction, favors a particular viewpoint on labor relations in the Perry schools * * * : the teachers inevitably will receive from [the petitioner] self-laudatory descriptions of its activities on their behalf and will be denied the critical perspective offered by [the respondents]." Perry Local Educators' Assn. v. Hohlt, 652 F.2d at 1296. * * *

On a practical level, the only reason for the petitioner to seek an exclusive-access policy is to deny its rivals access to an effective channel of communication. No other group is explicitly denied access to the mail system. * * * The very argument the petitioner advances in support of the policy, the need to preserve labor peace, also indicates that the access policy is not viewpoint-neutral.

In short, the exclusive-access policy discriminates against the respondents based on their viewpoint. The Board has agreed to amplify the speech of the petitioner, while repressing the speech of the respondents based on the respondents' point of view. This sort of discrimination amounts to censorship and infringes the First Amendment rights of the respondents. In this light, the policy can survive only if the petitioner can justify it.

* * *

The petitioner attempts to justify the exclusive-access provision based on its status as the exclusive bargaining representative for the teachers and on the State's interest in efficient communication between collective-bargaining representatives and the members of the unit. The petitioner's status and the State's interest in efficient communication are important considerations. They are not sufficient, however, to sustain the exclusive-access policy.

As the Court of Appeals pointed out, the exclusive-access policy is both "overinclusive and underinclusive" as a means of serving the State's interest in the efficient discharge of the petitioner's legal duties to the teachers. * * * The policy is overinclusive because it does not strictly limit the petitioner's use of the mail system to performance of its special legal duties and underinclusive because the Board permits outside organizations with no special duties to the teachers, or to the students, to use the system. * * * The Court of Appeals also suggested that even if the Board had attempted to tailor the policy more carefully by denying outside groups access to the system and by expressly limiting the petitioner's use of the system to messages relating to its official duties, "the fit would still be questionable, for it might be difficult—both in practice and in principle—effectively to separate 'necessary' communications from propaganda." * * * The Court of Appeals was justly concerned with this problem, because the scope of the petitioner's "legal duties" might be difficult, if not impossible, to define with precision. * * *

* * *

The petitioner also argues, and the Court agrees, * * *, that the exclusive-access policy is justified by the State's interest in preserving labor peace. * * *

Although the State's interest in preserving labor peace in the schools in order to prevent disruption is unquestionably substantial, merely articulating the interest is not enough to sustain the exclusive-access policy in this case. There must be some showing that the asserted interest is advanced by the policy. In the absence of such a showing, the exclusive-access policy must fail.[13]

C

Because the grant to the petitioner of exclusive access to the internal school mail system amounts to viewpoint discrimination that infringes the respondents' First Amendment rights and because the petitioner has failed to show that the policy furthers any substantial state interest, the policy must be invalidated as violative of the First Amendment.

* * *

CORNELIUS v. NAACP LEGAL DEFENSE & EDUCATIONAL FUND

Supreme Court of the United States, 1985.
473 U.S. 788, 105 S.Ct. 3439, 87 L.Ed.2d 567.

JUSTICE O'CONNOR delivered the opinion of the Court.

This case requires us to decide whether the Federal Government violates the First Amendment when it excludes legal defense and political advocacy organizations from participation in the Combined Federal Campaign (CFC or Campaign), a charity drive aimed at federal employees. The United States District Court for the District of Columbia held that the respondent organizations could not be excluded from the CFC, and the Court of Appeals affirmed. * * * We granted certiorari, * * *, and we now reverse.

I

The CFC is an annual charitable fundraising drive conducted in the federal workplace during working hours largely through the voluntary efforts of federal employees. At all times relevant to this litigation,

---

13. The Court also cites the availability of alternative channels of communication in support of the "reasonableness" of the exclusive-access policy. * * * In a detailed discussion, the Court of Appeals properly concluded that the other channels of communication available to the respondents were "not nearly as effective as the internal mail system." Perry Local Educators' Assn. v. Hohlt, 652 F.2d, at 1299. See also id., at 1299–1300. In addition, the Court apparently disregards the principle that "one is not to have the exercise of his liberty of expression in appropriate places abridged on the plea that it may be exercised in some other place." Schneider v. State, 308 U.S. 147, 163 (1939). In this case, the existence of inferior alternative channels of communication does not affect the conclusion that the petitioner has failed to justify the viewpoint-discriminatory exclusive-access policy.

participating organizations confined their fundraising activities to a 30-word statement submitted by them for inclusion in the Campaign literature. Volunteer federal employees distribute to their coworkers literature describing the Campaign and the participants along with pledge cards. * * * Contributions may take the form of either a payroll deduction or a lump-sum payment made to a designated agency or to the general Campaign fund. * * * Undesignated contributions are distributed on the local level by a private umbrella organization to certain participating organizations. * * * Designated funds are paid directly to the specified recipient. Through the CFC, the Government employees contribute in excess of $100 million to charitable organizations each year. * * *

The CFC is a relatively recent development. Prior to 1957, charitable solicitation in the federal workplace occurred on an ad hoc basis. Federal managers received requests from dozens of organizations seeking endorsements and the right to solicit contributions from federal employees at their worksites. * * * Eventually, the increasing number of entities seeking access to federal buildings and the multiplicity of appeals disrupted the work environment and confused employees who were unfamiliar with the groups seeking contributions. * * *

* * * From 1963 until 1982, the CFC was implemented by guidelines set forth in the Civil Service Commission's Manual on Fund-Raising. Only tax-exempt, nonprofit charitable organizations that were supported by contributions from the public and that provided direct health and welfare services to individuals were eligible to participate in the CFC. * * *

Respondents in this case are the NAACP Legal Defense and Educational Fund, Inc., the Sierra Club Legal Defense Fund, the Puerto Rican Legal Defense and Education Fund, the Federally Employed Women Legal Defense and Education Fund, the Indian Law Resource Center, the Lawyers' Committee for Civil Rights under Law, and the Natural Resources Defense Council. Each of the respondents attempts to influence public policy through one or more of the following means: political activity, advocacy, lobbying, or litigation on behalf of others. * * *

In the first action the Legal Defense Funds challenged the "direct services" requirement on the grounds that it violated the First Amendment and the equal protection component of the Fifth Amendment. * * * The District Court did not reach the equal protection challenge, because it found that the "direct services" requirement as formulated in the Manual on Fund-Raising was too vague to satisfy the strict standards of specificity required by the First Amendment. * * * The Government did not appeal the District Court's decision, and the plaintiffs, along with other legal defense funds, were allowed to participate in the 1982 and 1983 Campaigns and receive funds designated for their use by federal employees.

In the second proceeding, the Legal Defense Funds challenged the decision of the Director of OPM to authorize local federal coordinating groups to determine what share, if any, of the undesignated funds to allocate to organizations classified [as national service associations]. * * *

In response to the District Court's decision in *NAACP I,* President Reagan took several steps to restore the CFC to what he determined to be its original purpose. In 1982, the President issued Executive Order No. 12353, 3 CFR 139 (1983), to replace the 1961 Executive Order which had established the CFC. * * * The Order limited participation to "voluntary, charitable, health and welfare agencies that provide or support direct health and welfare services to individuals or their families," * * * and specifically excluded those "[a]gencies that seek to influence the outcomes of elections or the determination of public policy through political activity or advocacy, lobbying, or litigation on behalf of parties other than themselves." * * *

Respondents brought this action challenging their threatened exclusion under the new Executive Order. They argued that the denial of the right to seek designated funds violates their First Amendment right to solicit charitable contributions and that the denial of the right to participate in undesignated funds violates their rights under the equal protection component of the Fifth Amendment. * * *

* * *

II

The issue presented is whether respondents have a First Amendment right to solicit contributions that was violated by their exclusion from the CFC. To resolve this issue we must first decide whether solicitation in the context of the CFC is speech protected by the First Amendment, for, if it is not, we need go no further. Assuming that such solicitation is protected speech, we must identify the nature of the forum, because the extent to which the Government may limit access depends on whether the forum is public or nonpublic. Finally, we must assess whether the justifications for exclusion from the relevant forum satisfy the requisite standard. Applying this analysis, we find that respondents' solicitation is protected speech occurring in the context of a nonpublic forum and that the Government's reasons for excluding respondents from the CFC appear, at least facially, to satisfy the reasonableness standard. We express no opinion on the question whether petitioner's explanation is merely a pretext for viewpoint discrimination. Accordingly, we reverse and remand for further proceedings consistent with this opinion.

A

Charitable solicitation of funds has been recognized by this Court as a form of protected speech. In Village of Schaumburg v. Citizens for a Better Environment, 444 U.S. 620 (1980), the Court observed:

> "[S]oliciting funds involves interests protected by the First Amendment's guarantee of freedom of speech. Virginia Pharmacy Board v. Virginia Citizens Consumer Council, 425 U.S. 748, 761 (1976). * * *" *Id.,* at 629.

"Soliciting financial support is undoubtedly subject to reasonable regulation but the latter must be undertaken with due regard for the reality that solicitation is characteristically intertwined with informative and perhaps persuasive speech seeking support for particular causes or for particular views * * * and for the reality that without solicitation the flow of such information and advocacy would likely cease. * * * Furthermore, * * *, it has not been dealt with in our cases as a variety of purely commercial speech." * * *

* * *

Although *Village of Schaumburg* establishes that noncommercial solicitation is protected by the First Amendment, petitioner argues that solicitation within the confines of the CFC is entitled to a lesser degree of protection. This argument is premised on the inherent differences between the face-to-face solicitation involved in *Village of Schaumburg* and the 30-word written statements at issue here. In a face-to-face encounter there is a greater opportunity for the exchange of ideas and the propagation of views than is available in the CFC. * * *

Notwithstanding the significant distinctions between inperson solicitation and solicitation in the abbreviated context of the CFC, we find that the latter deserves First Amendment protection. The brief statements in the CFC literature directly advance the speaker's interest in informing readers about its existence and its goals. Moreover, an employee's contribution in response to a request for funds functions as a general expression of support for the recipient and its views.

B

The conclusion that the solicitation which occurs in the CFC is protected speech merely begins our inquiry. Even protected speech is not equally permissible in all places and at all times. Nothing in the Constitution requires the Government freely to grant access to all who wish to exercise their right to free speech on every type of Government property without regard to the nature of the property or to the disruption that might be caused by the speaker's activities. * * * Recognizing that the Government, "no less than a private owner of property, has power to preserve the property under its control for the use to which it is lawfully dedicated," Greer v. Spock, 424 U.S. 828, 836 (1976), the Court has adopted a forum analysis as a means of determining when the Government's interest in limiting the use of its property to its intended purpose outweighs the interest of those wishing to use the property for other purposes. Accordingly, the extent to which the Government can control access depends on the nature of the relevant forum. Because a principal purpose of traditional public fora is the free exchange of ideas, speakers can be excluded from a public forum only when the exclusion is necessary to serve a compelling state interest and the exclusion is narrowly drawn to achieve that interest. See Perry Education Assn. v. Perry Local Educators' Assn., 460 U.S., at 45. Similarly, when the Government has intentionally designated a place or means of communication as a public forum speakers cannot be excluded without a compelling governmental interest. Access to a nonpublic forum, however, can be restricted as long as the restrictions are "reasonable and [are] not an effort to suppress expression merely because public officials oppose the speaker's view." * * *

To determine whether the First Amendment permits the Government to exclude respondents from the CFC, we must first decide whether the forum consists of the federal workplace, as petitioner contends, or the CFC, as respondents maintain. * * *

* * *

We agree with respondents that the relevant forum for our purposes is the CFC. Although petitioner is correct that as an initial matter a speaker must seek access to public property or to private property dedicated to public use to evoke First Amendment concerns, forum analysis is not completed merely by identifying the government property at issue. * * * Here, as in *Perry Education Assn.*, respondents seek access to a particular means of communication. Consistent with the approach taken in prior cases, we find that the CFC, rather than the federal workplace, is the forum. This conclusion does not mean, however, that the Court will ignore the special nature and function of the federal workplace in evaluating the limits that may be imposed on an organization's right to participate in the CFC. * * *

Having identified the forum as the CFC, we must decide whether it is nonpublic or public in nature. Most relevant in this regard, of course, is *Perry Education Assn.* There the Court identified three types of fora: the traditional public forum, the public forum created by government designation, and the nonpublic forum. Traditional public fora are those places which "by long tradition or by government fiat have been devoted to assembly and debate." 460 U.S., at 45. Public streets and parks fall into this category. See Hague v. CIO, 307 U.S. 496, 515 (1939). In addition to traditional public fora, a public forum may be created by government designation of a place or channel of communication for use by the public at large for assembly and speech, for use by certain speakers, or for the discussion of certain subjects. *Perry Education Assn., supra,* at 45 and 46, n. 7. Of course, the government "is not required to indefinitely retain the open character of the facility." *Id.,* at 46.

The government does not create a public forum by inaction or by permitting limited discourse, but only by intentionally opening a nontraditional forum for public discourse. *Ibid.* Accordingly, the Court has looked to the policy and practice of the government to ascertain whether it intended to designate a place not traditionally open to assembly and debate as a public forum. *Ibid.* The Court has also examined the nature of the property and its compatibility with expressive activity to discern the government's intent. For example, in Widmar v. Vincent, 454 U.S. 263 (1981), we found that a state university that had an express policy of making its meeting facilities available to registered student groups had created a public forum for their use. *Id.,* at 267. The policy evidenced a clear intent to create a public forum, notwithstanding the University's erroneous conclusion that the Establishment Clause required the exclusion of groups meeting for religious purposes. Additionally, we noted that a university campus, at least as to its students, possesses many of the characteristics of a traditional public forum. *Id.,* at 267, n. 5. And in Madison Joint School District v. Wisconsin Employment Relations Comm'n, 429 U.S. 167 (1976), the Court held that a forum for citizen involvement was created by a state statute providing for open school board meetings. *Id.,* at 174, n. 6. Similarly, the Court found a public forum where a municipal auditorium and a city-leased theater were designed for and dedicated to expressive activities. Southeastern Promotions, Ltd. v. Conrad, 420 U.S. 546, 555 (1975).

Not every instrumentality used for communication, however, is a traditional public forum or a public forum by designation. * * *

Here the parties agree that neither the CFC nor the federal workplace is a traditional public forum. Respondents argue, however, that the Government created a limited public forum for use by all charitable organizations to solicit funds from federal employees. Petitioner contends, and we agree, that neither its practice nor its policy is consistent with an intent to designate the CFC as a public forum open to all tax-exempt organizations. In 1980, an estimated 850,000 organizations qualified for tax-exempt status. * * *

Nor does the history of the CFC support a finding that the Government was motivated by an affirmative desire to provide an open forum for charitable solicitation in the federal workplace when it began the Campaign. The historical background indicates that the Campaign was designed to minimize the disruption to the workplace that had resulted from unlimited ad hoc solicitation activities by lessening the amount of expressive activity occurring on federal property. * * *

An examination of the nature of the Government property involved strengthens the conclusion that the CFC is a nonpublic forum. * * * The federal workplace, like any place of employment, exists to accomplish the business of the employer. * * * In light of the Government policy in creating the CFC and its practice in limiting access, we conclude that the CFC is a nonpublic forum.

C

Control over access to a nonpublic forum can be based on subject matter and speaker identity so long as the distinctions drawn are reasonable in light of the purpose served by the forum and are viewpoint neutral. *Perry Education Assn., supra,* at 49. Although a speaker may be excluded from a nonpublic forum if he wishes to address a topic not encompassed within the purpose of the forum, see Lehman v. City of Shaker Heights, 418 U.S. 298 (1974), or if he is not a member of the class of speakers for whose especial benefit the forum was created, see *Perry Education Assn., supra,* the government violates the First Amendment when it denies access to a speaker solely to suppress the point of view he espouses on an otherwise includible subject. The Court of Appeals found it unnecessary to resolve whether the government's denial of access to respondents was viewpoint based, because it determined that respondents' exclusion was unreasonable in light of the purpose served by the CFC.

Petitioner maintains that the purpose of the CFC is to provide a means for traditional health and welfare charities to solicit contributions in the federal workplace, while at the same time maximizing private support of social programs that would otherwise have to be supported by Government funds and minimizing costs to the Federal Government by controlling the time that federal employees expend on the Campaign. Petitioner posits that excluding agencies that attempt to influence the outcome of political elections or the determination of public policy is reasonable in light of this purpose. First, petitioner contends that there is likely to be a general consensus among employees that traditional health and welfare charities are worthwhile, as compared with the more diverse views concerning the goals of organizations like respondents. Limiting participation to widely accepted groups is likely to contribute significantly to employees' acceptance of the Campaign and consequently to its ultimate success. In addition, because the CFC is conducted largely through the efforts of federal employees during their working hours, any controversy surrounding the CFC would produce unwelcome disruption. Finally, the President determined that agencies seeking to affect the outcome of elections or the determination of public policy should be denied access to the CFC in order to avoid the reality and the appearance of Government favoritism or entanglement with particular viewpoints. In such circumstances, petitioner contends that the decision to deny access to such groups was reasonable.

In respondents' view, the reasonableness standard is satisfied only when there is some basic incompatibility between the communication at issue and the principal activity occurring on the Government property. Respondents contend that the purpose of the CFC is to permit solicitation by groups that provide health and welfare services. By permitting such solicitation to take place in the federal workplace, respondents maintain, the Government has concluded that such activity is consistent with the activities usually conducted here. Because respondents are seeking to solicit such contributions and their activities result in direct, tangible benefits to the groups they represent, the Government's attempt to exclude them is unreasonable. Respondents reject petitioner's justifications on the ground that they are unsupported by the record.

The Court of Appeals accepted the position advanced by respondents. When the excluded and included speakers share a similar "status," the court asserted that a heightened reasonableness inquiry is appropriate. Here the status of respondents, in the court's view, is analogous to that of traditional health and welfare organizations, because both provide direct health and welfare services and are tax exempt under 26 U.S.C. § 501(c)(3). * * *

* * *

Based on the present record, we disagree and conclude that respondents may be excluded from the CFC. The Court of Appeals' conclusion to the contrary fails to reflect the nature of a nonpublic forum. The Government's decision to restrict access to a nonpublic forum need only be reasonable; it need not be the most reasonable or the only reasonable limitation. In contrast to a public forum, a finding of strict incompatibility between the nature of the speech or the identity of the speaker and the functioning of the nonpublic forum is not mandated. * * * Even if some incompatibility with general expressive activity were required, the CFC would meet the requirement because it would be administratively unmanageable if access could not be curtailed in a reasonable manner. Nor is there a requirement that the restriction be narrowly tailored or that the Government's interest be compelling. The First Amendment does not demand unrestricted access to a nonpublic forum merely because use of that forum may be the most efficient means of delivering the speaker's message. See United States Postal Service v. Council of Greenburgh Civic Assns., 453 U.S., at 129. Rarely will a nonpublic forum provide the only means of contact with a particular audience. Here, as in *Perry Education Assn., supra,* at 53–54, the speakers have access to alternative channels, including direct mail and in-person solicitation outside the workplace, to solicit contributions from federal employees.

The reasonableness of the Government's restriction of access to a nonpublic forum must be assessed in the light of the purpose of the forum and all the surrounding circumstances. Here the President could reasonably conclude that a dollar directly spent on providing food or shelter to the needy is more beneficial than a dollar spent on litigation that might or might not result in aid to the needy. Moreover, avoiding the appearance of political favoritism is a valid justification for limiting speech in a nonpublic forum. See Greer v. Spock, 424 U.S., at 839; *Lehman v. City of Shaker Heights, supra,* at 304. In furthering this interest, the Government is not bound by decisions of other executive agencies made in other contexts. Thus, respondents' tax status, while perhaps relevant, does not determine the reasonableness of the Government's conclusion that participation by such agencies in the CFC will create the appearance of favoritism.

* * *

Finally, the record amply supports an inference that respondents' participation in the CFC jeopardized the success of the Campaign. OPM submitted a number of letters from federal employees and managers, as well as from Chairmen of local Federal Coordinating Committees and Members of Congress expressing concern about the inclusion of groups termed "political" or "nontraditional" in the CFC. * * * [T]he record adequately supported petitioner's position that respondents' continued participation in the Campaign would be detrimental to the Campaign and disruptive of the federal workplace. Although the avoidance of controversy is not a valid ground for restricting speech in a public forum, a nonpublic forum by definition is not dedicated to general debate or the free exchange of ideas. The First Amendment does not forbid a viewpoint-neutral exclusion of speakers who would disrupt a nonpublic forum and hinder its effectiveness for its intended purpose.

D

* * *

Petitioner argues that a decision to exclude all advocacy groups, regardless of political or philosophical orientation, is by definition viewpoint neutral. Brief for Petitioner 30. Exclusion of groups advocating the use of litigation is not viewpoint-based, petitioner asserts, because litigation is a means of promoting a viewpoint, not a viewpoint in itself. *Id.*, at 30–31, n. 23. While we accept the validity and reasonableness of the justifications offered by petitioner for excluding advocacy groups from the CFC, those justifications cannot save an exclusion that is in fact based on the desire to suppress a particular point of view. * * *

* * * We decline to decide in the first instance whether the exclusion of respondents was impermissibly motivated by a desire to suppress a particular point of view. Respondents are free to pursue this contention on remand.

III

We conclude that the Government does not violate the First Amendment when it limits participation in the CFC in order to minimize disruption to the federal workplace, to ensure the success of the fundraising effort, or to avoid the appearance of political favoritism without regard to the viewpoint of the excluded groups. Accordingly, we reverse the judgment of the Court of Appeals that the exclusion of respondents was unreasonable, and we remand this case for further proceedings consistent with this opinion.

It is so ordered.

JUSTICE MARSHALL took no part in the consideration or decision of this case. JUSTICE POWELL took no part in the decision of this case.

JUSTICE BLACKMUN, with whom JUSTICE BRENNAN joins, dissenting.

I agree with the Court that the Combined Federal Campaign (CFC) is not a traditional public forum. I also agree with the Court that our precedents indicate that the Government may create a "forum by designation" (or, to use the term our cases have adopted, a "limited public forum") by allowing public property that traditionally has not been available for assembly and debate to be used as a place for expressive activity by certain speakers or about certain subjects. I cannot accept, however, the Court's circular reasoning that the CFC is not a limited public forum because the Government intended to limit the forum to a particular class of speakers. Nor can I agree with the Court's conclusion that distinctions the Government makes between speakers in defining the limits of a forum need not be narrowly tailored and necessary to achieve a compelling governmental interest. Finally, I would hold that the exclusion of the several respondents from the CFC was, on its face, viewpoint-based discrimination. Accordingly, I dissent.

I

The Court recognizes that its decisions regarding the right of a citizen to engage in expressive activity on public property generally have divided public property into three categories—public forums, limited public forums, and nonpublic forums. The Court also concedes, as it must, that "a public forum * * * created by government designation of a place or channel of communication for use by the public at large for assembly and speech, for use by certain speakers, or for the discussion of certain subjects" is a limited public forum. * * * It nevertheless goes on to find that the CFC is not a limited public forum precisely because the "Government's consistent policy has been to limit participation in the CFC" to certain speakers. * * * Because the Government intended to exclude some speakers from the CFC, the Court continues, the Government may exclude any speaker from the CFC on any "reasonable" ground, except viewpoint discrimination. In essence, the Court today holds that the First Amendment's guarantee of free speech and assembly, a "fundamental principle of the American government," Whitney v. California, 274 U.S. 357, 375 (1927) (BRANDEIS, J., concurring), reduces to this: when the Government acts as the holder of public property other than streets, parks, and similar places, the Government may do whatever it reasonably intends to do, so long as it does not intend to suppress a particular viewpoint.

The Court's analysis transforms the First Amendment into a mere ban on viewpoint censorship, ignores the principles underlying the public forum doctrine, flies in the face of the decisions in which the Court has identified property as a limited public forum, and empties the limited-public-forum concept of all its meaning.

A

The public forum doctrine arose out of the Court's efforts to address the recurring and troublesome issue of when the First Amendment gives an individual or group the right to engage in expressive activity on government property. * * *

Access to government property can be crucially important to those who wish to exercise their First Amendment rights. Government property often provides the only space suitable for large gatherings, and it often attracts audiences that are otherwise difficult to reach. Access to government property permits the use of the less costly means of communication so "essential to the poorly financed causes of little people," Martin v. Struthers, 319 U.S. 141, 146 (1943), and "allow[s] challenge to governmental action at its locus." Cass, First Amendment Access to Government Facilities, 65 Va.L.Rev. 1287, 1288 (1979).

* * *

At the same time, however, expressive activity on government property may interfere with other important activities for which the property is used. Accordingly, in answering the question whether a person has a right to engage in expressive activity on government property, the Court has recognized that the person's right to speak and the interests that such speech serves for society as a whole must be balanced against the "other interests inhering in the uses to which the public property is normally put." * * *

* * * Broad generalizations about the proper balance are, for the most part, impossible. The Court has stated one firm guideline, however: the First Amendment does not guarantee that one may engage in expressive activity on government property when the expressive activity would be incompatible with important purposes of the property. * * *

In applying that principle, the Court has found that public places generally may be divided into three categories. The first, the "quintessential public forums," includes those places "which by long tradition or by government fiat have been devoted to assembly and debate," such as parks, streets, and sidewalks. * * *

* * * In a limited public forum, it is not history or tradition, but the government's own acquiescence in the use of the property as a forum for expressive activity that tells us that such activity is compatible with the uses to which the place is normally put.

In both public and limited public forums, because at least some types of expressive activity obviously are compatible with the normal uses of the property, the Court has recognized that people generally have a First Amendment right to engage in expressive activity upon the property. As noted above, however, the Court has observed that the right to engage in expressive activity on public property is not absolute, and must be balanced against interests served by the other uses to which the property is put. Accordingly, the Court has held that the government may regulate the time, place, and manner of the expressive activity in order to accommodate the "interest of all" members of the public to enjoy the use of the public space, Hague v. CIO, 307 U.S., at 516, and in order to treat fairly all those who have an equal right to speak on the property. Cox v. New Hampshire, 312 U.S., at 574. Such restrictions must be "justified without reference to the content of the regulated speech," be "narrowly tailored to serve a significant governmental interest," and "leave open ample alternative channels for communication." Clark v. Community for Creative Non-Violence, 468 U.S. 288, 293 (1984); United States v. Grace, 461 U.S., at 177; *Perry,* 460 U.S., at 45; *Heffron,* 452 U.S., at 647–648.

The Court has held that regulations other than time, place, and manner restrictions must be necessary to serve a compelling governmental interest and must be narrowly tailored to achieve that purpose. *Perry,* 460 U.S., at 45; see also Carey v. Brown, 447 U.S., at 465; Police Department of Chicago v. Mosley, 408 U.S., at 96–97. Again, however, because First Amendment rights must be "applied in light of the special characteristics of the * * * environment," *Tinker,* 393 U.S., at 506, the Court has recognized that a regulation that would not survive scrutiny if applied in the context of a public forum sometimes will be allowed in the context of a limited public forum. Restrictions based on the subject matter of the speech, for example, will almost never be justified in a public forum such as a park, but will more often be justified as necessary to reserve the limited public forum to expressive activity compatible with the property. See, e.g., *Madison Joint School District,* 429 U.S., at 175, n. 8. In a traditional public forum, the government rarely could offer as a compelling interest the need to reserve the property for its normal uses, because expressive activity of all types traditionally has been a normal use of the property. In a limited public forum, on the other hand, the need to confine expressive activity on the property to that which is compatible with the intended uses of the property will be a compelling interest that may justify distinctions made between speakers.

* * *

The line between limited public forums and nonpublic forums "may blur at the edges," and is really more in the nature of a continuum than a definite demarcation. * * *

Further, the three categories are not exclusive. There are instances in which property has not traditionally been used for a particular form of expressive activity, and the government has not acquiesced, but the Court's examination of the nature of the forum and the nature of the expressive activity led it to conclude that the activity was compatible with normal uses of the property and was to be allowed. See, e.g., Brown v. Louisiana, 383 U.S. 131, 142 (1966) (plurality opinion); *id.,* at 148 (BRENNAN, J., concurring in judgment); *id.,* at 150 (WHITE, J., concurring in result).

Thus, the public forum, limited-public-forum, and nonpublic forum categories are but analytical shorthand for the principles that have guided the Court's decisions regarding claims to access to public property for expressive activity. The interests served by the expressive activity must be balanced against the interests served by the uses for which the property was intended and the interests of all citizens to enjoy the property. Where an examination of all the relevant interests indicates that certain expressive activity is not compatible with the normal uses of the property, the First Amendment does not require the government to allow that activity.

The Court's analysis, it seems to me, turns these principles on end. Rather than recognize that a nonpublic forum is a place where expressive activity would be incompatible with the purposes the property is intended to serve, the Court states that a nonpublic forum is a place where we need not even be concerned about whether expressive activity is incompatible with the purposes of the property. Rather than taking the nature of the property into account in balancing the First Amendment interests of the speaker and society's interests in freedom of speech against the interests served by reserving the property to its normal use, the Court simply labels the property and dispenses with the balancing.

* * * The Court offers no explanation why attaching the label "nonpublic forum" to particular property frees the Government of the more stringent constraints imposed by the First Amendment in other contexts. The Government's interests in being able to use the property for the purposes for which it was intended obviously are important; that is why a compatibility requirement is imposed. * * * Similarly, the mere fact that the Government acts as property owner should not exempt it from the First Amendment.

Nor should tradition or governmental "designation" be completely determinative of the rights of a citizen to speak on public property. Many places that are natural sites for expressive activity have no long tradition of use for expressive activity. Airports, for example, are a relatively recent phenomenon, as are government-sponsored shopping centers. Other public places may have no history of expressive activity because only recently have they become associated with the issue that citizens wish to use the property to discuss. It is likely that the library in *Brown v. Louisiana, supra,* historically had not been used for demonstrations for the obvious reason that its association with the subject of segregation became a topic of public protest only during the civil rights movement.[2] Another reason a particular parcel of property may have little history of expressive use is that the Government has excluded expressive activity from the property unjustifiably. Cf. United States v. Grace, 461 U.S., at 180.

The guarantees of the First Amendment should not turn entirely on either an accident of history or the grace of the Government. Thus, the fact that the Government "owns" the property to which a citizen seeks access for expressive activity does not dispose of the First Amendment claim; it requires that we balance the First Amendment interests of those who seek access for expressive activity against the interests of the other users of the property and the interests served by reserving the property for its intended uses. The Court's analysis forsakes that balancing, and abandons the compatibility test that always has served as a threshold indicator of the proper balance.

B

Not only does the Court err in labeling the CFC a nonpublic forum without first engaging in a compatibility inquiry, but it errs as well in reasoning that the CFC is not a limited public forum because the Government permitted only "limited discourse," rather than "intentionally opening" the CFC for "public discourse." * * * That reasoning is at odds with the cases in which the Court has found public property to be a limited public forum. Just as the Government's "consistent policy has been to limit participation in the CFC to 'appropriate' voluntary agencies and to require agencies seeking admission to obtain permission" from the relevant officials, * * *, the theater in Southeastern Promotions, Ltd. v. Conrad, 420 U.S. 546 (1975), limited the use of its facilities to "clean, healthful entertainment which will make for the upbuilding of a better citizenship" and required productions wishing to use the theater to obtain permission of the relevant officials. See *id.,* at 549, n. 4. Under the Court's reasoning, therefore, the theater in *Southeastern Promotions* would not have been a limited public forum. * * *

* * *

The Court would point to three "justifications" for the exclusion of respondents. First, the Court states that "the President could reason-

---

2. See generally Note, A Unitary Approach to Claims of First Amendment Access to Publicly Owned Property, 35 Stan. L.Rev. 121, 137 (1982).

ably conclude that a dollar directly spent on providing food or shelter to the needy is more beneficial than a dollar spent on litigation that might or might not result in aid to the needy." * * * I fail to see how the President's view of the relative benefits obtained by various charitable activities translates into a compelling governmental interest. The Government may have a compelling interest in increasing charitable contributions because charities provide services that the Government otherwise would have to provide. But that interest does not justify the exclusion of respondents, for respondents work to enforce the rights of minorities, women, and others through litigation, a task that various Government agencies otherwise might be called upon to undertake.

In any event, the fact that the President or his advisers may believe the money is best "directly spent on providing food or shelter to the needy" starkly fails to explain why respondents are excluded from the CFC while other groups that do not spend money to provide food or shelter directly to the needy are allowed to be included. * * *

The Court next states that "avoiding the appearance of political favoritism is a valid justification for limiting speech in a nonpublic forum." * * * The Court, however, flatly has rejected that justification in the context of limited public forums. Widmar v. Vincent, 454 U.S., at 274. In addition, petitioner's proffered justification again fails to explain why respondents are excluded when other groups, such as the National Right to Life Educational Trust Fund and Planned Parenthood, at least one of which the Government presumably would wish to avoid the appearance of supporting, are allowed to participate. And petitioner offers no explanation why a simple disclaimer in the brochure would not suffice to achieve the Government's interest in avoiding the appearance of support.

Nor is the Government's "interest in avoiding controversy" a compelling state interest that would justify the exclusion of respondents. The managers of the theater in *Southeastern Promotions* no doubt thought the exclusion of the rock musical "Hair" was necessary to avoid controversy, see 420 U.S., at 563–564 (DOUGLAS, J., dissenting in part and concurring in result in part); and the school officials in *Tinker* thought their exclusion of students protesting the activities of the United States in Vietnam was necessary to avoid controversy, see 393 U.S., at 509–510. Yet in those cases, both of which involved limited public forums, the Court did not accept the mere avoidance of controversy as a compelling governmental interest. Rather, the Court in *Tinker* held that in order to justify the exclusion of particular expressive activity, the government "must be able to show that its action was caused by something more than a mere desire to avoid the discomfort and unpleasantness that always accompany an unpopular viewpoint." 393 U.S., at 509. The government instead must show that the excluded speech would " 'materially and substantially interfere' " with the other activities for which the public property was intended. * * *

No such showing has been made here. * * *

Further, even if the avoidance of controversy in the forum itself could ever serve as a legitimate governmental purpose, the record here does not support a finding that the inclusion of respondents in the CFC threatened a material and substantial disruption. In fact, the evidence shows that contributions to the CFC increased during each of the years respondents participated in the Campaign. See Brief for Respondents 34 and sources cited therein. The "hundreds" of phone calls and letters expressing a preference that groups other than "traditional" charities be excluded from the CFC reflect nothing more than the discomfort that can be expected whenever a change is made, and whenever any opinion is expressed on a topic of concern to the huge force in 1983 of some 2.7 million civilian federal employees. The letters objecting to the inclusion of respondents in the Campaign must be considered against the fact that many federal employees obviously supported their inclusion in the CFC, as is evidenced by the substantial contributions respondents received through the Campaign.

It is true that unions organized boycotts of the CFC in some areas because of their opposition to the participation in the CFC of the National Right to Work Legal Defense and Education Fund, and that, in those areas, contributions sometimes declined. But the evidence also showed that after some initial confusion regarding whether the organization the unions found objectionable was receiving undesignated contributions, the major unions urged their members simply to designate their contributions so that none went to that group. * * *

* * *

I would affirm the judgment of the Court of Appeals.

JUSTICE STEVENS, dissenting. [Omitted.]

HAZELWOOD SCHOOL DISTRICT v. KUHLMEIER

Supreme Court of the United States, 1988.
484 U.S. 260, 108 S.Ct. 562, 98 L.Ed.2d 592.

JUSTICE WHITE delivered the opinion of the Court.

This case concerns the extent to which educators may exercise editorial control over the contents of a high school newspaper produced as part of the school's journalism curriculum.

I

Petitioners are the Hazelwood School District in St. Louis County, Missouri; various school officials; Robert Eugene Reynolds, the principal of Hazelwood East High School, and Howard Emerson, a teacher in the school district. Respondents are three former Hazelwood East students who were staff members of Spectrum, the school newspaper. They contend that school officials violated their First Amendment rights by deleting two pages of articles from the May 13, 1983, issue of Spectrum.

Spectrum was written and edited by the Journalism II class at Hazelwood East. The newspaper was published every three weeks or so during the 1982–1983 school year. More than 4,500 copies of the newspaper were distributed during that year to students, school personnel, and members of the community.

The Board of Education allocated funds from its annual budget for the printing of Spectrum. These funds were supplemented by proceeds from sales of the newspaper. The printing expenses during the 1982–1983 school year totaled $4,668.50; revenue from sales was $1,166.84. The other costs associated with the newspaper—such as supplies, textbooks, and a portion of the journalism teacher's salary—were borne entirely by the Board.

The Journalism II course was taught by Robert Stergos for most of the 1982–1983 academic year. Stergos left Hazelwood East to take a job in private industry on April 29, 1983, when the May 13 edition of Spectrum was nearing completion, and petitioner Emerson took his place as newspaper adviser for the remaining weeks of the term.

The practice at Hazelwood East during the spring 1983 semester was for the journalism teacher to submit page proofs of each Spectrum issue to Principal Reynolds for his review prior to publication. On May 10, Emerson delivered the proofs of the May 13 edition to Reynolds, who objected to two of the articles scheduled to appear in that edition. One of the stories described three Hazelwood East students' experiences with pregnancy; the other discussed the impact of divorce on students at the school.

Reynolds was concerned that, although the pregnancy story used false names "to keep the identity of these girls a secret," the pregnant students still might be identifiable from the text. He also believed that the article's references to sexual activity and birth control were inappropriate for some of the younger students at the school. In addition, Reynolds was concerned that a student identified by name in the divorce story had complained that her father "wasn't spending enough time with my mom, my sister and I" prior to the divorce, "was always out of town on business or out late playing cards with the guys," and "always argued about everything" with her mother. App. to Pet. for Cert. 38. Reynolds believed that the student's parents should have been given an opportunity to respond to these remarks or to consent to their publication. He was unaware that Emerson had deleted the student's name from the final version of the article.

Reynolds believed that there was no time to make the necessary changes in the stories before the scheduled press run and that the newspaper would not appear before the end of the school year if printing were delayed to any significant extent. He concluded that his only options under the circumstances were to publish a four-page newspaper instead of the planned six-page newspaper, eliminating the two pages on which the offending stories appeared, or to publish no newspaper at all. Accordingly, he directed Emerson to withhold from publication the two pages containing the stories on pregnancy and divorce.[1] He informed his superiors of the decision, and they concurred.

1. The two pages deleted from the newspaper also contained articles on teen-

Respondents subsequently commenced this action in the United States District Court for the Eastern District of Missouri seeking a declaration that their First Amendment rights had been violated, injunctive relief, and monetary damages. After a bench trial, the District Court denied an injunction, holding that no First Amendment violation had occurred. 607 F.Supp. 1450 (1985).

* * *

The Court of Appeals for the Eighth Circuit reversed. 795 F.2d 1368 (1986). The court held at outset that Spectrum was not only "a part of the school adopted curriculum," *id.*, at 1373, but also a public forum, because the newspaper was "intended to be and operated as a conduit for student viewpoint." *Id.* at 1372. * * *

* * *

We granted certiorari, * * *, and we now reverse.

* * *

We deal first with the question whether Spectrum may appropriately be characterized as a forum for public expression. The public schools do not possess all of the attributes of streets, parks, and other traditional public forums that "time out of mind, have been used for purposes of assembly, communicating thoughts between citizens, and discussing public questions." Hague v. CIO, 307 U.S. 496, 515 (1939). Cf. Widmar v. Vincent, 454 U.S. 263, 267–268, n. 5 (1981). Hence, school facilities may be deemed to be public forums only if school authorities have "by policy or by practice" opened those facilities "for indiscriminate use by the general public," Perry Education Assn. v. Perry Local Educators' Assn., 460 U.S. 37, 47 (1983), or by some segment of the public, such as student organizations. If the facilities have instead been reserved for other intended purposes, "communicative or otherwise," then no public forum has been created, and school officials may impose reasonable restrictions on the speech of students, teachers, and other members of the school community. * * *

* * *

The evidence relied upon by the Court of Appeals in finding Spectrum to be a public forum, see 795 F.2d, at 1372–1373, is equivocal at best. For example, Board Policy 348.51, which stated in part that "[s]chool sponsored student publications will not restrict free expression or diverse viewpoints within the rules of responsible journalism," also stated that such publications were "developed within the adopted curriculum and its educational implications." App. 22. One might reasonably infer from the full text of Policy 348.51 that school officials retained ultimate control over what constituted "responsible journalism" in a school-sponsored newspaper. Although the Statement of Policy published in the September 14, 1982, issue of Spectrum declared that "Spectrum, as a student-press publication, accepts all rights im-

---

age marriage, runaways, and juvenile delinquents, as well as a general article on teenage pregnancy. Reynolds testified that he had no objection to these articles and that they were deleted only because they appeared on the same pages as the two objectionable articles.

plied by the First Amendment," this statement, understood in the context of the paper's role in the school's curriculum, suggests at most that the administration will not interfere with the students' exercise of those First Amendment rights that attend the publication of a school-sponsored newspaper. It does not reflect an intent to expand those rights by converting a curricular newspaper into a public forum. Finally, that students were permitted to exercise some authority over the contents of Spectrum was fully consistent with the Curriculum Guide objective of teaching the Journalism II students "leadership responsibilities as issue and page editors." App. 11. A decision to teach leadership skills in the context of a classroom activity hardly implies a decision to relinquish school control over that activity. In sum, the evidence relied upon by the Court of Appeals fails to demonstrate the "clear intent to create a public forum," *Cornelius,* 473 U.S., at 802, that existed in cases in which we found public forums to have been created. * * * Instead, they "reserve[d] the forum for its intended purpos[e]," *id.,* at 46, as a supervised learning experience for journalism students. Accordingly, school officials were entitled to regulate the contents of Spectrum in any reasonable manner. It is this standard, rather than our decision in *Tinker,* that governs this case.

B

The question whether the First Amendment requires a school to tolerate particular student speech—the question that we addressed in *Tinker*—is different from the question whether the First Amendment requires a school affirmatively to promote particular student speech. The former question addresses educators' ability to silence a student's personal expression that happens to occur on the school premises. The latter question concerns educators' authority over school-sponsored publications, theatrical productions, and other expressive activities that students, parents, and members of the public might reasonably perceive to bear the imprimatur of the school. These activities may fairly be characterized as part of the school curriculum, whether or not they occur in a traditional classroom setting, so long as they are supervised by faculty members and designed to impart particular knowledge or skills to student participants and audiences.[3]

Educators are entitled to exercise greater control over this second form of student expression to assure that participants learn whatever lessons the activity is designed to teach, that readers or listeners are not exposed to material that may be inappropriate for their level of maturity, and that the views of the individual speaker are not erroneously attributed to the school. * * * A school must also retain the authority to refuse to sponsor student speech that might reasonably be perceived to advocate drug or alcohol use, irresponsible sex, or conduct otherwise inconsistent with "the shared values of a civilized social order," *Fraser, supra,* [478 U.S.], at 683 or to associate the school with

---

3. The distinction that we draw between speech that is sponsored by the school and speech that is not is fully consistent with Papish v. Board of Curators, 410 U.S. 667 (1973) (per curiam), which involved an off-campus "underground" newspaper that school officials merely had allowed to be sold on a state university campus.

any position other than neutrality on matters of political controversy. * * *

Accordingly, we conclude that the standard articulated in *Tinker* for determining when a school may punish student expression need not also be the standard for determining when a school may refuse to lend its name and resources to the dissemination of student expression. Instead, we hold that educators do not offend the First Amendment by exercising editorial control over the style and content of student speech in school-sponsored expressive activities so long as their actions are reasonably related to legitimate pedagogical concerns.

This standard is consistent with our oft-expressed view that the education of the Nation's youth is primarily the responsibility of parents, teachers, and state and local school officials and not of federal judges. * * * It is only when the decision to censor a school-sponsored publication, theatrical production, or other vehicle of student expression has no valid educational purpose that the First Amendment is so "directly and sharply implicate[d]," *ibid.*, as to require judicial intervention to protect students' constitutional rights.[7]

We also conclude that Principal Reynolds acted reasonably in requiring the deletion from the May 13 issue of Spectrum of the pregnancy article, the divorce article, and the remaining articles that were to appear on the same pages of the newspaper.

The initial paragraph of the pregnancy article declared that "[a]ll names have been changed to keep the identity of these girls a secret." The principal concluded that the students' anonymity was not adequately protected, however, given the other identifying information in the article and the small number of pregnant students at the school. Indeed, a teacher at the school credibly testified that she could positively identify at least one of the girls and possibly all three. It is likely that many students at Hazelwood East would have been at least as successful in identifying the girls. Reynolds therefore could reasonably have feared that the article violated whatever pledge of anonymity had been given to the pregnant students. In addition, he could reasonably have been concerned that the article was not sufficiently sensitive to the privacy interests of the students' boyfriends and parents, who were discussed in the article but who were given no opportunity to consent to its publication or to offer a response. The article did not contain graphic accounts of sexual activity. The girls did comment in the article, however, concerning their sexual histories and their use or nonuse of birth control. It was not unreasonable for the principal to have concluded that such frank talk was inappropriate in a school-sponsored publication distributed to 14-year-old freshmen and presumably taken home to be read by students' even younger brothers and sisters.

The student who was quoted by name in the version of the divorce article seen by Principal Reynolds made comments sharply critical of her father. The principal could reasonably have concluded that an

---

7. * * * We need not now decide whether the same degree of deference is appropriate with respect to school-sponsored expressive activities at the college and university level.

individual publicly identified as an inattentive parent—indeed, as one who chose "playing cards with the guys" over home and family—was entitled to an opportunity to defend himself as a matter of journalistic fairness. These concerns were shared by both of Spectrum's faculty advisers for the 1982–1983 school year, who testified that they would not have allowed the article to be printed without deletion of the student's name.[8]

Principal Reynolds testified credibly at trial that, at the time that he reviewed the proofs of the May 13 issue during an extended telephone conversation with Emerson, he believed that there was no time to make any changes in the articles, and that the newspaper had to be printed immediately or not at all. It is true that Reynolds did not verify whether the necessary modifications could still have been made in the articles, and that Emerson did not volunteer the information that printing could be delayed until the changes were made. We nonetheless agree with the District Court that the decision to excise the two pages containing the problematic articles was reasonable given the particular circumstances of this case. These circumstances included the very recent replacement of Stergos by Emerson, who may not have been entirely familiar with Spectrum editorial and production procedures, and the pressure felt by Reynolds to make an immediate decision so that students would not be deprived of the newspaper altogether.

In sum, we cannot reject as unreasonable Principal Reynolds' conclusion that neither the pregnancy article nor the divorce article was suitable for publication in Spectrum. Reynolds could reasonably have concluded that the students who had written and edited these articles had not sufficiently mastered those portions of the Journalism II curriculum that pertained to the treatment of controversial issues and personal attacks, the need to protect the privacy of individuals whose most intimate concerns are to be revealed in the newspaper, and "the legal, moral, and ethical restrictions imposed upon journalists within [a] school community" that includes adolescent subjects and readers. Finally, we conclude that the principal's decision to delete two pages of Spectrum, rather than to delete only the offending articles or to require that they be modified, was reasonable under the circumstances as he understood them. Accordingly, no violation of First Amendment rights occurred.[9]

---

8. The reasonableness of Principal Reynolds' concerns about the two articles was further substantiated by the trial testimony of Martin Duggan, a former editorial page editor of the St. Louis Globe Democrat and a former college journalism instructor and newspaper adviser. Duggan testified that the divorce story did not meet journalistic standards of fairness and balance because the father was not given an opportunity to respond, and that the pregnancy story was not appropriate for publication in a high school newspaper because it was unduly intrusive into the privacy of the girls, their parents, and their boyfriends. The District Court found Duggan to be "an objective and independent witness" whose testimony was entitled to significant weight. 607 F.Supp. 1450, 1461 (ED Mo.1985).

9. It is likely that the approach urged by the dissent would as a practical matter have far more deleterious consequences for the student press than does the approach that we adopt today. The dissent correctly acknowledges "[t]he State's prerogative to dissolve the student newspaper entirely." * * * It is likely that many public schools would do just that rather than open their newspapers to all student expression that does not threaten "materia[l] disrup[tion

The judgment of the Court of Appeals for the Eighth Circuit is therefore

Reversed.

JUSTICE BRENNAN, with whom JUSTICE MARSHALL and JUSTICE BLACKMUN join, dissenting.

* * *

Public education serves vital national interests in preparing the Nation's youth for life in our increasingly complex society and for the duties of citizenship in our democratic Republic. See Brown v. Board of Education, 347 U.S. 483, 493 (1954). The public school conveys to our young the information and tools required not merely to survive in, but to contribute to, civilized society. It also inculcates in tomorrow's leaders the "fundamental values necessary to the maintenance of a democratic political system * * *." Ambach v. Norwick, 441 U.S. 68, 77 (1979). All the while, the public educator nurtures students' social and moral development by transmitting to them an official dogma of "'community values.'" Board of Education v. Pico, 457 U.S. 853, 864 (1982) (plurality opinion) (citation omitted).

The public educator's task is weighty and delicate indeed. It demands particularized and supremely subjective choices among diverse curricula, moral values, and political stances to teach or inculcate in students, and among various methodologies for doing so. Accordingly, we have traditionally reserved the "daily operation of school systems" to the States and their local school boards. * * * We have not, however, hesitated to intervene where their decisions run afoul of the Constitution. * * *

Free student expression undoubtedly sometimes interferes with the effectiveness of the school's pedagogical functions. Some brands of student expression do so by directly preventing the school from pursuing its pedagogical mission: The young polemic who stands on a soapbox during calculus class to deliver an eloquent political diatribe interferes with the legitimate teaching of calculus. * * * Other student speech, however, frustrates the school's legitimate pedagogical purposes merely by expressing a message that conflicts with the school's, without directly interfering with the school's expression of its message: A student who responds to a political science teacher's question with the retort, "Socialism is good," subverts the school's inculcation of the message that capitalism is better. Even the maverick who sits in class passively sporting a symbol of protest against a government policy, cf. *Tinker,* 393 U.S. 503 (1969), or the gossip who sits in the student commons swapping stories of sexual escapade could readily muddle a clear official message condoning the government policy or condemning teenage sex. Likewise, the student newspaper that, like Spectrum, conveys a moral position at odds with the school's

of] classwork" or violation of "rights that are protected by law," * * *, regardless of how sexually explicit, racially intemperate, or personally insulting that expression otherwise might be.

official stance might subvert the administration's legitimate inculcation of its own perception of community values.

If mere incompatibility with the school's pedagogical message were a constitutionally sufficient justification for the suppression of student speech, school officials could censor each of the students or student organizations in the foregoing hypotheticals, converting our public schools into "enclaves of totalitarianism," *id.*, at 511, that "strangle the free mind at its source," *West Virginia State Board of Education v. Barnette, supra,* at 637. The First Amendment permits no such blanket censorship authority. * * * [P]ublic educators must accommodate some student expression even if it offends them or offers views or values that contradict those the school wishes to inculcate.

* * *

* * * The Court today casts no doubt on *Tinker*'s vitality. Instead it erects a taxonomy of school censorship, concluding that *Tinker* applies to one category and not another. On the one hand is censorship "to silence a student's personal expression that happens to occur on the school premises." * * * On the other hand is censorship of expression that arises in the context of "school-sponsored * * * expressive activities that students, parents, and members of the public might reasonably perceive to bear the imprimatur of the school."

The Court does not, for it cannot, purport to discern from our precedents the distinction it creates. * * *

Nor has this Court ever intimated a distinction between personal and school-sponsored speech in any other context. Particularly telling is this Court's heavy reliance on *Tinker* in two cases of First Amendment infringement on state college campuses. See Papish v. University of Missouri Board of Curators, 410 U.S. 667, 671, n. 6 (1973) (per curiam); Healy v. James, 408 U.S. 169, 180, 189, and n. 18, 191 (1972). One involved the expulsion of a student for lewd expression in a newspaper that she sold on campus pursuant to university authorization, * * *, and the other involved the denial of university recognition and concomitant benefits to a political student organization, * * *. Tracking *Tinker*'s analysis, the Court found each act of suppression unconstitutional. In neither case did this Court suggest the distinction, which the Court today finds dispositive, between school-sponsored and incidental student expression.

II

Even if we were writing on a clean slate, I would reject the Court's rationale for abandoning *Tinker* in this case. The Court offers no more than an obscure tangle of three excuses to afford educators "greater control" over school-sponsored speech than the *Tinker* test would permit: the public educator's prerogative to control curriculum; the pedagogical interest in shielding the high school audience from objectionable viewpoints and sensitive topics; and the school's need to dissociate itself from student expression. * * * None of the excuses, once disentangled, supports the distinction that the Court draws. *Tinker* fully addresses the first concern; the second is illegitimate; and the third is readily achievable through less oppressive means.

A
* * *

The Court relies on bits of testimony to portray the principal's conduct as a pedagogical lesson to Journalism II students who "had not sufficiently mastered those portions of the ... curriculum that pertained to the treatment of controversial issues and personal attacks, the need to protect the privacy of individuals * * *, and 'the legal, moral, and ethical restrictions imposed upon journalists....'" * * *

But the principal never consulted the students before censoring their work. "[T]hey learned of the deletions when the paper was released * * *." 795 F.2d, at 1371. Further, he explained the deletions only in the broadest of generalities. * * * The Court's supposition that the principal intended (or the protesters understood) those generalities as a lesson on the nuances of journalistic responsibility is utterly incredible. If he did, a fact that neither the District Court nor the Court of Appeals found, the lesson was lost on all but the psychic Spectrum staffer.

B

The Court's second excuse for deviating from precedent is the school's interest in shielding an impressionable high school audience from material whose substance is "unsuitable for immature audiences." * * * Specifically, the majority decrees that we must afford educators authority to shield high school students from exposure to "potentially sensitive topics" (like "the particulars of teenage sexual activity") or unacceptable social viewpoints (like the advocacy of "irresponsible se[x] or conduct otherwise inconsistent with 'the shared values of a civilized social order'") through school-sponsored student activities. * * *

Tinker teaches us that the state educator's undeniable, and undeniably vital, mandate to inculcate moral and political values is not a general warrant to act as "thought police" stifling discussion of all but state-approved topics and advocacy of all but the official position. * * *

The mere fact of school sponsorship does not, as the Court suggests, license such thought control in the high school, whether through school suppression of disfavored viewpoints or through official assessment of topic sensitivity. The former would constitute unabashed and unconstitutional viewpoint discrimination, see Board of Education v. Pico, 457 U.S., at 878–879 (BLACKMUN, J., concurring in part and concurring in judgment), as well as an impermissible infringement of the students' "'right to receive information and ideas,'" *id.,* at 867 * * * The State's prerogative to dissolve the student newspaper entirely (or to limit its subject matter) no more entitles it to dictate which viewpoints students may express on its pages, than the State's prerogative to close down the schoolhouse entitles it to prohibit the nondisruptive expression of antiwar sentiment within its gates.

Official censorship of student speech on the ground that it addresses "potentially sensitive topics" is, for related reasons, equally impermissible. I would not begrudge an educator the authority to limit the substantive scope of a school-sponsored publication to a certain, objectively definable topic, such as literary criticism, school sports, or an overview of the school year. Unlike those determinate limitations, "potential topic sensitivity" is a vaporous nonstandard—like " 'public welfare, peace, safety, health, decency, good order, morals or convenience,' " * * *—that invites manipulation to achieve ends that cannot permissibly be achieved through blatant viewpoint discrimination and chills student speech to which school officials might not object. * * *

The case before us aptly illustrates how readily school officials (and courts) can camouflage viewpoint discrimination as the "mere" protection of students from sensitive topics. Among the grounds that the Court advances to uphold the principal's censorship of one of the articles was the potential sensitivity of "teenage sexual activity." * * * If topic sensitivity were the true basis of the principal's decision, the two articles should have been equally objectionable. It is much more likely that the objectionable article was objectionable because of the viewpoint it expressed: It might have been read (as the majority apparently does) to advocate "irresponsible sex." * * *

C

The sole concomitant of school sponsorship that might conceivably justify the distinction that the Court draws between sponsored and nonsponsored student expression is the risk "that the views of the individual speaker [might be] erroneously attributed to the school." * * *

* * * Dissociative means short of censorship are available to the school. It could, for example, require the student activity to public a disclaimer, such as the "Statement of Policy" that Spectrum published each school year announcing that "[a]ll * * * editorials appearing in this newspaper reflect the opinions of the Spectrum staff, which are not necessarily shared by the administrators or faculty of Hazelwood East," * * *

III

* * * Nor did the censorship fall within the category that *Tinker* described as necessary to prevent student expression from "inva[ding] the rights of others," * * *. If that term is to have any content, it must be limited to rights that are protected by law. * * * And, as the Court of Appeals correctly reasoned, whatever journalistic impropriety these articles may have contained, they could not conceivably be tortious, much less criminal. * * *

Finally, even if the majority were correct that the principal could constitutionally have censored the objectionable material, I would emphatically object to the brutal manner in which he did so. Where "[t]he separation of legitimate from illegitimate speech calls for more sensitive tools" Speiser v. Randall, 357 U.S. 513, 525 (1958); * * * the principal used a paper shredder. He objected to some material in two articles, but excised six entire articles. He did not so much as inquire into obvious alternatives, such as precise deletions or additions (one of which had already been made), rearranging the layout, or delaying publication. Such unthinking contempt for individual rights is intolerable from any state official. It is particularly insidious from one to whom the public entrusts the task of inculcating in its youth an appreciation for the cherished democratic liberties that our Constitution guarantees.

* * *

* * * The young men and women of Hazelwood East expected a civics lesson, but not the one the Court teaches them today.

I dissent.

4. A "Forum" Discussion and Review

The Court's recent decisions appear to trifurcate first amendment review of restrictions on publicly-held property according to "forum analysis." Additionally, these cases clearly suggest a threshold problem not previously seen as such under "time, place, and manner" standards of review. The new analysis implies that one must take a step *preceding* the application of time, place, and manner, regulation review. For if the public property in question is not judicially regarded as some kind of public forum,[52] even the moderately protective standards of "time, place, and manner" first amendment review appear not to apply, i.e. they need not be met by the state.[53] As recently as 1987, moreover, a majority of the Supreme Court has reiterated the position that this three-forum threshold approach is correct:[54]

> In balancing the government's interest in limiting the use of its property against the interests of those who wish to use the property for expressive activity, the Court has identified three types of fora: the traditional public forum, the public forum created by government designation, and the nonpublic forum. [citing *Perry*] *The proper First Amendment analysis differs depending on whether the area in question falls in one category rather than another.*

---

52. Whether "traditional" or "dedicated," or whether "limited" rather than unlimited.

53. E.g., where the government-held property is a "nonpublic forum," the interest deemed sufficient to exclude a wide range of speech uses need not be "compelling" but merely not prohibited, and the regulation need not be "narrowly tailored," but merely rationally related. There is no question regarding ample alternative means for communicating elsewhere. And likewise, the regulation need not be content neutral, or speaker neutral. It is enough that the regulation is (a) viewpoint neutral, (b) rationally related to preserving the facility for its (lawful) use, and (c) not enacted from a mere desire to suppress expression or speech as such. (Consistent with the *Perry Education Association* case, moreover, by no means is it certain that the favored speech uses need necessarily be viewpoint neutral in determining the messages to be conveyed.)

54. Board of Airport Comm'rs v. Jews for Jesus, Inc., 482 U.S. 569, 582–83, 107 S.Ct. 2568, 2571, 96 L.Ed.2d 500, 505–06 (1987) (Emphasis added.)

Some public agencies have responded quite aggressively to this development of forum categorization; they have done so by restricting general access and speech uses of certain kinds of publicly-held premises more sharply than previously, encouraged by the apparent clarity the suggested distinctions the Court's newer opinions seem to invite. Immediately following the Supreme Court's decision in *Perry Education Association,* for instance, on July 13, 1983, the Board of Airport Commissioners for the Los Angeles International Airport adopted a resolution applicable to the entirety of the Los Angeles International Airport Terminal. It withdrew whatever invitation may have been previously implied to access-seekers and speech users of the terminal, whether by tradition or by acquiescence. The new regulation provided, rather, that "the Central Terminal Area of Los Angeles International Airport is not open for First Amendment activities by any individual and/or entity." Its object was to make the entire interior of the terminal a "nonpublic forum," i.e. a place restricted to the services incidental to travel, putting an end to various kinds of solicitations, petitions, leafletting activities, and the like, by banishing them all. Plainly the new rule sought to avoid the perplexities of "time, place, and manner" restrictions, and the unwelcome task of drawing fine lines.

In the actual case as it came to the Supreme Court, the Airport Authority's particular attempt to clear the airport of speech-users was held to fail. Tested in the Court "on its face," rather than "as applied," the regulation was held to be void on overbreadth grounds (the idea that *all* "first amendment activities" were forbidden was readily found to be quite absurd).[55] But the decision is otherwise inconclusive on the main point for which it was originally meant to be reviewed (namely, the extent to which a government-owned terminal might or might not be sheltered as a "nonpublic forum" subject only to the Court's least demanding kind of forum test).

On the other hand, the case may also cause one to pause over the usefulness of the "three-kinds-of-forum"[56] approach the Court appears

---

55. The Court unanimously held the regulation void on its face for overbreadth; on its face, the regulation was addressed to literally all first amendment activity and thus appeared to cover "even talking (politics) and reading (newspapers), or the wearing of campaign buttons or symbolic clothing" while in the terminal. 482 U.S. at 575, 107 S.Ct. at 2572, 96 L.Ed.2d at 507–08. Even treating the whole of the terminal as a nonpublic forum—the Court expressly declined to say whether it was—the Court held that "no conceivable governmental interest would justify an absolute prohibition of speech" within the terminal of the sort just illustrated; i.e. the regulation lacked even a rational nexus with a proper purpose, viewed this way, and so was invalid per se. Conceding for the sake of the argument that the regulation might possibly be construed as inapplicable to first amendment activity solely incidental to "airport-related activity" (e.g., activity such as reading a newspaper or chatting about politics while waiting for a plane), the Court held that that interpretation, combined with the expectation of trusting to the discretion of airport officials to decide ad hoc which speech activity was or was not sufficiently "airport related," was too vague a standard to be tolerated on first amendment, prior restraint grounds. 482 U.S. at 576, 107 S.Ct. at 2572–73, 96 L.Ed.2d at 508–09.

56. Or is it, rather, a four-forum approach ((a) traditional public forum, (b) dedicated public forum, (c) limited public forum, (d) nonpublic forum)?) Are (a) and (b) treated identically under the first amendment, in the first instance? If so, what is the distinction, if any, between the two? (Is the distinction between (a) and (b)

Ch. 3   GOVT.'S MANAGEMENT OF PUBLIC PROPERTY   483

to have adopted, as either a very exacting or as a wholly reliable new tool. For instance, note that in this case, *Jews for Jesus, Inc.*, while the Court expressly declined to decide whether the entirety of a major airport terminal could be cordoned off as a nonpublic forum, the Court nonetheless added that, assuming it could be, even then, in some measure, some confrontational forms of unwanted political speech might still be protected from regulations prohibiting some forms of such speech.[57] But if that is so, might there may be less actual clarity and certainty gained from the overall "forum" categories the Court has proposed than one might first have supposed, after all?[58] Yet, surely, these advantages (i.e. greater categorical clarity and greater regulatory certainty) were among the principal objects meant to be secured by this new approach.

Taking the new approach seriously, consider the following case. Does the outcome turn on what kind of forum is involved? The court deciding the case thought it did (it divided two-to-one on the basis of that very point). What different result, if any, if addressed pursuant to the standards of "time, place, and manner" review?[59]

---

the distinction that the first kind is not subject to more than time, place, and manner regulations, but that the second kind, while subject only to the same kinds of regulations while it remains "dedicated" as a public forum, can be withdrawn as such when government so elects (an option not applicable to the first kind)?) Similarly, what difference in first amendment review standards distinguishes (c) from (d)? And is there any first amendment limitation forbidding government from moving a (b) forum to a (c) forum, and/or a (c) forum to (d)?

57. Specifically, Justice O'Connor wrote (482 U.S. at 576, 107 S.Ct. at 2572–73, 96 L.Ed.2d at 508–09): "Much nondisruptive speech—such as the wearing of a T-shirt or button that contains a political message—may not be 'airport related,' *but is still protected speech even in a nonpublic forum*." Citing Cohen v. California, 403 U.S. 15, 91 S.Ct. 1780, 29 L.Ed.2d 284 (1971) (the "Fuck the draft" California Los Angeles Courthouse case) (Emphasis added).

58. For a post hoc refinement, consider again the *Taxpayers for Vincent* case, reproduced *supra*, and decided at the time under a "time, place, and manner" rationale (sustaining the complete ban of election posters on public utility poles or lines, solely on aesthetic grounds, though the lines were along the public streets, the posters were conventional political posters,

the city disclaimed safety concerns, a less restrictive regulation requiring removal within so many hours or days following the relevant election was not deemed required on first amendment grounds, nor a more narrowly drawn restriction deemed required, either). Under an application of the *PLEA* and *Cornelius* cases, would it have been plausible to argue that the "forum" to which Taxpayers for Vincent sought "access" was not the traditional forum of the public streets and sidewalks, but, rather, the lesser part thereof consisting of the utility lines and poles—and, as to these, they were neither traditional public fora, dedicated public fora, nor limited public fora, but nonpublic fora such that the flat ban, being viewpoint neutral, and rationally related to a legitimate police power interest in aesthetics, as imposed on a nonpublic forum is valid, whether or not related to a "substantial" or "compelling" government objective, whether or not "narrowly" tailored?

59. In turn, why or why not might the "*O'Brien*" standard of first amendment review be applied to this case? (In the taxonomy of first amendment categories of view, e.g., the *Brandenburg* test, the *Dennis* test, the *O'Brien* test, the time, place, and manner test, or "forum analysis," is there some hazard that one's view of the forest (so to speak) can become obscured in worrying overly much about the trees?

UNITED STATES v. KOKINDA

United States Court of Appeals, Fourth Circuit, 1989.
866 F.2d 699 (4th Cir.1989), rev'd, 497 U.S. ___, 110 S.Ct. 3115, 111 L.Ed.2d 571 (1990).

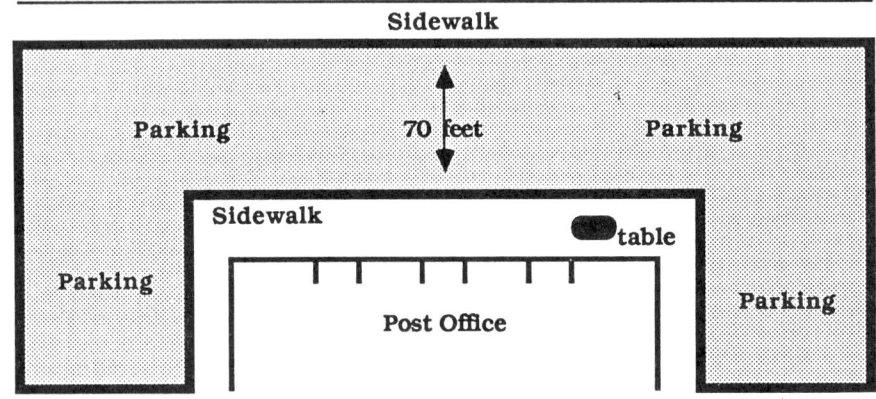

1. The public street and sidewalks [top of figure] are city owned.

2. The premises are otherwise U.S. government owned, including the sidewalk forming a perimeter to the U.S. Post Office.

3. The U.S. Post Office regulation re postal service property provides:

    "Soliciting alms and contributions, campaigning for election to any public office, collecting private debts, commercial solicitation and vending, and displaying or distributing commercial advertising on postal premises is prohibited."

4. Defendants are volunteers for the National Democratic Policy Committee who set up a table on the sidewalk nearby an entry to the Post Office, from which they distribute literature warning of an economic "blow out," calling for an end to the "Aids cover-up," and discussing problems of drug abuse in government, and soliciting subscriptions to the National Democratic Policy Committee's newspaper, *New Solidarity*.

The Postmaster, after seeing defendants' table and after receiving complaints from postal customers, advised defendants of the postal regulation and asked defendants to leave. Following their refusal to do so, defendants were charged with:

1. Violating the quoted regulation for soliciting contributions on postal service property;
2. Refusal to comply with the lawful direction of postal authorities;
3. Refusal to leave the grounds of a public building.

Defendants admit to the offenses but contend that, as applied, the regulations violate their first amendment rights. Upon proper joining of this issue in federal district court where their prosecution is pending, what result and why?

Consider the following points:

1. The regulation is "viewpoint neutral," i.e. it does not ration use of the immediate perimeter sidewalk according to the political affiliation or ideology of candidates seeking to campaign there or according to the pro or con position on some policy for which contributions are solicited. Rather, it "neutrally" forbids these activities altogether.

2. The regulation, moreover, may be "reasonably related" to the lawful purpose of providing the perimeter sidewalk solely as a convenient access route to and from the inside of the Post Office, from the service area of the surrounding parking area. The prohibition likewise serves the purpose to dispel third party impressions that might otherwise arise (and apparently did arise) that such persons who might solicit or distribute at this location do so with the active approval of the Post Office.

—Under "nonpublic forum" doctrine, these may be the sole tests that the regulation need clear in order to be sustained. (See, e.g., the Court's discussion in the *PLEA* case and discussion in *Cornelius*). That it is arguably not as narrowly tailored as it might be, consistent with maintaining the sidewalk as a useful walkway, is not per se a sufficient objection if this is a nonpublic forum; likewise, whether or not the public sidewalk seventy feet away may not be an ample alternative location, is also not consequential, under these tests. These elements would be crucial only if it—the inner perimeter sidewalk—were a traditional or dedicated public forum in which it might then be subject solely to narrowly tailored time, place, and manner [60] speech regulations serving substantial governmental interests, sustainable if ample alternative means of expression remain unaffected.

Neither, arguably, is it necessarily even a limited public forum— that would be some kind of publicly held property which is neither a traditional nor a dedicated general public forum, but some kind of property made available as a "forum," albeit relevantly limited by subject and perhaps by speaker identification, but nothing more, and as such subject only to reasonable time, place, and manner regulations.[61]

---

60. E.g., regulations forbidding the use of stationary tables as such, or regulations forbidding standing in a manner likely to obstruct the entry or block post office users, or shouting at persons to get their attention, or (even) leaving stacks of material at the entryways, likely to be blown away or scattered.

61. (An example of a limited public forum by subject, one might say, is a city hall meeting chamber—where speakers may be restricted by subject (e.g., to mat-

As in *Cornelius,* nothing here suggests that when the sidewalk was constructed, it was meant to serve as a public forum, i.e. it is decidedly unlike the civic auditorium in the *Conrad* case, or the meeting chamber in a city hall. Even if, until the regulation was adopted, some forum uses were previously allowed, moreover, strong dicta in the Supreme Court's case law suggest that the mere prior tolerance of such uses did not per se constitute the perimeter sidewalk as a dedicated public forum. Additionally, unless the perimeter sidewalk is also a traditional public forum, even if in some limited way it had previously been some sort of dedicated public forum, it may nonetheless evidently be withdrawn as a dedicated public forum if the government so elects, at least if not as a mere pretext to suppress a particular point of view. See *Cornelius, supra.* Accordingly, if this analysis is sound, the restriction may be valid and the criminal convictions of the noncomplying defendants may be affirmed. If, oppositely, "time, place, and manner" review standards are applied, what different result (if any), is indicated on the facts of the case?

5. Who Owns the Airwaves?

RED LION BROADCASTING CO. v. FCC

Supreme Court of the United States, 1969.
395 U.S. 367, 89 S.Ct. 1794, 23 L.Ed.2d 371.

MR. JUSTICE WHITE delivered the opinion of the Court.

* * *

The Red Lion Broadcasting Company is licensed to operate a Pennsylvania radio station, WGCB. On November 27, 1964, WGCB carried a 15–minute broadcast by the Reverend Billy James Hargis as part of a "Christian Crusade" series. A book by Fred J. Cook entitled "Goldwater—Extremist on the Right" was discussed by Hargis, who said that Cook had been fired by a newspaper for making false charges against city officials; that Cook had then worked for a Communist-affiliated publication; that he had defended Alger Hiss and attacked J. Edgar Hoover and the Central Intelligence Agency; and that he had now written a "book to smear and destroy Barry Goldwater." When Cook heard of the broadcast he concluded that he had been personally attacked and demanded free reply time, which the station refused. After an exchange of letters among Cook, Red Lion, and the FCC, the FCC declared that the Hargis broadcast constituted a personal attack

---

ters pending before or pertinent to the city council's agenda and jurisdiction), but where the locus is meant to serve as a forum nonetheless. An example of limited public forum by speaker identification, on the other hand, may be public school premises; they may be put off limits to general citizens during the school day, but available to students otherwise lawfully present. See, e.g., Tinker v. Des Moines School Dist., 393 U.S. 503, 89 S.Ct. 733, 21 L.Ed.2d 731 (1969).)

(Suppose also a revision of *Tinker* in the following manner: a revision of the school rule forbidding the wearing of armbands or other sorts of political buttons or insignia in the classrooms during classroom hours, but not on the campus overall. Consider it under "forum analysis.")

on Cook; that Red Lion had failed to meet its obligation under the fairness doctrine as expressed in Times–Mirror Broadcasting Co., 24 P & F Radio Reg. 404 (1962), to send a tape, transcript, or summary of the broadcast to Cook and offer him reply time; and that the station must provide reply time whether or not Cook would pay for it. * * *

* * *

As they now stand amended, the regulations read as follows:

"Personal attacks; political editorials.

"(a) When, during the presentation of views on a controversial issue of public importance, an attack is made upon the honesty, character, integrity or like personal qualities of an identified person or group, the licensee shall, within a reasonable time and in no event later than 1 week after the attack, transmit to the person or group attacked (1) notification of the date; time and identification of the broadcast; (2) a script or tape (or an accurate summary if a script or tape is not available) of the attack and (3) an offer of a reasonable opportunity to respond over the licensee's facilities.

* * *

The history of the emergence of the fairness doctrine and of the related legislation shows that the Commission's action in the Red Lion case did not exceed its authority, and that in adopting the new regulations the Commission was implementing congressional policy rather than embarking on a frolic of its own.

* * *

The broadcasters challenge the fairness doctrine and its specific manifestations in the personal attack and political editorial rules on conventional First Amendment grounds, alleging that the rules abridge their freedom of speech and press. Their contention is that the First Amendment protects their desire to use their allotted frequencies continuously to broadcast whatever they choose, and to exclude whomever they choose from ever using that frequency. No man may be prevented from saying or publishing what he thinks, or from refusing in his speech or other utterances to give equal weight to the views of his opponents. This right, they say, applies equally to broadcasters.

A.

Although broadcasting is clearly a medium affected by a First Amendment interest, United States v. Paramount Pictures, Inc., 334 U.S. 131, 166 (1948), differences in the characteristics of new media justify differences in the First Amendment standards applied to them. * * *

* * *

* * * The lack of know-how and equipment may keep many from the air, but only a tiny fraction of those with resources and intelligence can hope to communicate by radio at the same time if intelligible

communication is to be had, even if the entire radio spectrum is utilized in the present state of technology.

* * *

Where there are substantially more individuals who want to broadcast than there are frequencies to allocate, it is idle to posit an unabridgeable First Amendment right to broadcast comparable to the right of every individual to speak, write, or publish. If 100 persons want broadcast licenses but there are only 10 frequencies to allocate, all of them may have the same "right" to a license; but if there is to be any effective communication by radio, only a few can be licensed and the rest must be barred from the airwaves. It would be strange if the First Amendment, aimed at protecting and furthering communications, prevented the Government from making radio communication possible by requiring licenses to broadcast and by limiting the number of licenses so as not to overcrowd the spectrum.

* * *

By the same token, as far as the First Amendment is concerned those who are licensed stand no better than those to whom licenses are refused. A license permits broadcasting, but the licensee has no constitutional right to be the one who holds the license or to monopolize a radio frequency to the exclusion of his fellow citizens. There is nothing in the First Amendment which prevents Government from requiring a licensee to share his frequency with others and to conduct himself as a proxy or fiduciary with obligations to present those views and voices which are representative of his community and which would otherwise, by necessity, be barred from the airwaves.

* * *

B.

Rather than confer frequency monopolies on a relatively small number of licensees, in a Nation of 200,000,000, the Government could surely have decreed that each frequency should be shared among all or some of those who wish to use it, each being assigned a portion of the broadcast day or the broadcast week. The ruling and regulations at issue here do not go quite so far. They assert that under specified circumstances, a licensee must offer to make available a reasonable amount of broadcast time to those who have a view different from that which has already been expressed on his station. The expression of a political endorsement, or of a personal attack while dealing with a controversial public issue, simply triggers this time sharing. As we have said, the First Amendment confers no right on licensees to prevent others from broadcasting on "their" frequencies and no right to an unconditional monopoly of a scarce resource which the Government has denied others the right to use.

Nor can we say that it is inconsistent with the First Amendment goal of producing an informed public capable of conducting its own affairs to require a broadcaster to permit answers to personal attacks occurring in the course of discussing controversial issues, or to require that the political opponents of those endorsed by the station be given a chance to communicate with the public.[18] Otherwise, station owners and a few networks would have unfettered power to make time available only to the highest bidders, to communicate only their own views on public issues, people and candidates, and to permit on the air only those with whom they agreed. There is no sanctuary in the First Amendment for unlimited private censorship operating in a medium not open to all. "Freedom of the press from governmental interference under the First Amendment does not sanction repression of that freedom by private interests." Associated Press v. United States, 326 U.S. 1, 20 (1945).

C.

It is strenuously argued, however, that if political editorials or personal attacks will trigger an obligation in broadcasters to afford the opportunity for expression to speakers who need not pay for time and whose views are unpalatable to the licensees, then broadcasters will be irresistibly forced to self-censorship and their coverage of controversial public issues will be eliminated or at least rendered wholly ineffective. Such a result would indeed be a serious matter, for should licensees actually eliminate their coverage of controversial issues, the purposes of the doctrine would be stifled.

At this point, however, as the Federal Communications Commission has indicated, that possibility is at best speculative. The communications industry, and in particular the networks, have taken pains to present controversial issues in the past, and even now they do not assert that they intend to abandon their efforts in this regard. It would be better if the FCC's encouragement were never necessary to induce the broadcasters to meet their responsibility. And if experience with the administration of these doctrines indicates that they have the net effect of reducing rather than enhancing the volume and quality of coverage, there will be time enough to reconsider the constitutional implications. The fairness doctrine in the past has had no such overall effect.

That this will occur now seems unlikely, however, since if present licensees should suddenly prove timorous, the Commission is not powerless to insist that they give adequate and fair attention to public issues. It does not violate the First Amendment to treat licensees given the privilege of using scarce radio frequencies as proxies for the entire community, obligated to give suitable time and attention to matters of great public concern. To condition the granting or renewal of licenses on a willingness to present representative community views on controversial issues is consistent with the ends and purposes of those constitutional provisions forbidding the abridgment of freedom of speech and

---

18. The expression of views opposing those which broadcasters permit to be aired in the first place need not be confined solely to the broadcasters themselves as proxies. "Nor is it enough that he should hear the arguments of adversaries from his own teachers, presented as they state them, and accompanied by what they offer as refutations. That is not the way to do justice to the arguments, or bring them into real contact with his own mind. He must be able to hear them from persons who actually believe them; who defend them in earnest, and do their very utmost for them." J. Mill, On Liberty 32 (R. McCallum ed. 1947).

freedom of the press. Congress need not stand idly by and permit those with licenses to ignore the problems which beset the people or to exclude from the airways anything but their own views of fundamental questions. The statute, long administrative practice, and cases are to this effect.

* * *

We need not and do not now ratify every past and future decision by the FCC with regard to programming. There is no question here of the Commission's refusal to permit the broadcaster to carry a particular program or to publish his own views; of a discriminatory refusal to require the licensee to broadcast certain views which have been denied access to the airwaves; of government censorship of a particular program contrary to § 326; or of the official government view dominating public broadcasting. Such questions would raise more serious First Amendment issues. But we do hold that the Congress and the Commission do not violate the First Amendment when they require a radio or television station to give reply time to answer personal attacks and political editorials.

E.

It is argued that even if at one time the lack of available frequencies for all who wished to use them justified the Government's choice of those who would best serve the public interest by acting as proxy for those who would present differing views, or by giving the latter access directly to broadcast facilities, this condition no longer prevails so that continuing control is not justified. To this there are several answers.

Scarcity is not entirely a thing of the past. Advances in technology, such as microwave transmission, have led to more efficient utilization of the frequency spectrum but uses for that spectrum have also grown apace. * * *

* * *

In view of the scarcity of broadcast frequencies, the Government's role in allocating those frequencies, and the legitimate claims of those unable without governmental assistance to gain access to those frequencies for expression of their views, we hold the regulations and ruling at issue here are both authorized by statute and constitutional. The judgment of the Court of Appeals in *Red Lion* is affirmed and that in *RTNDA* reversed and the causes remanded for proceedings consistent with this opinion.

It is so ordered.

Not having heard oral argument in these cases, MR. JUSTICE DOUGLAS took no part in the Court's decision.

---

6. Notes on *Red Lion* and "Public Forum" Use

Red Lion Broadcasting Co. v. FCC, should at once raise a sharp comparison for contrast with *Miami Herald Publishing Co. v. Tornillo*.

There, as you will recall, a unanimous Supreme Court held that the first amendment forbids a state created right-of-reply entitlement, even for a candidate for public office whose character has been assailed in the columns of a newspaper, just prior to a pending election, and under circumstances where the impugned person may have no practical equivalent forum to rebut the disparagements or mischaracterizations the newspaper editorial contained. Moreover, whatever the self-censoring effect the Court felt was implicit in the Florida right-of-reply statute, surely it is at least as great in a *Red Lion* kind of case.[62] How are the cases best explained? To be sure, *Tornillo* did involve a newspaper rather than a radio or television station, of course, and perhaps the case is thought to be influenced by the express separate mention in the first amendment of "the freedom of the press." Yet, by itself, that distinction seems extremely weak.

It is obvious that CBS, NBC, ABC, CNN, etc., provide news coverage and other features of a like sort. In many other first amendment settings (e.g., first amendment limitations on the application of libel laws), moreover, we have seen that media defendants are treated without distinction under *New York Times v. Sullivan:* radio and television news and commentary are equally protected under the first amendment as news and commentary that appears in print. It would be odd at this late date to suppose a constitutional distinction would turn upon an adventitious distinction that radio and television were unknown in 1791 (the date of the first amendment's ratification), but that newspapers were already a well established fact of life. Moreover, in other areas of constitutional adjudication (e.g., fourth amendment privacy protection), the Bill of Rights has not been arrested by the state of the existing technology of the era.[63] Neither has the first amendment otherwise been limited to some time-bound notion of the communicative state of the art.[64] For that matter, neither did the Court in *Red Lion* deny the full relevance of the first amendment to communication by airwave. So this suggested distinction would not appear to explain the difference between the two cases, at all.

Rather, the case is expressly distinguished on two other grounds noted in the opinion by Justice White. Both grounds of distinction apparently are closely tied to the subject we have been considering here, namely, government-owned or government-managed *public* property, and the rules that may govern *that* property as such.

First, the Court noted that, strictly speaking, no private property is permitted to exist in the airwaves, by fiat of federal law. In that strict sense, the airwaves are more appropriately thought of as "socialized" property, i.e. they belong to us all, as a common resource, held in public

---

62. See discussion in note 74 *infra*.

63. See, e.g., Katz v. United States, 389 U.S. 347, 88 S.Ct. 507, 19 L.Ed.2d 576 (1967) (fourth amendment is applicable to telephone wiretaps though telephones did not exist when the fourth amendment was framed, and though the wiretap may not involve any act of trespass upon the premises of the property of the person whose messages are intercepted and recorded), overruling Olmstead v. United States, 277 U.S. 438, 48 S.Ct. 564, 72 L.Ed. 944 (1928).

64. Again, the public figure libel cases and the like treatment of television reports with newspaper reports on public figures, come to mind.

trust. They are thus also akin to a public park, held in public trust, subject to rationing by permit, issued by the FCC. Second, in awarding an exclusive three-year license to the Red Lion Broadcasting company, respecting the use of a given FM signal of a given transmitting strength, the government has thereby presumed to lock out all other would-be users of the same broadcast frequency thus withdrawing *any* use of that same "forum" (i.e. use of that FM frequency), during the whole time of the licensee's grant. From then on, during the time of the license, the public forum is severely restricted by government fiat, and restricted by mere "speaker identity" alone. What the government has done is to appoint a speaker to put in charge of a public forum and grant him or her virtual carte blanche power to admit or deny anyone else the privilege to speak in that forum. Its hubris in doing so, i.e. in generally forbidding others to broadcast over the same frequency without the licensee's permission, is merely palliated in moderating the licensee's monopoly by the minor restraints of the fairness doctrine. In the end, the licensee is still a vastly more privileged party, vis-a-vis others, in the use advantage the licensee has in the monopoly use right to a public forum (the FM broadcast frequency) the licensee retains, after satisfying every title and jot of the fairness doctrine as such.

In contrast, no similar thing can be said in respect to the *Miami Herald* case. There, there is no "public forum" advantage granted to the Miami Herald at all. Whatever the cost barriers (to starting up a newspaper), or whatever other problems faced by Pat Tornillo in getting his own message across by means of a newspaper or a pamphlet (or even a handbill), into the hands of those who subscribed to the Miami Herald, they are strictly problems faced by anyone else equally. They are not the result of any state action conferring any advantage in respect to the allocation of any public property or public "forum" vesting exclusive speaking rights in that forum in a single company for a three year, renewable term.[65] Rather, in the *Miami Herald* case, there was no public property specially committed to the newspaper's exclusive use, and no public forum with respect to which the Miami Herald was granted any privileged use.

Additionally, though the matter was not particularly emphasized by the Court in *Red Lion*, note that the grant of the public property speech monopoly-privilege (i.e. exclusive broadcast rights to a given broadcast frequency for three years renewable), was also made by the FCC to the Red Lion Broadcasting Company rent free.[66] May not this

---

65. Neither did the state or the city favor the Miami Herald in granting it any advantage in respect to any "public forum" means for delivering its publication (for instance, through the network of public streets) such that only the Miami Herald, and no one else, could distribute its messages by an exclusive license of that kind. Whatever sort of newspaper, pamphlet, handbill, etc., Pat Tornillo or those favorably disposed to him might have the means and will to put together, then whatever public property the Miami Herald had access to in distributing its newspaper (e.g., the streets and sidewalks), the same public property was unrestrictedly available for the same purpose to Tornillo and to anyone else.

66. If full market price value had been charged, would the outcome then be different? Suppose the Miami Herald happens to rent the property on which it constructs its editorial offices and/or publishing plant from the City of Miami. Would the additional datum of the city's relationship to the Miami Herald as "landlord" have been

also make some difference in the case? First, Red Lion Broadcasting Company received a privileged use of a natural public forum.[67] And for this exclusionary advantage vis-a-vis others who might want to broadcast from time to time over the same frequency, whether to reply to some message Red Lion broadcast or simply to present some original programs of their own, Red Lion had paid absolutely nothing at all.[68]

In the *Miami Herald* case, there is no equivalent public forum argument to be made. The government does not lock out anyone from the use of any public property or "public forum," and, obviously, neither is there any foregone rent so to favor a given publisher in the (rent free) exclusive use of a scarce public good.[69] In essence, then, from this perspective, *Red Lion* is both a distinguishable, and a very modest, Supreme Court case. The government has taken a natural forum (the public property of an airwave broadcast frequency), which formerly anyone might have used, and made it into a very limited public forum. Indeed, rent free it is made available to a single user (the licensee), except to the extent of providing an assurance of access to that limited forum when one otherwise denied access to it is specifically mentioned in a disparaging way and, albeit at a later time than the original broadcast, he or she may appear briefly to make some reply. Viewed this way, the case seems easy and right.[70] Indeed, viewed this way, perhaps several other questions might be raised.

at all persuasive to the Supreme Court in determining whether the state right-of-reply statute was valid as applied?

67. I.e. the FM "forum" frequency it was assigned.

68. Whether the actual rent value of the particular FCC license involved in the *Red Lion* case was large or small, the case does not enable us to say. (Obviously the rent value of particular broadcast frequencies may differ greatly, from an estimated several million dollars in certain top ten VHF television markets, down to virtually nothing for certain rural AM radio frequencies, even as sometimes evidenced insofar as some available frequencies may even go unclaimed for lack of a suitable applicant convinced that there is any money to be made by setting up a suitable broadcast facility and incurring the costs necessary to operate the station, though the license is free. The surer way of determining the real value of an FCC license would be to modify the current system and allocate licenses according to open market, competitive, sealed bids. A good proxy, absent the institution of a real bid auction system, is nonetheless available simply by determining what whole sum a transferee of an FCC license (the transfer of which the FCC approves prior to the closing of the deal) pays the transferor for the broadcast facilities the transferee purchases from the transferor, and by subtracting such amount as one can fairly determine to represent the fair market value merely of the facilities as such; the difference reflects the value of the license. (Consider buying a used taxicab in New York City, on the one hand, and an identical used taxicab-with-medallion-included, on the other hand. The latter purchase is likely to cost about $100,000 more.)

69. In contrast, arguably, were the state to charge full market price in allocating the airwaves (as in a bid auction system), it may be argued that the price paid by the successful bidder would make the "property" private property for first amendment purposes. (In paying full market price, for the property rental, the buyer is made to internalize the costs of his own freedom of speech preferences in respect to that property, just as The Miami Herald, The National Review, The Durham Morning Herald, Ms. Magazine, or any other private publisher does, with theirs.) See also discussion *infra*, note 75.

70. Note, however, in contrast, that this kind of public forum analysis will not work to rationalize certain other kinds of FCC rules such as those that forbid profanity, indecency, or vulgarity by broadcasters. Such rules obviously do not enlarge the opportunities for free speech. Neither do they compensate those lacking licenses, by providing some opportunity for them to address issues they might wish to present, in the manner they think best to do. Rather, the rules substantively restrict what may be said, regardless of by whom,

1. For instance, is it even arguable that were the fairness doctrine dropped by the FCC (as it might be),[71] the first amendment would itself mandate third party rights of access to a broadcast frequency in circumstances like those in *Red Lion,*—on the basis that it—the frequency—is public property and a natural public forum, with respect to which the government cannot, constitutionally, discriminate by "speaker identity" in this totally exclusionary (i.e. licensee-favoring) way?[72]

2. To what extent might the favored "forum status" of an FCC licensee support the statutory imposition of even *greater* (if different) restrictions on the licensee, such as common carrier obligations, i.e. rules obliging them to carry third party programs without discrimination because of their content whether the licensee finds them absolutely contrary to the licensee's own program preferences, economic interests, or point of view, and although clearly no such obligations could be imposed upon the ordinary private press?[73]

3. On the other hand, to what extent may the Fairness Doctrine in its current form nonetheless in fact tend to induce self-censorship[74] and thus merely add to general tendencies of industry risk-averseness in broadcasting, providing less diversity than one might reasonably otherwise expect were the doctrine either dropped or (as in the *Miami Herald* case) deemed unconstitutional per se?

4. In the domain of the (private) print media, note that the paradigm of "freedom of the press" is that each publisher marches solely to his or her own tune, leaving each other publisher—large or small, mainstream or idiosyncratic—to march solely to theirs. Their

---

and regardless of listener or viewer interest (which may in fact be very substantial). Nothing in the reasoning of *Red Lion* explains any such case at all. (Cf. FCC v. Pacifica Found., 438 U.S. 726, 98 S.Ct. 3026, 57 L.Ed.2d 1073 (1978).)

71. On August 4, 1987, the FCC unanimously moved to repeal the fairness doctrine, pointing to evidence that it chilled broadcasters from presenting controversial subjects (see also discussion note 74 *infra*), and relying also on evidence of enhanced diversity of communicative means (e.g., cable tv with vastly expanded carrying capacity of channels), and concluding on first amendment grounds that different standards from those applicable to newspapers were unwarranted. Efforts by Congress to derail the FCC Hearings pursuant to which repeal was proposed, succumbed to a presidential veto on first amendment grounds, on June 19, 1987. In 1989, Congress once again moved to mandate the fairness doctrine by statute. By the Spring of 1991, the legislative outcome was still uncertain.

72. Cf. CBS v. Democratic Nat. Committee, 412 U.S. 94, 93 S.Ct. 2080, 36 L.Ed.2d 772 (1973) (in light of fairness doctrine, first amendment does not require broadcast licensee otherwise to yield air time to third party requests). See Note, Constitutional Ramifications of a Repeal of the Fairness Doctrine, 64 Geo.L.J. 1293 (1976).

73. See, e.g., Geller & Lampert, Cable, Content Regulation and the First Amendment, 32 Cath.U.L.Rev. 603 (1983).

74. Note that unless an identifiable person is mentioned in a disparaging fashion in the course of the broadcast of a controversial social or political issue, there of course arises no duty to furnish free air time for a reply. The access right is thus triggered only by the broadcaster's own broadcast; to avoid having to subsidize the reply (a shadow cost to be added to the cost of the original broadcast), the broadcaster need merely be prudent and keep still. Note also that setting aside equal air time for a reply may also be far more expensive in terms of opportunity cost to a licensee broadcaster, than furnishing "reply space" in a newspaper. The medium is strictly limited (i.e. a fixed number of broadcast minutes), unlike the flexibility of pages, print size, width of margins, and columns in print. The resulting shadow cost may therefore be proportionately higher and the disincentive of controversy comparatively great. See Lange, The Role of the Access Doctrine in the Regulation of the Mass Media: A Critical Review and Assessment, 51 N.C.L.Rev. 1 (1973).

success or failure is, in turn, principally contingent on finding subscribers or at least willing readers (without whom they will ordinarily lack advertisers and thus will go broke). And, accordingly, Ms. Magazine is not expected to look like, or read like, The National Review. Those who "tune in" to either Ms. or to The National Review, moreover, may not be the same ones who prefer Playboy, or those who prefer Commentary, or those who prefer Elijah Speaks, though one may, if one wants, seek to subscribe to all five (why not?). Neither the selection of the subjects covered in any of these journals, nor the slant, the presentation, or the "fairness" of the publisher matters in resisting any effort by government to make them more alike, or more moderate, or more uplifting, or more in "the public interest" (whatever that is). Indeed, as to each, the point of the first amendment is that, as to all such matters, the government is to keep out of the way.

The paradigm of private speech property is freedom to publish whatever one thinks best (or can find a market to satisfy),—and the reciprocal freedom of each to read what one wants, however narrow, one-sided, and satisfying to oneself it may be, culled from a blizzard of alternative publishers, unleavened by what some agency of government deems consistent with the public interest. It is ultimately from the competition of this ideological marketplace, each publication having its own pronounced attitude, format, features, and editorial preferences, that "truth," popularity and success are in some sense sorted out. Consumers subscribe to, read, reject, boycott, or pick what they want, whether of the right, the center, or the left, whether the good, the bad, or the profane. It is in this unchecked diversity, itself subject principally to the sole check of marketplace failure—failure against the appeal for subscribers and advertisers by rivals—that seems to be the general first amendment rule.

Comparing that model with the "social" model of the FCC, given the proliferation of cable, of UHF, VHF, AM, FM, FAX, etc. (and given, too, their substantial overlapping communications markets with the print media as well), is there any principled distinction for treating the airwaves in the manner the *Red Lion* case presumes to do?[75]

---

75. Cf. the following view by Justice Douglas, writing separately in CBS v. Democratic Nat. Committee, 412 U.S. at 148–161, 93 S.Ct. at 2109–16, 36 L.Ed.2d at 809–17 (1973): "I did not participate in [*Red Lion*] and, with all respect, would not support it. * * * The struggle for liberty has been a struggle against Government * * * [I]t is anathema to the First Amendment to allow Government any role of censorship over newspapers, magazines, books, art, music, TV, radio, or any other aspect of the press." (Justice Douglas would have confined the FCC principally to (a) application of antitrust responsibilities and (b) facilitating new broadcast technologies; he would have taken the FCC out of program content controls virtually altogether). See also discussion at note 74 *supra.* Insofar as a licensee derives any advantage from having a license "rent free," consider the proposal to offset any such advantage by extracting a fair, market price rent, putting the ensuing risks entirely on the license holder—just as they are with Ms. Magazine, Time, or anyone else who must internalize the costs of what they publish, according to whatever position or positions they choose to take. (See, e.g., B. Owen, Economics and Freedom of Expression: Media Structure and the First Amendment (1975); Coase, Evaluation of Public Policy Relating to Radio and Television Broadcasting: Social and Economic Issues, 41 Land Econ. 161 (1965); Coase, The Federal Communications Commission, 2 J.L. & Econ. 1 (1959); Note, Reconciling Red Lion and Tornillo: A Consistent Theory of Media Regulation, 28 Stan.L.Rev. 563 (1976); Fowler & Brenner, A Marketplace Ap-

5. Consider also the following radical[76] idea. "Newsprint" is what newspapers are printed on (it is "inexpensive paper made from wood pulp, used chiefly for printing newspapers")[77] but it is also, like the airwaves, not a free good. To the extent one cannot afford to buy newsprint, to the same extent one may not be able to have the same practical influence as someone who can, for one will lack the same stock of material to use to print one's message in bulk to sell or give away, whether on a simple handbill or on the full equivalent of the New York Times.

Suppose, on this account, that newsprint were effectively *socialized* in the United States[78] (as the airwaves were socialized in the nineteen twenties by Act of Congress, and have remained so in contemplation of basic property ownership theory ever since). What then? The rationale for doing so, incidentally, might be that, as with airwaves, newsprint is a scarce good: that at any point in time, it is finite and its finitude matters, i.e. the relatively greater amounts demanded by those wanting it and the relatively lesser amounts then physically available, the relatively higher price the market price becomes for any stated quantity, and, correspondingly, the less equal each person's ability to have as much as someone else has on any given day or month or year. The fundamental reason for socializing newsprint is to recognize that all who might want it cannot simultaneously be supplied at the zero (or near zero) price level necessary to put it within the reach of all on equal terms, and the accompanying social resolve that access to newsprint ought not rest on inequalities of ability to pay.

The "real" value of newsprint, one may say, is its value in the printing of newspapers, just as the "real" value of airwaves is their value in facilitating broadcast speech. By first making some, most, or all newsprint a form of *public* property (as the airwaves are public property, or a public park is public property), we can better allocate free press rights more equitably than a price system allegedly does,

proach to Broadcast Regulation, 60 Tex.L. Rev. 207 (1982).) Nor (to anticipate the obvious objection) does this approach neglect "diversity," for what one will aim at in markets already saturated with tuned-in, mere ordinary audience appeal fare will be to provide a specialized niche—by capturing an element previously not as well served by others on the airwaves, one maximizes the highest possible use of the channel or frequency on which one seeks to bid. (In a word, the invisible hand works.)

For example, it may be that in Durham, North Carolina, the highest bid for an FM radio frequency, given what is already on the air, would in fact be submitted by a small company intending to devote the entirety of its programming to the black community, and absolutely *nothing* else; that proposed format may give it a product edge, so to speak, i.e. bring with it an array of advertisers, given the listening audience those advertisers find they now reach more effectively per dollar charged than on any other medium through which they might try to promote sales. (In what way is the black radio station different from a black magazine, in this regard?) Note, too, that in this circumstance, it has received no subsidy (for it is paying full rent for the airwave.) And why should its legal duty to afford access, reply, balance, etc., be any different from a black magazine subscribed to by those who think it just fine as it is?

76. (Not really.)

77. The American Heritage Dictionary 885 (1971 ed.)

78. It might be done by government purchase of all forests in which trees useful as newsprint can be grown, constitutionally pursued by the eminent domain clause in the fifth amendment. Alternatively, it might be done by establishing the government as a monopsonist (monopoly buyer) of all newsprint produced in the United States or permitted to be imported with its approval and consent.

where the queue of applicants for newsprint is simply sorted out by letting the price rise in light of demand until at the marginal price, the effective demand (i.e. ability-plus-willingness-to-buy) establishes an equilibrium between price and supply. We do not allocate the airwaves by a price system though we obviously could.[79] So why should we allocate newsprint by a price system, either? Rather, why not collectively acquire [(a) some, (b) most, or (c) all of][80] the existing supply of newsprint, even while providing incentives for additional sources of newsprint to be developed, as well. And, having publicly reserved or acquired [(a) some, (b) most, or (c) all of] the existing supply of newsprint, might one also establish an NNLC,[81] patterned on the existing FCC?

If one thought well of the model of the FCC, the NNLC could similarly provide for the issuance of licenses, each good for a three-year, renewable term, pursuant to which the licensee might pay merely in keeping with their ability to do so, for such stock as may be issued for their newsprint use. To the extent that the existing newsprint stock were too limited to meet all demand on this basis (as seems likely) then, in keeping with the FCC example, newsprint stock will be issued to licensees pursuant to comparative license application hearings under standards not unlike those now used by the FCC, including the feature upheld in *Red Lion*.[82] Among the several questions one might want to raise about such a proposal, consider these:

    A. If the proposed NNLC somehow strikes one as too closely resembling a system of government licensed presses (i.e. licensing with strings attached) to withstand first amendment scrutiny even under the conservative (i.e. Blackstone) understanding of that amendment, how is it distinguishable from the airwaves and the FCC?

    B. If the treatment of the airwaves we currently have is constitutional (as certainly the Court in *Red Lion* assumes), however, why would it be any less constitutional to proceed with the proposal just described, in respect to such newsprint stock as the government may either acquire or control?

---

79. See discussion and references in note 75 *supra*.

80. (Select a), b), or c).).

81. National Newsprint Licensing Commission.

82. E.g., a rule that such newsprint as one receives pursuant to application to the NNLC, will be impressed with a duty to notify in advance any person whom the recipient intends to identify and criticize, and provide free space for reply, in a column of equal length and prominence as the critical column in which they are disparaged.

7. The First Amendment as a "Freedom of Information Act"

HOUCHINS v. KQED, INC.
Supreme Court of the United States, 1978.
438 U.S. 1, 98 S.Ct. 2588, 57 L.Ed.2d 553.

MR. CHIEF JUSTICE BURGER announced the judgment of the Court and delivered an opinion, in which MR. JUSTICE WHITE and MR. JUSTICE REHNQUIST joined.

The question presented is whether the news media have a constitutional right of access to a county jail, over and above that of other persons, to interview inmates and make sound recordings, films, and photographs for publication and broadcasting by newspapers, radio, and television.

I

Petitioner Houchins, as Sheriff of Alameda County, Cal., controls all access to the Alameda County Jail at Santa Rita. Respondent KQED operates licensed television and radio broadcasting stations which have frequently reported newsworthy events relating to penal institutions in the San Francisco Bay Area. On March 31, 1975, KQED reported the suicide of a prisoner in the Greystone portion of the Santa Rita jail. The report included a statement by a psychiatrist that the conditions at the Greystone facility were responsible for the illnesses of his patient-prisoners there, and a statement from petitioner denying that prison conditions were responsible for the prisoners' illnesses.

KQED requested permission to inspect and take pictures within the Greystone facility. After permission was refused, KQED and the Alameda and Oakland branches of the National Association for the Advancement of Colored People (NAACP) filed suit under 42 U.S.C. § 1983. They alleged that petitioner had violated the First Amendment by refusing to permit media access and failing to provide any effective means by which the public could be informed of conditions prevailing in the Greystone facility or learn of the prisoners' grievances. Public access to such information was essential, they asserted, in order for NAACP members to participate in the public debate on jail conditions in Alameda County. They further asserted that television coverage of the conditions in the cells and facilities was the most effective way of informing the public of prison conditions.

The complaint requested a preliminary and permanent injunction to prevent petitioner from "excluding KQED news personnel from the Greystone cells and Santa Rita facilities and generally preventing full and accurate news coverage of the conditions prevailing therein." On June 17, 1975, when the complaint was filed, there appears to have been no formal policy regarding public access to the Santa Rita jail. However, according to petitioner, he had been in the process of planning a program of regular monthly tours since he took office six months earlier. On July 8, 1975, he announced the program and invited all interested persons to make arrangements for the regular public tours.

News media were given notice in advance of the public and presumably could have made early reservations.

Six monthly tours were planned and funded by the county at an estimated cost of $1,800. The first six scheduled tours were filled within a week after the July 8 announcement. A KQED reporter and several other reporters were on the first tour on July 14, 1975.

Each tour was limited to 25 persons and permitted only limited access to the jail. The tours did not include the disciplinary cells or the portions of the jail known as "Little Greystone," the scene of alleged rapes, beatings, and adverse physical conditions. Photographs of some parts of the jail were made available, but no cameras or tape recorders were allowed on the tours. Those on the tours were not permitted to interview inmates, and inmates were generally removed from view.

* * *

After considering the testimony, affidavits, and documentary evidence presented by the parties, the District Court preliminarily enjoined petitioner from denying KQED news personnel and "responsible representatives" of the news media access to the Santa Rita facilities, including Greystone, "at reasonable times and hours" and "from preventing KQED news personnel and responsible representatives of the news media from utilizing photographic and sound equipment or from utilizing inmate interviews in providing full and accurate coverage of the Santa Rita facilities."

On interlocutory appeal from the District Court's order, * * * [t]he Court of Appeals * * * concluded, albeit in three separate opinions, that the public and the media had a First and Fourteenth Amendment right of access to prisons and jails, and sustained the District Court's order.

* * *

III

We can agree with many of the respondents' generalized assertions; conditions in jails and prisons are clearly matters "of great public importance." * * * Penal facilities are public institutions which require large amounts of public funds, and their mission is crucial in our criminal justice system. Each person placed in prison becomes, in effect, a ward of the state for whom society assumes broad responsibility. It is equally true that with greater information, the public can more intelligently form opinions about prison conditions. Beyond question, the role of the media is important; acting as the "eyes and ears" of the public, they can be a powerful and constructive force, contributing to remedial action in the conduct of public business. They have served that function since the beginning of the Republic, but like all other components of our society media representatives are subject to limits.

The media are not a substitute for or an adjunct of government and, like the courts, they are "ill equipped" to deal with problems of prison administration. * * *

The public importance of conditions in penal facilities and the media's role of providing information afford no basis for reading into the Constitution a right of the public or the media to enter these institutions, with camera equipment, and take moving and still pictures of inmates for broadcast purposes. This Court has never intimated a First Amendment guarantee of a right of access to all sources of information within government control. Nor does the rationale of the decisions upon which respondents rely lead to the implication of such a right.

Grosjean v. American Press Co., * * *, and *Mills v. Alabama,* * * *, emphasized the importance of informed public opinion and the traditional role of a free press as a source of public information. But an analysis of those cases reveals that the Court was concerned with the freedom of the media to communicate information once it is obtained; neither case intimated that the Constitution compels the government to provide the media with information or access to it on demand. *Grosjean* involved a challenge to a state tax on advertising revenues of newspapers, the "plain purpose" of which was to penalize the publishers and curtail the publication of a selected group of newspapers. * * *

* * *

Mills involved a statute making it a crime to publish an editorial about election issues on election day. In striking down the statute, the Court noted that "a major purpose of [the First] Amendment was to protect the free discussion of governmental affairs," * * *. The Court also discussed the role of the media "as a powerful antidote to any abuses of power by governmental officials and as a constitutionally chosen means for keeping officials elected by the people responsible to all the people whom they were selected to serve." * * * As in *Grosjean,* however, the Court did not remotely imply a constitutional right guaranteeing anyone access to government information beyond that open to the public generally.

* * *

The right to receive ideas and information is not the issue in this case. See, e.g., Virginia Pharmacy Board v. Virginia Citizens Consumer Council, 425 U.S. 748 (1976); Procunier v. Martinez, 416 U.S., at 408–409; Kleindienst v. Mandel, 408 U.S. 753, 762–763 (1972). The issue is a claimed special privilege of access which the Court rejected in *Pell* and *Saxbe,* a right which is not essential to guarantee the freedom to communicate or publish.

IV

The respondents' argument is flawed, not only because it lacks precedential support and is contrary to statements in this Court's opinions, but also because it invites the Court to involve itself in what is clearly a legislative task which the Constitution has left to the political processes. Whether the government should open penal institutions in the manner sought by respondents is a question of policy which a legislative body might appropriately resolve one way or the other.

* * *

Unarticulated but implicit in the assertion that media access to the jail is essential for informed public debate on jail conditions is the assumption that media personnel are the best qualified persons for the task of discovering malfeasance in public institutions. But that assumption finds no support in the decisions of this Court or the First Amendment. Editors and newsmen who inspect a jail may decide to publish or not to publish what information they acquire. Cf. Columbia Broadcasting System, Inc. v. Democratic National Committee, 412 U.S. 94, 124 (1973); Miami Herald Publishing Co. v. Tornillo, 418 U.S. 241 (1974); Note, The Rights of the Public and the Press To Gather Information, 87 Harv.L.Rev. 1505, 1508, 1513 (1974). Public bodies and public officers, on the other hand, may be coerced by public opinion to disclose what they might prefer to conceal. No comparable pressures are available to anyone to compel publication by the media of what they might prefer not to make known.

There is no discernible basis for a constitutional duty to disclose, or for standards governing disclosure of or access to information. Because the Constitution affords no guidelines, absent statutory standards, hundreds of judges would, under the Court of Appeals' approach, be at large to fashion ad hoc standards, in individual cases, according to their own ideas of what seems "desirable" or "expedient." We, therefore, reject the Court of Appeals' conclusory assertion that the public and the media have a First Amendment right to government information regarding the conditions of jails and their inmates and presumably all other public facilities such as hospitals and mental institutions.

> "There is no constitutional right to have access to particular government information, or to require openness from the bureaucracy. [Citing *Pell v. Procunier, supra.*] The public's interest in knowing about its government is protected by the guarantee of a Free Press, but the protection is indirect. The Constitution itself is neither a Freedom of Information Act nor an Official Secrets Act.
>
> "The Constitution, in other words, establishes the contest, not its resolution. Congress may provide a resolution, at least in some instances, through carefully drawn legislation. For the rest, we must rely, as so often in our system we must, on the tug and pull of the political forces in American society." Stewart, "Or of the Press," 26 Hastings L.J. 631, 636 (1975).

Petitioner cannot prevent respondents from learning about jail conditions in a variety of ways, albeit not as conveniently as they might prefer. Respondents have a First Amendment right to receive letters from inmates criticizing jail officials and reporting on conditions. See Procunier v. Martinez, 416 U.S., at 413–418. Respondents are free to interview those who render the legal assistance to which inmates are entitled. See *id.*, at 419. They are also free to seek out former inmates, visitors to the prison, public officials, and institutional personnel, as they sought out the complaining psychiatrist here.

Moreover, California statutes currently provide for a prison Board of Corrections that has the authority to inspect jails and prisons and must provide a public report at regular intervals. * * * Following the reports of the suicide at the jail involved here, the County Board of Supervisors called for a report from the County Administrator; held a public hearing on the report, which was open to the media; and called for further reports when the initial report failed to describe the conditions in the cells in the Greystone portion of the jail.

Neither the First Amendment nor the Fourteenth Amendment mandates a right of access to government information or sources of information within the government's control. Under our holdings in *Pell v. Procunier, supra,* and *Saxbe v. Washington Post Co., supra,* until the political branches decree otherwise, as they are free to do, the media have no special right of access to the Alameda County Jail different from or greater than that accorded the public generally.

The judgment of the Court of Appeals is reversed, and the case is remanded for further proceedings.

Reversed and remanded.

Mr. Justice Marshall and Mr. Justice Blackmun took no part in the consideration or decision of this case.

Mr. Justice Stewart, concurring in the judgment.

I agree that the preliminary injunction issued against the petitioner was unwarranted, and therefore concur in the judgment. In my view, however, KQED was entitled to injunctive relief of more limited scope.

The First and Fourteenth Amendments do not guarantee the public a right of access to information generated or controlled by government, nor do they guarantee the press any basic right of access superior to that of the public generally. The Constitution does no more than assure the public and the press equal access once government has opened its doors. Accordingly, I agree substantially with what the opinion of The Chief Justice has to say on that score.

We part company, however, in applying these abstractions to the facts of this case. Whereas he appears to view "equal access" as meaning access that is identical in all respects, I believe that the concept of equal access must be accorded more flexibility in order to accommodate the practical distinctions between the press and the general public.

When on assignment, a journalist does not tour a jail simply for his own edification. He is there to gather information to be passed on to others, and his mission is protected by the Constitution for very specific reasons. * * *

That the First Amendment speaks separately of freedom of speech and freedom of the press is no constitutional accident, but an acknowledgment of the critical role played by the press in American society. The Constitution requires sensitivity to that role, and to the special needs of the press in performing it effectively. A person touring Santa Rita jail can grasp its reality with his own eyes and ears. But if a television reporter is to convey the jail's sights and sounds to those who cannot personally visit the place, he must use cameras and sound equipment. In short, terms of access that are reasonably imposed on individual members of the public may, if they impede effective reporting without sufficient justification, be unreasonable as applied to journalists who are there to convey to the general public what the visitors see.

Under these principles, KQED was clearly entitled to some form of preliminary injunctive relief. At the time of the District Court's decision, members of the public were permitted to visit most parts of the Santa Rita jail, and the First and Fourteenth Amendments required the Sheriff to give members of the press effective access to the same areas. The Sheriff evidently assumed that he could fulfill this obligation simply by allowing reporters to sign up for tours on the same terms as the public. I think he was mistaken in this assumption, as a matter of constitutional law.

* * *

In two respects, however, the District Court's preliminary injunction was overbroad. It ordered the Sheriff to permit reporters into the Little Greystone facility and it required him to let them interview randomly encountered inmates. In both these respects, the injunction gave the press access to areas and sources of information from which persons on the public tours had been excluded, and thus enlarged the scope of what the Sheriff and Supervisors had opened to public view. The District Court erred in concluding that the First and Fourteenth Amendments compelled this broader access for the press.

Because the preliminary injunction exceeded the requirements of the Constitution in these respects, I agree that the judgment of the Court of Appeals affirming the District Court's order must be reversed. But I would not foreclose the possibility of further relief for KQED on remand. In my view, the availability and scope of future permanent injunctive relief must depend upon the extent of access then permitted the public, and the decree must be framed to accommodate equitably the constitutional role of the press and the institutional requirements of the jail.

MR. JUSTICE STEVENS, with whom MR. JUSTICE BRENNAN and MR. JUSTICE POWELL join, dissenting.

The Court holds that the scope of press access to the Santa Rita jail required by the preliminary injunction issued against petitioner is inconsistent with the holding in Pell v. Procunier, 417 U.S. 817, 834, that "newsmen have no constitutional right of access to prisons or their inmates beyond that afforded the general public" and therefore the injunction was an abuse of the District Court's discretion. I respectfully disagree.

Respondent KQED, Inc., has televised a number of programs about prison conditions and prison inmates, and its reporters have been granted access to various correctional facilities in the San Francisco Bay area, including San Quentin State Prison, Soledad Prison, and the San Francisco County Jails at San Bruno and San Francisco, to prepare program material. They have taken their cameras and recording equipment inside the walls of those institutions and interviewed inmates. No disturbances or other problems have occurred on those occasions.

KQED has also reported newsworthy events involving the Alameda County Jail in Santa Rita, including a 1972 newscast reporting a decision of the United States District Court finding that the "shocking and debasing conditions which prevailed [at Santa Rita] constituted cruel and unusual punishment for man or beast as a matter of law."[1]

* * *

* * *

An evidentiary hearing on the motion for a preliminary injunction was held after the first four guided tours had taken place. The evidence revealed the inadequacy of the tours as a means of obtaining information about the inmates and their conditions of confinement for transmission to the public. The tours failed to enter certain areas of the jail.[9] They afforded no opportunity to photograph conditions within the facility, and the photographs which the county offered for sale to tour visitors omitted certain jail characteristics, such as catwalks above the cells from which guards can observe the inmates.[10] The tours provided no opportunity to question randomly encountered inmates about jail conditions. Indeed, to the extent possible, inmates were kept out of sight during the tour, preventing the tour visitors from obtaining a realistic picture of the conditions of confinement within the jail. In addition, the fixed scheduling of the tours prevented coverage of newsworthy events at the jail.

Of most importance, all of the remaining tours were completely booked, and there was no assurance that any tour would be conducted after December 1975. The District Court found that KQED had no access to the jail and that the broad restraints on access were not required by legitimate penological interests.

* * *

For two reasons, which will be discussed separately, the decisions in *Pell* and *Saxbe* do not control the propriety of the District Court's preliminary injunction. First, the unconstitutionality of petitioner's policies which gave rise to this litigation does not rest on the premise that the press has a greater right of access to information regarding prison conditions than do other members of the public. Second, relief tailored to the needs of the press may properly be awarded to a representative of the press which is successful in proving that it has

---

1. See Brenneman v. Madigan, 343 F.Supp. 128, 132–133 (ND Cal.1972). Based on a personal visit to the facility, Judge Zirpoli reached the "inescapable conclusion * * * that Greystone should be razed to the ground."

9. The tour did not include Little Greystone, which was the subject of reports of beatings, rapes, and poor conditions, or the disciplinary cells.

10. There were also no photos of the women's cells, of the "safety cell," of the "disciplinary cells," or of the interior of Little Greystone. In addition, the photograph of the dayroom omits the television monitor that maintains continuous observation of the inmates and the open urinals.

been harmed by a constitutional violation and need not await the grant of relief to members of the general public who may also have been injured by petitioner's unconstitutional access policy but have not yet sought to vindicate their rights.

* * *

In Pell v. Procunier, 417 U.S., at 834, the Court stated that "newsmen have no constitutional right of access to prisons or their inmates beyond that afforded the general public." But the Court has never intimated that a nondiscriminatory policy of excluding entirely both the public and the press from access to information about prison conditions would avoid constitutional scrutiny.[15] * * *

* * *

* * * What *Pell* does indicate is that the question whether respondents established a probability of prevailing on their constitutional claim is inseparable from the question whether petitioner's policies unduly restricted the opportunities of the general public to learn about the conditions of confinement in Santa Rita jail. As in *Pell*, in assessing its adequacy, the total access of the public and the press must be considered.

Here, the broad restraints on access to information regarding operation of the jail that prevailed on the date this suit was instituted are plainly disclosed by the record. * * *

II

The preservation of a full and free flow of information to the general public has long been recognized as a core objective of the First Amendment to the Constitution.

It is for this reason that the First Amendment protects not only the dissemination but also the receipt of information and ideas. * * *

In addition to safeguarding the right of one individual to receive what another elects to communicate, the First Amendment serves an essential societal function. Our system of self-government assumes the existence of an informed citizenry. As Madison wrote:

> "A popular Government, without popular information, or the means of acquiring it, is but a Prologue to a Farce or a Tragedy; or, perhaps both. Knowledge will forever govern ignorance: And a people who mean to be their own Governors, must arm themselves with the power which knowledge gives."
> 9 Writings of James Madison 103 (G. Hunt ed. 1910).

---

15. In Zemel v. Rusk, 381 U.S. 1, 17, the Court said:

"The right to speak and publish does not carry with it the unrestrained right to gather information." (Emphasis added.) And in Branzburg v. Hayes, 408 U.S. 665, 681:

"We do not question the significance of free speech, press, or assembly to the country's welfare. Nor is it suggested that news gathering does not qualify for First Amendment protection; without some protection for seeking out the news, freedom of the press could be eviscerated."

Both statements imply that there is a right to acquire knowledge that derives protection from the First Amendment. See *id.*, at 728 n. 4 (STEWART, J., dissenting).

It is not sufficient, therefore, that the channels of communication be free of governmental restraints. Without some protection for the acquisition of information about the operation of public institutions such as prisons by the public at large, the process of self-governance contemplated by the Framers would be stripped of its substance.[22]

For that reason information gathering is entitled to some measure of constitutional protection. * * * As this Court's decisions clearly indicate, however, this protection is not for the private benefit of those who might qualify as representatives of the "press" but to insure that the citizens are fully informed regarding matters of public interest and importance. * * *

* * *

* * * The question is whether petitioner's policies, which cut off the flow of information at its source, abridged the public's right to be informed about those conditions.

The answer to that question does not depend upon the degree of public disclosure which should attend the operation of most governmental activity. Such matters involve questions of policy which generally must be resolved by the political branches of government. Moreover, there are unquestionably occasions when governmental activity may properly be carried on in complete secrecy. For example, the public and the press are commonly excluded from "grand jury proceedings, our own conferences, [and] the meetings of other official bodies gathered in executive session * * *." Branzburg v. Hayes, 408 U.S., at 684; Pell v. Procunier, 417 U.S., at 834. In addition, some functions of government—essential to the protection of the public and indeed our country's vital interests—necessarily require a large measure of secrecy, subject to appropriate legislative oversight. In such situations the reasons for withholding information from the public are both apparent and legitimate.

* * *

In this case, the record demonstrates that both the public and the press had been consistently denied any access to the inner portions of the Santa Rita jail, that there had been excessive censorship of inmate correspondence, and that there was no valid justification for these broad restraints on the flow of information. An affirmative answer to the question whether respondents established a likelihood of prevailing on the merits did not depend, in final analysis, on any right of the press to special treatment beyond that accorded the public at large. Rather, the probable existence of a constitutional violation rested upon the

---

22. Admittedly, the right to receive or acquire information is not specifically mentioned in the Constitution. But "the protection of the Bill of Rights goes beyond the specific guarantees to protect from * * * abridgement those equally fundamental personal rights necessary to make the express guarantees fully meaningful. * * * The dissemination of ideas can accomplish nothing if otherwise willing addressees are not free to receive and consider them. It would be a barren marketplace of ideas that had only sellers and no buyers." Lamont v. Postmaster General, 381 U.S., at 308 (BRENNAN, J., concurring). It would be an even more barren marketplace that had willing buyers and sellers and no meaningful information to exchange.

special importance of allowing a democratic community access to knowledge about how its servants were treating some of its members who have been committed to their custody. An official prison policy of concealing such knowledge from the public by arbitrarily cutting off the flow of information at its source abridges the freedom of speech and of the press protected by the First and Fourteenth Amendments to the Constitution.

III

The preliminary injunction entered by the District Court granted relief to KQED without providing any specific remedy for other members of the public. Moreover, it imposed duties on petitioner that may not be required by the Constitution itself. The injunction was not an abuse of discretion for either of these reasons.

If a litigant can prove that he has suffered specific harm from the application of an unconstitutional policy, it is entirely proper for a court to grant relief tailored to his needs without attempting to redress all the mischief that the policy may have worked on others. Though the public and the press have an equal right to receive information and ideas, different methods of remedying a violation of that right may sometimes be needed to accommodate the special concerns of the one or the other. Preliminary relief could therefore appropriately be awarded to KQED on the basis of its proof of how it was affected by the challenged policy without also granting specific relief to the general public. Indeed, since our adversary system contemplates the adjudication of specific controversies between specific litigants, it would have been improper for the District Court to attempt to provide a remedy to persons who have not requested separate relief. Accordingly, even though the Constitution provides the press with no greater right of access to information than that possessed by the public at large, a preliminary injunction is not invalid simply because it awards special relief to a successful litigant which is a representative of the press.

* * *

RICHMOND NEWSPAPERS, INC. v. VIRGINIA
Supreme Court of the United States, 1980.
448 U.S. 555, 100 S.Ct. 2814, 65 L.Ed.2d 973.

MR. CHIEF JUSTICE BURGER announced the judgment of the Court and delivered an opinion, in which MR. JUSTICE WHITE and MR. JUSTICE STEVENS joined.

The narrow question presented in this case is whether the right of the public and press to attend criminal trials is guaranteed under the United States Constitution.

I

In March 1976, one Stevenson was indicted for the murder of a hotel manager who had been found stabbed to death on December 2,

1975. Tried promptly in July 1976, Stevenson was convicted of second-degree murder in the Circuit Court of Hanover County, Va. The Virginia Supreme Court reversed the conviction in October 1977, holding that a bloodstained shirt reportedly belonging to Stevenson had been improperly admitted into evidence. Stevenson v. Commonwealth, 218 Va. 462, 237 S.E.2d 779.

Stevenson was retried in the same court. This second trial ended in a mistrial on May 30, 1978, when a juror asked to be excused after trial had begun and no alternate was available.[1]

A third trial, which began in the same court on June 6, 1978, also ended in a mistrial. It appears that the mistrial may have been declared because a prospective juror had read about Stevenson's previous trials in a newspaper and had told other prospective jurors about the case before the retrial began. * * *

Stevenson was tried in the same court for a fourth time beginning on September 11, 1978. Present in the courtroom when the case was called were appellants Wheeler and McCarthy, reporters for appellant Richmond Newspapers, Inc. Before the trial began, counsel for the defendant moved that it be closed to the public:

"[T]here was this woman that was with the family of the deceased when we were here before. She had sat in the Courtroom. I would like to ask that everybody be excluded from the Courtroom because I don't want any information being shuffled back and forth when we have a recess as to what—who testified to what." * * *

The trial judge, who had presided over two of the three previous trials, asked if the prosecution had any objection to clearing the courtroom. The prosecutor stated he had no objection and would leave it to the discretion of the court. * * * Presumably referring to Va.Code § 19.2–266 (Supp.1980), the trial judge then announced: "[T]he statute gives me that power specifically and the defendant has made the motion." He then ordered "that the Courtroom be kept clear of all parties except the witnesses when they testify." * * * The record does not show that any objections to the closure order were made by anyone present at the time, including appellants Wheeler and McCarthy.

Later that same day, however, appellants sought a hearing on a motion to vacate the closure order. The trial judge granted the request and scheduled a hearing to follow the close of the day's proceedings. When the hearing began, the court ruled that the hearing was to be treated as part of the trial; accordingly, he again ordered the reporters to leave the courtroom, and they complied. At the closed hearing, counsel for appellants observed that no evidentiary findings had been made by the court prior to the entry of its closure order and pointed out that the court had failed to consider any other, less drastic measures

---

1. A newspaper account published the next day reported the mistrial and went on to note that "[a] key piece of evidence in Stevenson's original conviction was a bloodstained shirt obtained from Stevenson's wife soon after the killing. The Virginia Supreme Court, however, ruled that the shirt was entered into evidence improperly." App. 34a.

within its power to ensure a fair trial. * * * Counsel for appellants argued that constitutional considerations mandated that before ordering closure, the court should first decide that the rights of the defendant could be protected in no other way.

Counsel for defendant Stevenson pointed out that this was the fourth time he was standing trial. He also referred to "difficulty with information between the jurors," and stated that he "didn't want information to leak out," be published by the media, perhaps inaccurately, and then be seen by the jurors. Defense counsel argued that these things, plus the fact that "this is a small community," made this a proper case for closure. * * *

* * * The court denied the motion to vacate and ordered the trial to continue the following morning "with the press and public excluded."

What transpired when the closed trial resumed the next day was disclosed in the following manner by an order of the court entered September 12, 1978:

> "[I]n the absence of the jury, the defendant by counsel made a Motion that a mistrial be declared, which motion was taken under advisement.
>
> "At the conclusion of the Commonwealth's evidence, the attorney for the defendant moved the Court to strike the Commonwealth's evidence on grounds stated to the record, which Motion was sustained by the Court.
>
> "And the jury having been excused, the Court doth find the accused NOT GUILTY of Murder, as charged in the Indictment, and he was allowed to depart." Id., at 22a.[3]

On September 27, 1978, the trial court granted appellants' motion to intervene *nunc pro tunc* in the Stevenson case. Appellants then petitioned the Virginia Supreme Court for writs of mandamus and prohibition and filed an appeal from the trial court's closure order. On July 9, 1979, the Virginia Supreme Court dismissed the mandamus and prohibition petitions and, finding no reversible error, denied the petition for appeal. * * *

* * *

Since the Virginia Supreme Court declined plenary review, it is reasonably foreseeable that other trials may be closed by other judges without any more showing of need than is presented on this record. More often than not, criminal trials will be of sufficiently short duration that a closure order "will evade review, or at least considered plenary review in this Court." *Nebraska Press, supra,* at 547. Accordingly, we turn to the merits.

II

We begin consideration of this case by noting that the precise issue presented here has not previously been before this Court for decision.

---

3. At oral argument, it was represented to the Court that tapes of the trial were available to the public as soon as the trial terminated.

In *Gannett Co. v. DePasquale, supra,* the Court was not required to decide whether a right of access to trials, as distinguished from hearings on pretrial motions, was constitutionally guaranteed. The Court held that the Sixth Amendment's guarantee to the accused of a public trial gave neither the public nor the press an enforceable right of access to a pretrial suppression hearing. One concurring opinion specifically emphasized that "a hearing on a motion before trial to suppress evidence is not a trial...." 443 U.S., at 394 (BURGER, C.J., concurring). Moreover, the Court did not decide whether the First and Fourteenth Amendments guarantee a right of the public to attend trials * * *.

* * * But here for the first time the Court is asked to decide whether a criminal trial itself may be closed to the public upon the unopposed request of a defendant, without any demonstration that closure is required to protect the defendant's superior right to a fair trial, or that some other overriding consideration requires closure.

* * *

As we have shown, and as was shown in both the Court's opinion and the dissent in *Gannett,* 443 U.S., at 384, 386, n. 15, 418–425, the historical evidence demonstrates conclusively that at the time when our organic laws were adopted, criminal trials both here and in England had long been presumptively open. This is no quirk of history; rather, it has long been recognized as an indispensable attribute of an Anglo-American trial. Both Hale in the 17th century and Blackstone in the 18th saw the importance of openness to the proper functioning of a trial; it gave assurance that the proceedings were conducted fairly to all concerned, and it discouraged perjury, the misconduct of participants, and decisions based on secret bias or partiality. * * *

* * *

Looking back, we see that when the ancient "town meeting" form of trial became too cumbersome, 12 members of the community were delegated to act as its surrogates, but the community did not surrender its right to observe the conduct of trials. The people retained a "right of visitation" which enabled them to satisfy themselves that justice was in fact being done.

People in an open society do not demand infallibility from their institutions, but it is difficult for them to accept what they are prohibited from observing. When a criminal trial is conducted in the open, there is at least an opportunity both for understanding the system in general and its workings in a particular case:

> "The educative effect of public attendance is a material advantage. Not only is respect for the law increased and intelligent acquaintance acquired with the methods of government, but a strong confidence in judicial remedies is secured which could never be inspired by a system of secrecy." 6 Wigmore, *supra,* at 438. See also 1 J. Bentham, Rationale of Judicial Evidence, at 525.

In earlier times, both in England and America, attendance at court was a common mode of "passing the time." See, e.g., 6 Wigmore, *supra,* at 436; Mueller, *supra,* at 6. With the press, cinema, and electronic media now supplying the representations or reality of the real life drama once available only in the courtroom, attendance at court is no longer a widespread pastime. Yet "[i]t is not unrealistic even in this day to believe that public inclusion affords citizens a form of legal education and hopefully promotes confidence in the fair administration of justice." State v. Schmit, 273 Minn. 78, 87–88, 139 N.W.2d 800, 807 (1966). Instead of acquiring information about trials by firsthand observation or by word of mouth from those who attended, people now acquire it chiefly through the print and electronic media. In a sense, this validates the media claim of functioning as surrogates for the public. While media representatives enjoy the same right of access as the public, they often are provided special seating and priority of entry so that they may report what people in attendance have seen and heard. This "contribute[s] to public understanding of the rule of law and to comprehension of the functioning of the entire criminal justice system * * *." Nebraska Press Assn. v. Stuart, 427 U.S., at 587 (BRENNAN J., concurring in judgment).

C

From this unbroken, uncontradicted history, supported by reasons as valid today as in centuries past, we are bound to conclude that a presumption of openness inheres in the very nature of a criminal trial under our system of justice. * * *

Despite the history of criminal trials being presumptively open since long before the Constitution, the State presses its contention that neither the Constitution nor the Bill of Rights contains any provision which by its terms guarantees to the public the right to attend criminal trials. Standing alone, this is correct, but there remains the question whether, absent an explicit provision, the Constitution affords protection against exclusion of the public from criminal trials.

III

A

The First Amendment, in conjunction with the Fourteenth, prohibits governments from "abridging the freedom of speech, or of the press; or the right of the people peaceably to assemble, and to petition the Government for a redress of grievances." These expressly guaranteed freedoms share a common core purpose of assuring freedom of communication on matters relating to the functioning of government. Plainly it would be difficult to single out any aspect of government of higher concern and importance to the people than the manner in which criminal trials are conducted; as we have shown, recognition of this pervades the centuries-old history of open trials and the opinions of this Court. * * *

The Bill of Rights was enacted against the backdrop of the long history of trials being presumptively open. Public access to trials was then regarded as an important aspect of the process itself; the conduct of trials "before as many of the people as chuse to attend" was regarded as one of "the inestimable advantages of a free English constitution of government." 1 Journals 106, 107. In guaranteeing freedoms such as those of speech and press, the First Amendment can be read as protecting the right of everyone to attend trials so as to give meaning to those explicit guarantees. "[T]he First Amendment goes beyond protection of the press and the self-expression of individuals to prohibit government from limiting the stock of information from which members of the public may draw." First National Bank of Boston v. Bellotti, 435 U.S. 765, 783 (1978). * * *

It is not crucial whether we describe this right to attend criminal trials to hear, see, and communicate observations concerning them as a "right of access," cf. *Gannett, supra,* at 397 (POWELL, J., concurring); Saxbe v. Washington Post Co., 417 U.S. 843 (1974); Pell v. Procunier, 417 U.S. 817 (1974),[11] or a "right to gather information," for we have recognized that "without some protection for seeking out the news, freedom of the press could be eviscerated." Branzburg v. Hayes, 408 U.S. 665, 681 (1972). The explicit, guaranteed rights to speak and to publish concerning what takes place at a trial would lose much meaning if access to observe the trial could, as it was here, be foreclosed arbitrarily.[12]

B

The right of access to places traditionally open to the public, as criminal trials have long been, may be seen as assured by the amalgam of the First Amendment guarantees of speech and press; and their affinity to the right of assembly is not without relevance. From the outset, the right of assembly was regarded not only as an independent right but also as a catalyst to augment the free exercise of the other First Amendment rights with which it was deliberately linked by the draftsmen.[13] "The right of peaceable assembly is a right cognate to

---

11. *Procunier* and *Saxbe* are distinguishable in the sense that they were concerned with penal institutions which, by definition, are not "open" or public places. Penal institutions do not share the long tradition of openness, although traditionally there have been visiting committees of citizens, and there is no doubt that legislative committees could exercise plenary oversight and "visitation rights." * * *

12. That the right to attend may be exercised by people less frequently today when information as to trials generally reaches them by way of print and electronic media in no way alters the basic right. Instead of relying on personal observation or reports from neighbors as in the past, most people receive information concerning trials through the media whose representatives "are entitled to the same rights [to attend trials] as the general public." * * *

13. When the First Congress was debating the Bill of Rights, it was contended that there was no need separately to assert the right of assembly because it was subsumed in freedom of speech. Mr. Sedgwick of Massachusetts argued that inclusion of "assembly" among the enumerated rights would tend to make the Congress "appear trifling in the eyes of their constituents. * * * If people freely converse together, they must assemble for that purpose; it is a self-evident, unalienable right which the people possess; it is certainly a thing that never would be called in question. * * *" 1 Annals of Cong. 731 (1789). Since the right existed independent of any written guarantee, Sedgwick went on to argue that if it were the drafting committee's purpose to protect all inherent rights of the people by listing them, "they might have gone into a very lengthy enumeration of rights," but this was unnecessary, he said, "in a Government where none of them were intended to be infringed." *Id.,* at 732.

Mr. Page of Virginia responded, however, that at times "such rights have been opposed," and that "people have * * * been prevented from assembling together on their lawful occasions":

"[T]herefore it is well to guard against such stretches of authority, by inserting

those of free speech and free press and is equally fundamental." De Jonge v. Oregon, 299 U.S. 353, 364 (1937). People assemble in public places not only to speak or to take action, but also to listen, observe, and learn; indeed, they may "assembl[e] for any lawful purpose," Hague v. CIO, 307 U.S. 496, 519 (1939) (opinion of Stone, J.). Subject to the traditional time, place, and manner restrictions, see, e.g., Cox v. New Hampshire, 312 U.S. 569 (1941); see also Cox v. Louisiana, 379 U.S. 559, 560–564 (1965), streets, sidewalks, and parks are places traditionally open, where First Amendment rights may be exercised, see *Hague v. CIO, supra,* at 515 (opinion of Roberts, J.); a trial courtroom also is a public place where the people generally—and representatives of the media—have a right to be present, and where their presence historically has been thought to enhance the integrity and quality of what takes place.[14]

C

The State argues that the Constitution nowhere spells out a guarantee for the right of the public to attend trials, and that accordingly no such right is protected. The possibility that such a contention could be made did not escape the notice of the Constitution's draftsmen; they were concerned that some important rights might be thought disparaged because not specifically guaranteed. It was even argued that because of this danger no Bill of Rights should be adopted. See, e.g., The Federalist No. 84 (A. Hamilton). In a letter to Thomas Jefferson in October 1788, James Madison explained why he, although "in favor of a bill of rights," had "not viewed it in an important light" up to that time: "I conceive that in a certain degree * * * the rights in question are reserved by the manner in which the federal powers are granted." He went on to state that "there is great reason to fear that a positive declaration of some of the most essential rights could not be obtained in the requisite latitude." 5 Writings of James Madison 271 (G. Hunt ed. 1904).[15]

---

the privilege in the declaration of rights. If the people could be deprived of the power of assembling under any pretext whatsoever, they might be deprived of every other privilege contained in the clause." *Ibid.* The motion to strike "assembly" was defeated. *Id.,* at 733.

14. It is of course true that the right of assembly in our Bill of Rights was in large part drafted in reaction to restrictions on such rights in England. See, e.g., 1 Geo. 1, stat. 2, ch. 5 (1714); cf. 36 Geo. 3, ch. 8 (1795). As we have shown, the right of Englishmen to attend trials was not similarly limited; but it would be ironic indeed if the very historic openness of the trial could militate against protection of the right to attend it. The Constitution guarantees more than simply freedom from those abuses which led the Framers to single out particular rights. The very purpose of the First Amendment is to guarantee all facets of each right described; its draftsmen sought both to protect the "rights of Englishmen" and to enlarge their scope. See Bridges v. California, 314 U.S. 252, 263–265 (1941).

"There are no contrary implications in any part of the history of the period in which the First Amendment was framed and adopted. No purpose in ratifying the Bill of Rights was clearer than that of securing for the people of the United States much greater freedom of religion, expression, assembly, and petition than the people of Great Britain had ever enjoyed." *Id.,* at 265.

15. Madison's comments in Congress also reveal the perceived need for some sort of constitutional "saving clause," which, among other things, would serve to foreclose application to the Bill of Rights of the maxim that the affirmation of particular rights implies a negation of those not expressly defined. See 1 Annals of Cong.

But arguments such as the State makes have not precluded recognition of important rights not enumerated. Notwithstanding the appropriate caution against reading into the Constitution rights not explicitly defined, the Court has acknowledged that certain unarticulated rights are implicit in enumerated guarantees. For example, the rights of association and of privacy, the right to be presumed innocent, and the right to be judged by a standard of proof beyond a reasonable doubt in a criminal trial, as well as the right to travel, appear nowhere in the Constitution or Bill of Rights. Yet these important but unarticulated rights have nonetheless been found to share constitutional protection in common with explicit guarantees. The concerns expressed by Madison and others have thus been resolved; fundamental rights, even though not expressly guaranteed, have been recognized by the Court as indispensable to the enjoyment of rights explicitly defined.

We hold that the right to attend criminal trials [17] is implicit in the guarantees of the First Amendment; without the freedom to attend such trials, which people have exercised for centuries, important aspects of freedom of speech and "of the press could be eviscerated." *Branzburg*, 408 U.S., at 681.

D

Having concluded there was a guaranteed right of the public under the First and Fourteenth Amendments to attend the trial of Stevenson's case, we return to the closure order challenged by appellants. The Court in *Gannett* made clear that although the Sixth Amendment guarantees the accused a right to a public trial, it does not give a right to a private trial. 443 U.S., at 382. Despite the fact this was the fourth trial of the accused, the trial judge made no findings to support closure; no inquiry was made as to whether alternative solutions would have met the need to ensure fairness; there was no recognition of any right under the Constitution for the public or press to attend the trial. * * * There was no suggestion that any problems with witnesses could not have been dealt with by their exclusion from the courtroom or their sequestration during the trial. * * * Nor is there anything to indicate that sequestration of the jurors would not have guarded against their being subjected to any improper information. All of the alternatives admittedly present difficulties for trial courts, but none of the factors relied on here was beyond the realm of the manageable. Absent an overriding interest articulated in findings, the trial of a criminal case must be open to the public. Accordingly, the judgment under review is

Reversed.

MR. JUSTICE POWELL took no part in the consideration or decision of this case.

438–440 (1789). See also, e.g., 2 J. Story, Commentaries on the Constitution of the United States 651 (5th ed. 1891). Madison's efforts, culminating in the Ninth Amendment, served to allay the fears of those who were concerned that expressing certain guarantees could be read as excluding others.

17. Whether the public has a right to attend trials of civil cases is a question not raised by the case, but we note that historically both civil and criminal trials have been presumptively open.

MR. JUSTICE WHITE, concurring.

This case would have been unnecessary had Gannett Co. v. DePasquale, 443 U.S. 368 (1979), construed the Sixth Amendment to forbid excluding the public from criminal proceedings except in narrowly defined circumstances. But the Court there rejected the submission of four of us to this effect, thus requiring that the First Amendment issue involved here be addressed. On this issue, I concur in the opinion of The Chief Justice.

MR. JUSTICE STEVENS, concurring.

This is a watershed case. Until today the Court has accorded virtually absolute protection to the dissemination of information or ideas, but never before has it squarely held that the acquisition of newsworthy matter is entitled to any constitutional protection whatsoever. An additional word of emphasis is therefore appropriate.

Twice before, the Court has implied that any governmental restriction on access to information, no matter how severe and no matter how unjustified, would be constitutionally acceptable so long as it did not single out the press for special disabilities not applicable to the public at large. In a dissent joined by Mr. Justice Brennan and Mr. Justice Marshall in Saxbe v. Washington Post Co., 417 U.S. 843, 850, Mr. Justice Powell unequivocally rejected the conclusion that "any governmental restriction on press access to information, so long as it is nondiscriminatory, falls outside the purview of First Amendment concern." *Id.,* at 857 (emphasis in original). And in Houchins v. KQED, Inc., 438 U.S. 1, 19–40, I explained at length why Mr. Justice Brennan, Mr. Justice Powell, and I were convinced that "[a]n official prison policy of concealing * * * knowledge from the public by arbitrarily cutting off the flow of information at its source abridges the freedom of speech and of the press protected by the First and Fourteenth Amendments to the Constitution." * * * Since Mr. Justice Marshall and Mr. Justice Blackmun were unable to participate in that case, a majority of the Court neither accepted nor rejected that conclusion or the contrary conclusion expressed in the prevailing opinions. Today, however, for the first time, the Court unequivocally holds that an arbitrary interference with access to important information is an abridgment of the freedom of speech and of the press protected by the First Amendment.

It is somewhat ironic that the Court should find more reason to recognize a right of access today than it did in *Houchins.* For *Houchins* involved the plight of a segment of society least able to protect itself, an attack on a long-standing policy of concealment, and an absence of any legitimate justification for abridging public access to information about how government operates. In this case we are protecting the interests of the most powerful voices in the community, we are concerned with an almost unique exception to an established tradition of openness in the conduct of criminal trials, and it is likely that the closure order was motivated by the judge's desire to protect the individual defendant from the burden of a fourth criminal trial.

In any event, for the reasons stated in Part II of my *Houchins* opinion, 438 U.S., at 30–38, as well as those stated by The Chief Justice today, I agree that the First Amendment protects the public and the press from abridgment of their rights of access to information about the operation of their government, including the Judicial Branch; given the total absence of any record justification for the closure order entered in this case, that order violated the First Amendment.

MR. JUSTICE BRENNAN, with whom MR. JUSTICE MARSHALL joins, concurring in the judgment. [Omitted.]

* * *

MR. JUSTICE STEWART, concurring in the judgment. [Omitted.]

* * *

MR. JUSTICE BLACKMUN, concurring in the judgment.

* * *

* * * I remain convinced that the right to a public trial is to be found where the Constitution explicitly placed it—in the Sixth Amendment.

* * *

MR. JUSTICE REHNQUIST, dissenting.

In the Gilbert and Sullivan operetta "Iolanthe," the Lord Chancellor recites:

"The Law is the true embodiment of everything that's excellent, It has no kind of fault or flaw, And I, my Lords, embody the Law."

It is difficult not to derive more than a little of this flavor from the various opinions supporting the judgment in this case. * * *

For the reasons stated in my separate concurrence in Gannett Co. v. DePasquale, 443 U.S. 368, 403 (1979), I do not believe that either the First or Sixth Amendment, as made applicable to the States by the Fourteenth, requires that a State's reasons for denying public access to a trial, where both the prosecuting attorney and the defendant have consented to an order of closure approved by the judge, are subject to any additional constitutional review at our hands. And I most certainly do not believe that the Ninth Amendment confers upon us any such power to review orders of state trial judges closing trials in such situations. * * *

* * *

The issue here is not whether the "right" to freedom of the press conferred by the First Amendment to the Constitution overrides the defendant's "right" to a fair trial conferred by other Amendments to the Constitution; it is instead whether any provision in the Constitution may fairly be read to prohibit what the trial judge in the Virginia state-court system did in this case. Being unable to find any such prohibition in the First, Sixth, Ninth, or any other Amendment to the United States Constitution, or in the Constitution itself, I dissent.

8. The Blurred Boundary Between Private and Public Property

MARSH v. ALABAMA
Supreme Court of the United States, 1946.
326 U.S. 501, 66 S.Ct. 276, 90 L.Ed. 265.

MR. JUSTICE BLACK delivered the opinion of the Court.

In this case we are asked to decide whether a State, consistently with the First and Fourteenth Amendments, can impose criminal punishment on a person who undertakes to distribute religious literature on the premises of a company-owned town contrary to the wishes of the town's management. The town, a suburb of Mobile, Alabama, known as Chickasaw, is owned by the Gulf Shipbuilding Corporation. Except for that it has all the characteristics of any other American town. The property consists of residential buildings, streets, a system of sewers, a sewage disposal plant and a "business block" on which business places are situated. A deputy of the Mobile County Sheriff, paid by the company, serves as the town's policeman. Merchants and service establishments have rented the stores and business places on the business block and the United States uses one of the places as a post office from which six carriers deliver mail to the people of Chickasaw and the adjacent area. The town and the surrounding neighborhood, which can not be distinguished from the Gulf property by anyone not familiar with the property lines, are thickly settled, and according to all indications the residents use the business block as their regular shopping center. * * *

Appellant, a Jehovah's Witness, came onto the sidewalk we have just described, stood near the post office and undertook to distribute religious literature. In the stores the corporation had posted a notice which read as follows: "This is Private Property, and Without Written Permission, No Street, or House Vendor, Agent or Solicitation of Any Kind Will Be Permitted." Appellant was warned that she could not distribute the literature without a permit and told that no permit would be issued to her. She protested that the company rule could not be constitutionally applied so as to prohibit her from distributing religious writings. When she was asked to leave the sidewalk and Chickasaw she declined. The deputy sheriff arrested her and she was charged in the state court with violating Title 14, § 426 of the 1940 Alabama Code which makes it a crime to enter or remain on the premises of another after having been warned not to do so. * * *

Had the title to Chickasaw belonged not to a private but to a municipal corporation and had appellant been arrested for violating a municipal ordinance rather than a ruling by those appointed by the corporation to manage a company town it would have been clear that appellant's conviction must be reversed. Under our decision in Lovell v. Griffin, 303 U.S. 444 and others which have followed that case, neither a State nor a municipality can completely bar the distribution of literature containing religious or political ideas on its streets, sidewalks and public places or make the right to distribute dependent on a flat license tax or permit to be issued by an official who could deny it at will. * * * Our question then narrows down to this: Can those people who live in or come to Chickasaw be denied freedom of press and religion simply because a single company has legal title to all the town? For it is the State's contention that the mere fact that all the property interests in the town are held by a single company is enough to give that company power, enforceable by a state statute, to abridge these freedoms.

We do not agree that the corporation's property interests settle the question. The State urges in effect that the corporation's right to control the inhabitants of Chickasaw is coextensive with the right of a homeowner to regulate the conduct of his guests. We cannot accept that contention. Ownership does not always mean absolute dominion. The more an owner, for his advantage, opens up his property for use by the public in general, the more do his rights become circumscribed by the statutory and constitutional rights of those who use it. * * * Thus, the owners of privately held bridges, ferries, turnpikes and railroads may not operate them as freely as a farmer does his farm. Since these facilities are built and operated primarily to benefit the public and since their operation is essentially a public function, it is subject to state regulation. * * *

* * * Whether a corporation or a municipality owns or possesses the town the public in either case has an identical interest in the functioning of the community in such manner that the channels of communication remain free. As we have heretofore stated, the town of Chickasaw does not function differently from any other town. * * *

* * *

When we balance the Constitutional rights of owners of property against those of the people to enjoy freedom of press and religion, as we must here, we remain mindful of the fact that the latter occupy a preferred position. As we have stated before, the right to exercise the liberties safeguarded by the First Amendment "lies at the foundation of free government by free men" and we must in all cases "weigh the circumstances and * * * appraise the * * * reasons * * * in support of the regulation * * * of the rights." Schneider v. State, 308 U.S. 147, 161. In our view the circumstance that the property rights to the premises where the deprivation of liberty, here involved, took place, were held by others than the public, is not sufficient to justify the State's permitting a corporation to govern a community of citizens so as to restrict their fundamental liberties and the enforcement of such restraint by the application of a state statute. Insofar as the State has attempted to impose criminal punishment on appellant for undertaking to distribute religious literature in a company town, its action cannot stand. The case is reversed and the cause remanded for further proceedings not inconsistent with this opinion.

Reversed and remanded.

MR. JUSTICE JACKSON took no part in the consideration or decision of this case.

Mr. Justice Frankfurter, concurring.

* * *

A company-owned town gives rise to a net-work of property relations. As to these, the judicial organ of a State has the final say. But a company-owned town is a town. In its community aspects it does not differ from other towns. These community aspects are decisive in adjusting the relations now before us, and more particularly in adjudicating the clash of freedoms which the Bill of Rights was designed to resolve—the freedom of the community to regulate its life and the freedom of the individual to exercise his religion and to disseminate his ideas. Title to property as defined by State law controls property relations; it cannot control issues of civil liberties which arise precisely because a company town is a town as well as a congeries of property relations. And similarly the technical distinctions on which a finding of "trespass" so often depends are too tenuous to control decision regarding the scope of the vital liberties guaranteed by the Constitution.

Accordingly, as I have already indicated, so long as the scope of the guarantees of the Due Process Clause of the Fourteenth Amendment by absorption of the First remains that which the Court gave to it in the series of cases in the October Term, 1942, the circumstances of the present case seem to me clearly to fall within it. * * *

Mr. Justice Reed, dissenting.

* * * This is the first case to extend by law the privilege of religious exercises beyond public places or to private places without the assent of the owner. * * *

As the rule now announced permits this intrusion, without possibility of protection of the property by law, and apparently is equally applicable to the freedom of speech and the press, it seems appropriate to express a dissent to this, to us, novel Constitutional doctrine. Of course, such principle may subsequently be restricted by this Court to the precise facts of this case—that is to private property in a company town where the owner for his own advantage has permitted a restricted public use by his licensees and invitees. Such distinctions are of degree and require new arbitrary lines, judicially drawn, instead of those hitherto established by legislation and precedent. While the power of this Court, as the interpreter of the Constitution to determine what use of real property by the owner makes that property subject, at will, to the reasonable practice of religious exercises by strangers, cannot be doubted, we find nothing in the principles of the First Amendment, adopted now into the Fourteenth, which justifies their application to the facts of this case.

* * *

* * * Appellant was distributing religious pamphlets on a privately owned passway or sidewalk thirty feet removed from a public highway of the State of Alabama and remained on these private premises after an authorized order to get off. We do not understand from the record that there was objection to appellant's use of the nearby public highway and under our decisions she could rightfully have continued her activities a few feet from the spot she insisted upon using. An owner of property may very well have been willing for the public to use the private passway for business purposes and yet have been unwilling to furnish space for street trades or a location for the practice of religious exhortations by itinerants. The passway here in question was not put to any different use than other private passways that lead to privately owned areas, amusement places, resort hotels or other businesses. There had been no dedication of the sidewalk to the public use, express or implied. Alabama so decided and we understand that this Court accepts that conclusion. Alabama, also, decided that appellant violated by her activities the above-quoted state statute.

* * *

* * * The right to communicate ideas was expressed by us in Jamison v. Texas, 318 U.S. 413, 416, as follows: "But one who is rightfully on a street which the state has left open to the public carries with him there as elsewhere the Constitutional right to express his views in an orderly fashion."

Our Constitution guarantees to every man the right to express his views in an orderly fashion. An essential element of "orderly" is that the man shall also have a right to use the place he chooses for his exposition. The rights of the owner, which the Constitution protects as well as the right of free speech, are not outweighed by the interests of the trespasser, even though he trespasses in behalf of religion or free speech. We cannot say that Jehovah's Witnesses can claim the privilege of a license, which has never been granted, to hold their meetings in other private places, merely because the owner has admitted the public to them for other limited purposes. * * *

The CHIEF JUSTICE and MR. JUSTICE BURTON join in this dissent.

NOTE

I. There are several different points of emphasis in *Marsh v. Alabama*. Which do you find most persuasive?[83] Why?

A. At the beginning and again at the end, the Court emphasizes the state's own reviewable action as follows:

> In this case, we are asked to decide whether a State, consistently with the First and Fourteenth Amendments, can impose criminal sanctions on a person who undertakes to distribute religious literature on the premises of a company-

---

83. Cf. Harlan, J., dissenting in Evans v. Newton, 382 U.S. 297, 319, 86 S.Ct. 486, 498–99, 15 L.Ed.2d 373, 388 (1966) (describing *Marsh* as "a shaky precedent"), and see also his general objection, dissenting opinion in Burton v. Wilmington Parking Auth., 365 U.S. 715, 728, 81 S.Ct. 856, 864, 6 L.Ed.2d 45, 54 (1961). ("The Court's opinion, by a process of first undiscriminatingly throwing together various factual bits and pieces and then undermining the resulting structure by an equally vague disclaimer, seems to me to leave completely at sea just what it is in this record that satisfies the requirement of 'state action.' ")

owned town contrary to the wishes of the town's management. * * * Insofar as the State has attempted to impose criminal punishment on appellant for undertaking to distribute religious literature in a company town, its action cannot stand.

Is it, then, the use of state power to describe the conduct of the defendant as a crime, and its actions in imposing criminal sanctions, that violates the first amendment? Why?

1. A person who enters or remains on the premises of another for the purpose of distributing religious literature after having been warned not to do so, is guilty of criminal trespass and subject to 30 days in jail, $500 fine, or both.

2. A person who enters or remains on the premises of another after having been warned not to do so, is guilty of criminal trespass and subject to 30 days in jail, $500 fine, or both.[84]

B. If it is the state's use of criminal sanctions, and not the company's policy per se that offends the fourteenth amendment, what follows from that? Suppose the next week Marsh returned to Chickasaw, again to distribute Jehovah's Witness pamphlets in the same place as before. On this occasion, too, an authorized agent of the company, after pointing to the same signs as before (still in place) again asks Marsh to leave. Suppose Marsh refuses, following which the company sues Marsh in state court for civil trespass, but not pressing any criminal charge. Would state court recognition of the validity of the plaintiff's privately brought common law civil trespass action violate the first amendment? Why?[85]

C. In *Marsh,* the entirety of the town was under one corporate ownership, with power akin to that of a city council. But what if it were not so clear a case? Suppose the Gulf Shipbuilding Company, requiring capital to stay in the shipbuilding business, sells off half of its property such that an independent company (e.g., RJR Nabisco) becomes sole owner of all the land, buildings, streets, etc., on one half of Main Street, Gulf now being owner of merely the remaining half. Gulf

---

84. In case 1, the state's position seems to be that of disfavoring acts of trespass by criminal sanction only if they involve religious speech (for only one who attempts to distribute religious literature contrary to the owner's wishes is subject to arrest and no one else). Cf. Burton v. Wilmington Parking Auth., 365 U.S. at 728, 81 S.Ct. at 864, 6 L.Ed.2d at 54 (Stewart, J., concurring) (a state law generally disallowing restaurants to refuse service to customers of good deportment but nonetheless permitting them to refuse such service on grounds of race is violative of the fourteenth amendment). In case 2, the state's position is strictly a general position of protecting "private property rights." If it is nonetheless unconstitutional as applied, what makes it so?

85. Alternatively, suppose merely that employees of the company used minimum reasonable self-help to eject Marsh following Marsh's refusal to leave as requested, and Marsh sued the company for civil assault and battery (or sued for an injunction); if the state court acknowledged that the company's nonviolent ejection of Marsh was privileged under its common law (or refused an injunction), would the state court's acceptance of the defense of privilege be deemed to violate the fourteenth amendment? (Does *Marsh v. Alabama* stand for the proposition that unless the state affirmatively sides with Marsh, i.e. to enable Marsh to distribute her pamphlets at the time, in the place, and in the manner she sought to do, the state is guilty of abridging Marsh's freedom of speech?)

retains the same signage as before. It has nothing to say as to how RJR Nabisco admits or does not admit solicitors to its property. Marsh seeks to distribute Jehovah's Witness pamphlets on Gulf property. As before, Gulf says "no." How will this case come out?[86]

II. In many communities, the downtown area has been pretty well deserted such that efforts to engage residents by handing them leaflets, by engaging them in conversation, or by peaceful demonstration or soapbox talks in the town plaza, may go relatively unnoticed. Businesses have moved out to the suburbs and to large shopping malls surrounded by extensive parking aprons, taking the activity of the community to the malls. To what extent may the first amendment extend free speech easements to these locations as well? Consider the following principal cases.[87]

HUDGENS v. NLRB

Supreme Court of the United States, 1976.
424 U.S. 507, 96 S.Ct. 1029, 47 L.Ed.2d 196.

MR. JUSTICE STEWART delivered the opinion of the Court.

* * *

I

The petitioner, Scott Hudgens, is the owner of the North DeKalb Shopping Center, located in suburban Atlanta, Ga. The center consists of a single large building with an enclosed mall. Surrounding the building is a parking area which can accommodate 2,640 automobiles. The shopping center houses 60 retail stores leased to various businesses. One of the lessees is the Butler Shoe Co. Most of the stores, including Butler's, can be entered only from the interior mall.

In January 1971, warehouse employees of the Butler Shoe Co. went on strike to protest the company's failure to agree to demands made by their union in contract negotiations. The strikers decided to picket not only Butler's warehouse but its nine retail stores in the Atlanta area as well, including the store in the North DeKalb Shopping Center. On January 22, 1971, four of the striking warehouse employees entered the center's enclosed mall carrying placards which read: "Butler Shoe Warehouse on Strike, AFL–CIO, Local 315." The general manager of

---

86. Will it make a difference that RJR Nabisco may have no equivalent "no trespass" policy, i.e. it may welcome such activity, such that Marsh could have handed out her pamphlets just a few feet away?— Suppose RJR Nabisco and Gulf both subsequently sell off half of each of their respective holdings, such that each now does not control either a town or half a town, but a quarter "town." At what point will *Marsh* no longer control? Why?

87. See Wechsler, Toward Neutral Principles of Constitutional Law, 173 Harv. L.Rev. 1, 31 (1959). ("Many understandably would like to perceive in [cases such as *Marsh*] a principle susceptible of broad extension, applying to the other power aggregates in our society limitations of the kind the Constitution has imposed on government.") (Citing Berle, Constitutional Limitations on Corporate Activity—Protection of Personal Rights From Invasion Through Economic Power, 100 U.Pa.L.Rev. 933 (1952).)

the shopping center informed the employees that they could not picket within the mall or on the parking lot and threatened them with arrest if they did not leave. The employees departed but returned a short time later and began picketing in an area of the mall immediately adjacent to the entrances of the Butler store. After the picketing had continued for approximately 30 minutes, the shopping center manager again informed the pickets that if they did not leave they would be arrested for trespassing. The pickets departed.

The union subsequently filed with the Board an unfair labor practice charge against Hudgens, alleging interference with rights protected by § 7 of the Act, 29 U.S.C. § 157. Relying on this Court's decision in Food Employees v. Logan Valley Plaza, 391 U.S. 308, the Board entered a cease-and-desist order against Hudgens, reasoning that because the warehouse employees enjoyed a First Amendment right to picket on the shopping center property, the owner's threat of arrest violated § 8(a)(1) of the Act, 29 U.S.C. § 158(a)(1). * * *

II

It is, of course, a commonplace that the constitutional guarantee of free speech is a guarantee only against abridgment by government, federal or state. * * * Thus, while statutory or common law may in some situations extend protection or provide redress against a private corporation or person who seeks to abridge the free expression of others, no such protection or redress is provided by the Constitution itself.

This elementary proposition is little more than a truism. But even truisms are not always unexceptionably true, and an exception to this one was recognized almost 30 years ago in Marsh v. Alabama, 326 U.S. 501. In *Marsh,* a Jehovah's Witness who had distributed literature without a license on a sidewalk in Chickasaw, Ala., was convicted of criminal trespass. Chickasaw was a so-called company town, wholly owned by the Gulf Shipbuilding Corp. * * *

The Court pointed out that if the "title" to Chickasaw had "belonged not to a private but to a municipal corporation and had appellant been arrested for violating a municipal ordinance rather than a ruling by those appointed by the corporation to manage a company town it would have been clear that appellant's conviction must be reversed." * * * Concluding that Gulf's "property interests" should not be allowed to lead to a different result in Chickasaw, which did "not function differently from any other town," * * *, the Court invoked the First and Fourteenth Amendments to reverse the appellant's conviction.

It was the *Marsh* case that in 1968 provided the foundation for the Court's decision in Amalgamated Food Employees Union v. Logan Valley Plaza, 391 U.S. 308. That case involved peaceful picketing within a large shopping center near Altoona, Pa. One of the tenants of the shopping center was a retail store that employed a wholly nonunion staff. Members of a local union picketed the store, carrying signs proclaiming that it was nonunion and that its employees were not receiving union wages or other union benefits. The picketing took place on the shopping center's property in the immediate vicinity of the store. * * * This Court held that the doctrine of the *Marsh* case required reversal of that judgment.

* * *

The Court's opinion then reviewed the *Marsh* case in detail, emphasized the similarities between the business block in Chickasaw, Ala., and the Logan Valley shopping center, and unambiguously concluded:

> "The shopping center here is clearly the functional equivalent of the business district of Chickasaw involved in Marsh."
> * * *

Upon the basis of that conclusion, the Court held that the First and Fourteenth Amendments required reversal of the judgment of the Pennsylvania Supreme Court.

There were three dissenting opinions in the *Logan Valley* case, one of them by the author of the Court's opinion in *Marsh,* Mr. Justice Black. His disagreement with the Court's reasoning was total:

* * *

> "The question is, Under what circumstances can private property be treated as though it were public? The answer that *Marsh* gives is when that property has taken on all the attributes of a town, i.e. 'residential buildings, streets, a system of sewers, a sewage disposal plant and a "business block" on which business places are situated.' 326 U.S., at 502. I can find nothing in *Marsh* which indicates that if one of these features is present, e.g., a business district, this is sufficient for the Court to confiscate a part of an owner's private property and give its use to people who want to picket on it." * * *

* * *

Four years later the Court had occasion to reconsider the *Logan Valley* doctrine in Lloyd Corp. v. Tanner, 407 U.S. 551. That case involved a shopping center covering some 50 acres in downtown Portland, Ore. On a November day in 1968 five young people entered the mall of the shopping center and distributed handbills protesting the then ongoing American military operations in Vietnam. Security guards told them to leave, and they did so, "to avoid arrest." *Id.,* at 556. They subsequently brought suit in a Federal District Court, seeking declaratory and injunctive relief. The trial court ruled in their favor, holding that the distribution of handbills on the shopping center's property was protected by the First and Fourteenth Amendments. The Court of Appeals for the Ninth Circuit affirmed the judgment, 446 F.2d 545, expressly relying on this Court's *Marsh* and *Logan Valley* decisions. This Court reversed the judgment of the Court of Appeals.

The Court in its *Lloyd* opinion did not say that it was overruling the *Logan Valley* decision. Indeed, a substantial portion of the Court's opinion in *Lloyd* was devoted to pointing out the differences between the two cases, noting particularly that, in contrast to the handbilling in

Lloyd, the picketing in *Logan Valley* had been specifically directed to a store in the shopping center and the pickets had had no other reasonable opportunity to reach their intended audience. * * * But the fact is that the reasoning of the Court's opinion in *Lloyd* cannot be squared with the reasoning of the Court's opinion in *Logan Valley.*

* * *

If a large self-contained shopping center is the functional equivalent of a municipality, as *Logan Valley* held, then the First and Fourteenth Amendments would not permit control of speech within such a center to depend upon the speech's content. For while a municipality may constitutionally impose reasonable time, place, and manner regulations on the use of its streets and sidewalks for First Amendment purposes, see Cox v. New Hampshire, 312 U.S. 569; Poulos v. New Hampshire, 345 U.S. 395, and may even forbid altogether such use of some of its facilities, see Adderley v. Florida, 385 U.S. 39; what a municipality may not do under the First and Fourteenth Amendments is to discriminate in the regulation of expression on the basis of the content of that expression, Erznoznik v. City of Jacksonville, 422 U.S. 205. "[A]bove all else, the First Amendment means that government has no power to restrict expression because of its message, its ideas, its subject matter, or its content." Police Dept. of Chicago v. Mosley, 408 U.S. 92, 95. It conversely follows, therefore, that if the respondents in the *Lloyd* case did not have a First Amendment right to enter that shopping center to distribute handbills concerning Vietnam, then the pickets in the present case did not have a First Amendment right to enter this shopping center for the purpose of advertising their strike against the Butler Shoe Co.

We conclude, in short, that under the present state of the law the constitutional guarantee of free expression has no part to play in a case such as this.

* * *

For the reasons stated in this opinion, the judgment is vacated and the case is remanded to the Court of Appeals with directions to remand to the National Labor Relations Board, so that the case may be there considered under the statutory criteria of the National Labor Relations Act alone.

It is so ordered.

Mr. Justice Stevens took no part in the consideration or decision of this case.

Mr. Justice Powell, with whom The Chief Justice joins, concurring.

Although I agree with Mr. Justice White's view concurring in the result that Lloyd Corp. v. Tanner, 407 U.S. 551 (1972), did not overrule Food Employees v. Logan Valley Plaza, 391 U.S. 308 (1968), and that the present case can be distinguished narrowly from *Logan Valley,* I nevertheless have joined the opinion of the Court today.

The law in this area, particularly with respect to whether First Amendment or labor law principles are applicable, has been less than clear since *Logan Valley* analogized a shopping center to the "company town" in Marsh v. Alabama, 326 U.S. 501. Mr. Justice Black, the author of the Court's opinion in *Marsh,* thought the decisions were irreconcilable. I now agree with Mr. Justice Black that the opinions in these cases cannot be harmonized in a principled way. Upon more mature thought, I have concluded that we would have been wiser in *Lloyd Corp.* to have confronted this disharmony rather than draw distinctions based upon rather attenuated factual differences.

The Court's opinion today clarifies the confusion engendered by these cases by accepting Mr. Justice Black's reading of *Marsh* and by recognizing more sharply the distinction between the First Amendment and labor law issues that may arise in cases of this kind. It seems to me that this clarification of the law is desirable.

Mr. Justice White, concurring in the result.

While I concur in the result reached by the Court, I find it unnecessary to inter Food Employees v. Logan Valley Plaza, 391 U.S. 308, and therefore do not join the Court's opinion. I agree that "the constitutional guarantee of free expression has no part to play in a case such as this," *ante,* at 521; but Lloyd Corp. v. Tanner, 407 U.S. 551, did not overrule *Logan Valley,* either expressly or implicitly, and I would not, somewhat after the fact, say that it did.

Mr. Justice Marshall, with whom Mr. Justice Brennan joins, dissenting.

* * *

* * * I continue to believe that the First Amendment principles underlying *Logan Valley* are sound, and were unduly limited in *Lloyd.* But accepting *Lloyd,* I am not convinced that *Logan Valley* must be overruled.

The foundation of *Logan Valley* consisted of this Court's decisions recognizing a right of access to streets, sidewalks, parks, and other public places historically associated with the exercise of First Amendment rights. * * *

The Court adopts the view that *Marsh* has no bearing on this case because the privately owned property in *Marsh* involved all the characteristics of a typical town. But there is nothing in *Marsh* to suggest that its general approach was limited to the particular facts of that case. The underlying concern in *Marsh* was that traditional public channels of communication remain free, regardless of the incidence of ownership. Given that concern, the crucial fact in *Marsh* was that the company owned the traditional forums essential for effective communication; it was immaterial that the company also owned a sewer system and that its property in other respects resembled a town.

In *Logan Valley* we recognized what the Court today refuses to recognize—that the owner of the modern shopping center complex, by dedicating his property to public use as a business district, to some extent displaces the "State" from control of historical First Amendment forums, and may acquire a virtual monopoly of places suitable for effective communication. The roadways, parking lots, and walkways of the modern shopping center may be as essential for effective speech as the streets and sidewalks in the municipal or company-owned town. I simply cannot reconcile the Court's denial of any role for the First Amendment in the shopping center with *Marsh*'s recognition of a full role for the First Amendment on the streets and sidewalks of the company-owned town.

* * *

PRUNEYARD SHOPPING CENTER v. ROBINS
Supreme Court of the United States, 1980.
447 U.S. 74, 100 S.Ct. 2035, 64 L.Ed.2d 741.

MR. JUSTICE REHNQUIST delivered the opinion of the Court.

We postponed jurisdiction of this appeal from the Supreme Court of California to decide the important federal constitutional questions it presented. Those are whether state constitutional provisions, which permit individuals to exercise free speech and petition rights on the property of a privately owned shopping center to which the public is invited, violate the shopping center owner's property rights under the Fifth and Fourteenth Amendments or his free speech rights under the First and Fourteenth Amendments.

I

Appellant PruneYard is a privately owned shopping center in the city of Campbell, Cal. It covers approximately 21 acres—5 devoted to parking and 16 occupied by walkways, plazas, sidewalks, and buildings that contain more than 65 specialty shops, 10 restaurants, and a movie theater. The PruneYard is open to the public for the purpose of encouraging the patronizing of its commercial establishments. It has a policy not to permit any visitor or tenant to engage in any publicly expressive activity, including the circulation of petitions, that is not directly related to its commercial purposes. This policy has been strictly enforced in a nondiscriminatory fashion. The PruneYard is owned by appellant Fred Sahadi.

Appellees are high school students who sought to solicit support for their opposition to a United Nations resolution against "Zionism." On a Saturday afternoon they set up a card table in a corner of PruneYard's central courtyard. They distributed pamphlets and asked passersby to sign petitions, which were to be sent to the President and Members of Congress. Their activity was peaceful and orderly and so far as the record indicates was not objected to by PruneYard's patrons.

Soon after appellees had begun soliciting signatures, a security guard informed them that they would have to leave because their activity violated PruneYard regulations. The guard suggested that they move to the public sidewalk at the PruneYard's perimeter. Appellees immediately left the premises and later filed this lawsuit in the California Superior Court of Santa Clara County. They sought to enjoin appellants from denying them access to the PruneYard for the purpose of circulating their petitions.

The Superior Court held that appellees were not entitled under either the Federal or California Constitution to exercise their asserted rights on the shopping center property. * * * It concluded that there were "adequate, effective channels of communication for [appellees] other than soliciting on the private property of the [PruneYard]." * * * The California Court of Appeal affirmed.

The California Supreme Court reversed, holding that the California Constitution protects "speech and petitioning, reasonably exercised, in shopping centers even when the centers are privately owned." * * * It concluded that appellees were entitled to conduct their activity on PruneYard property. * * * Before this Court, appellants contend that their constitutionally established rights under the Fourteenth Amendment to exclude appellees from adverse use of appellants' private property cannot be denied by invocation of a state constitutional provision or by judicial reconstruction of a State's laws of private property. We postponed consideration of the question of jurisdiction until the hearing of the case on the merits. * * * We now affirm.

* * *

Appellants first contend that Lloyd Corp. v. Tanner, 407 U.S. 551 (1972), prevents the State from requiring a private shopping center owner to provide access to persons exercising their state constitutional rights of free speech and petition when adequate alternative avenues of communication are available. *Lloyd* dealt with the question whether under the Federal Constitution a privately owned shopping center may prohibit the distribution of handbills on its property when the handbilling is unrelated to the shopping center's operations. * * * Respondents in *Lloyd* argued that because the shopping center was open to the public, the First Amendment prevents the private owner from enforcing the handbilling restriction on shopping center premises. * * * In rejecting this claim we substantially repudiated the rationale of Food Employees v. Logan Valley Plaza, 391 U.S. 308 (1968), which was later overruled in Hudgens v. NLRB, 424 U.S. 507 (1976). We stated that property does not "lose its private character merely because the public is generally invited to use it for designated purposes," and that "[t]he essentially private character of a store and its privately owned abutting property does not change by virtue of being large or clustered with other stores in a modern shopping center." * * *

Our reasoning in *Lloyd,* however, does not *ex proprio vigore* limit the authority of the State to exercise its police power or its sovereign right to adopt in its own Constitution individual liberties more expansive than those conferred by the Federal Constitution. * * * It is, of course, well established that a State in the exercise of its police power may adopt reasonable restrictions on private property so long as the restrictions do not amount to a taking without just compensation or contravene any other federal constitutional provision. * * *

IV

Appellants next contend that a right to exclude others underlies the Fifth Amendment guarantee against the taking of property without just compensation and the Fourteenth Amendment guarantee against the deprivation of property without due process of law.

It is true that one of the essential sticks in the bundle of property rights is the right to exclude others. *Kaiser Aetna v. United States*, 444 U.S. 164, 179–180 (1979). And here there has literally been a "taking" of that right to the extent that the California Supreme Court has interpreted the State Constitution to entitle its citizens to exercise free expression and petition rights on shopping center property.[6] But it is well established that "not every destruction or injury to property by governmental action has been held to be a 'taking' in the constitutional sense." *Armstrong v. United States*, 364 U.S. 40, 48 (1960). Rather, the determination whether a state law unlawfully infringes a landowner's property in violation of the Taking Clause requires an examination of whether the restriction on private property "forc[es] some people alone to bear public burdens which, in all fairness and justice, should be borne by the public as a whole." *Id.*, at 49. This examination entails inquiry into such factors as the character of the governmental action, its economic impact, and its interference with reasonable investment-backed expectations. *Kaiser Aetna v. United States, supra*, at 175. When "regulation goes too far it will be recognized as a taking." *Pennsylvania Coal Co. v. Mahon*, 260 U.S. 393, 415 (1922).

Here the requirement the appellants permit appellees to exercise state-protected rights of free expression and petition on shopping center property clearly does not amount to an unconstitutional infringement of appellants' property rights under the Taking Clause. There is nothing to suggest that preventing appellants from prohibiting this sort of activity will unreasonably impair the value or use of their property as a shopping center. The PruneYard is a large commercial complex that covers several city blocks, contains numerous separate business establishments, and is open to the public at large. The decision of the California Supreme Court makes it clear that the PruneYard may restrict expressive activity by adopting time, place, and manner regulations that will minimize any interference with its commercial functions. Appellees were orderly, and they limited their activity to the common areas of the shopping center. In these circumstances, the fact that they may have "physically invaded" appellants' property cannot be viewed as determinative.

* * *

---

6. The term "property" as used in the Taking Clause includes the entire "group of rights inhering in the citizen's [ownership]." United States v. General Motors Corp., 323 U.S. 373 (1945). It is not used in the "vulgar and untechnical sense of the physical thing with respect to which the citizen exercises rights recognized by law. [Instead, it] denote[s] the group of rights inhering in the citizen's relation to the physical thing, as the right to possess, use and dispose of it * * *. The constitutional provision is addressed to every sort of interest the citizen may possess." *Id.*, at 377–378.

There is also little merit to appellants' argument that they have been denied their property without due process of law. In Nebbia v. New York, 291 U.S. 502 (1934), this Court stated:

> "[N]either property rights nor contract rights are absolute.... Equally fundamental with the private right is that of the public to regulate in the common interest....
>
> * * *
>
> "... [T]he guaranty of due process, as has often been held, demands only that the law shall not be unreasonable, arbitrary or capricious, and that the means selected shall have a real and substantial relation to the objective sought to be attained." Id., at 523, 525.

See also Railway Express Agency v. New York, 336 U.S. 106 (1949); Exxon Corp. v. Governor of Maryland, 437 U.S. 117, 124–125 (1978). Appellants have failed to provide sufficient justification for concluding that this test is not satisfied by the State's asserted interest in promoting more expansive rights of free speech and petition than conferred by the Federal Constitution.

V

Appellants finally contend that a private property owner has a First Amendment right not to be forced by the State to use his property as a forum for the speech of others. They state that in Wooley v. Maynard, 430 U.S. 705 (1977), this Court concluded that a State may not constitutionally require an individual to participate in the dissemination of an ideological message by displaying it on his private property in a manner and for the express purpose that it be observed and read by the public. This rationale applies here, they argue, because the message of *Wooley* is that the State may not force an individual to display any message at all.

Wooley, however, was a case in which the government itself prescribed the message, required it to be displayed openly on appellee's personal property that was used "as part of his daily life," and refused to permit him to take any measures to cover up the motto even though the Court found that the display of the motto served no important state interest. Here, by contrast, there are a number of distinguishing factors. Most important, the shopping center by choice of its owner is not limited to the personal use of appellants. It is instead a business establishment that is open to the public to come and go as they please. The views expressed by members of the public in passing out pamphlets or seeking signatures for a petition thus will not likely be identified with those of the owner. Second, no specific message is dictated by the State to be displayed on appellants' property. There consequently is no danger or governmental discrimination for or against a particular message. Finally, as far as appears here appellants can expressly disavow any connection with the message by simply posting signs in the area where the speakers or handbillers stand. Such signs, for example, could disclaim any sponsorship of the message and could explain that the persons are communicating their own messages by virtue of state law.

Appellants also argue that their First Amendment rights have been infringed in light of West Virginia State Board of Education v. Barnette, 319 U.S. 624 (1943), and Miami Herald Publishing Co. v. Tornillo, 418 U.S. 241 (1974). *Barnette* is inapposite because it involved the compelled recitation of a message containing an affirmation of belief. This Court held such compulsion unconstitutional because it "require[d] the individual to communicate by word and sign his acceptance" of government-dictated political ideas, whether or not he subscribed to them. 319 U.S., at 633. Appellants are not similarly being compelled to affirm their belief in any governmentally prescribed position or view, and they are free to publicly dissociate themselves from the views of the speakers or handbillers.

Tornillo struck down a Florida statute requiring a newspaper to publish a political candidate's reply to criticism previously published in that newspaper. It rests on the principle that the State cannot tell a newspaper what it must print. The Florida statute contravened this principle in that it "exact[ed] a penalty on the basis of the content of a newspaper." 418 U.S., at 256. There also was a danger in *Tornillo* that the statute would "dampe[n] the vigor and limi[t] the variety of public debate" by deterring editors from publishing controversial political statements that might trigger the application of the statute. *Id.,* at 257. Thus, the statute was found to be an "intrusion into the function of editors." *Id.,* at 258. These concerns obviously are not present here.

We conclude that neither appellants' federally recognized property rights nor their First Amendment rights have been infringed by the California Supreme Court's decision recognizing a right of appellees to exercise state-protected rights of expression and petition on appellants' property. The judgment of the Supreme Court of California is therefore

Affirmed.

* * *

Mr. Justice Marshall, concurring.

* * *

* * *

I continue to believe that *Logan Valley* was rightly decided, and that both *Lloyd* and *Hudgens* were incorrect interpretations of the First and Fourteenth Amendments. State action was present in all three cases. In all of them the shopping center owners had opened their centers to the public at large, effectively replacing the State with respect to such traditional First Amendment forums as streets, sidewalks, and parks. The State had in turn made its laws of trespass available to shopping center owners, enabling them to exclude those who wished to engage in expressive activity on their premises.[1] * * *

---

1. In this respect the cases resembled Shelley v. Kraemer, 334 U.S. 1 (1948), and New York Times Co. v. Sullivan, 376 U.S. 254 (1964), in which the common-law rules

* * *

Appellants' claim in this case amounts to no less than a suggestion that the common law of trespass is not subject to revision by the State, notwithstanding the California Supreme Court's finding that state-created rights of expressive activity would be severely hindered if shopping centers were closed to expressive activities by members of the public. If accepted, that claim would represent a return to the era of Lochner v. New York, 198 U.S. 45 (1905), when common-law rights were also found immune from revision by State or Federal Government. Such an approach would freeze the common law as it has been constructed by the courts, perhaps at its 19th-century state of development. It would allow no room for change in response to changes in circumstance. The Due Process Clause does not require such a result.

On the other hand, I do not understand the Court to suggest that rights of property are to be defined solely by state law, or that there is no federal constitutional barrier to the abrogation of common-law rights by Congress or a state government. The constitutional terms "life, liberty, and property" do not derive their meaning solely from the provisions of positive law. They have a normative dimension as well, establishing a sphere of private autonomy which government is bound to respect.[2] Quite serious constitutional questions might be raised if a legislature attempted to abolish certain categories of common-law rights in some general way. Indeed, our cases demonstrate that there are limits on governmental authority to abolish "core" common-law rights, including rights against trespass, at least without a compelling showing of necessity or a provision for a reasonable alternative remedy.

* * *

MR. JUSTICE WHITE, concurring in part and concurring in the judgment.

I join MR. JUSTICE POWELL'S concurring opinion but with these additional remarks.

* * *

I agree that on the record before us there was not an unconstitutional infringement of appellants' property rights. But it bears pointing out that the Federal Constitution does not require that a shopping center permit distributions or solicitations on its property. Indeed, Hudgens v. NLRB, 424 U.S. 507 (1976), and Lloyd Corp. v. Tanner, 407 U.S. 551 (1972), hold that the First and Fourteenth Amendments do not prevent the property owner from excluding those who would demonstrate or communicate on his property. Insofar as the Federal Constitution is concerned, therefore, a State may decline to construe its own

of contract and tort were held to constitute state action for Fourteenth Amendment purposes.

2. This understanding is embodied in cases in the procedural due process area holding that at least some "grievous losses" amount to deprivation of "liberty" or "property" within the meaning of the Due Process Clause, even if those losses are not protected by statutory or common law. See Vitek v. Jones, 445 U.S. 480, 488–489 (1980), and cases cited; Mathews v. Eldridge, 424 U.S. 319, 333 (1976). See also Meachum v. Fano, 427 U.S. 215, 229 (1976) (STEVENS, J., dissenting).

constitution so as to limit the property rights of the shopping center owner.

The Court also affirms the California Supreme Court's implicit holding that appellants' own free-speech rights under the First and Fourteenth Amendments were not infringed by requiring them to provide a forum for appellees to communicate with the public on shopping center property. I concur in this judgment, but I agree with Mr. Justice Powell that there are other circumstances that would present a far different First Amendment issue. May a State require the owner of a shopping center to subsidize any and all political, religious, or social-action groups by furnishing a convenient place for them to urge their views on the public and to solicit funds from likely prospects? Surely there are some limits on state authority to impose such requirements; and in this respect, I am not in entire accord with Part V of the Court's opinion.

Mr. Justice Powell, with whom Mr. Justice White joins, concurring in part and in the judgment.

* * *

I

Restrictions on property use, like other state laws, are invalid if they infringe the freedom of expression and belief protected by the First and Fourteenth Amendments. In Part V of today's opinion, the Court rejects appellants' contention that "a private property owner has a First Amendment right not to be forced by the State to use his property as a forum for the speech of others." * * *. I agree that the owner of this shopping center has failed to establish a cognizable First Amendment claim in this case. But some of the language in the Court's opinion is unnecessarily and perhaps confusingly broad. In my view, state action that transforms privately owned property into a forum for the expression of the public's views could raise serious First Amendment questions.

* * *

The selection of material for publication is not generally a concern of shopping centers. But similar speech interests are affected when listeners are likely to identify opinions expressed by members of the public on commercial property as the views of the owner. If a state law mandated public access to the bulletin board of a freestanding store, hotel, office, or small shopping center, customers might well conclude that the messages reflect the view of the proprietor. The same would be true if the public were allowed to solicit or distribute pamphlets in the entrance area of a store or in the lobby of a private building. The property owner or proprietor would be faced with a choice: he either could permit his customers to receive a mistaken impression or he could disavow the messages. Should he take the first course, he effectively has been compelled to affirm someone else's belief. Should he choose the second, he has been forced to speak when he would prefer to remain silent. In short, he has lost control over his freedom to speak or not to speak on certain issues. The mere fact that he is free to dissociate himself from the views expressed on his property, * * *, cannot restore his "right to refrain from speaking at all." *Wooley v. Maynard, supra,* at 714.

A property owner also may be faced with speakers who wish to use his premises as a platform for views that he finds morally repugnant. Numerous examples come to mind. A minority-owned business confronted with leaflet distributors from the American Nazi Party or the Ku Klux Klan, a church-operated enterprise asked to host demonstrations in favor of abortion, or a union compelled to supply a forum to right-to-work advocates could be placed in an intolerable position if state law requires it to make its private property available to anyone who wishes to speak. The strong emotions evoked by speech in such situations may virtually compel the proprietor to respond.

The pressure to respond is particularly apparent when the owner has taken a position opposed to the view being expressed on his property. But an owner who strongly objects to some of the causes to which the state-imposed right of access would extend may oppose ideological activities "of any sort" that are not related to the purposes for which he has invited the public onto his property. See Abood v. Detroit Board of Education, 431 U.S. 209, 213, 241 (1977). To require the owner to specify the particular ideas he finds objectionable enough to compel a response would force him to relinquish his "freedom to maintain his own beliefs without public disclosure." * * * Thus, the right to control one's own speech may be burdened impermissibly even when listeners will not assume that the messages expressed on private property are those of the owner.

II

One easily can identify other circumstances in which a right of access to commercial property would burden the owner's First and Fourteenth Amendment right to refrain from speaking. But appellants have identified no such circumstance. Nor did appellants introduce evidence that would support a holding in their favor under either of the legal theories outlined above.

* * *

Because appellants have not shown that the limited right of access held to be afforded by the California Constitution burdened their First and Fourteenth Amendment rights in the circumstances presented, I join the judgment of the Court. I do not interpret our decision today as a blanket approval for state efforts to transform privately owned commercial property into public forums. Any such state action would raise substantial federal constitutional questions not present in this case.

F. Coerced Expression and Freedom Not to Speak

The extent to which persons may be made to express or support the expression of views by government which views they do not hold and may, rather, oppose.

WEST VIRGINIA BOARD OF EDUCATION v. BARNETTE
Supreme Court of the United States, 1943.
319 U.S. 624, 63 S.Ct. 1178, 87 L.Ed. 1628.

Mr. Justice Jackson delivered the opinion of the Court.

Following the decision by this Court on June 3, 1940, in Minersville School District v. Gobitis, 310 U.S. 586 * * *.

The Board of Education on January 9, 1942, adopted a resolution containing recitals taken largely from the Court's *Gobitis* opinion and ordering that the salute to the flag become "a regular part of the program of activities in the public schools," that all teachers and pupils "shall be required to participate in the salute honoring the Nation represented by the Flag; provided, however, that refusal to salute the Flag be regarded as an act of insubordination, and shall be dealt with accordingly."

* * *

Failure to conform is "insubordination" dealt with by expulsion. Readmission is denied by statute until compliance. Meanwhile the expelled child is "unlawfully absent" and may be proceeded against as a delinquent. His parents or guardians are liable to prosecution, and if convicted are subject to fine not exceeding $50 and jail term not exceeding thirty days.

Appellees, citizens of the United States and of West Virginia, brought suit in the United States District Court for themselves and others similarly situated asking its injunction to restrain enforcement of these laws and regulations against Jehovah's Witnesses. The Witnesses are an unincorporated body teaching that the obligation imposed by law of God is superior to that of laws enacted by temporal government. Their religious beliefs include a literal version of Exodus, Chapter 20, verses 4 and 5, which says: "Thou shalt not make unto thee any graven image, or any likeness of anything that is in heaven above, or that is in the earth beneath, or that is in the water under the earth; thou shalt not bow down thyself to them nor serve them." They consider that the flag is an "image" within this command. For this reason they refuse to salute it.

Children of this faith have been expelled from school and are threatened with exclusion for no other cause. Officials threaten to send them to reformatories maintained for criminally inclined juveniles. Parents of such children have been prosecuted and are threatened with prosecution for causing delinquency.

The Board of Education moved to dismiss the complaint setting forth these facts and alleging that the law and regulations are an unconstitutional denial of religious freedom, and of freedom of speech, and are invalid under the "due process" and "equal protection" clauses of the Fourteenth Amendment to the Federal Constitution. The cause was submitted on the pleadings to a District Court of three judges. It restrained enforcement as to the plaintiffs and those of that class. The Board of Education brought the case here by direct appeal.

This case calls us to reconsider a precedent decision, as the Court throughout its history often has been required to do.[10] Before turning to the *Gobitis* case, however, it is desirable to notice certain characteristics by which this controversy is distinguished.

The freedom asserted by these appellees does not bring them into collision with rights asserted by any other individual. It is such conflicts which most frequently require intervention of the State to determine where the rights of one end and those of another begin. But the refusal of these persons to participate in the ceremony does not interfere with or deny rights of others to do so. Nor is there any question in this case that their behavior is peaceable and orderly. The sole conflict is between authority and rights of the individual. The State asserts power to condition access to public education on making a prescribed sign and profession and at the same time to coerce attendance by punishing both parent and child. The latter stand on a right of self-determination in matters that touch individual opinion and personal attitude.

As the present Chief Justice said in dissent in the *Gobitis* case, the State may "require teaching by instruction and study of all in our history and in the structure and organization of our government, including the guaranties of civil liberty, which tend to inspire patriotism and love of country." 310 U.S., at 604. Here, however, we are dealing with a compulsion of students to declare a belief. They are not merely made acquainted with the flag salute so that they may be informed as to what it is or even what it means. The issue here is whether this slow and easily neglected route to aroused loyalties constitutionally may be short-cut by substituting a compulsory salute and slogan. This issue is not prejudiced by the Court's previous holding that where a State, without compelling attendance, extends college facilities to pupils who voluntarily enroll, it may prescribe military training as part of the course without offense to the Constitution. It was held that those who take advantage of its opportunities may not on ground of conscience refuse compliance with such conditions. Hamilton v. Regents, 293 U.S. 245. In the present case attendance is not optional. That case is also to be distinguished from the present one because, independently of college privileges or requirements, the State has power to raise militia and impose the duties of service therein upon its citizens.

---

10. See authorities cited in Helvering v. Griffiths, 318 U.S. 371, 401, note 52.

There is no doubt that, in connection with the pledges, the flag salute is a form of utterance. Symbolism is a primitive but effective way of communicating ideas. The use of an emblem or flag to symbolize some system, idea, institution, or personality, is a short cut from mind to mind. Causes and nations, political parties, lodges and ecclesiastical groups seek to knit the loyalty of their followings to a flag or banner, a color or design. The State announces rank, function, and authority through crowns and maces, uniforms and black robes; the church speaks through the Cross, the Crucifix, the altar and shrine, and clerical raiment. Symbols of State often convey political ideas just as religious symbols come to convey theological ones. Associated with many of these symbols are appropriate gestures of acceptance or respect: a salute, a bowed or bared head, a bended knee. A person gets from a symbol the meaning he puts into it, and what is one man's comfort and inspiration is another's jest and scorn.

Over a decade ago Chief Justice Hughes led this Court in holding that the display of a red flag as a symbol of opposition by peaceful and legal means to organized government was protected by the free speech guaranties of the Constitution. Stromberg v. California, 283 U.S. 359. Here it is the State that employs a flag as a symbol of adherence to government as presently organized. It requires the individual to communicate by word and sign his acceptance of the political ideas it thus bespeaks. Objection to this form of communication when coerced is an old one, well known to the framers of the Bill of Rights.[13]

It is also to be noted that the compulsory flag salute and pledge requires affirmation of a belief and an attitude of mind. It is not clear whether the regulation contemplates that pupils forego any contrary convictions of their own and become unwilling converts to the prescribed ceremony or whether it will be acceptable if they simulate assent by words without belief and by a gesture barren of meaning. It is now a commonplace that censorship or suppression of expression of opinion is tolerated by our Constitution only when the expression presents a clear and present danger of action of a kind the State is empowered to prevent and punish. It would seem that involuntary affirmation could be commanded only on even more immediate and urgent grounds than silence. But here the power of compulsion is invoked without any allegation that remaining passive during a flag salute ritual creates a clear and present danger that would justify an effort even to muffle expression. To sustain the compulsory flag salute we are required to say that a Bill of Rights which guards the individual's right to speak his own mind, left it open to public authorities to compel him to utter what is not in his mind.

13. Early Christians were frequently persecuted for their refusal to participate in ceremonies before the statue of the emperor or other symbol of imperial authority. The story of William Tell's sentence to shoot an apple off his son's head for refusal to salute a bailiff's hat is an ancient one. 21 Encyclopedia Britannica (14th ed.) 911–912. The Quakers, William Penn included, suffered punishment rather than uncover their heads in deference to any civil authority. Braithwaite, The Beginnings of Quakerism (1912) 200, 229–230, 232–233, 447, 451; Fox, Quakers Courageous (1941) 113.

Whether the First Amendment to the Constitution will permit officials to order observance of ritual of this nature does not depend upon whether as a voluntary exercise we would think it to be good, bad or merely innocuous. Any credo of nationalism is likely to include what some disapprove or to omit what others think essential, and to give off different overtones as it takes on different accents or interpretations.[14] If official power exists to coerce acceptance of any patriotic creed, what it shall contain cannot be decided by courts, but must be largely discretionary with the ordaining authority, whose power to prescribe would no doubt include power to amend. Hence validity of the asserted power to force an American citizen publicly to profess any statement of belief or to engage in any ceremony of assent to one, presents questions of power that must be considered independently of any idea we may have as to the utility of the ceremony in question.

Nor does the issue as we see it turn on one's possession of particular religious views or the sincerity with which they are held. While religion supplies appellees' motive for enduring the discomforts of making the issue in this case, many citizens who do not share these religious views hold such a compulsory rite to infringe constitutional liberty of the individual. It is not necessary to inquire whether non-conformist beliefs will exempt from the duty to salute unless we first find power to make the salute a legal duty.

The *Gobitis* decision, however, *assumed,* as did the argument in that case and in this, that power exists in the State to impose the flag salute discipline upon school children in general. The Court only examined and rejected a claim based on religious beliefs of immunity from an unquestioned general rule. The question which underlies the flag salute controversy is whether such a ceremony so touching matters of opinion and political attitude may be imposed upon the individual by official authority under powers committed to any political organization under our Constitution. We examine rather than assume existence of this power and, against this broader definition of issues in this case, reëxamine specific grounds assigned for the *Gobitis* decision.

1. It was said that the flag-salute controversy confronted the Court with "the problem which Lincoln cast in memorable dilemma: 'Must a government of necessity be too *strong* for the liberties of its people, or too *weak* to maintain its own existence?'" and that the answer must be in favor of strength. *Minersville School District v. Gobitis, supra,* at 596.

We think these issues may be examined free of pressure or restraint growing out of such considerations.

It may be doubted whether Mr. Lincoln would have thought that the strength of government to maintain itself would be impressively vindicated by our confirming power of the State to expel a handful of

---

14. For example: Use of "Republic," if rendered to distinguish our government from a "democracy," or the words "one Nation," if intended to distinguish it from a "federation," open up old and bitter controversies in our political history; "liberty and justice for all," if it must be accepted as descriptive of the present order rather than an ideal, might to some seem an overstatement.

children from school. Such oversimplification, so handy in political debate, often lacks the precision necessary to postulates of judicial reasoning. If validly applied to this problem, the utterance cited would resolve every issue of power in favor of those in authority and would require us to override every liberty thought to weaken or delay execution of their policies.

Government of limited power need not be anemic government. Assurance that rights are secure tends to diminish fear and jealousy of strong government, and by making us feel safe to live under it makes for its better support. Without promise of a limiting Bill of Rights it is doubtful if our Constitution could have mustered enough strength to enable its ratification. To enforce those rights today is not to choose weak government over strong government. It is only to adhere as a means of strength to individual freedom of mind in preference to officially disciplined uniformity for which history indicates a disappointing and disastrous end.

The subject now before us exemplifies this principle. Free public education, if faithful to the ideal of secular instruction and political neutrality, will not be partisan or enemy of any class, creed, party, or faction. If it is to impose any ideological discipline, however, each party or denomination must seek to control, or failing that, to weaken the influence of the educational system. Observance of the limitations of the Constitution will not weaken government in the field appropriate for its exercise.

2. It was also considered in the *Gobitis* case that functions of educational officers in States, counties and school districts were such that to interfere with their authority "would in effect make us the school board for the country." *Id.* at 598.

The Fourteenth Amendment, as now applied to the States, protects the citizen against the State itself and all of its creatures—Boards of Education not excepted. These have, of course, important, delicate, and highly discretionary functions, but none that they may not perform within the limits of the Bill of Rights. That they are educating the young for citizenship is reason for scrupulous protection of Constitutional freedoms of the individual, if we are not to strangle the free mind at its source and teach youth to discount important principles of our government as mere platitudes.

* * *

The very purpose of a Bill of Rights was to withdraw certain subjects from the vicissitudes of political controversy, to place them beyond the reach of majorities and officials and to establish them as legal principles to be applied by the courts. One's right to life, liberty, and property, to free speech, a free press, freedom of worship and assembly, and other fundamental rights may not be submitted to vote: they depend on the outcome of no elections.

* * * It is important to note that while it is the Fourteenth Amendment which bears directly upon the State it is the more specific limiting principles of the First Amendment that finally govern this case.

Nor does our duty to apply the Bill of Rights to assertions of official authority depend upon our possession of marked competence in the field where the invasion of rights occurs. True, the task of translating the majestic generalities of the Bill of Rights, conceived as part of the pattern of liberal government in the eighteenth century, into concrete restraints on officials dealing with the problems of the twentieth century, is one to disturb self-confidence. These principles grew in soil which also produced a philosophy that the individual was the center of society, that his liberty was attainable through mere absence of governmental restraints, and that government should be entrusted with few controls and only the mildest supervision over men's affairs. We must transplant these rights to a soil in which the *laissez-faire* concept or principle of noninterference has withered at least as to economic affairs, and social advancements are increasingly sought through closer integration of society and through expanded and strengthened governmental controls. These changed conditions often deprive precedents of reliability and cast us more than we would choose upon our own judgment. But we act in these matters not by authority of our competence but by force of our commissions. We cannot, because of modest estimates of our competence in such specialities as public education, withhold the judgment that history authenticates as the function of this Court when liberty is infringed.

4. Lastly, and this is the very heart of the *Gobitis* opinion, it reasons that "National unity is the basis of national security," that the authorities have "the right to select appropriate means for its attainment," and hence reaches the conclusion that such compulsory measures toward "national unity" are constitutional. *Id.* at 595. Upon the verity of this assumption depends our answer in this case.

National unity as an end which officials may foster by persuasion and example is not in question. The problem is whether under our Constitution compulsion as here employed is a permissible means for its achievement.

Struggles to coerce uniformity of sentiment in support of some end thought essential to their time and country have been waged by many good as well as by evil men. Nationalism is a relatively recent phenomenon but at other times and places the ends have been racial or territorial security, support of a dynasty or regime, and particular plans for saving souls. As first and moderate methods to attain unity have failed, those bent on its accomplishment must resort to an ever-increasing severity. As governmental pressure toward unity becomes greater, so strife becomes more bitter as to whose unity it shall be. Probably no deeper division of our people could proceed from any provocation than from finding it necessary to choose what doctrine and whose program public educational officials shall compel youth to unite in embracing. Ultimate futility of such attempts to compel coherence is the lesson of every such effort from the Roman drive to stamp out Christianity as a disturber of its pagan unity, the Inquisition, as a means to religious and dynastic unity, the Siberian exiles as a means to Russian unity, down to the fast failing efforts of our present totalitarian enemies. Those who begin coercive elimination of dissent soon find themselves exterminating dissenters. Compulsory unification of opinion achieves only the unanimity of the graveyard.

It seems trite but necessary to say that the First Amendment to our Constitution was designed to avoid these ends by avoiding these beginnings. There is no mysticism in the American concept of the State or of the nature or origin of its authority. We set up government by consent of the governed, and the Bill of Rights denies those in power any legal opportunity to coerce that consent. Authority here is to be controlled by public opinion, not public opinion by authority.

The case is made difficult not because the principles of its decision are obscure but because the flag involved is our own. Nevertheless, we apply the limitations of the Constitution with no fear that freedom to be intellectually and spiritually diverse or even contrary will disintegrate the social organization. To believe that patriotism will not flourish if patriotic ceremonies are voluntary and spontaneous instead of a compulsory routine is to make an unflattering estimate of the appeal of our institutions to free minds. We can have intellectual individualism and the rich cultural diversities that we owe to exceptional minds only at the price of occasional eccentricity and abnormal attitudes. When they are so harmless to others or to the State as those we deal with here, the price is not too great. But freedom to differ is not limited to things that do not matter much. That would be a mere shadow of freedom. The test of its substance is the right to differ as to things that touch the heart of the existing order.

If there is any fixed star in our constitutional constellation, it is that no official, high or petty, can prescribe what shall be orthodox in politics, nationalism, religion, or other matters of opinion or force citizens to confess by word or act their faith therein. If there are any circumstances which permit an exception, they do not now occur to us.[19]

We think the action of the local authorities in compelling the flag salute and pledge transcends constitutional limitations on their power and invades the sphere of intellect and spirit which it is the purpose of the First Amendment to our Constitution to reserve from all official control.

The decision of this Court in *Minersville School District v. Gobitis* and the holdings of those few *per curiam* decisions which preceded and foreshadowed it are overruled, and the judgment enjoining enforcement of the West Virginia Regulation is

Affirmed.

MR. JUSTICE ROBERTS and MR. JUSTICE REED adhere to the views expressed by the Court in Minersville School District v. Gobitis, 310

---

19. The Nation may raise armies and compel citizens to give military service. *Selective Draft Law Cases,* 245 U.S. 366. It follows, of course, that those subject to military discipline are under many duties and may not claim many freedoms that we hold inviolable as to those in civilian life.

U.S. 586, and are of the opinion that the judgment below should be reversed.

MR. JUSTICE BLACK and MR. JUSTICE DOUGLAS, concurring.

* * *

MR. JUSTICE FRANKFURTER, dissenting.

One who belongs to the most vilified and persecuted minority in history is not likely to be insensible to the freedoms guaranteed by our Constitution. Were my purely personal attitude relevant I should wholeheartedly associate myself with the general libertarian views in the Court's opinion, representing as they do the thought and action of a lifetime. But as judges we are neither Jew nor Gentile, neither Catholic nor agnostic. We owe equal attachment to the Constitution and are equally bound by our judicial obligations whether we derive our citizenship from the earliest or the latest immigrants to these shores. As a member of this Court I am not justified in writing my private notions of policy into the Constitution, no matter how deeply I may cherish them or how mischievous I may deem their disregard. The duty of a judge who must decide which of two claims before the Court shall prevail, that of a State to enact and enforce laws within its general competence or that of an individual to refuse obedience because of the demands of his conscience, is not that of the ordinary person. It can never be emphasized too much that one's own opinion about the wisdom or evil of a law should be excluded altogether when one is doing one's duty on the bench. The only opinion of our own even looking in that direction that is material is our opinion whether legislators could in reason have enacted such a law. In the light of all the circumstances, including the history of this question in this Court, it would require more daring than I possess to deny that reasonable legislators could have taken the action which is before us for review. * * *

* * *

The precise scope of the question before us defines the limits of the constitutional power that is in issue. The State of West Virginia requires all pupils to share in the salute to the flag as part of school training in citizenship. The present action is one to enjoin the enforcement of this requirement by those in school attendance. We have not before us any attempt by the State to punish disobedient children or visit penal consequences on their parents. All that is in question is the right of the State to compel participation in this exercise by those who choose to attend the public school.

* * *

An act compelling profession of allegience to a religion, no matter how subtly or tenuously promoted, is bad. But an act promoting good citizenship and national allegiance is within the domain of governmental authority and is therefore to be judged by the same considerations of power and of constitutionality as those involved in the many claims of immunity from civil obedience because of religious scruples.

* * *

We are told that a flag salute is a doubtful substitute for adequate understanding of our institutions. The states that require such a school exercise do not have to justify it as the only means for promoting good citizenship in children, but merely as one of diverse means for accomplishing a worthy end. We may deem it a foolish measure, but the point is that this Court is not the organ of government to resolve doubts as to whether it will fulfill its purpose. Only if there be no doubt that any reasonable mind could entertain can we deny to the states the right to resolve doubts their way and not ours.

* * *

The right of West Virginia to utilize the flag salute as part of its educational process is denied because, so it is argued, it cannot be justified as a means of meeting a "clear and present danger" to national unity. In passing it deserves to be noted that the four cases which unanimously sustained the power of states to utilize such an educational measure arose and were all decided before the present World War. But to measure the state's power to make such regulations as are here resisted by the imminence of national danger is wholly to misconceive the origin and purpose of the concept of "clear and present danger." To apply such a test is for the Court to assume, however unwittingly, a legislative responsibility that does not belong to it. To talk about "clear and present danger" as the touchstone of allowable educational policy by the states whenever school curricula may impinge upon the boundaries of individual conscience, is to take a felicitous phrase out of the context of the particular situation where it arose and for which it was adapted. Mr. Justice Holmes used the phrase "clear and present danger" in a case involving mere speech as a means by which alone to accomplish sedition in time of war. By that phrase he meant merely to indicate that, in view of the protection given to utterance by the First Amendment, in order that mere utterance may not be proscribed, "the words used are used in such circumstances and are of such a nature as to create a clear and present danger that they will bring about the substantive evils that Congress has a right to prevent." * * *

* * * Saluting the flag suppresses no belief nor curbs it. Children and their parents may believe what they please, avow their belief and practice it. It is not even remotely suggested that the requirement for saluting the flag involves the slightest restriction against the fullest opportunity on the part both of the children and of their parents to disavow as publicly as they choose to do so the meaning that others attach to the gesture of salute. All channels of affirmative free expression are open to both children and parents. Had we before us any act of the state putting the slightest curbs upon such free expression, I should not lag behind any member of this Court in striking down such an invasion of the right to freedom of thought and freedom of speech protected by the Constitution.

I am fortified in my view of this case by the history of the flag salute controversy in this Court. Five times has the precise question now before us been adjudicated. Four times the Court unanimously found that the requirement of such a school exercise was not beyond the powers of the states. Indeed in the first three cases to come before the Court the constitutional claim now sustained was deemed so clearly unmeritorious that this Court dismissed the appeals for want of a substantial federal question. * * *

WOOLEY v. MAYNARD

Supreme Court of the United States, 1977.
430 U.S. 705, 97 S.Ct. 1428, 51 L.Ed.2d 752.

MR. CHIEF JUSTICE BURGER delivered the opinion of the Court.

The issue on appeal is whether the State of New Hampshire may constitutionally enforce criminal sanctions against persons who cover the motto "Live Free or Die" on passenger vehicle license plates because that motto is repugnant to their moral and religious beliefs.

(1)

Since 1969 New Hampshire has required that noncommercial vehicles bear license plates embossed with the state motto, "Live Free or Die." N.H.Rev.Stat.Ann. § 263:1 (Supp.1975). Another New Hampshire statute makes it a misdemeanor "knowingly [to obscure] * * * the figures or letters on any number plate." N.H.Rev.Stat.Ann. § 262:27–c (Supp.1975). The term "letters" in this section has been interpreted by the State's highest court to include the state motto. State v. Hoskin, 112 N.H. 332, 295 A.2d 454 (1972).

Appellees George Maynard and his wife Maxine are followers of the Jehovah's Witnesses faith. The Maynards consider the New Hampshire State motto to be repugnant to their moral, religious, and political beliefs,[2] and therefore assert it objectionable to disseminate this message by displaying it on their automobiles. Pursuant to these beliefs, the Maynards began early in 1974 to cover up the motto on their license plates.

On November 27, 1974, Mr. Maynard was issued a citation for violation § 262:27–c. * * *

On December 28, 1974, Mr. Maynard was again charged with violating § 262:27–c. He appeared in court on January 31, 1975, and again chose to represent himself; he was found guilty, fined $50, and sentenced to six months in the Grafton County House of Corrections. The court suspended the jail sentence but ordered Mr. Maynard to also pay the $25 fine for the first offense. Maynard informed the court

---

2. Mr. Maynard described his objection to the state motto:

"[B]y religious training and belief, I believe my 'government'—Jehovah's Kingdom—offers everlasting life. It would be contrary to that belief to give up my life for the state, even if it meant living in bondage. Although I obey all laws of the State not in conflict with my conscience, this slogan is directly at odds with my deep religious convictions.

" * * * I also disagree with the motto on political grounds. I believe that life is more precious than freedom." Affidavit of George Maynard, App. 3.

that, as a matter of conscience, he refused to pay the two fines. The court thereupon sentenced him to jail for a period of 15 days. He has served the full sentence.

* * *

(2)

On March 4, 1975, appellees brought the present action pursuant to 42 U.S.C. § 1983 in the United States District Court for the District of New Hampshire. They sought injunctive and declaratory relief against enforcement of N.H.Rev.Stat.Ann. § 262:27–c, 263:1, insofar as these required displaying the state motto on their vehicle license plates, and made it a criminal offense to obscure the motto. * * *

* * *

The District Court held that by covering up the state motto "Live Free or Die" on his automobile license plate, Mr. Maynard was engaging in symbolic speech and that "New Hampshire's interest in the enforcement of its defacement statute is not sufficient to justify the restriction on [appellee's] constitutionally protected expression." 406 F.Supp., at 1389. We find it unnecessary to pass on the "symbolic speech" issue, since we find more appropriate First Amendment grounds to affirm the judgment of the District Court.[10] We turn instead to what in our view is the essence of appellees' objection to the requirement that they display the motto "Live Free or Die" on their automobile license plates. This is succinctly summarized in the statement made by Mr. Maynard in his affidavit filed with the District Court:

> "I refuse to be coerced by the State into advertising a slogan which I find morally, ethically, religiously and politically abhorrent." App. 5.

We are thus faced with the question of whether the State may constitutionally require an individual to participate in the dissemination of an ideological message by displaying it on his private property in a manner and for the express purpose that it be observed and read by the public. We hold that the State may not do so.

A

We begin with the proposition that the right of freedom of thought protected by the First Amendment against state action includes both the right to speak freely and the right to refrain from speaking at all. See Board of Education v. Barnette, 319 U.S. 624, 633–634 (1943); *id.*, at 645 (MURPHY, J., concurring). * * *

---

10. We note that appellees' claim of symbolic expression is substantially undermined by their prayer in the District Court for issuance of special license plates not bearing the state motto. See n. 5, *supra*. This is hardly consistent with the stated intent to communicate affirmative opposition to the motto. Whether or not we view appellees' present practice of covering the motto with tape as sufficiently communicative to sustain a claim of symbolic expression, display of the "expurgated" plates requested by appellees would surely not satisfy that standard. See n. 1, *supra*; Spence v. Washington, 418 U.S. 405, 410–411 (1974); United States v. O'Brien, 391 U.S. 367, 376 (1968). (Mr. Justice Brennan does not join in this note.)

The Court in *Barnette, supra,* was faced with a state statute which required public school students to participate in daily public ceremonies by honoring the flag both with words and traditional salute gestures. In overruling its prior decision in Minersville District v. Gobitis, 310 U.S. 586 (1940), the Court held that "a ceremony so touching matters of opinion and political attitude may [not] be imposed upon the individual by official authority under powers committed to any political organization under our Constitution." 319 U.S., at 636. Compelling the affirmative act of a flag salute involved a more serious infringement upon personal liberties than the passive act of carrying the state motto on a license plate, but the difference is essentially one of degree. Here, as in *Barnette,* we are faced with a state measure which forces an individual, as part of his daily life—to be an instrument for fostering public adherence to an ideological point of view he finds unacceptable. In doing so, the State "invades the sphere of intellect and spirit which it is the purpose of the First Amendment to our Constitution to reserve from all official control." *Id.,* at 642.

New Hampshire's statute in effect requires that appellees use their private property as a "mobile billboard" for the State's ideological message—or suffer a penalty, as Maynard already has. As a condition to driving an automobile—a virtual necessity for most Americans—the Maynards must display "Live Free or Die" to hundreds of people each day.[11] The fact that most individuals agree with the thrust of New Hampshire's motto is not the test; most Americans also find the flag salute acceptable. The First Amendment protects the right of individuals to hold a point of view different from the majority and to refuse to foster, in the way New Hampshire commands, an idea they find morally objectionable.

B

Identifying the Maynards' interests as implicating First Amendment protections does not end our inquiry however. We must also determine whether the State's countervailing interest is sufficiently compelling to justify requiring appellees to display the state motto on their license plates. See, e.g., United States v. O'Brien, 391 U.S. 367, 376–377 (1968). The two interests advanced by the State are that display of the motto (1) facilitates the identification of passenger vehicles,[12] and (2) promotes appreciation of history, individualism, and state pride.

The State first points out that passenger vehicles, but not commercial, trailer, or other vehicles are required to display the state motto.

---

11. Some States require that certain documents bear the seal of the State or some other official stamp for purposes of recordation. Such seals might contain, albeit obscurely, a symbol or motto having political or philosophical implications. The purpose of such seal, however, is not to advertise the message it bears but simply to authenticate the document by showing the authority of its origin.

12. The Chief of Police of Lebanon, N.H., testified that "enforcement of the motor vehicle laws is facilitated by the State Motto appearing on non-commercial license plates, the benefits being the ease of distinguishing New Hampshire license plates from those of similar colors of other states and the ease of discovering misuse of license plates, for instance, the use of a 'trailer' license plate on a non-commercial vehicle." Brief for Appellants 20.

Thus, the argument proceeds, officers of the law are more easily able to determine whether passenger vehicles are carrying the proper plates. However, the record here reveals that New Hampshire passenger license plates normally consist of a specific configuration of letters and numbers, which makes them readily distinguishable from other types of plates, even without reference to the state motto. Even were we to credit the State's reasons and "even though the governmental purpose be legitimate and substantial, that purpose cannot be pursued by means that broadly stifle fundamental personal liberties when the end can be more narrowly achieved. The breadth of legislative abridgment must be viewed in the light of less drastic means for achieving the same basic purpose." Shelton v. Tucker, 364 U.S. 479, 488 (1960) (footnotes omitted).

The State's second claimed interest is not ideologically neutral. The State is seeking to communicate to others an official view as to proper appreciation of history, state pride, and individualism. Of course, the State may legitimately pursue such interests in any number of ways. However, where the State's interest is to disseminate an ideology, no matter how acceptable to some, such interest cannot outweigh an individual's First Amendment right to avoid becoming the courier of such message.

We conclude that the State of New Hampshire may not require appellees to display the state motto [15] upon their vehicle license plates; and accordingly, we affirm the judgment of the District Court.

Affirmed.

MR. JUSTICE REHNQUIST, with whom MR. JUSTICE BLACKMUN joins, dissenting.

* * *

I not only agree with the Court's implicit recognition that there is no protected "symbolic speech" in this case, but I think that that conclusion goes far to undermine the Court's ultimate holding that there is an element of protected expression here. The State has not forced appellees to "say" anything; and it has not forced them to communicate ideas with nonverbal actions reasonably likened to "speech," such as wearing a lapel button promoting a political candidate or waiving a flag as a symbolic gesture. The State has simply required that *all* non-commercial automobiles bear license tags with the state motto, "Live Free or Die." Appellees have not been forced to affirm or reject that motto; they are simply required by the State, under its police power, to carry a state auto license tag for identification and registration purposes.

---

15. It has been suggested that today's holding be read as sanctioning the obliteration of the national motto, "In God We Trust" from United States coins and currency. That question is not before us today but we note that currency, which is passed from hand to hand, differs in significant respects from an automobile, which is readily associated with its operator. Currency is generally carried in a purse or pocket and need not be displayed to the public. The bearer of currency is thus not required to publicly advertise the national motto.

In Part 4–A, the Court relies almost solely on Board of Education v. Barnette, 319 U.S. 624 (1943). The Court cites *Barnette* for the proposition that there is a constitutional right, in some cases, to "refrain from speaking." *Ante*, at 714. What the Court does not demonstrate is that there is any "speech" or "speaking" in the context of this case. The Court also relies upon the "right to decline to foster [religious, political, and ideological] concepts," *ibid.*, and treats the state law in this case as if it were forcing appellees to proselytize, or to advocate an ideological point of view. But this begs the question. The issue, confronted by the Court, is whether appellees, in displaying as they are required to do, state license tags, the format of which is known to all as having been prescribed by the State, would be considered to be advocating political or ideological views.

The Court recognizes, as it must, that this case substantially differs from *Barnette*, in which schoolchildren were forced to recite the pledge of allegiance while giving the flag salute. *Ante*. However, the Court states "the difference is essentially one of degree." *Ante*. But having recognized the rather obvious differences between these two cases, the Court does not explain why the same result should obtain. The Court suggests that the test is whether the individual is forced "to be an instrument for fostering public adherence to an ideological point of view he finds unacceptable." *Ibid.* But, once again, these are merely conclusory words, barren of analysis. For example, were New Hampshire to erect a multitude of billboards, each proclaiming "Live Free or Die," and tax all citizens for the cost of erection and maintenance, clearly the message would be "fostered" by the individual citizen-taxpayers and just as clearly those individuals would be "instruments" in that communication. Certainly, however, that case would not fall within the ambit of *Barnette*. In that case, as in this case, there is no *affirmation* of belief. For First Amendment principles to be implicated, the State must place the citizen in the position of either apparently or actually "asserting as true" the message. This was the focus of *Barnette*, and clearly distinguishes this case from that one.

In holding that the New Hampshire statute does not run afoul of our holding in *Barnette*, the New Hampshire Supreme Court in *Hoskin, supra*, at 295 A.2d, at 457, aptly articulated why there is no required affirmation of belief in this case:

> "The defendants' membership in a class of persons required to display plates bearing the State motto carries no implication and is subject to no requirement that they endorse that motto or profess to adopt it as matter of belief."

As found by the New Hampshire Supreme Court in *Hoskin*, there is nothing in state law which precludes appellees from displaying their disagreement with the state motto as long as the methods used do not obscure the license plates. Thus appellees could place on their bumper a conspicuous bumper sticker explaining in no uncertain terms that they do not profess the motto "Live Free or Die" and that they violently disagree with the connotations of that motto. Since any implication that they affirm the motto can be so easily displaced, I cannot agree that the state statutory system for motor vehicle identification and tourist promotion may be invalidated under the fiction that appellees are unconstitutionally forced to affirm, or profess belief in, the state motto.

The logic of the Court's opinion leads to startling, and I believe totally unacceptable, results. For example, the mottoes "In God We Trust" and "E Pluribus Unum" appear on the coin and currency of the United States. I cannot imagine that the statutes, see 18 U.S.C. §§ 331 and 333, proscribing defacement of United States currency impinge upon the First Amendment rights of an atheist. The fact that an atheist carries and uses United States currency does not, in any meaningful sense, convey any affirmation of belief on his part in the motto "In God We Trust." Similarly, there is no affirmation of belief involved in the display of state license tags upon the private automobiles involved here.

I would reverse the judgment of the District Court.

ABOOD v. DETROIT BOARD OF EDUCATION

Supreme Court of the United States, 1977.*
431 U.S. 209, 97 S.Ct. 1782, 52 L.Ed.2d 261.

MR. JUSTICE STEWART delivered the opinion of the Court.

The State of Michigan has enacted legislation authorizing a system for union representation of local governmental employees. A union and a local government employer are specifically permitted to agree to an "agency shop" arrangement, whereby every employee represented by a union—even though not a union member—must pay to the union, as a condition of employment, a service fee equal in amount to union dues. The issue before us is whether this arrangement violates the constitutional rights of government employees who object to public-sector unions as such or to various union activities financed by the compulsory service fees.

I

After a secret ballot election, the Detroit Federation of Teachers (Union) was certified in 1967 pursuant to Michigan law as the exclusive representative of teachers employed by the Detroit Board of Education (Board). The Union and the Board thereafter concluded a collective-bargaining agreement effective from July 1, 1969, to July 1, 1971. Among the agreement's provisions was an "agency shop" clause, requiring every teacher who had not become a Union member within 60 days of hire (or within 60 days of January 26, 1970, the effective date of the clause) to pay the Union a service charge equal to the regular dues required of Union members. A teacher who failed to meet this obli-

---

* See also Keller v. State Bar of California, 495 U.S. ___, 110 S.Ct. 2228, 110 L.Ed.2d 1 (1990). [Ed. note.]

gation was subject to discharge. Nothing in the agreement, however, required any teacher to join the Union, espouse the cause of unionism, or participate in any other way in Union affairs.

On November 7, 1969—more than two months before the agency-shop clause was to become effective—Christine Warczak and a number of other named teachers filed a class action in a state court, naming as defendants the Board, the Union, and several Union officials. Their complaint, as amended, alleged that they were unwilling or had refused to pay dues and that they opposed collective bargaining in the public sector. The amended complaint further alleged that the Union "carries on various social activities for the benefit of its members which are not available to non-members as a matter of right," and that the Union is engaged

> "in a number and variety of activities and programs which are economic, political, professional, scientific and religious in nature of which Plaintiffs do not approve, and in which they will have no voice, and which are not and will not be collective bargaining activities, i.e., the negotiation and administration of contracts with Defendant Board, and that a substantial part of the sums required to be paid under Agency Shop Clause are used and will continue to be used for the support of such activities and programs, and not solely for the purpose of defraying the cost of Defendant Federation of its activities as bargaining agent for teachers employed by Defendant Board.

The complaint prayed that the agency-shop clause be declared invalid under state law and also under the United States Constitution as a deprivation of, *inter alia,* the plaintiffs' freedom of association protected by the First and Fourteenth Amendments, and for such further relief as might be deemed appropriate.

Upon the defendants' motion for summary judgment, the trial court dismissed the action for failure to state a claim upon which relief could be granted. * * *

II

A

Consideration of the question whether an agency-shop provision in a collective-bargaining agreement covering governmental employees is, as such, constitutionally valid must begin with two cases in this Court that on their face go far toward resolving the issue. The cases are *Railway Employes' Dept. v. Hanson, supra,* and Machinists v. Street, 367 U.S. 740.

In the *Hanson* case a group of railroad employees brought an action in a Nebraska court to enjoin enforcement of a union-shop agreement.[10] * * *

10. Under a union-shop agreement, an employee must become a member of the union within a specified period of time after hire, and must as a member pay whatever union dues and fees are uniformly required. Under both the National Labor Relations Act and the Railway Labor Act, "[i]t is permissible to condition em-

The record in *Hanson* contained no evidence that union dues were used to force ideological conformity or otherwise to impair the free expression of employees, and the Court noted that "[i]f 'assessments' are in fact imposed for purposes not germane to collective bargaining, a different problem would be presented." * * * But the Court squarely held that "the requirement for financial support of the collective-bargaining agency by all who receive the benefits of its work * * * does not violate * * * the First * * * Amendmen[t]." *Id.*

The Court faced a similar question several years later in the *Street* case, which also involved a challenge to the constitutionality of a union shop authorized by the Railway Labor Act. In *Street*, however, the record contained findings that the union treasury to which all employees were required to contribute had been used "to finance the campaigns of candidates for federal and state offices whom [the plaintiffs] opposed, and to promote the propagation of political and economic doctrines, concepts and ideologies with which [they] disagreed." * * *

The Court recognized * * * that these findings presented constitutional "questions of the utmost gravity" not decided in *Hanson*, and therefore considered whether the Act could fairly be construed to avoid these constitutional issues. 367 U.S., at 749–750.[13] The Court concluded that the Act could be so construed, since only expenditures related to the union's functions in negotiating and administering the collective-bargaining agreement and adjusting grievances and disputes fell within "the reasons * * * accepted by Congress why authority to make union-shop agreements was justified," *id.*, at 768. The Court ruled, therefore, that the use of compulsory union dues for political purposes violated the Act itself. Nonetheless, it found that an injunction against enforcement of the union-shop agreement as such was impermissible under *Hanson*, and remanded the case to the Supreme Court of Georgia so that a more limited remedy could be devised.

* * *

The designation of a union as exclusive representative carries with it great responsibilities. The tasks of negotiating and administering a collective-bargaining agreement and representing the interests of employees in settling disputes and processing grievances are continuing and difficult ones. They often entail expenditure of much time and money. * * * The services of lawyers, expert negotiators, economists, and a research staff, as well as general administrative personnel, may

ployment upon membership, but membership, insofar as it has significance to employment rights, may in turn be conditioned only upon payment of fees and dues." * * *

Hanson was concerned simply with the requirement of financial support for the union, and did not focus on the question whether the additional requirement of a union-shop arrangement that each employee formally join the union is constitutionally permissible. * * * See *NLRB v. General Motors*, ("Such a difference between the union and agency shop may be of great importance in some contexts * * * ") * * * As the agency shop before us does not impose that additional requirement, we have no occasion to address that question.

13. In suggesting that *Street* "significantly undercut," and constituted a "rethinking" of, *Hanson*, * * *, the opinion concurring in the judgment loses sight of the fact that the record in *Street*, unlike that in *Hanson*, potentially presented constitutional questions arising from union expenditures for ideological purposes unrelated to collective bargaining.

be required. Moreover, in carrying out these duties, the union is obliged "fairly and equitably to represent all employees * * *, union and non-union," within the relevant unit. * * * A union-shop arrangement has been thought to distribute fairly the cost of these activities among those who benefit, and it counteracts the incentive that employees might otherwise have to become "free riders"—to refuse to contribute to the union while obtaining benefits of union representation that necessarily accrue to all employees. * * *

To compel employees financially to support their collective-bargaining representative has an impact upon their First Amendment interests. An employee may very well have ideological objections to a wide variety of activities undertaken by the union in its role as exclusive representative. His moral or religious views about the desirability of abortion may not square with the union's policy in negotiating a medical benefits plan. One individual might disagree with a union policy of negotiating limits on the right to strike, believing that to be the road of serfdom for the working class, while another might have economic or political objections to unionism itself. An employee might object to the union's wage policy because it violates guidelines designed to limit inflation, or might object to the union's seeking a clause in the collective-bargaining agreement proscribing racial discrimination. The examples could be multiplied. To be required to help finance the union as a collective-bargaining agent might well be thought, therefore, to interfere in some way with an employee's freedom to associate for the advancement of ideas, or to refrain from doing so, as he sees fit. But the judgment clearly made in *Hanson* and *Street* is that such interference as exists is constitutionally justified by the legislative assessment of the important contribution by the union shop to the system of labor relations established by Congress. "The furtherance of the common cause leaves some leeway for the leadership of the group. As long as they act to promote the cause which justified bringing the group together, the individual cannot withdraw his financial support merely because he disagrees with the group's strategy. If that were allowed, we would be reversing the *Hanson* case, *sub silentio*." Machinists v. Street, 367 U.S., at 778 (DOUGLAS, J., concurring).

B

* * *

Our province is not to judge the wisdom of Michigan's decision to authorize the agency shop in public employment. Rather, it is to adjudicate the constitutionality of that decision. The same important government interests recognized in the *Hanson* and *Street* cases presumptively support the impingement upon associational freedom created by the agency shop here at issue. Thus, insofar as the service charge is used to finance expenditures by the Union for the purposes of collective bargaining, contract administration, and grievance adjustment, those two decisions of this Court appear to require validation of the agency-shop agreement before us.

While recognizing the apparent precedential weight of the *Hanson* and *Street* cases, the appellants advance two reasons why those decisions should not control decision of the present case. First, the appellants note that it is *government employment* that is involved here, thus directly implicating constitutional guarantees, in contrast to the private employment that was the subject of the *Hanson* and *Street* decisions. Second, the appellants say that in the public sector collective bargaining itself is inherently "political," and that to require them to give financial support to it is to require the "ideological conformity" that the Court expressly found absent in the *Hanson* case. * * * We find neither argument persuasive.

Because it is employment by the State that is here involved, the appellants suggest that this case is governed by a long line of decisions holding that public employment cannot be conditioned upon the surrender of First Amendment rights. But, while the actions of public employers surely constitute "state action," the union shop, as authorized by the Railway Labor Act, also was found to result from governmental action in *Hanson*. The plaintiffs' claims in *Hanson* failed, not because there was no governmental action, but because there was no First Amendment violation. The appellants' reliance on the "unconstitutional conditions" doctrine is therefore misplaced.

* * * We conclude that the Michigan Court of Appeals was correct in viewing this Court's decisions in *Hanson* and *Street* as controlling in the present case insofar as the service charges are applied to collective-bargaining, contract administration, and grievance-adjustment purposes.

C

Because the Michigan Court of Appeals ruled that state law "sanctions the use of nonunion members' fees for purposes other than collective bargaining," * * * and because the complaints allege that such expenditures were made, this case presents constitutional issues not decided in *Hanson* and *Street*. * * *

Our decisions establish with unmistakable clarity that the freedom of an individual to associate for the purpose of advancing beliefs and ideas is protected by the First and Fourteenth Amendments. * * * Equally clear is the proposition that a government may not require an individual to relinquish rights guaranteed him by the First Amendment as a condition of public employment. * * * The appellants argue that they fall within the protection of these cases because they have been prohibited, not from actively associating, but rather from refusing to associate. They specifically argue that they may constitutionally prevent the Union's spending a part of their required service fees to contribute to political candidates and to express political views unrelated to its duties as exclusive bargaining representative. We have concluded that this argument is a meritorious one.

* * *

The fact that the appellants are compelled to make, rather than prohibited from making, contributions for political purposes works no

less an infringement of their constitutional rights.[31] For at the heart of the First Amendment is the notion that an individual should be free to believe as he will, and that in a free society one's beliefs should be shaped by his mind and his conscience rather than coerced by the State.
* * *

These principles prohibit a State from compelling any individual to affirm his belief in God, Torcaso v. Watkins, 367 U.S. 488, or to associate with a political party, *Elrod v. Burns, supra;* see 427 U.S., at 363–364, n. 17, as a condition of retaining public employment. They are no less applicable to the case at bar, and they thus prohibit the appellees from requiring any of the appellants to contribute to the support of an ideological cause he may oppose as a condition of holding a job as a public school teacher.

We do not hold that a union cannot constitutionally spend funds for the expression of political views, on behalf of political candidates, or toward the advancement of other ideological causes not germane to its duties as collective-bargaining representative. Rather, the Constitution requires only that such expenditures be financed from charges, dues, or assessments paid by employees who do not object to advancing those ideas and who are not coerced into doing so against their will by the threat of loss of governmental employment.

There will, of course, be difficult problems in drawing lines between collective-bargaining activities, for which contributions may be compelled, and ideological activities unrelated to collective bargaining, for which such compulsion is prohibited.[33] The Court held in *Street,* as a matter of statutory construction, that a similar line must be drawn under the Railway Labor Act, but in the public sector the line may be somewhat hazier. The process of establishing a written collective-bargaining agreement prescribing the terms and conditions of public employment may require not merely concord at the bargaining table, but subsequent approval by other public authorities; related budgetary and appropriations decisions might be seen as an integral part of the bargaining process. We have no occasion in this case, however, to try to define such a dividing line. * * * All that we decide is that the general allegations in the complaints, if proved, establish a cause of action under the First and Fourteenth Amendments.

---

31. This view has long been held. James Madison, the First Amendment's author, wrote in defense of religious liberty: "Who does not see * * * [t]hat the same authority which can force a citizen to contribute three pence only of his property for the support of any one establishment, may force him to conform to any other establishment in all cases whatsoever?" 2 The Writings of James Madison 186 (Hunt ed. 1901). Thomas Jefferson agreed that " 'to compel a man to furnish contributions of money for the propagation of opinions which he disbelieves, is sinful and tyrannical.' " I. Brant, James Madison: The Nationalist 354 (1948).

33. The appellants' complaints also alleged that the Union carries on various "social activities" which are not open to nonmembers. It is unclear to what extent such activities fall outside the Union's duties as exclusive representative or involve constitutionally protected rights of association. Without greater specificity in the description of such activities and the benefit of adversary argument, we leave these questions in the first instance to the Michigan courts.

III

In determining what remedy will be appropriate if the appellants prove their allegations, the objective must be to devise a way of preventing compulsory subsidization of ideological activity by employees who object thereto without restricting the Union's ability to require every employee to contribute to the cost of collective-bargaining activities.[35] * * *

The judgment is vacated, and the case is remanded for further proceedings not inconsistent with this opinion.

It is so ordered.

* * *

MR. JUSTICE STEVENS, concurring.

By joining the opinion of the Court, including its discussion of possible remedies, I do not imply—nor do I understand the Court to imply—that the remedies described in Machinists v. Street, 367 U.S. 740, and Railway Clerks v. Allen, 373 U.S. 113, would necessarily be adequate in this case or in any other case. More specifically, the Court's opinion does not foreclose the argument that the Union should not be permitted to exact a service fee from nonmembers without first establishing a procedure which will avoid the risk that their funds will be used, even temporarily, to finance ideological activities unrelated to collective bargaining. Any final decision on the appropriate remedy must await the full development of the facts at trial.

MR. JUSTICE POWELL, with whom THE CHIEF JUSTICE and MR. JUSTICE BLACKMUN join, concurring in the judgment.

The Court today holds that a State cannot constitutionally compel public employees to contribute to union political activities which they oppose. On this basis the Court concludes that "the general allegations in the complaints, if proved, establish a cause of action under the First and Fourteenth Amendments." *Ante.* With this much of the Court's opinion I agree, and I therefore join the Court's judgment remanding this case for further proceedings.

But the Court's holding and judgment are but a small part of today's decision. Working from the novel premise that public employ-

---

35. It is plainly not an adequate remedy to limit the use of the actual dollars collected from dissenting employees to collective-bargaining purposes:

"[Such a limitation] is of bookkeeping significance only rather than a matter of real substance. It must be remembered that the service fee is admittedly the exact equal of membership initiation fees and monthly dues * * * and that * * * dues collected from members may be used for a 'variety of purposes, in addition to meeting the union's costs of collective bargaining.' Unions 'rather typically' use their membership dues 'to do those things which the members authorize the union to do in their interest and on their behalf.' If the union's total budget is divided between collective bargaining and institutional expenses and if nonmember payments, equal to those of a member, go entirely for collective bargaining costs, the nonmember will pay more of these expenses than his pro rata share. The member will pay less and to that extent a portion of his fees and dues is available to pay institutional expenses. The union's budget is balanced. By paying a larger share of collective bargaining costs the nonmember subsidizes the union's institutional activities." Retail Clerks v. Schermerhorn, 373 U.S. 746, 753–754.

ers are under no greater constitutional constraints than their counterparts in the private sector, the Court apparently rules that public employees can be compelled by the State to pay full union dues to a union with which they disagree, subject only to a possible rebate or reduction if they are willing to step forward, declare their opposition to the union, and initiate a proceeding to establish that some portion of their dues has been spent on "ideological activities unrelated to collective bargaining." *Ante.* Such a sweeping limitation of First Amendment rights by the Court is not only unnecessary on the record; it is in my view unsupported by either precedent or reason.

* * *

The Court's extensive reliance on *Hanson* and *Street* requires it to rule that there is no constitutional distinction between what the government can require of its own employees and what it can permit private employers to do. To me the distinction is fundamental. Under the First Amendment the government may authorize private parties to enter into voluntary agreements whose terms it could not adopt as its own.

We stressed the importance of this distinction only recently, in Jackson v. Metropolitan Edison Co., 419 U.S. 345. There a New York resident had brought suit against a private utility, claiming that she had been denied due process when the utility terminated her service without notice or a hearing and alleging that the utility's summary termination procedures had been "specifically authorized and approved" by the State. In sustaining dismissal of the complaint, we held that authorization and approval did not transform the procedures of the company into the procedures of the State:

> "The nature of governmental regulation of private utilities is such that a utility may frequently be required by the state regulatory scheme to obtain approval for practices a business regulated in less detail would be free to institute without any approval from a regulatory body. Approval by a state utility commission of such a request from a regulated utility, where the commission has not put its own weight on the side of the proposed practice by ordering it, does not transmute a practice initiated by the utility and approved by the commission into 'state action.'" *Id.,* at 357.

Had the State itself adopted the procedures it approved for the utility, it would have been subject to the full constraints of the Constitution.

* * *

The State in this case has not merely authorized agency-shop agreements between willing parties; it has negotiated and adopted such an agreement itself. Acting through the Detroit Board of Education, the State has undertaken to compel employees to pay full fees equal in amount to dues to a union as a condition of employment. Accordingly, the Board's collective-bargaining agreement, like any other enactment of state law, is fully subject to the constraints that the Constitution imposes on coercive governmental regulation.

* * *

Before today it had been well established that when state law intrudes upon protected speech, the State itself must shoulder the burden of proving that its action is justified by overriding state interests. See *Elrod v. Burns, supra,* at 363; Healy v. James, 408 U.S. 169, 184; Speiser v. Randall, 357 U.S. 513, 525–526. The Court, for the first time in a First Amendment case, simply reverses this principle. Under today's decision a nonunion employee who would vindicate his First Amendment rights apparently must initiate a proceeding to prove that the union has allocated some portion of its budget to "ideological activities unrelated to collective bargaining." *Ante.* I would adhere to established First Amendment principles and require the State to come forward and demonstrate, as to each union expenditure for which it would exact support from minority employees, that the compelled contribution is necessary to serve overriding governmental objectives. This placement of the burden of litigation, not the Court's, gives appropriate protection to First Amendment rights without sacrificing ends of government that may be deemed important.

NOTE

1. Following *Abood* (and *Keller*), suppose that a student enrolled at the University of Illinois files suit to enjoin the university from requiring a payment of a $25 student activity fee a portion of which is allocated by the Student Government Association to a student Public Interest Research Group (PIRG). The Student PIRG is an organization on campus, open to all students, that devotes some organizational efforts to lobby in Springfield, Illinois, where the state legislature meets, for causes the student PIRG believes to be in the public interest: higher minimum wages for workers, state-financed abortion assistance for low income women, additional laws limiting cigarette smoking, community service by students in lieu of tuition fees at state schools. What should the outcome of this case be? [88]

2. Suppose a state legislature concludes that further labor organization in the state may adversely affect the state's general economy by discouraging capital investment and driving new companies either to other states or, indeed, to relocate outside the United States. The state currently has a "Right to Work" law, disallowing union shops. The legislature believes this legislation to be sound. Nevertheless, trade union organizational and political activity in the state is at such a level that members of the state legislature feel under pressure to repeal that law, a move a clear majority of the legislature believes would be extremely unwise.

---

88. As a variation, suppose the mandatory $25 student activity fee is also allocated through the student government association partly to fund the student campus newspaper—a paper that operates under its own student staff, with the editor-in-chief being chosen each year by election within the student staff. The newspaper decides its own editorial policy. Generally, that policy has been "center left." What, if anything, may students who disagree with that policy do?

Convinced that the repeal of the state right to work law would be damaging to the state's economy, and convinced, too, that the public does not understand how capital markets operate and how trade union practices can (in the legislature's view) lead to their own serious abuses (e.g., misappropriation of members' dues by union officials, infiltration by organized crime), the legislature appropriates $50 million to be allocated to the State Department of Development specifically to enter into contracts with private advertising firms that will undertake to prepare newspaper and television advertisements. The aim of the advertisements is to bring to public attention the negative aspects of trade unions and the negative aspects of repealing the right to work law, nothing more or less. The purpose, of course, is to serve the public interest as the legislature sees that interest. Is there a first amendment basis to seek to enjoin the expenditure? Who may bring such an action? Where? On what theory might it be based? What relief, if any, are they entitled to receive? [89]

Is it the case that the first amendment permits a faction not merely to take control of the legislative process when they succeed through fair and open elections, but that it permits them thereby to harness the power of government to levy taxes to finance tax-funded, government sponsored propaganda [90] respecting the proper attitude toward, response to and treatment of social, political, and economic issues, in keeping with its views on those issues, i.e. of how those issues ought to be seen and understood, and how one ought to think and behave? [91]

---

89. Is it, at most, that no objecting taxpayer may be denied such pro rata refund of such state taxes as they are otherwise required to pay as may be reflected by this appropriation, or is there a stronger first amendment objection to be made (e.g., that the first amendment disallows "domestic partisan ideological speech" under official government auspices in the United States)?

90. "Propaganda" merely in the sense of a selective culling, arrangement, and presentation of information done in a manner designed to achieve an effect (i.e. the material presented need not itself be false per se).

91. For some attempts to come to terms with this kind of question, see T. Emerson, The System of Free Expression 697–716 (1970); M. Yudof, When Governments Speak: Politics, Law and Government Expression in America (1983); Kamenshine, The First Amendment's Implied Establishment Clause, 67 Calif.L.Rev. 1104 (1979); Nowak, Using the Press Clause to Limit Government Speech, 30 Ariz.L.Rev. 1 (1988); Shiffrin, Government Speech, 27 U.C.L.A. L.Rev. 656 (1980), Yudof, Personal Speech and Government Expression, 30 Ariz.L.Rev. 671 (1988); Ziegler, Government Speech and the Constitution: The

G. EQUALIZING FREEDOM OF SPEECH BY LEVELLING EXPENDITURES AND CONTRIBUTIONS—REGULATING THE USES OF MONEY AND SPEECH

BUCKLEY v. VALEO

Supreme Court of the United States, 1976.*
424 U.S. 1, 96 S.Ct. 612, 46 L.Ed.2d 659.

Per curiam opinion, in the "case or controversy" part of which * * * all participating Members joined; and as to all other parts of which BRENNAN, STEWART and POWELL, JJ., joined; MARSHALL, J., joined in all but Part I–C–2; BLACKMUN, J., joined in all but Part I–B; REHNQUIST, J., joined in all but Part III–B–1; BURGER, C.J., joined in Parts I–C and IV (except insofar as it accords de facto validity for the Commission's past acts); and WHITE, J., joined in Part III. BURGER, C.J., * * *, WHITE, J., * * *, MARSHALL, J., * * *, BLACKMUN, J., * * *, and REHNQUIST, J., * * *, filed opinions concurring in part and dissenting in part. STEVENS, J., took no part in the consideration or decision of the cases.

* * *

PER CURIAM.

These appeals present constitutional challenges to the key provisions of the Federal Election Campaign Act of 1971, (Act) and related provisions of the Internal Revenue Code of 1954, all as amended in 1974.

The Court of Appeals, in sustaining the legislation in large part against various constitutional challenges,[2] viewed it as "by far the most comprehensive reform legislation [ever] passed by Congress concerning the election of the President, Vice–President, and members of Congress." 171 U.S.App.D.C. 172, 82, 519 F.2d 821, 831 (1975). The statutes at issue summarized in broad terms, contain the following provisions: (a) individual political contributions are limited to $1,000 to any single candidate per election, with an overall annual limitation of $25,000 by any contributor; independent expenditures by individuals and groups "relative to a clearly identified candidate" are limited to $1,000 a year; campaign spending by candidates for various federal offices and spending for national conventions by political parties are subject to prescribed limits; (b) contributions and expenditures above certain threshold levels must be reported and publicly disclosed; (c) a system for public funding of Presidential campaign activities is established by Subtitle H of the Internal Revenue Code;[3] and (d) a Federal

Limits of Official Partisanship, 21 B.C.L. Rev. 578 (1980).

* 294 pages. [Ed. note.]

2. 171 U.S.App.D.C. 172, 519 F.2d 821 (1975).

3. The Revenue Act of 1971, Title VIII, 85 Stat. 562, as amended, 87 Stat. 138, and further amended by the Federal Election Campaign Act Amendments of 1974, § 403 et seq., 88 Stat. 1291. This Subtitle consists of two parts: Chapter 95 deals with funding national party conventions and general election campaigns for President, and Chapter 96 deals with matching funds for Presidential primary campaigns.

Election Commission is established to administer and enforce the legislation.

This suit was originally filed by appellants in the United States District Court for the District of Columbia. Plaintiffs included a candidate for the Presidency of the United States, a United States Senator who is a candidate for re-election, a potential contributor, the Committee for a Constitutional Presidency—McCarthy '76, the Conservative Party of the State of New York, the Mississippi Republican Party, the Libertarian Party, the New York Civil Liberties Union, Inc., the American Conservative Union, the Conservative Victory Fund, and Human Events, Inc. * * *

* * *

On plenary review, a majority of the Court of Appeals rejected, for the most part, appellants' constitutional attacks. * * *

In this Court, appellants argue that the Court of Appeals failed to give this legislation the critical scrutiny demanded under accepted First Amendment and equal protection principles. In appellants' view, limiting the use of money for political purposes constitutes a restriction on communication violative of the First Amendment, since virtually all meaningful political communications in the modern setting involve the expenditure of money. Further, they argue that the reporting and disclosure provisions of the Act unconstitutionally impinge on their right to freedom of association. Appellants also view the federal subsidy provisions of Subtitle H as violative of the General Welfare Clause, and as inconsistent with the First and Fifth Amendments. Finally, appellants renew their attack on the Commission's composition and powers.

* * *

I. CONTRIBUTION AND EXPENDITURE LIMITATIONS

The intricate statutory scheme adopted by Congress to regulate federal election campaigns includes restrictions on political contributions and expenditures that apply broadly to all phases of and all participants in the election process. The major contribution and expenditure limitations in the Act prohibit individuals from contributing more than $25,000 in a single year or more than $1,000 to any single candidate for an election campaign and from spending more than $1,000 a year "relative to a clearly identified candidate." Other provisions restrict a candidate's use of personal and family resources in his campaign and limit the overall amount that can be spent by a candidate in campaigning for federal office.

* * *

A. General Principles

The Act's contribution and expenditure limitations operate in an area of the most fundamental First Amendment activities. Discussion of public issues and debate on the qualifications of candidates are integral to the operation of the system of government established by our Constitution. The First Amendment affords the broadest protection to such political expression in order "to assure [the] unfettered interchange of ideas for the bringing about of political and social changes desired by the people." Roth v. United States, 354 U.S. 476, 484 (1957). Although First Amendment protections are not confined to "the exposition of ideas," Winters v. New York, 333 U.S. 507, 510 (1948), "there is practically universal agreement that a major purpose of that Amendment was to protect the free discussion of governmental affairs, * * * of course includ[ing] discussions of candidates. * * *" Mills v. Alabama, 384 U.S. 214, 218 (1966). * * *

* * *

It is with these principles in mind that we consider the primary contentions of the parties with respect to the Act's limitations upon the giving and spending of money in political campaigns. Those conflicting contentions could not more sharply define the basic issues before us. Appellees contend that what the Act regulates is conduct, and that its effect on speech and association is incidental at most. Appellants respond that contributions and expenditures are at the very core of political speech, and that the Act's limitations thus constitute restraints on First Amendment liberty that are both gross and direct.

In upholding the constitutional validity of the Act's contribution and expenditure provisions on the ground that those provisions should be viewed as regulating conduct not speech, the Court of Appeals relied upon United States v. O'Brien, 391 U.S. 367 (1968). * * * The *O'Brien* case involved a defendant's claim that the First Amendment prohibited his prosecution for burning his draft card because his act was "'symbolic speech'" engaged in as a "'demonstration against the war and against the draft.'" 391 U.S., at 376. On the assumption that "the alleged communicative element in O'Brien's conduct [was] sufficient to bring into play the First Amendment," the Court sustained the conviction because it found "a sufficiently important governmental interest in regulating the nonspeech element" that was "unrelated to the suppression of free expression" and that had an "incidental restriction on alleged First Amendment freedoms * * * no greater than [was] essential to the furtherance of that interest." *Id.*, at 376–377. The Court expressly emphasized that *O'Brien* was not a case "where the alleged governmental interest in regulating conduct arises in some measure because the communication allegedly integral to the conduct is itself thought to be harmful." *Id.*, at 382.

We cannot share the view that the present Act's contribution and expenditure limitations are comparable to the restrictions on conduct upheld in *O'Brien*. * * *

Even if the categorization of the expenditure of money as conduct were accepted, the limitations challenged here would not meet the *O'Brien* test because the governmental interests advanced in support of the Act involve "suppressing communication." The interests served by the Act include restricting the voices of people and interest groups who have money to spend and reducing the overall scope of federal election campaigns. Although the Act does not focus on the ideas expressed by persons or groups subjected to its regulations, it is aimed in part at equalizing the relative ability of all voters to affect electoral outcomes by placing a ceiling on expenditures for political expression by citizens and groups. Unlike *O'Brien,* where the Selective Service System's administrative interest in the preservation of draft cards was wholly unrelated to their use as a means of communication, it is beyond dispute that the interest in regulating the alleged "conduct" of giving or spending money "arises in some measure because the communication allegedly integral to the conduct is itself thought to be harmful." * * *

* * *

The expenditure limitations contained in the Act represent substantial rather than merely theoretical restraints on the quantity and diversity of political speech. The $1,000 ceiling on spending "relative to a clearly identified candidate," 18 U.S.C. § 608(e)(1) (1970 ed., Supp. IV), would appear to exclude all citizens and groups except candidates, political parties, and the institutional press from any significant use of the most effective modes of communication.[20] * * *

By contrast with a limitation upon expenditures for political expression, a limitation upon the amount that any one person or group may contribute to a candidate or political committee entails only a marginal restriction upon the contributor's ability to engage in free communication. A contribution serves as a general expression of support for the candidate and his views, but does not communicate the underlying basis for the support. The quantity of communication by the contributor does not increase perceptibly with the size of his contribution, since the expression rests solely on the undifferentiated, symbolic act of contributing. At most, the size of the contribution provides a very rough index of the intensity of the contributor's support for the candidate. A limitation on the amount of money a person may give to a candidate or campaign organization thus involves little direct restraint on his political communication, for it permits the symbolic expression of support evidenced by a contribution but does not in any way infringe the contributor's freedom to discuss candidates and issues. While contributions may result in political expression if spent by a candidate or an association to present views to the voters, the transformation of contributions into political debate involves speech by someone other than the contributor.

Given the important role of contributions in financing political campaigns, contribution restrictions could have a severe impact on political dialogue if the limitations prevented candidates and political committees from amassing the resources necessary for effective advocacy. There is no indication, however, that the contribution limitations imposed by the Act would have any dramatic adverse effect on the funding of campaigns and political associations. * * *

---

20. The record indicates that, as of January 1, 1975, one full-page advertisement in a daily edition of a certain metropolitan newspaper cost $6,971.04—almost seven times the annual limit on expenditures "relative to" a particular candidate imposed on the vast majority of individual citizens and associations by § 608(e)(1).

The Act's contribution and expenditure limitations also impinge on protected associational freedoms. Making a contribution, like joining a political party, serves to affiliate a person with a candidate. In addition, it enables like-minded persons to pool their resources in furtherance of common political goals. The Act's contribution ceilings thus limit one important means of associating with a candidate or committee, but leave the contributor free to become a member of any political association and to assist personally in the association's efforts on behalf of candidates. And the Act's contribution limitations permit associations and candidates to aggregate large sums of money to promote effective advocacy. By contrast, the Act's $1,000 limitation on independent expenditures "relative to a clearly identified candidate" precludes most associations from effectively amplifying the voice of their adherents, the original basis for the recognition of First Amendment protection of the freedom of association. See NAACP v. Alabama, 357 U.S., at 460. * * *

In sum, although the Act's contribution and expenditure limitations both implicate fundamental First Amendment interests, its expenditure ceilings impose significantly more severe restrictions on protected freedoms of political expression and association than do its limitations on financial contributions.

B. Contribution Limitations

1. The $1,000 Limitation on Contributions by Individuals and Groups to Candidates and Authorized Campaign Committees

Section 608(b) provides, with certain limited exceptions, that "no person shall make contributions to any candidate with respect to any election for Federal office which, in the aggregate, exceed $1,000." The statute defines "person" broadly to include "an individual, partnership, committee, association, corporation or any other organization or group of persons." * * *

Appellants contend that the $1,000 contribution ceiling unjustifiably burdens First Amendment freedoms, employs overbroad dollar limits, and discriminates against candidates opposing incumbent officeholders and against minor-party candidates in violation of the Fifth Amendment. We address each of these claims of invalidity in turn.

(a)

* * *

Appellees argue that the Act's restrictions on large campaign contributions are justified by three governmental interests. According to the parties and *amici,* the primary interest served by the limitations and, indeed, by the Act as a whole, is the prevention of corruption and the appearance of corruption spawned by the real or imagined coercive influence of large financial contributions on candidates' positions and on their actions if elected to office. Two "ancillary" interests underlying the Act are also allegedly furthered by the $1,000 limits on contributions. First, the limits serve to mute the voices of affluent persons and groups in the election process and thereby to equalize the relative ability of all citizens to affect the outcome of elections.[26] Second, it is argued, the ceilings may to some extent act as a brake on the skyrocketing cost of political campaigns and thereby serve to open the political system more widely to candidates without access to sources of large amounts of money.[27]

It is unnecessary to look beyond the Act's primary purpose—to limit the actuality and appearance of corruption resulting from large individual financial contributions—in order to find a constitutionally sufficient justification for the $1,000 contribution limitation. Under a system of private financing of elections, a candidate lacking immense personal or family wealth must depend on financial contributions from others to provide the resources necessary to conduct a successful campaign. The increasing importance of the communications media and sophisticated mass-mailing and polling operations to effective campaigning make the raising of large sums of money an ever more essential ingredient of an effective candidacy. To the extent that large contributions are given to secure political *quid pro quo* from current and potential office holders, the integrity of our system of representative democracy is undermined. Although the scope of such pernicious practices can never be reliably ascertained, the deeply disturbing examples surfacing after the 1972 election demonstrate that the problem is not an illusory one.[28]

Of almost equal concern as the danger of actual *quid pro quo* arrangements is the impact of the appearance of corruption stemming from public awareness of the opportunities for abuse inherent in a regime of large individual financial contributions. In *CSC v. Letter Carriers, supra,* the Court found that the danger to "fair and effective government" posed by partisan political conduct on the part of federal employees charged with administering the law was a sufficiently important concern to justify broad restrictions on the employees' right of partisan political association. Here, as there, Congress could legitimately conclude that the avoidance of the appearance of improper influence "is also critical * * * if confidence in the system of representative Government is not to be eroded to a disastrous extent." 413 U.S., at 565.

Appellants contend that the contribution limitations must be invalidated because bribery laws and narrowly drawn disclosure requirements constitute a less restrictive means of dealing with "proven and

---

26. Contribution limitations alone would not reduce the greater potential voice of affluent persons and well-financed groups, who would remain free to spend unlimited sums directly to promote candidates and policies they favor in an effort to persuade voters.

27. Yet, a ceiling on the size of contributions would affect only indirectly the costs of political campaigns by making it relatively more difficult for candidates to raise large amounts of money. In 1974, for example, 94.9% of the funds raised by candidates for Congress came from contributions of $1,000 or less, see n. 23, *supra.*

Presumably, some or all of the contributions in excess of $1,000 could have been replaced through efforts to raise additional contributions from persons giving less than $1,000. It is the Act's campaign expenditure limitations, § 608(c), not the contribution limits, that directly address the overall scope of federal election spending.

28. The Court of Appeals' opinion in this case discussed a number of the abuses uncovered after the 1972 elections. See U.S.App.D.C., at 190–191, and nn. 36–38, 519 F.2d, at 839–840, and nn. 36–38.

suspected *quid pro quo* arrangements." But laws making criminal the giving and taking of bribes deal with only the most blatant and specific attempts of those with money to influence governmental action. And while disclosure requirements serve the many salutary purposes discussed elsewhere in this opinion, Congress was surely entitled to conclude that disclosure was only a partial measure, and that contribution ceilings were a necessary legislative concomitant to deal with the reality or appearance of corruption inherent in a system permitting unlimited financial contributions, even when the identities of the contributors and the amounts of their contributions are fully disclosed.

The Act's $1,000 contribution limitation focuses precisely on the problem of large campaign contributions—the narrow aspect of political association where the actuality and potential for corruption have been identified—while leaving persons free to engage in independent political expression, to associate actively through volunteering their services, and to assist to a limited but nonetheless substantial extent in supporting candidates and committees with financial resources. Significantly, the Act's contribution limitations in themselves do not undermine to any material degree the potential for robust and effective discussion of candidates and campaign issues by individual citizens, associations, the institutional press, candidates, and political parties.

We find that, under the rigorous standard of review established by our prior decisions, the weighty interests served by restricting the size of financial contributions to political candidates are sufficient to justify the limited effect upon First Amendment freedoms caused by the $1,000 contribution ceiling.

* * *

(c)

Apart from these First Amendment concerns, appellants argue that the contribution limitations work such an invidious discrimination between incumbents and challengers that the statutory provisions must be declared unconstitutional on their face. In considering this contention, it is important at the outset to note that the Act applies the same limitations on contributions to all candidates regardless of their present occupations, ideological views, or party affiliations. * * *

There is no such evidence to support the claim that the contribution limitations in themselves discriminate against major-party challengers to incumbents. * * * And, to the extent that incumbents generally are more likely than challengers to attract very large contributions, the Act's $1,000 ceiling has the practical effect of benefiting challengers as a class.[37] * * *

The charge of discrimination against minor-party and independent candidates is more troubling, but the record provides no basis for concluding that the Act invidiously disadvantages such candidates. As noted above, the Act on its face treats all candidates equally with

---

37. Of the $3,781,254 in contributions raised in 1974 by congressional candidates over and above a $1,000–per–contributor limit, almost twice as much money went to incumbents as to major-party challengers.

regard to contribution limitations. And the restriction would appear to benefit minor-party and independent candidates relative to their major-party opponents because major-party candidates receive far more money in large contributions. * * *

In view of these considerations, we conclude that the impact of the Act's $1,000 contribution limitation on major-party challengers and on minor-party candidates does not render the provision unconstitutional on its face.

* * *

C. EXPENDITURE LIMITATIONS

The Act's expenditure ceilings impose direct and substantial restraints on the quantity of political speech. The most drastic of the limitations restricts individuals and groups, including political parties that fail to place a candidate on the ballot, to an expenditure of $1,000 "relative to a clearly identified candidate during a calendar year." * * * The restrictions, while neutral as to the ideas expressed, limit political expression "at the core of our electoral process and of the First Amendment freedoms." Williams v. Rhodes, 393 U.S. 23, 32 (1968).

1. The $1,000 Limitation on Expenditures "Relative to a Clearly Identified Candidate"

* * * The plain effect of § 608(e)(1) is to prohibit all individuals, who are neither candidates nor owners of institutional press facilities, and all groups, except political parties and campaign organizations, from voicing their views "relative to a clearly identified candidate" through means that entail aggregate expenditures of more than $1,000 during a calendar year. The provision, for example, would make it a federal criminal offense for a person or association to place a single one-quarter page advertisement "relative to a clearly identified candidate" in a major metropolitan newspaper.

Before examining the interests advanced in support of § 608(e)(1)'s expenditure ceiling, consideration must be given to appellants' contention that the provision is unconstitutionally vague. * * *

* * * The use of so indefinite a phrase as "relative to" a candidate fails to clearly mark the boundary between permissible and impermissible speech, unless other portions of § 608(e)(1) make sufficiently explicit the range of expenditures covered by the limitation. The section prohibits "any expenditure ... relative to a clearly identified candidate during a calendar year which, *when added to all other expenditures* * * * *advocating the election or defeat of such candidate,* exceeds $1,000." (Emphasis added.) This context clearly permits, if indeed it does not require, the phrase "relative to" a candidate to be read to mean "advocating the election or defeat of" a candidate.

But while such a construction of § 608(e)(1) refocuses the vagueness question, the Court of Appeals was mistaken in thinking that this construction eliminates the problem of unconstitutional vagueness altogether. 171 U.S.App.D.C., at 204, 519 F.2d, at 853. For the distinction between discussion of issues and candidates and advocacy of election or defeat of candidates may often dissolve in practical application. Candidates, especially incumbents, are intimately tied to public issues involving legislative proposals and governmental actions. Not only do candidates campaign on the basis of their positions on various public issues, but campaigns themselves generate issues of public interest. * * *

* * * We agree that in order to preserve the provision against invalidation on vagueness grounds, § 608(e)(1) must be construed to apply only to expenditures for communications that in express terms advocate the election or defeat of a clearly identified candidate for federal office.[52]

We turn then to the basic First Amendment question—whether § 608(e)(1) even as thus narrowly and explicitly construed, impermissibly burdens the constitutional right of free expression. The Court of Appeals summarily held the provision constitutionally valid on the ground that "section 608(e) is a loophole-closing provision only" that is necessary to prevent circumvention of the contribution limitations. * * * We cannot agree.

The discussion in Part I–A, *supra,* explains why the Act's expenditure limitations impose far greater restraints on the freedom of speech and association than do its contribution limitations. The markedly greater burden on basic freedoms caused by § 608(e)(1) thus cannot be sustained simply by invoking the interest in maximizing the effectiveness of the less intrusive contribution limitations. Rather, the constitutionality of § 608(e)(1) turns on whether the governmental interests advanced in its support satisfy the exacting scrutiny applicable to limitations on core First Amendment rights of political expression.

We find that the governmental interest in preventing corruption and the appearance of corruption is inadequate to justify § 608(e)(1)'s ceiling on independent expenditures. First, assuming, *arguendo,* that large independent expenditures pose the same dangers of actual or apparent *quid pro quo* arrangements as do large contributions, § 608(e)(1) does not provide an answer that sufficiently relates to the elimination of those dangers. Unlike the contribution limitations' total ban on the giving of large amounts of money to candidates, § 608(e)(1) prevents only some large expenditures. So long as persons and groups eschew expenditures that in express terms advocate the election or defeat of a clearly identified candidate, they are free to spend as much as they want to promote the candidate and his views. The exacting interpretation of the statutory language necessary to avoid unconstitutional vagueness thus undermines the limitation's effectiveness as a loophole-closing provision by facilitating circumvention by those seeking to exert improper influence upon a candidate or officeholder. * * *

Second, quite apart from the shortcomings of § 608(e)(1) in preventing any abuses generated by large independent expenditures, the independent advocacy restricted by the provision does not presently appear

---

52. This construction would restrict the application of § 608(e)(1) to communications containing express words of advocacy of election or defeat, such as "vote for," "elect," "support," "cast your ballot for," "Smith for Congress," "vote against," "defeat," "reject."

to pose dangers of real or apparent corruption comparable to those identified with large campaign contributions. The parties defending § 608(e)(1) contend that it is necessary to prevent would-be contributors from avoiding the contribution limitations by the simple expedient of paying directly for media advertisements or for other portions of the candidate's campaign activities. They argue that expenditures controlled by or coordinated with the candidate and his campaign might well have virtually the same value to the candidate as a contribution and would pose similar dangers of abuse. Yet such controlled or coordinated expenditures are treated as contributions rather than expenditures under the Act. Section 608(b)'s contribution ceilings rather than § 608(e)(1)'s independent expenditure limitation prevent attempts to circumvent the Act through prearranged or coordinated expenditures amounting to disguised contributions. By contrast, § 608(e)(1) limits expenditures for express advocacy of candidates made totally independently of the candidate and his campaign. * * * Rather than preventing circumvention of the contribution limitations, § 608(e)(1) severely restricts all independent advocacy despite its substantially diminished potential for abuse.

While the independent expenditure ceiling thus fails to serve any substantial governmental interest in stemming the reality or appearance of corruption in the electoral process, it heavily burdens core First Amendment expression. * * * Advocacy of the election or defeat of candidates for federal office is no less entitled to protection under the First Amendment than the discussion of political policy generally or advocacy of the passage or defeat of legislation.

It is argued, however, that the ancillary governmental interest in equalizing the relative ability of individuals and groups to influence the outcome of elections serves to justify the limitation on express advocacy of the election or defeat of candidates imposed by § 608(e)(1)'s expenditure ceiling. But the concept that government may restrict the speech of some elements of our society in order to enhance the relative voice of others is wholly foreign to the First Amendment, which was designed "to secure 'the widest possible dissemination of information from diverse and antagonistic sources,'" and "'to assure unfettered interchange of ideas for the bringing about of political and social changes desired by the people.'" *New York Times Co. v. Sullivan, supra,* at 266, 269, quoting Associated Press v. United States, 326 U.S. 1, 20 (1945), and Roth v. United States, 354 U.S., at 484. * * *

* * * In *Mills*, the Court addressed the question whether "a State, consistently with the United States Constitution, can make it a crime for the editor of a daily newspaper to write and publish an editorial on election day urging people to vote a certain way on issues submitted to them." 384 U.S., at 215 (emphasis in original). We held that "no test of reasonableness can save [such] a state law from invalidation as a violation of the First Amendment." *Id.,* at 220. Yet the prohibition of election-day editorials invalidated in *Mills* is clearly a lesser intrusion on constitutional freedom than a $1,000 limitation on the amount of money any person or association can spend during an entire election year in advocating the election or defeat of a candidate for public office.

More recently in *Tornillo,* the Court held that Florida could not constitutionally require a newspaper to make space available for a political candidate to reply to its criticism. Yet under the Florida statute, every newspaper was free to criticize any candidate as much as it pleased so long as it undertook the modest burden of printing his reply. * * *

For the reasons stated, we conclude that § 608(e)(1)'s independent expenditure limitation is unconstitutional under the First Amendment.

2. Limitation on Expenditures by Candidates from Personal or Family Resources

The Act also sets limits on expenditures by a candidate "from his personal funds, or the personal funds of his immediate family, in connection with his campaigns during any calendar year." § 608(a)(1). These ceilings vary from $50,000 for Presidential or Vice Presidential candidates to $35,000 for senatorial candidates, and $25,000 for most candidates for the House of Representatives.

* * * The candidate, no less than any other person, has a First Amendment right to engage in the discussion of public issues and vigorously and tirelessly to advocate his own election and the election of other candidates. Indeed, it is of particular importance that candidates have the unfettered opportunity to make their views known so that the electorate may intelligently evaluate the candidates' personal qualities and their positions on vital public issues before choosing among them on election day. Mr. Justice Brandeis' observation that in our country "public discussion is a political duty," Whitney v. California, 274 U.S. 357, 375 (1927) (concurring opinion), applies with special force to candidates for public office. Section 608(a)'s ceiling on personal expenditures by a candidate in furtherance of his own candidacy thus clearly and directly interferes with constitutionally protected freedoms.

The primary governmental interest served by the Act—the prevention of actual and apparent corruption of the political process—does not support the limitation on the candidate's expenditure of his own personal funds. As the Court of Appeals concluded: "Manifestly, the core problem of avoiding undisclosed and undue influence on candidates from outside interests has lesser application when the monies involved come from the candidate himself or from his immediate family." 171 U.S.App.D.C., at 206, 519 F.2d, at 855. Indeed, the use of personal funds reduces the candidate's dependence on outside contributions and thereby counteracts the coercive pressures and attendant risks of abuse to which the Act's contribution limitations are directed.

The ancillary interest in equalizing the relative financial resources of candidates competing for elective office, therefore, provides the sole relevant rationale for § 608(a)'s expenditure ceiling. That interest is clearly not sufficient to justify the provision's infringement of fundamental First Amendment rights. First, the limitation may fail to promote financial equality among candidates. A candidate who spends less of his personal resources on his campaign may nonetheless outspend his rival as a result of more successful fundraising efforts.

Indeed, a candidate's personal wealth may impede his efforts to persuade others that he needs their financial contributions or volunteer efforts to conduct an effective campaign. Second, and more fundamentally, the First Amendment simply cannot tolerate § 608(a)'s restriction upon the freedom of a candidate to speak without legislative limit on behalf of his own candidacy. We therefore hold that § 608(a)'s restriction on a candidate's personal expenditures is unconstitutional.

3. Limitations on Campaign Expenditures

* * *

No governmental interest that has been suggested is sufficient to justify the restriction on the quantity of political expression imposed by § 608(c)'s campaign expenditure limitations. The major evil associated with rapidly increasing campaign expenditures is the danger of candidate dependence on large contributions. The interest in alleviating the corrupting influence of large contributions is served by the Act's contribution limitations and disclosure provisions rather than by § 608(c)'s campaign expenditure ceilings. * * *

The interest in equalizing the financial resources of candidates competing for federal office is no more convincing a justification for restricting the scope of federal election campaigns. Given the limitation on the size of outside contributions, the financial resources available to a candidate's campaign, like the number of volunteers recruited, will normally vary with the size and intensity of the candidate's support.[63] There is nothing invidious, improper, or unhealthy in permitting such funds to be spent to carry the candidate's message to the electorate.[64] Moreover, the equalization of permissible campaign expenditures might serve not to equalize the opportunities of all candidates but to handicap a candidate who lacked substantial name recognition or exposure of his views before the start of the campaign.

The campaign expenditure ceilings appear to be designed primarily to serve the governmental interests in reducing the allegedly skyrocketing costs of political campaigns. Appellees and the Court of Appeals stressed statistics indicating that spending for federal election campaigns increased almost 300% between 1952 and 1972 in comparison with a 57.6% rise in the consumer price index during the same period. Appellants respond that during these years the rise in campaign spending lagged behind the percentage increase in total expenditures for commercial advertising and the size of the gross national product. In any event, the mere growth in the cost of federal election campaigns in and of itself provides no basis for governmental restrictions on the quantity of campaign spending and the resulting limitation on the scope of federal campaigns. The First Amendment denies government the power to determine that spending to promote one's political views is

---

63. This normal relationship may not apply where the candidate devotes a large amount of his personal resources to his campaign.

64. As an opinion dissenting in part from decision below noted: "If a senatorial candidate can raise $1 from each voter, what evil is exacerbated by allowing that candidate to use all that money for political communication? I know of none." 171 U.S.App.D.C., at 268, 519 F.2d, at 917 (Tamm, J.)

wasteful, excessive, or unwise. In the free society ordained by our Constitution it is not the government but the people—individually as citizens and candidates and collectively as associations and political committees—who must retain control over the quantity and range of debate on public issues in a political campaign.

For these reasons we hold that § 608(c) is constitutionally invalid.

In sum, the provisions of the Act that impose a $1,000 limitation on contributions to a single candidate, § 608(b)(1), a $5,000 limitation on contributions by a political committee to a single candidate, § 608(b)(2), and a $25,000 limitation on total contributions by an individual during any calendar year, § 608(b)(3), are constitutionally valid. * * * By contrast, the First Amendment requires the invalidation of the Act's independent expenditure ceiling, § 608(e)(1), its limitation on a candidate's expenditures from his own personal funds, § 608(a), and its ceilings on overall campaign expenditures, § 608(c). These provisions place substantial and direct restrictions on the ability of candidates, citizens, and associations to engage in protected political expression, restrictions that the First Amendment cannot tolerate.

II. REPORTING AND DISCLOSURE REQUIREMENTS

Unlike the limitations on contributions and expenditures imposed by 18 U.S.C. § 608 * * *, the disclosure requirements of the Act, 2 U.S.C. § 431 *et seq.* * * *, are not challenged by appellants as per se unconstitutional restrictions on the exercise of First Amendment freedoms of speech and association.[69] Indeed, appellants argue that "narrowly drawn disclosure requirements are the proper solution to virtually all of the evils Congress sought to remedy." * * * The particular requirements embodied in the Act are attacked as overbroad—both in their application to minor-party and independent candidates and in their extension to contributions as small as $11 or $101. * * *

* * *

A. General Principles

* * *

We long have recognized that significant encroachments on First Amendment rights of the sort that compelled disclosure imposes cannot be justified by a mere showing of some legitimate governmental interest. Since *NAACP v. Alabama* we have required that the subordinating interests of the State must survive exacting scrutiny. We also have insisted that there be a "relevant correlation" or "substantial relation" between the governmental interest and the information required to be disclosed. See Pollard v. Roberts, 283 F.Supp. 248, 257 (ED Ark.1968) (three-judge court), *aff'd*, 393 U.S. 14 (1968) (*per curiam*). This type of scrutiny is necessary even if any deterrent effect on the exercise of First Amendment rights arises, not through direct government action, but indirectly as an unintended but inevitable result of the govern-

---

69. Appellants do contend that there should be a blanket exemption from the disclosure provisions for minor parties. See Part II–B–2, *infra*.

ment's conduct in requiring disclosure. *NAACP v. Alabama, supra,* at 461. * * *

* * *

The strict test established by *NAACP v. Alabama* is necessary because compelled disclosure has the potential for substantially infringing the exercise of First Amendment rights. But we have acknowledged that there are governmental interests sufficiently important to outweigh the possibility of infringement, particularly when the "free functioning of our national institutions" is involved. Communist Party v. Subversive Activities Control Bd., 367 U.S. 1, 97 (1961).

The governmental interests sought to be vindicated by the disclosure requirements are of this magnitude. They fall into three categories. First, disclosure provides the electorate with information "as to where political campaign money comes from and how it is spent by the candidate" in order to aid the voters in evaluating those who seek federal office. It allows voters to place each candidate in the political spectrum more precisely than is often possible solely on the basis of party labels and campaign speeches. The sources of a candidate's financial support also alert the voter to the interests to which a candidate is most likely to be responsive and thus facilitate predictions of future performance in office.

Second, disclosure requirements deter actual corruption and avoid the appearance of corruption by exposing large contributions and expenditures to the light of publicity. This exposure may discourage those who would use money for improper purposes either before or after the election. * * *

Third, and not least significant, recordkeeping, reporting, and disclosure requirements are an essential means of gathering the data necessary to detect violations of the contribution limitations described above.

The disclosure requirements, as a general matter, directly serve substantial governmental interests. In determining whether these interests are sufficient to justify the requirements we must look to the extent of the burden that they place on individual rights.

It is undoubtedly true that public disclosure of contributions to candidates and political parties will deter some individuals who otherwise might contribute. In some instances, disclosure may even expose contributors to harassment or retaliation. These are not insignificant burdens on individual rights, and they must be weighed carefully against the interests which Congress has sought to promote by this legislation. In this process, we note and agree with appellants' concession that disclosure requirements—certainly in most applications—appear to be the least restrictive means of curbing the evils of campaign ignorance and corruption that Congress found to exist. Appellants argue, however, that the balance tips against disclosure when it is required of contributors to certain parties and candidates. We turn now to this contention.

B. Application to Minor Parties and Independents

* * *

1. Requisite Factual Showing

* * *

It is true that the governmental interest in disclosure is diminished when the contribution in question is made to a minor party with little chance of winning an election. As minor parties usually represent definite and publicized viewpoints, there may be less need to inform the voters of the interests that specific candidates represent. Major parties encompass candidates of greater diversity. In many situations the label "Republican" or "Democrat" tells a voter little. The candidate who bears it may be supported by funds from the far right, the far left, or any place in between on the political spectrum. It is less likely that a candidate of, say, the Socialist Labor Party will represent interests that cannot be discerned from the party's ideological position.

* * *

We are not unmindful that the damage done by disclosure to the associational interests of the minor parties and their members and to supporters of independents could be significant. These movements are less likely to have a sound financial base and thus are more vulnerable to falloffs in contributions. In some instances fears of reprisal may deter contributions to the point where the movement cannot survive. The public interest also suffers if that result comes to pass, for there is a consequent reduction in the free circulation of ideas both within and without the political arena.

* * *

2. Blanket Exemption

Appellants agree that "the record here does not reflect the kind of focused and insistent harassment of contributors and members that existed in the NAACP cases." * * * They argue, however, that a blanket exemption for minor parties is necessary lest irreparable injury be done before the required evidence can be gathered.

* * *

We recognize that unduly strict requirements of proof could impose a heavy burden, but it does not follow that a blanket exemption for minor parties is necessary. Minor parties must be allowed sufficient flexibility in the proof of injury to assure a fair consideration of their claim. The evidence offered need show only a reasonable probability that the compelled disclosure of a party's contributors' names will subject them to threats, harassment, or reprisals from either Government officials or private parties. The proof may include, for example, specific evidence of past or present harassment of members due to their associational ties, or of harassment directed against the organization itself. A pattern of threats or specific manifestations of public hostility may be sufficient. New parties that have no history upon which to draw may be able to offer evidence of reprisals and threats directed against individuals or organizations holding similar views.

* * *

C. Section 434(e)

Section 434(e) requires "[e]very person (other than a political committee or candidate) who makes contributions or expenditures" aggregating over $100 in a calendar year "other than by contribution to a political committee or candidate" to file a statement with the Commission. Unlike the other disclosure provisions, this section does not seek the contribution list of any association. Instead, it requires direct disclosure of what an individual or group contributes or spends.

* * *

Appellants attack § 434(e) as a direct intrusion on privacy of belief, in violation of Talley v. California, 362 U.S. 60 (1960), and as imposing "very real, practical burdens * * * certain to deter individuals from making expenditures for their independent political speech" analogous to those held to be impermissible in Thomas v. Collins, 323 U.S. 516 (1945).

* * *

* * * To insure that the reach of § 434(e) is not impermissibly broad, we construe "expenditure" for purposes of that section in the same way we construed the terms of § 608(e)—to reach only funds used for communications that expressly advocate the election or defeat of a clearly identified candidate. This reading is directed precisely to that spending that is unambiguously related to the campaign of a particular federal candidate.

In summary, § 434(e) as construed, imposes independent reporting requirements on individuals and groups that are not candidates or political committees only in the following circumstances: (1) when they make contributions earmarked for political purposes or authorized or requested by a candidate or his agent, to some person other than a candidate or political committee, and (2) when they make expenditures for communications that expressly advocate the election or defeat of a clearly identified candidate.

Unlike 18 U.S.C. § 608(e)(1) (1970 ed., Supp. IV), § 434(e), as construed, bears a sufficient relationship to a substantial governmental interest. As narrowed, § 434(e), like § 608(e)(1), does not reach all partisan discussion for it only requires disclosure of those expenditures that expressly advocate a particular election result. This might have been fatal if the only purpose of § 434(e) were to stem corruption or its appearance by closing a loophole in the general disclosure requirements. But the disclosure provisions, including § 434(e), serve another, informational interest, and even as construed § 434(e) increases the fund of information concerning those who support the candidates.
* * *

* * *

D. Thresholds

Appellants' third contention, based on alleged overbreadth, is that the monetary thresholds in the recordkeeping and reporting provisions lack a substantial nexus with the claimed governmental interests, for the amounts involved are too low even to attract the attention of the candidate, much less have a corrupting influence.

* * *

The $10 and $100 thresholds are indeed low. Contributors of relatively small amounts are likely to be especially sensitive to recording or disclosure of their political preferences. These strict requirements may well discourage participation by some citizens in the political process, a result that Congress hardly could have intended. Indeed, there is little in the legislative history to indicate that Congress focused carefully on the appropriate level at which to require recording and disclosure. Rather, it seems merely to have adopted the thresholds existing in similar disclosure laws since 1910. But we cannot require Congress to establish that it has chosen the highest reasonable threshold. The line is necessarily a judgmental decision, best left in the context of this complex legislation to congressional discretion. We cannot say, on this bare record, that the limits designated are wholly without rationality.

* * *

In summary, we find no constitutional infirmities in the recordkeeping, reporting, and disclosure provisions of the Act.

III. PUBLIC FINANCING OF PRESIDENTIAL ELECTION CAMPAIGNS

* * *

A. Summary of Subtitle H

Section 9006 establishes a Presidential Election Campaign Fund (Fund), financed from general revenues in the aggregate amount designated by individual taxpayers, under § 6096, who on their income tax returns may authorize payment to the Fund of one dollar of their tax liability in the case of an individual return or two dollars in the case of a joint return. The Fund consists of three separate accounts to finance (1) party nominating conventions, § 9008(a), (2) general election campaigns, § 9006(a), and (3) primary campaigns, § 9037(a).[117]

Chapter 95 of Title 26, which concerns financing of party nominating conventions and general election campaigns, distinguishes among "major," "minor," and "new" parties. A major party is defined as a party whose candidate for President in the most recent election received 25% or more of the popular vote. § 9002(6). A minor party is defined as a party whose candidate received at least 5% but less than 25% of the vote at the most recent election. § 9002(7). All other

---

117. Priorities are established when the Fund is insufficient to satisfy all entitlements in any election year: the amount in the Fund is first allocated to convention funding, then to financing the general election, and finally to primary matching assistance. See §§ 9008(a), 9037(a). * * *

parties are new parties, § 9002(8), including both newly created parties and those receiving less than 5% of the vote in the last election.

Major parties are entitled to $2,000,000 to defray their national committee Presidential nominating convention expenses, must limit total expenditures to that amount, § 9008(d), and may not use any of this money to benefit a particular candidate or delegate, § 9008(c). A minor party receives a portion of the major-party entitlement determined by the ratio of the votes received by the party's candidate in the last election to the average of the votes received by the major-parties' candidates. § 9008(b)(2). The amounts given to the parties and the expenditure limit are adjusted for inflation, using 1974 as the base year. § 9008(b)(5). No financing is provided for new parties, nor is there any express provision for financing independent candidates or parties not holding a convention.

For expenses in the general election campaign, § 9004(a)(1) entitles each major-party candidate to $20,000,000. This amount is also adjusted for inflation. See § 9004(a)(1). To be eligible for funds the candidate must pledge not to incur expenses in excess of the entitlement under § 9004(a)(1) and not to accept private contributions except to the extent that the fund is insufficient to provide the full entitlement. § 9003(b). Minor-party candidates are also entitled to funding, again based on the ratio of the vote received by the party's candidate in the preceding election to the average of the major-party candidates. § 9004(a)(2)(A). Minor-party candidates must certify that they will not incur campaign expenses in excess of the major-party entitlement and that they will accept private contributions only to the extent needed to make up the difference between that amount and the public funding grant. § 9003(c). New-party candidates receive no money prior to the general election, but any candidate receiving 5% or more of the popular vote in the election is entitled to post-election payments according to the formula applicable to minor-party candidates. § 9004(a)(3). Similarly, minor-party candidates are entitled to post-election funds if they receive a greater percentage of the average major-party vote than their party's candidate did in the preceding election; the amount of such payments is the difference between the entitlement based on the preceding election and that based on the actual vote in the current election. § 9004(a)(3). A further eligibility requirement for minor- and new-party candidates is that the candidate's name must appear on the ballot, or electors pledged to the candidate must be on the ballot, in at least 10 States.

Chapter 96 establishes a third account in the Fund, the Presidential Primary Matching Payment Account. § 9037(a). This funding is intended to aid campaigns by candidates seeking Presidential nomination "by a political party," § 9033(b)(2), in "primary elections," § 9032(7). The threshold eligibility requirement is that the candidate raise at least $5,000 in each of 20 States, counting only the first $250 from each person contributing to the candidate. §§ 9033(b)(3), (4). In addition, the candidate must agree to abide by the spending limits in § 9035. See § 9033(b)(1). Funding is provided according to a matching formula: each qualified candidate is entitled to a sum equal to the total private contributions received, disregarding contributions from any person to the extent that total contributions to the candidate by that person exceed $250. § 9034(a). Payments to any candidate under Chapter 96 may not exceed 50% of the overall expenditure ceiling accepted by the candidate. § 9034(b).

B. Constitutionality of Subtitle H

Appellants argue that Subtitle H is invalid (1) as "contrary to the 'general welfare,'" Art. I, § 8, (2) because any scheme of public financing of election campaigns is inconsistent with the First Amendment, and (3) because Subtitle H invidiously discriminates against certain interests in violation of the Due Process Clause of the Fifth Amendment. We find no merit in these contentions.

Appellants' "general welfare" contention erroneously treats the General Welfare Clause as a limitation upon congressional power. It is rather a grant of power, the scope of which is quite expansive, particularly in view of the enlargement of power by the Necessary and Proper Clause. * * *

Appellants' challenge to the dollar check-off provision (§ 6096) fails for the same reason. They maintain that Congress is required to permit taxpayers to designate particular candidates or parties as recipients of their money. But the appropriation to the Fund in § 9006 is like any other appropriation from the general revenue except that its amount is determined by reference to the aggregate of the one- and two-dollar authorization on taxpayers' income tax returns. This detail does not constitute the appropriation any less an appropriation by Congress.[124] The fallacy of appellants' argument is therefore apparent; every appropriation made by Congress uses public money in a manner to which some taxpayers object.[125]

Appellants next argue that "by analogy" to the Religion Clauses of the First Amendment public financing of election campaigns, however meritorious, violates the First Amendment. We have, of course, held that the Religion Clauses—"Congress shall make no law respecting an establishment of religion, or prohibiting the free exercise thereof"—require Congress, and the States through the Fourteenth Amendment, to

---

124. The scheme involves no compulsion upon individuals to finance the dissemination of ideas with which they disagree, Lathrop v. Donohue, 367 U.S. 820, 871, 882 (1961) (Black, J. dissenting); id., at 822 (Douglas, J., dissenting); Machinists v. Street, 367 U.S. 740, 778 (1961) (Douglas, J., concurring); id., at 788–792 (Black, J., dissenting). The § 6096 check-off is simply the means by which Congress determines the amount of its appropriation.

125. Some proposals for public financing would give taxpayers the opportunity to designate the candidate or party to receive the dollar, and § 6096 initially offered this choice. See n. 114, supra. The voucher system proposed by Senator Metcalf, as amicus curiae here, also allows taxpayers this option. But Congress need not provide a mechanism for allowing taxpayers to designate the means in which their particular tax dollars are spent. See n. 124, supra. Further, insofar as these proposals are offered as less restrictive means, Congress had legitimate reasons for rejecting both. The designation option was criticized on privacy grounds, 119 Cong. Rec. 22598, 22396 (1973), and also because the identity of all candidates would not be known by April 15, the filing day for annual individual and joint tax returns. Senator Metcalf's proposal has also been criticized as possibly leading to black markets and to coercion to obtain vouchers and as administratively impractical.

remain neutral in matters of religion. E.g., Abington School Dist. v. Schempp, 374 U.S. 203, 222–226 (1963). The government may not aid one religion to the detriment of others or impose a burden on one religion that is not imposed on others, and may not even aid all religions. *E.g.,* Everson v. Board of Education, 330 U.S. 1, 15–16 (1947). See Kurland, Of Church and State and the Supreme Court, 29 U.Chi.L. Rev. 1, 96 (1961). But the analogy is patently inapplicable to our issue here. Although "Congress shall make no law * * * abridging the freedom of speech, or of the press," Subtitle H is a congressional effort, not to abridge, restrict, or censor speech, but rather to use public money to facilitate and enlarge public discussion and participation in the electoral process, goals vital to a self-governing people.[126] Thus, Subtitle H furthers, not abridges, pertinent First Amendment values.[127] Appellants argue, however, that as constructed public financing invidiously discriminates in violation of the Fifth Amendment. We turn therefore to that argument.

* * * Any disadvantage suffered by operation of the eligibility formulae under Subtitle H is thus limited to the claimed denial of the enhancement of opportunity to communicate with the electorate that the formulae afford eligible candidates. But eligible candidates suffer a countervailing denial. As we more fully develop later, acceptance of public financing entails voluntary acceptance of an expenditure ceiling. Noneligible candidates are not subject to that limitation. Accordingly, we conclude that public financing is generally less restrictive of access to the electoral process than the ballot-access regulations dealt with in prior cases. * * *

* * *

CONCLUSION

In summary, we sustain the individual contribution limits, the disclosure and reporting provisions, and the public financing scheme. We conclude, however, that the limitations on campaign expenditures, on independent expenditures by individuals and groups, and on expend-

---

126. Appellants voice concern that public funding will lead to governmental control of the internal affairs of political parties, and thus to a significant loss of political freedom. The concern is necessarily wholly speculative and hardly a basis for invalidation of the public financing scheme on its face. Congress has expressed its determination to avoid the possibility. S.Rep. No. 93–689, pp. 9–10 (1974).

127. The historical bases of the Religion and Speech Clauses are markedly different. Intolerable persecutions throughout history led to the Framers' firm determination that religious worship—both in method and belief—must be strictly protected from government intervention. "Another purpose of the Establishment Clause rested upon an awareness of the historical fact that governmentally established religions and religious persecutions go hand in hand." Engel v. Vitale, 370 U.S. 421, 432 (1962) (footnote omitted). See Everson v. Board of Education, 330 U.S. 1, 8–15 (1947). But the central purpose of the Speech and Press Clauses was to assure a society in which "uninhibited, robust, and wide-open" public debate concerning matters of public interest would thrive, for only in such a society can a healthy representative democracy flourish. New York Times Co. v. Sullivan, 376 U.S. 254, 270 (1964). Legislation to enhance these First Amendment values is the rule, not the exception. Our statute books are replete with laws providing financial assistance to the exercise of free speech, such as aid to public broadcasting and other forms of educational media, 47 U.S.C. §§ 390–399, and preferential postal rates and antitrust exemptions for newspapers, 39 CFR § 132.2 (1975); 15 U.S.C. §§ 1801–1804.

itures by a candidate from his personal funds are constitutionally infirm. Finally, we hold that most of the powers conferred by the Act upon the Federal Election Commission can be exercised only by "Officers of the United States," appointed in conformity with Art. II, § 2, cl. 2, of the Constitution, and therefore cannot be exercised by the Commission as presently constituted.

In No. 75–436, the judgment of the Court of Appeals is affirmed in part and reversed in part. The judgment of the District Court in No. 75–437 is affirmed. The mandate shall issue forthwith, except that our judgment is stayed, for a period of 30 days, insofar as it affects the authority of the Commission to exercise the duties and powers granted it under the Act.

So ordered.

* * *

MR. CHIEF JUSTICE BURGER, concurring in part and dissenting in part.

For reasons set forth more fully later, I dissent from those parts of the Court's holding sustaining the statutory provisions (a) for disclosure of small contributions, (b) for limitations on contributions, and (c) for public financing of Presidential campaigns. In my view, the Act's disclosure scheme is impermissibly broad and violative of the First Amendment as it relates to reporting contributions in excess of $10 and $100. The contribution limitations infringe on First Amendment liberties and suffer from the same infirmities that the Court correctly sees in the expenditure ceilings. The system for public financing of Presidential campaigns is, in my judgment, an impermissible intrusion by the Government into the traditionally private political process.

More broadly, the Court's result does violence to the intent of Congress in this comprehensive scheme of campaign finance. By dissecting the Act bit by bit, and casting off vital parts, the Court fails to recognize that the whole of this Act is greater than the sum of its parts. Congress intended to regulate all aspects of federal campaign finances, but what remains after today's holding leaves no more than a shadow of what Congress contemplated. I question whether the residue leaves a workable program.

* * *

The public right to know ought not be absolute when its exercise reveals private political convictions. Secrecy, like privacy, is not per se criminal. On the contrary, secrecy and privacy as to political preferences and convictions are fundamental in a free society. For example, one of the great political reforms was the advent of the secret ballot as a universal practice. Similarly, the enlightened labor legislation of our time has enshrined the secrecy of choice of a bargaining representative for workers. In other contexts, this Court has seen to it that governmental power cannot be used to force a citizen to disclose his private affiliations, NAACP v. Button, 371 U.S. 415 (1963), even without a record reflecting any systematic harassment or retaliation, as in Shelton v. Tucker, 364 U.S. 479 (1960). For me it is far too late in the day to recognize an ill-defined "public interest" to breach the historic safeguards guaranteed by the First Amendment.

* * *

In light of these views, it seems to me that the threshold limits fixed at $10 and $100 for anonymous contributions are constitutionally impermissible on their face. As the Court's opinion notes, * * *, Congress gave little or no thought, one way or the other, to these limits, but rather lifted figures out of a 65–year–old statute. As we are all painfully aware, the 1976 dollar is not what it used to be and is surely not the dollar of 1910. Ten dollars in 1976 will, for example, purchase only what $1.68 would buy in 1910. United States Dept. of Labor, Handbook of Labor Statistics 1975, p. 313 (Dec.1975). To argue that a 1976 contribution of $10 or $100 entails a risk of corruption or its appearance is simply too extravagant to be maintained. No public right to know justifies the compelled disclosure of such contributions, at the risk of discouraging them. There is, in short, no relation whatever between the means used and the legitimate goal of ventilating possible undue influence. Congress has used a shotgun to kill wrens as well as hawks.

* * *

Finally, no legitimate public interest has been shown in forcing the disclosure of modest contributions that are the prime support of new, unpopular, or unfashionable political causes. There is no realistic possibility that such modest donations will have a corrupting influence especially on parties that enjoy only "minor" status. Major parties would not notice them; minor parties need them. Furthermore, as the Court candidly recognizes, * * *, minor parties and new parties tend to be sharply ideological in character, and the public can readily discern where such parties stand, without resorting to the indirect device of recording the names of financial supporters. To hold, as the Court has, that privacy must sometimes yield to congressional investigations of alleged subversion, is quite different from making domestic political partisans give up privacy. * * *

I would therefore hold unconstitutional the provisions requiring reporting of contributions of more than $10 and to make a public record of the name, address, and occupation of a contributor of more than $100.

(2)

CONTRIBUTION AND EXPENDITURE

I agree fully with that part of the Court's opinion that holds unconstitutional the limitations the Act puts on campaign expenditures which "place substantial and direct restrictions on the ability of candidates, citizens, and associations to engage in protected political expression, restrictions that the First Amendment cannot tolerate." * * * Yet when it approves similarly stringent limitations on contributions, the Court ignores the reasons it finds so persuasive in the context of expenditures. For me contributions and expenditures are two sides of the same First Amendment coin.

* * *

The Court's attempt to distinguish the communication inherent in political contributions from the speech aspects of political expenditures simply "will not wash." We do little but engage in word games unless we recognize that people—candidates and contributors—spend money on political activity because they wish to communicate ideas, and their constitutional interest in doing so is precisely the same whether they or someone else utters the words.

* * *

* * * I see only two possible ways in which money differs from volunteer work, endorsements, and the like. Money can be used to buy favors, because an unscrupulous politician can put it to personal use; second, giving money is a less visible form of associational activity. With respect to the first problem, the Act does not attempt to do any more than the bribery laws to combat this sort of corruption. In fact, the Act does not reach at all, and certainly the contribution limits do not reach, forms of "association" that can be fully as corrupt as a contribution intended as a *quid pro quo*—such as the eleventh-hour endorsement by a former rival, obtained for the promise of a federal appointment. This underinclusiveness is not a constitutional flaw, but it demonstrates that the contribution limits do not clearly focus on this first distinction. To the extent Congress thought that the second problem, the lesser visibility of contributions, required that money be treated differently from other forms of associational activity, disclosure laws are the simple and wholly efficacious answer; they make the invisible apparent.

(3)
PUBLIC FINANCING

I dissent from Part III sustaining the constitutionality of the public financing provisions of Subtitle H.

Since the turn of this century when the idea of Government subsidies for political campaigns first was broached, there has been no lack of realization that the use of funds from the public treasury to subsidize political activity of private individuals would produce substantial and profound questions about the nature of our democratic society.
* * *

The Court chooses to treat this novel public financing of political activity as simply another congressional appropriation whose validity is "necessary and proper" to Congress' power to regulate and reform elections and primaries, relying on United States v. Classic, 313 U.S. 299 (1941), and Burroughs v. United States, 290 U.S. 534 (1934). No holding of this Court is directly in point, because no federal scheme allocating public funds in a comparable manner has ever been before us. * * *

* * * The public monies at issue here are not being employed simply to police the integrity of the electoral process or to provide a forum for the use of all participants in the political dialogue, as would,

for example, be the case if free broadcast time were granted. Rather, we are confronted with the Government's actual financing, out of general revenues, a segment of the political debate itself. * * *

* * *

I agree with Mr. Justice Rehnquist that the scheme approved by the Court today invidiously discriminates against minor parties. Assuming, *arguendo,* the constitutionality of the overall scheme, there is a legitimate governmental interest in requiring a group to make a "preliminary showing of a significant modicum of support." Jenness v. Fortson, 403 U.S. 431, 442 (1971). But the present system could preclude or severely hamper access to funds before a given election by a group or an individual who might, at the time of the election, reflect the views of a major segment or even a majority of the electorate. The fact that there have been few drastic realignments in our basic two-party structure in 200 years is no constitutional justification for freezing the status quo of the present major parties at the expense of such future political movements. Cf. discussion, *ante,* * * *. When and if some minority party achieves majority status, Congress can readily deal with any problems that arise. In short, I see grave risks in legislation, enacted by incumbents of the independent candidates. This Court has, until today, been particularly cautious when dealing with enactments that tend to perpetuate those who control legislative power. See Reynolds v. Sims, 377 U.S. 533, 570 (1964).

I would also find unconstitutional the system of matching grants which makes a candidate's ability to amass private funds the sole criterion for eligibility for public funds. Such an arrangement can put at serious disadvantage a candidate with a potentially large, widely diffused—but poor—constituency. The ability of a candidate's supporters to help pay for his campaign cannot be equated with their willingness to cast a ballot for him. See Lubin v. Panish, 415 U.S. 709 (1974); Bullock v. Carter, 405 U.S. 134 (1972).

* * *

Mr. Justice White, concurring in part and dissenting in part.

* * *

The disclosure requirements and the limitations on contributions and expenditures are challenged as invalid abridgments of the right of free speech protected by the First Amendment. I would reject these challenges. I agree with the Court's conclusion and much of its opinion with respect to sustaining the disclosure provisions. I am also in agreement with the Court's judgment upholding the limitations on contributions. I dissent, however, from the Court's view that the expenditure limitations of 18 U.S.C. §§ 608(c) and (e) (1970 ed., Supp. IV) violate the First Amendment.

* * *

Let us suppose that each of two brothers spends $1 million on TV spot announcements that he has individually prepared and in which he appears, urging the election of the same named candidate in identical words. One brother has sought and obtained the approval of the candidate; the other has not. The former may validly be prosecuted under § 608(e); under the Court's view, the latter may not, even though the candidate could scarcely help knowing about and appreciating the expensive favor. For constitutional purposes it is difficult to see the difference between the two situations. I would take the word of those who know—that limiting independent expenditures is essential to prevent transparent and widespread evasion of the contribution limits.

In sustaining the contribution limits, the Court recognizes the importance of avoiding public misapprehension about a candidate's reliance on large contributions. It ignores that consideration in invalidating § 608(e). In like fashion, it says that Congress was entitled to determine that the criminal provisions against bribery and corruption, together with the disclosure provisions, would not in themselves be adequate to combat the evil and that limits on contributions should be provided. Here, the Court rejects the identical kind of judgment made by Congress as to the need for and utility of expenditure limits. I would not do so.

* * *

It is also important to restore and maintain public confidence in federal elections. It is critical to obviate or dispel the impression that federal elections are purely and simply a function of money, that federal offices are bought and sold or that political races are reserved for those who have the facility—and the stomach—for doing whatever it takes to bring together those interests, groups, and individuals that can raise or contribute large fortunes in order to prevail at the polls.

The ceiling on candidate expenditures represents the considered judgment of Congress that elections are to be decided among candidates none of whom has overpowering advantage by reason of a huge campaign war chest. At least so long as the ceiling placed upon the candidates is not plainly too low, elections are not to turn on the difference in the amounts of money that candidates have to spend. This seems an acceptable purpose and the means chosen a commonsense way to achieve it. The Court nevertheless holds that a candidate has a constitutional right to spend unlimited amounts of money, mostly that of other people, in order to be elected. The holding perhaps is not that federal candidates have the constitutional right to purchase their election, but many will so interpret the Court's conclusion in this case. I cannot join the Court in this respect.

I also disagree with the Court's judgment that § 608(a), which limits the amount of money that a candidate or his family may spend on his campaign, violates the Constitution. Although it is true that this provision does not promote any interest in preventing the corruption of candidates, the provision does, nevertheless, serve salutary purposes related to the integrity of federal campaigns. By limiting the importance of personal wealth, § 608(a) helps to assure that only individuals with a modicum of support from others will be viable candidates. This in turn would tend to discourage any notion that the outcome of elections is primarily a function of money. Similarly, § 608(a) tends to equalize access to the political arena, encouraging the less wealthy, unable to bankroll their own campaigns, to run for political office.

As with the campaign expenditure limits, Congress was entitled to determine that personal wealth ought to play a less important role in political campaigns than it has in the past. Nothing in the First Amendment stands in the way of that determination.

* * *

Mr. Justice Marshall, concurring in part and dissenting in part.

I join in all of the Court's opinion except Part I–C–2, which deals with 18 U.S.C. § 608(a) (1970 ed., Supp. IV). That section limits the amount a candidate may spend from his personal funds, or family funds under his control, in connection with his campaigns during any calendar year. * * * The Court invalidates § 608(a) as violative of the candidate's First Amendment rights. "[T]he First Amendment," the Court explains, "simply cannot tolerate § 608(a)'s restriction upon the freedom of a candidate to speak without legislative limit on behalf of his own candidacy." * * * I disagree.

To be sure, § 608(a) affects the candidate's exercise of his First Amendment rights. But unlike the other expenditure limitations contained in the Act and invalidated by the Court—the limitation on independent expenditures relative to a clearly identified candidate, § 608(e), and the limitations on overall candidate expenditures, § 608(c)—the limitations on expenditures by candidates from personal resources contained in § 608(a) need never prevent the speaker from spending another dollar to communicate his ideas. Section 608(a) imposes no overall limit on the amount a candidate can spend; it simply limits the "contribution" a candidate may make to his own campaign. The candidate remains free to raise an unlimited amount in contributions from others. So long as the candidate does not contribute to his campaign more than the amount specified in § 608(a), and so long as he does not accept contributions from others in excess of the limitations imposed by § 608(b), he is free to spend without limit on behalf of his campaign.

It is significant, moreover, that the ceilings imposed by § 608(a) on candidate expenditures from personal resources are substantially higher than the $1,000 limit imposed by § 608(e) on independent expenditures by noncandidates. Presidential and Vice Presidential candidates may contribute $50,000 of their own money to their campaigns, Senate candidates $35,000, and most House candidates $25,000. Those ceilings will not affect most candidates. But they will admittedly limit the availability of personal funds for some candidates, and the question is whether that limitation is justified.

The Court views "[t]he ancillary interest in equalizing the relative financial resources of candidates" as the relevant rationale for § 608(a), and deems that interest insufficient to justify § 608(a). * * * In my view the interest is more precisely the interest in promoting the reality and appearance of equal access to the political arena. * * *

* * *

In view of § 608(b)'s limitations on contributions, then, § 608(a) emerges not simply as a device to reduce the natural advantage of the wealthy candidate, but as a provision providing some symmetry to a regulatory scheme that otherwise enhances the natural advantage of the wealthy. Regardless of whether the goal of equalizing access would justify a legislative limit on personal candidate expenditures standing by itself, I think it clear that that goal justifies § 608(a)'s limits when they are considered in conjunction with the remainder of the Act. I therefore respectfully dissent from the Court's invalidation of § 608(a).

MR. JUSTICE BLACKMUN, concurring in part and dissenting in part.

I am not persuaded that the Court makes, or indeed is able to make, a principled constitutional distinction between the contribution limitations, on the one hand, and the expenditure limitations, on the other, that are involved here. I therefore do not join Part I–B of the Court's opinion or those portions of Part I–A that are consistent with Part I–B. As to those, I dissent.

* * *

MR. JUSTICE REHNQUIST, concurring in part and dissenting in part.

I concur in Parts I, II, and IV of the Court's opinion. I concur in so much of Part III of the Court's opinion as holds that the public funding of the cost of a Presidential election campaign is a permissible exercise of congressional authority under the power to tax and spend granted by Art. I, but dissent from Part III–B–1 of the Court's opinion, which holds that certain aspects of the statutory treatment of minor parties and independent candidates are constitutionally valid. I state as briefly as possible my reasons for so doing.

* * *

For the reasons stated in the dissenting opinion of Mr. Justice Jackson in Beauharnais v. Illinois, 343 U.S. 250, 288–295 (1952), and by Mr. Justice Harlan in his dissenting opinion in Roth v. United States, 354 U.S. 476, 500–503 (1957), I am of the opinion that not all of the strictures which the First Amendment imposes upon Congress are carried over against the States by the Fourteenth Amendment, but rather that it is only the "general principle" of free speech, Gitlow v. New York, 268 U.S. 652, 672 (1925) (Holmes J., dissenting), that the latter incorporates. See Palko v. Connecticut, 302 U.S. 319, 324–325 (1937).

Given this view, cases which deal with state restrictions on First Amendment freedoms are not fungible with those which deal with restrictions imposed by the Federal Government, and cases which deal with the government as employer or proprietor are not fungible with those which deal with the government as a lawmaker enacting criminal statutes applying to the population generally. The statute before us was enacted by Congress, not with the aim of managing the Government's property nor of regulating the conditions of Government employment, but rather with a view to the regulation of the citizenry as a whole. The case for me, then, presents the First Amendment interests of the appellants at their strongest, and the legislative authority of

Congress in the position where it is most vulnerable to First Amendment attacks.

* * *

While I am not sure that I agree with the Court's comment, * * *, that "public financing is generally less restrictive of access to the electoral process than the ballot-access regulations dealt with in prior cases," in any case that is not, under my view, an adequate answer to appellants' claim. The electoral laws relating to ballot access which were examined in Lubin v. Panish, 415 U.S. 709, 716 (1974); American Party of Texas v. White, 415 U.S. 767, 780 (1974); and Storer v. Brown, 415 U.S. 724, 729 730 (1974), all arose out of state efforts to regulate minor party candidacies and the actual physical size of the ballot. If the States are to afford a republican form of government, they must by definition provide for general elections and for some standards as to the contents of the official ballots which will be used at those elections. The decision of the state legislature to enact legislation embodying such regulations is therefore not in any sense an optional one; there must be some standards, however few, which prescribe the contents of the official ballot if the popular will is to be translated into a choice among candidates. Dealing thus by necessity with these issues, the States have strong interests in "limiting places on the ballot to those candidates who demonstrate substantial popular support," * * *. They have a like interest in discouraging "splintered parties and unrestrained factionalism" which might proliferate the number of candidates on a state ballot so as to make it virtually unintelligible to the average voter. *Storer v. Brown, supra,* at 736.

Congress, on the other hand, while undoubtedly possessing the legislative authority to undertake the task if it wished, is not obliged to address the question of public financing of Presidential elections at all. When it chooses to legislate in this area, so much of its action as may arguably impair First Amendment rights lacks the same sort of mandate of necessity as does a State's regulation of ballot access.

Congress, of course, does have an interest in not "funding hopeless candidacies with large sums of public money," * * *, and may for that purpose legitimately require "'some preliminary showing of a significant modicum of support,' Jenness v. Fortson, [403 U.S. 431, 442 (1971),] as an eligibility requirement for public funds." * * * But Congress in this legislation has done a good deal more than that. It has enshrined the Republican and Democratic Parties in a permanently preferred position, and has established requirements for funding minor-party and independent candidates to which the two major parties are not subject. Congress would undoubtedly be justified in treating the Presidential candidates of the two major parties differently from minor-party or independent Presidential candidates, in view of the long demonstrated public support of the former. But because of the First Amendment overtones of the appellants' Fifth Amendment equal protection claim, something more than a merely rational basis for the difference in treatment must be shown, as the Court apparently recognizes. I find it impossible to subscribe to the Court's reasoning that because no third party has posed a credible threat to the two major parties in Presidential elections since 1860, Congress may by law attempt to assure that this pattern will endure forever.

I would hold that, as to general election financing, Congress has not merely treated the two major parties differently from minor parties and independents, but has discriminated in favor of the former in such a way as to run afoul of the Fifth and First Amendments to the United States Constitution.

CITIZENS AGAINST RENT CONTROL v. BERKELEY

Supreme Court of the United States, 1981.
454 U.S. 290, 102 S.Ct. 434, 70 L.Ed.2d 492.

CHIEF JUSTICE BURGER delivered the opinion of the Court.

The issue on appeal is whether a limitation of $250 on contributions to committees formed to support or oppose ballot measures violates the First Amendment.

I

The voters of Berkeley, Cal., adopted the Election Reform Act of 1974, Ord. No. 4700–N.S., by initiative. The campaign ordinance so enacted placed limits on expenditures and contributions in campaigns involving both candidates and ballot measures.[1] Section 602 of the ordinance provides:

> "No person shall make, and no campaign treasurer shall solicit or accept, any contribution which will cause the total amount contributed by such person with respect to a single election in support of or in opposition to a measure to exceed two hundred and fifty dollars ($250)." [2]

Appellant Citizens Against Rent Control is an unincorporated association formed to oppose a ballot measure at issue in the April 19, 1977, election. The ballot measure would have imposed rent control on many of Berkeley's rental units. To make its views on the ballot measure known, Citizens Against Rent Control raised more than $108,000 from approximately 1,300 contributors. It accepted nine contribu-

---

1. Section 217 of the ordinance defines "measure" as "any City Charter amendment, ordinance or other propositions submitted to a popular vote at an election, whether by initiative, referendum or recall procedure or otherwise, or circulated for the purposes of submission to a popular vote at any election, whether or not the proposition qualifies for the ballot."

2. It was not clear in 1977 whether § 602 would be enforced. The prohibition on contributions to ballot measure campaign committees by corporations and labor unions, § 605, was invalidated in Pacific Gas & Electric Co. v. City of Berkeley, 60 Cal.App.3d 123, 131 Cal.Rptr. 350 (1976). Following Buckley v. Valeo, 424 U.S. 1 (1976), the city repealed a number of sections of the ordinance, such as § 513, which limited expenditures in support of or in opposition to a ballot measure to the lesser of $7,500 or 10 cents times the number of registered voters. When revising the ordinance to comply with these changes, the city mistakenly labeled § 602, the section challenged in this case, with the notation "do not enforce," but it corrected this error approximately three months before the election involved in this case.

tions over the $250 limit. Those nine contributions totaled $20,850, or $18,600 more than if none of the contributions exceeded $250. Pursuant to § 604 of the ordinance,[3] appellee Berkeley Fair Campaign Practices Commission, 20 days before the election, ordered appellant Citizens Against Rent Control to pay $18,600 into the city treasury.

Two weeks before the election, Citizens Against Rent Control sought and obtained a temporary restraining order prohibiting enforcement of §§ 602 and 604. The ballot measure relating to rent control was defeated. The Superior Court subsequently granted Citizens Against Rent Control's motion for summary judgment, declaring that § 602 was invalid on its face because it violated the First Amendment of the United States Constitution and Art. I, § 2, of the California Constitution. A panel of the California Court of Appeal unanimously affirmed that conclusion.

The California Supreme Court, dividing 4–3, reversed. * * *

We noted probable jurisdiction, 450 U.S. 908 (1981), and we reverse.

* * *

There are, of course, some activities, legal if engaged in by one, yet illegal if performed in concert with others, but political expression is not one of them. To place a Spartan limit—or indeed any limit—on individuals wishing to band together to advance their views on a ballot measure, while placing none on individuals acting alone, is clearly a restraint on the right of association. Section 602 does not seek to mute the voice of one individual, and it cannot be allowed to hobble the collective expressions of a group.

Buckley identified a single narrow exception to the rule that limits on political activity were contrary to the First Amendment. The exception relates to the perception of undue influence of large contributors to a *candidate:* * * *

Federal Courts of Appeals have recognized that *Buckley* does not support limitations on contributions to committees formed to favor or oppose *ballot measures.* * * *

* * *

Whatever may be the state interest or degree of that interest in regulating and limiting contributions to or expenditures of a candidate or a candidate's committees there is no significant state or public interest in curtailing debate and discussion of a ballot measure. Placing limits on contributions which in turn limit expenditures plainly impairs freedom of expression. The integrity of the political system will be adequately protected if contributors are identified in a public filing revealing the amounts contributed; if it is thought wise, legislation can outlaw anonymous contributions.

---

3. Section 604 states: "If any person is found guilty of violating the terms of this chapter, each campaign treasurer who received part or all of the contribution or contributions which constitute the violation shall pay promptly, from available campaign funds, if any, the amount received from such persons in excess of the amount permitted by this chapter to City Auditor for deposit in the General fund of the City."

IV

* * *

Reversed and remanded.

JUSTICE REHNQUIST, concurring.

I agree that the judgment of the Supreme Court of California must be reversed in this case. Unlike the factual situation in First National Bank of Boston v. Bellotti, 435 U.S. 765 (1978), the Berkeley ordinance was not aimed only at corporations, but sought to impose an across-the-board limitation on the size of contributions to committees formed to support or oppose ballot measure referenda. While one of the appellants here, Mason–McDuffie, is a California corporation, there is no indication that the Berkeley ordinance was aimed at corporations as opposed to individuals. Therefore, my dissenting opinion in *First National Bank of Boston v. Bellotti, supra,* which relied on the corporate shield which the State had granted to corporations as a form of *quid pro quo* for the limitation does not come into play. Buckley v. Valeo, 424 U.S. 1 (1976), holds that in this situation there is no state interest which could justify a limitation on the exercise of rights guaranteed under the First and Fourteenth Amendments to the United States Constitution.

JUSTICE MARSHALL, concurring in the judgment.

The Court today holds that a local ordinance restricting the amount of money that an individual can contribute to a committee organized to support or oppose a ballot measure violates the right to freedom of speech and association guaranteed by the First Amendment. In reaching this conclusion, however, the Court fails to indicate whether or not it attaches any constitutional significance to the fact that the Berkeley ordinance seeks to limit contributions as opposed to direct expenditures. * * *

Because the Court's opinion is silent on the standard of review it is applying to this contributions limitation, I must assume that the Court is following our consistent position that this type of governmental action is subjected to less rigorous scrutiny than a direct restriction on expenditures. The city of Berkeley seeks to justify its ordinance on the ground that it is necessary to maintain voter confidence in government. If I found that the record before the California Supreme Court disclosed sufficient evidence to justify the conclusion that large contributions to ballot measure committees undermined the "confidence of the citizenry in government," First National Bank of Boston v. Bellotti, 435 U.S. 765, 790 (1978), I would join Justice White in dissent on the ground that the State had demonstrated a sufficient governmental interest to sustain the indirect infringement on First Amendment interests resulting from the operation of the Berkeley ordinance. Like Justices Blackmun and O'Connor, however, I find no such evidentiary support in this record. I therefore concur in the judgment.

JUSTICE BLACKMUN and JUSTICE O'CONNOR, concurring in the judgment. [Omitted.]

* * *

JUSTICE WHITE, dissenting.

* * * I would have upheld the expenditure limitations at issue in *Buckley* and the restrictions contested in *Bellotti*.

This case poses a less encompassing regulation on campaign activity, one tailored to the odd measurements of *Buckley* and *Bellotti*. Precisely because it reflects these decisions, the ordinance regulates contributions but not expenditures and does not prohibit corporate spending. * * *

I

* * *

The Court reaches the conclusion that the ordinance is unconstitutional only by giving *Buckley* the most extreme reading and by essentially giving the Berkeley ordinance no reading at all. It holds that the contributions involved here are "beyond question a very significant form of political expression." * * * Yet in Buckley the Court found that contribution limitations "entai[l] only a marginal restriction upon the contributor's ability to engage in free communication." 424 U.S., at 20–21. As with contributions to candidates, ballot measure contributions "involv[e] speech by someone other than the contributor" and a limitation on such donations "does not in any way infringe the contributor's freedom to discuss candidates and issues." * * *

* * *

It is bad enough that the Court overstates the extent to which First Amendment interests are implicated. But the Court goes on to assert that the ordinance furthers no legitimate public interest and cannot survive "any degree of scrutiny." Apparently the Court assumes this to be so because the ordinance is not directed at *quid pro quos* between large contributors and candidates for office, "the single narrow exception" for regulation that it viewed Buckley as endorsing. * * *

* * *

By restricting the size of contributions, the Berkeley ordinance requires major contributors to communicate directly with the voters. * * * Of course, entities remain free to make major direct expenditures. But because political communications must state the source of funds, voters will be able to identify the source of such messages and recognize that the communication reflects, for example, the opinion of a single powerful corporate interest rather than the views of a large number of individuals. * * *

* * *

II

* * * When the infringement is as slight and ephemeral as it is here, the requisite state interest to justify the regulation need not be so high.

* * *

FEDERAL ELECTION COMMISSION v. NATIONAL CONSERVATIVE POLITICAL ACTION COMMITTEE

Supreme Court of the United States, 1985.
470 U.S. 480, 105 S.Ct. 1459, 84 L.Ed.2d 455.

JUSTICE REHNQUIST delivered the opinion of the Court.[††]

The Presidential Election Campaign Fund Act (Fund Act), 26 U.S.C. § 9001 *et seq.*, offers the Presidential candidates of major political parties the option of receiving public financing for their general election campaigns. If a Presidential candidate elects public financing, § 9012(f) makes it a criminal offense for independent "political committees," such as appellees National Conservative Political Action Committee (NCPAC) and Fund For A Conservative Majority (FCM), to expend more than $1,000 to further that candidate's election. A three-judge District Court for the Eastern District of Pennsylvania, in companion lawsuits brought respectively by the Federal Election Commission (FEC) and by the Democratic Party of the United States and the Democratic National Committee (DNC), held § 9012(f) unconstitutional on its face because it violated the First Amendment to the United States Constitution. * * *

The present litigation began in May 1983 when the Democratic Party, the DNC, and Edward Mezvinsky, Chairman of the Pennsylvania Democratic State Committee, in his individual capacity as a citizen eligible to vote for President of the United States[1] (collectively, the Democrats), filed suit against NCPAC and FCM (the PACs), who had announced their intention to spend large sums of money to help bring about the reelection of President Ronald Reagan in 1984. Their amended complaint sought a declaration that § 9012(f), which they believed would prohibit the PACs' intended expenditures, was constitutional. The FEC intervened for the sole purpose of moving, along with the PACs, to dismiss the complaint for lack of standing.

In June 1983, the FEC brought a separate action against the same defendants seeking identical declaratory relief. * * *

* * *

In view of our conclusion that the Democrats lack standing under the statute, there is no need to reach the Art. III issue decided by the District Court. Therefore, we turn to the merits of the FEC's appeal of its unsuccessful declaratory judgment action against the PACs.

II

NCPAC is a nonprofit, nonmembership corporation formed under the District of Columbia Nonprofit Corporation Act in August 1975 and

---

[††] Justice Brennan joins only Part II of this opinion.

[1]. Mezvinsky did not pursue an appeal in this Court, though his name was inadvertently included in the notice of appeal filed by the Democratic Party and the DNC.

registered with the FEC as a political committee. Its primary purpose is to attempt to influence directly or indirectly the election or defeat of candidates for federal, state, and local offices by making contributions and by making its own expenditures. It is governed by a three-member board of directors which is elected annually by the existing board. The board's chairman and the other two members make all decisions concerning which candidates to support or oppose, the strategy and methods to employ, and the amounts of money to spend. Its contributors have no role in these decisions. It raises money by general and specific direct mail solicitations. It does not maintain separate accounts for the receipts from its general and specific solicitations, nor is it required by law to do so.

FCM is incorporated under the laws of Virginia and is registered with the FEC as a multi-candidate political committee. In all material respects it is identical to NCPAC.

Both NCPAC and FCM are self-described ideological organizations with a conservative political philosophy. They solicited funds in support of President Reagan's 1980 campaign, and they spent money on such means as radio and television advertisements to encourage voters to elect him President. On the record before us, these expenditures were "independent" in that they were not made at the request of or in coordination with the official Reagan election campaign committee or any of its agents. Indeed, there are indications that the efforts of these organizations were at times viewed with disfavor by the official campaign as counterproductive to its chosen strategy. NCPAC and FCM expressed their intention to conduct similar activities in support of President Reagan's reelection in 1984, and we may assume that they did so.

* * *

In these cases we consider provisions of the Fund Act that make it a criminal offense for political committees such as NCPAC and FCM to make independent expenditures in support of a candidate who has elected to accept public financing. Specifically, § 9012(f) provides:

> "(1) * * * it shall be unlawful for any political committee which is not an authorized committee with respect to the eligible candidates of a political party for President and Vice President in a presidential election knowingly and willfully to incur expenditures to further the election of such candidates, which would constitute qualified campaign expenses if incurred by an authorized committee of such candidates, in an aggregate amount exceeding $1,000."

* * *

* * * We conclude that the PACs' independent expenditures at issue in this case are squarely prohibited by § 9012(f), and we proceed to consider whether that prohibition violates the First Amendment.

There can be no doubt that the expenditures at issue in this case produce speech at the core of the First Amendment. * * *

The PACs in this case, of course, are not lone pamphleteers or street corner orators in the Tom Paine mold; they spend substantial amounts of money in order to communicate their political ideas through sophisticated media advertisements. And of course the criminal sanction in question is applied to the expenditure of money to propagate political views, rather than to the propagation of those views unaccompanied by the expenditure of money. But for purposes of presenting political views in connection with a nationwide Presidential election, allowing the presentation of views while forbidding the expenditure of more than $1,000 to present them is much like allowing a speaker in a public hall to express his views while denying him the use of an amplifying system. The Court said in *Buckley v. Valeo, supra:*

> "A restriction on the amount of money a person or group can spend on political communication during a campaign necessarily reduces the quantity of expression by restricting the number of issues discussed, the depth of their exploration, and the size of the audience reached. This is because virtually every means of communicating ideas in today's mass society requires the expenditure of money. The distribution of the humblest handbill or leaflet entails printing, paper, and circulation costs. Speeches and rallies generally necessitate hiring a hall and publicizing the event. The electorate's increasing dependence on television, radio, and other mass media for news and information has made these expensive modes of communication indispensable instruments of effective political speech." 424 U.S., at 19.

We also reject the notion that the PACs' form of organization or method of solicitation diminishes their entitlement to First Amendment protection. The First Amendment freedom of association is squarely implicated in these cases. NCPAC and FCM are mechanisms by which large numbers of individuals of modest means can join together in organizations which serve to "amplif[y] the voice of their adherents." Buckley v. Valeo, 424 U.S., at 22; NAACP v. Alabama, 357 U.S. 449, 460 (1958); Citizens Against Rent Control v. Berkeley, 454 U.S. 290, 295–296 (1981). It is significant that in 1979–1980 approximately 101,000 people contributed an average of $75 each to NCPAC and in 1980 approximately 100,000 people contributed an average of $25 each to FCM.

The FEC urges that these contributions do not constitute individual speech, but merely "speech by proxy," see California Medical Assn. v. FEC, 453 U.S. 182, 196 (1981) (MARSHALL, J.) (plurality opinion), because the contributors do not control or decide upon the use of the funds by the PACs or the specific content of the PACs' advertisements and other speech. The plurality emphasized in that case, however, that nothing in the statutory provision in question "limits the amount [an unincorporated association] or any of its members may independently expend in order to advocate political views," but only the amount it may contribute to a multi-candidate political committee. *Id.,* at 195. Unlike *California Medical Assn.,* the present cases involve limitations on expenditures by PACs, not on the contributions they receive; and in any event these contributions are predominantly small and thus do not raise the same concerns as the sizable contributions involved in *California Medical Assn.*

Another reason the "proxy speech" approach is not useful in this case is that the contributors obviously like the message they are hearing from these organizations and want to add their voices to that message; otherwise they would not part with their money. To say that their collective action in pooling their resources to amplify their voices is not entitled to full First Amendment protection would subordinate the voices of those of modest means as opposed to those sufficiently wealthy to be able to buy expensive media ads with their own resources.

* * *

Having concluded that the PACs' expenditures are entitled to full First Amendment protection, we now look to see if there is a sufficiently strong governmental interest served by § 9012(f)'s restriction on them and whether the section is narrowly tailored to the evil that may legitimately be regulated. * * *

We held in *Buckley* and reaffirmed in *Citizens Against Rent Control* that preventing corruption or the appearance of corruption are the only legitimate and compelling government interests thus far identified for restricting campaign finances. In *Buckley* we struck down the FECA's limitation on individuals' independent expenditures because we found no tendency in such expenditures, uncoordinated with the candidate or his campaign, to corrupt or to give the appearance of corruption. * * *

* * *

We think the same conclusion must follow here. It is contended that, because the PACs may by the breadth of their organizations spend larger amounts than the individuals in *Buckley,* the potential for corruption is greater. But precisely what the "corruption" may consist of we are never told with assurance. The fact that candidates and elected officials may alter or reaffirm their own positions on issues in response to political messages paid for by the PACs can hardly be called corruption, for one of the essential features of democracy is the presentation to the electorate of varying points of view. It is of course hypothetically possible here, as in the case of the independent expenditures forbidden in *Buckley,* that candidates may take notice of and reward those responsible for PAC expenditures by giving official favors to the latter in exchange for the supporting messages. But here, as in *Buckley,* the absence of prearrangement and coordination undermines the value of the expenditure to the candidate, and thereby alleviates the danger that expenditures will be given as a *quid pro quo* for improper commitments from the candidate. On this record, such an exchange of political favors for uncoordinated expenditures remains a hypothetical possibility and nothing more.

Even were we to determine that the large pooling of financial resources by NCPAC and FCM did pose a potential for corruption or the appearance of corruption, § 9012(f) is a fatally overbroad response to that evil. It is not limited to multimillion dollar war chests; its terms apply equally to informal discussion groups that solicit neighborhood contributions to publicize their views about a particular Presidential candidate.

Several reasons suggest that we are not free to adopt a limiting construction that might isolate wealthy PACs, even if such a construction might save the statute. First, Congress plainly intended to prohibit just what § 9012(f) prohibits—independent expenditures over $1,000 by all political committees, large and small. Even if it did not intend to cover small neighborhood groups, there is also no evidence in the statute or the legislative history that it would have looked favorably upon a construction of the statute limiting § 9012(f) only to very successful PACs. Secondly, we cannot distinguish in principle between a PAC that has solicited 1,000 $25 contributions and one that has solicited 100,000 $25 contributions. Finally, it has been suggested that § 9012(f) could be narrowed by limiting its prohibition to political committees in which the contributors have no voice in the use to which the contributions are put. Again, there is no indication in the statute or the legislative history that Congress would be content with such a construction. More importantly, as observed by the District Court, such a construction is intolerably vague. At what point, for example, does a neighborhood group that solicits some outside contributions fall within § 9012(f)? How active do the group members have to be in setting policy to satisfy the control test? Moreover, it is doubtful that the members of a large association in which each have a vote on policy have substantially more control in practice than the contributors to NCPAC and FCM: the latter will surely cease contributing when the message those organizations deliver ceases to please them.

* * *

Finally, the FEC urges us to uphold § 9012(f) as a prophylactic measure deemed necessary by Congress, which has far more expertise than the Judiciary in campaign finance and corrupting influences. In *NRWC,* 459 U.S., at 210, we stated:

> "While [2 U.S.C.] § 441b restricts the solicitation of corporations and labor unions without great financial resources, as well as those more fortunately situated, we accept Congress' judgment that it is the potential for such influence that demands regulation. Nor will we second-guess a legislative determination as to the need for prophylactic measures where corruption is the evil feared."

Here, however, the groups and associations in question, designed expressly to participate in political debate, are quite different from the traditional corporations organized for economic gain. In *NRWC* we rightly concluded that Congress might include, along with labor unions and corporations traditionally prohibited from making contributions to political candidates, membership corporations, though contributions by the latter might not exhibit all of the evil that contributions by traditional economically organized corporations exhibit. But this proper deference to a congressional determination of the need for a prophylactic rule where the evil of potential corruption had long been recognized does not suffice to establish the validity of § 9012(f), which indiscriminately lumps with corporations any "committee, association or organization." Indeed, the FEC in its briefs to this Court does not even make an effort to defend the statute under a construction limited in reach to corporations.

While in *NRWC* we held that the compelling governmental interest in preventing corruption supported the restriction of the influence of political war chests funneled through the corporate form, in the present cases we do not believe that a similar finding is supportable: when the First Amendment is involved, our standard of review is "rigorous," Buckley v. Valeo, 424 U.S., at 29, and the effort to link either corruption or the appearance of corruption to independent expenditures by PACs, whether large or small, simply does not pass this standard of review. Even assuming that Congress could fairly conclude that large-scale PACs have a sufficient tendency to corrupt, the overbreadth of § 9012(f) in these cases is so great that the section may not be upheld. We are not quibbling over fine-tuning of prophylactic limitations, but are concerned about wholesale restriction of clearly protected conduct. See Broadrick v. Oklahoma, 413 U.S. 601 (1973).

The judgment of the District Court is affirmed as to the constitutionality of § 9012(f), but is reversed on the issue of the Democrats' standing, with instructions to dismiss their complaint for lack of standing.

It is so ordered.

JUSTICE STEVENS, concurring in part and dissenting in part.

* * * I join only Part II of the Court's opinion.

JUSTICE WHITE, dissenting.

* * *

II

Section 9012(f) of the Internal Revenue Code limits to $1,000 the annual independent expenditures a PAC can make to further the election of a candidate receiving public funds. Because these expenditures "produce speech at the core of the First Amendment," * * *, the majority concludes that they can only be regulated in order to avoid real or apparent corruption. Perceiving no such danger, since the money does not go directly to political candidates or their committees, it strikes down § 9012(f).

My disagreements with this analysis, which continues this Court's dismemberment of congressional efforts to regulate campaign financing, are many. First, I continue to believe that Buckley v. Valeo, 424 U.S. 1 (1976), was wrongly decided. Congressional regulation of the amassing and spending of money in political campaigns without doubt involves First Amendment concerns, but restrictions such as the one at issue here are supported by governmental interests—including, but not limited to, the need to avoid real or apparent corruption—sufficiently compelling to withstand scrutiny. Second, even were *Buckley* correct, I consider today's holding a mistaken application of that precedent. The provision challenged here more closely resembles the contribution limitations that were upheld in *Buckley,* and later cases, than the limitations on uncoordinated individual expenditures that were struck down. Finally, even if *Buckley* requires that in general PACs be allowed to make independent expenditures, I do not think that that proposition applies to § 9012(f). As part of an integrated and complex system of public funding for Presidential campaigns, § 9012(f) is supported by governmental interests that were absent in *Buckley,* which was premised on a system of private campaign financing.

* * *

As in *Buckley,* I am convinced that it is pointless to limit the amount that can be contributed to a candidate or spent with his approval without also limiting the amounts that can be spent on his behalf. In the Fund Act, Congress limited contributions, direct or coordinated, to zero. It is nonsensical to allow the purposes of this limitation to be entirely defeated by allowing the sort of "independent" expenditures at issue here, and the First Amendment does not require us to do so.

B

Even if I accepted *Buckley* as binding precedent, I nonetheless would uphold § 9012(f). *Buckley* distinguished "direct political expression," which could not be curtailed, from financial contributions, which could. 424 U.S., at 21–22. Limitations on expenditures were considered direct restraints on the right to speak one's mind on public issues and to engage in advocacy protected by the First Amendment. *Id.,* at 48. The majority views the challenged provision as being in that category. I disagree.

The majority never explicitly identifies whose First Amendment interests it believes it is protecting. However, its concern for rights of association and the effective political speech of those of modest means, * * *, indicates that it is concerned with the interests of the PACs' contributors. But the "contributors" are exactly that—contributors, rather than speakers. Every reason the majority gives for treating § 9012(f) as a restraint on speech relates to the effectiveness with which the donors can make their voices heard. In other words, what the majority purports to protect is the right of the contributors to make contributions.

But the contributors are not engaging in speech; at least, they are not engaging in speech to any greater extent than are those who contribute directly to political campaigns. *Buckley* explicitly distinguished between, on the one hand, using one's own money to express one's views, and, on the other, giving money to someone else in the expectation that that person will use the money to express views with which one is in agreement. This case falls within the latter category. As the *Buckley* Court stated with regard to contributions to campaigns, "the transformation of contributions into political debate involves speech by someone other than the contributor." 424 U.S., at 21. The majority does not explain the metamorphosis of donated dollars from money into speech by virtue of the identity of the donee.

* * *

These cases are in any event different enough from *Buckley* that that decision is not dispositive. The challenged provision is not part of the FECA, whose expenditure limitations were struck down in *Buckley*. Rather, it is part of the Fund Act, which was, to the extent it was before the Court, upheld.

* * *

Because it is an indispensable component of the public funding scheme, § 9012(f) is supported by governmental interests absent in *Buckley*. Rather than forcing Congress to abandon public financing because it is unworkable without constitutionally prohibited restrictions on independent spending, I would hold that § 9012(f) is permissible precisely because it is a necessary, narrowly drawn means to a constitutional end. The need to make public financing, with its attendant benefits, workable is a constitutionally sufficient additional justification for the burden on First Amendment rights.

* * *

JUSTICE MARSHALL, dissenting.

In Buckley v. Valeo, 424 U.S. 1 (1976) (*per curiam*), this Court upheld congressional limitations on contributions to candidates for federal office but struck down limitations on independent expenditures made on behalf of such candidates. In upholding the former, the Court stated that "the weighty interests served by restricting the size of financial contributions to political candidates are sufficient to justify the limited effect upon First Amendment freedoms caused by the $1,000 contribution ceiling." *Id.* at 29. In striking down the latter, the Court noted that an expenditure limitation "fails to serve any substantial interest in stemming the reality or appearance of corruption in the electoral process," and that "it heavily burdens core First Amendment expression." *Id.*, at 47–48. Relying on *Buckley,* the Court today strikes down a limitation on expenditures by "political committees." Although I joined the portion of the *Buckley per curiam* that distinguished contributions from independent expenditures for First Amendment purposes, I now believe that the distinction has no constitutional significance.

* * *

Undoubtedly, when an individual interested in obtaining the proverbial ambassadorship had the option of either contributing directly to a candidate's campaign or doing so indirectly through independent expenditures, he gave money directly. It does not take great imagination, however, to see that, when the possibility for direct financial assistance is severely limited, as it is in light of *Buckley*'s decision to uphold the contribution limitation, such an individual will find other ways to financially benefit the candidate's campaign. It simply belies reality to say that a campaign will not reward massive financial assistance provided in the only way that is legally available. And the possibility of such a reward provides a powerful incentive to channel an independent expenditure into an area that a candidate will appreciate. Surely an eager supporter will be able to discern a candidate's needs and desires; similarly, a willing candidate will notice the supporter's efforts. To the extent that individuals are able to make independent expenditures as part of a *quid pro quo,* they succeed in undermining completely the first rationale for the distinction made in *Buckley.*

* * *

NOTE

In the last case, *FEC v. NCPAC,* the Court sustained the first amendment claim of independent political action committees (PACS) to operate as nonprofit, nonmembership corporations, soliciting funds from others to be spent as the directors of the Political Action Committee approve for media advertising urging the election or defeat of presidential candidates, including candidates already receiving federal funds. As in *Buckley v. Valeo,* in the Court's review of expenditure restrictions on individuals and political advocacy associations (e.g., the ACLU), the fact that these expenditures were not subject to the direction, control, or coordination of the candidate or of his or her campaign committee supplied the distinguishing key. Third party first amendment rights cannot be made to turn on whether a given candidate accepts or does not accept public funds.[92]

Would it make any constitutional difference if the limit on such candidate specific expenditures were a limit applied only to ordinary business corporations, e.g., publicly traded common stock companies primarily in business to produce or to sell certain goods or services—such as General Motors or American Tel. & Tel.? Even assuming no public funding of candidates, might a state statute restricting ordinary commercial corporations from authorizing their boards of directors to use general corporate funds [93] to buy media advertisements to support or oppose any candidate for local or state elected office be valid despite *Buckley* and *NCPAC?*[94]

If the Supreme Court upheld the corporation's first amendment claim in respect to such expenditures when directed to advertising

---

92. Consistent with the reasoning in *Buckley,* the candidate can decide whether he or she is better off by accepting public campaign funds and accepting limits on spending his or her own funds (and those of any committee working with the candidate); whatever the candidate's calculus, however, it cannot act to limit the independent first amendment rights of others to "speak" as they wish.

93. As distinct from such funds as the company may gain by means of specially soliciting shareholders to contribute to a segregated corporate fund.

94. Is there a constitutionally-viable distinction insofar as the corporation is a for-profit, commercially owned company, owned by multitudes of shareholders who buy and sell principally (perhaps solely) for investment reasons and not for any reason of political interest? Even though the corporation's articles of incorporation permit the directors to make decisions of this sort, and even though any shareholder personally offended by the corporation's choice of candidates to support or oppose in this way, may sell his or her shares and take their money elsewhere at any time?

campaigns urging the adoption or defeat of a ballot measure,[95] would you expect the result to be any different in respect to such expenditures relative to identified candidates for office instead?[96]—Though these pro- or anti-candidate expenditures are wholly independent of any expenditures made by the candidate or the candidate's campaign committee? If the outcome were different, on what basis, if any, could such a difference be proposed?[97]

---

95. See First Nat. Bank of Boston v. Bellotti, 435 U.S. 765, 98 S.Ct. 1407, 55 L.Ed.2d 707 (1978). (And consider also Citizens Against Rent Control v. Berkeley, 454 U.S. 290, 102 S.Ct. 434, 70 L.Ed.2d 492 (1981).)

96. Suppose the for-profit, large corporation is itself a "media" company, e.g., a newspaper such as the Miami Herald, devoting free space in its own publications to express its endorsement for candidates it wants to see elected. (The outcome here is quite clear, is it not?)

97. See Austin v. Michigan Chamber of Commerce, 494 U.S. ___, 110 S.Ct. 1391, 108 L.Ed.2d 652 (1990) (five-to-four). For two (of many) substantial and contrasting reviews on the general questions raised in the *Buckley* line of cases (i.e. various bills on public financing, election "reform," and limitations on money and speech), compare Wright, Money and the Pollution of Politics: Is the First Amendment an Obstacle to Political Equality?, 82 Colum.L.Rev. 609 (1982), with Fleischman & McCorkle, Level-Up Rather than Level-Down: Toward a New Theory of Campaign Finance Reform, 1 J.Law & Pol. 211 (1984).

Chapter 4

THE FIRST AMENDMENT AND THE LESSER PROTECTION OF NONPOLITICAL SPEECH IN THE UNITED STATES

A. Commercial Speech

The extent to which advertising is assimilated within ordinary standards of economic due process review and the uncertainties of distinguishing what is or is not "commercial speech."

1. "Commercial Speech" in the Supreme Court

In an early footnote tucked away in the Introduction to these materials, an example of "commercial speech" was used to check one's impulse to adhere to an absolute view of free speech (i.e. the view that Congress is forbidden to enact *any* restriction of speech in the United States). The example was one of commercial fraud involving an interstate seller of pork bellies who deliberately misstates the nutritional value of his product, and a Federal Trade Commission cease-and-desist order banning the misleading advertisement following a full, fair, adversary proceeding, complete with clear and convincing evidence establishing the factual falsity of the advertiser's profit-seeking misrepresentations. We now return to the general area represented by that hypothetical, to review it in greater detail and with far more discernment and case-by-case care.

I

The original case was put in the setting of an FTC false advertising proceeding, in order to relate the case to congressional powers of regulation, as distinct from those severally possessed by the states. But, now noting that, generally speaking the Supreme Court does not significantly distinguish the application of the first amendment via the fourteenth amendment in respect to such subjects as the states have power to regulate pursuant to their police power interests, here we can generalize the example, can we not? So, the case could as easily be a case of a local drug store *truthfully* advertising cut-rate prescription retail drug prices, and a state law or local ordinance either regulating or even prohibiting such advertisements altogether, and a fourteenth amendment challenge to that state or local law. How would/should the fourteenth amendment question be addressed? More specifically, should it be addressed [merely] in terms of fourteenth amendment, economic substantive due process judicial review, or shall it be addressed as a case of free speech?

In the FTC case, as we first proposed it, what was forbidden was solely advertising that was alleged to be false or at least highly misleading. And we imagined a carefully wrought administrative procedure for responding to consumer concerns, a fair hearing, a heavy burden-of-proof on the government, etc.,—all aimed at suggesting that first amendment concerns, such as they might be, have all been duly fitted into place. But our case need not have been modeled in this way. Rather, the case may in fact be one in which Congress enacts a ban on advertising a given service or product, whether through the mails or in any interstate medium, period. In such a case, from the congressional view, the absence of falsehood in the advertisement would make no difference at all. (Indeed, the truth of the advertisement might make it "worse.")[1] Does the first amendment permit Congress to keep consumers ignorant of services and products otherwise available to them? Even when trade in those products or services is itself wholly lawful? If so, why, and to what extent? (And, moreover, just what shall be deemed to be "commercial" speech?) Would it matter that the advertisement might be one placed by an attorney?—An advertisement drawing attention to his specialty as a personal injury lawyer, and advertising copy explaining that he or she is available on the basis of a purely contingent fee ("no success, no charge!")?

II.

In Con Law I, we did in fact engage several Supreme Court cases touching on this subject. Among the most notable was *Railway Express Agency v. New York*.[2] The *Railway Express Agency* case sustained a prohibition of advertising vehicles on the streets of New York City, exempting only business delivery vehicles advertising the "usual business" of the owner, thus disallowing an REA vehicle otherwise lawfully on the city streets from substituting poster ads for a local radio station (WOR) and for Camel Cigarettes, for poster ads for REA itself. The Supreme Court was unanimous in finding no (economic) substantive due process violation insofar as REA complained that the restriction was an unconstitutional restraint of its liberty and property interests as

1. E.g., suppose this case. Widgets, a handy item one might find in many homes, formerly cost $3 to produce. X corp. has discovered a new way of manufacturing widgets for $1, and is eager to promote sales by truthfully advertising the new reduced price at which it will sell widgets. Congress, not favoring any increased consumption of widgets, and having by statute already forbidden any advertisement of widgets in any medium "affecting commerce," obviously X corp. cannot, consistent with the pre-existing act of Congress, advertise the new and much lower price of its product. Here the very truthfulness (rather than any suggestion of falsehood) of what it proposes to say in its ads makes the "danger" identified by Congress (namely the purchase and use of widgets) even greater than were the proposed advertisement utterly false. Consumers are kept ignorant of the newly available lower price of widgets solely by the act of Congress. They are being misled (by that act) to believe widgets still presumably sell at $3, and they are thus deceived (as a consequence of the act of Congress) about a matter of interest to them on a matter the X corp. would bring to their attention (by truthful informational advertising) but for the act of Congress that threatens the X corp. with heavy fines.

2. 336 U.S. 106, 69 S.Ct. 463, 93 L.Ed. 533 (1949).

a commercial enterprise. Justice Jackson wrote a famous, barely concurring, opinion as to REA's equal protection complaint.[3] Even so, one will recall that no *"heightened scrutiny"* was given either to REA's due process claim or to REA's equal protection claim in the majority opinion for the Supreme Court. And no first amendment distinctive review was even implied in the opinions you read at the time.

Indeed, in the *Railway Express Agency* case, it appears to have been taken for granted that advertising-as-an-incident-of-commerce is wholly subsumed in "mere" economic substantive due process (and mere economic equal protection) review. In brief, the framework yielded nothing identified to the first amendment, though advertising is certainly "speech" of a sort.

III.

The *Railway Express Agency* decision was representative of "commercial speech" cases in general. The latitude of regulatory state power in respect to commercial speech or commercial advertising generally was treated by the Supreme Court as an included part of the latitude of regulatory state power over the general "liberty" (and "property") freedoms of entrepreneurs, following the repudiation of *Lochner v. New York*. The Supreme Court had freely sustained that larger field of substantive regulation, with minimal substantive review in respect to the states, beginning with *Nebbia v. New York,* in 1934. (It did likewise, in *United States v. Carolene Products,* vis-a-vis Congress, in 1938). In brief, commercial speech was, as well illustrated by *Railway Express* itself, treated mostly as "commerce," and little (if at all) as "speech," for purposes of substantive constitutional review. In textual Bill of Rights terms, the dispositive clause was the fifth amendment (substantive) due process clause—not the first amendment free speech clause. Commercial speech was thus principally a subset of economic due process, rather than a subset of (first amendment) free speech, review.

The cases immediately ahead in these materials begin from this point. But, just as with the assumptions prior to (but not after) *New York Times v. Sullivan,* in respect to libel—that "libel" raises no first amendment questions (yet today "libel" bristles with first amendment questions)—commercial speech also has become a specialized subset of first amendment case law. The principal cases we examine here, moving from *Valentine v. Chrestensen,* describe these developments up to date.

---

3. The ordinance did not equally restrict the fixed display advertisements for all the same products, though these displays fronted on the same city streets, i.e. none of them were confined to advertising merely the usual business of the owner of the business premises on which these (much more garish) advertisements were displayed. As between an ad carried for Camel Cigarettes on a REA truck (vis-a-vis the same ad carried on a Reynolds Tobacco delivery vehicle, or on a fixed display, etc.), moreover, REA argued that there was no rational distinction to be made at all.

VALENTINE v. CHRESTENSEN

Supreme Court of the United States, 1942.
316 U.S. 52, 62 S.Ct. 920, 86 L.Ed. 1262.

Mr. Justice Roberts delivered the opinion of the Court.

The respondent, a citizen of Florida, owns a former United States Navy submarine which he exhibits for profit. In 1940 he brought it to New York City and moored it at a State pier in the East River. He prepared and printed a handbill advertising the boat and soliciting visitors for a stated admission fee. On his attempting to distribute the bill in the city streets, he was advised by the petitioner, as Police Commissioner, that this activity would violate § 318 of the Sanitary Code, which forbids distribution in the streets of commercial and business advertising matter, but was told that he might freely distribute handbills solely devoted to "information or a public protest."

Respondent thereupon prepared and showed to the petitioner, in proof form, a double-faced handbill. On one side was a revision of the original, altered by the removal of the statement as to admission fee but consisting only of commercial advertising. On the other side was a protest against the action of the City Dock Department in refusing the respondent wharfage facilities at a city pier for the exhibition of his submarine, but no commercial advertising. The Police Department advised that distribution of a bill containing only the protest would not violate § 318, and would not be restrained, but that distribution of the double-faced bill was prohibited. The respondent, nevertheless, proceeded with the printing of his proposed bill and started to distribute it. He was restrained by the police.

Respondent then brought this suit to enjoin the petitioner from interfering with the distribution. In his complaint he alleged diversity of citizenship; an amount in controversy in excess of $3,000; the acts and threats of the petitioner under the purported authority of § 318; asserted a consequent violation of § 1 of the Fourteenth Amendment of the Constitution; and prayed an injunction. The District Court granted an interlocutory injunction, and after trial on a stipulation from which the facts appear as above recited, granted a permanent injunction. The Circuit Court of Appeals, by a divided court, affirmed.

The question is whether the application of the ordinance to the respondent's activity was, in the circumstances, an unconstitutional abridgement of the freedom of the press and of speech.

1. This court has unequivocally held that the streets are proper places for the exercise of the freedom of communicating information and disseminating opinion and that, though the states and municipalities may appropriately regulate the privilege in the public interest, they may not unduly burden or proscribe its employment in these public thoroughfares. We are equally clear that the Constitution imposes no such restraint on government as respects purely commercial advertising. Whether, and to what extent, one may promote or pursue a gainful occupation in the streets, to what extent such activity shall be adjudged a derogation of the public right of user, are matters for

legislative judgment. The question is not whether the legislative body may interfere with the harmless pursuit of a lawful business, but whether it must permit such pursuit by what it deems an undesirable invasion of, or interference with, the full and free use of the highways by the people in fulfillment of the public use to which streets are dedicated. If the respondent was attempting to use the streets of New York by distributing commercial advertising, the prohibition of the code provision was lawfully invoked against his conduct.

2. The respondent contends that, in truth, he was engaged in the dissemination of matter proper for public information, none the less so because there was inextricably attached to the medium of such dissemination commercial advertising matter. The court below appears to have taken this view, since it adverts to the difficulty of apportioning, in a given case, the contents of the communication as between what is of public interest and what is for private profit. We need not indulge nice appraisal based upon subtle distinctions in the present instance nor assume possible cases not now presented. It is enough for the present purpose that the stipulated facts justify the conclusion that the affixing of the protest against official conduct to the advertising circular was with the intent, and for the purpose, of evading the prohibition of the ordinance. If that evasion were successful, every merchant who desires to broadcast advertising leaflets in the streets need only append a civil appeal, or a moral platitude, to achieve immunity from the law's command.

The decree is

Reversed.

BIGELOW v. VIRGINIA

Supreme Court of the United States, 1975.
421 U.S. 809, 95 S.Ct. 2222, 44 L.Ed.2d 600.

Mr. Justice Blackmun delivered the opinion of the Court.

* * *

I

The Virginia Weekly was a newspaper published by the Virginia Weekly Associates of Charlottesville. It was issued in that city and circulated in Albemarle County, with particular focus on the campus of the University of Virginia. Appellant, Jeffrey C. Bigelow, was a director and the managing editor and responsible officer of the newspaper.[1]

On February 8, 1971, the Weekly's Vol. V, No. 6, was published and circulated under the direct responsibility of the appellant. On page 2 of that issue was the following advertisement:

---

1. His brief describes the publication as an "underground newspaper." Brief for Appellant 3. The appellee states that there is no evidence in the record to support that description. Brief for Appellee 3 n. 1.

"UNWANTED PREGNANCY LET US HELP YOU
Abortions are now legal in New York.
There are no residency requirements.
FOR IMMEDIATE PLACEMENT IN ACCREDITED
HOSPITALS AND CLINICS AT LOW COST
Contact
WOMEN'S PAVILION
515 Madison Avenue
New York, N.Y. 10022
or call any time
(212) 371–6670 or (212) 371–6650
AVAILABLE 7 DAYS A WEEK
STRICTLY CONFIDENTIAL. We will make all arrangements
for you and help you with information and counseling."

* * *

On May 13 Bigelow was charged with violating Va.Code Ann. § 18.1–63 (1960). The statute at that time read:

"If any person, by publication, lecture, advertisement, or by the sale or circulation of any publication, or in any other manner, encourage or prompt the procuring of abortion or miscarriage, he shall be guilty of a misdemeanor."

* * *

The Supreme Court of Virginia granted review and, by a 4–2 vote, affirmed Bigelow's conviction. * * * The court first rejected the appellant's claim that the advertisement was purely informational and thus was not within the "encourage or prompt" language of the statute. It held, instead, that the advertisement "clearly exceeded an informational status" and "constituted an active offer to perform a service, rather than a passive statement of fact." * * * It then rejected Bigelow's First Amendment claim. This, the court said, was a "commercial advertisement" and, as such, "may be constitutionally prohibited by the state," particularly "where, as here, the advertising relates to the medical-health field." * * * The issue, in the court's view, was whether the statute was a valid exercise of the State's police power. It answered this question in the affirmative, noting that the statute's goal was "to ensure that pregnant women in Virginia who decided to have abortions come to their decisions without the commercial advertising pressure usually incidental to the sale of a box of soap powder." * * * The court then turned to Bigelow's claim of overbreadth. It held that because the appellant himself lacked a legitimate First Amendment interest, inasmuch as his activity "was of a purely commercial nature," he had no "standing to rely upon the hypothetical rights of those in the non-commercial zone." * * *

Bigelow took a timely appeal to this Court. During the pendency of his appeal, Roe v. Wade, 410 U.S. 113 (1973), and Doe v. Bolton, 410 U.S. 179 (1973), were decided. We subsequently vacated Bigelow's judgment of conviction and remanded the case for further consideration in the light of *Roe* and *Doe*. * * *

The Supreme Court of Virginia, on such reconsideration, but without further oral argument, again affirmed appellant's conviction, observing that neither *Roe* nor *Doe* "mentioned the subject of abortion advertising" and finding nothing in those decisions "which in any way affects our earlier view."[5] * * * Once again, Bigelow appealed. We noted probable jurisdiction in order to review the important First Amendment issue presented. * * *

* * *

In view of the statute's amendment since Bigelow's conviction in such a way as "effectively to repeal" its prior application, there is no possibility now that the statute's pre-1972 form will be applied again to appellant or will chill the rights of others. As a practical matter, the issue of its overbreadth has become moot for the future. We therefore decline to rest our decision on overbreadth and we pass on to the further inquiry, of greater moment not only for Bigelow but for others, whether the statute as applied to appellant infringed constitutionally protected speech.

* * *

The appellee, as did the Supreme Court of Virginia, relies on Valentine v. Chrestensen, 316 U.S. 52 (1942), where a unanimous Court, in a brief opinion, sustained an ordinance which had been interpreted to ban the distribution of a handbill advertising the exhibition of a submarine. The handbill solicited customers to tour the ship for a fee. The promoter-advertiser had first attempted to distribute a single-faced handbill consisting only of the advertisement, and was denied permission to do so. He then had printed, on the reverse side of the handbill, a protest against official conduct refusing him the use of wharfage facilities. The Court found that the message of asserted "public interest" was appended solely for the purpose of evading the ordinance and therefore did not constitute an "exercise of the freedom of communicating information and disseminating opinion." *Id.,* at 54. It said:

> "We are equally clear that the Constitution imposes no such restraint on government as respects purely commercial advertising." *Ibid.*

But the holding is distinctly a limited one: the ordinance was upheld as a reasonable regulation of the manner in which commercial advertising could be distributed. The fact that it had the effect of banning a particular handbill does not mean that *Chrestensen* is authority for the proposition that all statutes regulating commercial advertising are immune from constitutional challenge. The case obviously does not support any sweeping proposition that advertising is unprotected per se.

* * *

B. The legitimacy of appellant's First Amendment claim in the present case is demonstrated by the important differences between the advertisement presently at issue and those involved in *Chrestensen* and

---

5. Virginia asserts, rightfully we feel, that this is "a First Amendment case" and "not an abortion case." Brief for Appellee 15 n. 6; Tr. of Oral Arg. 26.

in *Pittsburgh Press*. The advertisement published in appellant's newspaper did more than simply propose a commercial transaction. It contained factual material of clear "public interest." Portions of its message, most prominently the lines, "Abortions are now legal in New York. There are no residency requirements," involve the exercise of the freedom of communicating information and disseminating opinion. Viewed in its entirety, the advertisement conveyed information of potential interest and value to a diverse audience—not only to readers possibly in need of the services offered, but also to those with a general curiosity about, or genuine interest in, the subject matter or the law of another State and its development, and to readers seeking reform in Virginia. The mere existence of the Women's Pavilion in New York City, with the possibility of its being typical of other organizations there, and the availability of the services offered, were not unnewsworthy. Also, the activity advertised pertained to constitutional interests. See Roe v. Wade, 410 U.S. 113 (1973), and Doe v. Bolton, 410 U.S. 179 (1973). Thus, in this case, appellant's First Amendment interests coincided with the constitutional interests of the general public.

Moreover, the placement services advertised in appellant's newspaper were legally provided in New York at that time. The Virginia Legislature could not have regulated the advertiser's activity in New York, and obviously could not have proscribed the activity in that State. * * * Neither could Virginia prevent its residents from traveling to New York to obtain those services or, as the State conceded, Tr. of Oral Arg. 29, prosecute them for going there. See United States v. Guest, 383 U.S. 745, 757–759 (1966); Shapiro v. Thompson, 394 U.S. 618, 629–631 (1969); Doe v. Bolton, 410 U.S., at 200. Virginia possessed no authority to regulate the services provided in New York—the skills and credentials of the New York physicians and of the New York professionals who assisted them, the standards of the New York hospitals and clinics to which patients were referred, or the practices and charges of the New York referral services.

A State does not acquire power or supervision over the internal affairs of another State merely because the welfare and health of its own citizens may be affected when they travel to that State. It may seek to disseminate information so as to enable its citizens to make better informed decisions when they leave. But it may not, under the guise of exercising internal police powers, bar a citizen of another State from disseminating information about an activity that is legal in that State.

C. We conclude, therefore, that the Virginia courts erred in their assumptions that advertising, as such, was entitled to no First Amendment protection and that appellant Bigelow had no legitimate First Amendment interest. We need not decide in this case the precise extent to which the First Amendment permits regulation of advertising that is related to activities the State may legitimately regulate or even prohibit.

* * *

We conclude that Virginia could not apply Va.Code Ann. § 18.1–63 (1960), as it read in 1971, to appellant's publication of the advertisement in question without unconstitutionally infringing upon his First Amendment rights. The judgment of the Supreme Court of Virginia is therefore reversed.

It is so ordered.

MR. JUSTICE REHNQUIST, with whom MR. JUSTICE WHITE joins, dissenting.

The Court's opinion does not confront head-on the question which this case poses, but makes contact with it only in a series of verbal sideswipes. The result is the fashioning of a doctrine which appears designed to obtain reversal of this judgment, but at the same time to save harmless from the effects of that doctrine the many prior cases of this Court which are inconsistent with it.

I am in agreement with the Court, * * *, that Virginia's statute cannot properly be invalidated on grounds of overbreadth,[1] given that the sole prosecution which has ever been brought under this now substantially altered statute is that now in issue. * * *

* * *

If the Court's decision does, indeed, turn upon its conclusion that the advertisement here in question was protected by the First and Fourteenth Amendments, the subject of the advertisement ought to make no difference. It will not do to say, as the Court does, that this advertisement conveyed information about the "subject matter or the law of another State and its development" to those "seeking reform in Virginia," and that it "related to abortion," as if these factors somehow put it on a different footing from other commercial advertising. This was a proposal to furnish services on a commercial basis, and since we have always refused to distinguish for First Amendment purposes on the basis of content, it is no different from an advertisement for a bucket shop operation or a Ponzi scheme which has its headquarters in New York. If Virginia may not regulate advertising of commercial abortion agencies because of the interest of those seeking to reform Virginia's abortion laws, it is difficult to see why it is not likewise precluded from regulating advertising for an out-of-state bucket shop on the ground that such information might be of interest to those interested in repealing Virginia's "blue sky" laws.

* * *

* * * Beginning at least with our decision in Delamater v. South Dakota, 205 U.S. 93, 100 (1907), we have consistently recognized that irrespective of a State's power to regulate extraterritorial commercial transactions in which its citizens participate it retains an independent power to regulate the business of commercial solicitation and advertis-

---

1. The Court, * * *, states that the Virginia Supreme Court placed no limiting interpretation on its statute and that it implied that the statute might apply to doctors, husbands, and lecturers. The Court is in error: the Virginia Supreme Court stated that it would not interpret the statute to encompass such situations. 213 Va. 191, 198, 191 S.E.2d 173, 177 (1972).

ing within its borders. Thus, for example, in Head v. New Mexico Board, 374 U.S. 424 (1963), we upheld the power of New Mexico to prohibit commercial advertising by a New Mexico radio station of optometric services provided in Texas. Mr. Justice Brennan, concurring in that opinion, noted that a contrary result might well produce "a 'no-man's land' * * * in which there would be at best selective policing of the various advertising abuses and excesses which are now very extensively regulated by state law." *Id.,* at 446. See, e.g., Packer Corp. v. Utah, 285 U.S. 105 (1932); Breard v. Alexandria, 341 U.S. 622 (1951).

Were the Court's statements taken literally, they would presage a standard of the lowest common denominator for commercial ethics and business conduct. Securities issuers could circumvent the established blue-sky laws of States which had carefully drawn such laws for the protection of their citizens by establishing as a situs for transactions those States without such regulations, while spreading offers throughout the country. Loan sharks might well choose States with unregulated small loan industries, luring the unwary with immune commercial advertisements. And imagination would place the only limit on the use of such a "no-man's land" together with artificially created territorial contacts to bilk the public and circumvent long-established state schemes of regulation.

Since the Court saves harmless from its present opinion our prior cases in this area, * * *, it may be fairly inferred that it does not intend the results which might otherwise come from a literal reading of its opinion. But solely on the facts before it, I think the Court today simply errs in assessing Virginia's interest in its statute because it does not focus on the impact of the practices in question on the State. Cf. Young v. Masci, 289 U.S. 253 (1933). Although the commercial referral agency, whose advertisement in Virginia was barred, was physically located outside the State, this physical contact says little about Virginia's concern for the touted practices. Virginia's interest in this statute lies in preventing commercial exploitation of the health needs of its citizens. So long as the statute bans commercial advertising by publications within the State, the extraterritorial location at which the services are actually provided does not diminish that interest.

Since the statute in question is a "reasonable regulation that serves a legitimate public interest," * * *, I would affirm the judgment of the Supreme Court of Virginia.

VIRGINIA STATE BOARD OF PHARMACY v. VIRGINIA CITIZENS CONSUMER COUNCIL

Supreme Court of the United States, 1976.
425 U.S. 748, 96 S.Ct. 1817, 48 L.Ed.2d 346.

Mr. Justice Blackmun delivered the opinion of the Court.

The plaintiff-appellees in this case attack, as violative of the First and Fourteenth Amendments, that portion of § 54–524.35 of Va.Code

Ann. (1974), which provides that a pharmacist licensed in Virginia is guilty of unprofessional conduct if he "(3) publishes, advertises or promotes, directly or indirectly, in any manner whatsoever, any amount, price, fee, premium, discount, rebate or credit terms * * * for any drugs which may be dispensed only by prescription." [2] The three-judge District Court declared the quoted portion of the statute "void and of no effect," Jurisdictional Statement, App. 1, and enjoined the defendant-appellants, the Virginia State Board of Pharmacy and the individual members of that Board, from enforcing it. * * * We noted probable jurisdiction of the appeal. * * *

I

Since the challenged restraint is one that peculiarly concerns the licensed pharmacist in Virginia, we begin with a description of that profession as it exists under Virginia law.

The "practice of pharmacy" is statutorily declared to be "a professional practice affecting the public health, safety and welfare," and to be "subject to regulation and control in the public interest." Va.Code Ann. § 54–524.2(a) (1974).[3] Indeed, the practice is subject to extensive regulation aimed at preserving high professional standards. The regulatory body is the appellant Virginia State Board of Pharmacy.

The Board is broadly charged by statute with various responsibilities, including the "[m]aintenance of the quality, quantity, integrity, safety and efficacy of drugs or devices distributed, dispensed or administered." § 54–524.16(a). It also is to concern itself with "[m]aintaining the integrity of, and public confidence in, the profession and improving the delivery of quality pharmaceutical services to the citizens of Virginia." § 54–524.16(d). The Board is empowered to "make such bylaws, rules and regulations . . . as may be necessary for the lawful exercise of its powers."

The Board is also the licensing authority. It may issue a license, necessary for the practice of pharmacy in the State, only upon evidence that the applicant is "of good moral character," is a graduate in pharmacy of a school approved by the Board, and has had "a suitable period of experience [the period required not to exceed 12 months] acceptable to the Board." § 54–524.21. The applicant must pass the examination prescribed by the Board. *Ibid.* One approved school is the School of Pharmacy of the Medical College of Virginia, where the curriculum is for three years following two years of college. Prescribed

---

2. Section 54–524.35 provides in full:

"Any pharmacist shall be considered guilty of unprofessional conduct who (1) is found guilty of any crime involving grave moral turpitude, or is guilty of fraud or deceit in obtaining a certificate of registration; or (2) issues, publishes, broadcasts by radio, or otherwise, or distributes or uses in any way whatsoever advertising matter in which statements are made about his professional service which have a tendency to deceive or defraud the public, contrary to the public health and welfare; or (3) publishes, advertises or promotes, directly or indirectly, in any manner whatsoever, any amount, price, fee, premium, discount, rebate or credit terms for professional services or for drugs containing narcotics or for any drugs which may be dispensed only by prescription."

3. The parties, also, have stipulated that pharmacy "is a profession." Stipulation of Facts ¶ 11, App. 11.

prepharmacy courses, such as biology and chemistry, are to be taken in college, and study requirements at the school itself include courses in organic chemistry, biochemistry, comparative anatomy, physiology, and pharmacology. Students are also trained in the ethics of the profession, and there is some clinical experience in the school's hospital pharmacies and in the medical center operated by the Medical College. This is "a rigid, demanding curriculum in terms of what the pharmacy student is expected to know about drugs."

Once licensed, a pharmacist is subject to a civil monetary penalty, or to revocation or suspension of his license, if the Board finds that he "is not of good moral character," or has violated any of a number of stated professional standards (among them that he not be "negligent in the practice of pharmacy" or have engaged in "fraud or deceit upon the consumer * * * in connection with the practice of pharmacy"), or is guilty of "unprofessional conduct." § 54–524.22:1. "Unprofessional conduct" is specifically defined in § 54–524.35, n. 2, *supra*, the third numbered phrase of which relates to advertising of the price for any prescription drug, and is the subject of this litigation.

Inasmuch as only a licensed pharmacist may dispense prescription drugs in Virginia, § 54–524.48,[5] advertising or other affirmative dissemination of prescription drug price information is effectively forbidden in the State. Some pharmacies refuse even to quote prescription drug prices over the telephone. The Board's position, however, is that this would not constitute an unprofessional publication. It is clear, nonetheless, that all advertising of such prices, in the normal sense, is forbidden. The prohibition does not extend to nonprescription drugs, but neither is it confined to prescriptions that the pharmacist compounds himself. Indeed, about 95% of all prescriptions now are filled with dosage forms prepared by the pharmaceutical manufacturer.

II

* * *

The present, * * *, attack on the statute is one made not by one directly subject to its prohibition, that is, a pharmacist, but by prescription drug consumers who claim that they would greatly benefit if the prohibition were lifted and advertising freely allowed. The plaintiffs are an individual Virginia resident who suffers from diseases that require her to take prescription drugs on a daily basis, and two nonprofit organizations.[10] Their claim is that the First Amendment entitles the user of prescription drugs to receive information that pharmacists wish to communicate to them through advertising and other promotional means, concerning the prices of such drugs.

---

5. Exception is made for "legally qualified" practitioners of medicine, dentistry, osteopathy, chiropody, and veterinary medicine.

10. The organizations are the Virginia Citizens Consumer Council, Inc., and the Virginia State AFL–CIO. Each has a substantial membership (approximately 150,000 and 69,000, respectively) many of whom are users of prescription drugs. * * * The American Association of Retired Persons and the National Retired Teachers Association, also claiming many members who "depend substantially on prescription drugs for their well-being," Brief 2, are among those who have filed briefs *amici curiae* in support of the appellees.

Certainly that information may be of value. Drug prices in Virginia, for both prescription and nonprescription items, strikingly vary from outlet to outlet even within the same locality. It is stipulated, for example, that in Richmond "the cost of 40 Achromycin tablets ranges from $2.59 to $6.00, a difference of 140% [*sic*]," and that in the Newport News–Hampton area the cost of tetracycline ranges from $1.20 to $9.00, a difference of 650%.[11]

* * *

III

The question first arises whether, even assuming that First Amendment protection attaches to the flow of drug price information, it is a protection enjoyed by the appellees as recipients of the information, and not solely, if at all, by the advertisers themselves who seek to disseminate that information.

Freedom of speech presupposes a willing speaker. But where a speaker exists, as is the case here,[14] the protection afforded is to the communication, to its source and to its recipients both. * * *

IV

The appellants contend that the advertisement of prescription drug prices is outside the protection of the First Amendment because it is "commercial speech." There can be no question that in past decisions the Court has given some indication that commercial speech is unprotected. * * *

* * *

Last Term, in Bigelow v. Virginia, 421 U.S. 809 (1975), the notion of unprotected "commercial speech" all but passed from the scene. We reversed a conviction for violation of a Virginia statute that made the circulation of any publication to encourage or promote the processing of an abortion in Virginia a misdemeanor. The defendant had published in his newspaper the availability of abortions in New York. The advertisement in question, in addition to announcing that abortions were legal in New York, offered the services of a referral agency in that State. We rejected the contention that the publication was unprotected because it was commercial. *Chrestensen*'s continued validity was questioned, and its holding was described as "distinctly a limited one" that merely upheld "a reasonable regulation of the manner in which commercial advertising could be distributed." 421 U.S., at 819. We concluded that "the Virginia courts erred in their assumptions that advertising, as such, was entitled to no First Amendment protection," and we observed that the "relationship of speech to the marketplace of

---

11. Stipulation of Facts ¶¶ 22(b) and (c), App. 14. The phenomenon of widely varying drug prices is apparently national in scope. The American Medical Association conducted a survey in Chicago that showed price differentials in that city of up to 1200% for the same amounts of a specific drug. * * *

14. "In the absence of Section 54–524.-35(3), some pharmacies in Virginia would advertise, publish and promote price information regarding prescription drugs." Stipulation of Facts P 26, App. 15.

products or of services does not make it valueless in the marketplace of ideas." *Id.,* at 825–826.

Some fragment of hope for the continuing validity of a "commercial speech" exception arguably might have persisted because of the subject matter of the advertisement in *Bigelow.* We noted that in announcing the availability of legal abortions in New York, the advertisement "did more than simply propose a commercial transaction. It contained factual material of clear 'public interest.'" *Id.,* at 822. And, of course, the advertisement related to activity with which, at least in some respects, the State could not interfere. See Roe v. Wade, 410 U.S. 113 (1973); Doe v. Bolton, 410 U.S. 179 (1973). Indeed, we observed: "We need not decide in this case the precise extent to which the First Amendment permits regulation of advertising that is related to activities the State may legitimately regulate or even prohibit." 421 U.S., at 825.

Here, in contrast, the question whether there is a First Amendment exception for "commercial speech" is squarely before us. Our pharmacist does not wish to editorialize on any subject, cultural, philosophical, or political. He does not wish to report any particularly newsworthy fact, or to make generalized observations even about commercial matters. The "idea" he wishes to communicate is simply this: "I will sell you the X prescription drug at the Y price." Our question, then, is whether this communication is wholly outside the protection of the First Amendment.

V

We begin with several propositions that already are settled or beyond serious dispute. It is clear, for example, that speech does not lose its First Amendment protection because money is spent to project it, as in a paid advertisement of one form or another. Buckley v. Valeo, 424 U.S. 1, 35–59 (1976); * * * Speech likewise is protected even though it is carried in a form that is "sold" for profit, Smith v. California, 361 U.S. 147, 150 (1959) (books); Joseph Burstyn, Inc. v. Wilson, 343 U.S. 495, 501 (1952) (motion pictures); Murdock v. Pennsylvania, 319 U.S., at 111 (religious literature), and even though it may involve a solicitation to purchase or otherwise pay or contribute money. *New York Times Co. v. Sullivan, supra;* NAACP v. Button, 371 U.S. 415, 429 (1963); Jamison v. Texas, 318 U.S., at 417; Cantwell v. Connecticut, 310 U.S. 296, 306–307 (1940).

If there is a kind of commercial speech that lacks all First Amendment protection, therefore, it must be distinguished by its content. Yet the speech whose content deprives it of protection cannot simply be speech on a commercial subject. No one would contend that our pharmacist may be prevented from being heard on the subject of whether, in general, pharmaceutical prices should be regulated, or their advertisement forbidden. Nor can it be dispositive that a commercial advertisement is noneditorial, and merely reports a fact. Purely factual matter of public interest may claim protection. Bigelow v. Virginia, 421 U.S., at 822; Thornhill v. Alabama, 310 U.S. 88, 102 (1940).

Our question is whether speech which does "no more than propose a commercial transaction," Pittsburgh Press Co. v. Human Relations Comm'n, 413 U.S., at 385, is so removed from any "exposition of ideas," Chaplinsky v. New Hampshire, 315 U.S. 568, 572 (1942), and from " 'truth, science, morality, and arts in general, in its diffusion of liberal sentiments on the administration of Government,' " Roth v. United States, 354 U.S. 476, 484 (1957), that it lacks all protection. Our answer is that it is not.

Focusing first on the individual parties to the transaction that is proposed in the commercial advertisement, we may assume that the advertiser's interest is a purely economic one. That hardly disqualifies him from protection under the First Amendment. The interests of the contestants in a labor dispute are primarily economic, but it has long been settled that both the employee and the employer are protected by the First Amendment when they express themselves on the merits of the dispute in order to influence its outcome. See, e.g., NLRB v. Gissel Packing Co., 395 U.S. 575, 617–618 (1969); * * *

As to the particular consumer's interest in the free flow of commercial information, that interest may be as keen, if not keener by far, than his interest in the day's most urgent political debate. Appellees' case in this respect is a convincing one. Those whom the suppression of prescription drug price information hits the hardest are the poor, the sick, and particularly the aged. A disproportionate amount of their income tends to be spent on prescription drugs; yet they are the least able to learn, by shopping from pharmacist to pharmacist, where their scarce dollars are best spent. When drug prices vary as strikingly as they do, information as to who is charging what becomes more than a convenience. It could mean the alleviation of physical pain or the enjoyment of basic necessities.

Generalizing, society also may have a strong interest in the free flow of commercial information. Even an individual advertisement, though entirely "commercial," may be of general public interest. The facts of decided cases furnish illustrations: advertisements stating that referral services for legal abortions are available, *Bigelow v. Virginia, supra;* that a manufacturer of artificial furs promotes his product as an alternative to the extinction by his competitors of fur-bearing mammals, see Fur Information & Fashion Council, Inc. v. E.F. Timme & Son, 364 F.Supp. 16 (SDNY 1973); and that a domestic producer advertises his product as an alternative to imports that tend to deprive American residents of their jobs, cf. Chicago Joint Board v. Chicago Tribune Co., 435 F.2d 470 (CA7 1970), cert. denied, 402 U.S. 973 (1971). Obviously, not all commercial messages contain the same or even a very great public interest element. There are few to which such an element, however, could not be added. Our pharmacist, for example, could cast himself as a commentator on store-to-store disparities in drug prices, giving his own and those of a competitor as proof. We see little point in requiring him to do so, and little difference if he does not.

Moreover, there is another consideration that suggests that no line between publicly "interesting" or "important" commercial advertising and the opposite kind could ever be drawn. Advertising, however tasteless and excessive it sometimes may seem, is nonetheless dissemination of information as to who is producing and selling what product, for what reason, and at what price. So long as we preserve a predominantly free enterprise economy, the allocation of our resources in large measure will be made through numerous private economic decisions. It is a matter of public interest that those decisions, in the aggregate, be intelligent and well informed. To this end, the free flow of commercial information is indispensable. * * * And if it is indispensable to the proper allocation of resources in a free enterprise system, it is also indispensable to the formation of intelligent opinions as to how that system ought to be regulated or altered. Therefore, even if the First Amendment were thought to be primarily an instrument to enlighten public decisionmaking in a democracy, we could not say that the free flow of information does not serve that goal.[20]

Arrayed against these substantial individual and societal interests are a number of justifications for the advertising ban. These have to do principally with maintaining a high degree of professionalism on the part of licensed pharmacists.[21] Indisputably, the State has a strong interest in maintaining that professionalism. It is exercised in a number of ways for the consumer's benefit. There is the clinical skill involved in the compounding of drugs, although, as has been noted, these now make up only a small percentage of the prescriptions filled. Yet, even with respect to manufacturer-prepared compounds, there is room for the pharmacist to serve his customer well or badly. Drugs kept too long on the shelf may lose their efficacy or become adulterated. They can be packaged for the user in such a way that the same results occur. The expertise of the pharmacist may supplement that of the prescribing physician, if the latter has not specified the amount to be dispensed or the directions that are to appear on the label. The pharmacist, a specialist in the potencies and dangers of drugs, may even be consulted by the physician as to what to prescribe. * * *

---

20. Pharmaceuticals themselves provide a not insignificant illustration. The parties have stipulated that expenditures for prescription drugs in the United States in 1970 were estimated at $9.14 billion. Stipulation of Facts ¶ 17, App. 12. It has been said that the figure for drugs and drug sundries in 1974 was $9.695 billion, with that amount estimated to be increasing about $700 million per year. Worthington, National Health Expenditures 1929-1974, 38 Social Security Bull., No. 2, p. 9 (1975). The task of predicting the effect that a free flow of drug price information would have on the production and consumption of drugs obviously is a hazardous and speculative one. It was recently undertaken, however, by the staff of the Federal Trade Commission in the course of its report, n. 11 *supra*, on the merits of a possible Commission rule that would outlaw drug price advertising restrictions. The staff concluded that consumer savings would be "of a very substantial magnitude, amounting to many millions of dollars per year." Staff Report, *supra*, n. 11, at 181.

21. An argument not advanced by the Board, either in its brief or in the testimony proffered prior to summary judgment, but which on occasion has been made to other courts, see, e.g., Pennsylvania State Board of Pharmacy v. Pastor, 441 Pa. 186, 272 A.2d 487 (1971), is that the advertisement of low drug prices will result in overconsumption and in abuse of the advertised drugs. The argument prudently has been omitted. By definition, the drugs at issue here may be sold only on a physician's prescription. We do not assume, as apparently the dissent does, that simply because low prices will be freely advertised, physicians will overprescribe, or that pharmacists will ignore the prescription requirement.

Price advertising, it is argued, will place in jeopardy the pharmacist's expertise and, with it, the customer's health. It is claimed that the aggressive price competition that will result from unlimited advertising will make it impossible for the pharmacist to supply professional services in the compounding, handling, and dispensing of prescription drugs. Such services are time consuming and expensive; if competitors who economize by eliminating them are permitted to advertise their resulting lower prices, the more painstaking and conscientious pharmacist will be forced either to follow suit or to go out of business. It is also claimed that prices might not necessarily fall as a result of advertising. If one pharmacist advertises, others must, and the resulting expense will inflate the cost of drugs. It is further claimed that advertising will lead people to shop for their prescription drugs among the various pharmacists who offer the lowest prices, and the loss of stable pharmacist-customer relationships will make individual attention—and certainly the practice of monitoring—impossible. Finally, it is argued that damage will be done to the professional image of the pharmacist. This image, that of a skilled and specialized craftsman, attracts talent to the profession and reinforces the better habits of those who are in it. Price advertising, it is said, will reduce the pharmacist's status to that of a mere retailer.

The strength of these proffered justifications is greatly undermined by the fact that high professional standards, to a substantial extent, are guaranteed by the close regulation to which pharmacists in Virginia are subject. And this case concerns the retail sale by the pharmacist more than it does his professional standards. Surely, any pharmacist guilty of professional dereliction that actually endangers his customer will promptly lose his license. At the same time, we cannot discount the Board's justifications entirely. The Court regarded justifications of this type sufficient to sustain the advertising bans challenged on due process and equal protection grounds in *Head v. New Mexico Board, supra; Williamson v. Lee Optical Co., supra;* and *Semler v. Dental Examiners, supra.*

The challenge now made, however, is based on the First Amendment. This casts the Board's justifications in a different light, for on close inspection it is seen that the State's protectiveness of its citizens rests in large measure on the advantages of their being kept in ignorance. The advertising ban does not directly affect professional standards one way or the other. It affects them only through the reactions it is assumed people will have to the free flow of drug price information. There is no claim that the advertising ban in any way prevents the cutting of corners by the pharmacist who is so inclined. That pharmacist is likely to cut corners in any event. The only effect the advertising ban has on him is to insulate him from price competition and to open the way for him to make a substantial, and perhaps even excessive, profit in addition to providing an inferior service. The more painstaking pharmacist is also protected but, again, it is a protection based in large part on public ignorance.

It appears to be feared that if the pharmacist who wishes to provide low cost, and assertedly low quality, services is permitted to advertise, he will be taken up on his offer by too many unwitting customers. They will choose the low-cost, low-quality service and drive the "professional" pharmacist out of business. They will respond only to costly and excessive advertising, and end up paying the price. They will go from one pharmacist to another, following the discount, and destroy the pharmacist-customer relationship. They will lose respect for the profession because it advertises. All this is not in their best interests, and all this can be avoided if they are not permitted to know who is charging what.

There is, of course, an alternative to this highly paternalistic approach. That alternative is to assume that this information is not in itself harmful, that people will perceive their own best interests if only they are well enough informed, and that the best means to that end is to open the channels of communication rather than to close them. If they are truly open, nothing prevents the "professional" pharmacist from marketing his own assertedly superior product, and contrasting it with that of the low-cost, high-volume prescription drug retailer. But the choice among these alternative approaches is not ours to make or the Virginia General Assembly's. It is precisely this kind of choice, between the dangers of suppressing information, and the dangers of its misuse if it is freely available, that the First Amendment makes for us. Virginia is free to require whatever professional standards it wishes of its pharmacists; it may subsidize them or protect them from competition in other ways. Cf. Parker v. Brown, 317 U.S. 341 (1943). But it may not do so by keeping the public in ignorance of the entirely lawful terms that competing pharmacists are offering. In this sense, the justifications Virginia has offered for suppressing the flow of prescription drug price information, far from persuading us that the flow is not protected by the First Amendment, have reinforced our view that it is. We so hold.

VI

In concluding that commercial speech, like other varieties, is protected, we of course do not hold that it can never be regulated in any way. Some forms of commercial speech regulation are surely permissible. We mention a few only to make clear that they are not before us and therefore are not foreclosed by this case. There is no claim, for example, that the prohibition on prescription drug price advertising is a mere time, place, and manner restriction. We have often approved restrictions of that kind provided that they are justified without reference to the content of the regulated speech, that they serve a significant governmental interest, and that in so doing they leave open ample alternative channels for communication of the information. * * *

Nor is there any claim that prescription drug price advertisements are forbidden because they are false or misleading in any way. Untruthful speech, commercial or otherwise, has never been protected for its own sake. Gertz v. Robert Welch, Inc., 418 U.S. 323, 340 (1974); Konigsberg v. State Bar, 366 U.S. 36, 49, and n. 10 (1961). Obviously, much commercial speech is not provably false, or even wholly false, but only deceptive or misleading. We foresee no obstacle to a State's dealing effectively with this problem.[24] The First Amendment, as we construe it today, does not prohibit the State from insuring that the stream of commercial information flow cleanly as well as freely. See, for example, Va.Code Ann. § 18.2–216 (1975).

Also, there is no claim that the transactions proposed in the forbidden advertisements are themselves illegal in any way. Cf. Pittsburgh Press Co. v. Human Relations Comm'n, 413 U.S. 376 (1973); United States v. Hunter, 459 F.2d 205 (CA4), cert. denied, 409 U.S. 934 (1972). Finally, the special problems of the electronic broadcast media are likewise not in this case. Cf. Capitol Broadcasting Co. v. Mitchell, 333 F.Supp. 582 (DC 1971), aff'd *sub nom.* Capitol Broadcasting Co. v. Acting Attorney General, 405 U.S. 1000 (1972). What is at issue is whether a State may completely suppress the dissemination of concededly truthful information about entirely lawful activity, fearful of that information's effect upon its disseminators and its recipients. Reserving other questions,[25] we conclude that the answer to this one is in the negative.

The judgment of the District Court is affirmed.

It is so ordered.

MR. JUSTICE STEVENS took no part in the consideration or decision of this case.

---

24. In concluding that commercial speech enjoys First Amendment protection, we have not held that it is wholly undifferentiable from other forms. There are commonsense differences between speech that does "no more than propose a commercial transaction," Pittsburgh Press Co. v. Human Relations Comm'n, 413 U.S., at 385, and other varieties. Even if the differences do not justify the conclusion that commercial speech is valueless, and thus subject to complete suppression by the State, they nonetheless suggest that a different degree of protection is necessary to insure that the flow of truthful and legitimate commercial information is unimpaired. The truth of commercial speech, for example, may be more easily verifiable by its disseminator than, let us say, news reporting or political commentary, in that ordinarily the advertiser seeks to disseminate information about a specific product or service that he himself provides and presumably knows more about than anyone else. Also, commercial speech may be more durable than other kinds. Since advertising is the *sine qua non* of commercial profits, there is little likelihood of its being chilled by proper regulation and forgone entirely.

Attributes such as these, the greater objectivity and hardiness of commercial speech, may make it less necessary to tolerate inaccurate statements for fear of silencing the speaker. Compare New York Times Co. v. Sullivan, 376 U.S. 254 (1964), with Dun & Bradstreet, Inc. v. Grove, 404 U.S. 898 (1971). They may also make it appropriate to require that a commercial message appear in such a form, or include such additional information, warnings, and disclaimers, as are necessary to prevent its being deceptive. Compare Miami Herald Publishing Co. v. Tornillo, 418 U.S. 241 (1974), with Banzhaf v. FCC, 132 U.S.App. D.C. 14, 405 F.2d 1082 (1968), cert. denied *sub nom.* Tobacco Institute, Inc. v. FCC, 396 U.S. 842 (1969). Cf. United States v. 95 Barrels of Vinegar, 265 U.S. 438, 443 (1924) ("It is not difficult to choose statements, designs and devices which will not deceive"). They may also make inapplicable the prohibition against prior restraints. Compare New York Times Co. v. United States, 403 U.S. 713 (1971), with Donaldson v. Read Magazine, 333 U.S. 178, 189–191 (1948); FTC v. Standard Education Society, 302 U.S. 112 (1937); E.F. Drew & Co. v. FTC, 235 F.2d 735, 739–740 (CA2 1956), cert. denied, 352 U.S. 969 (1957).

25. We stress that we have considered in this case the regulation of commercial advertising by pharmacists. Although we express no opinion as to other professions, the distinctions, historical and functional, between professions, may require consideration of quite different factors. Physicians and lawyers, for example, do not dispense standardized products; they render professional services of almost infinite variety and nature, with the consequent enhanced possibility for confusion and deception if they were to undertake certain kinds of advertising.

Mr. Chief Justice Burger, concurring. [Omitted.]

* * *

Mr. Justice Stewart, concurring.

* * *

Today the Court ends the anomalous situation created by *Chrestensen* and holds that a communication which does no more than propose a commercial transaction is not "wholly outside the protection of the First Amendment." * * *. But since it is a cardinal principle of the First Amendment that "government has no power to restrict expression because of its message, its ideas, its subject matter, or its content," the Court's decision calls into immediate question the constitutional legitimacy of every state and federal law regulating false or deceptive advertising. I write separately to explain why I think today's decision does not preclude such governmental regulation.

* * *

The principles recognized in the libel decisions suggest that government may take broader action to protect the public from injury produced by false or deceptive price or product advertising than from harm caused by defamation. In contrast to the press, which must often attempt to assemble the true facts from sketchy and sometimes conflicting sources under the pressure of publication deadlines, the commercial advertiser generally knows the product or service he seeks to sell and is in a position to verify the accuracy of his factual representations before he disseminates them. The advertiser's access to the truth about his product and its price substantially eliminates any danger that governmental regulation of false or misleading price or product advertising will chill accurate and nondeceptive commercial expression. There is, therefore, little need to sanction "some falsehood in order to protect speech that matters." *Id.,* at 341.

* * *

The Court's determination that commercial advertising of the kind at issue here is not "wholly outside the protection of" the First Amendment indicates by its very phrasing that there are important differences between commercial price and product advertising, on the one hand, and ideological communication on the other. * * * Ideological expression, be it oral, literary, pictorial, or theatrical, is integrally related to the exposition of thought—thought that may shape our concepts of the whole universe of man. Although such expression may convey factual information relevant to social and individual decision-making, it is protected by the Constitution, whether or not it contains factual representations and even if it includes inaccurate assertions of fact. Indeed, disregard of the "truth" may be employed to give force to the underlying idea expressed by the speaker.[6] "Under the First

---

6. As the Court observed in Cantwell v. Connecticut, 310 U.S. 296, 310 (1940): "To persuade others to his own point of view, the pleader, as we know, at times, resorts to exaggeration, to vilification of men who have been, or are, prominent in church or state, and even to false statement. But the people of this nation have ordained in the light of history, that, in spite of the probability of excesses and

Amendment there is no such thing as a false idea," and the only way that ideas can be suppressed is through "the competition of other ideas," Gertz v. Robert Welch, Inc., 418 U.S., at 339–340.

Commercial price and product advertising differs markedly from ideological expression because it is confined to the promotion of specific goods or services. The First Amendment protects the advertisement because of the "information of potential interest and value" conveyed, Bigelow v. Virginia, 421 U.S. 809, 822 (1975), rather than because of any direct contribution to the interchange of ideas. * * *[8] Since the factual claims contained in commercial price or product advertisements relate to tangible goods or services, they may be tested empirically and corrected to reflect the truth without in any manner jeopardizing the free dissemination of thought. Indeed, the elimination of false and deceptive claims serves to promote the one facet of commercial price and product advertising that warrants First Amendment protection— its contribution to the flow of accurate and reliable information relevant to public and private decision-making.

MR. JUSTICE REHNQUIST, dissenting.

The logical consequences of the Court's decision in this case, a decision which elevates commercial intercourse between a seller hawking his wares and a buyer seeking to strike a bargain to the same plane as has been previously reserved for the free marketplace of ideas, are far reaching indeed. Under the Court's opinion the way will be open not only for dissemination of price information but for active promotion of prescription drugs, liquor, cigarettes, and other products the use of which it has previously been thought desirable to discourage. Now, however, such promotion is protected by the First Amendment so long as it is not misleading or does not promote an illegal product or enterprise. In coming to this conclusion, the Court has overruled a legislative determination that such advertising should not be allowed and has done so on behalf of a consumer group which is not directly disadvantaged by the statute in question. This effort to reach a result which the Court obviously considers desirable is a troublesome one, for two reasons. It extends standing to raise First Amendment claims beyond the previous decisions of this Court. It also extends the protection of that Amendment to purely commercial endeavors which its most vigorous champions on this Court had thought to be beyond its pale.

I

I do not find the question of the appellees' standing to urge the claim which the Court decides quite as easy as the Court does. The Court finds standing on the part of the consumer appellees based upon a "right to 'receive information.'" * * * Yet it has been stipulated in

---

abuses, these liberties are, in the long view, essential to enlightened opinion and right conduct on the part of the citizens of a democracy."

8. The information about price and product conveyed by commercial advertisements may, of course, stimulate thought and debate about political questions. The drug price information at issue in the present case might well have an impact, for instance, on a person's views concerning price control issues, government subsidy proposals, or special health care, consumer protection, or tax legislation.

this case that the challenged statute does not prohibit anyone from receiving this information either in person or by phone. * * * The statute forbids "only publish[ing], advertis[ing] or promot[ing]" prescription drugs.

While it may be generally true that publication of information by its source is essential to effective communication, it is surely less true, where, as here, the potential recipients of the information have, in the Court's own words, a "keen, if not keener by far," interest in it than "in the day's most urgent political debate." * * * Appellees who have felt so strongly about their right to receive information as to litigate the issue in this lawsuit must also have enough residual interest in the matter to call their pharmacy and inquire.

The statute, in addition, only forbids *pharmacists* to publish this price information. There is no prohibition against a consumer group, such as appellees, collecting and publishing comparative price information as to various pharmacies in an area. Indeed they have done as much in their briefs in this case. Yet, though appellees could both receive and publish the information in question the Court finds that they have standing to protest that pharmacists are not allowed to advertise. Thus, contrary to the assertion of the Court, appellees are not asserting their "right to receive information" at all but rather the right of some third party to publish. In the cases relied upon by the Court, * * *, the plaintiffs asserted their right to receive information which would not be otherwise reasonably available to them. They did not seek to assert the right of a third party, not before the Court, to disseminate information. Here, the only group truly restricted by this statute, the pharmacists, have not even troubled to join in this litigation and may well feel that the expense and competition of advertising is not in their interest.

II

Thus the issue on the merits is not, as the Court phrases it, whether "[o]ur pharmacist" may communicate the fact that he "will sell you the X prescription drug at the Y price." No pharmacist is asserting any such claim to so communicate. The issue is rather whether appellee consumers may override the legislative determination that pharmacists should not advertise even though the pharmacists themselves do not object. In deciding that they may do so, the Court necessarily adopts a rule which cannot be limited merely to dissemination of price alone, and which cannot possibly be confined to pharmacists but must likewise extend to lawyers, doctors, and all other professions.

The Court speaks of the consumer's interest in the free flow of commercial information, particularly in the case of the poor, the sick, and the aged. It goes on to observe that "society also may have a strong interest in the free flow of commercial information." * * * One need not disagree with either of these statements in order to feel that they should presumptively be the concern of the Virginia Legislature, which sits to balance these and other claims in the process of making laws such as the one here under attack. The Court speaks of the importance in a "predominantly free enterprise economy" of intelligent and well-informed decisions as to allocation of resources. * * * While there is again much to be said for the Court's observation as a matter of desirable public policy, there is certainly nothing in the United States Constitution which requires the Virginia Legislature to hew to the teachings of Adam Smith in its legislative decisions regulating the pharmacy profession. E.g., Nebbia v. New York, 291 U.S. 502 (1934); Olsen v. Nebraska, 313 U.S. 236 (1941).

As Mr. Justice Black, writing for the Court, observed in Ferguson v. Skrupa, 372 U.S. 726, 730 (1963):

> "The doctrine * * * that due process authorizes courts to hold laws unconstitutional when they believe the legislature has acted unwisely—has long since been discarded. We have returned to the original constitutional proposition that courts do not substitute their social and economic beliefs for the judgment of legislative bodies who are elected to pass laws."

Similarly in Williamson v. Lee Optical Co., 348 U.S. 483 (1955), the Court, in dealing with a state prohibition against the advertisement of eyeglass frames, held: "We see no constitutional reason why a State may not treat all who deal with the human eye as members of a profession who should use no merchandising methods for obtaining customers." *Id.*, at 490.

The Court addresses itself to the valid justifications which may be found for the Virginia statute, and apparently discounts them because it feels they embody a "highly paternalistic approach." * * * It concludes that the First Amendment requires that channels of advertising communication with respect to prescription drugs must be opened, and that Virginia may not keep "the public in ignorance of the entirely lawful terms that competing pharmacists are offering." *Ibid.*

The Court concedes that legislatures may prohibit false and misleading advertisements, and may likewise prohibit advertisements seeking to induce transactions which are themselves illegal. In a final footnote the opinion tosses a bone to the traditionalists in the legal and medical professions by suggesting that because they sell services rather than drugs the holding of this case is not automatically applicable to advertising in those professions. But if the sole limitation on permissible state proscription of advertising is that it may not be false or misleading, surely the difference between pharmacists' advertising and lawyers' and doctors' advertising can be only one of degree and not of kind. I cannot distinguish between the public's right to know the price of drugs and its right to know the price of title searches or physical examinations or other professional services for which standardized fees are charged. Nor is it apparent how the pharmacists in this case are less engaged in a regulatable profession than were the opticians in *Williamson, supra.*

* * *

There are undoubted difficulties with an effort to draw a bright line between "commercial speech" on the one hand and "protected speech" on the other, and the Court does better to face up to these difficulties than to attempt to hide them under labels. In this case, however, the Court has unfortunately substituted for the wavering line previously thought to exist between commercial speech and protected speech a no more satisfactory line of its own—that between "truthful" commercial speech, on the one hand, and that which is "false and misleading" on the other. The difficulty with this line is not that it wavers, but on the contrary that it is simply too Procrustean to take into account the congeries of factors which I believe could, quite consistently with the First and Fourteenth Amendments, properly influence a legislative decision with respect to commercial advertising.

The Court insists that the rule it lays down is consistent even with the view that the First Amendment is "primarily an instrument to enlighten public decisionmaking in a democracy." * * * I had understood this view to relate to public decisionmaking as to political, social, and other public issues, rather than the decision of a particular individual as to whether to purchase one or another kind of shampoo. It is undoubtedly arguable that many people in the country regard the choice of shampoo as just as important as who may be elected to local, state, or national political office, but that does not automatically bring information about competing shampoos within the protection of the First Amendment. It is one thing to say that the line between strictly ideological and political commentaries and other kinds of commentary is difficult to draw, and that the mere fact that the former may have in it an element of commercialism does not strip it of First Amendment protection. See New York Times Co. v. Sullivan, 376 U.S. 254 (1964). But it is another thing to say that because that line is difficult to draw, we will stand at the other end of the spectrum and reject out of hand the observation of so dedicated a champion of the First Amendment as Mr. Justice Black that the protections of that Amendment do not apply to a " 'merchant' who goes from door to door 'selling pots.' " Breard v. City of Alexandria, 341 U.S. 622, 650 (1951) (dissenting).

In the case of "our" hypothetical pharmacist, he may now presumably advertise not only the prices of prescription drugs, but may attempt to energetically promote their sale so long as he does so truthfully. Quite consistently with Virginia law requiring prescription drugs to be available only through a physician, "our" pharmacist might run any of the following representative advertisements in a local newspaper:

> "Pain getting you down? Insist that your physician prescribe Demerol. You pay a little more than for aspirin, but you get a lot more relief."
>
> "Can't shake the flu? Get a prescription for Tetracycline from your doctor today."
>
> "Don't spend another sleepless night. Ask your doctor to prescribe Seconal without delay."

Unless the State can show that these advertisements are either actually untruthful or misleading, it presumably is not free to restrict in any way commercial efforts on the part of those who profit from the sale of prescription drugs to put them in the widest possible circulation. But such a line simply makes no allowance whatever for what appears to have been a considered legislative judgment in most States that while prescription drugs are a necessary and vital part of medical care and treatment, there are sufficient dangers attending their widespread use that they simply may not be promoted in the same manner as hair creams, deodorants, and toothpaste. The very real dangers that general advertising for such drugs might create in terms of encouraging, even though not sanctioning, illicit use of them by individuals for whom they have not been prescribed, or by generating patient pressure upon physicians to prescribe them, are simply not dealt with in the Court's opinion. If prescription drugs may be advertised, they may be advertised on television during family viewing time. Nothing we know about the acquisitive instincts of those who inhabit every business and profession to a greater or lesser extent gives any reason to think that such persons will not do everything they can to generate demand for these products in much the same manner and to much the same degree as demand for other commodities has been generated.

Both Congress and state legislatures have by law sharply limited the permissible dissemination of information about some commodities because of the potential harm resulting from those commodities, even though they were not thought to be sufficiently demonstrably harmful to warrant outright prohibition of their sale. Current prohibitions on television advertising of liquor and cigarettes are prominent in this category, but apparently under the Court's holding so long as the advertisements are not deceptive they may no longer be prohibited.

* * *

ZAUDERER v. OFFICE OF DISCIPLINARY COUNSEL OF THE SUPREME COURT OF OHIO

Supreme Court of the United States, 1985.
471 U.S. 626, 105 S.Ct. 2265, 85 L.Ed.2d 652.

JUSTICE WHITE delivered the opinion of the Court.

* * *

I

Appellant is an attorney practicing in Columbus, Ohio. Late in 1981, he sought to augment his practice by advertising in local newspapers. His first effort was a modest one: he ran a small advertisement in the Columbus Citizen Journal advising its readers that his law firm would represent defendants in drunken driving cases and that his clients' "[f]ull legal fee [would be] refunded if [they were] convicted of DRUNK DRIVING." The advertisement appeared in the Journal for two days; on the second day, Charles Kettlewell, an attorney employed by the Office of Disciplinary Counsel of the Supreme Court of Ohio (appellee) telephoned appellant and informed him that the advertisement appeared to be an offer to represent criminal defendants on a contingent-fee basis, a practice prohibited by Disciplinary Rule 2–106(C) of the Ohio Code of Professional Responsibility. Appellant immediately withdrew the advertisement and in a letter to Kettlewell apologized for running it, also stating in the letter that he would decline to accept employment by persons responding to the ad.

Appellant's second effort was more ambitious. In the spring of 1982, appellant placed an advertisement in 36 Ohio newspapers publicizing his willingness to represent women who had suffered injuries resulting from their use of a contraceptive device known as the Dalkon Shield Intrauterine Device. The advertisement featured a line drawing of the Dalkon Shield accompanied by the question, "DID YOU USE THIS IUD?" The advertisement then related the following information:

> "The Dalkon Shield Interuterine [sic] Device is alleged to have caused serious pelvic infections resulting in hospitalizations, tubal damage, infertility, and hysterectomies. It is also alleged to have caused unplanned pregnancies ending in abortions, miscarriages, septic abortions, tubal or ectopic pregnancies, and full-term deliveries. If you or a friend have had a similar experience do not assume it is too late to take legal action against the Shield's manufacturer. Our law firm is presently representing women on such cases. The cases are handled on a contingent-fee basis of the amount recovered. If there is no recovery, no legal fees are owed by our clients."

The ad concluded with the name of appellant's law firm, its address, and a phone number that the reader might call for "free information."

The advertisement was successful in attracting clients: appellant received well over 200 inquiries regarding the advertisement, and he initiated lawsuits on behalf of 106 of the women who contacted him as a result of the advertisement. The ad, however, also aroused the interest of the Office of Disciplinary Counsel. On July 29, 1982, the Office filed a complaint against appellant charging him with a number of disciplinary violations arising out of both the drunken driving and Dalkon Shield advertisements.

The complaint, as subsequently amended, alleged that the drunken driving ad violated Ohio Disciplinary Rule 2–101(A) in that it was "false, fraudulent, misleading, and deceptive to the public" because it offered representation on a contingent-fee basis in a criminal case—an offer that could not be carried out under Disciplinary Rule 2–106(C). With respect to the Dalkon Shield advertisement, the complaint alleged that in running the ad and accepting employment by women responding to it, appellant had violated the following Disciplinary Rules: DR 2–101(B), which prohibits the use of illustrations in advertisements run by attorneys, requires that ads by attorneys be "dignified," and limits the information that may be included in such ads to a list of 20 items; DR 2–103(A), which prohibits an attorney from "recommend[ing] employment, as a private practitioner, of himself, his partner, or associate to a non-lawyer who has not sought his advice regarding employment of a lawyer"; and DR 2–104(A), which provides (with certain exceptions not applicable here) that "[a] lawyer who has given unsolicited advice to a layman that he should obtain counsel or take legal action shall not accept employment resulting from that advice."

The complaint also alleged that the advertisement violated DR 2–101(B)(15), which provides that any advertisement that mentions contingent-fee rates must "disclos[e] whether percentages are computed before or after deduction of court costs and expenses," and that the ad's failure to inform clients that they would be liable for costs (as opposed to legal fees) even if their claims were unsuccessful rendered the advertisement "deceptive" in violation of DR 2–101(A). The complaint did not allege that the Dalkon Shield advertisement was false or deceptive in any respect other than its omission of information relating to the contingent-fee arrangement; indeed, the Office of Disciplinary Counsel stipulated that the information and advice regarding Dalkon Shield litigation was not false, fraudulent, misleading, or deceptive and that the drawing was an accurate representation of the Dalkon Shield.

The charges against appellant were heard by a panel of the Board of Commissioners on Grievances and Discipline of the Supreme Court of Ohio. Appellant's primary defense to the charges against him was that Ohio's rules restricting the content of advertising by attorneys were unconstitutional under this Court's decisions in Bates v. State Bar of Arizona, 433 U.S. 350 (1977), and *In re* R.M.J., 455 U.S. 191 (1982). In support of his contention that the State had not provided justification for its rules sufficient to withstand the First Amendment scrutiny called for by those decisions, appellant proffered the testimony of expert witnesses that unfettered advertising by attorneys was economically beneficial and that appellant's advertising in particular was socially valuable in that it served to inform members of the public of their legal rights and of the potential health hazards associated with the Dalkon Shield. Appellant also put on the stand two of the women who had responded to his advertisements, both of whom testified that they would not have learned of their legal claims had it not been for appellant's advertisement.

The panel found that appellant's use of advertising had violated a number of Disciplinary Rules. The panel accepted the contention that the drunken driving advertisement was deceptive, but its reasoning differed from that of the Office of Disciplinary Counsel: the panel concluded that because the advertisement failed to mention the common practice of plea bargaining in drunken driving cases, it might be deceptive to potential clients who would be unaware of the likelihood that they would both be found guilty (of a lesser offense) and be liable for attorney's fees (because they had not been convicted of drunken driving). The panel also found that the use of an illustration in appellant's Dalkon Shield advertisement violated DR 2–101(B), that the ad's failure to disclose the client's potential liability for costs even if her suit were unsuccessful violated both DR 2–101(A) and DR 2–101(B)(15), that the advertisement constituted self-recommendation in violation of

DR 2–103(A), and that appellant's acceptance of offers of employment resulting from the advertisement violated DR 2–104(A).[5]

The panel rejected appellant's arguments that Ohio's regulations regarding the content of attorney advertising were unconstitutional as applied to him. The panel noted that neither *Bates* nor *In re R.M.J.* had forbidden all regulation of attorney advertising and that both of those cases had involved advertising regulations substantially more restrictive than Ohio's. The panel also relied heavily on Ohralik v. Ohio State Bar Assn., 436 U.S. 447 (1978), in which this Court upheld Ohio's imposition of discipline on an attorney who had engaged in in-person solicitation. The panel apparently concluded that the interests served by the application of Ohio's rules to advertising that contained legal advice and solicited clients to pursue a particular legal claim were as substantial as the interests at stake in *Ohralik*. Accordingly, the panel rejected appellant's constitutional defenses and recommended that he be publicly reprimanded for his violations. The Board of Commissioners adopted the panel's findings in full, but recommended the sanction of indefinite suspension from the practice of law rather than the more lenient punishment proposed by the panel.

The Supreme Court of Ohio, in turn, adopted the Board's findings that appellant's advertisements had violated the Disciplinary Rules specified by the hearing panel. * * * Having determined that appellant's advertisements violated Ohio's Disciplinary Rules and that the First Amendment did not forbid the application of those rules to appellant, the court concluded that appellant's conduct warranted a public reprimand.

Contending that Ohio's Disciplinary Rules violate the First Amendment insofar as they authorize the State to discipline him for the content of his Dalkon Shield advertisement, appellant filed this appeal. Appellant also claims that the manner in which he was disciplined for running his drunken driving advertisement violated his right to due process. We noted probable jurisdiction, 469 U.S. 813 (1984), and now affirm in part and reverse in part.

II

There is no longer any room to doubt that what has come to be known as "commercial speech" is entitled to the protection of the First Amendment, albeit to protection somewhat less extensive than that afforded "noncommercial speech." Bolger v. Youngs Drug Products Corp., 463 U.S. 60 (1983); *In re* R.M.J., 455 U.S. 191 (1982); Central Hudson Gas & Electric Corp. v. Public Service Comm'n of New York, 447 U.S. 557 (1980). More subject to doubt, perhaps, are the precise bounds of the category of expression that may be termed commercial speech, but it is clear enough that the speech at issue in this case—advertising pure and simple—falls within those bounds.

---

5. The panel did not find that the advertisement's alleged lack of "dignity" or its inclusion of information not allowed by DR 2–101(B)(1)–(20) constituted an independent violation.

Our general approach to restrictions on commercial speech is also by now well settled. The States and the Federal Government are free to prevent the dissemination of commercial speech that is false, deceptive, or misleading, see Friedman v. Rogers, 440 U.S. 1 (1979), or that proposes an illegal transaction, see Pittsburgh Press Co. v. Human Relations Comm'n, 413 U.S. 376 (1973). Commercial speech that is not false or deceptive and does not concern unlawful activities, however, may be restricted only in the service of a substantial governmental interest, and only through means that directly advance that interest. *Central Hudson Gas & Electric, supra,* at 566. Our application of these principles to the commercial speech of attorneys has led us to conclude that blanket bans on price advertising by attorneys and rules preventing attorneys from using nondeceptive terminology to describe their fields of practice are impermissible, see Bates v. State Bar of Arizona, 433 U.S. 350 (1977); *In re R.M.J., supra,* but that rules prohibiting in-person solicitation of clients by attorneys are, at least under some circumstances, permissible, see Ohralik v. Ohio State Bar Assn., 436 U.S. 447 (1978). To resolve this appeal, we must apply the teachings of these cases to three separate forms of regulation Ohio has imposed on advertising by its attorneys: prohibitions on soliciting legal business through advertisements containing advice and information regarding specific legal problems; restrictions on the use of illustrations in advertising by lawyers; and disclosure requirements relating to the terms of contingent fees.

III

* * *

The interest served by the application of the Ohio self-recommendation and solicitation rules to appellant's advertisement is not apparent from a reading of the opinions of the Ohio Supreme Court and its Board of Commissioners. The advertisement's information and advice concerning the Dalkon Shield were, as the Office of Disciplinary Counsel stipulated, neither false nor deceptive: in fact, they were entirely accurate. The advertisement did not promise readers that lawsuits alleging injuries caused by the Dalkon Shield would be successful, nor did it suggest that appellant had any special expertise in handling such lawsuits other than his employment in other such litigation. Rather, the advertisement reported the indisputable fact that the Dalkon Shield has spawned an impressive number of lawsuits [10] and advised readers that appellant was currently handling such lawsuits and was willing to represent other women asserting similar claims. In addition, the

---

10. By 1979, it was "estimated that 2500 claims [had] been made * * * for injuries allegedly caused by [the Dalkon Shield]." Van Dyke, The Dalkon Shield: A "Primer" in IUD Liability, 6 West.St.U. L.Rev. 1, 3, n. 7 (1978). By mid–1980, the number of lawsuits had risen to 4,000. Bamford, Dalkon Shield Starts Losing in Court, 2 American Lawyer 31 (July 1980). By the end of 1984 it was reported that the manufacturer had settled or satisfied judgments in 6,289 cases and that over 3,600 cases were still pending. See Robins Mounts Drive to Settle Dalkon Suits, National Law Journal, Dec. 24, 1984, p. 1, col. 3. Plaintiffs have succeeded in winning favorable settlements and jury verdicts against the Shield's manufacturer. See, e.g., Worsham v. A.H. Robins Co., 734 F.2d 676 (CA11 1984) (affirming jury verdict); Gardiner v. A.H. Robins Co., 747 F.2d 1180 (CA8 1984) (noting settlement of cases).

advertisement advised women that they should not assume that their claims were time-barred—advice that seems completely unobjectionable in light of the trend in many States toward a "discovery rule" for determining when a cause of action for latent injury or disease accrues. The State's power to prohibit advertising that is "inherently misleading," see *In re* R.M.J., 455 U.S., at 203, thus cannot justify Ohio's decision to discipline appellant for running advertising geared to persons with a specific legal problem.

Because appellant's statements regarding the Dalkon Shield were not false or deceptive, our decisions impose on the State the burden of establishing that prohibiting the use of such statements to solicit or obtain legal business directly advances a substantial governmental interest. * * * Our decision in *Ohralik* was largely grounded on the substantial differences between face-to-face solicitation and the advertising we had held permissible in *Bates*. In-person solicitation by a lawyer, we concluded, was a practice rife with possibilities for overreaching, invasion of privacy, the exercise of undue influence, and outright fraud. *Ohralik*, 436 U.S., at 464–465. In addition, we noted that in-person solicitation presents unique regulatory difficulties because it is "not visible or otherwise open to public scrutiny." * * *. These unique features of in-person solicitation by lawyers, we held, justified a prophylactic rule prohibiting lawyers from engaging in such solicitation for pecuniary gain, but we were careful to point out that "in-person solicitation of professional employment by a lawyer does not stand on a par with truthful advertising about the availability and terms of routine legal services." *Id.,* at 455.

It is apparent that the concerns that moved the Court in *Ohralik* are not present here. Although some sensitive souls may have found appellant's advertisement in poor taste, it can hardly be said to have invaded the privacy of those who read it. More significantly, appellant's advertisement—and print advertising generally—poses much less risk of overreaching or undue influence. Print advertising may convey information and ideas more or less effectively, but in most cases, it will lack the coercive force of the personal presence of a trained advocate. In addition, a printed advertisement, unlike a personal encounter initiated by an attorney, is not likely to involve pressure on the potential client for an immediate yes-or-no answer to the offer of representation. Thus, a printed advertisement is a means of conveying information about legal services that is more conducive to reflection and the exercise of choice on the part of the consumer than is personal solicitation by an attorney. Accordingly, the substantial interests that justified the ban on in-person solicitation upheld in *Ohralik* cannot justify the discipline imposed on appellant for the content of his advertisement.

Nor does the traditional justification for restraints on solicitation—the fear that lawyers will "stir up litigation"—justify the restriction imposed in this case. In evaluating this proffered justification, it is important to think about what it might mean to say that the State has an interest in preventing lawyers from stirring up litigation. It is possible to describe litigation itself as an evil that the State is entitled to combat: after all, litigation consumes vast quantities of social resources to produce little of tangible value but much discord and unpleasantness. "[A]s a litigant," Judge Learned Hand once observed, "I should dread a lawsuit beyond almost anything else short of sickness and death." L. Hand, The Deficiencies of Trials to Reach the Heart of the Matter, in 3 Association of the Bar of the City of New York, Lectures on Legal Topics 89, 105 (1926).

But we cannot endorse the proposition that a lawsuit, as such, is an evil. Over the course of centuries, our society has settled upon civil litigation as a means for redressing grievances, resolving disputes, and vindicating rights when other means fail. There is no cause for consternation when a person who believes in good faith and on the basis of accurate information regarding his legal rights that he has suffered a legally cognizable injury turns to the courts for a remedy: "We cannot accept the notion that it is always better for a person to suffer a wrong silently than to redress it by legal action." Bates v. State Bar of Arizona, 433 U.S., at 376. That our citizens have access to their civil courts is not an evil to be regretted; rather, it is an attribute of our system of justice in which we ought to take pride. The State is not entitled to interfere with that access by denying its citizens accurate information about their legal rights. Accordingly, it is not sufficient justification for the discipline imposed on appellant that his truthful and nondeceptive advertising had a tendency to or did in fact encourage others to file lawsuits.

* * *

The State's argument proceeds from the premise that it is intrinsically difficult to distinguish advertisements containing legal advice that is false or deceptive from those that are truthful and helpful, much more so than is the case with other goods or services.[12] This notion is belied by the facts before us: appellant's statements regarding Dalkon Shield litigation were in fact easily verifiable and completely accurate. Nor is it true that distinguishing deceptive from nondeceptive claims in advertising involving products other than legal services is a comparatively simple and straightforward process. * * *

* * * The First Amendment protections afforded commercial speech would mean little indeed if such arguments were allowed to

---

12. The State's argument may also rest in part on a suggestion that even completely accurate advice regarding the legal rights of the advertiser's audience may lead some members of the audience to initiate meritless litigation against innocent defendants. To the extent that this is the State's contention, it is unavailing. To be sure, some citizens, accurately informed of their legal rights, may file lawsuits that ultimately turn out not to be meritorious. But the State is not entitled to prejudge the merits of its citizens' claims by choking off access to information that may be useful to its citizens in deciding whether to press those claims in court. As we observed in Bates v. State Bar of Arizona, 433 U.S., at 375, n. 31, if the State's concern is with abuse of process, it can best achieve its aim by enforcing sanctions against vexatious litigation. In addition, there would be no impediment to a rule forbidding attorneys to use advertisements soliciting clients for nuisance suits—meritless claims filed solely to harass a defendant or coerce a settlement. Because a client has no legal right to file such a claim knowingly, advertisements designed to stir up such litigation may be forbidden because they propose an "illegal transaction." See Pittsburgh Press Co. v. Human Relations Comm'n, 413 U.S. 376 (1973).

prevail. Our recent decisions involving commercial speech have been grounded in the faith that the free flow of commercial information is valuable enough to justify imposing on would-be regulators the costs of distinguishing the truthful from the false, the helpful from the misleading, and the harmless from the harmful. The value of the information presented in appellant's advertising is no less than that contained in other forms of advertising—indeed, insofar as appellant's advertising tended to acquaint persons with their legal rights who might otherwise be shut off from effective access to the legal system, it was undoubtedly more valuable than many other forms of advertising. * * * An attorney may not be disciplined for soliciting legal business through printed advertising containing truthful and nondeceptive information and advice regarding the legal rights of potential clients.

IV

The application of DR 2–101(B)'s restriction on illustrations in advertising by lawyers to appellant's advertisement fails for much the same reasons as does the application of the self-recommendation and solicitation rules. The use of illustrations or pictures in advertisements serves important communicative functions: it attracts the attention of the audience to the advertiser's message, and it may also serve to impart information directly. Accordingly, commercial illustrations are entitled to the First Amendment protections afforded verbal commercial speech: restrictions on the use of visual media of expression in advertising must survive scrutiny under the *Central Hudson* test. Because the illustration for which appellant was disciplined is an accurate representation of the Dalkon Shield and has no features that are likely to deceive, mislead, or confuse the reader, the burden is on the State to present a substantial governmental interest justifying the restriction as applied to appellant and to demonstrate that the restriction vindicates that interest through the least restrictive available means.

* * *

* * * Given the possibility of policing the use of illustrations in advertisements on a case-by-case basis, the prophylactic approach taken by Ohio cannot stand; hence, appellant may not be disciplined for his use of an accurate and nondeceptive illustration.

V

Appellant contends that assessing the validity of the Ohio Supreme Court's decision to discipline him for his failure to include in the Dalkon Shield advertisement the information that clients might be liable for significant litigation costs even if their lawsuits were unsuccessful entails precisely the same inquiry as determining the validity of the restrictions on advertising content discussed above. * * *

Appellant, however, overlooks material differences between disclosure requirements and outright prohibitions on speech. In requiring attorneys who advertise their willingness to represent clients on a contingent-fee basis to state that the client may have to bear certain expenses even if he loses, Ohio has not attempted to prevent attorneys from conveying information to the public; it has only required them to provide somewhat more information than they might otherwise be inclined to present. We have, to be sure, held that in some instances compulsion to speak may be as violative of the First Amendment as prohibitions on speech. See, e.g., Wooley v. Maynard, 430 U.S. 705 (1977); Miami Herald Publishing Co. v. Tornillo, 418 U.S. 241 (1974). Indeed, in West Virginia State Bd. of Ed. v. Barnette, 319 U.S. 624 (1943), the Court went so far as to state that "involuntary affirmation could be commanded only on even more immediate and urgent grounds than silence." *Id.*, at 633.

But the interests at stake in this case are not of the same order as those discussed in *Wooley, Tornillo,* and *Barnette.* Ohio has not attempted to "prescribe what shall be orthodox in politics, nationalism, religion, or other matters of opinion or force citizens to confess by word or act their faith therein." 319 U.S., at 642. The State has attempted only to prescribe what shall be orthodox in commercial advertising, and its prescription has taken the form of a requirement that appellant include in his advertising purely factual and uncontroversial information about the terms under which his services will be available. Because the extension of First Amendment protection to commercial speech is justified principally by the value to consumers of the information such speech provides, see Virginia Pharmacy Board v. Virginia Citizens Consumer Council, Inc., 425 U.S. 748 (1976), appellant's constitutionally protected interest in not providing any particular factual information in his advertising is minimal. Thus, in virtually all our commercial speech decisions to date, we have emphasized that because disclosure requirements trench much more narrowly on an advertiser's interests than do flat prohibitions on speech, "warning[s] or disclaimer[s] might be appropriately required * * * in order to dissipate the possibility of consumer confusion or deception." *In re* R.M.J., 455 U.S., at 201. Accord, *Central Hudson Gas & Electric,* 447 U.S., at 565; *Bates v. State Bar of Arizona,* 433 U.S., at 384; *Virginia Pharmacy Bd., supra,* at 772, n. 24.

We do not suggest that disclosure requirements do not implicate the advertiser's First Amendment rights at all. We recognize that unjustified or unduly burdensome disclosure requirements might offend the First Amendment by chilling protected commercial speech. But we hold that an advertiser's rights are adequately protected as long as disclosure requirements are reasonably related to the State's interest in preventing deception of consumers.[14]

* * * The State's position that it is deceptive to employ advertising that refers to contingent-fee arrangements without mentioning the

---

14. We reject appellant's contention that we should subject disclosure requirements to a strict "least restrictive means" analysis under which they must be struck down if there are other means by which the State's purposes may be served. Although we have subjected outright prohibitions on speech to such analysis, all our discussions of restraints on commercial speech have recommended disclosure requirements as one of the acceptable less restrictive alternatives to actual suppression of speech.

client's liability for costs is reasonable enough to support a requirement that information regarding the client's liability for costs be disclosed.

* * *

The Supreme Court of Ohio issued a public reprimand incorporating by reference its opinion finding that appellant had violated Disciplinary Rules 2–101(A), 2–101(B), 2–101(B)(15), 2–103(A), and 2–104(A). That judgment is affirmed to the extent that it is based on appellant's advertisement involving his terms of representation in drunken driving cases and on the omission of information regarding his contingent-fee arrangements in his Dalkon Shield advertisement. But insofar as the reprimand was based on appellant's use of an illustration in his advertisement in violation of DR 2–101(B) and his offer of legal advice in his advertisement in violation of DR 2–103(A) and 2–104(A), the judgment is reversed.

It is so ordered.

JUSTICE POWELL took no part in the decision of this case.

JUSTICE BRENNAN, with whom JUSTICE MARSHALL joins, concurring in part, concurring in the judgment in part, and dissenting in part. [Omitted.]

* * *

JUSTICE O'CONNOR, with whom THE CHIEF JUSTICE and JUSTICE REHNQUIST join, concurring in part, concurring in the judgment in part, and dissenting in part.

* * * I dissent from Part III of the Court's opinion. In my view, the use of unsolicited legal advice to entice clients poses enough of a risk of overreaching and undue influence to warrant Ohio's rule.

* * *

The issue posed and decided in Part III of the Court's opinion is whether such a rule can be applied to punish the use of legal advice in a printed advertisement soliciting business. The majority's conclusion is a narrow one: "An attorney may not be disciplined for soliciting legal business through printed advertising containing truthful and nondeceptive * * * advice regarding the legal rights of potential clients." * * *

* * *

In my view, a State could reasonably determine that the use of unsolicited legal advice "as bait with which to obtain agreement to represent [a client] for a fee," *Ohralik*, 436 U.S., at 458, poses a sufficient threat to substantial state interests to justify a blanket prohibition. As the Court recognized in *Ohralik*, the State has a significant interest in preventing attorneys from using their professional expertise to overpower the will and judgment of laypeople who have not sought their advice. While it is true that a printed advertisement presents a lesser risk of overreaching than a personal encounter, the former is only one step removed from the latter. When legal advice is employed within an advertisement, the layperson may well conclude there is no means to judge its validity or applicability short of consulting the lawyer who placed the advertisement. This is particularly true where, as in appellant's Dalkon Shield advertisement, the legal advice is phrased in uncertain terms. A potential client who read the advertisement would probably be unable to determine whether "it is too late to take legal action against the * * * manufacturer" without directly consulting the appellant. And at the time of that consultation, the same risks of undue influence, fraud, and overreaching that were noted in *Ohralik* are present.

The State also has a substantial interest in requiring that lawyers consistently exercise independent professional judgment on behalf of their clients. Given the exigencies of the marketplace, a rule permitting the use of legal advice in advertisements will encourage lawyers to present that advice most likely to bring potential clients into the office, rather than that advice which it is most in the interest of potential clients to hear. In a recent case in New York, for example, an attorney wrote unsolicited letters to victims of a massive disaster advising them that, in his professional opinion, the liability of the potential defendants is clear. * * * Of course, under the Court's opinion claims like this might be reached by branding the advice misleading or by promulgating a state rule requiring extensive disclosure of all relevant liability rules whenever such a claim is advanced. But even if such a claim were completely accurate—even if liability were in fact clear and the attorney actually thought it to be so—I believe the State could reasonably decide that a professional should not accept employment resulting from such unsolicited advice. See *Ohralik, supra,* at 461 (noting that DR 2–104(A) serves "to avoid situations where the lawyer's exercise of judgment on behalf of the client will be clouded by his own pecuniary self-interest"). Ohio and other States afford attorneys ample opportunities to inform members of the public of their legal rights. See, e.g., Ohio DR 2–104(A)(4) (permitting attorneys to speak and write publicly on legal topics as long as they do not emphasize their own experience or reputation). Given the availability of alternative means to inform the public of legal rights, Ohio's rule against legal advice in advertisements is an appropriate means to assure the exercise of independent professional judgment by attorneys. A State might rightfully take pride that its citizens have access to its civil courts, * * *, while at the same time opposing the use of self-interested legal advice to solicit clients. In the face of these substantial and legitimate state concerns, I cannot agree with the majority that Ohio DR 2–104(A) is unnecessary to the achievement of those interests. The Ohio rule may sweep in some advertisements containing helpful legal advice within its general prohibition. Nevertheless, I am not prepared to second-guess Ohio's longstanding and careful balancing of legitimate state interests merely because appellant here can invent a less restrictive rule. As the Iowa Supreme Court recently observed, "[t]he professional disciplinary system would be in chaos if violations could be defended on the ground the lawyer involved could think of a better rule." Committee on Professional Ethics and Conduct of Ohio State Bar Assn. v. Humphrey, 355 N.W.2d 565, 569 (1984), cert. pending, No. 84–1150. Because I would defer to the judgment of the States that have chosen to preclude use of unsolicited legal advice to entice clients, I respectfully dissent from Part III of the Court's opinion.

CENTRAL HUDSON GAS & ELECTRIC CORPORATION v. PUBLIC SERVICE COMMISSION OF NEW YORK

Supreme Court of the United States, 1980.
447 U.S. 557, 100 S.Ct. 2343, 65 L.Ed.2d 341.

MR. JUSTICE POWELL delivered the opinion of the Court.

This case presents the question whether a regulation of the Public Service Commission of the State of New York violates the First and Fourteenth Amendments because it completely bans promotional advertising by an electrical utility.

I

In December 1973, the Commission, appellee here, ordered electric utilities in New York State to cease all advertising that "promot[es] the use of electricity." * * * The order was based on the Commission's finding that "the interconnected utility system in New York State does not have sufficient fuel stocks or sources of supply to continue furnishing all customer demands for the 1973–1974 winter." * * *

Three years later, when the fuel shortage had eased, the Commission requested comments from the public on its proposal to continue the ban on promotional advertising. Central Hudson Gas & Electric Corp., the appellant in this case, opposed the ban on First Amendment grounds. * * * After reviewing the public comments, the Commission extended the prohibition in a Policy Statement issued on February 25, 1977.

The Policy Statement divided advertising expenses "into two broad categories: promotional—advertising intended to stimulate the purchase of utility services—and institutional and informational, a broad category inclusive of all advertising not clearly intended to promote sales." * * * The Commission declared all promotional advertising contrary to the national policy of conserving energy. It acknowledged that the ban is not a perfect vehicle for conserving energy. For example, the Commission's order prohibits promotional advertising to develop consumption during periods when demand for electricity is low. By limiting growth in "off-peak" consumption, the ban limits the "beneficial side effects" of such growth in terms of more efficient use of existing powerplants. * * * And since oil dealers are not under the Commission's jurisdiction and thus remain free to advertise, it was recognized that the ban can achieve only "piecemeal conservationism." Still, the Commission adopted the restriction because it was deemed likely to "result in some dampening of unnecessary growth" in energy consumption. * * *

The Commission's order explicitly permitted "informational" advertising designed to encourage "shifts of consumption" from peak demand times to periods of low electricity demand. * * * Informational advertising would not seek to increase aggregate consumption, but would invite a leveling of demand throughout any given 24-hour period. The agency offered to review "specific proposals by the companies for specifically described [advertising] programs that meet these criteria." * * *

* * *

Appellant challenged the order in state court, arguing that the Commission had restrained commercial speech in violation of the First and Fourteenth Amendments. The Commission's order was upheld by the trial court and at the intermediate appellate level. The New York Court of Appeals affirmed. * * * We noted probable jurisdiction, 444 U.S. 962 (1979), and now reverse.

II

The Commission's order restricts only commercial speech, that is, expression related solely to the economic interests of the speaker and its audience. Virginia Pharmacy Board v. Virginia Citizens Consumer Council, 425 U.S. 748, 762 (1976); Bates v. State Bar of Arizona, 433 U.S. 350, 363–364 (1977); Friedman v. Rogers, 440 U.S. 1, 11 (1979). The First Amendment, as applied to the States through the Fourteenth Amendment, protects commercial speech from unwarranted governmental regulation. *Virginia Pharmacy Board,* 425 U.S., at 761–762. Commercial expression not only serves the economic interest of the speaker, but also assists consumers and furthers the societal interest in the fullest possible dissemination of information. In applying the First Amendment to this area, we have rejected the "highly paternalistic" view that government has complete power to suppress or regulate commercial speech. "[P]eople will perceive their own best interests if only they are well enough informed, and * * * the best means to that end is to open the channels of communication, rather than to close them. * * *" *Id.,* at 770; see Linmark Associates, Inc. v. Willingboro, 431 U.S. 85, 92 (1977). Even when advertising communicates only an incomplete version of the relevant facts, the First Amendment presumes that some accurate information is better than no information at all. *Bates v. State Bar of Arizona, supra,* at 374.

Nevertheless, our decisions have recognized "the 'commonsense' distinction between speech proposing a commercial transaction, which occurs in an area traditionally subject to government regulation, and other varieties of speech."[5] The Constitution therefore accords a lesser

---

5. In an opinion concurring in the judgment, Mr. Justice Stevens suggests that the Commission's order reaches beyond commercial speech to suppress expression that is entitled to the full protection of the First Amendment. * * * We find no support for this claim in the record of this case. The Commission's Policy Statement excluded "institutional and informational" messages from the advertising ban, which was restricted to all advertising "clearly intended to promote sales." * * * Nevertheless, the concurring opinion of Mr. Justice Stevens views the Commission's order as suppressing more than commercial speech because it would outlaw, for example, advertising that promoted electricity consumption by touting the environmental benefits of such uses. * * * Apparently the opinion would accord full First Amendment protection to all promotional advertising that includes claims "relating to . . .

protection to commercial speech than to other constitutionally guaranteed expression. 436 U.S., at 456, 457. The protection available for particular commercial expression turns on the nature both of the expression and of the governmental interests served by its regulation.

The First Amendment's concern for commercial speech is based on the informational function of advertising. See *First National Bank of Boston v. Bellotti*, 435 U.S. 765, 783 (1978). Consequently, there can be no constitutional objection to the suppression of commercial messages that do not accurately inform the public about lawful activity. The government may ban forms of communication more likely to deceive the public than to inform it. *Friedman v. Rogers, supra,* at 13, 15–16; *Ohralik v. Ohio State Bar Assn., supra,* at 464–465, or commercial speech related to illegal activity, *Pittsburgh Press Co. v. Human Relations Comm'n,* 413 U.S. 376, 388 (1973).

If the communication is neither misleading nor related to unlawful activity, the government's power is more circumscribed. The State must assert a substantial interest to be achieved by restrictions on commercial speech. Moreover, the regulatory technique must be in proportion to that interest. The limitation on expression must be designed carefully to achieve the State's goal. Compliance with this requirement may be measured by two criteria. First, the restriction must directly advance the state interest involved; the regulation may not be sustained if it provides only ineffective or remote support for the government's purpose. Second, if the governmental interest could be served as well by a more limited restriction on commercial speech, the excessive restrictions cannot survive.

Under the first criterion, the Court has declined to uphold regulations that only indirectly advance the state interest involved. In both *Bates* and *Virginia Pharmacy Board,* the Court concluded that an advertising ban could not be imposed to protect the ethical or performance standards of a profession. The Court noted in *Virginia Pharmacy Board* that "[t]he advertising ban does not directly affect professional standards one way or the other." * * *

The second criterion recognizes that the First Amendment mandates that speech restrictions be "narrowly drawn." *In re* Primus, 436 U.S. 412, 438 (1978).[8] The regulatory technique may extend only as far

questions frequently discussed and debated by our political leaders." * * *

Although this approach responds to the serious issues surrounding our national energy policy as raised in this case, we think it would blur further the line the Court has sought to draw in commercial speech cases. It would grant broad constitutional protection to any advertising that links a product to a current public debate. But many, if not most, products may be tied to public concerns with the environment, energy, economic policy, or individual health and safety. We rule today in *Consolidated Edison Co. v. Public Service Comm'n,* * * *, that utilities enjoy the full panoply of First Amendment protections for their direct comments on public issues. There is no reason for providing similar constitutional protection when such statements are made only in the context of commercial transactions. * * *

8. This analysis is not an application of the "overbreadth" doctrine. The latter theory permits the invalidation of regulations on First Amendment grounds even when the litigant challenging the regulation has engaged in no constitutionally protected activity. *E.g.,* Kunz v. New York, 340 U.S. 290 (1951). The overbreadth doctrine derives from the recognition that unconstitutional restriction of expression

as the interest it serves. The State cannot regulate speech that poses no danger to the asserted state interest, see *First National Bank of Boston v. Bellotti, supra,* at 794–795, nor can it completely suppress information when narrower restrictions on expression would serve its interest as well. For example, in *Bates* the Court explicitly did not "foreclose the possibility that some limited supplementation, by way of warning or disclaimer or the like, might be required" in promotional materials. 433 U.S., at 384. See *Virginia Pharmacy Board, supra,* at 773. And in Carey v. Population Services International, 431 U.S. 678, 701–702 (1977), we held that the State's "arguments * * * do not justify the total suppression of advertising concerning contraceptives." This holding left open the possibility that the State could implement more carefully drawn restrictions. See *id.,* at 712 (POWELL, J., concurring in part and in judgment); *id.,* at 716–717 (STEVENS, J., concurring in part and in judgment).[9]

In commercial speech cases, then, a four-part analysis has developed. At the outset, we must determine whether the expression is protected by the First Amendment. For commercial speech to come within that provision, it at least must concern lawful activity and not be misleading. Next, we ask whether the asserted governmental interest is substantial. If both inquiries yield positive answers, we must determine whether the regulation directly advances the governmental interest asserted, and whether it is not more extensive than is necessary to serve that interest.

III

We now apply this four-step analysis for commercial speech to the Commission's arguments in support of its ban on promotional advertising.

A

The Commission does not claim that the expression at issue either is inaccurate or relates to unlawful activity. Yet the New York Court of Appeals questioned whether Central Hudson's advertising is protected commercial speech. Because appellant holds a monopoly over the sale of electricity in its service area, the state court suggested that the Commission's order restricts no commercial speech of any worth. The

---

may deter protected speech by parties not before the court and thereby escape judicial review. Broadrick v. Oklahoma, 413 U.S. 601, 612–613 (1973); see Note, The First Amendment Overbreadth Doctrine, 83 Harv.L.Rev. 844, 853–858 (1970). This restraint is less likely where the expression is linked to "commercial well-being" and therefore is not easily deterred by "overbroad regulation." *Bates v. State Bar of Arizona, supra,* at 381.

In this case, the Commission's prohibition acts directly against the promotional activities of Central Hudson, and to the extent the limitations are unnecessary to serve the State's interest, they are invalid.

9. We review with special care regulations that entirely suppress commercial speech in order to pursue a nonspeech-related policy. In those circumstances, a ban on speech could screen from public view the underlying governmental policy. See *Virginia Pharmacy Board,* 425 U.S., at 780, n. 8 (STEWART, J., concurring). Indeed, in recent years this Court has not approved a blanket ban on commercial speech unless the expression itself was flawed in some way, either because it was deceptive or related to unlawful activity.

court stated that advertising in a "noncompetitive market" could not improve the decisionmaking of consumers. 47 N.Y.2d, at 110, 390 N.E.2d, at 757. The court saw no constitutional problem with barring commercial speech that it viewed as conveying little useful information.

This reasoning falls short of establishing that appellant's advertising is not commercial speech protected by the First Amendment. Monopoly over the supply of a product provides no protection from competition with substitutes for that product. Electric utilities compete with suppliers of fuel oil and natural gas in several markets, such as those for home heating and industrial power. * * * For consumers in those competitive markets, advertising by utilities is just as valuable as advertising by unregulated firms.

Even in monopoly markets, the suppression of advertising reduces the information available for consumer decisions and thereby defeats the purpose of the First Amendment. The New York court's argument appears to assume that the providers of a monopoly service or product are willing to pay for wholly ineffective advertising. Most businesses—even regulated monopolies—are unlikely to underwrite promotional advertising that is of no interest or use to consumers. Indeed, a monopoly enterprise legitimately may wish to inform the public that it has developed new services or terms of doing business. A consumer may need information to aid his decision whether or not to use the monopoly service at all, or how much of the service he should purchase. In the absence of factors that would distort the decision to advertise, we may assume that the willingness of a business to promote its products reflects a belief that consumers are interested in the advertising.[11] Since no such extraordinary conditions have been identified in this case, appellant's monopoly position does not alter the First Amendment's protection for its commercial speech.

B

The Commission offers two state interests as justifications for the ban on promotional advertising. The first concerns energy conservation. Any increase in demand for electricity—during peak or off-peak periods—means greater consumption of energy. The Commission argues, and the New York court agreed, that the State's interest in conserving energy is sufficient to support suppression of advertising designed to increase consumption of electricity. In view of our country's dependence on energy resources beyond our control, no one can doubt the importance of energy conservation. Plainly, therefore, the state interest asserted is substantial.

The Commission also argues that promotional advertising will aggravate inequities caused by the failure to base the utilities' rates on marginal cost. The utilities argued to the Commission that if they

---

11. There may be a greater incentive for a utility to advertise if it can use promotional expenses in determining its rate of return, rather than pass those costs on solely to shareholders. That practice, however, hardly distorts the economic decision whether to advertise. Unregulated businesses pass on promotional costs to consumers, and this Court expressly approved the practice for utilities in West Ohio Gas Co. v. Public Utilities Comm'n, 294 U.S. 63, 72 (1935).

could promote the use of electricity in periods of low demand, they would improve their utilization of generating capacity. The Commission responded that promotion of off-peak consumption also would increase consumption during peak periods. If peak demand were to rise, the absence of marginal cost rates would mean that the rates charged for the additional power would not reflect the true costs of expanding production. Instead, the extra costs would be borne by all consumers through higher overall rates. Without promotional advertising, the Commission stated, this inequitable turn of events would be less likely to occur. The choice among rate structures involves difficult and important questions of economic supply and distributional fairness. The State's concern that rates be fair and efficient represents a clear and substantial governmental interest.

C

Next, we focus on the relationship between the State's interests and the advertising ban. Under this criterion, the Commission's laudable concern over the equity and efficiency of appellant's rates does not provide a constitutionally adequate reason for restricting protected speech. The link between the advertising prohibition and appellant's rate structure is, at most, tenuous. The impact of promotional advertising on the equity of appellant's rates is highly speculative. Advertising to increase off-peak usage would have to increase peak usage, while other factors that directly affect the fairness and efficiency of appellant's rates remained constant. Such conditional and remote eventualities simply cannot justify silencing appellant's promotional advertising.

In contrast, the State's interest in energy conservation is directly advanced by the Commission order at issue here. There is an immediate connection between advertising and demand for electricity. Central Hudson would not contest the advertising ban unless it believed that promotion would increase its sales. Thus, we find a direct link between the state interest in conservation and the Commission's order.

D

We come finally to the critical inquiry in this case: whether the Commission's complete suppression of speech ordinarily protected by the First Amendment is no more extensive than necessary to further the State's interest in energy conservation. The Commission's order reaches all promotional advertising, regardless of the impact of the touted service on overall energy use. But the energy conservation rationale, as important as it is, cannot justify suppressing information about electric devices or services that would cause no net increase in total energy use. In addition, no showing has been made that a more limited restriction on the content of promotional advertising would not serve adequately the State's interests.

Appellant insists that but for the ban, it would advertise products and services that use energy efficiently. These include the "heat pump," which both parties acknowledge to be a major improvement in electric heating, and the use of electric heat as a "backup" to solar and other heat sources. Although the Commission has questioned the efficiency of electric heating before this Court, neither the Commission's Policy Statement nor its order denying rehearing made findings on this issue. In the absence of authoritative findings to the contrary, we must credit as within the realm of possibility the claim that electric heat can be an efficient alternative in some circumstances.

The Commission's order prevents appellant from promoting electric services that would reduce energy use by diverting demand from less efficient sources, or that would consume roughly the same amount of energy as do alternative sources. In neither situation would the utility's advertising endanger conservation or mislead the public. To the extent that the Commission's order suppresses speech that in no way impairs the State's interest in energy conservation, the Commission's order violates the First and Fourteenth Amendments and must be invalidated. * * *

The Commission also has not demonstrated that its interest in conservation cannot be protected adequately by more limited regulation of appellant's commercial expression. To further its policy of conservation, the Commission could attempt to restrict the format and content of Central Hudson's advertising. It might, for example, require that the advertisements include information about the relative efficiency and expense of the offered service, both under current conditions and for the foreseeable future.[13] * * *

IV

Our decision today in no way disparages the national interest in energy conservation. We accept without reservation the argument that conservation, as well as the development of alternative energy sources, is an imperative national goal. Administrative bodies empowered to regulate electric utilities have the authority—and indeed the duty—to take appropriate action to further this goal. When, however, such action involves the suppression of speech, the First and Fourteenth Amendments require that the restriction be no more extensive than is necessary to serve the state interest. In this case, the record before us fails to show that the total ban on promotional advertising meets this requirement.

Accordingly, the judgment of the New York Court of Appeals is

Reversed.

MR. JUSTICE BRENNAN, concurring in the judgment.

One of the major difficulties in this case is the proper characterization of the Commission's Policy Statement. I find it impossible to

---

13. The Commission also might consider a system of previewing advertising campaigns to insure that they will not defeat conservation policy. It has instituted such a program for approving "informational" advertising under the Policy Statement challenged in this case. * * * We have observed that commercial speech is such a sturdy brand of expression that traditional prior restraint doctrine may not apply to it. Virginia Pharmacy Board v. Virginia Citizens Consumer Council, 425 U.S., at 771–772, n. 24. And in other areas of speech regulation, such as obscenity, we have recognized that a prescreening arrangement can pass constitutional muster if it includes adequate procedural safeguards. Freedman v. Maryland, 380 U.S. 51 (1965).

determine on the present record whether the Commission's ban on all "promotional" advertising, in contrast to "institutional and informational" advertising, * * *, is intended to encompass more than "commercial speech." I am inclined to think that Mr. Justice Stevens is correct that the Commission's order prohibits more than mere proposals to engage in certain kinds of commercial transactions, and therefore I agree with his conclusion that the ban surely violates the First and Fourteenth Amendments. But even on the assumption that the Court is correct that the Commission's order reaches only commercial speech, I agree with Mr. Justice Blackmun that "[n]o differences between commercial speech and other protected speech justify suppression of commercial speech in order to influence public conduct through manipulation of the availability of information." * * *

Accordingly, with the qualifications implicit in the preceding paragraph, I join the opinions of MR. JUSTICE BLACKMUN and MR. JUSTICE STEVENS concurring in the judgment.

MR. JUSTICE BLACKMUN, with whom MR. JUSTICE BRENNAN joins, concurring in the judgment.

I agree with the Court that the Public Service Commission's ban on promotional advertising of electricity by public utilities is inconsistent with the First and Fourteenth Amendments. I concur only in the Court's judgment, however, because I believe the test now evolved and applied by the Court is not consistent with our prior cases and does not provide adequate protection for truthful, nonmisleading, noncoercive commercial speech.

* * * I agree with the Court that this level of intermediate scrutiny is appropriate for a restraint on commercial speech designed to protect consumers from misleading or coercive speech, or a regulation related to the time, place, or manner of commercial speech. I do not agree, however, that the Court's four-part test is the proper one to be applied when a State seeks to suppress information about a product in order to manipulate a private economic decision that the State cannot or has not regulated or outlawed directly.

Since the Court, without citing empirical data or other authority, finds a "direct link" between advertising and energy consumption, it leaves open the possibility that the State may suppress advertising of electricity in order to lessen demand for electricity. I, of course, agree with the Court that, in today's world, energy conservation is a goal of paramount national and local importance. I disagree with the Court, however, when it says that suppression of speech may be a permissible means to achieve that goal. Mr. Justice Stevens appropriately notes: "The justification for the regulation is nothing more than the expressed fear that the audience may find the utility's message persuasive. Without the aid of any coercion, deception, or misinformation, truthful communication may persuade some citizens to consume more electricity than they otherwise would." * * *

The Court recognizes that we have never held that commercial speech may be suppressed in order to further the State's interest in discouraging purchases of the underlying product that is advertised.

* * * Permissible restraints on commercial speech have been limited to measures designed to protect consumers from fraudulent, misleading, or coercive sales techniques. Those designed to deprive consumers of information about products or services that are legally offered for sale consistently have been invalidated.

I seriously doubt whether suppression of information concerning the availability and price of a legally offered product is ever a permissible way for the State to "dampen" demand for or use of the product. Even though "commercial" speech is involved, such a regulatory measure strikes at the heart of the First Amendment. This is because it is a covert attempt by the State to manipulate the choices of its citizens, not by persuasion or direct regulation, but by depriving the public of the information needed to make a free choice. As the Court recognizes, the State's policy choices are insulated from the visibility and scrutiny that direct regulation would entail and the conduct of citizens is molded by the information that government chooses to give them. * * *

* * *

* * * We have not suggested that the "commonsense differences" between commercial speech and other speech justify relaxed scrutiny of restraints that suppress truthful, nondeceptive, noncoercive commercial speech. The differences articulated by the Court, * * *, justify a more permissive approach to regulation of the manner of commercial speech for the purpose of protecting consumers from deception or coercion, and these differences explain why doctrines designed to prevent "chilling" of protected speech are inapplicable to commercial speech. No differences between commercial speech and other protected speech justify suppression of commercial speech in order to influence public conduct through manipulation of the availability of information. * * *

It appears that the Court would permit the State to ban all direct advertising of air conditioning, assuming that a more limited restriction on such advertising would not effectively deter the public from cooling its homes. In my view, our cases do not support this type of suppression. If a governmental unit believes that use or overuse of air conditioning is a serious problem, it must attack that problem directly, by prohibiting air conditioning or regulating thermostat levels. Just as the Commonwealth of Virginia may promote professionalism of pharmacists directly, so too New York may not promote energy conservation "by keeping the public in ignorance." *Virginia Pharmacy Board*, 425 U.S., at 770.

MR. JUSTICE STEVENS, with whom MR. JUSTICE BRENNAN joins, concurring in the judgment.

Because "commercial speech" is afforded less constitutional protection than other forms of speech, it is important that the commercial speech concept not be defined too broadly lest speech deserving of greater constitutional protection be inadvertently suppressed. The issue in this case is whether New York's prohibition on the promotion of the use of electricity through advertising is a ban on nothing but commercial speech.

In my judgment one of the two definitions the Court uses in addressing that issue is too broad and the other may be somewhat too narrow. The Court first describes commercial speech as "expression related solely to the economic interests of the speaker and its audience." * * * Although it is not entirely clear whether this definition uses the subject matter of the speech or the motivation of the speaker as the limiting factor, it seems clear to me that it encompasses speech that is entitled to the maximum protection afforded by the First Amendment. Neither a labor leader's exhortation to strike, nor an economist's dissertation on the money supply, should receive any lesser protection because the subject matter concerns only the economic interests of the audience. Nor should the economic motivation of a speaker qualify his constitutional protection; even Shakespeare may have been motivated by the prospect of pecuniary reward. Thus, the Court's first definition of commercial speech is unquestionably too broad.

The Court's second definition refers to " 'speech proposing a commercial transaction.' " * * * A saleman's solicitation, a broker's offer, and a manufacturer's publication of a price list or the terms of his standard warranty would unquestionably fit within this concept. Presumably, the definition is intended to encompass advertising that advises possible buyers of the availability of specific products at specific prices and describes the advantages of purchasing such items. Perhaps it also extends to other communications that do little more than make the name of a product or a service more familiar to the general public. Whatever the precise contours of the concept, and perhaps it is too early to enunciate an exact formulation, I am persuaded that it should not include the entire range of communication that is embraced within the term "promotional advertising."

This case involves a governmental regulation that completely bans promotional advertising by an electric utility. This ban encompasses a great deal more than mere proposals to engage in certain kinds of commercial transactions. It prohibits all advocacy of the immediate or future use of electricity. It curtails expression by an informed and interested group of persons of their point of view on questions relating to the production and consumption of electrical energy—questions frequently discussed and debated by our political leaders. For example, an electric company's advocacy of the use of electric heat for environmental reasons, as opposed to wood-burning stoves, would seem to fall squarely within New York's promotional advertising ban and also within the bounds of maximum First Amendment protection. The breadth of the ban thus exceeds the boundaries of the commercial speech concept, however that concept may be defined.

The justification for the regulation is nothing more than the expressed fear that the audience may find the utility's message persuasive. Without the aid of any coercion, deception, or misinformation, truthful communication may persuade some citizens to consume more electricity than they otherwise would. I assume that such a consequence would be undesirable and that government may therefore prohibit and punish the unnecessary or excessive use of electricity.

But if the perceived harm associated with greater electrical usage is not sufficiently serious to justify direct regulation, surely it does not constitute the kind of clear and present danger that can justify the suppression of speech.

* * *

In sum, I concur in the result because I do not consider this to be a "commercial speech" case. Accordingly, I see no need to decide whether the Court's four-part analysis, * * *, adequately protects commercial speech—as properly defined—in the face of a blanket ban of the sort involved in this case.

MR. JUSTICE REHNQUIST, dissenting.

* * *

The Court's analysis in my view is wrong in several respects. Initially, I disagree with the Court's conclusion that the speech of a state-created monopoly, which is the subject of a comprehensive regulatory scheme, is entitled to protection under the First Amendment. I also think that the Court errs here in failing to recognize that the state law is most accurately viewed as an economic regulation and that the speech involved (if it falls within the scope of the First Amendment at all) occupies a significantly more subordinate position in the hierarchy of First Amendment values than the Court gives it today. Finally, the Court in reaching its decision improperly substitutes its own judgment for that of the State in deciding how a proper ban on promotional advertising should be drafted. With regard to this latter point, the Court adopts as its final part of a four-part test a "no more extensive than necessary" analysis that will unduly impair a state legislature's ability to adopt legislation reasonably designed to promote interests that have always been rightly thought to be of great importance to the State.

* * *

The state-created monopoly status of a utility arises from the unique characteristics of the services that a utility provides. As recognized in Cantor v. Detroit Edison Co., 428 U.S. 579, 595–596 (1976), "public utility regulation typically assumes that the private firm is a natural monopoly and that public controls are necessary to protect the consumer from exploitation." The consequences of this natural monopoly in my view justify much more wide-ranging supervision and control of a utility under the First Amendment than this Court held in *Bellotti* to be permissible with regard to ordinary corporations. Corporate status is generally conferred as a result of a State's determination that the corporate characteristics "enhance its efficiency as an economic entity." *First National Bank of Boston v. Bellotti, supra*, at 825–826 (REHNQUIST, J., dissenting). A utility, by contrast, fulfills a function that serves special public interests as a result of the natural monopoly of the service provided. Indeed, the extensive regulations governing decision-making by public utilities suggest that for purposes of First Amendment analysis, a utility is far closer to a state-controlled enterprise than is an ordinary corporation. Accordingly, I think a State has broad discretion in determining the statements that a utility may make in that such statements emanate from the entity created by the State to provide important and unique public services. * * *

* * *

The Court today holds not only that commercial speech is entitled to First Amendment protection, but also that when it is protected a State may not regulate it unless its reason for doing so amounts to a "substantial" governmental interest, its regulation "directly advances" that interest, and its manner of regulation is "not more extensive than necessary" to serve the interest. * * * The test adopted by the Court thus elevates the protection accorded commercial speech that falls within the scope of the First Amendment to a level that is virtually indistinguishable from that of noncommercial speech. I think the Court in so doing has effectively accomplished the "devitalization" of the First Amendment that it counseled against in *Ohralik*. I think it has also, by labeling economic regulation of business conduct as a restraint on "free speech," gone far to resurrect the discredited doctrine of cases such as *Lochner* and Tyson & Brother v. Banton, 273 U.S. 418 (1927). New York's order here is in my view more akin to an economic regulation to which virtually complete deference should be accorded by this Court.

* * *

While it is true that an important objective of the First Amendment is to foster the free flow of information, identification of speech that falls within its protection is not aided by the metaphorical reference to a "marketplace of ideas." There is no reason for believing that the marketplace of ideas is free from market imperfections any more than there is to believe that the invisible hand will always lead to optimum economic decisions in the commercial market. See, e.g., Baker, Scope of the First Amendment, Freedom of Speech, 25 UCLA L.Rev. 964, 967–981 (1978). * * *

* * * Nor do I think there is any basis for concluding that individual citizens of the State will recognize the need for and act to promote energy conservation to the extent the government deems appropriate, if only the channels of communication are left open. Thus, even if I were to agree that commercial speech is entitled to some First Amendment protection, I would hold here that the State's decision to ban promotional advertising, in light of the substantial state interest at stake, is a constitutionally permissible exercise of its power to adopt regulations designed to promote the interests of its citizens.

* * *

Two ideas are here at war with one another, and their resolution, although it be on a judicial battlefield, will be a very difficult one. The sort of "advocacy" of which Mr. Justice Brandeis spoke was not the advocacy on the part of a utility to use more of its product. Nor do I think those who won our independence, while declining to "exalt order at the cost of liberty," would have viewed a merchant's unfettered freedom to advertise in hawking his wares as a "liberty" not subject to extensive regulation in light of the government's substantial interest in attaining "order" in the economic sphere.

* * *

I remain of the view that the Court unlocked a Pandora's Box when it "elevated" commercial speech to the level of traditional political speech by according it First Amendment protection in Virginia Pharmacy Board v. Virginia Citizens Consumer Council, 425 U.S. 748 (1976). The line between "commercial speech," and the kind of speech that those who drafted the First Amendment had in mind, may not be a technically or intellectually easy one to draw, but it surely produced far fewer problems than has the development of judicial doctrine in this area since *Virginia Pharmacy Board.* For in the world of political advocacy and its marketplace of ideas, there is no such thing as a "fraudulent" idea: there may be useless proposals, totally unworkable schemes, as well as very sound proposals that will receive the imprimatur of the "marketplace of ideas" through our majoritarian system of election and representative government. The free flow of information is important in this context not because it will lead to the discovery of any objective "truth," but because it is essential to our system of self-government.

* * *

III

The Court concedes that the state interest in energy conservation is plainly substantial, * * *, as is the State's concern that its rates be fair and efficient. * * * It also concedes that there is a direct link between the Commission's ban on promotional advertising and the State's interest in conservation. * * * The Court nonetheless strikes down the ban on promotional advertising because the Commission has failed to demonstrate, under the final part of the Court's four-part test, that its regulation is no more extensive than necessary to serve the State's interest. * * * In reaching this conclusion, the Court conjures up potential advertisements that a utility might make that conceivably would result in net energy savings. The Court does not indicate that the New York Public Service Commission has in fact construed its ban on "promotional" advertising to preclude the dissemination of information that clearly would result in a net energy savings, nor does it even suggest that the Commission has been confronted with and rejected such an advertising proposal. * * *

* * * The Court's analysis in this regard is in my view fundamentally misguided because it fails to recognize that the beneficial side effects of "more efficient use" may be inconsistent with the goal of energy conservation. Indeed, the Commission explicitly found that the promotion of off-peak consumption would impair conservation efforts. The Commission stated:

> "Increased off-peak generation, ... while conferring some beneficial side effects, also consumes valuable energy resources and, if it is the result of increased sales, necessarily creates incremental air pollution and thermal discharges to water-

ways. More important, any increase in off-peak generation from most of the major companies producing electricity in this state would not, at this time, be produced from coal or nuclear resources, but would require the use of oil-fired generating facilities. The increased requirement for fuel oil to serve the incremental off-peak load created by promotional advertising would aggravate the nation's already unacceptably high level of dependence on foreign sources of supply and would, in addition, frustrate rather than encourage conservation efforts."

* * * Until I have mastered electrical engineering and marketing, I am not prepared to contradict by virtue of my judicial office those who assume that the ban will be successful in making a substantial contribution to conservation efforts. And I doubt that any of this Court's First Amendment decisions justify striking down the Commission's order because more steps toward conservation could have been made. This is especially true when, as here, the Commission lacks authority over oil dealers.

The Court concludes that the Commission's ban on promotional advertising must be struck down because it is more extensive than necessary: it may result in the suppression of advertising by utilities that promotes the use of electrical devices or services that cause no net increase in total energy use. The Court's reasoning in this regard, however, is highly speculative. The Court provides two examples that it claims support its conclusion. It first states that both parties acknowledge that the "heat pump" will be "a major improvement in electric heating," and that but for the ban the utilities would advertise this type of "energy efficien[t]" product. The New York Public Service Commission, however, considered the merits of the heat pump and concluded that it would most likely result in an overall increase in electric energy consumption. The Commission stated:

> "[I]nstallation of a heat pump means also installation of central air-conditioning. To this extent, promotion of off-peak electric space heating involves promotion of on-peak summer air-conditioning as well as on-peak usage of electricity for water heating. And the price of electricity to most consumers in the State does not now fully reflect the much higher marginal costs of on-peak consumption in summer peaking markets. In these circumstances, there would be a subsidization of consumption on-peak, and consequently, higher subsidization of peak consumption not only may encourage the use of scarce energy resources during peak periods, but also may lead to larger reserve generating capacity requirements for the State."

The Court next asserts that electric heating as a backup to solar and other heat may be an efficient alternative energy source. * * * The Court fails to establish, however, that an advertising proposal of this sort was properly presented to the Commission. * * *

* * *

It is in my view inappropriate for the Court to invalidate the State's ban on commercial advertising here, based on its speculation that in some cases the advertising may result in a net savings in electrical energy use, and in the cases in which it is clear a net energy savings would result from utility advertising, the Public Service Commission would apply its ban so as to proscribe such advertising. Even assuming that the Court's speculation is correct, I do not think it follows that facial invalidation of the ban is the appropriate course. As stated in Parker v. Levy, 417 U.S. 733, 760 (1974), "even if there are marginal applications in which a statute would infringe on First Amendment values, facial invalidation is inappropriate if the 'remainder of the statute * * * covers a whole range of easily identifiable and constitutionally proscribable * * * conduct. * * *' CSC v. Letter Carriers, 413 U.S. 548, 580–581 (1973)." This is clearly the case here.

For the foregoing reasons, I would affirm the judgment of the New York Court of Appeals.

BOLGER v. YOUNGS DRUG PRODUCTS CORPORATION

Supreme Court of the United States, 1983.
463 U.S. 60, 103 S.Ct. 2875, 77 L.Ed.2d 469.

JUSTICE MARSHALL delivered the opinion of the Court.

Title 39 U.S.C. § 3001(e)(2) prohibits the mailing of unsolicited advertisements for contraceptives. The District Court held that, as applied to appellee's mailings, the statute violates the First Amendment. We affirm.

I

Section 3001(e)(2) states that "[a]ny unsolicited advertisement of matter which is designed, adapted, or intended for preventing conception is nonmailable matter, shall not be carried or delivered by mail, and shall be disposed of as the Postal Service directs * * *."[1] As interpreted by Postal Service regulations, the statutory provision does not apply to unsolicited advertisements in which the mailer has no commercial interest. In addition to the civil consequences of a violation of § 3001(e)(2), 18 U.S.C. § 1461 makes it a crime knowingly to use the mails for anything declared by § 3001(e) to be nonmailable.

Appellee Youngs Drug Products Corp. (Youngs) is engaged in the manufacture, sale, and distribution of contraceptives. Youngs markets its products primarily through sales to chain warehouses and wholesale distributors, who in turn sell contraceptives to retail pharmacists, who then sell those products to individual customers. Appellee publicizes

1. Section 3001(e)(2) contains express limitations. In particular, an advertisement is not deemed unsolicited "if it is contained in a publication for which the addressee has paid or promised to pay a consideration or which he has otherwise indicated he desires to receive." In addition, the provision does not apply to advertisements mailed to certain recipients such as a manufacturer of contraceptives, a licensed physician, or a pharmacist. See §§ 3001(e)(2)(A) and (B).

the availability and desirability of its products by various methods. This litigation resulted from Youngs' decision to undertake a campaign of unsolicited mass mailings to members of the public. In conjunction with its wholesalers and retailers, Youngs seeks to mail to the public on an unsolicited basis three types of materials:

—multi-page, multi-item flyers promoting a large variety of products available at a drug-store, including prophylactics;

—flyers exclusively or substantially devoted to promoting prophylactics;

—informational pamphlets discussing the desirability and availability of prophylactics in general or Youngs' products in particular.[4]

* * *

The District Court determined that § 3001(e)(2), by its plain language, prohibited all three types of proposed mailings. The court then addressed the constitutionality of the statute as applied to these mailings. Finding all three types of materials to be commercial solicitations, the court considered the constitutionality of the statute within the framework established by this Court for analyzing restrictions imposed on commercial speech. The court concluded that the statutory prohibition was more extensive than necessary to the interests asserted by the Government, and it therefore held that the statute's absolute ban on the three types of mailings violated the First Amendment.

* * *

II

Beginning with Bigelow v. Virginia, 421 U.S. 809 (1975), this Court extended the protection of the First Amendment to commercial speech.[6] Nonetheless, our decisions have recognized "the 'common-sense' distinction between speech proposing a commercial transaction, which occurs in an area traditionally subject to government regulation, and other varieties of speech." Ohralik v. Ohio State Bar Assn., 436 U.S. 447, 455–456 (1978). Thus, we have held that the Constitution accords less protection to commercial speech than to other constitutionally safeguarded forms of expression. * * *

For example, as a general matter, "the First Amendment means that government has no power to restrict expression because of its message, its ideas, its subject matter, or its content." Police Department of Chicago v. Mosley, 408 U.S. 92, 95 (1972). With respect to

---

4. In the District Court, Youngs offered two examples of informational pamphlets. See Record, Complaint, Group Exhibit C. The first, entitled "Condoms and Human Sexuality," is a 12–page pamphlet describing the use, manufacture, desirability, and availability of condoms, and providing detailed descriptions of various Trojan-brand condoms manufactured by Youngs. The second, entitled "Plain Talk about Venereal Disease," is an eight-page pamphlet discussing at length the problem of venereal disease and the use and advantages of condoms in aiding the prevention of venereal disease. The only identification of Youngs or its products is at the bottom of the last page of the pamphlet, which states that the pamphlet has been contributed as a public service by Youngs, the distributor of Trojan-brand prophylactics.

6. Before that time, purely commercial advertising received no First Amendment protection. See Valentine v. Chrestensen, 316 U.S. 52, 54 (1942).

noncommercial speech, this Court has sustained content-based restrictions only in the most extraordinary circumstances. See Consolidated Edison Co. v. Public Service Comm'n of New York, 447 U.S. 530, 538–539 (1980); Stone, Restrictions of Speech Because of its Content: The Peculiar Case of Subject–Matter Restrictions, 46 U.Chi.L.Rev. 81, 82 (1978). By contrast, regulation of commercial speech based on content is less problematic. In light of the greater potential for deception or confusion in the context of certain advertising messages, see *In re* R.M.J., 455 U.S. 191, 200 (1982), content-based restrictions on commercial speech may be permissible. See Friedman v. Rogers, 440 U.S. 1 (1979) (upholding prohibition on use of trade names by optometrists).

Because the degree of protection afforded by the First Amendment depends on whether the activity sought to be regulated constitutes commercial or noncommercial speech, we must first determine the proper classification of the mailings at issue here. * * *

Most of appellee's mailings fall within the core notion of commercial speech—"speech which does 'no more than propose a commercial transaction.'" *Virginia Pharmacy Board v. Virginia Citizens Consumer Council, Inc., supra,* at 762, quoting Pittsburgh Press Co. v. Human Relations Comm'n, 3 U.S. 376, 385 (1973).[12] Youngs' informational pamphlets, however, cannot be characterized merely as proposals to engage in commercial transactions. Their proper classification as commercial or noncommercial speech thus presents a closer question. The mere fact that these pamphlets are conceded to be advertisements clearly does not compel the conclusion that they are commercial speech. See New York Times Co. v. Sullivan, 376 U.S. 254, 265–266 (1964). Similarly, the reference to a specific product does not by itself render the pamphlets commercial speech.[13] * * * Finally, the fact that Youngs has an economic motivation for mailing the pamphlets would clearly be insufficient by itself to turn the materials into commercial speech. See Bigelow v. Virginia, 421 U.S., at 818; Ginzburg v. United States, 383 U.S. 463, 474 (1966); Thornhill v. Alabama, 310 U.S. 88 (1940).

---

12. For example, the drugstore flyer consists primarily of price and quantity information.

13. One of the informational pamphlets, "Condoms and Human Sexuality," specifically refers to a number of Trojan-brand condoms manufactured by appellee and describes the advantages of each type.

The other informational pamphlet, "Plain Talk about Venereal Disease," repeatedly discusses condoms without any specific reference to those manufactured by appellee. The only reference to appellee's products is contained at the very bottom of the last page, where appellee is identified as the distributor of Trojan-brand prophylactics. That a product is referred to generically does not, however, remove it from the realm of commercial speech. For example, a company with sufficient control of the market for a product may be able to promote the product without reference to its own brand names. Or a trade association may make statements about a product without reference to specific brand names. See, e.g., National Comm'n on Egg Nutrition v. FTC, 570 F.2d 157 (CA7 1977) (enforcing in part a Federal Trade Commission order prohibiting false and misleading advertising by an egg industry trade association concerning the relationship between cholesterol, eggs, and heart disease). In this case, Youngs describes itself as "the leader in the manufacture and sale" of contraceptives. Brief for Appellee 3.

The combination of all these characteristics, however, provides strong support for the District Court's conclusion that the informational pamphlets are properly characterized as commercial speech. The mailings constitute commercial speech notwithstanding the fact that they contain discussions of important public issues such as venereal disease and family planning. We have made clear that advertising which "links a product to a current public debate" is not thereby entitled to the constitutional protection afforded noncommercial speech. Central Hudson Gas & Electric Corp. v. Public Service Comm'n of New York, 447 U.S., at 563, n. 5. A company has the full panoply of protections available to its direct comments on public issues, so there is no reason for providing similar constitutional protection when such statements are made in the context of commercial transactions. See *ibid.* Advertisers should not be permitted to immunize false or misleading product information from government regulation simply by including references to public issues. Cf. Metromedia, Inc. v. San Diego, 453 U.S. 490, 540 (1981) (BRENNAN, J., concurring in judgment).

We conclude, therefore, that all of the mailings in this case are entitled to the qualified but nonetheless substantial protection accorded to commercial speech.

III

* * * In *Central Hudson* we adopted a four-part analysis for assessing the validity of restrictions on commercial speech. First, we determine whether the expression is constitutionally protected. For commercial speech to receive such protection, "it at least must concern lawful activity and not be misleading." *Id.,* at 566. Second, we ask whether the governmental interest is substantial. If so, we must then determine whether the regulation directly advances the government interest asserted, and whether it is not more extensive than necessary to serve that interest. *Ibid.* Applying this analysis, we conclude that § 3001(e)(2) is unconstitutional as applied to appellee's mailings.

We turn first to the protection afforded by the First Amendment. The State may deal effectively with false, deceptive, or misleading sales techniques. * * * In this case, however, appellants have never claimed that Youngs' proposed mailings fall into any of these categories. To the contrary, advertising for contraceptives not only implicates "substantial individual and societal interests" in the free flow of commercial information, but also relates to activity which is protected from unwarranted state interference. See Carey v. Population Services International, 431 U.S. 678, 700–701 (1977), quoting *Virginia Pharmacy Board, supra,* at 760, 763–766.[17] Youngs' proposed commercial speech is therefore clearly protected by the First Amendment. Indeed, where—as in this case—a speaker desires to convey truthful information relevant to important social issues such as family planning and the prevention of venereal disease, we have previously found the First Amendment

---

17. See also Eisenstadt v. Baird, 405 U.S. 438, 453 (1972); Griswold v. Connecticut, 381 U.S. 479 (1965).

interest served by such speech paramount. See *Carey v. Population Services International, supra; Bigelow v. Virginia, supra.*[18]

We must next determine whether the Government's interest in prohibiting the mailing of unsolicited contraceptive advertisements is a substantial one. The prohibition in § 3001(e)(2) originated in 1873 as part of the Comstock Act, a criminal statute designed "for the suppression of Trade in and Circulation of obscene Literature and Articles of immoral Use." * * * Appellants do not purport to rely on justifications for the statute offered during the 19th Century.[20] Instead, they advance interests that concededly were not asserted when the prohibition was enacted into law. This reliance is permissible since the insufficiency of the original motivation does not diminish other interests that the restriction may now serve. * * *

In particular, appellants assert that the statute (1) shields recipients of mail from materials that they are likely to find offensive and (2) aids parents' efforts to control the manner in which their children become informed about sensitive and important subjects such as birth control. The first of these interests carries little weight. In striking down a state prohibition of contraceptive advertisements in *Carey v. Population Services International, supra,* we stated that offensiveness was "classically not [a] justificatio[n] validating the suppression of expression protected by the First Amendment. At least where obscenity is not involved, we have consistently held that the fact that protected speech may be offensive to some does not justify its suppression." 431 U.S., at 701. We specifically declined to recognize a distinction between commercial and noncommercial speech that would render this interest a sufficient justification for a prohibition of commercial speech. * * *

Recognizing that their reliance on this interest is "problematic," appellants attempt to avoid the clear import of *Carey* by emphasizing that § 3001(e)(2) is aimed at the mailing of materials to the home. We have, of course, recognized the important interest in allowing addressees to give notice to a mailer that they wish no further mailings which, in their sole discretion, they believe to be erotically arousing or sexually provocative. * * * But we have never held that the Government itself can shut off the flow of mailings to protect those recipients who might potentially be offended. * * * Consequently, the "short, though regular, journey from mail box to trash can * * * is an acceptable burden, at least so far as the Constitution is concerned." Lamont v. Commissioner of Motor Vehicles, 269 F.Supp. 880, 883 (SDNY), summarily aff'd, 386 F.2d 449 (CA2 1967), cert. denied, 391 U.S. 915 (1968).

18. Appellants argue that § 3001(e)(2) does not interfere "significantly" with free speech because the statute applies only to unsolicited mailings and does not bar other channels of communication. See Brief for Appellants 16–24. However, this Court has previously declared that "one is not to have the exercise of his liberty of expression in appropriate places abridged on the plea that it may be exercised in some other place." Schneider v. State, 308 U.S. 147, 163 (1939). * * *

20. The party seeking to uphold a restriction on commercial speech carries the burden of justifying it. See Central Hudson Gas & Electric Corp. v. Public Service Comm'n of New York, 447 U.S. 557, 570 (1980); *Linmark Associates, Inc. v. Willingboro, supra,* at 95.

The second interest asserted by appellants—aiding parents' efforts to discuss birth control with their children—is undoubtedly substantial. "[P]arents have an important 'guiding role' to play in the upbringing of their children * * * which presumptively includes counseling them on important decisions." H.L. v. Matheson, 450 U.S. 398, 410 (1981), quoting Bellotti v. Baird, 443 U.S. 622, 637 (1979). As a means of effectuating this interest, however, § 3001(e)(2) fails to withstand scrutiny.

To begin with, § 3001(e)(2) provides only the most limited incremental support for the interest asserted. We can reasonably assume that parents already exercise substantial control over the disposition of mail once it enters their mailboxes. Under 39 U.S.C. § 3008, parents can also exercise control over information that flows into their mailboxes. And parents must already cope with the multitude of external stimuli that color their children's perception of sensitive subjects.[26] Under these circumstances, a ban on unsolicited advertisements serves only to assist those parents who desire to keep their children from confronting such mailings, who are otherwise unable to do so, and whose children have remained relatively free from such stimuli.

This marginal degree of protection is achieved by purging all mailboxes of unsolicited material that is entirely suitable for adults. We have previously made clear that a restriction of this scope is more extensive than the Constitution permits, for the government may not "reduce the adult population * * * to reading only what is fit for children." Butler v. Michigan, 352 U.S. 380, 383 (1957).[27] The level of discourse reaching a mailbox simply cannot be limited to that which would be suitable for a sandbox. * * *

Section 3001(e)(2) is also defective because it denies to parents truthful information bearing on their ability to discuss birth control and to make informed decisions in this area.

IV

We thus conclude that the justifications offered by appellants are insufficient to warrant the sweeping prohibition on the mailing of unsolicited contraceptive advertisements. As applied to appellee's mailings, § 3001(e)(2) is unconstitutional. The judgment of the District Court is therefore

Affirmed.

JUSTICE BRENNAN took no part in the decision of this case.

---

26. For example, many magazines contain advertisements for contraceptives. See M. Redford, G. Duncan, & D. Prager, The Condom: Increasing Utilization in the United States 145 (1974) (ads accepted in Family Health, Psychology Today, and Ladies' Home Journal in 1970). Section 3001(e)(2) itself permits the mailing of publications containing contraceptive advertisements to subscribers. Similarly, drugstores commonly display contraceptives. And minors taking a course in sex education will undoubtedly be exposed to the subject of contraception.

27. In *Butler* this Court declared unconstitutional a Michigan statute that banned reading materials inappropriate for children. The legislation was deemed not "reasonably restricted" to the evil it sought to address; rather, the effect of the statute was "to burn the house to roast the pig." 352 U.S., at 383.

JUSTICE REHNQUIST, with whom JUSTICE O'CONNOR joins, concurring in the judgment.

I agree that the judgment should be affirmed, but my reasoning differs from that of the Court. The right to use the mails is undoubtedly protected by the First Amendment, Blount v. Rizzi, 400 U.S. 410 (1971). But because the home mailbox has features which distinguish it from a public hall or public park, where it may be assumed that all who are present wish to hear the views of the particular speaker then on the rostrum, it cannot be totally assimilated for purposes of analysis with these traditional public forums. Several people within a family or living group may have free access to a mailbox, including minor children; and obviously not every piece of mail received has been either expressly or impliedly solicited. It is the unsolicited mass mailings sent by appellee designed to promote the use of condoms that gives rise to this litigation.

* * *

The material that Youngs seeks to mail concerns lawful activity and is not misleading. The Postal Service does not contend otherwise.

The Postal Service does contend that the Government has substantial interests in "aiding parents' efforts to discuss sensitive and important subjects such as birth control with their children," * * *, and in preventing material that the recipient may find offensive from entering the home on an unsolicited basis. * * * The Government is entitled, the argument goes, to help individuals shield their families and homes from advertisements for contraceptives.

The first of these interests is undoubtedly substantial. * * *

The second interest advanced by the Postal Service is also substantial. We have often recognized that individuals have a legitimate "right to be left alone" "in the privacy of the home," FCC v. Pacifica Foundation, 438 U.S. 726, 748 (1978), "the one place where people ordinarily have the right not to be assaulted by uninvited and offensive sights and sounds." *Id.,* at 759 (opinion of POWELL, J.). Accord, Rowan v. Post Office Dept., 397 U.S. 728, 736–738 (1970). The Government may properly act to protect people from unreasonable intrusions into their homes.

The questions whether § 3001(e)(2) directly advances these interests, and whether it is more extensive than necessary, are more problematic. Under 39 U.S.C. § 3008, an individual can have his name removed from Youngs' mailing list if he so wishes. See *Rowan v. Post Office Dept., supra* (holding § 3008 constitutional). Thus, individuals are able to avoid the information in Youngs' advertisements after one exposure. Furthermore, as we noted in Consolidated Edison Co. v. Public Service Comm'n of New York, 447 U.S. 530, 542 (1980), the recipient of Youngs' advertising "may escape exposure to objectionable material simply by transferring [it] from envelope to wastebasket." Therefore a mailed advertisement is significantly less intrusive than the daytime broadcast at issue in *Pacifica* or the sound truck at issue in Kovacs v. Cooper, 336 U.S. 77 (1949). See *Consolidated Edison,* 447

U.S., at 542–543. Where the recipients can "'effectively avoid further bombardment of their sensibilities simply by averting their eyes,'" *id.*, at 542, quoting Cohen v. California, 403 U.S. 15, 21 (1971), a more substantial governmental interest is necessary to justify restrictions on speech.

* * *

Section 3001(e)(2) is also broader than is necessary because it completely bans from the mail unsolicited materials that are suitable for adults. The Government may not "reduce that adult population * * * to reading only what is fit for children." Butler v. Michigan, 352 U.S. 380, 383 (1957). Narrower restrictions, such as the provisions of 39 U.S.C. § 3008 and restrictions of the kind suggested by the District Court in this case, can fully serve the Government's interests.

* * *

JUSTICE STEVENS, concurring in the judgment.

Two aspects of the Court's opinion merit further comment: (1) its conclusion that all of the communications at issue are properly classified as "commercial speech" * * *; and (2) its virtually complete rejection of offensiveness as a possibly legitimate justification for the suppression of speech * * *. My views are somewhat different from the Court's on both of these matters.

I

Even if it may not intend to do so, the Court's opinion creates the impression that "commercial speech" is a fairly definite category of communication that is protected by a fairly definite set of rules that differ from those protecting other categories of speech. That impression may not be wholly warranted. * * *

* * *

Appellee's pamphlet entitled "Plain Talk about Venereal Disease" highlights the classification problem. On the one hand, the pamphlet includes statements that implicitly extol the quality of the appellee's products. A law that protects the public from suffering commercial harm as a result of such statements would appropriately be evaluated as a regulation of commercial speech. On the other hand, most of the pamphlet is devoted to a discussion of the symptoms, significant risks, and possibility of treatment for venereal disease. That discussion does not appear to endanger any commercial interest whatsoever; it serves only to inform the public about a medical issue of regrettably great significance.

I have not yet been persuaded that the commercial motivation of an author is sufficient to alter the state's power to regulate speech. Anthony Comstock surely had a constitutional right to speak out against the use of contraceptives in his day. Like Comstock, many persons today are morally opposed to contraception, and the First Amendment commands the government to allow them to express their views in appropriate ways and in appropriate places. I believe that Amendment affords the same protection to this appellee's views regarding the hygienic and family planning advantages of its contraceptive products.

Because significant speech so often comprises both commercial and noncommercial elements, it may be more fruitful to focus on the nature of the challenged regulation rather than the proper label for the communication. Cf. Farber, Commercial Speech and First Amendment Theory, 74 NW. U.L. Rev. 372, 386–390 (1979). The statute at issue in this case prohibits the mailing of "[a]ny unsolicited advertisement of matter which is designed, adapted, or intended for preventing conception." Any legitimate interests the statute may serve are unrelated to the prevention of harm to participants in commercial exchanges. Thus, because it restricts speech by the appellee that has a significant noncommercial component, I have scrutinized this statute in the same manner as I would scrutinize a prohibition on unsolicited mailings by an organization with absolutely no commercial interest in the subject.

II

Assuming that this case deals only with commercial speech, the Court implies, if it does not actually hold, that the fact that protected speech may be offensive to some persons is not a "sufficient justification for a prohibition of commercial speech." * * * I think it essential to emphasize once again, however, that:

> "a communication may be offensive in two different ways. Independently of the message the speaker intends to convey, the form of his communication may be offensive—perhaps because it is too loud or too ugly in a particular setting. Other speeches, even though elegantly phrased in dulcet tones, are offensive simply because the listener disagrees with the speaker's message." Consolidated Edison Co. v. Public Service Comm'n of New York, 447 U.S. 530, 546–548 (1980) (STEVENS, J., concurring in judgment) (footnotes omitted).

It matters whether a law regulates communications for their ideas or for their style. Governmental suppression of a specific point of view strikes at the core of First Amendment values. In contrast, regulations of form and context may strike a constitutionally appropriate balance between the advocate's right to convey a message and the recipient's interest in the quality of his environment:

> "The fact that the advertising of a particular subject matter is sometimes offensive does not deprive all such advertising of First Amendment protection; but it is equally clear to me that the existence of such protection does not deprive the State of all power to regulate such advertising in order to minimize its offensiveness. A picture which may appropriately be included in an instruction book may be excluded from a billboard." Carey v. Population Services International, 431 U.S. 678, 717 (1977) (opinion of STEVENS, J.).

The statute at issue in this case censors ideas, not style. It prohibits appellee from mailing any unsolicited advertisement of contraceptives, no matter how unobtrusive and tactful; yet it permits anyone to mail unsolicited advertisements of devices intended to facilitate conception, no matter how coarse or grotesque. It thus excludes one advocate from a forum to which adversaries have unlimited access. I concur in the Court's judgment that the First Amendment prohibits the application of the statute to these materials.

POSADAS DE PUERTO RICO ASSOCIATES v. TOURISM COMPANY OF PUERTO RICO

Supreme Court of the United States, 1986.
478 U.S. 328, 106 S.Ct. 2968, 92 L.Ed.2d 266.

JUSTICE REHNQUIST delivered the opinion of the Court.
* * *

In 1948, the Puerto Rico Legislature legalized certain forms of casino gambling. The Games of Chance Act of 1948, * * *, authorized the playing of roulette, dice, and card games in licensed "gambling rooms." § 2, codified, as amended, at P.R. Laws Ann., Tit. 15, § 71 (1972). Bingo and slot machines were later added to the list of authorized games of chance under the Act. * * * The legislature's intent was set forth in the Act's Statement of Motives:

> "The purpose of this Act is to contribute to the development of tourism by means of the authorization of certain games of chance which are customary in the recreation places of the great tourist centers of the world, and by the establishment of regulations for and the strict surveillance of said games by the government, in order to ensure for tourists the best possible safeguards, while at the same time opening for the Treasurer of Puerto Rico an additional source of income." Games of Chance Act of 1948, Act No. 221 of May 15, 1948, § 1.

The Act also provided that "[n]o gambling room shall be permitted to advertise or otherwise offer their facilities to the public of Puerto Rico." § 8, codified, as amended, at P.R. Laws Ann., Tit. 15, § 77 (1972).

The Act authorized the Economic Development Administration of Puerto Rico to issue and enforce regulations implementing the various provisions of the Act. * * * Appellee Tourism Company of Puerto Rico, a public corporation, assumed the regulatory powers of the Economic Development Administration under the Act in 1970. * * * The two regulations at issue in this case were originally issued in 1957 for the purpose of implementing the advertising restrictions contained in § 8 of the Act. * * * Regulation 76a–1(7), as amended in 1971, provides in pertinent part:

> "No concessionaire, nor his agent or employee is authorized to advertise the gambling parlors to the public in Puerto Rico. The advertising of our games of chance is hereby authorized through newspapers, magazines, radio, television and other publicity media outside Puerto Rico subject to the prior editing and approval by the Tourism Development Company of

the advertisement to be submitted in draft to the Company."
* * *

In 1975, appellant Posadas de Puerto Rico Associates, a partnership organized under the laws of Texas, obtained a franchise to operate a gambling casino and began doing business under the name Condado Holiday Inn Hotel and Sands Casino. In 1978, appellant was twice fined by the Tourism Company for violating the advertising restrictions in the Act and implementing regulations. Appellant protested the fines in a series of letters to the Tourism Company. On February 16, 1979, the Tourism Company issued to all casino franchise holders a memorandum setting forth the following interpretation of the advertising restrictions:

> "This prohibition includes the use of the word 'casino' in matchbooks, lighters, envelopes, inter-office and/or external correspondence, invoices, napkins, brochures, menus, elevators, glasses, plates, lobbies, banners, flyers, paper holders, pencils, telephone books, directories, bulletin boards or in any hotel dependency or object which may be accessible to the public in Puerto Rico." App. 7a.

Pursuant to this administrative interpretation, the Tourism Company assessed additional fines against appellant. The Tourism Company ordered appellant to pay the outstanding total of $1,500 in fines by March 18, 1979, or its gambling franchise would not be renewed. Appellant continued to protest the fines, but ultimately paid them without seeking judicial review of the decision of the Tourism Company. In July 1981, appellant was again fined for violating the advertising restrictions. Faced with another threatened nonrenewal of its gambling franchise, appellant paid the $500 fine under protest.

Appellant then filed a declaratory judgment action against the Tourism Company in the Superior Court of Puerto Rico, San Juan Section, seeking a declaration that the Act and implementing regulations, both facially and as applied by the Tourism Company, violated appellant's commercial speech rights under the United States Constitution. * * * [T]he court issued a narrowing construction of the statute, declaring that "the only advertisement prohibited by the law originally is that which is contracted with an advertising agency, for consideration, to attract the resident to bet at the dice, card, roulette and bingo tables." * * * The court also issued the following narrowing construction of Regulation 76a–1(7):

> "... Advertisements of the casinos in Puerto Rico are prohibited in the local publicity media addressed to inviting the residents of Puerto Rico to visit the casinos.
>
> * * * * *
>
> "We hereby allow, within the jurisdiction of Puerto Rico, advertising by the casinos addressed to tourists, provided they do not invite the residents of Puerto Rico to visit the casino, even though said announcements may incidentally reach the hands of a resident. * * * [T]he ads of casinos in magazines

for distribution primarily in Puerto Rico to the tourist, including the official guide of the Tourism Company 'Que Pasa in Puerto Rico' and any other tourist facility guide in Puerto Rico, even though said magazines may be available to the residents and in movies, television, radio, newspapers and trade magazines which may be published, taped, or filmed in the exterior for tourism promotion in the exterior even though they may be exposed or incidentally circulated in Puerto Rico. For example: an advertisement in the New York Times, an advertisement in CBS which reaches us through Cable TV, whose main objective is to reach the potential tourist.

"We hereby authorize advertising in the mass communication media of the country, where the trade name of the hotel is used even though it may contain a reference to the casino provided that the word casino is never used alone nor specified. * * *

"The direct promotion of the casinos within the premises of the hotels is allowed. In-house guests and clients may receive any type of information and promotion regarding the location of the casino, its schedule and the procedure of the games as well as magazines, souvenirs, stirrers, matchboxes, cards, dice, chips, T-shirts, hats, photographs, postcards and similar items used by the tourism centers of the world. "Since a clausus enumeration of this regulation is unforeseeable, any other situation or incident relating to the legal restriction must be measured in light of the public policy of promoting tourism. If the object of the advertisement is the tourist, it passes legal scrutiny." * * *

* * *

Before turning to the merits of appellant's First Amendment claim, we must address an additional preliminary matter. Although we have not heretofore squarely addressed the issue in the context of a case originating in Puerto Rico, we think it obvious that, in reviewing the facial constitutionality of the challenged statute and regulations, we must abide by the narrowing constructions announced by the Superior Court and approved *sub silentio* by the Supreme Court of Puerto Rico. This would certainly be the rule in a case originating in one of the 50 States. * * *

* * * Under *Central Hudson,* commercial speech receives a limited form of First Amendment protection so long as it concerns a lawful activity and is not misleading or fraudulent. Once it is determined that the First Amendment applies to the particular kind of commercial speech at issue, then the speech may be restricted only if the government's interest in doing so is substantial, the restrictions directly advance the government's asserted interest, and the restrictions are no more extensive than necessary to serve that interest. * * *

The particular kind of commercial speech at issue here, namely, advertising of casino gambling aimed at the residents of Puerto Rico, concerns a lawful activity and is not misleading or fraudulent, at least in the abstract. We must therefore proceed to the three remaining steps of the *Central Hudson* analysis in order to determine whether Puerto Rico's advertising restrictions run afoul of the First Amendment. The first of these three steps involves an assessment of the strength of the government's interest in restricting the speech. The interest at stake in this case, as determined by the Superior Court, is the reduction of demand for casino gambling by the residents of Puerto Rico. * * * The Tourism Company's brief before this Court explains the legislature's belief that "[e]xcessive casino gambling among local residents * * * would produce serious harmful effects on the health, safety and welfare of the Puerto Rican citizens, such as the disruption of moral and cultural patterns, the increase in local crime, the fostering of prostitution, the development of corruption, and the infiltration of organized crime." * * * These are some of the very same concerns, of course, that have motivated the vast majority of the 50 States to prohibit casino gambling. We have no difficulty in concluding that the Puerto Rico Legislature's interest in the health, safety, and welfare of its citizens constitutes a "substantial" governmental interest. * * *

The last two steps of the *Central Hudson* analysis basically involve a consideration of the "fit" between the legislature's ends and the means chosen to accomplish those ends. Step three asks the question whether the challenged restrictions on commercial speech "directly advance" the government's asserted interest. In the instant case, the answer to this question is clearly "yes." The Puerto Rico Legislature obviously believed, when it enacted the advertising restrictions at issue here, that advertising of casino gambling aimed at the residents of Puerto Rico would serve to increase the demand for the product advertised. We think the legislature's belief is a reasonable one, and the fact that appellant has chosen to litigate this case all the way to this Court indicates that appellant shares the legislature's view. * * *

* * *

We also think it clear beyond peradventure that the challenged statute and regulations satisfy the fourth and last step of the *Central Hudson* analysis, namely, whether the restrictions on commercial speech are no more extensive than necessary to serve the government's interest. The narrowing constructions of the advertising restrictions announced by the Superior Court ensure that the restrictions will not affect advertising of casino gambling aimed at tourists, but will apply only to such advertising when aimed at the residents of Puerto Rico. * * * Appellant contends, however, that the First Amendment requires the Puerto Rico Legislature to reduce demand for casino gambling among the residents of Puerto Rico not by suppressing commercial speech that might *encourage* such gambling, but by promulgating additional speech designed to *discourage* it. We reject this contention. We think it is up to the legislature to decide whether or not such a "counterspeech" policy would be as effective in reducing the demand for casino gambling as a restriction on advertising. * * *

In short, we conclude that the statute and regulations at issue in this case, as construed by the Superior Court, pass muster under each prong of the *Central Hudson* test. We therefore hold that the Supreme Court of Puerto Rico properly rejected appellant's First Amendment claim.

Appellant argues, however, that the challenged advertising restrictions are constitutionally defective under our decisions in Carey v. Population Services International, 431 U.S. 678 (1977), and Bigelow v. Virginia, 421 U.S. 809 (1975). In *Carey,* this Court struck down a ban on any "advertisement or display" of contraceptives, 431 U.S., at 700–702, and in *Bigelow,* we reversed a criminal conviction based on the advertisement of an abortion clinic. We think appellant's argument ignores a crucial distinction between the *Carey* and *Bigelow* decisions and the instant case. In *Carey* and *Bigelow,* the underlying conduct that was the subject of the advertising restrictions was constitutionally protected and could not have been prohibited by the State. Here, on the other hand, the Puerto Rico Legislature surely could have prohibited casino gambling by the residents of Puerto Rico altogether. In our view, the greater power to completely ban casino gambling necessarily includes the lesser power to ban advertising of casino gambling, and *Carey* and *Bigelow* are hence inapposite.

Appellant also makes the related argument that, having chosen to legalize casino gambling for residents of Puerto Rico, the legislature is prohibited by the First Amendment from using restrictions on advertising to accomplish its goal of reducing demand for such gambling. We disagree. In our view, appellant has the argument backwards. As we noted in the preceding paragraph, it is precisely *because* the government could have enacted a wholesale prohibition of the underlying conduct that it is permissible for the government to take the less intrusive step of allowing the conduct, but reducing the demand through restrictions on advertising. It would surely be a Pyrrhic victory for casino owners such as appellant to gain recognition of a First Amendment right to advertise their casinos to the residents of Puerto Rico, only to thereby force the legislature into banning casino gambling by residents altogether. It would just as surely be a strange constitutional doctrine which would concede to the legislature the authority to totally ban a product or activity, but deny to the legislature the authority to forbid the stimulation of demand for the product or activity through advertising on behalf of those who would profit from such increased demand. Legislative regulation of products or activities deemed harmful, such as cigarettes, alcoholic beverages, and prostitution, has varied from outright prohibition on the one hand, see, e.g., Cal. Penal Code Ann. § 647(b) (West Supp.1986) (prohibiting soliciting or engaging in act of prostitution), to legalization of the product or activity with restrictions on stimulation of its demand on the other hand, see, e.g., Nev.Rev.Stat. §§ 244.345(1), (8) (1986) (authorizing licensing of houses of prostitution except in counties with more than 250,000 population), §§ 201.430, 201.440 (prohibiting advertising of houses of prostitution "[i]n any public theater, on the public streets of any city or town, or on any public highway," or "in [a] place of business").¹⁰ To rule out the latter, intermediate kind of response would require more than we find in the First Amendment.

* * * Viewed in light of that construction, and particularly with the interpretive assistance of the implementing regulations as modified by the Superior Court, we do not find the statute unconstitutionally vague.

For the foregoing reasons, the decision of the Supreme Court of Puerto Rico that, as construed by the Superior Court, § 8 of the Games of Chance Act of 1948 and the implementing regulations do not facially violate the First Amendment or the due process or equal protection guarantees of the Constitution, is affirmed.¹¹

It is so ordered.

JUSTICE BRENNAN, with whom JUSTICE MARSHALL and JUSTICE BLACKMUN join, dissenting.

* * * I do not believe that Puerto Rico constitutionally may suppress truthful commercial speech in order to discourage its residents from engaging in lawful activity.

I

It is well settled that the First Amendment protects commercial speech from unwarranted governmental regulation. * * *

* * *

The Court asserts that the Commonwealth has a legitimate and substantial interest in discouraging its residents from engaging in casino gambling. * * * Neither the statute on its face nor the legislative history indicates that the Puerto Rico Legislature thought that serious harm would result if residents were allowed to engage in casino gambling; indeed, the available evidence suggests exactly the opposite. Puerto Rico has legalized gambling casinos, and permits its residents to

---

10. See also 15 U.S.C. § 1335 (prohibiting cigarette advertising "on any medium of electronic communication subject to the jurisdiction of the Federal Communications Commission"), upheld in Capital Broadcasting Co. v. Mitchell, 333 F.Supp. 582 (DC 1971), summarily aff'd sub nom. Capital Broadcasting Co. v. Acting Attorney General, 405 U.S. 1000 (1972); Fla.Stat. § 561.42(10)–(12) (1985) (prohibiting all signs except for one sign per product in liquor store windows); Mass.Gen.Laws § 138:24 (1974) (authorizing Alcoholic Beverages Control Commission to regulate liquor advertising); Miss.Code Ann. § 67-1-85 (Supp.1985) (prohibiting most forms of liquor sign advertising), upheld in Dunagin v. City of Oxford, Miss., supra; Ohio Rev.Code Ann. §§ 4301.03(E), 4301.-211 (1982) (authorizing Liquor Control Commission to regulate liquor advertising and prohibiting off-premises advertising of beer prices), upheld in Queensgate Investment Co. v. Liquor Control Comm'n, 69 Ohio St.2d 361, 433 N.E.2d 138, appeal dism'd for want of a substantial federal question, 459 U.S. 807 (1982); Okla.Const., Art. 27, § 5, and Okla.Stat., Tit. 37, § 516 (1981) (prohibiting all liquor advertising except for one storefront sign), upheld in Oklahoma Telecasters Assn. v. Crisp, 699 F.2d 490 (CA10 1983), rev'd on other grounds sub nom. Capital Cities Cable, Inc. v. Crisp, 467 U.S. 691 (1984); Utah Code Ann. §§ 32-7-26 to 32-7-28 (1974) (repealed 1985) (prohibiting all liquor advertising except for one storefront sign).

11. Justice Stevens claims that the Superior Court's narrowing construction creates an impermissible "prior restraint" on protected speech, because that court required the submission of certain casino advertising to appellee for its prior approval. See post, at 361. This argument was not raised by appellant either below or in this Court, and we therefore express no view on the constitutionality of the particular portion of the Superior Court's narrowing construction cited by Justice Stevens.

patronize them. Thus, the Puerto Rico Legislature has determined that permitting residents to engage in casino gambling will not produce the "serious harmful effects" that have led a majority of States to ban such activity. Residents of Puerto Rico are also permitted to engage in a variety of other gambling activities—including horse racing, "picas," cockfighting, and the Puerto Rico lottery—all of which are allowed to advertise freely to residents. Indeed, it is surely not farfetched to suppose that the legislature chose to restrict casino advertising not because of the "evils" of casino gambling, but because it preferred that Puerto Ricans spend their gambling dollars on the Puerto Rico lottery. In any event, in light of the legislature's determination that serious harm will not result if residents are permitted and encouraged to gamble, I do not see how Puerto Rico's interest in discouraging its residents from engaging in casino gambling can be characterized as "substantial," even if the legislature had actually asserted such an interest which, of course, it has not. * * *

The Court nevertheless sustains Puerto Rico's advertising ban because the legislature could have determined that casino gambling would seriously harm the health, safety, and welfare of the Puerto Rican citizens. * * *[4] This reasoning is contrary to this Court's long-established First Amendment jurisprudence. When the government seeks to place restrictions upon commercial speech, a court may not, as the Court implies today, simply speculate about valid reasons that the government might have for enacting such restrictions. Rather, the government ultimately bears the burden of justifying the challenged regulation, and it is incumbent upon the government to prove that the interests it seeks to further are real and substantial. See *Zauderer,* 471 U.S., at 641; *In re R.M.J.,* 455 U.S., at 205–206; *Friedman,* 440 U.S., at 15. In this case, appellee has not shown that "serious harmful effects" will result if Puerto Rico residents gamble in casinos, and the legislature's decision to legalize such activity suggests that it believed the opposite to be true. In short, appellees have failed to show that a substantial government interest supports Puerto Rico's ban on protected expression.

B

Even assuming that appellee could show that the challenged restrictions are supported by a substantial governmental interest, this would not end the inquiry into their constitutionality. See *Linmark*

---

4. The Court reasons that because Puerto Rico could legitimately decide to prohibit casino gambling entirely, it may also take the "less intrusive step" of legalizing casino gambling but restricting speech. * * * According to the Court, it would "surely be a strange constitutional doctrine which would concede to the legislature the authority to totally ban [casino gambling] but deny to the legislature the authority to forbid the stimulation of demand for [casino gambling]" by banning advertising. *Ibid.* I do not agree that a ban on casino advertising is "less intrusive" than an outright prohibition of such activity. A majority of States have chosen not to legalize casino gambling, and we have never suggested that this might be unconstitutional. However, having decided to legalize casino gambling, Puerto Rico's decision to ban truthful speech concerning entirely lawful activity raises serious First Amendment problems. Thus, the "constitutional doctrine" which bans Puerto Rico from banning advertisements concerning lawful casino gambling is not so strange a restraint—it is called the First Amendment.

Associates, 431 U.S., at 94; *Virginia Pharmacy Board,* 425 U.S., at 766. Appellee must still demonstrate that the challenged advertising ban directly advances Puerto Rico's interest in controlling the harmful effects allegedly associated with casino gambling. *Central Hudson,* 447 U.S., at 564. The Court proclaims that Puerto Rico's legislature "obviously believed * * * that advertising of casino gambling aimed at the residents of Puerto Rico would serve to increase the demand for the product advertised." * * * However, even assuming that an advertising ban would effectively reduce residents' patronage of gambling casinos,[5] it is not clear how it would directly advance Puerto Rico's interest in controlling the "serious harmful effects" the Court associates with casino gambling. In particular, it is unclear whether banning casino advertising aimed at residents would affect local crime, prostitution, the development of corruption, or the infiltration of organized crime. Because Puerto Rico actively promotes its casinos to tourists, these problems are likely to persist whether or not residents are also encouraged to gamble. Absent some showing that a ban on advertising aimed only at residents will directly advance Puerto Rico's interest in controlling the harmful effects allegedly associated with casino gambling, Puerto Rico may not constitutionally restrict protected expression in that way.

C

Finally, appellees have failed to show that Puerto Rico's interest in controlling the harmful effects allegedly associated with casino gambling "cannot be protected adequately by more limited regulation of appellant's commercial expression." *Central Hudson, supra,* at 570. Rather than suppressing constitutionally protected expression, Puerto Rico could seek directly to address the specific harms thought to be associated with casino gambling. Thus, Puerto Rico could continue carefully to monitor casino operations to guard against "the development of corruption, and the infiltration of organized crime." * * * It could vigorously enforce its criminal statutes to combat "the increase in local crime [and] the fostering of prostitution." *Ibid.* It could establish limits on the level of permissible betting, or promulgate additional speech designed to discourage casino gambling among residents, in order to avoid the "disruption of moral and cultural patterns," *ibid.,* that might result if residents were to engage in excessive casino gambling. Such measures would directly address the problems appellee associates with casino gambling, while avoiding the First Amendment problems raised where the government seeks to ban constitutionally protected speech.

The Court fails even to acknowledge the wide range of effective alternatives available to Puerto Rico, and addresses only appellant's claim that Puerto Rico's legislature might choose to reduce the demand

---

5. Unlike the Court, I do not read the fact that appellant has chosen to litigate the case here to necessarily indicate that appellant itself believes that Puerto Rico residents would respond to casino advertising. In light of appellees' arbitrary and capricious application of § 8, appellant could justifiably have believed that, notwithstanding the Superior Court's "narrowing" construction, its First Amendment rights could be safeguarded effectively only if the Act was invalidated on its face.

for casino gambling among residents by "promulgating additional speech designed to discourage it." * * * The Court rejects this alternative, asserting that "it is up to the legislature to decide whether or not such a 'counterspeech' policy would be as effective in reducing the demand for casino gambling as a restriction on advertising." *Ibid.* This reasoning ignores the commands of the First Amendment. Where the government seeks to restrict speech in order to advance an important interest, it is not, contrary to what the Court has stated, "up to the legislature" to decide whether or not the government's interest might be protected adequately by less intrusive measures. Rather, it is incumbent upon the government to prove that more limited means are not sufficient to protect its interests, and for a court to decide whether or not the government has sustained this burden. * * *

The Court believes that Puerto Rico constitutionally may prevent its residents from obtaining truthful commercial speech concerning otherwise lawful activity because of the effect it fears this information will have. However, "[i]t is precisely this kind of choice between the dangers of suppressing information, and the dangers of its misuse if it is freely available, that the First Amendment makes for us." *Virginia Pharmacy Board,* 425 U.S., at 770. * * * Accordingly, I would hold that Puerto Rico may not suppress the dissemination of truthful information about entirely lawful activity merely to keep its residents ignorant. The Court, however, would allow Puerto Rico to do just that, thus dramatically shrinking the scope of First Amendment protection available to commercial speech, and giving government officials unprecedented authority to eviscerate constitutionally protected expression. I respectfully dissent.

JUSTICE STEVENS, with whom JUSTICE MARSHALL and JUSTICE BLACKMUN join, dissenting. [Omitted.]

NOTE

I. Suppose in New York where casino gambling is not permitted, that Acme Casino, a company profitably operating casinos in New Jersey (where such casinos are lawful), buys ad space in The New York Times, in which it says:

"Let's vote to make casino gambling lawful in New York."

Would a state law forbidding the Times to carry such an advertisement be subject to the *Posadas* rationale?

II. What are the ramifications of the Court's view in *Posadas* that to the extent a state legislature could constitutionally restrict or eliminate a particular kind of commercial service (e.g., gambling) or product (e.g., tobacco), it may do the lesser thing of restricting or eliminating advertisements of that service or product?

A. Suppose in a jurisdiction where casino gambling is lawful, the Acme Company takes out the following advertisement in a newspaper of general circulation:

As residents of this state already know, casino gambling is lawful for everyone over the age of eighteen. What you may not know is this. Standardly, in casino establishments the roulette wheel odds in rouge et noir (i.e. betting on red or betting on black) favor the house by four percent. At Acme, however, the roulette wheel odds in rouge et noir favor the house by only half as much, i.e. by a mere two percent. For better value, consider the odds and consider ACME.

Would a state law forbidding any such notice be valid under the *Posadas* case? Assuming you conclude that it might be valid, would it also be valid as applied to a news story in the same newspaper, i.e. a news story reporting on rouge et noir odds at the various casinos, reporting that only at Acme is the house favored by a mere two percent?—Would it (should it) make any difference whether the newspaper published the information: (a) because it regarded the furnishing of such information of news interest and of consumer interest in the same fashion as it might from time to time publish information of which gas stations were selling gasoline at prices lower than it was being offered at other stations; (b) because by publishing such information it believed it would sell more newspapers (and thus also more advertising the rates of which are driven by its circulation figures); (c) because of a combination of (a) and (b)?

B. If, consistent with *Posadas,* one thinks the commercial advertisement placed by Acme could be forbidden (because clearly the state could forbid commercial gambling itself), what distinctions, if any, can you propose for the following variations:

1. Consistent with fourteenth amendment economic substantive due process, suppose it to be the case that a state might forbid the sale of prescription drugs at discount,[4] but the state legislature has not in fact done so. As a compromise measure, however, the legislature forbids any advertisement of prescription drugs at discounted prices. Is the measure: (a) invalid under *Virginia State Board of Pharmacy;* (b) valid under *Posadas;* (c) controlled rather by the *Central Hudson* test—in which case it is ....?

2. In *Posadas,* Justice Rehnquist distinguished from *Posadas* commercial speech of products or services not within the power of legislatures to disallow (e.g., contraceptive devices, medically safe abortion services), unlike the power to disallow gambling and probably sale of tobacco products or sale of motorcycles, etc. Presumably the same distinction would apply in respect to first amendment goods and services as well (e.g., that the state could not forbid publication, distribution, or sale of Marx's *Das Kapital,* and, correspondingly, could not regulate commercial advertisements promoting sales of the book, except narrowly in ways consistent with *Central Hudson* and related cases). Consist-

---

4. I.e. that a minimum price law would be sustained against constitutional objection, just as such a law was sustained as long ago as 1934, in Nebbia v. New York, 291 U.S. 502, 54 S.Ct. 505, 78 L.Ed. 940 (1934) (state law forbidding retail sale of milk at less than nine cents a quart, *sustained* as applied to small grocer who sold two quarts for eighteen cents but included a "free" loaf of bread, the Court disallowing a fourteenth amendment due process liberty and property claim).

ent with this distinction, presumably the rendering of legal professional service would also be treated in a similar fashion, i.e. the state could not forbid such services (consistent with the due process clause itself and the guarantees of right to counsel furnished by the Constitution). Accordingly, the lawyer advertising cases (e.g., *Bates, Ohralik, Zauderer*) would appear to be governed by the *Central Hudson* formula and not by the implications of *Posadas*.

Consider, however, the following case and decide whether the state law would be (a) invalid under *Bates*, or (b) valid under *Posadas*: a prohibition on lawyer advertising of legal services available on a contingent fee basis.[5]—More generally, to what extent does the *Posadas* test require one to address an uncertain, partly advisory constitutional question (namely, the extent to which such legislation may or may not outlaw a particular kind of product, service, or commercial practice), to determine which commercial speech doctrine may or may not apply? Where *Posadas* does apply, to what extent is its effect to return the constitutional protection of commercial speech to the same place it held under *Valentine v. Chrestensen*, in 1942?[6]

B. The Uncertainties of Regulating or Criminalizing the "Obscene"

1. "Obscenity"[7] and the First Amendment

In a 1942 case previously noted in these materials, *Chaplinsky v. New Hampshire*,[8] the Supreme Court sustained the conviction of a Jehovah Witness for addressing a police officer as a "God damned racketeer" and "a damned fascist," in the heat of being led away from a spot on the public street where he had been aggressively trying to proselytize passersby. The charge against Chaplinsky was not based on

---

5. Invalid under *Bates* (and related lawyer advertising decisions) assuming only clarity, accuracy, no misleading omissions, etc. in the statements respecting the contingent fee option, or valid under *Posadas*—if the state could constitutionally forbid this form of offering legal services (as generally is still the case in England and elsewhere, where contingent fee contracts are often disallowed as a form of barratry, champerty, or maintenance)?

6. For several critical reviews of *Posadas* and of the commercial speech cases generally, see Barrett, "The Unchartered Area"—Commercial Speech and the First Amendment, 13 U.C.Davis L.Rev. 175 (1980); Farber, Commercial Speech and First Amendment Theory, 74 Nw.U.L.Rev. 372 (1979); Jackson & Jeffries, Commercial Speech: Economic Due Process and the First Amendment, 65 Va.L.Rev. 1 (1979); McGowan, A Critical Analysis of Commercial Speech, 78 Calif.L.Rev. 359 (1990); Schauer, Commercial Speech and the Architecture of the First Amendment, 56 U.Cin.L.Rev. 1181 (1988); Shiffrin, The First Amendment and Economic Regulation: Away from a General Theory of the First Amendment, 78 N.W.U.L.Rev. 1212 (1983).

7. "*Obscene:* 1. Offensive to accepted standards of decency or modesty. 2. Inciting lustful feelings; indecent; lewd. 3. Offensive or repulsive to the senses; loathsome. [Old French, from Latin *obscenus, obscaenus*, ill-boding, inauspicious, repulsive.]" American Heritage Dictionary (1971 ed.)] Cf. "*pornographic:* written or graphic forms of communication intended to excite lascivious feelings. [From Greek *pornographos*, writing about prostitutes."]

8. 315 U.S. 568, 62 S.Ct. 766, 86 L.Ed. 1031 (1942).

his annoyance of the pedestrians,[9] but on his use of epithets, face-to-face, addressed to the policeman. It was not brought under a state anti-obscenity statute, but under an act forbidding anyone to address "any offensive, derisive or annoying word to any other person" lawfully in a public place. Nevertheless, in the course of his opinion for the Court upholding the statute as applied in this case, Justice Murphy also included the following, much more general paragraph:

> There are certain well-defined and narrowly limited classes of speech, the prevention and punishment of which have never been thought to raise any Constitutional problem. *These include the lewd and obscene,* the profane, the libelous, and the insulting or "fighting" words—those which by their very utterance inflict injury or tend to incite an immediate breach of the peace. [S]uch utterances are no essential part of any exposition of ideas, and are of such slight social value as a step to truth that any benefit that may be derived from them is clearly outweighed by the social interest in order and morality.[10]

To be sure, other portions of the Court's opinion in the case suggested that this paragraph might not mean literally what it appeared to say.[11] But it has been taken to say that certain named categories of speech are wholly excluded from the first amendment.[12] "Lewd and obscene" speech are examples of such first amendment-excluded categories, "the prevention and punishment of which have never been thought to raise any Constitutional problem," *Chaplinsky* declares. Accordingly, if that is so, the correct approach to this subject would be a one-step approach, nothing more, because insofar as the speech in question were either lewd or obscene, the government could

---

9. Cantwell v. Connecticut, 310 U.S. 296, 60 S.Ct. 900, 84 L.Ed. 1213 (1940), overturned a conviction in just such a case, sheltering street proselytizing in accordance with the felt obligations of one's religion, even when conducted aggressively, with condemnation of other faiths. *Cantwell* is significant aside from its general usefulness as a strong first amendment case. It is the first case holding that the free exercise of religion clause of the first amendment fully applies—via the due process clause—to the states. Several earlier cases had presaged that holding, e.g., Pierce v. Society of the Sisters, 268 U.S. 510, 45 S.Ct. 571, 69 L.Ed. 1070 (1925) ("liberty" in the fourteenth amendment's due process clause includes freedom of religion.)

10. *Id.* (emphasis added). See also Cantwell v. Connecticut, 310 U.S. 296, 60 S.Ct. 900, 84 L.Ed. 1213 (1940) (dictum); Z. Chafee, Free Speech in the United States 149–50 (1942) ("[O]bscenity, profanity, and gross libels of individuals * * * fall outside the protection of the free speech clauses as I have defined them.")

11. Much of the balance of the full opinion, as well as one not unreasonable reading of this excerpt, is merely consistent with a Learned Hand style of general first amendment test, rather than with the view that the first amendment has no application at all. The Court noted that the words were not part of the defendant's street corner remarks, rather, they were addressed personally and directly to the arresting officer, away from the forum, and spoken as words of immediate personal abuse; the case might have been reasoned in terms of whether police officers must, because of the first amendment, be made to accept an unmitigated amount of verbal abuse as part of their work—and refrain from striking back, or whether the avoidance of provoking the arresting officer or subjecting him to personal humiliation in the circumstances would justify the restriction on the citizen under the circumstances, consistent with the first amendment, rather than on the theory that the first amendment has no application at all.

12. See, e.g., the quotation from Chafee, note 9 *supra*, in accord with this view.

enter a demurrer to any claim of first amendment protection in respect to such speech, and thereby prevail in the case at hand even with no showing of danger or of evil or of harm. The state would but cite *Chaplinsky* in support of its demurrer. Once it is determined that the speech was "obscene" speech, the defendant cannot invoke the first amendment (for this is just what is meant in saying that a given class of utterances is excluded from the first amendment, is it not?).

We have seen this approach in earlier areas of our first amendment investigations, but in each previous instance in which we encountered it, it did not long endure. In the just completed section of our work on "commercial" speech, we noted that the same thing was once also said to be true there as well. *Valentine v. Chrestensen,* also decided in 1942, conveyed just such a suggestion respecting ordinary commercial advertising. Any such advertising was treated as but an incident of the ordinary trade or business practice of the entrepreneur and, as such, it was deemed equally subject to such regulation as the state might choose to impose consistent solely with a "minimum rationality," substantive due process test, with no special first amendment claim at all. *Railway Express Agency v. New York* (1949) likewise treated commercial advertising as merely an incident of economic activity protected by mere minimum, substantive due process review. But as we learned, beginning not later than the *Virginia State Board of Pharmacy* decision, in 1976, no such exclusionary first amendment boundary now cordons off commercial speech. Rather, as we have noted in the previous section of our work, the first amendment now applies to this field generally, pursuant to the *Central Hudson* four-part test.

Similarly, prior to *New York Times v. Sullivan* (1964), the whole class of utterances called "libel" was also allegedly outside the first amendment—just as the quoted paragraph from *Chaplinsky* declared.[13] Yet, beginning with *New York Times v. Sullivan* itself, the view has become altogether different in respect to criminal or civil actions for libel, as well as in respect to commercial speech.[14]

"Libel," we have seen, even as "commercial" speech, is now understood to embrace quite a complex first amendment subject.[15] Indeed, on reflection, the evolved, specialized first amendment treatment of each of those subjects has but mirrored the consistent pattern of every other subject we have reviewed in this course. That pattern has become virtually a matter of predictable routine. It has run pretty much in

---

13. (I.e. "libel" is listed with the "lewd," the "obscene," the "profane," and with "fighting words," as presumptively raising no constitutional problem at all).

14. To recall the critical quotation from *New York Times v. Sullivan,* "[L]ibel can claim no talismanic immunity from constitutional limitations. It must be measured by standards that satisfy the First Amendment." (Emphasis added.) To recall the parallel observation in the *Virginia Pharmacy* case, "Last term, in *Bigelow v. Virginia* [citation omitted], the notion of unprotected 'commercial speech' all but passed from the scene."

15. E.g., it now matters to ask "libel" of whom? (A public figure, limited public figure, nonpublic figure?) "Libel" in reference to *what kind of subject*? (A subject of public interest or not?) "Libel" in *what manner of medium*? "Libel" with *what degree of scienter,* with *what kind of damages* in mind, etc., all of these now regarded as each presenting highly pertinent questions driven by first amendment concerns.

the following way. First, at "time one," a subject is said not to raise first amendment problems at all.[16] Somewhat later, that categorical denial is withdrawn.[17] Eventually the first amendment becomes systematically applied, i.e. applied to the once-orphaned field, albeit with a particular contour of doctrine somewhat formulaically shaped.[18] And so it has gone for us, at *every* stage of our unhurried first amendment review.

In keeping with these other developments that we have already traced, e.g., on commercial speech and on libel, as we begin our work here one might expect to see a parallel development in the case law of "obscenity." In brief, one might expect that sometime after 1942,[19] the Court would certainly find that "obscenity" is not unprotected by the first amendment but, rather, the first amendment extent of protection (as with libel or as with commercial speech) would be worked out on a case by case basis, perhaps in keeping with time, place, and manner doctrines we have examined in related areas, but presumably not much more.[20] Surprisingly, however, that has not in fact happened. Surprisingly, in a literal sense the *Chaplinsky* dictum is still the law. Narrowly speaking, the first amendment law of obscenity, 1942–1990, can be summarized in the following way.

---

16. The first cases we examined appeared to take this view in respect to restrictions on public employees (e.g., McAuliffe v. Mayor of New Bedford, 155 Mass. 216, 29 N.E. 517 (1892); Scopes v. State, 154 Tenn. 105, 289 S.W. 363 (1927); Bailey v. Richardson, 341 U.S. 918, 71 S.Ct. 669, 95 L.Ed. 1352 (1951). Likewise the first cases we examined appeared to take the very same view respecting restrictive uses of publicly-owned property as well (e.g., Davis v. Massachusetts, 167 U.S. 43, 17 S.Ct. 731, 42 L.Ed. 71 (1897)). Each of these subjects, like "libel," and like "commercial speech," had no significant first amendment standing, though each is now a principal source of ongoing dispute.

17. E.g., as in Pickering v. Board of Educ., 391 U.S. 563, 88 S.Ct. 1731, 20 L.Ed.2d 811 (1968) (in respect to public employees) and as in Hague v. CIO, 307 U.S. 954, 59 S.Ct. 954, 83 L.Ed. 1423 (1939) (in respect to publicly-owned parks).

18. E.g., the "four part" (commercial) speech test of *Central Hudson*, the *Pickering–Connick–Mt. Healthy* "test" (of public employee speech), the "forum" (public property) analysis outlined in the *Cornelius* case, the four-part *O'Brien* "test," the complex web of libel analysis, etc.

19. The date of the oft-repeated *Chaplinsky* dictum.

20. So, even as to "fighting words" themselves (i.e. the immediate subject of the Supreme Court's pronouncements in *Chaplinsky*), it is an oversimplification to regard such speech as excluded from the first amendment. Crude, insulting speech, including a great deal that may stir others to anger, is not now excluded from full first amendment protection, depending upon the place where it occurs, whether it has an ideological content, how captive the persons subjected to it may or may not be, and a variety of other things as well. (See, e.g., Hustler Magazine v. Falwell, 485 U.S. 46, 108 S.Ct. 876, 99 L.Ed.2d 41 (1988) (disallowing personal tort remedy for intentional infliction of emotional distress); Cohen v. California, 403 U.S. 15, 91 S.Ct. 1780, 29 L.Ed.2d 284 (1971) (disallowing disorderly conduct charge for failure on officer's request to remove jacket with "Fuck The Draft" within courthouse corridors trafficked by women and children); Kunz v. New York, 340 U.S. 290, 71 S.Ct. 312, 95 L.Ed. 280 (1951) reviewed in these materials previously. See also Rosenfeld v. New Jersey, 408 U.S. 901, 92 S.Ct. 2479, 33 L.Ed.2d 321 (1972); Lewis v. New Orleans, 408 U.S. 913, 92 S.Ct. 2499, 33 L.Ed.2d 321 (1972); Brown v. Oklahoma, 408 U.S. 914, 92 S.Ct. 2507, 33 L.Ed.2d 326 (1972); Gooding v. Wilson, 405 U.S. 518, 92 S.Ct. 1103, 31 L.Ed.2d 408 (1972); Terminiello v. Chicago, 337 U.S. 1, 69 S.Ct. 894, 93 L.Ed. 1131 (1949); Cantwell v. Connecticut, 310 U.S. 296, 60 S.Ct. 900, 84 L.Ed. 1213 (1940); H. Kalven, A Worthy Tradition 80–118 (1988). An especially strong state case disallowing a "fighting words" rationale even in circumstances of extreme provocation and targeted insult, despite *Chaplinsky*, is Skokie v. National Socialist Party, 69 Ill.2d 605, 14 Ill.Dec. 890, 373 N.E.2d 21 (1978).

In 1958, sixteen years after *Chaplinsky*, the Supreme Court again held that "obscenity" derives *no* protection from the first amendment. It did so on the basis of its conclusion that the first amendment deemed such speech to have no value at all.[21] Nine years later, in 1967, the Court concluded that obscenity still derives no protection from the first amendment, but only if it has no redeeming value, a requirement moreover, the government must establish affirmatively in each case.[22]— Otherwise, it then held, that which may well be "obscene" (in the ordinary dictionary sense) may nonetheless be protected by the first amendment, albeit still subject to some degree of social control principally according to time, place, manner, and age.[23]

This shift *de facto,* although not *de jure,*[24] obviously was a very major shift indeed. For without repudiating the general position (i.e. that "obscenity" has no first amendment protection), practically speaking the first amendment was brought into the field albeit by a back door approach. The back door approach was to admit at least some relevance of standard first amendment review via the three-part special definition of "obscenity" the Court deemed somehow required by the strictures of the first amendment itself, despite what it had previously declared (i.e. that implicit in the history of the first amendment was the rejection of obscenity as of so little value as to require no weighing or balancing at all), with the Court itself undertaking to monitor the

---

21. *Roth–Alberts:* "[I]mplicit in the history of the first amendment is the rejection of obscenity as utterly without redeeming social importance. * * * [We] hold that obscenity is not within the area of constitutionally protected speech or press." Compare, however, what might equally be said of "libel" or of "fighting words," (e.g., "implicit in the history of the first amendment is the rejection of libel as utterly without redeeming social importance. * * * [We] hold that libel is not within the area of constitutionally protected speech or press"). The latter sentence reads as compellingly as the former, surely. Why, then, is "libel" often within—rather than never within—the area of constitutionally protected speech or press? Why, correspondingly, may not "obscenity" at least be sometimes within, rather than never within, the first amendment as well? According to the general view of the first amendment, moreover, who decides whether certain speech may or may not have some kind of "value," e.g., the founding fathers, today's legislators, the Supreme Court, or each individual for himself or herself? Is it the lack of alleged value that subjects speech to regulation consistent with the first amendment, or, rather, the felt need to avoid or redress certain harms? In the case of "obscenity," vis-a-vis "libel," "criminal solicitation," "advocacy of violence," etc., what is the alleged harm? Surely these are not idle questions, but, note, insofar as "obscenity" is regarded as excluded from the first amendment, they evidently need not even be addressed.

22. *Memoirs*: "[In order for published material to be treated as obscene and therefore excluded from the protection of the first amendment] it must be established that (a) the dominant theme of the material taken as a whole appeals to a prurient interest in sex; (b) the material is patently offensive because it affronts contemporary community standards relating to the description or representation of sexual matters; *and* (c) the material is utterly without redeeming social value." (The emphasis added is meant to highlight the Court's departure respecting its definition of "obscenity" from the ordinary dictionary definition (note 1, *supra*). The dictionary definition is unconcerned with the personal or "social value" of obscenity, such as such value may or may not be, i.e. the dictionary definition has nothing resembling part (c) of the Supreme Court's *Memoirs* test.)

23. See, e.g., Redrup v. New York, 386 U.S. 767, 87 S.Ct. 1414, 18 L.Ed.2d 515 (1967) and Stanley v. Georgia, 394 U.S. 557, 89 S.Ct. 1243, 22 L.Ed.2d 542 (1969) decisions, *infra* in the materials in this section.

24. I.e. *de jure* it remained at all times true that if the utterance, speech, or other material were "obscene," then it received no first amendment protection.

manner in which that three-part definition was applied by judges and juries, virtually from case to case. In 1969, a majority of the Court appeared to be ready to abandon the position that "obscenity" has no first amendment protection, moreover, such that the issue, as with libel, the uses of public property, etc., would then become not whether, but, rather, how much? [25]

In 1973, however, the Court backed off. It concluded again that obscenity derives no protection from the first amendment, and this time it held that that is so even assuming there may be some redeeming value of some sort. In doing so, it substantially reversed the contrary trend of the decisional law that had occurred during the previous fifteen years.[26] And, from that time to this time through 1991, this has remained the prevailing view within the Supreme Court. We shall examine several cases to help determine how the current standard actually works. Here, in completing an introductory overview of the field, we shall note but a few features along the way.

First, the reason for the principal 1973 modification (namely, that some slight modicum of alleged literary, artistic, political, or scientific value may not be enough to pull otherwise-obscene material within the protection of the first amendment), may come from concerns reflected in the *Ginzburg* case, a case also presented in these materials. The marketing of the particular magazine involved in the case emphasized its promise of prurient content. Included within the magazine, however, were some features and reprinted bawdy literary tales such that at least those parts of the magazine could fairly be said by reliable experts on literature to have redeeming literary value. The Court's decision, sustaining Ginzburg's conviction, evidently meant to permit the government to head off what it (the Court as well as the government) regarded as mere evasions of otherwise valid anti-obscenity laws by entrepreneurs who would take due commercial care to pad the publication with some passing gesture to a serious idea, discussion, editorial, etc., to frustrate any prosecutorial attempt. The *Miller* modification of the *Memoirs* standard (requiring the prosecution to convince judge and jury the material is "utterly" lacking in redeeming literary, artistic, political, or scientific value) was almost certainly made largely to bring this sort of commercial charade to an end, but it may apply even when, in contrast to *Ginzburg*, the facts show no deliberate deviousness on the producer's or exhibitor's part.[27]

---

25. Stanley v. Georgia, 394 U.S. 557, 89 S.Ct. 1243, 22 L.Ed.2d 542 (1969), is just such a case. The Court accepted the government's view that the material in question was "obscene" even according to its own, three-part test, yet reversed the conviction of the accused.

26. *Miller*: "A state offense must * * * be limited to works which, taken as a whole, appeal to the prurient interest in sex, which portray sexual conduct in a patently offensive way, and which, taken as a whole, do not have *serious* literary, artistic, political, or scientific value." (Emphasis added.) (A modicum of literary, artistic, political, or scientific value may not suffice. Moreover, evidently some other kind of "value" (e.g., value personal to the consumer) may not count, if the material is otherwise "obscene," though the Court is unclear why this is so.)

27. Note also that the *Miller* standard makes one other change of the same kind; it speaks of "works * * * taken as a whole," rather than (as in both *Roth* and *Memoirs*) of "*the dominant theme* of the material taken as a whole." (Emphasis added.) The shift may seem trivial, but it

Second, the *Miller–Slaton* standard, announced in 1973, moreover, is itself not conclusive as to material that may be found obscene. So, for example, even if the material in question would *not* be obscene as a general matter,[28] it may still be regulated as such, and successful criminal prosecutions brought, if found obscene (by the *Miller–Slaton* test) in terms of some targeted subset of the population to whom it is sent for its appeal. If obscene "for children" (though not for adults), the material may be criminalized as to its distribution to children.[29] If obscene "for homosexuals" (though not for others),[30] it may be criminalized as to that targeted market as well.[31]

Conversely, on the other hand, the fact that material may be obscene only as to juveniles will not sustain a regulation banning the material from others on that account.[32] In other words, a general ban may not be sustained by a "most vulnerable member(s) of the community" test.[33] This much was itself settled originally in *Roth–Alberts*, rejecting the *Regina v. Hicklin* most-vulnerable-member-of-the-community standard of the older common law. Rather, differentiating statutes (e.g., disallowing commercial motion picture exhibitors to admit persons under 17 to films "obscene" for minors, but not otherwise forbidding the films to be shown) may be permitted and applied.[34]

is meant to cope with a defense strategy similar to the strategy (some redeeming value) in *Ginzburg*. That strategy was keyed to using a moral theme, as it were, as the dominant theme of the obscene work, i.e., to suggest in the text accompanying the otherwise obscene film, magazine, etc., that the dissolute, wayward, freewheeling sexual promiscuity of the described (fictitious) characters was, in the end, their undoing. So, the "theme" was that the depicted licentiousness reaped a bad outcome, after all. *Miller* is meant to cut off this device for salvaging an otherwise "obscene" cheaply-produced commercial flick or sex magazine.

28. It might not be obscene even under *Miller–Slaton*, because, for example, so far as the average adult person in the relevant contemporary community may be concerned, taken as a whole the film or magazine does not engender a prurient response; alternatively, though it evokes a prurient response, the particular portrayal of sexual conduct might not flunk the "patently offensive," independent, second part of the test.

29. Ginsberg v. New York, 390 U.S. 629, 88 S.Ct. 1274, 20 L.Ed.2d 195 (1968). This issue is separate and additional to the criminalization of the use of minors even in the production of nonobscene, but sexually explicit, materials, sustained in New York v. Ferber, 458 U.S. 747, 102 S.Ct. 3348, 73 L.Ed.2d 1113 (1982). The basis of that decision is the protection of minors from "exploitation" as such, period. (Akin to a child labor law.) The *Ferber* doctrine does not, on the other hand, sanction laws outlawing pedophilia material per se. Such material remains subject to prohibition only if, as such, it is obscene under the *Miller–Slayton* standards, adjusted by the targeted-audience rationale we have already noted.

30. —Because, for instance, it lacks capacity to stimulate in nonhomosexual persons any erotic response (and thus, while still possibly patently offensive as to them, it has no prurient appeal for them).

31. Mishkin v. New York, 383 U.S. 502, 86 S.Ct. 958, 16 L.Ed.2d 56 (1966).

32. Butler v. Michigan, 352 U.S. 380, 77 S.Ct. 524, 1 L.Ed.2d 412 (1957). The state may not reduce the adult population [to] reading only what is fit for children. See also Sable Communications of Cal., Inc. v. FCC, 492 U.S. 115, 109 S.Ct. 2829, 106 L.Ed.2d 93 (1989) (Congressional ban on "indecent" dial-a-porn telephone services, to protect children, held invalid as unconstitutionally overbroad (because the ban affects adults and the ban was not limited to such dial-a-porn messages as would satisfy the *Miller–Slaton* test)). (But see dicta in case, suggesting that if the total ban were the only efficient way such calls could be made unavailable to juveniles, then it might be sustained *despite its invasion of adult first amendment rights.*)

33. See also Pinkus v. United States, 436 U.S. 293, 98 S.Ct. 1808, 53 L.Ed.2d 293 (1978) (*Butler v. Michigan* applied).

Mere parity of reasoning should provide, conversely, of course, that specialized audiences (e.g., Kinsey Institute personnel, Johnson & Masters users) would, in turn, be able to invoke a successful first amendment claim even assuming the material otherwise fails the *Miller–Slaton* test. Arguably, that should be so, because in specific context the material has met the "serious redeeming value" requirement to qualify the material for first amendment protection in such settings, though not in general commercial markets. There appears to be no direct Supreme Court decision on the point, but it is strongly arguable that even producers or senders of "obscene" materials should be fully protected insofar as the delivery were limited to such "redeeming-use" audiences as those just described.[35]

These sorts of special problems aside, moreover, because of the still-prevailing majority view (i.e. that if the material is "obscene" it receives no first amendment protection—thus no usual first amendment proof of actual harm need be met by the state),[36] some real strains are felt at the margin of uncertainty as to whether particular works are or are not obscene. Since so much rides on the right guess respecting the nonobscenity of the material in question, one's uncertainty may per

---

34. This may be a suitable place to note and distinguish, the "rating" system (P, PG, PG–13, R, NC–17) the film industry uses. These ratings are not ratings based on first amendment criteria (e.g., the fact that a film may have a PG–13 rating does not mean that it could not therefore be seen by youngsters under thirteen, a film rated NC–17 does not mean that it would necessarily be subject to successful criminal prosecution even assuming persons under the age of seventeen may be admitted; a state law presuming to mimic the rating system would therefore not be constitutional as such. It is nonetheless true that the rating system practically affects which films are available (exhibitors were very chary of taking X-rated films, partly from fear of inviting criminal prosecution), so its de facto influence is quite strong. (Note, however, there is no obligation on a film producer to submit its film to the rating system; accordingly, a number of films will carry no rating at all.)

35. An interesting variation of the example might be one we ourselves could provide: to distribute within this classroom examples of work otherwise held to be suppressible (because found to be "obscene"), in order that, as lawyers in training, one be able to compare material which has been upheld vis-a-vis material that has not been upheld in the courts. *Query,* whether a criminal prosecution for such limited use of the materials, in this class, could, consistent with the first amendment, be sustained. Assuming it could not be sustained, to what extent might one extend the example itself? E.g., if one is free to inspect and discuss such material in a first amendment law school course, ought not one also be able to secure a copy of such material from a willing supplier, with the supplier equally being protected in having made it available for such classroom use, with reliance upon the first amendment as against any attempt to prosecute the supplier himself? Cf. Lamont v. Postmaster General, 381 U.S. 301, 85 S.Ct. 1983, 14 L.Ed.2d 398 (1965).

36. Though note, again, that whether particular material is "obscene" is not a function inherent in the material itself but is, rather, partly contingent upon the community in which it appears (e.g., the film, *The Devil in Miss Jones,* may be obscene in one state or one town, but not obscene in a different state or a different town, or not obscene in the District of Columbia), although, to be found obscene even in the most restrictive community the material must separately meet the minimum qualifications of "obscene" speech as set in *Miller–Slaton.* (See, e.g., Jenkins v. Georgia, 418 U.S. 153, 94 S.Ct. 2750, 41 L.Ed.2d 642 (1974) (film *Carnal Knowledge* judged by Georgia jury to be obscene pursuant to *Miller–Slaton* jury instruction held, not obscene as a matter of constitutional law, because the manner in which intimate erotic sexual acts were depicted lacked sufficient coarseness as such as not to be deemable as patently offensive, as a matter of law).

se produce a large chilling effect.[37]

Two principal cases in the following materials illustrate the problem in the obscenity area, and the Supreme Court's response to each: *Freedman v. Maryland,* (1965) and *Smith v. California,* (1959). The *Smith* case holds that in order that one be criminally accountable under an anti-obscenity law, one must at least know or have reason to know the content of the books or journals comprising the inventory of one's retail shop. The scienter requirement of the *Smith* case lifts the chilling effect that might otherwise result from being unable to stock any larger assortment of printed materials that one had the time (or the means of paying employees) to read.[38]

Freedman v. Maryland, relatedly, is twice significant. First, it is a "hostile" case in approving a form of prior restraint—requiring submission of commercial films to some kind of local film clearance board may not per se violate the first amendment, though a strong contrary argument can surely be made that it does.[39] (One might plausibly have thought that such preview clearance boards would be prohibited,[40] given the usual first amendment presumption against a regime of prior restraint). Second, however, because the orientation of the censor is presumed to be such that in close cases he or she will be prone to err in favor of protecting the public rather than the exhibitor, *Freedman* mandates special safeguards insofar as film clearance procedures are

---

37. The problem has an obvious kinship with the overbreadth doctrine we have encountered before, i.e. speech-specific statutes on their face forbidding speech not within the constitutional authority of the state to forbid, are subject to attack even by a party whose speech could clearly have been reached under a more narrowly drawn statute. (The "guilty" go free in order that the "innocent" not be unduly "chilled.") The problem has an obvious kinship, as well, with the chilling effect rationale for protecting libel as strongly as it is protected under the *New York Times v. Sullivan* rule. (Newspapers are given a first amendment immunity for public figure libel even when false and damaging statements are negligently researched and published, in order that there be adequate "breathing space" for publishers who might otherwise be too fearful to publish critical stories.)

38. If *Smith* imports a special scienter requirement (as it does) in order that protected materials not be suppressed, might it not likewise be argued that the first amendment may require some limitation on the magnitude of penalty or punishment the state may impose, since at least as chilling an effect inhibiting book sellers to carry close-to-the-edge books (or film exhibitors carrying close-to-the-edge films), must surely result when the criminal sanction for an obscenity law violation is very great (e.g., up to five years in prison, or forfeiture of one's store—for having sold "criminal contraband")? Bearing in mind that, consistent with *Roth–Alberts–Miller* doctrine, "obscenity" having been formally excluded from the first amendment (such that the state need make no conventional showing of any strong reason for disallowing it in the first place), with the result that so much is made to depend upon sorting the "obscene" from the "nonobscene" in terms of one's liability, a strong argument along these lines would seem to be sound. Thus far, however, a majority of the Supreme Court has given it no acceptance. (The latest rejection is Fort Wayne Books, Inc. v. Indiana, 489 U.S. 46, 109 S.Ct. 916, 103 L.Ed.2d 34 (1989).) Correspondingly, some state anti-obscenity laws have been revised upwards in recent years, to impose very heavy sanctions, akin to dealing in drugs.

39. *Freedman* is not new in this respect. See Times Film Corp. v. Chicago, 365 U.S. 43, 81 S.Ct. 391, 5 L.Ed.2d 403 (1961) (film clearance municipal ordinance sustained as not invalid per se, five-to-four (Warren–Black–Douglas–Brennan, JJ., dissenting).

40. See, e.g., Bantam Books, Inc. v. Sullivan, 372 U.S. 58, 83 S.Ct. 631, 9 L.Ed.2d 584 (1963) (prior restraint systems are presumed to be invalid). (And see prior discussion, beginning even with Blackstone, all the way through *Pentagon Papers* and *Nebraska Press.*)

used at all. Accordingly, it requires that the relevant standards must be both specifically and narrowly defined, the time within which the censor must decide (or failing which, the film may be shown) must be short, and if the censorship decision is adverse to the film, an expeditious review must be provided in the courts in which it is the censor's burden to go forward to sustain the adverse censorship decision—not the film exhibitor's burden to show the decision was in error. The *Freedman* standards, moreover, have been carried over into other prior restraints environments, noted in our previous work.[41]

ROTH v. UNITED STATES
ALBERTS v. CALIFORNIA

Supreme Court of the United States, 1957.
354 U.S. 476, 77 S.Ct. 1304, 1 L.Ed.2d 1498.

MR. JUSTICE BRENNAN delivered the opinion of the Court.

The constitutionality of a criminal obscenity statute is the question in each of these cases. In *Roth*, the primary constitutional question is whether the federal obscenity statute[1] violates the provision of the First Amendment that "Congress shall make no law * * * abridging the freedom of speech, or of the press * * *" In *Alberts*, the primary constitutional question is whether the obscenity provisions of the California Penal Code[2] invade the freedoms of speech and press as they

---

41. See, e.g., Carroll v. President and Com'rs of Princess Anne, 393 U.S. 175, 89 S.Ct. 347, 21 L.Ed.2d 325 (1968) (ten-day ex parte injunction against imminent public political meeting held void for failure to satisfy *Freedman* standards). For a general review, see Monaghan, First Amendment Due Process, 83 Harv.L.Rev. 518 (1970).

1. The federal obscenity statute provided, in pertinent part:

"Every obscene, lewd, lascivious, or filthy book, pamphlet, picture, paper, letter, writing, print, or other publication of an indecent character; and—

* * *

"Every written or printed card, letter, circular, book, pamphlet, advertisement, or notice of any kind giving information, directly or indirectly, where, or how, or from whom, or by what means any of such mentioned matters, articles, or things may be obtained or made, * * * whether sealed or unsealed * * *

* * *

"Is declared to be nonmailable matter and shall not be conveyed in the mails or delivered from any post office or by any letter carrier.

"Whoever knowingly deposits for mailing or delivery, anything declared by this section to be nonmailable, or knowingly takes the same from the mails for the purpose of circulating or disposing thereof, or of aiding in the circulation or disposition thereof, shall be fined not more than $5,000 or imprisoned not more than five years, or both." 18 U.S.C.A. § 1461.

* * *

2. The California Penal Code provides, in pertinent part:

"Every person who wilfully and lewdly, either:

* * *

"3. Writes, composes, stereotypes, prints, publishes, sells, distributes, keeps for sale, or exhibits any obscene or indecent writing, paper, or book; or designs, copies, draws, engraves, paints, or otherwise prepares any obscene or indecent picture or print; or molds, cuts, casts, or otherwise makes any obscene or indecent figure; or,

"4. Writes, composes, or publishes any notice or advertisement of any such writing, paper, book, picture, print or figure;
* * *

* * *

may be incorporated in the liberty protected from state action by the Due Process Clause of the Fourteenth Amendment.

Other constitutional questions are: whether these statutes violate due process, because too vague to support conviction for crime; whether power to punish speech and press offensive to decency and morality is in the States alone, so that the federal obscenity statute violates the Ninth and Tenth Amendments (raised in *Roth*); and whether Congress, by enacting the federal obscenity statute, under the power delegated by Art. I, § 8, cl. 7, to establish post offices and post roads, pre-empted the regulation of the subject matter (raised in *Alberts*).

Roth conducted a business in New York in the publication and sale of books, photographs and magazines. He used circulars and advertising matter to solicit sales. He was convicted by a jury in the District Court for the Southern District of New York upon 4 counts of a 26–count indictment charging him with mailing obscene circulars and advertising, and an obscene book, in violation of the federal obscenity statute. His conviction was affirmed by the Court of Appeals for the Second Circuit. We granted certiorari.

Alberts conducted a mail-order business from Los Angeles. He was convicted by the Judge of the Municipal Court of the Beverly Hills Judicial District (having waived a jury trial) under a misdemeanor complaint which charged him with lewdly keeping for sale obscene and indecent books, and with writing, composing and publishing an obscene advertisement of them, in violation of the California Penal Code. The conviction was affirmed by the Appellate Department of the Superior Court of the State of California in and for the County of Los Angeles. We noted probable jurisdiction.

The dispositive question is whether obscenity is utterance within the area of protected speech and press.[8] Although this is the first time the question has been squarely presented to this Court, either under the First Amendment or under the Fourteenth Amendment, expressions found in numerous opinions indicate that this Court has always assumed that obscenity is not protected by the freedoms of speech and press. * * *

The guaranties of freedom of expression in effect in 10 of the 14 States which by 1792 had ratified the Constitution, gave no absolute protection for every utterance. Thirteen of the 14 States provided for the prosecution of libel, and all of those States made either blasphemy or profanity, or both, statutory crimes. As early as 1712, Massachusetts made it criminal to publish "any filthy, obscene, or profane song, pamphlet, libel or mock sermon" in imitation or mimicking of religious services. * * *

In light of this history, it is apparent that the unconditional phrasing of the First Amendment was not intended to protect every utterance. This phrasing did not prevent this Court from concluding

"6. * * * is guilty of a misdemeanor. * * *"

8. No issue is presented in either case concerning the obscenity of the material involved.

that libelous utterances are not within the area of constitutionally protected speech. * * * At the time of the adoption of the First Amendment, obscenity law was not as fully developed as libel law, but there is sufficiently contemporaneous evidence to show that obscenity, too, was outside the protection intended for speech and press.

The protection given speech and press was fashioned to assure unfettered interchange of ideas for the bringing about of political and social changes desired by the people. * * *

All ideas having even the slightest redeeming social importance—unorthodox ideas, controversial ideas, even ideas hateful to the prevailing climate of opinion—have the full protection of the guaranties, unless excludable because they encroach upon the limited area of more important interests. But implicit in the history of the First Amendment is the rejection of obscenity as utterly without redeeming social importance. This rejection for that reason is mirrored in the universal judgment that obscenity should be restrained, reflected in the international agreement of over 50 nations, in the obscenity laws of all of the 48 States, and in the 20 obscenity laws enacted by the Congress from 1842 to 1956. This is the same judgment expressed by this Court in Chaplinsky v. New Hampshire, 315 U.S. 568, 571–572:

> " * * * There are certain well-defined and narrowly limited classes of speech, the prevention and punishment of which have never been thought to raise any Constitutional problem. *These include the lewd and obscene * * * It has been well observed that such utterances are no essential part of any exposition of ideas, and are of such slight social value as a step to truth that any benefit that may be derived from them is clearly outweighed by the social interest in order and morality.* * * * " (Emphasis added.)

We hold that obscenity is not within the area of constitutionally protected speech or press.

It is strenuously urged that these obscenity statutes offend the constitutional guaranties because they punish incitation to impure sexual *thoughts*, not shown to be related to any overt antisocial conduct which is or may be incited in the persons stimulated to such thoughts. In *Roth*, the trial judge instructed the jury: "The words 'obscene, lewd and lascivious' as used in the law, signify that form of immorality which has relation to sexual impurity and has a tendency to excite lustful *thoughts.*" (Emphasis added.) In *Alberts*, the trial judge applied the test laid down in People v. Wepplo, 78 Cal.App.2d Supp. 959, 178 P.2d 853, namely, whether the material has "a substantial tendency to deprave or corrupt its readers by inciting *lascivious* thoughts or arousing lustful desires." (Emphasis added.) It is insisted that the constitutional guaranties are violated because convictions may be had without proof either that obscene material will perceptibly create a clear and present danger of anti-social conduct, or will probably induce its recipients to such conduct. But, in light of our holding that obscenity is not protected speech, the complete answer to this argument is in the holding of this Court in *Beauharnais v. Illinois, supra*, at 266:

"Libelous utterances not being within the area of constitutionally protected speech, it is unnecessary, either for us or for the State courts, to consider the issues behind the phrase 'clear and present danger.' Certainly no one would contend that obscene speech, for example, may be punished only upon a showing of such circumstances. Libel, as we have seen, is in the same class."

However, sex and obscenity are not synonymous. Obscene material is material which deals with sex in a manner appealing to prurient interest.[20] The portrayal of sex, e.g., in art, literature and scientific works, is not itself sufficient reason to deny material the constitutional protection of freedom of speech and press. Sex, a great and mysterious motive force in human life, has indisputably been a subject of absorbing interest to mankind through the ages; it is one of the vital problems of human interest and public concern. * * *

The fundamental freedoms of speech and press have contributed greatly to the development and well-being of our free society and are indispensable to its continued growth. Ceaseless vigilance is the watchword to prevent their erosion by Congress or by the States. The door barring federal and state intrusion into this area cannot be left ajar; it must be kept tightly closed and opened only the slightest crack necessary to prevent encroachment upon more important interests. It is therefore vital that the standards for judging obscenity safeguard the protection of freedom of speech and press for material which does not treat sex in a manner appealing to prurient interest.

The early leading standard of obscenity allowed material to be judged merely by the effect of an isolated excerpt upon particularly susceptible persons. Regina v. Hicklin, [1868] L.R. 3 Q.B. 360. Some American courts adopted this standard but later decisions have rejected it and substituted this test: whether to the average person, applying contemporary community standards, the dominant theme of the material taken as a whole appeals to prurient interest. The *Hicklin* test, judging obscenity by the effect of isolated passages upon the most susceptible persons, might well encompass material legitimately treating with sex, and so it must be rejected as unconstitutionally restrictive of the freedoms of speech and press. On the other hand, the substituted standard provides safeguards adequate to withstand the charge of constitutional infirmity.

---

20. I.e., material having a tendency to excite lustful thoughts. Webster's New International Dictionary (Unabridged, 2d ed., 1949) defines prurient, in pertinent part, as follows:

" * * * Itching; longing; uneasy with desire or longing; of persons, having itching, morbid, or lascivious longings; of desire, curiosity, or propensity, lewd. * * * "

Pruriency is defined, in pertinent part, as follows:

" * * * Quality of being prurient; lascivious desire or thought. * * * "

* * *

We perceive no significant difference between the meaning of obscenity developed in the case law and the definition of the A.L.I., Model Penal Code, § 207.10(2) (Tent. Draft No. 6, 1957), viz.:

" * * * A thing is obscene if, considered as a whole, its predominant appeal is to prurient interest, i.e., a shameful or morbid interest in nudity, sex, or excretion, and if it goes substantially beyond customary limits of candor in description or representation of such matters. * * * "

Both trial courts below sufficiently followed the proper standard. Both courts used the proper definition of obscenity. * * *

It is argued that the statutes do not provide reasonably ascertainable standards of guilt and therefore violate the constitutional requirements of due process. Winters v. People of State of New York, 333 U.S. 507. The federal obscenity statute makes punishable the mailing of material that is "obscene, lewd, lascivious, or filthy * * * or other publications of an indecent character."[28] The California statute makes punishable, *inter alia,* the keeping for sale or advertising material that is "obscene or indecent." The thrust of the argument is that these words are not sufficiently precise because they do not mean the same thing to all people, all the time, everywhere.

Many decisions have recognized that these terms of obscenity statutes are not precise. This Court, however, has consistently held that lack of precision is not itself offensive to the requirements of due process. " * * * [T]he Constitution does not require impossible standards"; all that is required is that the language "conveys sufficiently definite warning as to the proscribed conduct when measured by common understanding and practices * * *." *United States v. Petrillo,* 332 U.S. 1, 7–8. These words applied according to the proper standard for judging obscenity, already discussed, give adequate warning of the conduct proscribed and mark " * * * boundaries sufficiently distinct for judges and juries fairly to administer the law * * *. That there may be marginal cases in which it is difficult to determine the side of the line on which a particular fact situation falls is no sufficient reason to hold the language too ambiguous to define a criminal offense * * *." *Id.,* at 332 U.S., at 7. * * *

In summary, then, we hold that these statutes, applied according to the proper standard for judging obscenity, do not offend constitutional safeguards against convictions based upon protected material, or fail to give men in acting adequate notice of what is prohibited.

Roth's argument that the federal obscenity statute unconstitutionally encroaches upon the powers reserved by the Ninth and Tenth Amendments to the States and to the people to punish speech and press where offensive to decency and morality is hinged upon his contention that obscenity is expression not excepted from the sweep of the provision of the First Amendment that "*Congress* shall make *no law* * * * abridging the freedom of speech, or of the press * * * " (Emphasis added.) That argument falls in light of our holding that obscenity is not expression protected by the First Amendment.[31] We therefore hold that the federal obscenity statute punishing the use of the mails for

---

28. This Court, as early as 1896, said of the federal obscenity statute:

" * * * Every man who uses the mails of the United States for carrying papers or publications must take notice of what, in this enlightened age, is meant by decency, purity, and chastity in social life, and what must be deemed obscene, lewd, and lascivious." * * *

31. For the same reason, we reject, in this case, the argument that there is greater latitude for state action under the word "liberty" under the Fourteenth Amendment than is allowed to Congress by the language of the First Amendment.

obscene material is a proper exercise of the postal power delegated to Congress by Art. I, § 8, cl. 7. * * *

* * *

The judgments are

Affirmed.

Mr. Chief Justice Warren, concurring in the result.

I agree with the result reached by the Court in these cases, but, because we are operating in a field of expression and because broad language used here may eventually be applied to the arts and sciences and freedom of communication generally, I would limit our decision to the facts before us and to the validity of the statutes in question as applied.

Appellant Alberts was charged with wilfully, unlawfully and lewdly disseminating obscene matter. Obscenity has been construed by the California courts to mean having a substantial tendency to corrupt by arousing lustful desires. * * * Petitioner Roth was indicted for unlawfully, wilfully and knowingly mailing obscene material that was calculated to corrupt and debauch the minds and morals of those to whom it was sent. Each was accorded all the protections of a criminal trial. Among other things, they contend that the statutes under which they were convicted violate the constitutional guarantees of freedom of speech, press and communication.

That there is a social problem presented by obscenity is attested by the expression of the legislatures of the forty-eight States as well as the Congress. To recognize the existence of a problem, however, does not require that we sustain any and all measures adopted to meet that problem. The history of the application of laws designed to suppress the obscene demonstrates convincingly that the power of government can be invoked under them against great art or literature, scientific treatises, or works exciting social controversy. Mistakes of the past prove that there is a strong countervailing interest to be considered in the freedoms guaranteed by the First and Fourteenth Amendments.

The line dividing the salacious or pornographic from literature or science is not straight and unwavering. Present laws depend largely upon the effect that the materials may have upon those who receive them. It is manifest that the same object may have a different impact, varying according to the part of the community it reached. But there is more to these cases. It is not the book that is on trial; it is a person. The conduct of the defendant is the central issue, not the obscenity of a book or picture. The nature of the materials is, of course, relevant as an attribute of the defendant's conduct, but the materials are thus placed in context from which they draw color and character. A wholly different result might be reached in a different setting.

The personal element in these cases is seen most strongly in the requirement of *scienter*. Under the California law, the prohibited activity must be done "wilfully and lewdly." The federal statute limits the crime to acts done "knowingly." In his charge to the jury, the district judge stated that the matter must be "calculated" to corrupt or debauch. The defendants in both these cases were engaged in the business of purveying textual or graphic matter openly advertised to appeal to the erotic interest of their customers. They were plainly engaged in the commercial exploitation of the morbid and shameful craving for materials with prurient effect. I believe that the State and Federal Governments can constitutionally punish such conduct. That is all that these cases present to us, and that is all we need to decide.

I agree with the Court's decision in its rejection of the other contentions raised by these defendants.

MR. JUSTICE HARLAN, concurring in the result in No. 61, and dissenting in No. 582.

I regret not to be able to join the Court's opinion. I cannot do so because I find lurking beneath its disarming generalizations a number of problems which not only leave me with serious misgivings as to the future effect of today's decisions, but which also, in my view, call for different results in these two cases.

I.

My basic difficulties with the Court's opinion are three-fold. First, the opinion paints with such a broad brush that I fear it may result in a loosening of the tight reins which state and federal courts should hold upon the enforcement of obscenity statutes. Second, the Court fails to discriminate between the different factors which, in my opinion, are involved in the constitutional adjudication of state and federal obscenity cases. Third, relevant distinctions between the two obscenity statutes here involved, and the Court's own definition of "obscenity," are ignored.

In final analysis, the problem presented by these cases is how far, and on what terms, the state and federal governments have power to punish individuals for disseminating books considered to be undesirable because of their nature or supposed deleterious effect upon human conduct. Proceeding from the premise that "no issue is presented in either case, concerning the obscenity of the material involved," the Court finds the "dispositive question" to be "whether obscenity is utterance within the area of protected speech and press," and then holds that "obscenity" is not so protected because it is "utterly without redeeming social importance." This sweeping formula appears to me to beg the very question before us. The Court seems to assume that "obscenity" is a peculiar *genus* of "speech and press," which is as distinct, recognizable, and classifiable as poison ivy is among other plants. On this basis the *constitutional* question before us simply becomes, as the Court says, whether "obscenity," as an abstraction, is protected by the First and Fourteenth Amendments, and the question whether a *particular* book may be suppressed becomes a mere matter of classification, of "fact," to be entrusted to a fact-finder and insulated from independent constitutional judgment. But surely the problem cannot be solved in such a generalized fashion. Every communication has an individuality and "value" of its own. The suppression of a particular writing or other tangible form of expression is, therefore, an *individual* matter, and in the nature of things every such suppression raises an individual constitutional problem, in which a reviewing court must determine for itself whether the attacked expression is suppressible within constitutional standards. Since those standards do not readily lend themselves to generalized definitions, the constitutional problem in the last analysis becomes one of particularized judgments which appellate courts must make for themselves.

I do not think that reviewing courts can escape this responsibility by saying that the trier of the facts, be it a jury or a judge, has labeled the questioned matter as "obscene," for, if "obscenity" is to be suppressed, the question whether a particular work is of that character involves not really an issue of fact but a question of constitutional *judgment* of the most sensitive and delicate kind. Many juries might find that Joyce's "Ulysses" or Bocaccio's [sic] "Decameron" was obscene, and yet the conviction of a defendant for selling either book would raise, for me, the gravest constitutional problems, for no such verdict could convince me, without more, that these books are "utterly without redeeming social importance." In short, I do not understand how the Court can resolve the constitutional problems now before it without making its own independent judgment upon the character of the material upon which these convictions were based. I am very much afraid that the broad manner in which the Court has decided these cases will tend to obscure the peculiar responsibilities resting on state and federal courts in this field and encourage them to rely on easy labeling and jury verdicts as a substitute for facing up to the tough individual problems of constitutional judgment involved in every obscenity case.

My second reason for dissatisfaction with the Court's opinion is that the broad strides with which the Court has proceeded has led it to brush aside with perfunctory ease the vital constitutional considerations which, in my opinion, differentiate these two cases. It does not seem to matter to the Court that in one case we balance the power of a State in this field against the restrictions of the Fourteenth Amendment, and in the other the power of the Federal Government against the limitations of the First Amendment. I deal with this subject more particularly later.

Thirdly, the Court has not been bothered by the fact that the two cases involve different statutes. In California the book must have a "tendency to deprave or corrupt its readers"; under the federal statute it must tend "to stir sexual impulses and lead to sexually impure thoughts." The two statutes do not seem to me to present the same problems. Yet the Court compounds confusion when it superimposes on these two statutory definitions a third, drawn from the American Law Institute's Model Penal Code, Tentative Draft No. 6: "A thing is obscene if, considered as a whole, its predominant appeal is to prurient interest." The bland assurance that this definition is the same as the ones with which we deal flies in the face of the authors' express rejection of the "deprave and corrupt" and "sexual thoughts" tests:

"Obscenity [in the Tentative Draft] is defined in terms of material which appeals predominantly to prurient interest in sexual matters and which goes beyond customary freedom of expression in these matters. We reject the prevailing test of tendency to arouse lustful thoughts or desires because it is unrealistically broad for a society that plainly tolerates a great deal of erotic interest in literature, advertising, and art, and because regulation of thought or desire, unconnected with overt misbehavior, raises the most acute constitutional as well as practical difficulties. We likewise reject the common definition of obscene as that which 'tends to corrupt or debase.' If this means anything different from tendency to arouse lustful thought and desire, it suggests that change of character or actual misbehavior follows from contact with obscenity. Evidence of such consequences is lacking * * * On the other hand, 'appeal to prurient interest' refers to qualities of the material itself: the capacity to attract individuals eager for a forbidden look * * * "

As this passage makes clear, there is a significant distinction between the definitions used in the prosecutions before us, and the American Law Institute formula. If, therefore, the latter is the correct standard, as my Brother Brennan elsewhere intimates, then these convictions should surely be reversed. Instead, the Court merely assimilates the various tests into one indiscriminate potpourri.

I now pass to the consideration of the two cases before us.

II.

I concur in the judgment of the Court in No. 61, *Alberts v. California.*

The question in this case is whether the defendant was deprived of liberty without due process of law when he was convicted for selling certain materials found by the judge to be obscene because they would have a "tendency to deprave or corrupt its readers by exciting lascivious thoughts or arousing lustful desire." In judging the constitutionality of this conviction, we should remember that our function in reviewing state judgments under the Fourteenth Amendment is a narrow one. We do not decide whether the policy of the State is wise, or whether it is based on assumptions scientifically substantiated. We can inquire only whether the state action so subverts the fundamental liberties implicit in the Due Process Clause that it cannot be sustained as a rational exercise of power. See Jackson, J., dissenting in Beauharnais v. Illinois, 343 U.S. 250, 287. The States' power to make printed words criminal is, of course, confined by the Fourteenth Amendment, but only insofar as such power is inconsistent with our concepts of "ordered liberty." Palko v. Connecticut, 302 U.S. 319, 324–325.

What, then, is the purpose of this California statute? Clearly the state legislature has made the judgment that printed words can "deprave or corrupt" the reader—that words can incite to antisocial or immoral action. The assumption seems to be that the distribution of certain types of literature will induce criminal or immoral sexual conduct. It is well known, of course, that the validity of this assumption is a matter of dispute among critics, sociologists, psychiatrists, and penologists. There is a large school of thought, particularly in the scientific community, which denies any causal connection between the reading of pornography and immorality, crime, or delinquency. Others disagree. Clearly it is not our function to decide this question. That function belongs to the state legislature. Nothing in the Constitution requires California to accept as truth the most advanced and sophisticated psychiatric opinion. It seems to me clear that it is not irrational, in our present state of knowledge, to consider that pornography can induce a type of sexual conduct which a State may deem obnoxious to the moral fabric of society. In fact the very division of opinion on the subject counsels us to respect the choice made by the State.

Furthermore, even assuming that pornography cannot be deemed ever to cause, in an immediate sense, criminal sexual conduct, other interests within the proper cognizance of the States may be protected by the prohibition placed on such materials. The State can reasonably draw the inference that over a long period of time the indiscriminate dissemination of materials, the essential character of which is to degrade sex, will have an eroding effect on moral standards. And the State has a legitimate interest in protecting the privacy of the home against invasion of unsolicited obscenity.

Above all stands the realization that we deal here with an area where knowledge is small, data are insufficient, and experts are divided. Since the domain of sexual morality is pre-eminently a matter of state concern, this Court should be slow to interfere with state legislation calculated to protect that morality. It seems to me that nothing in the broad and flexible command of the Due Process Clause forbids California to prosecute one who sells books whose dominant tendency might be to "deprave or corrupt" a reader. I agree with the Court, of course, that the books must be judged as a whole and in relation to the normal adult reader.

What has been said, however, does not dispose of the case. It still remains for us to decide whether the state court's determination that this material should be suppressed is consistent with the Fourteenth Amendment; and that, of course, presents a federal question as to which we, and not the state court, have the ultimate responsibility. And so, in the final analysis, I concur in the judgment because, upon an independent perusal of the material involved, and in light of the considerations discussed above, I cannot say that its suppression would so interfere with the communication of "ideas" in any proper sense of that term that it would offend the Due Process Clause. I therefore agree with the Court that appellant's conviction must be affirmed.

III.

I dissent in No. 582, *Roth v. United States*.

We are faced here with the question whether the federal obscenity statute, as construed and applied in this case, violates the First Amendment to the Constitution. To me, this question is of quite a different order than one where we are dealing with state legislation under the Fourteenth Amendment. I do not think it follows that state and federal powers in this area are the same, and that just because the State may suppress a particular utterance, it is automatically permissible for the Federal Government to do the same. I agree with Mr. Justice Jackson that the historical evidence does not bear out the claim that the Fourteenth Amendment "incorporates" the First in any literal sense. See *Beauharnais v. Illinois, supra.* But laying aside any consequences which might flow from that conclusion, cf. Mr. Justice Holmes in Gitlow v. New York, 268 U.S. 652, 672, I prefer to rest my views about this case on broader and less abstract grounds.

The Constitution differentiates between those areas of human conduct subject to the regulation of the States and those subject to the powers of the Federal Government. The substantive powers of the two governments, in many instances, are distinct. And in every case where we are called upon to balance the interest in free expression against other interests, it seems to me important that we should keep in the forefront the question of whether those other interests are state or federal. Since under our constitutional scheme the two are not necessarily equivalent, the balancing process must needs often produce different results. Whether a particular limitation on speech or press is to be upheld because it subserves a paramount governmental interest must, to a large extent, I think, depend on whether that government has, under the Constitution, a direct substantive interest, that is, the power to act, in the particular area involved.

The Federal Government has, for example, power to restrict seditious speech directed against it, because that Government certainly has the substantive authority to protect itself against revolution. * * * But in dealing with obscenity we are faced with the converse situation, for the interests which obscenity statutes purportedly protect are primarily entrusted to the care, not of the Federal Government, but of the States. Congress has no substantive power over sexual morality. Such powers as the Federal Government has in this field are but incidental to its other powers, here the postal power, and are not of the same nature as those possessed by the States, which bear direct responsibility for the protection of the local moral fabric.[5] * * *

Not only is the federal interest in protecting the Nation against pornography attenuated, but the dangers of federal censorship in this field are far greater than anything the States may do. It has often been said that one of the great strengths of our federal system is that we have, in the forty-eight States, forty-eight experimental social laboratories. "State statutory law reflects predominantly this capacity of a legislature to introduce novel techniques of social control. The federal system has the immense advantage of providing forty-eight separate

---

5. The hoary dogma of *Ex parte* Jackson, 96 U.S. 727, and Public Clearing House v. Coyne, 194 U.S. 497, that the use of the mails is a privilege on which the Government may impose such conditions as it chooses, has long since evaporated. See Brandeis, J., dissenting, in Milwaukee Social Democratic Publishing Co. v. Burleson, 255 U.S. 407, 430–433; * * *

centers for such experimentation." Different States will have different attitudes toward the same work of literature. The same book which is freely read in one State might be classed as obscene in another.[7] And it seems to me that no overwhelming danger to our freedom to experiment and to gratify our tastes in literature is likely to result from the suppression of a borderline book in one of the States, so long as there is no uniform nation-wide suppression of the book, and so long as other States are free to experiment with the same or bolder books.

Quite a different situation is presented, however, where the Federal Government imposes the ban. The danger is perhaps not great if the people of one State, through their legislature, decide that "Lady Chatterley's Lover" goes so far beyond the acceptable standards of candor that it will be deemed offensive and non-sellable, for the State next door is still free to make its own choice. At least we do not have one uniform standard. But the dangers to free thought and expression are truly great if the Federal Government imposes a blanket ban over the Nation on such a book. The prerogative of the States to differ on their ideas of morality will be destroyed, the ability of States to experiment will be stunted. The fact that the people of one State cannot read some of the works of D.H. Lawrence seems to me, if not wise or desirable, at least acceptable. But that no person in the United States should be allowed to do so seems to me to be intolerable, and violative of both the letter and spirit of the First Amendment.

I judge this case, then, in view of what I think is the attenuated federal interest in this field, in view of the very real danger of a deadening uniformity which can result from nation-wide federal censorship, and in view of the fact that the constitutionality of this conviction must be weighed against the First and not the Fourteenth Amendment. So viewed, I do not think that this conviction can be upheld. The petitioner was convicted under a statute which, under the judge's charge, makes it criminal to sell books which "tend to stir sexual impulses and lead to sexually impure thoughts." I cannot agree that any book which tends to stir sexual impulses and lead to sexually impure thoughts necessarily is "utterly without redeeming social importance." Not only did this charge fail to measure up to the standards which I understand the Court to approve, but as far as I can see, much of the great literature of the world could lead to conviction under such a view of the statute. Moreover, in no event do I think that the limited federal interest in this area can extend to mere "thoughts." The Federal Government has no business, whether under the postal or commerce power, to bar the sale of books because they might lead to any kind of "thoughts."

It is no answer to say, as the Court does, that obscenity is not protected speech. The point is that this statute, as here construed, defines obscenity so widely that it encompasses matters which might

---

7. To give only a few examples: Edmund Wilson's "Memoirs of Hecate County" was found obscene in New York, see Doubleday & Co. v. New York, 335 U.S. 848; a bookseller indicted for selling the same book was acquitted in California. "God's Little Acre" was held to be obscene in Massachusetts, not obscene in New York and Pennsylvania.

very well be protected speech. I do not think that the federal statute can be constitutionally construed to reach other than what the Government has termed as "hard-core" pornography. Nor do I think the statute can fairly be read as directed only at *persons* who are engaged in the business of catering to the prurient minded, even though their wares fall short of hard-core pornography. Such a statute would raise constitutional questions of a different order. That being so, and since in my opinion the material here involved cannot be said to be hard-core pornography, I would reverse this case with instructions to dismiss the indictment.

MR. JUSTICE DOUGLAS, with whom MR. JUSTICE BLACK concurs, dissenting.

When we sustain these convictions, we make the legality of a publication turn on the purity of thought which a book or tract instills in the mind of the reader. I do not think we can approve that standard and be faithful to the command of the First Amendment, which by its terms is a restraint on Congress and which by the Fourteenth is a restraint on the States.

In the *Roth* case the trial judge charged the jury that the statutory words "obscene, lewd and lascivious" describe "that form of immorality which has relation to sexual impurity and has a tendency to excite lustful thoughts." He stated that the term "filthy" in the statute pertains "to that sort of treatment of sexual matters in such a vulgar and indecent way, so that it tends to arouse a feeling of disgust and revulsion." He went on to say that the material "must be calculated to corrupt and debauch the minds and morals" of "the average person in the community," not those of any particular class. "You judge the circulars, pictures and publications which have been put in evidence by present-day standards of the community. You may ask yourselves does it offend the common conscience of the community by present-day standards."

The trial judge who, sitting without a jury, heard the *Alberts* case and the appellate court that sustained the judgment of conviction, took California's definition of "obscenity" from People v. Wepplo, 78 Cal. App.2d Supp. 959, 961, 178 P.2d 853, 855. That case held that a book is obscene "if it has a substantial tendency to deprave or corrupt its readers by inciting lascivious thoughts or arousing lustful desire."

By these standards punishment is inflicted for thoughts provoked, not for overt acts nor antisocial conduct. This test cannot be squared with our decisions under the First Amendment. Even the ill-starred *Dennis* case conceded that speech to be punishable must have some relation to action which could be penalized by government. Dennis v. United States, 341 U.S. 494, 502–511. * * * This issue cannot be avoided by saying that obscenity is not protected by the First Amendment. The question remains, what is the constitutional test of obscenity?

The tests by which these convictions were obtained require only the arousing of sexual thoughts. Yet the arousing of sexual thoughts and desires happens every day in normal life in dozens of ways. Nearly 30 years ago a questionnaire sent to college and normal school women graduates asked what things were most stimulating sexually. Of 409 replies, 9 said "music"; 18 said "pictures"; 29 said "dancing"; 40 said "drama"; 95 said "books"; and 218 said "man." Alpert, Judicial Censorship of Obscene Literature, 52 Harv.L.Rev. 40, 73.

The test of obscenity the Court endorses today gives the censor free range over a vast domain. To allow the State to step in and punish mere speech or publication that the judge or the jury thinks has an *undesirable* impact on thoughts but that is not shown to be a part of unlawful action is drastically to curtail the First Amendment. As recently stated by two of our outstanding authorities on obscenity, "The danger of influencing a change in the current moral standards of the community, or of shocking or offending readers, or of stimulating sex thoughts or desires apart from objective conduct, can never justify the losses to society that result from interference with literary freedom." Lockhart & McClure, Literature, The Law of Obscenity, and the Constitution, 38 Minn.L.Rev. 295, 387.

* * *

As noted, the trial judge in the *Roth* case charged the jury in the alternative that the federal obscenity statute outlaws literature dealing with sex which offends "the common conscience of the community." That standard is, in my view, more inimical still to freedom of expression.

The standard of what offends "the common conscience of the community" conflicts, in my judgment, with the command of the First Amendment that "Congress shall make no law ... abridging the freedom of speech, or of the press." Certainly that standard would not be an acceptable one if religion, economics, politics or philosophy were involved. How does it become a constitutional standard when literature treating with sex is concerned?

Any test that turns on what is offensive to the community's standards is too loose, too capricious, too destructive of freedom of expression to be squared with the First Amendment. Under that test, juries can censor, suppress, and punish what they don't like, provided the matter relates to "sexual impurity" or has a tendency "to excite lustful thoughts." This is community censorship in one of its worst forms. It creates a regime where in the battle between the literati and the Philistines, the Philistines are certain to win. If experience in this field teaches anything, it is that "censorship of obscenity has almost always been both irrational and indiscriminate." Lockhart & McClure, *op. cit. supra,* at 371. The test adopted here accentuates that trend.

* * *

I can understand (and at times even sympathize) with programs of civic groups and church groups to protect and defend the existing moral standards of the community. I can understand the motives of the Anthony Comstocks who would impose Victorian standards on the community. When speech alone is involved, I do not think that government, consistently with the First Amendment, can become the sponsor of any of these movements. I do not think that government, consistently with the First Amendment, can throw its weight behind one school or another. * * *

* * *

The Court today suggests a third standard. It defines obscene material as that "which deals with sex in a manner appealing to prurient interest." Like the standards applied by the trial judges below, that standard does not require any nexus between the literature which is prohibited and action which the legislature can regulate or prohibit. Under the First Amendment, that standard is no more valid than those which the courts below adopted.

* * *

* * * I reject too the implication that problems of freedom of speech and of the press are to be resolved by weighing against the values of free expression, the judgment of the Court that a particular form of that expression has "no redeeming social importance." The First Amendment, its prohibition in terms absolute, was designed to preclude courts as well as legislatures from weighing the values of speech against silence. The First Amendment puts free speech in the preferred position.

Freedom of expression can be suppressed if, and to the extent that, it is so closely brigaded with illegal action as to be an inseparable part of it. * * * As a people, we cannot afford to relax that standard. For the test that suppresses a cheap tract today can suppress a literary gem tomorrow. All it need do is to incite a lascivious thought or arouse a lustful desire. The list of books that judges or juries can place in that category is endless.

I would give the broad sweep of the First Amendment full support. I have the same confidence in the ability of our people to reject noxious literature as I have in their capacity to sort out the true from the false in theology, economics, politics, or any other field.

SMITH v. CALIFORNIA

Supreme Court of the United States, 1959.
361 U.S. 147, 80 S.Ct. 215, 4 L.Ed.2d 205.

MR. JUSTICE BRENNAN delivered the opinion of the Court.

Appellant, the proprietor of a bookstore, was convicted in a California Municipal Court under a Los Angeles City ordinance which makes it unlawful "for any person to have in his possession any obscene or indecent writing, [or] book * * * [in] any place of business where * * * books * * * are sold or kept for sale." The offense was defined by the Municipal Court, and by the Appellate Department of the Superior Court, which affirmed the Municipal Court judgment imposing a jail sentence on appellant, as consisting solely of the possession, in the appellant's bookstore, of a certain book found upon judicial investigation to be obscene. The definition included no element of scienter—knowledge by appellant of the contents of the book—and thus the ordinance was construed as imposing a "strict" or "absolute" criminal liability. The appellant made timely objection below that if the ordinance were so construed it would be in conflict with the Constitution of the United States. This contention, together with other contentions based on the Constitution, was rejected, and the case comes here on appeal. * * *

* * *

California here imposed a strict or absolute criminal responsibility on appellant not to have obscene books in his shop. "The existence of a *mens rea* is the rule of, rather than the exception to, the principles of Anglo–American criminal jurisprudence." Dennis v. United States, 341 U.S. 494, 500. Still, it is doubtless competent for the States to create strict criminal liabilities by defining criminal offenses without any element of scienter—though even where no freedom-of-expression question is involved, there is precedent in this Court that this power is not without limitations. See Lambert v. California, 355 U.S. 225. But the question here is as to the validity of this ordinance's elimination of the scienter requirement—an elimination which may tend to work a substantial restriction on the freedom of speech and of the press. Our decisions furnish examples of legal devices and doctrines, in most applications consistent with the Constitution, which cannot be applied in settings where they have the collateral effect of inhibiting the freedom of expression, by making the individual the more reluctant to exercise it. The States generally may regulate the allocation of the burden of proof in their courts, and it is a common procedural device to impose on a taxpayer the burden of proving his entitlement to exemptions from taxation, but where we conceived that this device was being applied in a manner tending to cause even a self-imposed restriction of free expression, we struck down its application. Speiser v. Randall, 357 U.S. 513. * * * Very much to the point here, where the question is the elimination of the mental element in an offense, is this Court's holding in Wieman v. Updegraff, 344 U.S. 183. There an oath as to past freedom from membership in subversive organizations, exacted by a State as a qualification for public employment, was held to violate the Constitution in that it made no distinction between members who had, and those who had not, known of the organization's character. The Court said of the elimination of scienter in this context: "To thus inhibit individual freedom of movement is to stifle the flow of democratic expression and controversy at one of its chief sources." *Id.*, at 191.

These principles guide us to our decision here. We have held that obscene speech and writings are not protected by the constitutional guarantees of freedom of speech and the press. Roth v. United States, 354 U.S. 476. The ordinance here in question, to be sure, only imposes criminal sanctions on a bookseller if in fact there is to be found in his shop an obscene book. But our holding in *Roth* does not recognize any state power to restrict the dissemination of books which are not obscene; and we think this ordinance's strict liability feature would tend seriously to have that effect, by penalizing booksellers, even though they had not the slightest notice of the character of the books they sold. The appellee and the court below analogize this strict liability penal ordinance to familiar forms of penal statutes which dispense with any element of knowledge on the part of the person charged, food and drug legislation being a principal example. We find the analogy instructive in our examination of the question before us. The usual rationale for such statutes is that the public interest in the purity of its food is so great as to warrant the imposition of the highest standard of care on distributors—in fact an absolute standard which will not hear the distributor's plea as to the amount of care he has used. * * * His ignorance of the character of the food is irrelevant. There is no specific constitutional inhibition against making the distributors of food the strictest censors of their merchandise, but the constitutional guarantees of the freedom of speech and of the press stand in the way of imposing a similar requirement on the bookseller. By dispensing with any requirement of knowledge of the contents of the book on the part of the seller, the ordinance tends to impose a severe limitation on the public's access to constitutionally protected matter. For if the bookseller is criminally liable without knowledge of the contents, and the ordinance fulfills its purpose, he will tend to restrict the books he sells to those he has inspected; and thus the State will have imposed a restriction upon the distribution of constitutionally protected as well as obscene literature. It has been well observed of a statute construed as dispensing with any requirement of scienter that: "Every bookseller would be placed under an obligation to make himself aware of the contents of every book in his shop. It would be altogether unreasonable to demand so near an approach to omniscience." The King v. Ewart, 25 N.Z.L.R. 709, 729 (C.A.). And the bookseller's burden would become the public's burden, for by restricting him the public's access to reading matter would be restricted. If the contents of bookshops and periodical stands were restricted to material of which their proprietors had made an inspection, they might be depleted indeed. The bookseller's limitation in the amount of reading material with which he could familiarize himself, and his timidity in the face of his absolute criminal liability, thus would tend to restrict the public's access to forms of the printed word which the State could not constitutionally suppress directly. The bookseller's self-censorship, compelled by the State, would be a censorship affecting the whole public, hardly less virulent for being privately administered. Through it, the distribution of all books, both obscene and not obscene, would be impeded.

It is argued that unless the scienter requirement is dispensed with, regulation of the distribution of obscene material will be ineffective, as booksellers will falsely disclaim knowledge of their books' contents or falsely deny reason to suspect their obscenity. We might observe that it has been some time now since the law viewed itself as impotent to explore the actual state of a man's mind. See Pound, The Role of the Will in Law, 68 Harv.L.Rev. 1. Cf. American Communications Assn. v. Douds, 339 U.S. 382, 411. Eyewitness testimony of a bookseller's perusal of a book hardly need be a necessary element in proving his awareness of its contents. The circumstances may warrant the inference that he was aware of what a book contained, despite his denial.

We need not and most definitely do not pass today on what sort of mental element is requisite to a constitutionally permissible prosecution of a bookseller for carrying an obscene book in stock; whether honest mistake as to whether its contents in fact constituted obscenity need be an excuse; whether there might be circumstances under which the State constitutionally might require that a bookseller investigate further, or might put on him the burden of explaining why he did not, and what such circumstances might be. Doubtless any form of criminal obscenity statute applicable to a bookseller will induce some tendency to self-censorship and have some inhibitory effect on the dissemination of material not obscene, but we consider today only one which goes to the extent of eliminating all mental elements from the crime.

Reversed.

MR. JUSTICE BLACK, concurring.

The appellant was sentenced to prison for possessing in his bookstore an "obscene" book in violation of a Los Angeles city ordinance. I concur in the judgment holding that ordinance unconstitutional, but not for the reasons given in the Court's opinion.

The Court invalidates the ordinance solely because it penalizes a bookseller for mere possession of an "obscene" book, even though he is unaware of its obscenity. The grounds on which the Court draws a constitutional distinction between a law that punishes possession of a book with knowledge of its "obscenity" and a law that punishes without such knowledge are not persuasive to me. Those grounds are that conviction of a bookseller for possession of an "obscene" book when he is unaware of its obscenity "will tend to restrict the books he sells to those he has inspected," and therefore "may tend to work a substantial restriction on freedom of speech." The fact is, of course, that prison sentences for possession of "obscene" books will seriously burden freedom of the press whether punishment is imposed with or without knowledge of the obscenity. The Court's opinion correctly points out how little extra burden will be imposed on prosecutors by requiring proof that a bookseller was aware of a book's contents when he possessed it. And if the Constitution's requirement of knowledge is so easily met, the result of this case is that one particular bookseller gains his freedom, but the way is left open for state censorship and punishment of all other booksellers by merely adding a few new words to old censorship laws. Our constitutional safeguards for speech and press therefore gain little. Their victory, if any, is a Pyrrhic one. Cf. Beauharnais v. Illinois, 343 U.S. 250, 267, at 275 (dissenting opinion).

* * *

MR. JUSTICE FRANKFURTER, concurring.

* * *

I am no friend of deciding a case beyond what the immediate controversy requires, particularly when the limits of constitutional power are at stake. On the other hand, a case before this Court is not just a case. Inevitably its disposition carries implications and gives directions beyond its particular facts. Were the Court holding that this kind of prosecution for obscenity requires proof of the guilty mind associated with the concept of crimes deemed infamous, that would be that and no further elucidation would be needed. But if the requirement of scienter in obscenity cases plays a role different from the normal role of *mens rea* in the definition of crime, a different problem confronts the Court. If, as I assume, the requirement of scienter in an obscenity prosecution like the one before us does not mean that the bookseller must have read the book or must substantially know its contents on the one hand, nor on the other that he can exculpate himself by studious avoidance of knowledge about its contents, then, I submit, invalidating an obscenity statute because a State dispenses altogether with the requirement of scienter does require some indication of the scope and quality of scienter that is required. It ought at least to be made clear, and not left for future litigation, that the Court's decision in its practical effect is not intended to nullify the conceded power of the State to prohibit booksellers from trafficking in obscene literature.

* * *

* * * Out of regard for the State's interest, the Court suggests an unguiding, vague standard for establishing "awareness" by the bookseller of the contents of a challenged book in contradiction of his disclaimer of knowledge of its contents. A bookseller may, of course, be well aware of the nature of a book and its appeal without having opened its cover, or, in any true sense, having knowledge of the book. As a practical matter therefore the exercise of the constitutional right of a State to regulate obscenity will carry with it some hazard to the dissemination by a bookseller of non-obscene literature. Such difficulties or hazards are inherent in many domains of the law for the simple reason that law cannot avail itself of factors ascertained quantitatively or even wholly impersonally.

* * *

Mr. Justice Douglas, concurring.

I need not repeat here all I said in my dissent in Roth v. United States, 354 U.S. 476, 508, to underline my conviction that neither the author nor the distributor of this book can be punished under our Bill of Rights for publishing or distributing it. * * *

* * *

Yet my view is in the minority; and rather fluid tests of obscenity prevail which require judges to read condemned literature and pass judgment on it. This role of censor in which we find ourselves is not an edifying one. But since by the prevailing school of thought we must perform it, I see no harm, and perhaps some good, in the rule fashioned by the Court which requires a showing of scienter. For it recognizes implicitly that these First Amendment rights, by reason of the strict command in that Amendment—a command that carries over to the States by reason of the Due Process Clause of the Fourteenth Amendment—are preferred rights. What the Court does today may possibly provide some small degree of safeguard to booksellers by making those who patrol bookstalls proceed less high-handedly than has been their custom.

Mr. Justice Harlan, concurring in part and dissenting in part.

The striking down of local legislation is always serious business for this Court. In my opinion in the *Roth* case, 354 U.S., at 503–508, I expressed the view that state power in the obscenity field has a wider scope than federal power. The question whether *scienter* is a constitutionally required element in a criminal obscenity statute is intimately related to the constitutional scope of the power to bar material as obscene, for the impact of such a requirement on effective prosecution may be one thing where the scope of the power to proscribe is broad and quite another where the scope is narrow. Proof of scienter may entail no great burden in the case of obviously obscene material; it may, however, become very difficult where the character of the material is more debatable. In my view then, the scienter question involves considerations of a different order depending on whether a state or a federal statute is involved. We have here a state ordinance, and on the meagre data before us I would not reach the question whether the absence of a scienter element renders the ordinance unconstitutional. I must say, however, that the generalities in the Court's opinion striking down the ordinance leave me unconvinced.

From the point of view of the free dissemination of constitutionally protected ideas, the Court invalidates the ordinance on the ground that its effect may be to induce booksellers to restrict their offerings of nonobscene literary merchandise through fear of prosecution for unwittingly having on their shelves an obscene publication. From the point of view of the State's interest in protecting its citizens against the dissemination of obscene material, the Court in effect says that proving the state of a man's mind is little more difficult than proving the state of his digestion, but also intimates that a relaxed standard of *mens rea* would satisfy constitutional requirements. This is for me too rough a balancing of the competing interests at stake. Such a balancing is unavoidably required in this kind of constitutional adjudication, notwithstanding that it arises in the domain of liberty of speech and press. A more critical appraisal of both sides of the constitutional balance, not possible on the meagre material before us, seems to me required before the ordinance can be struck down on this ground. For, as the concurring opinions of my Brothers Black and Frankfurter show, the conclusion that this ordinance, but not one embodying some element of scienter, is likely to restrict the dissemination of legitimate literature seems more dialectical than real.

* * *

KINGSLEY INTERNATIONAL PICTURES CORPORATION v. REGENTS OF THE UNIVERSITY OF THE STATE OF NEW YORK

Supreme Court of the United States, 1959.
360 U.S. 684, 79 S.Ct. 1362, 3 L.Ed.2d 1512.

Mr. Justice Stewart delivered the opinion of the Court.

Once again the Court is required to consider the impact of New York's motion picture licensing law upon First Amendment liberties, protected by the Fourteenth Amendment from infringement by the States. Cf. Joseph Burstyn, Inc. v. Wilson, 343 U.S. 495.

The New York statute makes it unlawful "to exhibit, or to sell, lease or lend for exhibition at any place of amusement for pay or in connection with any business in the state of New York, any motion picture film or reel [with certain exceptions not relevant here], unless there is at the time in full force and effect a valid license or permit therefor of the education department. * * *" The law provides that a license shall issue "unless such film or a part thereof is obscene, indecent, immoral, inhuman, sacrilegious, or is of such a character that its exhibition would tend to corrupt morals or incite to crime. * * *" A recent statutory amendment provides that, "the term 'immoral' and the phrase 'of such a character that its exhibition would tend to corrupt morals' shall denote a motion picture film or part thereof, the dominant purpose or effect of which is erotic or pornographic; or which portrays acts of sexual immorality, perversion, or lewdness, or which expressly or impliedly presents such acts as desirable, acceptable or proper patterns of behavior."

As the distributor of a motion picture entitled "Lady Chatterley's Lover," the appellant Kingsley submitted that film to the Motion Picture Division of the New York Education Department for a license. Finding three isolated scenes in the film " 'immoral' within the intent of our Law," the Division refused to issue a license until the scenes in question were deleted. The distributor petitioned the Regents of the University of the State of New York for a review of that ruling. The Regents upheld the denial of a license, but on the broader ground that "the whole theme of this motion picture is immoral under said law, for that theme is the presentation of adultery as a desirable, acceptable and proper pattern of behavior."

* * *

The Court of Appeals unanimously and explicitly rejected any notion that the film is obscene. * * * Rather, the court found that the picture as a whole "alluringly portrays adultery as proper behavior." As Chief Judge Conway's prevailing opinion emphasized, therefore, the only portion of the statute involved in this case is that part of §§ 122 and 122–a of the Education Law requiring the denial of a license to motion pictures "which are immoral in that they portray 'acts of sexual immorality * * * as desirable, acceptable or proper patterns of behavior." * * *

* * * That construction, we emphasize, gives to the term "sexual immorality" a concept entirely different from the concept embraced in words like "obscenity" or "pornography." Moreover, it is not suggested that the film would itself operate as an incitement to illegal action. Rather, the New York Court of Appeals tells us that the relevant portion of the New York Education Law requires the denial of a license to any motion picture which approvingly portrays an adulterous relationship, quite without reference to the manner of its portrayal.

What New York has done, therefore, is to prevent the exhibition of a motion picture because that picture advocates an idea—that adultery under certain circumstances may be proper behavior. Yet the First Amendment's basic guarantee is of freedom to advocate ideas. The State, quite simply, has thus struck at the very heart of constitutionally protected liberty.

It is contended that the State's action was justified because the motion picture attractively portrays a relationship which is contrary to the moral standards, the religious precepts, and the legal code of its citizenry. This argument misconceives what it is that the Constitution protects. Its guarantee is not confined to the expression of ideas that are conventional or shared by a majority. It protects advocacy of the opinion that adultery may sometimes be proper, no less than advocacy of socialism or the single tax. And in the realm of ideas it protects expression which is eloquent no less than that which is unconvincing.

Advocacy of conduct proscribed by law is not, as Mr. Justice Brandeis long ago pointed out, "a justification for denying free speech where the advocacy falls short of incitement and there is nothing to indicate that the advocacy would be immediately acted on." Whitney v. California, 274 U.S. 357, at 376 (concurring opinion). * * *

The inflexible command which the New York Court of Appeals has attributed to the State Legislature thus cuts so close to the core of constitutional freedom as to make it quite needless in this case to examine the periphery. Specifically, there is no occasion to consider the appellant's contention that the State is entirely without power to require films of any kind to be licensed prior to their exhibition. Nor need we here determine whether, despite problems peculiar to motion pictures, the controls which a State may impose upon this medium of expression are precisely coextensive with those allowable for newspapers, books, or individual speech. It is enough for the present case to reaffirm that motion pictures are within the First and Fourteenth Amendments' basic protection. Joseph Burstyn, Inc. v. Wilson, 343 U.S. 495.

Reversed.

[Concurring opinions omitted.]

A BOOK NAMED "JOHN CLELAND'S MEMOIRS OF A WOMAN OF PLEASURE" v. ATTORNEY GENERAL OF MASSACHUSETTS

Supreme Court of the United States, 1966.
383 U.S. 413, 86 S.Ct. 975, 16 L.Ed.2d 1.

MR. JUSTICE BRENNAN announced the judgment of the Court and delivered an opinion in which THE CHIEF JUSTICE and MR. JUSTICE FORTAS join.

This is an obscenity case in which *Memoirs of a Woman of Pleasure* (commonly known as *Fanny Hill*), written by John Cleland in about 1750, was adjudged obscene in a proceeding that put on trial the book itself, and not its publisher or distributor. The proceeding was a civil equity suit brought by the Attorney General of Massachusetts, pursuant to General Laws of Massachusetts, Chapter 272, §§ 28C–28H, to have the book declared obscene. Section 28C requires that the petition commencing the suit be "directed against [the] book by name" and that an order to show cause "why said book should not be judicially determined to be obscene" be published in a daily newspaper and sent by registered mail "to all persons interested in the publication." Publication of the order in this case occurred in a Boston daily newspaper, and a copy of the order was sent by registered mail to G.P. Putnam's Sons, alleged to be the publisher and copyright holder of the book.

As authorized by § 28D, G.P. Putnam's Sons intervened in the proceedings in behalf of the book, but it did not claim the right provided by that section to have the issue of obscenity tried by a jury. At the hearing before a justice of the Superior Court, which was conducted, under § 28F, "in accordance with the usual course of proceedings in equity," the court received the book in evidence and also, as allowed by the section, heard the testimony of experts [2] and accepted other evidence, such as book reviews, in order to assess the literary, cultural, or educational character of the book. This constituted the entire evidence, as neither side availed itself of the opportunity provided by the section to introduce evidence "as to the manner and form of its publication, advertisement, and distribution." The trial justice entered a final decree, which adjudged *Memoirs* obscene and declared that the book "is not entitled to the protection of the First and Fourteenth Amendments to the Constitution of the United States against action by the Attorney General or other law enforcement officer pursuant to the provisions of * * * § 28B, or otherwise." The

---

2. * * * "In the view of one or another or all of the following viz., the chairman of the English department at Williams College, a professor of English at Harvard College, an associate professor of English literature at Boston University, an associate professor of English at Massachusetts Institute of Technology, and an assistant professor of English and American literature at Brandeis University, the book is a minor 'work of art' having 'literary merit' and 'historical value' and containing a good deal of 'deliberate, calculated comedy.' It is a piece of 'social history of interest to anyone who is interested in fiction as a way of understanding society in the past.'" * * *

"* * * In the opinion of the other academic witness, the headmaster of a private school, whose field is English literature, the book is without literary merit and is obscene, impure, hard core pornography, and is patently offensive."

Massachusetts Supreme Judicial Court affirmed the decree. * * * We noted probable jurisdiction. 382 U.S. 900. We reverse.

I.

* * *

We defined obscenity in *Roth* in the following terms: "[Whether] to the average person, applying contemporary community standards, the dominant theme of the material taken as a whole appeals to prurient interest." 354 U.S., at 489. Under this definition, as elaborated in subsequent cases, three elements must coalesce: it must be established that (a) the dominant theme of the material taken as a whole appeals to a prurient interest in sex; (b) the material is patently offensive because it affronts contemporary community standards relating to the description or representation of sexual matters; and (c) the material is utterly without redeeming social value.

The Supreme Judicial Court purported to apply the *Roth* definition of obscenity and held all three criteria satisfied. We need not consider the claim that the court erred in concluding that *Memoirs* satisfied the prurient appeal and patent offensiveness criteria; for reversal is required because the court misinterpreted the social value criterion. The court applied the criterion in this passage:

> "It remains to consider whether the book can be said to be 'utterly without social importance.' We are mindful that there was expert testimony, much of which was strained, to the effect that *Memoirs* is a structural novel with literary merit; that the book displays a skill in characterization and a gift for comedy; that it plays a part in the history of the development of the English novel; and that it contains a moral, namely, that sex with love is superior to sex in a brothel. But the fact that the testimony may indicate this book has some minimal literary value does not mean it is of any social importance. We do not interpret the 'social importance' test as requiring that a book which appeals to prurient interest and is patently offensive must be unqualifiedly worthless before it can be deemed obscene." * * *

The Supreme Judicial Court erred in holding that a book need not be "unqualifiedly worthless before it can be deemed obscene." A book cannot be proscribed unless it is found to be *utterly* without redeeming social value. This is so even though the book is found to possess the requisite prurient appeal and to be patently offensive. Each of the three federal constitutional criteria is to be applied independently; the social value of the book can neither be weighed against nor canceled by its prurient appeal or patent offensiveness. Hence, even on the view of the court below that *Memoirs* possessed only a modicum of social value, its judgment must be reversed as being founded on an erroneous interpretation of a federal constitutional standard.

II.

It does not necessarily follow from this reversal that a determination that *Memoirs* is obscene in the constitutional sense would be improper under all circumstances. On the premise, which we have no occasion to assess, that *Memoirs* has the requisite prurient appeal and is patently offensive, but has only a minimum of social value, the circumstances of production, sale, and publicity are relevant in determining whether or not the publication or distribution of the book is constitutionally protected. Evidence that the book was commercially exploited for the sake of prurient appeal, to the exclusion of all other values, might justify the conclusion that the book was utterly without redeeming social importance. It is not that in such a setting the social value test is relaxed so as to dispense with the requirement that a book be utterly devoid of social value, but rather that, as we elaborate in *Ginzburg v. United States,* * * *, where the purveyor's sole emphasis is on the sexually provocative aspects of his publications, a court could accept his evaluation at its face value. In this proceeding, however, the courts were asked to judge the obscenity of *Memoirs* in the abstract, and the declaration of obscenity was neither aided nor limited by a specific set of circumstances of production, sale, and publicity. All possible uses of the book must therefore be considered, and the mere risk that the book might be exploited by panderers because it so pervasively treats sexual matters cannot alter the fact—given the view of the Massachusetts court attributing to *Memoirs* a modicum of literary and historical value—that the book will have redeeming social importance in the hands of those who publish or distribute it on the basis of that value.

Reversed.

* * *

Mr. Justice Douglas, concurring in the judgment.

Memoirs of a Woman of Pleasure, or, as it is often titled, *Fanny Hill,* concededly is an erotic novel. It was first published in about 1749 and has endured to this date, despite periodic efforts to suppress it.[1]

* * *

In 1963, an American publishing house undertook the publication of *Memoirs.* The record indicates that an unusually large number of orders were placed by universities and libraries; the Library of Congress requested the right to translate the book into Braille. But the Commonwealth of Massachusetts instituted the suit that ultimately found its way here, praying that the book be declared obscene so that the citizens of Massachusetts might be spared the necessity of determining for themselves whether or not to read it.

* * *

Four of the seven Justices of the Massachusetts Supreme Judicial Court conclude that *Fanny Hill* is obscene. * * * Four of the seven judges of the New York Court of Appeals conclude that it is not obscene. Larkin v. Putnam's Sons, 14 N.Y.2d 399, 200 N.E.2d 760. To

---

1. *Memoirs* was the subject of what is generally regarded as the first recorded suppression of a literary work in this country on grounds of obscenity. See Commonwealth v. Holmes, 17 Mass. 336. The edition there condemned differed from the present volume in that it contained apparently erotic illustrations.

outlaw the book on such a voting record would be to let majorities rule where minorities were thought to be supreme. The Constitution forbids abridgment of "freedom of speech, or of the press." Censorship is the most notorious form of abridgment. It substitutes majority rule where minority tastes or viewpoints were to be tolerated.

It is to me inexplicable how a book that concededly has social worth can nonetheless be banned because of the manner in which it is advertised and sold. However florid its cover, whatever the pitch of its advertisements, the contents remain the same.

Every time an obscenity case is to be argued here, my office is flooded with letters and postal cards urging me to protect the community or the Nation by striking down the publication. The messages are often identical even down to commas and semicolons. The inference is irresistible that they were all copied from a school or church blackboard. Dozens of postal cards often are mailed from the same precinct. The drives are incessant and the pressures are great. Happily we do not bow to them. I mention them only to emphasize the lack of popular understanding of our constitutional system. Publications and utterances were made immune from majoritarian control by the First Amendment, applicable to the States by reason of the Fourteenth. No exceptions were made, not even for obscenity. The Court's contrary conclusion in *Roth*, where obscenity was found to be "outside" the First Amendment, is without justification.

* * *

It is true, as the Court observed in *Roth*, that obscenity laws appeared on the books of a handful of States at the time the First Amendment was adopted. But the First Amendment was, until the adoption of the Fourteenth, a restraint only upon federal power. Moreover, there is an absence of any *federal* cases or laws relative to obscenity in the period immediately after the adoption of the First Amendment. Congress passed no legislation relating to obscenity until the middle of the nineteenth century. Neither reason nor history warrants exclusion of any particular class of expression from the protection of the First Amendment on nothing more than a judgment that it is utterly without merit. We faced the difficult questions the First Amendment poses with regard to libel in New York Times v. Sullivan, 376 U.S. 254, 269, where we recognized that "libel can claim no talismanic immunity from constitutional limitations." We ought not to permit fictionalized assertions of constitutional history to obscure those questions here. Were the Court to undertake that inquiry, it would be unable, in my opinion, to escape the conclusion that no interest of society with regard to suppression of "obscene" literature could override the First Amendment to justify censorship.

The censor is always quick to justify his function in terms that are protective of society. But the First Amendment, written in terms that are absolute, deprives the States of any power to pass on the value, the propriety, or the morality of a particular expression. Cf. Kinglsey Int'l Pictures Corp. v. Regents, 360 U.S. 684, 688–689; Joseph Burstyn, Inc. v. Wilson, 343 U.S. 495. Perhaps the most frequently assigned justification for censorship is the belief that erotica produce antisocial sexual conduct. But that relationship has yet to be proven. Indeed, if one were to make judgments on the basis of speculation, one might guess that literature of the most pornographic sort would, in many cases, provide a substitute—not a stimulus—for antisocial sexual conduct. See Murphy, The Value of Pornography, 10 Wayne L.Rev. 655, 661 and n. 19 (1964). As I read the First Amendment, judges cannot gear the literary diet of an entire nation to whatever tepid stuff is incapable of triggering the most demented mind. The First Amendment demands more than a horrible example or two of the perpetrator of a crime of sexual violence, in whose pocket is found a pornographic book, before it allows the Nation to be saddled with a regime of censorship.[11]

Whatever may be the reach of the power to regulate *conduct*, I stand by my view in *Roth v. United States, supra,* that the First Amendment leaves no power in government over *expression of ideas.*

* * *

MR. JUSTICE CLARK, dissenting.

It is with regret that I write this dissenting opinion. However, the public should know of the continuous flow of pornographic material reaching this Court and the increasing problem States have in controlling it. *Memoirs of a Woman of Pleasure,* the book involved here, is typical. I have "stomached" past cases for almost 10 years without much outcry. Though I am not known to be a purist—or a shrinking violet—this book is too much even for me. It is important that the Court has refused to declare it obscene and thus affords it further circulation. In order to give my remarks the proper setting I have been obliged to portray the book's contents, which causes me embarrassment. However, quotations from typical episodes would so debase our Reports that I will not follow that course.

* * *

* * * I repeat that I regret having to depict the sordid episodes of this book.

---

11. It would be a futile effort even for a censor to attempt to remove all that might possibly stimulate antisocial sexual conduct:

"The majority [of individuals], needless to say, are somewhere between the over-scrupulous extremes of excitement and frigidity * * * Within this variety, it is impossible to define 'hard-core' pornography, as if there were some singly lewd concept from which all profane ideas passed by imperceptible degrees into that sexuality called holy. But there is no 'hard-core.' Everything, every idea, is capable of being obscene if the personality perceiving it so apprehends it.

"It is for this reason that books, pictures, charades, ritual, the spoken word, can and do lead directly to conduct harmful to the self indulging in it and to others. Heinrich Pommerenke, who was a rapist, abuser, and mass slayer of women in Germany, was prompted to his series of ghastly deeds by Cecil B. DeMille's *The Ten Commandments.* During the scene of the Jewish women dancing about the Golden Calf, all the doubts of his life came clear: Women were the source of the world's trouble and it was his mission to both punish them for this and to execute them. Leaving the theater, he slew his first victim in a park nearby. John George Haigh, the British vampire who sucked his victims' blood through soda straws and dissolved their drained bodies in acid baths, first had his murder-inciting dreams and vampire-longings from watching the 'voluptuous' procedure of—an Anglican High Church Service!" Murphy, *supra,* at 668.

III.

Memoirs is nothing more than a series of minutely and vividly described sexual episodes. The book starts with Fanny Hill, a young 15-year-old girl, arriving in London to seek household work. She goes to an employment office where through happenstance she meets the mistress of a bawdy house. This takes 10 pages. The remaining 200 pages of the book detail her initiation into various sexual experiences, from a lesbian encounter with a sister prostitute to all sorts and types of sexual debauchery in bawdy houses and as the mistress of a variety of men. This is presented to the reader through an uninterrupted succession of descriptions by Fanny, either as an observer or participant, of sexual adventures so vile that one of the male expert witnesses in the case was hesitant to repeat any one of them in the courtroom. These scenes run the gamut of possible sexual experience such as lesbianism, female masturbation, homosexuality between young boys, the destruction of a maidenhead with consequent gory descriptions, the seduction of a young virgin boy, the flagellation of male by female, and vice versa, followed by fervid sexual engagement, and other abhorrent acts, including over two dozen separate bizarre descriptions of different sexual intercourses between male and female characters. In one sequence four girls in a bawdy house are required in the presence of one another to relate the lurid details of their loss of virginity and their glorification of it. This is followed the same evening by "public trials" in which each of the four girls engages in sexual intercourse with a different man while the others witness, with Fanny giving a detailed description of the movement and reaction of each couple.

* * *

* * * It is true that Fanny's perverse experiences finally bring from her the observation that "the heights of [sexual] enjoyment cannot be achieved until true affection prepares the bed of passion." But this merely emphasizes that sex, wherever and however found, remains the sole theme of *Memoirs*. In my view, the book's repeated and unrelieved appeals to the prurient interest of the average person leave it utterly without redeeming social importance.

IV.

In his separate concurrence, my Brother Douglas asserts there is no proof that obscenity produces antisocial conduct. I had thought that this question was foreclosed by the determination in *Roth* that obscenity was not protected by the First Amendment. I find it necessary to comment upon Brother Douglas' views, however, because of the new requirement engrafted upon *Roth* by Brother Brennan, i.e., that material which "appeals to a prurient interest" and which is "patently offensive" may still not be suppressed unless it is "utterly without redeeming social value." The question of antisocial effect thus becomes relevant to the more limited question of social value. * * *

Psychological and physiological studies clearly indicate that many persons become sexually aroused from reading obscene material. While erotic stimulation caused by pornography may be legally insignificant in itself, there are medical experts who believe that such stimulation frequently manifests itself in criminal sexual behavior or other antisocial conduct. For example, Dr. George W. Henry of Cornell University has expressed the opinion that obscenity, with its exaggerated and morbid emphasis on sex, particularly abnormal and perverted practices, and its unrealistic presentation of sexual behavior and attitudes, may induce antisocial conduct by the average person. A number of sociologists think that this material may have adverse effects upon individual mental health, with potentially disruptive consequences for the community.

* * *

But this is not all that Massachusetts courts might consider. I believe it can be established that the book "was commercially exploited for the sake of prurient appeal, to the exclusion of all other values" and should therefore be declared obscene under the test of commercial exploitation announced today in *Ginzburg* and *Mishkin*.

* * *

MR. JUSTICE HARLAN, dissenting.

* * *

My premise is that in the area of obscenity the Constitution does not bind the States and the Federal Government in precisely the same fashion. This approach is plainly consistent with the language of the First and Fourteenth Amendments and, in my opinion, more responsive to the proper functioning of a federal system of government in this area. * * *

Federal suppression of allegedly obscene matter should, in my view, be constitutionally limited to that often described as "hard-core pornography." To be sure, that rubric is not a self-executing standard, but it does describe something that most judges and others will "know * * * when [they] see it" (STEWART, J., in Jacobellis v. Ohio, 378 U.S. 184, 197) and that leaves the smallest room for disagreement between those of varying tastes. To me it is plain, for instance, that *Fanny Hill* does not fall within this class and could not be barred from the federal mails. If further articulation is meaningful, I would characterize as "hard-core" that prurient material that is patently offensive or whose indecency is self-demonstrating and I would describe it substantially as does Mr. Justice Stewart's opinion in *Ginzburg,* * * *. The Federal Government may be conceded a limited interest in excluding from the mails such gross pornography, almost universally condemned in this country. But I believe the dangers of national censorship and the existence of primary responsibility at the state level amply justify drawing the line at this point.

State obscenity laws present problems of quite a different order. The varying conditions across the country, the range of views on the need and reasons for curbing obscenity, and the traditions of local self-government in matters of public welfare all favor a far more flexible attitude in defining the bounds for the States. From my standpoint, the Fourteenth Amendment requires of a State only that it apply criteria rationally related to the accepted notion of obscenity and that it reach results not wholly out of step with current American standards. * * *

* * * I think it more satisfactory to acknowledge that on this record the book has been shown to have some quantum of social value, that it may at the same time be deemed offensive and salacious, and that the State's decision to weigh these elements and to ban this particular work does not exceed constitutional limits.

* * * I venture to say that the Court's burden of decision would be ameliorated under the constitutional principles that I have advocated. "Hard-core pornography" for judging federal cases is one of the more tangible concepts in the field. As to the States, the due latitude my approach would leave them ensures that only the unusual case would require plenary review and correction by this Court.

There is plenty of room, I know, for disagreement in this area of constitutional law. Some will think that what I propose may encourage States to go too far in this field. Others will consider that the Court's present course unduly restricts state experimentation with the still elusive problem of obscenity. For myself, I believe it is the part of wisdom for those of us who happen currently to possess the "final word" to leave room for such experimentation, which indeed is the underlying genius of our federal system.

On the premises set forth in this opinion, supplementing what I have earlier said in my opinions in *Roth, supra,* Manual Enterprises, Inc. v. Day, 370 U.S. 478, and Jacobellis v. Ohio, 378 U.S., at 203, I would affirm the judgment of the Massachusetts Supreme Judicial Court.

MR. JUSTICE WHITE, dissenting.

In *Roth v. United States,* 354 U.S. 476, the Court held a publication to be obscene if its predominant theme appeals to the prurient interest in a manner exceeding customary limits of candor. Material of this kind, the Court said, is "utterly without redeeming social importance" and is therefore unprotected by the First Amendment.

To say that material within the *Roth* definition of obscenity is nevertheless not obscene if it has some redeeming social value is to reject one of the basic propositions of the *Roth* case—that such material is not protected because it is inherently and utterly without social value.

If "social importance" is to be used as the prevailing opinion uses it today, obscene material, however far beyond customary limits of candor, is immune if it has any literary style, if it contains any historical references or language characteristic of a bygone day, or even if it is printed or bound in an interesting way. Well written, especially effective obscenity is protected; the poorly written is vulnerable. And why shouldn't the fact that some people buy and read such material prove its "social value"?

* * *

In my view, "social importance" is not an independent test of obscenity but is relevant only to determining the predominant prurient interest of the material, a determination which the court or the jury will make based on the material itself and all the evidence in the case, expert or otherwise.

Application of the *Roth* test, as I understand it, necessarily involves the exercise of judgment by legislatures, courts and juries. But this does not mean that there are no limits to what may be done in the name of *Roth*. Cf. Jacobellis v. Ohio, 378 U.S. 184. *Roth* does not mean that a legislature is free to ban books simply because they deal with sex or because they appeal to the prurient interest. Nor does it mean that if books like *Fanny Hill* are unprotected, their non-prurient appeal is necessarily lost to the world. Literary style, history, teachings about sex, character description (even of a prostitute) or moral lessons need not come wrapped in such packages. The fact that they do impeaches their claims to immunity from legislative censure.

Finally, it should be remembered that if the publication and sale of *Fanny Hill* and like books are proscribed, it is not the Constitution that imposes the ban. Censure stems from a legislative act, and legislatures are constitutionally free to embrace such books whenever they wish to do so. But if a State insists on treating *Fanny Hill* as obscene and forbidding its sale, the First Amendment does not prevent it from doing so.

I would affirm the judgment below.

GINZBURG v. UNITED STATES

Supreme Court of the United States, 1966.
383 U.S. 463, 86 S.Ct. 942, 16 L.Ed.2d 31.

MR. JUSTICE BRENNAN delivered the opinion of the Court.

A judge sitting without a jury in the District Court for the Eastern District of Pennsylvania convicted petitioner Ginzburg and three corporations controlled by him upon all 28 counts of an indictment charging violation of the federal obscenity statute, 18 U.S.C. § 3237 (1964 ed.). * * * Each count alleged that a resident of the Eastern District received mailed matter, either one of three publications challenged as obscene, or advertising telling how and where the publications might be obtained. The Court of Appeals for the Third Circuit affirmed, 338 F.2d 12. We granted certiorari, 380 U.S. 961. We affirm. Since petitioners do not argue that the trial judge misconceived or failed to apply the standards we first enunciated in Roth v. United States, 354 U.S. 476,[3] the only serious question is whether those standards were

---

3. We are not, however, to be understood as approving all aspects of the trial judge's exegesis of *Roth*, for example his remarks that "the community as a whole is the proper consideration. In this community, our society, we have children of all ages, psychotics, feeble-minded and other susceptible elements. Just as they cannot set the pace for the average adult reader's taste, they cannot be overlooked as part of

correctly applied.[4]

In the cases in which this Court has decided obscenity questions since *Roth,* it has regarded the materials as sufficient in themselves for the determination of the question. In the present case, however, the prosecution charged the offense in the context of the circumstances of production, sale, and publicity and assumed that, standing alone, the publications themselves might not be obscene. We agree that the question of obscenity may include consideration of the setting in which the publications were presented as an aid to determining the question of obscenity, and assume without deciding that the prosecution could not have succeeded otherwise. * * *

The three publications were EROS, a hard-cover magazine of expensive format; Liaison, a bi-weekly newsletter; and The Housewife's Handbook on Selective Promiscuity (hereinafter the *Handbook*), a short book. The issue of EROS specified in the indictment, Vol. 1, No. 4, contains 15 articles and photo-essays on the subject of love, sex, and sexual relations. The specified issue of Liaison, Vol. 1, No. 1, contains a prefatory "letter from the Editors" announcing its dedication to "keeping sex an art and preventing it from becoming a science." The remainder of the issue consists of digests of two articles concerning sex and sexual relations which had earlier appeared in professional journals and a report of an interview with a psychotherapist who favors the broadest license in sexual relationships. As the trial judge noted, "[w]hile the treatment is largely superficial, it is presented entirely without restraint of any kind. According to defendants' own expert, it is entirely without literary merit." 224 F.Supp., at 134. The *Handbook* purports to be a sexual autobiography detailing with complete candor the author's sexual experiences from age 3 to age 36. The text includes, and prefatory and concluding sections of the book elaborate, her views on such subjects as sex education of children, law regulating private consensual adult sexual practices, and the equality of women in sexual relationships. It was claimed at trial that women would find the book valuable, for example as a marriage manual or as an aid to the sex education of their children.

Besides testimony as to the merit of the material, there was abundant evidence to show that each of the accused publications was originated or sold as stock in trade of the sordid business of pandering —"the business of purveying textual or graphic matter openly advertised to appeal to the erotic interest of their customers." EROS early sought mailing privileges from the postmasters of Intercourse and Blue Ball, Pennsylvania. The trial court found the obvious, that these hamlets were chose only for the value of their names would have in furthering petitioners' efforts to sell their publications on the basis of salacious appeal; the facilities of the post offices were inadequate to handle the anticipated volume of mail, and the privileges were denied.

---

the community." 224 F.Supp., at 137. Compare Butler v. Michigan, 352 U.S. 380.

4. The Government stipulated at trial that the circulars advertising the publications were not themselves obscene; therefore the convictions on the counts for mailing the advertising stand only if the mailing of the publications offended the statute.

Mailing privileges were then obtained from the postmaster of Middlesex, New Jersey. EROS and Liaison thereafter mailed several million circulars soliciting subscriptions from that post office; over 5,500 copies of the *Handbook* were mailed.

The "leer of the sensualist" also permeates the advertising for the three publications. The circulars sent for EROS and Liaison stressed the sexual candor of the respective publications, and openly boasted that the publishers would take full advantage of what they regarded as an unrestricted license allowed by law in the expression of sex and sexual matters. * * *

This evidence, in our view, was relevant in determining the ultimate question of obscenity and, in the context of this record, serves to resolve all ambiguity and doubt. The deliberate representation of petitioners' publications as erotically arousing, for example, stimulated the reader to accept them as prurient; he looks for titillation, not for saving intellectual content. Similarly, such representation would tend to force public confrontation with the potentially offensive aspects of the work; the brazenness of such an appeal heightens the offensiveness of the publications to those who are offended by such material. And the circumstances of presentation and dissemination of material are equally relevant to determining whether social importance claimed for material in the courtroom was, in the circumstances, pretense or reality—whether it was the basis upon which it was traded in the marketplace or a spurious claim for litigation purposes. Where the purveyors sole emphasis is on the sexually provocative aspects of his publications, that fact may be decisive in the determination of obscenity. * * *

* * *

We perceive no threat to First Amendment guarantees in thus holding that in close cases evidence of pandering may be probative with respect to the nature of the material in question and thus satisfy the *Roth* test. No weight is ascribed to the fact that petitioners have profited from the sale of publications which we have assumed but do not hold cannot themselves be adjudged obscene in the abstract; to sanction consideration of this fact might indeed induce self-censorship, and offend the frequently stated principle that commercial activity, in itself, is no justification for narrowing the protection of expression secured by the First Amendment. Rather, the fact that each of these publications was created or exploited entirely on the basis of its appeal to prurient interests strengthens the conclusion that the transactions here were sales of illicit merchandise, not sales of constitutionally protected matter. * * *

It is important to stress that this analysis simply elaborates the test by which the obscenity vel non of the material must be judged. Where an exploitation of interests in titillation by pornography is shown with respect to material lending itself to such exploitation through pervasive treatment or description of sexual matters, such evidence may support the determination that the material is obscene even though in other contexts the material would escape such condemnation.

* * *

Affirmed.

MR. JUSTICE BLACK, dissenting.

Only one stark fact emerges with clarity out of the confusing welter of opinions and thousands of words written in this and two other cases today. That fact is that Ginzburg, petitioner here, is now finally and authoritatively condemned to serve five years in prison for distributing printed matter about sex which neither Ginzburg nor anyone else could possibly have known to be criminal. Since, as I have said many times, I believe the Federal Government is without any power whatever under the Constitution to put any type of burden on speech and expression of ideas of any kind (as distinguished from conduct), I agree with part II of the dissent of my Brother Douglas in this case, and I would reverse Ginzburg's conviction on this ground alone. Even assuming, however, that the Court is correct in holding today that Congress does have power to clamp official censorship on some subjects selected by the Court, in some ways approved by it, I believe that the federal obscenity statute as enacted by Congress and as enforced by the Court against Ginzburg in this case should be held invalid on two other grounds.

I.

* * *

I agree with my Brother Harlan that the Court has in effect rewritten the federal obscenity statute and thereby imposed on Ginzburg standards and criteria that Congress never thought about; or if it did think about them, certainly it did not adopt them. Consequently, Ginzburg is, as I see it, having his conviction and sentence affirmed upon the basis of a statute amended by this Court for violation of which amended statute he was not charged in the courts below. Such an affirmance we have said violate due process. * * *

* * *

MR. JUSTICE DOUGLAS, dissenting.

Today's condemnation of the use of sex symbols to sell literature engrafts another exception on First Amendment rights that is as unwarranted as the judge-made exception concerning obscenity. This new exception condemns an advertising technique as old as history, the advertisements of our best magazines are chock-full of thighs, ankles, calves, bosoms, eyes, and hair, to draw the potential buyer's attention to lotions, tires, food, liquor, clothing, autos, and even insurance policies. The sexy advertisement neither adds to nor detracts from the quality of the merchandise being offered for sale. And I do not see how it adds to or detracts one whit from the legality of the book being distributed. A book should stand on its own, irrespective of the reasons why it was written or the wiles used in selling it. I cannot imagine any promotional effort that would make chapters 7 and 8 of the Song of

Solomon any less or any more worthy of First Amendment protection than does their unostentatious inclusion in the average edition of the Bible.

* * *

Some of the tracts for which publishers go to prison concern normal sex, some homosexuality, some the masochistic yearning that is probably present in everyone and dominant in some. Masochism is a desire to be punished or subdued. In the broad frame of reference the desire may be expressed in the longing to be whipped and lashed, bound and gagged, and cruelly treated. Why is it unlawful to cater to the needs of this group? They are, to be sure, somewhat offbeat, nonconformist, and odd. But we are not in the realm of criminal conduct, only ideas and tastes. Some like Chopin, others like "rock and roll." Some are "normal," some are masochistic, some deviant in other respects, such as the homosexual. Another group also represented here translates mundane articles into sexual symbols. This group, like those embracing masochism, are anathema to the so-called stable majority. But why is freedom of the press and expression denied them? Are they to be barred from communicating in symbolisms important to them? When the Court today speaks of "social value," does it mean a "value" to the majority? Why is not a minority "value" cognizable? The masochistic group is one; the deviant group is another. Is it not important that members of those groups communicate with each other? Why is communication by the "written word" forbidden? If we were wise enough, we might know that communication may have greater therapeutical value than any sermon that those of the "normal" community can ever offer, but if the communication is of value to the masochistic community or to others of the deviant community, how can it be said to be "utterly without redeeming social importance"? "Redeeming" to whom? "Importance" to whom?

* * *

Man was not made in a fixed mold. If a publication caters to the idiosyncrasies of a minority, why does it not have some "social importance"? Each of us is a very temporary transient with likes and dislikes that cover the spectrum. However plebian my tastes may be, who am I to say that others' tastes must be so limited and that other tastes have no "social importance"? How can we know enough to probe the mysteries of the subconscious of our people and say that this is good for them and that is not? Catering to the most eccentric taste may have "social importance" in giving that minority an opportunity to express itself rather than to repress its inner desires, as I suggest in my separate opinion in *Memoirs v. Massachusetts,* * * * How can we know that this expression may not *prevent antisocial* conduct?

I find it difficult to say that a publication has no "social importance" because it caters to the taste of the most unorthodox amongst us. We members of this Court should be among the last to say what should be orthodox in literature. An omniscience would be required which few in our whole society possess.

II.

This leads me to the conclusion, previously noted, that the First Amendment allows all ideas to be expressed—whether orthodox, popular, offbeat, or repulsive. I do not think it permissible to draw lines between the "good" and the "bad" and be true to the constitutional mandate to let all ideas alone. If our Constitution permitted "reasonable" regulation of freedom of expression, as do the constitutions of some nations, we would be in a field where the legislative and the judiciary would have much leeway. But under our charter all regulation or control of expression is barred. Government does not sit to reveal where the "truth" is. People are left to pick and choose between competing offerings. There is no compulsion to take and read what is repulsive any more than there is to spend one's time poring over government bulletins, political tracts, or theological treatises. The theory is that people are mature enough to pick and choose, to recognize trash when they see it, to be attracted to the literature that satisfies their deepest need, and, hopefully, to move from plateau to plateau and finally reach the world of enduring ideas.

I think this is the ideal of the Free Society written into our Constitution. We have no business acting as censors or endowing any group with censorship powers. It is shocking to me for us to send to prison anyone for publishing anything, especially tracts so distant from any incitement to action as the ones before us.

* * *

Mr. Justice Harlan, dissenting.

I would reverse the convictions of Ginzburg and his three corporate co-defendants. The federal obscenity statute under which they were convicted, 18 U.S.C. § 1461 (1964 ed.), is concerned with unlawful shipment of "nonmailable" matter. In my opinion announcing the judgment of the Court in Manual Enterprises, Inc. v. Day, 370 U.S. 478, the background of the statute was assessed, and its focus was seen to be solely on the character of the material in question. That too has been the premise on which past cases in this Court arising under this statute was assessed, and its focus was seen to be solely on the character of the material in question. * * *

* * *

Although it is not clear whether the majority views the panderer test as a statutory gloss or as constitutional doctrine, I read the opinion to be in the latter category. The First Amendment, in the obscenity area, no longer fully protects material on its face nonobscene, for such material must now also be examined in the light of the defendant's conduct, attitude, motives. This seems to me a mere euphemism for allowing punishment of a person who mails otherwise constitutionally protected material just because a jury or a judge may not find him or his business agreeable. Were a State to enact a "panderer" statute under its police power, I have little doubt that—subject to clear drafting to avoid attacks on vagueness and equal protection grounds—such a statute would be constitutional. Possibly the same might be true of the

Federal Government acting under its postal or commerce powers. What I fear the Court has done today is in effect to write a new statute, but without the sharply focused definitions and standards necessary in such a sensitive area. Casting dubious gloss over a straightforward 101-year old statute * * * is for me an astonishing piece of judicial improvisation.

It seems perfectly clear that the theory on which these convictions are now sustained is quite different from the basis on which the case was tried and decided by the District Court and affirmed by the Court of Appeals. * * *

If there is anything to this new pandering dimension to the mailing statute, the Court should return the case for a new trial, for petitioners are at least entitled to a day in court on the question on which their guilt has ultimately come to depend. * * *

* * *

* * * In addition, I think such a test for obscenity is impermissibly vague, and unwarranted by anything in the First Amendment or in 18 U.S.C. § 1461.

I would reverse the judgments below.

Mr. Justice Stewart, dissenting.

Ralph Ginzburg has been sentenced to five years in prison for sending through the mail copies of a magazine, a pamphlet, and a book. There was testimony at his trial that these publications possess artistic and social merit. Personally, I have a hard time discerning any. Most of the material strikes me as both vulgar and unedifying. But if the First Amendment means anything, it means that a man cannot be sent to prison merely for distributing publications which offend a judge's esthetic sensibilities, mine or any other's.

Censorship reflects a society's lack of confidence in itself. It is a hallmark of an authoritarian regime. Long ago those who wrote our First Amendment charted a different course. They believed a society can be truly strong only when it is truly free. In the realm of expression they put their faith, for better or for worse, in the enlightened choice of the people, free from the interference of a policeman's intrusive thumb or a judge's heavy hand. So it is that the Constitution protects coarse expression as well as refined, and vulgarity no less than elegance. A book worthless to me may convey something of value to my neighbor. In the free society to which our Constitution has committed us, it is for each to choose for himself.

Because such is the mandate of our Constitution, there is room for only the most restricted view of this Court's decision in Roth v. United States, 354 U.S. 476. * * *

There does exist a distinct and easily identifiable class of material in which all of these elements coalesce. It is that, and that alone, which I think government may constitutionally suppress, whether by criminal or civil sanctions. I have referred to such material before as hard-core pornography, without trying further to define it. Jacobellis

v. Ohio, 378 U.S. 184, at 197 (concurring opinion). In order to prevent any possible misunderstanding, I have set out in the margin a description, borrowed from the Solicitor General's brief, of the kind of thing to which I have reference.[3] * * *

Although arguments can be made to the contrary, I accept the proposition that the general dissemination of matter of this description may be suppressed under valid laws. That has long been the almost universal judgment of our society. * * * But material of this sort is wholly different from the publications mailed by Ginzburg in the present case, and different not in degree but in kind.

The Court today appears to concede that the materials Ginzburg mailed were themselves protected by the First Amendment. But, the Court says, Ginzburg can still be sentenced to five years in prison for mailing them. Why? Because, says the Court, he was guilty of "commercial exploitation," of "pandering," and of "titillation." But Ginzburg was not charged with "commercial exploitation"; he was not charged with "pandering"; he was not charged with "titillation." Therefore, to affirm his conviction now on any of those grounds, even if otherwise valid, is to deny him due process of law. * * *

For me, however, there is another aspect of the Court's opinion in this case that is even more regrettable. Today the Court assumes the power to deny Ralph Ginzburg the protection of the First Amendment because it disapproves of his "sordid business." That is a power the Court does not possess. For the First Amendment protects us all with an even hand. It applies to Ralph Ginzburg with no less completeness and force than to G.P. Putnam's Sons. In upholding and enforcing the Bill of Rights, this Court has no power to pick or to choose. When we lose sight of that fixed star of constitutional adjudication, we lose our way. For then we forsake a government of law and are left with government by Big Brother.

I dissent.

MISHKIN v. NEW YORK
Supreme Court of the United States, 1966.
383 U.S. 502, 86 S.Ct. 958, 16 L.Ed.2d 56.

Mr. Justice Brennan delivered the opinion of the Court.

This case, like *Ginzburg v. United States*, * * *, also decided today, involves convictions under a criminal obscenity statute. A panel of

---

3. "* * * Such materials include photographs, both still and motion picture, with no pretense of artistic value, graphically depicting acts of sexual intercourse, including various acts of sodomy and sadism, and sometimes involving several participants in scenes of orgy-like character. They also include strips of drawings in comic-book format grossly depicting similar activities in an exaggerated fashion. There are, in addition, pamphlets and booklets, sometimes with photographic illustrations, verbally describing such activities in a bizarre manner with no attempt whatsoever to afford portrayals of character or situation and with no pretense to literary value. All of this material * * * cannot conceivably be characterized as embodying communication of ideas or artistic values inviolate under the First Amendment. * * *"

three judges of the Court of Special Sessions of the City of New York found appellant guilty of violating § 1141 of the New York Penal Law [1] by hiring others to prepare obscene books with intent to sell them. * * *

Appellant was not prosecuted for anything he said or believed, but for what he did, for his dominant role in several enterprises engaged in producing and selling allegedly obscene books. Fifty books are involved in this case. They portray sexuality in many guises. Some depict relatively normal heterosexual relations, but more depict such deviations as sado-masochism, fetishism, and homosexuality. Many have covers with drawings of scantily clad women being whipped, beaten, tortured, or abused. Many, if not most, are photo-offsets of typewritten books written and illustrated by authors and artists according to detailed instructions given by the appellant. Typical of appellant's instructions was that related by one author who testified that appellant insisted that the books be "full of sex scenes and lesbian scenes. * * * [T]he sex had to be very strong, it had to be rough, it had to be clearly spelled out. * * * I had to write sex very bluntly, make the sex scenes between men and women, and women and women, and men and men. * * * [H]e wanted scenes in which women were making love with women. * * * [H]e wanted sex scenes * * * in which there were lesbian scenes. He didn't call it lesbian, but he described women making love to women and men * * * making love to men, and there were spankings and scenes—sex in an abnormal and irregular fashion." Another author testified that appellant instructed him "to deal very graphically with * * * the darkening of the flesh under flagellation. * * *" Artists testified in similar vein as to appellant's instructions regarding illustrations and covers for the books.

All the books are cheaply prepared paperbound "pulps" with imprinted sales prices that are several thousand percent above costs. * * *

---

1. Section 1141 of the Penal Law, in pertinent part, reads as follows:

"1. A person who * * * has in his possession with intent to sell, lend, distribute * * * any obscene, lewd, lascivious, filthy, indecent, sadistic, masochistic or disgusting book * * * or who * * * prints, utters, publishes, or in any manner manufactures, or prepares any such book * * * or who

"2. In any manner, hires, employs, uses or permits any person to do or assist in doing any act or thing mentioned in this section, or any of them,

"Is guilty of a misdemeanor. * * *

* * *

"4. The possession by any person of six or more identical or similar articles coming within the provisions of subdivision one of this section is presumptive evidence of a violation of this section.

"5. The publication for sale of any book, magazine or pamphlet designed, composed or illustrated as a whole to appeal to and commercially exploit prurient interest by combining covers, pictures, drawings, illustrations, caricatures, cartoons, words, stories and advertisements or any combination or combinations thereof devoted to the description, portrayal or deliberate suggestion of illicit sex, including adultery, prostitution, fornication, sexual crime and sexual perversion or to the exploitation of sex and nudity by the presentation of nude or partially nude female figures, posed, photographed or otherwise presented in a manner calculated to provoke or incite prurient interest, or any combination or combinations thereof, shall be a violation of this section."

I.

Appellant attacks § 1141 as invalid on its face, contending that it exceeds First Amendment limitations by proscribing publications that are merely sadistic or masochistic, that the terms "sadistic" and "masochistic" are impermissibly vague, and that the term "obscene" is also impermissibly vague. We need not decide the merits of the first two contentions, for the New York courts held in this case that the terms "sadistic" and "masochistic," as well as the other adjectives used in § 1141 to describe proscribed books, are "synonymous with 'obscene.' " * * *

* * *

* * * [A]ppellant's sole contention regarding the nature of the material is that some of the books involved in this prosecution, those depicting various deviant sexual practices, such as flagellation, fetishism, and lesbianism, do not satisfy the prurient-appeal requirement because they do not appeal to a prurient interest of the "average person" in sex, that "instead of stimulating the erotic, they disgust and sicken." We reject this argument as being founded on an unrealistic interpretation of the prurient-appeal requirement.

Where the material is designed for and primarily disseminated to a clearly defined deviant sexual group, rather than the public at large, the prurient-appeal requirement of the *Roth* test is satisfied if the dominant theme of the material taken as a whole appeals to the prurient interest in sex of the members of that group. The reference to the "average" or "normal" person in *Roth,* * * *, does not foreclose this holding. In regard to the prurient-appeal requirement, the concept of the "average" or "normal" person was employed in *Roth* to serve the essentially negative purpose of expressing our rejection of that aspect of the *Hicklin* test, Regina v. Hicklin, [1868] L.R.3.Q.B. 360, that made the impact on the most susceptible person determinative. We adjust the prurient-appeal requirement to social realities by permitting the appeal of this type of material to be assessed in terms of the sexual interests of its intended and probable recipient group; and since our holding requires that the recipient group be defined with more specificity than in terms of sexually immature persons, it also avoids the inadequacy of the most-susceptible-person facet of the *Hicklin* test.

No substantial claim is made that the books depicting sexually deviant practices are devoid of prurient appeal to sexually deviant groups. The evidence fully establishes that these books were specifically conceived and marketed for such groups. * * *

* * *

Affirmed.

[The concurring opinion of MR. JUSTICE HARLAN, and dissenting opinion by JUSTICES BLACK, DOUGLAS and STEWART, have been omitted.]

REDRUP v. NEW YORK

Supreme Court of the United States, 1967.
386 U.S. 767, 87 S.Ct. 1414, 18 L.Ed.2d 515.

PER CURIAM.

These three cases arise from a recurring conflict—the conflict between asserted state power to suppress the distribution of books and magazines through criminal or civil proceedings, and the guarantees of the First and Fourteenth Amendments of the United States Constitution.

I.

In No. 3, *Redrup v. New York,* the petitioner was a clerk at a New York City newsstand. A plainclothes patrolman approached the newsstand, saw two paperback books on a rack—Lust Pool, and Shame Agent—and asked for them by name. The petitioner handed him the books and collected the price of $1.65. As a result of this transaction, the petitioner was charged in the New York City Criminal Court with violating a state criminal law. He was convicted, and the conviction was affirmed on appeal.

In No. 16, *Austin v. Kentucky,* the petitioner owned and operated a retail bookstore and newsstand in Paducah, Kentucky. A woman resident of Paducah purchased two magazines from a salesgirl in the petitioner's store, after asking for them by name—High Heels, and Spree. As a result of this transaction the petitioner stands convicted in the Kentucky courts for violating a criminal law of that State.

In No. 50, *Gent v. Arkansas,* the prosecuting attorney of the Eleventh Judicial District of Arkansas brought a civil proceeding under a state statute to have certain issues of various magazines declared obscene, to enjoin their distribution and to obtain a judgment ordering their surrender and destruction. The magazines proceeded against were: Gent, Swank, Bachelor, Modern Man, Cavalcade, Gentleman, Ace, and Sir. The County Chancery Court entered the requested judgment after a trial with an advisory jury, and the Supreme Court of Arkansas affirmed, with minor modifications.

In none of the cases was there a claim that the statute in question reflected a specific and limited state concern for juveniles. See Prince v. Massachusetts, 321 U.S. 158; cf. Butler v. Michigan, 352 U.S. 380. In none was there any suggestion of an assault upon individual privacy by publication in a manner so obtrusive as to make it impossible for an unwilling individual to avoid exposure to it. * * * And in none was there evidence of the sort of "pandering" which the Court found significant in Ginzburg v. United States, 383 U.S. 463.

II.

The Court originally limited review in these cases to certain particularized questions, upon the hypothesis that the material involved in each case was of a character described as "obscene in the constitutional sense" in Memoirs v. Massachusetts, 383 U.S. 413, 418. But we have concluded that the hypothesis upon which the Court originally proceeded was invalid, and accordingly that the cases can and should be decided upon a common and controlling fundamental constitutional basis, without prejudice to the questions upon which review was originally granted. We have concluded, in short, that the distribution of the publications in each of these cases is protected by the First and Fourteenth Amendments from governmental suppression, whether criminal or civil, *in personam* or *in rem.*

Two members of the Court have consistently adhered to the view that a State is utterly without power to suppress, control, or punish the distribution of any writings or pictures upon the ground of their "obscenity." A third has held to the opinion that a State's power in this area is narrowly limited to a distinct and clearly identifiable class of material. Others have subscribed to a not dissimilar standard, holding that a State may not constitutionally inhibit the distribution of literary material as obscene unless "(a) the dominant theme of the material taken as a whole appeals to a prurient interest in sex; (b) the material is patently offensive because it affronts contemporary community standards relating to the description or representation of sexual matters; and (c) the material is utterly without redeeming social value," emphasizing that the "three elements must coalesce," and that no such material can "be proscribed unless it is found to be utterly without redeeming social value." Memoirs v. Massachusetts, 383 U.S. 413, 418–419. Another Justice has not viewed the "social value" element as an independent factor in the judgment of obscenity. *Id.,* at 460–462 (dissenting opinion).

Whichever of these constitutional views is brought to bear upon the cases before us, it is clear that the judgments cannot stand. Accordingly, the judgment in each case is reversed.

It is so ordered.

MR. JUSTICE HARLAN, whom MR. JUSTICE CLARK joins, dissenting.

Two of these cases, *Redrup v. New York* and *Austin v. Kentucky,* were taken to consider the standards governing the application of the scienter requirement announced in Smith v. California, 361 U.S. 147, for obscenity prosecutions. There it was held that a defendant criminally charged with purveying obscene material must be shown to have had some kind of knowledge of the character of such material; the quality of that knowledge, however, was not defined. The third case, *Gent v. Arkansas,* was taken to consider the validity of a comprehensive Arkansas anti-obscenity statute, in light of the doctrines of "vagueness" and "prior restraint." The writs of certiorari in *Redrup* and *Austin,* and the notation of probable jurisdiction in Gent, were respectively limited to these issues, thus laying aside, for the purposes of these cases, the permissibility of the state determinations as to the obscenity of the challenged publications. Accordingly, the obscenity *vel non* of these publications was not discussed in the briefs or oral arguments of any of the parties.

The three cases were argued together at the beginning of this Term. Today, the Court rules that the materials could not constitutionally be adjudged obscene by the States, thus rendering adjudication of the other issues unnecessary. In short, the Court disposes of the cases on the issue that was deliberately excluded from review, and refuses to pass on the questions that brought the cases here.

In my opinion these dispositions do not reflect well on the processes of the Court, and I think the issues for which the cases were taken should be decided. Failing that, I prefer to cast my vote to dismiss the writs in *Redrup* and *Austin* as improvidently granted and, in the circumstances, to dismiss the appeal in *Gent* for lack of a substantial federal question. I deem it more appropriate to defer an expression of my own views on the questions brought here until an occasion when the Court is prepared to come to grips with such issues.

STANLEY v. GEORGIA

Supreme Court of the United States, 1969.
394 U.S. 557, 89 S.Ct. 1243, 22 L.Ed.2d 542.

MR. JUSTICE MARSHALL delivered the opinion of the Court.

An investigation of appellant's alleged bookmaking activities led to the issuance of a search warrant for appellant's home. Under authority of this warrant, federal and state agents secured entrance. They found very little evidence of bookmaking activity, but while looking through a desk drawer in an upstairs bedroom, one of the federal agents, accompanied by a state officer, found three reels of eight-millimeter film. Using a projector and screen found in an upstairs living room, they viewed the films. The state officer concluded that they were obscene and seized them. Since a further examination of the bedroom indicated that appellant occupied it, he was charged with possession of obscene matter and placed under arrest. He was later indicted for "knowingly [having] possession of * * * obscene matter" in violation of Georgia law. Appellant was tried before a jury and convicted. The Supreme Court of Georgia affirmed. Stanley v. State, 224 Ga. 259, 161 S.E.2d 309 (1968). We noted probable jurisdiction of an appeal brought under 28 U.S.C. § 1257(2). 393 U.S. 819 (1968).

Appellant raises several challenges to the validity of his conviction.[2] We find it necessary to consider only one. Appellant argues here, and argued below, that the Georgia obscenity statute, insofar as it punishes mere private possession of obscene matter, violates the First Amendment, as made applicable to the States by the Fourteenth Amendment. For reasons set forth below, we agree that the mere private possession of obscene matter cannot constitutionally be made a crime.

The court below saw no valid constitutional objection to the Georgia statute, even though it extends further than the typical statute forbidding commercial sales of obscene material. It held that "[it] is

---

2. Appellant does not argue that the films are not obscene. For the purpose of this opinion, we assume that they are obscene under any of the tests advanced by members of this Court. See Redrup v. New York, 386 U.S. 767 (1967).

not essential to an indictment charging one with possession of obscene matter that it be alleged that such possession was 'with intent to sell, expose or circulate the same.'" Stanley v. State, *supra,* at 261, 161 S.E.2d, at 311. The State and appellant both agree that the question here before us is whether "a statute imposing criminal sanctions upon the mere [knowing] possession of obscene matter" is constitutional. In this context, Georgia concedes that the present case appears to be one of "first impression * * * on this exact point," but contends that since "obscenity is not within the area of constitutionally protected speech or press," Roth v. United States, 354 U.S. 476, 485 (1957), the States are free, subject to the limits of other provisions of the Constitution, see, *e.g.,* Ginsberg v. New York, 390 U.S. 629, 637–645 (1968), to deal with it any way deemed necessary, just as they may deal with possession of other things thought to be detrimental to the welfare of their citizens. If the State can protect the body of a citizen, may it not, argues Georgia, protect his mind?

It is true that Roth does declare, seemingly without qualification, that obscenity is not protected by the First Amendment. That statement has been repeated in various forms in subsequent cases. See, e.g., Smith v. California, 361 U.S. 147, 152 (1959); Jacobellis v. Ohio, 378 U.S. 184, 186–187 (1964) (opinion of BRENNAN, J.); *Ginsberg v. New York, supra,* at 635. However, neither *Roth* nor any subsequent decision of this Court dealt with the precise problem involved in the present case. Roth was convicted of mailing obscene circulars and advertising, and an obscene book, in violation of a federal obscenity statute. The defendant in a companion case, Alberts v. California, 354 U.S. 476 (1957), was convicted of "lewdly keeping for sale obscene and indecent books, and [of] writing, composing and publishing an obscene advertisement of them. * * *" *Id.,* at 481. None of the statements cited by the Court in *Roth* for the proposition that "this Court has always assumed that obscenity is not protected by the freedoms of speech and press" were made in the context of a statute punishing mere private possession of obscene material; the cases cited deal for the most part with use of the mails to distribute objectionable material or with some form of public distribution or dissemination. Moreover, none of this Court's decisions subsequent to *Roth* involved prosecution for private possession of obscene materials. Those cases dealt with the power of the State and Federal Governments to prohibit or regulate certain public actions taken or intended to be taken with respect to obscene matter. Indeed, with one exception, we have been unable to discover any case in which the issue in the present case has been fully considered.

In this context, we do not believe that this case can be decided simply by citing *Roth. Roth* and its progeny certainly do mean that the First and Fourteenth Amendments recognize a valid governmental interest in dealing with the problem of obscenity. But the assertion of that interest cannot, in every context, be insulated from all constitutional protections. Neither *Roth* nor any other decision of this Court reaches that far. As the Court said in *Roth* itself, "[ceaseless] vigilance is the watchword to prevent * * * erosion [of First Amendment rights] by Congress or by the States. The door barring federal and state intrusion into this area cannot be left ajar; it must be kept tightly closed and opened only the slightest crack necessary to prevent encroachment upon more important interests." 354 U.S., at 488. *Roth* and the cases following it discerned such an "important interest" in the regulation of commercial distribution of obscene material. That holding cannot foreclose an examination of the constitutional implications of a statute forbidding mere private possession of such material. It is now well established that the Constitution protects the right to receive information and ideas. "This freedom [of speech and press] * * * necessarily protects the right to receive. * * *" Martin v. City of Struthers, 319 U.S. 141, 143 (1943); see Griswold v. Connecticut, 381 U.S. 479, 482 (1965); Lamont v. Postmaster General, 381 U.S. 301, 307–308 (1965) (BRENNAN, J., concurring); cf. Pierce v. Society of Sisters, 268 U.S. 510 (1925). This right to receive information and ideas, regardless of their social worth, see Winters v. New York, 333 U.S. 507, 510 (1948), is fundamental to our free society. Moreover, in the context of this case—a prosecution for mere possession of printed or filmed matter in the privacy of a person's own home—that right takes on an added dimension. For also fundamental is the right to be free, except in very limited circumstances, from unwanted governmental intrusions into one's privacy.

> "The makers of our Constitution undertook to secure conditions favorable to the pursuit of happiness. They recognized the significance of man's spiritual nature, of his feelings and of his intellect. They knew that only a part of the pain, pleasure and satisfactions of life are to be found in material things. They sought to protect Americans in their beliefs, their thoughts, their emotions and their sensations. They conferred, as against the Government, the right to be let alone—the most comprehensive of rights and the right most valued by civilized man." Olmstead v. United States, 277 U.S. 438, 478 (1928) (BRANDEIS, J., dissenting).

See *Griswold v. Connecticut, supra;* cf. NAACP v. Alabama, 357 U.S. 449, 462 (1958).

These are the rights that appellant is asserting in the case before us. He is asserting the right to read or observe what he pleases—the right to satisfy his intellectual and emotional needs in the privacy of his own home. He is asserting the right to be free from state inquiry into the contents of his library. Georgia contends that appellant does not have these rights, that there are certain types of materials that the individual may not read or even possess. Georgia justifies this assertion by arguing that the films in the present case are obscene. But we think that mere categorization of these films as "obscene" is insufficient justification for such a drastic invasion of personal liberties guaranteed by the First and Fourteenth Amendments. Whatever may be the justifications for other statutes regulating obscenity, we do not think they reach into the privacy of one's own home. If the First Amendment means anything, it means that a State has no business telling a man, sitting alone in his own house, what books he may read or what films he may watch. Our whole constitutional heritage rebels at the thought of giving government the power to control men's minds.

And yet, in the face of these traditional notions of individual liberty, Georgia asserts the right to protect the individual's mind from the effects of obscenity. We are not certain that this argument amounts to anything more than the assertion that the State has the right to control the moral content of a person's thoughts. To some, this may be a noble purpose, but it is wholly inconsistent with the philosophy of the First Amendment. As the Court said in Kingsley International Pictures Corp. v. Regents, 360 U.S. 684, 688–689 (1959), "[this] argument misconceives what it is that the Constitution protects. Its guarantee is not confined to the expression of ideas that are conventional or shared by a majority. * * * And in the realm of ideas it protects expression which is eloquent no less than that which is unconvincing." Cf. Joseph Burstyn, Inc. v. Wilson, 343 U.S. 495 (1952). Nor is it relevant that obscene materials in general, or the particular films before the Court, are arguably devoid of any ideological content. The line between the transmission of ideas and mere entertainment is much too elusive for this Court to draw, if indeed such a line can be drawn at all. See *Winters v. New York, supra,* at 510. Whatever the power of the state to control public dissemination of ideas inimical to the public morality, it cannot constitutionally premise legislation on the desirability of controlling a person's private thoughts.

Perhaps recognizing this, Georgia asserts that exposure to obscene materials may lead to deviant sexual behavior or crimes of sexual violence. There appears to be little empirical basis for that assertion. But more important, if the State is only concerned about printed or filmed materials inducing antisocial conduct, we believe that in the context of private consumption of ideas and information we should adhere to the view that "[among] free men, the deterrents ordinarily to be applied to prevent crime are education and punishment for violations of the law. * * *" Whitney v. California, 274 U.S. 357, 378 (1927) (BRANDEIS, J., concurring). See Emerson, Toward a General Theory of the First Amendment, 72 Yale L.J. 877, 938 (1963). Given the present state of knowledge, the State may no more prohibit mere possession of obscene matter on the ground that it may lead to antisocial conduct than it may prohibit possession of chemistry books on the ground that they may lead to the manufacture of homemade spirits.

It is true that in *Roth* this Court rejected the necessity of proving that exposure to obscene material would create a clear and present danger of antisocial conduct or would probably induce its recipients to such conduct. 354 U.S., at 486–487. But that case dealt with public distribution of obscene materials and such distribution is subject to different objections. For example, there is always the danger that obscene material might fall into the hands of children, see *Ginsberg v. New York, supra,* or that it might intrude upon the sensibilities or privacy of the general public. See Redrup v. New York, 386 U.S. 767, 769 (1967). No such dangers are present in this case.

Finally, we are faced with the argument that prohibition of possession of obscene materials is a necessary incident to statutory schemes prohibiting distribution. That argument is based on alleged difficulties of proving an intent to distribute or in producing evidence of actual distribution. We are not convinced that such difficulties exist, but even if they did we do not think that they would justify infringement of the individual's right to read or observe what he pleases. Because that right is so fundamental to our scheme of individual liberty, its restriction may not be justified by the need to ease the administration of otherwise valid criminal laws. See Smith v. California, 361 U.S. 147 (1959).

We hold that the First and Fourteenth Amendments prohibit making mere private possession of obscene material a crime.[11] *Roth* and the cases following that decision are not impaired by today's holding. As we have said, the States retain broad power to regulate obscenity; that power simply does not extend to mere possession by the individual in the privacy of his own home. Accordingly, the judgment of the court below is reversed and the case is remanded for proceedings not inconsistent with this opinion.

It is so ordered.

Mr. Justice Black, concurring.

I agree with the Court that the mere possession of reading matter or movie films, whether labeled obscene or not, cannot be made a crime by a State without violating the First Amendment, made applicable to the States by the Fourteenth. My reasons for this belief have been set out in many of my prior opinions, as for example, Smith v. California, 361 U.S. 147, 155 (1959) (concurring opinion), and Ginzburg v. United States, 383 U.S. 463, 476 (1966) (dissenting opinion).

Mr. Justice Stewart, with whom Mr. Justice Brennan and Mr. Justice White join, concurring in the result.

Before the commencement of the trial in this case, the appellant filed a motion to suppress the films as evidence upon the ground that they had been seized in violation of the Fourth and Fourteenth Amendments. The motion was denied, and the films were admitted in evidence at the trial. In affirming the appellant's conviction, the Georgia Supreme Court specifically determined that the films had been lawfully seized. The appellant correctly contends that this determination was clearly wrong under established principles of constitutional law. But the Court today disregards this preliminary issue in its hurry

---

11. What we have said in no way infringes upon the power of the State or Federal Government to make possession of other items, such as narcotics, firearms, or stolen goods, a crime. Our holding in the present case turns upon the Georgia statute's infringement of fundamental liberties protected by the First and Fourteenth Amendments. No First Amendment rights are involved in most statutes making mere possession criminal.

Nor do we mean to express any opinion on statutes making criminal possession of other types of printed, filmed, or recorded materials. See, e.g., 18 U.S.C. § 793(d), which makes criminal the otherwise lawful possession of materials which "the possessor has reason to believe could be used to the injury of the United States or to the advantage of any foreign nation. * * *" In such cases, compelling reasons may exist for overriding the right of the individual to possess those materials.

to move on to newer constitutional frontiers. I cannot so readily overlook the serious inroads upon Fourth Amendment guarantees countenanced in this case by the Georgia courts.

The Fourth Amendment provides that "no Warrants shall issue, but upon probable cause, supported by Oath or affirmation, and particularly describing the place to be searched, and the persons or things to be seized." The purpose of these clear and precise words was to guarantee to the people of this Nation that they should forever be secure from the general searches and unrestrained seizures that had been a hated hallmark of colonial rule under the notorious writs of assistance of the British Crown. See Stanford v. Texas, 379 U.S. 476, 481 (1965). This most basic of Fourth Amendment guarantees was frustrated in the present case, I think, in a manner made the more pernicious by its very subtlety. For what happened here was that a search that began as perfectly lawful became the occasion for an unwarranted and unconstitutional seizure of the films.

The state and federal officers gained admission to the appellant's house under the authority of a search warrant issued by a United States Commissioner. The warrant described "the place to be searched" with particularity. With like particularity, it described the "things to be seized"—equipment, records, and other material used in or derived from an illegal wagering business. And the warrant was issued only after the Commissioner had been apprised of more than adequate probable cause to issue it.

There can be no doubt, therefore, that the agents were lawfully present in the appellant's house, lawfully authorized to search for any and all of the items specified in the warrant, and lawfully empowered to seize any such items they might find. It follows, therefore, that the agents were acting within the authority of the warrant when they proceeded to the appellant's upstairs bedroom and pulled open the drawers of his desk. But when they found in one of those drawers not gambling material but moving picture films, the warrant gave them no authority to seize the films.

* * *

This is not a case where agents in the course of a lawful search came upon contraband, criminal activity, or criminal evidence in plain view. For the record makes clear that the contents of the films could not be determined by mere inspection. And this is not a case that presents any questions as to the permissible scope of a search made incident to a lawful arrest. For the appellant had not been arrested when the agents found the films. After finding them, the agents spent some 50 minutes exhibiting them by means of the appellant's projector in another upstairs room. Only then did the agents return downstairs and arrest the appellant.

Even in the much-criticized case of United States v. Rabinowitz, 339 U.S. 56 (1950), the Court emphasized that "exploratory searches * * * cannot be undertaken by officers with or without a warrant." *Id.,* at 62. This record presents a bald violation of that basic constitutional rule. To condone what happened here is to invite a government official to use a seemingly precise and legal warrant only as a ticket to get into a man's home, and, once inside, to launch forth upon unconfined searches and indiscriminate seizures as if armed with all the unbridled and illegal power of a general warrant.

Because the films were seized in violation of the Fourth and Fourteenth Amendments, they were inadmissible in evidence at the appellant's trial. Mapp v. Ohio, 367 U.S. 643 (1961). Accordingly, the judgment of conviction must be reversed.

MILLER v. CALIFORNIA
Supreme Court of the United States, 1973.
413 U.S. 15, 93 S.Ct. 2607, 37 L.Ed.2d 419.

MR. CHIEF JUSTICE BURGER delivered the opinion of the Court.

* * *

Appellant conducted a mass mailing campaign to advertise the sale of illustrated books, euphemistically called "adult" material. After a jury trial, he was convicted of violating California Penal Code § 311.2(a), a misdemeanor, by knowingly distributing obscene matter, and the Appellate Department, Superior Court of California, County of Orange, summarily affirmed the judgment without opinion. Appellant's conviction was specifically based on his conduct in causing five unsolicited advertising brochures to be sent through the mail in an envelope addressed to a restaurant in Newport Beach, California. The envelope was opened by the manager of the restaurant and his mother. They had not requested the brochures; they complained to the police.

The brochures advertise four books entitled "Intercourse," "Man-Woman," "Sex Orgies Illustrated," and "An Illustrated History of Pornography," and a film entitled "Marital Intercourse." While the brochures contain some descriptive printed material, primarily they consist of pictures and drawings very explicitly depicting men and women in groups of two or more engaging in a variety of sexual activities, with genitals often prominently displayed.

I

This case involves the application of a State's criminal obscenity statute to a situation in which sexually explicit materials have been thrust by aggressive sales action upon unwilling recipients who had in no way indicated any desire to receive such materials. This Court has recognized that the States have a legitimate interest in prohibiting dissemination or exhibition of obscene material [2] when the mode of

---

2. This Court has defined "obscene material" as "material which deals with sex in a manner appealing to prurient interest," *Roth v. United States, supra,* at 487, but the *Roth* definition does not reflect the precise meaning of "obscene" as traditionally used in the English language. Derived from the Latin *obscaenus, ob,* to, plus *caenum,* filth, "obscene" is defined in the Webster's Third New International Dictionary (Unabridged 1969) as "1a: disgusting to the senses * * * b: grossly repugnant to the generally accepted notions of what is appropriate * * * 2: offensive or revolting

dissemination carries with it a significant danger of offending the sensibilities of unwilling recipients or of exposure to juveniles. * * * It is in this context that we are called on to define the standards which must be used to identify obscene material that a State may regulate without infringing on the First Amendment as applicable to the States through the Fourteenth Amendment.

The dissent of Mr. Justice Brennan reviews the background of the obscenity problem, but since the Court now undertakes to formulate standards more concrete than those in the past, it is useful for us to focus on two of the landmark cases in the somewhat tortured history of the Court's obscenity decisions. In Roth v. United States, 354 U.S. 476 (1957), the Court sustained a conviction under a federal statute punishing the mailing of "obscene, lewd, lascivious or filthy * * *" materials. The key to that holding was the Court's rejection of the claim that obscene materials were protected by the First Amendment. * * *

Nine years later, in Memoirs v. Massachusetts, 383 U.S. 413 (1966), the Court veered sharply away from the *Roth* concept and, with only three Justices in the plurality opinion, articulated a new test of obscenity. The plurality held that under the *Roth* definition

> "as elaborated in subsequent cases, three elements must coalesce: it must be established that (a) the dominant theme of the material taken as a whole appeals to a prurient interest in sex; (b) the material is patently offensive because it affronts contemporary community standards relating to the description or representation of sexual matters; and (c) the material is utterly without redeeming social value." * * *

The sharpness of the break with *Roth,* represented by the third element of the *Memoirs* test and emphasized by Mr. Justice White's dissent, * * *, was further underscored when the *Memoirs* plurality went on to state:

> "The Supreme Judicial Court erred in holding that a book need not be 'unqualifiedly worthless before it can be deemed obscene.' A book cannot be proscribed unless it is found to be utterly without redeeming social value." *Id.,* at 419 (emphasis in original).

---

as countering or violating some ideal or principle." The Oxford English Dictionary (1933 ed.) gives a similar definition, "[o]ffensive to the senses, or to taste or refinement; disgusting, repulsive, filthy, foul, abominable, loathsome."

The material we are discussing in this case is more accurately defined as "pornography" or "pornographic material." "Pornography" derives from the Greek (*pornè,* harlot, and *graphos,* writing). The word now means "1: a description of prostitutes or prostitution 2: a depiction (as in writing or painting) of licentiousness or lewdness: a portrayal of erotic behavior designed to cause sexual excitement." Webster's Third New International Dictionary, *supra.* Pornographic material which is obscene forms a sub-group of all "obscene" expression, but not the whole, at least as the word "obscene" is now used in our language. We note, therefore, that the words "obscene material," as used in this case, have a specific judicial meaning which derives from the *Roth* case, i.e., obscene material "which deals with sex." *Roth, supra,* at 487. See also ALI Model Penal Code § 251.4(*l*) "Obscene Defined." (Official Draft 1962.)

While *Roth* presumed "obscenity" to be "utterly without redeeming social importance," *Memoirs* required that to prove obscenity it must be affirmatively established that the material is "*utterly* without redeeming social value." Thus, even as they repeated the words of *Roth*, the *Memoirs* plurality produced a drastically altered test that called on the prosecution to prove a negative, i.e., that the material was "utterly without redeeming social value"—a burden virtually impossible to discharge under our criminal standards of proof. * * *

The case we now review was tried on the theory that the California Penal Code § 311 approximately incorporates the three-stage *Memoirs* test, *supra*. But now the *Memoirs* test has been abandoned as unworkable by its author,[4] and no Member of the Court today supports the *Memoirs* formulation.

II

This much has been categorically settled by the Court, that obscene material is unprotected by the First Amendment. * * * We acknowledge, however, the inherent dangers of undertaking to regulate any form of expression. State statutes designed to regulate obscene materials must be carefully limited. * * * As a result, we now confine the permissible scope of such regulation to works which depict or describe sexual conduct. That conduct must be specifically defined by the applicable state law, as written or authoritatively construed.[6] A state offense must also be limited to works which, taken as a whole, appeal to the prurient interest in sex, which portray sexual conduct in a patently offensive way, and which, taken as a whole, do not have serious literary, artistic, political, or scientific value.

The basic guidelines for the trier of fact must be: (a) whether "the average person, applying contemporary community standards" would find that the work, taken as a whole, appeals to the prurient interest, * * *; (b) whether the work depicts or describes, in a patently offensive way, sexual conduct specifically defined by the applicable state law; and (c) whether the work, taken as a whole, lacks serious literary, artistic, political, or scientific value. We do not adopt as a constitutional standard the "*utterly* without redeeming social value" test of *Memoirs v. Massachusetts*, * * *; that concept has never commanded the adherence of more than three Justices at one time.[7] If a state law that regulates obscene material is thus limited, as written or construed, the First Amendment values applicable to the States through the Four-

---

4. See the dissenting opinion of Mr. Justice Brennan in *Paris Adult Theatre I v. Slaton*, [413 U.S. 49].

6. See, e.g., Oregon Laws 1971, c. 743, Art. 29, §§ 255–262, and Hawaii Penal Code, Tit. 37, §§ 1210–1216, 1972 Hawaii Session Laws, Act 9, c. 12, pt. II, pp. 126–129, as examples of state laws directed at depiction of defined physical conduct, as opposed to expression. Other state formulations could be equally valid in this respect. In giving the Oregon and Hawaii statutes as examples, we do not wish to be understood as approving of them in all other respects nor as establishing their limits as the extent of state power.

We do not hold, as Mr. Justice Brennan intimates, that all States other than Oregon must now enact new obscenity statutes. Other existing state statutes, as construed heretofore or hereafter, may well be adequate. * * *

7. * * * We also reject, as a constitutional standard, the ambiguous concept of "social importance." * * *

teenth Amendment are adequately protected by the ultimate power of appellate courts to conduct an independent review of constitutional claims when necessary. * * *

We emphasize that it is not our function to propose regulatory schemes for the States. That must await their concrete legislative efforts. It is possible, however, to give a few plain examples of what a state statute could define for regulation under part (b) of the standard announced in this opinion, *supra:*

(a) Patently offensive representations or descriptions of ultimate sexual acts, normal or perverted, actual or simulated.

(b) Patently offensive representations or descriptions of masturbation, excretory functions, and lewd exhibition of the genitals.

Sex and nudity may not be exploited without limit by films or pictures exhibited or sold in places of public accommodation any more than live sex and nudity can be exhibited or sold without limit in such public places.[8] At a minimum, prurient, patently offensive depiction or description of sexual conduct must have serious literary, artistic, political, or scientific value to merit First Amendment protection. * * * For example, medical books for the education of physicians and related personnel necessarily use graphic illustrations and descriptions of human anatomy. In resolving the inevitably sensitive questions of fact and law, we must continue to rely on the jury system, accompanied by the safeguards that judges, rules of evidence, presumption of innocence, and other protective features provide, as we do with rape, murder, and a host of other offenses against society and its individual members.[9]

Mr. Justice Brennan * * * has abandoned his former position and now maintains that no formulation of this Court, the Congress, or the States can adequately distinguish obscene material unprotected by the First Amendment from protected expression, *Paris Adult Theatre I v. Slaton,* [413 U.S. 49, 73] (BRENNAN, J., dissenting). Paradoxically, Mr. Justice Brennan indicates that suppression of unprotected obscene material is permissible to avoid exposure to unconsenting adults, as in this case, and to juveniles, although he gives no indication of how the division between protected and nonprotected materials may be drawn with greater precision for these purposes than for regulation of commercial exposure to consenting adults only. Nor does he indicate where in the Constitution he finds the authority to distinguish between a willing "adult" one month past the state law age of majority and a willing "juvenile" one month younger.

Under the holdings announced today, no one will be subject to prosecution for the sale or exposure of obscene materials unless these materials depict or describe patently offensive "hard core" sexual conduct specifically defined by the regulating state law, as written or

---

8. Although we are not presented here with the problem of regulating lewd public conduct itself, the States have greater power to regulate nonverbal, physical conduct than to suppress depictions or descriptions of the same behavior. * * *

9. The mere fact juries may reach different conclusions as to the same material does not mean that constitutional rights are abridged. * * *

construed. We are satisfied that these specific prerequisites will provide fair notice to a dealer in such materials that his public and commercial activities may bring prosecution. * * * If the inability to define regulated materials with ultimate, god-like precision altogether removes the power of the States or the Congress to regulate, then "hard core" pornography may be exposed without limit to the juvenile, the passerby, and the consenting adult alike, as, indeed, Mr. Justice Douglas contends. * * * In this belief, however, Mr. Justice Douglas now stands alone.

Mr. Justice Brennan also emphasizes "institutional stress" in justification of his change of view. Noting that "[t]he number of obscenity cases on our docket gives ample testimony to the burden that has been placed upon this Court," he quite rightly remarks that the examination of contested materials "is hardly a source of edification to the members of this Court." *Paris Adult Theatre I v. Slaton,* [413 U.S., at] 92, 93. He also notes, and we agree, that "uncertainty of the standards creates a continuing source of tension between state and federal courts...." "The problem is ... that one cannot say with certainty that material is obscene until at least five members of this Court, applying inevitably obscure standards, have pronounced it so." * * *

It is certainly true that the absence, since *Roth,* of a single majority view of this Court as to proper standards for testing obscenity has placed a strain on both state and federal courts. But today, for the first time since *Roth* was decided in 1957, a majority of this Court has agreed on concrete guidelines to isolate "hard core" pornography from expression protected by the First Amendment. Now we may abandon the casual practice of Redrup v. New York, 386 U.S. 767 (1967), and attempt to provide positive guidance to federal and state courts alike.

* * *

III

Under a National Constitution, fundamental First Amendment limitations on the powers of the States do not vary from community to community, but this does not mean that there are, or should or can be, fixed, uniform national standards of precisely what appeals to the "prurient interest" or is "patently offensive." These are essentially questions of fact, and our Nation is simply too big and too diverse for this Court to reasonably expect that such standards could be articulated for all 50 States in a single formulation, even assuming the prerequisite consensus exists. When triers of fact are asked to decide whether "the average person, applying contemporary community standards" would consider certain materials "prurient," it would be unrealistic to require that the answer be based on some abstract formulation. The adversary system, with lay jurors as the usual ultimate factfinders in criminal prosecutions, has historically permitted triers of fact to draw on the standards of their community, guided always by limiting instructions on the law. To require a State to structure obscenity proceedings around evidence of a *national* "community standard" would be an exercise in futility.

As noted before, this case was tried on the theory that the California obscenity statute sought to incorporate the tripartite test of *Memoirs*. This, a "national" standard of First Amendment protection enumerated by a plurality of this Court, was correctly regarded at the time of trial as limiting state prosecution under the controlling case law. The jury, however, was explicitly instructed that, in determining whether the "dominant theme of the material as a whole * * * appeals to the prurient interest" and in determining whether the material "goes substantially beyond customary limits of candor and affronts contemporary community standards of decency," it was to apply "contemporary community standards of the State of California."

During the trial, both the prosecution and the defense assumed that the relevant "community standards" in making the factual determination of obscenity were those of the State of California, not some hypothetical standard of the entire United States of America. Defense counsel at trial never objected to the testimony of the State's expert on community standards or to the instructions of the trial judge on "statewide" standards. On appeal to the Appellate Department, Superior Court of California, County of Orange, appellant for the first time contended that application of state, rather than national, standards violated the First and Fourteenth Amendments.

We conclude that neither the State's alleged failure to offer evidence of "national standards," nor the trial court's charge that the jury consider state community standards, were constitutional errors. Nothing in the First Amendment requires that a jury must consider hypothetical and unascertainable "national standards" when attempting to determine whether certain materials are obscene as a matter of fact. * * * It is neither realistic nor constitutionally sound to read the First Amendment as requiring that the people of Maine or Mississippi accept public depiction of conduct found tolerable in Las Vegas, or New York City.[13] * * *. People in different States vary in their tastes and attitudes, and this diversity is not to be strangled by the absolutism of imposed uniformity. As the Court made clear in *Mishkin v. New York*, 383 U.S., at 508–509, the primary concern with requiring a jury to apply the standard of "the average person, applying contemporary community standards" is to be certain that, so far as material is not

---

13. In Jacobellis v. Ohio, 378 U.S. 184 (1964), two Justices argued that application of "local" community standards would run the risk of preventing dissemination of materials in some places because sellers would be unwilling to risk criminal conviction by testing variations in standards from place to place. *Id.*, at 193–195 (opinion of BRENNAN, J., joined by GOLDBERG, J.). The use of "national" standards, however, necessarily implies that materials found tolerable in some places, but not under the "national" criteria, will nevertheless be unavailable where they are acceptable. Thus, in terms of danger to free expression, the potential for suppression seems at least as great in the application of a single nationwide standard as in allowing distribution in accordance with local tastes, a point which Mr. Justice Harlan often emphasized. * * *

Appellant also argues that adherence to a "national standard" is necessary "in order to avoid unconscionable burdens on the free flow of interstate commerce." * * * Appellant's argument would appear without substance in any event. Obscene material may be validly regulated by a State in the exercise of its traditional local power to protect the general welfare of its population despite some possible incidental effect on the flow of such materials across state lines. * * *

aimed at a deviant group, it will be judged by its impact on an average person, rather than a particularly susceptible or sensitive person—or indeed a totally insensitive one. * * * We hold that the requirement that the jury evaluate the materials with reference to "contemporary standards of the State of California" serves this protective purpose and is constitutionally adequate.

IV

The dissenting Justices sound the alarm of repression. But, in our view, to equate the free and robust exchange of ideas and political debate with commercial exploitation of obscene material demeans the grand conception of the First Amendment and its high purposes in the historic struggle for freedom. It is a "misuse of the great guarantees of free speech and free press. * * *" *Breard v. Alexandria,* 341 U.S., at 645. The First Amendment protects works which, taken as a whole, have serious literary, artistic, political, or scientific value, regardless of whether the government or a majority of the people approve of the ideas these works represent. "The protection given speech and press was fashioned to assure unfettered interchange of ideas for the bringing about of political and social changes desired by the people," *Roth v. United States, supra,* at 484 (emphasis added). * * * But the public portrayal of hard core sexual conduct for its own sake, and for the ensuing commercial gain, is a different matter.

There is no evidence, empirical or historical, that the stern 19th century American censorship of public distribution and display of material relating to sex, * * * in any way limited or affected expression of serious literary, artistic, political, or scientific ideas. On the contrary, it is beyond any question that the era following Thomas Jefferson to Theodore Roosevelt was an "extraordinarily vigorous period," not just in economics and politics, but in belles lettres and in "the outlying fields of social and political philosophies."[16] We do not see the harsh hand of censorship of ideas—good or bad, sound or unsound-and "repression" of political liberty lurking in every state regulation of commercial exploitation of human interest in sex.

Mr. Justice Brennan finds "it is hard to see how state-ordered regimentation of our minds can ever be forestalled." *Paris Adult Theatre I v. Slaton,* [413 U.S.] at 110 (BRENNAN, J., dissenting). These doleful anticipations assume that courts cannot distinguish commerce in ideas, protected by the First Amendment, from commercial exploitation of obscene material. Moreover, state regulation of hard core pornography so as to make it unavailable to nonadults, a regulation which Mr. Justice Brennan finds constitutionally permissible, has all the elements of "censorship" for adults; indeed even more rigid enforcement techniques may be called for with such dichotomy of regulation. * * * One can concede that the "sexual revolution" of recent years may have had useful byproducts in striking layers of prudery from a subject long irrationally kept from needed ventilation. But it

---

16. See 2 V. Parrington, Main Currents in American Thought ix et seq. (1930).
* * *

does not follow that no regulation of patently offensive "hard core" materials is needed or permissible; civilized people do not allow unregulated access to heroin because it is a derivative of medicinal morphine.

In sum, we (a) reaffirm the *Roth* holding that obscene material is not protected by the First Amendment; (b) hold that such material can be regulated by the States, subject to the specific safeguards enunciated above, without a showing that the material is "*utterly* without redeeming social value"; and (c) hold that obscenity is to be determined by applying "contemporary community standards," * * * not "national standards." The judgment of the Appellate Department of the Superior Court, Orange County, California, is vacated and the case remanded to that court for further proceedings not inconsistent with the First Amendment standards established by this opinion. * * *

Vacated and remanded.

Mr. Justice Douglas, dissenting.

I

Today we leave open the way for California to send a man to prison for distributing brochures that advertise books and a movie under freshly written standards defining obscenity which until today's decision were never the part of any law.

* * *

Today the Court retreats from the earlier formulations of the constitutional test and undertakes to make new definitions. This effort, like the earlier ones, is earnest and well intentioned. The difficulty is that we do not deal with constitutional terms, since "obscenity" is not mentioned in the Constitution or Bill of Rights. And the First Amendment makes no such exception from "the press" which it undertakes to protect nor, as I have said on other occasions, is an exception necessarily implied, for there was no recognized exception to the free press at the time the Bill of Rights was adopted which treated "obscene" publications differently from other types of papers, magazines, and books. So there are no constitutional guidelines for deciding what is and what is not "obscene." The Court is at large because we deal with tastes and standards of literature. What shocks me may be sustenance for my neighbor. What causes one person to boil up in rage over one pamphlet or movie may reflect only his neurosis, not shared by others. We deal here with a regime of censorship which, if adopted, should be done by constitutional amendment after full debate by the people.

Obscenity cases usually generate tremendous emotional outbursts. They have no business being in the courts. If a constitutional amendment authorized censorship, the censor would probably be an administrative agency. Then criminal prosecutions could follow as, if, and when publishers defied the censor and sold their literature. Under that regime a publisher would know when he was on dangerous ground. Under the present regime—whether the old standards or the new ones are used—the criminal law becomes a trap. A brand new test would put a publisher behind bars under a new law improvised by the courts after the publication. That was done in *Ginzburg* and has all the evils of an *ex post facto* law.

* * *

II

If a specific book, play, paper, or motion picture has in a civil proceeding been condemned as obscene and review of that finding has been completed, and thereafter a person publishes, shows, or displays that particular book or film, then a vague law has been made specific. There would remain the underlying question whether the First Amendment allows an implied exception in the case of obscenity. I do not think it does and my views on the issue have been stated over and over again. But at least a criminal prosecution brought at that juncture would not violate the time-honored void-for-vagueness test.

No such protective procedure has been designed by California in this case. Obscenity—which even we cannot define with precision—is a hodge-podge. To send men to jail for violating standards they cannot understand, construe, and apply is a monstrous thing to do in a Nation dedicated to fair trials and due process.

III

While the right to know is the corollary of the right to speak or publish, no one can be forced by government to listen to disclosure that he finds offensive. * * * There is no "captive audience" problem in these obscenity cases. No one is being compelled to look or to listen. Those who enter newsstands or bookstalls may be offended by what they see. But they are not compelled by the State to frequent those places; and it is only state or governmental action against which the First Amendment, applicable to the States by virtue of the Fourteenth, raises a ban.

The idea that the First Amendment permits government to ban publications that are "offensive" to some people puts an ominous gloss on freedom of the press. That test would make it possible to ban any paper or any journal or magazine in some benighted place. The First Amendment was designed "to invite dispute," to induce "a condition of unrest," to "create dissatisfaction with conditions as they are," and even to stir "people to anger." Terminiello v. Chicago, 337 U.S. 1, 4. The idea that the First Amendment permits punishment for ideas that are "offensive" to the particular judge or jury sitting in judgment is astounding. No greater leveler of speech or literature has ever been designed. To give the power to the censor, as we do today, is to make a sharp and radical break with the traditions of a free society. The First Amendment was not fashioned as a vehicle for dispensing tranquilizers to the people. Its prime function was to keep debate open to "offensive" as well as to "staid" people. The tendency throughout history has been to subdue the individual and to exalt the power of government. The use of the standard "offensive" gives authority to government that cuts the very vitals out of the First Amendment. As is intimated by the Court's opinion, the materials before us may be garbage. But so is much of what is said in political campaigns, in the daily press, on TV, or over the radio. By reason of the First Amendment—and solely because of it—speakers and publishers have not been threatened or subdued because their thoughts and ideas may be "offensive" to some.

* * *

If there are to be restraints on what is obscene, then a constitutional amendment should be the way of achieving the end. There are societies where religion and mathematics are the only free segments. It would be a dark day for America if that were our destiny. But the people can make it such if they choose to write obscenity into the Constitution and define it.

We deal with highly emotional, not rational, questions. To many the Song of Solomon is obscene. I do not think we, the judges, were ever given the constitutional power to make definitions of obscenity. If it is to be defined, let the people debate and decide by a constitutional amendment what they want to ban as obscene and what standards they want the legislatures and the courts to apply. Perhaps the people will decide that the path towards a mature, integratedsociety requires that all ideas competing for acceptance must have no censor. Perhaps they will decide otherwise. Whatever the choice, the courts will have some guidelines. Now we have none except our own predilections.

Mr. Justice Brennan, with whom Mr. Justice Stewart and Mr. Justice Marshall join, dissenting. [Omitted.]

PARIS ADULT THEATRE I v. SLATON
Supreme Court of the United States, 1973.
413 U.S. 49, 93 S.Ct. 2628, 37 L.Ed.2d 446.

Mr. Chief Justice Burger delivered the opinion of the Court.

Petitioners are two Atlanta, Georgia, movie theaters and their owners and mangers, operating in the style of "adult" theaters. On December 28, 1970, respondents, the local state district attorney and the solicitor for the local state trial court, filed civil complaints in that court alleging that petitioners were exhibiting to the public for paid admission two allegedly obscene films, contrary to Georgia Code Ann. § 26–2101.[1] The two films in question, "Magic Mirror" and "It All Comes Out in the End," depict sexual conduct characterized by the Georgia Supreme Court as "hard core pornography" leaving "little to the imagination."

* * *

On January 13, 1971, 15 days after the proceedings began, the films were produced by petitioners at a jury-waived trial. Certain photographs, also produced at trial, were stipulated to portray the single entrance to both Paris Adult Theatre I and Paris Adult Theatre II as it

---

1. This is a civil proceeding. Georgia Code Ann. § 26–2101 defines a criminal offense, but the exhibition of materials found to be "obscene" as defined by that statute may be enjoined in a civil proceeding under Georgia law. * * *

appeared at the time of the complaints. These photographs show a conventional, inoffensive theater entrance, without any pictures, but with signs indicating the theaters exhibit "Atlanta's Finest Mature Feature Films." On the door itself is a sign saying: "Adult Theatre— You must be 21 and able to prove it. If viewing the nude body offends you. Please Do Not Enter."

The two films were exhibited to the trial court. The only other state evidence was testimony by criminal investigators that they had paid admission to see the films and that nothing on the outside of the theater indicated the full nature of what was shown. In particular, nothing indicated that the films depicted—as they did—scenes of simulated fellatio, cunnilingus, and group sex intercourse. There was no evidence presented that minors had ever entered the theaters. Nor was there evidence presented that petitioners had a systematic policy of barring minors, apart from posting signs at the entrance. On April 12, 1971, the trial judge dismissed respondents' complaints. He assumed "that obscenity is established," but stated:

> "It appears to the Court that the display of these films in a commercial theatre, when surrounded by requisite notice to the public of their nature and by reasonable protection against the exposure of these films to minors, is constitutionally permissible."

On appeal, The Georgia Supreme Court unanimously reversed. * * * It assumed that the adult theaters in question barred minors and gave a full warning to the general public of the nature of the films shown, but held that the films were without protection under the First Amendment. * * *

I

It should be clear from the outset that we do not undertake to tell the States what they must do, but rather to define the area in which they may chart their own course in dealing with obscene material. This Court has consistently held that obscene material is not protected by the First Amendment as a limitation on the state police power by virtue of the Fourteenth Amendment. Miller v. California, 413 U.S. 15 * * *.

* * * Today, in *Miller v. California, supra,* we have sought to clarify the constitutional definition of obscene material subject to regulation by the States, and we vacate and remand this case for reconsideration in light of *Miller.*

* * *

We categorically disapprove the theory, apparently adopted by the trial judge, that obscene, pornographic films acquire constitutional immunity from state regulation simply because they are exhibited for consenting adults only. This holding was properly rejected by the Georgia Supreme Court. Although we have often pointedly recognized the high importance of the state interest in regulating the exposure of obscene materials to juveniles and unconsenting adults, * * *, this Court has never declared these to be the only legitimate state interests permitting regulation of obscene material. The States have a long-recognized legitimate interest in regulating the use of obscene material in local commerce and in all places of public accommodation as long as these regulations do not run afoul of specific constitutional prohibitions. * * *

In particular, we hold that there are legitimate state interests at stake in stemming the tide of commercialized obscenity, even assuming it is feasible to enforce effective safeguards against exposure to juveniles and to passersby. * * * These include the interest of the public in the quality of life and the total community environment, the tone of commerce in the great city centers, and, possibly, the public safety itself. The Hill–Link Minority Report of the Commission on Obscenity and Pornography indicates that there is at least an arguable correlation between obscene material and crime. * * *

But, it is argued, there are no scientific data which conclusively demonstrate that exposure to obscene material adversely affects men and women or their society. It is urged on behalf of the petitioners that, absent such a demonstration, any kind of state regulation is "impermissible." We reject this argument. It is not for us to resolve empirical uncertainties underlying state legislation, save in the exceptional case where that legislation plainly impinges upon rights protected by the Constitution itself. * * * Although there is no conclusive proof of a connection between antisocial behavior and obscene material, the legislature of Georgia could quite reasonably determine that such a connection does or might exist. In deciding *Roth*, this Court implicitly accepted that a legislature could legitimately act on such a conclusion to protect *"the social interest in order and morality."*

* * *

If we accept the unprovable assumption that a complete education requires the reading of certain books, * * *, and the well nigh universal belief that good books, plays, and art lift the spirit, improve the mind, enrich the human personality, and develop character, can we then say that a state legislature may not act on the corollary assumption that commerce in obscene books, or public exhibitions focused on obscene conduct, have a tendency to exert a corrupting and debasing impact leading to antisocial behavior? * * * The sum of experience, including that of the past two decades, affords an ample basis for legislatures to conclude that a sensitive, key relationship of human existence, central to family life, community welfare, and the development of human personality, can be debased and distorted by crass commercial exploitation of sex. Nothing in the Constitution prohibits a State from reaching such a conclusion and acting on it legislatively simply because there is no conclusive evidence or empirical data.

* * *

Finally, petitioners argue that conduct which directly involves "consenting adults" only has, for that sole reason, a special claim to constitutional protection. Our Constitution establishes a broad range of conditions on the exercise of power by the States, but for us to say that our Constitution incorporates the proposition that conduct involving consenting adults only is always beyond state regulation,[14] is a step we are unable to take.[15] Commercial exploitation of depictions, descriptions, or exhibitions of obscene conduct on commercial premises open to the adult public falls within a State's broad power to regulate commerce and protect the public environment. The issue in this context goes beyond whether someone, or even the majority, considers the conduct depicted as "wrong" or "sinful." The States have the power to make a morally neutral judgment that public exhibition of obscene material, or commerce in such material, has a tendency to injure the community as a whole, to endanger the public safety, or to jeopardize in Mr. Chief Justice Warren's words, the States' "right * * * to maintain a decent society." Jacobellis v. Ohio, 378 U.S., at 199 (dissenting opinion).

To summarize, we have today reaffirmed the basic holding of *Roth v. United States, supra,* that obscene material has no protection under the First Amendment. * * * We have directed our holdings, not at thoughts or speech, but at depiction and description of specifically defined sexual conduct that States may regulate within limits designed to prevent infringement of First Amendment rights. We have also reaffirmed the holdings of *United States v. Reidel, supra,* and *United States v. Thirty-Seven Photographs, supra,* that commerce in obscene material is unprotected by any constitutional doctrine of privacy. * * * In this case we hold that the States have a legitimate interest in regulating commerce in obscene material and in regulating exhibition of obscene material in places of public accommodation, including so-called "adult" theaters from which minors are excluded. In light of these holdings, nothing precludes the State of Georgia from the regulation of the allegedly obscene material exhibited in Paris Adult Theatre I or II, provided that the applicable Georgia law, as written or authoritatively interpreted by the Georgia courts, meets the First Amendment standards set forth in *Miller v. California, supra,* 413 U.S., at 23–25. The judgment is vacated and the case is remanded to the Georgia Supreme Court for further proceedings not inconsistent with this opinion and *Miller v. California, supra.* * * *

Vacated and remanded.

MR. JUSTICE BRENNAN, with whom MR. JUSTICE STEWART and MR. JUSTICE MARSHALL join, dissenting.

This case requires the Court to confront once again the vexing problem of reconciling state efforts to suppress sexually oriented expression with the protections of the First Amendment, as applied to the States through the Fourteenth Amendment. No other aspect of the First Amendment has, in recent years, demanded so substantial a commitment of our time, generated such disharmony of views, and

---

14. Cf. J. Mill, On Liberty 13 (1955 ed.).

15. The state statute books are replete with constitutionally unchallenged laws against prostitution, suicide, voluntary self-mutilation, brutalizing "bare fist" prize fights, and duels, although these crimes may only directly involve "consenting adults." Statutes making bigamy a crime surely cut into an individual's freedom to associate but few today seriously claim such statutes violate the First Amendment or any other constitutional provision.

remained so resistant to the formulation of stable and manageable standards. I am convinced that the approach initiated 16 years ago in Roth v. United States, 354 U.S. 476 (1957), and culminating in the Court's decision today, cannot bring stability to this area of the law without jeopardizing fundamental First Amendment values, and I have concluded that the time has come to make a significant departure from that approach.

* * *

* * * The decision of the Georgia Supreme Court rested squarely on its conclusion that the State could constitutionally suppress these films even if they were displayed only to persons over the age of 21 who were aware of the nature of their contents and who had consented to viewing them. For the reasons set forth in this opinion, I am convinced of the invalidity of that conclusion of law, and I would therefore vacate the judgment of the Georgia Supreme Court. I have no occasion to consider the extent of state power to regulate the distribution of sexually oriented materials to juveniles or to unconsenting adults.
* * *

* * *

* * * By 1967 the following views had emerged: Mr. Justice Black and Mr. Justice Douglas consistently maintained that government is wholly powerless to regulate any sexually oriented matter on the ground of its obscenity. * * * Mr. Justice Harlan on the other hand, believed that the Federal Government in the exercise of its enumerated powers could control the distribution of "hard core" pornography, while the States were afforded more latitude to "[ban] any material which, taken as a whole, has been reasonably found in state judicial proceedings to treat with sex in a fundamentally offensive manner, under rationally established criteria for judging such material." * * * Mr. Justice Stewart regarded "hard core" pornography as the limit of both federal and state power. * * *

The view that, until today, enjoyed the most, but not majority, support was an interpretation of *Roth* * * * adopted by Mr. Chief Justice Warren, Mr. Justice Fortas, and the author of this opinion in Memoirs v. Massachusetts, 383 U.S. 413. We expressed the view that Federal or State Governments could control the distribution of material where "three elements * * * coalesce: it must be established that (a) the dominant theme of the material taken as a whole appeals to a prurient interest in sex; (b) the material is patently offensive because it affronts contemporary community standards relating to the description or representation of sexual matters; and (c) the material is utterly without redeeming social value." * * *Even this formulation, however, concealed difference of opinion. * * * Moreover, it did not provide a definition covering all situations. See Mishkin v. New York, 383 U.S. 502 (prurient appeal defined in terms of a deviant sexual group); *Ginzburg v. United States, supra* ("pandering" probative evidence of obscenity in close cases). See also Ginsberg v. New York, 390 U.S. 629 (obscenity for juveniles). Nor, finally, did it ever command a majority of the Court. * * *

In the face of this divergence of opinion the Court began the practice in Redrup v. New York, 386 U.S. 767, of *per curiam* reversals of convictions for the dissemination of materials that at least five members of the Court, applying their separate tests, deemed not to be obscene.[8] This approach capped the attempt in *Roth* to separate all forms of sexually oriented expression into two categories—the one subject to full governmental suppression and the other beyond the reach of governmental regulation to the same extent as any other protected form of speech or press. * * *

* * *

Our experience since *Roth* requires us not only to abandon the effort to pick out obscene materials on a case-by-case basis, but also to reconsider a fundamental postulate of *Roth:* that there exists a definable class of sexually oriented expression that may be totally suppressed by the Federal and State Governments. Assuming that such a class of expression does in fact exist, I am forced to conclude that the concept of "obscenity" cannot be defined with sufficient specificity and clarity to provide fair notice to persons who create and distribute sexually oriented materials, to prevent substantial erosion of protected speech as a byproduct of the attempt to suppress unprotected speech, and to avoid very costly institutional harms. Given these inevitable side effects of state efforts to suppress what is assumed to be *unprotected* speech, we must scrutinize with care the state interest that is asserted to justify the suppression. For in the absence of some very substantial interest in suppressing such speech, we can hardly condone the ill effects that seem to flow inevitably from the effort.

* * *

Because we assumed—incorrectly, as experience has proved—that obscenity could be separated from other sexually oriented expression without significant costs either to the First Amendment or to the judicial machinery charged with the task of safeguarding First Amendment freedoms, we had no occasion in *Roth* to probe the asserted state interest in curtailing unprotected, sexually oriented speech. Yet, as we have increasingly come to appreciate the vagueness of the concept of obscenity, we have begun to recognize and articulate the state interests at stake. * * *

The opinions in *Redrup* and *Stanley* reflected our emerging view that the state interests in protecting children and in protecting unconsenting adults may stand on a different footing from the other asserted state interests. It may well be, as one commentator has argued, that "exposure to [erotic material] is for some persons an intense emotional experience. A communication of this nature, imposed upon a person contrary to his wishes, has all the characteristics of a physical assault. * * * [And it] constitutes an invasion of his privacy * * *. But cf. Cohen v. California, 403 U.S., at 21–22. Similarly, if children are "not possessed of that full capacity for individual choice which is the presupposition of the First Amendment guarantees," Ginsberg v. New

---

8. No fewer than 31 cases have been disposed of in this fashion. * * *

York, 390 U.S. at 649–650 (STEWART, J., concurring), then the State may have a substantial interest in precluding the flow of obscene materials even to consenting juveniles. * * *

But, whatever the strength of the state interests in protecting juveniles and unconsenting adults from exposure to sexually oriented materials, those interests cannot be asserted in defense of the holding of the Georgia Supreme Court in this case. That court assumed for the purposes of its decision that the films in issue were exhibited only to persons over the age of 21 who viewed them willingly and with prior knowledge of the nature of their contents. And on that assumption the state court held that the films could still be suppressed. The justification for the suppression must be found, therefore, in some independent interest in regulating the reading and viewing habits of consenting adults.

* * *

* * * I would hold * * * that at least in the absence of distribution to juveniles or obtrusive exposure to unconsenting adults, the First and Fourteenth Amendments prohibit the State and Federal Governments from attempting wholly to suppress sexually oriented materials on the basis of their allegedly "obscene" contents. Nothing in this approach precludes those governments from taking action to serve what may be strong and legitimate interests through regulation of the manner of distribution of sexually oriented material.

VI

* * * Since the Supreme Court of Georgia erroneously concluded that the State has power to suppress sexually oriented material even in the absence of distribution to juveniles or exposure to unconsenting adults, I would reverse that judgment and remand the case to that court for further proceedings not inconsistent with this opinion.

MR. JUSTICE DOUGLAS, dissenting. [Omitted.]

NEW YORK v. FERBER

Supreme Court of the United States, 1982.
458 U.S. 747, 102 S.Ct. 3348, 73 L.Ed.2d 1113.

JUSTICE WHITE delivered the opinion of the Court.

At issue in this case is the constitutionality of a New York criminal statute which prohibits persons from knowingly promoting sexual performances by children under the age of 16 by distributing material which depicts such performances.

I

In recent years, the exploitive use of children in the production of pornography has become a serious national problem.[1] The Federal

---

1. "[C]hild pornography and child prostitution have become highly organized,

Government and 47 States have sought to combat the problem with statutes specifically directed at the production of child pornography. At least half of such statutes do not require that the materials produced be legally obscene. Thirty-five States and the United States Congress have also passed legislation prohibiting the distribution of such materials; 20 States prohibit the distribution of material depicting children engaged in sexual conduct without requiring that the material be legally obscene.

New York is one of the 20. In 1977, the New York Legislature enacted Article 263 of its Penal Law. N.Y.Penal Law, Art. 263 (McKinney 1980). Section 263.05 criminalizes as a class C felony the use of a child in a sexual performance:

> "A person is guilty of the use of a child in a sexual performance if knowing the character and content thereof he employs, authorizes or induces a child less than sixteen years of age to engage in a sexual performance or being a parent, legal guardian or custodian of such child, he consents to the participation by such child in a sexual performance."

A "[s]exual performance" is defined as "any performance or part thereof which includes sexual conduct by a child less than sixteen years of age." * * * "Sexual conduct" is in turn defined in § 263.00(3):

> "'Sexual conduct' means actual or simulated sexual intercourse, deviate sexual intercourse, sexual bestiality, masturbation, sado-masochistic abuse, or lewd exhibition of the genitals.'"

A performance is defined as "any play, motion picture, photograph or dance" or "any other visual representation exhibited before an audience." § 263.00(4).

At issue in this case is § 263.15, defining a class D felony:[3]

> "A person is guilty of promoting a sexual performance by a child when, knowing the character and content thereof, he produces, directs or promotes any performance which includes sexual conduct by a child less than sixteen years of age."

To "promote" is also defined:

> "'Promote' means to procure, manufacture, issue, sell, give, provide, lend, mail, deliver, transfer, transmute, publish, dis-

multimillion dollar industries that operate on a nationwide scale." S.Rep. No. 95–438, p. 5 (1977). One researcher has documented the existence of over 260 different magazines which depict children engaging in sexually explicit conduct. *Ibid.* "Such magazines depict children, some as young as three to five years of age. * * * The activities featured range from lewd poses to intercourse, fellatio, cunnilingus, masturbation, rape, incest and sado-masochism." *Id.*, at 6. In Los Angeles alone, police reported that 30,000 children have been sexually exploited. Sexual Exploitation of Children, Hearings before the Subcommittee on Select Education of the House Committee on Education and Labor, 95th Cong., 1st Sess., 41–42 (1977).

3. Class D felonies carry a maximum punishment for up to seven years as to individuals, and as to corporations a fine of up to $10,000. N.Y.Penal Law §§ 70.00, 80.10 (McKinney 1975). Respondent Ferber was sentenced to 45 days in prison.

tribute, circulate, disseminate, present, exhibit or advertise, or to offer or agree to do the same." * * *

A companion provision bans only the knowing dissemination of obscene material.

This case arose when Paul Ferber, the proprietor of a Manhattan bookstore specializing in sexually oriented products, sold two films to an undercover police officer. The films are devoted almost exclusively to depicting young boys masturbating. Ferber was indicted on two counts of violating § 263.10 and two counts of violating § 263.15, the two New York laws controlling dissemination of child pornography. After a jury trial, Ferber was acquitted of the two counts of promoting an obscene sexual performance, but found guilty of the two counts under § 263.15, which did not require proof that the films were obscene. * * *

The New York Court of Appeals reversed, holding that § 263.15 violated the First Amendment. 52 N.Y.2d 674, 422 N.E.2d 523 (1981). * * * Although the court recognized the State's "legitimate interest in protecting the welfare of minors" and noted that this "interest may transcend First Amendment concerns," * * *, it nevertheless found two fatal defects in the New York statute. Section 263.15 was underinclusive because it discriminated against visual portrayals of children engaged in sexual activity by not also prohibiting the distribution of films of other dangerous activity. It was also overbroad because it prohibited the distribution of materials produced outside the State, as well as materials, such as medical books and educational sources, which "deal with adolescent sex in a realistic but nonobscene manner." * * * Two judges dissented. We granted the State's petition for certiorari, * * * presenting the single question:

> "To prevent the abuse of children who are made to engage in sexual conduct for commercial purposes, could the New York State Legislature, consistent with the First Amendment, prohibit the dissemination of material which shows children engaged in sexual conduct, regardless of whether such material is obscene?"

II

The Court of Appeals proceeded on the assumption that the standard of obscenity incorporated in § 263.10, which follows the guidelines enunciated in Miller v. California, 413 U.S. 15 (1973), constitutes the appropriate line dividing protected from unprotected expression by which to measure a regulation directed at child pornography. * * *

The Court of Appeals' assumption was not unreasonable in light of our decisions. This case, however, constitutes our first examination of a statute directed at and limited to depictions of sexual activity involving children. We believe our inquiry should begin with the question of whether a State has somewhat more freedom in proscribing works which portray sexual acts or lewd exhibitions of genitalia by children.

A

In Chaplinsky v. New Hampshire, 315 U.S. 568 (1942), the Court laid the foundation for the excision of obscenity from the realm of constitutionally protected expression:

> "There are certain well-defined and narrowly limited classes of speech, the prevention and punishment of which have never been thought to raise any Constitutional problem. These include the lewd and obscene. * * * It has been well observed that such utterances are no essential part of any exposition of ideas, and are of such slight social value as a step to truth that any benefit that may be derived from them is clearly outweighed by the social interest in order and morality." *Id.*, at 571–572 (footnotes omitted).

Embracing this judgment, the Court squarely held in Roth v. United States, 354 U.S. 476 (1957), that "obscenity is not within the area of constitutionally protected speech or press." *Id.*, at 485. The Court recognized that "rejection of obscenity as utterly without redeeming social importance" was implicit in the history of the First Amendment: The original States provided for the prosecution of libel, blasphemy, and profanity and the "universal judgment that obscenity should be restrained [is] reflected in the international agreement of over 50 nations, in the obscenity laws of all of the 48 states, and in the 20 obscenity laws enacted by Congress from 1842 to 1956." *Id.*, at 484–485 (footnotes omitted).

Roth was followed by 15 years during which this Court struggled with "the intractable obscenity problem." Interstate Circuit, Inc. v. Dallas, 390 U.S. 676, 704 (1968) (opinion of HARLAN, J.). See, e.g., Redrup v. New York, 386 U.S. 767 (1967). Despite considerable vacillation over the proper definition of obscenity, a majority of the Members of the Court remained firm in the position that "the States have a legitimate interest in prohibiting dissemination or exhibition of obscene material when the mode of dissemination carries with it a significant danger of offending the sensibilities of unwilling recipients or of exposure to juveniles." *Miller v. California, supra,* at 18–19 (footnote omitted); Stanley v. Georgia, 394 U.S. 557, 567 (1967); Ginsberg v. New York, 390 U.S. 629, 637–643 (1968); *Interstate Circuit, Inc. v. Dallas, supra,* at 690; *Redrup v. New York, supra,* at 769; Jacobellis v. Ohio, 378 U.S. 184, 195 (1964).

Throughout this period, we recognized "the inherent dangers of undertaking to regulate any form of expression." *Miller v. California, supra,* at 23. Consequently, our difficulty was not only to assure that statutes designed to regulate obscene materials sufficiently defined what was prohibited, but also to devise substantive limits on what fell within the permissible scope of regulation. In *Miller v. California, supra,* a majority of the Court agreed that a "state offense must also be limited to works which, taken as a whole, appeal to the prurient interest in sex, which portray sexual conduct in a patently offensive way, and which, taken as a whole, do not have serious literary, artistic, political, or scientific value." *Id.,* at 24. Over the past decade, we have adhered to the guidelines expressed in *Miller,* which subsequently has been followed in the regulatory schemes of most States.

B

The *Miller* standard, like its predecessors, was an accommodation between the State's interests in protecting the "sensibilities of unwilling recipients" from exposure to pornographic material and the dangers of censorship inherent in unabashedly content-based laws. Like obscenity statutes, laws directed at the dissemination of child pornography run the risk of suppressing protected expression by allowing the hand of the censor to become unduly heavy. For the following reasons, however, we are persuaded that the States are entitled to greater leeway in the regulation of pornographic depictions of children.

First. It is evident beyond the need for elaboration that a State's interest in "safeguarding the physical and psychological well-being of a minor" is "compelling." Globe Newspaper Co. v. Superior Court, 457 U.S. 596, 607 (1982). "A democratic society rests, for its continuance, upon the healthy, well-rounded growth of young people into full maturity as citizens." Prince v. Massachusetts, 321 U.S. 158, 168 (1944). Accordingly, we have sustained legislation aimed at protecting the physical and emotional well-being of youth even when the laws have operated in the sensitive area of constitutionally protected rights. In *Prince v. Massachusetts, supra,* the Court held that a statute prohibiting use of a child to distribute literature on the street was valid notwithstanding the statute's effect on a First Amendment activity. In *Ginsberg v. New York, supra,* we sustained a New York law protecting children from exposure to nonobscene literature. Most recently, we held that the Government's interest in the "well-being of its youth" justified special treatment of indecent broadcasting received by adults as well as children. FCC v. Pacifica Foundation, 438 U.S. 726 (1978).

The prevention of sexual exploitation and abuse of children constitutes a government objective of surpassing importance. * * *

* * * The legislative judgment, as well as the judgment found in the relevant literature, is that the use of children as subjects of pornographic materials is harmful to the physiological, emotional, and mental health of the child. That judgment, we think, easily passes muster under the First Amendment.

Second. The distribution of photographs and films depicting sexual activity by juveniles is intrinsically related to the sexual abuse of children in at least two ways. First, the materials produced are a permanent record of the children's participation and the harm to the child is exacerbated by their circulation. Second, the distribution network for child pornography must be closed if the production of material which requires the sexual exploitation of children is to be effectively controlled. Indeed, there is no serious contention that the legislature was unjustified in believing that it is difficult, if not impossible, to halt the exploitation of children by pursuing only those who produce the photographs and movies. While the production of pornographic materials is a low-profile, clandestine industry, the need to market the resulting products requires a visible apparatus of distribution. The most expeditious if not the only practical method of law enforcement may be to dry up the market for this material by imposing severe criminal penalties on persons selling, advertising, or otherwise promoting the product. Thirty-five States and Congress have concluded that restraints on the distribution of pornographic materials are required in order to effectively combat the problem, and there is a body of literature and testimony to support these legislative conclusions. * * *

Respondent does not contend that the State is unjustified in pursuing those who distribute child pornography. Rather, he argues that it is enough for the State to prohibit the distribution of materials that are legally obscene under the *Miller* test. While some States may find that this approach properly accommodates its interests, it does not follow that the First Amendment prohibits a State from going further. The *Miller* standard, like all general definitions of what may be banned as obscene, does not reflect the State's particular and more compelling interest in prosecuting those who promote the sexual exploitation of children. Thus, the question under the Miller test of whether a work, taken as a whole, appeals to the prurient interest of the average person bears no connection to the issue of whether a child has been physically or psychologically harmed in the production of the work. Similarly, a sexually explicit depiction need not be "patently offensive" in order to have required the sexual exploitation of a child for its production. In addition, a work which, taken on the whole, contains serious literary, artistic, political, or scientific value may nevertheless embody the hardest core of child pornography. "It is irrelevant to the child [who has been abused] whether or not the material * * * has a literary, artistic, political or social value." Memorandum of Assemblyman Lasher in Support of § 263.15. We therefore cannot conclude that the *Miller* standard is a satisfactory solution to the child pornography problem.

Third. The advertising and selling of child pornography provide an economic motive for and are thus an integral part of the production of such materials, an activity illegal throughout the Nation. * * *

Fourth. The value of permitting live performances and photographic reproductions of children engaged in lewd sexual conduct is exceedingly modest, if not *de minimis*. We consider it unlikely that visual depictions of children performing sexual acts or lewdly exhibiting their genitals would often constitute an important and necessary part of a literary performance or scientific or educational work. As a state judge in this case observed, if it were necessary for literary or artistic value, a person over the statutory age who perhaps looked younger could be utilized. Simulation outside of the prohibition of the statute could provide another alternative. Nor is there any question here of censoring a particular literary theme or portrayal of sexual activity. The First Amendment interest is limited to that of rendering the portrayal somewhat more "realisitc" by utilizing or photographing children.

Fifth. Recognizing and classifying child pornography as a category of material outside the protection of the First Amendment is not incompatible with our earlier decisions. "The question whether speech is, or is not, protected by the First Amendment often depends on the content of the speech." Young v. American Mini Theatres, Inc., 427 U.S. 50, 66 (1976) (opinion of STEVENS, J., joined by BURGER, C.J., and WHITE and REHNQUIST, JJ.). See also FCC v. Pacifica Foundation, 438 U.S. 726, 742–748 (1978) (opinion of STEVENS, J., joined by BURGER, C.J., and REHNQUIST, J.). "[I]t is the content of [an] utterance that determines whether it is a protected epithet or an unprotected 'fighting comment.'" *Young v. American Mini Theatres, Inc., supra,* at 66. See Chaplinsky v. New Hampshire, 315 U.S. 568 (1942). Leaving aside the special considerations when public officials are the target, New York Times Co. v. Sullivan, 376 U.S. 254 (1964), a libelous publication is not protected by the Constitution. Beauharnais v. Illinois, 343 U.S. 250 (1952). Thus, it is not rare that a content-based classification of speech has been accepted because it may be appropriately generalized that within the confines of the given classification, the evil to be restricted so overwhelmingly outweighs the expressive interests, if any, at stake, that no process of case-by-case adjudication is required. When a definable class of material, such as that covered by § 263.15, bears so heavily and pervasively on the welfare of children engaged in its production, we think the balance of competing interests is clearly struck and that it is permissible to consider these materials as without the protection of the First Amendment.

C

There are, of course, limits on the category of child pornography which, like obscenity, is unprotected by the First Amendment. As with all legislation in this sensitive area, the conduct to be prohibited must be adequately defined by the applicable state law, as written or authoritatively construed. Here the nature of the harm to be combated requires that the state offense be limited to works that *visually* depict sexual conduct by children below a specified age.[17] The category of "sexual conduct" proscribed must also be suitably limited and described.

The test for child pornography is separate from the obscenity standard enunciated in *Miller,* but may be compared to it for purpose of clarity. The *Miller* formulation is adjusted in the following respects: A trier of fact need not find that the material appeals to the prurient interest of the average person; it is not required that sexual conduct portrayed be done so in a patently offensive manner; and the material at issue need not be considered as a whole. We note that the distribution of descriptions or other depictions of sexual conduct, not otherwise obscene, which do not involve live performance or photographic or other visual reproduction of live performances, retains First Amendment protection. As with obscenity laws, criminal responsibility may

---

17. Sixteen States define a child as a person under age 18. Four States define a child as under 17 years old. The federal law and 16 States, including New York, define a child as under 16. * * *

not be imposed without some element of scienter on the part of the defendant. Smith v. California, 361 U.S. 147 (1959); Hamling v. United States, 418 U.S. 87 (1974).

* * *

It remains to address the claim that the New York statute is unconstitutionally overbroad because it would forbid the distribution of material with serious literary, scientific, or educational value or material which does not threaten the harms sought to be combated by the State. Respondent prevailed on that ground below, and it is to that issue that we now turn.

The New York Court of Appeals recognized that overbreadth scrutiny has been limited with respect to conduct-related regulation, Broadrick v. Oklahoma, 413 U.S. 601 (1973), but it did not apply the test enunciated in *Broadrick* because the challenged statute, in its view, was directed at "pure speech." The court went on to find that § 263.15 was fatally overbroad: "[T]he statute would prohibit the showing of any play or movie in which a child portrays a defined sexual act, real or simulated, in a nonobscene manner. It would also prohibit the sale, showing, or distributing of medical or educational materials containing photographs of such acts. Indeed, by its terms, the statute would prohibit those who oppose such portrayals from providing illustrations of what they oppose." * * *

While the construction that a state court gives a state statute is not a matter subject to our review, Wainwright v. Stone, 414 U.S. 21, 22–23 (1973) * * *, this Court is the final arbiter of whether the Federal Constitution necessitated the invalidation of a state law. * * *

* * *

The scope of the First Amendment overbreadth doctrine, like most exceptions to established principles, must be carefully tied to the circumstances in which facial invalidation of a statute is truly warranted. Because of the wide-reaching effects of striking down a statute on its face at the request of one whose own conduct may be punished despite the First Amendment, we have recognized that the overbreadth doctrine is "strong medicine" and have employed it with hesitation, and then "only as a last resort." *Broadrick*, 413 U.S., at 613. We have, in consequence, insisted that the overbreadth involved be "substantial" before the statute involved will be invalidated on its face.[24]

* * *

---

24. When a federal court is dealing with a federal statute challenged as overbroad, it should, of course, construe the statute to avoid constitutional problems, if the statute is subject to such a limiting construction. * * * Furthermore, if the federal statute is not subject to a narrowing construction and is impermissibly overbroad, it nevertheless should not be stricken down on its face; if it is severable, only the unconstitutional portion is to be invalidated. United States v. Thirty–seven Photographs, 402 U.S. 363 (1971). A state court is also free to deal with a state statute in the same way. If the invalid reach of the law is cured, there is no longer reason for proscribing the statute's application to unprotected conduct. Here, of course, we are dealing with a state statute on direct review of a state-court decision that has construed the statute. Such a construction is binding on us.

Applying these principles, we hold that § 263.15 is not substantially overbroad. We consider this the paradigmatic case of a state statute whose legitimate reach dwarfs its arguably impermissible applications. New York, as we have held, may constitutionally prohibit dissemination of material specified in § 263.15. While the reach of the statute is directed at the hard core of child pornography, the Court of Appeals was understandably concerned that some protected expression, ranging from medical textbooks to pictorials in the National Geographic would fall prey to the statute. How often, if ever, it may be necessary to employ children to engage in conduct clearly within the reach of § 263.15 in order to produce educational, medical, or artistic works cannot be known with certainty. Yet we seriously doubt, and it has not been suggested, that these arguably impermissible applications of the statute amount to more than a tiny fraction of the materials within the statute's reach. Nor will we assume that the New York courts will widen the possibly invalid reach of the statute by giving an expansive construction to the proscription on "lewd exhibition[s] of the genitals." Under these circumstances, § 263.15 is "not substantially overbroad and * * * whatever overbreadth may exist should be cured through case-by-case analysis of the fact situations to which its sanctions, assertedly, may not be applied." Broadrick v. Oklahoma, 413 U.S., at 615–616.

IV

Because § 263.15 is not substantially overbroad, it is unnecessary to consider its application to material that does not depict sexual conduct of a type that New York may restrict consistent with the First Amendment. As applied to Paul Ferber and to others who distribute similar material, the statute does not violate the First Amendment as applied to the States through the Fourteenth. The decision of the New York Court of Appeals is reversed, and the case is remanded to that court for further proceedings not inconsistent with this opinion.

So ordered.

JUSTICE O'CONNOR, concurring.

Although I join the Court's opinion, I write separately to stress that the Court does not hold that New York must except "material with serious literary, scientific, or educational value," *ante,* at 766, from its statute. The Court merely holds that, even if the First Amendment shelters such material, New York's current statute is not sufficiently overbroad to support respondent's facial attack. The compelling interests identified in today's opinion, * * * suggest that the Constitution might in fact permit New York to ban knowing distribution of works depicting minors engaged in explicit sexual conduct, regardless of the social value of the depictions. For example, a 12-year-old child photographed while masturbating surely suffers the same psychological harm whether the community labels the photograph "edifying" or "tasteless." The audience's appreciation of the depiction is simply irrelevant to New York's asserted interest in protecting children from psychological, emotional, and mental harm.

An exception for depictions of serious social value, moreover, would actually increase opportunities for the content-based censorship disfavored by the First Amendment. As drafted, New York's statute does not attempt to suppress the communication of particular ideas. The statute permits discussion of child sexuality, forbidding only attempts to render the "portrayal[s] somewhat more 'realistic' by utilizing or photographing children." * * * Thus, the statute attempts to protect minors from abuse without attempting to restrict the expression of ideas by those who might use children as live models.

On the other hand, it is quite possible that New York's statute is overbroad because it bans depictions that do not actually threaten the harms identified by the Court. For example, clinical pictures of adolescent sexuality, such as those that might appear in medical textbooks, might not involve the type of sexual exploitation and abuse targeted by New York's statute. Nor might such depictions feed the poisonous "kiddie porn" market that New York and other States have attempted to regulate. Similarly, pictures of children engaged in rites widely approved by their cultures, such as those that might appear in issues of the National Geographic, might not trigger the compelling interests identified by the Court. It is not necessary to address these possibilities further today, however, because this potential overbreadth is not sufficiently substantial to warrant facial invalidation of New York's statute.

JUSTICE BRENNAN, with whom JUSTICE MARSHALL joins, concurring in the judgment.

* * *

JUSTICE STEVENS, concurring in the judgment.

Two propositions seem perfectly clear to me. First, the specific conduct that gave rise to this criminal prosecution is not protected by the Federal Constitution; second, the state statute that respondent violated prohibits some conduct that is protected by the First Amendment. The critical question, then, is whether this respondent, to whom the statute may be applied without violating the Constitution, may challenge the statute on the ground that it conceivably may be applied unconstitutionally to others in situations not before the Court. I agree with the Court's answer to this question but not with its method of analyzing the issue.

Before addressing that issue, I shall explain why respondent's conviction does not violate the Constitution. The two films that respondent sold contained nothing more than lewd exhibition; there is no claim that the films included any material that had literary, artistic, scientific, or educational value.[1] Respondent was a willing participant in a commercial market that the State of New York has a legitimate interest in suppressing. The character of the State's interest in protecting children from sexual abuse justifies the imposition of criminal sanctions against those who profit, directly or indirectly, from the

---

1. Respondent's counsel conceded at oral argument that a finding that the films are obscene would have been consistent with the *Miller* definition. Tr. of Oral Arg. 41.

promotion of such films. In this respect my evaluation of this case is different from the opinion I have expressed concerning the imposition of criminal sanctions for the promotion of obscenity in other contexts.

A holding that respondent may be punished for selling these two films does not require us to conclude that other users of these very films, or that other motion pictures containing similar scenes, are beyond the pale of constitutional protection. Thus, the exhibition of these films before a legislative committee studying a proposed amendment to a state law, or before a group of research scientists studying human behavior, could not, in my opinion, be made a crime. Moreover, it is at least conceivable that a serious work of art, a documentary on behavioral problems, or a medical or psychiatric teaching device, might include a scene from one of these films and, when viewed as a whole in a proper setting, be entitled to constitutional protection. The question whether a specific act of communication is protected by the First Amendment always requires some consideration of both its content and its context.

The Court's holding that this respondent may not challenge New York's statute as overbroad follows its discussion of the contours of the category of nonobscene child pornography that New York may legitimately prohibit. Having defined that category in an abstract setting,[3] the Court makes the empirical judgment that the arguably impermissible application of the New York statute amounts to only a "tiny fraction of the materials within the statute's reach." * * * Even assuming that the Court's empirical analysis is sound,[4] I believe a more conservative approach to the issue would adequately vindicate the State's interest in protecting its children and cause less harm to the federal interest in free expression.

A hypothetical example will illustrate my concern. Assume that the operator of a New York motion picture theater specializing in the exhibition of foreign feature films is offered a full-length movie containing one scene that is plainly lewd if viewed in isolation but that nevertheless is part of a serious work of art. If the child actor resided abroad, New York's interest in protecting its young from sexual exploitation would be far less compelling than in the case before us. The federal interest in free expression would, however, be just as strong as

3. "The test for child pornography is separate from the obscenity standard enunciated in *Miller*, but may be compared to it for the purpose of clarity. The *Miller* formulation is adjusted in the following respects: A trier of fact need not find that the material appeals to the prurient interest of the average person; it is not required that sexual conduct portrayed be done so in a patently offensive manner; and the material at issue need not be considered as a whole." * * *

4. The Court's analysis is directed entirely at the permissibility of the statute's coverage of nonobscene material. Its empirical evidence, however, is drawn substantially from congressional Committee Reports that ultimately reached the conclusion that a prohibition against obscene child pornography—coupled with sufficiently stiff sanctions—is an adequate response to this social problem. The Senate Committee on the Judiciary concluded that "virtually all of the materials that are normally considered child pornography are obscene under the current standards," and that "[i]n comparison with this blatant pornography, non-obscene materials that depict children are very few and very inconsequential." * * *

if an adult actor had been used. There are at least three different ways to deal with the statute's potential application to that sort of case.

First, at one extreme and as the Court appears to hold, the First Amendment inquiry might be limited to determining whether the offensive scene, viewed in isolation, is lewd. When the constitutional protection is narrowed in this drastic fashion, the Court is probably safe in concluding that only a tiny fraction of the materials covered by the New York statute is protected. And with respect to my hypothetical exhibitor of foreign films, he need have no uncertainty about the permissible application of the statute; for the one lewd scene would deprive the entire film of any constitutional protection.

Second, at the other extreme and as the New York Court of Appeals correctly perceived, the application of this Court's cases requiring that an obscenity determination be based on the artistic value of a production taken as a whole would afford the exhibitor constitutional protection and result in a holding that the statute is invalid because of its overbreadth. Under that approach, the rationale for invalidating the entire statute is premised on the concern that the exhibitor's understanding about its potential reach could cause him to engage in self-censorship. This Court's approach today substitutes broad, unambiguous, state-imposed censorship for the self-censorship that an overbroad statute might produce.

Third, as an intermediate position, I would refuse to apply overbreadth analysis for reasons unrelated to any prediction concerning the relative number of protected communications that the statute may prohibit. Specifically, I would postpone decision of my hypothetical case until it actually arises. Advocates of a liberal use of overbreadth analysis could object to such postponement on the ground that it creates the risk that the exhibitor's uncertainty may produce self-censorship. But that risk obviously interferes less with the interest in free expression than does an abstract, advance ruling that the film is simply unprotected whenever it contains a lewd scene, no matter how brief.

My reasons for avoiding overbreadth analysis in this case are more qualitative than quantitative. When we follow our traditional practice of adjudicating difficult and novel constitutional questions only in concrete factual situations, the adjudications tend to be crafted with greater wisdom. Hypothetical rulings are inherently treacherous and prone to lead us into unforeseen errors; they are qualitatively less reliable than the products of case-by-case adjudication.

Moreover, it is probably safe to assume that the category of speech that is covered by the New York statute generally is of a lower quality than most other types of communication. On a number of occasions, I have expressed the view that the First Amendment affords some forms of speech more protection from governmental regulation than other forms of speech. Today the Court accepts this view, putting the category of speech described in the New York statute in its rightful place near the bottom of this hierarchy. * * * Although I disagree with the Court's position that such speech is totally without First Amendment protection, I agree that generally marginal speech does not warrant the extraordinary protection afforded by the overbreadth doctrine.

Because I have no difficulty with the statute's application in this case, I concur in the Court's judgment.

JENKINS v. GEORGIA

Supreme Court of the United States, 1974.
418 U.S. 153, 94 S.Ct. 2750, 41 L.Ed.2d 642.

MR. JUSTICE REHNQUIST delivered the opinion of the Court.

Appellant was convicted in Georgia of the crime of distributing obscene material. His conviction, in March 1972, was for showing the film "Carnal Knowledge" in a movie theater in Albany, Georgia. The jury that found appellant guilty was instructed on obscenity pursuant to the Georgia statute, which defines obscene material in language similar to that of the definition of obscenity set forth in this Court's plurality opinion in Memoirs v. Massachusetts, 383 U.S. 413, 418 (1966)
* * *

We hold today in *Hamling v. United States*, * * *, that defendants convicted prior to the announcement of our *Miller* decisions but whose convictions were on direct appeal at that time should receive any benefit available to them from those decisions. We conclude here that the film "Carnal Knowledge" is not obscene under the constitutional standards announced in Miller v. California, 413 U.S. 15 (1973), and that the First and Fourteenth Amendments therefore require that the judgment of the Supreme Court of Georgia affirming appellant's conviction be reversed.

* * *

We agree with the Supreme Court of Georgia's implicit ruling that the Constitution does not require that juries be instructed in state obscenity cases to apply the standards of a hypothetical statewide community. *Miller* approved the use of such instructions; it did not mandate their use. What *Miller* makes clear is that state juries need not be instructed to apply "national standards." We also agree with the Supreme Court of Georgia's implicit approval of the trial court's instructions directing jurors to apply "community standards" without specifying what "community." *Miller* held that it was constitutionally permissible to permit juries to rely on the understanding of the community from which they came as to contemporary community standards, and the States have considerable latitude in framing statutes under this element of the *Miller* decision. A State may choose to define an obscenity offense in terms of "contemporary community standards" as defined in *Miller* without further specification, as was done here, or it may choose to define the standards in more precise geographic terms, as was done by California in *Miller*.

We now turn to the question of whether appellant's exhibition of the film was protected by the First and Fourteenth Amendments, a question which appellee asserts is not properly before us because appellant did not raise it on his state appeal. But whether or not appellant argued this constitutional issue below, it is clear that the Supreme Court of Georgia reached and decided it. That is sufficient under our practice. * * *

There is little to be found in the record about the film "Carnal Knowledge" other than the film itself.[5] However, appellant has supplied a variety of information and critical commentary, the authenticity of which appellee does not dispute. The film appeared on many "Ten Best" lists for 1971, the year in which it was released. Many but not all of the reviews were favorable. * * *

Appellee contends essentially that under Miller the obscenity *vel non* of the film "Carnal Knowledge" was a question for the jury, and that the jury having resolved the question against appellant, and there being some evidence to support its findings, the judgment of conviction should be affirmed. We turn to the language of *Miller* to evaluate appellee's contention.

Miller states that the questions of what appeals to the "prurient interest" and what is "patently offensive" under the obscenity test which it formulates are "essentially questions of fact." 413 U.S., at 30 "When triers of fact are asked to decide whether 'the average person, applying contemporary community standards' would consider certain materials 'prurient' it would be unrealistic to require that the answer be based on some abstract formulation. * * * To require a State to structure obscenity proceedings around evidence of a national 'community standard' would be an exercise in futility." *Ibid.* We held in Paris Adult Theatre I v. Slaton, 413 U.S. 49 (1973), decided on the same day, that expert testimony as to obscenity is not necessary when the films at issue are themselves placed in evidence. *Id.,* at 56.

But all of this does not lead us to agree with the Supreme Court of Georgia's apparent conclusion that the jury's verdict against appellant virtually precluded all further appellate review of appellant's assertion that his exhibition of the film was protected by the First and Fourteenth Amendments. Even though questions of appeal to the "prurient interest" or of patent offensiveness are "essentially questions of fact," it would be a serious misreading of *Miller* to conclude that juries have unbridled discretion in determining what is "patently offensive." Not only did we there say that "the First Amendment values applicable to the State through the Fourteenth Amendment are adequately protected by the ultimate power of appellate courts to conduct an independent review of constitutional claims when necessary," 413 U.S., at 25, but we made it plain that under that holding "no one will be subject to prosecution for the sale or exposure of obscene materials unless these materials depict or describe patently offensive 'hard core' sexual conduct. * * *" *Id.,* at 27.

---

5. Appellant testified that the film was "critically acclaimed as one of the ten best pictures of 1971 and Ann Margaret has received an Academy Award nomination for her performance in the picture." He further testified that "Carnal Knowledge" had played in 29 towns in Georgia and that it was booked in 50 or 60 more theaters for spring and summer showing. App. 24.

We also took pains in *Miller* to "give a few plain examples of what a state statute could define for regulation under part (b) of the standard announced," that is, the requirement of patent offensiveness. *Id.,* at 25. These examples included "representations or descriptions of ultimate sexual acts, normal or perverted, actual or simulated," and "representations or descriptions of masturbation, excretory functions, and lewd exhibition of the genitals." *Ibid.* While this did not purport to be an exhaustive catalog of what juries might find patently offensive, it was certainly intended to fix substantive constitutional limitations, deriving from the First Amendment, on the type of material subject to such a determination. It would be wholly at odds with this aspect of *Miller* to uphold an obscenity conviction based upon a defendant's depiction of a woman with a bare midriff, even though a properly charged jury unanimously agreed on a verdict of guilty.

Our own viewing of the film satisfies us that "Carnal Knowledge" could not be found under the *Miller* standards to depict sexual conduct in a patently offensive way. Nothing in the movie falls within either of the two examples given in *Miller* of material which may constitutionally be found to meet the "patently offensive" element of those standards, nor is there anything sufficiently similar to such material to justify similar treatment. While the subject matter of the picture is, in a broader sense, sex, and there are scenes in which sexual conduct including "ultimate sexual acts" is to be understood to be taking place, the camera does not focus on the bodies of the actors at such times. There is no exhibition whatever of the actors' genitals, lewd or otherwise, during these scenes. There are occasional scenes of nudity, but nudity alone is not enough to make material legally obscene under the *Miller* standards.

Appellant's showing of the film "Carnal Knowledge" is simply not the "public portrayal of hard core sexual conduct for its own sake, and for the ensuing commercial gain" which we said was punishable in *Miller*. *Id.,* at 35. We hold that the film could not, as a matter of constitutional law, be found to depict sexual conduct in a patently offensive way, and that it is therefore not outside the protection of the First and Fourteenth Amendments because it is obscene. No other basis appearing in the record upon which the judgment of conviction can be sustained, we reverse the judgment of the Supreme Court of Georgia.

Reversed.

Mr. Justice Douglas, being of the view that any ban on obscenity is prohibited by the First Amendment, made applicable to the States through the Fourteenth, concurs in the reversal of this conviction. * * *

Mr. Justice Brennan, with whom Mr. Justice Stewart and Mr. Justice Marshall join, concurring in the result.

* * * Today's decision confirms my observation in Paris Adult Theatre I v. Slaton, 413 U.S. 49 (1973), that the Court's new formulation does not extricate us from the mire of case-by-case determinations of obscenity. * * *

After the Court's decision today, there can be no doubt that Miller requires appellate courts—including this Court—to review independently the constitutional fact of obscenity. Moreover, the Court's task is not limited to reviewing a jury finding under part (c) of the Miller test that "the work, taken as a whole, lack[ed] serious literary, artistic, political, or scientific value." 413 U.S., at 24. Miller also requires independent review of a jury's determination under part (b) of the Miller test that "the work depicts or describes, in a patently offensive way, sexual conduct specifically defined by the applicable state law."
* * *

In order to make the review mandated by *Miller*, the Court was required to screen the film "Carnal Knowledge" and make an independent determination of obscenity *vel non*. Following that review, the Court holds that "Carnal Knowledge" "could not, as a matter of constitutional law, be found to depict sexual conduct in a patently offensive way, and that it is therefore not outside the protection of the First and Fourteenth Amendments because it is obscene." * * *

Thus, it is clear that as long as the *Miller* test remains in effect "one cannot say with certainty that material is obscene until at least five members of this Court, applying inevitably obscure standards, have pronounced it so." Paris Adult Theatre I v. Slaton, 413 U.S., at 92 (BRENNAN, J., dissenting). Because of the attendant uncertainty of such a process and its inevitable institutional stress upon the judiciary, I continue to adhere to my view that, "at least in the absence of distribution to juveniles or obstrusive exposure to unconsenting adults, the First and Fourteenth Amendments prohibit the State and Federal Governments from attempting wholly to suppress sexually oriented materials on the basis of their allegedly 'obscene' contents." *Id.,* at 113. It is clear that, tested by that constitutional standard, the Georgia obscenity statutes under which appellant Jenkins was convicted are constitutionally overbroad and therefore facially invalid. I therefore concur in the result in the Court's reversal of Jenkins' conviction.

A CONCLUDING NOTE
EXCERPTS FROM CERTAIN BAWDY VERSES

Your rounded thighs are like jewels,
the work of a master hand.
Your navel is a rounded bowl
that never lacks mixed wine.
Your belly is a heap of wheat,
encircled with lilies.
Your two breasts are like two fawns,
twins of a gazelle

* * *

> How fair and pleasant you are,
> O loved one, delectable maiden!
> You are stately as a palm tree,
> and your breasts are like its clusters.
> I say I will climb the palm tree
> and lay hold of its branches.
> Oh, may your breasts be like
> clusters of the vine,
> and the scent of your breath like apples,
> and your kisses like the best wine
> that goes down smoothly
> gliding over lips and teeth.
>
> * * *
>
> O that you were like a brother to me,
> that nursed at my mother's breast!
> I would give you spiced wine to drink
> the juice of my pomegranates.
> Make haste, my beloved,
> and be like a gazelle
> or a young stag
> upon the mountain of spices.

---

1. Are these verses "obscene?"[42] What is the proper test to be applied?—What part of that test (*Miller–Slaton–Jenkins*), necessarily precludes the conclusion that these verses can be found "obscene"?

2. Suppose these verses are accompanied by illustrations graphically depicting the artist's rendering of these verses; at least then may the work as a whole, inclusive of these verses, be "obscene"?[43]

3. If with accompanying illustrations these and similar bawdy verses are collected in a slick commercial magazine featuring the lurid magazine title *Concupiscent Sex,* and the magazine is ordered from a New York mailhouse by a postal inspector in Provo, Utah, responding to a mailed leaflet soliciting orders for the magazine for $3.50,—could a federal criminal conviction for mailing nonmailable material be sus-

---

42. Alternatively (by way of review), might they be suppressible:

  a) by public school board decision disallowing their inclusion in any book or written materials used in grades K through 12;

  b) pursuant to a public university anti-harassment rule as applied to a student with these verses printed on a T shirt (s)he wears on campus or in class;

  c) pursuant to a Title VII action brought by a female co-worker or the EEOC to enjoin workplace discrimination against the company failing to discipline a male co-worker for the display of these verses in large print on a poster above his desk in an office she also shares.

43. To what extent, if any, may it matter that the "artist" providing the graphics is famous or not famous? Suppose the illustrations are crude but the artist is nonetheless famous. What difference may it make? (Should a famous illustrator's signature provide a first amendment safe harbor? How famous, in his day, was Van Gogh?)

tained or not?[44] Whose "contemporary community" standards apply? —New York (the state in which the magazine was put into the mail)? Utah (the state in which it is taken from the mail and read)? Provo (the immediate community to which the magazine was directed and in which it was taken from the mail? The United States overall (because it was a federal statute, and not a state statute or local ordinance)?[45]

4. Suppose these verses were spoken in heavy rhythm, accented with strong body movements and accompanied by evocative sounds ("rap" fashion). Would a criminal prosecution for exhibiting "obscenity" be sustainable against first amendment objections, under a state or local anti-obscenity law as applied to a nightclub or cabaret?[46] Would the result be different if the same performance were instead rendered in Carnegie Hall?[47]

5. Of what consequence would it be were these verses not described as "bawdy" verses? Would it make any difference if instead one described them as "prurient" or "lewd"—or as an example of "pandering to male stereotype" (i.e., sexual images of women as erotic objects craving to be possessed)?[48] However they strike you on first impression, is it of any consequence to learn that they are in fact verses from Holy Scripture, passages from the Old Testament, and thus (?) not bawdy verses at all?[49] Would this datum make any difference in respect to the proper outcome of any of the cases hypothesized *supra*? Why?

44. See Ginzburg v. United States, 383 U.S. 463, 86 S.Ct. 942, 16 L.Ed.2d 31 (1966).

45. —For a decision by the Court that the "literary, artistic, political, or scientific value" factor is not to be measured by local community standards but by "whether a reasonable person [?] would find such value in the material, taken as a whole", see Pope v. Illinois, 481 U.S. 497, 107 S.Ct. 1918, 95 L.Ed.2d 439 (1987). Given that that may be so, is it a question of fact for the jury to determine whether a reasonable person would so conclude, a question of law addressed to the trial (and appellate) court, or a mixed question of law and fact, or a question of constitutional fact? Compare the Court's treatment of the second factor ("patent offensiveness") on this question, in Jenkins v. Georgia, 418 U.S. 153, 94 S.Ct. 2750, 41 L.Ed.2d 642 (1974). Note that in Miller v. California, 413 U.S. 15, 25 n. 7, 93 S.Ct. 2607, 2615 n. 7, 37 L.Ed. 419, 431 n. 7 (1973), Chief Justice Burger excludes the consideration of "social importance" as distinct from literary, artistic, political, or scientific value, under part three of the test. Why is that?

46. As a variation, would such a prosecution be upheld insofar as the statute or ordinance is limited to such establishments as are licensed to serve alcoholic beverages? (See City of Newport v. Iacobucci, 479 U.S. 92, 107 S.Ct. 383, 93 L.Ed.2d 334 (1986); New York State Liquor Auth. v. Bellanca, 452 U.S. 714, 101 S.Ct. 2599, 69 L.Ed.2d 357 (1981); California v. LaRue, 409 U.S. 109, 93 S.Ct. 390, 34 L.Ed.2d 342 (1972).) As a further variation, would such a prosecution be upheld insofar as the statute or ordinance is limited to such establishments admitting persons under the age of seventeen? (See Ginsberg v. New York, 390 U.S. 629, 88 S.Ct. 1274, 20 L.Ed.2d 195 (1968).)

47. If so, why? Because the booking of the act at Carnegie Hall per se proves "serious * * * artistic * * * value"?

48. See C. MacKinnon, Feminism Unmodified 146–228 (1987); S. Brownmiller, Against Our Will: Men, Women and Rape 394 (1975) ("Pornography is the undiluted essence of antifemale propaganda."); Sunstein, Pornography and the First Amendment, 1986 Duke L.J. 589 (1986). (Cf. Kingsley Intern. Pictures Corp. v. Regents of N.Y.U., 360 U.S. 684, 79 S.Ct. 1362, 3 L.Ed.2d 1512 (1959); American Booksellers Ass'n, Inc. v. Hudnut, 771 F.2d 323 (7th Cir.1985), summarily aff'd, 475 U.S. 1001, 106 S.Ct. 1172, 89 L.Ed.2d 291 (1986).)

49. Old Testament, The Song of Solomon, chapters 7 & 8. (See the opinions by Douglas, J., dissenting in Ginzburg v. United States, 383 U.S. at 482–92, 86 S.Ct. at 969–75, 16 L.Ed.2d at 45–50 and in Miller v. California, 413 U.S. at 37–47, 86 S.Ct. at 2622–27, 37 L.Ed.2d at 439–44, providing references to these passages.)

6. If in one or more of the above settings a prosecution or a civil action for injunction were brought not under an anti-obscenity law but instead under an anti-blasphemy law,[50] how would you expect the first amendment to be applied?[51]

7. Given that the various proceedings hypothesized *supra*, were not brought under an anti-blasphemy law, but under an anti-obscenity law, even so, why should the outcome be different? What is the "governmental interest" (i.e. the "harm" to be avoided) sufficient to override the first amendment claims?[52]

---

50. The point of this alternative prosecution being that a recognized religion's verses of religious scripture are used in a manner or setting that distorts them and makes a vile, inflammatory misappropriation belittling their sacredness and profaning their true meaning, presenting a false image of holy text. (Cf. the call for the death of Salman Rushdie, following publication of *The Satanic Verses*.)

51. See Burstyn, Inc. v. Wilson, 343 U.S. 495, 72 S.Ct. 777, 96 L.Ed. 1098 (1952). See also Kingsley Intern. Pictures Corp. v. Regents of Univ. State of N.Y., 360 U.S. 684, 79 S.Ct. 1362, 3 L.Ed.2d 1512 (1959) (ideological obscenity fully protected).

52. Is the thought that pornography (i.e. "true" pornography) acts not on the mind even in the usual way of highly affective speech (e.g., Cohen v. California, 403 U.S. 15, 91 S.Ct. 1780, 29 L.Ed.2d 284 (1971) ("Fuck The Draft"), or on the mind even as dangerous ideological speech, but rather that it acts—and is meant to act—much more directly on the senses more in the manner of an injected chemical stimulus or as a product made and marketed for stimulative sexual use? —So that it ought, therefore, to be treated for purposes of constitutional analysis essentially as regulable as "nonspeech," i.e. on the same terms as sexual products may be regulated, or as prescription or nonprescription drugs may be regulated, rather than as "speech"? (Compare Mishkin v. New York, 383 U.S. 502, 86 S.Ct. 958, 16 L.Ed.2d 56 (1966) and Bowers v. Hardwick, 478 U.S. 186, 106 S.Ct. 2841, 92 L.Ed.2d 140 (1986). But see Stanley v. Georgia, 394 U.S. 557, 89 S.Ct. 1243, 22 L.Ed.2d 542 (1969) *supra*.) For development of arguments of this sort (generally, and with reference to obscenity specifically), see Schauer, Speech and "Speech"—Obscenity and "Obscenity": An Exercise in the Interpretation of Constitutional Language, 67 Geo.L.J. 899 (1979); Schauer, Response: Pornography and the First Amendment, 40 U.Pitt.L.Rev. 605 (1979). But if the "harm" to be avoided is sexual excitement per se, then even assuming that other modes of stimulating such excitement may be regulated or forbidden (e.g., vibrators, dildos, aphrodisiacs etc.), presumably it is so *only* because they are not speech but rather are nonspeech products subject only to extremely weak substantive fifth and fourteenth amendment ("commercial products") due process review. Is Professor Schauer's point that The Song of Solomon, Eros, Lust Pool, or Shame Agent, may not be speech, and not products of a free press? If not, what are they? Is this an area where one can attempt to apply even the reasoning derived from United States v. O'Brien, 391 U.S. 370, 88 S.Ct. 1833, 20 L.Ed.2d 853 (1968)? (Is either writing or reading even a thoroughly "hard core" pornographic book "the same" as tearing in two the pages of that book?) Some state supreme courts do not now exclude "obscene" speech from ordinary first amendment review pursuant to state constitutional free speech provisions. See, e.g., State v. Henry, 302 Or. 510, 732 P.2d 9 (1987). As a general alternative to the Court's current approach, see also Redrup v. New York, 386 U.S. 767, 87 S.Ct. 1414, 18 L.Ed.2d 515 (1967) (supra).

Chapter 5

AN INTRODUCTION TO THE CHURCH–STATE CLAUSES OF THE FIRST AMENDMENT

When we became reacquainted with the first amendment, in the Introduction in Chapter 1, we began with the reminder that students enrolling in this course already had been introduced to the first amendment indirectly, in Con Law I.[1] We begin with the church-state clauses of the same amendment in exactly the same easy fashion as well. In Con Law I, we were in fact provided some insight into the first amendment establishment clause, just as had happened, albeit in a different manner, in respect to the clause on freedom of speech and of the press.

In respect to the establishment clause, the occasion arose in the course of coming to terms with article III of the Constitution and with requirements of standing to sue. That question of standing, i.e. of who could bring a case or controversy within the judicial power of article III courts to resolve, was part of the constitutional inquiry respecting what constituted a "case or controversy" as such. The discussion proceeded roughly along these lines.

I.

In Con Law I, the article III idea of "case or controversy" generally required: (a) two or more parties who are genuinely adverse; (b) a concrete sets of facts; (c) some kind of injury-in-fact either threatened or already inflicted; and (d) a request for a form of relief that would lift

---

1. So, as to the free speech and press clause, the reminder from Con Law I was, roughly, this: cases such as *Griswold v. Connecticut* analyzed certain substantive due process claims in a special way ("strict scrutiny" judicial review). They proceeded by way of analogy to certain specially favored rights, such as those of freedom of speech and of the press, rights explicitly protected by the first amendment itself. In offering the analogy, the Court adverted to the "penumbra" of first amendment protection, and then proceeded from there. E.g., one's interest in the privacy of one's *political* affiliation, the Court noted in *Griswold*, was itself protected by the first amendment from compulsory disclosure in certain circumstances; the observation was offered as a point of departure for developing a more general thesis, in *Griswold*, for privacy rights, as such. Even in Con Law I, therefore, one was made aware of the fact that express first amendment rights would not be subject to mere "rationality" review. Similarly, in those sections of Con Law I where article III concepts of "standing" were examined, the exceptional treatment of first amendment standing was also noted—standing to challenge an act as facially invalid on grounds of overbreadth or on grounds of vagueness, despite the standard rule applicable to *ius tertii* claims. So, in this respect, additionally, we were already on notice before beginning the course on the First Amendment that laws adversely affecting freedom of speech or of the press were exceptionally treated under much more rigorous standards of judicial review, than we found to be true of many other sorts of constitutional claims.

the threat of injury or provide adequate redress. The judicial determination of the case, moreover, must be final and not merely advisory to the parties or to someone else. Indeed, the merely *advisory* opinion was just what the Supreme Court early declared lay beyond the article III authority of federal courts, i.e. it was a service proposed for, but expressly rejected for, federal courts.[2]

By moving through a variety of pertinent Supreme Court cases, between the extremes of a "purely advisory opinion" on the one hand,[3] and the tightest example of "a litigable case" on the other hand,[4] one gradually came to terms with virtually all of the more mannered or particularized requirements of an article III "case." For example, such elements as "ripeness,"[5] as well as "lack of mootness,"[6] and even such refinements as "independent and adequate state grounds,"[7] were all laid into place in just this way.

In respect to the article III requirement of "standing" to sue, one will recall that the general article III rule is that one must assert some kind of injury that is *definite, material,* and *particular to oneself,* i.e.

---

2. The point was itself interestingly raised in the presidential campaign of 1988, between Governor Dukakis of Massachusetts and Vice President George Bush. Mr. Bush faulted Mr. Dukakis for declining to sign an act of the Massachusetts legislature requiring all public school teachers to lead the Pledge of Allegiance recitation at the beginning of each day's opening class. The Governor had declined to do so after the Massachusetts Supreme Court rendered an advisory opinion that such a requirement would not be enforceable in light of the U.S. Supreme Court's rulings in cases such as *West Virginia Bd. of Educ. v. Barnette, Wooley v. Maynard,* and several related lower federal court decisions. Because of the state supreme court's five-to-two ruling, the Governor returned the bill to the legislature for reconsideration in light of what the state supreme court had held. The state supreme court's ruling, of course, was itself not subject to further review in the U.S. Supreme Court at the time, since it arose under a procedure not satisfying article III "case or controversy" demands. Critics of Dukakis noted that he was legally free to sign the law despite the state supreme court's opinion. Others strongly defended the procedure he followed at the time. (*Query,* incidentally: was the Massachusetts Supreme Court correct, or incorrect, on the substantive first amendment point?)

3. E.g., an individual legislator, lobbyist, citizen, or President, interested in drafting and submitting some sort of bill and desirous of expert judicial assistance to help draft it, and who thus writes an article III court to ask how it might be best done, but who, assuming the court complied with the request, may nonetheless change his mind as he likes and give the whole matter no further thought.

4. E.g., a person about to be executed for an alleged crime with no hope other than his or her pending habeas petition in federal court, alleging that a lethal injection is about to be administered though no trial has been held determining guilt, much less whether the statute employed pursuant to which they were sentenced to death violates the first amendment.

5. I.e. the more prematurely the case has been brought, the more the case resembles the solicitation of an advisory opinion insofar as there is no demonstration of imminent and unalterable certainty of injury unless a court intervenes and adjudicates the plaintiff's questions of law pursuant to which he or she seeks abatement of the alleged threat.

6. I.e. the more obvious it is that the once-threatened injury is no longer imminent nor likely to be renewed, or the more obvious it is that in light of the relief originally requested it is now too late, so also the clearer it becomes that an adjudication can now furnish no more than the satisfaction of the plaintiff's (moot) interest in the legal questions as such.

7. I.e. if the injury the plaintiff seeks to avert cannot be avoided even assuming the lower court utterly erred in ruling against the plaintiff on his or her constitutional objection—because the decision against the plaintiff rested additionally on a consideration of state law the plaintiff is unable to show is erroneous on federal grounds—then, again, deciding the federal question would do no more than satisfy the plaintiff's curiosity and not affect the outcome of the case.

that it must not be merely an injury to another (unless one is able to assert some sort of special legal relationship enabling one to sue on the other person's behalf). Nor may it merely be an injury of a *de minimis* sort or of a kind so indiscriminately borne by others such that the grievance sounds more frankly political than legal, at least as article III courts are likely so to hold.

Distinctions of this last sort were not always clear. Nonetheless, a leading example of the last sort, was provided by one principal case, *Frothingham v. Mellon.* The *Frothingham* case was an individual federal taxpayer's suit against the Secretary of the Treasury, brought to challenge the constitutionality of certain congressionally authorized expenditures of federal funds, wherein the Supreme Court held it had no authority to address the plaintiff's claims.[8] The taxpayer's claim of injury was thought to be too attenuated (her objection was not to the tax imposed on her but went solely to the expenditure rather than to the tax), and perhaps too minuscule (no more than a matter of pennies of hers could be involved), and in any event, too indifferent to distinguish her from countless other taxpayers. At least these seemed to be the principal points the Supreme Court stressed. The Court regarded Mrs. Frothingham as wanting to settle the substantive constitutionality of an act of Congress not really differentially affecting her in any significant (*non de minimis*) fashion. The Court declined to hear the case, remanding her instead to the political process where, it implied, such general objections to certain expenditures properly belonged.

In 1968, however, despite *Frothingham v. Mellon,* a different result was reached on the standing of an otherwise identically situated mere taxpayer in a case also reviewed in Con Law I. In this later case, *Flast v. Cohen,*[9] there was little to help one see how Flast was in any

---

8. You will recall that the expenditures were challenged on the basis that: (a) they were not within the enumerated objects listed in article I, Section 8, for which Congress was authorized to make expenditures from taxes levied by the United States; (b) since they were not authorized by the Constitution, the taxes from which the expenditures were appropriated were not levied lawfully, either, but were, rather, a taking of property invalid under the fifth amendment; and (c) the expenditures were not merely constitutionally unauthorized, rather, they sought also to interfere with subjects reserved by the tenth amendment solely to the states. Thus, on all three grounds, the complaint averred, the Secretary of the Treasury should be appropriately enjoined.

9. 392 U.S. 83, 88 S.Ct. 1942, 20 L.Ed.2d 947 (1968). And recall, too, that the Supreme Court correspondingly limited the reach of *Flast v. Cohen,* by its subsequent decision in Valley Forge Christian College v. Americans United, 454 U.S. 464, 102 S.Ct. 752, 70 L.Ed.2d 700 (1982) (taxpayer standing fails where the allegedly improper government assistance to a religious organization inheres in the proposed giveaway of federal property, rather than the disbursement of funds to which the plaintiff taxpayer may have been compelled to contribute). As of 1989, moreover, except for the very narrow exception represented by *Flast v. Cohen,* itself, the Court has declined to find any other exception to *Frothingham,* at all (i.e. only the establishment clause has been identified as sufficient to anchor taxpayer standing to litigate expenditures not provided for within the same statute levying the tax). (*Query,* however: would a taxpayer suit to enjoin spending measures objected to on free speech grounds be treated more like *Flast* than like *Frothingham?* E.g., suppose an act of Congress authorizing the Pentagon to spend $100 million to buy TV network advertising slots to press the alleged need for invading Iraq. Who, if anyone, would have standing to sue to enjoin the Pentagon on a first amendment claim that the first amendment disallows the government to attempt to influence the direction or outcome of political debate in the United States by harnessing the tax-and-spend powers to generate domestic political prop-

important way distinguishable from Mrs. Frothingham as a mere ordinary Form 1040 general income taxpayer. Even so, Flast was deemed to have standing to challenge proposed disbursements to be made by Sheldon Cohen, the Secretary of Health, Education, and Welfare—disbursements inclusive of certain parochial schools and church-related universities. The distinction drawn between *Frothingham* and *Flast* was itself an introduction to the church-state first amendment clauses. The distinction arose in the course of attempting to answer the more general question, namely, *why* was Flast allowed to go forward in an article III court against Secretary Cohen, when Ms. Frothingham (who in her day certainly paid more in taxes than Mr. Flast had paid in his day) had been barred against Secretary Mellon?

What the Warren Court appeared to hold in *Flast v. Cohen*, was that a federal [10] taxpayer's standing to seek injunctive relief against a proposed federal expenditure did not depend on the amount he or she may have personally paid in taxes, *but on which constitutional clause the plaintiff relied upon* in framing his or her complaint. If the complaint were framed in terms of "specific constitutional limitations imposed upon the exercise of the congressional taxing and spending power and not simply that the enactment is generally beyond the powers delegated to Congress by Art. I, Section 8," then the plaintiff's standing *qua* taxpayer might suffice.[11] Because the Court viewed the clause Flast relied upon as such a clause—whereas the clauses invoked by Mrs. Frothingham were not viewed as such clauses—Flast succeeded in his claim of standing to sue although Mrs. Frothingham did not.

II.

For many, however, the distinction the Supreme Court drew in the *Flast* case, to distinguish it from *Frothingham*, seemed difficult to comprehend. The problem was not so much an intellectual one, i.e. in the basic idea,[12] but, rather, in the seeming arbitrariness of the Court's disposition to say which clauses were clauses imposing "specific" limitations on taxing and spending, as distinct from other clauses (such as

aganda?) (To be sure, as we saw in *Buckley v. Valeo,* the Court has held that private persons cannot be limited in spending as much as they may have the personal means and the personal will so to spend, to speak for or against such issues or candidates as they wish; but does the basis of that decision apply also to allow *the government* to spend as much coercively-collected taxpayer money as it wishes to try to influence the direction of political discussion? That important question is not foreclosed by the *Buckley* case, is it?)

10. In the case of a state or local taxpayer the rule pertinent to standing may be somewhat different, but that need not trouble us here.

11. The phrases quoted in this sentence are quoted from the Court's opinion in *Flast*.

12. The basic idea is to relate the kind of injury one relies upon for standing (injury to one as a taxpayer) to some clause evidently meant to protect one specially as a taxpayer, even if the protection is protection from certain *uses* of the funds coerced from one by way of taxation, and not from anything else. Suppose a clause expressly provided that "no person shall be taxed in order to support another person's religious practices," and that Congress proposed to use tax monies to subsidize religious practices. The standing of the taxpayer would be clear, would it not: the clause just quoted itself describes as an injury to a taxpayer the "injury" of having such money as may be taken from him as taxes given to subsidize someone else's religion. Suing to restrain the disbursing agent from making any such payment is, accordingly, just what one would expect.

those on which Mrs. Frothingham relied) which do not meet that test. What was unclear in *Flast,* in part, was what it was that made the Court treat the clause Flast relied upon as more of a specific limitation on expenditures than any of the several clauses on which Mrs. Frothingham relied?

In framing her objections to the proposed expenditures by Secretary Mellon, Mrs. Frothingham relied upon three clauses: the tax-and-spend clause in article I, the tenth amendment, and the fifth amendment due process clause. Mr. Flast, on the other hand, relied merely upon this clause in the first amendment:

> Congress shall make no law respecting an establishment of religion.[13]

In what special way, if any, was this clause a special taxpayer protection clause? Nothing on its face suggests that it is.[14] Yet, the Warren Court treated it as such, and made that treatment *the* critical distinction for purposes of Flast's standing to sue. On what basis did the Warren Court so presume?—It did so on the basis of some earlier cases that had previously engaged the same clause in the Supreme Court, cases that in turn relied upon statements identified to church-state controversies in which James Madison and Thomas Jefferson had been engaged near the time the first amendment was proposed. The Warren Court believed that that history was thus germane to an understanding of the establishment clause, and germane to Flast's theory of standing as well.

In 1777, the Court noted in *Flast,* Jefferson had drafted A Bill for Establishing Religious Freedom, in Virginia. Among its passages, there were several directed to the impropriety of government coercing any person's financial support of a religion, whether his own or one with whose doctrines he disagreed:

> [T]o compel a man to furnish contributions of money for the propagation of opinions he disbelieves and abhors, is sinful and tyrannical; * * * even the forcing him to support this or that teacher of his own religious persuasion [is wrong].

In Jefferson's view, financial support of religion should be forthcoming from voluntary contributions alone, i.e. by those devoted to its particular creed and theology and ministers, and not furnished via the state. Likewise, in remonstrating in Virginia against a proposed bill to provide tax support for religious teachers, a bill ultimately abandoned under protest, Madison had taken the view that no matter how small the tax, its imposition was objectionable in principle:

---

13. The full clause, of course, is more inclusive: "Congress shall make no law respecting an establishment of religion, or prohibiting the free exercise thereof * * * " But Flast was not relying upon the latter part of the clause.

14. Many are inclined to read the clause as merely interdicting the establishment of a national religion, or single nationally-preferred religion, a reading the clause will of course bear. (Chief Justice Rehnquist tends to hold this view, as you will see from the cases assigned in this chapter of our work; and so may as many as three other members of the 1990 Supreme Court.)

Who does not see that * * * the same authority which can force a citizen to contribute three pence only of his property for the support of any one establishment, may force him to conform to any other establishment in all cases whatsoever?

And the balance of Madison's Memorial and Remonstrance went on to criticize the effects, historically, of linking *any* church or religion with state fiscal supports, claiming that it at once made those thus supported both dependent on, as well as forever entangled with, the state—consequences in Madison's view fraught with disaster for the freedom of religion as well as the neutrality of civil government.

Believing this history to be germane, the Court in *Flast* identified to the "no-law-respecting-an-establishment of religion" clause the thesis that this clause was, among other things, a clause meant for the protection of taxpayers as such, as against any form of national religious assistance from national taxes. No amount would be *de minimis*—not even "three pence." [15] Not the amount, but the proposed use—a forbidden use, was the injury Flast, accordingly, had standing—as a taxpayer—to assert.

III.

Implicit in *Flast*, there was thus contained a larger proposition respecting the interpretation of the establishment clause, of which the case's own point (on standing to sue) is just an example in application. The larger proposition is that the Supreme Court generally accepts the first amendment's church-state clauses with an orientation derived from James Madison's and Thomas Jefferson's views, rather than the views of those clauses others might think to be preferable or more correct.[16] This interpretive stance by the Court is of no small moment.

---

15. After leaving the Presidency, Madison reflected the following thoughts on the appointment, use, and payment of congressional chaplains:

Is the appointment of Chaplains to the two Houses of Congress consistent with the Constitution, and with the pure principles of religious freedom? * * * In strictness the answer on both points must be in the negative. The Constitution of the U.S. forbids everything like an establishment of a national religion. The law appointing Chaplains establishes a religious worship for the national representatives, to be performed by Ministers of religion, elected by a majority of them; and these are to be paid out of the national taxes. * * * If Religion consists in voluntary acts of individuals, singly, or voluntarily associated, and [if] it be proper that public functionaries, as well as their Constituents should discharge their religious duties, let them like their Constituents, do so at their own expense.

Madison, Aspects of Monopoly One Hundred Years Ago, Harper's Mag. 489, 493 (1914), quoted in 1A Stokes, Church and State in the United States, 346–47 (1950). (Cf. Marsh v. Chambers, 463 U.S. 783, 103 S.Ct. 3330, 77 L.Ed.2d 1019 (1983) (use of tax funds to pay state legislative chaplains sustained, STEVENS, BRENNAN, and MARSHALL, JJ., dissenting).

16. The argument has been made forcefully that the Jefferson–Madison position in Virginia is "totally incorrect" as being descriptive of the framing of the first amendment which was, rather, on this different accounting, concerned only with "the establishment of a national church, and perhaps the preference of one religious sect over another." (REHNQUIST, J., dissenting, in Wallace v. Jaffree, 472 U.S. 38, 105 S.Ct. 2479, 86 L.Ed.2d 29 (1985).) For a work strongly supporting that view (cited and relied upon by Justice Rehnquist), see R. Cord, Separation of Church and State: Historical Fact and Current Fiction (1982). For some contrary views, however, see, e.g., T. Curry, The First Freedoms: Church and State in America to the Passage of the First Amendment (1986); L. Levy, The Establishment Clause: Religion and The First Amendment (1986); W. Miller, The

The phrasing of this part of the first amendment is somewhat awkward and ambiguous (i.e. not "no law respecting religion," but "no law respecting an establishment of religion"). A wide range of very different interpretations are compatible with the text.[17] The states did not all treat religion in the same separationist manner as was settled in Virginia in the 1780s—several provided religious subsidies of various substantial types, and some states were virtually founded by religions.[18] Moreover, there had been virtually no useful discussion of the clause at all, in 1789, when Madison submitted his original draft of the Bill of Rights in Congress, and not until 1947, did the Supreme Court provide any serious direct address to the clause.[19] We start our class efforts there, with *Everson v. Board of Education.* It is *Everson* that provides the constitutional theory of *Flast v. Cohen.*

First Liberty: Religion and The American Republic (1985).

17. See, e.g., J. Story, II Commentaries on the Constitution of the United States 627–34 (5th ed. 1891) ("[I]t is impossible for those who believe in the truth of Christianity as a divine revelation to doubt that it is the especial duty of government to foster and encourage it among all the citizens and subjects. * * * The real difficulty lies in ascertaining the limits to which government may rightfully go in fostering and encouraging religion. * * * The real object of the amendment was not to countenance, much less to advance, Mahometanism, or Judaism, or infidelity, by prostrating Christianity; but to exclude all rivalry among Christian sects, and to prevent any national ecclesiastical establishment which should give to a hierarchy the exclusive patronage of the national government.")

18. Indeed, it is arguable that in part, at least, the first amendment was agreeable to those states that did maintain religious establishment laws because it would bar Congress from interfering with their own state constitutional treatment of religion just as it would likewise bar Congress from interfering with the different arrangement reached in each other state. See Van Alstyne, Trends in the Supreme Court: Mr. Jefferson's Crumbling Wall—A Comment on *Lynch v. Donnelly,* 1984 Duke L.J. 770, 772–79.

19. Even then, in point of fact, the Supreme Court was not dealing with the first amendment but, rather, with the fourteenth amendment—that has no such express clause at all. Everson v. Board of Education, 330 U.S. 1, 67 S.Ct. 504, 91 L.Ed. 711 (1947). (The relationship of the fourteenth and first amendments is one we previously examined with respect to free speech, but the same question is even muddier so far as the church-state clauses are concerned.)

Chapter 6

"CONGRESS SHALL MAKE NO LAW RESPECTING AN ESTABLISHMENT OF RELIGION * * *"

A. The General Test(s)

EVERSON v. BOARD OF EDUCATION

Supreme Court of the United States, 1947.
330 U.S. 1, 67 S.Ct. 504, 91 L.Ed. 711.

MR. JUSTICE BLACK delivered the opinion of the Court.

A New Jersey statute authorizes its local school districts to make rules and contracts for the transportation of children to and from schools.[1] The appellee, a township board of education, acting pursuant to this statute, authorized reimbursement to parents of money expended by them for the bus transportation of their children on regular busses operated by the public transportation system. Part of this money was for the payment of transportation of some children in the community to Catholic parochial schools. These church schools give their students, in addition to secular education, regular religious instruction conforming to the religious tenets and modes of worship of the Catholic Faith. The superintendent of these schools is a Catholic priest.

The appellant, in his capacity as a district taxpayer, filed suit in a state court challenging the right of the Board to reimburse parents of parochial school students. He contended that the statute and the resolution passed pursuant to it violated both the State and the Federal Constitutions. That court held that the legislature was without power to authorize such payment under the state constitution. * * * The New Jersey Court of Errors and Appeals reversed, holding that neither the statute nor the resolution passed pursuant to it was in conflict with

---

1. "Whenever in any district there are children living remote from any schoolhouse, the board of education of the district may make rules and contracts for the transportation of such children to and from school, including the transportation of school children to and from school other than a public school, except such school as is operated for profit in whole or in part.

"When any school district provides any transportation for public school children to and from school, transportation from any point in such established school route to any other point in such established school route shall be supplied to school children residing in such school district in going to and from school other than a public school, except such school as is operated for profit in whole or in part." New Jersey Laws, 1941, c. 191, p. 581; N.J.R.S.Cum.Supp., tit. 18, c. 14, § 8.

the State constitution or the provisions of the Federal Constitution in issue. * * * The case is here on appeal * * *.

Since there has been no attack on the statute on the ground that a part of its language excludes children attending private schools operated for profit from enjoying State payment for their transportation, we need not consider this exclusionary language; it has no relevancy to any constitutional question here presented.[2] Furthermore, if the exclusion clause had been properly challenged, we do not know whether New Jersey's highest court would construe its statutes as precluding payment of the school transportation of any group of pupils, even those of a private school run for profit.[3] Consequently, we put to one side the question as to the validity of the statute against the claim that it does not authorize payment for the transportation generally of schoolchildren in New Jersey.

The only contention here is that the state statute and the resolution, insofar as they authorized reimbursement to parents of children attending parochial schools, violate the Federal Constitution in these two respects, which to some extent overlap. *First.* They authorize the State to take by taxation the private property of some and bestow it upon others, to be used for their own private purposes. This, it is alleged, violates the due process clause of the Fourteenth Amendment. *Second.* The statute and the resolution forced inhabitants to pay taxes to help support and maintain schools which are dedicated to, and which regularly teach, the Catholic Faith. This is alleged to be a use of state power to support church schools contrary to the prohibition of the First Amendment which the Fourteenth Amendment made applicable to the states.

* * *

It is much too late to argue that legislation intended to facilitate the opportunity of children to get a secular education serves no public purpose. * * * The same thing is no less true of legislation to reimburse needy parents, or all parents, for payment of the fares of their children so that they can ride in public busses to and from schools

---

2. Appellant does not challenge the New Jersey statute or the resolution on the ground that either violates the equal protection clause of the Fourteenth Amendment by excluding payment for the transportation of any pupil who attends a "private school run for profit." Although the township resolution authorized reimbursement only for parents of public and Catholic school pupils, appellant does not allege, nor is there anything in the record which would offer the slightest support to an allegation, that there were any children in the township who attended or would have attended, but for want of transportation, any but public and Catholic schools. It will be appropriate to consider the exclusion of students of private schools operated for profit when and if it is proved to have occurred, is made the basis of a suit by one in a position to challenge it, and New Jersey's highest court has ruled adversely to the challenger. Striking down a state law is not a matter of such light moment that it should be done by a federal court *ex mero motu* on a postulate neither charged nor proved, but which rests on nothing but a possibility. Cf. Liverpool, N.Y. & P.S.S. Co. v. Comm'rs of Emigration, 113 U.S. 33, 39.

3. It might hold the excepting clause to be invalid, and sustain the statute with that clause excised. N.J.R.S., tit. 1, c. 1, § 10, provides with regard to any statute that if "any provision thereof, shall be declared to be unconstitutional * * * in whole or in part, by a court of competent jurisdiction, such * * * article * * * shall, to the extent that it is not unconstitutional, * * * be enforced. * * *" * * *.

rather than run the risk of traffic and other hazards incident to walking or "hitchhiking." See *Barbier v. Connolly, supra,* at 31. * * *

Insofar as the second phase of the due process argument may differ from the first, it is by suggesting that taxation for transportation of children to church schools constitutes support of a religion by the State. But if the law is invalid for this reason, it is because it violates the First Amendment's prohibition against the establishment of religion by law. This is the exact question raised by appellant's second contention, to consideration of which we now turn.

* * * The First Amendment, as made applicable to the states by the Fourteenth, Murdock v. Pennsylvania, 319 U.S. 105, commands that a state "shall make no law respecting an establishment of religion, or prohibiting the free exercise thereof. * * * " These words of the First Amendment reflected in the minds of early Americans a vivid mental picture of conditions and practices which they fervently wished to stamp out in order to preserve liberty for themselves and for their posterity. Doubtless their goal has not been entirely reached; but so far has the Nation moved toward it that the expression "law respecting an establishment of religion," probably does not so vividly remind present-day Americans of the evils, fears, and political problems that caused that expression to be written into our Bill of Rights. Whether this New Jersey law is one respecting an "establishment of religion" requires an understanding of the meaning of that language, particularly with respect to the imposition of taxes. Once again,[4] therefore, it is not inappropriate briefly to review the background and environment of the period in which that constitutional language was fashioned and adopted.

A large proportion of the early settlers of this country came here from Europe to escape the bondage of laws which compelled them to support and attend government-favored churches. The centuries immediately before and contemporaneous with the colonization of America had been filled with turmoil, civil strife, and persecutions, generated in large part by established sects determined to maintain their absolute political and religious supremacy. With the power of government supporting them, at various times and places, Catholics had persecuted Protestants, Protestants had persecuted Catholics, Protestant sects had persecuted other Protestant sects, Catholics of one shade of belief had persecuted Catholics of another shade of belief, and all of these had from time to time persecuted Jews. In efforts to force loyalty to whatever religious group happened to be on top and in league with the government of a particular time and place, men and women had been fined, cast in jail, cruelly tortured, and killed. Among the offenses for which these punishments had been inflicted were such things as speaking disrespectfully of the views of ministers of government-established churches, non-attendance at those churches, expressions of non-belief in their doctrines, and failure to pay taxes and tithes to support them.[5]

4. See Reynolds v. United States, 98 U.S. 145, 162; * * *.

5. See e.g., Macaulay, History of England (1849) I, cc. 2, 4; The Cambridge Modern History (1908) V, cc. V, IX, XI; Beard,

These practices of the old world were transplanted to and began to thrive in the soil of the new America. The very charters granted by the English Crown to the individuals and companies designated to make the laws which would control the destinies of the colonials authorized these individuals and companies to erect religious establishments which all, whether believers or non-believers, would be required to support and attend.[6] * * *

These practices became so commonplace as to shock the freedom-loving colonials into a feeling of abhorrence.[9] The imposition of taxes to pay ministers' salaries and to build and maintain churches and church property aroused their indignation. It was these feelings which found expression in the First Amendment. No one locality and no one group throughout the Colonies can rightly be given entire credit for having aroused the sentiment that culminated in adoption of the Bill of Rights' provisions embracing religious liberty. But Virginia, where the established church had achieved a dominant influence in political affairs and where many excesses attracted wide public attention, provided a great stimulus and able leadership for the movement. * * *

The movement toward this end reached its dramatic climax in Virginia in 1785–86 when the Virginia legislative body was about to renew Virginia's tax levy for the support of the established church. Thomas Jefferson and James Madison led the fight against this tax. Madison wrote his great Memorial and Remonstrance against the law. In it, he eloquently argued that a true religion did not need the support of law; that no person, either believer or non-believer, should be taxed to support a religious institution of any kind; that the best interest of a society required that the minds of men always be wholly free; and that cruel persecutions were the inevitable result of government-established religions. Madison's Remonstrance received strong support throughout Virginia, and the Assembly postponed consideration of the proposed tax measure until its next session. When the proposal came up for consideration at that session, it not only died in committee, but the Assembly enacted the famous "Virginia Bill for Religious Liberty" originally written by Thomas Jefferson. * * *

This Court has previously recognized that the provisions of the First Amendment, in the drafting and adoption of which Madison and

---

Rise of American Civilization (1933) I, 60; Cobb, Rise of Religious Liberty in America (1902) c. II; Sweet, The Story of Religion in America (1939) c. II; Sweet, Religion in Colonial America (1942) 320–322.

6. See, e.g., the charter of the colony of Carolina which gave the grantees the right of "patronage and advowsons of all the churches and chapels * * * together with licence and power to build and found churches, chapels and oratories * * * and to cause them to be dedicated and consecrated, according to the ecclesiastical laws of our kingdom of England." * * *

9. Madison wrote to a friend in 1774: "That diabolical, hell-conceived principle of persecution rages among some * * * This vexes me the worst of anything whatever. There are at this time in the adjacent country not less than five or six well-meaning men in close jail for publishing their religious sentiments, which in the main are very orthodox. I have neither patience to hear, talk, or think of anything relative to this matter; for I have squabbled and scolded, abused and ridiculed, so long about it to little purpose, that I am without common patience. So I must beg you to pity me, and pray for liberty of conscience to all." I Writings of James Madison (1900) 18, 21.

Jefferson played such leading roles, had the same objective and were intended to provide the same protection against governmental intrusion on religious liberty as the Virginia statute. *Reynolds v. United States, supra* at 164; * * *. Prior to the adoption of the Fourteenth Amendment, the First Amendment did not apply as a restraint against the state. Most of them did soon provide similar constitutional protections for religious liberty. But some states persisted for about half a century in imposing restraints upon the free exercise of religion and in discriminating against particular religious groups. In recent years, so far as the provision against the establishment of a religion is concerned, the question has most frequently arisen in connection with proposed state aid to church schools and efforts to carry on religious teachings in the public schools in accordance with the tenets of a particular sect. * * * The state courts, in the main, have remained faithful to the language of their own constitutional provisions designed to protect religious freedom and to separate religions and governments. Their decisions, however, show the difficulty in drawing the line between tax legislation which provides funds for the welfare of the general public and that which is designed to support institutions which teach religion.

The meaning and scope of the First Amendment, preventing establishment of religion or prohibiting the free exercise thereof, in the light of its history and the evils it was designed forever to suppress, have been several times elaborated by the decisions of this Court prior to the application of the First Amendment to the states by the Fourteenth. The broad meaning given the Amendment by these earlier cases has been accepted by this Court in its decisions concerning an individual's religious freedom rendered since the Fourteenth Amendment was interpreted to make the prohibitions of the First applicable to state action abridging religious freedom. There is every reason to give the same application and broad interpretation to the "establishment of religion" clause. The interrelation of these complementary clauses was well summarized in a statement of the Court of Appeals of South Carolina,[23] quoted with approval by this Court in Watson v. Jones, 80 U.S. 679, 730: "The structure of our government has, for the preservation of civil liberty, rescued the temporal institutions from religious interference. On the other hand, it has secured religious liberty from the invasion of the civil authority."

The "establishment of religion" clause of the First Amendment means at least this: Neither a state nor the Federal Government can set up a church. Neither can pass laws which aid one religion, aid all religions, or prefer one religion over another. Neither can force nor influence a person to go to or to remain away from church against his will or force him to profess a belief or disbelief in any religion. No person can be punished for entertaining or professing religious beliefs or disbeliefs, for church attendance or non-attendance. No tax in any amount, large or small, can be levied to support any religious activities or institutions, whatever they may be called, or whatever form they may adopt to teach or practice religion. Neither a state nor the

---

23. Harmon v. Dreher, Speer's Equity Reports (S.C., 1843), 87, 120.

Federal Government can, openly or secretly, participate in the affairs of any religious organizations or groups and vice versa. In the words of Jefferson, the clause against establishment of religion by law was intended to erect "a wall of separation between church and State." *Reynolds v. United States, supra* at 164.

We must consider the New Jersey statute in accordance with the foregoing limitations imposed by the First Amendment. But we must not strike that state statute down if it is within the State's constitutional power even though it approaches the verge of that power. * * * New Jersey cannot consistently with the "establishment of religion" clause of the First Amendment contribute tax-raised funds to the support of an institution which teaches the tenets and faith of any church. On the other hand, other language of the amendment commands that New Jersey cannot hamper its citizens in the free exercise of their own religion. Consequently, it cannot exclude individual Catholics, Lutherans, Mohammedans, Baptists, Jews, Methodists, Non-believers, Presbyterians, or the members of any other faith, *because of their faith, or lack of it,* from receiving the benefits of public welfare legislation. While we do not mean to intimate that a state could not provide transportation only to children attending public schools, we must be careful, in protecting the citizens of New Jersey against state-established churches, to be sure that we do not inadvertently prohibit New Jersey from extending its general state law benefits to all its citizens without regard to their religious belief.

Measured by these standards, we cannot say that the First Amendment prohibits New Jersey from spending tax-raised funds to pay the bus fares of parochial school pupils as a part of a general program under which it pays the fares of pupils attending public and other schools. It is undoubtedly true that children are helped to get to church schools. There is even a possibility that some of the children might not be sent to the church schools if the parents were compelled to pay their children's bus fares out of their own pockets when transportation to a public school would have been paid for by the State. The same possibility exists where the state requires a local transit company to provide reduced fares to school children including those attending parochial schools,[24] or where a municipally owned transportation system undertakes to carry all school children free of charge. Moreover, state-paid policemen, detailed to protect children going to and from church schools from the very real hazards of traffic, would serve much the same purpose and accomplish much the same result as state provisions intended to guarantee free transportation of a kind which the state deems to be best for the school children's welfare. And parents might refuse to risk their children to the serious danger of traffic accidents going to and from parochial schools, the approaches to which were not protected by policemen. Similarly, parents might be

---

24. New Jersey long ago permitted public utilities to charge school children reduced rates. See Public S.R. Co. v. Public Utility Comm'rs, 81 N.J.L. 363, 80 A. 27; see also *Interstate Ry. v. Massachusetts, supra.* The District of Columbia Code requires that the new charter of the District public transportation company provide a three-cent fare "for school children * * * going to and from public, parochial, or like schools. * * *" 47 Stat. 752, 759.

reluctant to permit their children to attend schools which the state had cut off from such general government services as ordinary police and fire protection, connections for sewage disposal, public highways and sidewalks. Of course, cutting off church schools from these services, so separate and so indisputably marked off from the religious function, would make it far more difficult for the schools to operate. But such is obviously not the purpose of the First Amendment. That Amendment requires the state to be a neutral in its relations with groups of religious believers and non-believers; it does not require the state to be their adversary. State power is no more to be used so as to handicap religions than it is to favor them.

This Court has said that parents may, in the discharge of their duty under state compulsory education laws, send their children to a religious rather than a public school if the school meets the secular educational requirements which the state has power to impose. See Pierce v. Society of Sisters, 268 U.S. 510. It appears that these parochial schools meet New Jersey's requirements. The State contributes no money to the schools. It does not support them. Its legislation, as applied, does no more than provide a general program to help parents get their children, regardless of their religion, safely and expeditiously to and from accredited schools.

The First Amendment has erected a wall between church and state. That wall must be kept high and impregnable. We could not approve the slightest breach. New Jersey has not breached it here.

Affirmed.

MR. JUSTICE JACKSON, dissenting.

I find myself, contrary to first impressions, unable to join in this decision. I have a sympathy, though it is not ideological, with Catholic citizens who are compelled by law to pay taxes for public schools, and also feel constrained by conscience and discipline to support other schools for their own children. Such relief to them as this case involves is not in itself a serious burden to taxpayers and I had assumed it to be as little serious in principle. Study of this case convinces me otherwise. The Court's opinion marshals every argument in favor of state aid and puts the case in its most favorable light, but much of its reasoning confirms my conclusions that there are no good grounds upon which to support the present legislation. In fact, the undertones of the opinion, advocating complete and uncompromising separation of Church from State, seem utterly discordant with its conclusion yielding support to their commingling in educational matters. The case which irresistibly comes to mind as the most fitting precedent is that of Julia who, according to Byron's reports, "whispering 'I will ne'er consent,'—consented."

I.

The Court sustains this legislation by assuming two deviations from the facts of this particular case; first, it assumes a state of facts the record does not support, and secondly, it refuses to consider facts which are inescapable on the record.

The Court concludes that this "legislation, as applied, does no more than provide a general program to help parents get their children, regardless of their religion, safely and expeditiously to and from accredited schools," and it draws a comparison between "state provisions intended to guarantee free transportation" for school children with services such as police and fire protection, and implies that we are here dealing with "laws authorizing new types of public services * * *" This hypothesis permeates the opinion. The facts will not bear that construction.

The Township of Ewing is not furnishing transportation to the children in any form; it is not operating school busses itself or contracting for their operation; and it is not performing any public service of any kind with this taxpayer's money. All school children are left to ride as ordinary paying passengers on the regular busses operated by the public transportation system. What the Township does, and what the taxpayer complains of, is at stated intervals to reimburse parents for the fares paid, provided the children attend either public schools or Catholic Church schools. * * *

* * *

The New Jersey Act in question makes the character of the school, not the needs of the children, determine the eligibility of parents to reimbursement. * * *

Of course, this case is not one of a Baptist or a Jew or an Episcopalian or a pupil of a private school complaining of discrimination. It is one of a taxpayer urging that he is being taxed for an unconstitutional purpose. I think he is entitled to have us consider the Act just as it is written. * * * As applied to this taxpayer by the action he complains of, certainly the Act does not authorize reimbursement to those who choose any alternative to the public school except Catholic Church schools.

If we are to decide this case on the facts before us, our question is simply this: Is it constitutional to tax this complainant to pay the cost of carrying pupils to Church schools of one specified denomination?

II.

Whether the taxpayer constitutionally can be made to contribute aid to parents of students because of their attendance at parochial schools depends upon the nature of those schools and their relation to the Church. * * *

* * * Under the rubric "Catholic Schools," the Canon Law of the Church, by which all Catholics are bound, provides:

> "1215. Catholic children are to be educated in schools where not only nothing contrary to Catholic faith and morals is taught, but rather in schools where religious and moral training occupy the first place. * * * (Canon 1372.)" * * *
>
> * * *
>
> "1217. Catholic children shall not attend non-Catholic, indifferent, schools that are mixed, that is to say, schools open

to Catholics and non-Catholics alike. The bishop of the diocese only has the right, in harmony with the instructions of the Holy See, to decide under what circumstances, and with what safeguards to prevent loss of faith, it may be tolerated that Catholic children go to such schools. (Canon 1374.)"

* * *

I should be surprised if any Catholic would deny that the parochial school is a vital, if not the most vital, part of the Roman Catholic Church. If put to the choice, that venerable institution, I should expect, would forego its whole service for mature persons before it would give up education of the young, and it would be a wise choice. Its growth and cohesion, discipline and loyalty, spring from its schools. Catholic education is the rock on which the whole structure rests, and to render tax aid to its Church school is indistinguishable to me from rendering the same aid to the Church itself.

III.

It is of no importance in this situation whether the beneficiary of this expenditure of tax-raised funds is primarily the parochial school and incidentally the pupil, or whether the aid is directly bestowed on the pupil with indirect benefits to the school. The state cannot maintain a Church and it can no more tax its citizens to furnish free carriage to those who attend a Church. The prohibition against establishment of religion cannot be circumvented by a subsidy, bonus or reimbursement of expense to individuals for receiving religious instruction and indoctrination.

* * * Of course, the state may pay out tax-raised funds to relieve pauperism, but it may not under our Constitution do so to induce or reward piety. It may spend funds to secure old age against want, but it may not spend funds to secure religion against skepticism. It may compensate individuals for loss of employment, but it cannot compensate them for adherence to a creed.

It seems to me that the basic fallacy in the Court's reasoning, which accounts for its failure to apply the principles it avows, is in ignoring the essentially religious test by which beneficiaries of this expenditure are selected. A policeman protects a Catholic, of course—but not because he is a Catholic; it is because he is a man and a member of our society. The fireman protects the Church school—but not because it is a Church school; it is because it is property, part of the assets of our society. Neither the fireman nor the policeman has to ask before he renders aid "Is this man or building identified with the Catholic Church?" But before these school authorities draw a check to reimburse for a student's fare they must ask just that question, and if the school is a Catholic one they may render aid because it is such, while if it is of any other faith or is run for profit, the help must be withheld. To consider the converse of the Court's reasoning will best disclose its fallacy. That there is no parallel between police and fire protection and this plan of reimbursement is apparent from the incongruity of the limitation of this Act if applied to police and fire service.

Could we sustain an Act that said the police shall protect pupils on the way to or from public schools and Catholic schools but not while going to and coming from other schools, and firemen shall extinguish a blaze in public or Catholic school buildings but shall not put out a blaze in Protestant Church schools or private schools operated for profit? That is the true analogy to the case we have before us and I should think it pretty plain that such a scheme would not be valid.

* * * There is no answer to the proposition, more fully expounded by Mr. Justice Rutledge, that the effect of the religious freedom Amendment to our Constitution was to take every form of propagation of religion out of the realm of things which could directly or indirectly be made public business and thereby be supported in whole or in part at taxpayers' expense. That is a difference which the Constitution sets up between religion and almost every other subject matter of legislation, a difference which goes to the very root of religious freedom and which the Court is overlooking today. This freedom was first in the Bill of Rights because it was first in the forefathers' minds; it was set forth in absolute terms, and its strength is its rigidity. It was intended not only to keep the states' hands out of religion, but to keep religion's hands off the state, and, above all, to keep bitter religious controversy out of public life by denying to every denomination any advantage from getting control of public policy or the public purse. Those great ends I cannot but think are immeasurably compromised by today's decision.

This policy of our Federal Constitution has never been wholly pleasing to most religious groups. They all are quick to invoke its protections; they all are irked when they feel its restraints. This Court has gone a long way, if not an unreasonable way, to hold that public business of such paramount importance as maintenance of public order, protection of the privacy of the home, and taxation may not be pursued by a state in a way that even indirectly will interfere with religious proselyting. See dissent in Douglas v. Jeannette, 319 U.S. 157, 166; Murdock v. Pennsylvania, 319 U.S. 105; Martin v. Struthers, 319 U.S. 141; Jones v. Opelika, 316 U.S. 584, reversed on rehearing, 319 U.S. 103.

But we cannot have it both ways. Religious teaching cannot be a private affair when the state seeks to impose regulations which infringe on it indirectly, and a public affair when it comes to taxing citizens of one faith to aid another, or those of no faith to aid all. If these principles seem harsh in prohibiting aid to Catholic education, it must not be forgotten that it is the same Constitution that alone assures Catholics the right to maintain these schools at all when predominant local sentiment would forbid them. Pierce v. Society of Sisters, 268 U.S. 510. Nor should I think that those who have done so well without this aid would want to see this separation between Church and State broken down. If the state may aid these religious schools, it may therefore regulate them. * * *

* * *

Mr. Justice Frankfurter joins in this opinion.

MR. JUSTICE RUTLEDGE, with whom MR. JUSTICE FRANKFURTER, MR. JUSTICE JACKSON and MR. JUSTICE BURTON agree, dissenting.

"Congress shall make no law respecting an establishment of religion, or prohibiting the free exercise thereof * * *" U.S. Const., Amend. I.

"Well aware that Almighty God hath created the mind free; * * * that to compel a man to furnish contributions of money for the propagation of opinions which he disbelieves, is sinful and tyrannical; . . .

"*We, the General Assembly, do enact,* That no man shall be compelled to frequent or support any religious worship, place, or ministry whatsoever, nor shall be enforced, restrained, molested, or burthened in his body or goods, nor shall otherwise suffer, on account of his religious opinions or belief * * *"[1]

I cannot believe that the great author of those words, or the men who made them law, could have joined in this decision. Neither so high nor so impregnable today as yesterday is the wall raised between church and state by Virginia's great statute of religious freedom and the First Amendment, now made applicable to all the states by the Fourteenth. * * *

This case forces us to determine squarely for the first time what was "an establishment of religion" in the First Amendment's conception; and by that measure to decide whether New Jersey's action violates its command. The facts may be stated shortly, to give setting and color to the constitutional problem.

* * *

Named parents have paid the cost of public conveyance of their children from their homes in Ewing to three public high schools and four parochial schools outside the district. Semi-annually the Board has reimbursed the parents from public school funds raised by general taxation. Religion is taught as part of the curriculum in each of the four private schools, as appears affirmatively by the testimony of the superintendent of parochial schools in the Diocese of Trenton.

* * *

I.

Not simply an established church, but any law respecting an establishment of religion is forbidden. The Amendment was broadly but not loosely phrased. It is the compact and exact summation of its author's views formed during his long struggle for religious freedom. In Madison's own words characterizing Jefferson's Bill for Establishing Religious Freedom, the guaranty he put in our national charter, like

---

1. "A Bill for Establishing Religious Freedom," enacted by the General Assembly of Virginia, January 19, 1786. See 1 Randall, The Life of Thomas Jefferson (1858) 219–220; XII Hening's Statutes of Virginia (1823) 84.

the bill he piloted through the Virginia Assembly, was "a Model of technical precision, and perspicuous brevity." Madison could not have confused "church" and "religion," or "an established church" and "an establishment of religion."

The Amendment's purpose was not to strike merely at the official establishment of a single sect, creed or religion, outlawing only a formal relation such as had prevailed in England and some of the colonies. Necessarily it was to uproot all such relationships. But the object was broader than separating church and state in this narrow sense. It was to create a complete and permanent separation of the spheres of religious activity and civil authority by comprehensively forbidding every form of public aid or support for religion. In proof the Amendment's wording and history unite with this Court's consistent utterances whenever attention has been fixed directly upon the question.

"Religion" appears only once in the Amendment. But the word governs two prohibitions and governs them alike. It does not have two meanings, one narrow to forbid "an establishment" and another, much broader, for securing "the free exercise thereof." "Thereof" brings down "religion" with its entire and exact content, no more and no less, from the first into the second guaranty, so that Congress and now the states are as broadly restricted concerning the one as they are regarding the other.

* * *

"Religion" has the same broad significance in the twin prohibition concerning "an establishment." The Amendment was not duplicitous. "Religion" and "establishment" were not used in any formal or technical sense. The prohibition broadly forbids state support, financial or other, of religion in any guise, form or degree. It outlaws all use of public funds for religious purposes.

II.

No provision of the Constitution is more closely tied to or given content by its generating history than the religious clause of the First Amendment. It is at once the refined product and the terse summation of that history. The history includes not only Madison's authorship and the proceedings before the First Congress, but also the long and intensive struggle for religious freedom in America, more especially in Virginia, of which the Amendment was the direct culmination. * * *

* * *

* * * As a member of the General Assembly in 1779 he threw his full weight behind Jefferson's historic Bill for Establishing Religious Freedom. That bill was a prime phase of Jefferson's broad program of democratic reform undertaken on his return from the Continental Congress in 1776 and submitted for the General Assembly's consideration in 1779 as his proposed revised Virginia code. With Jefferson's departure for Europe in 1784, Madison became the Bill's prime sponsor. Enactment failed in successive legislatures from its introduction in June, 1779, until its adoption in January, 1786. But during all this time the fight for religious freedom moved forward in Virginia on

various fronts with growing intensity. Madison led throughout, against Patrick Henry's powerful opposing leadership until Henry was elected governor in November, 1784.

The climax came in the legislative struggle of 1784–1785 over the Assessment Bill. * * * This was nothing more nor less than a taxing measure for the support of religion, designed to revive the payment of tithes suspended since 1777. So long as it singled out a particular sect for preference it incurred the active and general hostility of dissentient groups. It was broadened to include them, with the result that some subsided temporarily in their opposition. As altered, the bill gave to each taxpayer the privilege of designating which church should receive his share of the tax. In default of designation the legislature applied it to pious uses. But what is of the utmost significance here, "in its final form the bill left the taxpayer the option of giving his tax to education."

Madison was unyielding at all times, opposing with all his vigor the general and nondiscriminatory as he had the earlier particular and discriminatory assessments proposed. * * * And before the Assembly reconvened in the fall he issued his historic Memorial and Remonstrance.

This is Madison's complete, though not his only, interpretation of religious liberty. It is a broadside attack upon all forms of "establishment" of religion, both general and particular, nondiscriminatory or selective. Reflecting not only the many legislative conflicts over the Assessment Bill and the Bill for Establishing Religious Freedom but also, for example, the struggles for religious incorporations and the continued maintenance of the glebes, the Remonstrance is at once the most concise and the most accurate statement of the views of the First Amendment's author concerning what is "an establishment of religion." * * *

* * *

As the Remonstrance discloses throughout, Madison opposed every form and degree of official relation between religion and civil authority. For him religion was a wholly private matter beyond the scope of civil power either to restrain or to support. Denial or abridgment of religious freedom was a violation of rights both of conscience and of natural equality. State aid was no less obnoxious or destructive to freedom and to religion itself than other forms of state interference. "Establishment" and "free exercise" were correlative and coextensive ideas, representing only different facets of the single great and fundamental freedom. The Remonstrance, following the Virginia statute's example, referred to the history of religious conflicts and the effects of all sorts of establishments, current and historical, to suppress religion's free exercise. With Jefferson, Madison believed that to tolerate any fragment of establishment would be by so much to perpetuate restraint upon that freedom. Hence he sought to tear out the institution not partially but root and branch, and to bar its return forever.

In no phase was he more unrelentingly absolute than in opposing state support or aid by taxation. Not even "three pence" contribution was thus to be exacted from any citizen for such a purpose. * * *

* * *

Compulsory attendance upon religious exercises went out early in the process of separating church and state, together with forced observance of religious forms and ceremonies. Test oaths and religious qualification for office followed later.[37] These things none devoted to our great tradition of religious liberty would think of bringing back. Hence today, apart from efforts to inject religious training or exercises and sectarian issues into the public schools, the only serious surviving threat to maintaining that complete and permanent separation of religion and civil power which the First Amendment commands is through use of the taxing power to support religion, religious establishments, or establishments having a religious foundation whatever their form or special religious function.

Does New Jersey's action furnish support for religion by use of the taxing power? Certainly it does, if the test remains undiluted as Jefferson and Madison made it, that money taken by taxation from one is not to be used or given to support another's religious training or belief, or indeed one's own. * * *

* * * Here parents pay money to send their children to parochial schools and funds raised by taxation are used to reimburse them. This not only helps the children to get to school and the parents to send them. It aids them in a substantial way to get the very thing which they are sent to the particular school to secure, namely, religious training and teaching.

Believers of all faiths, and others who do not express their feeling toward ultimate issues of existence in any creedal form, pay the New Jersey tax. When the money so raised is used to pay for transportation to religious schools, the Catholic taxpayer to the extent of his proportionate share pays for the transportation of Lutheran, Jewish and otherwise religiously affiliated children to receive their non-Catholic religious instruction. Their parents likewise pay proportionately for the transportation of Catholic children to receive Catholic instruction. Each thus contributes to "the propagation of opinions which he disbelieves" in so far as their religions differ, as do others who accept no creed without regard to those differences. Each thus pays taxes also to support the teaching of his own religion, an exaction equally forbidden since it denies "the comfortable liberty" of giving one's contribution to the particular agency of instruction he approves.

New Jersey's action therefore exactly fits the type of exaction and the kind of evil at which Madison and Jefferson struck. Under the test they framed it cannot be said that the cost of transportation is no part of the cost of education or of the religious instruction given. That it is a substantial and a necessary element is shown most plainly by the continuing and increasing demand for the state to assume it. * * * And the very purpose of the state's contribution is to defray the cost of

---

37. "* * * but no religious Test shall ever be required as a Qualification to any Office or public Trust under the United States." Const., Art. VI, § 3. See also the two forms prescribed for the President's Oath or Affirmation. Const., Art. II, § 1. * * *

conveying the pupil to the place where he will receive not simply secular, but also and primarily religious, teaching and guidance.

Indeed the view is sincerely avowed by many of various faiths, that the basic purpose of all education is or should be religious, that the secular cannot be and should not be separated from the religious phase and emphasis. Hence, the inadequacy of public or secular education and the necessity for sending the child to a school where religion is taught. But whatever may be the philosophy or its justification, there is undeniably an admixture of religious with secular teaching in all such institutions. That is the very reason for their being. Certainly for purposes of constitutionality we cannot contradict the whole basis of the ethical and educational convictions of people who believe in religious schooling.

* * *

Finally, transportation, where it is needed, is as essential to education as any other element. Its cost is as much a part of the total expense, except at times in amount, as the cost of textbooks, of school lunches, of athletic equipment, of writing and other materials; indeed of all other items composing the total burden. * * *

For me, therefore, the feat is impossible to select so indispensable an item from the composite of total costs, and characterize it as not aiding, contributing to, promoting or sustaining the propagation of beliefs which it is the very end of all to bring about. Unless this can be maintained, and the Court does not maintain it, the aid thus given is outlawed. Payment of transportation is no more, nor is it any the less essential to education, whether religious or secular, than payment for tuitions, for teachers' salaries, or buildings, equipment and necessary materials. Nor is it any the less directly related, in a school giving religious instruction, to the primary religious objective all those essential items of cost are intended to achieve. * * *

* * *

Of course paying the cost of transportation promotes the general cause of education and the welfare of the individual. So does paying all other items of educational expense. And obviously, as the majority say, it is much too late to urge that legislation designed to facilitate the opportunities of children to secure a secular education serves no public purpose. Our nationwide system of public education rests on the contrary view, as do all grants in aid of education, public or private, which is not religious in character.

* * * The public function argument, by casting the issue in terms of promoting the general cause of education and the welfare of the individual, ignores the religious factor and its essential connection with the transportation, thereby leaving out the only vital element in the case. * * *

* * *

In truth this view contradicts the whole purpose and effect of the First Amendment as heretofore conceived. The "public function"—"public welfare"—"social legislation" argument seeks, in Madison's words, to "employ Religion [that is, here, religious education] as an engine of Civil policy." Remonstrance, Par. 5. It is of one piece with the Assessment Bill's preamble, although with the vital difference that it wholly ignores what that preamble explicitly states.

Our constitutional policy is exactly the opposite. It does not deny the value or the necessity for religious training, teaching or observance. Rather it secures their free exercise. But to that end it does deny that the state can undertake or sustain them in any form or degree. For this reason the sphere of religious activity, as distinguished from the secular intellectual liberties, has been given the twofold protection and, as the state cannot forbid, neither can it perform or aid in performing the religious function. The dual prohibition makes that function altogether private. It cannot be made a public one by legislative act. This was the very heart of Madison's Remonstrance, as it is of the Amendment itself.

* * *

* * * The great condition of religious liberty is that it be maintained free from sustenance, as also from other interferences, by the state. For when it comes to rest upon that secular foundation it vanishes with the resting. Id., Pars. 7, 8.[45] Public money devoted to payment of religious costs, educational or other, brings the quest for more. * * *

* * *

Notwithstanding the recognition that this two-way aid is given and the absence of any denial that religious teaching is thus furthered, the Court concludes that the aid so given is not "support" of religion. It is rather only support of education as such, without reference to its religious content, and thus becomes public welfare legislation. To this elision of the religious element from the case is added gloss in two respects, one that the aid extended partakes of the nature of a safety measure, the other that failure to provide it would make the state unneutral in religious matters, discriminating against or hampering such children concerning public benefits all others receive.

As will be noted, the one gloss is contradicted by the facts of record and the other is of whole cloth with the "public function" argument's excision of the religious factor. But most important is that this approach, if valid, supplies a ready method for nullifying the Amendment's guaranty, not only for this case and others involving small grants in aid for religious education, but equally for larger ones. The only thing needed will be for the Court again to transplant the "public welfare—public function" view from its proper nonreligious due process bearing to First Amendment application, holding that religious education is not "supported" though it may be aided by the appropriation, and that the cause of education generally is furthered by helping the pupil to secure that type of training.

---

45. "Because experience witnesseth that ecclesiastical establishments, instead of maintaining the purity and efficacy of Religion, have had a contrary operation." II Madison 183, 187.

This is not therefore just a little case over bus fares. * * * * * *

V.

No one conscious of religious values can be unsympathetic toward the burden which our constitutional separation puts on parents who desire religious instruction mixed with secular for their children. They pay taxes for others' children's education, at the same time the added cost of instruction for their own. Nor can one happily see benefits denied to children which others receive, because in conscience they or their parents for them desire a different kind of training others do not demand.

But if those feelings should prevail, there would be an end to our historic constitutional policy and command. No more unjust or discriminatory in fact is it to deny attendants at religious schools the cost of their transportation than it is to deny them tuitions, sustenance for their teachers, or any other educational expense which others receive at public cost. Hardship in fact there is which none can blink. But, for assuring to those who undergo it the greater, the most comprehensive freedom, it is one written by design and firm intent into our basic law.

Of course discrimination in the legal sense does not exist. The child attending the religious school has the same right as any other to attend the public school. * * *

* * *

The problem then cannot be cast in terms of legal discrimination or its absence. This would be true, even though the state in giving aid should treat all religious instruction alike. Thus, if the present statute and its application were shown to apply equally to all religious schools of whatever faith, yet in the light of our tradition it could not stand. For then the adherent of one creed still would pay for the support of another, the childless taxpayer with others more fortunate. Then too there would seem to be no bar to making appropriations for transportation and other expenses of children attending public or other secular schools, after hours in separate places and classes for their exclusively religious instruction. The person who embraces no creed also would be forced to pay for teaching what he does not believe. Again, it was the furnishing of "contributions of money for the propagation of opinions which he disbelieves" that the fathers outlawed. That consequence and effect are not removed by multiplying to all-inclusiveness the sects for which support is exacted. The Constitution requires, not comprehensive identification of state with religion, but complete separation.

* * *

Two great drives are constantly in motion to abridge, in the name of education, the complete division of religion and civil authority which our forefathers made. One is to introduce religious education and observances into the public schools. The other, to obtain public funds for the aid and support of various private religious schools. * * * In my opinion both avenues were closed by the Constitution. Neither should be opened by this Court. * * *

* * *

NOTES ON THE *EVERSON* OPINIONS

1. Other clauses regarding religion

Justice Rutledge, in his separate opinion in *Everson*, notes that aside from the first amendment—the focus of the Court in this case [1]—the Constitution makes some reference to religion in several *other* clauses. The other clauses include the following:

Article VI, cl. 3:

> The Senators and Representatives before mentioned, and the Members of the several State Legislatures, and all executive and judicial Officers, both of the United States and of the several States, shall be bound by *Oath or Affirmation,* to support this Constitution; *but no religious Test shall ever be required as a Qualification to any Office or public Trust under the United States.*

Article II, § 1, cl. 8:

> Before he [the President] enter on the Execution of his Office, he shall take the following *Oath or Affirmation:*—"I do solemnly *swear (or affirm)* that I will faithfully execute the Office of President of the United States, and will to the best of my Ability, preserve, protect and defend the Constitution of the United States." [2]

Article I, § 3, cl. 6:

> The Senate shall have the sole Power to try all Impeachments. When sitting for that Purpose, they shall be on *Oath or Affirmation.*

4th Amendment:

> * * * and no Warrants shall issue, but upon probable cause, supported by *Oath or affirmation,* and particularly describing the place to be searched and the persons or things to be seized.

—Note, then, that in these respects the Constitution seems to square overall with the broad consensus in *Everson*—i.e. that the Constitution itself reports some conscious effort to provide for a neutral civil national government quite distinct from the varying church-state arrange-

---

1. Albeit technically not the first amendment directly, but only indirectly (i.e., through the due process clause of the 14th amendment).

2. I.e. note that here (as in Article VI) the alternative of affirming (rather than subscribing by "oath") is provided for. Note also that there is no "so help me God" feature of the sentence expected to be said by the President.

ments within the several states forming the United States.³ So, for example: (1) the provision in Article VI disallows any religious test for holding office under the authority of the United States; (2) the oath or affirmation provided for the President is itself civil; (3) the several clauses otherwise providing for "oath"⁴ provide the alternative of merely affirming; (4) the Preamble⁵ to the Constitution is civil and secular,⁶ rather than religious.⁷

2. The Blaine amendment, state constitutions, and the controversy respecting the fourteenth amendment⁸

No state shall make any law respecting an establishment of religion or prohibiting the free exercise thereof; and, no money raised by taxation in any state for the support of public schools, or derived from any public fund therefore, nor any public lands devoted thereto, shall ever be under the control of any religious sect, nor shall any money so raised or lands so devoted be divided between religious sects or denominations.

---

3. Similarly, the original motto of the United States was "E Pluribus Unum," unchanged until the nineteen fifties (when it was altered by Congress to "In God We Trust"). ("In God We Trust" did not appear on American currency until the Lincoln administration and the Civil War. It did not become standard on all currency until the nineteen fifties, during the same decade—the Cold War with the Soviet Union—when the national motto was altered and "under God" was added to the Pledge of Allegiance as well.)

4. "Oath: A formal declaration or formal declaration or promise to fulfill a pledge, often calling upon God or some other sacred object as witness." American Heritage Dictionary 904 (W. Morris ed. 1971).

5. Cf. the theistic references in the Declaration of Independence ("to assume among the powers of the earth the separate and equal station to which the laws of nature and of nature's God entitle them * * * endowed by their Creator with certain inalienable rights * * * ").

6. See also article XI of the Treaty of Peace and Friendship, Nov. 4, 1796–Jan. 3, 1797, United States–Tripoli, 8 Stat. 154, 155, T.S. No. 358. ("As the government of the United States of America is not in any sense founded on the Christian religion—as it has in itself no character of enmity against the laws, religion, or tranquility of Musselmen * * * it is declared by the parties, that no pretext arising from religious opinions shall ever produce an interruption of the harmony existing between the two countries.")

7. On the other hand, consider Art. I, § 7, cl. 2. ("If any Bill shall not be returned by the President within ten Days (Sundays excepted) after it shall have been presented to him, the Same shall be a Law, in like Manner as if he had signed it, unless the Congress by their Adjournment prevent its Return, in which Case it shall not be a Law.") (Why "*Sundays* excepted"?) Note, also, that at the end of Article VII, the final sentence memorializing the date of the Constitution's own completion reads in the following way: "done in Convention by the Unanimous Consent of the States present the Seventeenth Day of September *in the Year of our Lord* one thousand seven hundred and Eighty seven * * * " See also Douglas, J., in Zorach v. Clauson, 343 U.S. 306, 72 S.Ct. 679, 96 L.Ed. 954 (1952) ("We are a religious people whose institutions presuppose a Supreme Being.")

8. See discussion in R. Smith, Public Prayer and the Constitution 163–69, 261–65 (1987). (The Blaine amendment was introduced in the House of Representatives by James Blaine, Representative from Maine, on the suggestion of President Ulysses S. Grant, in 1875. It passed in the House 180 to 7 (98 not voting). Following discussion and some changes in the Senate, it failed of sufficient two-thirds vote 28 to 16 (27 not voting). The antecedent address by Grant, Sept. 29, 1875, in Des Moines, Iowa, provided: "Let us all labor to add all needful guarantees for the security of free thought, free speech, a free press, pure morals, unfettered religious sentiments, and of equal right and privileges to all men, irrespective of nationality, color, or religion. * * * Leave the matter of religion to the family altar, the church, and the private school, supported entirely by private contributions. Keep the church and the state forever separate."

A version of the Blaine amendment was adopted by a number of states. The state supreme courts in some of these states have applied the relevant state constitutional clause to disallow the reimbursement arrangement sustained five-to-four in *Everson,* i.e. they have construed such a clause as a more complete and more stringent restriction on the state's use of tax revenue than the Supreme Court construed the shorter version of the first amendment in *Everson.*[9]

The failure of the Blaine amendment in Congress, on the other hand, is often offered as evidence of a contemporary understanding in Congress that the fourteenth amendment did *not* "incorporate" the establishment clause of the first amendment. If it did, why the proposal for an additional amendment, the entire first phrase of which is verbatim the same as the first amendment except that it speaks to what "no state" (rather than what no Congress) may do? The force of the argument has been discounted on several grounds:

a. Prior to the Blaine amendment, but subsequent to the fourteenth amendment, the Supreme Court decided the *Slaughterhouse Cases,* in 1873. That decision had eviscerated the privileges and immunities clause—the clause actually relied upon in Congress for the incorporation thesis.[10] Insofar as the Court subsequently merely corrected its own error—albeit through the due process rather than the privileges and immunities clause—the matter has simply come out approximately in the right way.

b. The form the Blaine amendment ultimately assumed in Congress was more detailed and complex than the first amendment's more succinct and simpler provision; the resistance it encountered in the Senate was due partly to uncertainty respecting the appropriateness and consequences of the added provisions which were controversial in their sheer detail.

c. The free exercise clause, like the establishment clause, is also a verbatim part of the Blaine amendment, and parity of reasoning would suggest that the fourteenth amendment thus does not propose any protection for the free exercise of religion from state abridgments either,—but far fewer persons believe this to be so.

d. An argument that the free exercise part of the first amendment is nonetheless picked up by the "liberty" portion of the due process clause, while the establishment clause is allegedly not similarly incorporated into the (substantive) due process clause of the fourteenth amendment, on the other hand, has no confirming support either in the associated history of the fourteenth amendment or in the treatment and fate of the Blaine amendment as such.

---

9. See C. Antieau, P. Carroll, & T. Burke, Religion Under the State Constitutions (1965).

10. See materials and discussion at pp. 54–65, *supra.*

It is true, however, that the modern Court's continuing reliance solely on the due process clause (*rather than on the privileges and immunities clause*), does give Court critics a textual basis for arguing that only such state practices regarding establishment of religion as might be inconsistent with the "liberty" of religion are forbidden by the fourteenth amendment. As we shall see, despite what is said in *Everson*, several Justices appear to subscribe to this view.[11]

3. The *Everson* test

In *Everson*, all nine Justices appear to concur in Justice Black's general explication of the first amendment and its full applicability to the states, in keeping with his understanding of the Madison–Jefferson view:

> The "establishment of religion" clause of the First Amendment means at least this: Neither a state nor the Federal Government can set up a church. Neither can pass laws which *aid one religion, aid all religions, or prefer one religion over another.* Neither can force nor influence a person to go to or to remain away from church against his will or force him to profess a belief or disbelief in any religion. No person can be punished for entertaining or professing religious beliefs or disbeliefs, for church attendance or non-attendance. *No tax in any amount, large or small, can be levied to support any religious activities or institutions, whatever they may be called, or whatever form they may adopt to teach or practice religion.* Neither a state nor the Federal Government can, openly or secretly, participate in the affairs of any religious organizations or groups and vice versa. In the words of Jefferson, the clause against establishment of religion by law was intended to "erect a wall of separation between church and State."

Given its unanimous agreement on this meaning of the "no establishment" clause, why (i.e. on what basis) does the Court nonetheless divide, five-to-four? More specifically:

1. In light of the italicized portions of the paragraph from Justice Black's opinion (*supra*), how does he nonetheless conclude that no tax herein involved provides support for any "religious institution?" (The parochial schools are surely religious institutions, are they not?)

    (i) Had the buses used for the parochial school students been owned and operated by those schools, with payment to the parents to reimburse them for such fares as the parochial school children might be required to pay to ride the parochial school buses (though not in excess of such fares as the regular buses might charge public

---

11. See, e.g., County of Allegheny v. ACLU, 492 U.S. 573, 109 S.Ct. 3086, 106 L.Ed.2d 472 (1989). (In brief, this view puts the dominant stress on the free exercise of religion; it reads the prohibition on laws respecting an establishment of religion as a restriction on such laws as may impair the free exercise of religion, but not otherwise.)

school riders), would the result have been the same? What difference, if any, would there be?

(ii) Had the parochial schools operated their own buses to insure the safe transport of parochial school children to travel to and from those schools at the beginning and close of each school day, with Ewing Township agreeing by contract to reimburse the schools for the cost of defraying such means of transportation, what difference then, if any?

2. What distinction, if any, underlies Justice Jackson's agreement that furnishing police protection inclusive of children en route to parochial school, or fire protection inclusive of churches and parochial schools, presents no issue under the "no establishment" clause? How does he characterize the actual reimbursement plan adopted by the Township Board of Education? What is Justice Black's treatment of that complaint?

3. The Court does not particularly note the extent to which the tax revenues used to support the reimbursement plan were contributed equally by those with children enrolled in parochial school. Assuming (as the Court appears to) that they are fully included in the tax base, is it arguable that failure to include them in the bus fare reimbursement plan would be invalid, either as a denial of equal protection or as a violation of the "free exercise" clause? All nine members of the Court appear to agree that no such question would arise. Do you agree? Why or why not?

Responding to *Everson* and other cases treated by the Supreme Court under the church-state clauses of the first amendment, Professor Philip Kurland proposed the following synthesis of the two clauses in 1961, as follows: [12]

[T]he thesis proposed here as the proper construction of the religion clause of the first amendment is that the freedom and separation clauses should be read as a single precept that government cannot utilize religion as a standard for action or inaction because these clauses prohibit classification in terms of religion either to confer a benefit or to impose a burden.

1. Is *Everson* consistent with this view?

2. What kinds of laws or practices might not be valid if this view were to be followed? E.g., state laws requiring businesses generally to close on Sundays? Draft laws providing for exemption from combatant training and service for those with conscientious objections? State or local laws providing tax exempt status for religiously-held property? Internal Revenue Code provisions providing for tax exempt status of income to churches, and tax deduction treatment of charitable contribu-

12. P. Kurland, Religion and the Law 18 (1961); Kurland, The Irrelevance of the Constitution: The Religion Clauses of the First Amendment and the Supreme Court, 24 Vill.L.Rev. 3, 24 (1978).

tions to religious organizations? Excusal from public school attendance of children to attend released time classes in religious instruction? Do the subsequent cases (infra) appear to fulfill Professor Kurland's suggestion? If not, in what respect do they represent a departure from his proposal and synthesis, i.e. what is the basic doctrine they tend to report?

ILLINOIS EX REL. MCCOLLUM v. BOARD OF EDUCATION OF SCHOOL DISTRICT NO. 71, CHAMPAIGN COUNTY, ILLINOIS

Supreme Court of the United States, 1948.
333 U.S. 203, 68 S.Ct. 461, 92 L.Ed. 649.

Mr. Justice Black delivered the opinion of the Court.

This case relates to the power of a state to utilize its tax-supported public school system in aid of religious instruction insofar as that power may be restricted by the First and Fourteenth Amendments to the Federal Constitution.

The appellant, Vashti McCollum, began this action for mandamus against the Champaign Board of Education in the Circuit Court of Champaign County, Illinois. Her asserted interest was that of a resident and taxpayer of Champaign and of a parent whose child was then enrolled in the Champaign public schools. Illinois has a compulsory education law which, with exceptions, requires parents to send their children, aged seven to sixteen, to its tax-supported public schools where the children are to remain in attendance during the hours when the schools are regularly in session. Parents who violate this law commit a misdemeanor punishable by fine unless the children attend private or parochial schools which meet educational standards fixed by the State. District boards of education are given general supervisory powers over the use of the public school buildings within the school districts. * * *

Appellant's petition for mandamus alleged that religious teachers, employed by private religious groups, were permitted to come weekly into the school buildings during the regular hours set apart for secular teaching, and then and there for a period of thirty minutes substitute their religious teaching for the secular education provided under the compulsory education law. The petitioner charged that this joint public-school religious-group program violated the First and Fourteenth Amendments to the United States Constitution. The prayer of her petition was that the Board of Education be ordered to "adopt and enforce rules and regulations prohibiting all instruction in and teaching of religious education in all public schools in Champaign School District Number 71, * * * and in all public school houses and buildings in said district when occupied by public schools."

* * *

Although there are disputes between the parties as to various inferences that may or may not properly be drawn from the evidence concerning the religious program, the following facts are shown by the record without dispute. In 1940 interested members of the Jewish, Roman Catholic, and a few of the Protestant faiths formed a voluntary association called the Champaign Council on Religious Education. They obtained permission from the Board of Education to offer classes in religious instruction to public school pupils in grades four to nine inclusive. Classes were made up of pupils whose parents signed printed cards requesting that their children be permitted to attend; they were held weekly, thirty minutes for the lower grades, forty-five minutes for the higher. The council employed the religious teachers at no expense to the school authorities, but the instructors were subject to the approval and supervision of the superintendent of schools. The classes were taught in three separate religious groups by Protestant teachers, Catholic priests, and a Jewish rabbi, although for the past several years there have apparently been no classes instructed in the Jewish religion. Classes were conducted in the regular classrooms of the school building. Students who did not choose to take the religious instruction were not released from public school duties; they were required to leave their classrooms and go to some other place in the school building for pursuit of their secular studies. On the other hand, students who were released from secular study for the religious instructions were required to be present at the religious classes. Reports of their presence or absence were to be made to their secular teachers.

The foregoing facts, without reference to others that appear in the record, show the use of tax-supported property for religious instruction and the close cooperation between the school authorities and the religious council in promoting religious education. The operation of the State's compulsory education system thus assists and is integrated with the program of religious instruction carried on by separate religious sects. Pupils compelled by law to go to school for secular education are released in part from their legal duty upon the condition that they attend the religious classes. This is beyond all question a utilization of the tax-established and tax-supported public school system to aid religious groups to spread their faith. And it falls squarely under the ban of the First Amendment (made applicable to the States by the Fourteenth) as we interpreted it in Everson v. Board of Education, 330 U.S. 1. * * *

* * *

Here not only are the State's tax-supported public school buildings used for the dissemination of religious doctrines. The State also affords sectarian groups an invaluable aid in that it helps to provide pupils for their religious classes through use of the State's compulsory public school machinery. This is not separation of Church and State.

The cause is reversed and remanded to the State Supreme Court for proceedings not inconsistent with this opinion.

Reversed and remanded.

Mr. Justice Frankfurter delivered the following opinion, in which Mr. Justice Jackson, Mr. Justice Rutledge and Mr. Justice Burton join.

* * *

We do not consider, as indeed we could not, school programs not before us which, though colloquially characterized as "released time," present situations differing in aspects that may well be constitutionally crucial. Different forms which "released time" has taken during more than thirty years of growth include programs which, like that before us, could not withstand the test of the Constitution; others may be found unexceptionable. We do not now attempt to weigh in the Constitutional scale every separate detail or various combination of factors which may establish a valid "released time" program. We find that the basic Constitutional principle of absolute Separation was violated when the State of Illinois, speaking through its Supreme Court, sustained the school authorities of Champaign in sponsoring and effectively furthering religious beliefs by its educational arrangement.

* * *

Mr. Justice Jackson, concurring. [Omitted.]

Mr. Justice Reed, dissenting.

* * *

* * * I find it difficult to extract from the opinions any conclusion as to what it is in the Champaign plan that is unconstitutional. Is it the use of school buildings for religious instruction; the release of pupils by the schools for religious instruction during school hours; the so-called assistance by teachers in handing out the request cards to pupils, in keeping lists of them for release and records of their attendance; or the action of the principals in arranging an opportunity for the classes and the appearance of the Council's instructors? None of the reversing opinions say whether the purpose of the Champaign plan for religious instruction during school hours is unconstitutional or whether it is some ingredient used in or omitted from the formula that makes the plan unconstitutional.

* * *

Mr. Jefferson, as one of the founders of the University of Virginia, a school which from its establishment in 1819 has been wholly governed, managed and controlled by the State of Virginia, was faced with the same problem that is before this Court today: the question of the constitutional limitation upon religious education in public schools. In his annual report as Rector, to the President and Directors of the Literary Fund, dated October 7, 1822, approved by the Visitors of the University of whom Mr. Madison was one, Mr. Jefferson set forth his views at some length. These suggestions of Mr. Jefferson were adopted and ch. II, § 1, of the Regulations of the University of October 4, 1824, provided that:

> "Should the religious sects of this State, or any of them, according to the invitation held out to them, establish within, or adjacent to, the precincts of the University, schools for instruction in the religion of their sect, the students of the University will be free, and expected to attend religious worship at the establishment of their respective sects, in the

morning, and in time to meet their school in the University at its stated hour."

Thus, the "wall of separation between church and State" that Mr. Jefferson built at the University which he founded did not exclude religious education from that school. The difference between the generality of his statements on the separation of church and state and the specificity of his conclusions on education are considerable. A rule of law should not be drawn from a figure of speech.

* * *

* * * Devotion to the great principle of religious liberty should not lead us into a rigid interpretation of the constitutional guarantee that conflicts with accepted habits of our people. This is an instance where, for me, the history of past practices is determinative of the meaning of a constitutional clause, not a decorous introduction to the study of its text. The judgment should be affirmed.

ZORACH v. CLAUSON

Supreme Court of the United States, 1952.
343 U.S. 306, 72 S.Ct. 679, 96 L.Ed. 954.

Mr. Justice Douglas delivered the opinion of the Court.

New York City has a program which permits its public schools to release students during the school day so that they may leave the school buildings and school grounds and go to religious centers for religious instruction or devotional exercises. A student is released on written request of his parents. Those not released stay in the classrooms. The churches make weekly reports to the schools, sending a list of children who have been released from public school but who have not reported for religious instruction.

This "released time" program involves neither religious instruction in public school classrooms nor the expenditure of public funds. All costs, including the application blanks, are paid by the religious organizations. The case is therefore unlike McCollum v. Board of Education, 333 U.S. 203, which involved a "released time" program from Illinois. In that case the classrooms were turned over to religious instructors. We accordingly held that the program violated the First Amendment which (by reason of the Fourteenth Amendment) prohibits the states from establishing religion or prohibiting its free exercise.

Appellants, who are taxpayers and residents of New York City and whose children attend its public schools, challenge the present law, contending it is in essence not different from the one involved in the *McCollum* case. Their argument, stated elaborately in various ways, reduces itself to this: the weight and influence of the school is put behind a program for religious instruction; public school teachers police it, keeping tab on students who are released; the classroom activities come to a halt while the students who are released for religious instruction are on leave; the school is a crutch on which the churches are leaning for support in their religious training; without the cooperation of the schools this "released time" program, like the one in the *McCollum* case, would be futile and ineffective. The New York Court of Appeals sustained the law against this claim of unconstitutionality. * * * The case is here on appeal. * * *

* * *

There is a suggestion that the system involves the use of coercion to get public school students into religious classrooms. There is no evidence in the record before us that supports that conclusion.[6] The present record indeed tells us that the school authorities are neutral in this regard and do no more than release students whose parents so request. If in fact coercion were used, if it were established that any one or more teachers were using their office to persuade or force students to take the religious instruction, a wholly different case would be presented. Hence we put aside that claim of coercion both as respects the "free exercise" of religion and "an establishment of religion" within the meaning of the First Amendment.

Moreover, apart from that claim of coercion, we do not see how New York by this type of "released time" program has made a law respecting an establishment of religion within the meaning of the First Amendment. * * *

* * *

We are a religious people whose institutions presuppose a Supreme Being. We guarantee the freedom to worship as one chooses. We make room for as wide a variety of beliefs and creeds as the spiritual needs of man deem necessary. We sponsor an attitude on the part of government that shows no partiality to any one group and that lets each flourish according to the zeal of its adherents and the appeal of its dogma. When the state encourages religious instruction or cooperates with religious authorities by adjusting the schedule of public events to sectarian needs, it follows the best of our traditions. For it then respects the religious nature of our people and accommodates the public service to their spiritual needs. To hold that it may not would be to find in the Constitution a requirement that the government show a callous indifference to religious groups. That would be preferring those who believe in no religion over those who do believe. Government may not finance religious groups nor undertake religious instruction nor blend secular and sectarian education nor use secular institutions to force one or some religion on any person. But we find no constitutional requirement which makes it necessary for government to be hostile to religion and to throw its weight against efforts to widen the effective scope of religious influence. The government must be neutral when it comes to competition between sects. It may not thrust any sect on any person. It may not make a religious observance compulsory. It may not coerce anyone to attend church, to observe a religious holiday, or to take religious instruction. But it can close its doors or suspend its operations as to those who want to repair to their

---

6. Nor is there any indication that the public schools enforce attendance at religious schools by punishing absentees from the released time programs for truancy.

religious sanctuary for worship or instruction. No more than that is undertaken here.

* * *

Affirmed.

MR. JUSTICE BLACK, dissenting.

* * *

I see no significant difference between the invalid Illinois system and that of New York here sustained. * * *

* * *

Difficulty of decision in the hypothetical situations mentioned by the Court, but not now before us, should not confuse the issues in this case. Here the sole question is whether New York can use its compulsory education laws to help religious sects get attendants presumably too unenthusiastic to go unless moved to do so by the pressure of this state machinery. That this is the plan, purpose, design and consequence of the New York program cannot be denied. The state thus makes religious sects beneficiaries of its power to compel children to attend secular schools. Any use of such coercive power by the state to help or hinder some religious sects or to prefer all religious sects over nonbelievers or vice versa is just what I think the First Amendment forbids. In considering whether a state has entered this forbidden field the question is not whether it has entered too far but whether it has entered at all. New York is manipulating its compulsory education laws to help religious sects get pupils. This is not separation but combination of Church and State.

The Court's validation of the New York system rests in part on its statement that Americans are "a religious people whose institutions presuppose a Supreme Being." * * * It was precisely because Eighteenth Century Americans were a religious people divided into many fighting sects that we were given the constitutional mandate to keep Church and State completely separate. Colonial history had already shown that, here as elsewhere zealous sectarians entrusted with governmental power to further their causes would sometimes torture, maim and kill those they branded "heretics," "atheists" or "agnostics." The First Amendment was therefore to insure that no one powerful sect or combination of sects could use political or governmental power to punish dissenters whom they could not convert to their faith. Now as then, it is only by wholly isolating the state from the religious sphere and compelling it to be completely neutral, that the freedom of each and every denomination and of all nonbelievers can be maintained. It is this neutrality the Court abandons today when it treats New York's coercive system as a program which merely "encourages religious instruction or cooperates with religious authorities." The abandonment is all the more dangerous to liberty because of the Court's legal exaltation of the orthodox and its derogation of unbelievers.

* * *

Mr. Justice FRANKFURTER, dissenting.

By way of emphasizing my agreement with Mr. Justice Jackson's dissent, I add a few words.

The Court tells us that in the maintenance of its public schools, "[The State government] can close its doors or suspend its operations" so that its citizens may be free for religious devotions or instruction. If that were the issue, it would not rise to the dignity of a constitutional controversy. Of course, a State may provide that the classes in its schools shall be dismissed, for any reason, or no reason, on fixed days, or for special occasions. The essence of this case is that the school system did not "close its doors" and did not "suspend its operations." There is all the difference in the world between letting the children out of school and letting some of them out of school into religious classes. If every one is free to make what use he will of time wholly unconnected from schooling required by law—those who wish sectarian instruction devoting it to that purpose, those who have ethical instruction at home, to that, those who study music, to that—then of course there is no conflict with the Fourteenth Amendment.

The pith of the case is that formalized religious instruction is substituted for other school activity which those who do not participate in the released-time program are compelled to attend. The school system is very much in operation during this kind of released time. If its doors are closed, they are closed upon those students who do not attend the religious instruction, in order to keep them within the school. That is the very thing which raises the constitutional issue. It is not met by disregarding it. Failure to discuss this issue does not take it out of the case.

* * *

Mr. Justice JACKSON, dissenting.

This released time program is founded upon a use of the State's power of coercion, which, for me, determines its unconstitutionality. Stripped to its essentials, the plan has two stages: first, that the State compel each student to yield a large part of his time for public secular education; and, second, that some of it be "released" to him on condition that he devote it to sectarian religious purposes.

No one suggests that the Constitution would permit the State directly to require this "released" time to be spent "under the control of a duly constituted religious body." This program accomplishes that forbidden result by indirection. If public education were taking so much of the pupils' time as to injure the public or the students' welfare by encroaching upon their religious opportunity, simply shortening everyone's school day would facilitate voluntary and optional attendance at Church classes. But that suggestion is rejected upon the ground that if they are made free many students will not go to the Church. Hence, they must be deprived of freedom for this period, with Church attendance put to them as one of the two permissible ways of using it.

The greater effectiveness of this system over voluntary attendance after school hours is due to the truant officer who, if the youngster fails to go to the Church school, dogs him back to the public schoolroom. Here schooling is more or less suspended during the "released time" so the nonreligious attendants will not forge ahead of the churchgoing absentees. But it serves as a temporary jail for a pupil who will not go to Church. It takes more subtlety of mind than I possess to deny that this is governmental constraint in support of religion. It is as unconstitutional, in my view, when exerted by indirection as when exercised forthrightly.

As one whose children, as a matter of free choice, have been sent to privately supported Church schools, I may challenge the Court's suggestion that opposition to this plan can only be antireligious, atheistic, or agnostic. My evangelistic brethren confuse an objection to compulsion with an objection to religion. It is possible to hold a faith with enough confidence to believe that what should be rendered to God does not need to be decided and collected by Caesar.

* * *

ENGEL v. VITALE
Supreme Court of the United States, 1962.
370 U.S. 421, 82 S.Ct. 1261, 8 L.Ed.2d 601.

Mr. Justice Black delivered the opinion of the Court.

The respondent Board of Education of Union Free School District No. 9, New Hyde Park, New York, acting in its official capacity under state law, directed the School District's principal to cause the following prayer to be said aloud by each class in the presence of a teacher at the beginning of each school day:

> "Almighty God, we acknowledge our dependence upon Thee, and we beg Thy blessings upon us, our parents, our teachers and our Country."

This daily procedure was adopted on the recommendation of the State Board of Regents, a governmental agency created by the State Constitution to which the New York Legislature has granted broad supervisory, executive, and legislative powers over the State's public school system. These state officials composed the prayer which they recommended and published as a part of their "Statement on Moral and Spiritual Training in the Schools," saying: "We believe that this Statement will be subscribed to by all men and women of good will, and we call upon all of them to aid in giving life to our program."

Shortly after the practice of reciting the Regents' prayer was adopted by the School District, the parents of ten pupils brought this action in a New York State Court insisting that use of this official prayer in the public schools was contrary to the beliefs, religions, or religious practices of both themselves and their children. * * * The New York Court of Appeals, over the dissents of Judges Dye and Fuld, sustained an order of the lower state courts which had upheld the power of New York to use the Regents' prayer as a part of the daily procedures of its public schools so long as the schools did not compel any pupil to join in the prayer over his or his parents' objection. We granted certiorari to review this important decision involving rights protected by the First and Fourteenth Amendments.

We think that by using its public school system to encourage recitation of the Regents' prayer, the State of New York has adopted a practice wholly inconsistent with the Establishment Clause. There can, of course, be no doubt that New York's program of daily classroom invocation of God's blessings as prescribed in the Regents' prayer is a religious activity. It is a solemn avowal of divine faith and supplication for the blessings of the Almighty. * * *

The petitioners contend among other things that the state laws requiring or permitting use of the Regents' prayer must be struck down as a violation of the Establishment Clause because that prayer was composed by governmental officials as a part of a governmental program to further religious beliefs. For this reason, petitioners argue, the State's use of the Regents' prayer in its public school system breaches the constitutional wall of separation between Church and State. We agree with that contention since we think that the constitutional prohibition against laws respecting an establishment of religion must at least mean that in this country it is no part of the business of government to compose official prayers for any group of the American people to recite as a part of a religious program carried on by government.

It is a matter of history that this very practice of establishing governmentally composed prayers for religious services was one of the reasons which caused many of our early colonists to leave England and seek religious freedom in America. * * *

It is an unfortunate fact of history that when some of the very groups which had most strenuously opposed the established Church of England found themselves sufficiently in control of colonial governments in this country to write their own prayers into law, they passed laws making their own religion the official religion of their respective colonies. Indeed, as late as the time of the Revolutionary War, there were established churches in at least eight of the thirteen former colonies and established religions in at least four of the other five. But the successful Revolution against English political domination was shortly followed by intense opposition to the practice of establishing religion by law. This opposition crystallized rapidly into an effective political force in Virginia where the minority religious groups such as Presbyterians, Lutherans, Quakers and Baptists had gained such strength that the adherents to the established Episcopal Church were actually a minority themselves. In 1785–1786, those opposed to the established Church, led by James Madison and Thomas Jefferson, who, though themselves not members of any of these dissenting religious groups, opposed all religious establishments by law on grounds of principle, obtained the enactment of the famous "Virginia Bill for Religious Liberty" by which all religious groups were placed on an equal footing so far as the State was concerned. * * *

By the time of the adoption of the Constitution, our history shows that there was a widespread awareness among many Americans of the dangers of a union of Church and State. * * * The First Amendment was added to the Constitution to stand as a guarantee that neither the power nor the prestige of the Federal Government would be used to control, support or influence the kinds of prayer the American people can say—that the people's religions must not be subjected to the pressures of government for change each time a new political administration is elected to office. Under that Amendment's prohibition against governmental establishment of religion, as reinforced by the provisions of the Fourteenth Amendment, government in this country, be it state or federal, is without power to prescribe by law any particular form of prayer which is to be used as an official prayer in carrying on any program of governmentally sponsored religious activity.

There can be no doubt that New York's state prayer program officially establishes the religious beliefs embodied in the Regents' prayer. The respondents' argument to the contrary, which is largely based upon the contention that the Regents' prayer is "non-denominational" and the fact that the program, as modified and approved by state courts, does not require all pupils to recite the prayer but permits those who wish to do so to remain silent or be excused from the room, ignores the essential nature of the program's constitutional defects. Neither the fact that the prayer may be denominationally neutral nor the fact that its observance on the part of the students is voluntary can serve to free it from the limitations of the Establishment Clause, as it might from the Free Exercise Clause, of the First Amendment, both of which are operative against the States by virtue of the Fourteenth Amendment. Although these two clauses may in certain instances overlap, they forbid two quite different kinds of governmental encroachment upon religious freedom. The Establishment Clause, unlike the Free Exercise Clause, does not depend upon any showing of direct governmental compulsion and is violated by the enactment of laws which establish an official religion whether those laws operate directly to coerce nonobserving individuals or not. This is not to say, of course, that laws officially prescribing a particular form of religious worship do not involve coercion of such individuals. When the power, prestige and financial support of government is placed behind a particular religious belief, the indirect coercive pressure upon religious minorities to conform to the prevailing officially approved religion is plain. But the purposes underlying the Establishment Clause go much further than that. Its first and most immediate purpose rested on the belief that a union of government and religion tends to destroy government and to degrade religion. The history of governmentally established religion, both in England and in this country, showed that whenever government had allied itself with one particular form of religion, the inevitable result had been that it had incurred the hatred, disrespect and even contempt of those who held contrary beliefs. That same history showed that many people had lost their respect for any religion that had relied upon the support of government to spread its faith. The

Establishment Clause thus stands as an expression of principle on the part of the Founders of our Constitution that religion is too personal, too sacred, too holy, to permit its "unhallowed perversion" by a civil magistrate.[15] * * *

It is true that New York's establishment of its Regents' prayer as an officially approved religious doctrine of that State does not amount to a total establishment of one particular religious sect to the exclusion of all others—that, indeed, the governmental endorsement of that prayer seems relatively insignificant when compared to the governmental encroachments upon religion which were commonplace 200 years ago. To those who may subscribe to the view that because the Regents' official prayer is so brief and general there can be no danger to religious freedom in its governmental establishment, however, it may be appropriate to say in the words of James Madison, the author of the First Amendment:

> "[It] is proper to take alarm at the first experiment on our liberties. * * * Who does not see that the same authority which can establish Christianity, in exclusion of all other Religions, may establish with the same ease any particular sect of Christians, in exclusion of all other Sects? That the same authority which can force a citizen to contribute three pence only of his property for the support of any one establishment, may force him to conform to any other establishment in all cases whatsoever?"

The judgment of the Court of Appeals of New York is reversed and the cause remanded for further proceedings not inconsistent with this opinion.

Reversed and remanded.

MR. JUSTICE FRANKFURTER took no part in the decision of this case.

MR. JUSTICE WHITE took no part in the consideration or decision of this case.

MR. JUSTICE DOUGLAS, concurring.

It is customary in deciding a constitutional question to treat it in its narrowest form. Yet at times the setting of the question gives it a form and content which no abstract treatment could give. The point for decision is whether the Government can constitutionally finance a religious exercise. Our system at the federal and state levels is presently honeycombed with such financing. Nevertheless, I think it is an unconstitutional undertaking whatever form it takes.

First, a word as to what this case does not involve.

Plainly, our Bill of Rights would not permit a State or the Federal Government to adopt an official prayer and penalize anyone who would not utter it. This, however, is not that case, for there is no element of

---

15. Memorial and Remonstrance against Religious Assessments, II Writings of Madison, at 187.

compulsion or coercion in New York's regulation requiring that public schools be opened each day with the following prayer:

> "Almighty God, we acknowledge our dependence upon Thee, and we beg Thy blessings upon us, our parents, our teachers and our Country."

* * * No student, however, is compelled to take part. The respondents have adopted a regulation which provides that "Neither teachers nor any school authority shall comment on participation or non-participation * * * nor suggest or request that any posture or language be used or dress be worn or be not used or not worn." Provision is also made for excusing children, upon written request of a parent or guardian, from the saying of the prayer or from the room in which the prayer is said. A letter implementing and explaining this regulation has been sent to each taxpayer and parent in the school district. As I read this regulation, a child is free to stand or not stand, to recite or not recite, without fear of reprisal or even comment by the teacher or any other school official.

In short, the only one who need utter the prayer is the teacher; and no teacher is complaining of it. * * *

* * *

The question presented by this case is therefore an extremely narrow one. It is whether New York oversteps the bounds when it finances a religious exercise.

What New York does on the opening of its public schools is what we do when we open court. Our Crier has from the beginning announced the convening of the Court and then added "God save the United States and this Honorable Court." That utterance is a supplication, a prayer in which we, the judges, are free to join, but which we need not recite any more than the students need recite the New York prayer.

What New York does on the opening of its public schools is what each House of Congress does at the opening of each day's business. Reverend Frederick B. Harris is Chaplain of the Senate; Reverend Bernard Braskamp is Chaplain of the House. Guest chaplains of various denominations also officiate.

In New York the teacher who leads in prayer is on the public payroll; and the time she takes seems minuscule as compared with the salaries appropriated by state legislatures and Congress for chaplains to conduct prayers in the legislative halls. Only a bare fraction of the teacher's time is given to reciting this short 22-word prayer, about the same amount of time that our Crier spends announcing the opening of our sessions and offering a prayer for this Court. Yet for me the principle is the same, no matter how briefly the prayer is said, for in each of the instances given the person praying is a public official on the public payroll, performing a religious exercise in a governmental institution.[6] * * *

6. The fact that taxpayers do not have standing in the federal courts to raise the

* * *

MR. JUSTICE STEWART, dissenting.

A local school board in New York has provided that those pupils who wish to do so may join in a brief prayer at the beginning of each school day, acknowledging their dependence upon God and asking His blessing upon them and upon their parents, their teachers, and their country. The Court today decides that in permitting this brief nondenominational prayer the school board has violated the Constitution of the United States. I think this decision is wrong.

The Court does not hold, nor could it, that New York has interfered with the free exercise of anybody's religion. For the state courts have made clear that those who object to reciting the prayer must be entirely free of any compulsion to do so, including any "embarrassments and pressures." Cf. West Virginia State Board of Education v. Barnette, 319 U.S. 624. But the Court says that in permitting school children to say this simple prayer, the New York authorities have established "an official religion."

With all respect, I think the Court has misapplied a great constitutional principle. I cannot see how an "official religion" is established by letting those who want to say a prayer say it. On the contrary, I think that to deny the wish of these school children to join in reciting this prayer is to deny them the opportunity of sharing in the spiritual heritage of our Nation.

* * *

At the opening of each day's Session of this Court we stand, while one of our officials invokes the protection of God. Since the days of John Marshall our Crier has said, "God save the United States and this Honorable Court." Both the Senate and the House of Representatives open their daily Sessions with prayer. Each of our Presidents, from George Washington to John F. Kennedy, has upon assuming his Office asked the protection and help of God.

* * * In 1954 Congress added a phrase to the Pledge of Allegiance to the Flag so that it now contains the words "one Nation under God, indivisible, with liberty and justice for all." In 1952 Congress enacted legislation calling upon the President each year to proclaim a National Day of Prayer. Since 1865 the words "IN GOD WE TRUST" have been impressed on our coins.

Countless similar examples could be listed, but there is no need to belabor the obvious.[9] It was all summed up by this Court just ten years

issue (Frothingham v. Mellon, 262 U.S. 447) is of course no justification for drawing a line between what is done in New York on the one hand and on the other what we do and what Congress does in this matter of prayer.

9. I am at a loss to understand the Court's unsupported *ipse dixit* that these official expressions of religious faith in and reliance upon a Supreme Being "bear no true resemblance to the unquestioned religious exercise that the State of New York has sponsored in this instance." * * *. I can hardly think that the Court means to say that the First Amendment imposes a lesser restriction upon the Federal Government than does the Fourteenth Amendment upon the States. Or is the Court suggesting that the Constitution permits judges and Congressmen and Presidents to

ago in a single sentence: "We are a religious people whose institutions presuppose a Supreme Being." Zorach v. Clauson, 343 U.S. 306, 313.

I do not believe that this Court, or the Congress, or the President has by the actions and practices I have mentioned established an "official religion" in violation of the Constitution. And I do not believe the State of New York has done so in this case. What each has done has been to recognize and to follow the deeply entrenched and highly cherished spiritual traditions of our Nation—traditions which come down to us from those who almost two hundred years ago avowed their "firm Reliance on the Protection of divine Providence" when they proclaimed the freedom and independence of this brave new world.

I dissent.

B. The General Test Refined

SCHOOL DISTRICT OF ABINGTON TP. v. SCHEMPP
Supreme Court of the United States, 1963.
374 U.S. 203, 83 S.Ct. 1560, 10 L.Ed.2d 844.

MR. JUSTICE BLACK delivered the opinion of the Court.

Once again we are called upon to consider the scope of the provision of the First Amendment to the United States Constitution which declares that "Congress shall make no law respecting an establishment of religion, or prohibiting the free exercise thereof. * * * " These companion cases present the issues in the context of state action requiring that schools begin each day with readings from the Bible. * * *

I.

* * * The Commonwealth of Pennsylvania by law, * * * requires that "At least ten verses from the Holy Bible shall be read, without comment, at the opening of each public school on each school day. Any child shall be excused from such Bible reading, or attending such Bible reading, upon the written request of his parent or guardian." The Schempp family, husband and wife and two of their three children, brought suit to enjoin enforcement of the statute, contending that their rights under the Fourteenth Amendment to the Constitution of the United States are, have been, and will continue to be violated unless this statute be declared unconstitutional as violative of these provisions of the First Amendment. They sought to enjoin the appellant school district, wherein the Schempp children attend school, and its officers and the Superintendent of Public Instruction of the Commonwealth from continuing to conduct such readings and recitation of the Lord's Prayer in the public schools of the district pursuant to the statute. * * *

* * *

join in prayer, but prohibits school children from doing so?

On each school day at the Abington Senior High School between 8:15 and 8:30 a.m., while the pupils are attending their home rooms or advisory sections, opening exercises are conducted pursuant to the statute. The exercises are broadcast into each room in the school building through an intercommunications system and are conducted under the supervision of a teacher by students attending the school's radio and television workshop. Selected students from this course gather each morning in the school's workshop studio for the exercises, which include readings by one of the students of 10 verses of the Holy Bible, broadcast to each room in the building. This is followed by the recitation of the Lord's Prayer, likewise over the intercommunications system, but also by the students in the various classrooms, who are asked to stand and join in repeating the prayer in unison. The exercises are closed with the flag salute and such pertinent announcements as are of interest to the students. Participation in the opening exercises, as directed by the statute, is voluntary. The student reading the verses from the Bible may select the passages and read from any version he chooses, although the only copies furnished by the school are the King James version, copies of which were circulated to each teacher by the school district. During the period in which the exercises have been conducted the King James, the Douay and the Revised Standard versions of the Bible have been used, as well as the Jewish Holy Scriptures. There are no prefatory statements, no questions asked or solicited, no comments or explanations made and no interpretations given at or during the exercises. The students and parents are advised that the student may absent himself from the classroom or, should he elect to remain, not participate in the exercises.

It appears from the record that in schools not having an intercommunications system the Bible reading and the recitation of the Lord's Prayer were conducted by the home-room teacher,[2] who chose the text of the verses and read them herself or had students read them in rotation or by volunteers. This was followed by a standing recitation of the Lord's Prayer, together with the Pledge of Allegiance to the Flag by the class in unison and a closing announcement of routine school items of interest.

At the first trial Edward Schempp and the children testified as to specific religious doctrines purveyed by a literal reading of the Bible "which were contrary to the religious beliefs which they held and to their familial teaching." * * * Edward Schempp testified at the second trial that he had considered having Roger and Donna excused from attendance at the exercises but decided against it for several reasons, including his belief that the children's relationships with their teachers and classmates would be adversely affected.

* * *

2. The statute as amended imposes no penalty upon a teacher refusing to obey its mandate. However, it remains to be seen whether one refusing could have his contract of employment terminated for "wilful violation of the school laws." 24 Pa.Stat. (Supp.1960) § 11–1122.

The trial court, in striking down the practices and the statute requiring them, made specific findings of fact that the children's attendance at Abington Senior High School is compulsory and that the practice of reading 10 verses from the Bible is also compelled by law. It also found that:

> "The reading of the verses, even without comment, possesses a devotional and religious character and constitutes in effect a religious observance. The devotional and religious nature of the morning exercises is made all the more apparent by the fact that the Bible reading is followed immediately by a recital in unison by the pupils of the Lord's Prayer. The fact that some pupils, or theoretically all pupils, might be excused from attendance at the exercises does not mitigate the obligatory nature of the ceremony for * * * Section 1516 * * * unequivocally requires the exercises to be held every school day in every school in the Commonwealth. The exercises are held in the school buildings and perforce are conducted by and under the authority of the local school authorities and during school sessions. Since the statute requires the reading of the 'Holy Bible,' a Christian document, the practice * * * prefers the Christian religion. The record demonstrates that it was the intention of * * * the Commonwealth * * * to introduce a religious ceremony into the public schools of the Commonwealth." * * *.

* * *

The wholesome "neutrality" of which this Court's cases speak * * * stems from a recognition of the teachings of history that powerful sects or groups might bring about a fusion of governmental and religious functions or a concert or dependency of one upon the other to the end that official support of the State or Federal Government would be placed behind the tenets of one or of all orthodoxies. This the Establishment Clause prohibits. And a further reason for neutrality is found in the Free Exercise Clause, which recognizes the value of religious training, teaching and observance and, more particularly, the right of every person to freely choose his own course with reference thereto, free of any compulsion from the state. This the Free Exercise Clause guarantees. Thus, as we have seen, the two clauses may overlap. As we have indicated, the Establishment Clause has been directly considered by this Court eight times in the past score of years and, with only one Justice dissenting on the point, it has consistently held that the clause withdrew all legislative power respecting religious belief or the expression thereof. The test may be stated as follows: what are the purpose and the primary effect of the enactment? If either is the advancement or inhibition of religion then the enactment exceeds the scope of legislative power as circumscribed by the Constitution. That is to say that to withstand the strictures of the Establishment Clause there must be a secular legislative purpose and a primary effect that neither advances nor inhibits religion. *Everson v. Board of Education, supra; McGowan v. Maryland, supra,* at 442. The Free Exercise Clause, likewise considered many times here, withdraws from legislative power, state and federal, the exertion of any restraint on the free exercise of religion. Its purpose is to secure religious liberty in the individual by prohibiting any invasions thereof by civil authority. Hence it is necessary in a free exercise case for one to show the coercive effect of the enactment as it operates against him in the practice of his religion. The distinction between the two clauses is apparent—a violation of the Free Exercise Clause is predicated on coercion while the Establishment Clause violation need not be so attended.

Applying the Establishment Clause principles to the cases at bar we find that the States are requiring the selection and reading at the opening of the school day of verses from the Holy Bible and the recitation of the Lord's Prayer by the students in unison. These exercises are prescribed as part of the curricular activities of students who are required by law to attend school. They are held in the school buildings under the supervision and with the participation of teachers employed in those schools. None of these factors, other than compulsory school attendance, was present in the program upheld in *Zorach v. Clauson*. The trial court in No. 142 has found that such an opening exercise is a religious ceremony and was intended by the State to be so. We agree with the trial court's finding as to the religious character of the exercises. Given that finding, the exercises and the law requiring them are in violation of the Establishment Clause.

There is no such specific finding as to the religious character of the exercises in No. 119, and the State contends (as does the State in No. 142) that the program is an effort to extend its benefits to all public school children without regard to their religious belief. Included within its secular purposes, it says, are the promotion of moral values, the contradiction to the materialistic trends of our times, the perpetuation of our institutions and the teaching of literature. The case came up on demurrer, of course, to a petition which alleged that the uniform practice under the rule had been to read from the King James version of the Bible and that the exercise was sectarian. The short answer, therefore, is that the religious character of the exercise was admitted by the State. But even if its purpose is not strictly religious, it is sought to be accomplished through readings, without comment, from the Bible. Surely the place of the Bible as an instrument of religion cannot be gainsaid, and the State's recognition of the pervading religious character of the ceremony is evident from the rule's specific permission of the alternative use of the Catholic Douay version as well as the recent amendment permitting nonattendance at the exercises. None of these factors is consistent with the contention that the Bible is here used either as an instrument for nonreligious moral inspiration or as a reference for the teaching of secular subjects.

The conclusion follows that in both cases the laws require religious exercises and such exercises are being conducted in direct violation of the rights of the appellees and petitioners.[9] Nor are these required

---

9. It goes without saying that the laws and practices involved here can be challenged only by persons having standing to complain. But the requirements for standing to challenge state action under the Establishment Clause, unlike those relat-

exercises mitigated by the fact that individual students may absent themselves upon parental request, for that fact furnishes no defense to a claim of unconstitutionality under the Establishment Clause. See *Engel v. Vitale, supra,* at 430. Further, it is no defense to urge that the religious practices here may be relatively minor encroachments on the First Amendment. The breach of neutrality that is today a trickling stream may all too soon become a raging torrent and, in the words of Madison, "it is proper to take alarm at the first experiment on our liberties." * * *.

It is insisted that unless these religious exercises are permitted a "religion of secularism" is established in the schools. We agree of course that the State may not establish a "religion of secularism" in the sense of affirmatively opposing or showing hostility to religion, thus "preferring those who believe in no religion over those who do believe." *Zorach v. Clauson, supra,* at 314. We do not agree, however, that this decision in any sense has that effect. In addition, it might well be said that one's education is not complete without a study of comparative religion or the history of religion and its relationship to the advancement of civilization. It certainly may be said that the Bible is worthy of study for its literary and historic qualities. Nothing we have said here indicates that such study of the Bible or of religion, when presented objectively as part of a secular program of education, may not be effected consistently with the First Amendment. But the exercises here do not fall into those categories. They are religious exercises, required by the States in violation of the command of the First Amendment that the Government maintain strict neutrality, neither aiding nor opposing religion.

Finally, we cannot accept that the concept of neutrality, which does not permit a State to require a religious exercise even with the consent of the majority of those affected, collides with the majority's right to free exercise of religion.[10] While the Free Exercise Clause clearly prohibits the use of state action to deny the rights of free exercise to anyone, it has never meant that a majority could use the machinery of the State to practice its beliefs. Such a contention was effectively answered by Mr. Justice Jackson for the Court in West Virginia Board of Education v. Barnette, 319 U.S. 624, 638 (1943):

> "The very purpose of a Bill of Rights was to withdraw certain subjects from the vicissitudes of political controversy, to place them beyond the reach of majorities and officials and to establish them as legal principles to be applied by the courts. One's right to * * * freedom of worship * * * and other fundamental rights may not be submitted to vote; they depend on the outcome of no elections."

ing to the Free Exercise Clause, do not include proof that particular religious freedoms are infringed.

10. We are not of course presented with and therefore do not pass upon a situation such as military service, where the Government regulates the temporal and geographic environment of individuals to a point that, unless it permits voluntary religious services to be conducted with the use of government facilities, military personnel would be unable to engage in the practice of their faiths.

The place of religion in our society is an exalted one, achieved through a long tradition of reliance on the home, the church and the inviolable citadel of the individual heart and mind. We have come to recognize through bitter experience that it is not within the power of government to invade that citadel, whether its purpose or effect be to aid or oppose, to advance or retard. In the relationship between man and religion, the State is firmly committed to a position of neutrality. Though the application of that rule requires interpretation of a delicate sort, the rule itself is clearly and concisely stated in the words of the First Amendment. Applying that rule to the facts of these cases, we affirm the judgment in No. 142. In No. 119, the judgment is reversed and the cause remanded to the Maryland Court of Appeals for further proceedings consistent with this opinion.

It is so ordered.

MR. JUSTICE DOUGLAS, concurring.

I join the opinion of the Court and add a few words in explanation.

While the Free Exercise Clause of the First Amendment is written in terms of what the State may not require of the individual, the Establishment Clause, serving the same goal of individual religious freedom, is written in different terms.

Establishment of a religion can be achieved in several ways. The church and state can be one; the church may control the state or the state may control the church; or the relationship may take one of several possible forms of a working arrangement between the two bodies. Under all of these arrangements the church typically has a place in the state's budget, and church law usually governs such matters as baptism, marriage, divorce and separation, at least for its members and sometimes for the entire body politic. Education, too, is usually high on the priority list of church interests. In the past schools were often made the exclusive responsibility of the church. Today in some state-church countries the state runs the public schools, but compulsory religious exercises are often required of some or all students. Thus, under the agreement Franco made with the Holy See when he came to power in Spain, "The Church regained its place in the national budget. It insists on baptizing all children and has made the catechism obligatory in state schools."

The vice of all such arrangements under the Establishment Clause is that the state is lending its assistance to a church's efforts to gain and keep adherents. Under the First Amendment it is strictly a matter for the individual and his church as to what church he will belong to and how much support, in the way of belief, time, activity or money, he will give to it. * * *

* * *

These regimes violate the Establishment Clause in two different ways. In each case the State is conducting a religious exercise; and, as the Court holds, that cannot be done without violating the "neutrality" required of the State by the balance of power between individual, church and state that has been struck by the First Amendment. But the Establishment Clause is not limited to precluding the State itself from conducting religious exercises. It also forbids the State to employ its facilities or funds in a way that gives any church, or all churches, greater strength in our society than it would have by relying on its members alone. Thus, the present regimes must fall under that clause for the additional reason that public funds, though small in amount, are being used to promote a religious exercise. Through the mechanism of the State, all of the people are being required to finance a religious exercise that only some of the people want and that violates the sensibilities of others.

The most effective way to establish any institution is to finance it; and this truth is reflected in the appeals by church groups for public funds to finance their religious schools. Financing a church either in its strictly religious activities or in its other activities is equally unconstitutional, as I understand the Establishment Clause. Budgets for one activity may be technically separable from budgets for others. But the institution is an inseparable whole, a living organism, which is strengthened in proselytizing when it is strengthened in any department by contributions from other than its own members.

Such contributions may not be made by the State even in a minor degree without violating the Establishment Clause. It is not the amount of public funds expended; as this case illustrates, it is the use to which public funds are put that is controlling. For the First Amendment does not say that some forms of establishment are allowed; it says that "no law respecting an establishment of religion" shall be made. What may not be done directly may not be done indirectly lest the Establishment Clause become a mockery.

MR. JUSTICE BRENNAN, concurring.

* * *

When John Locke ventured in 1689, "I esteem it above all things necessary to distinguish exactly the business of civil government from that of religion and to settle the just bounds that lie between the one and the other," he anticipated the necessity which would be thought by the Framers to require adoption of a First Amendment, but not the difficulty that would be experienced in defining those "just bounds." The fact is that the line which separates the secular from the sectarian in American life is elusive. The difficulty of defining the boundary with precision inheres in a paradox central to our scheme of liberty. While our institutions reflect a firm conviction that we are a religious people, those institutions by solemn constitutional injunction may not officially involve religion in such a way as to prefer, discriminate against, or oppress, a particular sect or religion. Equally the Constitution enjoins those involvements of religious with secular institutions which (a) serve the essentially religious activities of religious institutions; (b) employ the organs of government for essentially religious purposes; or (c) use essentially religious means to serve governmental ends where secular means would suffice. The constitutional mandate expresses a deliberate and considered judgment that such matters are to be left to the conscience of the citizen, and declares as a basic postulate of the relation between the citizen and his government that "the rights of conscience are, in their nature, of peculiar delicacy, and will little bear the gentlest touch of governmental hand * * *."

I join fully in the opinion and the judgment of the Court. I see no escape from the conclusion that the exercises called in question in these two cases violate the constitutional mandate. The reasons we gave only last Term in Engel v. Vitale, 370 U.S. 421, for finding in the New York Regents' prayer an impermissible establishment of religion, compel the same judgment of the practices at bar. The involvement of the secular with the religious is no less intimate here; and it is constitutionally irrelevant that the State has not composed the material for the inspirational exercises presently involved. It should be unnecessary to observe that our holding does not declare that the First Amendment manifests hostility to the practice or teaching of religion, but only applies prohibitions incorporated in the Bill of Rights in recognition of historic needs shared by Church and State alike. While it is my view that not every involvement of religion in public life is unconstitutional, I consider the exercises at bar a form of involvement which clearly violates the Establishment Clause.

The importance of the issue and the deep conviction with which views on both sides are held seem to me to justify detailing at some length my reasons for joining the Court's judgment and opinion.

I.

The First Amendment forbids both the abridgment of the free exercise of religion and the enactment of laws "respecting an establishment of religion." The two clauses, although distinct in their objectives and their applicability, emerged together from a common panorama of history. The inclusion of both restraints upon the power of Congress to legislate concerning religious matters shows unmistakably that the Framers of the First Amendment were not content to rest the protection of religious liberty exclusively upon either clause. "In assuring the free exercise of religion," Mr. Justice Frankfurter has said, "the Framers of the First Amendment were sensitive to the then recent history of those persecutions and impositions of civil disability with which sectarian majorities in virtually all of the Colonies had visited deviation in the matter of conscience. This protection of unpopular creeds, however, was not to be the full extent of the Amendment's guarantee of freedom from governmental intrusion in matters of faith. The battle in Virginia, hardly four years won, where James Madison had led the forces of disestablishment in successful opposition to Patrick Henry's proposed Assessment Bill levying a general tax for the support of Christian teachers, was a vital and compelling memory in 1789." McGowan v. Maryland, 366 U.S. 420, 464–465.

* * *

The exposition by this Court of the religious guarantees of the First Amendment has consistently reflected and reaffirmed the concerns which impelled the Framers to write those guarantees into the Constitution. It would be neither possible nor appropriate to review here the entire course of our decisions on religious questions. There emerge from those decisions, however, three principles of particular relevance to the issue presented by the cases at bar, and some attention to those decisions is therefore appropriate.

First. One line of decisions derives from contests for control of a church property or other internal ecclesiastical disputes. This line has settled the proposition that in order to give effect to the First Amendment's purpose of requiring on the part of all organs of government a strict neutrality toward theological questions, courts should not undertake to decide such questions. * * *

The mandate of judicial neutrality in theological controversies met its severest test in United States v. Ballard, 322 U.S. 78. That decision put in sharp relief certain principles which bear directly upon the questions presented in these cases. Ballard was indicted for fraudulent use of the mails in the dissemination of religious literature. He requested that the trial court submit to the jury the question of the truthfulness of the religious views he championed. The requested charge was refused, and we upheld that refusal, reasoning that the First Amendment foreclosed any judicial inquiry into the truth or falsity of the defendant's religious beliefs. * * *

The dilemma presented by the case was severe. While the alleged truthfulness of *nonreligious* publications could ordinarily have been submitted to the jury, Ballard was deprived of that defense only because the First Amendment forbids governmental inquiry into the verity of religious beliefs. In dissent Mr. Justice Jackson expressed the concern that under this construction of the First Amendment "[prosecutions] of this character easily could degenerate into religious persecution." 322 U.S., at 95. The case shows how elusive is the line which enforces the Amendment's injunction of strict neutrality, while manifesting no official hostility toward religion—a line which must be considered in the cases now before us. * * *

Second. It is only recently that our decisions have dealt with the question whether issues arising under the Establishment Clause may be isolated from problems implicating the Free Exercise Clause. Everson v. Board of Education, 330 U.S. 1, is in my view the first of our decisions which treats a problem of asserted unconstitutional involvement as raising questions purely under the Establishment Clause. A scrutiny of several earlier decisions said by some to have etched the contours of the clause shows that such cases neither raised nor decided any constitutional issues under the First Amendment. * * *

* * *

Third. It is true, as the Court says, that the "two clauses [Establishment and Free Exercise] may oerlap." Because of the overlap, however, our decisions under the Free Exercise Clause bear considerable relevance to the problem now before us, and should be briefly reviewed. The early free exercise cases generally involved the objections of religious minorities to the application to them of general nonreligious legislation governing conduct. * * *

* * *

The absorption of the Establishment Clause has, however, come later and by a route less easily charted. It has been suggested, with some support in history, that absorption of the First Amendment's ban against congressional legislation "respecting an establishment of religion" is conceptually impossible because the Framers meant the Establishment Clause also to foreclose any attempt by Congress to disestablish the existing official state churches. Whether or not such was the understanding of the Framers and whether such a purpose would have inhibited the absorption of the Establishment Clause at the threshold of the Nineteenth Century are questions not dispositive of our present inquiry. For it is clear on the record of history that the last of the formal state establishments was dissolved more than three decades before the Fourteenth Amendment was ratified, and thus the problem of protecting official state churches from federal encroachments could hardly have been any concern of those who framed the post-Civil War Amendments. Any such objective of the First Amendment, having become historical anachronism by 1868, cannot be thought to have deterred the absorption of the Establishment Clause to any greater degree than it would, for example, have deterred the absorption of the Free Exercise Clause. That no organ of the Federal Government possessed in 1791 any power to restrain the interference of the States in religious matters is indisputable. See Permoli v. New Orleans, 3 How. 589. It is equally plain, on the other hand, that the Fourteenth Amendment created a panoply of new federal rights for the protection of citizens of the various States. And among those rights was freedom from such state governmental involvement in the affairs of religion as the Establishment Clause had originally foreclosed on the part of Congress.

It has also been suggested that the "liberty" guaranteed by the Fourteenth Amendment logically cannot absorb the Establishment Clause because that clause is not one of the provisions of the Bill of Rights which in terms protects a "freedom" of the individual. See Corwin, A Constitution of Powers in a Secular State (1951), 113–116. The fallacy in this contention, I think, is that it underestimates the role of the Establishment Clause as a coguarantor, with the Free Exercise Clause, of religious liberty. The Framers did not entrust the liberty of religious beliefs to either clause alone. The Free Exercise Clause "was not to be the full extent of the Amendment's guarantee of freedom from governmental intrusion in matters of faith." *McGowan v. Maryland, supra,* at 464 (opinion of Frankfurter, J.).

Finally, it has been contended that absorption of the Establishment Clause is precluded by the absence of any intention on the part of the Framers of the Fourteenth Amendment to circumscribe the residual powers of the States to aid religious activities and institutions in ways which fell short of formal establishments.[21] That argument relies in

---

21. See Corwin, A Constitution of Powers in a Secular State (1951), 111–114; Fairman and Morrison, Does the Fourteenth Amendment Incorporate the Bill of Rights? 2 Stan.L.Rev. 5 (1949); Meyer, Comment, The Blaine Amendment and the

part upon the express terms of the abortive Blaine Amendment—proposed several years after the adoption of the Fourteenth Amendment—which would have added to the First Amendment a provision that "[no] State shall make any law respecting an establishment of religion. * * * " Such a restriction would have been superfluous, it is said, if the Fourteenth Amendment had already made the Establishment Clause binding upon the States.

The argument proves too much, for the Fourteenth Amendment's protection of the free exercise of religion can hardly be questioned; yet the Blaine Amendment would also have added an explicit protection against state laws abridging that liberty.[22] Even if we assume that the draftsmen of the Fourteenth Amendment saw no immediate connection between its protections against state action infringing personal liberty and the guarantees of the First Amendment, it is certainly too late in the day to suggest that their assumed inattention to the question dilutes the force of these constitutional guarantees in their application to the States. It is enough to conclude that the religious liberty embodied in the Fourteenth Amendment would not be viable if the Constitution were interpreted to forbid only establishments ordained by Congress.[24]

The issue of what particular activities the Establishment Clause forbids the States to undertake is our more immediate concern. In Everson v. Board of Education, 330 U.S. 1, 15–16, a careful study of the relevant history led the Court to the view, consistently recognized in decisions since *Everson*, that the Establishment Clause embodied the Framers' conclusion that government and religion have discrete interests which are mutually best served when each avoids too close a proximity to the other. It is not only the nonbeliever who fears the injection of sectarian doctrines and controversies into the civil policy, but in as high degree it is the devout believer who fears the seculariza-

---

Bill of Rights, 64 Harv.L.Rev. 939 (1951); Howe, Religion and Race in Public Education, 8 Buffalo L.Rev. 242, 245–247 (1959). Cf. Cooley, Principles of Constitutional Law (2d ed. 1891), 213–214. Compare Professor Freund's comment:

"Looking back, it is hard to see how the Court could have done otherwise, how it could have persisted in accepting freedom of contract as a guaranteed liberty without giving equal status to freedom of press and speech, assembly, and religious observance. What does not seem so inevitable is the inclusion within the Fourteenth Amendment of the concept of nonestablishment of religion in the sense of forbidding nondiscriminatory aid to religion, where there is no interference with freedom of religious exercise." Freund, The Supreme Court of the United States (1961), 58–59.

22. The Blaine Amendment, 4 Cong. Rec. 5580, included also a more explicit provision that "no money raised by taxation in any State for the support of public schools or derived from any public fund therefor, nor any public lands devoted thereto, shall ever be under the control of any religious sect or denomination. * * * " The Amendment passed the House but failed to obtain the requisite two-thirds vote in the Senate. See 4 Cong. Rec. 5595. * * *

24. * * *

Compare Thomas M. Cooley's exposition in the year in which the Fourteenth Amendment was ratified:

"Those things which are not lawful under any of the American constitutions may be stated thus:—

"1. Any law respecting an establishment of religion. * * *

"2. Compulsory support, by taxation or otherwise, of religious instruction. Not only is no one denomination to be favored at the expense of the rest, but all support of religious instruction must be entirely voluntary." Cooley, Constitutional Limitations (1st ed. 1868), 469.

tion of a creed which becomes too deeply involved with and dependent upon the government. * * *

* * *

I turn now to the cases before us. The religious nature of the exercises here challenged seems plain. Unless *Engel v. Vitale* is to be overruled, or we are to engage in wholly disingenuous distinction, we cannot sustain these practices. Daily recital of the Lord's Prayer and the reading of passages of Scripture are quite as clearly breaches of the command of the Establishment Clause as was the daily use of the rather bland Regents' Prayer in the New York public schools. Indeed, I would suppose that, if anything, the Lord's Prayer and the Holy Bible are more clearly sectarian, and the present violations of the First Amendment consequently more serious. But the religious exercises challenged in these cases have a long history. * * *

* * *

* * * Indeed, public pressures upon school administrators in many parts of the country would hardly have condoned abandonment of practices to which a century or more of private religious education had accustomed the American people. The controversy centered, in fact, principally about the elimination of plainly sectarian practices and textbooks, and led to the eventual substitution of nonsectarian, though still religious, exercises and materials.[35]

Statutory provision for daily religious exercises is, however, of quite recent origin. At the turn of this century, there was but one State—Massachusetts—which had a law making morning prayer or Bible reading obligatory. Statutes elsewhere either permitted such practices or simply left the question to local option. It was not until after 1910 that 11 more States, within a few years, joined Massachusetts in making one or both exercises compulsory. The Pennsylvania law with which we are concerned in the *Schempp* case, for example, took effect in 1913; and even the Rule of the Baltimore School Board involved in the *Murray* case dates only from 1905. In no State has there ever been a constitutional or statutory prohibition against the recital of prayers or the reading of Scripture, although a number of States have outlawed these practices by judicial decision or administrative order. What is noteworthy about the panoply of state and local regulations from which these cases emerge is the relative recency of the statutory codification of practices which have ancient roots, and the rather small number of States which have ever prescribed compulsory religious exercises in the public schools.

* * *

Almost from the beginning religious exercises in the public schools have been the subject of intense criticism, vigorous debate, and judicial or administrative prohibition. * * *

---

35. See 2 Stokes, Church and State in the United States (1950), 572–579; Greene, Religion and the State: The Making and Testing of an American Tradition (1941), 122–126.

Thus a great deal of controversy over religion in the public schools had preceded the debate over the Blaine Amendment, precipitated by President Grant's insistence that matters of religion should be left "to the family altar, the church, and the private school, supported entirely by private contributions." There was ample precedent, too, for Theodore Roosevelt's declaration that in the interest of "absolutely nonsectarian public schools" it was "not our business to have the Protestant Bible or the Catholic Vulgate or the Talmud read in those schools." The same principle appeared in the message of an Ohio Governor who vetoed a compulsory Bible-reading bill in 1925:

> "It is my belief that religious teaching in our homes, Sunday schools, churches, by the good mothers, fathers, and ministers of Ohio is far preferable to compulsory teaching of religion by the state. The spirit of our federal and state constitutions from the beginning * * * [has] been to leave religious instruction to the discretion of parents."

* * *

* * *

* * * I have previously suggested that *Torcaso* and the *Sunday Law Cases* forbid the use of religious means to achieve secular ends where nonreligious means will suffice. That principle is readily applied to these cases. It has not been shown that readings from the speeches and messages of great Americans, for example, or from the documents of our heritage of liberty, daily recitation of the Pledge of Allegiance, or even the observance of a moment of reverent silence at the opening of class, may not adequately serve the solely secular purposes of the devotional activities without jeopardizing either the religious liberties of any members of the community or the proper degree of separation between the spheres of religion and government. Such substitutes would, I think, be unsatisfactory or inadequate only to the extent that the present activities do in fact serve religious goals. While I do not question the judgment of experienced educators that the challenged practices may well achieve valuable secular ends, it seems to me that the State acts unconstitutionally if it either sets about to attain even indirectly religious ends by religious means, or if it uses religious means to serve secular ends where secular means would suffice.

Second, it is argued that the particular practices involved in the two cases before us are unobjectionable because they prefer no particular sect or sects at the expense of others. Both the Baltimore and Abington procedures permit, for example, the reading of any of several versions of the Bible, and this flexibility is said to ensure neutrality sufficiently to avoid the constitutional prohibition. One answer, which might be dispositive, is that any version of the Bible is inherently sectarian, else there would be no need to offer a system of rotation or alternation of versions in the first place, that is, to allow different sectarian versions to be used on different days. The sectarian character of the Holy Bible has been at the core of the whole controversy over religious practices in the public schools throughout its long and often bitter history. To vary the version as the Abington and Baltimore schools have done may well be less offensive than to read from the King James version every day, as once was the practice. But the result even of this relatively benign procedure is that majority sects are preferred in approximate proportion to their representation in the community and in the student body, while the smaller sects suffer commensurate discrimination. So long as the subject matter of the exercise is sectarian in character, these consequences cannot be avoided.

The argument contains, however, a more basic flaw. There are persons in every community—often deeply devout—to whom any version of the Judaeo–Christian Bible is offensive. * * *

* * *

It has been suggested that a tentative solution to these problems may lie in the fashioning of a "common core" of theology tolerable to all creeds but preferential to none. But as one commentator has recently observed, "[history] is not encouraging to" those who hope to fashion a "common denominator of religion detached from its manifestation in any organized church." Sutherland, Establishment According to *Engel,* 76 Harv.L.Rev. 25, 51 (1962). Thus, the notion of a "common core" litany or supplication offends many deeply devout worshippers who do not find clearly sectarian practices objectionable. Father Gustave Weigel has recently expressed a widely shared view: "The moral code held by each separate religious community can reductively be unified, but the consistent particular believer wants no such reduction." And, as the American Council on Education warned several years ago, "The notion of a common core suggests a watering down of the several faiths to the point where common essentials appear. This might easily lead to a new sect—a public school sect—which would take its place alongside the existing faiths and compete with them." * * *

A third element which is said to absolve the practices involved in these cases from the ban of the religious guarantees of the Constitution is the provision to excuse or exempt students who wish not to participate. Insofar as these practices are claimed to violate the Establishment Clause, I find the answer which the District Court gave after our remand of *Schempp* to be altogether dispositive:

> "The fact that some pupils, or theoretically all pupils, might be excused from attendance at the exercises does not mitigate the obligatory nature of the ceremony. * * * The exercises are held in the school buildings and perforce are conducted by and under the authority of the local school authorities and during school sessions. Since the statute requires the reading of the 'Holy Bible,' a Christian document, the practice, as we said in our first opinion, prefers the Christian religion. The record demonstrates that it was the intention of the General Assembly of the Commonwealth of Pennsylvania to introduce a religious ceremony into the public schools of the Commonwealth." 201 F.Supp., at 819.

Thus the short, and to me sufficient, answer is that the availability of excusal or exemption simply has no relevance to the establishment question, if it is once found that these practices are essentially religious exercises designed at least in part to achieve religious aims through the use of public school facilities during the school day.

The more difficult question, however, is whether the availability of excusal for the dissenting child serves to refute challenges to these practices under the Free Exercise Clause. While it is enough to decide these cases to dispose of the establishment questions, questions of free exercise are so inextricably interwoven into the history and present status of these practices as to justify disposition of this second aspect of the excusal issue. The answer is that the excusal procedure itself necessarily operates in such a way as to infringe the rights of free exercise of those children who wish to be excused. * * * [B]y requiring what is tantamount in the eyes of teachers and schoolmates to a profession of disbelief, or at least of nonconformity, the procedure may well deter those children who do not wish to participate for any reason based upon the dictates of conscience from exercising an indisputably constitutional right to be excused. Thus the excusal provision in its operation subjects them to a cruel dilemma. In consequence, even devout children may well avoid claiming their right and simply continue to participate in exercises distasteful to them because of an understandable reluctance to be stigmatized as atheists or nonconformists simply on the basis of their request.

Such reluctance to seek exemption seems all the more likely in view of the fact that children are disinclined at this age to step out of line or to flout "peer-group norms." Such is the widely held view of experts who have studied the behaviors and attitudes of children. * * * Also apposite is the answer given more than 70 years ago by the Supreme Court of Wisconsin to the argument that an excusal provision saved a public school devotional exercise from constitutional invalidation:

> " * * * the excluded pupil loses caste with his fellows, and is liable to be regarded with aversion, and subjected to reproach and insult. But it is a sufficient refutation of the argument that the practice in question tends to destroy the equality of the pupils which the constitution seeks to establish and protect, and puts a portion of them to serious disadvantage in many ways with respect to the others." State ex rel. Weiss v. District Board of School District No. 8, 76 Wis. 177, 200, 44 N.W. 967, 975.

* * *

To summarize my views concerning the merits of these two cases: The history, the purpose and the operation of the daily prayer recital and Bible reading leave no doubt that these practices standing by themselves constitute an impermissible breach of the Establishment Clause. Such devotional exercises may well serve legitimate nonreligious purposes. To the extent, however, that such purposes are really without religious significance, it has never been demonstrated that secular means would not suffice. Indeed, I would suggest that patriotic or other nonreligious materials might provide adequate substitutes—inadequate only to the extent that the purposes now served are indeed directly or indirectly religious. Under such circumstances, the States may not employ religious means to reach a secular goal unless secular means are wholly unavailing. I therefore agree with the Court that the judgment in *Schempp,* No. 142, must be affirmed, and that in *Murray,* No. 119, must be reversed.

* * *

MR. JUSTICE GOLDBERG, with whom MR. JUSTICE HARLAN joins, concurring.

As is apparent from the opinions filed today, delineation of the constitutionally permissible relationship between religion and government is a most difficult and sensitive task, calling for the careful exercise of both judicial and public judgment and restraint. The considerations which lead the Court today to interdict the clearly religious practices presented in these cases are to me wholly compelling; I have no doubt as to the propriety of the decision and therefore join the opinion and judgment of the Court. The singular sensitivity and concern which surround both the legal and practical judgments involved impel me, however, to add a few words in further explication, while at the same time avoiding repetition of the carefully and ably framed examination of history and authority by my Brethren.

The First Amendment's guarantees, as applied to the States through the Fourteenth Amendment, foreclose not only laws "respecting an establishment of religion" but also those "prohibiting the free exercise thereof." These two proscriptions are to be read together, and in light of the single end which they are designed to serve. The basic purpose of the religion clause of the First Amendment is to promote and assure the fullest possible scope of religious liberty and tolerance for all and to nurture the conditions which secure the best hope of attainment of that end.

The fullest realization of true religious liberty requires that government neither engage in nor compel religious practices, that it effect no favoritism among sects or between religion and nonreligion, and that it work deterrence of no religious belief. * * *

* * *

The practices here involved do not fall within any sensible or acceptable concept of compelled or permitted accommodation and involve the state so significantly and directly in the realm of the sectarian as to give rise to those very divisive influences and inhibitions of freedom which both religion clauses of the First Amendment preclude. The state has ordained and has utilized its facilities to engage in unmistakably religious exercises—the devotional reading and recitation of the Holy Bible—in a manner having substantial and significant import and impact. That it has selected, rather than written, a particular devotional liturgy seems to me without constitutional import. The pervasive religiosity and direct governmental involvement inhering in the prescription of prayer and Bible reading in the public schools, during and as part of the curricular day, involving young impressionable children whose school attendance is statutorily compelled, and utilizing the prestige, power, and influence of school administration, staff, and authority, cannot realistically be termed simply accommodation, and must fall within the interdiction of the First Amendment. I find nothing in the opinion of the Court which says more than this. * * *

Mr. Justice Stewart, dissenting.

I think the records in the two cases before us are so fundamentally deficient as to make impossible an informed or responsible determination of the constitutional issues presented. Specifically, I cannot agree that on these records we can say that the Establishment Clause has necessarily been violated.[1] But I think there exist serious questions under both that provision and the Free Exercise Clause—insofar as each is imbedded in the Fourteenth Amendment—which require the remand of these cases for the taking of additional evidence.

I.

The First Amendment declares that "Congress shall make no law respecting an establishment of religion, or prohibiting the free exercise thereof. * * * " It is, I think, a fallacious oversimplification to regard these two provisions as establishing a single constitutional standard of "separation of church and state," which can be mechanically applied in every case to delineate the required boundaries between government and religion. We err in the first place if we do not recognize, as a matter of history and as a matter of the imperatives of our free society, that religion and government must necessarily interact in countless ways. Secondly, the fact is that while in many contexts the Establishment Clause and the Free Exercise Clause fully complement each other, there are areas in which a doctrinaire reading of the Establishment Clause leads to irreconcilable conflict with the Free Exercise Clause.

A single obvious example should suffice to make the point. Spending federal funds to employ chaplains for the armed forces might be said to violate the Establishment Clause. Yet a lonely soldier stationed at some faraway outpost could surely complain that a government which did not provide him the opportunity for pastoral guidance was affirmatively prohibiting the free exercise of his religion. And such examples could readily be multiplied. The short of the matter is simply that the two relevant clauses of the First Amendment cannot accurately be reflected in a sterile metaphor which by its very nature may distort rather than illumine the problems involved in a particular case. Cf. *Sherbert v. Verner,* * * *.

* * *

It has become accepted that the decision in Pierce v. Society of Sisters, 268 U.S. 510, upholding the right of parents to send their children to nonpublic schools, was ultimately based upon the recognition of the validity of the free exercise claim involved in that situation.

---

1. It is instructive, in this connection, to examine the complaints in the two cases before us. Neither complaint attacks the challenged practices as "establishments." What both allege as the basis for their causes of actions are, rather, violations of religious liberty.

It might be argued here that parents who wanted their children to be exposed to religious influences in school could, under *Pierce,* send their children to private or parochial schools. But the consideration which renders this contention too facile to be determinative has already been recognized by the Court: "Freedom of speech, freedom of the press, freedom of religion are available to all, not merely to those who can pay their own way." Murdock v. Pennsylvania, 319 U.S. 105, 111.

It might also be argued that parents who want their children exposed to religious influences can adequately fulfill that wish off school property and outside school time. With all its surface persuasiveness, however, this argument seriously misconceives the basic constitutional justification for permitting the exercises at issue in these cases. For a compulsory state educational system so structures a child's life that if religious exercises are held to be an impermissible activity in schools, religion is placed at an artificial and state-created disadvantage. Viewed in this light, permission of such exercises for those who want them is necessary if the schools are truly to be neutral in the matter of religion. And a refusal to permit religious exercises thus is seen, not as the realization of state neutrality, but rather as the establishment of a religion of secularism, or at the least, as government support of the beliefs of those who think that religious exercises should be conducted only in private.

What seems to me to be of paramount importance, then, is recognition of the fact that the claim advanced here in favor of Bible reading is sufficiently substantial to make simple reference to the constitutional phrase "establishment of religion" as inadequate an analysis of the cases before us as the ritualistic invocation of the nonconstitutional phrase "separation of church and state." What these cases compel, rather, is an analysis of just what the "neutrality" is which is required by the interplay of the Establishment and Free Exercise Clauses of the First Amendment, as imbedded in the Fourteenth.

IV.

Our decisions make clear that there is no constitutional bar to the use of government property for religious purposes. On the contrary, this Court has consistently held that the discriminatory barring of religious groups from public property is itself a violation of First and Fourteenth Amendment guarantees. Fowler v. Rhode Island, 345 U.S. 67; Niemotko v. Maryland, 340 U.S. 268. A different standard has been applied to public school property, because of the coercive effect which the use by religious sects of a compulsory school system would necessarily have upon the children involved. McCollum v. Board of Education, 333 U.S. 203. But insofar as the *McCollum* decision rests on the Establishment rather than the Free Exercise Clause, it is clear that its effect is limited to religious instruction—to government support of proselytizing activities of religious sects by throwing the weight of secular authority behind the dissemination of religious tenets.

The dangers both to government and to religion inherent in official support of instruction in the tenets of various religious sects are absent in the present cases, which involve only a reading from the Bible unaccompanied by comments which might otherwise constitute instruction. Indeed, since, from all that appears in either record, any teacher who does not wish to do so is free not to participate, it cannot even be contended that some infinitesimal part of the salaries paid by the State are made contingent upon the performance of a religious function.

In the absence of evidence that the legislature or school board intended to prohibit local schools from substituting a different set of readings where parents requested such a change, we should not assume that the provisions before us—as actually administered—may not be construed simply as authorizing religious exercises, nor that the designations may not be treated simply as indications of the promulgating body's view as to the community's preference. We are under a duty to interpret these provisions so as to render them constitutional if reasonably possible. * * * In the *Schempp* case there is evidence which indicates that variations were in fact permitted by the very school there involved, and that further variations were not introduced only because of the absence of requests from parents. And in the *Murray* case the Baltimore rule itself contains a provision permitting another version of the Bible to be substituted for the King James version.

If the provisions are not so construed, I think that their validity under the Establishment Clause would be extremely doubtful, because of the designation of a particular religious book and a denominational prayer. But since, even if the provisions are construed as I believe they must be, I think that the cases before us must be remanded for further evidence on other issues—thus affording the plaintiffs an opportunity to prove that local variations are not in fact permitted—I shall for the balance of this dissenting opinion treat the provisions before us as making the variety and content of the exercises, as well as a choice as to their implementation, matters which ultimately reflect the consensus of each local school community. In the absence of coercion upon those who do not wish to participate—because they hold less strong beliefs, other beliefs, or no beliefs at all—such provisions cannot, in my view, be held to represent the type of support of religion barred by the Establishment Clause. For the only support which such rules provide for religion is the withholding of state hostility—a simple acknowledgment on the part of secular authorities that the Constitution does not require extirpation of all expression of religious belief.

V.

I have said that these provisions authorizing religious exercises are properly to be regarded as measures making possible the free exercise of religion. But it is important to stress that, strictly speaking, what is at issue here is a privilege rather than a right. In other words, the question presented is not whether exercises such as those at issue here are constitutionally compelled, but rather whether they are constitutionally invalid. And that issue, in my view, turns on the question of coercion.

It is clear that the dangers of coercion involved in the holding of religious exercises in a schoolroom differ qualitatively from those presented by the use of similar exercises or affirmations in ceremonies attended by adults. Even as to children, however, the duty laid upon government in connection with religious exercises in the public schools is that of refraining from so structuring the school environment as to put any kind of pressure on a child to participate in those exercises; it is not that of providing an atmosphere in which children are kept scrupulously insulated from any awareness that some of their fellows may want to open the school day with prayer, or of the fact that there exist in our pluralistic society differences of religious belief.

* * *

The governmental neutrality which the First and Fourteenth Amendments require in the cases before us, in other words, is the extension of evenhanded treatment of all who believe, doubt, or disbelieve—a refusal on the part of the State to weight the scales of private choice. In these cases, therefore, what is involved is not state action based on impermissible categories, but rather an attempt by the State to accommodate those differences which the existence in our society of a variety of religious beliefs makes inevitable. The Constitution requires that such efforts be struck down only if they are proven to entail the use of the secular authority of government to coerce a preference among such beliefs.

It may well be, as has been argued to us, that even the supposed benefits to be derived from noncoercive religious exercises in public schools are incommensurate with the administrative problems which they would create. The choice involved, however, is one for each local community and its school board, and not for this Court. For, as I have said, religious exercises are not constitutionally invalid if they simply reflect differences which exist in the society from which the school draws its pupils. They become constitutionally invalid only if their administration places the sanction of secular authority behind one or more particular religious or irreligious beliefs.

* * *

What our Constitution indispensably protects is the freedom of each of us, be he Jew or Agnostic, Christian or Atheist, Buddhist or Freethinker, to believe or disbelieve, to worship or not worship, to pray or keep silent, according to his own conscience, uncoerced and unrestrained by government. It is conceivable that these school boards, or even all school boards, might eventually find it impossible to administer a system of religious exercises during school hours in such a way as to meet this constitutional standard—in such a way as completely to free from any kind of official coercion those who do not affirmatively want to participate.[8] But I think we must not assume that school boards so lack the qualities of inventiveness and good will as to make impossible the achievement of that goal.

I would remand both cases for further hearings.

8. For example, if the record in the *Schempp* case contained proof (rather than mere prophecy) that the timing of morning announcements by the school was such as to handicap children who did not want to listen to the Bible reading, or that the excusal provision was so administered as to carry any overtones of social inferiority, then impermissible coercion would clearly exist.

LEMON v. KURTZMAN
Supreme Court of the United States, 1971.
403 U.S. 602, 91 S.Ct. 2105, 29 L.Ed.2d 745.

MR. CHIEF JUSTICE BURGER delivered the opinion of the Court.

These two appeals raise questions as to Pennsylvania and Rhode Island statutes providing state aid to church-related elementary and secondary schools. Both statutes are challenged as violative of the Establishment and Free Exercise Clauses of the First Amendment and the Due Process Clause of the Fourteenth Amendment.

Pennsylvania has adopted a statutory program that provides financial support to nonpublic elementary and secondary schools by way of reimbursement for the cost of teachers' salaries, textbooks, and instructional materials in specified secular subjects. Rhode Island has adopted a statute under which the State pays directly to teachers in nonpublic elementary schools a supplement of 15% of their annual salary. Under each statute state aid has been given to church-related educational institutions. We hold that both statutes are unconstitutional.

I

The Rhode Island Statute

The Rhode Island Salary Supplement Act was enacted in 1969. It rests on the legislative finding that the quality of education available in nonpublic elementary schools has been jeopardized by the rapidly rising salaries needed to attract competent and dedicated teachers. The Act authorizes state officials to supplement the salaries of teachers of secular subjects in non-public elementary schools by paying directly to a teacher an amount not in excess of 15% of his current annual salary. As supplemented, however, a nonpublic school teacher's salary cannot exceed the maximum paid to teachers in the State's public schools, and the recipient must be certified by the state board of education in substantially the same manner as public school teachers.

In order to be eligible for the Rhode Island salary supplement, the recipient must teach in a nonpublic school at which the average per-pupil expenditure on secular education is less than the average in the State's public schools during a specified period. Appellant State Commissioner of Education also requires eligible schools to submit financial data. If this information indicates a per-pupil expenditure in excess of the statutory limitation, the records of the school in question must be examined in order to assess how much of the expenditure is attributable to secular education and how much to religious activity.

The Act also requires that teachers eligible for salary supplements must teach only those subjects that are offered in the State's public schools. They must use "only teaching materials which are used in the public schools." Finally, any teacher applying for a salary supplement must first agree in writing "not to teach a course in religion for so long as or during such time as he or she receives any salary supplements" under the Act.

* * *

A three-judge federal court was convened pursuant to 28 U.S.C. §§ 2281, 2284. It found that Rhode Island's nonpublic elementary schools accommodated approximately 25% of the State's pupils. About 95% of these pupils attended schools affiliated with the Roman Catholic church. To date some 250 teachers have applied for benefits under the Act. All of them are employed by Roman Catholic schools.

* * *

The Pennsylvania Statute

Pennsylvania has adopted a program that has some but not all of the features of the Rhode Island program. The Pennsylvania Nonpublic Elementary and Secondary Education Act was passed in 1968 in response to a crisis that the Pennsylvania Legislature found existed in the State's nonpublic schools due to rapidly rising costs. * * *

The statute authorizes appellee state Superintendent of Public Instruction to "purchase" specified "secular educational services" from nonpublic schools. Under the "contracts" authorized by the statute, the State directly reimburses nonpublic schools solely for their actual expenditures for teachers' salaries, textbooks, and instructional materials. A school seeking reimbursement must maintain prescribed accounting procedures that identify the "separate" cost of the "secular educational service." These accounts are subject to state audit. The funds for this program were originally derived from a new tax on horse and harness racing, but the Act is now financed by a portion of the state tax on cigarettes.

There are several significant statutory restrictions on state aid. Reimbursement is limited to courses "presented in the curricula of the public schools." It is further limited "solely" to courses in the following "secular" subjects: mathematics, modern foreign languages, physical science, and physical education. Textbooks and instructional materials included in the program must be approved by the state Superintendent of Public Instruction. Finally, the statute prohibits reimbursement for any course that contains "any subject matter expressing religious teaching, or the morals or forms of worship of any sect."

The Act went into effect on July 1, 1968, and the first reimbursement payments to schools were made on September 2, 1969. It appears that some $5 million has been expended annually under the Act. The State has now entered into contracts with some 1,181 nonpublic elementary and secondary schools with a student population of some 535,215 pupils—more than 20% of the total number of students in the State. More than 96% of these pupils attend church-related schools, and most of these schools are affiliated with the Roman Catholic church.

* * *

In the absence of precisely stated constitutional prohibitions, we must draw lines with reference to the three main evils against which the Establishment Clause was intended to afford protection: "sponsorship, financial support, and active involvement of the sovereign in religious activity." Walz v. Tax Commission, 397 U.S. 664, 668 (1970).

Every analysis in this area must begin with consideration of the cumulative criteria developed by the Court over many years. Three such tests may be gleaned from our cases. First, the statute must have a secular legislative purpose; second, its principal or primary effect must be one that neither advances nor inhibits religion, Board of Education v. Allen, 392 U.S. 236, 243 (1968); finally, the statute must not foster "an excessive government entanglement with religion." *Walz, supra,* at 674.

Inquiry into the legislative purposes of the Pennsylvania and Rhode Island statutes affords no basis for a conclusion that the legislative intent was to advance religion. On the contrary, the statutes themselves clearly state that they are intended to enhance the quality of the secular education in all schools covered by the compulsory attendance laws. There is no reason to believe the legislatures meant anything else. * * *

* * * The legislatures of Rhode Island and Pennsylvania have concluded that secular and religious education are identifiable and separable. In the abstract we have no quarrel with this conclusion. The two legislatures, however, have also recognized that church-related elementary and secondary schools have a significant religious mission and that a substantial portion of their activities is religiously oriented. They have therefore sought to create statutory restrictions designed to guarantee the separation between secular and religious educational functions and to ensure that State financial aid supports only the former. All these provisions are precautions taken in candid recognition that these programs approached, even if they did not intrude upon, the forbidden areas under the Religion Clauses. We need not decide whether these legislative precautions restrict the principal or primary effect of the programs to the point where they do not offend the Religion Clauses, for we conclude that the cumulative impact of the entire relationship arising under the statutes in each State involves excessive entanglement between government and religion.

* * *

In order to determine whether the government entanglement with religion is excessive, we must examine the character and purposes of the institutions that are benefited, the nature of the aid that the State provides, and the resulting relationship between the government and the religious authority. * * *

* * *

In *Allen* the Court refused to make assumptions, on a meager record, about the religious content of the textbooks that the State would be asked to provide. We cannot, however, refuse here to recognize that teachers have a substantially different ideological character from books. In terms of potential for involving some aspect of faith or morals in secular subjects, a textbook's content is ascertainable, but a teacher's handling of a subject is not. We cannot ignore the danger that a teacher under religious control and discipline poses to the separation of the religious from the purely secular aspects of pre-college education. The conflict of functions inheres in the situation.

* * *

We need not and do not assume that teachers in parochial schools will be guilty of bad faith or any conscious design to evade the limitations imposed by the statute and the First Amendment. We simply recognize that a dedicated religious person, teaching in a school affiliated with his or her faith and operated to inculcate its tenets, will inevitably experience great difficulty in remaining religiously neutral. Doctrines and faith are not inculcated or advanced by neutrals. With the best of intentions such a teacher would find it hard to make a total separation between secular teaching and religious doctrine. What would appear to some to be essential to good citizenship might well for others border on or constitute instruction in religion. Further difficulties are inherent in the combination of religious discipline and the possibility of disagreement between teacher and religious authorities over the meaning of the statutory restrictions.

* * *

A comprehensive, discriminating, and continuing state surveillance will inevitably be required to ensure that these restrictions are obeyed and the First Amendment otherwise respected. Unlike a book, a teacher cannot be inspected once so as to determine the extent and intent of his or her personal beliefs and subjective acceptance of the limitations imposed by the First Amendment. These prophylactic contacts will involve excessive and enduring entanglement between state and church.

* * *

A broader base of entanglement of yet a different character is presented by the divisive political potential of these state programs. In a community where such a large number of pupils are served by church-related schools, it can be assumed that state assistance will entail considerable political activity. Partisans of parochial schools, understandably concerned with rising costs and sincerely dedicated to both the religious and secular educational missions of their schools, will inevitably champion this cause and promote political action to achieve their goals. Those who oppose state aid, whether for constitutional, religious, or fiscal reasons, will inevitably respond and employ all of the usual political campaign techniques to prevail. Candidates will be forced to declare and voters to choose. It would be unrealistic to ignore the fact that many people confronted with issues of this kind will find their votes aligned with their faith.

* * *

In *Walz* it was argued that a tax exemption for places of religious worship would prove to be the first step in an inevitable progression leading to the establishment of state churches and state religion. That claim could not stand up against more than 200 years of virtually universal practice imbedded in our colonial experience and continuing into the present.

The progression argument, however, is more persuasive here. We have no long history of state aid to church-related educational institutions comparable to 200 years of tax exemption for churches. Indeed, the state programs before us today represent something of an innovation. We have already noted that modern governmental programs have self-perpetuating and self-expanding propensities. These internal pressures are only enhanced when the schemes involve institutions whose legitimate needs are growing and whose interests have substantial political support. Nor can we fail to see that in constitutional adjudication some steps, which when taken were thought to approach "the verge," have become the platform for yet further steps. A certain momentum develops in constitutional theory and it can be a "downhill thrust" easily set in motion but difficult to retard or stop. * * *

* * *

* * * Under our system the choice has been made that government is to be entirely excluded from the area of religious instruction and churches excluded from the affairs of government. The Constitution decrees that religion must be a private matter for the individual, the family, and the institutions of private choice, and that while some involvement and entanglement are inevitable, lines must be drawn.

* * *

Mr. Justice Douglas, whom Mr. Justice Black joins, concurring.

* * *

The analysis of the constitutional objections to these two state systems of grants to parochial or sectarian schools must start with the admitted and obvious fact that the raison d'etre of parochial schools is the propagation of a religious faith. They also teach secular subjects; but they came into existence in this country because Protestant groups were perverting the public schools by using them to propagate their faith. The Catholics naturally rebelled. If schools were to be used to propagate a particular creed or religion, then Catholic ideals should also be served. Hence the advent of parochial schools.

* * *

Early in the 19th century the Protestants obtained control of the New York school system and used it to promote reading and teaching of the Scriptures as revealed in the King James version of the Bible.
* * *

* * *

The story of conflict and dissension is long and well known. The result was a state of so-called equilibrium where religious instruction was eliminated from public schools and the use of public funds to support religious schools was deemed to be banned.

But the hydraulic pressures created by political forces and by economic stress were great and they began to change the situation. Laws were passed—state and federal—that dispensed public funds to sustain religious schools and the plea was always in the educational frame of reference: education in all sectors was needed, from languages to calculus to nuclear physics. And it was forcefully argued that a linguist or mathematician or physicist trained in religious schools was just as competent as one trained in secular schools.

And so we have gradually edged into a situation where vast amounts of public funds are supplied each year to sectarian schools.

And the argument is made that the private parochial school system takes about $9 billion a year off the back of government—as if that were enough to justify violating the Establishment Clause.

While the evolution of the public school system in this country marked an escape from denominational control and was therefore admirable as seen through the eyes of those who think like Madison and Jefferson, it has disadvantages. The main one is that a state system may attempt to mold all students alike according to the views of the dominant group and to discourage the emergence of individual idiosyncrasies.

Sectarian education, however, does not remedy that condition. The advantages of sectarian education relate solely to religious or doctrinal matters. They give the church the opportunity to indoctrinate its creed delicately and indirectly, or massively through doctrinal courses.

* * *

When Madison in his Remonstrance attacked a taxing measure to support religious activities, he advanced a series of reasons for opposing it. One that is extremely relevant here was phrased as follows: "[I]t will destroy that moderation and harmony which the forbearance of our laws to intermeddle with Religion, has produced amongst its several sects." Intermeddling, to use Madison's word, or "entanglement," to use what was said in *Walz,* has two aspects. The intrusion of government into religious schools through grants, supervision, or surveillance may result in establishment of religion in the constitutional sense when what the State does enthrones a particular sect for overt or subtle propagation of its faith. Those activities of the State may also intrude on the Free Exercise Clause by depriving a teacher, under threats of reprisals, of the right to give sectarian construction or interpretation of, say, history and literature, or to use the teaching of such subjects to inculcate a religious creed or dogma.

* * *

In my view the taxpayers' forced contribution to the parochial schools in the present cases violates the First Amendment.

* * *

Mr. Justice Brennan.

I agree that the judgments in Nos. 569 and 570 must be affirmed. In my view the judgment in No. 89 must be reversed outright. I dissent in No. 153 insofar as the plurality opinion and the opinion of my Brother White sustain the constitutionality, as applied to sectarian institutions, of the Federal Higher Education Facilities Act of 1963, as amended, 77 Stat. 363, 20 U.S.C. § 711 et seq. (1964 ed. and Supp. V). In my view that Act is unconstitutional insofar as it authorizes grants of federal tax monies to sectarian institutions, but is unconstitutional only to that extent. I therefore think that our remand of the case should be limited to the direction of a hearing to determine whether the four institutional appellees here are sectarian institutions.

* * *

* * * In Walz, the passive aspect of the benefits conferred by a tax exemption, particularly since cessation of the exemptions might easily lead to impermissible involvements and conflicts, led me to conclude that exemptions were consistent with the First Amendment values. However, I contrasted direct government subsidies:

> "Tax exemptions and general subsidies, however, are qualitatively different. Though both provide economic assistance, they do so in fundamentally different ways. A subsidy involves the direct transfer of public monies to the subsidized enterprise and uses resources exacted from taxpayers as a whole. An exemption, on the other hand, involves no such transfer. It assists the exempted enterprise only passively, by relieving a privately funded venture of the burden of paying taxes. In other words, '[i]n the case of direct subsidy, the state forcibly diverts the income of both believers and nonbelievers to churches,' while '[i]n the case of an exemption, the state merely refrains from diverting to its own uses income independently generated by the churches through voluntary contributions.' Thus, 'the symbolism of tax exemption is significant as a manifestation that organized religion is not expected to support the state; by the same token the state is not expected to support the church.'" 397 U.S., at 690–691 (footnotes and citations omitted) (concurring opinion).

* * *

* * * The universality of state constitutional provisions forbidding such grants, as well as the weight of judicial authority disapproving such aid as a violation of our tradition of separation of church and state, reflects a time-tested judgment that such grants do indeed constitute impermissible aid to religion. * * *

* * *

* * * [T]he textbooks in *Allen* had been previously provided by the parents, and not the schools, 392 U.S., at 244 n. 6, no aid to the institution was involved. Rather, as in the case of the bus transportation in *Everson*, the general program of providing all children in the State with free secular textbooks assisted all parents in schooling their children. And as in *Everson*, there was undoubtedly the possibility that some parents might not have been able to exercise their constitutional

right to send their children to parochial school if the parents were compelled themselves to pay for textbooks. * * *

* * * The present cases, however, involve direct subsidies of tax monies to the schools themselves and we cannot blink the fact that the secular education those schools provide goes hand in hand with the religious mission that is the only reason for the schools' existence. Within the institution, the two are inextricably intertwined.

* * *

I conclude that, in using sectarian institutions to further goals in secular education, the three statutes do violence to the principle that "government may not employ religious means to serve secular interests, however legitimate they may be, at least without the clearest demonstration that nonreligious means will not suffice." *Schempp, supra,* at 265 (BRENNAN, J., concurring).

* * *

MR. JUSTICE WHITE, concurring in the judgments in * * * and dissenting * * *.

* * *

No one in these cases questions the constitutional right of parents to satisfy their state-imposed obligation to educate their children by sending them to private schools, sectarian or otherwise, as long as those schools meet minimum standards established for secular instruction. The States are not only permitted, but required by the Constitution, to free students attending private schools from any public school attendance obligation. * * *

Our prior cases have recognized the dual role of parochial schools in American society: they perform both religious and secular functions. * * *

* * *

It is enough for me that the States and the Federal Government are financing a separable secular function of overriding importance in order to sustain the legislation here challenged. That religion and private interests other than education may substantially benefit does not convert these laws into impermissible establishments of religion.

* * *

I do agree, however, that the complaint should not have been dismissed for failure to state a cause of action. Although it did not specifically allege that the schools involved mixed religious teaching with secular subjects, the complaint did allege that the schools were operated to fulfill religious purposes and one of the legal theories stated in the complaint was that the Pennsylvania Act "finances and participates in the blending of sectarian and secular instruction." At trial under this complaint, evidence showing such a blend in a course supported by state funds would appear to be admissible and, if credited, would establish financing of religious instruction by the State. Hence, I would reverse the judgment of the District Court and remand the case for trial, thereby holding the Pennsylvania legislation valid on its face but leaving open the question of its validity as applied to the particular facts of this case. * * * [2]

TILTON v. RICHARDSON

Supreme Court of the United States, 1971.
403 U.S. 672, 91 S.Ct. 2091, 29 L.Ed.2d 790.

MR. CHIEF JUSTICE BURGER announced the judgment of the Court and an opinion in which MR. JUSTICE HARLAN, MR. JUSTICE STEWART, and MR. JUSTICE BLACKMUN join.

This appeal presents important constitutional questions as to federal aid for church-related colleges and universities under Title I of the Higher Education Facilities Act of 1963, 77 Stat. 364, as amended, 20 U.S.C. §§ 711–721 (1964 ed. and Supp. V), which provides construction grants for buildings and facilities used exclusively for secular educational purposes. We must determine first whether the Act authorizes aid to such church-related institutions, and, if so, whether the Act violates either the Establishment or Free Exercise Clauses of the First Amendment.

* * *

Appellants are citizens and taxpayers of the United States and residents of Connecticut. They brought this suit for injunctive relief against the officials who administer the Act. Four church-related colleges and universities in Connecticut receiving federal construction grants under Title I were also named as defendants. Federal funds were used for five projects at these four institutions: (1) a library building at Sacred Heart University; (2) a music, drama, and arts building at Annhurst College; (3) a science building at Fairfield University; (4) a library building at Fairfield; and (5) a language laboratory at Albertus Magnus College.

* * *

II

We are satisfied that Congress intended the Act to include all colleges and universities regardless of any affiliation with or sponsorship by a religious body. * * *

* * *

Against this background we consider four questions: First, does the Act reflect a secular legislative purpose? Second, is the primary effect of the Act to advance or inhibit religion? Third, does the administra-

---

2. As a postscript I should note that both the federal and state cases are decided on specified Establishment Clause considerations, without reaching the questions that would be presented if the evidence in any of these cases showed that any of the involved schools restricted entry on racial or religious grounds or required all students gaining admission to receive instruction in the tenets of a particular faith. For myself, if such proof were made, the legislation would to that extent be unconstitutional.

tion of the Act foster an excessive government entanglement with religion? Fourth, does the implementation of the Act inhibit the free exercise of religion?

* * *

The Act itself was carefully drafted to ensure that the federally subsidized facilities would be devoted to the secular and not the religious function of the recipient institutions. It authorizes grants and loans only for academic facilities that will be used for defined secular purposes and expressly prohibits their use for religious instruction, training, or worship. These restrictions have been enforced in the Act's actual administration, and the record shows that some church-related institutions have been required to disgorge benefits for failure to obey them.

Finally, this record fully supports the findings of the District Court that none of the four church-related institutions in this case has violated the statutory restrictions. The institutions presented evidence that there had been no religious services or worship in the federally financed facilities, that there are no religious symbols or plaques in or on them, and that they had been used solely for nonreligious purposes. On this record, therefore, these buildings are indistinguishable from a typical state university facility. Appellants presented no evidence to the contrary.

Appellants instead rely on the argument that government may not subsidize any activities of an institution of higher learning that in some of its programs teaches religious doctrines. This argument rests on *Everson* where the majority stated that the Establishment Clause barred any "tax * * * levied to support any religious * * * institutions * * * whatever form they may adopt to teach or practice religion."
* * *

* * *

There is no evidence that religion seeps into the use of any of these facilities. Indeed, the parties stipulated in the District Court that courses at these institutions are taught according to the academic requirements intrinsic to the subject matter and the individual teacher's concept of professional standards. Although appellants introduced several institutional documents that stated certain religious restrictions on what could be taught, other evidence showed that these restrictions were not in fact enforced and that the schools were characterized by an atmosphere of academic freedom rather than religious indoctrination. All four institutions, for example, subscribe to the 1940 Statement of Principles on Academic Freedom and Tenure endorsed by the American Association of University Professors and the Association of American Colleges.

Rather than focus on the four defendant colleges and universities involved in this case, however, appellants seek to shift our attention to a "composite profile" that they have constructed of the "typical sectarian" institution of higher education. We are told that such a "composite" institution imposes religious restrictions on admissions, requires attendance at religious activities, compels obedience to the doctrines and dogmas of the faith, requires instruction in theology and doctrine, and does everything it can to propagate a particular religion. Perhaps some church-related schools fit the pattern that appellants describe. Indeed, some colleges have been declared ineligible for aid by the authorities that administer the Act. But appellants do not contend that these four institutions fall within this category. Individual projects can be properly evaluated if and when challenges arise with respect to particular recipients and some evidence is then presented to show that the institution does in fact possess these characteristics. We cannot, however, strike down an Act of Congress on the basis of a hypothetical "profile."

(b)

Although we reject appellants' broad constitutional arguments we do perceive an aspect in which the statute's enforcement provisions are inadequate to ensure that the impact of the federal aid will not advance religion. If a recipient institution violates any of the statutory restrictions on the use of a federally financed facility, § 754(b)(2) permits the Government to recover an amount equal to the proportion of the facility's present value that the federal grant bore to its original cost.

This remedy, however, is available to the Government only if the statutory conditions are violated "within twenty years after completion of construction." * * *

* * *

Limiting the prohibition for religious use of the structure to 20 years obviously opens the facility to use for any purpose at the end of that period. It cannot be assumed that a substantial structure has no value after that period and hence the unrestricted use of a valuable property is in effect a contribution of some value to a religious body.
* * *

To this extent the Act therefore trespasses on the Religion Clauses. The restrictive obligations of a recipient institution under § 751(a)(2) cannot, compatibly with the Religion Clauses, expire while the building has substantial value. * * *

IV

We next turn to the question of whether excessive entanglements characterize the relationship between government and church under the Act. * * *

In *DiCenso* the District Court found that the parochial schools in Rhode Island were "an integral part of the religious mission of the Catholic Church." There, the record fully supported the conclusion that the inculcation of religious values was a substantial if not the dominant purpose of the institutions. * * *

* * *

There are generally significant differences between the religious aspects of church-related institutions of higher learning and parochial elementary and secondary schools. The "affirmative if not dominant policy" of the instruction in pre-college church schools is "to assure future adherents to a particular faith by having control of their total education at an early age." *Walz v. Tax Comm'n, supra,* at 671. There is substance to the contention that college students are less impressionable and less susceptible to religious indoctrination. Common observation would seem to support that view, and Congress may well have entertained it. The skepticism of the college student is not an inconsiderable barrier to any attempt or tendency to subvert the congressional objectives and limitations. Furthermore, by their very nature, college and postgraduate courses tend to limit the opportunities for sectarian influence by virtue of their own internal disciplines. Many church-related colleges and universities are characterized by a high degree of academic freedom and seek to evoke free and critical responses from their students.

The record here would not support a conclusion that any of these four institutions departed from this general pattern. All four schools are governed by Catholic religious organizations, and the faculties and student bodies at each are predominantly Catholic. Nevertheless, the evidence shows that non-Catholics were admitted as students and given faculty appointments. Not one of these four institutions requires its students to attend religious services. Although all four schools require their students to take theology courses, the parties stipulated that these courses are taught according to the academic requirements of the subject matter and the teacher's concept of professional standards. The parties also stipulated that the courses covered a range of human religious experiences and are not limited to courses about the Roman Catholic religion. The schools introduced evidence that they made no attempt to indoctrinate students or to proselytize. Indeed, some of the required theology courses at Albertus Magnus and Sacred Heart are taught by rabbis. Finally, as we have noted, these four schools subscribe to a well-established set of principles of academic freedom, and nothing in this record shows that these principles are not in fact followed. In short, the evidence shows institutions with admittedly religious functions but whose predominant higher education mission is to provide their students with a secular education.

Since religious indoctrination is not a substantial purpose or activity of these church-related colleges and universities, there is less likelihood than in primary and secondary schools that religion will permeate the area of secular education. This reduces the risk that government aid will in fact serve to support religious activities. Correspondingly, the necessity for intensive government surveillance is diminished and the resulting entanglements between government and religion lessened. Such inspection as may be necessary to ascertain that the facilities are devoted to secular education is minimal and indeed hardly more than the inspections that States impose over all private schools within the reach of compulsory education laws.

The entanglement between church and state is also lessened here by the nonideological character of the aid that the Government provides. * * *

Finally, government entanglements with religion are reduced by the circumstance that, unlike the direct and continuing payments under the Pennsylvania program, and all the incidents of regulation and surveillance, the Government aid here is a one-time, single-purpose construction grant. There are no continuing financial relationships or dependencies, no annual audits, and no government analysis of an institution's expenditures on secular as distinguished from religious activities. Inspection as to use is a minimal contact.

No one of these three factors standing alone is necessarily controlling; cumulatively all of them shape a narrow and limited relationship with government which involves fewer and less significant contacts than the two state schemes before us in *Lemon* and *DiCenso*. The relationship therefore has less potential for realizing the substantive evils against which the Religion Clauses were intended to protect.

* * *

MR. JUSTICE DOUGLAS, with whom MR. JUSTICE BLACK and MR. JUSTICE MARSHALL concur, dissenting in part.

The correct constitutional principle for this case was stated by President Kennedy in 1961 when questioned as to his policy respecting aid to private and parochial schools:

"[T]he Constitution clearly prohibits aid to the school, to parochial schools. I don't think there is any doubt of that.

"The *Everson* case, which is probably the most celebrated case, provided only by a 5 to 4 decision was it possible for a local community to provide bus rides to nonpublic school children. But all through the majority and minority statements on that particular question there was a very clear prohibition against aid to the school direct. The Supreme Court made its decision in the *Everson* case by determining that the aid was to the child, not to the school. Aid to the school is—there isn't any room for debate on that subject. It is prohibited by the Constitution, and the Supreme Court has made that very clear. And therefore there would be no possibility of our recommending it."

* * *

The public purpose in secular education is, to be sure, furthered by the program. Yet the sectarian purpose is aided by making the parochial school system viable. The purpose is to increase "student enrollment" and the students obviously aimed at are those of the particular faith now financed by taxpayers' money. Parochial schools are not beamed at agnostics, atheists, or those of a competing sect. The more sophisticated institutions may admit minorities; but the dominant religious character is not changed.

* * *

What I have said in *Lemon* and in the *DiCenso* cases decided today is relevant here. The facilities financed by taxpayers' funds are not to be used for "sectarian" purposes. Religious teaching and secular teaching are so enmeshed in parochial schools that only the strictest supervision and surveillance would insure compliance with the condition. Parochial schools may require religious exercises, even in the classroom. A parochial school operates on one budget. Money not spent for one purpose becomes available for other purposes. Thus the fact that there are no religious observances in federally financed facilities is not controlling because required religious observances will take place in other buildings. * * * Once these schools become federally funded they become bound by federal standards (Ivanhoe Irrig. Dist. v. McCracken, 357 U.S. 275, 296 (1958); Rosado v. Wyman, 397 U.S. 397, 427 (1970) (concurring opinion); Simkins v. Moses H. Cone Memorial Hosp., 323 F.2d 959 (1963)) and accordingly adherence to *Engel* would require an end to required religious exercises. * * *

* * *

It is almost unbelievable that we have made the radical departure from Madison's Remonstrance memorialized in today's decision.

I dissent not because of any lack of respect for parochial schools but out of a feeling of despair that the respect which through history has been accorded the First Amendment is this day lost.

It should be remembered that in this case we deal with federal grants and with the command that "Congress shall make no law respecting an establishment of religion, or prohibiting the free exercise thereof." The million-dollar grants sustained today put Madison's miserable "three pence" to shame. But he even thought, as I do, that even a small amount coming out of the pocket of taxpayers and going into the coffers of a church was not in keeping with our constitutional ideal.

I would reverse the judgment below.

WALZ v. TAX COMMISSION OF THE CITY OF NEW YORK
Supreme Court of the United States, 1970.
397 U.S. 664, 90 S.Ct. 1409, 25 L.Ed.2d 697.

MR. JUSTICE BURGER delivered the opinion of the Court.

Appellant, owner of real estate in Richmond County, New York, sought an injunction in the New York courts to prevent the New York City Tax Commission from granting property tax exemptions to religious organizations for religious properties used solely for religious worship. The exemption from state taxes is authorized by Art. 16, § 1, of the New York Constitution, which provides in relevant part:

> "Exemptions from taxation may be granted only by general laws. Exemptions may be altered or repealed except those exempting real or personal property used exclusively for religious, educational or charitable purposes as defined by law and owned by any corporation or association organized or conducted exclusively for one or more of such purposes and not operating for profit."

The essence of appellant's contention was that the New York City Tax Commission's grant of an exemption to church property indirectly requires the appellant to make a contribution to religious bodies and thereby violates provisions prohibiting establishment of religion under the First Amendment which under the Fourteenth Amendment is binding on the States.

Appellee's motion for summary judgment was granted and the Appellate Division of the New York Supreme Court, and the New York Court of Appeals affirmed. We noted probable jurisdiction, 395 U.S. 957 (1969), and affirm.

* * *

The Court has struggled to find a neutral course between the two Religion Clauses, both of which are cast in absolute terms, and either of which, if expanded to a logical extreme, would tend to clash with the other. * * *

* * *

The course of constitutional neutrality in this area cannot be an absolutely straight line; rigidity could well defeat the basic purpose of these provisions, which is to insure that no religion be sponsored or favored, none commanded, and none inhibited. The general principle deducible from the First Amendment and all that has been said by the Court is this: that we will not tolerate either governmentally established religion or governmental interference with religion. Short of those expressly proscribed governmental acts there is room for play in the joints productive of a benevolent neutrality which will permit religious exercise to exist without sponsorship and without interference.

Each value judgment under the Religion Clauses must therefore turn on whether particular acts in question are intended to establish or interfere with religious beliefs and practices or have the effect of doing so. Adherence to the policy of neutrality that derives from an accommodation of the Establishment and Free Exercise Clauses has prevented the kind of involvement that would tip the balance toward government control of churches or governmental restraint on religious practice.

* * *

* * * [I]f as in *Everson* buses can be provided to carry and policemen to protect church school pupils, we fail to see how a broader range of police and fire protection given equally to all churches, along with nonprofit hospitals, art galleries, and libraries receiving the same tax exemption, is different for purposes of the Religion Clauses.

* * *

The legislative purpose of the property tax exemption is neither the advancement nor the inhibition of religion; it is neither sponsorship nor hostility. New York, in common with the other States, has determined that certain entities that exist in a harmonious relationship to the community at large, and that foster its "moral or mental improvement," should not be inhibited in their activities by property taxation or the hazard of loss of those properties for nonpayment of taxes. It has not singled out one particular church or religious group or even churches as such; rather, it has granted exemption to all houses of religious worship within a broad class of property owned by nonprofit, quasi-public corporations which include hospitals, libraries, playgrounds, scientific, professional, historical, and patriotic groups. The State has an affirmative policy that considers these groups as beneficial and stabilizing influences in community life and finds this classification useful, desirable, and in the public interest. Qualification for tax exemption is not perpetual or immutable; some tax-exempt groups lose that status when their activities take them outside the classification and new entities can come into being and qualify for exemption.

Governments have not always been tolerant of religious activity, and hostility toward religion has taken many shapes and forms—economic, political, and sometimes harshly oppressive. Grants of exemption historically reflect the concern of authors of constitutions and statutes as to the latent dangers inherent in the imposition of property taxes; exemption constitutes a reasonable and balanced attempt to guard against those dangers. The limits of permissible state accommodation to religion are by no means co-extensive with the noninterference mandated by the Free Exercise Clause. To equate the two would be to deny a national heritage with roots in the Revolution itself. See Sherbert v. Verner, 374 U.S. 398, 423 (1963) (HARLAN, J., dissenting); Braunfeld v. Brown, 366 U.S. 599, 608 (1961). See generally Kauper, The Constitutionality of Tax Exemptions for Religious Activities in The Wall Between Church and State 95 (D.Oaks ed. 1963). We cannot read New York's statute as attempting to establish religion; it is simply sparing the exercise of religion from the burden of property taxation levied on private profit institutions.

We find it unnecessary to justify the tax exemption on the social welfare services or "good works" that some churches perform for parishioners and others—family counselling, aid to the elderly and the infirm, and to children. Churches vary substantially in the scope of such services; programs expand or contract according to resources and need. As public-sponsored programs enlarge, private aid from the church sector may diminish. The extent of social services may vary, depending on whether the church serves an urban or rural, a rich or poor constituency. To give emphasis to so variable an aspect of the work of religious bodies would introduce an element of governmental evaluation and standards as to the worth of particular social welfare programs, thus producing a kind of continuing day-to-day relationship which the policy of neutrality seeks to minimize. Hence, the use of a social welfare yardstick as a significant element to qualify for tax exemption could conceivably give rise to confrontations that could escalate to constitutional dimensions.

Determining that the legislative purpose of tax exemption is not aimed at establishing, sponsoring, or supporting religion does not end the inquiry, however. We must also be sure that the end result—the effect—is not an excessive government entanglement with religion. The test is inescapably one of degree. Either course, taxation of churches or exemption, occasions some degree of involvement with religion. Elimination of exemption would tend to expand the involvement of government by giving rise to tax valuation of church property, tax liens, tax foreclosures, and the direct confrontations and conflicts that follow in the train of those legal processes.

Granting tax exemptions to churches necessarily operates to afford an indirect economic benefit and also gives rise to some, but yet a lesser, involvement than taxing them. In analyzing either alternative the questions are whether the involvement is excessive, and whether it is a continuing one calling for official and continuing surveillance leading to an impermissible degree of entanglement. Obviously a direct money subsidy would be a relationship pregnant with involvement and, as with most governmental grant programs, could encompass sustained and detailed administrative relationships for enforcement of statutory or administrative standards, but that is not this case. The hazards of churches supporting government are hardly less in their potential than the hazards of government supporting churches;[3] each relationship carries some involvement rather than the desired insulation and separation. We cannot ignore the instances in history when church support of government led to the kind of involvement we seek to avoid.

The grant of a tax exemption is not sponsorship since the government does not transfer part of its revenue to churches but simply abstains from demanding that the church support the state. No one has ever suggested that tax exemption has converted libraries, art galleries, or hospitals into arms of the state or put employees "on the public payroll." There is no genuine nexus between tax exemption and establishment of religion. As Mr. Justice Holmes commented in a related context "a page of history is worth a volume of logic." New York Trust Co. v. Eisner, 256 U.S. 345, 349 (1921). The exemption creates only a minimal and remote involvement between church and state and far less than taxation of churches. It restricts the fiscal relationship between church and state, and tends to complement and reinforce the desired separation insulating each from the other.

Separation in this context cannot mean absence of all contact; the complexities of modern life inevitably produce some contact and the fire and police protection received by houses of religious worship are no more than incidental benefits accorded all persons or institutions within a State's boundaries, along with many other exempt organizations. The appellant has not established even an arguable quantitative correlation between the payment of an ad valorem property tax and the receipt of these municipal benefits.

All of the 50 States provide for tax exemption of places of worship, most of them doing so by constitutional guarantees. For so long as federal income taxes have had any potential impact on churches—over

---

3. The support of religion with direct allocation of public revenue was a common colonial practice. See C. Antieau, A. Downey, & E. Roberts, Freedom from Federal Establishment cc. 1 and 2 (1964). A general assessment proposed in the Virginia Legislature in 1784 prompted the writing of James Madison's Remonstrance. See opinion of Mr. Justice Douglas dissenting, * * *.

75 years—religious organizations have been expressly exempt from the tax. Such treatment is an "aid" to churches no more and no less in principle than the real estate tax exemption granted by States. Few concepts are more deeply embedded in the fabric of our national life, beginning with pre-Revolutionary colonial times, than for the government to exercise at the very least this kind of benevolent neutrality toward churches and religious exercise generally so long as none was favored over others and none suffered interference.

It is significant that Congress, from its earliest days, has viewed the Religion Clauses of the Constitution as authorizing statutory real estate tax exemption to religious bodies. * * *

It is obviously correct that no one acquires a vested or protected right in violation of the Constitution by long use, even when that span of time covers our entire national existence and indeed predates it. Yet an unbroken practice of according the exemption to churches, openly and by affirmative state action, not covertly or by state inaction, is not something to be lightly cast aside. Nearly 50 years ago Mr. Justice Holmes stated:

> "If a thing has been practised for two hundred years by common consent, it will need a strong case for the Fourteenth Amendment to affect it...." Jackman v. Rosenbaum Co., 260 U.S. 22, 31 (1922).

Nothing in this national attitude toward religious tolerance and two centuries of uninterrupted freedom from taxation has given the remotest sign of leading to an established church or religion and on the contrary it has operated affirmatively to help guarantee the free exercise of all forms of religious belief. * * *

* * *

It appears that at least up to 1885 this Court, reflecting more than a century of our history and uninterrupted practice, accepted without discussion the proposition that federal or state grants of tax exemption to churches were not a violation of the Religion Clauses of the First Amendment. As to the New York statute, we now confirm that view.

Affirmed.

MR. JUSTICE BRENNAN, concurring.

I concur for reasons expressed in my opinion in Abington School Dist. v. Schempp, 374 U.S. 203, 230 (1963). I adhere to the view there stated that to give concrete meaning to the Establishment Clause,

> "the line we must draw between the permissible and the impermissible is one which accords with history and faithfully reflects the understanding of the Founding Fathers. It is a line which the Court has consistently sought to mark in its decisions expounding the religious guarantees of the First Amendment. What the Framers meant to foreclose, and what our decisions under the Establishment Clause have forbidden, are those involvements of religious with secular institutions which (a) serve the essentially religious activities of religious

institutions; (b) employ the organs of government for essentially religious purposes; or (c) use essentially religious means to serve governmental ends, where secular means would suffice. When the secular and religious institutions become involved in such a manner, there inhere in the relationship precisely those dangers—as much to church as to state—which the Framers feared would subvert religious liberty and the strength of a system of secular government. On the other hand, there may be myriad forms of involvements of government with religion which do not import such dangers and therefore should not, in my judgment, be deemed to violate the Establishment Clause." *Id.,* at 294–295.

Thus, in my view, the history, purpose, and operation of real property tax exemptions for religious organizations must be examined to determine whether the Establishment Clause is breached by such exemptions. * * *

II

Government has two basic secular purposes for granting real property tax exemptions to religious organizations. First, these organizations are exempted because they, among a range of other private, nonprofit organizations contribute to the well-being of the community in a variety of nonreligious ways, and thereby bear burdens that would otherwise either have to be met by general taxation, or be left undone, to the detriment of the community. * * *

Appellant seeks to avoid the force of this secular purpose of the exemptions by limiting his challenge to "exemptions from real property taxation to religious organizations on real property used exclusively for religious purposes." Appellant assumes, apparently, that church-owned property is used for exclusively religious purposes if it does not house a hospital, orphanage, weekday school, or the like. Any assumption that a church building itself is used for exclusively religious activities, however, rests on a simplistic view of ordinary church operations. As the appellee's brief cogently observes, "the public welfare activities and the sectarian activities of religious institutions are * * * intertwined * * *. Often a particular church will use the same personnel, facilities and source of funds to carry out both its secular and religious activities." Thus, the same people who gather in church facilities for religious worship and study may return to these facilities to participate in Boy Scout activities, to promote antipoverty causes, to discuss public issues, or to listen to chamber music. Accordingly, the funds used to maintain the facilities as a place for religious worship and study also maintain them as a place for secular activities beneficial to the community as a whole. Even during formal worship services, churches frequently collect the funds used to finance their secular operations and make decisions regarding their nature.

Second, government grants exemptions to religious organizations because they uniquely contribute to the pluralism of American society by their religious activities. Government may properly include religious institutions among the variety of private, nonprofit groups that receive tax exemptions, for each group contributes to the diversity of association, viewpoint, and enterprise essential to a vigorous, pluralistic society. * * *

* * *

Against the background of this survey of the history, purpose, and operation of religious tax exemptions, I must conclude that the exemptions do not "serve the essentially religious activities of religious institutions." Their principal effect is to carry out secular purposes—the encouragement of public service activities and of a pluralistic society. During their ordinary operations, most churches engage in activities of a secular nature that benefit the community; and all churches by their existence contribute to the diversity of association, viewpoint, and enterprise so highly valued by all of us.

Nor do I find that the exemptions "employ the organs of government for essentially religious purposes." To the extent that the exemptions further secular ends, they do not advance "essentially religious purposes." To the extent that purely religious activities are benefited by the exemptions, the benefit is passive. Government does not affirmatively foster these activities by exempting religious organizations from taxes, as it would were it to subsidize them. The exemption simply leaves untouched that which adherents of the organization bring into being and maintain.

Finally, I do not think that the exemptions "use essentially religious means to serve governmental ends, where secular means would suffice." The means churches use to carry on their public service activities are not "essentially religious" in nature. They are the same means used by any purely secular organization—money, human time and skills, physical facilities. It is true that each church contributes to the pluralism of our society through its purely religious activities, but the state encourages these activities not because it champions religion per se but because it values religion among a variety of private, nonprofit enterprises that contribute to the diversity of the Nation. Viewed in this light, there is no nonreligious substitute for religion as an element in our societal mosaic, just as there is no nonliterary substitute for literary groups.

* * *

Opinion of MR. JUSTICE HARLAN.

While I entirely subscribe to the result reached today and find myself in basic agreement with what The Chief Justice has written, I deem it appropriate, in view of the radiations of the issues involved, to state those considerations that are, for me, controlling in this case and lead me to conclude that New York's constitutional provision, as implemented by its real property law, does not offend the Establishment Clause. Preliminarily, I think it relevant to face up to the fact that it is far easier to agree on the purpose that underlies the First Amendment's Establishment and Free Exercise Clauses than to obtain agreement on the standards that should govern their application. What is at stake as a matter of policy is preventing that kind and degree of government involvement in religious life that, as history teaches us, is apt to lead to strife and frequently strain a political system to the breaking point.

I

Two requirements frequently articulated and applied in our cases for achieving this goal are "neutrality" and "voluntarism." E.g., see Abington School Dist. v. Schempp, 374 U.S. 203, 305 (1963) (concurring opinion of Mr. Justice Goldberg); Engel v. Vitale, 370 U.S. 421 (1962). These related and mutually reinforcing concepts are short-form for saying that the Government must neither legislate to accord benefits that favor religion over nonreligion, nor sponsor a particular sect, nor try to encourage participation in or abnegation of religion. Mr. Justice Goldberg's concurring opinion in Abington which I joined set forth these principles: "The fullest realization of true religious liberty requires that government neither engage in nor compel religious practices, that it effect no favoritism among sects or between religion and nonreligion, and that it work deterrence of no religious belief." 374 U.S., at 305. The Court's holding in Torcaso v. Watkins, 367 U.S. 488, 495 (1961), is to the same effect: the State cannot "constitutionally pass laws or impose requirements which aid all religions as against non-believers, and neither can [it] aid those religions based on a belief in the existence of God as against those religions founded on different beliefs." In the vast majority of cases the inquiry, albeit an elusive one, can end at this point. Neutrality and voluntarism stand as barriers against the most egregious and hence divisive kinds of state involvement in religious matters.

II

This legislation neither encourages nor discourages participation in religious life and thus satisfies the voluntarism requirement of the First Amendment. Unlike the instances of school prayers, *Abington School Dist. v. Schempp, supra,* and *Engel v. Vitale, supra,* or "released time" programs, Zorach v. Clauson, 343 U.S. 306 (1952), and McCollum v. Board of Education, 333 U.S. 203 (1948), the State is not "utilizing the prestige, power, and influence" of a public institution to bring religion into the lives of citizens. 374 U.S., at 307 (GOLDBERG, J., concurring).

The statute also satisfies the requirement of neutrality. Neutrality in its application requires an equal protection mode of analysis. The Court must survey meticulously the circumstances of governmental categories to eliminate, as it were, religious gerrymanders. In any particular case the critical question is whether the circumference of legislation encircles a class so broad that it can be fairly concluded that religious institutions could be thought to fall within the natural perimeter.

The statute that implements New York's constitutional provision for tax exemptions to religious organizations has defined a class of nontaxable entities whose common denominator is their nonprofit pursuit of activities devoted to cultural and moral improvement and the doing of "good works" by performing certain social services in the community that might otherwise have to be assumed by government. Included are such broad and divergent groups as historical and literary societies and more generally associations "for the moral or mental improvement of men." The statute by its terms grants this exemption in furtherance of moral and intellectual diversity and would appear not to omit any organization that could be reasonably thought to contribute to that goal.

To the extent that religious institutions sponsor the secular activities that this legislation is designed to promote, it is consistent with neutrality to grant them an exemption just as other organizations devoting resources to these projects receive exemptions. I think, moreover, in the context of a statute so broad as the one before us, churches may properly receive an exemption even though they do not themselves sponsor the secular-type activities mentioned in the statute but exist merely for the convenience of their interested members. As long as the breadth of exemption includes groups that pursue cultural, moral, or spiritual improvement in multifarious secular ways, including, I would suppose, groups whose avowed tenets may be antitheological, atheistic, or agnostic, I can see no lack of neutrality in extending the benefit of the exemption to organized religious groups.[1]

* * *

I agree with my Brother Douglas that exemptions do not differ from subsidies as an economic matter. Aside from the longstanding tradition behind exemptions there are other differences, however. Subsidies, unlike exemptions, must be passed on periodically and thus invite more political controversy than exemptions. Moreover, subsidies or direct aid, as a general rule, are granted on the basis of enumerated and more complicated qualifications and frequently involve the state in administration to a higher degree, though to be sure, this is not necessarily the case.

Whether direct aid or subsidies entail that degree of involvement that is prohibited by the Constitution is a question that must be reserved for a later case upon a record that fully develops all the pertinent considerations such as the significance and character of subsidies in our political system and the role of the government in administering the subsidy in relation to the particular program aided. It may also be that the States, while bound to observe strict neutrality, should be freer to experiment with involvement—on a neutral basis—than the Federal Government. Cf., e.g., my separate opinion in Roth v. United States, 354 U.S. 476, 496 (1957).

I recognize that for those who seek inflexible solutions this tripartite analysis provides little comfort. It is always possible to shrink

---

1. While I would suppose most churches devote part of their resources to secular community projects and conventional charitable activities, it is a question of fact, a fact that would only be relevant if we had before us a statute framed more narrowly to include only "charities" or a limited class of organizations, and churches. In such a case, depending on the administration of the exemption, it might be that the granting of an exemption to religion would turn out to be improper. * * *

from a first step lest the momentum will plunge the law into pitfalls that lie in the trail ahead. I, for one, however, do not believe that a "slippery slope" is necessarily without a constitutional toehold. Like The Chief Justice I am of the view that it is the task of this tribunal to "draw distinctions, including fine ones, in the process of interpreting the Constitution." * * * The prospect of difficult questions of judgment in constitutional law should not be the basis for prohibiting legislative action that is constitutionally permissible. I think this one is, and on the foregoing premises join with the Court in upholding this New York statute.

MR. JUSTICE DOUGLAS, dissenting.

Petitioner is the owner of real property in New York and is a Christian. But he is not a member of any of the religious organizations, "rejecting them as hostile." The New York statute exempts from taxation real property "owned by a corporation or association organized exclusively for * * * religious * * * purposes" and used "exclusively for carrying out" such purposes. Yet non-believers who own realty are taxed at the usual rate. The question in the case therefore is whether believers—organized in church groups—can be made exempt from real estate taxes, merely because they are believers, while nonbelievers, whether organized or not, must pay the real estate taxes.

My Brother Harlan says he "would suppose" that the tax exemption extends to "groups whose avowed tenets may be antitheological, atheistic, or agnostic." * * *. If it does, then the line between believers and nonbelievers has not been drawn. But, with all respect, there is not even a suggestion in the present record that the statute covers property used exclusively by organizations for "antitheological purposes," "atheistic purposes," or "agnostic purposes."

* * *

With all due respect the governing principle is not controlled by *Everson v. Board of Education, supra.* Everson involved the use of public funds to bus children to parochial as well as to public schools. Parochial schools teach religion; yet they are also educational institutions offering courses competitive with public schools. They prepare students for the professions and for activities in all walks of life. Education in the secular sense was combined with religious indoctrination at the parochial schools involved in *Everson.* Even so, the *Everson* decision was five to four and, though one of the five, I have since had grave doubts about it, because I have become convinced that grants to institutions teaching a sectarian creed violate the Establishment Clause. See *Engel v. Vitale, supra,* at 443–444 (DOUGLAS, J., concurring).

This case, however, is quite different. Education is not involved. The financial support rendered here is to the church, the place of worship. A tax exemption is a subsidy. Is my Brother Brennan correct in saying that we would hold that state or federal grants to churches, say, to construct the edifice itself would be unconstitutional? What is the difference between that kind of subsidy and the present subsidy?

* * *

If believers are entitled to public financial support, so are nonbelievers. A believer and nonbeliever under the present law are treated differently because of the articles of their faith. Believers are doubtless comforted that the cause of religion is being fostered by this legislation. Yet one of the mandates of the First Amendment is to promote a viable, pluralistic society and to keep government neutral, not only between sects, but also between believers and nonbelievers. The present involvement of government in religion may seem *de minimis*. But it is, I fear, a long step down the Establishment path. Perhaps I have been misinformed. But as I have read the Constitution and its philosophy, I gathered that independence was the price of liberty.

I conclude that this tax exemption is unconstitutional.

* * *

BOARD OF EDUCATION OF CENTRAL SCHOOL DISTRICT v. ALLEN

Supreme Court of the United States, 1968.
392 U.S. 236, 88 S.Ct. 1923, 20 L.Ed.2d 1060.

Mr. Justice White delivered the opinion of the Court.

A law of the State of New York requires local public school authorities to lend textbooks free of charge to all students in grades seven through 12; students attending private schools are included. This case presents the question whether this statute is a "law respecting an establishment of religion, or prohibiting the free exercise thereof," and so in conflict with the First and Fourteenth Amendments to the Constitution, because it authorizes the loan of textbooks to students attending parochial schools. We hold that the law is not in violation of the Constitution.

* * * Beginning with the 1966–1967 school year, local school boards were required to purchase textbooks and lend them without charge "to all children residing in such district who are enrolled in grades seven to twelve of a public or private school which complies with the compulsory education law." The books now loaned are "text-books which are designated for use in any public, elementary or secondary schools of the state or are approved by any boards of education," and which—according to a 1966 amendment—"a pupil is required to use as a text for a semester or more in a particular class in the school he legally attends."

* * *

Everson v. Board of Education, 330 U.S. 1 (1947), is the case decided by this Court that is most nearly in point for today's problem. New Jersey reimbursed parents for expenses incurred in busing their children to parochial schools. The Court stated that the Establishment Clause bars a State from passing "laws which aid one religion, aid all religions, or prefer one religion over another," and bars too any "tax in any amount, large or small * * * levied to support any religious activities or institutions, whatever they may be called, or whatever form they may adopt to teach or practice religion." * * *. Nevertheless, said the Court, the Establishment Clause does not prevent a State from extending the benefits of state laws to all citizens without regard for their religious affiliation and does not prohibit "New Jersey from spending tax-raised funds to pay the bus fares of parochial school pupils as a part of a general program under which it pays the fares of pupils attending public and other schools." The statute was held to be valid even though one of its results was that "children are helped to get to church schools" and "some of the children might not be sent to the church schools if the parents were compelled to pay their children's bus fares out of their own pockets." * * *. As with public provision of police and fire protection, sewage facilities, and streets and sidewalks, payment of bus fares was of some value to the religious school, but was nevertheless not such support of a religious institution as to be a prohibited establishment of religion within the meaning of the First Amendment.

Everson and later cases have shown that the line between state neutrality to religion and state support of religion is not easy to locate. * * * Abington School District v. Schempp, 374 U.S. 203 (1963), fashioned a test subscribed to by eight Justices for distinguishing between forbidden involvements of the State with religion and those contacts which the Establishment Clause permits:

> "The test may be stated as follows: what are the purpose and the primary effect of the enactment? If either is the advancement or inhibition of religion then the enactment exceeds the scope of legislative power as circumscribed by the Constitution. That is to say that to withstand the strictures of the Establishment Clause there must be a secular legislative purpose and a primary effect that neither advances nor inhibits religion. Everson v. Board of Education.* * *" 374 U.S., at 222.

This test is not easy to apply, but the citation of *Everson* by the *Schempp* Court to support its general standard made clear how the *Schempp* rule would be applied to the facts of *Everson*. The statute upheld in Everson would be considered a law having "a secular legislative purpose and a primary effect that neither advances nor inhibits religion." We reach the same result with respect to the New York law requiring school books to be loaned free of charge to all students in specified grades. The express purpose of § 701 was stated by the New York Legislature to be furtherance of the educational opportunities available to the young. Appellants have shown us nothing about the necessary effects of the statute that is contrary to its stated purpose. The law merely makes available to all children the benefits of a general program to lend school books free of charge. Books are furnished at the request of the pupil and ownership remains, at least technically, in the State. Thus no funds or books are furnished to parochial schools, and the financial benefit is to parents and children, not to schools.[6] Perhaps free books make it more likely that some children choose to attend a sectarian school, but that was true of the state-paid bus fares in *Everson* and does not alone demonstrate an unconstitutional degree of support for a religious institution.

Of course books are different from buses. Most bus rides have no inherent religious significance, while religious books are common. However, the language of § 701 does not authorize the loan of religious books, and the State claims no right to distribute religious literature. Although the books loaned are those required by the parochial school for use in specific courses, each book loaned must be approved by the public school authorities; only secular books may receive approval. The law was construed by the Court of Appeals of New York as "merely making available secular textbooks at the request of the individual student," *supra*, and the record contains no suggestion that religious books have been loaned. Absent evidence, we cannot assume that school authorities, who constantly face the same problem in selecting textbooks for use in the public schools, are unable to distinguish between secular and religious books or that they will not honestly discharge their duties under the law. In judging the validity of the statute on this record we must proceed on the assumption that books loaned to students are books that are not unsuitable for use in the public schools because of religious content.

The major reason offered by appellants for distinguishing free textbooks from free bus fares is that books, but not buses, are critical to the teaching process, and in a sectarian school that process is employed to teach religion. However this Court has long recognized that religious schools pursue two goals, religious instruction and secular education. In the leading case of Pierce v. Society of Sisters, 268 U.S. 510 (1925), the Court held that although it would not question Oregon's power to compel school attendance or require that the attendance be at an institution meeting State-imposed requirements as to quality and nature of curriculum, Oregon had not shown that its interest in secular education required that all children attend publicly operated schools. A premise of this holding was the view that the State's interest in education would be served sufficiently by reliance on the secular teaching that accompanied religious training in the schools maintained by the Society of Sisters. Since *Pierce,* a substantial body of case law has confirmed the power of the States to insist that attendance at private schools, if it is to satisfy state compulsory-attendance laws, be at institutions which provide minimum hours of instruction, employ

---

6. While the record and the state court opinions in this case contained no information about how the books are in fact transferred from the Boards of Education to individual students, both parties suggested in their briefs and on oral argument before this Court that New York permits private schools to submit to boards of education summaries of the requests for textbooks filed by individual students, and also permits private schools to store on their premises the textbooks being loaned by the Board of Education to the students. This interpretation of the State's administrative procedure is supported by an "Opinion of Counsel" made available by the Board of Regents and the State Department of Education to local school superintendents.

teachers of specified training, and cover prescribed subjects of instruction. * * *

Underlying these cases, and underlying also the legislative judgments that have preceded the court decisions, has been a recognition that private education has played and is playing a significant and valuable role in raising national levels of knowledge, competence, and experience. Americans care about the quality of the secular education available to their children. They have considered high quality education to be an indispensable ingredient for achieving the kind of nation, and the kind of citizenry, that they have desired to create. Considering this attitude, the continued willingness to rely on private school systems, including parochial systems, strongly suggests that a wide segment of informed opinion, legislative and otherwise, has found that those schools do an acceptable job of providing secular education to their students. This judgment is further evidence that parochial schools are performing, in addition to their sectarian function, the task of secular education.

Against this background of judgment and experience, unchallenged in the meager record before us in this case, we cannot agree with appellants either that all teaching in a sectarian school is religious or that the processes of secular and religious training are so intertwined that secular textbooks furnished to students by the public are in fact instrumental in the teaching of religion. This case comes to us after summary judgment entered on the pleadings. Nothing in this record supports the proposition that all textbooks, whether they deal with mathematics, physics, foreign languages, history, or literature, are used by the parochial schools to teach religion. No evidence has been offered about particular schools, particular courses, particular teachers, or particular books. We are unable to hold, based solely on judicial notice, that this statute results in unconstitutional involvement of the State with religious instruction or that § 701, for this or the other reasons urged, is a law respecting the establishment of religion within the meaning of the First Amendment.

Appellants also contend that § 701 offends the Free Exercise Clause of the First Amendment. However, "it is necessary in a free exercise case for one to show the coercive effect of the enactment as it operates against him in the practice of his religion," Abington School District v. Schempp, 374 U.S. 203, 223 (1963), and appellants have not contended that the New York law in any way coerces them as individuals in the practice of their religion.

The judgment is affirmed.

Mr. Justice Harlan, concurring.

Although I join the opinion and judgment of the Court, I wish to emphasize certain of the principles which I believe to be central to the determination of this case, and which I think are implicit in the Court's decision.

The attitude of government toward religion must, as this Court has frequently observed, be one of neutrality. Neutrality is, however, a coat of many colors. It requires that "government neither engage in nor compel religious practices, that it effect no favoritism among sects or between religion and nonreligion, and that it work deterrence of no religious belief." Abington School District v. Schempp, 374 U.S. 203, 305 (concurring opinion of GOLDBERG, J.). * * * I would hold that where the contested governmental activity is calculated to achieve nonreligious purposes otherwise within the competence of the State, and where the activity does not involve the State "so significantly and directly in the realm of the sectarian as to give rise to * * * divisive influences and inhibitions of freedom," *id.*, at 307, it is not forbidden by the religious clauses of the First Amendment.

In my opinion, § 701 of the Education Law of New York does not employ religion as its standard for action or inaction, and is not otherwise inconsistent with these principles.

MR. JUSTICE BLACK, dissenting.

The Court here affirms a judgment of the New York Court of Appeals which sustained the constitutionality of a New York law providing state tax-raised funds to supply school books for use by pupils in schools owned and operated by religious sects. I believe the New York law held valid is a flat, flagrant, open violation of the First and Fourteenth Amendments which together forbid Congress or state legislatures to enact any law "respecting an establishment of religion." For that reason I would reverse the New York Court of Appeals' judgment. This, I am confident, would be in keeping with the deliberate statement we made in Everson v. Board of Education, 330 U.S. 1, 15–16 (1947), * * *

The *Everson* and *McCollum* cases plainly interpret the First and Fourteenth Amendments as protecting the taxpayers of a State from being compelled to pay taxes to their government to support the agencies of private religious organizations the taxpayers oppose. To authorize a State to tax its residents for such church purposes is to put the State squarely in the religious activities of certain religious groups that happen to be strong enough politically to write their own religious preferences and prejudices into the laws. This links state and churches together in controlling the lives and destinies of our citizenship—a citizenship composed of people of myriad religious faiths, some of them bitterly hostile to and completely intolerant of the others. It was to escape laws precisely like this that a large part of the Nation's early immigrants fled to this country. It was also to escape such laws and such consequences that the First Amendment was written in language strong and clear barring passage of any law "respecting an establishment of religion."

It is true, of course, that the New York law does not as yet formally adopt or establish a state religion. But it takes a great stride in that direction and coming events cast their shadows before them. The same powerful sectarian religious propagandists who have succeeded in securing passage of the present law to help religious schools carry on their sectarian religious purposes can and doubtless will continue their propaganda, looking toward complete domination and supremacy of their particular brand of religion. * * *

* * *

As my Brother Douglas, so forcefully shows, in an argument with which I fully agree, upholding a State's power to pay bus or streetcar fares for school children cannot provide support for the validity of a state law using tax-raised funds to buy school books for a religious school. The First Amendment's bar to establishment of religion must preclude a State from using funds levied from all of its citizens to purchase books for use by sectarian schools, which, although "secular," realistically will in some way inevitably tend to propagate the religious views of the favored sect. Books are the most essential tool of education since they contain the resources of knowledge which the educational process is designed to exploit. In this sense it is not difficult to distinguish books, which are the heart of any school, from bus fares, which provide a convenient and helpful general public transportation service. With respect to the former, state financial support actively and directly assists the teaching and propagation of sectarian religious viewpoints in clear conflict with the First Amendment's establishment bar; with respect to the latter, the State merely provides a general and nondiscriminatory transportation service in no way related to substantive religious views and beliefs.

This New York law, it may be said by some, makes but a small inroad and does not amount to complete state establishment of religion. But that is no excuse for upholding it. It requires no prophet to foresee that on the argument used to support this law others could be upheld providing for state or federal government funds to buy property on which to erect religious school buildings or to erect the buildings themselves, to pay the salaries of the religious school teachers, and finally to have the sectarian religious groups cease to rely on voluntary contributions of members of their sects while waiting for the Government to pick up all the bills for the religious schools. * * *

I still subscribe to the belief that tax-raised funds cannot constitutionally be used to support religious schools, buy their school books, erect their buildings, pay their teachers, or pay any other of their maintenance expenses, even to the extent of one penny. The First Amendment's prohibition against governmental establishment of religion was written on the assumption that state aid to religion and religious schools generates discord, disharmony, hatred, and strife among our people, and that any government that supplies such aids is to that extent a tyranny. And I still believe that the only way to protect minority religious groups from majority groups in this country is to keep the wall of separation between church and state high and impregnable as the First and Fourteenth Amendments provide. The Court's affirmance here bodes nothing but evil to religious peace in this country.

Mr. Justice Douglas, dissenting.

* * *

The statute on its face empowers each parochial school to determine for itself which textbooks will be eligible for loans to its students, for the Act provides that the only text which the State may provide is "a book which a pupil is required to use as a text for a semester or more in a particular class in the school he legally attends." New York Education Law § 701, subd. 2. This initial and crucial selection is undoubtedly made by the parochial school's principal or its individual instructors, who are, in the case of Roman Catholic schools, normally priests or nuns. The next step under the Act is an "individual request" for an eligible textbook (§ 701, subd. 3), but the State Education Department has ruled that a pupil may make his request to the local public board of education through a "private school official." Local boards have accordingly provided for those requests to be made by the individual or "by groups or classes." And forms for textbook requisitions to be filled out by the head of the private school are provided.

The role of the local public school board is to decide whether to veto the selection made by the parochial school. This is done by determining first whether the text has been or should be "approved" for use in public schools and second whether the text is "secular," "nonreligious," or "non-sectarian." The local boards apparently have broad discretion in exercising this veto power.

Thus the statutory system provides that the parochial school will ask for the books that it wants. Can there be the slightest doubt that the head of the parochial school will select the book or books that best promote its sectarian creed?

If the board of education supinely submits by approving and supplying the sectarian or sectarian-oriented textbooks, the struggle to keep church and state separate has been lost. If the board resists, then the battle line between church and state will have been drawn and the contest will be on to keep the school board independent or to put it under church domination and control.

Whatever may be said of *Everson,* there is nothing ideological about a bus. There is nothing ideological about a school lunch, or a public nurse, or a scholarship. The constitutionality of such public aid to students in parochial schools turns on considerations not present in this textbook case. The textbook goes to the very heart of education in a parochial school. It is the chief, although not solitary, instrumentality for propagating a particular religious creed or faith. How can we possibly approve such state aid to a religion? A parochial school textbook may contain many, many more seeds of creed and dogma than a prayer. * * *

Judge Van Voorhis, joined by Chief Judge Fuld and Judge Breitel, dissenting below, said that the difficulty with the textbook loan program "is that there is no reliable standard by which secular and religious textbooks can be distinguished from each other." 20 N.Y.2d, at 122, 228 N.E.2d, at 798, 281 N.Y.S.2d, at 809. The New York Legislature felt that science was a non-sectarian subject (* * *, *supra*). Does this mean that any general science textbook intended for use in grades 7–12 may be provided by the State to parochial school students?

May John M. Scott's Adventures in Science (1963) be supplied under the textbook loan program? This book teaches embryology in the following manner:

> "To you an animal usually means a mammal, such as a cat, dog, squirrel, or guinea pig. The new animal or embryo develops inside the body of the mother until birth. The fertilized egg becomes an embryo or developing animal. Many cell divisions take place. In time some cells become muscle cells, others nerve cells or blood cells, and organs such as eyes, stomach, and intestine are formed.
>
> "The body of a human being grows in the same way, but it is much more remarkable than that of any animal, for the embryo has a human soul infused into the body by God. Human parents are partners with God in creation. They have very great powers and great responsibilities, for through their cooperation with God souls are born for heaven." (At 618–619.) [7]

* * *

Father Peter O'Reilly put the matter succinctly when he disclosed what was happening in one Catholic school: "On February 24, 1954, Rev. Cyril F. Meyer, C.M., then Vice President of the University, sent the following letter to all the faculty, both Catholics and non-Catholics, even those teaching law, science, and mathematics:

"'Dear Faculty Member:

"'As a result of several spirited discussions in the Academic Senate, a resolution was passed by that body that a self-evaluation be made of the effectiveness with which we are achieving in our classrooms the stated objectives of the University. * * * The primacy of the spiritual is the reason for a Christian university. Our goal is not merely to equip students with marketable skills. It is far above this—to educate man, the whole man, the theocentric man. As you are well aware, we strive to educate not only for personal and social success in secular society, but far more for leadership toward a theocentric society. * * *

"'May I, therefore, respectfully request that you submit answers as specific as possible to the following questions:

"'1. What do you do to make your particular courses theocentric?

* * *

"'Please try to have your answers, using this size paper, returned to me by March 10.'"

---

7. Although the author of this textbook is a priest, the text contains no imprimatur and no *nihil obstat*. Although published by a Catholic press, the Loyola University Press, Chicago, it is not marked in any manner as a "denominational edition," but is simply the general edition of the book. Accordingly, under Opinion of Counsel No. 181, the only document approaching a "regulation" on the issue involved here, Adventures in Science would qualify as "non-sectarian." * * *

* * *

The initiative to select and requisition "the books desired" is with the parochial school. Powerful religious-political pressures will therefore be on the state agencies to provide the books that are desired.

These then are the battlegrounds where control of textbook distribution will be won or lost. Now that "secular" textbooks will pour into religious schools, we can rest assured that a contest will be on to provide those books for religious schools which the dominant religious group concludes best reflect the theocentric or other philosophy of the particular church.

* * *

Even if I am wrong in that basic premise, we still should not affirm the judgment below. Judge Van Voorhis, dissenting in the New York Court of Appeals, thought that the result of tying parochial school textbooks to public funds would be to put nonsectarian books into religious schools, which in the long view would tend towards state domination of the church. 20 N.Y.2d, at 123, 228 N.E.2d, at 798, 281 N.Y.S.2d, at 810. That would, indeed, be the result if the school boards did not succumb to "sectarian" pressure or control. So, however, the case be viewed—whether sectarian groups win control of school boards or do not gain such control—the principle of separation of church and state, inherent in the Establishment Clause of the First Amendment, is violated by what we today approve.

* * *

Mr. Justice Fortas, dissenting.

The majority opinion of the Court upholds the New York statute by ignoring a vital aspect of it. Public funds are used to buy, for students in sectarian schools, textbooks which are selected and prescribed by the sectarian schools themselves. As my Brother Douglas points out, despite the transparent camouflage that the books are furnished to students, the reality is that they are selected and their use is prescribed by the sectarian authorities. The child must use the prescribed book. He cannot use a different book prescribed for use in the public schools. The State cannot choose the book to be used. It is true that the public school boards must "approve" the book selected by the sectarian authorities; but this has no real significance. The purpose of these provisions is to hold out promise that the books will be "secular" (but cf. Douglas, J., dissenting, *ante,*); but the fact remains that the books are chosen by and for the sectarian schools.

It is misleading to say, as the majority opinion does, that the New York "law merely makes available to all children the benefits of a general program to lend school books free of charge." * * * This is not a "general" program. It is a specific program to use state funds to buy books prescribed by sectarian schools which, in New York, are primarily Catholic, Jewish, and Lutheran sponsored schools. It could be called a "general" program only if the school books made available to all children were precisely the same—the books selected for and used in the public schools. But this program is not one in which all children are treated alike, regardless of where they go to school. This program, in its unconstitutional features, is hand-tailored to satisfy the specific needs of sectarian schools. Children attending such schools are given special books—books selected by the sectarian. How can this be other than the use of public money to aid those sectarian establishments?

It is also beside the point, in my opinion, to "assume," as the majority opinion does, that "books loaned to students are books that are not unsuitable for use in the public schools because of religious content." * * * The point is that the books furnished to students of sectarian schools are selected by the religious authorities and are prescribed by them.

This case is not within the principle of Everson v. Board of Education, 330 U.S. 1 (1947). Apart from the differences between textbooks and bus rides, the present statute does not call for extending to children attending sectarian schools the same service or facility extended to children in public schools. This statute calls for furnishing special, separate, and particular books, specially, separately, and particularly chosen by religious sects or their representatives for use in their sectarian schools. This is the infirmity, in my opinion. This is the feature that makes it impossible, in my view, to reach any conclusion other than that this statute is an unconstitutional use of public funds to support an establishment of religion.

This is the feature of the present statute that makes it totally inaccurate to suggest, as the majority does here, that furnishing these specially selected books for use in sectarian schools is like "public provision of police and fire protection, sewage facilities, and streets and sidewalks." * * * These are furnished to all alike. They are not selected on the basis of specification by a religious sect. And patrons of any one sect do not receive services or facilities different from those accorded members of other religions or agnostics or even atheists. I would reverse the judgment below.

WOLMAN v. WALTER

Supreme Court of the United States, 1977.
433 U.S. 229, 97 S.Ct. 2593, 53 L.Ed.2d 714.

Mr. Justice Blackmun delivered the opinion of the Court (Parts I, V, VI, VII, and VIII), together with an opinion (Parts II, III, and IV), in which The Chief Justice, Mr. Justice Stewart, and Mr. Justice Powell joined.

This is still another case presenting the recurrent issue of the limitations imposed by the Establishment Clause of the First Amendment, made applicable to the States by the Fourteenth Amendment, Meek v. Pittenger, 421 U.S. 349, 351 (1975), on state aid to pupils in church-related elementary and secondary schools. Appellants are citizens and taxpayers of Ohio. They challenge all but one of the provisions of Ohio Rev. Code Ann. § 3317.06 (Supp.1976) which authorize various forms of aid. * * * A three judge court was convened. It held the statute constitutional in all respects. Wolman v. Essex, 417 F.Supp. 1113 (ND Ohio 1976). We noted probable jurisdiction. 429 U.S. 1037 (1977).

I

* * * In broad outline, the statute authorizes the State to provide nonpublic school pupils with books, instructional materials and equipment, standardized testing and scoring, diagnostic services, therapeutic services, and field trip transportation.

The initial biennial appropriation by the Ohio Legislature for implementation of the statute was the sum of $88,800,000. App. 27. Funds so appropriated are paid to the State's public school districts and are then expended by them. All disbursements made with respect to nonpublic schools have their equivalents in disbursements for public schools, and the amount expended per pupil in nonpublic schools may not exceed the amount expended per pupil in the public schools.

The parties stipulated that during the 1974–1975 school year there were 720 chartered nonpublic schools in Ohio. Of these, all but 29 were sectarian. More than 96% of the nonpublic enrollment attended sectarian schools, and more than 92% attended Catholic schools. * * *

* * *

The mode of analysis for Establishment Clause questions is defined by the three-part test that has emerged from the Court's decisions. In order to pass muster, a statute must have a secular legislative purpose, must have a principal or primary effect that neither advances nor inhibits religion, and must not foster an excessive government entanglement with religion. * * *

In the present case we have no difficulty with the first prong of this three-part test. We are satisfied that the challenged statute reflects Ohio's legitimate interest in protecting the health of its youth and in providing a fertile educational environment for all the school children of the State. As is usual in our cases, the analytical difficulty has to do with the effect and entanglement criteria.

We have acknowledged before, and we do so again here, that the wall of separation that must be maintained between church and state "is a blurred, indistinct, and variable barrier depending on all the circumstances of a particular relationship." *Lemon,* 403 U.S., at 614. Nonetheless, the Court's numerous precedents "have become firmly rooted," *Nyquist,* 413 U.S., at 761, and now provide substantial guidance. We therefore turn to the task of applying the rules derived from our decisions to the respective provisions of the statute at issue.

III
Textbooks

* * *

This system for the loan of textbooks to individual students bears a striking resemblance to the systems approved in Board of Education v. Allen, 392 U.S. 236 (1968), * * *

* * * Accordingly, we conclude that § 3317.06(A) is constitutional.

IV
Testing and Scoring

Section 3317.06 authorizes expenditure of funds:

"(J) To supply for use by pupils attending nonpublic schools within the district such standardized tests and scoring services as are in use in the public schools of the state."

These tests "are used to measure the progress of students in secular subjects." App. 48. Nonpublic school personnel are not involved in either the drafting or scoring of the tests. 417 F.Supp., at 1124. The statute does not authorize any payment to nonpublic school personnel for the costs of administering the tests.

* * *

Under the section at issue, the State provides both the schools and the school district with the means of ensuring that the minimum standards are met. The nonpublic school does not control the content of the test or its result. This serves to prevent the use of the test as a part of religious teaching, and thus avoids that kind of direct aid to religion found present in *Levitt*. Similarly, the inability of the school to control the test eliminates the need for the supervision that gives rise to excessive entanglement. We therefore agree with the District Court's conclusion that § 3317.06(J) is constitutional.

V
Diagnostic Services

Section 3317.06 authorizes expenditures of funds:

"(D) To provide speech and hearing diagnostic services to pupils attending nonpublic schools within the district. Such service shall be provided in the nonpublic school attended by the pupil receiving the service.

* * *

"(F) To provide diagnostic psychological services to pupils attending nonpublic schools within the district. Such services shall be provided in the school attended by the pupil receiving the service."

It will be observed that these speech and hearing and psychological diagnostic services are to be provided within the nonpublic school. It is stipulated, however, that the personnel (with the exception of physicians) who perform the services are employees of the local board of education; that physicians may be hired on a contract basis; that the purpose of these services is to determine the pupil's deficiency or need of assistance; and that treatment of any defect so found would take place off the nonpublic school premises. * * *

* * *

The reason for considering diagnostic services to be different from teaching or counseling is readily apparent. First, diagnostic services, unlike teaching or counseling, have little or no educational content and are not closely associated with the educational mission of the nonpublic school. Accordingly, any pressure on the public diagnostician to allow the intrusion of sectarian views is greatly reduced. Second, the diagnostician has only limited contact with the child, and that contact involves chiefly the use of objective and professional testing methods to detect students in need of treatment. The nature of the relationship between the diagnostician and the pupil does not provide the same opportunity for the transmission of sectarian views as attends the relationship between teacher and student or that between counselor and student.

We conclude that providing diagnostic services on the nonpublic school premises will not create an impermissible risk of the fostering of ideological views. It follows that there is no need for excessive surveillance, and there will not be impermissible entanglement. We therefore hold that §§ 3317.06(D) and (F) are constitutional.

* * *

Instructional Materials and Equipment

Sections 3317.06(B) and (C) authorize expenditures of funds for the purchase and loan to pupils or their parents upon individual request of instructional materials and instructional equipment of the kind in use in the public schools within the district and which is "incapable of diversion to religious use." Section 3317.06 also provides that the materials and equipment may be stored on the premises of a nonpublic school and that publicly hired personnel who administer the lending program may perform their services upon the nonpublic school premises when necessary "for efficient implementation of the lending program."

Although the exact nature of the material and equipment is not clearly revealed, the parties have stipulated: "It is expected that materials and equipment loaned to pupils or parents under the new law will be similar to such former materials and equipment except that to the extent that the law requires that materials and equipment capable of diversion to religious issues will not be supplied." * * * Equipment provided under the predecessor statute, * * *, included projectors, tape recorders, record players, maps and globes, science kits, weather forecasting charts, and the like. The District Court, * * *, found the * * * statute, * * *, constitutional because the court could not distinguish the loan of material and equipment from the textbook provisions upheld in *Meek,* 421 U.S., at 359–362, and in *Allen,* 392 U.S., at 248.

In *Meek,* however, the Court considered the constitutional validity of a direct loan to nonpublic schools of instructional material and equipment, and, despite the apparent secular nature of the goods, held the loan impermissible. Mr. Justice Stewart, in writing for the Court, stated:

"The very purpose of many of those schools is to provide an integrated secular and religious education; the teaching process is, to a large extent, devoted to the inculcation of religious values and belief. See Lemon v. Kurtzman, 403 U.S., at 616–617. Substantial aid to the educational function of such schools, accordingly, necessarily results in aid to the sectarian school enterprise as a whole. '[T]he secular education those schools provide goes hand in hand with the religious mission that is the only reason for the schools' existence. Within the institution, the two are inextricably intertwined.' *Id.*, at 657 (opinion of BRENNAN, J.)." 421 U.S., at 366.

Thus, even though the loan ostensibly was limited to neutral and secular instructional material and equipment, it inescapably had the primary effect of providing a direct and substantial advancement of the sectarian enterprise.

Appellees seek to avoid *Meek* by emphasizing that it involved a program of direct loans to nonpublic schools. In contrast, the material and equipment at issue under the Ohio statute are loaned to the pupil or his parent. In our view, however, it would exalt form over substance if this distinction were found to justify a result different from that in *Meek*. Before *Meek* was decided by this Court, Ohio authorized the loan of material and equipment directly to the nonpublic schools. Then, in light of *Meek*, the state legislature decided to channel the goods through the parents and pupils. Despite the technical change in legal bailee, the program in substance is the same as before: The equipment is substantially the same; it will receive the same use by the students; and it may still be stored and distributed on the nonpublic school premises. In view of the impossibility of separating the secular education function from the sectarian, the state aid inevitably flows in part in support of the religious role of the schools.

* * * Accordingly, we hold §§ 3317.06(B) and (C) to be unconstitutional.

VIII
Field Trips

Section 3317.06 also authorizes expenditures of funds:

"(L) To provide such field trip transportation and services to nonpublic school students as are provided to public school students in the district. School districts may contract with commercial transportation companies for such transportation service if school district busses are unavailable."

There is no restriction on the timing of field trips; the only restriction on number lies in the parallel the statute draws to field trips provided to public school students in the district. The parties have stipulated that the trips "would consist of visits to governmental, industrial, cultural, and scientific centers designed to enrich the secular studies of students." App. 49. The choice of destination, however, will be made by the nonpublic school teacher from a wide range of locations.

The District Court, 417 F.Supp., at 1124–1125, held this feature to be constitutionally indistinguishable from that with which the Court was concerned in Everson v. Board of Education, 330 U.S. 1 (1947). We do not agree. In *Everson* the Court approved a system under which a New Jersey board of education reimbursed parents for the costs of sending their children to and from school, public or parochial, by public carrier. * * *

The Ohio situation is in sharp contrast. First, the nonpublic school controls the timing of the trips and, within a certain range, their frequency and destinations. Thus, the schools, rather than the children, truly are the recipients of the service and, as this Court has recognized, this fact alone may be sufficient to invalidate the program as impermissible direct aid. See Lemon v. Kurtzman, 403 U.S., at 621. Second, although a trip may be to a location that would be of interest to those in public schools, it is the individual teacher who makes a field trip meaningful. The experience begins with the study and discussion of the place to be visited; it continues on location with the teacher pointing out items of interest and stimulating the imagination; and it ends with a discussion of the experience. The field trips are an integral part of the educational experience, and where the teacher works within and for a sectarian institution, an unacceptable risk of fostering of religion is an inevitable byproduct. * * *

* * *

We hold § 3317.06(L) to be unconstitutional.

IX

In summary, we hold constitutional those portions of the Ohio statute authorizing the State to provide nonpublic school pupils with books, standardized testing and scoring, diagnostic services, and therapeutic and remedial services. We hold unconstitutional those portions relating to instructional materials and equipment and field trip services.

The judgment of the District Court is therefore affirmed in part and reversed in part.

It is so ordered.

The Chief Justice dissents from Parts VII and VIII of the Court's opinion.

* * *

Mr. Justice Brennan, concurring in part and dissenting. [Omitted.]
* * *

Mr. Justice Marshall, concurring in part and dissenting in part.
* * *

The court upholds the textbook loan provision, § 3317.06(A), on the precedent of Board of Education v. Allen, 392 U.S. 236 (1968). * * *. It also recognizes, however, that there is "a tension" between *Allen* and the reasoning of the Court in Meek v. Pittenger, 421 U.S. 349 (1975). I would resolve that tension by overruling *Allen*. I am now convinced that *Allen* is largely responsible for reducing the "high and impregnable" wall between church and state erected by the First Amendment, Everson v. Board of Education, 330 U.S. 1, 18 (1947), to "a blurred, indistinct, and variable barrier," Lemon v. Kurtzman, 403 U.S. 602, 614 (1971), incapable of performing its vital functions of protecting both church and state.

* * *

It is, of course, unquestionable that textbooks are central to the educational process. Under the rationale of *Meek*, therefore, they should not be provided by the State to sectarian schools because "[substantial] aid to the educational function of such schools * * * necessarily results in aid to the sectarian school enterprise as a whole."
* * *

Mr. Justice Powell, concurring in part, concurring in the judgment in part, and dissenting in part. [Omitted.]

* * *

Mr. Justice Stevens, concurring in part and dissenting in part.

The distinction between the religious and the secular is a fundamental one. To quote from Clarence Darrow's argument in the *Scopes* case:

> "The realm of religion * * * is where knowledge leaves off, and where faith begins, and it never has needed the arm of the State for support, and wherever it has received it, it has harmed both the public and the religion that it would pretend to serve."

The line drawn by the Establishment Clause of the First Amendment must also have a fundamental character. It should not differentiate between direct and indirect subsidies, or between instructional materials like globes and maps on the one hand and instructional materials like textbooks on the other. For that reason, rather than the three-part test described in Part II of the plurality's opinion, I would adhere to the test enunciated for the Court by Mr. Justice Black:

> "No tax in any amount, large or small, can be levied to support any religious activities or institutions, whatever they may be called, or whatever form they may adopt to teach or practice religion." Everson v. Board of Education, 330 U.S. 1, 16 (1947).

Under that test, a state subsidy of sectarian schools is invalid regardless of the form it takes. The financing of buildings, field trips, instructional materials, educational tests, and schoolbooks are all equally invalid. For all give aid to the school's educational mission, which at heart is religious. On the other hand, I am not prepared to exclude the possibility that some parts of the statute before us may be administered in a constitutional manner. The State can plainly provide public health services to children attending nonpublic schools. The diagnostic and therapeutic services described in Parts V and VI of the Court's opinion may fall into this category. Although I have some misgivings on this point, I am not prepared to hold this part of the statute invalid on its face.

* * *

C. The General Test Modified and in Dispute

MUELLER v. ALLEN

Supreme Court of the United States, 1983.
463 U.S. 388, 103 S.Ct. 3062, 77 L.Ed.2d 721.

JUSTICE REHNQUIST delivered the opinion of the Court.

Minnesota allows taxpayers, in computing their state income tax, to deduct certain expenses incurred in providing for the education of their children. Minn.Stat. § 290.09, subd. 22 (1982).[1] * * *

Minnesota, like every other State, provides its citizens with free elementary and secondary schooling. Minn.Stat. §§ 120.06, 120.72 (1982). It seems to be agreed that about 820,000 students attended this school system in the most recent school year. During the same year, approximately 91,000 elementary and secondary students attended some 500 privately supported schools located in Minnesota, and about 95% of these students attended schools considering themselves to be sectarian.

* * *

Petitioners—certain Minnesota taxpayers—sued in the United States District Court for the District of Minnesota claiming that § 290.09, subd. 22, violated the Establishment Clause by providing financial assistance to sectarian institutions. They named as defendants, respondents here, the Commissioner of the Department of Revenue of Minnesota and several parents who took advantage of the tax deduction for expenses incurred in sending their children to parochial schools. The District Court granted respondents' motion for summary judgment, holding that the statute was "neutral on its face and in its application and does not have a primary effect of either advancing or

---

1. Minnesota Stat. § 290.09, subd. 22 (1982), permits a taxpayer to deduct from his or her computation of gross income the following:

"Tuition and transportation expense. The amount he has paid to others, not to exceed $500 for each dependent in grades K to 6 and $700 for each dependent in grades 7 to 12, for tuition, textbooks and transportation of each dependent in attending an elementary or secondary school situated in Minnesota, North Dakota, South Dakota, Iowa, or Wisconsin, wherein a resident of this state may legally fulfill the state's compulsory attendance laws, which is not operated for profit, and which adheres to the provisions of the Civil Rights Act of 1964 and chapter 363. As used in this subdivision, 'textbooks' shall mean and include books and other instructional materials and equipment used in elementary and secondary schools in teaching only those subjects legally and commonly taught in public elementary and secondary schools in this state and shall not include instructional books and materials used in the teaching of religious tenets, doctrines or worship, the purpose of which is to inculcate such tenets, doctrines or worship, nor shall it include such books or materials for, or transportation to, extracurricular activities including sporting events, musical or dramatic events, speech activities, driver's education, or programs of a similar nature."

inhibiting religion." 514 F.Supp. 998, 1003 (Minn.1981). On appeal, the Court of Appeals affirmed, concluding that the Minnesota statute substantially benefited a "broad class of Minnesota citizens." 676 F.2d 1195, 1205 (CA8 1982).

* * *

* * * In this case we are asked to decide whether Minnesota's tax deduction bears greater resemblance to those types of assistance to parochial schools we have approved, or to those we have struck down. Petitioners place particular reliance on our decision in *Committee for Public Education v. Nyquist, supra,* where we held invalid a New York statute providing public funds for the maintenance and repair of the physical facilities of private schools and granting thinly disguised "tax benefits," actually amounting to tuition grants, to the parents of children attending private schools. As explained below, we conclude that § 290.09, subd. 22, bears less resemblance to the arrangement struck down in *Nyquist* than it does to assistance programs upheld in our prior decisions and those discussed with approval in *Nyquist*.

The general nature of our inquiry in this area has been guided, since the decision in *Lemon v. Kurtzman, supra,* by the "three-part" test laid down in that case:

> "First, the statute must have a secular legislative purpose; second, its principal or primary effect must be one that neither advances nor inhibits religion * * *; finally, the statute must not foster 'an excessive government entanglement with religion.'" *Id.,* at 612–613.

While this principle is well settled, our cases have also emphasized that it provides "no more than [a] helpful signpos[t]" in dealing with Establishment Clause challenges. *Hunt v. McNair, supra,* at 741. With this caveat in mind, we turn to the specific challenges raised against § 290.09, subd. 22, under the *Lemon* framework.

Little time need be spent on the question of whether the Minnesota tax deduction has a secular purpose. Under our prior decisions, governmental assistance programs have consistently survived this inquiry even when they have run afoul of other aspects of the *Lemon* framework. See, *e.g., Lemon v. Kurtzman, supra; Meek v. Pittenger, supra,* at 363; *Wolman v. Walter, supra,* at 236. This reflects, at least in part, our reluctance to attribute unconstitutional motives to the States, particularly when a plausible secular purpose for the State's program may be discerned from the face of the statute.

A State's decision to defray the cost of educational expenses incurred by parents—regardless of the type of schools their children attend—evidences a purpose that is both secular and understandable. An educated populace is essential to the political and economic health of any community, and a State's efforts to assist parents in meeting the rising cost of educational expenses plainly serves this secular purpose of ensuring that the State's citizenry is well educated. Similarly, Minnesota, like other States, could conclude that there is a strong public interest in assuring the continued financial health of private schools, both sectarian and nonsectarian. By educating a substantial number of students such schools relieve public schools of a correspondingly great burden—to the benefit of all taxpayers. In addition, private schools may serve as a benchmark for public schools, in a manner analogous to the "TVA yardstick" for private power companies. As Justice Powell has remarked:

> "Parochial schools, quite apart from their sectarian purpose, have provided an educational alternative for millions of young Americans; they often afford wholesome competition with our public schools; and in some States they relieve substantially the tax burden incident to the operation of public schools. The State has, moreover, a legitimate interest in facilitating education of the highest quality for all children within its boundaries, whatever school their parents have chosen for them."
> *Wolman v. Walter, supra,* at 262 (POWELL, J., concurring in part, concurring in judgment in part, and dissenting in part).

All these justifications are readily available to support § 290.09, subd. 22, and each is sufficient to satisfy the secular purpose inquiry of *Lemon.*

We turn therefore to the more difficult but related question whether the Minnesota statute has "the primary effect of advancing the sectarian aims of the nonpublic schools." Committee for Public Education v. Regan, 444 U.S. 646, 662 (1980); Lemon v. Kurtzman, 403 U.S., at 612–613. In concluding that it does not, we find several features of the Minnesota tax deduction particularly significant. First, an essential feature of Minnesota's arrangement is the fact that § 290.09, subd. 22, is only one among many deductions—such as those for medical expenses, § 290.09, subd. 10, and charitable contributions, § 290.21, subd. 3—available under the Minnesota tax laws. Our decisions consistently have recognized that traditionally "[l]egislatures have especially broad latitude in creating classifications and distinctions in tax statutes," * * *

* * * Most importantly, the deduction is available for educational expenses incurred by all parents, including those whose children attend public schools and those whose children attend nonsectarian private schools or sectarian private schools. Just as in Widmar v. Vincent, 454 U.S. 263, 274 (1981), where we concluded that the State's provision of a forum neutrally "available to a broad class of nonreligious as well as religious speakers" does not "confer any imprimatur of state approval," *ibid.,* so here: "[t]he provision of benefits to so broad a spectrum of groups is an important index of secular effect." * * *

In this respect, as well as others, this case is vitally different from the scheme struck down in *Nyquist.* There, public assistance amounting to tuition grants, was provided only to parents of children in *nonpublic* schools. * * *

We also agree with the Court of Appeals that, by channeling whatever assistance it may provide to parochial schools through individual parents, Minnesota has reduced the Establishment Clause objections to which its action is subject. It is true, of course, that financial assistance provided to parents ultimately has an economic effect comparable to that of aid given directly to the schools attended by their children. It is also true, however, that under Minnesota's arrangement public funds become available only as a result of numerous, private choices of individual parents of school-age children. For these reasons, we recognized in *Nyquist* that the means by which state assistance flows to private schools is of some importance: we said that "the fact that aid is disbursed to parents rather than to * * * schools" is a material consideration in Establishment Clause analysis, albeit "only one among many factors to be considered." * * *

* * * The Establishment Clause of course extends beyond prohibition of a state church or payment of state funds to one or more churches. We do not think, however, that its prohibition extends to the type of tax deduction established by Minnesota. The historic purposes of the Clause simply do not encompass the sort of attenuated financial benefit, ultimately controlled by the private choices of individual parents, that eventually flows to parochial schools from the neutrally available tax benefit at issue in this case.

Petitioners argue that, notwithstanding the facial neutrality of § 290.09, subd. 22, in application the statute primarily benefits religious institutions. Petitioners rely, as they did below, on a statistical analysis of the type of persons claiming the tax deduction. They contend that most parents of public school children incur no tuition expenses, see Minn.Stat. § 120.06 (1982), and that other expenses deductible under § 290.09, subd. 22, are negligible in value; moreover, they claim that 96% of the children in private schools in 1978–1979 attended religiously affiliated institutions. Because of all this, they reason, the bulk of deductions taken under § 290.09, subd. 22, will be claimed by parents of children in sectarian schools. Respondents reply that petitioners have failed to consider the impact of deductions for items such as transportation, summer school tuition, tuition paid by parents whose children attended schools outside the school districts in which they resided, rental or purchase costs for a variety of equipment, and tuition for certain types of instruction not ordinarily provided in public schools.

We need not consider these contentions in detail. We would be loath to adopt a rule grounding the constitutionality of a facially neutral law on annual reports reciting the extent to which various classes of private citizens claimed benefits under the law. * * *

* * * More fundamentally, whatever unequal effect may be attributed to the statutory classification can fairly be regarded as a rough return for the benefits, discussed above, provided to the State and all taxpayers by parents sending their children to parochial schools. In the light of all this, we believe it wiser to decline to engage in the type of empirical inquiry into those persons benefited by state law which petitioners urge.

Thus, we hold that the Minnesota tax deduction for educational expenses satisfies the primary effect inquiry of our Establishment Clause cases.

Turning to the third part of the *Lemon* inquiry, we have no difficulty in concluding that the Minnesota statute does not "excessively entangle" the State in religion. The only plausible source of the "comprehensive, discriminating, and continuing state surveillance," 403 U.S., at 619, necessary to run afoul of this standard would lie in the fact that state officials must determine whether particular textbooks qualify for a deduction. In making this decision, state officials must disallow deductions taken for "instructional books and materials used in the teaching of religious tenets, doctrines or worship, the purpose of which is to inculcate such tenets, doctrines or worship." Minn.Stat. § 290.09, subd. 22 (1982). Making decisions such as this does not differ substantially from making the types of decisions approved in earlier opinions of this Court. In Board of Education v. Allen, 392 U.S. 236 (1968), for example, the Court upheld the loan of secular textbooks to parents or children attending nonpublic schools; though state officials were required to determine whether particular books were or were not secular, the system was held not to violate the Establishment Clause.

* * *

For the foregoing reasons, the judgment of the Court of Appeals is Affirmed.

JUSTICE MARSHALL, with whom JUSTICE BRENNAN, JUSTICE BLACKMUN, and JUSTICE STEVENS join, dissenting.

The Establishment Clause of the First Amendment prohibits a State from subsidizing religious education, whether it does so directly or indirectly. In my view, this principle of neutrality forbids not only the tax benefits struck down in Committee for Public Education v. Nyquist, 413 U.S. 756 (1973), but any tax benefit, including the tax deduction at issue here, which subsidizes tuition payments to sectarian schools. I also believe that the Establishment Clause prohibits the tax deductions that Minnesota authorizes for the cost of books and other instructional materials used for sectarian purposes.

I

The majority today does not question the continuing vitality of this Court's decision in *Nyquist*. That decision established that a State may not support religious education either through direct grants to parochial schools or through financial aid to parents of parochial school students. * * * *Nyquist* also established that financial aid to parents of students attending parochial schools is no more permissible if it is provided in the form of a tax credit than if provided in the form of cash payments. * * *

A

In calculating their net income for state income tax purposes, Minnesota residents are permitted to deduct the cost of their children's tuition, subject to a ceiling of $500 or $700 per child. By taking this deduction, a taxpayer reduces his tax bill by a sum equal to the amount of tuition multiplied by his rate of tax. Although this tax benefit is available to any parents whose children attend schools which charge tuition, the vast majority of the taxpayers who are eligible to receive the benefit are parents whose children attend religious schools. In the 1978–1979 school year, 90,000 students were enrolled in nonpublic schools charging tuition; over 95% of those students attended sectarian schools. Although the statute also allows a deduction for the tuition expenses of children attending public schools, Minnesota public schools are generally prohibited by law from charging tuition. * * * Public schools may assess tuition charges only for students accepted from outside the district. * * * In the 1978–1979 school year, only 79 public school students fell into this category. The parents of the remaining 815,000 students who attended public schools were ineligible to receive this tax benefit.

* * *

As we recognized in *Nyquist,* direct government subsidization of parochial school tuition is impermissible because "the effect of the aid is unmistakably to provide desired financial support for nonpublic, sectarian institutions." 413 U.S., at 783. "[A]id to the educational function of [parochial] schools * * * necessarily results in aid to the sectarian school enterprise as a whole" because "[t]he very purpose of many of those schools is to provide an integrated secular and religious education." *Meek v. Pittenger, supra,* at 366. For this reason, aid to sectarian schools must be restricted to ensure that it may be not used to further the religious mission of those schools. See, e.g., *Wolman v. Walter, supra,* at 250–251. While "services such as police and fire protection, sewage disposal, highways, and sidewalks," may be provided to parochial schools in common with other institutions, because this type of assistance is clearly "'marked off from the religious function'" of those schools, *Nyquist, supra,* at 781–782, quoting Everson v. Board of Education, 330 U.S. 1, 18 (1947), unrestricted financial assistance, such as grants for the maintenance and construction of parochial schools, may not be provided. * * *

* * *

The majority attempts to distinguish *Nyquist* by pointing to two differences between the Minnesota tuition-assistance program and the program struck down in *Nyquist.* Neither of these distinctions can withstand scrutiny.

1

The majority first attempts to distinguish *Nyquist* on the ground that Minnesota makes all parents eligible to deduct up to $500 or $700 for each dependent, whereas the New York law allowed a deduction only for parents whose children attended nonpublic schools. Although Minnesota taxpayers who send their children to local public schools may not deduct tuition expenses because they incur none, they may deduct other expenses, such as the cost of gym clothes, pencils, and notebooks, which are shared by all parents of school-age children. This, in the majority's view, distinguishes the Minnesota scheme from the law at issue in *Nyquist.*

That the Minnesota statute makes some small benefit available to all parents cannot alter the fact that the most substantial benefit provided by the statute is available only to those parents who send their children to schools that charge tuition. It is simply undeniable that the single largest expense that may be deducted under the Minnesota statute is tuition. The statute is little more than a subsidy of tuition masquerading as a subsidy of general educational expenses. The other deductible expenses are *de minimis* in comparison to tuition expenses.

* * *

* * * The only factual inquiry necessary is the same as that employed in *Nyquist* and Sloan v. Lemon, 413 U.S. 825 (1973): whether the deduction permitted for tuition expenses primarily benefits those who send their children to religious schools. * * *

* * *

2

The majority also asserts that the Minnesota statute is distinguishable from the statute struck down in *Nyquist* in another respect: the tax benefit available under Minnesota law is a "genuine tax deduction," whereas the New York law provided a benefit which, while nominally a deduction, also had features of a "tax credit." * * * Under the Minnesota law, the amount of the benefit varies directly with the amount of the expenditure. Under the New York law, the amount of deduction was not dependent upon the amount actually paid for tuition but was a predetermined amount which depended on the tax bracket of each taxpayer. The deduction was designed to yield roughly the same amount of tax "forgiveness" for each taxpayer.

This is a distinction without a difference. Our prior decisions have rejected the relevance of the majority's formalistic distinction between tax deductions and the tax benefit at issue in *Nyquist.* * * *

* * *

C

The majority incorrectly asserts that Minnesota's tax deduction for tuition expenses "bears less resemblance to the arrangement struck down in *Nyquist* than it does to assistance programs upheld in our prior decisions and those discussed with approval in *Nyquist.*" * * * One might as well say that a tangerine bears less resemblance to an orange than to an apple. The two cases relied on by the majority, Board of Education v. Allen, 392 U.S. 236 (1968), and Everson v. Board of Education, 330 U.S. 1 (1947), are inapposite today for precisely the same reasons that they were inapposite in *Nyquist.*

We distinguished these cases in *Nyquist, supra,* at 781–782, and again in *Sloan v. Lemon, supra,* at 832. Financial assistance for tuition payments has a consequence that

> "is quite unlike the sort of 'indirect' and 'incidental' benefits that flowed to sectarian schools from programs aiding all

parents by supplying bus transportation and secular textbooks for their children. Such benefits were carefully restricted to the purely secular side of church-affiliated institutions and provided no special aid for those who had chosen to support religious schools. Yet such aid approached the 'verge' of the constitutionally impermissible." *Sloan v. Lemon, supra,* at 832 (latter emphasis added).

As previously noted, *supra,* * * *, the Minnesota tuition tax deduction is not available to all parents, but only to parents whose children attend schools that charge tuition, which are comprised almost entirely of sectarian schools. More importantly, the assistance that flows to parochial schools as a result of the tax benefit is not restricted, and cannot be restricted, to the secular functions of those schools.

II

In my view, Minnesota's tax deduction for the cost of textbooks and other instructional materials is also constitutionally infirm. The majority is simply mistaken in concluding that a tax deduction, unlike a tax credit or a direct grant to parents, promotes religious education in a manner that is only "attenuated." * * * A tax deduction has a primary effect that advances religion if it is provided to offset expenditures which are not restricted to the secular activities of parochial schools.

The instructional materials which are subsidized by the Minnesota tax deduction plainly may be used to inculcate religious values and belief. In Meek v. Pittenger, 421 U.S., at 366, we held that even the use of "wholly neutral, secular instructional material and equipment" by church-related schools contributes to religious instruction because " '[t]he secular education those schools provide goes hand in hand with the religious mission that is the only reason for the schools' existence.' " In Wolman v. Walter, 433 U.S., at 249–250, we concluded that precisely the same impermissible effect results when the instructional materials are loaned to the pupil or his parent, rather than directly to the schools. We stated that "it would exalt form over substance if this distinction were found to justify a result different from that in *Meek.*" *Id.,* at 250. It follows that a tax deduction to offset the cost of purchasing instructional materials for use in sectarian schools, like a loan of such materials to parents, "necessarily results in aid to the sectarian school enterprise as a whole" and is therefore a "substantial advancement of religious activity" that "constitutes an impermissible establishment of religion." *Meek v. Pittenger, supra,* at 366.

There is no reason to treat Minnesota's tax deduction for textbooks any differently. Secular textbooks, like other secular instructional materials, contribute to the religious mission of the parochial schools that use those books. Although this Court upheld the loan of secular textbooks to religious schools in *Board of Education v. Allen, supra,* the Court believed at that time that it lacked sufficient experience to determine "based solely on judicial notice" that "the processes of secular and religious training are so intertwined that secular textbooks furnished to students by the public [will always be] instrumental in the teaching of religion." 392 U.S., at 248. This basis for distinguishing secular instructional materials and secular textbooks is simply untenable, and is inconsistent with many of our more recent decisions concerning state aid to parochial schools. See Wolman v. Walter, 433 U.S., at 257–258 (MARSHALL, J., concurring in part and dissenting in part); *id.*, at 264–266 (STEVENS, J., concurring in part and dissenting in part); *Meek v. Pittenger, supra*, at 378 (BRENNAN, J., concurring in part and dissenting in part).

In any event, the Court's assumption in *Allen* that the textbooks at issue there might be used only for secular education was based on the fact that those very books had been chosen by the State for use in the public schools. 392 U.S., at 244–245. In contrast, the Minnesota statute does not limit the tax deduction to those books which the State had approved for use in public schools. Rather, it permits a deduction for books that are chosen by the parochial schools themselves. Indeed, under the Minnesota statutory scheme, textbooks chosen by parochial schools but not used by public schools are likely to be precisely the ones purchased by parents for their children's use. * * *

III

* * *

In my view, the lines drawn in *Nyquist* were drawn on a reasoned basis with appropriate regard for the principles of neutrality embodied by the Establishment Clause. I do not believe that the same can be said of the lines drawn by the majority today. For the first time, the Court has upheld financial support for religious schools without any reason at all to assume that the support will be restricted to the secular functions of those schools and will not be used to support religious instruction. This result is flatly at odds with the fundamental principle that a State may provide no financial support whatsoever to promote religion. As the Court stated in *Everson,* 330 U.S., at 16, and has often repeated, see, e.g., Meek v. Pittenger, 421 U.S., at 359; *Nyquist,* 413 U.S., at 780:

> "No tax in any amount, large or small, can be levied to support any religious activities or institutions, whatever they may be called, or whatever form they may adopt to teach or practice religion."

I dissent.

NOTES ON THE ESTABLISHMENT CLAUSE AND "THEOCRACY" [32]

1. Enforcing God's laws as the law of the civil state

The cases thus far reviewed go to show the extent to which the no establishment clause has been construed to draw lines between laws

---

32. "Theocracy: 1. Government by a God regarded as the ruling power or by priests or officials claiming divine sanction 2. A state so governed. [Greek *theokra-*

"accommodating" religious needs [33] and those "aiding" or "advancing" religion, i.e. laws "establishing" religion through some kind of government support.[34] A different form of the same problem may arise when civil government enacts positive law the very predicate of which is that "the law of God should also be the law of the state"—to be enforced against believers and nonbelievers alike. Government by such rule is usually identified to theocratic states.[35]

The establishment clause, plus the Article VI clause forbidding any religious test as a qualification of office or trust under the authority of the United States, plus the "support and defend" oath requirement of Article VI—the oath to support and defend the Constitution (including the establishment clause as part of the Constitution one is pledged to support and defend)—are the principal clauses directed to concerns of this kind. In some measure, of course, the free exercise clause may also be relevant as well.

In some states, particular state constitutional provisions may also be pertinent—i.e. we have already noted that state constitutional clauses antedating or modeled on the Blaine amendment have sometimes been given a wider scope than the establishment clause itself.[36] In some states there have been explicit state constitutional limitations on office holding by members of the clergy; the majority of these provisions have reflected a strong view that members of the clergy ought not share power in legislative bodies while simultaneously holding office as ministers or as priests bound by vows as keepers of a sectarian faith.

In 1978, in *McDaniel v. Paty*,[37] however, the Supreme Court held that a state constitutional provision disqualifying "ministers of the gospel" from eligibility for election to the state legislature was unconstitutional under the 14th amendment.[38] The state constitutional pro-

tia]" American Heritage Dictionary 1334 (1971 ed.)

33. E.g., *Pierce, Zorach, Allen, Walz, Mueller, Tilton.*

34. E.g., *McCollum, Engel, Schempp, Wolman, Lemon, Nyquist.*

35. See the definition, note 32 *supra*. See also K. Greenawalt, Religious Convictions and Political Choices (1988); Greenawalt, Religious Convictions and Lawmaking, 84 Mich.L.Rev. 352, 401 (1985) ("[T]o demand that other people act in accord with dominant religious beliefs is to promote or impose those beliefs in an impermissible way.") Cf. J. Noonan, The Believer and the Powers That Are (1987); Berman, The Challenge of the Modern State, in Articles of Faith, Articles of Peace 47 (J. Hunter & O. Guinness eds. 1990) ("[In 1787 religion played a guiding role, and government an implementing role, in family law and criminal law.")

36. In a number of states, arrangements of the sort narrowly sustained in *Everson* had been held invalid under such state constitutional clauses. See, e.g., Judd v. Board of Educ. of Union Free Sch. Dist., 278 N.Y. 200, 15 N.E.2d 576 (1938). (*Everson*-type appropriation of local tax funds to furnish bus transport to private and parochial schools, additional to public schools, held invalid pursuant to state constitutional provision providing: "Neither the State nor any subdivision thereof, shall use its property or credit or any public money * * * directly or indirectly, in aid * * * of any school * * * wholly or in part under the control or direction of any religious denomination * * *.")

37. 435 U.S. 618, 98 S.Ct. 1322, 55 L.Ed.2d 593 (1978).

38. The immediate issue before the Court involved a state statutory restriction on candidate eligibility to serve as a delegate to the state's limited constitutional convention,—rather than eligibility to serve in the state legislature. The constitutional convention delegate eligibility standard, however, was set by state law by reference to the state constitution provision regarding eligibility for election to the House of Representatives of the Tennessee

vision involved in the case was very old, established in the Tennessee Constitution, dating from 1796. It was of a kind fairly common to a number of states during the nineteenth century. The general purpose of such elective office restrictions "was primarily to assure the success of a new political experiment, the separation of church and state." [39] Provisions of this kind had in fact been supported by John Locke and Thomas Jefferson, and originally by James Madison as well.

In *McDaniel v. Paty*, the Court held that even assuming the state had a substantial interest in adopting office holding eligibility standards to provide some assurance that such acts as its General Assembly might adopt would not seek to enact sectarian religious interests (but would, rather, be guided by the separation principles of the "no establishment" clause),[40] the state's categorical presumption that ordained ministers would be unable to abide by the civil oath required of them—to support and defend the Constitution—was unwarranted. So the flat ban on legislative eligibility was struck down.[41] The Court acknowledged that such notables as John Locke and Thomas Jefferson had supported such limitations. It also noted that James Madison originally agreed with that view but that Madison came to believe otherwise (i.e. that such restrictions were not really necessary and were, moreover, quite unfair)—and eventually, so had every state except Tennessee, the last state still to retain such a limitation on ordained ministers or priests and eligibility for legislative election.

The Court's decision in *McDaniel v. Paty* serves as a reminder that priests, ministers, mullahs, rabbis, etc. may not be deemed ineligible for

---

General Assembly, and the Court therefore directly addressed the latter provision as well. The state supreme court had held that the restriction on ordained ministers from holding legislative office did not violate the fourteenth amendment, insofar as the disqualification was not based on religious belief but more narrowly, on vocational status as an ordained minister; it upheld the limitation in light of the constitutional interest to separate legislative action from religious action in "the lawmaking process of government—*where religious action is absolutely prohibited by the establishment clause* * * *" 547 S.W.2d 897, 903 (1977) (Emphasis added).

39. 435 U.S. at 622, 98 S.Ct. at 1325, 55 L.Ed.2d at 598.

40. See note 38, *supra*.

41. The plurality opinion was written by Chief Justice Burger for himself, Powell, Rehnquist, and Stevens. A concurring opinion by Brennan, (for himself and Marshall) treated the state constitutional provision as a form of unconstitutional condition, i.e. requiring one who is an ordained minister (one form of exercising one's freedom of religion) either to give up his office as a minister or to be deemed ineligible for elective offices open to others. Justice Brennan, 435 U.S. at 642, 98 S.Ct. at 1326, 55 L.Ed.2d at 611), relied on "judicial enforcement of the Establishment Clause" to provide the necessary safeguard against such sectarian actions ministers-as-legislators might be tempted to take, to the extent that they might not themselves live up to the oath of office otherwise required of them—to support and defend the Constitution (including the establishment clause). Stewart concurred separately on the basis that disqualification from office because of one's religious vocation (as a minister) was indistinguishable from disqualification on grounds of religious belief or lack of religious belief, a kind of disqualification the Court had earlier held to be unconstitutional in Torcaso v. Watkins, 367 U.S. 488, 81 S.Ct. 1680, 6 L.Ed.2d 982 (1961). White concurred separately on the basis of the fourteenth amendment equal protection clause, opining that the disqualification swept too broadly (and thus was overinclusive) since it disqualified ministers whose religious beliefs would not necessarily prevent them from properly discharging their obligations in office.

elective office.[42] And of course each person is free to support whomever they wish for elective office, according to their own preference for such legislation they desire to see enacted—including that based on a strongly-held religious conviction that the civil law ought to report what scripture and/or religious teaching prescribes—including laws characteristic of theocratic states.

The principal safeguards against tendencies of a theocratic state, therefore, are *not* safeguards limiting office-holding eligibility to non-clergy, or limitations on first amendment rights to form parties committed to certain religious aims, or limitations on how people choose to vote. Rather, such as they are, they arise from the Article VI requirement nominally binding federal and state officials to support and defend the Constitution in their role as civil legislators, executives, and judges, and from the judicial enforcement of the establishment clause itself—directly as to Congress and indirectly (i.e. via the fourteenth amendment) as to the states.[43] But how is this latter "safeguard" expected to work?

As a hypothetical example, suppose it is contrary to the tenets of a particular religion to eat pork. And suppose, moreover, that the eating of pork is deemed by the scriptures of that religion to be a sin generally, condemned in the sight of God. Suppose the religion is or becomes of controlling influence within a given state legislature such that a general law is enacted of the following sort: —a law forbidding the sale of pork for human consumption, punishing those who do eat it as criminal misdemeanants, by criminal fines up to $500 or jail up to thirty days. Insofar as the predicate for this legislation is that "the human consumption of pork is an abomination in the sight of God, and therefore on that account is to be forbidden in a community founded on God's will," it would seem to be vulnerable pursuant to the "no establishment" clause of the first amendment. Accordingly, one might expect that a person prosecuted for violating such a law would have a valid constitutional defense. —The defense would not be that the law abridges the defendant's freedom of religion (the defendant's religion, if he or she has one, may say nothing one way or the other about eating pork). Rather, it would be that the law violates the establishment clause's separation of the civil from the theocratic state.

Perhaps the following is another suitable example. In the Book of Exodus, chapt. 20, the following Commandment appears:

> Remember the sabbath day, to keep it holy. Six days you shall labor, and do all your work; but the seventh day is a sabbath to the Lord your god; in it you shall not do any work * * *

Consistent with the "no establishment" clause, may the civil state require all to conform according to the dictates of this religious text on

---

42. Neither could any restriction of eligibility for election to the House, the Senate, presidency, or vice presidency disqualify religious leaders, heads of churches, clergy, ministers, etc. for such offices. See, e.g., Powell v. McCormack, 395 U.S. 486, 89 S.Ct. 1944, 23 L.Ed.2d 491 (1969) (the criteria of eligibility for election to the House provided in the Constitution are exclusive, i.e. no other criteria may constitutionally be required).

43. See, e.g., the quotation by Brennan, in *McDaniel v. Paty, supra* note 41.

pain of fine or jail? And more generally, to whatever extent the state attempts to carry into positive law "God's will" in prescribing (and proscribing) what may (and may not) be done,[44] isn't this a manifestation of a "theocratic," rather than a "civil," state?[45] Isn't the legislative predicate of a theocratic state at odds with the no establishment clause of the first amendment?[46] Consider the following reported case. How does one disentangle a "religious" from a "civil" or "secular" predicate for legislative action? How will the three-part *Lemon* establishment clause test apply?[47]

McGOWAN v. MARYLAND
Supreme Court of the United States, 1961.
366 U.S. 420, 81 S.Ct. 1101, 6 L.Ed.2d 393.

Mr. Chief Justice WARREN delivered the opinion of the Court.

The issues in this case concern the constitutional validity of Maryland criminal statutes, commonly known as Sunday Closing Laws or Sunday Blue Laws. These statutes, with exceptions to be noted hereafter, generally proscribe all labor, business and other commercial activities on Sunday. The questions presented are whether the classifications within the statutes bring about a denial of equal protection of the law, whether the laws are so vague as to fail to give reasonable notice of the forbidden conduct and therefore violate due process, and whether

---

44. Does it matter whether the legislators are themselves ministers, priests, or ayatollahs or whether, though they are not themselves ministers, priests, or ayatollahs, they nonetheless legislate according to the dictates of the politically dominant religion either because they agree with its tenets, or though disagreeing, nevertheless vote in accord with its tenets to avoid losing elections in favor of others who will?

45. If "sodomy" is criminalized "because it is an abomination in the sight of God" (according to the tenets of the religion dominantly of influence with the particular legislature criminalizing it), does not its criminalization thereby enact the compulsory observance of the religious tenets of the dominant faith? Is this not to establish a religion (i.e. its tenets) under secular auspices, enacting a theocracy on the installment plan? Cf. Bowers v. Hardwick, 478 U.S. 186, 106 S.Ct. 2841, 92 L.Ed.2d (1986) If the reading or willing viewing of obscenity is condemned as a "sin"—and for that reason made criminal, how does one describe the foundation of the law in nontheocratic terms? See Henkin, Morals and the Constitution: The Sin of Obscenity, 63 Colum.L.Rev. 391 (1963). See also Webster v. Reproductive Health Services, 492 U.S. ___, 109 S.Ct. 3040, 3079, 106 L.Ed.2d 410 (1989) (Stevens, J., dissenting) (finding no non-religious legislative basis to distinguish a gamete and a zygote, for purposes of drawing any constitutional distinction for an anti-abortion act applicable at the moment of conception as distinct from a later time in the gestation of the fetus).

46. But see Douglas, J., in *Zorach v. Clauson, supra* ("We are a religious people whose institutions presuppose a Supreme Being.")

47. Cf. Stone v. Graham, 449 U.S. 39, 101 S.Ct. 192, 66 L.Ed.2d 199 (1980) (state legislatively mandated posting of the Ten Commandments on public classroom walls, held unconstitutional as serving solely a religious purpose (and no secular purpose), despite required notation printed at the bottom of each posted copy declaring: "The secular application of the Ten Commandments is clearly seen in its adoption as the fundamental legal code of Western Civilization and the Common Law of the United States"). See also Epperson v. Arkansas, 393 U.S. 97, 89 S.Ct. 266, 21 L.Ed.2d 228 (1968) (legislative ban on public school instruction on evolution held invalid as applied to high school biology teacher, on "no establishment" grounds, failing the "secular purpose" prong of the three-part *Lemon* test).

the statutes are laws respecting an establishment of religion or prohibiting the free exercise thereof.

Appellants are seven employees of a large discount department store located on a highway in Anne Arundel County, Maryland. They were indicted for the Sunday sale of a three-ring loose-leaf binder, a can of floor wax, a stapler and staples, and a toy submarine in violation of Md.Ann.Code, Art. 27, § 521. Generally, this section prohibited, throughout the State, the Sunday sale of all merchandise except the retail sale of tobacco products, confectioneries, milk, bread, fruits, gasoline, oils, greases, drugs and medicines, and newspapers and periodicals. Recently amended, this section also now excepts from the general prohibition the retail sale in Anne Arundel County of all foodstuffs, automobile and boating accessories, flowers, toilet goods, hospital supplies and souvenirs. * * *

* * *

Among other things, appellants contended at the trial that the Maryland statutes under which they were charged were contrary to the Fourteenth Amendment for the reasons stated at the outset of this opinion. Appellants were convicted and each was fined five dollars and costs. The Maryland Court of Appeals affirmed, * * *; on appeal brought under 28 U.S.C. § 1257(2), we noted probable jurisdiction. * * *

I.

Appellants argue that the Maryland statutes violate the "Equal Protection" Clause of the Fourteenth Amendment on several counts. First, they contend that the classifications contained in the statutes concerning which commodities may or may not be sold on Sunday are without rational and substantial relation to the object of the legislation. Specifically, appellants allege that the statutory exemptions for the Sunday sale of the merchandise mentioned above render arbitrary the statute under which they were convicted. Appellants further allege that § 521 is capricious because of the exemptions for the operation of the various amusements that have been listed and because slot machines, pin-ball machines, and bingo are legalized and are freely played on Sunday.

The standards under which this proposition is to be evaluated have been set forth many times by this Court. Although no precise formula has been developed, the Court has held that the Fourteenth Amendment permits the States a wide scope of discretion in enacting laws which affect some groups of citizens differently than others. The constitutional safeguard is offended only if the classification rests on grounds wholly irrelevant to the achievement of the State's objective. State legislatures are presumed to have acted within their constitutional power despite the fact that, in practice, their laws result in some inequality. A statutory discrimination will not be set aside if any state of facts reasonably may be conceived to justify it. * * *

* * *

The final questions for decision are whether the Maryland Sunday Closing Laws conflict with the Federal Constitution's provisions for religious liberty. First, appellants contend here that the statutes applicable to Anne Arundel County violate the constitutional guarantee of freedom of religion in that the statutes' effect is to prohibit the free exercise of religion in contravention of the First Amendment, made applicable to the States by the Fourteenth Amendment. But appellants allege only economic injury to themselves; they do not allege any infringement of their own religious freedoms due to Sunday closing. In fact, the record is silent as to what appellants' religious beliefs are.
* * *

Secondly, appellants contend that the statutes violate the guarantee of separation of church and state in that the statutes are laws respecting an establishment of religion contrary to the First Amendment, made applicable to the States by the Fourteenth Amendment. If the purpose of the "establishment" clause was only to insure protection for the "free exercise" of religion, then what we have said above concerning appellants' standing to raise the "free exercise" contention would appear to be true here. However, the writings of Madison, who was the First Amendment's architect, demonstrate that the establishment of a religion was equally feared because of its tendencies to political tyranny and subversion of civil authority. Thus, in *Everson v. Board of Education, supra,* the Court permitted a district taxpayer to challenge, on "establishment" grounds, a state statute which authorized district boards of education to reimburse parents for fares paid for the transportation of their children to both public and Catholic schools. Appellants here concededly have suffered direct economic injury, allegedly due to the imposition on them of the tenets of the Christian religion.

The essence of appellants' "establishment" argument is that Sunday is the Sabbath day of the predominant Christian sects; that the purpose of the enforced stoppage of labor on that day is to facilitate and encourage church attendance; that the purpose of setting Sunday as a day of universal rest is to induce people with no religion or people with marginal religious beliefs to join the predominant Christian sects; that the purpose of the atmosphere of tranquility created by Sunday closing is to aid the conduct of church services and religious observance of the sacred day. In substantiating their "establishment" argument, appellants rely on the wording of the present Maryland statutes, on earlier versions of the current Sunday laws and on prior judicial characterizations of these laws by the Maryland Court of Appeals. Although only the constitutionality of § 521, the section under which appellants have been convicted, is immediately before us in this litigation, inquiry into the history of Sunday Closing Laws in our country, in addition to an examination of the Maryland Sunday closing statutes in their entirety and of their history, is relevant to the decision of whether the Maryland Sunday law in question is one respecting an establishment of religion. There is no dispute that the original laws which dealt with Sunday labor were motivated by religious forces. But what we must decide is whether present Sunday legislation, having undergone extensive changes from the earliest forms, still retains its religious character.

Sunday Closing Laws go far back into American history, having been brought to the colonies with a background of English legislation dating to the thirteenth century. In 1237, Henry III forbade the frequenting of markets on Sunday; the Sunday showing of wools at the staple was banned by Edward III in 1354; in 1409, Henry IV prohibited the playing of unlawful games on Sunday; Henry VI proscribed Sunday fairs in churchyards in 1444 and, four years later, made unlawful all fairs and markets and all showings of any goods or merchandise; Edward VI disallowed Sunday bodily labor by several injunctions in the mid-sixteenth century; various Sunday sports and amusements were restricted in 1625 by Charles I. * * * Observation of the above language, and of that of the prior mandates, reveals clearly that the English Sunday legislation was in aid of the established church.

The American colonial Sunday restrictions arose soon after settlement. Starting in 1650, the Plymouth Colony proscribed servile work, unnecessary travelling, sports, and the sale of alcoholic beverages on the Lord's day and enacted laws concerning church attendance. The Massachusetts Bay Colony and the Connecticut and New Haven Colonies enacted similar prohibitions, some even earlier in the seventeenth century. The religious orientation of the colonial statutes was equally apparent. For example, a 1629 Massachusetts Bay instruction began, "And to the end the Sabbath may be celebrated in a religious manner. * * * " A 1653 enactment spoke of Sunday activities "which things tend much to the dishonor of God, the reproach of religion, and the profanation of his holy Sabbath, the sanctification whereof is sometimes put for all duties immediately respecting the service of God. * * * " * * *

But, despite the strongly religious origin of these laws, beginning before the eighteenth century, nonreligious arguments for Sunday closing began to be heard more distinctly and the statutes began to lose some of their totally religious flavor. In the middle 1700's, Blackstone wrote, "[The] keeping one day in the seven holy, as a time of relaxation and refreshment as well as for public worship, is of admirable service to a state considered merely as a civil institution. It humanizes, by the help of conversation and society, the manners of the lower classes; which would otherwise degenerate into a sordid ferocity and savage selfishness of spirit; it enables the industrious workman to pursue his occupation in the ensuing week with health and cheerfulness." 4 Bl.Comm. 63. * * *

More recently, further secular justifications have been advanced for making Sunday a day of rest, a day when people may recover from the labors of the week just passed and may physically and mentally prepare for the week's work to come. In England, during the First World War, a committee investigating the health conditions of munitions workers reported that "if the maximum output is to be secured and maintained for any length of time, a weekly period of rest must be allowed. * * * On economic and social grounds alike this weekly period of rest is best provided on Sunday."

The proponents of Sunday closing legislation are no longer exclusively representatives of religious interests. * * *

* * * Some of our States now enforce their Sunday legislation through Departments of Labor, e.g., 6 S.C.Code Ann. (1952), § 64–5. Thus have Sunday laws evolved from the wholly religious sanctions that originally were enacted.

Moreover, litigation over Sunday closing laws is not novel. Scores of cases may be found in the state appellate courts relating to sundry phases of Sunday enactments. Religious objections have been raised there on numerous occasions but sustained only once, in *Ex parte Newman,* 9 Cal. 502 (1858); and that decision was overruled three years later, in *Ex parte Andrews,* 18 Cal. 678. * * *

* * *

But in order to dispose of the case before us, we must consider the standards by which the Maryland statutes are to be measured. * * *

* * *

An early commentator opined that the "real object of the amendment was * * * to prevent any national ecclesiastical establishment, which should give to an hierarchy the exclusive patronage of the national government." 3 Story, Commentaries on the Constitution of the United States, 728. But, the First Amendment, in its final form, did not simply bar a congressional enactment establishing a church; it forbade all laws respecting an establishment of religion. Thus, this Court has given the Amendment a "broad interpretation * * * in the light of its history and the evils it was designed forever to suppress. * * *" *Everson v. Board of Education, supra,* at pp. 14–15. It has found that the First and Fourteenth Amendments afford protection against religious establishment far more extensive than merely to forbid a national or state church. Thus, in McCollum v. Board of Education, 333 U.S. 203, the Court held that the action of a board of education, permitting religious instruction during school hours in public school buildings and requiring those children who chose not to attend to remain in their classrooms, to be contrary to the "Establishment" Clause.

However, it is equally true that the "Establishment" Clause does not ban federal or state regulation of conduct whose reason or effect merely happens to coincide or harmonize with the tenets of some or all religions. In many instances, the Congress or state legislatures conclude that the general welfare of society, wholly apart from any religious considerations, demands such regulation. Thus, for temporal purposes, murder is illegal. And the fact that this agrees with the dictates of the Judaeo–Christian religions while it may disagree with others does not invalidate the regulation. So too with the questions of adultery and polygamy. Davis v. Beason, 133 U.S. 333; *Reynolds v. United States, supra.* The same could be said of theft, fraud, etc., because those offenses were also proscribed in the Decalogue.

* * *

In light of the evolution of our Sunday Closing Laws through the centuries, and of their more or less recent emphasis upon secular considerations, it is not difficult to discern that as presently written and administered, most of them, at least, are of a secular rather than of a religious character, and that presently they bear no relationship to establishment of religion as those words are used in the Constitution of the United States.

Throughout this century and longer, both the federal and state governments have oriented their activities very largely toward improvement of the health, safety, recreation and general well-being of our citizens. Numerous laws affecting public health, safety factors in industry, laws affecting hours and conditions of labor of women and children, week-end diversion at parks and beaches, and cultural activities of various kinds, now point the way toward the good life for all. Sunday Closing Laws, like those before us, have become part and parcel of this great governmental concern wholly apart from their original purposes or connotations. The present purpose and effect of most of them is to provide a uniform day of rest for all citizens; the fact that this day is Sunday, a day of particular significance for the dominant Christian sects, does not bar the State from achieving its secular goals. To say that the States cannot prescribe Sunday as a day of rest for these purposes solely because centuries ago such laws had their genesis in religion would give a constitutional interpretation of hostility to the public welfare rather than one of mere separation of church and State.

We now reach the Maryland statutes under review. The title of the major series of sections of the Maryland Code dealing with Sunday closing—Art. 27, §§ 492–534C—is "Sabbath Breaking"; § 492 proscribes work or bodily labor on the "Lord's day," and forbids persons to "profane the Lord's day" by gaming, fishing et cetera; § 522 refers to Sunday as the "Sabbath day." As has been mentioned above, many of the exempted Sunday activities in the various localities of the State may only be conducted during the afternoon and late evening; most Christian church services, of course, are held on Sunday morning and early Sunday evening. Finally, as previously noted, certain localities do not permit the allowed Sunday activities to be carried on within one hundred yards of any church where religious services are being held. This is the totality of the evidence of religious purpose which may be gleaned from the face of the present statute and from its operative effect.

The predecessors of the existing Maryland Sunday laws are undeniably religious in origin. * * *

* * *

Considering the language and operative effect of the current statutes, we no longer find the blanket prohibition against Sunday work or bodily labor. To the contrary, we find that § 521 of Art. 27, the section which appellants violated, permits the Sunday sale of tobaccos and sweets and a long list of sundry articles which we have enumerated above; we find that § 509 of Art. 27 permits the Sunday operation of bathing beaches, amusement parks and similar facilities; we find that Art. 2B, § 28, permits the Sunday sale of alcoholic beverages, products strictly forbidden by predecessor statutes; we are told that Anne Arundel County allows Sunday bingo and the Sunday playing of pinball machines and slot machines, activities generally condemned by prior Maryland Sunday legislation. Certainly, these are not works of charity or necessity. Section 521's current stipulation that shops with only one employee may remain open on Sunday does not coincide with a religious purpose. These provisions, along with those which permit various sports and entertainments on Sunday, seem clearly to be fashioned for the purpose of providing a Sunday atmosphere of recreation, cheerfulness, repose and enjoyment. Coupled with the general proscription against other types of work, we believe that the air of the day is one of relaxation rather than one of religion.

The existing Maryland Sunday laws are not simply verbatim re-enactments of their religiously oriented antecedents. Only § 492 retains the appellation of "Lord's day" and even that section no longer makes recitation of religious purpose. It does talk in terms of "[profaning] the Lord's day," but other sections permit the activities previously thought to be profane. Prior denunciation of Sunday drunkenness is now gone. Contemporary concern with these statutes is evidenced by the dozen changes made in 1959 and by the recent enactment of a majority of the exceptions.

Finally, the relevant pronouncements of the Maryland Court of Appeals dispel any argument that the statutes' announced purpose is religious. * * * And the Maryland court declared in its decision in the instant case: "The legislative plan is plain. It is to compel a day of rest from work, permitting only activities which are necessary or recreational." *McGowan v. State, supra,* at p. 123, 151 A.2d, at 159. After engaging in the close scrutiny demanded of us when First Amendment liberties are at issue, we accept the State Supreme Court's determination that the statutes' present purpose and effect is not to aid religion but to set aside a day of rest and recreation.

But this does not answer all of appellants' contentions. We are told that the State has other means at its disposal to accomplish its secular purpose, other courses that would not even remotely or incidentally give state aid to religion. On this basis, we are asked to hold these statutes invalid on the ground that the State's power to regulate conduct in the public interest may only be executed in a way that does not unduly or unnecessarily infringe upon the religious provisions of the First Amendment. See *Cantwell v. Connecticut, supra,* at pp. 304–305. However relevant this argument may be, we believe that the factual basis on which it rests is not supportable. It is true that if the State's interest were simply to provide for its citizens a periodic respite from work, a regulation demanding that everyone rest one day in seven, leaving the choice of the day to the individual, would suffice.

However, the State's purpose is not merely to provide a one-day-in-seven work stoppage. In addition to this, the State seeks to set one day apart from all others as a day of rest, repose, recreation and tranquility—a day which all members of the family and community have the opportunity to spend and enjoy together, a day on which there exists relative quiet and disassociation from the everyday intensity of commercial activities, a day on which people may visit friends and relatives who are not available during working days.

Obviously, a State is empowered to determine that a rest-one-day-in-seven statute would not accomplish this purpose; that it would not provide for a general cessation of activity, a special atmosphere of tranquility, a day which all members of the family or friends and relatives might spend together. Furthermore, it seems plain that the problems involved in enforcing such a provision would be exceedingly more difficult than those in enforcing a common-day-of-rest provision.

Moreover, it is common knowledge that the first day of the week has come to have special significance as a rest day in this country. People of all religions and people with no religion regard Sunday as a time for family activity, for visiting friends and relatives, for late sleeping, for passive and active entertainments, for dining out, and the like. * * * It would seem unrealistic for enforcement purposes and perhaps detrimental to the general welfare to require a State to choose a common day of rest other than that which most persons would select of their own accord. For these reasons, we hold that the Maryland statutes are not laws respecting an establishment of religion.

The distinctions between the statutes in the case before us and the state action in *McCollum v. Board of Education, supra,* the only case in this Court finding a violation of the "Establishment" Clause, lend further substantiation to our conclusion. In *McCollum,* state action permitted religious instruction in public school buildings during school hours and required students not attending the religious instruction to remain in their classrooms during that time. The Court found that this system had the effect of coercing the children to attend religious classes; no such coercion to attend church services is present in the situation at bar. In *McCollum,* the only alternative available to the nonattending students was to remain in their classrooms; the alternatives open to nonlaboring persons in the instant case are far more diverse. In *McCollum,* there was direct cooperation between state officials and religious ministers; no such direct participation exists under the Maryland laws. In *McCollum,* tax-supported buildings were used to aid religion; in the instant case, no tax monies are being used in aid of religion.

Finally, we should make clear that this case deals only with the constitutionality of § 521 of the Maryland statute before us. We do not hold that Sunday legislation may not be a violation of the "Establishment" Clause if it can be demonstrated that its purpose—evidenced either on the face of the legislation, in conjunction with its legislative history, or in its operative effect—is to use the State's coercive power to aid religion.

Accordingly, the decision is

Affirmed.

* * *

Separate opinion of MR. JUSTICE FRANKFURTER, whom MR. JUSTICE HARLAN joins.

So deeply do the issues raised by these cases cut that it is not surprising that no one opinion can wholly express the views even of all the members of the Court who join in its result. * * *

* * *

Of course, the immediate object of the First Amendment's prohibition was the established church as it had been known in England and in most of the Colonies. But with foresight those who drafted and adopted the words, "Congress shall make no law respecting an establishment of religion" did not limit the constitutional proscription to any particular, dated form of state-supported theological venture. The Establishment Clause withdrew from the sphere of legitimate legislative concern and competence a specific, but comprehensive, area of human conduct: man's belief or disbelief in the verity of some transcendental idea and man's expression in action of that belief or disbelief. Congress may not make these matters, as such, the subject of legislation, nor, now, may any legislature in this country. Neither the National Government nor, under the Due Process Clause of the Fourteenth Amendment, a State may, by any device, support belief or the expression of belief for its own sake, whether from conviction of the truth of that belief, or from conviction that by the propagation of that belief the civil welfare of the State is served, or because a majority of its citizens, holding that belief, are offended when all do not hold it.

With regulations which have other objectives the Establishment Clause, and the fundamental separationist concept which it expresses, are not concerned. These regulations may fall afoul of the constitutional guarantee against infringement of the free exercise or observance of religion. Where they do, they must be set aside at the instance of those whose faith they prejudice. But once it is determined that a challenged statute is supportable as implementing other substantial interests than the promotion of belief, the guarantee prohibiting religious "establishment" is satisfied.

To ask what interest, what objective, legislation serves, of course, is not to psychoanalyze its legislators, but to examine the necessary effects of what they have enacted. If the primary end achieved by a form of regulation is the affirmation or promotion of religious doctrine —primary, in the sense that all secular ends which it purportedly serves are derivative from, not wholly independent of, the advancement of religion—the regulation is beyond the power of the state. This was the case in *McCollum*. Or if a statute furthers both secular and religious ends by means unnecessary to the effectuation of the secular ends alone—where the same secular ends could equally be attained by means which do not have consequences for promotion of religion—the statute cannot stand. A State may not endow a church although that church might inculcate in its parishioners moral concepts deemed to make them better citizens, because the very *raison d'etre* of a church, as opposed to any other school of civilly serviceable morals, is the predication of religious doctrine. However, inasmuch as individuals are free, if they will, to build their own churches and worship in them, the State may guard its people's safety by extending fire and police protection to the churches so built. It was on the reasoning that parents are also at liberty to send their children to parochial schools which meet the reasonable educational standards of the State, Pierce v. Society of Sisters, 268 U.S. 510, that this Court held in the *Everson* case that expenditure of public funds to assure that children attending every kind of school enjoy the relative security of buses, rather than being left to walk or hitchhike, is not an unconstitutional "establishment," even though such an expenditure may cause some children to go to parochial schools who would not otherwise have gone. The close division of the Court in *Everson* serves to show what nice questions are involved in applying to particular governmental action the proposition, undeniable in the abstract, that not every regulation some of whose practical effects may facilitate the observance of a religion by its adherents affronts the requirement of church-state separation.

* * *

In the present cases the Sunday retail sellers and their employees and customers, in attacking statutes banning various activities on a day which most Christian creeds consecrate, do assert that these statutes have no other purpose. * * *

* * *

But, whatever the nature of the propulsions underlying state-enforced Sunday labor stoppage during these centuries before the twentieth, it is clear that its effect was the creation of an institution of Sunday as a day apart. The origins of the institution were religious, certainly, but through long-established usage it had become a part of the life of the English people. It was a day of rest not merely in a physical, hygienic sense, but in the sense of a recurrent time in the cycle of human activity when the rhythms of existence changed, a day of particular associations which came to have their own autonomous value for life. When that value was threatened by the pressures of the Industrial Revolution, agitation began for new legislative action to preserve the traditional English Sunday.

* * *

* * * The bill was strongly supported by labor and trade groups and passed by an overwhelming margin.

Thus the English experience demonstrates the intimate relationship between civil Sunday regulation and the interest of a state in preserving to its people a recurrent time of mental and physical recuperation from the strains and pressures of their ordinary labors.
* * *

* * *

Legislation currently in force in forty-nine of the fifty States illegalizes on Sunday some form of conduct lawful if performed on weekdays. * * *

To be sure, the Massachusetts statute now before the Court, and statutes in Pennsylvania and Maryland, still call Sunday the "Lord's day" or the "Sabbath." So do the Sunday laws in many other States. But the continuation of seventeenth century language does not of itself prove the continuation of the purposes for which the colonial governments enacted these laws, or that these are the purposes for which their successors of the twentieth have retained them and modified them. We know, for example, that Committees of the New York Legislature, considering that State's Sabbath Laws on two occasions more than a century apart, twice recommended no repeal of those laws, both times on the ground that the laws did not involve "any partisan religious issue, but rather economic and health regulation of the activities of the people on a universal day of rest," and that a Massachusetts legislative committee rested on the same views. Sunday legislation has been supported not only by such clerical organizations as the Lord's Day Alliance, but also by labor and trade groups. * * *

It is urged, however, that if a day of rest were the legislative purpose, statutes to secure it would take some other form than the prohibition of activity on Sunday. Such statutes, it is argued, would provide for one day's labor stoppage in seven, leaving the choice of the day to the individual; or, alternatively, would fix a common day of rest on some other day—Monday or Tuesday. But, in all fairness, certainly, it would be impossible to call unreasonable a legislative finding that these suggested alternatives were unsatisfactory. A provision for one day's closing per week, at the option of every particular enterpriser, might be disruptive of families whose members are employed by different enterprises. Enforcement might be more difficult, both because violation would be less easily discovered and because such a law would not be seconded, as is Sunday legislation, by the community's moral temper. More important, one-day-a-week laws do not accomplish all that is accomplished by Sunday laws. They provide only a periodic physical rest, not that atmosphere of entire community repose which Sunday has traditionally brought and which, a legislature might reasonably believe, is necessary to the welfare of those who for many generations have been accustomed to its recuperative effects.

* * *

Appellees in the *Gallagher* case and appellants in the *Braunfeld* case contend that, as applied to them, Orthodox Jewish retailers and their Orthodox Jewish customers, the Massachusetts Lord's day statute and the Pennsylvania Sunday retail sales act violate the Due Process Clause of the Fourteenth Amendment because, in effect, the statutes deter the exercise and observance of their religion. The argument runs that by compelling the Sunday closing of retail stores and thus making unavailable for business and shopping uses one-seventh part of the week, these statutes force them either to give up the Sabbath observance—an essential part of their faith—or to forego advantages enjoyed by the non-Sabbatarian majority of the community. They point out, moreover, that because of the prevailing five-day working week of a large proportion of the population, Sunday is a day peculiarly profitable to retail sellers and peculiarly convenient to retail shoppers. The records in these cases support them in this. The claim which these litigants urge assumes a number of aspects. First, they argue that any one-common-day-of-closing regulation which selected a day other than their Sabbath would be *ipso facto* unconstitutional in its application to them because of its effect in preferring persons who observe no Sabbath, therefore creating economic pressures which urge Sabbatarians to give up their usage. The creation of this pressure by the Sunday statutes, it is said, is not so necessary a means to the achievement of the ends of day-of-rest legislation as to justify its employment when weighed against the injury to Sabbatarian religion which it entails. Six-day-week regulation, with the closing day left to individual choice, is urged as a more reasonable alternative.

Second, they argue that even if legitimate state interests justify the enforcement against persons generally of a single common day of rest, the choice of Sunday as that day violates the rights of religious freedom of the Sabbatarian minority. By choosing a day upon which Sunday-observing Christians worship and abstain from labor, the statutes are said to discriminate between religions. The Sunday observer may practice his faith and yet work six days a week, while the observer of the Jewish Sabbath, his competitor, may work only during five days, to the latter's obvious disadvantage. Orthodox Jewish shoppers whose jobs occupy a five-day week have no week-end shopping day, while Sunday-observing Christians do. * * *

* * *

In urging that an exception in favor of those who observe some other day as sacred would not defeat the ends of Sunday legislation, and therefore that failure to provide such an exception is an unnecessary—hence an unconstitutional—burden on Sabbatarians, the *Gallagher* appellees and *Braunfeld* appellants point to such exceptions in twenty-one of the thirty-four jurisdictions which have statutes banning labor or employment or the selling of goods on Sunday. Actually, in less than half of these twenty-one States does the exemption extend to sales activity as well as to labor. There are tenable reasons why a legislature might choose not to make such an exception. To whatever extent persons who come within the exception are present in a community, their activity would disturb the atmosphere of general repose and reintroduce into Sunday the business tempos of the week. Administration would be more difficult, with violations less evident and, in effect, two or more days to police instead of one. If it is assumed that the retail demand for consumer items is approximately equivalent on Saturday and on Sunday, the Sabbatarian, in proportion as he is less numerous, and hence the competition less severe, might incur through the exception a competitive advantage over the non-Sabbatarian, who would then be in a position, presumably, to complain of discrimination against his religion. Employers who wished to avail themselves of the exception would have to employ only their coreligionists, and there might be introduced into private employment practices an element of religious differentiation which a legislature could regard as undesirable.[106]

Finally, a relevant consideration which might cause a State's lawmakers to reject exception for observers of another day than Sunday is that administration of such a provision may require judicial inquiry into religious belief. A legislature could conclude that if all that is made requisite to qualify for the exemption is an abstinence from labor on some other day, there would be nothing to prevent an enterpriser from closing on his slowest business day, to take advantage of the whole of the profitable week-end trade, thereby converting the Sunday labor ban, in effect, into a day-of-rest-in-seven statute, with choice of the day left to the individual. All of the state exempting statutes seem to reflect this consideration. Ten of them require that a person claiming exception "conscientiously" believe in the sanctity of another day or "conscientiously: observe another day as the Sabbath. Five demand that he keep another day as "holy time." Three allow the exemption only to members of a "religious" society observing another day, and a fourth provides for proof of membership in such a society by the certificate of a preacher or of any three adherents. * * *

* * * Surely, in light of the delicate enforcement problems to which these provisions bear witness, the legislative choice of a blanket Sunday ban applicable to observers of all faiths cannot be held unreasonable. A legislature might in reason find that the alternative of exempting Sabbatarians would impede the effective operation of the Sunday statutes, produce harmful collateral effects, and entail, itself, a not inconsiderable intrusion into matters of religious faith. However preferable, personally, one might deem such an exception, I cannot find that the Constitution compels it.

* * *

MR. JUSTICE DOUGLAS, dissenting.

The question is not whether one day out of seven can be imposed by a State as a day of rest. The question is not whether Sunday can by force of custom and habit be retained as a day of rest. The question is whether a State can impose criminal sanctions on those who, unlike the Christian majority that makes up our society, worship on a different day or do not share the religious scruples of the majority.

* * *

* * * [T]hose who fashioned the First Amendment decided that if and when God is to be served, His service will not be motivated by coercive measures of government. "Congress shall make no law respecting an establishment of religion, or prohibiting the free exercise thereof"—such is the command of the First Amendment made applicable to the State by reason of the Due Process Clause of the Fourteenth. This means, as I understand it, that if a religious heaven is to be worked into the affairs of our people, it is to be done by individuals and groups, not by the Government. This necessarily means, *first*, that the

---

106. Both Pennsylvania and Massachusetts have fair employment practices acts prohibiting religious discrimination in hiring. * * *

dogma, creed, scruples, or practices of no religious group or sect are to be preferred over those of any others; *second,* that no one shall be interfered with by government for practicing the religion of his choice; *third,* that the State may not require anyone to practice a religion or even any religion; and *fourth,* that the State cannot compel one so to conduct himself as not to offend the religious scruples of another. The idea, as I understand it, was to limit the power of government to act in religious matters (*Board of Education v. Barnette, supra;* McCollum v. Board of Education, 333 U.S. 203), not to limit the freedom of religious men to act religiously nor to restrict the freedom of atheists or agnostics.

* * *

The Court picks and chooses language from various decisions to bolster its conclusion that these Sunday laws in the modern setting are "civil regulations." No matter how much is written, no matter what is said, the parentage of these laws is the Fourth Commandment; and they serve and satisfy the religious predispositions of our Christian communities. * * *

It seems to me plain that by these laws the States compel one, under sanction of law, to refrain from work or recreation on Sunday because of the majority's religious views about that day. The State by law makes Sunday a symbol of respect or adherence. Refraining from work or recreation in deference to the majority's religious feelings about Sunday is within every person's choice. By what authority can government compel it?

Cases are put where acts that are immoral by our standards but not by the standards of other religious groups are made criminal. That category of cases, until today, has been a very restricted one confined to polygamy (Reynolds v. United States, 98 U.S. 145) and other extreme situations. The latest example is Prince v. Massachusetts, 321 U.S. 158, which upheld a statute making it criminal for a child under twelve to sell papers, periodicals, or merchandise on a street or in any public place. It was sustained in spite of the finding that the child thought it was her religious duty to perform the act. But that was a narrow holding which turned on the effect which street solicitation might have on the child solicitor:

> "The state's authority over children's activities is broader than over like actions of adults. This is peculiarly true of public activities and in matters of employment. A democratic society rests, for its continuance, upon the healthy, well-rounded growth of young people into full maturity as citizens, with all that implies. It may secure this against impeding restraints and dangers within a broad range of selection. Among evils most appropriate for such action are the crippling effects of child employment, more especially in public places, and the possible harms arising from other activities subject to all the diverse influences of the street. It is too late now to doubt that legislation appropriately designed to reach such evils is within the state's police power, whether against the parent's claim to

control of the child or one that religious scruples dictate contrary action." *Id.,* 168–169.

None of the acts involved here implicates minors. None of the actions made constitutionally criminal today involves the doing of any act that any society has deemed to be immoral.

The conduct held constitutionally criminal today embraces the selling of pure, not impure, food; wholesome, not noxious, articles. Adults, not minors, are involved. The innocent acts, now constitutionally classified as criminal, emphasize the drastic break we make with tradition.

* * *

The State can, of course, require one day of rest a week: one day when every shop or factory is closed. Quite a few States make that requirement. Then the "day of rest" becomes purely and simply a health measure. But the Sunday laws operate differently. They force minorities to obey the majority's religious feelings of what is due and proper for a Christian community; they provide a coercive spur to the "weaker brethren," to those who are indifferent to the claims of a Sabbath through apathy or scruple. Can there be any doubt that Christians, now aligned vigorously in favor of these laws, would be as strongly opposed if they were prosecuted under a Moslem law that forbade them from engaging in secular activities on days that violated Moslem scruples?

There is an "establishment" of religion in the constitutional sense if any practice of any religious group has the sanction of law behind it. There is an interference with the "free exercise" of religion if what in conscience one can do or omit doing is required because of the religious scruples of the community. Hence I would declare each of those laws unconstitutional as applied to the complaining parties, whether or not they are members of a sect which observes as its Sabbath a day other than Sunday. When these laws are applied to Orthodox Jews, as they are in No. 11 and in No. 67, or to Sabbatarians their vice is accentuated. If the Sunday laws are constitutional, kosher markets are on a five-day week. Thus those laws put an economic penalty on those who observe Saturday rather than Sunday as the Sabbath. For the economic pressures on these minorities, created by the fact that our communities are predominantly Sunday-minded, there is no recourse. When, however, the State uses its coercive powers—here the criminal law—to compel minorities to observe a second Sabbath, not their own, the State undertakes to aid and "prefer one religion over another"—contrary to the command of the Constitution. See *Everson v. Board of Education,* * * *.

* * *

NOTE

In light of *McGowan v. Maryland, Stone v. Graham,* and *Epperson v. Arkansas,* consider the following case as reported in the New York

Times.[48]

SUPREME COURT LETS STAND A MISSOURI TOWN'S BAN ON SCHOOL DANCES

by Linda Greenhouse

Special to THE NEW YORK TIMES

Washington, April 16 [1990]:—A ban on school dances in a small Missouri town survived Supreme Court review today.

Without comment, the Court refused to hear a challenge by a group of students and their parents in Purdy, Mo., to the ban. They argued that the policy, reflecting the Christian fundamentalist view that social dancing is sinful, violated the constitutionally required separation of church and state.

Fundamentalist Christians make up a majority of Purdy's residents, and a group of ministers took the leading role in preserving the century old ban when school officials considered modifying it in 1986. * * * A school board official, asked at one community meeting whether he thought the ban might violate the separation of church and state, replied, "You better hope there's never a separation of God and school."

A Federal District Judge in Missouri, Russell G. Clark, ruled in 1988 that the ban amounted to an unconstitutional "establishment" of religion. But a three-judge panel of the United States Court of Appeals for the Eighth Circuit overturned the decision.

The appeals court said that dancing was a "secular" activity and that a prohibition against school dances could be defended as an appropriately "neutral" policy, whatever the motivation behind it.

"We simply do not believe elected government officials are required to check at the door whatever religious background they carry with them before they act on rules that are otherwise [un]objectionable," the appellate panel said.

The full Eighth Circuit voted 5 to 4 against rehearing the case. The dissenting judges declared that "this is a case about religious tyranny."

In their Supreme Court appeal, Clayton v. Place, No. 89–1348, the students argued that the appeals court had failed to give proper consideration to the religious motivation behind the ban. They said the decision indicated that "public school boards may endorse and promote the religious beliefs of a

---

48. For additional facts and discussion in the lower courts, see Clayton by Clayton v. Place, 690 F.Supp. 850 (W.D.Mo.1988), reh'g denied, 884 F.2d 376 (8th Cir.), reh'g en banc denied, 889 F.2d 192 (8th Cir.1989).

locally dominant religious sect as official school policy, so long as the school policy is 'facially neutral.'"

But the school board, in turn, warned the Justices that to strike down the dancing ban on church-state ground would call into question a number of other "public school rules and decisions which have their bases in traditional morality," like dress codes and rules against swearing.

The school board's brief continued: "All citizens are allowed to participate equally in public policy formulation. To exclude those who are informed in their moral vision by an underlying religious faith would deny them freedom of speech and their right to engage in the political process."

2. **Religion in government**

A different aspect of the theocratic state would reflect the installation of theology within government. An example might be provided by a government formally incorporating a distinctive theocratic commitment in its official self-description, e.g., "One Nation, Under Allah," thereby proclaiming to be a government subordinate to Allah, faithful to Allah, conducting itself according to Allah, and reflecting the will of Allah in its proceedings,—as well as explaining its laws in terms of what the Koran is alleged to require (e.g., to forbid charging interest on loans because to do so would be to permit that which is wrong in the sight of Allah).

A different hypothetical example might be a nation proclaiming itself "One Nation, Under God,"—wherein its legislative assemblies are also regularly called to order by ministers offering prayers within the assembly (ministers appointed under government auspices and paid from tax monies),—a nation also proclaiming "In God We Trust" as its national motto,—a nation administering theistic oaths as an incident of its elected officials taking public office, and administering the same theistic oath even to private citizens appearing as witnesses before its formal legislative committees or before its official courts. How does one reconcile the "no establishment" clause with installed government practices such as these?

MARSH v. CHAMBERS
Supreme Court of the United States, 1983.
463 U.S. 783, 103 S.Ct. 3330, 77 L.Ed.2d 1019.

CHIEF JUSTICE BURGER delivered the opinion of the Court.

The question presented is whether the Nebraska Legislature's practice of opening each legislative day with a prayer by a chaplain paid by the State violates the Establishment Clause of the First Amendment.

I

The Nebraska Legislature begins each of its sessions with a prayer offered by a chaplain who is chosen biennially by the Executive Board of the Legislative Council and paid out of public funds.¹ Robert E. Palmer, a Presbyterian minister, has served as chaplain since 1965 at a salary of $319.75 per month for each month the legislature is in session.

Ernest Chambers is a member of the Nebraska Legislature and a taxpayer of Nebraska. Claiming that the Nebraska Legislature's chaplaincy practice violates the Establishment Clause of the First Amendment, he brought this action under 42 U.S.C. § 1983, seeking to enjoin enforcement of the practice.² After denying a motion to dismiss on the ground of legislative immunity, the District Court held that the Establishment Clause was not breached by the prayers, but was violated by paying the chaplain from public funds. 504 F.Supp. 585 (Neb.1980). It therefore enjoined the legislature from using public funds to pay the chaplain; it declined to enjoin the policy of beginning sessions with prayers. Cross-appeals were taken.³

The Court of Appeals for the Eighth Circuit rejected arguments that the case should be dismissed on Tenth Amendment, legislative immunity, standing, or federalism grounds. On the merits of the chaplaincy issue, the court refused to treat respondent's challenges as separable issues as the District Court had done. Instead, the Court of Appeals assessed the practice as a whole because "[p]arsing out [the] elements" would lead to "an incongruous result." 675 F.2d 228, 233 (1982).

Applying the three-part test of Lemon v. Kurtzman, 403 U.S. 602, 612–613 (1971), as set out in Committee for Public Education & Religious Liberty v. Nyquist, 413 U.S. 756, 773 (1973), the court held that the chaplaincy practice violated all three elements of the test: the purpose and primary effect of selecting the same minister for 16 years and publishing his prayers was to promote a particular religious expression; use of state money for compensation and publication led to entanglement. 675 F.2d, at 234–235. Accordingly, the Court of Appeals modified the District Court's injunction and prohibited the State from engaging in any aspect of its established chaplaincy practice.

We granted certiorari limited to the challenge to the practice of opening sessions with prayers by a state-employed clergyman, 459 U.S. 966 (1982), and we reverse.

II

The opening of sessions of legislative and other deliberative public bodies with prayer is deeply embedded in the history and tradition of

1. Rules of the Nebraska Unicameral, Rules 1, 2, and 21. These prayers are recorded in the Legislative Journal and, upon the vote of the legislature, collected from time to time into prayerbooks, which are published at public expense. In 1975, 200 copies were printed; prayerbooks were also published in 1978 (200 copies), and 1979 (100 copies). In total, publication costs amounted to $458.56.

2. Respondent named as defendants State Treasurer Frank Marsh, Chaplain Palmer, and the members of the Executive Board of the Legislative Council in their official capacity. All appear as petitioners before us.

3. The District Court also enjoined the State from using public funds to publish the prayers holding that this practice violated the Establishment Clause. Petitioners have represented to us that they did not challenge this facet of the District Court's decision, Tr. of Oral Arg. 19–20. Accordingly, no issue as to publishing these prayers is before us.

this country. From colonial times through the founding of the Republic and ever since, the practice of legislative prayer has coexisted with the principles of disestablishment and religious freedom. In the very courtrooms in which the United States District Judge and later three Circuit Judges heard and decided this case, the proceedings opened with an announcement that concluded, "God save the United States and this Honorable Court." The same invocation occurs at all sessions of this Court.

The tradition in many of the Colonies was, of course, linked to an established church, but the Continental Congress, beginning in 1774, adopted the traditional procedure of opening its sessions with a prayer offered by a paid chaplain. * * * Although prayers were not offered during the Constitutional Convention, the First Congress, as one of its early items of business, adopted the policy of selecting a chaplain to open each session with prayer. * * * A statute providing for the payment of these chaplains was enacted into law on September 22, 1789. * * *

On September 25, 1789, three days after Congress authorized the appointment of paid chaplains, final agreement was reached on the language of the Bill of Rights, S. Jour., *supra*, at 88; H.R.Jour., *supra*, at 121. Clearly the men who wrote the First Amendment Religion Clause did not view paid legislative chaplains and opening prayers as a violation of that Amendment, for the practice of opening sessions with prayer has continued without interruption ever since that early session of Congress. It has also been followed consistently in most of the states, including Nebraska, where the institution of opening legislative sessions with prayer was adopted even before the State attained statehood. * * *

* * *

In Walz v. Tax Comm'n, 397 U.S. 664, 678 (1970), we considered the weight to be accorded to history:

> "It is obviously correct that no one acquires a vested or protected right in violation of the Constitution by long use, even when that span of time covers our entire national existence and indeed predates it. Yet an unbroken practice * * * is not something to be lightly cast aside."

No more is Nebraska's practice of over a century, consistent with two centuries of national practice, to be cast aside. It can hardly be thought that in the same week Members of the First Congress voted to appoint and to pay a chaplain for each House and also voted to approve the draft of the First Amendment for submission to the states, they intended the Establishment Clause of the Amendment to forbid what they had just declared acceptable. In applying the First Amendment to the states through the Fourteenth Amendment, Cantwell v. Connecticut, 310 U.S. 296 (1940), it would be incongruous to interpret that Clause as imposing more stringent First Amendment limits on the states than the draftsmen imposed on the Federal Government.

This unique history leads us to accept the interpretation of the First Amendment draftsmen who saw no real threat to the Establishment Clause arising from a practice of prayer similar to that now challenged. We conclude that legislative prayer presents no more potential for establishment than the provision of school transportation, Everson v. Board of Education, 330 U.S. 1 (1947), beneficial grants for higher education, Tilton v. Richardson, 403 U.S. 672 (1971), or tax exemptions for religious organizations, *Walz, supra.*

* * *

In light of the unambiguous and unbroken history of more than 200 years, there can be no doubt that the practice of opening legislative sessions with prayer has become part of the fabric of our society. To invoke Divine guidance on a public body entrusted with making the laws is not, in these circumstances, an "establishment" of religion or a step toward establishment; it is simply a tolerable acknowledgment of beliefs widely held among the people of this country. As Justice Douglas observed, "[w]e are a religious people whose institutions presuppose a Supreme Being." Zorach v. Clauson, 343 U.S. 306, 313 (1952).

III

We turn then to the question of whether any features of the Nebraska practice violate the Establishment Clause. Beyond the bare fact that a prayer is offered, three points have been made: first, that a clergyman of only one denomination—Presbyterian—has been selected for 16 years; second, that the chaplain is paid at public expense; and third, that the prayers are in the Judeo–Christian tradition. Weighed against the historical background, these factors do not serve to invalidate Nebraska's practice.

The Court of Appeals was concerned that Palmer's long tenure has the effect of giving preference to his religious views. We cannot, any more than Members of the Congresses of this century, perceive any suggestion that choosing a clergyman of one denomination advances the beliefs of a particular church. To the contrary, the evidence indicates that Palmer was reappointed because his performance and personal qualities were acceptable to the body appointing him. * * *

Nor is the compensation of the chaplain from public funds a reason to invalidate the Nebraska Legislature's chaplaincy; remuneration is grounded in historic practice initiated, as we noted earlier, * * *, by the same Congress that drafted the Establishment Clause of the First Amendment. * * * The content of the prayer is not of concern to judges where, as here, there is no indication that the prayer opportunity has been exploited to proselytize or advance any one, or to disparage any other, faith or belief. That being so, it is not for us to embark on a sensitive evaluation or to parse the content of a particular prayer.

We do not doubt the sincerity of those, who like respondent, believe that to have prayer in this context risks the beginning of the establishment the Founding Fathers feared. But this concern is not well founded, for as Justice Goldberg aptly observed in his concurring opinion in *Abington*, 374 U.S., at 308:

> "It is of course true that great consequences can grow from small beginnings, but the measure of constitutional adjudication is the ability and willingness to distinguish between real threat and mere shadow."

The unbroken practice for two centuries in the National Congress, for more than a century in Nebraska and in many other states, gives abundant assurance that there is no real threat "while this Court sits," Panhandle Oil Co. v. Mississippi ex rel. Knox, 277 U.S. 218, 223 (1928) (HOLMES, J., dissenting).

The judgment of the Court of Appeals is

Reversed.

JUSTICE BRENNAN, with whom JUSTICE MARSHALL joins, dissenting.

The Court today has written a narrow and, on the whole, careful opinion. In effect, the Court holds that officially sponsored legislative prayer, primarily on account of its "unique history," * * *, is generally exempted from the First Amendment's prohibition against "an establishment of religion." The Court's opinion is consistent with dictum in at least one of our prior decisions, and its limited rationale should pose little threat to the overall fate of the Establishment Clause. Moreover, disagreement with the Court requires that I confront the fact that some 20 years ago, in a concurring opinion in one of the cases striking down official prayer and ceremonial Bible reading in the public schools, I came very close to endorsing essentially the result reached by the Court today.[2] Nevertheless, after much reflection, I have come to the conclusion that I was wrong then and that the Court is wrong today. I now believe that the practice of official invocational prayer, as it exists in Nebraska and most other state legislatures, is unconstitutional. It is contrary to the doctrine as well as the underlying purposes of the Establishment Clause, and it is not saved either by its history or by any of the other considerations suggested in the Court's opinion.

I respectfully dissent.

I

The Court makes no pretense of subjecting Nebraska's practice of legislative prayer to any of the formal "tests" that have traditionally structured our inquiry under the Establishment Clause. That it fails to do so is, in a sense, a good thing, for it simply confirms that the Court is carving out an exception to the Establishment Clause rather than reshaping Establishment Clause doctrine to accommodate legislative prayer. For any purposes, however, I must begin by demonstrating what should be obvious: that, if the Court were to judge legislative

---

2. "The saying of invocational prayers in legislative chambers, state or federal, and the appointment of legislative chaplains, might well represent no involvements of the kind prohibited by the Establishment Clause. Legislators, federal and state, are mature adults who may presumably absent themselves from such public and ceremonial exercises without incurring any penalty, direct or indirect." *Schempp, supra,* at 299–300 (BRENNAN, J., concurring) (footnote omitted).

prayer through the unsentimental eye of our settled doctrine, it would have to strike it down as a clear violation of the Establishment Clause.

The most commonly cited formulation of prevailing Establishment Clause doctrine is found in Lemon v. Kurtzman, 403 U.S. 602 (1971):

> "Every analysis in this area must begin with consideration of the cumulative criteria developed by the Court over many years. Three such tests may be gleaned from our cases. First, the statute [at issue] must have a secular legislative purpose; second, its principal or primary effect must be one that neither advances nor inhibits religion; finally, the statute must not foster 'an excessive government entanglement with religion.'"
>
> *Id.*, at 612–613 (citations omitted).

That the "purpose" of legislative prayer is pre-eminently religious rather than secular seems to me to be self-evident. "To invoke Divine guidance on a public body entrusted with making the laws," * * *, is nothing but a religious act. Moreover, whatever secular functions legislative prayer might play—formally opening the legislative session, getting the members of the body to quiet down, and imbuing them with a sense of seriousness and high purpose—could so plainly be performed in a purely nonreligious fashion that to claim a secular purpose for the prayer is an insult to the perfectly honorable individuals who instituted and continue the practice.

* * *

Finally, there can be no doubt that the practice of legislative prayer leads to excessive "entanglement" between the State and religion. *Lemon* pointed out that "entanglement" can take two forms: First, a state statute or program might involve the state impermissibly in monitoring and overseeing religious affairs. 403 U.S., at 614–622. In the case of legislative prayer, the process of choosing a "suitable" chaplain, whether on a permanent or rotating basis, and insuring that the chaplain limits himself or herself to "suitable" prayers, involves precisely the sort of supervision that agencies of government should if at all possible avoid.

Second, excessive "entanglement" might arise out of "the divisive political potential" of a state statute or program. 403 U.S., at 622.

> "Ordinarily political debate and division, however vigorous or even partisan, are normal and healthy manifestations of our democratic system of government, but political division along religious lines was one of the principal evils against which the First Amendment was intended to protect. The potential divisiveness of such conflict is a threat to the normal political process." *Ibid.* (citations omitted).

In this case, this second aspect of entanglement is also clear. The controversy between Senator Chambers and his colleagues, which had reached the stage of difficulty and rancor long before this lawsuit was brought, has split the Nebraska Legislature precisely on issues of religion and religious conformity. App. 21–24. The record in this case also reports a series of instances, involving legislators other than

Senator Chambers, in which invocations by Reverend Palmer and others led to controversy along religious lines. And in general, the history of legislative prayer has been far more eventful—and divisive—than a hasty reading of the Court's opinion might indicate.[10]

In sum, I have no doubt that, if any group of law students were asked to apply the principles of *Lemon* to the question of legislative prayer, they would nearly unanimously find the practice to be unconstitutional.

* * *

Nor should it be thought that this view of the Establishment Clause is a recent concoction of an overreaching judiciary. Even before the First Amendment was written, the Framers of the Constitution broke with the practice of the Articles of Confederation and many state constitutions, and did not invoke the name of God in the document. This "omission of a reference to the Deity was not inadvertent; nor did it remain unnoticed."[18] Moreover, Thomas Jefferson and Andrew Jackson, during their respective terms as President, both refused on Establishment Clause grounds to declare national days of thanksgiving or fasting.[19] And James Madison, writing subsequent to his own Presidency on essentially the very issue we face today, stated:

> "Is the appointment of Chaplains to the two Houses of Congress consistent with the Constitution, and with the pure principle of religious freedom?
>
> "In strictness, the answer on both points must be in the negative. The Constitution of the U.S. forbids everything like an establishment of a national religion. The law appointing Chaplains establishes a religious worship for the national representatives, to be performed by Ministers of religion, elected

---

10. * * *

In more recent years, particular prayers and particular chaplains in the state legislatures have periodically led to serious political divisiveness along religious lines. See, e.g., The Oregonian, Apr. 1, 1983, p. C8 ("Despite protests from at least one representative, a follower of an Indian guru was allowed to give the prayer at the start of Thursday's [Oregon] House [of Representatives] session. Shortly before Ma Anand Sheela began the invocation, about a half-dozen representatives walked off the House floor in apparent protest of the prayer"); Cal.Senate Jour., 37th Sess., 171–173, 307–308 (1907) (discussing request by a State Senator that State Senate Chaplain not use the name of Christ in legislative prayer, and response by one local clergyman claiming that the legislator who made the request had committed a "crowning infamy" and that his "words were those of an irreverent and godless man"). * * *

18. Pfeffer, The Deity in American Constitutional History, 23 J. Church & State 215, 217 (1981). See also 1 Stokes 523.

19. See L. Pfeffer, Church, State, and Freedom 266 (rev. ed. 1967) (hereinafter Pfeffer). Jefferson expressed his views as follows: "'I consider the government of the United States as interdicted by the Constitution from intermeddling with religious institutions, their doctrines, discipline, or exercises. [I]t is only proposed that I should recommend not prescribe a day of fasting and prayer. [But] I do not believe it is for interest of religion to invite the civil magistrate to direct its exercises, its discipline, or its doctrine. * * * Fasting and prayer are religious exercises; the enjoining of them an act of discipline. Every religious society has a right to determine for itself the times for these exercises, and the objects proper for them, according to their own particular tenets; and the right can never be safer than in their hands, where the Constitution has deposited it.'" *Ibid.*, quoting 11 Jefferson's Writings 428–430 (Monticello ed. 1905).

by a majority of them; and these are to be paid out of the national taxes. Does not this involve the principle of a national establishment, applicable to a provision for a religious worship for the Constituent as well as of the representative Body, approved by the majority, and conducted by Ministers of religion paid by the entire nation." Fleet, Madison's "Detached Memoranda," 3 Wm. & Mary Quarterly 534, 558 (1946).

C

Legislative prayer clearly violates the principles of neutrality and separation that are embedded within the Establishment Clause. It is contrary to the fundamental message of *Engel* and *Schempp*. It intrudes on the right to conscience by forcing some legislators either to participate in a "prayer opportunity," * * *, with which they are in basic disagreement, or to make their disagreement a matter of public comment by declining to participate. It forces all residents of the State to support a religious exercise that may be contrary to their own beliefs. It requires the State to commit itself on fundamental theological issues. It has the potential for degrading religion by allowing a religious call to worship to be intermeshed with a secular call to order. And it injects religion into the political sphere by creating the potential that each and every selection of a chaplain, or consideration of a particular prayer, or even reconsideration of the practice itself, will provoke a political battle along religious lines and ultimately alienate some religiously identified group of citizens.

* * *

* * * I sympathize with the Court's reluctance to strike down a practice so prevalent and so ingrained as legislative prayer. I am, however, unconvinced by the Court's arguments, and cannot shake my conviction that legislative prayer violates both the letter and the spirit of the Establishment Clause.

A

The Court's main argument for carving out an exception sustaining legislative prayer is historical. The Court cannot—and does not—purport to find a pattern of "undeviating acceptance," *Walz, supra,* at 681 (BRENNAN, J., concurring), of legislative prayer. * * * It also disclaims exclusive reliance on the mere longevity of legislative prayer. * * * The Court does, however, point out that, only three days before the First Congress reached agreement on the final wording of the Bill of Rights, it authorized the appointment of paid chaplains for its own proceedings, * * *, and the Court argues that in light of this "unique history," * * *, the actions of Congress reveal its intent as to the meaning of the Establishment Clause, * * *. I agree that historical practice is "of considerable import in the interpretation of abstract constitutional language," *Walz,* 397 U.S., at 681 (BRENNAN, J., concurring). This is a case, however, in which—absent the Court's invocation of history—there would be no question that the practice at issue was unconstitutional. And despite the surface appeal of the Court's argument, there are at least three reasons why specific historical practice should not in this case override that clear constitutional imperative.[30]

First, it is significant that the Court's historical argument does not rely on the legislative history of the Establishment Clause itself. Indeed, that formal history is profoundly unilluminating on this and most other subjects. Rather, the Court assumes that the Framers of the Establishment Clause would not have themselves authorized a practice that they thought violated the guarantees contained in the Clause. * * * This assumption, however, is questionable. Legislators, influenced by the passions and exigencies of the moment, the pressure of constituents and colleagues, and the press of business, do not always pass sober constitutional judgment on every piece of legislation they enact, and this must be assumed to be as true of the Members of the First Congress as any other. Indeed, the fact that James Madison, who voted for the bill authorizing the payment of the first congressional chaplains, * * *, later expressed the view that the practice was unconstitutional, * * *, is instructive on precisely this point. * * *

* * *

Finally, and most importantly, the argument tendered by the Court is misguided because the Constitution is not a static document whose meaning on every detail is fixed for all time by the life experience of the Framers. We have recognized in a wide variety of constitutional contexts that the practices that were in place at the time any particular guarantee was enacted into the Constitution do not necessarily fix forever the meaning of that guarantee. To be truly faithful to the Framers, "our use of the history of their time must limit itself to broad purposes, not specific practices." Abington School Dist. v. Schempp, 374 U.S., at 241 (BRENNAN, J., concurring). Our primary task must be to translate "the majestic generalities of the Bill of Rights, conceived as part of the pattern of liberal government in the eighteenth century, into concrete restraints on officials dealing with the problems of the twentieth century. * * * " West Virginia Bd. of Education v. Barnette, 319 U.S. 624, 639 (1943).

The inherent adaptability of the Constitution and its amendments is particularly important with respect to the Establishment Clause. "[O]ur religious composition makes us a vastly more diverse people than were our forefathers. * * * In the face of such profound changes, practices which may have been objectionable to no one in the time of Jefferson and Madison may today be highly offensive to many persons, the deeply devout and the nonbelievers alike." *Schempp, supra*, at 240–241 (BRENNAN, J., concurring). * * * Indeed, a proper respect for the Framers themselves forbids us to give so static and lifeless a

---

30. Indeed, the sort of historical argument made by the Court should be advanced with some hesitation in light of certain other skeletons in the congressional closet. See, e.g., An Act for the Punishment of Certain Crimes Against the United States, § 16, 1 Stat. 116 (1790) (enacted by the First Congress and requiring that persons convicted of certain theft offenses "be publicly whipped, not exceeding thirty-nine stripes"); Act of July 23, 1866, 14 Stat. 216 (reaffirming the racial segregation of the public schools in the District of Columbia; enacted exactly one week after Congress proposed Fourteenth Amendment to the States).

meaning to their work. To my mind, the Court's focus here on a narrow piece of history is, in a fundamental sense, a betrayal of the lessons of history.

* * *

JUSTICE STEVENS, dissenting.

In a democratically elected legislature, the religious beliefs of the chaplain tend to reflect the faith of the majority of the lawmakers' constituents. Prayers may be said by a Catholic priest in the Massachusetts Legislature and by a Presbyterian minister in the Nebraska Legislature, but I would not expect to find a Jehovah's Witness or a disciple of Mary Baker Eddy or the Reverend Moon serving as the official chaplain in any state legislature. * * *

The Court declines to "embark on a sensitive evaluation or to parse the content of a particular prayer." * * *. Perhaps it does so because it would be unable to explain away the clearly sectarian content of some of the prayers given by Nebraska's chaplain.[2] Or perhaps the Court is unwilling to acknowledge that the tenure of the chaplain must inevitably be conditioned on the acceptability of that content to the silent majority.

I would affirm the judgment of the Court of Appeals.

LYNCH, MAYOR OF PAWTUCKET v. DONNELLY

Supreme Court of the United States, 1984.
465 U.S. 668, 104 S.Ct. 1355, 79 L.Ed.2d 604.

CHIEF JUSTICE BURGER delivered the opinion of the Court.

We granted certiorari to decide whether the Establishment Clause of the First Amendment prohibits a municipality from including a crèche, or Nativity scene, in its annual Christmas display.

I

Each year, in cooperation with the downtown retail merchants' association, the city of Pawtucket, R.I., erects a Christmas display as part of its observance of the Christmas holiday season. The display is situated in a park owned by a nonprofit organization and located in the heart of the shopping district. The display is essentially like those to be found in hundreds of towns or cities across the Nation—often on public grounds—during the Christmas season. The Pawtucket display

---

2. On March 20, 1978, for example, Chaplain Palmer gave the following invocation:

"Father in heaven, the suffering and death of your son brought life to the whole world moving our hearts to praise your glory. The power of the cross reveals your concern for the world and the wonder of Christ crucified.

"The days of his life-giving death and glorious resurrection are approaching. This is the hour when he triumphed over Satan's pride; the time when we celebrate the great event of our redemption."

* * *

comprises many of the figures and decorations traditionally associated with Christmas, including, among other things, a Santa Claus house, reindeer pulling Santa's sleigh, candy-striped poles, a Christmas tree, carolers, cutout figures representing such characters as a clown, an elephant, and a teddy bear, hundreds of colored lights, a large banner that reads "SEASONS GREETINGS," and the crèche at issue here. All components of this display are owned by the city.

The crèche, which has been included in the display for 40 or more years, consists of the traditional figures, including the Infant Jesus, Mary and Joseph, angels, shepherds, kings, and animals, all ranging in height from 5" to 5'. In 1973, when the present crèche was acquired, it cost the city $1,365; it now is valued at $200. The erection and dismantling of the crèche costs the city about $20 per year; nominal expenses are incurred in lighting the crèche. No money has been expended on its maintenance for the past 10 years.

Respondents, Pawtucket residents and individual members of the Rhode Island affiliate of the American Civil Liberties Union, and the affiliate itself, brought this action in the United States District Court for Rhode Island, challenging the city's inclusion of the crèche in the annual display. The District Court held that the city's inclusion of the crèche in the display violates the Establishment Clause, 525 F.Supp. 1150, 1178 (1981), which is binding on the states through the Fourteenth Amendment. The District Court found that, by including the crèche in the Christmas display, the city has "tried to endorse and promulgate religious beliefs," * * *, and that "erection of the crèche has the real and substantial effect of affiliating the City with the Christian beliefs that the crèche represents." * * *. This "appearance of official sponsorship," it believed, "confers more than a remote and incidental benefit on Christianity." * * * Last, although the court acknowledged the absence of administrative entanglement, it found that excessive entanglement has been fostered as a result of the political divisiveness of including the crèche in the celebration. * * *. The city was permanently enjoined from including the crèche in the display.

A divided panel of the Court of Appeals for the First Circuit affirmed. 691 F.2d 1029 (1982). We granted certiorari, 460 U.S. 1080 (1983), and we reverse.

II

A

This Court has explained that the purpose of the Establishment and Free Exercise Clauses of the First Amendment is

> "to prevent, as far as possible, the intrusion of either [the church or the state] into the precincts of the other." Lemon v. Kurtzman, 403 U.S. 602, 614 (1971).

At the same time, however, the Court has recognized that

"total separation is not possible in an absolute sense. Some relationship between government and religious organizations is inevitable." *Ibid.*

In every Establishment Clause case, we must reconcile the inescapable tension between the objective of preventing unnecessary intrusion of either the church or the state upon the other, and the reality that, as the Court has so often noted, total separation of the two is not possible.

The Court has sometimes described the Religion Clauses as erecting a "wall" between church and state, see, e.g., Everson v. Board of Education, 330 U.S. 1, 18 (1947). The concept of a "wall" of separation is a useful figure of speech probably deriving from views of Thomas Jefferson. The metaphor has served as a reminder that the Establishment Clause forbids an established church or anything approaching it. But the metaphor itself is not a wholly accurate description of the practical aspects of the relationship that in fact exists between church and state.

No significant segment of our society and no institution within it can exist in a vacuum or in total or absolute isolation from all the other parts, much less from government. "It has never been thought either possible or desirable to enforce a regime of total separation. * * *" Committee for Public Education & Religious Liberty v. Nyquist, 413 U.S. 756, 760 (1973). Nor does the Constitution require complete separation of church and state; it affirmatively mandates accommodation, not merely tolerance, of all religions, and forbids hostility toward any. * * *

B

* * * In Marsh v. Chambers, 463 U.S. 783 (1983), we noted that 17 Members of that First Congress had been Delegates to the Constitutional Convention where freedom of speech, press, and religion and antagonism toward an established church were subjects of frequent discussion. We saw no conflict with the Establishment Clause when Nebraska employed members of the clergy as official legislative Chaplains to give opening prayers at sessions of the state legislature. *Id.,* at 791.

The interpretation of the Establishment Clause by Congress in 1789 takes on special significance in light of the Court's emphasis that the First Congress

> "was a Congress whose constitutional decisions have always been regarded, as they should be regarded, as of the greatest weight in the interpretation of that fundamental instrument," Myers v. United States, 272 U.S. 52, 174–175 (1926).

It is clear that neither the 17 draftsmen of the Constitution who were Members of the First Congress, nor the Congress of 1789, saw any establishment problem in the employment of congressional Chaplains to offer daily prayers in the Congress, a practice that has continued for nearly two centuries. It would be difficult to identify a more striking example of the accommodation of religious belief intended by the Framers.

C

There is an unbroken history of official acknowledgment by all three branches of government of the role of religion in American life from at least 1789. Seldom in our opinions was this more affirmatively expressed than in Justice Douglas' opinion for the Court validating a program allowing release of public school students from classes to attend off-campus religious exercise. Rejecting a claim that the program violated the Establishment Clause, the Court asserted pointedly:

"We are a religious people whose institutions presuppose a Supreme Being." *Zorach v. Clauson, supra,* at 313.

See also Abington School District v. Schempp, 374 U.S. 203, 213 (1963).

Our history is replete with official references to the value and invocation of Divine guidance in deliberations and pronouncements of the Founding Fathers and contemporary leaders. Beginning in the early colonial period long before Independence, a day of Thanksgiving was celebrated as a religious holiday to give thanks for the bounties of Nature as gifts from God. President Washington and his successors proclaimed Thanksgiving, with all its religious overtones, a day of national celebration and Congress made it a National Holiday more than a century ago. Ch. 167, 16 Sat. 168. That holiday has not lost its theme of expressing thanks for Divine aid any more than has Christmas lost its religious significance.

Executive Orders and other official announcements of Presidents and of the Congress have proclaimed both Christmas and Thanksgiving National Holidays in religious terms. And, by Acts of Congress, it has long been the practice that federal employees are released from duties on these National Holidays, while being paid from the same public revenues that provide the compensation of the Chaplains of the Senate and the House and the military services. See J.Res. 5, 23 Stat. 516. Thus, it is clear that Government has long recognized—indeed it has subsidized—holidays with religious significance.

Other examples of reference to our religious heritage are found in the statutorily prescribed national motto "In God We Trust," 36 U.S.C. § 186, which Congress and the President mandated for our currency, see 31 U.S.C. § 5112(d)(1) (1982 ed.), and in the language "One nation under God," as part of the Pledge of Allegiance to the American flag. That pledge is recited by many thousands of public school children—and adults—every year.

Art galleries supported by public revenues display religious paintings of the 15th and 16th centuries, predominantly inspired by one religious faith. The National Gallery in Washington, maintained with Government support, for example, has long exhibited masterpieces with religious messages, notably the Last Supper, and paintings depicting the Birth of Christ, the Crucifixion, and the Resurrection, among many others with explicit Christian themes and messages.[4] The very cham-

---

4. The National Gallery regularly exhibits more than 200 similar religious paintings.

ber in which oral arguments on this case were heard is decorated with a notable and permanent—not seasonal—symbol of religion: Moses with the Ten Commandments. Congress has long provided chapels in the Capitol for religious worship and meditation.

There are countless other illustrations of the Government's acknowledgment of our religious heritage and governmental sponsorship of graphic manifestations of that heritage. Congress has directed the President to proclaim a National Day of Prayer each year "on which [day] the people of the United States may turn to God in prayer and meditation at churches, in groups, and as individuals." 36 U.S.C. § 169h. Our Presidents have repeatedly issued such Proclamations. * * * One cannot look at even this brief résumé without finding that our history is pervaded by expressions of religious beliefs such as are found in *Zorach*. Equally pervasive is the evidence of accommodation of all faiths and all forms of religious expression, and hostility toward none. Through this accommodation, as Justice Douglas observed, governmental action has "follow[ed] the best of our traditions" and "respect[ed] the religious nature of our people." 343 U.S., at 314.

III

This history may help explain why the Court consistently has declined to take a rigid, absolutist view of the Establishment Clause. We have refused "to construe the Religion Clauses with a literalness that would undermine the ultimate constitutional objective as illuminated by history." Walz v. Tax Comm'n, 397 U.S. 664, 671 (1970) (emphasis added). In our modern, complex society, whose traditions and constitutional underpinnings rest on and encourage diversity and pluralism in all areas, an absolutist approach in applying the Establishment Clause is simplistic and has been uniformly rejected by the Court.

* * *

In this case, the focus of our inquiry must be on the crèche in the context of the Christmas season. See, e.g., Stone v. Graham, 449 U.S. 39 (1980) (*per curiam*); Abington School District v. Schempp, 374 U.S. 203 (1963). In *Stone*, for example, we invalidated a state statute requiring the posting of a copy of the Ten Commandments on public classroom walls. But the Court carefully pointed out that the Commandments were posted purely as a religious admonition, not "integrated into the school curriculum, where the Bible may constitutionally be used in an appropriate study of history, civilization, ethics, comparative religion, or the like." 449 U.S., at 42. Similarly, in *Abington,* although the Court struck down the practices in two States requiring daily Bible readings in public schools, it specifically noted that nothing in the Court's holding was intended to "indicat[e] that such study of the Bible or of religion, when presented objectively as part of a secular program of education, may not be effected consistently with the First Amendment." 374 U.S., at 225. Focus exclusively on the religious component of any activity would inevitably lead to its invalidation under the Establishment Clause.

The District Court inferred from the religious nature of the crèche that the city has no secular purpose for the display. In so doing, it rejected the city's claim that its reasons for including the crèche are essentially the same as its reasons for sponsoring the display as a whole. The District Court plainly erred by focusing almost exclusively on the crèche. When viewed in the proper context of the Christmas Holiday season, it is apparent that, on this record, there is insufficient evidence to establish that the inclusion of the crèche is a purposeful or surreptitious effort to express some kind of subtle governmental advocacy of a particular religious message. In a pluralistic society a variety of motives and purposes are implicated. The city, like the Congresses and Presidents, however, has principally taken note of a significant historical religious event long celebrated in the Western World. The crèche in the display depicts the historical origins of this traditional event long recognized as a National Holiday. * * *

The narrow question is whether there is a secular purpose for Pawtucket's display of the crèche. The display is sponsored by the city to celebrate the Holiday and to depict the origins of that Holiday. These are legitimate secular purposes.[6] The District Court's inference, drawn from the religious nature of the crèche, that the city has no secular purpose was, on this record, clearly erroneous.[7]

The District Court found that the primary effect of including the crèche is to confer a substantial and impermissible benefit on religion in general and on the Christian faith in particular. Comparisons of the relative benefits to religion of different forms of governmental support are elusive and difficult to make. But to conclude that the primary effect of including the crèche is to advance religion in violation of the Establishment Clause would require that we view it as more beneficial to and more an endorsement of religion, for example, than expenditure of large sums of public money for textbooks supplied throughout the country to students attending church-sponsored schools, *Board of Education v. Allen, supra;* expenditure of public funds for transportation of students to church-sponsored schools, *Everson v. Board of Education, supra;* federal grants for college buildings of church-sponsored institutions of higher education combining secular and religious education, Tilton v. Richardson, 403 U.S. 672 (1971); noncategorical grants to church-sponsored colleges and universities, Roemer v. Board of Public Works, 426 U.S. 736 (1976); and the tax exemptions for church properties sanctioned in Walz v. Tax Comm'n, 397 U.S. 664 (1970). It would also require that we view it as more of an endorsement of religion than the Sunday Closing Laws upheld in McGowan v. Maryland, 366 U.S. 420 (1961); the release time program for religious training in Zorach v.

---

6. The city contends that the purposes of the display are "exclusively secular." We hold only that Pawtucket has a secular purpose for its display, which is all that Lemon v. Kurtzman, 403 U.S. 602 (1971), requires. Were the test that the government must have "exclusively secular" objectives, much of the conduct and legislation this Court has approved in the past would have been invalidated.

7. Justice Brennan argues that the city's objectives could have been achieved without including the crèche in the display, * * *. True or not, that is irrelevant. The question is whether the display of the crèche violates the Establishment Clause.

Clauson, 343 U.S. 306 (1952); and the legislative prayers upheld in Marsh v. Chambers, 463 U.S. 783 (1983).

We are unable to discern a greater aid to religion deriving from inclusion of the crèche than from these benefits and endorsements previously held not violative of the Establishment Clause. * * *

* * *

The dissent asserts some observers may perceive that the city has aligned itself with the Christian faith by including a Christian symbol in its display and that this serves to advance religion. We can assume, *arguendo*, that the display advances religion in a sense; but our precedents plainly contemplate that on occasion some advancement of religion will result from governmental action. * * * Here, whatever benefit there is to one faith or religion or to all religions, is indirect, remote, and incidental; display of the crèche is no more an advancement or endorsement of religion than the Congressional and Executive recognition of the origins of the Holiday itself as "Christ's Mass," or the exhibition of literally hundreds of religious paintings in governmentally supported museums.

The District Court found that there had been no administrative entanglement between religion and state resulting from the city's ownership and use of the crèche. 525 F.Supp., at 1179. But it went on to hold that some political divisiveness was engendered by this litigation. Coupled with its finding of an impermissible sectarian purpose and effect, this persuaded the court that there was "excessive entanglement." The Court of Appeals expressly declined to accept the District Court's finding that inclusion of the crèche has caused political divisiveness along religious lines, and noted that this Court has never held that political divisiveness alone was sufficient to invalidate government conduct.

Entanglement is a question of kind and degree. In this case, however, there is no reason to disturb the District Court's finding on the absence of administrative entanglement. There is no evidence of contact with church authorities concerning the content or design of the exhibit prior to or since Pawtucket's purchase of the crèche. No expenditures for maintenance of the crèche have been necessary; and since the city owns the crèche, now valued at $200, the tangible material it contributes is *de minimis*. In many respects the display requires far less ongoing, day-to-day interaction between church and state than religious paintings in public galleries. There is nothing here, of course, like the "comprehensive, discriminating, and continuing state surveillance" or the "enduring entanglement" present in *Lemon*, 403 U.S., at 619–622.

The Court of Appeals correctly observed that this Court has not held that political divisiveness alone can serve to invalidate otherwise permissible conduct. And we decline to so hold today. This case does not involve a direct subsidy to church-sponsored schools or colleges, or other religious institutions, and hence no inquiry into potential political divisiveness is even called for, Mueller v. Allen, 463 U.S. 388, 403–404, n. 11 (1983). * * *

We are satisfied that the city has a secular purpose for including the crèche, that the city has not impermissibly advanced religion, and that including the crèche does not create excessive entanglement between religion and government.

IV

* * *

Of course the crèche is identified with one religious faith but no more so than the examples we have set out from prior cases in which we found no conflict with the Establishment Clause. See, e.g., McGowan v. Maryland, 366 U.S. 420 (1961); Marsh v. Chambers, 463 U.S. 783 (1983). It would be ironic, however, if the inclusion of a single symbol of a particular historic religious event, as part of a celebration acknowledged in the Western World for 20 centuries, and in this country by the people, by the Executive Branch, by the Congress, and the courts for 2 centuries, would so "taint" the city's exhibit as to render it violative of the Establishment Clause. To forbid the use of this one passive symbol—the crèche—at the very time people are taking note of the season with Christmas hymns and carols in public schools and other public places, and while the Congress and legislatures open sessions with prayers by paid chaplains would be a stilted overreaction contrary to our history and to our holdings. If the presence of the crèche in this display violates the Establishment Clause, a host of other forms of taking official note of Christmas, and of our religious heritage, are equally offensive to the Constitution.

The Court has acknowledged that the "fears and political problems" that gave rise to the Religion Clauses in the 18th century are of far less concern today. *Everson,* 330 U.S., at 8. We are unable to perceive the Archbishop of Canterbury, the Bishop of Rome, or other powerful religious leaders behind every public acknowledgment of the religious heritage long officially recognized by the three constitutional branches of government. Any notion that these symbols pose a real danger of establishment of a state church is farfetched indeed.

* * *

* * * Accordingly, the judgment of the Court of Appeals is reversed.

It is so ordered.

JUSTICE O'CONNOR, concurring.

I concur in the opinion of the Court. I write separately to suggest a clarification of our Establishment Clause doctrine. The suggested approach leads to the same result in this case as that taken by the Court, and the Court's opinion, as I read it, is consistent with my analysis.

I

The Establishment Clause prohibits government from making adherence to a religion relevant in any way to a person's standing in the political community. Government can run afoul of that prohibition in two principal ways. One is excessive entanglement with religious institutions, which may interfere with the independence of the institutions, give the institutions access to government or governmental powers not fully shared by nonadherents of the religion, and foster the creation of political constituencies defined along religious lines. *E.g.,* Larkin v. Grendel's Den, Inc., 459 U.S. 116 (1982). The second and more direct infringement is government endorsement or disapproval of religion. Endorsement sends a message to nonadherents that they are outsiders, not full members of the political community, and an accompanying message to adherents that they are insiders, favored members of the political community. Disapproval sends the opposite message. See generally Abington School District v. Schempp, 374 U.S. 203 (1963).

Our prior cases have used the three-part test articulated in Lemon v. Kurtzman, 403 U.S. 602, 612–613 (1971), as a guide to detecting these two forms of unconstitutional government action. It has never been entirely clear, however, how the three parts of the test relate to the principles enshrined in the Establishment Clause. Focusing on institutional entanglement and on endorsement or disapproval of religion clarifies the *Lemon* test as an analytical device.

II

In this case, as even the District Court found, there is no institutional entanglement. Nevertheless, the respondents contend that the political divisiveness caused by Pawtucket's display of its crèche violates the excessive-entanglement prong of the *Lemon* test. * * * In my view, political divisiveness along religious lines should not be an independent test of constitutionality.

Although several of our cases have discussed political divisiveness under the entanglement prong of *Lemon,* see, e.g., Committee for Public Education & Religious Liberty v. Nyquist, 413 U.S. 756, 796 (1973); *Lemon v. Kurtzman, supra,* at 623, we have never relied on divisiveness as an independent ground for holding a government practice unconstitutional. Guessing the potential for political divisiveness inherent in a government practice is simply too speculative an enterprise, in part because the existence of the litigation, as this case illustrates, itself may affect the political response to the government practice. Political divisiveness is admittedly an evil addressed by the Establishment Clause. Its existence may be evidence that institutional entanglement is excessive or that a government practice is perceived as an endorsement of religion. But the constitutional inquiry should focus ultimately on the character of the government activity that might cause such divisiveness, not on the divisiveness itself. The entanglement prong of the *Lemon* test is properly limited to institutional entanglement.

III

The central issue in this case is whether Pawtucket has endorsed Christianity by its display of the crèche. To answer that question, we must examine both what Pawtucket intended to communicate in displaying the crèche and what message the city's display actually conveyed. The purpose and effect prongs of the *Lemon* test represent these two aspects of the meaning of the city's action.

The meaning of a statement to its audience depends both on the intention of the speaker and on the "objective" meaning of the statement in the community. Some listeners need not rely solely on the words themselves in discerning the speaker's intent: they can judge the intent by, for example, examining the context of the statement or asking questions of the speaker. Other listeners do not have or will not seek access to such evidence of intent. They will rely instead on the words themselves; for them the message actually conveyed may be something not actually intended. If the audience is large, as it always is when government "speaks" by word or deed, some portion of the audience will inevitably receive a message determined by the "objective" content of the statement, and some portion will inevitably receive the intended message. Examination of both the subjective and the objective components of the message communicated by a government action is therefore necessary to determine whether the action carries a forbidden meaning.

The purpose prong of the *Lemon* test asks whether government's actual purpose is to endorse or disapprove of religion. The effect prong asks whether, irrespective of government's actual purpose, the practice under review in fact conveys a message of endorsement or disapproval. An affirmative answer to either question should render the challenged practice invalid.

A

The purpose prong of the *Lemon* test requires that a government activity have a secular purpose. That requirement is not satisfied, however, by the mere existence of some secular purpose, however dominated by religious purposes. * * * The proper inquiry under the purpose prong of *Lemon*, I submit, is whether the government intends to convey a message of endorsement or disapproval of religion.

Applying that formulation to this case, I would find that Pawtucket did not intend to convey any message of endorsement of Christianity or disapproval of non-Christian religions. The evident purpose of including the crèche in the larger display was not promotion of the religious content of the crèche but celebration of the public holiday through its traditional symbols. Celebration of public holidays, which have cultural significance even if they also have religious aspects, is a legitimate secular purpose.

The District Court's finding that the display of the crèche had no secular purpose was based on erroneous reasoning. The District Court believed that it should ascertain the city's purpose in displaying the crèche separate and apart from the general purpose in setting up the display. It also found that, because the tradition-celebrating purpose was suspect in the court's eyes, the city's use of an unarguably religious symbol "raises an inference" of intent to endorse. When viewed in light of correct legal principles, the District Court's finding of unlawful purpose was clearly erroneous.

B

Focusing on the evil of government endorsement or disapproval of religion makes clear that the effect prong of the *Lemon* test is properly interpreted not to require invalidation of a government practice merely because it in fact causes, even as a primary effect, advancement or inhibition of religion. * * * What is crucial is that a government practice not have the effect of communicating a message of government endorsement or disapproval of religion. It is only practices having that effect, whether intentionally or unintentionally, that make religion relevant, in reality or public perception, to status in the political community.

Pawtucket's display of its crèche, I believe, does not communicate a message that the government intends to endorse the Christian beliefs represented by the crèche. Although the religious and indeed sectarian significance of the crèche, as the District Court found, is not neutralized by the setting, the overall holiday setting changes what viewers may fairly understand to be the purpose of the display—as a typical museum setting, though not neutralizing the religious content of a religious painting, negates any message of endorsement of that content. The display celebrates a public holiday, and no one contends that declaration of that holiday is understood to be an endorsement of religion. The holiday itself has very strong secular components and traditions. Government celebration of the holiday, which is extremely common, generally is not understood to endorse the religious content of the holiday, just as government celebration of Thanksgiving is not so understood. The crèche is a traditional symbol of the holiday that is very commonly displayed along with purely secular symbols, as it was in Pawtucket.

* * *

The city of Pawtucket is alleged to have violated the Establishment Clause by endorsing the Christian beliefs represented by the crèche included in its Christmas display. Giving the challenged practice the careful scrutiny it deserves, I cannot say that the particular crèche display at issue in this case was intended to endorse or had the effect of endorsing Christianity. I agree with the Court that the judgment below must be reversed.

JUSTICE BRENNAN, with whom JUSTICE MARSHALL, JUSTICE BLACKMUN, and JUSTICE STEVENS join, dissenting.

The principles announced in the compact phrases of the Religion Clauses have, as the Court today reminds us, * * *, proved difficult to apply. Faced with that uncertainty, the Court properly looks for guidance to the settled test announced in Lemon v. Kurtzman, 403 U.S. 602 (1971), for assessing whether a challenged governmental practice involves an impermissible step toward the establishment of religion. * * * Applying that test to this case, the Court reaches an essentially narrow result which turns largely upon the particular holiday context in which the city of Pawtucket's nativity scene appeared. The Court's decision implicitly leaves open questions concerning the constitutionality of the public display on public property of a crèche standing alone, or the public display of other distinctively religious symbols such as a cross. Despite the narrow contours of the Court's opinion, our precedents in my view compel the holding that Pawtucket's inclusion of a life-sized display depicting the biblical description of the birth of Christ as part of its annual Christmas celebration is unconstitutional. Nothing in the history of such practices or the setting in which the city's crèche is presented obscures or diminishes the plain fact that Pawtucket's action amounts to an impermissible governmental endorsement of a particular faith.

I

Last Term, I expressed the hope that the Court's decision in Marsh v. Chambers, 463 U.S. 783 (1983), would prove to be only a single, aberrant departure from our settled method of analyzing Establishment Clause cases. *Id.,* at 796 (BRENNAN, J., dissenting). That the Court today returns to the settled analysis of our prior cases gratifies that hope. At the same time, the Court's less-than-vigorous application of the *Lemon* test suggests that its commitment to those standards may only be superficial. After reviewing the Court's opinion, I am convinced that this case appears hard not because the principles of decision are obscure, but because the Christmas holiday seems so familiar and agreeable. Although the Court's reluctance to disturb a community's chosen method of celebrating such an agreeable holiday is understandable, that cannot justify the Court's departure from controlling precedent. * * *

* * *

* * * To be found constitutional, Pawtucket's seasonal celebration must at least be non-denominational and not serve to promote religion. The inclusion of a distinctively religious element like the crèche, however, demonstrates that a narrower sectarian purpose lay behind the decision to include a nativity scene. That the crèche retained this religious character for the people and municipal government of Pawtucket is suggested by the Mayor's testimony at trial in which he stated that for him, as well as others in the city, the effort to eliminate the nativity scene from Pawtucket's Christmas celebration "is a step towards establishing another religion, non-religion that it may be." * * *. Plainly, the city and its leaders understood that the inclusion of the crèche in its display would serve the wholly religious purpose of "keep[ing] 'Christ in Christmas.' " 525 F.Supp. 1150, 1173 (D.R.I. 1981). From this record, therefore, it is impossible to say with the kind of confidence that was possible in McGowan v. Maryland, 366 U.S. 420, 445 (1961), that a wholly secular goal predominates.

The "primary effect" of including a nativity scene in the city's display is, as the District Court found, to place the government's imprimatur of approval on the particular religious beliefs exemplified by the crèche. Those who believe in the message of the nativity receive the unique and exclusive benefit of public recognition and approval of their views. For many, the city's decision to include the crèche as part of its extensive and costly efforts to celebrate Christmas can only mean that the prestige of the government has been conferred on the beliefs associated with the crèche, thereby providing "a significant symbolic benefit to religion. * * *" *Larkin v. Grendel's Den, Inc., supra*, at 125–126. The effect on minority religious groups, as well as on those who may reject all religion, is to convey the message that their views are not similarly worthy of public recognition nor entitled to public support. It was precisely this sort of religious chauvinism that the Establishment Clause was intended forever to prohibit. In this case, as in *Engel v. Vitale*, "[w]hen the power, prestige and financial support of government is placed behind a particular religious belief, the indirect coercive pressure upon religious minorities to conform to the prevailing officially approved religion is plain." * * *

* * *

The American historical experience concerning the public celebration of Christmas, if carefully examined, provides no support for the Court's decision. * * *

* * *

* * * Two features of this history are worth noting. First, at the time of the adoption of the Constitution and the Bill of Rights, there was no settled pattern of celebrating Christmas, either as a purely religious holiday or as a public event. Second, the historical evidence, such as it is, offers no uniform pattern of widespread acceptance of the holiday and indeed suggests that the development of Christmas as a public holiday is a comparatively recent phenomenon.[25]

* * *

Many of the same religious sects that were devotedly opposed to the celebration of Christmas on purely religious grounds, were also some of the most vocal and dedicated foes of established religions in the period just prior to the Revolutionary War. The Puritans, and later the Presbyterians, Baptists, and Methodists, generally associated the celebration of Christmas with the elaborate and, in their view, sacrilegious celebration of the holiday by the Church of England, and also with, for them, the more sinister theology of "Popery." In the eyes of these dissenting religious sects, therefore, the groups most closely associated with established religion—the Churches of England and of Rome—were also most closely linked to the profane practice of publicly celebrating Christmas. * * *

* * *

In sum, there is no evidence whatsoever that the Framers would have expressly approved a federal celebration of the Christmas holiday including public displays of a nativity scene; accordingly, the Court's

---

25. The Court's insistence upon pursuing this vague historical analysis is especially baffling since even the petitioners and their supporting *amici* concede that no historical evidence equivalent to that relied upon in *Marsh, McGowan*, or *Walz* supports publicly sponsored Christmas displays. At oral argument, counsel for petitioners was asked whether there is "anything we can refer to to let us know how long it has been the practice in this country for public bodies to have nativity scenes displayed?" Counsel responded: "Specifically, I cannot * * *. The recognition of Christmas [as a public holiday] began in the middle part of the last century * * * but specifically with respect to the use of the nativity scene, we have been unable to locate that data."

repeated invocation of the decision in *Marsh,* see *ante,* at 673–674, 682, 685–686, is not only baffling, it is utterly irrelevant. Nor is there any suggestion that publicly financed and supported displays of Christmas crèches are supported by a record of widespread, undeviating acceptance that extends throughout our history. Therefore, our prior decisions which relied upon concrete, specific historical evidence to support a particular practice simply have no bearing on the question presented in this case. Contrary to today's careless decision, those prior cases have all recognized that the "illumination" provided by history must always be focused on the particular practice at issue in a given case. Without that guiding principle and the intellectual discipline it imposes, the Court is at sea, free to select random elements of America's varied history solely to suit the views of five members of this Court.

IV

* * *

I dissent.

JUSTICE BLACKMUN, with whom JUSTICE STEVENS joins, dissenting.

As Justice Brennan points out, the logic of the Courts decision in *Lemon v. Kurtzman,* 403 U.S. 602, 612–613 (1971) (which The Chief Justice would say has been applied by this Court "often," * * *, but which Justice O'Connor acknowledges with the words, "Our prior cases have used the three-part test articulated in *Lemon,* " * * *), compels an affirmance here. If that case and its guidelines mean anything, the presence of Pawtucket's crèche in a municipally sponsored display must be held to be a violation of the First Amendment.

Not only does the Court's resolution of this controversy make light of our precedents, but also, ironically, the majority does an injustice to the crèche and the message it manifests. While certain persons, including the Mayor of Pawtucket, undertook a crusade to "keep 'Christ' in Christmas," * * *, the Court today has declared that presence virtually irrelevant. The majority urges that the display, "with or without a crèche," "recall[s] the religious nature of the Holiday," and "engenders a friendly community spirit of goodwill in keeping with the season." * * * Before the District Court, an expert witness for the city made a similar, though perhaps more candid, point, stating that Pawtucket's display invites people "to participate in the Christmas spirit, brotherhood, peace, and let loose with their money." See 525 F.Supp. 1150, 1161 (RI1981). The crèche has been relegated to the role of a neutral harbinger of the holiday season, useful for commercial purposes, but devoid of any inherent meaning and incapable of enhancing the religious tenor of a display of which it is an integral part. The city has its victory—but it is a Pyrrhic one indeed.

The import of the Court's decision is to encourage use of the crèche in a municipally sponsored display, a setting where Christians feel constrained in acknowledging its symbolic meaning and non-Christians feel alienated by its presence. Surely, this is a misuse of a sacred symbol. Because I cannot join the Court in denying either the force of our precedents or the sacred message that is at the core of the crèche, I dissent and join Justice Brennan's opinion.

COUNTY OF ALLEGHENY v. AMERICAN CIVIL LIBERTIES UNION

Supreme Court of the United States, 1989.
492 U.S. 573, 109 S.Ct. 3086, 106 L.Ed.2d 472.

MR. JUSTICE BLACKMUN announced the judgment of the Court and delivered the opinion of the Court with respect to Parts III–A, IV, and V, in which BRENNAN, MARSHALL, STEVENS, and O'CONNOR, JJ., joined, an opinion with respect to Parts I and II, in which O'CONNOR and STEVENS, JJ., joined, an opinion with respect to Part III–B, in which STEVENS, J., joined, and an opinion with respect to Part VI. O'CONNOR, J., filed an opinion concurring in part and concurring in the judgment, in Part II of which BRENNAN and STEVENS, JJ., joined. BRENNAN, J., filed an opinion concurring in part and dissenting in part, in which MARSHALL and STEVENS, JJ., joined. STEVENS, J., filed an opinion concurring in part and dissenting in part, in which BRENNAN and MARSHALL, JJ., joined. KENNEDY, J., filed an opinion concurring in the judgment in part and dissenting in part, in which REHNQUIST, C.J., and WHITE and SCALIA, JJ., joined.

* * *

This litigation concerns the constitutionality of two recurring holiday displays located on public property in downtown Pittsburgh. The first is a crèche placed on the Grand Staircase of the Allegheny County Courthouse. The second is a Chanukah menorah placed just outside the City–County Building, next to a Christmas tree and a sign saluting liberty. The Court of Appeals for the Third Circuit ruled that each display violates the Establishment Clause of the First Amendment because each has the impermissible effect of endorsing religion. 842 F.2d 655 (1988). We agree that the crèche display has that unconstitutional effect but reverse the Court of Appeals' judgment regarding the menorah display.

I

A

The County Courthouse is owned by Allegheny County and is its seat of government. It houses the offices of the County Commissioners, Controller, Treasurer, Sheriff, and Clerk of Court. Civil and criminal trials are held there. App. 69. The "main," "most beautiful," and "most public" part of the courthouse is its Grand Staircase, set into one arch and surrounded by others, with arched windows serving as a backdrop. * * *

Since 1981, the county has permitted the Holy Name Society, a Roman Catholic group, to display a crèche in the County Courthouse during the Christmas holiday season. App. 164. Christmas, we note perhaps needlessly, is the holiday when Christians celebrate the birth of Jesus of Nazareth, whom they believe to be the Messiah. Western churches have celebrated Christmas Day on December 25 since the fourth century. As observed in this Nation, Christmas has a secular as well as a religious dimension.

The crèche in the County Courthouse, like other crèches, is a visual representation of the scene in the manger in Bethlehem shortly after the birth of Jesus, as described in the Gospels of Luke and Matthew. The crèche includes figures of the infant Jesus, Mary, Joseph, farm animals, shepherds, and wise men, all placed in or before a wooden representation of a manger, which has at its crest an angel bearing a banner that proclaims "Gloria in Excelsis Deo!"

During the 1986–87 holiday season, the crèche was on display on the Grand Staircase from November 26 to January 9. App. 59. It had a wooden fence on three sides and bore a plaque stating: "This Display Donated by the Holy Name Society." Sometime during the week of December 2, the county placed red and white poinsettia plants around the fence. * * * The county also placed a small evergreen tree, decorated with a red bow, behind each of the two endposts of the fence. * * * These trees stood alongside the manger backdrop, and were slightly shorter than it was. The angel thus was at the apex of the crèche display. Altogether, the crèche, the fence, the poinsettias, and the trees occupied a substantial amount of space on the Grand Staircase. No figures of Santa Claus or other decorations appeared on the Grand Staircase. * * * Cf. Lynch v. Donnelly, 465 U.S. 668, 671 (1984). * * *

B

The City–County Building is separate and a block removed from the County Courthouse and, as the name implies, is jointly owned by the city of Pittsburgh and Allegheny County. The city's portion of the building houses the city's principal offices, including the Mayor's. * * * The city is responsible for the building's Grant Street entrance which has three rounded arches supported by columns. * * *

For a number of years, the city has had a large Christmas tree under the middle arch outside the Grant Street entrance. Following this practice, city employees on November 17, 1986, erected a 45-foot tree under the middle arch and decorated it with lights and ornaments. * * * A few days later, the city placed at the foot of the tree a sign bearing the Mayor's name and entitled "Salute to Liberty." Beneath the title, the sign stated:

> "During this holiday season, the City of Pittsburgh salutes liberty. Let these festive lights remind us that we are the keepers of the flame of liberty and our legacy of freedom."
> * * *

At least since 1982, the city has expanded its Grant Street holiday display to include a symbolic representation of Chanukah, an 8-day Jewish holiday that begins on the 25th day of the Jewish lunar month of Kislev. App. 138. The 25th of Kislev usually occurs in December, and thus Chanukah is the annual Jewish holiday that falls closest to Christmas Day each year. * * *

* * *

On December 22 of the 1986 holiday season, the city placed at the Grant Street entrance to the City–County Building an 18–foot Chanukah menorah of an abstract tree-and-branch design. The menorah was placed next to the city's 45–foot Christmas tree, against one of the columns that supports the arch into which the tree was set. The menorah is owned by Chabad, a Jewish group,[35] but is stored, erected, and removed each year by the city. * * * The tree, the sign, and the menorah were all removed on January 13. * * *

II

This litigation began on December 10, 1986, when respondents, the Greater Pittsburgh Chapter of the American Civil Liberties Union and seven local residents, filed suit against the county and the city, seeking permanently to enjoin the county from displaying the crèche in the County Courthouse and the city from displaying the menorah in front of the City–County Building. Respondents claim that the displays of the crèche and the menorah each violate the Establishment Clause of the First Amendment, made applicable to state governments by the Fourteenth Amendment. * * *

On May 8, 1987, the District Court denied respondent's request for a permanent injunction. * * *

Respondents appealed, and a divided panel of the Court of Appeals reversed. 842 F.2d 655 (CA3 1988). Distinguishing *Lynch v. Donnelly*, the panel majority determined that the crèche and the menorah must be understood as endorsing Christianity and Judaism. * * *

III

A

This Nation is heir to a history and tradition of religious diversity that dates from the settlement of the North American continent. Sectarian differences among various Christian denominations were central to the origins of our Republic. Since then, adherents of religions too numerous to name have made the United States their home, as have those whose beliefs expressly exclude religion.

Precisely because of the religious diversity that is our national heritage, the Founders added to the Constitution a Bill of Rights, the very first words of which declare: "Congress shall make no law respecting an establishment of religion, or prohibiting the free exercise thereof. * * *" Perhaps in the early days of the Republic these words were understood to protect only the diversity within Christianity, but today they are recognized as guaranteeing religious liberty and equality to

---

35. Chabad, also known as Lubavitch, is an organization of Hasidic Jews who follow the teachings of a particular Jewish leader, the Lubavitch Rebbe. * * * The Lubavitch movement is a branch of Hasidism, which itself is a branch of orthodox Judaism. * * * Pittsburgh has a total population of 45,000 Jews; of these, 100 to 150 families attend synagogue at Pittsburgh's Lubavitch Center. * * *

"the infidel, the atheist, or the adherent of a non-Christian faith such as Islam or Judaism." Wallace v. Jaffree, 472 U.S. 38, 52 (1985). It is settled law that no government official in this Nation may violate these fundamental constitutional rights regarding matters of conscience. *Id.*, at 49.

In the course of adjudicating specific cases, this Court has come to understand the Establishment Clause to mean that government may not promote or affiliate itself with any religious doctrine or organization, may not discriminate among persons on the basis of their religious beliefs and practices, may not delegate a governmental power to a religious institution, and may not involve itself too deeply in such an institution's affairs. * * *

In *Lemon v. Kurtzman, supra,* the Court sought to refine these principles by focusing on three "tests" for determining whether a government practice violates the Establishment Clause. Under the *Lemon* analysis, a statute or practice which touches upon religion, if it is to be permissible under the Establishment Clause, must have a secular purpose; it must neither advance nor inhibit religion in its principal or primary effect; and it must not foster an excessive entanglement with religion. 403 U.S., at 612–613. This trilogy of tests has been applied regularly in the Court's later Establishment Clause cases.

Our subsequent decisions further have refined the definition of governmental action that unconstitutionally advances religion. In recent years, we have paid particularly close attention to whether the challenged governmental practice either has the purpose or effect of "endorsing" religion, a concern that has long had a place in our Establishment Clause jurisprudence. * * *

Of course, the word "endorsement" is not self-defining. Rather, it derives its meaning from other words that this Court has found useful over the years in interpreting the Establishment Clause. Thus, it has been noted that the prohibition against governmental endorsement of religion "preclude[s] government from conveying or attempting to convey a message that religion or a particular religious belief is favored or preferred." Wallace v. Jaffree, 472 U.S., at 70 (O'Connor, J., concurring in judgment) (emphasis added). * * *

Whether the key word is "endorsement," "favoritism," or "promotion," the essential principle remains the same. The Establishment Clause, at the very least, prohibits government from appearing to take a position on questions of religious belief or from "making adherence to a religion relevant in any way to a person's standing in the political community." Lynch v. Donnelly, 465 U.S., at 687 (O'Connor, J., concurring).

* * *

Although Justice O'Connor joined the majority opinion in Lynch, she wrote a concurrence that differs in significant respects from the majority opinion. The main difference is that the concurrence provides a sound analytical framework for evaluating governmental use of religious symbols.

First and foremost, the concurrence squarely rejects any notion that this Court will tolerate some government endorsement of religion. Rather, the concurrence recognizes any endorsement of religion as "invalid," *id.,* at 690, because it "sends a message to nonadherents that they are outsiders, not full members of the political community, and an accompanying message to adherents that they are insiders, favored members of the political community." *Id.,* at 688.

Second, the concurrence articulates a method for determining whether the government's use of an object with religious meaning has the effect of endorsing religion. The effect of the display depends upon the message that the government's practice communicates: the question is "what viewers may fairly understand to be the purpose of the display." *Id.,* at 692. That inquiry, of necessity, turns upon the context in which the contested object appears: "a typical museum setting, though not neutralizing the religious content of a religious painting, negates any message of endorsement of that content." *Ibid.* The concurrence thus emphasizes that the constitutionality of the crèche in that case depended upon its "particular physical setting," *ibid.,* and further observes: "Every government practice must be judged in its unique circumstances to determine whether it [endorses] religion." *Id.,* at 694.

* * *

Under the Court's holding in *Lynch,* the effect of a crèche display turns on its setting. Here, unlike in *Lynch,* nothing in the context of the display detracts from the crèche's religious message. The *Lynch* display comprised a series of figures and objects, each group of which had its own focal point. Santa's house and his reindeer were objects of attention separate from the crèche, and had their specific visual story to tell. Similarly, whatever a "talking" wishing well may be, it obviously was a center of attention separate from the crèche. Here, in contrast, the crèche stands alone: it is the single element of the display on the Grand Staircase.

The floral decoration surrounding the crèche cannot be viewed as somehow equivalent to the secular symbols in the overall *Lynch* display. The floral frame, like all good frames, serves only to draw one's attention to the message inside the frame. The floral decoration surrounding the crèche contributes to, rather than detracts from, the endorsement of religion conveyed by the crèche. It is as if the county had allowed the Holy Name Society to display a cross on the Grand Staircase at Easter, and the county had surrounded the cross with Easter lilies. The county could not say that surrounding the cross with traditional flowers of the season would negate the endorsement of Christianity conveyed by the cross on the Grand Staircase. Its contention that the traditional Christmas greens negate the endorsement effect of the crèche fares no better.

Nor does the fact that the crèche was the setting for the county's annual Christmas carol-program diminish its religious meaning. First, the carol program in 1986 lasted only from December 3 to December 23 and occupied at most two hours a day. * * * The effect of the crèche on those who viewed it when the choirs were not singing—the vast majority of the time—cannot be negated by the presence of the choir program. Second, because some of the carols performed at the site of the crèche were religious in nature, those carols were more likely to augment the religious quality of the scene than to secularize it.

Furthermore, the crèche sits on the Grand Staircase, the "main" and "most beautiful part" of the building that is the seat of county government. App. 157. No viewer could reasonably think that it occupies this location without the support and approval of the government. Thus, by permitting the "display of the crèche in this particular physical setting." *Lynch,* 465 U.S., at 692 (O'CONNOR, J., concurring), the county sends an unmistakable message that it supports and promotes the Christian praise to God that is the crèche's religious message.

The fact that the crèche bears a sign disclosing its ownership by a Roman Catholic organization does not alter this conclusion. On the contrary, the sign simply demonstrates that the government is endorsing the religious message of that organization, rather than communicating a message of its own. * * *

* * *

In sum, *Lynch* teaches that government may celebrate Christmas in some manner and form, but not in a way that endorses Christian doctrine. Here, Allegheny County has transgressed this line. It has chosen to celebrate Christmas in a way that has the effect of endorsing a patently Christian message: Glory to God for the birth of Jesus Christ. Under *Lynch,* and the rest of our cases, nothing more is required to demonstrate a violation of the Establishment Clause. The display of the crèche in this context, therefore, must be permanently enjoined.

* * *

* * * Justice Kennedy, however, argues that *Marsh* legitimates all "practices with no greater potential for an establishment of religion" than those "accepted traditions dating back to the Founding." * * * Otherwise, the Justice asserts, such practices as our national motto ("In God We Trust") and our Pledge of Allegiance (with the phrase "under God," added in 1954, Pub.L. 396, 68 Stat. 249) are in danger of invalidity.

Our previous opinions have considered in dicta the motto and the pledge, characterizing them as consistent with the proposition that government may not communicate an endorsement of religious belief. *Lynch,* 465 U.S., at 693 (O'CONNOR, J., concurring); *id.,* at 716–717 (BRENNAN, J., dissenting). We need not return to the subject of "ceremonial deism," see n. 46, *supra,* because there is an obvious distinction between crèche displays and references to God in the motto and the pledge. However history may affect the constitutionality of nonsectarian references to religion by the government,[52] history cannot legitimate

---

52. It is worth noting that just because *Marsh* sustained the validity of legislative prayer, it does not necessarily follow that practices like proclaiming a National Day of Prayer are constitutional. * * * Legislative prayer does not urge citizens to en-

practices that demonstrate the government's allegiance to a particular sect or creed.

Indeed, in *Marsh* itself, the Court recognized that not even the "unique history" of legislative prayer, 463 U.S., at 791, can justify contemporary legislative prayers that have the effect of affiliating the government with any one specific faith or belief. *Id.,* at 794–795. The legislative prayers involved in *Marsh* did not violate this principle because the particular chaplain had "removed all references to Christ." * * *

* * *

Indeed, not even under Justice Kennedy's preferred approach can the Establishment Clause be transformed into an exception to this rule. The Justice would substitute the term "proselytization" for "endorsement," * * *, but his "proselytization" test suffers from the same "defect," if one must call it that, of requiring close factual analysis. Justice Kennedy "ha[s] no doubt, for example, that the [Establishment] Clause would forbid a city to permit the permanent erection of a large Latin cross on the roof of city hall * * * because such an obtrusive year-round religious display would pace the government's weight behind an obvious effort to proselytize on behalf of a particular religion." * * * He also suggests that a city would demonstrate an unconstitutional preference for Christianity if it displayed a Christian symbol during every major Christian holiday but did not display the religious symbols of other faiths during other religious holidays. * * * But, for Justice Kennedy, would it be enough of a preference for Christianity if that city each year displayed a crèche for 40 days during the Christmas season and a cross for 40 days during Lent (and never the symbols of other religions)? If so, then what if there were no cross but the 40-day crèche display contained a sign exhorting the city's citizens "to offer up their devotions to God their Creator, and his Son Jesus Christ, the Redeemer of the world"? * * *

* * *

The display of the Chanukah menorah in front of the City–County Building may well present a closer constitutional question. The menorah, one must recognize, is a religious symbol: it serves to commemorate the miracle of the oil as described in the Talmud. But the menorah's message is not exclusively religious. The menorah is the primary visual symbol for a holiday that, like Christmas, has both religious and secular dimensions.

Moreover, the menorah here stands next to a Christmas tree and a sign saluting liberty. While no challenge has been made here to the display of the tree and the sign, their presence is obviously relevant in determining the effect of the menorah's display. * * *

* * *

gage in religious practices, and on that basis could well be distinguishable from an exhortation from government to the people that they engage in religious conduct. But, as this practice is not before us, we express no judgment about its constitutionality.

The conclusion here that, in this particular context, the menorah's display does not have an effect of endorsing religious faith does not foreclose the possibility that the display of the menorah might violate either the "purpose" or "entanglement" prong of the *Lemon* analysis. These issues were not addressed by the Court of Appeals and may be considered by that court on remand.

There is also some suggestion in the record that Chabad advocates the public display of menorahs as part of its own proselytizing mission, but again there have been no relevant factual findings that would enable this Court to conclude that Pittsburgh has endorsed Chabad's particular proselytizing message. Of course, nothing in this opinion forecloses a challenge to a menorah display based on such factual findings.

VII

Lynch v. Donnelly confirms, and in no way repudiates, the long-standing constitutional principle that government may not engage in a practice that has the effect of promoting or endorsing religious beliefs. The display of the crèche in the County Courthouse has this unconstitutional effect. The display of the menorah in front of the City–County Building, however, does not have this effect, given its "particular physical setting." The judgment of the Court of Appeals is affirmed in part and reversed in part, and the cases are remanded for further proceedings.

It is so ordered.

JUSTICE O'CONNOR, with whom JUSTICE BRENNAN and JUSTICE STEVENS join as to Part II, concurring in part and concurring in the judgment.

* * *

The constitutionality of the two displays at issue in this case turns on how we interpret and apply the holding in Lynch v. Donnelly, 465 U.S. 668 (1984), in which we rejected an Establishment Clause challenge to the city of Pawtucket's inclusion of a crèche in its annual Christmas holiday display. * * *

* * *

In my concurrence in *Lynch,* I suggest a clarification of our Establishment Clause doctrine to reinforce the concept that the Establishment Clause "prohibits government from making adherence to a religion relevant in any way to a person's standing in the political community." *Id.,* at 687. The government violates this prohibition if it endorses or disapproves of religion. *Id.,* at 688. "Endorsement sends a message to nonadherents that they are outsiders, not full members of the political community, and an accompanying message to adherents that they are insiders, favored members of the political community." *Ibid.* Disapproval of religion conveys the opposite message. Thus, in my view, the central issue in *Lynch* was whether the city of Pawtucket had endorsed Christianity by displaying a crèche as part of a larger exhibit of traditional secular symbols of the Christmas holiday season.

In *Lynch,* I concluded that the city's display of a crèche in its larger holiday exhibit in a private park in the commercial district had neither the purpose nor the effect of conveying a message of government endorsement of Christianity or disapproval of other religions. The purpose of including the crèche in the larger display was to celebrate the public holiday through its traditional symbols, not to promote the religious content of the crèche. *Id.,* at 691. Nor, in my view, did Pawtucket's display of the crèche along with secular symbols of the Christmas holiday objectively convey a message of endorsement of Christianity. *Id.,* at 692.

For the reasons stated in Part IV of the Court's opinion in this case, I agree that the crèche displayed on the Grand Staircase of the Allegheny County Courthouse, the seat of county government, conveys a message to nonadherents of Christianity that they are not full members of the political community, and a corresponding message to Christians that they are favored members of the political community. In contrast to the crèche in *Lynch,* which was displayed in a private park in the city's commercial district as part of a broader display of traditional secular symbols of the holiday season, this crèche stands alone in the County Courthouse. The display of religious symbols in public areas of core government buildings runs a special risk of "mak[ing] religion relevant, in reality or public perception, to status in the political community." *Lynch, supra,* at 692 (concurring opinion). See also American Jewish Congress v. City of Chicago, 827 F.2d 120, 128 (CA7 1987) ("[b]ecause City Hall is so plainly under government ownership and control, every display and activity in the building is implicitly marked with the stamp of government approval. The presence of a nativity scene in the lobby, therefore, inevitably creates a clear and strong impression that the local government tacitly endorses Christianity"). The Court correctly concludes that placement of the central religious symbol of the Christmas holiday season at the Allegheny County Courthouse has the unconstitutional effect of conveying a government endorsement of Christianity.

* * *

For reasons which differ somewhat from those set forth in Part VI of Justice Blackmun's opinion, I also conclude that the city of Pittsburgh's combined holiday display of a Chanukah menorah, a Christmas tree, and a sign saluting liberty does not have the effect of conveying an endorsement of religion. * * *

* * * In my view, the relevant question for Establishment Clause purposes is whether the city of Pittsburgh's display of the menorah, the religious symbol of a religious holiday, next to a Christmas tree and a sign saluting liberty sends a message of government endorsement of Judaism or whether it sends a message of pluralism and freedom to choose one's own beliefs.

* * *

JUSTICE BRENNAN, with whom JUSTICE MARSHALL and JUSTICE STEVENS join, concurring in part and dissenting in part.

I have previously explained at some length my views on the relationship between the Establishment Clause and government-sponsored celebrations of the Christmas holiday. See Lynch v. Donnelly, 465 U.S. 668, 694–726 (1984) (dissenting opinion). I continue to believe that the display of an object that "retains a specifically Christian [or other] religious meaning," *id.*, at 708, is incompatible with the separation of church and state demanded by our Constitution. I therefore agree with the Court that Allegheny County's display of a crèche at the county courthouse signals an endorsement of the Christian faith in violation of the Establishment Clause, and join Parts III–A, IV, and V of the Court's opinion. I cannot agree, however, that the city's display of a 45–foot Christmas tree and an 18–foot Chanukah menorah at the entrance to the building housing the Mayor's office shows no favoritism towards Christianity, Judaism, or both. Indeed, I should have thought that the answer as to the first display supplied the answer to the second.

* * *

* * * The menorah is indisputably a religious symbol, used ritually in a celebration that has deep religious significance. That, in my view, is all that need be said. Whatever secular practices the holiday of Chanukah has taken on in its contemporary observance are beside the point.

Indeed, at the very outset of his discussion of the menorah display, Justice Blackmun recognizes that the menorah is a religious symbol. * * * That should have been the end of the case. But, as did the Court in *Lynch*, Justice Blackmun, "by focusing on the holiday 'context' in which the [menorah] appeared, seeks to explain away the clear religious import of the [menorah]. * * *" 465 U.S., at 705 (BRENNAN, J., dissenting). By the end of the opinion, the menorah has become but a coequal symbol, with the Christmas tree, of "the winter-holiday season." * * * Pittsburgh's secularization of an inherently religious symbol, aided and abetted here by Justice Blackmun's opinion, recalls the effort in *Lynch* to render the crèche a secular symbol. * * *

* * *

JUSTICE STEVENS, with whom JUSTICE BRENNAN and JUSTICE MARSHALL join, concurring in part and dissenting in part.

* * *

In my opinion the Establishment Clause should be construed to create a strong presumption against the display of religious symbols on public property. There is always a risk that such symbols will offend nonmembers of the faith being advertised as well as adherents who consider the particular advertisement disrespectful. Some devout Christians believe that the crèche should be placed only in reverential settings, such as a church or perhaps a private home; they do not countenance its use as an aid to commercialization of Christ's birthday. Cf. *Lynch*, 465 U.S., at 726–727 (BLACKMUN, J., dissenting).[8] In this very

---

8. The point is reiterated here by *amicus* the Governing Board of the National

case, members of the Jewish faith firmly opposed the use of which the menorah was put by the particular sect that sponsored the display at Pittsburgh's City–County Building.[9] Even though "[p]assersby who disagree with the message conveyed by these displays are free to ignore them, or even turn their backs," * * * (KENNEDY, J., concurring in judgment in part and dissenting in part), displays of this kind inevitably have a greater tendency to emphasize sincere and deeply felt differences among individuals than to achieve an ecumenical goal. The Establishment Clause does not allow public bodies to foment such disagreement.[10]

* * *

I cannot agree with the Court's conclusion that the display at Pittsburgh's City–County Building was constitutional. Standing alone in front of a governmental headquarters, a lighted 45-foot evergreen tree might convey holiday greetings linked too tenuously to Christianity to have constitutional moment. Juxtaposition of this tree with an 18-foot menorah does not make the latter secular, as Justice Blackmun contends, * * *. Rather, the presence of the Chanukah menorah, unquestionably a religious symbol, gives religious significance to the Christmas tree. The overall display thus manifests governmental approval of the Jewish and Christian religions. * * *

* * *

JUSTICE KENNEDY, with whom THE CHIEF JUSTICE, JUSTICE WHITE, and JUSTICE SCALIA join, concurring in the judgment in part and dissenting in part.

* * *

I

In keeping with the usual fashion of recent years, the majority applies the *Lemon* test to judge the constitutionality of the holiday displays here in question. I am content for present purposes to remain within the *Lemon* framework, but do not wish to be seen as advocating, let alone adopting, that test as our primary guide in this difficult area. Persuasive criticism of *Lemon* has emerged. * * * Substantial revision of our Establishment Clause doctrine may be in order, but it is unnecessary to undertake that task today, for even the *Lemon* test, when applied with proper sensitivity to our traditions and our caselaw,

---

Counsel of Churches of Christ in the U.S.A., which argues that "government acceptance of a crèche on public property * * * secularizes and degrades a sacred symbol of Christianity," Brief for American Jewish Committee et al. as *Amici Curiae* ii. See also *Engel,* 370 U.S., at 431. Indeed two Roman Catholics testified before the District Court in this case that the crèche display offended them. App. 79–80, 93–96.

9. See Brief for American Jewish Committee et al. as *Amici Curiae* i–ii; Brief for American Jewish Congress et al. as *Amici Curiae* 1–2; Tr. of Oral Arg. 44.

10. This case illustrates the danger that governmental displays of religious symbols may give rise to unintended divisiveness, for the net result of the Court's disposition is to disallow the display of the crèche but to allow the display of the menorah. Laypersons unfamiliar with the intricacies of Establishment Clause jurisprudence may reach the wholly unjustified conclusion that the Court itself is preferring one faith over another. * * *

supports the conclusion that both the crèche and the menorah are permissible displays in the context of the holiday season.

The only *Lemon* factor implicated in this case directs us to inquire whether the "principal or primary effect" of the challenged government practice is "one that neither advances nor inhibits religion." 403 U.S., at 612. The requirement of neutrality inherent in that formulation has sometimes been stated in categorical terms. For example, in Everson v. Board of Education, 330 U.S. 1 (1947), the first case in our modern Establishment Clause jurisprudence, Justice Black wrote that the Clause forbids laws "which aid one religion, aid all religions, or prefer one religion over another." *Id.*, at 15–16. We have stated that government "must be neutral in matters of religious theory, doctrine, and practice" and "may not aid, foster, or promote one religion or religious theory against another or even against the militant opposite." * * *

These statements must not give the impression of a formalism that does not exist. Taken to its logical extreme, some of the language quoted above would require a relentless extirpation of all contact between government and religion. But that is not the history or the purpose of the Establishment Clause. Government policies of accommodation, acknowledgment, and support for religion are an accepted part of our political and cultural heritage. * * *

Rather than requiring government to avoid any action that acknowledges or aids religion, the Establishment Clause permits government some latitude in recognizing and accommodating the central role religion plays in our society. * * *

* * *

The ability of the organized community to recognize and accommodate religion in a society with a pervasive public sector requires diligent observance of the border between accommodation and establishment. Our cases disclose two limiting principles: government may not coerce anyone to support or participate in any religion or its exercise; and it may not, in the guise of avoiding hostility or callous indifference, give direct benefits to religion in such a degree that it in fact "establishes a [state] religion or religious faith, or tends to do so." *Lynch v. Donnelly, supra*, at 678. These two principles, while distinct, are not unrelated, for it would be difficult indeed to establish a religion without some measure of more or less subtle coercion, be it in the form of taxation to supply the substantial benefits that would sustain a state-established faith, direct compulsion to observance, or governmental exhortation to religiosity that amounts in fact to proselytizing.

* * *

As Justice Blackmun observes, * * *, some of our recent cases reject the view that coercion is the sole touchstone of an Establishment Clause violation. * * * That may be true if by "coercion" is meant *direct* coercion in the classic sense of an establishment of religion that the Framers knew. But coercion need not be a direct tax in aid of religion or a test oath. Symbolic recognition or accommodation of religious faith may violate the Clause in an extreme case. I doubt not,

for example, that the Clause forbids a city to permit the permanent erection of a large Latin cross on the roof of city hall. This is not because government speech about religion is per se suspect, as the majority would have it, but because such an obtrusive year-round religious display would place the government's weight behind an obvious effort to proselytize on behalf of a particular religion. * * *
* * *

* * * Non-coercive government action within the realm of flexible accommodation or passive acknowledgment of existing symbols does not violate the Establishment Clause unless it benefits religion in a way more direct and more substantial than practices that are accepted in our national heritage.

II

These principles are not difficult to apply to the facts of the case before us. In permitting the displays on government property of the menorah and the crèche, the city and county sought to do no more than "celebrate the season," Brief for Petitioner County of Allegheny in No. 87–2050, p. 27, and to acknowledge, along with many of their citizens, the historical background and the religious as well as secular nature of the Chanukah and Christmas holidays. This interest falls well within the tradition of government accommodation and acknowledgment of religion that has marked our history from the beginning. * * *
* * *

There is no suggestion here that the government's power to coerce has been used to further the interests of Christianity or Judaism in any way. No one was compelled to observe or participate in any religious ceremony or activity. Neither the city nor the county contributed significant amounts of tax money to serve the cause of one religious faith. The crèche and the menorah are purely passive symbols of religious holidays. Passersby who disagree with the message conveyed by these displays are free to ignore them, or even to turn their backs, just as they are free to do when they disagree with any other form of government speech.

There is no realistic risk that the crèche or the menorah represent an effort to proselytize or are otherwise the first step down the road to an establishment of religion. *Lynch* is dispositive of this claim with respect to the crèche, and I find no reason for reaching a different result with respect to the menorah. Both are the traditional symbols of religious holidays that over time have acquired a secular component.
* * *

* * *

Nor can I comprehend why it should be that placement of a government-owned crèche on private land is lawful while placement of a privately owned crèche on public land is not.[5] If anything, I should have thought government ownership of a religious symbol presented

---

5. The crèche in *Lynch* was owned by Pawtucket. Neither the crèche nor the menorah at issue in this case is owned by a governmental entity.

the more difficult question under the Establishment Clause, but as *Lynch* resolved that question to sustain the government action, the sponsorship here ought to be all the easier to sustain. In short, nothing about the religious displays here distinguishes them in any meaningful way from the crèche we permitted in *Lynch*.

If *Lynch* is still good law—and until today it was—the judgment below cannot stand. I accept and indeed approve both the holding and the reasoning of Chief Justice Burger's opinion in *Lynch*, and so I must dissent from the judgment that the crèche display is unconstitutional. On the same reasoning, I agree that the menorah display is constitutional.

III

* * * Even if *Lynch* did not control, I would not commit this Court to the test applied by the majority today. The notion that cases arising under the Establishment Clause should be decided by an inquiry into whether a " 'reasonable observer' " may " 'fairly understand' " government action to " 'sen[d] a message to nonadherents that they are outsiders, not full members of the political community,' " is a recent, and in my view most unwelcome, addition to our tangled Establishment Clause jurisprudence. * * *

* * *

If the endorsement test, applied without artificial exceptions for historical practice, reached results consistent with history, my objections to it would have less force. But, as I understand that test, the touchstone of an Establishment Clause violation is whether nonadherents would be made to feel like "outsiders" by government recognition or accommodation of religion. Few of our traditional practices recognizing the part religion plays in our society can withstand scrutiny under a faithful application of this formula.

* * *

* * * Either the endorsement test must invalidate scores of traditional practices recognizing the place religion holds in our culture, or it must be twisted and stretched to avoid inconsistency with practices we know to have been permitted in the past, while condemning similar practices with no greater endorsement effect simply by reason of their lack of historical antecedent. Neither result is acceptable.

* * *

The approach adopted by the majority contradicts important values embodied in the Clause. Obsessive, implacable resistance to all but the most carefully scripted and secularized forms of accommodation requires this Court to act as a censor, issuing national decrees as to what is orthodox and what is not. What is orthodox, in this context, means what is secular; the only Christmas the State can acknowledge is one in which references to religion have been held to a minimum. The Court thus lends its assistant to an Orwellian rewriting of history as many understand it. I can conceive of no judicial function more antithetical to the First Amendment.

A further contradiction arises from the majority's approach, for the Court also assumes the difficult and inappropriate task of saying what every religious symbol means. Before studying this case, I had not known the full history of the menorah, and I suspect the same was true of my colleagues. More important, this history was, and is, likely unknown to the vast majority of people of all faiths who saw the symbol displayed in Pittsburgh. Even if the majority is quite right about the history of the menorah, it hardly follows that this same history informed the observers' view of the symbol and the reason for its presence. This Court is ill-equipped to sit as a national theology board, and I question both the wisdom and the constitutionality of its doing so. Indeed, were I required to choose between the approach taken by the majority and a strict separationist view, I would have to respect the consistency of the latter.

The case before us is admittedly a troubling one. It must be conceded that, however neutral the purpose of the city and county, the eager proselytizer may seek to use these symbols for his own ends. The urge to use them to teach or to taunt is always present. It is also true that some devout adherents of Judaism or Christianity may be as offended by the holiday display as are nonbelievers, if not more so. To place these religious symbols in a common hallway or sidewalk, where they may be ignored or even insulted, must be distasteful to many who cherish their meaning.

For these reasons, I might have voted against installation of these particular displays were I a local legislative official. But we have no jurisdiction over matters of taste within the realm of constitutionally permissible discretion. Our role is enforcement of a written Constitution. In my view, the principles of the Establishment Clause and our Nation's historic traditions of diversity and pluralism allow communities to make reasonable judgments respecting the accommodation or acknowledgment of holidays with both cultural and religious aspects. No constitutional violation occurs when they do so by displaying a symbol of the holiday's religious origins.

I dissent.

NOTE

Against the background of these cases, reporting the judicial effort to reconcile tradition and historical practices in the United States with some sensitivity to the first amendment,[49] consider the following hypothetical case:

---

49. See W. Miller, The Moral Project of the American Founders, in Articles of Faith, Articles of Peace 36 (J. Hunter & O. Guinness eds. 1990). ("Whereas later believers look back at the founding through the screen of the evangelical revivals and of their own sympathies to find more piety than there was in early America, the cultured among the despisers look back through the screen of their unbelief to find only Thomas Jefferson and Tom Paine and more unabashed secularism than there really was.") For comment on the *Lynch* and *Allegheny County* cases, see Van Alstyne, Trends in the Supreme Court: Mr. Jefferson's Crumbling Wall, 1984 Duke

In Collander County, Idaho, during the past thirty years a major population change has occurred. The earlier residents, discouraged by farm conditions, have tended to move away. New, darker skinned residents, with customs of their own, principally from different parts of Southeast Asia, Indonesia, and Pakistan have tended to move in. By 1991, they had become a majority of the voting age population in Collander County. By 1992, a majority of the elected county commissioners reflected the new political success of the newer residents of Collander County.

Thinking it appropriate to have the county reflect the recent changes, in 1993 the county commissioners voted in favor of reflecting the different traditions of the newer, rather than of the older, residents. Formerly, the county commission had opened with a prayer provided by a local Presbyterian minister, paid an annual $500 fee for his service, from the county fund. In 1993, the county commission let the local minister's contract lapse, in favor of extending the same arrangement instead to a resident mullah (a Moslem teacher or religious leader), to lead the commission, when meeting in public session, in Islamic prayer.

Concurrently, the county commission meeting chamber was redone. Where formerly there had been several painted pictures and scenes on the walls, mosaic patterns were substituted (pictures being regarded as inappropriate to the tradition of Islam). Where formerly the motif up behind the semi-circular dais in the commission public chamber reported the motto "In God We Trust," it was replaced with letters merely of the same size reporting "Allah Akbar" ("God Is Great").

The majority of the residents being Moslem, moreover, the day previously established by county ordinance as a day requiring most businesses to close (Sunday) was determined to be less convenient than once it was. This, because Sunday was a relatively indifferent day for most of the current residents, many of whom spent much of Friday as the Moslem day for prayer, and accordingly, for whom missing work also on Sunday was an unwelcome loss. Consistent still with providing one uniform day free from required employment by businesses for more than six consecutive days, the county commissioners voted affirmatively to repeal the Sunday closing law and enact the same county ordinance exactly, except shifting to a uniform Friday closing day, instead.

By state law, in Idaho, the consumption and sale of alcoholic beverages has always been subject to local option, i.e. determined by county commission choice. Collander County has generally been a "dry" county, i.e. possession, sale, or consumption of alcoholic beverages except for medicinal uses (on a doctor's written prescription) is generally forbidden, though the ordinance, while not actually providing any other express exception, had not been en-

L.J. 770; Van Alstyne, A Judicial Postscript to the Church–State Debates of 1989: How Porous the Wall, How Civil the State?, 4 Notre Dame J. Law, Ethics & Pub. Pol'y 559 (1990).

forced in respect to the mere use of sacramental wine as part of holy communion, at the local Catholic church. The new county commission, however, took the county ordinance somewhat more seriously than had their predecessors. They fully agreed with Collander County being a dry county (Islam is as much opposed to the use of alcohol as the more fundamentalist Christian groups have traditionally been), so they fully endorsed the current ordinance. They saw no reason for continuing the de facto exemption of wine use inconsistent with the ordinance, however, and directed the county sheriff to give notice that hereafter it would be uniformly enforced.

These changes in Collander County have not been free of controversy. Indeed, a number of residents previously satisfied with things as they were, are now angry and in a serious litigative mood. Accordingly, the following actions have been filed in state court. Your task is to assess their likelihood of success or failure, and briefly to indicate on what basis each might have been brought in first amendment terms, and the grounds on which they may fail or succeed:

1. An action by the priest of the local Catholic church, on his own behalf and on behalf of resident Catholic communicants, naming the county prosecutor as defendant, for declaratory relief against threatened criminal enforcement of the alcohol prohibition ordinance;

2. An action by a local businessman, a practicing Protestant, on his own behalf and on behalf of his employees and customers, naming the County Commission as defendant, for declaratory judgment voiding the Friday closing law;

3. An action by a local resident for declaratory judgment and mandatory injunction, naming the County Commission as defendant, to direct the commission to remove the new motto from the rear wall of the public county commission chamber, to modify the mosaic motif, to desist from paying or permitting the mullah (also named as defendant) to commence public commission sessions with Islamic prayer;

4. An action by the nonrenewed Presbyterian minister for mandatory injunction against the County Commission as defendant to reinstate the previous arrangement he had with the county; in the alternative, an injunction requiring that he be paid and treated in rotation of service on equal terms as the commission provides to the mullah.

Chapter 7

"* * * OR PROHIBITING THE FREE EXERCISE THEREOF."

A. The General Test

REYNOLDS v. UNITED STATES
Supreme Court of the United States, 1878.
98 U.S. 145, 23 L.Ed. 244.

Mr. Chief Justice Waite delivered the opinion of the court.

* * *

On the trial, the plaintiff in error, the accused, proved that at the time of his alleged second marriage he was, and for many years before had been, a member of the Church of Jesus Christ of Latter-Day Saints, commonly called the Mormon Church, and a believer in its doctrines; that it was an accepted doctrine of that church "that it was the duty of male members of said church, circumstances permitting, to practise polygamy; * * * that this duty was enjoined by different books which the members of said church believed to be of divine origin, and among others the Holy Bible, and also that the members of the church believed that the practice of polygamy was directly enjoined upon the male members thereof by the Almight God, in a revelation to Joseph Smith, the founder and prophet of said church; that the failing or refusing to practise polygamy by such male members of said church, when circumstances would admit, would be punished, and that the penalty for such failure and refusal would be damnation in the life to come." He also proved "that he had received permission from the recognized authorities in said church to enter into polygamous marriage; * * * that Daniel H. Wells, one having authority in said church to perform the marriage ceremony, married the said defendant on or about the time the crime is alleged to have been committed, to some woman by the name of Schofield, and that such marriage ceremony was performed under and pursuant to the doctrines of said church."

Upon this proof he asked the court to instruct the jury that if they found from the evidence that he "was married as charged—if he was married—in pursuance of and in conformity with what he believed at the time to be a religious duty, that the verdict must be 'not guilty.'" This request was refused, and the court did charge "that there must have been a criminal intent, but that if the defendant, under the influence of a religious belief that it was right,—under an inspiration, if you please, that it was right,—deliberately married a second time, having a first wife living, the want of consciousness of evil intent—the want of understanding on his part that he was committing a crime—did not excuse him; but the law inexorably in such case implies the criminal intent."

Upon this charge and refusal to charge the question is raised, whether religious belief can be accepted as a justification of an overt act made criminal by the law of the land. The inquiry is not as to the power of Congress to prescribe criminal laws for the Territories, but as to the guilt of one who knowingly violates a law which has been properly enacted, if he entertains a religious belief that the law is wrong.

Congress cannot pass a law for the government of the Territories which shall prohibit the free exercise of religion. The first amendment to the Constitution expressly forbids such legislation. Religious freedom is guaranteed everywhere throughout the United States, so far as congressional interference is concerned. The question to be determined is, whether the law now under consideration comes within this prohibition.

The word "religion" is not defined in the Constitution. We must go elsewhere, therefore, to ascertain its meaning, and nowhere more appropriately, we think, than to the history of the times in the midst of which the provision was adopted. The precise point of the inquiry is, what is the religious freedom which has been guaranteed.

Before the adoption of the Constitution, attempts were made in some of the colonies and States to legislate not only in respect to the establishment of religion, but in respect to its doctrines and precepts as well. The people were taxed, against their will, for the support of religion, and sometimes for the support of particular sects to whose tenets they could not and did not subscribe. Punishments were prescribed for a failure to attend upon public worship, and sometimes for entertaining heretical opinions. The controversy upon this general subject was animated in many of the States, but seemed at last to culminate in Virginia. In 1784, the House of Delegates of that State having under consideration "a bill establishing provision for teachers of the Christian religion," postponed it until the next session, and directed that the bill should be published and distributed, and that the people be requested "to signify their opinion respecting the adoption of such a bill at the next session of assembly."

This brought out a determined opposition. Amongst others, Mr. Madison prepared a "Memorial and Remonstrance," which was widely circulated and signed, and in which he demonstrated "that religion, or the duty we owe the Creator," was not within the cognizance of civil government. * * * At the next session the proposed bill was not only defeated, but another, "for establishing religious freedom," drafted by Mr. Jefferson, was passed. 1 Jeff. Works, 45; 2 Howison, Hist. of Va. 298. In the preamble of this act (12 Hening's Stat. 84) religious freedom is defined; and after a recital "that to suffer the civil magistrate to intrude his powers into the field of opinion, and to restrain the profession or propagation of principles on supposition of their ill tendency, is a dangerous fallacy which at once destroys all religious liberty," it is declared "that it is time enough for the rightful purposes of civil government for its officers to interfere when principles break out into overt acts against peace and good order." In these two sentences is found the true distinction between what properly belongs to the church and what to the State.

In a little more than a year after the passage of this statute the convention met which prepared the "Constitution of the United States." Of this convention Mr. Jefferson was not a member, he being then absent as minister to France. As soon as he saw the draft of the Constitution proposed for adoption, he, in a letter to a friend, expressed his disappointment at the absence of an express declaration insuring the freedom of religion (2 Jeff. Works, 355), but was willing to accept it as it was, trusting that the good sense and honest intentions of the people would bring about the necessary alterations. 1 Jeff. Works, 79. Five of the States, while adopting the Constitution, proposed amendments. Three—New Hampshire, New York, and Virginia—included in one form or another a declaration of religious freedom in the changes they desired to have made, as did also North Carolina, where the convention at first declined to ratify the Constitution until the proposed amendments were acted upon. Accordingly, at the first session of the first Congress the amendment now under consideration was proposed with others by Mr. Madison. It met the views of the advocates of religious freedom, and was adopted. Mr. Jefferson afterwards, in reply to an address to him by a committee of the Danbury Baptist Association (8 id. 113), took occasion to say: "Believing with you that religion is a matter which lies solely between man and his God; that he owes account to none other for his faith or his worship; that the legislative powers of the government reach actions only, and not opinions,—I contemplate with sovereign reverence that act of the whole American people which declared that their legislature should 'make no law respecting an establishment of religion or prohibiting the free exercise thereof,' thus building a wall of separation between church and State. Adhering to this expression of the supreme will of the nation in behalf of the rights of conscience, I shall see with sincere satisfaction the progress of those sentiments which tend to restore man to all his natural rights, convinced he has no natural right in opposition to his social duties." Coming as this does from an acknowledged leader of the advocates of the measure, it may be accepted almost as an authoritative declaration of the scope and effect of the amendment thus secured. Congress was deprived of all legislative power over mere opinion, but was left free to reach actions which were in violation of social duties or subversive of good order.

Polygamy has always been odious among the northern and western nations of Europe, and, until the establishment of the Mormon Church, was almost exclusively a feature of the life of Asiatic and of African people. * * *

By the statute of 1 James I. (c. 11), the offence, if committed in England or Wales, was made punishable in the civil courts, and the penalty was death. As this statute was limited in its operation to England and Wales, it was at a very early period re-enacted, generally with some modifications, in all the colonies. In connection with the case we are now considering, it is a significant fact that on the 8th of December, 1788, after the passage of the act establishing religious freedom, and after the convention of Virginia had recommended as an amendment to the Constitution of the United States the declaration in a bill of rights that 'all men have an equal, natural, and unalienable right to the free exercise of religion, according to the dictates of conscience,' the legislature of that State substantially enacted the statute of James I., death penalty included, because, as recited in the preamble, "it hath been doubted whether bigamy or polygamy be punishable by the laws of this Commonwealth." 12 Hening's Stat. 691. From that day to this we think it may safely be said there never has been a time in any State of the Union when polygamy has not been an offence against society, cognizable by the civil courts and punishable with more or less severity. In the face of all this evidence, it is impossible to believe that the constitutional guaranty of religious freedom was intended to prohibit legislation in respect to this most important feature of social life. Marriage, while from its very nature a sacred obligation, is nevertheless, in most civilized nations, a civil contract, and usually regulated by law. Upon it society may be said to be built, and out of its fruits spring social relations and social obligations and duties, with which government is necessarily required to deal. In fact, according as monogamous or polygamous marriages are allowed, do we find the principles on which the government of the people, to a greater or less extent, rests. Professor Lieber says, polygamy leads to the patriarchal principle, and which, when applied to large communities, fetters the people in stationary despotism, while that principle cannot long exist in connection with monogamy. * * *

In our opinion, the statute immediately under consideration is within the legislative power of Congress. It is constitutional and valid as prescribing a rule of action for all those residing in the Territories, and in places over which the United States have exclusive control. This being so, the only question which remains is, whether those who make polygamy a part of their religion are excepted from the operation of the statute. If they are, then those who do not make polygamy a part of their religious belief may be found guilty and punished, while those who do, must be acquitted and go free. This would be introducing a new element into criminal law. Laws are made for the government of actions, and while they cannot interfere with mere religious belief and opinions, they may with practices. Suppose one believed that human sacrifices were a necessary part of religious worship, would it be seriously contended that the civil government under which he lived could not interfere to prevent a sacrifice? Or if a wife religiously believed it was her duty to burn herself upon the funeral pile of her dead husband, would it be beyond the power of the civil government to prevent her carrying her belief into practice?

So here, as a law of the organization of society under the exclusive dominion of the United States, it is provided that plural marriages shall not be allowed. Can a man excuse his practices to the contrary because of his religious belief? To permit this would be to make the professed doctrines of religious belief superior to the law of the land, and in effect to permit every citizen to become a law unto himself. Government could exist only in name under such circumstances.

A criminal intent is generally an element of crime, but every man is presumed to intend the necessary and legitimate consequences of what he knowingly does. Here the accused knew he had been once married, and that his first wife was living. He also knew that his second marriage was forbidden by law. When, herefore, he married the second time, he is presumed to have intended to break the law. And the breaking of the law is the crime. Every act necessary to constitute the crime was knowingly done, and the crime was therefore knowingly committed. Ignorance of a fact may sometimes be taken as evidence of a want of criminal intent, but not ignorance of the law. The only defence of the accused in this case is his belief that the law ought not to have been enacted. It matters not that his belief was a part of his professed religion: it was still belief, and belief only.

In Regina v. Wagstaff (10 Cox Crim. Cases, 531), the parents of a sick child, who omitted to call in medical attendance because of their religious belief that what they did for its cure would be effective, were held not to be guilty of manslaughter, while it was said the contrary would have been the result if the child had actually been starved to death by the parents, under the notion that it was their religious duty to abstain from giving it food. But when the offence consists of a positive act which is knowingly done, it would be dangerous to hold that the offender might escape punishment because he religiously believed the law which he had broken ought never to have been made. No case, we believe, can be found that has gone so far.

* * *

Upon a careful consideration of the whole case, we are satisfied that no error was committed by the court below.

Judgment affirmed.

CANTWELL v. CONNECTICUT
Supreme Court of the United States, 1940.
310 U.S. 296, 60 S.Ct. 900, 84 L.Ed. 1213.

MR. JUSTICE ROBERTS delivered the opinion of the Court.

Newton Cantwell and his two sons, Jesse and Russell, members of a group known as Jehovah's Witnesses, and claiming to be ordained ministers, were arrested in New Haven, Connecticut, and each was charged by information in five counts, with statutory and common law offenses. After trial in the Court of Common Pleas of New Haven County each of them was convicted on the third count, which charged a violation of § 6294 of the General Statutes of Connecticut, and on the fifth count, which charged commission of the common law offense of inciting a breach of the peace. On appeal to the Supreme Court the conviction of all three on the third count was affirmed. The conviction of Jesse Cantwell, on the fifth count, was also affirmed * * *.

* * *

The facts adduced to sustain the convictions on the third count follow. On the day of their arrest the appellants were engaged in going singly from house to house on Cassius Street in New Haven. They were individually equipped with a bag containing books and pamphlets on religious subjects, a portable phonograph and a set of records, each of which, when played, introduced, and was a description of, one of the books. Each appellant asked the person who responded to his call for permission to play one of the records. If permission was granted he asked the person to buy the book described and, upon refusal, he solicited such contribution towards the publication of the pamphlets as the listener was willing to make. If a contribution was received a pamphlet was delivered upon condition that it would be read.

Cassius Street is in a thickly populated neighborhood, where about ninety per cent of the residents are Roman Catholics. A phonograph record, describing a book entitled "Enemies," included an attack on the Catholic religion. None of the persons interviewed were members of Jehovah's Witnesses.

The statute under which the appellants were charged provides:

"No person shall solicit money, services, subscriptions or any valuable thing for any alleged religious, charitable or philanthropic cause, from other than a member of the organization for whose benefit such person is soliciting or within the county in which such person or organization is located unless such cause shall have been approved by the secretary of the public welfare council. Upon application of any person in behalf of such cause, the secretary shall determine whether such cause is a religious one or is a bona fide object of charity or philanthropy and conforms to reasonable standards of efficiency and integrity, and, if he shall so find, shall approve the same and issue to the authority in charge a certificate to that effect. Such certificate may be revoked at any time. Any person violating any provision of this section shall be fined not more than one hundred dollars or imprisoned not more than thirty days or both."

The appellants claimed that their activities were not within the statute but consisted only of distribution of books, pamphlets, and periodicals. The State Supreme Court construed the finding of the trial court to be that "in addition to the sale of the books and the distribution of the pamphlets the defendants were also soliciting contributions or donations of money for an alleged religious cause, and thereby came within the purview of the statute." It overruled the contention that the Act, as applied to the appellants, offends the due process clause of the Fourteenth Amendment, because it abridges or denies religious freedom and liberty of speech and press. The court stated that it was the solicitation that brought the appellants within the sweep of the Act and not their other activities in the dissemination of literature. It declared the legislation constitutional as an effort by the State to protect the public against fraud and imposition in the solicitation of funds for what purported to be religious, charitable, or philanthropic causes.

The facts which were held to support the conviction of Jesse Cantwell on the fifth count were that he stopped two men in the street, asked, and received, permission to play a phonograph record, and played the record "Enemies," which attacked the religion and church of the two men, who were Catholics. Both were incensed by the contents of the record and were tempted to strike Cantwell unless he went away. On being told to be on his way he left their presence. There was no evidence that he was personally offensive or entered into any argument with those he interviewed.

The court held that the charge was not assault or breach of the peace or threats on Cantwell's part, but invoking or inciting others to breach of the peace, and that the facts supported the conviction of that offense.

First. We hold that the statute, as construed and applied to the appellants, deprives them of their liberty without due process of law in contravention of the Fourteenth Amendment. The fundamental concept of liberty embodied in that Amendment embraces the liberties guaranteed by the First Amendment. The First Amendment declares that Congress shall make no law respecting an establishment of religion or prohibiting the free exercise thereof. The Fourteenth Amendment has rendered the legislatures of the states as incompetent as Congress to enact such laws. The constitutional inhibition of legislation on the subject of religion has a double aspect. On the one hand, it forestalls compulsion by law of the acceptance of any creed or the practice of any form of worship. Freedom of conscience and freedom to adhere to such religious organization or form of worship as the individual may choose cannot be restricted by law. On the other hand, it safeguards the free exercise of the chosen form of religion. Thus the Amendment embraces two concepts,—freedom to believe and freedom to act. The first is absolute but, in the nature of things, the second cannot be. Conduct remains subject to regulation for the protection of society.[4] The freedom to act must have appropriate definition to preserve the enforcement of that protection. In every case the power to regulate must be so exercised as not, in attaining a permissible end, unduly to infringe the protected freedom. No one would contest the proposition that a State may not, by statute, wholly deny the right to preach or to disseminate religious views. Plainly such a previous and absolute restraint would violate the terms of the guarantee. It is equally clear that a State may by general and non-discriminatory legislation regulate the times, the places, and the manner of soliciting upon its streets, and of holding meetings thereon; and may in other respects safeguard the peace, good order and comfort of the community, without unconstitutionally invading the liberties protected by the Fourteenth Amendment. The appellants are right in their insistence that the Act in question is not such a regulation. If a certificate is procured,

---

4. Reynolds v. United States, 98 U.S. 145; Davis v. Beason, 133 U.S. 333.

solicitation is permitted without restraint but, in the absence of a certificate, solicitation is altogether prohibited.

The appellants urge that to require them to obtain a certificate as a condition of soliciting support for their views amounts to a prior restraint on the exercise of their religion within the meaning of the Constitution. The State insists that the Act, as construed by the Supreme Court of Connecticut, imposes no previous restraint upon the dissemination of religious views or teaching but merely safeguards against the perpetration of frauds under the cloak of religion. Conceding that this is so, the question remains whether the method adopted by Connecticut to that end transgresses the liberty safeguarded by the Constitution.

The general regulation, in the public interest, of solicitation, which does not involve any religious test and does not unreasonably obstruct or delay the collection of funds, is not open to any constitutional objection, even though the collection be for a religious purpose. Such regulation would not constitute a prohibited previous restraint on the free exercise of religion or interpose an inadmissible obstacle to its exercise.

It will be noted, however, that the Act requires an application to the secretary of the public welfare council of the State; that he is empowered to determine whether the cause is a religious one, and that the issue of a certificate depends upon his affirmative action. If he finds that the cause is not that of religion, to solicit for it becomes a crime. He is not to issue a certificate as a matter of course. His decision to issue or refuse it involves appraisal of facts, the exercise of judgment, and the formation of an opinion. He is authorized to withhold his approval if he determines that the cause is not a religious one. Such a censorship of religion as the means of determining its right to survive is a denial of liberty protected by the First Amendment and included in the liberty which is within the protection of the Fourteenth.

The State asserts that if the licensing officer acts arbitrarily, capriciously, or corruptly, his action is subject to judicial correction. Counsel refer to the rule prevailing in Connecticut that the decision of a commission or an administrative official will be reviewed upon a claim that "it works material damage to individual or corporate rights, or invades or threatens such rights, or is so unreasonable as to justify judicial intervention, or is not consonant with justice, or that a legal duty has not been performed." It is suggested that the statute is to be read as requiring the officer to issue a certificate unless the cause in question is clearly not a religious one; and that if he violates his duty his action will be corrected by a court.

To this suggestion there are several sufficient answers. The line between a discretionary and a ministerial act is not always easy to mark and the statute has not been construed by the state court to impose a mere ministerial duty on the secretary of the welfare council. Upon his decision as to the nature of the cause, the right to solicit depends. Moreover, the availability of a judicial remedy for abuses in the system of licensing still leaves that system one of previous restraint which, in the field of free speech and press, we have held inadmissible. A statute authorizing previous restraint upon the exercise of the guaranteed freedom by judicial decision after trial is as obnoxious to the Constitution as one providing for like restraint by administrative action.[7]

Nothing we have said is intended even remotely to imply that, under the cloak of religion, persons may, with impunity, commit frauds upon the public. Certainly penal laws are available to punish such conduct. Even the exercise of religion may be at some slight inconvenience in order that the State may protect its citizens from injury. Without doubt a State may protect its citizens from fraudulent solicitation by requiring a stranger in the community, before permitting him publicly to solicit funds for any purpose, to establish his identity and his authority to act for the cause which he purports to represent. The State is likewise free to regulate the time and manner of solicitation generally, in the interest of public safety, peace, comfort or convenience. But to condition the solicitation of aid for the perpetuation of religious views or systems upon a license, the grant of which rests in the exercise of a determination by state authority as to what is a religious cause, is to lay a forbidden burden upon the exercise of liberty protected by the Constitution.

Second. We hold that, in the circumstances disclosed, the conviction of Jesse Cantwell on the fifth count must be set aside. Decision as to the lawfulness of the conviction demands the weighing of two conflicting interests. The fundamental law declares the interest of the United States that the free exercise of religion be not prohibited and that freedom to communicate information and opinion be not abridged. The State of Connecticut has an obvious interest in the preservation and protection of peace and good order within her borders. We must determine whether the alleged protection of the State's interest, means to which end would, in the absence of limitation by the Federal Constitution, lie wholly within the State's discretion, has been pressed, in this instance, to a point where it has come into fatal collision with the overriding interest protected by the federal compact.

* * *

The offense known as breach of the peace embraces a great variety of conduct destroying or menacing public order and tranquility. It includes not only violent acts but acts and words likely to produce violence in others. No one would have the hardihood to suggest that the principle of freedom of speech sanctions incitement to riot or that religious liberty connotes the privilege to exhort others to physical attack upon those belonging to another sect. When clear and present danger of riot, disorder, interference with traffic upon the public streets, or other immediate threat to public safety, peace, or order, appears, the power of the State to prevent or punish is obvious. Equally obvious is it that a State may not unduly suppress free communication of views, religious or other, under the guise of conserv-

---

7. Near v. Minnesota, 283 U.S. 697.

ing desirable conditions. Here we have a situation analogous to a conviction under a statute sweeping in a great variety of conduct under a general and indefinite characterization, and leaving to the Executive and Judicial branches too wide a discretion in its application.

Having these considerations in mind, we note that Jesse Cantwell, on April 26, 1938, was upon a public street, where he had a right to be, and where he had a right peacefully to impart his views to others. There is no showing that his deportment was noisy, truculent, overbearing or offensive. He requested of two pedestrians permission to play to them a phonograph record. The permission was granted. It is not claimed that he intended to insult or affront the hearers by playing the record. It is plain that he wished only to interest them in his propaganda. The sound of the phonograph is not shown to have disturbed residents of the street, to have drawn a crowd, or to have impeded traffic. Thus far he had invaded no right or interest of the public or of the men accosted.

The record played by Cantwell embodies a general attack on all organized religious systems as instruments of Satan and injurious to man; it then singles out the Roman Catholic Church for strictures couched in terms which naturally would offend not only persons of that persuasion, but all others who respect the honestly held religious faith of their fellows. The hearers were in fact highly offended. One of them said he felt like hitting Cantwell and the other that he was tempted to throw Cantwell off the street. The one who testified he felt like hitting Cantwell said, in answer to the question "Did you do anything else or have any other reaction?" "No, sir, because he said he would take the victrola and he went." The other witness testified that he told Cantwell he had better get off the street before something happened to him and that was the end of the matter as Cantwell picked up his books and walked up the street.

* * *

We find in the instant case no assault or threatening of bodily harm, no truculent bearing, no intentional discourtesy, no personal abuse. On the contrary, we find only an effort to persuade a willing listener to buy a book or to contribute money in the interest of what Cantwell, however misguided others may think him, conceived to be true religion.

In the realm of religious faith, and in that of political belief, sharp differences arise. In both fields the tenets of one man may seem the rankest error to his neighbor. To persuade others to his own point of view, the pleader, as we know, at times, resorts to exaggeration, to vilification of men who have been, or are, prominent in church or state, and even to false statement. But the people of this nation have ordained in the light of history, that, in spite of the probability of excesses and abuses, these liberties are, in the long view, essential to enlightened opinion and right conduct on the part of the citizens of a democracy.

The essential characteristic of these liberties is, that under their shield many types of life, character, opinion and belief can develop unmolested and unobstructed. Nowhere is this shield more necessary than in our own country for a people composed of many races and of many creeds. There are limits to the exercise of these liberties. The danger in these times from the coercive activities of those who in the delusion of racial or religious conceit would incite violence and breaches of the peace in order to deprive others of their equal right to the exercise of their liberties, is emphasized by events familiar to all. These and other transgressions of those limits the States appropriately may punish.

Although the contents of the record not unnaturally aroused animosity, we think that, in the absence of a statute narrowly drawn to define and punish specific conduct as constituting a clear and present danger to a substantial interest of the State, the petitioner's communication, considered in the light of the constitutional guarantees, raised no such clear and present menace to public peace and order as to render him liable to conviction of the common law offense in question.[10] The judgment affirming the convictions on the third and fifth counts is reversed and the cause is remanded for further proceedings not inconsistent with this opinion.

Reversed.

PRINCE v. MASSACHUSETTS

Supreme Court of the United States, 1944.
321 U.S. 158, 64 S.Ct. 438, 88 L.Ed. 645.

MR. JUSTICE RUTLEDGE delivered the opinion of the court.

The case brings for review another episode in the conflict between Jehovah's Witnesses and state authority. This time Sarah Prince appeals from convictions for violating Massachusetts' child labor laws, by acts said to be a rightful exercise of her religious convictions.

When the offenses were committed she was the aunt and custodian of Betty M. Simmons, a girl nine years of age. Originally there were three separate complaints. They were, shortly, for (1) refusal to disclose Betty's identity and age to a public officer whose duty was to enforce the statutes; (2) furnishing her with magazines, knowing she was to sell them unlawfully, that is, on the street; and (3) as Betty's custodian, permitting her to work contrary to law. The complaints were made, respectively, pursuant to §§ 79, 80 and 81 of Chapter 149, Gen.Laws of Mass. (Ter.Ed.). The Supreme Judicial Court reversed the conviction under the first complaint on state grounds; but sustained the judgments founded on the other two. 313 Mass. 223, 46 N.E.2d 755. They present the only questions for our decision. These are whether §§ 80 and 81, as applied, contravene the Fourteenth Amendment by denying or abridging appellant's freedom of religion and by denying to her the equal protection of the laws.

---

10. Compare Schenck v. United States, 249 U.S. 47, 52; Herndon v. Lowry, 301 U.S. 242, 256; *Thornhill v. Alabama,* * * *.

Sections 80 and 81 form parts of Massachusetts' comprehensive child labor law. They provide methods for enforcing the prohibitions of § 69, which is as follows:

"No boy under twelve and no girl under eighteen shall sell, expose or offer for sale any newspapers, magazines, periodicals or any other articles of merchandise of any description, or exercise the trade of bootblack or scavenger, or any other trade, in any street or public place."

Sections 80 and 81, so far as pertinent, read:

"Whoever furnishes or sells to any minor any article of any description with the knowledge that the minor intends to sell such article in violation of any provision of sections sixty-nine to seventy-three, inclusive, or after having received written notice to this effect from any officer charged with the enforcement thereof, or knowingly procures or encourages any minor to violate any provisions of said sections, shall be punished by a fine of not less than ten nor more than two hundred dollars or by imprisonment for not more than two months, or both." § 80.

"Any parent, guardian or custodian having a minor under his control who compels or permits such minor to work in violation of any provision of sections sixty to seventy-four, inclusive, * * * shall for a first offence be punished by a fine of not less than two nor more than ten dollars or by imprisonment for not more than five days, or both; * * *." § 81.

The story told by the evidence has become familiar. It hardly needs repeating, except to give setting to the variations introduced through the part played by a child of tender years. Mrs. Prince, living in Brockton, is the mother of two young sons. She also has legal custody of Betty Simmons who lives with them. The children too are Jehovah's Witnesses and both Mrs. Prince and Betty testified they were ordained ministers. The former was accustomed to go each week on the streets of Brockton to distribute "Watchtower" and "Consolation," according to the usual plan.[4] She had permitted the children to engage in this activity previously, and had been warned against doing so by the school attendance officer, Mr. Perkins. But, until December 18, 1941, she generally did not take them with her at night.

That evening, as Mrs. Prince was preparing to leave her home, the children asked to go. She at first refused. Childlike, they resorted to tears and, motherlike, she yielded. Arriving downtown, Mrs. Prince permitted the children "to engage in the preaching work with her upon the sidewalks." That is, with specific reference to Betty, she and Mrs. Prince took positions about twenty feet apart near a street intersection. Betty held up in her hand, for passersby to see, copies of "Watchtower" and "Consolation." From her shoulder hung the usual canvas maga-

---

4. Cf. the facts as set forth in Jamison v. Texas, 318 U.S. 413; Largent v. Texas, 318 U.S. 418; Murdock v. Pennsylvania, 319 U.S. 105; Busey v. District of Columbia, 75 U.S.App.D.C. 352, 129 F.2d 24. A common feature is that specified small sums are generally asked and received but the publications may be had without the payment if so desired.

zine bag, on which was printed "Watchtower and Consolation 5¢ per copy." No one accepted a copy from Betty that evening and she received no money. Nor did her aunt. But on other occasions, Betty had received funds and given out copies.

Mrs. Prince and Betty remained until 8:45 p.m. A few minutes before this Mr. Perkins approached Mrs. Prince. A discussion ensued. He inquired and she refused to give Betty's name. However, she stated the child attended the Shaw School. Mr. Perkins referred to his previous warnings and said he would allow five minutes for them to get off the street. Mrs. Prince admitted she supplied Betty with the magazines and said, "[N]either you nor anybody else can stop me * * *. This child is exercising her God-given right and her constitutional right to preach the gospel, and no creature has a right to interfere with God's commands." However, Mrs. Prince and Betty departed. She remarked as she went, "I'm not going through this any more. We've been through it time and time again. I'm going home and put the little girl to bed." It may be added that testimony, by Betty, her aunt and others, was offered at the trials, and was excluded, to show that Betty believed it was her religious duty to perform this work and failure would bring condemnation "to everlasting destruction at Armageddon."

* * *

Appellant does not stand on freedom of the press. Regarding it as secular, she concedes it may be restricted as Massachusetts has done. Hence, she rests squarely on freedom of religion under the First Amendment, applied by the Fourteenth to the states. She buttresses this foundation, however, with a claim of parental right as secured by the due process clause of the latter Amendment. Cf. Meyer v. Nebraska, 262 U.S. 390. These guarantees, she thinks, guard alike herself and the child in what they have done. Thus, two claimed liberties are at stake. One is the parent's, to bring up the child in the way he should go, which for appellant means to teach him the tenets and the practices of their faith. The other freedom is the child's, to observe these; and among them is "to preach the gospel * * * by public distribution" of "Watchtower" and "Consolation," in conformity with the scripture: "A little child shall lead them."

If by this position appellant seeks for freedom of conscience a broader protection than for freedom of the mind, it may be doubted that any of the great liberties insured by the First Article can be given higher place than the others. All have preferred position in our basic scheme. * * *

To make accommodation between these freedoms and an exercise of state authority always is delicate. It hardly could be more so than in such a clash as this case presents. On one side is the obviously earnest claim for freedom of conscience and religious practice. With it is allied the parent's claim to authority in her own household and in the rearing of her children. The parent's conflict with the state over control of the child and his training is serious enough when only secular matters are concerned. It becomes the more so when an element of religious conviction enters. Against these sacred private interests, basic in a democracy, stand the interests of society to protect the welfare of children, and the state's assertion of authority to that end, made here in a manner conceded valid if only secular things were involved. * * *

The rights of children to exercise their religion, and of parents to give them religious training and to encourage them in the practice of religious belief, as against preponderant sentiment and assertion of state power voicing it, have had recognition here, most recently in West Virginia State Board of Education v. Barnette, 319 U.S. 624. Previously in Pierce v. Society of Sisters, 268 U.S. 510, this Court had sustained the parent's authority to provide religious with secular schooling, and the child's right to receive it, as against the state's requirement of attendance at public schools. And in Meyer v. Nebraska, 262 U.S. 390, children's rights to receive teaching in languages other than the nation's common tongue were guarded against the state's encroachment. It is cardinal with us that the custody, care and nurture of the child reside first in the parents, whose primary function and freedom include preparation for obligations the state can neither supply nor hinder. *Pierce v. Society of Sisters, supra.* And it is in recognition of this that these decisions have respected the private realm of family life which the state cannot enter.

But the family itself is not beyond regulation in the public interest, as against a claim of religious liberty. Reynolds v. United States, 98 U.S. 145 * * * Thus, he cannot claim freedom from compulsory vaccination for the child more than for himself on religious grounds.[12] The right to practice religion freely does not include liberty to expose the community or the child to communicable disease or the latter to ill health or death. * * * The catalogue need not be lengthened. It is sufficient to show what indeed appellant hardly disputes, that the state has a wide range of power for limiting parental freedom and authority in things affecting the child's welfare; and that this includes, to some extent, matters of conscience and religious conviction.

But it is said the state cannot do so here. This, first, because when state action impinges upon a claimed religious freedom, it must fall unless shown to be necessary for or conducive to the child's protection against some clear and present danger, cf. Schenck v. United States, 249 U.S. 47; and, it is added, there was no such showing here. The child's presence on the street, with her guardian, distributing or offering to distribute the magazines, it is urged, was in no way harmful to her, nor in any event more so than the presence of many other children at the same time and place, engaged in shopping and other activities not prohibited. Accordingly, in view of the preferred position the freedoms of the First Article occupy, the statute in its present application must fall. It cannot be sustained by any presumption of validity. Cf. Schneider v. State, 308 U.S. 147. And, finally, it is said, the statute is, as to children, an absolute prohibition, not merely a reasonable regulation, of the denounced activity.

Concededly a statute or ordinance identical in terms with Section 69, except that it is applicable to adults or all persons generally, would

12. Jacobson v. Massachusetts, 197 U.S. 11.

be invalid. * * * But the mere fact a state could not wholly prohibit this form of adult activity, whether characterized locally as a "sale" or otherwise, does not mean it cannot do so for children. Such a conclusion granted would mean that a state could impose no greater limitation upon child labor than upon adult labor. * * *

The state's authority over children's activities is broader than over like actions of adults. This is peculiarly true of public activities and in matters of employment. A democratic society rests, for its continuance, upon the healthy, well-rounded growth of young people into full maturity as citizens, with all that implies. It may secure this against impeding restraints and dangers, within a broad range of selection. Among evils most appropriate for such action are the crippling effects of child employment, more especially in public places, and the possible harms arising from other activities subject to all the diverse influences of the street. It is too late now to doubt that legislation appropriately designed to reach such evils is within the state's police power, whether against the parents claim to control of the child or one that religious scruples dictate contrary action.

* * *

Street preaching, whether oral or by handing out literature, is not the primary use of the highway, even for adults. While for them it cannot be wholly prohibited, it can be regulated within reasonable limits in accommodation to the primary and other incidental uses.[17] But, for obvious reasons, notwithstanding appellant's contrary view,[18] the validity of such a prohibition applied to children not accompanied by an older person hardly would seem open to question. The case reduces itself therefore to the question whether the presence of the child's guardian puts a limit to the state's power. That fact may lessen the likelihood that some evils the legislation seeks to avert will occur. But it cannot forestall all of them. The zealous though lawful exercise of the right to engage in propagandizing the community, whether in religious, political or other matters, may and at times does create situations difficult enough for adults to cope with and wholly inappropriate for children, especially of tender years, to face. Other harmful possibilities could be stated, of emotional excitement and psychological or physical injury. Parents may be free to become martyrs themselves. But it does not follow they are free, in identical circumstances, to make martyrs of their children before they have reached the age of full and legal discretion when they can make that choice for themselves. Massachusetts has determined that an absolute prohibition, though one limited to streets and public places and to the incidental uses proscribed, is necessary to accomplish its legitimate objectives. Its power to attain them is broad enough to reach these peripheral instances in which the parent's supervision may reduce but cannot eliminate entire-

17. Cox v. New Hampshire, 312 U.S. 569; Chaplinsky v. New Hampshire, 315 U.S. 568.

18. Although the argument points to the guardian's presence as showing the child's activities here were not harmful, it is nowhere conceded in the briefs that the statute could be applied, consistently with the guaranty of religious freedom, if the facts had been altered only by the guardian's absence.

ly the ill effects of the prohibited conduct. We think that with reference to the public proclaiming of religion, upon the streets and in other similar public places, the power of the state to control the conduct of children reaches beyond the scope of its authority over adults, as is true in the case of other freedoms, and the rightful boundary of its power has not been crossed in this case.

* * *

Our ruling does not extend beyond the facts the case presents. We neither lay the foundation "for any [that is, every] state intervention in the indoctrination and participation of children in religion" which may be done "in the name of their health and welfare" nor give warrant for "every limitation on their religious training and activities." The religious training and indoctrination of children may be accomplished in many ways, some of which, as we have noted, have received constitutional protection through decisions of this Court. These and all others except the public proclaiming of religion on the streets, if this may be taken as either training or indoctrination of the proclaimer, remain unaffected by the decision.

The judgment is affirmed.

Affirmed.

MR. JUSTICE MURPHY, dissenting.

This attempt by the state of Massachusetts to prohibit a child from exercising her constitutional right to practice her religion on the public streets cannot, in my opinion, be sustained.

The record makes clear the basic fact that Betty Simmons, the nine-year old child in question, was engaged in a genuine religious, rather than commercial, activity. * * * There was no expectation of pecuniary profit to herself or to appellant. It is undisputed, furthermore, that she did this of her own desire and with appellant's consent. She testified that she was motivated by her love of the Lord and that He commanded her to distribute this literature; this was, she declared, her way of worshipping God. She was occupied, in other words, in "an age-old form of missionary evangelism" with a purpose "as evangelical as the revival meeting." Murdock v. Pennsylvania, 319 U.S. 105, 108, 109.

Religious training and activity, whether performed by adult or child, are protected by the Fourteenth Amendment against interference by state action, except insofar as they violate reasonable regulations adopted for the protection of the public health, morals and welfare. Our problem here is whether a state, under the guise of enforcing its child labor laws, can lawfully prohibit girls under the age of eighteen and boys under the age of twelve from practicing their religious faith insofar as it involves the distribution or sale of religious tracts on the public streets.

As the opinion of the Court demonstrates, the power of the state lawfully to control the religious and other activities of children is greater than its power over similar activities of adults. But that fact is no more decisive of the issue posed by this case than is the obvious fact that the family itself is subject to reasonable regulation in the public interest. We are concerned solely with the reasonableness of this particular prohibition of religious activity by children.

In dealing with the validity of statutes which directly or indirectly infringe religious freedom and the right of parents to encourage their children in the practice of a religious belief, we are not aided by any strong presumption of the constitutionality of such legislation. United States v. Carolene Products Co., 304 U.S. 144, 152, note 4. On the contrary, the human freedoms enumerated in the First Amendment and carried over into the Fourteenth Amendment are to be presumed to be invulnerable and any attempt to sweep away those freedoms is prima facie invalid. It follows that any restriction or prohibition must be justified by those who deny that the freedoms have been unlawfully invaded. The burden was therefore on the state of Massachusetts to prove the reasonableness and necessity of prohibiting children from engaging in religious activity of the type involved in this case.

* * * If the right of a child to practice its religion in that manner is to be forbidden by constitutional means, there must be a convincing proof that such a practice constitutes a grave and immediate danger to the state or to the health, morals or welfare of the child. West Virginia State Board of Education v. Barnette, 319 U.S. 624, 639. The vital freedom of religion, which is "of the very essence of a scheme of ordered liberty," Palko v. Connecticut, 302 U.S. 319, 325, cannot be erased by slender references to the state's power to restrict the more secular activities of children.

The state, in my opinion, has completely failed to sustain its burden of proving the existence of any grave or immediate danger to any interest which it may lawfully protect. There is no proof that Betty Simmons' mode of worship constituted a serious menace to the public. It was carried on in an orderly, lawful manner at a public street corner. And "one who is rightfully on a street which the state has left open to the public carries with him there as elsewhere the constitutional right to express his views in an orderly fashion. This right extends to the communication of ideas by handbills and literature as well as by the spoken word." Jamison v. Texas, 318 U.S. 413, 416. The sidewalk, no less than the cathedral or the evangelist's tent, is a proper place, under the Constitution, for the orderly worship of God. Such use of the streets is as necessary to the Jehovah's Witnesses, the Salvation Army and others who practice religion without benefit of conventional shelters as is the use of the streets for purposes of passage.

It is claimed, however, that such activity was likely to affect adversely the health, morals and welfare of the child. Reference is made in the majority opinion to "the crippling effects of child employment, more especially in public places, and the possible harms arising from other activities subject to all the diverse influences of the street." To the extent that they flow from participation in ordinary commercial activities, these harms are irrelevant to this case. And the bare possibility that such harms might emanate from distribution of religious literature is not, standing alone, sufficient justification for restricting freedom of conscience and religion. Nor can parents or guardians be subjected to criminal liability because of vague possibilities that their teachings might cause injury to the child. The evils must be grave, immediate, substantial. Cf. Bridges v. California, 314 U.S. 252, 262. * * *

No chapter in human history has been so largely written in terms of persecution and intolerance as the one dealing with religious freedom. From ancient times to the present day, the ingenuity of man has known no limits in its ability to forge weapons of oppression for use against those who dare to express or practice unorthodox religious beliefs. And the Jehovah's Witnesses are living proof of the fact that even in this nation, conceived as it was in the ideals of freedom, the right to practice religion in unconventional ways is still far from secure. Theirs is a militant and unpopular faith, pursued with a fanatical zeal. They have suffered brutal beatings; their property has been destroyed; they have been harassed at every turn by the resurrection and enforcement of little used ordinances and statutes. See Mulder and Comisky, "Jehovah's Witnesses Mold Constitutional Law," 2 Bill of Rights Review, No. 4, p. 262. To them, along with other present-day religious minorities, befalls the burden of testing our devotion to the ideals and constitutional guarantees of religious freedom. We should therefore hesitate before approving the application of a statute that might be used as another instrument of oppression. Religious freedom is too sacred a right to be restricted or prohibited in any degree without convincing proof that a legitimate interest of the state is in grave danger.

* * *

UNITED STATES v. BALLARD
Supreme Court of the United States, 1944.
322 U.S. 78, 64 S.Ct. 882, 88 L.Ed. 1148.

MR. JUSTICE DOUGLAS delivered the opinion of the court.

Respondents were indicted and convicted for using, and conspiring to use, the mails to defraud. * * * The indictment was in twelve counts. It charged a scheme to defraud by organizing and promoting the I Am movement through the use of the mails. The charge was that certain designated corporations were formed, literature distributed and sold, funds solicited, and memberships in the I Am movement sought "by means of false and fraudulent representations, pretenses and promises". The false representations charged were eighteen in number. It is sufficient at this point to say that they covered respondents' alleged religious doctrines or beliefs. They were all set forth in the first count. The following are representative:

> that Guy W. Ballard, now deceased, alias Saint Germain, Jesus, George Washington, and Godfre Ray King, had been selected and thereby designated by the alleged "ascertained

masters," Saint Germain, as a divine messenger; and that the words of "ascended masters" and the words of the alleged divine entity, Saint Germain, would be transmitted to mankind through the medium of the said Guy W. Ballard;

that Guy W. Ballard, during his lifetime, and Edna W. Ballard, and Donald Ballard, by reason of their alleged high spiritual attainments and righteous conduct, had been selected as divine messengers through which the words of the alleged "ascended masters," including the alleged Saint Germain, would be communicated to mankind under the teachings commonly known as the "I Am" movement;

that Guy W. Ballard, during his lifetime, and Edna W. Ballard and Donald Ballard had, by reason of supernatural attainments, the power to heal persons of ailments and diseases and to make well persons afflicted with any diseases, injuries, or ailments, and did falsely represent to persons intended to be defrauded that the three designated persons had the ability and power to cure persons of those diseases normally classified as curable and also of diseases which are ordinarily classified by the medical profession as being incurable diseases; and did further represent that the three designated persons had in fact cured either by the activity of one, either, or all of said persons, hundreds of persons afflicted with diseases and ailments;

Each of the representations enumerated in the indictment was followed by the charge that respondents "well knew" it was false. After enumerating the eighteen misrepresentations the indictment also alleged:

At the time of making all of the afore-alleged representations by the defendants, and each of them, the defendants, and each of them, well knew that all of said aforementioned representations were false and untrue and were made with the intention on the part of the defendants, and each of them, to cheat, wrong, and defraud persons intended to be defrauded, and to obtain from persons intended to be defrauded by the defendants, money, property, and other things of value and to convert the same to the use and the benefit of the defendants, and each of them;

* * * Early in the trial, * * *, objections were raised to the admission of certain evidence concerning respondents' religious beliefs. The court conferred with counsel in absence of the jury and with the acquiescence of counsel for the United States and for respondents confined the issues on this phase of the case to the question of the good faith of respondents. At the request of counsel for both sides the court advised the jury of that action in the following language:

Now, gentlemen, here is the issue in this case:

First, the defendants in this case made certain representations of belief in a divinity and in a supernatural power. Some of the teachings of the defendants, representations, might seem extremely improbable to a great many people. For instance, the appearance of Jesus to dictate some of the works that we have had introduced in evidence, as testified to here at the opening transcription, or shaking hands with Jesus, to some people that might seem highly improbable. I point that out as one of the many statements.

Whether that is true or not is not the concern of this Court and is not the concern of the jury—and they are going to be told so in their instructions. As far as this Court sees the issue, it is immaterial what these defendants preached or wrote or taught in their classes. They are not going to be permitted to speculate on the actuality of the happening of those incidents. Now, I think I have made that as clear as I can. Therefore, the religious beliefs of these defendants cannot be an issue in this court.

The issue is: Did these defendants honestly and in good faith believe those things? If they did, they should be acquitted. I cannot make it any clearer than that.

* * * As we have said, counsel for the defense acquiesced in this treatment of the matter, made no objection to it during the trial, and indeed treated it without protest as the law of the case throughout the proceedings prior to the verdict. Respondents did not change their position before the District Court after verdict and contend that the truth or verity of their religious doctrines or beliefs should have been submitted to the jury. In their motion for new trial they did contend, however, that the withdrawal of these issues from the jury was error because it was in effect an amendment of the indictment. That was also one of their specifications of errors on appeal.

The Circuit Court of Appeals reversed the judgment of conviction and granted a new trial, one judge dissenting. * * * Its reason was that the scheme to defraud alleged in the indictment was that respondents made the eighteen alleged false representations; and that to prove that defendants devised the scheme described in the indictment "it was necessary to prove that they schemed to make some, at least, of the (eighteen) representations * * * and that some, at least, of the representations which they schemed to make were false." 138 F.2d 545. * * *

* * *

* * * A careful reading of the whole charge leads us to agree with the Circuit Court of Appeals on this phase of the case that the only issue submitted to the jury was the question as stated by the District Court, of respondents' "belief in their representations and promises."

The United States contends that respondents acquiesced in the withdrawal from the jury of the truth of their religious doctrines or beliefs and that their consent bars them from insisting on a different course once that one turned out to be unsuccessful. * * * In fairness to respondents that principle cannot be applied here. The real objection of respondents is not that the truth of their religious doctrines or beliefs should have been submitted to the jury. Their demurrer and motion to quash made clear their position that that issue should be withheld from the jury on the basis of the First Amendment. Moreover, their position at all times was and still is that the court should have gone the whole way and withheld from the jury both that issue and the issue of their good faith. Their demurrer and motion to quash asked for dismissal of the entire indictment. Their argument that the truth of their religious doctrines or beliefs should have gone to the jury when the question of their good faith was submitted was and is merely an alternative argument. * * *

As we have noted, the Circuit Court of Appeals held that the question of the truth of the representations concerning respondent's religious doctrines or beliefs should have been submitted to the jury. And it remanded the case for a new trial. It may be that the Circuit Court of Appeals took that action because it did not think that the indictment could be properly construed as charging a scheme to defraud by means other than misrepresentations of respondents' religious doctrines or beliefs. Or that court may have concluded that the withdrawal of the issue of the truth of those religious doctrines or beliefs was unwarranted because it resulted in a substantial change in the character of the crime charged. But on whichever basis that court rested its action, we do not agree that the truth or verity of respondents' religious doctrines or beliefs should have been submitted to the jury. Whatever this particular indictment might require, the First Amendment precludes such a course, as the United States seems to concede. * * * Heresy trials are foreign to our Constitution. Men may believe what they cannot prove. They may not be put to the proof of their religious doctrines or beliefs. Religious experiences which are as real as life to some may be incomprehensible to others. Yet the fact that they may be beyond the ken of mortals does not mean that they can be made suspect before the law. Many take their gospel from the New Testament. But it would hardly be supposed that they could be tried before a jury charged with the duty of determining whether those teachings contained false representations. The miracles of the New Testament, the Divinity of Christ, life after death, the power of prayer are deep in the religious convictions of many. If one could be sent to jail because a jury in a hostile environment found those teachings false, little indeed would be left of religious freedom. The Fathers of the Constitution were not unaware of the varied and extreme views of religious sects, of the violence of disagreement among them, and of the lack of any one religious creed on which all men would agree. They fashioned a charter of government which envisaged the widest possible toleration of conflicting views. Man's relation to his God was made no concern of the state. He was granted the right to worship as he pleased and to answer to no man for the verity of his religious views. The religious views espoused by respondents might seem incredible, if not preposterous, to most people. But if those doctrines are subject to trial before a jury charged with finding their truth or falsity, then the same can be done with the religious beliefs of any sect. When the triers of fact undertake that task, they enter a forbidden domain. The First

Amendment does not select any one group or any one type of religion for preferred treatment. It puts them all in that position. * * * So we conclude that the District Court ruled properly when it withheld from the jury all questions concerning the truth or falsity of the religious beliefs or doctrines of respondents.

The judgment is reversed and the cause is remanded to the Circuit Court of Appeals for further proceedings in conformity to this opinion.

Reversed.

Mr. Chief Justice Stone, dissenting.

* * *

The indictment charges respondents' use of the mails to defraud and a conspiracy to commit that offense by false statements of their religious experiences which had not in fact occurred. But it also charged that the representations were "falsely and fraudulently" made, that respondents "well knew" that these representations were untrue, and that they were made by respondents with the intent to cheat and defraud those to whom they were made. With the assent of the prosecution and the defense the trial judge withdrew from the consideration of the jury the question whether the alleged religious experiences had in fact occurred, but submitted to the jury the single issue whether petitioners honestly believed that they had occurred, with the instruction that if the jury did not so find, then it should return a verdict of guilty. On this issue the jury, on ample evidence that respondents were without belief in the statements which they had made to their victims, found a verdict of guilty. The state of one's mind is a fact as capable of fraudulent misrepresentation as is one's physical condition or the state of his bodily health. See Seven Cases v. United States, 239 U.S. 510, 517; cf. Durland v. United States, 161 U.S. 306, 313. There are no exceptions to the charge and no contention that the trial court rejected any relevant evidence which petitioners sought to offer. Since the indictment and the evidence support the conviction, it is irrelevant whether the religious experiences alleged did or did not in fact occur or whether that issue could or could not, for constitutional reasons, have been rightly submitted to the jury. Certainly none of respondents' constitutional rights are violated if they are prosecuted for the fraudulent procurement of money by false representations as to their beliefs, religious or otherwise.

Obviously if the question whether the religious experiences in fact occurred could not constitutionally have been submitted to the jury the court rightly withdrew it. If it could have been submitted I know of no reason why the parties could not, with the advice of counsel, assent to its withdrawal from the jury. And where, as here, the indictment charges two sets of false statements, each independently sufficient to sustain the conviction, I cannot accept respondents' contention that the withdrawal of one set and the submission of the other to the jury amounted to an amendment of the indictment.

An indictment is amended when it is so altered as to charge a different offense from that found by the grand jury. Ex parte Bain, 121

U.S. 1. But here there was no alteration of the indictment, Salinger v. United States, 272 U.S. 542, 549, nor did the court's action, in effect, add anything to it by submitting to the jury matters which it did not charge. United States v. Norris, 281 U.S. 619, 622. In *Salinger v. United States, supra,* 548–549, we explicitly held that where an indictment charges several offenses, or the commission of one offense in several ways, the withdrawal from the jury's consideration of one offense or one alleged method of committing it does not constitute a forbidden amendment of the indictment. See also Goto v. Lane, 265 U.S. 393, 402–403; Ford v. United States, 273 U.S. 593, 602. Were the rule otherwise the common practice of withdrawing from the jury's consideration one count of an indictment while submitting others for its verdict, sustained in Dealy v. United States, 152 U.S. 539, 542, would be a fatal error.

We may assume that under some circumstances the submission to the jury of part only of the matters alleged in the indictment might result in such surprise to the defendant as to amount to the denial of a fair trial. But, as in the analogous case of a variance between pleading and proof, a conviction can be reversed only upon a showing of injury to the "substantial rights" of the accused. Berger v. United States, 295 U.S. 78, 82. Here no claim of surprise has been or could be made. The indictment plainly charged both falsity of, and lack of good faith belief in the representations made, and it was agreed at the outset of the trial, without objection from the defendants, that only the issue of respondents' good faith belief in the representations of religious experiences would be submitted to the jury. Respondents, who were represented by counsel, at no time in the course of the trial offered any objection to this limitation of the issues, or any contention that it would result in a prohibited amendment of the indictment. So far as appears from the record before us the point was raised for the first time in the specifications of errors in the Circuit Court of Appeals. It is asserted that it was argued to the District Court on motions for new trial and in arrest of judgment. If so, there was still no surprise by a ruling to which, as we have said, respondents' counsel assented when it was made.

On the issue submitted to the jury in this case it properly rendered a verdict of guilty. As no legally sufficient reason for disturbing it appears, I think the judgment below should be reversed and that of the District Court reinstated.

MR. JUSTICE ROBERTS and MR. JUSTICE FRANKFURTER join in this opinion.

MR. JUSTICE JACKSON, dissenting.

I should say the defendants have done just that for which they are indicted. If I might agree to their conviction without creating a precedent, I cheerfully would do so. I can see in their teachings nothing but humbug, untainted by any trace of truth. But that does not dispose of the constitutional question whether misrepresentation of religious experience or belief is prosecutable; it rather emphasizes the danger of such prosecutions.

The Ballard family claimed miraculous communication with the spirit world and supernatural power to heal the sick. They were brought to trial for mail fraud on an indictment which charged that their representations were false and that they "well knew" they were false. The trial judge, obviously troubled, ruled that the court could not try whether the statements were untrue, but could inquire whether the defendants knew them to be untrue; and, if so, they could be convicted.

I find it difficult to reconcile this conclusion with our traditional religious freedoms.

In the first place, as a matter of either practice or philosophy I do not see how we can separate an issue as to what is believed from considerations as to what is believable. The most convincing proof that one believes his statements is to show that they have been true in his experience. Likewise, that one knowingly falsified is best proved by showing that what he said happened never did happen. How can the Government prove these persons knew something to be false which it cannot prove to be false? If we try religious sincerity severed from religious verity, we isolate the dispute from the very considerations which in common experience provide its most reliable answer.

* * * When one comes to trial which turns on any aspect of religious belief or representation, unbelievers among his judges are likely not to understand and are almost certain not to believe him.

And then I do not know what degree of skepticism or disbelief in a religious representation amounts to actionable fraud. James points out that "Faith means belief in something concerning which doubt is theoretically possible."[2] Belief in what one may demonstrate to the senses is not faith. All schools of religious thought make enormous assumptions, generally on the basis of revelations authenticated by some sign or miracle. The appeal in such matters is to a very different plane of credulity than is invoked by representations of secular fact in commerce. Some who profess belief in the Bible read literally what others read as allegory or metaphor, as they read Aesop's fables. Religious symbolism is even used by some with the same mental reservations one has in teaching of Santa Claus or Uncle Sam or Easter bunnies or dispassionate judges. It is hard in matters so mystical to say how literally one is bound to believe the doctrine he teaches and even more difficult to say how far it is reliance upon a teacher's literal belief which induces followers to give him money.

There appear to be persons—let us hope not many—who find refreshment and courage in the teachings of the "I Am" cult. If the members of the sect get comfort from the celestial guidance of their "Saint Germain," however doubtful it seems to me, it is hard to say that they do not get what they pay for. Scores of sects flourish in this country by teaching what to me are queer notions. It is plain that there is wide variety in American religious taste. The Ballards are not alone in catering to it with a pretty dubious product.

---

2. William James, The Will to Believe, p. 90.

The chief wrong which false prophets do to their following is not financial. The collections aggregate a tempting total, but individual payments are not ruinous. I doubt if the vigilance of the law is equal to making money stick by over-credulous people. But the real harm is on the mental and spiritual plane. There are those who hunger and thirst after higher values which they feel wanting in their humdrum lives. They live in mental confusion or moral anarchy and seek vaguely for truth and beauty and moral support. When they are deluded and then disillusioned, cynicism and confusion follow. The wrong of these things, as I see it, is not in the money the victims part with half so much as in the mental and spiritual poison they get. But that is precisely the thing the Constitution put beyond the reach of the prosecutor, for the price of freedom of religion or of speech or of the press is that we must put up with, and even pay for, a good deal of rubbish.

Prosecutions of this character easily could degenerate into religious persecution. I do not doubt that religious leaders may be convicted of fraud for making false representations on matters other than faith or experience, as for example if one represents that funds are being used to construct a church when in fact they are being used for personal purposes. But that is not this case, which reaches into wholly dangerous ground. When does less than full belief in a professed credo become actionable fraud if one is soliciting gifts or legacies? Such inquiries may discomfort orthodox as well as unconventional religious teachers, for even the most regular of them are sometimes accused of taking their orthodoxy with a grain of salt.

I would dismiss the indictment and have done with this business of judicially examining other people's faiths.

B. The General Test Refined and in Dispute
WISCONSIN v. YODER

Supreme Court of the United States, 1972.
406 U.S. 205, 92 S.Ct. 1526, 32 L.Ed.2d 15.

MR. CHIEF JUSTICE BURGER delivered the opinion of the Court.

On petition of the State of Wisconsin, we granted the writ of certiorari in this case to review a decision of the Wisconsin Supreme Court holding that respondents' convictions for violating the State's compulsory school-attendance law were invalid under the Free Exercise Clause of the First Amendment to the United States Constitution made applicable to the States by the Fourteenth Amendment. For the reasons hereafter stated we affirm the judgment of the Supreme Court of Wisconsin.

Respondents Jonas Yoder and Wallace Miller are members of the Old Order Amish religion, and respondent Adin Yutzy is a member of the Conservative Amish Mennonite Church. They and their families are residents of Green County, Wisconsin. Wisconsin's compulsory school-attendance law required them to cause their children to attend public or private school until reaching age 16 but the respondents declined to send their children, ages 14 and 15, to public school after they complete the eighth grade. The children were not enrolled in any private school, or within any recognized exception to the compulsory-attendance law, and they are conceded to be subject to the Wisconsin statute.

On complaint of the school district administrator for the public schools, respondents were charged, tried, and convicted of violating the compulsory-attendance law in Green County Court and were fined the sum of $5 each. * * * The trial testimony showed that respondents believed, in accordance with the tenets of Old Order Amish communities generally, that their children's attendance at high school, public or private, was contrary to the Amish religion and way of life. They believed that by sending their children to high school, they would not only expose themselves to the danger of the censure of the church community, but, as found by the county court, also endanger their own salvation and that of their children. The State stipulated that respondents' religious beliefs were sincere.

In support of their position, respondents presented as expert witnesses scholars on religion and education whose testimony is uncontradicted. They expressed their opinions on the relationship of the Amish belief concerning school attendance to the more general tenets of their religion, and described the impact that compulsory high school attendance could have on the continued survival of Amish communities as they exist in the United States today. The history of the Amish sect was given in some detail, beginning with the Swiss Anabaptists of the 16th century who rejected institutionalized churches and sought to return to the early, simple, Christian life de-emphasizing material success, rejecting the competitive spirit, and seeking to insulate themselves from the modern world. As a result of their common heritage, Old Order Amish communities today are characterized by a fundamental belief that salvation requires life in a church community separate and apart from the world and worldly influence. This concept of life aloof from the world and its values is central to their faith.

A related feature of Old Order Amish communities is their devotion to a life in harmony with nature and the soil, as exemplified by the simple life of the early Christian era that continued in America during much of our early national life. Amish beliefs require members of the community to make their living by farming or closely related activities.
* * *

Amish objection to formal education beyond the eighth grade is firmly grounded in these central religious concepts. They object to the high school, and higher education generally, because the values they teach are in marked variance with Amish values and the Amish way of life; they view secondary school education as an impermissible exposure of their children to a "worldly" influence in conflict with their beliefs. The high school tends to emphasize intellectual and scientific accomplishments, self-distinction, competitiveness, worldly success, and social life with other students. Amish society emphasizes informal learning-through-doing; a life of "goodness," rather than a life of intellect; wisdom, rather than technical knowledge, community welfare, rather than competition; and separation from, rather than integration with, contemporary worldly society.

* * *

* * * In the Amish belief higher learning tends to develop values they reject as influences that alienate man from God.

On the basis of such considerations, Dr. Hostetler testified that compulsory high school attendance could not only result in great psychological harm to Amish children, because of the conflicts it would produce, but would also, in his opinion, ultimately result in the destruction of the Old Order Amish church community as it exists in the United States today. The testimony of Dr. Donald A. Erickson, an expert witness on education, also showed that the Amish succeed in preparing their high school age children to be productive members of the Amish community. He described their system of learning through doing the skills directly relevant to their adult roles in the Amish community as "ideal" and perhaps superior to ordinary high school education. The evidence also showed that the Amish have an excellent record as law-abiding and generally self-sufficient members of society.

Although the trial court in its careful findings determined that the Wisconsin compulsory school-attendance law "does interfere with the freedom of the Defendants to act in accordance with their sincere religious belief" it also concluded that the requirement of high school attendance until age 16 was a "reasonable and constitutional" exercise of governmental power, and therefore denied the motion to dismiss the charges. The Wisconsin Circuit Court affirmed the convictions. The Wisconsin Supreme Court, however, sustained respondents' claim under the Free Exercise Clause of the First Amendment and reversed the convictions. A majority of the court was of the opinion that the State had failed to make an adequate showing that its interest in "establishing and maintaining an educational system overrides the defendants' right to the free exercise of their religion." * * *

I

There is no doubt as to the power of a State, having a high responsibility for education of its citizens, to impose reasonable regulations for the control and duration of basic education. See, e.g., Pierce v. Society of Sisters, 268 U.S. 510, 534 (1925). Providing public schools ranks at the very apex of the function of a State. Yet even this paramount responsibility was, in *Pierce*, made to yield to the right of parents to provide an equivalent education in a privately operated system. There the Court held that Oregon's statute compelling attendance in a public school from age eight to age 16 unreasonably interfered with the interest of parents in directing the rearing of their off-spring, including their education in church-operated schools. As that case suggests, the values of parental direction of the religious upbringing and education of their children in their early and formative years have a high place in our society. * * * Thus, a State's interest in universal education, however highly we rank it, is not totally free from a balancing process when it impinges on fundamental rights and interests, such as those specifically protected by the Free Exercise Clause of the First Amendment, and the traditional interest of parents with respect to the religious upbringing of their children so long as they, in the words of *Pierce,* "prepare [them] for additional obligations." 268 U.S., at 535.

It follows that in order for Wisconsin to compel school attendance beyond the eighth grade against a claim that such attendance interferes with the practice of a legitimate religious belief, it must appear either that the State does not deny the free exercise of religious belief by its requirement, or that there is a state interest of sufficient magnitude to override the interest claiming protection under the Free Exercise Clause. * * *

The essence of all that has been said and written on the subject is that only those interests of the highest order and those not otherwise served can overbalance legitimate claims to the free exercise of religion. We can accept it as settled, therefore, that, however strong the State's interest in universal compulsory education, it is by no means absolute to the exclusion or subordination of all other interests. * * *

II

We come then to the quality of the claims of the respondents concerning the alleged encroachment of Wisconsin's compulsory school-attendance statute on their rights and the rights of their children to the free exercise of the religious beliefs they and their forebears have adhered to for almost three centuries. In evaluating those claims we must be careful to determine whether the Amish religious faith and their mode of life are, as they claim, inseparable and interdependent. A way of life, however virtuous and admirable, may not be interposed as a barrier to reasonable state regulation of education if it is based on purely secular considerations; to have the protection of the Religion Clauses, the claims must be rooted in religious belief. Although a determination of what is a "religious" belief or practice entitled to constitutional protection may present a most delicate question, the very concept of ordered liberty precludes allowing every person to make his own standards on matters of conduct in which society as a whole has important interests. Thus, if the Amish asserted their claims because of their subjective evaluation and rejection of the contemporary secular values accepted by the majority, much as Thoreau rejected the social values of his time and isolated himself at Walden Pond, their claims would not rest on a religious basis. Thoreau's choice was philosophical and personal rather than religious, and such belief does not rise to the demands of the Religion Clauses.

Giving no weight to such secular considerations, however, we see that the record in this case abundantly supports the claim that the traditional way of life of the Amish is not merely a matter of personal preference, but one of deep religious conviction, shared by an organized group, and intimately related to daily living. That the Old Order Amish daily life and religious practice stem from their faith is shown by the fact that it is in response to their literal interpretation of the Biblical injunction from the Epistle of Paul to the Romans, "be not conformed to this world. * * * " This command is fundamental to the Amish faith. Moreover, for the Old Order Amish, religion is not simply a matter of theocratic belief. As the expert witnesses explained, the Old Order Amish religion pervades and determines virtually their entire way of life, regulating it with the detail of the Talmudic diet through the strictly enforced rules of the church community.

* * * Their rejection of telephones, automobiles, radios, and television, their mode of dress, of speech, their habits of manual work do indeed set them apart from much of contemporary society; these customs are both symbolic and practical.

As the society around the Amish has become more populous, urban, industrialized, and complex, particularly in this century, government regulation of human affairs has correspondingly become more detailed and pervasive. The Amish mode of life has thus come into conflict increasingly with requirements of contemporary society exerting a hydraulic insistence on conformity to majoritarian standards. So long as compulsory education laws were confined to eight grades of elementary basic education imparted in a nearby rural schoolhouse, with a large proportion of students of the Amish faith, the Old Order Amish had little basis to fear that school attendance would expose their children to the worldly influence they reject. But modern compulsory secondary education in rural areas is now largely carried on in a consolidated school, often remote from the student's home and alien to his daily home life. As the record so strongly shows, the values and programs of the modern secondary school are in sharp conflict with the fundamental mode of life mandated by the Amish religion; * * * The conclusion is inescapable that secondary schooling, by exposing Amish children to worldly influences in terms of attitudes, goals, and values contrary to beliefs, and by substantially interfering with the religious development of the Amish child and his integration into the way of life of the Amish faith community at the crucial adolescent stage of development, contravenes the basic religious tenets and practice of the Amish faith, both as to the parent and the child.

* * *

In sum, the unchallenged testimony of acknowledged experts in education and religious history, almost 300 years of consistent practice, and strong evidence of a sustained faith pervading and regulating respondents' entire mode of life support the claim that enforcement of the State's requirement of compulsory formal education after the eighth grade would gravely endanger if not destroy the free exercise of respondents' religious beliefs.

III

* * *

Wisconsin concedes that under the Religion Clauses religious beliefs are absolutely free from the State's control, but it argues that "actions," even though religiously grounded, are outside the protection of the First Amendment. But our decisions have rejected the idea that religiously grounded conduct is always outside the protection of the Free Exercise Clause. It is true that activities of individuals, even when religiously based, are often subject to regulation by the States in the exercise of their undoubted power to promote the health, safety, and general welfare, or the Federal Government in the exercise of its delegated powers. * * * But to agree that religiously grounded conduct must often be subject to the broad police power of the State is not to deny that there are areas of conduct protected by the Free Exercise Clause of the First Amendment and thus beyond the power of the State to control, even under regulations of general applicability. * * *

Nor can this case be disposed of on the grounds that Wisconsin's requirement for school attendance to age 16 applies uniformly to all citizens of the State and does not, on its face, discriminate against religions or a particular religion, or that it is motivated by legitimate secular concerns. A regulation neutral on its face may, in its application, nonetheless offend the constitutional requirement for governmental neutrality if it unduly burdens the free exercise of religion. * * * The Court must not ignore the danger that an exception from a general obligation of citizenship on religious grounds may run afoul of the Establishment Clause, but that danger cannot be allowed to prevent any exception no matter how vital it may be to the protection of values promoted by the right of free exercise. * * *

The State advances two primary arguments in support of its system of compulsory education. It notes, as Thomas Jefferson pointed out early in our history, that some degree of education is necessary to prepare citizens to participate effectively and intelligently in our open political system if we are to preserve freedom and independence. Further, education prepares individuals to be self-reliant and self-sufficient participants in society. We accept these propositions.

However, the evidence adduced by the Amish in this case is persuasively to the effect that an additional one or two years of formal high school for Amish children in place of their long-established program of informal vocational education would do little to serve those interests. Respondents' experts testified at trial, without challenge, that the value of all education must be assessed in terms of its capacity to prepare the child for life. It is one thing to say that compulsory education for a year or two beyond the eighth grade may be necessary when its goal is the preparation of the child for life in modern society as the majority live, but it is quite another if the goal of education be viewed as the preparation of the child for life in the separated agrarian community that is the keystone of the Amish faith. * * *

The State attacks respondents' position as one fostering "ignorance" from which the child must be protected by the State. No one can question the State's duty to protect children from ignorance but this argument does not square with the facts disclosed in the record.

Whatever their idiosyncrasies as seen by the majority, this record strongly shows that the Amish community has been a highly successful social unit within our society, even if apart from the conventional "mainstream." Its members are productive and very law-abiding members of society; they reject public welfare in any of its usual modern forms. * * *

It is neither fair nor correct to suggests that the Amish are opposed to education beyond the eighth grade level. What this record shows is that they are opposed to conventional formal education of the type provided by a certified high school because it comes at the child's crucial adolescent period of religious development. Dr. Donald Erickson, for example, testified that their system of learning-by-doing was an "ideal system" of education in terms of preparing Amish children for life as adults in the Amish community, and that "I would be inclined to say they do a better job in this than most of the rest of us do." As he put it, "These people aren't purporting to be learned people, and it seems to me the self-sufficiency of the community is the best evidence I can point to—whatever is being done seems to function well."

We must not forget that in the Middle Ages important values of the civilization of the Western World were preserved by members of religious orders who isolated themselves from all worldly influences against great obstacles. There can be no assumption that today's majority is "right" and the Amish and others like them are "wrong." A way of life that is odd or even erratic but interferes with no rights or interests of others is not to be condemned because it is different.

The State, however, supports its interest in providing an additional one or two years of compulsory high school education to Amish children because of the possibility that some such children will choose to leave the Amish community, and that if this occurs they will be ill-equipped for life. The State argues that if Amish children leave their church they should not be in the position of making their way in the world without the education available in the one or two additional years the State requires. However, on this record, that argument is highly speculative. * * *

There is nothing in this record to suggest that the Amish qualities of reliability, self-reliance, and dedication to work would fail to find ready markets in today's society. Absent some contrary evidence supporting the State's position, we are unwilling to assume that persons possessing such valuable vocational skills and habits are doomed to become burdens on society should they determine to leave the Amish faith, nor is there any basis in the record to warrant a finding that an additional one or two years of formal school education beyond the eighth grade would serve to eliminate any such problem that might exist.

Insofar as the State's claim rests on the view that a brief additional period of formal education is imperative to enable the Amish to participate effectively and intelligently in our democratic process, it must fall. The Amish alternative to formal secondary school education has enabled them to function effectively in their day-to-day life under self-imposed limitations on relations with the world, and to survive and prosper in contemporary society as a separate, sharply identifiable and highly self-sufficient community for more than 200 years in this country. In itself this is strong evidence that they are capable of fulfilling the social and political responsibilities of citizenship without compelled attendance beyond the eighth grade at the price of jeopardizing their free exercise of religious belief.[13] When Thomas Jefferson emphasized the need for education as a bulwark of a free people against tyranny, there is nothing to indicate he had in mind compulsory education through any fixed age beyond a basic education. Indeed, the Amish communities singularly parallel and reflect many of the virtues of Jefferson's ideal of the "sturdy yeoman" who would form the basis of what he considered as the ideal of a democratic society. Even their idiosyncratic separateness exemplifies the diversity we profess to admire and encourage.

The requirement for compulsory education beyond the eighth grade is a relatively recent development in our history. * * *

We should also note that compulsory education and child labor laws find their historical origin in common humanitarian instincts, and that the age limits of both laws have been coordinated to achieve their related objectives. In the context of this case, such considerations, if anything, support rather than detract from respondents' position. The origins of the requirement for school attendance to age 16, an age falling after the completion of elementary school but before completion of high school, are not entirely clear. But to some extent such laws reflected the movement to prohibit most child labor under age 16 that culminated in the provisions of the Federal Fair Labor Standards Act of 1938. It is true, then, that the 16–year child labor age limit may to some degree derive from a contemporary impression that children should be in school until that age. But at the same time, it cannot be denied that, conversely, the 16–year education limit reflects, in substantial measure, the concern that children under that age not be employed under conditions hazardous to their health, or in work that should be performed by adults.

The requirement of compulsory schooling to age 16 must therefore be viewed as aimed not merely at providing educational opportunities for children, but as an alternative to the equally undesirable consequence of unhealthful child labor displacing adult workers, or, on the other hand, forced idleness. The two kinds of statutes—compulsory school attendance and child labor laws—tend to keep children of certain ages off the labor market and in school; this regimen in turn provides opportunity to prepare for a livelihood of a higher order than that which children could pursue without education and protects their health in adolescence.

---

13. All of the children involved in this case are graduates of the eighth grade. In the county court, the defense introduced a study by Dr. Hostetler indicating that Amish children in the eighth grade achieved comparably to non-Amish children in the basic skills. Supp.App. 9–11. * * *

In these terms, Wisconsin's interest in compelling the school attendance of Amish children to age 16 emerges as somewhat less substantial than requiring such attendance for children generally. For, while agricultural employment is not totally outside the legitimate concerns of the child labor laws, employment of children under parental guidance and on the family farm from age 14 to age 16 is an ancient tradition that lies at the periphery of the objectives of such laws. There is no intimation that the Amish employment of their children on family farms is in any way deleterious to their health or that Amish parents exploit children at tender years. Any such inference would be contrary to the record before us. Moreover, employment of Amish children on the family farm does not present the undesirable economic aspects of eliminating jobs that might otherwise be held by adults.

IV

Finally, the State, on authority of *Prince v. Massachusetts*, argues that a decision exempting Amish children from the State's requirement fails to recognize the substantive right of the Amish child to a secondary education, and fails to give due regard to the power of the State as *parens patriae* to extend the benefit of secondary education to children regardless of the wishes of their parents. Taken at its broadest sweep, the Court's language in *Prince*, might be read to give support to the State's position. However, the Court was not confronted in *Prince* with a situation comparable to that of the Amish as revealed in this record; this is shown by the Court's severe characterization of the evils that it thought the legislature could legitimately associate with child labor; even when performed in the company of an adult. * * *

This case, of course, is not one in which any harm to the physical or mental health of the child or to the public safety, peace, order, or welfare has been demonstrated or may be properly inferred. The record is to the contrary, and any reliance on that theory would find no support in the evidence.

Contrary to the suggestion of the dissenting opinion of Mr. Justice Douglas, our holding today in no degree depends on the assertion of the religious interest of the child as contrasted with that of the parents. It is the parents who are subject to prosecution here for failing to cause their children to attend school, and it is their right of free exercise, not that of their children, that must determine Wisconsin's power to impose criminal penalties on the parent. The dissent argues that a child who expresses a desire to attend public high school in conflict with the wishes of his parents should not be prevented from doing so. There is no reason for the Court to consider that point since it is not an issue in the case. The children are not parties to this litigation. The State has at no point tried this case on the theory that respondents were preventing their children from attending school against their expressed desires, and indeed the record is to the contrary.[21] The

---

21. The only relevant testimony in the record is to the effect that the wishes of the one child who testified corresponded with those of her parents. Testimony of Frieda Yoder, Tr. 92–94, to the effect that her personal religious beliefs guided her decision to discontinue school attendance

State's position from the outset has been that it is empowered to apply its compulsory-attendance law to Amish parents in the same manner as to other parents—that is, without regard to the wishes of the child. That is the claim we reject today.

Our holding in no way determines the proper resolution of possible competing interests of parents, children, and the State in an appropriate state court proceeding in which the power of the State is asserted on the theory that Amish parents are preventing their minor children from attending high school despite their expressed desires to the contrary. Recognition of the claim of the State in such a proceeding would, of course, call into question traditional concepts of parental control over the religious upbringing and education of their minor children recognized in this Court's past decisions. It is clear that such an intrusion by a State into family decisions in the area of religious training would give rise to grave questions of religious freedom comparable to those raised here and those presented in Pierce v. Society of Sisters, 268 U.S. 510 (1925). On this record we neither reach nor decide those issues.

* * *

However read, the Court's holding in *Pierce* stands as a charter of the rights of parents to direct the religious upbringing of their children. And, when the interests of parenthood are combined with a free exercise claim of the nature revealed by this record, more than merely a "reasonable relation to some purpose within the competency of the State" is required to sustain the validity of the State's requirement under the First Amendment. To be sure, the power of the parent, even when linked to a free exercise claim, may be subject to limitation under *Prince* if it appears that parental decisions will jeopardize the health or safety of the child, or have a potential for significant social burdens. But in this case, the Amish have introduced persuasive evidence undermining the arguments the State has advanced to support its claims in terms of the welfare of the child and society as a whole. The record strongly indicates that accommodating the religious objections of the Amish by forgoing one, or at most two, additional years of compulsory education will not impair the physical or mental health of the child, or result in an inability to be self-supporting or to discharge the duties and responsibilities of citizenship, or in any other way materially detract from the welfare of society.

In the face of our consistent emphasis on the central values underlying the Religion Clauses in our constitutional scheme of government, we cannot accept a *parens patriae* claim of such all-encompassing scope and with such sweeping potential for broad and unforseeable application as that urged by the State.

V

For the reasons stated we hold, with the Supreme Court of Wisconsin, that the First and Fourteenth Amendments prevent the State from compelling respondents to cause their children to attend formal high

after the eighth grade. The other children were not called by either side.

school to age 16. Our disposition of this case, however, in no way alters our recognition of the obvious fact that courts are not school boards or legislatures, and are ill-equipped to determine the "necessity" of discrete aspects of a State's program of compulsory education. This should suggest that courts must move with great circumspection in performing the sensitive and delicate task of weighing a State's legitimate social concern when faced with religious claims for exemption from generally applicable education requirements. It cannot be overemphasized that we are not dealing with a way of life and mode of education by a group claiming to have recently discovered some "progressive" or more enlightened process for rearing children for modern life.

* * *

Affirmed.

Mr. Justice Powell and Mr. Justice Rehnquist took no part in the consideration or decision of this case.

Mr. Justice Stewart, with whom Mr. Justice Brennan joins, concurring.

* * *

It is clear to me, * * *, that this record simply does not present the interesting and important issue discussed in Part II of the dissenting opinion of Mr. Justice Douglas. With this observation, I join the opinion and the judgment of the Court.

Mr. Justice White, with whom Mr. Justice Brennan and Mr. Justice Stewart join, concurring.

Cases such as this one inevitably call for a delicate balancing of important but conflicting interests. I join the opinion and judgment of the Court because I cannot say that the State's interest in requiring two more years of compulsory education in the ninth and tenth grades outweighs the importance of the concededly sincere Amish religious practice to the survival of that sect.

* * *

* * * A State has a legitimate interest not only in seeking to develop the latent talents of its children but also in seeking to prepare them for the life style that they may later choose, or at least to provide them with an option other than the life they have led in the past. In the circumstances of this case, although the question is close, I am unable to say that the State has demonstrated that Amish children who leave school in the eighth grade will be intellectually stulified or unable to acquire new academic skills later. The statutory minimum school attendance age set by the State is, after all, only 16.

* * *

Mr. Justice Douglas, dissenting in part.

I

I agree with the Court that the religious scruples of the Amish are opposed to the education of their children beyond the grade schools, yet

I disagree with the Court's conclusion that the matter is within the dispensation of parents alone. The Court's analysis assumes that the only interests at stake in the case are those of the Amish parents on the one hand, and those of the State on the other. The difficulty with this approach is that, despite the Court's claim, the parents are seeking to vindicate not only their own free exercise claims, but also those of their high-school-age children.

* * *

* * * If the parents in this case are allowed a religious exemption, the inevitable effect is to impose the parents' notions of religious duty upon their children. Where the child is mature enough to express potentially conflicting desires, it would be an invasion of the child's rights to permit such an imposition without canvassing his views. As in Prince v. Massachusetts, 321 U.S. 158, it is an imposition resulting from this very litigation. As the child has no other effective forum, it is in this litigation that his rights should be considered. And, if an Amish child desires to attend high school, and is mature enough to have that desire respected, the State may well be able to override the parents' religiously motivated objections.

Religion is an individual experience. It is not necessary, nor even appropriate, for every Amish child to express his views on the subject in a prosecution of a single adult. Crucial, however, are the views of the child whose parent is the subject of the suit. Frieda Yoder has in fact testified that her own religious views are opposed to high-school education. I therefore join the judgment of the Court as to respondent Jonas Yoder. But Frieda Yoder's views may not be those of Vernon Yutzy or Barbara Miller. I must dissent, therefore, as to respondents Adin Yutzy and Wallace Miller as their motion to dismiss also raised the question of their children's religious liberty.

II

This issue has never been squarely presented before today. Our opinions are full of talk about the power of the parents over the child's education. See Pierce v. Society of Sisters, 268 U.S. 510 (1925); Meyer v. Nebraska, 262 U.S. 390 (1923). And we have in the past analyzed similar conflicts between parent and State with little regard for the views of the child. See *Prince v. Massachusetts, supra.* Recent cases, however, have clearly held that the children themselves have constitutionally protectible interests. These children are "persons" within the meaning of the Bill of Rights. We have so held over and over again.
* * *

* * *

On this important and vital matter of education, I think the children should be entitled to be heard. While the parents, absent dissent, normally speak for the entire family, the education of the child is a matter on which the child will often have decided views. He may want to be a pianist or an astronaut or an oceanographer. To do so he will have to break from the Amish tradition.

It is the future of the student, not the future of the parents, that is imperiled by today's decision. If a parent keeps his child out of school beyond the grade school, then the child will be forever barred from entry into the new and amazing world of diversity that we have today. The child may decide that that is the preferred course, or he may rebel. It is the student's judgment, not his parents', that is essential if we are to give full meaning to what we have said about the Bill of Rights and of the right of students to be masters of their own destiny. If he is harnessed to the Amish way of life by those in authority over him and if his education is truncated, his entire life may be stunted and deformed. The child, therefore, should be given an opportunity to be heard before the State gives the exemption which we honor today.

The views of the two children in question were not canvassed by the Wisconsin courts. The matter should be explicitly reserved so that new hearings can be held on remand of the case.

III

I think the emphasis of the Court on the "law and order" record of this Amish group of people is quite irrelevant. A religion is a religion irrespective of what the misdemeanor or felony records of its members might be. I am not at all sure how the Catholics, Episcopalians, the Baptists, Jehovah's Witnesses, the Unitarians, and my own Presbyterians would make out if subjected to such a test. It is, of course, true that if a group or society was organized to perpetuate crime and if that is its motive, we would have rather startling problems akin to those that were raised when some years back a particular sect was challenged here as operating on a fraudulent basis. United States v. Ballard, 322 U.S. 78 (1944). But no such factors are present here, and the Amish, whether with a high or low criminal record, certainly qualify by all historic standards as a religion within the meaning of the First Amendment.

The Court rightly rejects the notion that actions, even though religiously grounded, are always outside the protection of the Free Exercise Clause of the First Amendment. In so ruling, the Court departs from the teaching of Reynolds v. United States, 98 U.S. 145, 164 (1878), where it was said concerning the reach of the Free Exercise Clause of the First Amendment, "Congress was deprived of all legislative power over mere opinion, but was left free to reach actions which were in violation of social duties or subversive of good order." In that case it was conceded that polygamy was a part of the religion of the Mormons. Yet the Court said, "It matters not that his belief [in polygamy] was a part of his professed religion: it was still belief and belief only." *Id.*, at 167.

Action, which the Court deemed to be antisocial, could be punished even though it was grounded on deeply held and sincere religious convictions. What we do today, at least in this respect, opens the way to give organized religion a broader base than it has ever enjoyed; and it even promises that in time *Reynolds* will be overruled.

In another way, however, the Court retreats when in reference to Henry Thoreau it says his "choice was philosophical and personal rather than religious, and such belief does not rise to the demands of the Religion Clauses." That is contrary to what we held in United States v. Seeger, 380 U.S. 163, where we were concerned with the meaning of the words "religious training and belief" in the Selective Service Act, which were the basis of many conscientious objector claims.

* * *

I adhere to these exalted views of "religion" and see no acceptable alternative to them now that we have become a Nation of many religions and sects, representing all of the diversities of the human race. United States v. Seeger, 380 U.S., at 192–193 (concurring opinion).

SHERBERT v. VERNER

Supreme Court of the United States, 1963.
374 U.S. 398, 83 S.Ct. 1790, 10 L.Ed.2d 965.

Mr. Justice Brennan delivered the opinion of the Court.

Appellant, a member of the Seventh-day Adventist Church was discharged by her South Carolina employer because she would not work on Saturday, the Sabbath Day of her faith.[1] When she was unable to obtain other employment because from conscientious scruples she would not take Saturday work,[2] she filed a claim for unemployment compensation benefits under the South Carolina Unemployment Compensation Act. That law provides that, to be eligible for benefits, a claimant must be "able to work and * * * is available for work"; and, further, that a claimant is ineligible for benefits "[i]f * * * he has failed, without good cause * * * to accept available suitable work when offered him by the employment office or the employer * * *." The appellee Employment Security Commission, in administrative proceedings under the statute, found that appellant's restriction upon her availability for Saturday work brought her within the provision disqualifying for benefits insured workers who fail, without good cause, to accept "suitable work when offered * * * by the employment office or

---

1. Appellant became a member of the Seventh-day Adventist Church in 1957, at a time when her employer, a textile-mill operator, permitted her to work a five-day week. It was not until 1959 that the work week was changed to six days, including Saturday, for all three shifts in the employer's mill. No question has been raised in this case concerning the sincerity of appellant's religious beliefs. Nor is there any doubt that the prohibition against Saturday labor is a basic tenet of the Seventh-day Adventist creed, based upon that religion's interpretation of the Holy Bible.

2. After her discharge, appellant sought employment with three other mills in the Spartanburg area, but found no suitable five-day work available at any of the mills. In filing her claim with the Commission, she expressed a willingness to accept employment at other mills, or even in another industry, so long as Saturday work was not required. The record indicates that of the 150 or more Seventh-day Adventists in the Spartanburg area, only appellant and one other have been unable to find suitable non-Saturday employment.

the employer * * *." The Commission's finding was sustained by the Court of Common Pleas for Spartanburg County. That court's judgment was in turn affirmed by the South Carolina Supreme Court, which rejected appellant's contention that, as applied to her, the disqualifying provisions of the South Carolina statute abridged her right to the free exercise of her religion secured under the Free Exercise Clause of the First Amendment through the Fourteenth Amendment. The State Supreme Court held specifically that appellant's ineligibility infringed no constitutional liberties because such a construction of the statute "places no restriction upon the appellant's freedom of religion nor does it in any way prevent her in the exercise of her right and freedom to observe her religious beliefs in accordance with the dictates of her conscience." 240 S.C. 286, 303–304, 125 S.E.2d 737, 746.[4] We noted probable jurisdiction of appellant's appeal. * * * We reverse the judgment of the South Carolina Supreme Court and remand for further proceedings not inconsistent with this opinion.

* * *

We turn first to the question whether the disqualification for benefits imposes any burden on the free exercise of appellant's religion. We think it is clear that it does. In a sense the consequences of such a disqualification to religious principles and practices may be only an indirect result of welfare legislation within the State's general competence to enact; it is true that no criminal sanctions directly compel appellant to work a six-day week. But this is only the beginning, not the end, of our inquiry.[5] For "[i]f the purpose or effect of a law is to impede the observance of one or all religions or is to discriminate invidiously between religions, that law is constitutionally invalid even though the burden may be characterized as being only indirect." *Braunfeld v. Brown, supra*, 366 U.S., at 607. Here not only is it apparent that appellant's declared ineligibility for benefits derives solely from the practice of her religion, but the pressure upon her to forego that practice is unmistakable. The ruling forces her to choose between following the precepts of her religion and forfeiting benefits, on the one hand, and abandoning one of the precepts of her religion in order to accept work, on the other hand. Governmental imposition of such a choice puts the same kind of burden upon the free exercise of religion as would a fine imposed against appellant for her Saturday worship.

---

4. It has been suggested that appellant is not within the class entitled to benefits under the South Carolina statute because her unemployment did not result from discharge or layoff due to lack of work. It is true that unavailability for work for some personal reasons not having to do with matters of conscience or religion has been held to be a basis of disqualification for benefits. * * * But appellant claims that the Free Exercise Clause prevents the State from basing the denial of benefits upon the "personal reason" she gives for not working on Saturday. * * *

5. In a closely analogous context, this Court said:

" * * * the fact that no direct restraint or punishment is imposed upon speech or assembly does not determine the free speech question. Under some circumstances, indirect 'discouragements' undoubtedly have the same coercive effect upon the exercise of First Amendment rights as imprisonment, fines, injunctions or taxes. A requirement that adherents of particular religious faiths or political parties wear identifying armbands, for example, is obviously of this nature."

Nor may the South Carolina court's construction of the statute be saved from constitutional infirmity on the ground that unemployment compensation benefits are not appellant's "right" but merely a "privilege." It is too late in the day to doubt that the liberties of religion and expression may be infringed by the denial of or placing of conditions upon a benefit or privilege. * * * In Speiser v. Randall, 357 U.S. 513, we emphasized that conditions upon public benefits cannot be sustained if they so operate, whatever their purpose, as to inhibit or deter the exercise of First Amendment freedoms. We there struck down a condition which limited the availability of a tax exemption to those members of the exempted class who affirmed their loyalty to the state government granting the exemption. While the State was surely under no obligation to afford such an exemption, we held that the imposition of such a condition upon even a gratuitous benefit inevitably deterred or discouraged the exercise of First Amendment rights of expression and thereby threatened to "produce a result which the State could not command directly." * * * Likewise, to condition the availability of benefits upon this appellant's willingness to violate a cardinal principle of her religious faith effectively penalizes the free exercise of her constitutional liberties.

Significantly South Carolina expressly saves the Sunday worshipper from having to make the kind of choice which we here hold infringes the Sabbatarian's religious liberty. When in times of "national emergency" the textile plants are authorized by the State Commissioner of Labor to operate on Sunday, "no employee shall be required to work on Sunday * * * who is conscientiously opposed to Sunday work; and if any employee should refuse to work on Sunday on account of conscientious * * * objections he or she shall not jeopardize his or her seniority by such refusal or be discriminated against in any other manner." S.C.Code, § 64–4. No question of the disqualification of a Sunday worshipper for benefits is likely to arise, since we cannot suppose that an employer will discharge him in violation of this statute. The unconstitutionality of the disqualification of the Sabbatarian is thus compounded by the religious discrimination which South Carolina's general statutory scheme necessarily effects.

III.

We must next consider whether some compelling state interest enforced in the eligibility provisions of the South Carolina statute justifies the substantial infringement of appellant's First Amendment right. It is basic that no showing merely of a rational relationship to some colorable state interest would suffice; in this highly sensitive constitutional area, "[o]nly the gravest abuses, endangering paramount interest, give occasion for permissible limitation," Thomas v. Collins, 323 U.S. 516, 530. No such abuse or danger has been advanced in the present case. The appellees suggest no more than a possibility that the filing of fraudulent claims by unscrupulous claimants feigning religious objections to Saturday work might not only dilute the unemployment compensation fund but also hinder the scheduling by employers of necessary Saturday work. But that possibility is not apposite here because no such objection appears to have been made before the South Carolina Supreme Court, and we are unwilling to assess the importance of an asserted state interest without the views of the state court. Nor, if the contention had been made below, would the record appear to sustain it; there is no proof whatever to warrant such fears of malingering or deceit as those which the respondents now advance. * * * For even if the possibility of spurious claims did threaten to dilute the fund and disrupt the scheduling of work, it would plainly be incumbent upon the appellees to demonstrate that no alternative forms of regulation would combat such abuses without infringing First Amendment rights.[7] * * *

In these respects, then, the state interest asserted in the present case is wholly dissimilar to the interests which were found to justify the less direct burden upon religious practices in *Braunfeld v. Brown, supra*. The Court recognized that the Sunday closing law which that decision sustained undoubtedly served "to make the practice of [the Orthodox Jewish merchants'] religious beliefs more expensive," 366 U.S., at 605. But the statute was nevertheless saved by a countervailing factor which finds no equivalent in the instant case—a strong state interest in providing one uniform day of rest for all workers. That secular objective could be achieved, the Court found, only by declaring Sunday to be that day of rest. Requiring exemptions for Sabbatarians, while theoretically possible, appeared to present an administrative problem of such magnitude, or to afford the exempted class so great a competitive advantage, that such a requirement would have rendered the entire statutory scheme unworkable. In the present case no such justifications underlie the determination of the state court that appellant's religion makes her ineligible to receive benefits.

IV.

In holding as we do, plainly we are not fostering the "establishment" of the Seventh-day Adventist religion in South Carolina, for the extension of unemployment benefits to Sabbatarians in common with Sunday worshippers reflects nothing more than the governmental obligation of neutrality in the face of religious differences, and does not represent that involvement of religious with secular institutions which it is the object of the Establishment Clause to forestall. See School District of Abington Township v. Schempp, 374 U.S. 203. Nor does the recognition of the appellant's right to unemployment benefits under the state statute serve to abridge any other person's religious liberties. Nor do we, by our decision today, declare the existence of a constitutional right to unemployment benefits on the part of all persons whose

---

7. We note that before the instant decision, state supreme courts had, without exception, granted benefits to persons who were physically available for work but unable to find suitable employment solely because of a religious prohibition against Saturday work. * * * Of the 47 States which have eligibility provisions similar to those of the South Carolina statute, only 28 appear to have given administrative rulings concerning the eligibility of persons whose religious convictions prevented them from accepting available work. Twenty-two of those States have held such persons entitled to benefits, although apparently only one such decision rests exclusively upon the federal constitutional ground which constitutes the basis of our decision. * * *

religious convictions are the cause of their unemployment. This is not a case in which an employee's religious convictions serve to make him a nonproductive member of society. See note 2, *supra*. Finally, nothing we say today constrains the States to adopt any particular form or scheme of unemployment compensation. Our holding today is only that South Carolina may not constitutionally apply the eligibility provisions so as to constrain a worker to abandon his religious convictions respecting the day of rest. This holding but reaffirms a principle that we announced a decade and a half ago, namely that no State may "exclude individual Catholics, Lutherans, Mohammedans, Baptists, Jews, Methodists, Non-believers, Presbyterians, or the members of any other faith, because of their faith, or lack of it, from receiving the benefits of public welfare legislation." Everson v. Board of Education, 330 U.S. 1, 16.

* * *

The judgment of the South Carolina Supreme Court is reversed and the case is remanded for further proceedings not inconsistent with this opinion. It is so ordered.

Reversed and remanded.

Mr. Justice Douglas, concurring.

* * *

This case is resolvable not in terms of what an individual can demand of government, but solely in terms of what government may not do to an individual in violation of his religious scruples. The fact that government cannot exact from me a surrender of one iota of my religious scruples does not, of course, mean that I can demand of government a sum of money, the better to exercise them. For the Free Exercise Clause is written in terms of what the government cannot do to the individual, not in terms of what the individual can exact from the government.

Those considerations, however, are not relevant here. If appellant is otherwise qualified for unemployment benefits, payments will be made to her not as a Seventh-day Adventist, but as an unemployed worker. Conceivably these payments will indirectly benefit her church, but no more so than does the salary of any public employee. Thus, this case does not involve the problems of direct or indirect state assistance to a religious organization—matters relevant to the Establishment Clause, not in issue here.

Mr. Justice Stewart, concurring in the result.

Although fully agreeing with the result which the Court reaches in this case, I cannot join the Court's opinion. This case presents a double-barreled dilemma, which in all candor I think the Court's opinion has not succeeded in papering over. The dilemma ought to be resolved.

* * *

Because the appellant refuses to accept available jobs which would require her to work on Saturdays, South Carolina has declined to pay unemployment compensation benefits to her. Her refusal to work on Saturdays is based on the tenets of her religious faith. The Court says that South Carolina cannot under these circumstances declare her to be not "available for work" within the meaning of its statute because to do so would violate her constitutional right to the free exercise of her religion.

Yet what this Court has said about the Establishment Clause must inevitably lead to a diametrically opposite result. If the appellant's refusal to work on Saturdays were based on indolence, or on a compulsive desire to watch the Saturday television programs, no one would say that South Carolina could not hold that she was not "available for work" within the meaning of its statute. That being so, the Establishment Clause as construed by this Court not only permits but affirmatively requires South Carolina equally to deny the appellant's claim for unemployment compensation when her refusal to work on Saturdays is based upon her religious creed. * * *
* * *

South Carolina would deny unemployment benefits to a mother unavailable for work on Saturdays because she was unable to get a babysitter.[3] Thus, we do not have before us a situation where a State provides unemployment compensation generally, and singles out for disqualification only those persons who are unavailable for work on religious grounds. This is not, in short, a scheme which operates so as to discriminate against religion as such. But the Court nevertheless holds that the State must prefer a religious over a secular ground for being unavailable for work—that state financial support of the appellant's religion is constitutionally required to carry out "the governmental obligation of neutrality in the face of religious differences * * *."

Yet in cases decided under the Establishment Clause the Court has decreed otherwise. It has decreed that government must blind itself to the differing religious beliefs and traditions of the people. With all respect, I think it is the Court's duty to face up to the dilemma posed by the conflict between the Free Exercise Clause of the Constitution and the Establishment Clause as interpreted by the Court. It is a duty, I submit, which we owe to the people, the States, and the Nation, and a duty which we owe to ourselves. * * *

II.

My second difference with the Court's opinion is that I cannot agree that today's decision can stand consistently with *Braunfeld v. Brown, supra*. The Court says that there was a "less direct burden upon religious practices" in that case than in this. With all respect, I think the Court is mistaken, simply as a matter of fact. The *Braunfeld* case involved a state criminal statute. The undisputed effect of that statute, as pointed out by Mr. Justice Brennan in his dissenting opinion in that case, was that " 'Plaintiff, Abraham Braunfeld, will be unable to

---

3. See Judson Mills v. South Carolina Unemployment Compensation Comm., 204 S.C. 37, 28 S.E.2d 535; Hartsville Cotton Mill v. South Carolina Employment Security Comm., 224 S.C. 407, 79 S.E.2d 381.

continue in his business if he may not stay open on Sunday and he will thereby lose his capital investment.' In other words, the issue in this case—and we do not understand either appellees or the Court to contend otherwise—is whether a State may put an individual to a choice between his business and his religion." 366 U.S., at 611.

The impact upon the appellant's religious freedom in the present case is considerably less onerous. We deal here not with a criminal statute, but with the particularized administration of South Carolina's Unemployment Compensation Act. Even upon the unlikely assumption that the appellant could not find suitable non-Saturday employment,[4] the appellant at the worst would be denied a maximum of 22 weeks of compensation payments. I agree with the Court that the possibility of that denial is enough to infringe upon the appellant's constitutional right to the free exercise of her religion. But it is clear to me that in order to reach this conclusion the Court must explicitly reject the reasoning of *Braunfeld v. Brown*. I think the *Braunfeld* case was wrongly decided and should be overruled, and accordingly I concur in the result reached by the Court in the case before us.

MR. JUSTICE HARLAN, whom MR. JUSTICE WHITE joins, dissenting.

Today's decision is disturbing both in its rejection of existing precedent and in its implications for the future. The significance of the decision can best be understood after an examination of the state law applied in this case.

South Carolina's Unemployment Compensation Law was enacted in 1936 in response to the grave social and economic problems that arose during the depression of that period. As stated in the statute itself:

> "Economic insecurity due to unemployment is a serious menace to health, morals and welfare of the people of this State; *involuntary unemployment* is therefore a subject of general interest and concern * * *; the achievement of social security requires protection against this greatest hazard of our economic life; this can be provided by encouraging the employers *to provide more stable employment and by the systematic accumulation of funds during periods of employment to provide benefits for periods of unemployment*, thus maintaining purchasing power and limiting the serious social consequences of poor relief assistance." § 68–38. (Emphasis added.)

Thus the purpose of the legislature was to tide people over, and to avoid social and economic chaos, during periods when *work was unavailable*. But at the same time there was clearly no intent to provide relief for those who for purely personal reasons were or became *unavailable for work*. In accordance with this design, the legislature provided, in § 68–113, that "[a]n unemployed insured worker shall be eligible to receive benefits with respect to any week *only* if the Commission finds that * * * [h]e is able to work and is available for work * * *." (Emphasis added.)

---

4. As noted by the Court, "The record indicates that of the 150 or more Seventh-day Adventists in the Spartanburg area, only appellant and one other have been unable to find suitable non-Saturday employment."

The South Carolina Supreme Court has uniformly applied this law in conformity with its clearly expressed purpose. It has consistently held that one is not "available for work" if his unemployment has resulted not from the inability of industry to provide a job but rather from personal circumstances, no matter how compelling. The reference to "involuntary unemployment" in the legislative statement of policy, whatever a sociologist, philosopher, or theologian might say, has been interpreted not to embrace such personal circumstances. * * *

In the present case all that the state court has done is to apply these accepted principles. Since virtually all of the mills in the Spartanburg area were operating on a six-day week, the appellant was "unavailable for work," and thus ineligible for benefits, when personal considerations prevented her from accepting employment on a full-time basis in the industry and locality in which she had worked. The fact that these personal considerations sprang from her religious convictions was wholly without relevance to the state court's application of the law. Thus in no proper sense can it be said that the State discriminated against the appellant on the basis of her religious beliefs or that she was denied benefits because she was a Seventh-day Adventist. She was denied benefits just as any other claimant would be denied benefits who was not "available for work" for personal reasons.[1]

With this background, this Court's decision comes into clearer focus. What the Court is holding is that if the State chooses to condition unemployment compensation on the applicant's availability for work, it is constitutionally compelled to carve out an exception— and to provide benefits—for those whose unavailability is due to their religious convictions.[2] Such a holding has particular significance in two respects.

First, despite the Court's protestations to the contrary, the decision necessarily overrules Braunfeld v. Brown, 366 U.S. 599 * * *

Second, the implications of the present decision are far more troublesome than its apparently narrow dimensions would indicate at first glance. The meaning of today's holding, as already noted, is that

---

1. I am completely at a loss to understand note 4 of the Court's opinion. Certainly the Court is not basing today's decision on the unsupported supposition that some day, the South Carolina Supreme Court may conclude that there is some personal reason for unemployment that may not disqualify a claimant for relief. In any event, I submit it is perfectly clear that South Carolina would not compensate persons who became unemployed for any personal reason, as distinguished from layoffs or lack of work, since the State Supreme Court's decisions make it plain that such persons would not be regarded as "available for work" within the manifest meaning of the eligibility requirements. * * *

2. The Court does suggest, in a rather startling disclaimer, * * *, that its holding is limited in applicability to those whose religious convictions do not make them "nonproductive" members of society, noting that most of the Seventh-day Adventists in the Spartanburg area are employed. But surely this disclaimer cannot be taken seriously, for the Court cannot mean that the case would have come out differently if none of the Seventh-day Adventists in Spartanburg had been gainfully employed, or if the appellant's religion had prevented her from working on Tuesdays instead of Saturdays. Nor can the Court be suggesting that it will make a value judgment in each case as to whether a particular individual's religious convictions prevent him from being "productive." I can think of no more inappropriate function for this Court to perform.

the State must furnish unemployment benefits to one who is unavailable for work if the unavailability stems from the exercise of religious convictions. The State, in other words, must single out for financial assistance those whose behavior is religiously motivated, even though it denies such assistance to others whose identical behavior (in this case, inability to work no Saturdays) is not religiously motivated.

It has been suggested that such singling out of religious conduct for special treatment may violate the constitutional limitations on state action. See Kurland, Of Church and State and the Supreme Court, 29 U. of Chi.L.Rev. 1 * * *. My own view, however, is that at least under the circumstances of this case it would be a permissible accommodation of religion for the State, if it *chose* to do so, to create an exception to its eligibility requirements for persons like the appellant. * * * There are too many instances in which no such course can be charted, too many areas in which the pervasive activities of the State justify some special provision for religion to prevent it from being submerged by an all-embracing secularism. The State violates its obligation of neutrality when, for example, it mandates a daily religious exercise in its public schools, with all the attendant pressures on the school children that such an exercise entails. See Engel v. Vitale, 370 U.S. 421; *School District of Abington Township v. Schempp, supra.* But there is, I believe, enough flexibility in the Constitution to permit a legislative judgment accommodating an unemployment compensation law to the exercise of religious beliefs such as appellant's.

For very much the same reasons, however, I cannot subscribe to the conclusion that the State is constitutionally compelled to carve out an exception to its general rule of eligibility in the present case. Those situations in which the Constitution may require special treatment on account of religion are, in my view, few and far between, and this view is amply supported by the course of constitutional litigation in this area. * * * Such compulsion in the present case is particularly inappropriate in light of the indirect, remote, and insubstantial effect of the decision below on the exercise of appellant's religion and in light of the direct financial assistance to religion that today's decision requires.

For these reasons I respectfully dissent from the opinion and judgment of the Court.[4]

AN EXTENDED NOTE ON *SHERBERT v. VERNER*

I. Note that *Sherbert v. Verner* is a case presenting no direct conflict between the plaintiff's religiously-felt obligation and the state law. It does not involve a free exercise clause claim frustrated by a law that commands one to do that which is forbidden by one's religion; neither does it involve a law forbidding one to do that which one's religion commands.—As the Court acknowledges, Ms. Sherbert was not

---

4. Since the Court states, * * *, that it does not reach the appellant's "equal protection" argument, based upon South Carolina's emergency Sunday-work provisions, §§ 64–4, 64–6, I do not consider it appropriate for me to do so.

confronted with the kind of dilemma presented by *Prince v. Massachusetts,* i.e. of either obeying God or obeying the law of the civil state, there being no possibility, however, of obeying both. Either of these arrangements, characteristic of the cases thus far examined [1] and of most others one will encounter, describes a direct conflict between the free exercise of religion and the civil state. Ms. Sherbert, however, was not required by state law to work on Saturday or, for that matter, on any other day. She breaks no law of the state by abstaining from work on Saturday, as she is free to do as she sees fit. Her dilemma, rather, is more like that of the Jewish merchant in *McGowan* or in *Braunfeld.* Moreover, the legal consequences of exercising her religious choice seem no different than the legal consequences of any nonreligious person exercising a like choice. Why, then, is the case treated as it is?

II. Is it the case, rather, that the statute operates in the mode of an "unconstitutional condition," as Justice Brennan's opinion suggests? —That if Ms. Sherbert adheres to her religion she will be made to forfeit an advantage provided to others, and while something similar was present for the observant Jewish merchant in *Braunfeld,* that was a very different case in that the resulting disadvantage was the consequence of the merchant's religion, but not a consequence of the law?— Whereas in this instance the law itself subjected her to a forfeiture (of unemployment compensation benefits) for what her religion requires her to do?[2]

But note that insofar as Ms. Sherbert declined to accept work on Saturday because it conflicted with her religion, she evidently was not treated differently than any other person declining such work for reasons that would be equally compelling to them albeit without reference to any particular religion or religious belief. How, then, is it appropriate to describe the case as one imposing a special cost or penalty or forfeiture, on the exercise of one's religious belief? Justice Stewart, while concurring in the Court's judgment, notes that unemployment benefits would also be unavailable under the South Carolina

---

1. Cf., e.g., *West Virginia Bd. of Education v. Barnette* (if one salutes the flag, one thereby directly breaks God's commandment not to do so; but if one fails to salute the flag, one will be suspended from school, be taken from one's home, and be placed in a place of detention for delinquent children under superintendence of the state). See also *Reynolds v. United States* and *Wisconsin v. Yoder* (each presenting an equivalent direct conflict under the law).

2. But this effort to distinguish *Braunfeld* is not correct, is it? The law which Braunfeld objected to, as applied to him, was the Sunday closing law which was itself the cause of the hardship to him insofar as he obeyed his religious obligation not to do business on Saturday, and the Sunday closing law forced him to miss two days of business vis-a-vis others who missed only one.—Consistent with the Court's free exercise clause decision in *Sherbert v. Verner,* may it now be the case that *Braunfeld* is no longer valid? How, if at all, is the case to be distinguished?—In *Everson,* as we noted, all nine Justices of the Supreme Court assumed it would be valid to subsidize the bus transport of public school students only (indeed, the Court divided five-to-four whether it was even allowable to include parochial school parents in the reimbursement plan). After *Sherbert,* would it be *unconstitutional* to limit bus fare reimbursement *solely* to parents of public school children? (Would such a law operate as an "unconstitutional condition" upon the free exercise of religion of those placing their children in parochial schools, working a forfeiture of bus transportation reimbursement eligibility insofar as they opt out of the public schools, albeit on religious grounds?)

act "to a mother unavailable for work on Saturdays because she was unable to get a babysitter." Justice Harlan, in dissent, is similarly emphatic—that Ms. Sherbert was denied benefits "just as any other claimant would be denied benefits who was not 'available for work' for personal reasons," [3] adding by way of footnote: "I submit it is perfectly clear that South Carolina would not compensate persons who became unemployed for any personal reason, as distinguished from layoffs or lack of work * * *." [4]

Insofar as this was the actual case, how then can the issue be described as one involving the doctrine of unconstitutional conditions in the usual sense of that doctrine's application, i.e., a case in which certain valuable benefits controlled by the state (here, rights to the unemployment compensation fund) will be withheld by a classificatory trait of ineligibility deemed specially protected by the Constitution—such as what political party one affiliates with, what social or political causes one supports, or what religion one may or may not profess—when no such classificatory standard was involved in this law?[5] Is this not, rather, an instance where one seeks an advantage of eligibility that others who are otherwise similarly situated *will be denied?*

It was not the case that Ms. Sherbert was deemed ineligible "because" she was a Seventh Day Adventist, or because of any religious practice or belief, was it? Rather, she was deemed ineligible "because" she was unavailable for work in the same sense as would characterize another who stayed at home to care for a dying relative, or another who moved away in order not to be separated from a spouse who found work somewhere else.[6] And insofar as this appears to have been the

---

3. See also the three later cases, following *Sherbert,* cited in note 15 *infra.* (In these cases also the statute made no distinction between religious and nonreligious reasons, i.e. the criterion of ineligibility was not tied to the exercise of any constitutional right.)

4. (Emphasis added.) The point was stressed both in the state's brief (at p. 21) and in the course of the state's oral argument in the Supreme Court. So, at oral argument the state attorney general drew the distinction and gave as an additional example:

"For instance, a workman, a worker having to care for children, having to care for a sick husband—a very laudable purpose that would require that she not be at her job. But nevertheless, in circumstances such as that, compensation is denied. * * * Cases involving the cessation of work by a wife when her husband has been transferred away from the site of her employment. She may from religious or other reasons feel compelled to be by the side of her husband, but nevertheless that is not held to be a suitable ground for ceasing work and in that case unemployment benefits are [also] withheld."

Oral Argument of Appellee, at p. 9, reprinted in 57 Landmark Briefs and Arguments of the Supreme Court of the United States: Constitutional Law 1282 (P. Kurland & G. Casper eds. 1975) [hereinafter Landmark Briefs].

5. See discussion and cases at pp. 292–301, *supra.*

6. See Wimberly v. Labor & Indus. Rel. Com'n, 479 U.S. 511, 107 S.Ct. 821, 93 L.Ed.2d 909 (1987). Following *Sherbert v. Verner,* compare these two cases: (a) Mrs. Smith stays away from work because her child is very young and she feels strongly the duty to be with and to nurture her child; (b) Mrs. Smith stays away from work because her child is very young *and* according to her religion it would be contrary to God's law were she not to be with and to nurture her child. Is it the case that in case (a) the state need not pay unemployment compensation benefits, but that in case (b) the free exercise clause *requires* such benefits to be paid? Insofar as no benefits are paid in case (a), how is the failure to pay benefits in case (b) an unconstitutional condition attached to the unemployment compensation law? (If, moreover, benefits are paid in case (b) but

case,[7] *Sherbert v. Verner* may not fit comfortably within the usual profile of unconstitutional conditions kinds of cases, whatever the scope of the doctrine may be.

In brief, there appears to have been no singling out here of religiously-actuated conduct as the trigger for the disqualification at stake. Applying the doctrine of unconstitutional conditions in this setting seems therefore to require something special *just on account of* the free exercise clause, namely, the special *affirmative* favoring of persons identified by their religious practice, in a manner and in a form denied to others who are otherwise like themselves. *It requires an affirmative payment of money to them and not merely an exemption from an otherwise valid regulation* (as was sought in *Braunfeld, Reynolds,* or *Prince*), moreover, though others who are otherwise similarly situated will not be eligible for the same financial payments to them.

The apparent tension[8] with the Court's own establishment clause cases is noted in the Stewart concurrence and in the Harlan dissent.[9] How does one reconcile the apparent contradiction of the Court's own previous views of what it is that the establishment clause forbids, on the one hand, and what the free exercise clause—according to *Sherbert* —requires?

Even assuming that it might not be inconsistent with those establishment clause decisions for the state to make an exception so to merely *permit* payments to be made to those unavailable for work due to religious dictates, even while withholding them from others who are unavailable for any other reason,[10] what is the basis for the holding that in fact the free exercise clause not only affords a suitable public purpose sufficient to permit such payments, but indeed *requires* the state to treat religious absentees better than others whom it will continue to regard as unavailable for work?—How is this different from a tax on some, to be paid to others, to enable them to practice their religious faith?[11]

III. *Sherbert v. Verner* has sometimes been thought to turn on the fact that South Carolina's unemployment compensation statute did not exist in a vacuum. The point is not that the preceding critical review

---

not in case (a), why is that not a breach of the "no establishment" clause?)

7. It was not in fact quite the case (e.g., in oral argument the state attorney general suggested that leaving work on account of pregnancy might not have disqualified the employee from eligibility for unemployment compensation), but overall the case was approximately this.

8. See note 6, *supra*.

9. The point was separately noted in the course of oral argument, by Justice Stewart: "The difficulty with your argument, so far as I'm concerned, Mr. Donnelly [counsel for appellant], is that if the State had done anything other than what it did in this case it would have violated the establishment clause [under the Court's own earlier exposition of the establishment clause, as Justice Stewart understood it to be] * * *." Oral argument at p. 5, reprinted in Landmark Briefs *supra*.

10. But it would be inconsistent, would it not?

11. See Choper, The Religion Clauses of the First Amendment: Reconciling the Conflict, 41 U.Pitt.L.Rev. 673, 698 (1980) (*Sherbert* irreconcilable insofar as it involves forced tax subsidy of religious practice); McConnell & Posner, An Economic Approach to Issues of Religious Freedom, 56 U.Chi.L.Rev. 1, 38–41 (1989). ("Under *Sherbert*, religious workers are insured [without additional charge] against an additional risk, not borne by nonreligious workers: the risk that their work may become unsuitable for religious reasons.")

misrepresents the unemployment compensation statute, but that it nonetheless leaves several other matters out of account. The point is to see whether these other matters properly affected the case, and to see also whether they may therefore limit it such that the tension with the establishment clause is not, after all, nearly so severe as the foregoing review makes it appear to be. It is worthwhile, therefore, to take these other matters into fuller account.

As Justice Brennan took care to note, side by side the unemployment compensation law, it was also true that South Carolina:

(a) maintained a general Sunday closing law such that, if merely as a consequence of that law, those bound by religious belief to do no work on Sunday would themselves *not* confront the need to choose between having to work on the day set aside by their religion, in violation of their religion, and being without work with no unemployment compensation;

(b) further provided that even when textile mills could lawfully operate on Sunday (namely in times of designated national emergency), no mill could discharge any employee for refusal to work on Sunday insofar as that particular employee was "conscientiously opposed to Sunday work." [12]—So Sunday observant religionists were already protected in a way Ms. Sherbert was not.

The majority in *Sherbert* noted that the state's Sunday closing law had the effect (if not the purpose) of benefitting some religious persons, notably mainline Protestants and Catholics: losing their job, without benefit of unemployment compensation, triggered by a conflict between a particular kind of religious duty and an employer's needs, was not a real possibility as to them in most circumstances. The effect of the two laws combined, moreover, virtually eliminated one kind of unemployment risk (the risk of unemployment due to one kind of religious conflict, i.e. a conflict affecting the day one might be unable to work), for all workers save only those like Ms. Sherbert. Restoring Ms. Sherbert to a position of compensation eligibility in *these* circumstances might thus be seen as warranted by the need to have her treated merely on approximately equal—not better—terms with them, as to the particular kind of unemployment risk only those in her position effectively incurred.[13]

IV. Influential as these considerations may or might have been in *Sherbert* itself, however, the case does not appear to have been reasoned in this way.[14] At least it is no longer so regarded by the Court as

12. The quoted language is taken from the pertinent South Carolina statute. (Cf. Estate of Thorton v. Caldor, 472 U.S. 703, 105 S.Ct. 2914, 86 L.Ed.2d 557 (1985) (state statute granting absolute protection from dismissal to any employee declining work on a day forbidden by their religion as a work day, *held*, unconstitutional under the establishment clause), distinguishing Trans World Airlines, Inc. v. Hardison, 432 U.S. 63, 97 S.Ct. 2264, 53 L.Ed.2d 113 (1977) (sustaining Act of Congress forbidding religious as well as sex, race, and national origin employment discrimination, and requiring "reasonable" accommodation of employee religiously-based concerns, held, not invalid under the establishment clause).)

13. Cf. McConnell and Posner, note 11, *supra*.

14. Nor of course is this analysis of the case necessarily a proper one, is it? (E.g., if the unemployment compensation law is

limiting the application of the decision itself. In three subsequent cases otherwise much like *Sherbert,* no use is made of these observations to limit the Court's holding in *Sherbert.* Indeed no equivalent form of "equality-among-religions" rationale was available to help explain two of these three subsequent cases, or relied upon in any of the cases decided so to require the payment of unemployment benefits.[15]

How then shall one describe the free exercise "test" as modified and applied in *Sherbert v. Verner?* In what other environments may it apply, and especially its involvement of the affirmative payment of tax funds, in order that one's free exercise of religion not be accompanied by personal financial loss?—Is *Everson* itself such a case? If not, why not?

GOLDMAN v. WEINBERGER
Supreme Court of the United States, 1986.
475 U.S. 503, 106 S.Ct. 1310, 89 L.Ed.2d 478.

JUSTICE REHNQUIST delivered the opinion of the Court.

Petitioner S. Simcha Goldman contends that the Free Exercise Clause of the First Amendment to the United States Constitution permits him to wear a yarmulke while in uniform, notwithstanding an Air Force regulation mandating uniform dress for Air Force personnel. The District Court for the District of Columbia permanently enjoined the Air Force from enforcing its regulation against petitioner and from penalizing him for wearing his yarmulke. The Court of Appeals for the District of Columbia Circuit reversed on the ground that the Air Force's strong interest in discipline justified the strict enforcement of its uniform dress requirements. We granted certiorari because of the importance of the question, * * * and now affirm.

---

otherwise valid, then even granted that the Sunday closing law has the effect of reducing the hazard of one possible kind of hardship for some religionists which one kind of hazard is not equally reduced for all other religionists, namely those in Ms. Sherbert's position, that may simply be an implicit consequence of the closing law as such—a consequence already sustained as it were in the Court's own decisions in *McGowan* and in *Braunfeld;* by itself it establishes no objection to the unemployment compensation law either on its face or as applied.) *Sherbert* may in fact represent an unusual extension of the free exercise clause in requiring payments facilitating religiously-motivated acts.

15. See Frazee v. Illinois Dept. of Employment Security, 489 U.S. 829, 109 S.Ct. 1514, 103 L.Ed.2d 914 (1989) (*Sunday* observer refused retail clerk position because it required Sunday work, *Sherbert* applied to require the state to treat the claimant as eligible for unemployment compensation); Hobbie v. Unemployment Com'n of Florida, 480 U.S. 136, 107 S.Ct. 1046, 94 L.Ed.2d 190 (1987) (convert to Seventh Day Adventist discharged after refusing to work on Saturdays, *Sherbert* applied to require state payment of unemployment compensation) (REHNQUIST, J., dissenting); Thomas v. Review Bd. of Ind. Employment Sec. Div., 450 U.S. 707, 101 S.Ct. 1425, 67 L.Ed.2d 624 (1981) (*Sherbert* applied to require unemployment compensation payments to religious person who quit for religious reasons not involving the day, but rather when he learned the steel production in which he was engaged was for armaments, Court held that unemployment compensation must nonetheless be paid, Rehnquist dissenting—and noting (*id.* at 725, 101 S.Ct. at 1435–36, 67 L.Ed.2d at 638–39) evident inconsistency with prior establishment clause cases which would, absent the *Sherbert* decision, forbid a state from doing that which the Court says the free exercise clause requires).

Petitioner Goldman is an Orthodox Jew and ordained rabbi. In 1973, he was accepted into the Armed Forces Health Professions Scholarship Program and placed on inactive reserve status in the Air Force while he studied clinical psychology at Loyola University of Chicago. During his three years in the scholarship program, he received a monthly stipend and an allowance for tuition, books, and fees. After completing his Ph.D. in psychology, petitioner entered active service in the United States Air Force as a commissioned officer, in accordance with a requirement that participants in the scholarship program serve one year of active duty for each year of subsidized education. Petitioner was stationed at March Air Force Base in Riverside, California, and served as a clinical psychologist at the mental health clinic on the base.

Until 1981, petitioner was not prevented from wearing his yarmulke on the base. He avoided controversy by remaining close to his duty station in the health clinic and by wearing his service cap over the yarmulke when out of doors. But in April 1981, after he testified as a defense witness at a court-martial wearing his yarmulke but not his service cap, opposing counsel lodged a complaint with Colonel Joseph Gregory, the Hospital Commander, arguing that petitioner's practice of wearing his yarmulke was a violation of Air Force Regulation (AFR) 35–10. This regulation states in pertinent part that "[h]eadgear will not be worn * * * [w]hile indoors except by armed security police in the performance of their duties." * * *.

* * *

Petitioner argues that AFR 35–10, as applied to him, prohibits religiously motivated conduct and should therefore be analyzed under the standard enunciated in Sherbert v. Verner, 374 U.S. 398 (1963). * * *

Our review of military regulations challenged on First Amendment grounds is far more deferential than constitutional review of similar laws or regulations designed for civilian society. The military need not encourage debate or tolerate protest to the extent that such tolerance is required of the civilian state by the First Amendment; to accomplish its mission the military must foster instinctive obedience, unity, commitment, and esprit de corps. * * *

These aspects of military life do not, of course, render entirely nugatory in the military context the guarantees of the First Amendment. * * * But "within the military community there is simply not the same [individual] autonomy as there is in the larger civilian community." *Parker v. Levy, supra,* at 751. In the context of the present case, when evaluating whether military needs justify a particular restriction on religiously motivated conduct, courts must give great deference to the professional judgment of military authorities concerning the relative importance of a particular military interest. * * *

The considered professional judgment of the Air Force is that the traditional outfitting of personnel in standardized uniforms encourages the subordination of personal preferences and identities in favor of the overall group mission. Uniforms encourage a sense of hierarchical unity by tending to eliminate outward individual distinctions except for those of rank. The Air Force considers them as vital during peacetime as during war because its personnel must be ready to provide an effective defense on a moment's notice; the necessary habits of discipline and unity must be developed in advance of trouble. We have acknowledged that "[t]he inescapable demands of military discipline and obedience to orders cannot be taught on battlefields; the habit of immediate compliance with military procedures and orders must be virtually reflex with no time for debate or reflection." *Chappell v. Wallace, supra,* at 300.

* * *

Petitioner Goldman contends that the Free Exercise Clause of the First Amendment requires the Air Force to make an exception to its uniform dress requirements for religious apparel unless the accoutrements create a "clear danger" of undermining discipline and esprit de corps. He asserts that in general, visible but "unobtrusive" apparel will not create such a danger and must therefore be accommodated. He argues that the Air Force failed to prove that a specific exception for his practice of wearing an unobtrusive yarmulke would threaten discipline. He contends that the Air Force's assertion to the contrary is mere *ipse dixit*, with no support from actual experience or a scientific study in the record, and is contradicted by expert testimony that religious exceptions to AFR 35–10 are in fact desirable and will increase morale by making the Air Force a more humane place.

But whether or not expert witnesses may feel that religious exceptions to AFR 35–10 are desirable is quite beside the point. The desirability of dress regulations in the military is decided by the appropriate military officials, and they are under no constitutional mandate to abandon their considered professional judgment. Quite obviously, to the extent the regulations do not permit the wearing of religious apparel such as a yarmulke, a practice described by petitioner as silent devotion akin to prayer, military life may be more objectionable for petitioner and probably others. But the First Amendment does not require the military to accommodate such practices in the face of its view that they would detract from the uniformity sought by the dress regulations. The Air Force has drawn the line essentially between religious apparel which is visible and that which is not, and we hold that those portions of the regulations challenged here reasonably and evenhandedly regulate dress in the interest of the military's perceived need for uniformity. The First Amendment therefore does not prohibit them from being applied to petitioner even though their effect is to restrict the wearing of the headgear required by his religious beliefs.

The judgment of the Court of Appeals is

Affirmed.

JUSTICE STEVENS, with whom JUSTICE WHITE and JUSTICE POWELL join, concurring.

Captain Goldman presents an especially attractive case for an exception from the uniform regulations that are applicable to all other

Air Force personnel. His devotion to his faith is readily apparent. The yarmulke is a familiar and accepted sight. In addition to its religious significance for the wearer, the yarmulke may evoke the deepest respect and admiration—the symbol of a distinguished tradition and an eloquent rebuke to the ugliness of anti-Semitism.[3] Captain Goldman's military duties are performed in a setting in which a modest departure from the uniform regulation creates almost no danger of impairment of the Air Force's military mission. Moreover, on the record before us, there is reason to believe that the policy of strict enforcement against Captain Goldman had a retaliatory motive—he had worn his yarmulke while testifying on behalf of a defendant in a court-martial proceeding. Nevertheless, as the case has been argued,[5] I believe we must test the validity of the Air Force's rule not merely as it applies to Captain Goldman but also as it applies to all service personnel who have sincere religious beliefs that may conflict with one or more military commands.

Justice Brennan is unmoved by the Government's concern "that while a yarmulke might not seem obtrusive to a Jew, neither does a turban to a Sikh, a saffron robe to a Satchidananda Ashram-Integral Yogi, nor do dreadlocks to a Rastafarian." * * *. He correctly points out that "turbans, saffron robes, and dreadlocks are not before us in this case," and then suggests that other cases may be fairly decided by reference to a reasonable standard based on "functional utility, health and safety considerations, and the goal of a polished, professional appearance." * * * As the Court has explained, this approach attaches no weight to the separate interest in uniformity itself. Because professionals in the military service attach great importance to that plausible interest, it is one that we must recognize as legitimate and rational even though personal experience or admiration for the performance of the "rag-tag band of soldiers" that won us our freedom in the revolutionary war might persuade us that the Government has exaggerated the importance of that interest.

The interest in uniformity, however, has a dimension that is of still greater importance for me. It is the interest in uniform treatment for the members of all religious faiths. The very strength of Captain Goldman's claim creates the danger that a similar claim on behalf of a Sikh or a Rastafarian might readily be dismissed as "so extreme, so unusual, or so faddish an image that public confidence in his ability to perform his duties will be destroyed." * * * If exceptions from dress code regulations are to be granted on the basis of a multifactored test such as that proposed by Justice Brennan, inevitably the decisionmak-

---

3. Cf. N. Belth, A Promise to Keep (1979) (recounting history of anti-Semitism in the United States). The history of intolerance in our own country can be glimpsed by reviewing Justice Story's observation that the purpose of the First Amendment was "not to countenance, much less to advance Mahometanism, or Judaism, or infidelity, by prostrating Christianity; but to exclude all rivalry among Christian sects," 2 J. Story, Commentaries on the Constitution of the United States § 1877, p. 594 (1851)—a view that the Court has, of course, explicitly rejected. See Wallace v. Jaffree, 472 U.S. 38, 52–55 (1985).

5. Captain Goldman has mounted a broad challenge to the prohibition on visible religious wear as it applies to yarmulkes. He has not argued the far narrower ground that, even if the general prohibition is valid, its application in his case was retaliatory and impermissible. * * *

er's evaluation of the character and the sincerity of the requestor's faith—as well as the probable reaction of the majority to the favored treatment of a member of that faith—will play a critical part in the decision. For the difference between a turban or a dreadlock on the one hand, and a yarmulke on the other, is not merely a difference in "appearance"—it is also the difference between a Sikh or a Rastafarian, on the one hand, and an Orthodox Jew on the other. The Air Force has no business drawing distinctions between such persons when it is enforcing commands of universal application.

As the Court demonstrates, the rule that is challenged in this case is based on a neutral, completely objective standard—visibility. It was not motivated by hostility against, or any special respect for, any religious faith. An exception for yarmulkes would represent a fundamental departure from the true principle of uniformity that supports that rule. For that reason, I join the Court's opinion and its judgment.

JUSTICE BRENNAN, with whom JUSTICE MARSHALL joins, dissenting.

Simcha Goldman invokes this Court's protection of his First Amendment right to fulfill one of the traditional religious obligations of a male Orthodox Jew—to cover his head before an omnipresent God. The Court's response to Goldman's request is to abdicate its role as principal expositor of the Constitution and protector of individual liberties in favor of credulous deference to unsupported assertions of military necessity. I dissent.

I

In ruling that the paramount interests of the Air Force override Dr. Goldman's free exercise claim, the Court overlooks the sincere and serious nature of his constitutional claim. It suggests that the desirability of certain dress regulations, rather than a First Amendment right, is at issue. The Court declares that in selecting dress regulations, "military officials are under no constitutional mandate to abandon their considered professional judgment." * * *. If Dr. Goldman wanted to wear a hat to keep his head warm or to cover a bald spot I would join the majority. Mere personal preferences in dress are not constitutionally protected. The First Amendment, however, restrains the Government's ability to prevent an Orthodox Jewish serviceman from, or punish him for, wearing a yarmulke.

The Court also attempts, unsuccessfully, to minimize the burden that was placed on Dr. Goldman's rights. The fact that "the regulations don't permit the wearing of * * * a yarmulke," does not simply render military life for observant Orthodox Jews "objectionable." * * *. It sets up an almost absolute bar to the fulfillment of a religious duty. Dr. Goldman spent most of his time in uniform indoors, where the dress code forbade him even from covering his head with his service cap. Consequently, he was asked to violate the tenets of his faith virtually every minute of every work day.

II

A

Dr. Goldman has asserted a substantial First Amendment claim, which is entitled to meaningful review by this Court. The Court, however, evades its responsibility by eliminating, in all but name only, judicial review of military regulations that interfere with the fundamental constitutional rights of service personnel.

* * *

Today the Court eschews its constitutionally mandated role. It adopts for review of military decisions affecting First Amendment rights a subrational-basis standard—absolute, uncritical "deference to the professional judgment of military authorities." * * *. If a branch of the military declares one of its rules sufficiently important to outweigh a service person's constitutional rights, it seems that the Court will accept that conclusion, no matter how absurd or unsupported it may be.

A deferential standard of review, however, need not, and should not, mean that the Court must credit arguments that defy common sense. When a military service burdens the free exercise rights of its members in the name of necessity, it must provide, as an initial matter and at a minimum, a credible explanation of how the contested practice is likely to interfere with the proffered military interest.[2] Unabashed *ipse dixit* cannot outweigh a constitutional right.

B

1

The Government maintains in its brief that discipline is jeopardized whenever exceptions to military regulations are granted. Service personnel must be trained to obey even the most arbitrary command reflexively. Non–Jewish personnel will perceive the wearing of a yarmulke by an Orthodox Jew as an unauthorized departure from the rules and will begin to question the principle of unswerving obedience. Thus shall our fighting forces slip down the treacherous slope toward unkempt appearance, anarchy, and, ultimately, defeat at the hands of our enemies.

The contention that the discipline of the armed forces will be subverted if Orthodox Jews are allowed to wear yarmulkes with their uniforms surpasses belief. It lacks support in the record of this case and the Air Force offers no basis for it as a general proposition. While the perilous slope permits the services arbitrarily to refuse exceptions requested to satisfy mere personal preferences, before the Air Force may burden free exercise rights it must advance, at the very least, a

---

2. I continue to believe that Government restraints on First Amendment rights, including limitations placed on military personnel, may be justified only upon showing a compelling state interest which is precisely furthered by a narrowly tailored regulation. See, e.g., Brown v. Glines, 444 U.S. 348, 367 (1980) (BRENNAN, J., dissenting). I think that any special needs of the military can be accommodated in the compelling interest prong of the test. My point here is simply that even under a more deferential test Dr. Goldman should prevail. In the present case, the Air Force asserts that its interests in discipline and uniformity would be undermined by an exception to the dress code permitting observant male Orthodox Jews to wear yarmulkes. The Court simply restates these assertions without offering any explanation how the exception Dr. Goldman requests reasonably could interfere with the Air Force's interests. Had the Court given actual consideration to Goldman's claim, it would have been compelled to decide in his favor.

rational reason for doing so. Furthermore, the Air Force cannot logically defend the content of its rule by insisting that discipline depends upon absolute adherence to whatever rule is established. If, as General Usher admitted at trial, App. 52, the dress code codified religious exemptions from the "no-headgear-indoors" regulation, then the wearing of a yarmulke would be sanctioned by the code and could not be considered an unauthorized deviation from the rules.

2

The Government also argues that the services have an important interest in uniform dress, because such dress establishes the preeminence of group identity, thus fostering esprit de corps and loyalty to the service that transcends individual bonds. In its brief, the Government characterizes the yarmulke as an assertion of individuality and as a badge of religious and ethnic identity, strongly suggesting that, as such, it could drive a wedge of divisiveness between members of the services.

* * *

I find totally implausible the suggestion that the overarching group identity of the Air Force would be threatened if Orthodox Jews were allowed to wear yarmulkes with their uniforms. To the contrary, a yarmulke worn with a United States military uniform is an eloquent reminder that the shared and proud identity of United States serviceman embraces and unites religious and ethnic pluralism.

Finally, the Air Force argues that while Dr. Goldman describes his yarmulke as an "un-obtrusive" addition to his uniform, obtrusiveness is a purely relative, standardless judgment. The Government notes that while a yarmulke might not seem obtrusive to a Jew, neither does a turban to a Sikh, a saffron robe to a Satchidananda Ashram–Integral Yogi, nor do dreadlocks to a Rastafarian. If the Court were to require the Air Force to permit yarmulkes, the service must also allow all of these other forms of dress and grooming.

The Government dangles before the Court a classic parade of horribles, the specter of a brightly-colored, "rag-tag band of soldiers." Brief for Respondents 20. Although turbans, saffron robes, and dreadlocks are not before us in this case and must each be evaluated against the reasons a service branch offers for prohibiting personnel from wearing them while in uniform, a reviewing court could legitimately give deference to dress and grooming rules that have a reasoned basis in, for example, functional utility, health and safety considerations, and the goal of a polished, professional appearance.[4] * * *

Furthermore, contrary to its intimations, the Air Force has available to it a familiar standard for determining whether a particular style of yarmulke is consistent with a polished, professional military appearance—the "neat and conservative" standard by which the service judges jewelry. AFR 35–10, P 1–12b.(1)(b) (1978). No rational

---

4. For example, the Air Force could no doubt justify regulations ordering troops to wear uniforms, prohibiting garments that could become entangled in machinery, and requiring hair to be worn short so that it may not be grabbed in combat and may be kept louse-free in field conditions.

reason exists why yarmulkes cannot be judged by the same criterion. Indeed, at argument Dr. Goldman declared himself willing to wear whatever style and color yarmulke the Air Force believes best comports with its uniform. * * *

3

Department of Defense Directive 1300.17 (June 18, 1985) grants commanding officers the discretion to permit service personnel to wear religious items and apparel that are not visible with the uniform, such as crosses, temple garments, and scapulars. Justice Stevens favors this "visibility test" because he believes that it does not involve the Air Force in drawing distinctions among faiths. * * * He rejects functional utility, health, and safety considerations, and similar grounds as criteria for religious exceptions to the dress code, because he fears that these standards will allow some service persons to satisfy their religious dress and grooming obligations, while preventing others from fulfilling theirs. * * * But, the visible/not visible standard has that same effect. Furthermore, it restricts the free exercise rights of a larger number of service persons. The visibility test permits only individuals whose outer garments and grooming are indistinguishable from those of mainstream Christians to fulfill their religious duties. In my view, the Constitution requires the selection of criteria that permit the greatest possible number of persons to practice their faiths freely.

Implicit in Justice Stevens' concurrence, and in the Government's arguments, is what might be characterized as a fairness concern. It would be unfair to allow Orthodox Jews to wear yarmulkes, while prohibiting members of other minority faiths with visible dress and grooming requirements from wearing their saffron robes, dreadlocks, turbans, and so forth. While I appreciate and share this concern for the feelings and the free exercise rights of members of these other faiths, I am baffled by this formulation of the problem. What puzzles me is the implication that a neutral standard that could result in the disparate treatment of Orthodox Jews and, for example, Sikhs is more troublesome or unfair than the existing neutral standard that does result in the different treatment of Christians, on the one hand, and Orthodox Jews and Sikhs on the other. Both standards are constitutionally suspect; before either can be sustained, it must be shown to be a narrowly tailored means of promoting important military interests.

* * *

It is not the province of the federal courts to second-guess the professional judgments of the military services, but we are bound by the Constitution to assure ourselves that there exists a rational foundation for assertions of military necessity when they interfere with the free exercise of religion. "The concept of military necessity is seductively broad," *Glines,* 444 U.S., at 369 (BRENNAN, J., dissenting), and military decisionmakers themselves are as likely to succumb to its allure as are the courts and the general public. Definitions of necessity are influenced by decisionmakers' experiences and values. As a consequence, in pluralistic societies such as ours, institutions dominated by a majority are inevitably, if inadvertently, insensitive to the needs and values of minorities when these needs and values differ from those of the majority. The military, with its strong ethic of conformity and unquestioning obedience, may be particularly impervious to minority needs and values. A critical function of the Religion Clauses of the First Amendment is to protect the rights of members of minority religions against quiet erosion by majoritarian social institutions that dismiss minority beliefs and practices as unimportant, because unfamiliar. It is the constitutional role of this Court to ensure that this purpose of the First Amendment be realized.

The Court and the military services have presented patriotic Orthodox Jews with a painful dilemma—the choice between fulfilling a religious obligation and serving their country. Should the draft be reinstated, compulsion will replace choice. Although the pain the services inflict on Orthodox Jewish servicemen is clearly the result of insensitivity rather than design, it is unworthy of our military because it is unnecessary. The Court and the military have refused these servicemen their constitutional rights; we must hope that Congress will correct this wrong.

JUSTICE BLACKMUN, dissenting.

I would reverse the judgment of the Court of Appeals, but for reasons somewhat different from those respectively enunciated by Justice Brennan and Justice O'Connor. I feel that the Air Force is justified in considering not only the costs of allowing Captain Goldman to cover his head indoors, but also the cumulative costs of accommodating constitutionally indistinguishable requests for religious exemptions. Because, however, the Government has failed to make any meaningful showing that either set of costs is significant, I dissent from the Court's rejection of Goldman's claim.

* * *

The problem with this argument, it seems to me, is not doctrinal but empirical. The Air Force simply has not shown any reason to fear that a significant number of enlisted personnel and officers would request religious exemptions that could not be denied on neutral grounds such as safety, let alone that granting these requests would noticeably impair the overall image of the service. Cf. Thomas v. Review Board of Indiana Employment Security Div., 450 U.S., at 719; Sherbert v. Verner, 374 U.S., at 407. The Air Force contends that the potential for such disruption was demonstrated at trial through the introduction of an Army publication discussing the beliefs and practices of a variety of religious denominations, some of which have traditions or requirements involving attire. See Department of the Army Pamphlet No. 165–13–1, Religious Requirements and Practices of Certain Selected Groups: A Handbook Supplement for Chaplains (1980). But that publication provides no indication whatsoever as to how many soldiers belong to the denominations it describes, or as to how many are likely to seek religious exemptions from the dress code.

In these circumstances, deference seems unwarranted. Reasoned military judgments, of course, are entitled to respect, but the military has failed to show that this particular judgment with respect to Captain

Goldman is a reasoned one. If, in the future, the Air Force is besieged with requests for religious exemptions from the dress code, and those requests cannot be distinguished on functional grounds from Goldman's, the service may be able to argue credibly that circumstances warrant a flat rule against any visible religious apparel. That, however, would be a case different from the one at hand.

JUSTICE O'CONNOR, with whom JUSTICE MARSHALL joins, dissenting.

The issue posed in this case is whether, consistent with the Free Exercise Clause of the First Amendment, the Air Force may prohibit Captain Goldman, an Orthodox Jewish psychologist, from wearing a yarmulke while he is in uniform on duty inside a military hospital.

* * *

I believe that the Court should attempt to articulate and apply an appropriate standard for a free exercise claim in the military context, and should examine Captain Goldman's claim in light of that standard.

Like the Court today in this case involving the military, the Court in the past has had some difficulty, even in the civilian context, in articulating a clear standard for evaluating free exercise claims that result from the application of general state laws burdening religious conduct. In Sherbert v. Verner, 374 U.S. 398 (1963), and Thomas v. Review Board, 450 U.S. 707 (1981), the Court required the States to demonstrate that their challenged policies were "the least restrictive means of achieving some compelling state interest" in order to deprive claimants of unemployment benefits when the refusal to work was based on sincere religious beliefs. *Thomas, supra,* at 718. See also *Sherbert, supra,* 374 U.S., at 406–408. In Wisconsin v. Yoder, 406 U.S. 205, 215 (1972), the Court noted that "only those interests of the highest order and those not otherwise served can overbalance legitimate claims to the free exercise of religion" in deciding that the Amish were exempt from a State's requirement that children attend school through the age of 16. * * *

These tests, though similar, are not identical. One can, however, glean at least two consistent themes from this Court's precedents. First, when the government attempts to deny a free exercise claim, it must show that an unusually important interest is at stake, whether that interest is denominated "compelling," "of the highest order," or "overriding." Second, the government must show that granting the requested exemption will do substantial harm to that interest, whether by showing that the means adopted is the "least restrictive" or "essential," or that the interest will not "otherwise be served." These two requirements are entirely sensible in the context of the assertion of a free exercise claim. First, because the government is attempting to override an interest specifically protected by the Bill of Rights, the government must show that the opposing interest it asserts is of especial importance before there is any chance that its claim can prevail. Second, since the Bill of Rights is expressly designed to protect the individual against the aggregated and sometimes intolerant powers of the state, the government must show that the interest asserted will in fact be substantially harmed by granting the type of exemption requested by the individual.

There is no reason why these general principles should not apply in the military, as well as the civilian, context. * * *

The first question that the Court should face here, therefore, is whether the interest that the Government asserts against the religiously based claim of the individual is of unusual importance. It is perfectly appropriate at this step of the analysis to take account of the special role of the military. The mission of our armed services is to protect our Nation from those who would destroy all our freedoms. * * * The need for military discipline and esprit de corps is unquestionably an especially important governmental interest.

But the mere presence of such an interest cannot, as the majority implicitly believes, end the analysis of whether a refusal by the Government to honor the free exercise of an individual's religion is constitutionally acceptable. A citizen pursuing even the most noble cause must remain within the bounds of the law. So, too, the Government may, even in pursuing its most compelling interests, be subject to specific restraints in doing so. The second question in the analysis of a Free Exercise claim under this Court's precedents must also be reached here: will granting an exemption of the type requested by the individual do substantial harm to the especially important governmental interest?

I have no doubt that there are many instances in which the unique fragility of military discipline and esprit de corps necessitates rigidity by the Government when similar rigidity to preserve an assertedly analogous interest would not pass constitutional muster in the civilian sphere. Compare Greer v. Spock, 424 U.S. 828 (1976) with Metromedia, Inc. v. San Diego, 453 U.S. 490 (1981) and West Virginia Board of Education v. Barnette, 319 U.S. 624, 630–634, (1943). Nonetheless, as Justice Brennan persuasively argues, the Government can present no sufficiently convincing proof in this case to support an assertion that granting an exemption of the type requested here would do substantial harm to military discipline and esprit de corps. * * *

First, the Government's asserted need for absolute uniformity is contradicted by the Government's own exceptions to its rule. As Justice Brennan notes, * * *, an Air Force dress code in force at the time of Captain Goldman's service states:

> "Neither the Air Force nor the public expects absolute uniformity of appearance. Each member has the right, within limits, to express individuality through his or her appearance. However, the image of a disciplined service member who can be relied on to do his or her job excludes the extreme, the unusual, and the fad." AFR 35–10, P 1–12.a.(2) (1978).

Furthermore, the Government does not assert, and could not plausibly argue, that petitioner's decision to wear his yarmulke while indoors at the hospital presents a threat to health or safety. And finally, the District Court found as fact that in this particular case, far from creating discontent or indiscipline in the hospital where Captain Goldman worked, "[f]rom September 1977 to May 7, 1981, *no objection* was raised to Goldman's wearing of his yarmulke while in uniform." See Goldman v. Secretary of Defense, 29 EPD P 32,753 (1982); Finding of Fact No. 4 (emphasis added).

In the rare instances where the military has not consistently or plausibly justified its asserted need for rigidity of enforcement, and where the individual seeking the exemption establishes that the assertion by the military of a threat to discipline or esprit de corps is in his or her case completely unfounded, I would hold that the Government's policy of uniformity must yield to the individual's assertion of the right of free exercise of religion. On the facts of this case, therefore, I would require the Government to accommodate the sincere religious belief of Captain Goldman. Napoleon may have been correct to assert that, in the military sphere, morale is to all other factors as three is to one,* but contradicted assertions of necessity by the military do not on the scales of justice bear a similarly disproportionate weight to sincere religious beliefs of the individual.

I respectfully dissent.

LYNG v. NORTHWEST INDIAN CEMETERY PROTECTIVE ASSOCIATION

Supreme Court of the United States, 1988.
485 U.S. 439, 108 S.Ct. 1319, 99 L.Ed.2d 534.

JUSTICE O'CONNOR delivered the opinion of the Court.

This case requires us to consider whether the First Amendment's Free Exercise Clause forbids the Government from permitting timber harvesting in, or constructing a road through, a portion of a National Forest that has traditionally been used for religious purposes by members of three American Indian tribes in northwestern California. We conclude that it does not.

I

As part of a project to create a paved 75–mile road linking two California towns, Gasquet and Orleans, the United States Forest Service has upgraded 49 miles of previously unpaved roads on federal land. In order to complete this project (the G–O road), the Forest Service must build a 6–mile paved segment through the Chimney Rock section of the Six Rivers National Forest. That section of the forest is situated between two other portions of the road that are already complete.

In 1977, the Forest Service issued a draft environmental impact statement that discussed proposals for upgrading an existing unpaved road that runs through the Chimney Rock area. In response to comments on the draft statement, the Forest Service commissioned a

---

* See Letter, Aug. 27, 1808 ("In war, moral considerations account for three-quarters, the balance of actual forces only for the other quarter"), as translated and quoted in J. Cohen & M. Cohen, The Penguin Dictionary of Quotations 268 (1962).

study of American Indian cultural and religious sites in the area. The Hoopa Valley Indian Reservation adjoins the Six Rivers National Forest, and the Chimney Rock area has historically been used for religious purposes by Yurok, Karok, and Tolowa Indians. * * * The study concluded that constructing a road along any of the available routes "would cause serious and irreparable damage to the sacred areas which are an integral and necessary part of the belief systems and lifeway of Northwest California Indian peoples." * * *. Accordingly, the report recommended that the G–O road not be completed.

In 1982, the Forest Service decided not to adopt this recommendation, and it prepared a final environmental impact statement for construction of the road. The Regional Forester selected a route that avoided archaeological sites and was removed as far as possible from the sites used by contemporary Indians for specific spiritual activities. Alternative routes that would have avoided the Chimney Rock area altogether were rejected because they would have required the acquisition of private land, had serious soil stability problems, and would in any event have traversed areas having ritualistic value to American Indians. * * * At about the same time, the Forest Service adopted a management plan allowing for the harvesting of significant amounts of timber in this area of the forest. The management plan provided for one-half mile protective zones around all the religious sites identified in the report that had been commissioned in connection with the G–O road.

After exhausting their administrative remedies, respondents—an Indian organization, individual Indians, nature organizations and individual members of those organizations, and the State of California—challenged both the road-building and timber-harvesting decisions in the United States District Court for the Northern District of California. * * *

After a trial, the District Court issued a permanent injunction forbidding the Government from constructing the Chimney Rock section of the G–O road or putting the timber-harvesting management plan into effect. See Northwest Indian Cemetery Protective Assn. v. Peterson, 565 F.Supp. 586 (ND Cal.1983). The court found that both actions would violate the Free Exercise Clause because they "would seriously damage the salient visual, aural, and environmental qualities of the high country." *Id.*, at 594–595. * * *

* * *

A panel of the Ninth Circuit affirmed in part. Northwest Indian Cemetery Protective Assn. v. Peterson, 795 F.2d 688 (1986). The panel unanimously rejected the District Court's conclusion that the Government's proposed actions would breach its trust responsibilities to Indians on the Hoopa Valley Reservation. The panel also vacated the injunction to the extent that it had been rendered moot by the California Wilderness Act, which now prevents timber harvesting in certain areas covered by the District Court's order. The District Court's decision, to the extent that it rested on statutory grounds, was otherwise unanimously affirmed.

By a divided decision, the District Court's constitutional ruling was also affirmed. * * *

* * *

I

We begin by noting that the courts below did not articulate the bases of their decisions with perfect clarity. A fundamental and long-standing principle of judicial restraint requires that courts avoid reaching constitutional questions in advance of the necessity of deciding them. * * *

* * *

Because it appears reasonably likely that the First Amendment issue was necessary to the decisions below, we believe that it would be inadvisable to vacate and remand without addressing that issue on the merits. This conclusion is strengthened by considerations of judicial economy. * * *

III

A

The Free Exercise Clause of the First Amendment provides that "Congress shall make no law * * * prohibiting the free exercise [of religion]." U.S. Const., Amdt. 1. It is undisputed that the Indian respondents' beliefs are sincere and that the Government's proposed actions will have severe adverse effects on the practice of their religion. Respondents contend that the burden on their religious practices is heavy enough to violate the Free Exercise Clause unless the Government can demonstrate a compelling need to complete the G–O road or to engage in timber harvesting in the Chimney Rock area. We disagree.

* * *

Whatever may be the exact line between unconstitutional prohibitions on the free exercise of religion and the legitimate conduct by government of its own affairs, the location of the line cannot depend on measuring the effects of a governmental action on a religious objector's spiritual development. * * *

Even if we assume that we should accept the Ninth Circuit's prediction, according to which the G–O road will "virtually destroy the Indians' ability to practice their religion," 795 F.2d, at 693 (opinion below), the Constitution simply does not provide a principle that could justify upholding respondents' legal claims. However much we might wish that it were otherwise, government simply could not operate if it were required to satisfy every citizen's religious needs and desires. * * *

* * * Respondents attempt to stress the limits of the religious servitude that they are now seeking to impose on the Chimney Rock area of the Six Rivers National Forest. While defending an injunction against logging operations and the construction of a road, they apparently do not *at present* object to the area's being used by recreational

visitors, other Indians, or forest rangers. Nothing in the principle for which they contend, however, would distinguish this case from another lawsuit in which they (or similarly situated religious objectors) might seek to exclude all human activity but their own from sacred areas of the public lands. The Indian respondents insist that "[p]rivacy during the power quests is required for the practitioners to maintain the purity needed for a successful journey." Brief for Indian Respondents 8 (emphasis added; citation to record omitted). Similarly: "The practices conducted in the high country entail intense meditation and require the practitioner to achieve a profound awareness of the natural environment. Prayer seats are oriented so there is an unobstructed view, and the practitioner must be surrounded by *undisturbed* naturalness." *Id.,* at 8, n. 4 (emphasis added) (citations to record omitted). No disrespect for these practices is implied when one notes that such beliefs could easily require *de facto* beneficial ownership of some rather spacious tracts of public property. Even without anticipating future cases, the diminution of the Government's property rights, and the concomitant subsidy of the Indian religion, would in this case be far from trivial: the District Court's order permanently forbade commercial timber harvesting, or the construction of a two-lane road, anywhere within an area covering a full 27 sections (i.e. more than 17,000 acres) of public land.

The Constitution does not permit government to discriminate against religions that treat particular physical sites as sacred, and a law forbidding the Indian respondents from visiting the Chimney Rock area would raise a different set of constitutional questions. Whatever rights the Indians may have to the use of the area, however, those rights do not divest the Government of its right to use what is, after all, its land. * * *

B

Nothing in our opinion should be read to encourage governmental insensitivity to the religious needs of any citizen. The Government's rights to the use of its own land, for example, need not and should not discourage it from accommodating religious practices like those engaged in by the Indian respondents. Cf. *Sherbert,* 374 U.S., at 422–423 (HARLAN, J., dissenting). * * *

* * *

The dissent proposes an approach to the First Amendment that is fundamentally inconsistent with the principles on which our decision rests. Notwithstanding the sympathy that we all must feel for the plight of the Indian respondents, it is plain that the approach taken by the dissent cannot withstand analysis. On the contrary, the path towards which it points us is incompatible with the text of the Constitution, with the precedents of this Court, and with a responsible sense of our own institutional role.

The dissent begins by asserting that the "constitutional guarantee we interpret today * * * is directed against *any* form of government action that frustrates or inhibits religious practice." * * * (emphasis added). The Constitution, however, says no such thing. Rather, it states: "Congress shall make no law * * * *prohibiting* the free exercise [of religion]." U.S. Const., Amdt. 1 (emphasis added).

As we explained above, *Bowen v. Roy* rejected a First Amendment challenge to government activities that the religious objectors sincerely believed would "'rob the spirit' of [their] daughter and prevent her from attaining greater spiritual power." * * * The dissent now offers to distinguish that case by saying that the Government was acting there "in a purely internal manner," whereas land-use decisions "are likely to have substantial external effects." * * * Whatever the source or meaning of the dissent's distinction, it has no basis in *Roy*. Robbing the spirit of a child, and preventing her from attaining greater spiritual power, is both a "substantial external effect" and one that is remarkably similar to the injury claimed by respondents in the case before us today. The dissent's reading of *Roy* would effectively overrule that decision, without providing any compelling justification for doing so.

The dissent also misreads Wisconsin v. Yoder, 406 U.S. 205 (1972). The statute at issue in that case prohibited the Amish parents, on pain of criminal prosecution, from providing their children with the kind of education required by the Amish religion. *Id.*, at 207–209, 223. The statute directly compelled the Amish to send their children to public high schools "contrary to the Amish religion and way of life." *Id.*, at 209. The Court acknowledged that the statute might be constitutional, despite its coercive nature, if the state could show with sufficient "particularity how its admittedly strong interest in compulsory education would be adversely affected by granting an exemption to the Amish." *Id.*, at 236 (citation omitted). The dissent's out-of-context quotations notwithstanding, there is nothing whatsoever in the *Yoder* opinion to support the proposition that the "impact" on the Amish religion would have been constitutionally problematic if the statute at issue had not been coercive in nature. * * *

Perceiving a "stress point in the longstanding conflict between two disparate cultures," the dissent attacks us for declining to "balanc[e] these competing and potentially irreconcilable interests, choosing instead to turn this difficult task over to the federal legislature." * * *. Seeing the Court as the arbiter, the dissent proposes a legal test under which it would decide which public lands are "central" or "indispensable" to which religions, and by implication which are "dispensable" or "peripheral," and would then decide which government programs are "compelling" enough to justify "infringement of those practices." * * *. We would accordingly be required to weigh the value of every religious belief and practice that is said to be threatened by any government program. Unless a "showing of 'centrality,'" * * *, is nothing but an assertion of centrality, * * *, the dissent thus offers us the prospect of this Court holding that some sincerely held religious beliefs and practices are not "central" to certain religions, despite protestations to the contrary from the religious objectors who brought the lawsuit. In other words, the dissent's approach would require us to rule that some religious adherents misunderstand their own religious beliefs. We think such an approach cannot be squared with the

Constitution or with our precedents, and that it would cast the judiciary in a role that we were never intended to play.

IV

The decision of the court below, according to which the First Amendment precludes the Government from completing the G–O road or from permitting timber harvesting in the Chimney Rock area, is reversed. In order that the District Court's injunction may be reconsidered in light of this holding, and in the light of any other relevant events that may have intervened since the injunction issued, the case is remanded for further proceedings consistent with this opinion.

It is so ordered.

JUSTICE KENNEDY took no part in the consideration or decision of this case.

JUSTICE BRENNAN, with whom JUSTICE MARSHALL and JUSTICE BLACKMUN join, dissenting.

" '[T]he Free Exercise Clause,' " the Court explains today, " 'is written in terms of what the government cannot do to the individual, not in terms of what the individual can exact from the government.' " * * * Pledging fidelity to this unremarkable constitutional principle, the Court nevertheless concludes that even where the Government uses federal land in a manner that threatens the very existence of a Native American religion, the Government is simply not "doing" anything to the practitioners of that faith. Instead, the Court believes that Native Americans who request that the Government refrain from destroying their religion effectively seek to exact from the Government de facto beneficial ownership of federal property. These two astonishing conclusions follow naturally from the Court's determination that federal land-use decisions that render the practice of a given religion impossible do not burden that religion in a manner cognizable under the Free Exercise Clause, because such decisions neither coerce conduct inconsistent with religious belief not penalize religious activity. The constitutional guarantee we interpret today, however, draws no such fine distinctions between types of restraints on religious exercise, but rather is directed against any form of governmental action that frustrates or inhibits religious practice. Because the Court today refuses even to acknowledge the constitutional injury respondents will suffer, and because this refusal essentially leaves Native Americans with absolutely no constitutional protection against perhaps the gravest threat to their religious practices, I dissent.

* * *

For respondent Indians, the most sacred of lands is the high country where, they believe, prehuman spirits moved with the coming of humans to the earth. Because these spirits are seen as the source of religious power, or "medicine," many of the tribes' rituals and practices require frequent journeys to the area. Thus, for example, religious leaders preparing for the complex of ceremonies that underlie the Tribes' World Renewal efforts must travel to specific sites in the high country in order to attain the medicine necessary for successful renewal. Similarly, individual tribe members may seek curative powers for the healing of the sick, or personal medicine for particular purposes such as good luck in singing, hunting, or love. A period of preparation generally precedes such visits, and individuals must select trails in the sacred area according to the medicine they seek and their abilities, gradually moving to increasingly more powerful sites, which are typically located at higher altitudes. Among the most powerful of sites are Chimney Rock, Doctor Rock, and Peak 8, all of which are elevated rock outcroppings.

According to the Theodoratus Report, the qualities "of silence, the aesthetic perspective, and the physical attributes, are an extension of the sacredness of [each] particular site." App. 148. The act of medicine making is akin to meditation: the individual must integrate physical, mental and vocal actions in order to communicate with the prehuman spirits. As a result, "successful use of the high country is dependent upon and facilitated by certain qualities of the physical environment, the most important of which are privacy, silence, and an undisturbed natural setting." *Id.,* at 181. Although few tribe members actually make medicine at the most powerful sites, the entire tribe's welfare hinges on the success of the individual practitioners.

* * *

* * * Recognizing that the high country is "indispensable" to the religious lives of the approximately 5,000 tribe members who reside in the area, Northwest Indian Cemetery Protective Assn. v. Peterson, 795 F.2d 688, 692 (CA9 1986), the court concluded "that the proposed government operations would *virtually destroy* the * * * Indians' ability to practice their religion." *Id.,* at 693 (emphasis added).[3] * * *

II

The Court does not for a moment suggest that the interests served by the G–O road are in any way compelling, or that they outweigh the destructive effect construction of the road will have on respondents' religious practices. Instead, the Court embraces the Government's contention that its prerogative as landowner should always take precedence over a claim that a particular use of federal property infringes religious practices. Attempting to justify this rule, the Court argues that the First Amendment bars only outright prohibitions, indirect coercion, and penalties on the free exercise of religion. All other "incidental effects of government programs," it concludes, even those "which may make it more difficult to practice certain religions but

---

3. Remarkably, the Court treats this factual determination as nothing more than an assumption or "prediction," * * *, and suggests that it is "less than certain that construction of the road will be so disruptive that it will doom [respondents'] religion." *Ibid.* Such speculation flies in the face of the most basic principles of appellate review, * * *. Even if our review were not governed by such rules, however, the mere fact that a handful of the Native Americans who reside in the effected area do not oppose the road in no way casts doubt upon the validity of the lower courts' amply supported factual findings, particularly where the members of this minority did not indicate whether their lack of objection reflected their assessment of the religious significance of the high country, or their own apathy towards religious matters generally.

which have no tendency to coerce individuals into acting contrary to their religious beliefs," simply do not give rise to constitutional concerns. * * * Since our recognition nearly half a century ago that restraints on religious conduct implicate the concerns of the Free Exercise Clause, see Prince v. Massachusetts, 321 U.S. 158 (1944), we have never suggested that the protections of the guarantee are limited to so narrow a range of governmental burdens. The land-use decision challenged here will restrain respondents from practicing their religion as surely and as completely as any of the governmental actions we have struck down in the past, and the Court's efforts simply to define away respondents' injury as nonconstitutional is both unjustified and ultimately unpersuasive.

* * *

I thus cannot accept the Court's premise that the form of the Government's restraint on religious practice, rather than its effect, controls our constitutional analysis. Respondents here have demonstrated that construction of the G–O road will completely frustrate the practice of their religion, for as the lower courts found, the proposed logging and construction activities will virtually destroy respondents' religion, and will therefore necessarily force them into abandoning those practices altogether. Indeed, the Government's proposed activities will restrain religious practice to a far greater degree here than in any of the cases cited by the Court today. None of the religious adherents in *Hobbie, Thomas,* and *Sherbert,* for example, claimed or could have claimed that the denial of unemployment benefits rendered the practice of their religions impossible; at most, the challenged laws made those practices more expensive. Here, in stark contrast, respondents have claimed—and proved—that the desecration of the high country will prevent religious leaders from attaining the religious power or medicine indispensable to the success of virtually all their rituals and ceremonies. Similarly, in *Yoder* the compulsory school law threatened to "undermin[e] the Amish community and religious practice," and thus to force adherents to "abandon belief * * * or * * * to migrate to some other and more tolerant region." * * *

Ultimately, the Court's coercion test turns on a distinction between governmental actions that compel affirmative conduct inconsistent with religious belief, and those governmental actions that prevent conduct consistent with religious belief. In my view, such a distinction is without constitutional significance. The crucial word in the constitutional text, as the Court itself acknowledges, is "prohibit," * * *, a comprehensive term that in no way suggests that the intended protection is aimed only at governmental actions that coerce affirmative conduct. Nor does the Court's distinction comport with the principles animating the constitutional guarantee: religious freedom is threatened no less by governmental action that makes the practice of one's chosen faith impossible than by governmental programs that pressure one to engage in conduct inconsistent with religious beliefs. The Court attempts to explain the line it draws by arguing that the protections of the Free Exercise Clause "cannot depend on measuring the effects of a governmental action on a religious objector's spiritual development,"

* * *, for in a society as diverse as ours, the Government cannot help but offend the "religious needs and desires" of some citizens. * * * While I agree that governmental action that simply offends religious sensibilities may not be challenged under the Clause, we have recognized that laws that affect spiritual development by impeding the integration of children into the religious community or by increasing the expense of adherence to religious principles—in short, laws that frustrate or inhibit religious *practice*—trigger the protections of the constitutional guarantee. Both common sense and our prior cases teach us, therefore, that governmental action that makes the practice of a given faith more difficult necessarily penalizes that practice and thereby tends to prevent adherence to religious belief. The harm to the practitioners is the same regardless of the manner in which the Government restrains their religious expression, and the Court's fear that an "effects" test will permit religious adherents to challenge governmental actions they merely find "offensive" in no way justifies its refusal to recognize the constitutional injury citizens suffer when governmental action not only offends but actually restrains their religious practices. Here, respondents have demonstrated that the Government's proposed activities will completely prevent them from practicing their religion, and such a showing, no less than those made out in *Hobbie, Thomas, Sherbert,* and *Yoder*, entitles them to the protections of the Free Exercise Clause.

B

Nor can I agree with the Court's assertion that respondents' constitutional claim is foreclosed by our decision in Bowen v. Roy, 476 U.S. 693 (1986). * * *

Today the Court professes an inability to differentiate *Roy* from the present case, suggesting that "[t]he building of a road or the harvesting of timber on publicly owned land cannot meaningfully be distinguished from the use of a Social Security number." * * * I find this inability altogether remarkable. In *Roy,* we repeatedly stressed the "internal" nature of the Government practice at issue: noting that *Roy* objected to "the widespread use of the social security number by the federal or state governments *in their computer systems,"* 476 U.S., at 697 (citation omitted; internal quotation marks omitted; emphasis added), we likened the use of such recordkeeping numbers to decisions concerning the purchase of office equipment. When the Government processes information, of course, it acts in a purely internal manner, and any free exercise challenge to such internal recordkeeping in effect seeks to dictate how the Government conducts its own affairs.

Federal land-use decisions, by contrast, are likely to have substantial external effects that government decisions concerning office furniture and information storage obviously will not, and they are correspondingly subject to public scrutiny and public challenge in a host of ways that office equipment purchases are not. * * *

* * *

C

In the final analysis, the Court's refusal to recognize the constitutional dimension of respondents' injuries stems from its concern that acceptance of respondents' claim could potentially strip the Government of its ability to manage and use vast tracts of federal property. * * * In addition, the nature of respondents' site-specific religious practices raises the specter of future suits in which Native Americans seek to exclude all human activity from such areas. * * * These concededly legitimate concerns lie at the very heart of this case, which represents yet another stress point in the longstanding conflict between two disparate cultures—the dominant western culture, which views land in terms of ownership and use, and that of Native Americans, in which concepts of private property are not only alien, but contrary to a belief system that holds land sacred. Rather than address this conflict in any meaningful fashion, however, the Court disclaims all responsibility for balancing these competing and potentially irreconcilable interests, choosing instead to turn this difficult task over to the federal legislature. Such an abdication is more than merely indefensible as an institutional matter: by defining respondents' injury as "nonconstitutional," the Court has effectively bestowed on one party to this conflict the unilateral authority to resolve all future disputes in its favor, subject only to the Court's toothless exhortation to be "sensitive" to affected religions. In my view, however, Native Americans deserve—and the Constitution demands—more than this.

* * *

Similarly, the Court's concern that the claims of Native Americans will place "religious servitudes" upon vast tracts of federal property cannot justify its refusal to recognize the constitutional injury respondents will suffer here. It is true, as the Court notes, that respondents' religious use of the high country requires privacy and solitude. The fact remains, however, that respondents have never asked the Forest Service to exclude others from the area. Should respondents or any other group seek to force the Government to protect their religious practices from the interference of private parties, such a demand would implicate not only the concerns of the Free Exercise Clause, but those of the Establishment Clause as well. That case, however, is most assuredly not before us today, and in any event cannot justify the Court's refusal to acknowledge that the injuries respondents will suffer as a result of the Government's proposed activities are sufficient to state a constitutional cause of action.

JIMMY SWAGGART MINISTRIES v. BOARD OF EQUALIZATION OF CALIFORNIA

Supreme Court of the United States, 1990.
493 U.S. 378, 110 S.Ct. 688, 107 L.Ed.2d 796.

JUSTICE O'CONNOR delivered the opinion of the Court.

This case presents the question whether the Religion Clauses of the First Amendment prohibit a State from imposing a generally applicable sales and use tax on the distribution of religious materials by a religious organization.

I

California's Sales and Use Tax Law requires retailers to pay a sales tax "[f]or the privilege of selling tangible personal property at retail." * * * A "sale" includes any transfer of title or possession of tangible personal property for consideration. * * *

The use tax, as a complement to the sales tax, reaches out-of-state purchases by residents of the State. It is "imposed on the storage, use, or other consumption in this state of tangible personal property purchased from any retailer," * * *, at the same rate as the sales tax (6 percent). Although the use tax is imposed on the purchaser, * * *, it is generally collected by the retailer at the time the sale is made. * * * Neither the State Constitution nor the State Sales and Use Tax Law exempts religious organizations from the sales and use tax, apart from a limited exemption for the serving of meals by religious organizations, * * *.

During the tax period in question (1974 to 1981), appellant Jimmy Swaggart Ministries was a religious organization incorporated as a Louisiana nonprofit corporation and recognized as such by the Internal Revenue Service pursuant to § 501(c)(3) of the Internal Revenue Code of 1954, as amended, 26 U.S.C. § 501(c)(3) (1982 ed.), and by the California State Controller pursuant to the Inheritance Tax and Gift Tax Laws of the State of California. Appellant's constitution and by-laws provide that it "is called for the purpose of establishing and maintaining an evangelistic outreach for the worship of Almighty God." App. 107. This outreach is to be performed "by all available means, both at home and in foreign lands," * * *

From 1974 to 1981, appellant conducted numerous "evangelistic crusades" in auditoriums and arenas across the country in cooperation with local churches. *Id.*, at 61. During this period, appellant held 23 crusades in California—each lasting one to three days, with one crusade lasting six days—for a total of 52 days. *Id.*, at 19–20. At the crusades, appellant conducted religious services that included preaching and singing. Some of these services were recorded for later sale or broadcast. Appellant also sold religious books, tapes, records, and other religious and nonreligious merchandise at the crusades.

Appellant also published a monthly magazine, "The Evangelist," which was sold nationwide by subscription. The magazine contained articles of a religious nature as well as advertisements for appellant's religious books, tapes, and records. The magazine included an order form listing the various items for sale in the particular issue and their unit price, with spaces for purchasers to fill in the quantity desired and the total price. * * *

In 1980, appellee Board of Equalization of the State of California (Board) informed appellant that religious materials were not exempt from the sales tax and requested appellant to register as a seller to facilitate reporting and payment of the tax. * * *

* * * Based on the sales figures for appellant's religious materials, the Board notified appellant that it owed sales and use taxes of $118,294.54, plus interest of $36,021.11, and a penalty of $11,829.45, for a total amount due of $166,145.10. * * * Appellant did not contest the Board's assessment of tax liability for the sale and use of certain nonreligious merchandise, including such items as "T-shirts with JSM logo, mugs, bowls, plates, replicas of crown of thorns, ark of the covenant, Roman coin, candlesticks, Bible stand, pen and pencil sets, prints of religious scenes, bud vase, and communion cups." * * *.

Appellant filed a petition for redetermination with the Board, reiterating its view that the tax on religious materials violated the First Amendment. Following a hearing and an appeal to the Board, the Board deleted the penalty but otherwise redetermined the matter without adjustment in the amount of $118,294.54 in taxes owing, plus $65,043.55 in interest. * * *

The trial court entered judgment for the Board, ruling that appellant was not entitled to a refund of any tax. The California Court of Appeal affirmed, * * *, and the California Supreme Court denied discretionary review. We noted probable jurisdiction * * * and now affirm.

II

Appellant's central contention is that the State's imposition of sales and use tax liability on its sale of religious materials contravenes the First Amendment's command, made applicable to the States by the Fourteenth Amendment, to "make no law respecting an establishment of religion, or prohibiting the free exercise thereof." Appellant challenges the sales and use tax law under both the Free Exercise and Establishment Clauses.

A

The Free Exercise Clause, we have noted, "withdraws from legislative power, state and federal, the exertion of any restraint on the free exercise of religion. Its purpose is to secure religious liberty in the individual by prohibiting any invasions thereof by civil authority." Abington School Dist. v. Schempp, 374 U.S. 203, 222–223 (1963). Indeed, "[a] regulation neutral on its face may, in its application, nonetheless offend the constitutional requirement for governmental neutrality if it unduly burdens the free exercise of religion." Wisconsin v. Yoder, 406 U.S. 205, 220 (1972). Our cases have established that "[t]he free exercise inquiry asks whether government has placed a substantial burden on the observation of a central religious belief or practice and, if so, whether a compelling governmental interest justifies the burden." * * *

Appellant relies almost exclusively on our decisions in Murdock v. Pennsylvania, 319 U.S. 105 (1943), and Follett v. McCormick, 321 U.S. 573, 576 (1944), for the proposition that a State may not impose a sales or use tax on the evangelical distribution of religious material by a religious organization. Appellant contends that the State's imposition of use and sales tax liability on it burdens its evangelical distribution of religious materials in a manner identical to the manner in which the evangelists in *Murdock* and *Follett* were burdened.

We reject appellant's expansive reading of *Murdock* and *Follett* as contrary to the decisions themselves. In *Murdock,* we considered the constitutionality of a city ordinance requiring all persons canvassing or soliciting within the city to procure a license by paying a flat fee. Reversing the convictions of Jehovah's Witnesses convicted under the ordinance of soliciting and distributing religious literature without a license, we explained:

> "The hand distribution of religious tracts is an age-old form of missionary evangelism * * * [and] has been a potent force in various religious movements down through the years. This form of evangelism is utilized today on a large scale by various religious sects whose colporteurs carry the Gospel to thousands upon thousands of homes and seek through personal visitations to win adherents to their faith. It is more than preaching; it is more than distribution of religious literature. It is a combination of both. Its purpose is as evangelical as the revival meeting. This form of religious activity occupies the same high estate under the First Amendment as do worship in the churches and preaching in the pulpits." 319 U.S., at 108–109 (footnotes omitted).

Accordingly, we held that "spreading one's religious beliefs or preaching the Gospel through distribution of religious literature and through personal visitation is an age-old type of evangelism with as high a claim to constitutional protection as the more orthodox types." * * *

We extended *Murdock* the following Term by invalidating, as applied to "one who earns his livelihood as an evangelist or preacher in his home town," an ordinance (similar to that involved in *Murdock*) that required all booksellers to pay a flat fee to procure a license to sell books. Follett v. McCormick, 321 U.S., at 576. * * *

Our decisions in these cases, however, resulted from the particular nature of the challenged taxes—flat license taxes that operated as a prior restraint on the exercise of religious liberty. In *Murdock,* for instance, we emphasized that the tax at issue was "a license tax—a flat tax imposed on the exercise of a privilege granted by the Bill of Rights," 319 U.S., at 113, and cautioned that "[w]e do not mean to say that religious groups and the press are free from all financial burdens of government. * * * We have here something quite different, for example, from a tax on the income of one who engages in religious activities or a tax on property used or employed in connection with those activities." * * * In *Follett,* we reiterated that a preacher is not "free from all financial burdens of government, including taxes on income or property" and, "like other citizens, may be subject to *general* taxation." 321 U.S., at 578 (emphasis added).

Significantly, we noted in both cases that a primary vice of the ordinances at issue was that they operated as prior restraints of constitutionally protected conduct:

"In all of these cases [in which license taxes have been invalidated] the issuance of the permit or license is dependent on the payment of a license tax. And the license tax is fixed in amount and unrelated to the scope of the activities of petitioners or to their realized revenues. It is not a nominal fee imposed as a regulatory measure to defray the expenses of policing the activities in question. It is in no way apportioned. It is a flat license tax levied and collected as a condition to the pursuit of activities whose enjoyment is guaranteed by the First Amendment. Accordingly, *it restrains in advance those constitutional liberties of press and religion and inevitably tends to suppress their exercise.* That is almost uniformly recognized as the inherent vice and evil of this flat license tax." *Murdock, supra,* at 113–114 (emphasis added).

* * * Thus, although *Murdock* and *Follett* establish that appellant's form of religious exercise has "as high a claim to constitutional protection as the more orthodox types," *Murdock, supra,* at 110, those cases are of no further help to appellant. Our concern in *Murdock* and *Follett*—that a flat license tax would act as a precondition to the free exercise of religious beliefs—is simply not present where a tax applies to all sales and uses of tangible personal property in the State.

Our reading of *Murdock* and *Follett* is confirmed by our decision in Minnesota Star & Tribune Co. v. Minnesota Commissioner of Revenue, 460 U.S. 575 (1983), where we considered a newspaper's First Amendment challenge to a state use tax on ink and paper products used in the production of periodic publications. In the course of striking down the tax, we rejected the newspaper's suggestion, premised on *Murdock* and *Follett,* that a generally applicable sales tax could not be applied to publications. Construing those cases as involving "a flat tax, unrelated to the receipts or income of the speaker or to the expenses of administering a valid regulatory scheme, as a *condition* of the right to speak," 460 U.S., at 587, n. 9 (emphasis in original), we noted:

"By imposing the tax as a condition of engaging in protected activity, the defendants in those cases imposed a form of prior restraint on speech, rendering the tax highly susceptible to constitutional challenge. In that regard, the cases cited by Star Tribune do not resemble a generally applicable sales tax. Indeed, our cases have consistently recognized that nondiscriminatory taxes on the receipts or income of newspapers would be permissible." *Ibid.* (citations omitted).

Accord Arkansas Writers' Project, Inc. v. Ragland, 481 U.S. 221, 229 (1987) ("a genuinely nondiscriminatory tax on the receipts of newspapers would be constitutionally permissible").

* * *

* * * California's generally applicable sales and use tax is not a flat tax, represents only a small fraction of any retail sale, and applies neutrally to all retail sales of tangible personal property made in California. California imposes its sales and use tax even if the seller or the purchaser is charitable, religious, nonprofit, or state or local governmental in nature. * * * Thus, the sales and use tax is not a tax on the right to disseminate religious information, ideas, or beliefs per se; rather, it is a tax on the privilege of making retail sales of tangible personal property and on the storage, use, or other consumption of tangible personal property in California. For example, California treats the sale of a bible by a religious organization just as it would treat the sale of a bible by a bookstore; as long as both are in-state retail sales of tangible personal property, they are both subject to the tax regardless of the motivation for the sale or the purchase. There is no danger that appellant's religious activity is being singled out for special and burdensome treatment.

Moreover, our concern in *Murdock* and *Follett* that flat license taxes operate as a precondition to the exercise of evangelistic activity is not present in this case, because the registration requirement, * * *, and the tax itself do not act as prior restraints—no fee is charged for registering, the tax is due regardless of preregistration, and the tax is not imposed as a precondition of disseminating the message. Thus, unlike the license tax in *Murdock,* which was "in no way apportioned" to the "realized revenues" of the itinerant preachers forced to pay the tax, 319 U.S., at 113–114; * * *

* * * There is no evidence in this case that collection and payment of the tax violates appellant's sincere religious beliefs. California's nondiscriminatory sales and use tax law requires only that appellant collect the tax from its California purchasers and remit the tax money to the State. The only burden on appellant is the claimed reduction in income resulting from the presumably lower demand for appellant's wares (caused by the marginally higher price) and from the costs associated with administering the tax. * * *

* * * At bottom, though we do not doubt the economic cost to appellant of complying with a generally applicable sales and use tax, such a tax is no different from other generally applicable laws and regulations—such as health and safety regulations—to which appellant must adhere.

Finally, because appellant's religious beliefs do not forbid payment of the sales and use tax, appellant's reliance on Sherbert v. Verner, 374 U.S. 398 (1963), and its progeny is misplaced, because in no sense has the State " 'condition[ed] receipt of an important benefit upon conduct proscribed by a religious faith, or * * * denie[d] such a benefit because of conduct mandated by religious belief, thereby putting substantial pressure on an adherent to modify his behavior and to violate his beliefs.' " * * * Appellant has never alleged that the mere act of paying the tax, by itself, violates its sincere religious beliefs.

We therefore conclude that the collection and payment of the generally applicable tax in this case imposes no constitutionally significant burden on appellant's religious practices or beliefs. The Free Exercise Clause accordingly does not require the State to grant appellant an exemption from its generally applicable sales and use tax. Although it is of course possible to imagine that a more onerous tax rate, even if generally applicable, might effectively choke off an adherent's religious practices, cf. *Murdock,* 319 U.S., at 115 (the burden of a flat tax could render itinerant evangelism "crushed and closed out by the sheer weight of the toll or tribute which is exacted town by town"), we face no such situation in this case. Accordingly, we intimate no views as to whether such a generally applicable tax might violate the Free Exercise Clause.

B

Appellant also contends that application of the sales and use tax to its sale of religious materials violates the Establishment Clause because it fosters "'an excessive government entanglement with religion,'" Lemon v. Kurtzman, 403 U.S. 602, 613 (1971) (quoting Walz v. Tax Comm'n of New York City, 397 U.S. 664, 674 (1970)). Appellant alleges, for example, that the present controversy has featured on-site inspections of appellant's evangelistic crusades, lengthy on-site audits, examinations of appellant's books and records, threats of criminal prosecution, and layers of administrative and judicial proceedings.

* * * The issue presented, therefore, is whether the imposition of sales and use tax liability in this case on appellant results in "excessive" involvement between appellant and the State and "continuing surveillance leading to an impermissible degree of entanglement."

At the outset, it is undeniable that a generally applicable tax has a secular purpose and neither advances nor inhibits religion, for the very essence of such a tax is that it is neutral and nondiscriminatory on questions of religious belief. * * *

Even applying the "excessive entanglement" prong of the *Lemon* test, however, we hold that California's imposition of sales and use tax liability on appellant threatens no excessive entanglement between church and state. First, we note that the evidence of administrative entanglement in this case is thin. Appellant alleges that collection and payment of the sales and use tax impose severe accounting burdens on it. The Court of Appeal, however, expressly found that the record did not support appellant's factual assertions, noting that appellant "had a sophisticated accounting staff and had recently computerized its accounting and that [appellant] in its own books and for purposes of obtaining a federal income tax exemption segregated 'retail sales' and 'donations.'" 204 Cal.App.3d, at 1289, 250 Cal.Rptr., at 905.

Second, even assuming that the tax imposes substantial administrative burdens on appellant, such administrative and recordkeeping burdens do not rise to a continually significant level. Collection and payment of the tax will of course require some contact between appellant and the State, but we have held that generally applicable administrative and recordkeeping regulations may be imposed on religious organization without running afoul of the Establishment Clause. See *Hernandez,* 490 U.S., at ___-___ ("[R]outine regulatory interaction [such as application of neutral tax laws] which involves no inquiries into religious doctrine, * * * no delegation of state power to a religious body, * * * and no 'detailed monitoring and close administrative contact' between secular and religious bodies, * * * does not of itself violate the nonentanglement command"); Tony and Susan Alamo Foundation v. Secretary of Labor, 471 U.S. 290, 305–306 (1985) ("The Establishment Clause does not exempt religious organizations from such secular governmental activity as fire inspections and building and zoning regulations, Lemon, supra, at 614, and the recordkeeping requirements of the Fair Labor Standards Act, while perhaps more burdensome in terms of paperwork, are not significantly more intrusive into religious affairs"). * * *

* * *

Most significantly, the imposition of the sales and use tax without an exemption for appellant does not require the State to inquire into the religious content of the items sold or the religious motivation for selling or purchasing the items, because the materials are subject to the tax regardless of content or motive. From the State's point of view, the critical question is not whether the materials are religious, but whether there is a sale or a use, a question which involves only a secular determination. * * * Although appellant asserts that donations often accompany payments made for the religious items and that items are sometimes given away without payment (or only nominal payment), it is plain that, in the first case, appellant's use of "order forms" and "price lists" renders illusory any difficulty in separating the two portions and that, in the second case, the question is only whether any particular transfer constitutes a "sale." Ironically, appellant's theory, under which government may not tax "religious core" activities but may tax "nonreligious" activities, would require government to do precisely what appellant asserts the Religion Clauses prohibit: "determine which expenditures are religious and which are secular." *Lemon,* 403 U.S., at 621–622.

Accordingly, because we find no excessive entanglement between government and religion in this case, we hold that the imposition of sales and use tax liability on appellant does not violate the Establishment Clause.

* * *

The judgment of the California Court of Appeal is affirmed.

EMPLOYMENT DIVISION, DEPARTMENT OF HUMAN RESOURCES OF OREGON v. SMITH

Supreme Court of the United States, 1990.
494 U.S. ___, 110 S.Ct. 1595, 108 L.Ed.2d 876.

Respondents Smith and Black were fired by a private drug rehabilitation organization because they ingested peyote, a hallucinogenic drug, for sacramental purposes at a ceremony of their Native American Church. Their applications for unemployment compensation were denied by the State of Oregon under a state law disqualifying employees discharged for work-related "misconduct." Holding that the denials violated respondents' First Amendment free exercise rights, the State

Court of Appeals reversed. The State Supreme Court affirmed, but this Court vacated the judgment and remanded for a determination whether sacramental peyote use is proscribed by the State's controlled substance law, which makes it a felony to knowingly or intentionally possess the drug. Pending that determination, the Court refused to decide whether such use is protected by the Constitution. On remand, the State Supreme Court held that sacramental peyote use violated, and was not excepted from, the state-law prohibition, but concluded that the prohibition was invalid under the Free Exercise Clause.

SCALIA, J., delivered the opinion of the Court, in which REHNQUIST, C.J., and WHITE, STEVENS, and KENNEDY, JJ., joined. O'CONNOR, J., filed an opinion concurring in the judgment, in Parts I and II of which BRENNAN, MARSHALL, and BLACKMUN, JJ., joined without concurring in the judgment. BLACKMUN, J., filed a dissenting opinion, in which BRENNAN and MARSHALL, JJ., joined.

ON WRIT OF CERTIORARI TO THE SUPREME COURT OF OREGON.

MR. JUSTICE SCALIA delivered the opinion of the Court.

This case requires us to decide whether the Free Exercise Clause of the First Amendment permits the State of Oregon to include religiously inspired peyote use within the reach of its general criminal prohibition on use of that drug, and thus permits the State to deny unemployment benefits to persons dismissed from their jobs because of such religiously inspired use.

* * *

The Free Exercise Clause of the First Amendment, which has been made applicable to the States by incorporation into the Fourteenth Amendment, see Cantwell v. Connecticut, 310 U.S. 296, 303 (1940), provides that "Congress shall make no law respecting an establishment of religion, or prohibiting the free exercise thereof. * * * " U.S. Const. Am. I * * *. The free exercise of religion means, first and foremost, the right to believe and profess whatever religious doctrine one desires. Thus, the First Amendment obviously excludes all "governmental regulation of religious beliefs as such." *Sherbert v. Verner, supra*, at 402. The government may not compel affirmation of religious belief, see Torcaso v. Watkins, 367 U.S. 488 (1961), punish the expression of religious doctrines it believes to be false, United States v. Ballard, 322 U.S. 78, 86–88 (1944), impose special disabilities on the basis of religious views or religious status, see McDaniel v. Paty, 435 U.S. 618 (1978); Fowler v. Rhode Island, 345 U.S. 67, 69 (1953); cf. Larson v. Valente, 456 U.S. 228, 245 (1982), or lend its power to one or the other side in controversies over religious authority or dogma, see Presbyterian Church v. Hull Church, 393 U.S. 440, 445–452 (1969); Kedroff v. St. Nicholas Cathedral, 344 U.S. 94, 95–119 (1952); Serbian Eastern Orthodox Diocese v. Milivojevich, 426 U.S. 696, 708–725 (1976).

But the "exercise of religion" often involves not only belief and profession but the performance of (or abstention from) physical acts: assembling with others for a worship service, participating in sacramental use of bread and wine, proselytizing, abstaining from certain foods or certain modes of transportation. It would be true, we think (though no case of ours has involved the point), that a state would be "prohibiting the free exercise [of religion]" if it sought to ban such acts or abstentions only when they are engaged in for religious reasons, or only because of the religious belief that they display. It would doubtless be unconstitutional, for example, to ban the casting of "statues that are to be used for worship purposes," or to prohibit bowing down before a golden calf.

Respondents in the present case, however, seek to carry the meaning of "prohibiting the free exercise [of religion]" one large step further. They contend that their religious motivation for using peyote places them beyond the reach of a criminal law that is not specifically directed at their religious practice, and that is concededly constitutional as applied to those who use the drug for other reasons. They assert, in other words, that "prohibiting the free exercise [of religion]" includes requiring any individual to observe a generally applicable law that requires (or forbids) the performance of an act that his religious belief forbids (or requires). As a textual matter, we do not think the words must be given that meaning. It is no more necessary to regard the collection of a general tax, for example, as "prohibiting the free exercise [of religion]" by those citizens who believe support of organized government to be sinful, than it is to regard the same tax as "abridging the freedom * * * of the press" of those publishing companies that must pay the tax as a condition of staying in business. It is a permissible reading of the text, in the one case as in the other, to say that if prohibiting the exercise of religion (or burdening the activity of printing) is not the object of the tax but merely the incidental effect of a generally applicable and otherwise valid provision, the First Amendment has not been offended. * * *

Our decisions reveal that the latter reading is the correct one. We have never held that an individual's religious beliefs excuse him from compliance with an otherwise valid law prohibiting conduct that the State is free to regulate. On the contrary, the record of more than a century of our free exercise jurisprudence contradicts that proposition. As described succinctly by Justice Frankfurter in Minersville School Dist. Bd. of Educ. v. Gobitis, 310 U.S. 586, 594–595 (1940): "Conscientious scruples have not, in the course of the long struggle for religious toleration, relieved the individual from obedience to a general law not aimed at the promotion or restriction of religious beliefs. The mere possession of religious convictions which contradict the relevant concerns of a political society does not relieve the citizen from the discharge of political responsibilities (footnote omitted)." We first had occasion to assert that principle in Reynolds v. United States, 98 U.S. 145 (1879), where we rejected the claim that criminal laws against polygamy could not be constitutionally applied to those whose religion commanded the practice. "Laws," we said, "are made for the government of actions, and while they cannot interfere with mere religious belief and opinions, they may with practices. * * * Can a man excuse his practices to the contrary because of his religious belief? To permit this would be to make the professed doctrines of religious belief superior to the law of the land, and in effect to permit every citizen to become a law unto himself." *Id.*, at 166–167.

Subsequent decisions have consistently held that the right of free exercise does not relieve an individual of the obligation to comply with a "valid and neutral law of general applicability on the ground that the law proscribes (or prescribes) conduct that his religion prescribes (or proscribes)." United States v. Lee, 455 U.S. 252, 263, n. 3 (1982) * * *.

The only decisions in which we have held that the First Amendment bars application of a neutral, generally applicable law to religiously motivated action have involved not the Free Exercise Clause alone, but the Free Exercise Clause in conjunction with other constitutional protections, such as freedom of speech and of the press, see Cantwell v. Connecticut, 310 U.S. at 304–307 * * * or the right of parents, acknowledged in Pierce v. Society of Sisters, 268 U.S. 510 (1925), to direct the education of their children, see Wisconsin v. Yoder, 406 U.S. 205 (1972) (invalidating compulsory school-attendance laws as applied to Amish parents who refused on religious grounds to send their children to school). * * *

Yoder said that "the Court's holding in *Pierce* stands as a charter of the rights of parents to direct the religious upbringing of their children. And, when the interests of parenthood are combined with a free exercise claim of the nature revealed by this record, more than merely a 'reasonable relation to some purpose within the competency of the State' is required to sustain the validity of the State's requirement under the First Amendment." 406 U.S., at 233.

The present case does not present such a hybrid situation, but a free exercise claim unconnected with any communicative activity or parental right. Respondents urge us to hold, quite simply, that when otherwise prohibitable conduct is accompanied by religious convictions, not only the convictions but the conduct itself must be free from governmental regulation. We have never held that, and decline to do so now. There being no contention that Oregon's drug law represents an attempt to regulate religious beliefs, the communication of religious beliefs, or the raising of one's children in those beliefs, the rule to which we have adhered ever since *Reynolds* plainly controls. * * *

B

Respondents argue that even though exemption from generally applicable criminal laws need not automatically be extended to religiously motivated actors, at least the claim for a religious exemption must be evaluated under the balancing test set forth in Sherbert v. Verner, 374 U.S. 398 (1963). * * * In recent years we have abstained from applying the *Sherbert* test (outside the unemployment compensation field) at all. * * *

Even if we were inclined to breathe into *Sherbert* some life beyond the unemployment compensation field, we would not apply it to require exemptions from a generally applicable criminal law. The *Sherbert* test, it must be recalled, was developed in a context that lent itself to individualized governmental assessment of the reasons for the relevant conduct. As a plurality of the Court noted in *Roy,* a distinctive feature of unemployment compensation programs is that their eligibility criteria invite consideration of the particular circumstances behind an applicant's unemployment: "The statutory conditions [in *Sherbert* and *Thomas*] provided that a person was not eligible for unemployment compensation benefits if, 'without good cause,' he had quit work or refused available work. The 'good cause' standard created a mechanism for individualized exemptions." * * *

Whether or not the decisions are that limited, they at least have nothing to do with an across-the-board criminal prohibition on a particular form of conduct. * * * We conclude today that the sounder approach, and the approach in accord with the vast majority of our precedents, is to hold the test inapplicable to such challenges. The government's ability to enforce generally applicable prohibitions of socially harmful conduct, like its ability to carry out other aspects of public policy, "cannot depend on measuring the effects of a governmental action on a religious objector's spiritual development." *Lyng, supra,* at 451. To make an individual's obligation to obey such a law contingent upon the law's coincidence with his religious beliefs, except where the State's interest is "compelling"—permitting him, by virtue of his beliefs, "to become a law unto himself," Reynolds v. United States, 98 U.S., at 167—contradicts both constitutional tradition and common sense.

The "compelling government interest" requirement seems benign, because it is familiar from other fields. But using it as the standard that must be met before the government may accord different treatment on the basis of race, see, e.g., Palmore v. Sidoti, 466 U.S. 429, 432 (1984), or before the government may regulate the content of speech, see, e.g., Sable Communications of California v. FCC, 492 U.S. ___, ___ (1989), is not remotely comparable to using it for the purpose asserted here. What it produces in those other fields—equality of treatment, and an unrestricted flow of contending speech—are constitutional norms; what it would produce here—a private right to ignore generally applicable laws—is a constitutional anomaly.[3]

---

3. Justice O'Connor suggests that "[t]here is nothing talismanic about neutral laws of general applicability," and that all laws burdening religious practices should be subject to compelling-interest scrutiny because "the First Amendment unequivocally makes freedom of religion, like freedom from race discrimination and freedom of speech, a 'constitutional norm,' not an 'anomaly.'" * * * (O'CONNOR, J., concurring). But this comparison with other fields supports, rather than undermines, the conclusion we draw today. Just as we subject to the most exacting scrutiny laws that make classifications based on race, see *Palmore v. Sidoti, supra,* or on the content of speech, see *Sable Communications, supra,* so too we strictly scrutinize governmental classifications based on religion, see McDaniel v. Paty, 435 U.S. 618 (1978); see also Torcaso v. Watkins, 367 U.S. 488 (1961). But we have held that race-neutral laws that have the effect of disproportionately disadvantaging a particular racial group do not thereby become subject to compelling-interest analysis under the Equal Protection Clause, see Washington v. Davis, 426 U.S. 229 (1976) (police employment examination); and we have held that generally applicable laws unconcerned with regulating speech that have the effect of interfering with speech do not thereby become subject to compelling-interest analysis under the First Amendment, * * *

Nor is it possible to limit the impact of respondents' proposal by requiring a "compelling state interest" only when the conduct prohibited is "central" to the individual's religion. Cf. *Lyng v. Northwest Indian Cemetery Protective Assn., supra,* * * * (BRENNAN, J., dissenting). It is no more appropriate for judges to determine the "centrality" of religious beliefs before applying a "compelling interest" test in the free exercise field, than it would be for them to determine the "importance" of ideas before applying the "compelling interest" test in the free speech field. What principle of law or logic can be brought to bear to contradict a believer's assertion that a particular act is "central" to his personal faith? Judging the centrality of different religious practices is akin to the unacceptable "business of evaluating the relative merits of differing religious claims." United States v. Lee, 455 U.S., at 263 n. 2 (STEVENS, J., concurring). * * *

Nor is this difficulty avoided by Justice Blackmun's assertion that "although courts should refrain from delving into questions of whether, as a matter of religious doctrine, a particular practice is 'central' to the religion, I do not think this means that the courts must turn a blind eye to the severe impact of a State's restrictions on the adherents of a minority religion." * * * (BLACKMUN, J., dissenting). As Justice Blackmun's opinion proceeds to make clear, inquiry into "severe impact" is no different from inquiry into centrality. He has merely substituted for the question "How important is X to the religious adherent?" the question "How great will be the harm to the religious adherent if X is taken away?" There is no material difference.

If the "compelling interest" test is to be applied at all, then, it must be applied across the board, to all actions thought to be religiously commanded. Moreover, if "compelling interest" really means what it says (and watering it down here would subvert its rigor in the other fields where it is applied), many laws will not meet the test. Any society adopting such a system would be courting anarchy, but that danger increases in direct proportion to the society's diversity of religious beliefs, and its determination to coerce or suppress none of them. Precisely because "we are a cosmopolitan nation made up of people of almost every conceivable religious preference," Braunfield v. Brown, 366 U.S., at 606, and precisely because we value and protect that religious divergence, we cannot afford the luxury of deeming presumptively invalid, as applied to the religious objector, every regulation of conduct that does not protect an interest of the highest order. The rule respondents favor would open the prospect of constitutionally required religious exemptions from civic obligations of almost every conceivable kind—ranging from compulsory military service, see, e.g., Gillette v. United States, 401 U.S. 437 (1971), to the payment of taxes, see, e.g., *United States v. Lee, supra;* to health and safety regulation such as manslaughter and child neglect laws, * * * and laws providing for equality of opportunity for the races, see, e.g., Bob Jones University v. United States, 461 U.S. 574, 603–604 (1983). The First Amendment's protection of religious liberty does not require this.[5]

---

5. Justice O'Connor contends that the "parade of horribles" in the text only "demonstrates * * * that courts have been

Values that are protected against government interference through enshrinement in the Bill of Rights are not thereby banished from the political process. Just as a society that believes in the negative protection accorded to the press by the First Amendment is likely to enact laws that affirmatively foster the dissemination of the printed word, so also a society that believes in the negative protection accorded to religious belief can be expected to be solicitous of that value in its legislation as well. It is therefore not surprising that a number of States have made an exception to their drug laws for sacramental peyote use. * * * But to say that a nondiscriminatory religious-practice exemption is permitted, or even that it is desirable, is not to say that it is constitutionally required, and that the appropriate occasions for its creation can be discerned by the courts. It may fairly be said that leaving accommodation to the political process will place at a relative disadvantage those religious practices that are not widely engaged in; but that unavoidable consequence of democratic government must be preferred to a system in which each conscience is a law unto itself or in which judges weigh the social importance of all laws against the centrality of all religious beliefs.

* * *

Because respondents' ingestion of peyote was prohibited under Oregon law, and because that prohibition is constitutional, Oregon may, consistent with the Free Exercise Clause, deny respondents unemployment compensation when their dismissal results from use of the drug. The decision of the Oregon Supreme Court is accordingly reversed.

It is so ordered.

JUSTICE O'CONNOR, with whom JUSTICE BRENNAN, JUSTICE MARSHALL, and JUSTICE BLACKMUN join as to Parts I and II, concurring in the judgment.

* * *

The Court today extracts from our long history of free exercise precedents the single categorical rule that "if prohibiting the exercise of religion * * * is * * * merely the incidental effect of a generally applicable and otherwise valid provision, the First Amendment has not been offended." * * * (citations omitted). Indeed, the Court holds that where the law is a generally applicable criminal prohibition, our usual free exercise jurisprudence does not even apply. * * * To reach this sweeping result, however, the Court must not only give a strained

quite capable of strik[ing] sensible balances between religious liberty and competing state interests." * * * (O'CONNOR, J., concurring). But the cases we cite have struck "sensible balances" only because they have all applied the general laws, despite the claims for religious exemption. In any event, Justice O'Connor mistakes the purpose of our parade: it is not to suggest that courts would necessarily permit harmful exemptions from these laws (though they might), but to suggest that courts would constantly be in the business of determining whether the "severe impact" of various laws on religious practice (to use Justice Blackmun's terminology) or the "constitutiona[l] significan[ce]" of the "burden on the particular plaintiffs" (to use Justice O'Connor's terminology) suffices to permit us to confer an exemption. It is a parade of horribles because it is horrible to contemplate that federal judges will regularly balance against the importance of general laws the significance of religious practice.

reading of the First Amendment but must also disregard our consistent application of free exercise doctrine to cases involving generally applicable regulations that burden religious conduct.

A.

The Free Exercise Clause of the First Amendment commands that "Congress shall make no law * * * prohibiting the free exercise [of religion]." In Cantwell v. Connecticut, 310 U.S. 296 (1940), we held that this prohibition applies to the States by incorporation into the Fourteenth Amendment and that it categorically forbids government regulation of religious beliefs. *Id.*, at 303. As the Court recognizes, however, the "free exercise" of religion often, if not invariably, requires the performance of (or abstention from) certain acts. * * * Because the First Amendment does not distinguish between religious belief and religious conduct, conduct motivated by sincere religious belief, like the belief itself, must therefore be at least presumptively protected by the Free Exercise Clause.

The Court today, however, interprets the Clause to permit the government to prohibit, without justification, conduct mandated by an individual's religious beliefs, so long as that prohibition is generally applicable. * * * But a law that prohibits certain conduct—conduct that happens to be an act of worship for someone—manifestly does prohibit that person's free exercise of his religion. A person who is barred from engaging in religiously motivated conduct is barred from freely exercising his religion. Moreover, that person is barred from freely exercising his religion regardless of whether the law prohibits the conduct only when engaged in for religious reasons, only by members of that religion, or by all persons. It is difficult to deny that a law that prohibits religiously motivated conduct, even if the law is generally applicable, does not at least implicate First Amendment concerns.

The Court responds that generally applicable laws are "one large step" removed from laws aimed at specific religious practices. * * * The First Amendment, however, does not distinguish between laws that are generally applicable and laws that target particular religious practices. Indeed, few States would be so naive as to enact a law directly prohibiting or burdening a religious practice as such. Our free exercise cases have all concerned generally applicable laws that had the effect of significantly burdening a religious practice. If the First Amendment is to have any vitality, it ought not be construed to cover only the extreme and hypothetical situation in which a State directly targets a religious practice. * * *

To say that a person's right to free exercise has been burdened, of course, does not mean that he has an absolute right to engage in the conduct. Under our established First Amendment jurisprudence, we have recognized that the freedom to act, unlike the freedom to believe, cannot be absolute. * * * Instead, we have respected both the First Amendment's express textual mandate and the governmental interest in regulation of conduct by requiring the Government to justify any substantial burden on religiously motivated conduct by a compelling state interest and by means narrowly tailored to achieve that interest.

* * * The compelling interest test effectuates the First Amendment's command that religious liberty is an independent liberty, that it occupies a preferred position, and that the Court will not permit encroachments upon this liberty, whether direct or indirect, unless required by clear and compelling governmental interests "of the highest order," *Yoder, supra,* at 215. * * *

The Court endeavors to escape from our decisions in *Cantwell* and *Yoder* by labeling them "hybrid" decisions, * * *, but there is no denying that both cases expressly relied on the Free Exercise Clause, see *Cantwell,* 310 U.S., at 303–307; *Yoder,* 406 U.S., at 219–229, and that we have consistently regarded those cases as part of the mainstream of our free exercise jurisprudence. Moreover, in each of the other cases cited by the Court to support its categorical rule, *ante,* * * *, we rejected the particular constitutional claims before us only after carefully weighing the competing interests. See Prince v. Massachusetts, 321 U.S. 158, 168–170 (1944) (state interest in regulating children's activities justifies denial of religious exemption from child labor laws); Braunfeld v. Brown, 366 U.S. 599, 608–609 (1961) (plurality opinion) (state interest in uniform day of rest justifies denial of religious exemption from Sunday closing law); * * *

B

Respondents, of course, do not contend that their conduct is automatically immune from all governmental regulation simply because it is motivated by their sincere religious beliefs. The Court's rejection of that argument, * * *, might therefore be regarded as merely harmless dictum. Rather, respondents invoke our traditional compelling interest test to argue that the Free Exercise Clause requires the State to grant them a limited exemption from its general criminal prohibition against the possession of peyote. The Court today, however, denies them even the opportunity to make that argument, concluding that "the sounder approach, and the approach in accord with the vast majority of our precedents, is to hold the [compelling interest] test inapplicable to" challenges to general criminal prohibitions. * * *

In my view, however, the essence of a free exercise claim is relief from a burden imposed by government on religious practices or beliefs, whether the burden is imposed directly through laws that prohibit or compel specific religious practices, or indirectly through laws that, in effect, make abandonment of one's own religious or conformity to the religious beliefs of others the price of an equal place in the civil community. * * *

Indeed, we have never distinguished between cases in which a State conditions receipt of a benefit on conduct prohibited by religious beliefs and cases in which a State affirmatively prohibits such conduct. The *Sherbert* compelling interest test applies in both kinds of cases. * * * I would reaffirm that principle today: a neutral criminal law prohibiting conduct that a State may legitimately regulate is, if anything, more burdensome than a neutral civil statute placing legitimate conditions on the award of a state benefit.

* * * Once it has been shown that a government regulation or criminal prohibition burdens the free exercise of religion, we have consistently asked the Government to demonstrate that unbending application of its regulation to the religious objector "is essential to accomplish an overriding governmental interest," *Lee, supra,* at 257–258, or represents "the least restrictive means of achieving some compelling state interest," *Thomas,* 450 U.S., at 718. * * * To me, the sounder approach—the approach more consistent with our role as judges to decide each case on its individual merits—is to apply this test in each case to determine whether the burden on the specific plaintiffs before us is constitutionally significant and whether the particular criminal interest asserted by the State before us is compelling. Even if, as an empirical matter, a government's criminal laws might usually serve a compelling interest in health, safety, or public order, the First Amendment at least requires a case-by-case determination of the question, sensitive to the facts of each particular claim. * * *

* * *

The Court today gives no convincing reason to depart from settled First Amendment jurisprudence. There is nothing talismanic about neutral laws of general applicability or general criminal prohibitions, for laws neutral toward religion can coerce a person to violate his religious conscience or intrude upon his religious duties just as effectively as laws aimed at religion. * * *

Finally, the Court today suggests that the disfavoring of minority religions is an "unavoidable consequence" under our system of government and that accommodation of such religions must be left to the political process. * * * In my view, however, the First Amendment was enacted precisely to protect the rights of those whose religious practices are not shared by the majority and may be viewed with hostility. The history of our free exercise doctrine amply demonstrates the harsh impact majoritarian rule has had on unpopular or emerging religious groups such as the Jehovah's Witnesses and the Amish. Indeed, the words of Justice Jackson in *West Virginia Board of Education v. Barnette* (overruling *Minersville School District v. Gobitis,* * * *) are apt:

> "The very purpose of a Bill of Rights was to withdraw certain subjects from the vicissitudes of political controversy, to place them beyond the reach of majorities and officials and to establish them as legal principles to be applied by the courts. One's right to life, liberty, and property, to free speech, a free press, freedom of worship and assembly, and other fundamental rights may not be submitted to vote; they depend on the outcome of no elections."

* * *

III

The Court's holding today not only misreads settled First Amendment precedent; it appears to be unnecessary to this case. I would

A

There is no dispute that Oregon's criminal prohibition of peyote places a severe burden on the ability of respondents to freely exercise their religion. Peyote is a sacrament of the Native American Church and is regarded as vital to respondents' ability to practice their religion. See O. Stewart, Peyote Religion: A History 327–336 (1987) * * * see also People v. Woody, 61 Cal.2d 716, 721–722, 394 P.2d 813, 817–818 (1964). As we noted in *Smith* I, the Oregon Supreme Court concluded that "the Native American Church is a recognized religion, that peyote is a sacrament of that church, and that respondent's beliefs were sincerely held." 485 U.S., at 667. Under Oregon law, as construed by that State's highest court, members of the Native American Church must choose between carrying out the ritual embodying their religious beliefs and avoidance of criminal prosecution. That choice is, in my view, more than sufficient to trigger First Amendment scrutiny.

There is also no dispute that Oregon has a significant interest in enforcing laws that control the possession and use of controlled substances by its citizens. * * * In light of our recent decisions holding that the governmental interests in the collection of income tax, *Hernandez,* 490 U.S., at ___, a comprehensive social security system, see *Lee,* 455 U.S., at 258–259, and military conscription, see *Gillette,* 401 U.S., at 460, are compelling, respondents do not seriously dispute that Oregon has a compelling interest in prohibiting the possession of peyote by its citizens.

B

Thus, the critical question in this case is whether exempting respondents from the State's general criminal prohibition "will unduly interfere with fulfillment of the governmental interest." *Lee, supra,* at 259; see also *Roy,* 476 U.S., at 727 ("[T]he Government must accommodate a legitimate free exercise claim unless pursuing an especially important interest by narrowly tailored means"); *Yoder,* 406 U.S., at 221; *Braunfeld,* 366 U.S., at 605–607. Although the question is close, I would conclude that uniform application of Oregon's criminal prohibition is "essential to accomplish" *Lee, supra,* at 257, its overriding interest in preventing the physical harm caused by the use of a Schedule I controlled substance. Oregon's criminal prohibition represents that State's judgment that the possession and use of controlled substances, even by only one person, is inherently harmful and dangerous. Because the health effects caused by the use of controlled substances exist regardless of the motivation of the user, the use of such substances, even for religious purposes, violates the very purpose of the laws that prohibit them. * * * Moreover, in view of the societal interest in preventing trafficking in controlled substances, uniform application of the criminal prohibition at issue is essential to the effectiveness of Oregon's stated interest in preventing any possession of peyote. * * *

For these reasons, I believe that granting a selective exemption in this case would seriously impair Oregon's compelling interest in prohibiting possession of peyote by its citizens. Under such circumstances, the Free Exercise Clause does not require the State to accommodate respondents' religiously motivated conduct. * * * Unlike in *Yoder,* where we noted that "[t]he record strongly indicates that accommodating the religious objections of the Amish by forgoing one, or at most two, additional years of compulsory education will not impair the physical or mental health of the child, or result in an inability to be self-supporting or to discharge the duties and responsibilities of citizenship, or in any other way materially detract from the welfare of society," * * *, a religious exemption in this case would be incompatible with the State's interest in controlling use and possession of illegal drugs.

Respondents contend that any incompatibility is belied by the fact that the Federal Government and several States provide exemptions for the religious use of peyote, * * * But other governments may surely choose to grant an exemption without Oregon, with its specific asserted interest in uniform application of its drug laws, being required to do so by the First Amendment. Respondents also note that the sacramental use of peyote is central to the tenets of the Native American Church, but I agree with the Court, * * *, that because "[i]t is not within the judicial ken to question the centrality of particular beliefs or practices to a faith," *Hernandez, supra,* at (slip op., at 17), our determination of the constitutionality of Oregon's general criminal prohibition cannot, and should not, turn on the centrality of the particular religious practice at issue. * * *

I would therefore adhere to our established free exercise jurisprudence and hold that the State in this case has a compelling interest in regulating peyote use by its citizens and that accommodating respondents' religiously motivated conduct "will unduly interfere with fulfillment of the governmental interest." *Lee,* 455 U.S., at 259. Accordingly, I concur in the judgment of the Court.

JUSTICE BLACKMUN, with whom JUSTICE BRENNAN and JUSTICE MARSHALL join, dissenting.

This Court over the years painstakingly has developed a consistent and exacting standard to test the constitutionality of a state statute that burdens the free exercise of religion. Such a statute may stand only if the law in general, and the State's refusal to allow a religious exemption in particular, are justified by a compelling interest that cannot be served by less restrictive means.

Until today, I thought this was a settled and inviolate principle of this Court's First Amendment jurisprudence. The majority, however, perfunctorily dismisses it as a "constitutional anomaly." * * * As carefully detailed in Justice O'Connor's concurring opinion, *ante,* the majority is able to arrive at this view only by mischaracterizing this Court's precedents. The Court discards leading free exercise cases such as Cantwell v. Connecticut, 310 U.S. 296 (1940), and Wisconsin v. Yoder, 406 U.S. 205 (1972), as "hybrid." * * * The Court cites cases in which, due to various exceptional circumstances, we found strict scrutiny inapposite, to hint that the Court has repudiated that standard altogether. * * * In short, it effectuates a wholesale overturning of settled law concerning the Religion Clauses of our Constitution. One hopes that the Court is aware of the consequences, and that its result is not a product of overreaction to the serious problems the country's drug crisis has generated.

* * * I do not believe the Founders thought their dearly bought freedom from religious persecution a "luxury," but an essential element of liberty—and they could not have thought religious intolerance "unavoidable," for they drafted the Religion Clauses precisely in order to avoid that intolerance.

For these reasons, I agree with Justice O'Connor's analysis of the applicable free exercise doctrine, and I join parts I and II of her opinion. As she points out, "the critical question in this case is whether exempting respondents from the State's general criminal prohibition 'will unduly interfere with fulfillment of the governmental interest.'" * * *, quoting United States v. Lee, 455 U.S. 252, 259 (1982). I do disagree, however, with her specific answer to that question.

I

In weighing respondents' clear interest in the free exercise of their religion against Oregon's asserted interest in enforcing its drug laws, it is important to articulate in precise terms the state interest involved. It is not the State's broad interest in fighting the critical "war on drugs" that must be weighed against respondents' claim, but the State's narrow interest in refusing to make an exception for the religious, ceremonial use of peyote. * * * Failure to reduce the competing interests to the same plane of generality tends to distort the weighing process in the State's favor. See Clark, Guidelines for the Free Exercise Clause, 83 Harv.L.Rev. 327, 330–331 (1969) ("The purpose of almost any law can be traced back to one or another of the fundamental concerns of government: public health and safety, public peace and order, defense, revenue. To measure an individual interest directly against one of these rarified values inevitably makes the individual interest appear the less significant"); Pound, A Survey of Social Interests, 57 Harv.L.Rev. 1, 2 (1943) ("When it comes to weighing or valuing claims or demands with respect to other claims or demands, we must be careful to compare them on the same plane * * * [or else] we may decide the question in advance in our very way of putting it").

It is surprising, to say the least, that this Court which so often prides itself about principles of judicial restraint and reduction of federal control over matters of state law would stretch its jurisdiction to the limit in order to reach, in this abstract setting, the constitutionality of Oregon's criminal prohibition of peyote use.

The State's interest in enforcing its prohibition, in order to be sufficiently compelling to outweigh a free exercise claim, cannot be merely abstract or symbolic. The State cannot plausibly assert that unbending application of a criminal prohibition is essential to fulfill any compelling interest, if it does not, in fact, attempt to enforce that prohibition. In this case, the State actually has not evinced any concrete interest in enforcing its drug laws against religious users of peyote. Oregon has never sought to prosecute respondents, and does not claim that it has made significant enforcement efforts against other religious users of peyote. * * *

Similarly, this Court's prior decisions have not allowed a government to rely on mere speculation about potential harms, but have demanded evidentiary support for a refusal to allow a religious exception. * * *

The fact that peyote is classified as a Schedule I controlled substance does not, by itself, show that any and all uses of peyote, in any circumstance, are inherently harmful and dangerous. The Federal Government, which created the classifications of unlawful drugs from which Oregon's drug laws are derived, apparently does not find peyote so dangerous as to preclude an exemption for religious use. * * *

Moreover, 23 States, including many that have significant Native American populations, have statutory or judicially crafted exemptions in their drug laws for religious use of peyote. * * * Although this does not prove that Oregon must have such an exception too, it is significant that these States, and the Federal Government, all find their (presumably compelling) interests in controlling the use of dangerous drugs compatible with an exemption for religious use of peyote. * * *

The carefully circumscribed ritual context in which respondents used peyote is far removed from the irresponsible and unrestricted recreational use of unlawful drugs.[6] * * *

Moreover, just as in *Yoder,* the values and interests of those seeking a religious exemption in this case are congruent, to a great degree, with those the State seeks to promote through its drug laws. * * * Not only does the Church's doctrine forbid nonreligious use of peyote; it also generally advocates self-reliance, familial responsibility, and abstinence from alcohol. * * * Far from promoting the lawless and irresponsible use of drugs, Native American Church members' spiritual code exemplifies values that Oregon's drug laws are presumably intended to foster.

The State also seeks to support its refusal to make an exception for religious use of peyote by invoking its interest in abolishing drug trafficking. There is, however, practically no illegal traffic in peyote. See *Olsen,* 878 F.2d, at 1463, 1467 (quoting DEA Final Order to the effect that total amount of peyote seized and analyzed by federal authorities between 1980 and 1987 was 19.4 pounds; in contrast, total amount of marijuana seized during that period was over 15 million pounds). Also, the availability of peyote for religious use, even if

---

6. In this respect, respondents' use of peyote seems closely analogous to the sacramental use of wine by the Roman Catholic Church. During Prohibition, the Federal Government exempted such use of wine from its general ban on possession and use of alcohol. See National Prohibition Act, Title II, § 3, 41 Stat. 308. However compelling the Government's then general interest in prohibiting the use of alcohol may have been, it could not plausibly have asserted an interest sufficiently compelling to outweigh Catholics' right to take communion.

Oregon were to allow an exemption from its criminal laws, would still be strictly controlled by federal regulations, see 21 U.S.C. §§ 821–823 (registration requirements for distribution of controlled substances); 21 CFR § 1307.31 (1989) (distribution of peyote to Native American Church subject to registration requirements), and by the State of Texas, the only State in which peyote grows in significant quantities. See Texas Health & Safety Code, § 481.111 (1990); Texas Admin.Code, Tit. 37, pt. 1, ch. 13, Controlled Substances Regulations, §§ 13.35–13.41 (1989); *Woody,* 61 Cal.2d, at 720, 394 P.2d, at 816 (peyote is "found in the Rio Grande Valley of Texas and northern Mexico"). Peyote simply is not a popular drug; its distribution for use in religious rituals has nothing to do with the vast and violent traffic in illegal narcotics that plagues this country.

Finally, the State argues that granting an exception for religious peyote use would erode its interest in the uniform, fair, and certain enforcement of its drug laws. The State fears that, if it grants an exemption for religious peyote use, a flood of other claims to religious exemptions will follow. It would then be placed in a dilemma, it says, between allowing a patchwork of exemptions that would hinder its law enforcement efforts, and risking a violation of the Establishment Clause by arbitrarily limiting its religious exemptions. This argument, however, could be made in almost any free exercise case. See Lupu, Where Rights Begin: The Problem of Burdens on the Free Exercise of Religion, 102 Harv.L.Rev. 933, 947 (1989) ("Behind every free exercise claim is a spectral march; grant this one, a voice whispers to each judge, and you will be confronted with an endless chain of exemption demands from religious deviants of every stripe"). This Court, however, consistently has rejected similar arguments in past free exercise cases, and it should do so here as well. See Frazee v. Illinois Dept. of Employment Security, 489 U.S. 829 (1989) (slip op. 6) (rejecting State's speculation concerning cumulative effect of many similar claims); *Thomas,* 450 U.S., at 719 (same); *Sherbert,* 374 U.S., at 407.

The State's apprehension of a flood of other religious claims is purely speculative. Almost half the States, and the Federal Government, have maintained an exemption for religious peyote use for many years, and apparently have not found themselves overwhelmed by claims to other religious exemptions.[8] * * *

III

Finally, although I agree with Justice O'Connor that courts should refrain from delving into questions of whether, as a matter of religious doctrine, a particular practice is "central" to the religion, * * *, I do not think this means that the courts must turn a blind eye to the severe impact of a State's restrictions on the adherents of a minority religion. Cf. *Yoder,* 406 U.S., at 219 (since "education is inseparable from and a

---

8. Over the years, various sects have raised free exercise claims regarding drug use. In no reported case, except those involving claims of religious peyote use, has the claimant prevailed. See, e.g., Olsen v. Iowa, 808 F.2d 652 (CA8 1986) (marijuana use by Ethiopian Zion Coptic Church); United States v. Rush, 738 F.2d 497 (CA1 1984), *cert. denied,* 470 U.S. 1004 (1985) (same); * * *

part of the basic tenets of their religion * * * [just as] baptism, the confessional, or a sabbath may be for others," enforcement of State's compulsory education law would "gravely endanger if not destroy the free exercise of respondents' religious beliefs").

Respondents believe, and their sincerity has never been at issue, that the peyote plant embodies their deity, and eating it is an act of worship and communion. Without peyote, they could not enact the essential ritual of their religion. * * *

If Oregon can constitutionally prosecute them for this act of worship, they, like the Amish, may be "forced to migrate to some other and more tolerant region." *Yoder,* 406 U.S., at 218. This potentially devastating impact must be viewed in light of the federal policy—reached in reaction to many years of religious persecution and intolerance—of protecting the religious freedom of Native Americans. * * *

* * *

For these reasons, I conclude that Oregon's interest in enforcing its drug laws against religious use of peyote is not sufficiently compelling to outweigh respondents' right to the free exercise of their religion. Since the State could not constitutionally enforce its criminal prohibition against respondents, the interests underlying the State's drug laws cannot justify its denial of unemployment benefits. Absent such justification, the State's regulatory interest in denying benefits for religiously motivated "misconduct," * * *, is indistinguishable from the state interests this Court has rejected in *Frazee, Hobbie, Thomas,* and *Sherbert.* The State of Oregon cannot, consistently with the Free Exercise Clause, deny respondents unemployment benefits.

I dissent.

Chapter 8

DEFINING "RELIGION"

INTRODUCTORY NOTE

How is "religion" to be understood within the first amendment?—Exactly how generously or how stringently shall the differentiating key noun be taken in the clause that provides:

Congress shall make no law respecting an establishment of [*religion*], or prohibiting the free exercise thereof.

Consider the following assortment of dictionary definitions. Does the religion clause embrace them all?—If not, at what point does it stop?

religion:[1] 1. the personal commitment to and serving of God or a god with worshipful devotion, conduct in accord with divine commands esp. as found in accepted sacred writings or declared by authoritative teachers, a way of life recognized as incumbent on true believers, and typically the relating of oneself to an organized body of beliefs; 2. one of the systems of faith and worship; 3. a personal awareness of or conviction of the existence of a supreme being or of supernatural powers or influences controlling one's own, humanity's, or all nature's destiny—the access of such an awareness or conviction accompanied by or arousing reverence and a sense of duty to obey; 4. the body of institutionalized expressions of sacred beliefs, observances, and social practices found within a given cultural context; 5. a value held to be of supreme importance, a cause, principle, system of tenets held with ardor, devotion, conscientiousness, and faith; 6. any objective attended to or pursued with zeal or conscientious devotion.

A. The usual presumption rebuttably applicable in constitutional interpretation is the presumption of generous construction. Assuredly this presumption was applied to the free speech and press clauses, was it not? Applied here, that presumption might readily embrace *all* of these dictionary meanings, even if some of these were not necessarily

---

1. The noun "religion" is from Latin, derived from the verb *ligare,* meaning "to tie" or "to bind." We recognize it more familiarly in the noun "ligature"—something that ties (like a cord, a fastening, a binding). With the prefix *re* (also Latin), it is *religare,* to "tie back." One will find the same etymology in dictionaries under "rely" as well as under "religion," i.e. both "rely" and "religion" are traced to "religare," to tie back, *to bind to something preceding itself.* Compare also the noun "religion" with the adjective "religious." The adjective springs even freer (in usage) than the noun, i.e. it ascribes a quality of attitude that struggles to close the distance between the actual (the *is*) and the ideal (the *ought*),—of holding with something that ties and that binds one, that identifies oneself with some value one holds even in the face of futility, even when one is alone.

generally recognized in common usage in 1787 or 1789. Is this what the first amendment does?

Note that some of these meanings are quite earth bound, i.e. they are secular and even anti-spiritual. Marxism may be a religion within definition 5. or at least within definition 6., and this despite its own denunciation of immanence or of anything "up there" or "out there" which Marxism does not draw on but, rather, eschews. Definition 4. in the random list collected from the dictionary is easily sufficient to include mere cults.[2] Are these also within the "religion" of the first amendment's purview? Definition 3. itself does not rigorously require any sense of divinity or of God, whether personal or impersonal; it is enough that one hold some belief in "supernatural * * * influences controlling one's * * * destiny." Such a definition is quite consistent with one common view of astrology—without God, church, or any particularized articles of faith. Does the free exercise of astrology, and equally of Marxism on the other hand, bring the "religion" clauses of the first amendment into play?

B. Because the establishment clause may be thought to be principally concerned with disallowing government acts tending toward "*establishment* of religion," i.e. establishment of religion under government auspices, as distinct from the more general protection of "freedom of conscience,"[3]—the preserve more particularly (though not exclusively) of the free exercise clause—there has been some inclination to view the word "religion" somewhat differently depending upon *which* clause is invoked, i.e. the establishment clause or the free exercise clause.[4]

---

2. *Cf.* Africa v. Pennsylvania, 662 F.2d 1025 (3d Cir.1981), cert. denied, 456 U.S. 908, 102 S.Ct. 1756, 72 L.Ed.2d 65 (1982) (discussing and delimiting "religion").

3. For works generally arguing for this construction of "religion" as protected by the first amendment, see R. Dworkin, Taking Rights Seriously 200–201 (1977); D. Richards, Toleration and the Constitution 136–46, 238 (1986); M. Konvitz, Religious Liberty and Conscience (1967). Historically oriented scholarship tends to reject these claims, requiring at a minimum a belief in *some* transcendental extrapersonal or otherworldly source of personal duty, even if not identified to a concrete notion of God. Ingber, Religion and Ideology: A Needed Clarification of the Religion Clauses, 41 Stan.L.Rev. 233 (1989); McConnell, The Origins and Historical Understanding of Free Exercise of Religion, 103 Harv.L. Rev. 1409, 1488–1500 (1990). Professor (and Dean) Jesse Choper, a principal commentator on the religion clauses, suggests an additional requirement to qualify a free exercise claim—that the law would require an act or forbid an act the performance of which (on the one hand) or the forbearance from which (on the other hand) would at once imperil one in some extratemporal manner, i.e. that it would carry post-death consequences which the state cannot control. Choper, Defining "Religion" in the First Amendment, 1981 U.Ill.L.Rev. 579. Similar though not the same is M. Sandel, Freedom of Conscience or Freedom of Choice, in Articles of Faith, Articles of Peace 74 (J. Hunter & O. Guiness eds. 1990) (the religiously impelled person does not choose, i.e. he or she feels no freedom to do so; rather the religious person is an "encumbered" self.) Sandel does not use the phrase, but his essay is insightful even in the literal definition of "religion" and *religare*, noted *supra*, in the sense of being literally tied, and not possessing choice. The reasoning person, idealized by the Enlightenment, may choose the good and wager all—including death itself—on its account. The dividing line is with the person who feels no power of election, i.e. the matter (for them) is literally out of their hands.

4. E.g., Members or representatives of a group may sometimes designate the group as nonreligious (e.g., as "Science") to avoid the strictures of the establishment clause, —to qualify for inclusion in public school curricula, or to qualify for federal grants. See, e.g., Edwards v. Aguillard, 482 U.S. 578, 107 S.Ct. 2573, 96 L.Ed.2d 510 (1987) (holding invalid pursuant to the establishment clause a state statute mandating

The notion here is fairly obvious: the first clause seems to be principally concerned with ecclesiastical organizations, with churches, with official articles of faith, practice, and worship; the second clause may seem more spacious, i.e. more concerned with liberty—"religious" liberty—freedom of belief and of personal conscience needing breathing room from callous disregard by the secular state. So, for instance, it has been suggested that:

> [All] that is *"arguably religious"* should be considered religious in a free exercise analysis [and] anything *"arguably non-religious"* should not be considered religious in applying the establishment clause.[5]

Thus unless the state seems to seek to advance an organized church or a preferred religion or set of religions or their doctrines, the establishment clause should seldom be deemed to be drawn into play. But insofar as the thick layers of ordinary law may far more routinely create severe headwinds for conscience, often unnecessarily (or so it may be argued), the appropriate protection of the latter is conducive to a more generous view of "religion,"—more freely enabling one to state a free exercise claim.[6]

C. On the other hand, Justice Rutledge, in *Everson*, seemed to rule out this very bifurcation. He raised just this point in the following way:

> "Religion" appears only once in the [First] Amendment. But the word governs two prohibition and governs them alike. It does not have two meanings, one narrow to forbid "an establishment" and another, much broader, for securing "the free exercise thereof." "Thereof" brings down "religion" with its entire and exact content, no more and no less, from the first into the second guaranty, so that Congress and now the states are as broadly restricted concerning the one as they are regarding the other.

equal time for classroom instruction in "Creation Science" as for evolution). See also Malnak v. Yogi, 592 F.2d 197 (3d Cir. 1979) ("Science" of Creative Intelligence–Transcendental Meditation held to be essentially religious in character and thus ineligible for federal funds sought to sponsor TM in public schools). Quite oppositely, Scientology (founded by L. Ron Hubbard) became the "Church of Scientology," gaining thereby the protections and exemptions of religions under statutes and under the free exercise clause. See, e.g., Founding Church of Scientology v. United States, 409 F.2d 1146 (D.C.Cir.1969).

5. L. Tribe, American Constitutional Law 848 (1977). Cf. L. Tribe, American Constitutional Law 1186 (2d ed. 1988) (abandoning former position). See also Note, Toward a Constitutional Definition of Religion, 91 Harv.L.Rev. 1056 (1978) (likewise proposing a "bifurcated" definition, with "religion" defined as embracing matters deemed of "ultimate concern" to the individual, under the free exercise clause, a narrower definition being applied in reviewing establishment clause objections or claims). (The "ultimate concern" suggestion is taken from P. Tillich, The Shakings of Foundations 63–64 (1972); it is synonymous with whatever one "take[s] seriously without any reservation," whether or not related to any notion of God or of immanence as such.)

6. See also Van Alstyne, Constitutional Separation of Church and State: The Quest for a Coherent Position, 57 Amer. Pol.Sci.Rev. 865, 873–75 (1963) (de facto the Court has been more receptive toward a broad view of "religion" in qualifying free exercise claims than in validating establishment clause objections).

Perhaps it is just as well to turn to some few cases, to see what has become of this issue in the Supreme Court.[7]

TORCASO v. WATKINS

Supreme Court of the United States, 1961.
367 U.S. 488, 81 S.Ct. 1680, 6 L.Ed.2d 982.

MR. JUSTICE BLACK delivered the opinion of the Court.

Article 37 of the Declaration of Rights of the Maryland Constitution provides:

> "[N]o religious test ought ever to be required as a qualification for any office of profit or trust in this State, other than a declaration of belief in the existence of God * * *."

The appellant Torcaso was appointed to the office of Notary Public by the Governor of Maryland but was refused a commission to serve because he would not declare his belief in God. He then brought this action in a Maryland Circuit Court to compel issuance of his commission, charging that the State's requirement that he declare this belief violated "the First and Fourteenth Amendments to the Constitution of the United States * * *."[1] The Circuit Court rejected these federal constitutional contentions, and the highest court of the State, the Court of Appeals, affirmed. * * *

There is, and can be, no dispute about the purpose or effect of the Maryland Declaration of Rights requirement before us—it sets up a religious test which was designed to and, if valid, does bar every person who refuses to declare a belief in God from holding a public "office of profit or trust" in Maryland. The power and authority of the State of Maryland thus is put on the side of one particular sort of believers—those who are willing to say they believe in "the existence of God." It is true that there is much historical precedent for such laws. Indeed, it was largely to escape religious test oaths and declarations that a great many of the early colonists left Europe and came here hoping to worship in their own way. It soon developed, however, that many of those who had fled to escape religious test oaths turned out to be perfectly willing, when they had the power to do so, to force dissenters

---

7. For additional suggestions and approaches, see Freeman, The Misguided Search for the Constitutional Definition of "Religion," 71 Geo.L.J. 1519 (1983); Greenawalt, Religion as a Concept of Constitutional Law, 72 Calif.L.Rev. 753 (1984); Hall, The Sacred and the Profane: A First Amendment Definition of Religion, 61 Tex. L.Rev. 1239 (1982); Merel, The Protection of Individual Choice: A Consistent Understanding of Religion Under the First Amendment, 45 U.Chi.L.Rev. 805 (1978). More generally, see J. Dewey, Intelligence in the Modern World 1036 (Ratner ed. 1939); J. Huxley, Religion Without Revelation 20, 194 (1957); W. James, Essays in Pragmatism 122–124 (Castell ed. 1952).

1. Appellant also claimed that the State's test oath requirement violates the provision of Art. VI of the Federal Constitution that "no religious Test shall ever be required as a Qualification to any Office or public Trust under the United States." Because we are reversing the judgment on other grounds, we find it unnecessary to consider appellant's contention that this provision applies to state as well as federal offices.

from their faith to take test oaths in conformity with that faith. This brought on a host of laws in the new Colonies imposing burdens and disabilities of various kinds upon varied beliefs depending largely upon what group happened to be politically strong enough to legislate in favor of its own beliefs. The effect of all this was the formal or practical "establishment" of particular religious faiths in most of the Colonies, with consequent burdens imposed on the free exercise of the faiths of nonfavored believers.

There were, however, wise and farseeing men in the Colonies—too many to mention—who spoke out against test oaths and all the philosophy of intolerance behind them. One of these, it so happens, was George Calvert (the first Lord Baltimore), who took a most important part in the original establishment of the Colony of Maryland. He was a Catholic and had, for this reason, felt compelled by his conscience to refuse to take the Oath of Supremacy in England at the cost of resigning from high governmental office. He again refused to take that oath when it was demanded by the Council of the Colony of Virginia, and as a result he was denied settlement in that Colony. A recent historian of the early period of Maryland's life has said that it was Calvert's hope and purpose to establish in Maryland a colonial government free from the religious persecutions he had known—one "securely beyond the reach of oaths * * *."

* * * Since prior cases in this Court have thoroughly explored and documented the history behind the First Amendment, the reasons for it, and the scope of the religious freedom it protects, we need not cover that ground again. * * *

* * *

We repeat and again reaffirm that neither a State nor the Federal Government can constitutionally force a person "to profess a belief or disbelief in any religion." Neither can constitutionally pass laws or impose requirements which aid all religions as against non-believers and neither can aid those religions based on a belief in the existence of God as against those religions founded on different beliefs.[11]

This Maryland religious test for public office unconstitutionally invades the appellant's freedom of belief and religion and therefore cannot be enforced against him.

The judgment of the Court of Appeals of Maryland is accordingly reversed and the cause is remanded for further proceedings not inconsistent with this opinion.

Reversed and remanded.

---

11. Among religions in this country which do not teach what would generally be considered a belief in the existence of God are Buddhism, Taoism, Ethical Culture, Secular Humanism and others. See Washington Ethical Society v. District of Columbia, 249 F.2d 127; Fellowship of Humanity v. County of Alameda, 153 Cal. App.2d 673, 315 P.2d 394; II Encyclopaedia of the Social Sciences 293; 4 Encyclopaedia Britannica (1957 ed.) 325–327; 21 id., at 797; Archer, Faiths Men Live By (2d ed. revised by Purinton), 120–138, 254–313; 1961 World Almanac 695, 712; Year Book of American Churches for 1961, at 29, 47.

Mr. Justice Frankfurter and Mr. Justice Harlan concur in the result.

UNITED STATES v. SEEGER

Supreme Court of the United States, 1965.
380 U.S. 163, 85 S.Ct. 850, 13 L.Ed.2d 733.

Mr. Justice Clark delivered the opinion of the Court.

These cases involve claims of conscientious objectors under § 6(j) of the Universal Military Training and Service Act, 50 U.S.C.App. § 456(j) (1958 ed.), which exempts from combatant training and service in the armed forces of the United States those persons who by reason of their religious training and belief are conscientiously opposed to participation in war in any form. The cases were consolidated for argument and we consider them together although each involves different facts and circumstances. The parties raise the basic question of the constitutionality of the section which defines the term "religious training and belief," as used in the Act, as "an individual's belief in a relation to a Supreme Being involving duties superior to those arising from any human relation, but (not including) essentially political, sociological, or philosophical views or a merely personal moral code." The constitutional attack is launched under the First Amendment's Establishment and Free Exercise Clauses and is twofold: (1) The section does not exempt nonreligious conscientious objectors; and (2) it discriminates between different forms of religious expression in violation of the Due Process Clause of the Fifth Amendment. * * *

THE FACTS IN THE CASE.

* * * Seeger was convicted in the District Court for the Southern District of New York of having refused to submit to induction in the armed forces. He was originally classified 1–A in 1953 by his local board, but this classification was changed in 1955 to 2–S (student) and he remained in this status until 1958 when he was reclassified 1–A. He first claimed exemption as a conscientious objector in 1957 after successive annual renewals of his student classification. Although he did not adopt verbatim the printed Selective Service System form, he declared that he was conscientiously opposed to participation in war in any form by reason of his "religious" belief; that he preferred to leave the question as to his belief in a Supreme Being open, "rather than answer 'yes' or 'no' "; that his "skepticism or disbelief in the existence of God" did "not necessarily mean lack of faith in anything whatsoever"; that his was a "belief in and devotion to goodness and virtue for their own sakes, and a religious faith in a purely ethical creed." * * *. He cited such personages as Plato, Aristotle and Spinoza for support of his ethical belief in intellectual and moral integrity "without belief in God, except in the remotest sense." * * *. His belief was found to be sincere, honest, and made in good faith; and his conscientious objection to be based upon individual training and belief, both of which included

research in religious and cultural fields. Seeger's claim, however, was denied solely because it was not based upon a "belief in a relation to a Supreme Being" as required by § 6(j) of the Act. At trial Seeger's counsel admitted that Seeger's belief was not in relation to a Supreme Being as commonly understood, but contended that he was entitled to the exemption because "under the present law Mr. Seeger's position would also include definitions of religion which have been stated more recently," * * *, and could be "accommodated" under the definition of religious training and belief in the Act, * * *. He was convicted and the Court of Appeals reversed, holding that the Supreme Being requirement of the section distinguished "between internally derived and externally compelled beliefs" and was, therefore, an "impermissible classification" under the Due Process Clause of the Fifth Amendment. * * *

* * *

BACKGROUND OF § 6(J).

* * *

Governmental recognition of the moral dilemma posed for persons of certain religious faiths by the call to arms came early in the history of this country. Various methods of ameliorating their difficulty were adopted by the Colonies, and were later perpetuated in state statutes and constitutions. Thus by the time of the Civil War there existed a state pattern of exempting conscientious objectors on religious grounds. * * *

The need for conscription did not again arise until World War I. The Draft Act of 1917, * * *, afforded exemptions to conscientious objectors who were affiliated with a "well-recognized religious sect or organization (then) organized and existing and whose existing creed or principles (forbade) its members to participate in war in any form * * *." The Act required that all persons be inducted into the armed services, but allowed the conscientious objectors to perform noncombatant service in capacities designated by the President of the United States. Although the 1917 Act excused religious objectors only, in December 1917, the Secretary of War instructed that "personal scruples against war" be considered as constituting "conscientious objection." * * *

In adopting the 1940 Selective Training and Service Act Congress broadened the exemption afforded in the 1917 Act by making it unnecessary to belong to a pacifist religious sect if the claimant's own opposition to war was based on "religious training and belief." * * *. Those found to be within the exemption were not inducted into the armed services but were assigned to noncombatant service under the supervision of the Selective Service System. The Congress recognized that one might be religious without belonging to an organized church just as surely as minority members of a faith not opposed to war might through religious reading reach a conviction against participation in war. * * *

Between 1940 and 1948 two courts of appeals held that the phrase "religious training and belief" did not include philosophical, social or political policy. Then in 1948 the Congress amended the language of the statute and declared that "religious training and belief" was to be defined as "an individual's belief in a relation to a Supreme Being involving duties superior to those arising from any human relation, but (not including) essentially political, sociological, or philosophical views or a merely personal moral code." * * *

INTERPRETATION OF § 6(J).

1. * * * The section excludes those persons who, disavowing religious belief, decide on the basis of essentially political, sociological or economic considerations that war is wrong and that they will have no part of it. These judgments have historically been reserved for the Government, and in matters which can be said to fall within these areas the conviction of the individual has never been permitted to override that of the state. *United States v. Macintosh, supra* (dissenting opinion). The statute further excludes those whose opposition to war stems from a "merely personal moral code," a phrase to which we shall have occasion to turn later in discussing the application of § 6(j) to these cases. We also pause to take note of what is not involved in this litigation. No party claims to be an atheist or attacks the statute on this ground. The question is not, therefore, one between theistic and atheistic beliefs. * * *

2. Few would quarrel, we think, with the proposition that in no field of human endeavor has the tool of language proved so inadequate in the communication of ideas as it has in dealing with the fundamental questions of man's predicament in life, in death or in final judgment and retribution. This fact makes the task of discerning the intent of Congress in using the phrase "Supreme Being" a complex one. Nor is it made the easier by the richness and variety of spiritual life in our country. Over 250 sects inhabit our land. Some believe in a purely personal God, some in a supernatural deity; others think of religion as a way of life envisioning as its ultimate goal the day when all men can live together in perfect understanding and peace. There are those who think of God as the depth of our being; others, such as the Buddhists, strive for a state of lasting rest through self-denial and inner purification; in Hindu philosophy, the Supreme Being is the transcendental reality which is truth, knowledge and bliss. * * *

* * *

* * * Under the 1940 Act it was necessary only to have a conviction based upon religious training and belief; we believe that is all that is required here. Within that phrase would come all sincere religious beliefs which are based upon a power or being, or upon a faith, to which all else is subordinate or upon which all else is ultimately dependent. The test might be stated in these words: A sincere and meaningful belief which occupies in the life of its possessor a place parallel to that filled by the God of those admittedly qualifying for the exemption comes within the statutory definition. This construction avoids imputing to Congress an intent to classify different religious beliefs, exempt-

ing some and excluding others, and is in accord with the well-established congressional policy of equal treatment for those whose opposition to service is grounded in their religious tenets.

* * *

5. We recognize the difficulties that have always faced the trier of fact in these cases. We hope that the test that we lay down proves less onerous. The examiner is furnished a standard that permits consideration of criteria with which he has had considerable experience. While the applicant's words may differ, the test is simple of application. It is essentially an objective one, namely, does the claimed belief occupy the same place in the life of the objector as an orthodox belief in God holds in the life of one clearly qualified for exemption? Moreover, it must be remembered that in resolving these exemption problems one deals with the beliefs of different individuals who will articulate them in a multitude of ways. In such an intensely personal area, of course, the claim of the registrant that his belief is an essential part of a religious faith must be given great weight. * * *

* * *

APPLICATION OF § 6(J) TO THE INSTANT CASES.

As we noted earlier, the statutory definition excepts those registrants whose beliefs are based on a "merely personal moral code." The records in these cases, however, show that at no time did any one of the applicants suggest that his objection was based on a "merely personal moral code." Indeed at the outset each of them claimed in his application that his objection was based on a religious belief. We have construed the statutory definition broadly and it follows that any exception to it must be interpreted narrowly. The use by Congress of the words "merely personal" seems to us to restrict the exception to a moral code which is not only personal but which is the sole basis for the registrant's belief and is in no way related to a Supreme Being. It follows, therefore, that if the claimed religious beliefs of the respective registrants in these cases meet the test that we lay down then their objections cannot be based on a "merely personal" moral code.

In *Seeger*, No. 50, the Court of Appeals failed to find sufficient "externally compelled beliefs." However, it did find that "it would seem impossible to say with assurance that [Seeger] is not bowing to 'external commands' in virtually the same sense as is the objector who defers to the will of a supernatural power." * * * It found little distinction between Jakobson's devotion to a mystical force of "Godness" and Seeger's compulsion to "goodness." Of course, as we have said, the statute does not distinguish between externally and internally derived beliefs. Such a determination would, as the Court of Appeals observed, prove impossible as a practical matter, and we have found that Congress intended no such distinction.

The Court of Appeals also found that there was no question of the applicant's sincerity. He was a product of a devout Roman Catholic home; he was a close student of Quaker beliefs from which he said "much of [his] thought is derived"; he approved of their opposition to war in any form; he devoted his spare hours to the American Friends Service Committee and was assigned to hospital duty.

In summary, Seeger professed "religious belief" and "religious faith." He did not disavow any belief "in a relation to a Supreme Being"; indeed he stated that "the cosmic order does, perhaps, suggest a creative intelligence." He decried the tremendous "spiritual" price man must pay for his willingness to destroy human life. In light of his beliefs and the unquestioned sincerity with which he held them, we think the Board, had it applied the test we propose today, would have granted him the exemption. We think it clear that the beliefs which prompted his objection occupy the same place in his life as the belief in a traditional deity holds in the lives of his friends, the Quakers. We are reminded once more of Dr. Tillich's thoughts:

> "And if that word [God] has not much meaning for you, translate it, and speak of the depths of your life, of the source of your being, or your ultimate concern, *of what you take seriously without any reservation.* Perhaps, in order to do so, you must forget everything traditional that you have learned about God * * *." Tillich, The Shaking of the Foundations. 57 (1948). (Emphasis supplied.)

It may be that Seeger did not clearly demonstrate what his beliefs were with regard to the usual understanding of the term "Supreme Being." But as we have said Congress did not intend that to be the test. We therefore affirm the judgment in No. 50.

* * *

It is so ordered.

Mr. Justice Douglas, concurring.

If I read the statute differently from the Court, I would have difficulties. For then those who embraced one religious faith rather than another would be subject to penalties; and that kind of discrimination, as we held in Sherbert v. Verner, 374 U.S. 398, would violate the Free Exercise Clause of the First Amendment. It would also result in a denial of equal protection by preferring some religions over others—an invidious discrimination that would run afoul of the Due Process Clause of the Fifth Amendment. See Bolling v. Sharpe, 347 U.S. 497.

The legislative history of this Act leaves much in the dark. But it is, in my opinion, not a *tour de force* if we construe the words "Supreme Being" to include the cosmos, as well as an anthropomorphic entity. If it is a *tour de force* so to hold, it is no more so than other instances where we have gone to extremes to construe an Act of Congress to save it from demise on constitutional grounds. In a more extreme case than the present one we said that the words of a statute may be strained "in the candid service of avoiding a serious constitutional doubt." United States v. Rumely, 345 U.S. 41.[1]

---

1. And see Crowell v. Benson, 285 U.S. 22, 62; Ullmann v. United States, 350 U.S. 422, 433; Ashwander v. TVA, 297 U.S. 288, 341, 348 (concurring opinion).

WELSH v. UNITED STATES

Supreme Court of the United States, 1970.
398 U.S. 333, 90 S.Ct. 1792, 26 L.Ed.2d 308.

MR. JUSTICE BLACK announced the judgment of the Court and delivered an opinion in which MR. JUSTICE DOUGLAS, MR. JUSTICE BRENNAN, and MR. JUSTICE MARSHALL join.

The petitioner, Elliott Ashton Welsh II, was convicted by a United States District Judge of refusing to submit to induction into the Armed Forces in violation of 50 U.S.C.App. § 462(a), and was on June 1, 1966, sentenced to imprisonment for three years. One of petitioner's defenses to the prosecution was that § 6(j) of the Universal Military Training and Service Act exempted him from combat and noncombat service because he was "by reason of religious training and belief * * * conscientiously opposed to participation in war in any form." * * * For the reasons to be stated, and without passing upon the constitutional arguments that have been raised, we vote to reverse this conviction because of its fundamental inconsistency with *United States v. Seeger,* * * *.

The controlling facts in this case are strikingly similar to those in *Seeger.* Both Seeger and Welsh were brought up in religious homes and attended church in their childhood, but in neither case was this church one which taught its members not to engage in war at any time for any reason. Neither Seeger nor Welsh continued his childhood religious ties into his young manhood, and neither belonged to any religious group or adhered to the teachings of any organized religion during the period of his involvement with the Selective Service System. At the time of registration for the draft, neither had yet come to accept pacifist principles. Their views on war developed only in subsequent years, but when their ideas did fully mature both made application to their local draft boards for conscientious objector exemptions from military service under § 6(j) of the Universal Military Training and Service Act. That section then provided, in part:

> "Nothing contained in this title shall be construed to require any person to be subject to combatant training and service in the armed forces of the United States who, by reason of religious training and belief, is conscientiously opposed to participation in war in any form. Religious training and belief in this connection means an individual's belief in a relation to a Supreme Being involving duties superior to those arising from any human relation, but does not include essentially political, sociological, or philosophical views or a merely personal moral code."

In filling out their exemption applications both Seeger and Welsh were unable to sign the statement that, as printed in the Selective Service form, stated "I am, by reason of my religious training and belief, conscientiously opposed to participation in war in any form." Seeger could sign only after striking the words "training and" and putting quotation marks around the word "religious." Welsh could sign only after striking the words "my religious training and." On those same applications, neither could definitely affirm or deny that he believed in a "Supreme Being," both stating that they preferred to leave the question open.[3] But both Seeger and Welsh affirmed on those applications that they held deep conscientious scruples against taking part in wars where people were killed. Both strongly believed that killing in war was wrong, unethical, and immoral, and their consciences forbade them to take part in such an evil practice. Their objection to participating in war in any form could not be said to come from a "still, small voice of conscience"; rather, for them that voice was so loud and insistent that both men preferred to go to jail rather than serve in the Armed Forces. There was never any question about the sincerity and depth of Seeger's convictions as a conscientious objector, and the same is true of Welsh. * * * Seeger's conscientious objector claim was denied "solely because it was not based upon a 'belief in a relation to a Supreme Being' as required by § 6(j) of the Act," * * * while Welsh was denied the exemption because his Appeal Board and the Department of Justice hearing officer "could find no religious basis for the registrant's beliefs, opinions and convictions." * * * Both Seeger and Welsh subsequently refused to submit to induction into the military and both were convicted of that offense.

In *Seeger* the Court was confronted, first, with the problem that § 6(j) defined "religious training and belief" in terms of a "belief in a relation to a Supreme Being * * *," a definition that arguably gave a preference to those who believed in a conventional God as opposed to those who did not. Noting the "vast panoply of beliefs" prevalent in our country, the Court construed the congressional intent as being in "keeping with its long-established policy of not picking and choosing among religious beliefs," * * *, and accordingly interpreted "the meaning of religious training and belief so as to embrace *all* religions. * * *" * * * But, having decided that all religious conscientious objectors were entitled to the exemption, we faced the more serious problem of determining which beliefs were "religious" within the meaning of the statute. This question was particularly difficult in the case of Seeger himself. Seeger stated that his was a "belief in and devotion to goodness and virtue for their own sakes, and a religious faith in a purely ethical creed." * * * In a letter to his draft board, he wrote:

> "My decision arises from what I believe to be considerations of validity from the standpoint of the welfare of humanity and the preservation of the democratic values which we in the United States are struggling to maintain. I have concluded that war, from the practical standpoint, is futile and self-de-

---

3. In his original application in April 1964, Welsh stated that he did not believe in a Supreme Being, but in a letter to his local board in June 1965, he requested that his original answer be stricken and the question left open. App. 29.

feating, and that from the more important moral standpoint, it is unethical." * * *

On the basis of these and similar assertions, the Government argued that Seeger's conscientious objection to war was not "religious" but stemmed from "essentially political, sociological, or philosophical views or a merely personal moral code."

In resolving the question whether Seeger and the other registrants in that case qualified for the exemption, the Court stated that "[the] task is to decide whether the beliefs professed by a registrant are sincerely held and whether they are, *in his own scheme of things*, religious." * * * The reference to the registrant's "own scheme of things" was intended to indicate that the central consideration in determining whether the registrant's beliefs are religious is whether these beliefs play the role of a religion and function as a religion in the registrant's life. The Court's principal statement of its test for determining whether a conscientious objector's beliefs are religious within the meaning of § 6(j) was as follows:

> "The test might be stated in these words: A sincere and meaningful belief which occupies in the life of its possessor a place parallel to that filled by the God of those admittedly qualifying for the exemption comes within the statutory definition." * * *

* * * What is necessary under *Seeger* for a registrant's conscientious objection to all war to be "religious" within the meaning of § 6(j) is that this opposition to war stem from the registrant's moral, ethical, or religious beliefs about what is right and wrong and that these beliefs be held with the strength of traditional religious convictions. Most of the great religions of today and of the past have embodied the idea of a Supreme Being or a Supreme Reality—a God—who communicates to man in some way a consciousness of what is right and should be done, of what is wrong and therefore should be shunned. If an individual deeply and sincerely holds beliefs that are purely ethical or moral in source and content but that nevertheless impose upon him a duty of conscience to refrain from participating in any war at any time, those beliefs certainly occupy in the life of that individual "a place parallel to that filled by * * * God" in traditionally religious persons. * * * The Court concluded:

> "We think it clear that the beliefs which prompted his objection occupy the same place in his life as the belief in a traditional deity holds in the lives of his friends, the Quakers."
> 380 U.S., at 187.

Accordingly, the Court found that Seeger should be granted conscientious objector status.

In the case before us the Government seeks to distinguish our holding in *Seeger* on basically two grounds, both of which were relied upon by the Court of Appeals in affirming Welsh's conviction. First, it is stressed that Welsh was far more insistent and explicit than Seeger in denying that his views were religious. For example, in filling out their conscientious objector applications, Seeger put quotation marks around the word "religious," but Welsh struck the word "religious' entirely and later characterized his beliefs as having been formed "by reading in the fields of history and sociology." * * * The Court of Appeals found that Welsh had "denied that his objection to war was premised on religious belief" and concluded that "[t]he Appeal Board was entitled to take him at his word." * * * We think this attempt to distinguish *Seeger* fails for the reason that it places undue emphasis on the registrant's interpretation of his own beliefs. * * * When a registrant states that his objections to war are "religious," that information is highly relevant to the question of the function his beliefs have in his life. But very few registrants are fully aware of the broad scope of the word "religious" as used in § 6(j), and accordingly a registrant's statement that his beliefs are nonreligious is a highly unreliable guide for those charged with administering the exemption. Welsh himself presents a case in point. Although he originally characterized his beliefs as nonreligious, he later upon reflection wrote a long and thoughtful letter to his Appeal Board in which he declared that his beliefs were "certainly religious in the ethical sense of the word." He explained:

> "I believe I mentioned taking of life as not being, for me, a religious wrong. Again, I assumed Mr. [Brady (the Department of Justice hearing officer)] was using the word 'religious' in the conventional sense, and, in order to be perfectly honest did not characterize my belief as 'religious'". * * *

The Government also seeks to distinguish *Seeger* on the ground that Welsh's views, unlike Seeger's, were "essentially political, sociological, or philosophical views or a merely personal moral code." As previously noted, the Government made the same argument about Seeger, and not without reason, for Seeger's views had a substantial political dimension. * * * In this case, Welsh's conscientious objection to war was undeniably based in part on his perception of world politics. In a letter to his local board, he wrote:

> "I can only act according to what I am and what I see. And I see that the military complex wastes both human and material resources, that it fosters disregard for (what I consider a paramount concern) human needs and ends; I see that the means we employ to 'defend' our 'way of life' profoundly change that way of life. I see that in our failure to recognize the political, social, and economic realities of the world, we, *as a nation,* fail our responsibility *as a nation.*" * * *

We certainly do not think that § 6(j)'s exclusion of those persons with "essentially political, sociological, or philosophical views or a merely personal moral code" should be read to exclude those who hold strong beliefs about our domestic and foreign affairs or even those whose conscientious objection to participation in all wars is founded to a substantial extent upon considerations of public policy. The two groups of registrants that obviously do fall within these exclusions from the exemption are those whose beliefs are not deeply held and those whose objection to war does not rest at all upon moral, ethical, or religious principle but instead rests solely upon considerations of policy, pragmatism, or expediency. * * *

* * * Welsh elaborated his beliefs in later communications with Selective Service officials. On the basis of these beliefs and the conclusion of the Court of Appeals that he held them "with the strength of more traditional religious convictions," * * * we think Welsh was clearly entitled to a conscientious objector exemption. Section 6(j) requires no more. That section exempts from military service all those whose consciences, spurred by deeply held moral, ethical, or religious beliefs, would give them no rest or peace if they allowed themselves to become a part of an instrument of war.

The judgment is

Reversed.

Mr. Justice Blackmun took no part in the consideration or decision of this case.

Mr. Justice Harlan, concurring in the result.

Candor requires me to say that I joined the Court's opinion in United States v. Seeger, 380 U.S. 163 (1965), only with the gravest misgivings as to whether it was a legitimate exercise in statutory construction, and today's decision convinces me that in doing so I made a mistake which I should now acknowledge.

* * *

In my opinion, the liberties taken with the statute both in *Seeger* and today's decision cannot be justified in the name of the familiar doctrine of construing federal statutes in a manner that will avoid possible constitutional infirmities in them. * * * I therefore find myself unable to escape facing the constitutional issue that this case squarely presents: whether § 6(j) in limiting this draft exemption to those opposed to war in general because of theistic beliefs runs afoul of the religious clauses of the First Amendment. For reasons later appearing I believe it does, and on that basis I concur in the judgment reversing this conviction, and adopt the test announced by Mr. Justice Black, not as a matter of statutory construction, but as the touchstone for salvaging a congressional policy of long standing that would otherwise have to be nullified.

* * *

The natural reading of § 6(j), which quite evidently draws a distinction between theistic and nontheistic religions, is the only one that is consistent with the legislative history. Section 5(g) of the 1940 Draft Act exempted individuals whose opposition to war could be traced to "religious training and belief," * * * without any allusion to a Supreme Being. In United States v. Kauten, 133 F.2d 703 (C.A.2d Cir.1943), the Second Circuit, speaking through Judge Augustus Hand, broadly construed "religious training and belief" to include a "belief finding expression in a conscience which categorically requires the believer to disregard elementary self-interest and to accept martyrdom in preference to transgressing its tenets." * * * This expansive interpretation of § 5(g) was rejected by a divided Ninth Circuit in Berman v. United States, 156 F.2d 377, 380–381 (1946):

> "It is our opinion that the expression 'by reason of religious training and belief' * * * was written into the statute for the specific purpose of distinguishing between a conscientious social belief, or a sincere devotion to a high moralistic philosophy, and one based upon an individual's belief in his responsibility to an authority higher and beyond any worldly one.
>
> * * *
>
> "[I]n United States v. Macintosh, 283 U.S. 605 * * * Mr. [Chief] Justice Hughes in his dissent * * * said: 'The essence of religion is belief in a relation to God involving duties superior to those arising from any human relation.'"

* * *

In the wake of this intercircuit dialogue, crystallized by the dissent in *Berman* which espoused the Second Circuit interpretation in *Kauten, supra,* Congress enacted § 6(j) in 1948. That Congress intended to anoint the Ninth Circuit's interpretation of § 5(g) would seem beyond question in view of the similarity of the statutory language to that used by Chief Justice Hughes in his dissenting opinion in *Macintosh* and quoted in *Berman* and the Senate report. The first half of the new language was almost word for word that of Chief Justice Hughes in *Macintosh,* and quoted by the *Berman* majority; and the Senate Committee report adverted to *Berman,* thus foreclosing any possible speculation as to whether Congress was aware of the possible alternatives. The report stated:

> "This section reenacts substantially the same provisions as were found in subsection 5(g) of the 1940 act. Exemption extends to anyone who, because of religious training and belief in his relationship to a Supreme Being, is conscientiously opposed to combatant military service or to both combatant and noncombatant military service. (See United States v. Berman [sic], 156 F. (2d) 377, certiorari denied, 329 U.S. 795.)" S.Rep. No. 1268, 80th Cong., 2d Sess., 14.

Against this legislative history it is a remarkable feat of judicial surgery to remove as did *Seeger,* the theistic requirement of § 6(j). * * *

* * *

I cannot subscribe to a wholly emasculated construction of a statute to avoid facing a latent constitutional question, in purported fidelity to the salutary doctrine of avoiding unnecessary resolution of constitutional issues, a principle to which I fully adhere. See Ashwander v. Tennessee Valley Authority, 297 U.S. 288, 348 (1936) (BRANDEIS, J., concurring). It is, of course, desirable to salvage by construction legislative enactments whenever there is good reason to believe that Congress did not intend to legislate consequences that are unconstitutional, but it is not permissible, in my judgment, to take a lateral step that robs legislation of all meaning in order to avert the collision between its plainly intended purpose and the commands of the Constitution.

* * *

* * * I therefore turn to the constitutional question.

The constitutional question that must be faced in this case is whether a statute that defers to the individual's conscience only when his views emanate from adherence to theistic religious beliefs is within the power of Congress. Congress, of course, could, entirely consistently with the requirements of the Constitution, eliminate all exemptions for conscientious objectors. Such a course would be wholly "neutral" and, in my view, would not offend the Free Exercise Clause, for reasons set forth in my dissenting opinion in Sherbert v. Verner, 374 U.S. 398, 418 (1963). See * * * Kurland, Of Church and State and the Supreme Court, 29 U.Chi.L.Rev. 1 (1961). However, having chosen to exempt, it cannot draw the line between theistic or nontheistic religious beliefs on the one hand and secular beliefs on the other. Any such distinctions are not, in my view, compatible with the Establishment Clause of the First Amendment. See my separate opinion in Walz v. Tax Comm'n, 397 U.S. 664, 694 (1970); * * * The implementation of the neutrality principle of these cases requires, in my view, as I stated in *Walz v. Tax Comm'n, supra,* "an equal protection mode of analysis. The Court must survey meticulously the circumstances of governmental categories to eliminate, as it were, religious gerrymanders. In any particular case the critical question is whether the scope of legislation encircles a class so broad that it can be fairly concluded that [all groups that] could be thought to fall within the natural perimeter [are included]." 397 U.S., at 696.

The "radius" of this legislation is the conscientiousness with which an individual opposes war in general, yet the statute, as I think it must be construed, excludes from its "scope" individuals motivated by teachings of nontheistic religions,[8] and individuals guided by an inner ethical voice that bespeaks secular and not "religious" reflection. It not only accords a preference to the "religious" but also disadvantages adherents of religions that do not worship a Supreme Being. The constitutional infirmity cannot be cured, moreover, even by an impermissible construction that eliminates the theistic requirement and simply draws the line between religious and nonreligious. This in my view offends the Establishment Clause and is that kind of classification that this Court has condemned. See my separate opinion in *Walz v. Tax Comm'n, supra; School District of Abington Township v. Schempp* (GOLDBERG, J., concurring), *supra; Engel v. Vitale, supra; Torcaso v. Watkins, supra.*

If the exemption is to be given application, it must encompass the class of individuals it purports to exclude, those whose beliefs emanate

---

8. This Court has taken notice of the fact that recognized "religions" exist that "do not teach what would generally be considered a belief in the existence of God," Torcaso v. Watkins, 367 U.S. 488, 495 n. 11, e.g., "Buddhism, Taoism, Ethical Culture, Secular Humanism and others."

from a purely moral, ethical, or philosophical source.[9] The common denominator must be the intensity of moral conviction with which a belief is held. Common experience teaches that among "religious" individuals some are weak and others strong adherents to tenets and this is no less true of individuals whose lives are guided by personal ethical considerations.

The Government enlists the *Selective Draft Law Cases*, 245 U.S. 366 (1918), as precedent for upholding the constitutionality of the religious conscientious objector provision. That case involved the power of Congress to raise armies by conscription and only incidentally the conscientious objector exemption. The language emphasized by the Government to the effect that the exemption for religious objectors and ministers constituted neither an establishment nor interference with free exercise of religion can only be considered an after-thought since the case did not involve any individuals who claimed to be nonreligious conscientious objectors. This conclusory assertion, unreasoned and unaccompanied by citation, surely cannot foreclose consideration of the question in a case that squarely presents the issue.

Other authorities assembled by the Government, far from advancing its case, demonstrate the unconstitutionality of the distinction drawn in § 6(j) between religious and nonreligious beliefs. Everson v. Board of Education, 330 U.S. 1 (1947), the *Sunday Closing Law Cases*, 366 U.S. 420, 582 599, and 617 (1961), and Board of Education v. Allen, 392 U.S. 236 (1968), all sustained legislation on the premise that it was neutral in its application and thus did not constitute an establishment, notwithstanding the fact that it may have assisted religious groups by giving them the same benefits accorded to non-religious groups.[12] To the extent that Zorach v. Clauson, 343 U.S. 306 (1952), and *Sherbert v.*

---

9. In Sherbert v. Verner, 374 U.S. 398 (1963), the Court held unconstitutional over my dissent a state statute that conditioned eligibility for unemployment benefits on being "able to work and * * * available for work" and further provided that a claimant was ineligible "[i]f * * * he has failed, without good cause * * * to accept available suitable work when offered him by the employment office or the employer * * *." This, the Court held, was a violation of the Free Exercise Clause as applied to Seventh Day Adventists whose religious background forced them as a matter of conscience to decline Saturday employment. My own conclusion, to which I still adhere, is that the Free Exercise Clause does not require a State to conform a neutral secular program to the dictates of religious conscience of any group. I suggested, however, that a State could constitutionally create exceptions to its program to accommodate religious scruples. That suggestion must, however, be qualified by the observation that any such exception in order to satisfy the Establishment Clause of the First Amendment, would have to be sufficiently broad to be religiously neutral. See my separate opinion in *Walz v. Tax Comm'n, supra*. This would require creating an exception for anyone who, as a matter of conscience, could not comply with the statute. * * *

12. * * * Section 6(j) speaks directly to belief divorced entirely from conduct. It evinces a judgment that individuals who hold the beliefs set forth by the statute should not be required to bear arms, and the statutory belief that qualifies is only a religious belief. * * * Congress, whether in response to political considerations or simply out of sensitivity for men of religious conscience, can of course decline to exercise its power to conscript to the fullest extent, but it cannot do so without equal regard for men of nonreligious conscience. It goes without saying that the First Amendment is perforce a guarantee that the conscience of religion may not be preferred simply because organized religious groups in general are more visible than the individual who practices morals and ethics on his own. Any view of the Free Exercise Clause that does not insist on this neutrality would engulf the Establishment Clause and render it vestigial.

Verner, supra, stand for the proposition that the Government may (*Zorach*), or must (*Sherbert*), shape its secular programs to accommodate the beliefs and tenets of religious groups, I think these cases unsound.[13] See generally Kurland, *supra.* To conform with the requirements of the First Amendment's religious clauses as reflected in the mainstream of American history, legislation must, at the very least, be neutral. * * *

Where a statute is defective because of underinclusion there exist two remedial alternatives: a court may either declare it a nullity and order that its benefits not extend to the class that the legislature intended to benefit, or it may extend the coverage of the statute to include those who are aggrieved by exclusion. * * *

The appropriate disposition of this case, which is a prosecution for refusing to submit to induction and not an action for a declaratory judgment on the constitutionality of § 6(j), is determined by the fact that at the time of Welsh's induction notice and prosecution the Selective Service was, as required by statute, exempting individuals whose beliefs were identical in all respects to those held by petitioner except that they derived from a religious source. Since this created a religious benefit not accorded to petitioner, it is clear to me that this conviction must be reversed under the Establishment Clause of the First Amendment unless Welsh is to go remediless. * * *

* * *

When a policy has roots so deeply embedded in history, there is a compelling reason for a court to hazard the necessary statutory repairs if they can be made within the administrative framework of the statute and without impairing other legislative goals, even though they entail, not simply eliminating an offending section, but rather building upon it. Thus I am prepared to accept the prevailing opinion's conscientious objector test, not as a reflection of congressional statutory intent but as patchwork of judicial making that cures the defect of underinclusion in § 6(j) and can be administered by local boards in the usual course of business. Like the prevailing opinion, I also conclude that petitioner's beliefs are held with the required intensity and consequently vote to reverse the judgment of conviction.

Mr. Justice White, with whom The Chief Justice and Mr. Justice Stewart join, dissenting.

---

13. That the "released-time" program in *Zorach* did not utilize classroom facilities for religious instruction, unlike McCollum v. Board of Education, 333 U.S. 203 (1948), is a distinction for me without Establishment Clause substance. At the very least the Constitution requires that the State not excuse students early for the purpose of receiving religious instruction when it does not offer to nonreligious students the opportunity to use school hours for spiritual or ethical instruction of a nonreligious nature. Moreover, whether a released-time program cast in terms of improving "conscience" to the exclusion of artistic or cultural pursuits, would be "neutral" and consistent with the requirement of "voluntarism," is by no means an easy question. Such a limited program is quite unlike the broad approach of the tax exemption statute, sustained in *Walz v. Tax Comm'n, supra,* which included literary societies, playgrounds, and associations "for the moral or mental improvement of men."

Whether or not United States v. Seeger, 380 U.S. 163 (1965), accurately reflected the intent of Congress in providing draft exemptions for religious conscientious objectors to war, I cannot join today's construction of § 6(j) extending draft exemption to those who disclaim religious objections to war and whose views about war represent a purely personal code arising not from religious training and belief as the statute requires but from readings in philosophy, history, and sociology.

For me that conclusion should end this case. Even if Welsh is quite right in asserting that exempting religious believers is an establishment of religion forbidden by the First Amendment, he nevertheless remains one of those persons whom Congress took pains not to relieve from military duty. Whether or not § 6(j) is constitutional, Welsh had no First Amendment excuse for refusing to report for induction. If it is contrary to the express will of Congress to exempt Welsh, as I think it is, then there is no warrant for saving the religious exemption and the statute by redrafting it in this Court to include Welsh and all others like him.

If the Constitution expressly provided that aliens should not be exempt from the draft, but Congress purported to exempt them and no others, Welsh, a citizen, could hardly qualify for exemption by demonstrating that exempting aliens is unconstitutional. By the same token, if the Constitution prohibits Congress from exempting religious believers, but Congress exempts them anyway, why should the invalidity of the exemption create a draft immunity for Welsh? * * *

If I am wrong in thinking that Welsh cannot benefit from invalidation of § 6(j) on Establishment Clause grounds, I would nevertheless affirm his conviction; for I cannot hold that Congress violated the Clause in exempting from the draft all those who oppose war by reason of religious training and belief. In exempting religious conscientious objectors, Congress was making one of two judgments, perhaps both. First, § 6(j) may represent a purely practical judgment that religious objectors, however admirable, would be of no more use in combat than many others unqualified for military service. Exemption was not extended to them to further religious belief or practice but to limit military service to those who were prepared to undertake the fighting that the armed services have to do. On this basis, the exemption has neither the primary purpose nor the effect of furthering religion. * * *

Second, Congress may have granted the exemption because otherwise religious objectors would be forced into conduct that their religions forbid and because in the view of Congress to deny the exemption would violate the Free Exercise Clause or at least raise grave problems in this respect. True, this Court has more than once stated its unwillingness to construe the First Amendment, standing alone, as requiring draft exemptions for religious believers. * * *

* * *

On the assumption, however, that the Free Exercise Clause of the First Amendment does not by its own force require exempting devout objectors from military service, it does not follow that § 6(j) is a law respecting an establishment of religion within the meaning of the First Amendment. * * * I would not frustrate congressional will by construing the Establishment Clause to condition the exemption for religionists upon extending the exemption also to those who object to war on nonreligious grounds.

We have said that neither support nor hostility, but neutrality, is the goal of the religion clauses of the First Amendment. "Neutrality," however, is not self-defining. If it is "favoritism" and not "neutrality" to exempt religious believers from the draft, is it "neutrality" and not "inhibition" of religion to compel religious believers to fight when they have special reasons for not doing so, reasons to which the Constitution gives particular recognition? * * *

* * *

The Establishment Clause as construed by this Court unquestionably has independent significance; its function is not wholly auxiliary to the Free Exercise Clause. It bans some involvements of the State with religion that otherwise might be consistent with the Free Exercise Clause. But when in the rationally based judgment of Congress free exercise of religion calls for shielding religious objectors from compulsory combat duty, I am reluctant to frustrate the legislative will by striking down the statutory exemption because it does not also reach those to whom the Free Exercise Clause offers no protection whatsoever.

I would affirm the judgment below.

INDEX

References are to Pages

ABORTION, 385 n. 35

ABRAMS v. UNITED STATES, 41

ABSOLUTE VIEW
See Views

ACADEMIC FREEDOM, 331, 379, 831, 833

ACCESS
Equal,
    Press, 502
    Public, 502
Selective, 450

ACCESS ADVOCATES, 207

ACCUSED
Publication of name, 181 n. 71

ACQUISITION OF NEWSWORTHY MATTER, 515

ACT
Symbolic, 225

ACTOR, 257

ADAMSON v. CALIFORNIA, 55

ADDRESSEES
Willing, 335

ADULTS
Consenting, 737

ADVERTISING
Ads,
    Opinions, 210
    Parody, 209, 211, 215
        Which viciously malign, 216
Bans,
    Being kept in ignorance, 617
    Challenged on due process and equal protection grounds, 617
Cigarettes, 625
Commercial, 162, 395 n. 3
Contraceptives, 650
Handbills, 604
Leaflets, 605
Liquor, 625
Obscene, 679
On vehicles, 602

ADVERTISING—Cont'd
Paid, 614
Previewing, 642 n. 13
Price, 617
Promotional, 636
Suppression of a specific point of view, 658
Truth of, 602
Unsolicited, 650

ADVOCACY, 33
Political, 155
    Independent, 567
Public, 170
Social, 29, 155

AFFIRMATION
Involuntary, 537

AFFRONT
Unwelcome,
    In public places, 156

"AGENCY SHOP" ARRANGEMENT, 549

AIRPORT TERMINAL, 482

AIRWAVES
See Media

ALIENS, 27 n. 62, 64

ALPERT
Judicial Censorship of Obscene Literature, 691

ALTERNATIVE MEASURES, 104

AMERICAN FLAG
See Flags

AMISH
See Religion

ANARCHY
Criminal, 49

ANDERSON
The Origins of the Press Clause, 17 n. 35

ANONYMITIES
Puny, 132

ANTIEAU, A. & E. ROBERTS
Freedom from Federal Establishment, 838 n. 3

APPROPRIATION
Of commercial value, 182 n. 72

ARCHER
Faiths Men Live By, 1026 n. 11

ARMBANDS, 3 n. 8, 224, 225, 252
Black, 227, 230
Regulation, 227 n. 4

ARRESTEES
Crime, 181 n. 71

ARSON, 274 n. 8

ASSASSINATION
Of President, 136

ASSEMBLY, 2
Freedom of, 231
Peaceable, 2, 27, 393
Right of, 512 & n. 13
Riotous, 26 n. 57
Stationary, 385

ASSOCIATION, 2
Right of, 354, 357, 588
    Guilt by, 355
    Political, 360

ATTORNEYS, 619 n. 25
Advertising, 625, 628
    Fees,
        Blanket bans on price, 629
        Contingent basis, 626
        Disclosure requirements, 629
Clients,
    In-person solicitation of, 629
    Solicitation of,
        Self-interested legal advice, 635

AUDIENCES
Captive, 151, 229, 262, 266 n. 2, 442
Hostile, 412
Specialized, 676

AVAILABILITY OF BENEFITS, 968

BACK DOOR APPROACH, 673

BAD TENDENCY
See Tendency

BAILIFF, 376

BALANCE, 16

BALANCING
Of interests, 315
Process, 5 n. 18
Sliding scale, 141 n. 51
Test, 324

BALLOTS
    See also Elections
Australian, 371 n. 11

BARGAINING REPRESENTATIVE
Exclusive, 453

BARRON v. MAYOR . . ., 18 n. 38

BELIEF
Freedom of, 360

BERGER, RAOUL, 62
The Fourteenth Amendment and the Bill of Rights, 62 n. 27

BERLE
Constitutional Limitations on Corporate Activity . . ., 522 n. 87

BILL FOR ESTABLISHING RELIGIOUS FREEDOM, 764, 777 n. 1

BILL OF RIGHTS
Incorporation clause, 55
Jot-for-jot, 57, n. 17
Relation with fourteenth amendment, 55
    Incorporation debate, 15 n. 27
Watered-down, 57 n. 17

BILLBOARDS, 424

BILLS OF ATTAINDER, 238 n. 30

BITTER WITH THE SWEET, 288

BLACK, C.
Structure and Relationship in Constitutional Law, 22 n. 43

BLACK, HUGO L., 5 n. 18, 13, 62, 112
No law means no law, 112

BLACKSTONE, WILLIAM, 15 n. 28, 16 n. 31, 20
Commentaries, 11, 15, 26 n. 57

BLAINE AMENDMENT, 785 & n. 8, 812 & n. 22

BLASI
The Checking Value in First Amendment Theory, 155 n. 54
Learned Hand and the First Amendment, 34 n. 10
The Pathological Perspective and the First Amendment, 155 n. 54
Prior Restraints on Demonstrations, 388 n. 44
Toward a Theory of Prior Restraints, 388 n. 44

BOCCACCIO, GIOVANNI
Decameron, 685

BOGEN, D.
Bulwark of Liberty . . ., 22 n. 44

BOMBS
Planting of, 136

BOOKS
    See also Libraries; Obscenity
Containing vulgarity and profanity,
    Removal of, 344, 347

BOOKS—Cont'd
Library,
    Removal of, 333

BOOKSELLERS
Private, 344

BOSTON COMMON, 387

BRADBURY, RAY
Dandelion Wine, 332
Farenheit 451, 332

BRANDEIS, LOUIS D., 29, 71, 175
The Right to Privacy, 180 n. 69

BRANDENBERG v. OHIO, 142
Test, 29, 156

BREATHING ROOM, 204

BREATHING SPACE, 187, 212, 215

BRIDGES v. CALIFORNIA, 75

BROADCASTING
See Media

BURR, AARON, 23 n. 50

CAMPER
Ordinary, 253

CAMPUS
See Schools

CANDIDATES
See Elections

CARICATURE, 213
Outrageous, 213

CARNAL KNOWLEDGE
See Motion Pictures

CAROLENE PRODUCTS CO.
Note 4, 945

CARTOONISTS
Political, 213

CARTOONS, 39, 213

CASS
First Amendment Access to Government Facilities, 387 n. 40

CELLOPHANE WRAPPER DOCTRINE, 253 n. 89

CENSORSHIP
Administrative, 397
Community, 691
Of motion pictures, 443
Self, 187

CENTRAL HUDSON
Four-part analysis, 653, 671

CHAFEE, Z.
Free Speech in the United States, 17 n. 35, 19 n. 40

CHAPLAINS
Federal,
    Armed forces,
        Spending federal funds to employ, 818
    Congressional, 765 n. 15, 895
        Historical practice, 896
        Prayers, 900
            Constitutional Convention, 891
            First Congress, 891
                Paid chaplains, 896
        History of, 892
            Skeletons in congressional closet, 897 n. 10
State,
    Compensation, 892
    Legislature, 890
        Prayers, 891, 893
            Degrading religion,
                Potential for, 896
        History and tradition, 890
        Published,
            Public funds, 890 n. 3

CHILD NEGLECT LAWS
See Church and State

CHILDRESS, ALICE, 333 n. 3

CHILLING EFFECT, 307, 677

CHOPER
The Religion Clause of the First Amendment ..., 977 n. 11

CHURCH AND STATE
Accommodation,
    Permissible, 974
"Ceremonial deism", 917
Children,
    Are "persons", 964
    Compulsory vaccination, 942
    Employment,
        Child labor laws, 960
        On family farms, 961
        Ordinary commercial activities, 945
    Family life, 942
    Grave and immediate danger to, 945
    Martyrs of, 943
    Neglect laws, 1011
    Parental rights, 941
    State authority over activities of, 943
    Welfare of, 942
Clergy,
    Elective office holding by, 870, 872 n. 42
        Ministers, 871
        Mullahs, 871
        Priests, 871
        Rabbis, 871
Combination of, 794
Government buildings,
    Chapels in Capitol, 902
    Displays in,
        Make religion relevant, 920
    Supreme Court,
        Decorations,
            Moses with Ten Commandments, 902

CHURCH AND STATE—Cont'd
Heresy trials, 949
Holidays,
    Chanukah,
        Menorah, 914, 918
        Endorsement,
            Judaism, 914
    Christmas,
        Appearance of official sponsorship, 899
        Municipal, 898
            Christmas display, 898
            Tree, 914
        Nativity scene, 898, 902
            Crèche,
                Banner,
                      "Gloria in Excelsis Deo!", 913
                Government,
                      Owned on private land, 924
                      Identified with one religious faith, 905
                      Privately owned on public land, 924
            Endorsement, 914
                Christianity, 914
            In county courthouse, 913
            Historical evidence, 910 n. 25
            "Keeping 'Christ in Christmas' ", 909
            Misuse of sacred symbol, 911
            Secularizes and degrades, 922 n. 8
        Political divisiveness, 904, 922 n. 10
    Thanksgiving, 895, 901
        National holiday, 901
"In the Year of our Lord", 785 n. 7
Law of God, 870
Mottoes,
    "Under God", 785 n. 3
    "In God We Trust", 549, 785 n. 3, 801, 901
        Currency, 901
    "E Pluribus Unum", 549, 785 n. 3
National Day of Prayer, 902, 917 n. 52
Religion in government, 889
    History and tradition, 926
    Sacramental wine, 928
    Slogans,
        "One Nation, Under Allah", 889
        "One Nation, Under God", 889
    Uniform Friday closing day, 927
Religious,
    Beliefs, 930
        As justification of overt act,
            Made criminal, 930
        Centrality of, 1011
        Divine messengers, 947
        Free exercise, 929
            In military context, 988
        General test, 929
        Human sacrifices, 932
        Judicial examination, 953
        Marriage, 932

CHURCH AND STATE—Cont'd
Religious—Cont'd
    Beliefs—Cont'd
        Marriage—Cont'd
            Civil contract, 932
            Negative protection, 1012
            Polygamy, 929, 931
                Patriarchal principle, 932
        Power to heal persons, 947
        Sincerity of, 952
        Truth or verity of, 948, 952
        Wife's duty to burn herself, 932
    Exemptions,
        From civic obligations, 1011
        Nondiscriminatory religious practice, 1012
    Experiences,
        False statements of, 950
            State of mind, 950
        Misrepresentation of, 951
    Merchandise, 1000
        Bowls, 1001
        Mugs, 1001
        Plates, 1001
        Tax,
            Flat license, 1002
            Sales and use, 1000, 1001
    Organizations,
        Assistance to,
            Direct, 970
            Indirect, 970
    Symbols,
        On public property, 921, 924
Routine regulatory interaction, 1005
Separation of, 772
    State,
        Law benefits, 772
        Neutral in relations, 773
State church, 905
Sundays,
    Sabbath day, 872
        Book of Exodus, 872
    Sunday closing laws, 873
        Economic injury, 875
        History of, 876
        Imposition of Christian religion, 875
        Maryland statutes,
            Coercion, 880
            "Sabbath Breaking", 878
            Tax monies, 880
        Moslem law, 887
        Secular justifications, 876
    "Sundays excepted", 785 n. 7
Taxes,
    Income, 1002
    License, 1002, 1003
    Neutral,
        Routine regulatory interaction, 1005
    Property, 1002
    Rate,
        Onerous, 1004
    Sales and use, 1000, 1001, 1003
Test oaths, 923
Theocratic state, 872
    Separation of civil from, 872

INDEX

CHURCH–STATE CLAUSES, 760
Standing to sue, 760 & n. 1

CITIZENSHIP
Rights of, 64
Schools,
    Training in, 542

CIVIC CENTER AUDITORIUM, 385

CIVIL SERVICE COMMISSION, 302

CLARK
Guidelines for the Free Exercise Clause, 1018

CLASSIFICATIONS
Based on race, 1010 n. 3
Based on religion, 1010 n. 3

CLASSROOMS
Compulsory environment of, 336
Orthodoxy over, 336

CLEAR AND PRESENT DANGER, 29, 31, 32, 76, 125, 942
Test, 31, 134, 146

CLEAVER, ELDRIDGE, 333 n. 3

CLELAND, JOHN, 700
See also *Memoirs*
Fanny Hill, 700

COASE
Evaluation of Public Policy Relating to Radio and Television Broadcasting ..., 495 n. 75
The Federal Communications Commission, 495 n. 75

COHEN v. CALIFORNIA, 149

COLLEGES
See Universities

COLONIES
American, 195

COMMON CARRIERS
Obligations of, 494

COMMON LAW
Rules, 531 n. 1
Standard, 32

COMMUNICATION
Cost of, 429
Statutes to suppress, 237

COMMUNISM, 138

COMMUNIST PARTY, 123, 354
Membership in, 357

COMPANY–OWNED TOWN
See Property

COMPELLED RECITATION, 531

COMPLAINTS
Privately expressed, 312

CONDUCT, 234
Disorderly, 147, 274 n. 8, 410
Expressive, 241
    Restricted, 271
Noncommunicative impact, 237
Nonexpressive,
    Ordinarily, 244 n. 7
Offensive, 149, 152
Partisan political,
    By federal employees, 303
Socially harmful,
    Applicable prohibitions, 1010
Unprofessional, 612

CONGRESS, 5
Judgment of, 132

CONSCIENTIOUS OBJECTORS, 1027
Anthropomorphic entity, 1031
Avoiding a serious constitutional doubt, 1031
Beliefs,
    Externally compelled, 1028
    Internally derived, 1028
    Line between theistic and nontheistic, 1038
    Secular, 1038
Buddhists, 1029
Compulsion to "goodness", 1030
Conscience of religion may not be preferred, 1039 n. 12
Cosmos, 1031
Intensity of moral conviction, 1039
Moral code,
    Personal, 1029
    War,
        Killing,
            Wrong, unethical, immoral, 1033
        Principles,
    Moral, ethical, religious, 1036
Mystical force of "Godness", 1030
Neutrality principle, 1038
Noncombatant, 1028
Nonreligious, 1027
Nontheistic religion, 1038
Relation to Supreme Being, 1027
Religion as way of life, 1029
Religious,
    Faith in purely ethical creed, 1027
        Plato, 1027
        Aristotle, 1027
        Spinoza, 1027
    Gerrymander, 1038
    Training and belief, 1027
Supreme Being, 1029
    Duties superior to those arising from any human relation, 1029
Welfare of humanity, 1033

CONSPIRACY
Law of, 134

CONSTITUTION
British (English), 3, 77
China, 3
Denmark, 4
Germany, 4
Norway, 3

INDEX
References are to Pages

CONSTITUTION—Cont'd
Qualified clauses, 4
Soviet Union, 3
United States, 4
    Article VI, 1025 n. 1

CONSTITUTIONAL
Interpretation,
    Presumption of generous construction, 1022
On its face, 238
Validity,
    Heavy presumption against, 100, 105 n. *, 111

CONSTITUTIONAL RAMIFICATIONS OF A REPEAL OF THE FAIRNESS DOCTRINE, 494 n. 72

CONTEMPT, 7
Of court, 75, 93
Publication as, 80

CONTENT-NEUTRAL, 242

CONTRACTS
Government, 373 n. 7

CONVERSATIONS
See Speech

COOLEY
Constitutional Limitations, 812 n. 24

CORD, R.
Separation of Church and State . . . , 765 n. 16

CORPORATIONS
First amendment standing of, 65 n. 33

CORWIN
A Constitution of Powers in a Secular State, 811 n. 21
The Doctrine of Due Process, 66 n. 34

COURTS
Power of, 72

CREDIT REPORTS, 205

CRIMINAL ATTEMPTS, 32 n. 1

CRIMINAL LIBEL
See Libel

CRIMINAL SYNDICALISM ACT, 70

CURRY, T.
The First Freedoms: Church and State in America . . . , 765 n. 16

CURTIS, MICHAEL, 62
No State Shall Abridge . . . , 62 n. 24

DAMAGES
Chilling danger of large awards, 204
General, 161
Presumed, 190, 200, 203
Punitive, 190, 191, 200, 203
    In libel action, 160

DAMNUM ABSQUE INJURIA, 172

DANBURY BAPTIST ASSOCIATION, 931

DANGER
See also Clear and Present Danger
Imminent, 73

DARROW, CLARENCE, 291

DARWIN, CHARLES
Origin of the Species, 291

DAUMIER, HONORE, 217 n. 79

DEBATES
Political, 211
Public, 170

DECENCY
Community standards of, 731

DECLARATION OF INDEPENDENCE, 785 n. 5

DEFAMATION
Absolute immunity, 173 n. 65
Absolute unconditional privilege, 169
Criminal, 171 n. 62, 299
Criticism of official conduct,
    Press,
        Absolute immunity of, 169, 170
False and defamatory statements not involving matters of public concern, 197
Liability without fault, 190
Nature of material, 196
Of government, 156
Of private citizen, 182
Of public figure, 188
Relating to private conduct, 171 n. 4
Tort law of, 157

DEFENSE FACILITY, 354

DE JONGE v. OREGON, 28 n. 64

DENNIS v. UNITED STATES, 122

DEPOSITIONS AND INTERROGATORIES
Pretrial, 109

DIAL-A-PORN TELEPHONE SERVICES
See Pornography

DICKENS, CHARLES, 217 n. 79

DISCOVERY, 108
Pretrial, 106

DISMISSALS
Absolute protection from, 978 n. 12
From employment, 299
Retaliatory, 298

DISRUPTION, 227

DISSENT
Symbolic, 224

DISTRIBUTION
Door-to-door, 250 n. 14

INDEX

DISTURBANCE
Fear of, 226, 320

DIVERSITY
Unchecked, 495

DRAFT
Card,
   Burning, 227 n. 4
   Mutilator, 253
Registration certificate, 236
Resistance to, 39

DRAMATIC PERFORMANCES
See Speech
See Speech

DRED SCOTT v. SANDFORD, 65 n. 34

DRUGS
Illegal
   Possession, 1017
Prescription,
   Prices, 612
      Advertising, 617
      Discount, 668
      Information, 668

DUE PROCESS
See also Fifth Amendment; First Amendment; Fourteenth Amendment
Clause, 68
Economic, 603
Substantive, 67
   Economic, 603

DUKER, W.
A Constitutional History of Habeas Corpus, 22 n. 46

DWORKIN
Taking Rights Seriously, 1023 n. 3

EASTERBROOK
... *The Court and the Economic System,* 255 n. 95

EASTERN R.R. PRESIDENTS CONF. v. NOERR MOTOR FREIGHT, 27 n. 63

EDITORIAL CHOICE, 181 n. 71

EDUCATION
See also Schools
Based on purely secular considerations, 956
Philosophy of,
   Conservative, 334
Public,
   Access to, 536
   Free, 539
Secondary,
   Inculcative function of, 336
Suitability, 337

EFFECTS
Chilling, 307
Dampening, 172

EFFECTS—Cont'd
Incidental,
   Of generally applicable and valid provision, 1008
Inhibiting, 355

ELECTIONS
Federal,
   Ballot-access regulations, 578
   Committees,
      Political,
         Independent, 591
   Contributions,
      Disclosure requirements, 565
      Limitations, 560, 565
   Eligibility, 872 n. 42
   Expenditures,
      Campaign, 570
      Candidates, 569
      Limitations, 560
         Independent, 563, 567
      Minor parties, 573, 582
   Organizations,
      Ideological, 592
   Restrictions,
      Business corporations, 599
      Political advocacy associations, 599
   Minor parties, 582
   Reporting and disclosure requirements, 571
   Spending, 564 n. 27
      To promote one's political views, 570
   Political action committees, 591
      Expenditures, 593
   Public financing,
      Presidential, 575
      Voucher system, 577 n. 125
   Public subsidization,
      Of private individuals, 581
Local,
   Contributions,
      To committees, 587
         Formed to favor or oppose ballot measures, 588
Precinct judges, 376

EMOTIONAL DISTRESS
Intentional infliction of, 209, 210, 211, 214, 216, 672 n. 20

EMPLOYEES
See also Employment
Deputies, 373
Dismissal,
   Absolute protection from, 978 n. 12
   On partisan basis, 359
Federal,
   Partisan conduct, 303
Government, 303
Hiring, 367 n. *
Nonpolicymaking, 326
Policymaking,
   Confidential, 372
Promotions, 367 n. *

EMPLOYEES—Cont'd
Public,
  Rights of, 319
  Speaks not as citizen, 315
Reasonable accommodation of religiously-based concerns, 978 n. 12
Rehiring, 367 n. *
Transfers, 367 n. *

EMPLOYMENT
See also Employees
Public, 296
  Conditioned on political faith, 360
  Denial of, 360
  Loss of, 554
  Need for confidentiality, 297 n. 3

ENDORSEMENT
Implicit, 341

EQUAL PROTECTION, 403
Clause, 384 n. 33, 446 n. 2, 448, 874

EQUALIZING RELATIVE ABILITY OF INDIVIDUALS AND GROUPS, 568

ESPIONAGE, 35 n. 1

ESPIONAGE ACT OF 1917, 29
As amended,
  May 1918, p. 41
1919 act, 389 n. 45

ESTABLISHMENT CLAUSE, 881, 1038
Absorption of, 811
Accommodating religious needs, 870
Advancing religion, 870
Adherence to religion, 905
As coguarantor, 811
Doctrine,
  Revision of, 922
Enforcing God's laws, 869
Religion, 767
Religious,
  Belief,
    Endorsement, 915
    Favoritism, 915
    Promotion, 915
    Proselytization, 918
  Education,
    Secular means, 816
    Subsidization prohibited, 865
Standing to sue, 760 & n. 1
Theocracy, 869
Three-part test, 855

EVIL
Gravity of, 29, 103, 126, 140
Serious,
  To be prevented, 73
Significant substantive, 424

EX POST CASE–SPECIFIC PERSPECTIVE, 254

EXAGGERATION, 164, 414

EXPRESSION
See also Obscenity
Coarse, 714

EXPRESSION—Cont'd
Coerced, 535
Forms not entitled to protection, 265
Political, 360
Suppression of, 244
Symbolic, 242

EXPRESSIVE CONDUCT
See Conduct

FACT
Questions of, 730
Triers of, 730

FAIRMAN, CHARLES, 62

FAIRNESS DOCTRINE, 487

FALSEHOODS
Defamatory, 209
Reckless, 177

FARBER & NOWAK
The Misleading Nature of Public Forum Analysis ..., 387 n. 40

FAVORITISM
Political,
  Avoiding appearance of, 464

FEAR
Undifferentiated, 320

FEDERAL
System, 194, 688
Tribunals, 193 n. 2

FEDERAL COMMUNICATIONS ACT OF 1934, p. 14 n. 26

FEDERAL COMMUNICATIONS COMMISSION (FCC), 14 n. 26, 486, 489

FEDERAL ELECTION CAMPAIGN ACT AMENDMENTS OF 1974, p. 559 n. 3

FEDERAL ELECTION COMMISSION, 591

FEDERAL TRADE COMMISSION (FTC), 17 n. 33, 19 n. 40, 601

FEDERALISM, 55 n. 14

FEDERALIST NO. 84, p. 18 n. 37

FERBER DOCTRINE, 675 n. 29

FICTION, 217 n. 79

FIFTH AMENDMENT, 58
Due process clause, 58, 764, 1027
  Substantive, 603
Equal protection component, 459

"FIGHTING WORDS"
See Language

FIRE
Falsely shouted in theater, 31
Regulations, 251 n. 83

FIRST AMENDMENT, 4, 448
Absolute view (Black, Hugo, J.), 85
And city councils, 5

FIRST AMENDMENT, 4, 448—Cont'd
And Congress, 5
And state legislatures, 5
As a "Freedom of Information Act", 498
Concentric circles, 155
Core expression, 568
Due process, 65 n. 33
Excluded categories, 670
Free speech doctrine, 85
Freedom of assembly clause, 231
Forms of expression not entitled to protection, 265
General test, 255 n. 97
Generous construction, 252 n. 87
Incorporated, 68
Introduction to, 1
Limitations on magnitude of penalty or punishment, 677 n. 38
Music,
  Protection of, 434
No heightened scrutiny, 110
No law means no law (Black, Hugo, J.), 112
No licensing view (Blackstone), 85
No protection, 673
Relationship with fourteenth amendment,
  Jot-for-jot, 69
Rights of students, 335

FLACK, HORACE, 62

FLAGS, 3 n. 8
Flying red, 245
United States, 245, 259, 260
  As public property, 260
  As symbol of national unity, 264
  Burning, 268, 276, 284
  Criticism of, 268
  Desecration, 269
    Statutes, 259, 284
      Improper use, 259
  Facial challenge, 269 n. 3
  Failure to show proper respect, 262
  In commercial context, 262 n. 7
  National property, 267
  On private property, 260
  Peace symbol on, 259, 260
  Personal use of, 267
  Political uses of, 284
  Regulations, 252
    State,
      Sensibilities of passersby, 262
  Salute, 535, 537, 541
    Compelled, 541
  Treatment,
    Precatory regulations, 277
  Upside down, 259

FLYNT, LARRY, 217 n. 79

FORUM
Analysis, 383, 481
  Discussion and review, 481
Four-forum approach, 482 n. 56
Nonpublic, 417, 451, 461
  Limiting speech in, 464
Public, 417, 427 n. 32, 492
  Doctrine, 383
  Limited, 462

FORUM—Cont'd
Public—Cont'd
  Quintessential, 449

FOURTEENTH AMENDMENT, 8, 58
Due process clause, 52
Privileges and immunities clause, 10, 15, 26, 60
Relation with Bill of Rights, 55

FOURTH AMENDMENT, 21 n. 43, 24

FOWLER & BRENNER
A Marketplace Approach to Broadcast Regulation, 495 n. 75

FRANKFURTER, FELIX, 55

FRATERNITIES
Greek letter, 231

FRAUD, 601

FREE EXERCISE CLAUSE, 1009
Hybrid situation, 1009

FREE REPLY TIME, 486

FREE SPEECH ACCESS
See Speech

FREEDMAN STANDARDS, 678

FREEDOM NOT TO SPEAK
See Speech

FREEDOM OF ASSEMBLY CLAUSE
See First Amendment

FREEDOM TO SPEAK ONE'S MIND
See Speech

FREEMAN
The Misguided Search for the Constitutional Definition of "Religion", 1025 n. 7

FREUND
The Debs Case and Freedom of Speech, 32 n. 3

FUNDS
Charitable,
  Solicitation of, 459

GELLER & LAMPERT
Cable, Content Regulation and the First Amendment, 494 n. 73

GERTZ v. ROBERT WELCH, INC., 201

GITLOW v. NEW YORK, 49, 54

GOLDBERGER
Judicial Scrutiny in Public Forum Cases ..., 251 n. 16
A Reconsideration of Cox v. New Hampshire ..., 385 n. 36

GOLDMAN, EMMA, 36

GOVERNMENT
As contractor, 287
As educator, 345, 347
As employer, 287, 347

GOVERNMENT—Cont'd
As monopsonist, 496 n. 78
As property owner, 347
As sovereign, 345, 347
Contracts, 373 n. 7
Funds, 376 n. 12
Neutrality, 969
Provider of benefits, 287
Purchaser of services, 287
Theology within, 889

GRAND JURY, 95
Proceedings, 506

GRAVITY OF EVIL
See Evil

GREENAWALT, K.
Religion as a Concept of Constitutional Law, 1025 n. 7
Relgious Convictions and Lawmaking, 870 n. 35
Religious Convictions and Political Choices, 870 n. 35

GRIEVANCE PROCEDURES, 298 n. 4

GRISWOLD v. CONNECTICUT, 1

GUNTHER
Learned Hand and the Origins of Modern First Amendment Doctrine . . . , 34 n. 10
Reflections on Robel . . . , 389 n. 45

HABEAS CORPUS, 20 n. 41, 22 n. 46

HAMILTON, ALEXANDER, 18 n. 37

HAND, LEARNED, 29, 34, 36, 126
Not improbable test, 146

HAND–BILLS, 394
Distribution, 436 n. 7

HARLAN, JOHN MARSHALL, 96

HATCH ACT, 301

HATRED, 212

HELLER, JOSEPH, 217 n. 79

HENKIN
Morals and the Constitution: The Sin of Obscenity, 873 n. 45

HERBLOCK (HERBERT LAWRENCE BLOCK), 217 n. 79

HIGH SCHOOLS
See Schools

HITLER, ADOLPH
Mein Kampf, 137, 217 n. 79

HOGARTH, WILLIAM, 217 n. 79

HOLMES, OLIVER WENDELL, 6, 46

HOMER
Iliad, 219

HORNUNG
The First Amendment Right to a Public Forum, 387 n. 40

HOWARD, SENATOR, 62

HUDON, E.
Freedom of Speech and Press in America, 17 n. 35

HUGHES, LANGSTON, 333 n. 3

HURST, J.
The Law of Treason in the United States, 23 n. 51

HUXLEY, J.
Religion Without Revelation, 1025 n. 7

IDEAS
Constitutionally protected,
  In books, 337
False, 186
Free trade in, 49
Marketplace of, 207, 222, 276
Official suppression of, 344
Political,
  Government-dictated, 531
Right to receive in school, 345
State discrimination between, 338

IDEOLOGY
Dissemination of,
  State interest in, 547

IGNORANCE
Of fact, 933
Of law, 933

ILL–WILL, 212

IMMUNITIES
Of citizens, 8

INFORMATION
Gathering, 506
Not in itself harmful, 618
Right to receive, 621
Suppression of, 618

INDIANS
See Native Americans

INGBER
Religion and Ideology . . . , 1023 n. 3

INJUNCTIVE RELIEF, 116, 366

INJURY
Actual, 191

INSULT
Personal
  Direct, 272

INTELLIGENCE
Classified, 349

INTENT
Common law, 32

INTERESTS
Balancing of, 315

INDEX

References are to Pages

INTERESTS—Cont'd
In aesthetics, 422
Plainly illegitimate, 423

INTERPRETATION
Statutory, 389 n. 45

IUS TERTII CLAIMS, 760 n. 1

JACKSON, ANDREW, 378, 895

JAILS
Local,
 Curtilage of, 383 n. 32
 Right to visit, 512 n. 11

JAMES, J.
The Framing of the Fourth Amendment, 62 n. 24

JAMES, W.
The Will to Believe, 952 n. 2

JAYWALKING, 251, 252, 253 n. 90

JEFFERSON, THOMAS, 15 n. 29, 72 n. 2, 79 n. 16, 378, 764, 895, 930, 931

JEHOVAH'S WITNESSES
See Religion

JOB CAPABILITY, 363

JOYCE, JAMES
Ulysses, 219, 685

JUDGMENT
Aesthetic,
 Subjective, 430
Artistic, 435
Content–based, 341
Summary, 202

JUDICIAL REVIEW
Burden of obtaining, 444
Case–by–case, 29

KALVEN
Ernest Freund and the First Amendment Tradition, 32 n. 3
The New York Times Case: A Note on "The Central Meaning" of the First Amendment, 155 n. 54
Privacy in Tort Law ..., 180 n. 68
A Worthy Tradition, 672 n. 20

KAMENSHINE
The First Amendment's Implied Establishment Clause, 387 n. 39

KAUPER
The Constitutionality of Tax Exemptions ..., 837

KENNEDY, JOHN F., 834

KEY, V.
Politics, Parties and Pressure Groups, 365 n. 21

KNOWLEDGE
Spectrum of available, 335

KONVITZ
Religious Liberty and Conscience, 1023 n. 3

KU KLUX KLAN, 325 n. 18

KURLAND, P., 788
Of Church and State and the Supreme Court, 974, 1038
The Irrelevance of the Constitution ..., 788 n. 12
Religion and the Law, 788 n. 12

LABOR
Peace, 456

LAFARGE, OLIVER, 333 n. 3

LANGE
The Role of the Access Doctrine in the Regulation of the Mass Media ..., 494 n. 74

LANGUAGE
See also Obscene; Speech
Ass, 343
Bloody Christ Killers, 343
"Fighting words", 147, 150, 214, 272, 281, 670, 672 n. 20
"Fuck the Draft", 149, 672 n. 20
"Fuck a white woman", 342
Goddamned, 343
Inciting words, 409
Insulting, 214, 281, 409
Lewd, 281
Libelous, 281
Never trust a Jew, 343
Obscene, 281
Pissing, 343
Profane, 281
Provocative, 409
Shitty, 343
Vulgar, 251

LAW–BREAKING
Advocacy of, 73

LAWYERS
See Attorneys

LEAFLETS, 415

LEAST INTRUSIVE MEANS, 435

LEAST RESTRICTIVE MEANS, 365, 366
Analysis, 633 n. 14

LEGISLATURES
Colonial, 195
Legislatures, 6

LEMON v. KURTZ, 906
Effect prong,
 Primary effect, 908
 Status in political community, 908
Excessive–entanglement prong,
 Institutional entanglement, 906
Purpose prong,
 Government's actual purpose, 907
 Some secular purpose, 907
Test, 909

INDEX
References are to Pages

LESS–RESTRICTIVE–ALTERNATIVE ANALYSIS, 435

LEVY, LEONARD, 16 n. 30, 17
Emergence of a Free Press, 16 n. 30
The Establishment Clause ..., 765 n. 16

LIABILITY
Without fault, 192

LIBEL, 155 & n. 53, 209
By vicious fiction, 217
Civil action, 180 n. 67
    Personal, 157 n. 59
Civil law tort of, 157
Criminal, 8, 11
Group, 223 n. 3
Per se, 163
Private actions,
    Dampening effects of, 172
Punitive damages,
    Civil action, 160
Retractions, 161
Seditious, 23 n. 51, 155, 157 n. 57
    Chilling prospects, 172
    Common law, 25 n. 53, 49
Tort law of, 157

LIBERTY, 67

LIBRARIES
Public,
    Anteroom, 383 n. 32
    Exclusion of Anti–American books, 339
School, 337
    Contents, 339
    Educational suitability, 337
    High school, 333
    Junior high school, 333
    Like assigned reading list, 342 n. 2
    Removal of books, 333, 334, 336
        Motivation behind, 337
        Profane, 344, 347
        Vulgar, 337, 344, 347
    Voluntary inquiry, 336

LICENSE PLATES
Passenger vehicle, 544
    Motto on,
        "Live Free or Die", 544
    Private property,
        Mobile billboard for State ideological message, 546

LICENSEE'S MONOPOLY, 492

LICENSING
Books, 12 n. *
Motion picture, 443
Officials, 403
Press, 14, 24
Systems, 14 n. 26, 16 n. 31, 24

LINCOLN, ABRAHAM, 378 n. 1

LINDE
Justice Douglas on Freedom in the Welfare State, 294 n. 23

LINDER
When Names Are Not News, They're Negligence ..., 181 n. 71

LISTENERS
Unwilling, 151

"LIVE FREE OR DIE", 544

LOCHNER v. NEW YORK, 67

LOCKE, JOHN, 808

LOCKHART & McCLURE
Literature, the Law of Obscenity, and the Constitution, 691

LUBELL, S.
The Future of American Politics, 369 n. 6

LUPU
Where Rights Begin ..., 1020

MADISON, JAMES, 5 n. 18, 18 n. 38, 77, 335, 505, 554 n. 31, 764, 770 n. 9, 930
Memorial and Remonstrance, 765, 770, 930

MAGNA CARTA, 82
Right to petition, 26

MAILS, 946
Fraud, 946
Unsolicited mass mailings, 651
Use of, 35 n. 1

MALAMUD, BERNARD, 333 n. 3

MALICE
Actual, 166, 214
Evidence of, 167

MALICIOUS MISCHIEF, 253 n. 90

MANSLAUGHTER, 1011

MARC ANTHONY, 34 n. 8

MARCHES
Protest, 227 n. 4

MARCUS v. SEARCH WARRANTS, 24 n. 52

MARKETING, 674

MARKETPLACE
Of products, 614
Of services, 614

MARSHALL, JOHN, 23 n. 50

MARX, KARL
Das Kapital, 217 n. 79

MARXIST–LENINIST DOCTRINE
Teaching of, 137

MASSES, THE, 36

MAYTON
Seditious Libel and the Lost Guarantee of a Freedom of Expression, 17 n. 35, 23 n. 49

McCONNELL
The Origins and Historical Understanding of Free Exercise of Religion, 1023 n. 3

McCONNELL & POSNER
An Economic Approach to Issues of Religious Freedom, 977 n. 11

McGOWAN
A Critical Analysis of Commercial Speech, 669 n. 6

McKITRICK, E.
Party Politics ..., 378 n. 1

MEANS
Least restrictive, 365
Less dramatic, 363

MEDIA
Access to the jail, 498, 501
Broadcast, 487
    Airwaves, 486
    Frequency monopolies, 488
    Radio, 491
        Scarcity of frequencies, 489, 490
    Television, 491
Defendants, 491
News, 498
Reply time, 486, 490
Right of reply, 206
Role of, 499

MEIKLEJOHN, ALEXANDER, 129 n. 5
Free Speech and Its Relation to Self-Government, 155 n. 54

MEMOIRS, 673 n. 22
    See also Cleland, John
Dominant theme of the material, 673 n. 27

MILITARY
    See also United States Armed Forces
Base, 383 n. 32
Reservation, 418
Service, 806 n. 10

MILL, JOHN STUART
On Liberty, 33 n. 6, 34 n. 11, 166 n. 19, 489 n. 18, 738 n. 14

MILLER, 674 n. 26
Works taken as a whole, 674 n. 27

MILLER, W.
The First Liberty ..., 765 n. 16
The Moral Project of the American Founders, 926 n. 49

MILLER-SLATON STANDARD, 675 n. 28
Works taken as a whole, 674 n. 27

MILTON, JOHN
Areopagitica, 12 n. *

MISCONDUCT
Of superiors, 319

MISREPRESENTATION
Of persons, 180 n. 68

MONAGHAN
First Amendment Due Process, 388 n. 44

MONEY AND SPEECH, 559

MONOPOLY, 526
Markets, 640

MORRIS, DESMOND
The Naked Ape, 333 n. 3

MOTION PICTURES
Carnal Knowledge, 676 n. 36, 753
Industry rating system, 676 n. 34
    X-rated, 676 n. 34
Lady Chatterley's Lover, 698
Licensing
    See Licensing
Preview clearance boards, 677
Sacrilegious, 698
That tend to corrupt morals, 698

MOTIVATION, 337

MOTIVES
Bad, 212
Legislative, 238 n. 30
Wrongful, 237

MOTTOES see CHURCH AND STATE

MS. MAGAZINE, 495

MULDER & COMISKY
Jehovah's Witnesses Mold Constitutional Law, 946

MURDER
Advocacy of, 142 n. 52

MURPHY
The Value of Pornography, 704

MURRAY & VEDLITZ
Party Voting on Lower-Level Electoral Contests, 381 n. 17

MUSIC
Amplified, 432
    Decibel limit, 432
First Amendment protection, 434

MUSSER v. UTAH, 33 n. 4

NARROW TAILORING REQUIREMENT, 438

NAST, THOMAS, 213, 217 n. 79

NATIONAL ASSOCIATION OF LETTER CARRIERS, 302

NATIONAL DEFENSE INDUSTRIES
Sabotage and espionage in, 355

NATIONAL PARK SERVICE
    See also Parks
Government interest,
    Unrelated to suppression of expression, 244
Regulations,
    Camping in certain parks, 240
    Fishing, 244 n. 7

NATIONAL PARK SERVICE—Cont'd
Regulations—Cont'd
   Flying model planes, 244 n. 7
   Gambling, 244 n. 7
   Grazing animals, 244 n. 7
   Hunting, 244 n. 7
   Setting off fireworks, 244 n. 7
   Sleeping, 240, 248
   Urination, 244 n. 7

NATIONAL REVIEW, 495

NATIONAL UNITY, 540

NATIVE AMERICANS, 990, 1021
Church, 1006
   Peyote, 1006
      Criminal prohibition, 1007
      Misconduct,
         Work-related, 1006
      Sacramental purposes, 1006
Federal land, 990
Government programs,
   Incidental effects, 996
Property rights, 993
Religious,
   Accommodating practices, 993
   Activity,
      Penalized, 995
   Conduct,
      Neither coerce, 995
   Practices,
      Government,
         Internal, 998
            Use of Social Security number, 998
      Laws,
         Frustrate, 998
         Inhibit, 998
   Servitude, 992
Sacred areas, 991

NEBRASKA PRESS ASS'N v. STUART, 99

NEGLIGENCE, 167, 181 n. 71

NEW YORK v. P.J. VIDEO, INC., 24 n. 52

NEW YORK TIMES v. SULLIVAN, 171
Standard, 192

NEWSPAPERS, 208, 389, 491
Nondiscriminatory taxes on receipts and income, 1003

NEWSPRINT
Access,
   Inequalities of ability to pay, 496
National Newsprint Licensing Commission, 497 n. 81
Socializing of, 496

NINTH AMENDMENT, 514 n. 16

NONPROFIT ORGANIZATIONS
   See also Religion
Art galleries, 836
Hospitals, 836
Libraries, 836

NOONAN, J.
The Believer and the Powers That Are, 870 n. 35

NOT IMPROBABLE TEST
See Hand, Learned

NOWAK
Using the Press Clause to Limit Government Speech, 558 n. 91

OATH
Religious test, 77, 1025

O'BRIEN, UNITED STATES v., 362 n. 17
Four-step analysis, 247 n. 6, 263 n. 8, 436
Treated as general first amendment test, 255 n. 97

OBSCENE
Advertisements, 679
Books,
   Absolute criminal responsibility, 693
   Concern for juveniles, 718
   Nation-wide suppression, 689
   Pandering, 718
   Patently offensive, 701
   "Pulps", 716
   Without redeeming social value, 701
Circulars, 679
Criminalizing,
   Uncertainties of, 669
Language, see Language
Magazines,
   Leer of sensualist, 710
Material,
   Possession of, 723
   Private possession of, 721
Regulating,
   Uncertainties of, 669
Remarks, 231

OBSCENITY, 69 n. 44, 442
   See also Pornography; Sex, Sexual
Appeal to erotic interest, 684
Arousing lustful desires, 683
Coarse expression, 714
Community standards, 701
   Contemporary, 681
   Hicklin test, 681
   Judged in the abstract, 702
   Nudity, 755
   Panderer test, 713
   Patently offensive material, 701
   Prurient interests, 681, 701
   Sodomy, 873 n. 45
Standards of decency,
   Community, 683
      Contemporary, 731, 753
   National, 731 n. 13
Susceptible persons, 681
Test of, 691

OCCUPATIONS
Gainful,
   In streets, 604

OLIPHANT, 217 n. 79

OLYMPIC
Commercial and promotional uses of word prohibited, 275 n. 10

OPINIONS, 216 & n. 76
Absolute right to propagate, 220
Advisory, 761
Article III cases,
    Adequate, 761
    Elements,
        Ripeness, 761
        Mootness, 761
        State grounds,
        Independent, 761
    Standing to sue, 760, 761
Compulsory unification of, 541
Expression of, 39
Pernicious, 186

ORTHODOX IN POLITICS
See Politics

ORTHODOXY
Over classroom, 336

OUTRAGEOUSNESS
See Political

OVERBREADTH, 306, 355, 609
Doctrine, 638 n. 8, 677 n. 37
Void on its face for, 482 n. 55

OVERBROAD ON ITS FACE, 356

OVERREGULATION
Incentives for, 250

OWEN, B.
Economics and Freedom of Expression . . ., 495 n. 75

PAMPHLETS, 394

PARADIGMS
Of "freedom of the press", 494
Of private speech property, 495

PARKS
    See also National Park Service
Lafayette, 245
Public, 384

PARLIAMENT, 14

PARODY, 209
Ad, 211, 215
    Which viciously maligns, 216

PASSPORT
Denial of, 358

PATRONAGE
Beneficiaries of, 368
Combined with civil service, 370
Dismissals, 359, 365
Hiring practices, 367, 370
Policymaking positions, 364
Political, 359
Practice as old as Republic, 368
Validated, 364

PATRONAGE—Cont'd
Wholesale, 364

PATTERSON v. COLORADO, 20, 78 n. 13

PEACE
Breach of, 404, 411 n. 2, 412
Disturbing, 149
Preserving, 272

PENAL INSTITUTIONS
See Jails

PENUMBRAS, 2, 3 n. 8, 760 n. 1

PERMITS
Administrative, 388 n. 44
Systems, 388 n. 44
    Void on its face, 388 n. 44
To hold public meetings, 390

PERNICIOUS TENDENCY, 12

PERSONAL ATTACKS, 488

PERSUASION
Conventional modes of, 250 n. 14
Financial means of, 250 n. 14

PETITION, 26
Addressed to Congress, 27
Tumultuous, 26 n. 57

PFEFFER, L.
Church, State, and Freedom, 895 n. 19

PHYSICIANS, 619 n. 25

PICKERING TEST, 319

PICKERING–CONNICK BALANCING TEST, 287

PICKETING, 417

PLEDGE OF ALLEGIANCE, 785 n. 3, 901
"One Nation under God", 801

POINT OF VIEW
Approved, 223

POLITICAL
Action committee, 591
    See also Elections
Activities,
    Off-the-job, 330 n. 26
Affiliation, 375
Belief and association, 360
Candidates,
    Right of reply, 206
    Right to equal space, 205
Community,
    Insiders, 906
    Outsiders, 906
Debates,
    Robust, 211
Discourse, 213
    Outrageousness in, 214
Parties,
    One-party system, 365 n. 26
    Strengthening, 369
Private convictions, 579

1058 INDEX
References are to Pages

POLITICAL—Cont'd
Two-party system, 365

POLITICS
Orthodox in, 220, 336

PORNOGRAPHY, 218, 669 n. 7
See also Obscenity; Sex, Sexual
As speech, 221
Child, 741 n. 1
Dial-a-porn telephone services, 675 n. 32
Distribution to children, 675
Erotic stimulation, 705
Hard-core, 706, 714, 754
Influences on attitudes, 218
Obscene for homosexuals, 675
Women, 218

POSADAS, 659

POST OFFICE, 387, 390

POSTAL OFFICIALS, 443

POSTAL RATES
Preferential, 578 n. 127

POUND
A Survey of Social Interests, 1018

POWER
Abuses of, 319
To declare truth, 222

PRESIDENT
Assassination of, 136

PRESIDENTIAL ELECTION CAMPAIGN FUND ACT, 591
See also Elections

PRESS
Free, 208
Freedom of, 495
Licensing, see Licensing

PREVIOUS RESTRAINTS, 8, 11

PRIOR RESTRAINT, 103, 105, 111, 220, 287, 388 n. 44, 406, 440, 442, 443
See also Speech
As applied to press, 122
No judicial, 116

PRIOR REVIEW, 24 n. 52

PRIVACY, 155, 178, 209
Actions, 179 n. 6
False light claims, 180 n. 68
Right of, 176

PRIVATE
Individuals, 189
Political convictions, 579

PRIVILEGE
Absolute, unconditional, 170
Executive, 23 n. 50

PRIVILEGES AND IMMUNITIES CLAUSE, 10, 60, 68, 787

PRODUCTS
Authority to totally ban, 663

PROFANITY, 331, 344

PROPAGANDA, 558 n. 90
Government sponsored, 558

PROPERTY
Blurred boundary between private and public, 517
Government,
    Access to, 427
    Held, 383, 387
Private, 386 n. 37
    Commercial, 534
    Farms, 386 n. 38
    Shopping centers, 386 n. 38
    Universities, 386 n. 38
Public, 481
    No favored group, 384 n. 33
Socialized, 491
Towns,
    Company-owned, 386 n. 38, 517
        Refusal to leave, 521 n. 85

PROSECUTORS, 377 n. 13

PROTECTION
Different degrees of, 619 n. 24

PROTECTIVE ORDERS, 107, 108, 110

PROTESTORS
Imposter problem, 246

PUBLIC
Buildings,
    Painting of, 265
Concern,
    Matters of, 318, 327
        Speech regarding, 323
        Private statement on, 323 n. 13
Defender,
    Assistant, 371
Discussion, 72
Employer,
    Dual role of, 322
Employment,
    "Free speech" claim, 328
Figures, 188, 192, 214
    Involuntary, 189
Forum, 417
    Doctrine, 28, 383
Importance,
    Matters of, 298
Interest,
    Factual material of clear, 608
    Matters of, 370
Places,
    Unwelcome affront in, 156
Safety measures, 251 n. 83
Trust, 491

PUBLICATION
Offensive, 212

PUBLICITY see also RIGHT
Pretrial, 101, 105

PURPOSE
Legislative, 238 n. 30
Wrongful, 237

INDEX

References are to Pages

QUALIFIED CLAUSES, 5

QUESTION OF LAW
For judge, 129

RABBAN
The Ahistorical Historian: Leonard Levy ..., 17 n. 35
The Emergence of Modern First Amendment Doctrine, 17 n. 35
The First Amendment in Its Forgotten Years, 32 n. 3

RECEPTION
Hostile, 407

REDRUP, 740

REGISTRATION CERTIFICATE
See Draft

REGULATIONS
Fire, 251 n. 83
Need not be judged solely by reference to demonstration at hand, 243
Reasonable, 395

REICH, C.
Individual Rights and Social Welfare, 288 n. 5
The New Property, 288 n. 5

RELIGION
See also Church and State; Establishment Clause
Amish, 957
  Mennonite, 953
  Old Order, 953, 956
    Compulsory school attendance laws, 954
      Accommodating religious objections, 962
      Balancing process, 956, 963
      Wishes of child, 962
  Talmudic diet, 957
Buddhism, 1026 n. 11, 1038 n. 8
Catholic,
  Communion, 1019 n. 6
Censorship, 936
Christianity,
  Nonadherents of, 920
Common denominator of, 815
Conduct, 958
Defined, 1022
  Astrology, 1023
  Cults, 1023
  Ethical Culture, 1026 n. 11, 1038 n. 8
  Marxism, 1023
  Secular Humanism, 1026 n. 11, 1038 n. 8
  Toward a Constitutional Definition of Religion, 1024 n. 5
Discrimination, 968
Encumbered self, 1023 n. 3
Excessive government entanglement, 837, 855

RELIGION—Cont'd
Federal courts,
  Prayers in,
    "God save the United States and this Honorable Court", 800
Free exercise, 1013
  Coercion, 793
  Conduct,
    Religiously grounded, 958
  Cumulative effect of similar claims, 1020
  Single categorical rule, 1012
  Unduly burdened, 958
Freedom,
  Of acceptance of any creed or practice, Compulsion by law, 935
  Of conscience, 935, 1023
  Of religious practice, 941
  Price for, 953
    Of rubbish, 953
  To act, 935
  To adhere to religious organization or form of worship, 935
  To believe, 935
Government finance of, 799
  Direct subsidy, 904
Incidental benefits, 838
  Fire protection, 838
  Police protection, 838
Interests of parenthood, 962
Jehovah's Witnesses, 399, 934
  And state authority, 939
    Child labor laws, 939
    Welfare of children, 942
  Breach of the peace, 933
  Parental right, 942
  Solicitation, 934
    Fraudulent, 937
    Time, place and manner, 935
Jews,
  Orthodox, 983
Liberty of, 787
Minority,
  Disfavoring of, 1015
  Indirect coercive pressure on, 798
  Severe impact of state restrictions, 1011
Neutrality, 842
No law respecting an establishment of, 767
  General tests, 767
Nondiscriminatory aid to, 812 n. 21
Political offices,
  No religious tests, 780 n. 37, 784, 1025
  President's oath, 780 n. 37
Post death consequences, 1023 n. 3
Propagation of, 776
Property,
  For religious instruction,
    Tax-supported, 790, 828
Realm of, 860
Sacramental uses of,
  Bread, 1007
  Wine, 1007, 1019 n. 6
Schools, see Schools
Science of Creative Intelligence–Transcendental Meditation, 1024 n. 4
Scientology, 1024 n. 4

INDEX
References are to Pages

RELIGION—Cont'd
Seventh–Day Adventist, 966
   Unemployment compensation benefits, 966
Special treatment, 974
Taoism, 1038 n. 8
Taxation,
   Affirmative payment of funds, 979
   Deduction treatment, 788
   Direct tax in aid of religion, 923
   Exempt status, 788, 825, 835, 840
      Excessive government entanglement, 837
      Passive aspect, 828
   Long use, 839
   To support religion, 977
Use of public funds, 778
Voluntarism, 842
Wall of separation, 772, 855, 900
Wholesale overturning of settled laws, 1018

RETRACTIONS, 161

REVIEW
Mere rationality, 384 n. 33
Prepublication, 349

REYNOLDS
Will be overruled, 965

RICHARDS, D.
Toleration and the Constitution, 1023 n. 3

RIGHT
Of association, 2, 357, 360
Of publicity,
   Appropriation of, 212
Of reply, 206
To be left alone, 180, 656, 722
To bury past, 180
To petition, 26
To publish,
   Absolute, unconditional, 169
To read, 722
To receive information and ideas, 335, 621, 722
To refrain from speaking, 545
To work law, 557

RIGHT–PRIVILEGE DISTINCTION, 287, 290 n. 10, 291, 362

RIGHTS
Legal,
   Accurate information about, 631

ROE v. WADE, 1

ROTH–ALBERTS, 673 n. 21
Dominant theme of material, 674 n. 27

ROTH v. UNITED STATES, 69 n. 44

RULE OF REASON, 134

RUTLEDGE, JOHN, 33

SABOTAGE
Teaching techniques of, 136

SALINGER, J.D.
The Catcher in the Rye, 332

SANDEL, M.
Freedom of Conscience or Freedom of Choice, 1023 n. 3

SATIRISTS
Political, 213

SCHENCK v. UNITED STATES, 29

SCHOOLS
And religion,
   Dances,
      Ban on, 888
      Religious motivation, 888
   Prayers,
      Coercion,
         Overtones of social inferiority, 821 n. 8
      Lord's Prayer, 803
      Official, 797
      Regents, 796
      Spiritual heritage of Nation, 801
   Released time programs, 791, 792
   Religion courses,
      Comparative religion, 806
      "Creation science", 1024 n. 4
      History of religion, 806
   Religious exercises, 806
      Daily readings from Bible, 802
      Religion of secularism, 806
   Ten Commandments,
      Posted in classrooms, 873 n. 47
Authorities, 224
Campus, 228
Citizenship,
   Training in, 542
Enclaves of totalitarianism, 478
Evolution,
   Ban on instruction, 873 n. 47
Interschool mail system,
   Teacher mailboxes, 447
Nonpublic/parochial-government support for, 768
   Bus transportation, 767
      Field trips, 858
      Reimbursement of parents for, 767
   Diagnostic services, 856
   Equipment, 857
   Expenses,
      Tax deductions for, 861
   Fire protection, 788
   General test modified and in dispute, 861
   General test refined and in dispute, 953
   Police protection, 788
   Public funds,
      Repair of physical facilities, 862
   Religious teaching, 776
   Statutes,
      Excessive government entanglement, 824
      Primary effect, 824
      Secular legislative purpose, 824
   Tax-raised funds, 850

SCHOOLS—Cont'd
Nonpublic/parochial-government support for—Cont'd
Teachers,
  Reimbursement of salaries, 822
Textbooks,
  Free secular, 828, 847
  Loan to students, 845, 856
  Parochial, 851
  Tax deduction for, 868
Officials, 232
Premises, 383 n. 32
  Hair style, 226
  Length of skirts, 226
  Regulations, 226
  Type of clothing, 226
Right to receive ideas in, 345
Secondary, 224
  Newspapers/publications, 557 n. 88
    As part of curriculum, 471, 474
    School financed,
      Censorship of, 331 n. 28
    School-sponsored, 474
Speech sponsored by school, 474 n. 3
State-operated, 227
Students, 225
  Activity fees,
    Mandatory, 557 n. 88
  First amendment rights of, 335
  Expression, 477
Teachers, 225
  As citizen, 296
  Contracts,
    Board's refusal to renew, 308
  Nontenured, 309

SCIENTER, 172 n. 63
Requirement, 677 & n. 38

SCOPES CASE, 330

SCRUTINY
Exacting, 274
Strict, 1, 384 n. 33

SCULPTURES, 3 n. 8

SEARCH WARRANT, 21 n. 43
General, 24

SECURITY
Breaches of, 350
Guards, 376

SEDITION ACT OF 1798, pp. 15, 16 n. 29, 49, 165

SEDITIOUS ACTS, 138

SELF-HELP, 521, n. 85

SEX, SEXUAL
See also Obscenity; Pornography
And obscenity, 681
Community standards, 701
Conduct,
  Hard-core, 754
  Portrayed in patently offensive way, 728
Criminal behavior, 706

SEX, SEXUAL—Cont'd
Deviant practices, 717
Double entendre, 209
Experiences,
  Fetishism, 716
  Flagellation, 705
  Heterosexual relations, 716
  Homosexuality, 705, 716
  Lesbianism, 705, 716
  Sado-masochism, 716
Morality,
  Congress has no substantive power over, 688
Patently offensive, 701
Prurient interest in, 681, 701
  Requirement, 717
Representation of, 701
Responses, 222
Taoism, 1026, n. 11
Thoughts, 680
Value,
  Artistic, 728
  Literary, 728
  Political, 728
  Scientific, 728

SHAKESPEARE, WILLIAM, 217 n. 79
Othello, 155, n. 53

SHERBERT TEST, 1009, 1014

SHIFFRIN, S.
The First Amendment, Democracy, and Romance, 328 n. 25
The First Amendment and Economic Regulation . . . , 669 n. 6
Government Speech, 386 n. 39, 558 n. 91

SHOPPING CENTERS AND MALLS, 522
Privately owned, 527

SIDEWALKS, 415
Public, 418

SIEBERT, F.
Freedom of The Press in England 1476–1776, p. 17 n. 35

SIGNS, 242
As visual clutter, 422
Posting of, 421
  On fire hydrants, 422
  On traffic signals, 422
  On utility poles, 421, 483 n. 58

SIT-IN, 245

SIXTH AMENDMENT, 24, 510

SLANDER, 155, n. 53
Tort law of, 157

SLAUGHTER-HOUSE CASES, 27

SMITH ACT, 122

SMITH, R.
Public Prayer and the Constitution, 785 n. 8

SMOLLA, RODNEY
Law of Defamation, 157 n. 61

SOCIAL ADVOCACY
See Advocacy

SOLICITATION
Fraudulent, 937

SONG OF SOLOMON, 735

SOVIET UNION, 4

SPEAKERS
Identity of, 492
Poor, 250 n. 14

SPECIAL VERDICT
See Trials

SPEECH
At office, 317
Brigaded with action, 146
By proxy, 593
Commercial, 266 n. 2, 275 n. 10, 601, 603
    Advertising, 603
    Definition of, 645
    Fraud, 601
    Four-part analysis, 639
    Intermediate scrutiny, 643
Content of, 219
Crude, 672 n. 20
Domestic partisan ideological, 558 n. 89
Dramatic performances, 257
Easement of access and use, 398
Elements, 271
Exercise of,
    Financial assistance to, 578 n. 127
Favoring some viewpoints, 423
Free,
    Access, 383
    Clauses relating to, 21
    Equalization of,
        By levelling contributions, 559
        By levelling expenditures, 559
    Public employment claim to, 328
    Value to political process, 182 n. 71
Freedom,
    Not to speak, 535, 545
    To speak one's mind, 211
Freezes, 103
Hostile reaction to, 151
Insulting, 672 n. 20
"Low value", 223
Nonpolitical,
    Lesser protection of, 601
Nonspeech,
    Elements, 235, 271
Of state-created monopoly, 646
Offensive, 214
On matter of public concern, 322
Political, 275 n. 10, 428
Political process, 155
    Values, 182 n. 71
Prior restraint on, 102, 103, 220
    Chills, 103
    Freezes, 103
Private conversations, 325

SPEECH—Cont'd
Promotional uses of word "Olympic", 275 n. 10
Pure,
    Akin to, 225, 284
    Entitled to comprehensive protection, 225
Right to refrain from, 545
Shocking, 214
"Sold" for profit, 614
Subordinating,
    Women, 220
Symbolic, 230, 235, 247, 545
Time, place and manner regulations, 251 n. 83
Vulgar, 214

SPEECH AND DEBATE CLAUSE, 22

STANDARDS
Lack of, 401

STANDING, 621

STANLEY, 740

STAR–CHAMBER, COURT OF, 12 n. *

STASIS, 223

STATE
Action,
    Pursuant to general police power, 292
As corporation, 291
As employer, 292, 296
As property owner, 344, 383
As proprietor, 292
Constitutional provisions, 527
Interest,
    Compelling, 968, 984 n. 2
        Furthered by narrowly tailored regulation, 984 n. 2
    Rational relationship, 968

STATEMENTS
Erroneous, 177
False, 164, 165 n. 19, 414
Judicial decrees, 202 n. 2
Of fact,
    False, 186, 212

STEWART
Or of the Press, 501

STOKES
Church and State in the United States, 765 n. 15

STONE
Fora Americana . . . , 387 n. 40

STORY, J.
II Commentaries on the Constitution of the United States, 766 n. 17

STREETS
Littering of, 397, 414 n. 9
Public, 396
Traffic signals, 422

INDEX
References are to Pages

STRONG, F.
Substantive Due Process, 66 n. 34

STUDENTS see SCHOOLS

SUBVERSIVE ACTIVITIES CONTROL ACT OF 1950, p. 354

SULLIVAN, K.
Unconstitutional Conditions, 291 n. 13

SUPPRESSION
Content-based, 430

SUPREME COURT
United States,
    Building, and on its grounds, violates the First Amendment, 415

SYMBOLIC
City, 242
Expression, 242
Speech, see Speech
Tents, 241

SYMBOLS OF STATE, 537

TAX-AND-SPEND CLAUSES, 764

TAXPAYER'S SUITS, 762
Local, 763 n. 10
State, 763 n. 10

TEACHERS
See Schools

TENDENCY, 31, 39
Bad, 29
Reasonable, 84
Toward formal complexity, 290 n. 9

TENTH AMENDMENT, 764

THEATERS
Adult, 735
Community-owned, 445
Municipal, 440, 444

THEATRICAL PRODUCTIONS, 257, 258

THOMAS, PIRI
Down These Mean Streets, 333 n. 3

THOREAU, HENRY DAVID
Philosophical rather than religious belief, 956

THOUGHT
Freedom of, 545

TILLICH, P., 1031
The Shakings of Foundations, 1024 n. 5, 1031
    Ultimate concern, 1031

TIME, PLACE, AND MANNER, 383
Regulations, 251 n. 83, 417
Restrictions, 241, 399, 438, 618
    Content-neutral, 417

TORT LAW, 155

TREASON, 23
Constructive, 23

TRESPASS, 274 n. 8
Advocacy of, 142 n. 52
Land, 74

TRIALS
Civil,
    Right to attend, 514 n. 17
Criminal,
    Right to attend, 507, 514
        Public and press, 507
Fair, 87
Jury, 24, 25, 128
    Special verdict, 25
Not a "free trade in ideas", 83
    See also Ideas
Not like elections, 91

TRIBUNALS
Federal, 193 n. 2

TRUTH
Competition of market, 49
Defense of, 187
Power to declare, 222

TUCKER, ST. GEORGE, 18 n. 37–38

TWAIN, MARK, 217 n. 79

TWO PARTY SYSTEM, 365

UNCONSTITUTIONAL
Conditions, 976
    Doctrine, 287, 290 n. 10, 292, 293 n. 22, 294 n. 23, 330 n. 26, 389
On its face, 243, 304

UNIFORMS
    See also United States Armed Forces
Military, 257

UNITED STATES ARMED FORCES
Military regulations, 980
    Deference to, 980
    Narrowly tailored, 986
    Religious exemptions,
        Cumulative costs of, 987
    Uniform dress requirements, 979
        Dreadlocks, 982
        Parade of horribles, 985
        Personal preference, 983
        Saffron robes, 982
        Turbans, 982
        Yarmulkes, 980, 981, 982

UNITED STATES ATTORNEYS, 379

UNITED STATES v. BURR, 23 n. 50

UNIVERSAL MILITARY TRAINING AND SERVICE ACT, 239

UNIVERSITIES
Academic freedom, 831, 833
Church-related,
    Federal aid, 830, 835
    Religious indoctrination, 831
    Theocentric man, 852
Expressive activities, 475 n. 7

UNIVERSITIES—Cont'd
State,
  Newspapers,
    Student, 331 n. 28
  University of Virginia, 791

UNSOLICITED MASS MAILINGS, 651

USES
Competing, 442

VAN ALSTYNE, WILLIAM
A Comment on the Inappropriate Uses of an Old Analogy, 294 n. 23
Congressional Power and Free Speech, 18 n. 38
Constitutional Separation of Church and State . . ., 1024 n. 6
The Demise of the Right–Privilege Distinction, 291 n. 13
A Judicial Postscript to the Church–State Debates of 1989 . . ., p. 927 n. 49
The Recrudescence of Property Rights, 250 n. 14, 398 n. 50
Trends in the Supreme Court: Mr. Jefferson's Crumbling Wall . . ., 766 n. 18, 926 n. 49

VEHICLE LICENSE PLATES see LICENSE PLATES

VENDORS
News, 385 n. 36

VERBAL CACOPHONY, 153

VICIOUS FICTION, 217

VICTIMS
Crime,
  Identification of, 181
    Rape, 181 n. 71
    Recovery on theory of negligence, 181 n. 7

VIEWPOINT
Discrimination,
  Pretext for, 459
Favored, 423
Neutral regulation, 423

VIEWS
Absolute, 85
Unpopular, 413
Suppression of specific point, 658

VILIFICATION, 164, 414

VISHINSKY, ANDRE, 139

VONNEGUT, KURT
Slaughterhouse Five, 331 n. 28, 333 n. 3

VULGARITY
One man's vulgarity is another's lyric, 153

WALKING, 252

WAR
Declaration of, 115, 240
Power, 115

WARRANTS OF SEARCH
See Search Warrant

WARREN, EARL, 175

WEALTH
Disparities in, 250 n. 14

WECHSLER
Toward Neutral Principles of Constitutional Law, 522 n. 87

WERHAN
The Supreme Court's Public Forum Doctrine . . ., 387 n. 40

WEST VIRGINIA BD. OF EDUC. v. BARNETTE, 68 n. 43

WHITNEY v. CALIFORNIA, 69

WILKES, JOHN, 24 n. 52

WOLFE, THOMAS, 217 n. 79

WOOD v. GEORGIA, 93

WORDS
See Language

WORKING RELATIONSHIPS
Close, 317

WRIGHT
Level–Up Rather Than Level–Down, 600 n. 97
Money and the Pollution of Politics . . ., 600 n. 97

WRIGHT, RICHARD, 333 n. 3

WRITS OF ASSISTANCE
General, 24

YATES v. UNITED STATES, 139 n. 47

YUDOF, M.
Personal Speech and Government Expression, 558 n. 91
When Governments Speak, . . ., 386 n. 39, 558 n. 91

ZENGER, PETER, 25 n. 53

ZIEGLER
Government Speech and the Constitution . . ., 558 n. 91

ZURCHER v. STANFORD DAILY, 22 n. 43